HANDBOOK OF CRITICAL STUDIES OF ARTIFICIAL INTELLIGENCE

Handbook of Critical Studies of Artificial Intelligence

Edited by

Simon Lindgren

Professor of Sociology and Director, DIGSUM Centre for Digital Social Research, Umeå University, Sweden

EE Edward Elgar
PUBLISHING

Cheltenham, UK · Northampton, MA, USA

Published by
Edward Elgar Publishing Limited
The Lypiatts
15 Lansdown Road
Cheltenham
Glos GL50 2JA
UK

Edward Elgar Publishing, Inc.
William Pratt House
9 Dewey Court
Northampton
Massachusetts 01060
USA

A catalogue record for this book
is available from the British Library

Library of Congress Control Number: 2023945122

This book is available electronically in the **Elgar**online
Sociology, Social Policy and Education subject collection
http://dx.doi.org/10.4337/9781803928562

ISBN 978 1 80392 855 5 (cased)
ISBN 978 1 80392 856 2 (eBook)
Printed and bound by CPI Group (UK) Ltd, Croydon, CR0 4YY

Contents

PART IV   AI TRANSPARENCY, ETHICS AND REGULATION

Contributors

Kendra Albert is a Clinical Instructor at the Cyberlaw Clinic at Harvard Law School and a Lecturer on Studies of Women, Gender, and Sexuality at Harvard University.

Fernando Avila is a PhD Candidate at the Centre for Criminology and Sociolegal Studies, University of Toronto, Canada.

Vian Bakir is Professor of Journalism and Political Communication for the School of History, Law and Social Sciences at Bangor University, UK.

Andrea Ballatore is a Lecturer in Social and Cultural Informatics at King's College London, UK.

Caroline Bassett is the Director of CDH (Cambridge Digital Humanities) and a Professor within the Faculty of English, University of Cambridge, UK.

Andreas Beinsteiner teaches media studies and philosophy at the Universities of Innsbruck and Vienna, Austria.

Anton Berg is a Doctoral Researcher at the Helsinki Institute for Social Sciences and Humanities, Helsinki University, Finland.

Sukanto Bhattacharya is a Senior Lecturer in the Department of Management at Deakin Business School, Deakin University, Australia.

Abeba Birhane is a Senior Fellow in Trustworthy AI at Mozilla Foundation and Adjunct Assistant Professor at the School of Computer Science and Statistics, Trinity College Dublin, Ireland.

Peter Bloom is a Professor of Management and Society at the University of Essex in the UK.

Saba Rebecca Brause is a PhD Candidate and Research Assistant at the Department of Communication and Media Research at the University of Zurich, Switzerland.

Benedetta Brevini is Senior Visiting Fellow at the London School of Economics, UK, and Associate Professor of Political Economy of Communication at the University of Sydney, Australia.

Laila M. Brown is a Librarian at Hawai'i Pacific University, USA.

Manuel Carabantes is affiliated to the Complutense University of Madrid, Spain.

Vanja Carlsson is Senior Lecturer in Public Administration at the University of Gothenburg, Sweden.

Janet Chan is Emeritus Professor at the Faculty of Law and Justice, UNSW Sydney, Australia.

Simona Chiodo is Professor of Philosophy at Politecnico di Milano, Italy.

Ching-Hua Chuan is an Assistant Professor of Interactive Media at School of Communication, University of Miami, USA.

Coppélie Cocq is Professor and Deputy Director at Humlab, Umeå University, Sweden.

Randy Connolly is Professor of Mathematics and Computing at Mount Royal University, Calgary, Canada.

Karin Danielsson is Associate Professor at the Department of Informatics and Director of Humlab, Umeå University, Sweden.

Maggie Delano is an Assistant Professor at the Department of Engineering at Swarthmore College.

Virginia Dignum is Professor of Artificial Intelligence at the Department of Computing Science, Umeå University, Sweden, and program director of WASP-HS, the Wallenberg Program on Humanities and Social Sciences for AI, Autonomous Systems and Software.

Anne Dippel is Associate Professor at Friedrich-Schiller-University Jena, Germany.

Lina Eklund is a Senior Lecturer in Human-Computer Interaction at the Department of Informatics and Media, Uppsala University, Sweden.

Niva Elkin-Koren is a Professor at Tel-Aviv University Faculty of Law in Israel and a Faculty Associate at the Berkman Klein Center for Internet and Society at Harvard University.

Severin Engelmann is a Research Associate at the Professorship of Cyber Trust, Department of Computer Science, Technical University of Munich, Germany.

Kalle Eriksson is a PhD Candidate at the Department of Political Science, Umeå University, Sweden.

Eran Fisher is an Associate Professor at the Department of Sociology, Political Science, and Communication at the Open University of Israel.

Johnathan Flowers is an Assistant Professor at the Department of Philosophy at California State University, Northridge. USA.

Anna Foka is Professor in Digital Humanities at the Department of ALM (Archives, Library and Information Science, Museum and Cultural Heritage Studies) at Uppsala University in Sweden.

Maria Forsgren is a Doctoral Researcher at the Department of Psychology, Umeå University, Sweden.

Eleonore Fournier-Tombs is Head of Anticipatory Action Research at United Nations University Centre for Policy Research.

João Gonçalves is Assistant Professor in Media and Communication at Erasmus University Rotterdam, Netherlands.

Dejan Grba is an Associate Professor at the Digital Art Program, Interdisciplinary Graduate Center, University of the Arts in Belgrade, Serbia.

Gabriele Griffin is Professor of Gender Research at Uppsala University and Extraordinary Professor of Gender and African Studies at the Free State University, South Africa.

Jens Hälterlein is a Research Associate at the Department of Media Studies at Paderborn University, Germany.

Kelly Hannah-Moffat is a Full Professor in Criminology and Sociolegal Studies and Sociology, and a Vice President at the University of Toronto, Canada.

Jenna Imad Harb is a Research Fellow at the School of Regulation and Global Governance (RegNet) at the Australian National University.

Kashyap Haresamudram is a WASP-HS Doctoral Researcher at the Department of Technology and Society, Lund University, Sweden.

Fredrik Heintz is a Professor at the Department of Computer and Information Science, Linköping University, Sweden, and program director of WASP-ED, the Wallenberg AI and Transformative Technologies Education Development Program.

Rasmus Helles is an Associate Professor at the Department of Communication, University of Copenhagen, Denmark.

Kathryn Henne is a Professor at the Australian National University (ANU), where she serves as Director of RegNet, the ANU School of Regulation and Global Governance, and the Justice and Technoscience Lab. She is also an Adjunct Professor at Arizona State University, USA.

Jan Hjelte is a Senior Lecturer at the Department of Social Work, Umeå University, Sweden.

Steve G. Hoffman is an Associate Professor of Sociology, University of Toronto, Canada.

Wolfgang Hofkirchner is a retired Professor at the Faculty of Informatics, TU Wien, and serves as Director of the independent Institute for a Global Sustainable Information Society, Vienna, Austria.

Charlotte Högberg is a PhD Candidate at The Department of Technology and Society, The Faculty of Engineering, Lund University, Sweden.

Robert Holton is Emeritus Professor of Sociology at Trinity College, Dublin, Ireland

Andre Holzapfel is Associate Professor at the Division of Media Technology and Interaction Design at KTH Royal Institute of Technology, Stockholm, Sweden.

Stefka Hristova is Associate Professor of Digital Media at Michigan Technological University, USA.

Anna Jobin is a Senior Lecturer and Researcher at the University of Fribourg, Switzerland, also affiliated with the Humboldt Institute for Internet and Society (HIIG), Berlin, Germany.

Walter G. Johnson is a PhD Scholar at the School of Regulation and Global Governance (RegNet) at the Australian National University.

Fabrice Jotterand is Professor of Bioethics and Medical Humanities, and Director of the Graduate Program in Bioethics at the Medical College of Wisconsin, Milwaukee, USA. He is also Senior Researcher at the Institute for Biomedical Ethics, University of Basel in Switzerland.

Kaisla Kajava is a Doctoral Researcher in the Department of Computer Science at Aalto University, Finland.

Christian Katzenbach is a Professor of Communication and Media Studies at the Centre for Media, Communication and Information Research (ZeMKI) at the University of Bremen, and Associated Researcher at the Humboldt Institute for Internet and Society (HIIG), Berlin, Germany.

Miroslav Kotásek is an Assistant Professor at the Faculty of Arts, Masaryk University Brno and at the Faculty of Electrical Engineering and Communication, Brno University of Technology, Czech Republic.

Hans-Jörg Kreowski is a retired Professor at the Faculty of Mathematics and Computer Science, Universität Bremen, and serves as board member of the Forum of Computer Professionals for Peace and Social Responsibility, Bremen, Germany.

Salla-Maaria Laaksonen is an Adjunct Professor and a Senior Researcher at the Centre for Consumer Society Research at the University of Helsinki, Finland.

Amanda Lagerkvist is a Professor of Media and Communication Studies at Uppsala University, Sweden.

Signe Sophus Lai is an Assistant Professor (tenure track) at the Department of Communication, University of Copenhagen, Denmark.

Yucong Lao is a PhD Student at the Department of Information Studies, the Research Unit of History, Culture and Communications, Faculty of Humanities, University of Oulu, Finland.

Stefan Larsson is a Senior Lecturer and Associate Professor in Technology and Social Change at Lund University, Sweden, Department of Technology and Society.

Ashlin Lee is a Research Scientist at the Commonwealth Science and Industrial Research Organisation in Canberra, Australia. He is also an Honorary Lecturer in sociology at the Australian National University's (ANU) School of Sociology, and a member of the Justice and Technoscience Lab at RegNet, the ANU's School of Regulation and Global Governance.

Megan LePere-Schloop, Ph.D., is an assistant professor of public and nonprofit management in the John Glenn College of Public Affairs at the Ohio State University. Her research focuses on language, using both traditional qualitative approaches and computational methods including machine learning to study community philanthropic foundations, sexual harassment in fundraising, and knowledge production in the fields of public affairs and organization studies.

Evelina Liliequist is an associate professor in digital humanities at Humlab, Umeå University, and a researcher at the Center for regional science, Umeå University.

Simon Lindgren is a Full Professor of Sociology and Director of DIGSUM Centre for Digital Social Research, Umeå University, Sweden.

Janina Loh (neé Sombetzki) is an ethicist (Stabsstelle Ethik) at Stiftung Liebenau in Meckenbeuren on Lake Constance, Germany, and Honorary Professor at Hochschule Bonn-Rhein-Sieg, University for Applied Studies, Centre for Ethics and Responsibility (ZEV).

Stine Lomborg is an Associate Professor at the Department of Communication, and director of Center for Tracking and Society, University of Copenhagen, Denmark.

Anders Sundnes Løvlie is an Associate Professor in the Center for Digital Play at the IT University of Copenhagen, Denmark.

Fenwick McKelvey is an Associate Professor in Communication Studies at Concordia University, Canada.

Andrew McStay is Professor of Technology & Society for the School of History, Law and Social Sciences at Bangor University, UK.

Samuel Merrill is an Associate Professor at the Department of Sociology, Umeå University, Sweden.

Shintaro Miyazaki is a Junior Professor (Tenure Track) of Digital Media and Computation, Department of Musicology and Media Studies, Humboldt-Universität zu Berlin, Germany.

Markus Naarttijärvi is a Professor of Law at the Department of Law, Umeå University, Sweden.

Simone Natale is an Associate Professor in Media Theory and History at the University of Turin, Italy, and an Editor of *Media, Culture & Society*.

Axel Nyström is a Doctoral Student at the Division of Occupational and Environmental Medicine, Lund University, Sweden.

Carl Öhman is an Associate Senior Lecturer at the Department of Government, Uppsala University, Sweden.

Emily Öhman is an Assistant Professor in Digital Humanities at Waseda University, Japan.

Andreas Öjehag-Pettersson is a Senior Lecturer in Political Science at Karlstad University, Sweden.

Chinasa T. Okolo is a PhD Candidate in the Department of Computer Science at Cornell University, USA.

Will Orr is a PhD Student at the Annenberg School for Communication at the University of Southern California, USA, and a Visiting Fellow at the School of Regulation and Global Governance (RegNet) at the Australian National University.

Juho Pääkkönen is a Doctoral Researcher in the Doctoral Programme in Social Sciences, University of Helsinki, Finland, and Project Coordinator at the Helsinki Institute for Social Sciences and Humanities.

Guy Paltieli is a Lecturer at the Cyber, Politics and Government Program at Tel Aviv University, Israel.

Orestis Papakyriakopoulos is Research Scientist in AI Ethics at Sony AI, Switzerland.

Jaana Parviainen is a Senior Researcher at the Faculty of Social Sciences, Tampere University, Finland.

Maayan Perel is an Assistant Professor at the Netanya Academic College, School of Law, Israel.

Arun Teja Polcumpally is a Doctoral Fellow at Jindal School of International Affairs, O. P. Jindal Global University, India.

Ana Pop Stefanija is a Doctoral Researcher at imec-SMIT, Vrije Universiteit Brussel, Belgium.

Lina Rahm is an Assistant Professor in the History of Media and Environment with specialisation in Artificial Intelligence and Autonomous Systems, KTH, Stockholm.

Tyler Reigeluth is Assistant Professor of Philosophy at the ETHICS Lab, Catholic University of Lille, France.

Bo Reimer is Professor of Media and Communication Studies at The School of Arts and Communication, Malmö University, Sweden.

Anais Resseguier is a philosopher and Research Manager in the Ethics, Human Rights and Emerging Technologies cluster, Trilateral Research, Ireland.

Vanessa Richter is a PhD Candidate at the Amsterdam School of Cultural Analysis at the University of Amsterdam, Netherlands, and a Research Assistant at the Centre for Media, Communication and Information Research (ZeMKI) at the University of Bremen, Germany.

Jonathan Roberge is Full Professor at the Institut National de la Recherche Scientifique (INRS) in Montreal, Canada.

Ben Roberts is a Senior Lecturer in Digital Humanities at the University of Sussex and co-Director of Sussex Humanities Lab.

Malin Rönnblom is Professor of Political Science at Karlstad University.

Rinat B. Rosenberg-Kima is an Assistant Professor and the head of the Mindful Learning Technologies Lab at the Faculty of Education in Science and Technology, Technion – Israel Institute of Technology.

Carrie B. Sanders is Professor of Criminology in the Department of Criminology at Wilfrid Laurier University, Canada.

Nitin Sawhney is Professor of Practice in the Department of Computer Science at Aalto University, Finland.

Mike S. Schäfer is Professor of Science Communication at the Department of Communication and Media Research at the University of Zurich, Switzerland.

Daniel S. Schiff is an Assistant Professor in Technology Policy at Purdue University, Indiana, USA, and Responsible AI Lead at JP Morgan Chase & Co.

Robyn Schimmer is a Postdoc Researcher at the Department of Psychology at Umeå University, Sweden.

Ralph Schroeder is Professor of Social Science of the Internet at the Oxford Internet Institute at the University of Oxford, UK.

Kasia Söderlund is a PhD Candidate at the Department of Technology and Society, the Faculty of Engineering, Lund University, Sweden.

James Steinhoff is an Assistant Professor in the School of Information and Communication Studies, University College Dublin, Ireland.

Andreas Stenling is an Associate Professor at the Department of Psychology, Umeå University, Sweden.

Michael Strange is Reader in International Relations, Department of Global Political Studies, Malmö University, Sweden. He coordinates a research group focused on democracy and healthcare, including the everyday politics of AI, and has been invited by Chatham House as an expert on participatory healthcare and AI.

Andreas Sudmann is Adjunct Professor of Media Studies at Bochum University, Germany. Furthermore, he is the scientific coordinator and principal investigator of the research group "How is artificial intelligence changing science? Research in the era of learning algorithms", funded by the VW Foundation.

Annika M. Svensson is an MD, PhD, MA and a consultant at Tournier Medical, Malmö, Sweden.

Susanne Tafvelin is an Associate Professor at the Department of Psychology, Umeå University, Sweden.

Zeerak Talat is an independent researcher.

Scott Timcke is a Senior Research Associate at Research ICT Africa, Cape Town, South Africa.

Vicenç Torra is Professor at the Department of Computing Science, Umeå University, Sweden.

Andrea Aler Tubella is a Senior Research Engineer at the Department of Computing Science, Umeå University, Sweden.

Jason Tucker is Assistant Professor at the Department of Global Political Studies, Malmö University, Sweden.

Katja Valaskivi is Professor in Religious Studies and Media Research at Helsinki Institute for Social Sciences and Humanities (HSSH), University of Helsinki, Finland.

Pieter Verdegem is Reader in Technology and Society, Westminster School of Media and Communication and member of CAMRI, University of Westminster, UK.

Mario Verdicchio is a researcher at the University of Bergamo, Italy, and a member of the Berlin Ethics Lab, Technische Universität Berlin, Germany.

Rosalie A. Waelen is a Doctoral Researcher in applied ethics at the University of Twente, Netherlands.

Ina Weber is a Doctoral Researcher at the Department of Communication Studies at the University of Antwerp, Belgium.

Mikael Wiberg is Professor of Informatics at Umeå University, Sweden.

Tanja Wiehn is a postdoc at the University of Copenhagen, Denmark.

Harry Yaojun Yan is a PhD Candidate in the National Science Foundation-Interdisciplinary Trainee (NSF-NRT) program, dual-majoring in Media Arts & Sciences at the Media School and Complex Networks & Systems (CNS) at Luddy School of Informatics, Computing, and Engineering, at Indiana University Bloomington, USA.

Kai-Cheng Yang is a PhD Candidate in Informatics at the Luddy School of Informatics, Computing, and Engineering at Indiana University Bloomington, USA.

Mike Zajko is an Assistant Professor at the Department of History and Sociology, University of British Columbia, Okanagan.

Jing Zeng is an Assistant Professor at the Department of Media and Culture Studies, Utrecht University, Netherlands.

Sandy Zook, Ph.D., is an assistant professor of public and nonprofit management in the School of Public Affairs at the University of Colorado Denver. Her research focuses on domestic and international perspectives of nonprofit governance, civil society development, and nonprofit/ NGO financial management and governance.

1. Introducing critical studies of artificial intelligence

Simon Lindgren

CRITICAL STUDIES OF AI: BEYOND AI ETHICS AND FAIRNESS

As artificial intelligence (AI) seeps into ever more areas of society and culture, critical perspectives of the technology are more urgent than ever before. While the AI industry is engaged in a race to develop models and tools better, faster, stronger, and more profitable, work that engages with AI ethics, AI fairness, AI transparency, AI auditing, and so on has become an industry in itself. Both inside and outside of academia, there is a lively and ongoing debate about the uses of AI and its future. Undoubtedly, scholarship interested in making AI ethical and responsible is thriving (Liu & Zheng, 2022; Vieweg, 2021). It can be argued, however, that much of the work that is done along these lines is not critical enough.

A substantial share of research on AI ethics is conducted in close proximity to the technological and economic processes where AI is produced. This closeness may have benefits, but a major downside is that perspectives that may be deemed "too critical" end up playing second fiddle to the heavy economic and technological drives to push forward no matter the consequences. In some literature, it is argued that the reason why we must make AI ethical is that "unfair decisions made by the systems [are] ultimately impacting the reputation of the product" and that "AI done correctly [...] is not just good for the user; it is good business too" (Agarwal & Mishra, 2021, p. 3).

This handbook offers a broad orientation in research that largely positions itself further away from the technical doing of AI. There is immense value in scholars being able to critique AI from the outside and standing on a platform that is independent of the needs of big business. As of today, clients are demanding that AI corporations ensure that their products are safe, and as a result, corporations hire responsible AI teams, which often include senior academics, and push for quick approval of the product. Tech journalist Melissa Heikkilä (2022) reports about how those academics often fall victim to burnout:

> Tech companies such as Meta have been forced by courts to offer compensation and extra mental-health support for employees such as content moderators, who often have to sift through graphic and violent content that can be traumatizing. But teams who work on responsible AI are often left to fend for themselves, [...] even though the work can be just as psychologically draining as content moderation. Ultimately, this can leave people in these teams feeling undervalued, which can affect their mental health and lead to burnout.

Other reports tell of inadequate AI audits that tend to cover up discrimination and other problems with AI systems that may be badly designed and carelessly implemented. Such audits are worthless and may create a structure of permission that offers excuses for the very same harms that were supposed to be mitigated in the first place (Goodman & Trehu, 2022). Ethical guidelines for AI—for example, those developed by the European Commission—have been criticized for being fuzzy and "half-arsed" (Davies, 2019) Philosopher Thomas Metzinger (2019) has called such work "conceptual nonsense" and explains that:

> Industry organizes and cultivates ethical debates to buy time—to distract the public and to prevent or at least delay effective regulation and policy-making. Politicians also like to set up ethics committees because it gives them a course of action when, given the complexity of the issues, they simply don't know what to do—and that's only human. At the same time, however, industry is building one "ethics washing machine" after another. [...] Because industry acts more quickly and efficiently than politics or the academic sector, there is a risk that, as with "Fake News", we will now also have a problem with fake ethics, including lots of conceptual smoke screens and mirrors, highly paid industrial philosophers, [and] self-invented quality seals [... I]t is high time that universities and civil society recapture the process and take the self-organized discussion out of the hands of industry. (Metzinger, 2019)

As argued by Virginia Dignum (2021), there can never be any "complete AI fairness". AI is not some magic, superhuman, system that we can tweak to some final and optimal setting. Rather, the results and societal consequences produced by AI are "fundamentally constrained by the convictions and expectations of those that build, manage, deploy and use it" (Dignum 2021, p. 1). What is seen as fair by some people may not be perceived to be fair by others, and the complex networked connections among people and technology in society mean that what ensures fairness for one group may produce unfairness for others. As algorithms are today mostly designed to be as accurate and efficient as possible, Dignum argues, we must take other criteria into account just as much—or even more. To achieve this, we need critical AI scholarship that is rooted in the humanities and the social sciences, carried out by scholars that have no stakes in the AI industry. In other words, critical studies of AI are significantly broader, and much deeper-cutting than the tech-driven fields where the lighter forms of critique that are carried out largely aim to build acceptance for, and legitimize, the rapidly implemented tools. This handbook, then, wants to emphasize the need of approaching AI from the perspective of cultural and social critique. As argued by Bassett and Roberts in their contribution to this handbook:

> Critical studies of artificial intelligence pick up where normative models of "responsible AI" end. The latter seeks to build acceptance for AI decision making by incorporating a form of "best practice" into AI techniques and machine learning models to ensure "equity" of some order (racial, gender, less often sexuality or disability, hardly ever class) through the avoidance of bias and [through] "transparency" in their operation. Responsible AI is, then, primarily a technical solution to technosocial problems. [...] As such, it fails to address the concerns about artificial intelligence that are bound up with wider social challenges, debates and anxieties, anxieties that are not simply technical in nature.

Sociologist Ben Agger (2013) explained that a critical social perspective rests on seven foundations. First, it opposes positivism. This means that it emphasizes that the world—and, by extension, also AI—is an active *social construction*, that necessarily makes certain assumptions about our reality. This means, again, that it is impossible for AI to be completely value free. The opposition to the positivist stance also means that AI interaction with society cannot be understood according to any simple or universal "natural" laws. Rather, society is not only affected by a range of historical and contextual factors—it is also structured according to power relations by which technology that is beneficial for some may be perilous for others. Such relations of power must be the object of study for critical studies of AI. Importantly, however, as Agger also points out, the opposition toward positivism does not mean that critical research on AI should be impressionistic or relativistic. Its task, rather, is to develop a sharp, valid, and theoretically grounded, critique of AI's social and cultural consequences.

Second, Agger posits, critical social theories are focused not on mere description, but on possibly addressing social problems to contribute to mitigating them. Critical analysis is characterized by its—direct or indirect—adherence to Max Horkheimer's (1972, p. 246) description of critical theory as "radically analyzing present social conditions", providing a "critique of the economy" (broadly conceived), and to put the finger on processes of power so that the research can be a "liberating [...] influence" with an emancipatory agenda "to create a world which satisfies the needs and powers" of humans. In line with this, Bohman et al. (2021) explain that:

> Because such theories aim to explain and transform all the circumstances that enslave human beings, many "critical theories" in the broader sense have been developed. They have emerged in connection with the many social movements that identify varied dimensions of the domination of human beings in modern societies. In both the broad and the narrow senses, however, a critical theory provides the descriptive and normative bases for social inquiry aimed at decreasing domination and increasing freedom in all their forms.

Agger (2006, p. 5) writes that analyses that draw on critical social theory make a distinction between the past and the present, with a focus on "domination, exploitation, and oppression, and a possible future rid of these phenomena". For AI studies then, the point of the critical perspective is to raise consciousness about negative consequences in terms of, for example, distortions, exploitation, discrimination, and other problems or injustices—and also to "demonstrate the possibility of a qualitatively different future society". This means, to varying degrees, that critical analysis is political:

> [It] is political in the sense that it participates in bringing about social change. Yet it is not simply or mechanically agitational: It steps back from society in order to appraise it and then offers its insights and analyses to people. (Agger, 2006, p. 5)

Third, critical analysis of AI will focus on the connection between the development and implementation of AI on the one hand, and social structures—the broader context of politics, economics, culture, discourse, race, gender, and so on. And fourth, it thus takes an interest in the role of ideology for AI. On the one hand, AI is indeed driven by ideology in the sense that certain ideas, which are connected to power relations in society, become construed as given truths and objectives of AI, even though many other truths and objectives might be possible (Lindgren, 2023). There is a constant repetition of this ideology in marketing talk, hyped conferences, tech evangelism, business manifestos, and overblown media coverage. AI certainly runs on a potent concoction of overlapping sets of ideas. Those ideas are defined in different terms by different thinkers, where some key notions include Californian ideology, libertarianism, technocracy, computational thinking, and innovationism (see Lindgren, 2023).

In AI ideology, we will often find relentless technological optimism, the belief that technological progress is an autonomous force and can save us all, and the tendency to delegate key decisions to opaque algorithms. One of the dangers of ideology is that once dominant views and priorities have been established, they can become naturalized, and therefore, appear legitimate and unquestionable. Nevertheless, we always have a choice. And that choice can be informed by critical analysis that dares ask critical questions about social and political repercussions of the machinery of innovation, progress, control, and efficiency. Agger's fifth point about critical analysis is that it avoids determinism. The sixth point is that the knowledge about structural conditions—produced through critical theoretical analysis—can help people transform society for the better. Finally, his seventh point is that critical analysis will help those who stand to lose out on—in our case—social implications of AI development and implementation, become more aware of this. Critical analysis rests on the view that social and technological progress must be achieved without sacrificing people's liberties.

Another critical part of AI research is that it must by necessity be multidisciplinary (Dignum, 2020). While there may still exist a clear polarization of perspectives in many respects, there is also in fact an increased openness and overlap between ethical/responsible AI scholarship and sociopolitically informed critical perspectives. In general, there is a growing interest in analyzing our age of AI in ways that are more clearly rooted in longstanding critical theories of power, politics, and technology, and which allow for a more far-reaching challenge of downsides and injustices related to AI, datafication, and automation (Dignum, 2022; Gunkel, 2012; Noble, 2018; O'Neil, 2016; Pasquale, 2020; Waelen, 2022).

But at the same time, AI is also big business, and there are limits to the openness. The rationale behind this handbook is that we need to push analyses of AI much further into critical territory than what is the case today. The handbook wants to contribute to an ongoing discussion about what critical studies of AI can entail—what questions it may pose, and what concepts it can offer to address them.

AI AND CRITICAL THEORY: CONCEPTUAL DISCUSSIONS

The first section of the handbook includes several chapters that all engage with conceptual issues that relate to how AI can be critically approached through scholarly analysis. Throughout these chapters, some of the key concepts are politics, ideology, governance, antagonism, epistemology, knowledge, habitus, intimacy, (de)coloniality, pragmatism, digital humanism, technological solutionism, and geopolitics.

In their chapter, Fenwick McKelvey and Jonathan Roberge argue that there is an increasing overlap between the study of AI and that of governmentality. They compare supporting discourses around two AI governance icons—Elon Musk and Kevin Kelly—and show how the concepts of dispositifs and doctrines can clarify how AI governmentality works, as well as depoliticizes itself. Peter Bloom's chapter offers a critical reframing of the issue of how AI and humans relate to one another, particularly highlighting the ways in which AI reproduces the dominant capitalist ideology in society. The chapter also addresses the issue of "trans-human relations" from a different direction by focusing on their more radical and counter-hegemonic potential. Bloom argues for the need of promoting forms of "counter-hegemonic intelligence" and "antagonistic machines".

Anna Jobin and Christian Katzenbach discuss, in their contribution, how AI takes shape as an important sociotechnical institution in present-day society. Their argument is that AI must be seen as not merely technologically driven, but that it relies just as much on other drivers such as economy, politics, and discourse. It is at the intersection of technological research, media discourse, and regulatory governance that AI comes into being as a powerful sociotechnical entity. Robert Holton's chapter makes the case that AI must be assessed critically by confronting it with the ever-present element of uncertainty in human affairs. Knowledge in sociotechnical systems must be addressed with a deep-cutting focus on epistemological weaknesses and limitations as regards the claims that are presently being made about AI progress. AI is still largely unable to respond to uncertainty in social life and institutions, which means that its uncritical application may create false visions of certainty where none exists.

Simona Chiodo's chapter problematizes the issue of trading human autonomy for technological automation. The chapter poses the question of why we use the term "autonomy" to describe technologies, particularly those based on AI, when this word has traditionally been used to describe the core of human identity in Western philosophy. Chiodo explores the possible reasons for this shift and how it changes our understanding of human identity in relation to technology. The focus on understandings of AI continues in the chapter by Caroline Bassett and Ben Roberts. They introduce the notion of "automation anxiety" and analyze it as a recurring phenomenon during the post-war era. The authors examine historical debates around automation, cybernetics, and the future of work to make the point that a critical history of automation anxiety can aid in understanding and, importantly, critiquing some of the claims currently made about the societal challenges offered up by AI.

The contribution by Eran Fisher stays with the issue of critical knowledge. The discussion here revolves around algorithmic decision-making systems and sees them as epistemic devices that contribute to processes of meaning-making around the self and the world. Fisher goes on, drawing on the critical theory of Habermas, to pose the question of what it actually means for AI to "know". What are the social and political repercussions of algorithms' modes of knowing and how do we view them? Turning from Habermas to Bourdieu, Stefka Hristova's chapter repurposes the sociological notion of "habitus" for the critical analysis of AI. This contribution problematizes the cultural and political effects of predictive algorithm assumptions about people's habitual behavior. Our embodied habitus is the product of cultural norms and social identity, which gets far-reaching consequences in the shape of naturalizing ideology, for example, in such cases where algorithms are used in job recruitment to decide "who we are" or who we should be allowed to be.

Another example of how AI's entanglement with our, even most intimate, lives can be critically analyzed is given in Tanja Wiehn's chapter. The chapter looks at new relationships developing between people and algorithmic systems. These involve technology, society, and economics, all interrelated to AI. Wiehn uses the concept of intimacy to understand how AI-driven relationships in digital spaces can perpetuate power dynamics. The chapter uses the example of chat labor on the platform OnlyFans to illustrate these concepts and aims to contribute to a trend in studying algorithms through power relations using interdisciplinary research.

We turn to the concepts of "coloniality" and "decoloniality" in Abeba Birhane and Zeerak Talat's chapter. Their focus is on how, recently, some scholars have suggested that machine learning perpetuates colonial thought patterns and that decolonization should be considered in future machine learning development. Birhane and Talat discuss the objectives of machine learning and decolonization and argue that they are conflicting. Machine learning is focused on abstraction and pattern recognition, while decolonization is focused on understanding and addressing historical marginalization. However, the tension between these goals can be reconciled by a critical rethinking of machine learning.

The theoretical perspective of pragmatism, drawing on philosopher John Dewey, sits at the center of Johnathan Flowers' chapter. Flowers introduces Dewey's view that technology and society are closely intertwined and mutually shape one another. The chapter goes on to apply

Dewey's theory of culture and technology to algorithmic platforms to demonstrate the importance of examining not just the platforms themselves, but also the data they use, as part of culture, to better comprehend the indirect and direct effects of their use and how they shape our experiences. Flowers argues that Dewey's philosophy highlights the need to consider the cultural context in which AI platforms are deployed to fully understand their impact on society. Yet another addition to the critical analytical framework provided throughout this part of the handbook comes from the field of digital humanism. As discussed in Wolfgang Hofkirchner and Jörg Kreowski's chapter on digital humanism and AI, there is much to gain from applying critical humanistic thinking to AI development and use. We need technologies that respect the common good, and given the current existential threats to humanity, digital humanism helps us recognize that the current logic of scientific and technological development needs to be reevaluated, as the current ways of interacting with nature and social relationships have proven problematic. We must, the authors argue, reset our understanding of cognition, communication, and cooperation to focus more strongly on conviviality. With the right "digital priorities", AI may be an essential tool for achieving such transformations.

In line with the discussion of how AI should be approached, and what perspectives should be prioritized, my own chapter co-authored with Virginia Dignum problematizes the fact that there currently seems to be a widespread assumption that the adoption of AI is inevitable and that its negative effects are easily managed. However, this view is misguided. The chapter challenges the idea that AI can be a one-size-fits-all solution for diverse and complex social issues such as unfair credit checks, racism, and sexism. We argue that AI's social issues should not be dealt with solely from a technological perspective, but rather, they require a multidisciplinary approach that combines technological expertise with critical social science and humanities analysis.

Moving the conceptual discussion in the direction of memory studies, Samuel Merrill's chapter provides a conceptual exploration of social memory in relation to AI. Merrill sees AI systems as memory-enhancing technologies and looks at how AI researchers and developers have primarily viewed memory in terms of storage. The chapter proposes a different perspective that allows for a more comprehensive and hybrid understanding of social memory in the age of AI. The chapter draws on the work of Donna J. Haraway and Bernard Stiegler to introduce the concepts of "cyborgian remembrance" and "AI mnemotechnics" to help understand the complex relationship between AI and social memory by shifting the focus away from human memory to allow for a more critical analysis of challenges and risks. Finally, in the concluding chapter of this section of the handbook, Arun Teja Polcumpally illustrates how we can make sense of AI-influenced geopolitics with the help of theories from the field of science, technology, and society studies (STS). The author shows how STS can be combined with analytical approaches from the area of international relations research to provide a deeper understanding of how AI can influence geopolitics.

AI IMAGINARIES AND DISCOURSES

AI is currently at the center of a wide range of social and political imaginings, from utopian to dystopian. These imaginings often focus on ideas of progress, profitability, improvement of the world, precision, and rationality. There are also conflicting ideas about robot apocalypses and disillusionment. Through its various forms, AI shapes our reality. The way we imagine AI affects what kinds of future lives and societies are considered possible. Amanda Lagerkvist (2020, p. 16) states that "In the present age, AI emerges as both a medium for and a message about (or even from) the future, eclipsing all other possible prospects".

The second section of the handbook deals with issues surrounding the social and symbolic construction of AI and how it relates to ideology. AI is driven by a set of ideas, often connected to power relations in society, that tend to be presented as objective truths and goals. The ideas often involve a belief in the potential of technology to save us all, and the tendency to hand over key decisions to opaque machinic processes. The danger is that these views and priorities are seen as unquestionable. Instead, there should be a focus on democratized decision-making and critical examination of the societal impact of AI.

Amanda Lagerkvist and Bo Reimer argue, in their chapter, that AI should be understood not only as a technology but also as a narrative about the potential future. This narrative is present in various industries, policies, and academic discussions, and often divides into binary perspectives of potential and risk, enhancement and replacement. They propose re-evaluating these binaries by considering AI as a form of anticipatory media that can allow for the unexpected, the unpredictable, and the uncanny. The authors draw on the philosophies of Jaspers, Derrida, and Bloch to explore ways to reimagine a more diverse and dynamic vision of AI's future in an urgent and productive way. The following chapter by Vanessa Richter, Christian Katzenbach, and Mike Schäfer also focuses on how the ways in which society imagines and perceives AI greatly influences its integration and trajectory. They propose using the concept of sociotechnical imaginaries to analyze the characteristics and impact of this process. They assert that AI is currently in a formative phase, where it is important to understand the role of these imaginaries in shaping economic, research, and political agendas, and which stakeholders are promoting them.

In the following contribution, Nitin Sawhney and Kaisla Kajava discuss and analyze the "language of algorithms" in AI Watch reports and stakeholder responses to the proposed AI Act in the European Union. Their analysis of language reveals how society conceptualizes and attributes agency to AI systems. The authors conclude that by critically examining AI discourses, it is possible to see how language shapes attitudes, influences practices and policies, and shapes future imaginaries around AI. Focusing further on the mythological aspects of AI, Andrea Ballatore and Simone Natale write of the historical fascination with, and debates around, creating a machine that can think like a human. Despite repeated failures and a resurgence of interest, some computer scientists, scientists, and philosophers argue that creating an AI that is equivalent or superior to human intelligence is impossible, while others continue to hold out hope for its achievement. In their chapter, these authors explore the issue of technological failure in the context of AI and examine how the debate surrounding its feasibility has persisted for decades, perpetuating the myth of the thinking machine.

Mario Verdicchio's contribution continues the exploration of definitional processes surrounding AI. Verdicchio's focus is on the metaphor of drawing lines: lines to define, lines to connect and compare, lines to separate, and lines to chart a path toward the future. In relation to AI, these lines are often blurred, as without a clear definition of intelligence, AI itself is difficult to define. Furthermore, the future of AI is often portrayed in science fiction scenarios with little connection to reality. AI's relationship to science fiction is discussed further in Miroslav Kotásek's contribution. Kotásek argues that science fiction has the potential to critically examine technology, particularly forms of artificiality such as A-life, artificial intelligence, eugenics, and gene manipulation. He suggests that science fiction can provide a valuable perspective on the future as it is openly fictional in contrast to discourses in areas such as economy, politics, and artificial intelligence. The chapter also explores the potential of artificial intelligence to change our understanding of the future and humanity, focusing on the subgenre of cyberpunk fiction.

Ching-Hua Chuan's contribution to this handbook has a particular focus on the role of news media in understandings of AI. The chapter shows how AI is portrayed and framed in news articles has a significant impact on public debates surrounding this technology. Chuan provides an in-depth review of existing studies on AI news framing to reveal the key issues, perspectives, and social forces that shape public opinion on AI. Staying with this topic, Saba Rebecca Brause, Jing Zeng, Mike Schäfer, and Christian Katzenbach, review more broadly the emerging field of research on media representations of AI, including its characteristics and findings. This chapter examines the aspects of AI that are studied, the countries and media that are focused on, and the methodologies that are used. Additionally, it identifies key findings and outlines directions for future research. The final chapter in this section of the handbook—Lina Rahm's contribution on educational imaginaries of AI—examines how problematizations and epistemic injustice in international educational and technological policies affect the understanding of what should be learned, and why, when it comes to AI.

THE POLITICAL ECONOMY OF AI: DATAFICATION AND SURVEILLANCE

Critical analyses of AI must consider the social, political, and economic contexts in which the technology is embedded, as well as the impact it has on these contexts. It is crucial to understand that technology is always entangled with political economy and should therefore never be considered as an autonomous or external force to society. Focusing on the political economy of AI, this section of the handbook takes an interest in how AI and automation as technologies are related—in their implementation and consequences—to societal hierarchies of domination and exploitation, particularly in the sphere of capital and labor. The introductory chapter by Pieter Verdegem discusses how using the perspective of critical political economy is an effective way to examine the hype around AI, as it provides a framework to understand how power and social inequalities are intertwined with AI's development and use. The chapter examines how AI's technical aspects, industrial structures, and social practices are shaped by power. The perspective of critical political economy allows for the analysis of both economic power, such as the concentration of AI industries and the tendency toward monopolization, and symbolic power, which refers to the influence of dominant ideas about the desired and necessary types of AI. The ensuing chapter by James Steinhoff keeps with the critical political economy perspective and gives an overview of the contemporary AI industry and its place within capitalism. It covers the scope of the AI industry, the products it produces, the labor that creates them, and one of the industry's unique features: its emphasis on automating automation.

Scott Timcke's contribution continues along similar lines of argument, showing how the development of AI is closely tied to the specific historical context of expansive global capitalism. Understanding this relationship can provide a counterpoint to futurist claims about AI's ability to free people from labor, especially when such claims are made without consideration of social class or the influence of capitalist reasoning on the development of AI. Timcke discusses how the work of critical theorists Lukács and Marcuse can be useful for scholars and researchers in the area of critical AI studies. In the same vein, Guy Paltieli examines how AI poses challenges to democratic politics and political theory. It is argued, in his chapter, that some current political theory concepts are not sufficient to grasp the risks that AI poses to democracy. The chapter focuses on two main challenges: the erosion of democratic politics caused by AI systems and the emergence of passive forms of political participation. To address these challenges, the chapter proposes the idea of a "liberal data republic" that would give citizens more control over AI.

The chapter by Mike Zajko looks more specifically at how AI and algorithmic decision-making may contribute to the perpetuation of social inequality. It also discusses the significance of surveillance studies in this context. Algorithms based on machine learning replicate existing inequalities found in their training data, whether these are inherent social inequalities or differences in visibility, where certain individuals are more likely to be targeted or excluded from data collection. Surveillance studies concentrate on the collection and extraction of data for governance purposes and how this reinforces power relations. The use of AI to govern inequality is not a departure from the past, but a continuation of longstanding bureaucratic, statistical, and algorithmic processes that have been used to monitor and manage people living in poverty. The issue of surveillance is also at the forefront of the chapter by Stine Lomborg, Rasmus Helles, and Signe Sophus Lai. Their contribution focuses on a key aspect of current AI advancements, namely digital tracking, which enables the collection and modeling of vast amounts of data in digital systems. The authors also connect digital tracking to the underlying material infrastructure of digital communication systems and examine how big tech companies' power has grown with their ability to track users. The chapter introduces the concept of infrastructural power, which is defined as the ability to exert control over the underlying infrastructure of an ecosystem.

This handbook section continues with a chapter by Michael Strange and Jason Tucker, who write on AI and the everyday political economy of global health. The focus is on the significantly increased use of AI in healthcare. Strange and Tucker argue that to fully understand the potential of AI health technologies, it is crucial to critically examine the global political economy that enables their development. It is important to view this political economy as embedded in the everyday relationships in which healthcare operates. This section of the handbook concludes with Chinasa Okolo's chapter, which widens the scope of the discussion, and problematizes the fact that those who are most economically powerful are best positioned to benefit from the spread of AI systems. To address global inequality, Western tech companies have taken steps to involve more diverse groups in the development and use of AI, such as hiring local talent and setting up data centers and laboratories in Africa, Asia, and South America. However, given that wealth tends to perpetuate itself and that top-down AI solutions often lack local knowledge, Okolo argues that more emphasis should be placed on redistributing power, rather than just including underrepresented groups.

AI TRANSPARENCY, ETHICS AND REGULATION

Scholars in critical AI studies may tend to see fields such as "ethical AI" and "responsible AI" as not being critical enough. But an important challenge to be faced has to do with how critical theory can benefit AI ethics instead of merely criticizing it. In the first chapter of this section of the handbook, Rosalie Waelen outlines the contours of a critical approach to AI ethics. Waelen sees similarities between critical theory's aim to help overcome social injustices on the one hand, and AI ethics' objective to identify and mitigate the normative implications of AI technologies. Given these similarities, Waelen argues for a critical approach to analyzing AI's ethical, social, and political repercussions. This approach requires an understanding of the power to identify and understand AI's impact, and an understanding of autonomy to normatively evaluate and address identified issues in the pursuit of emancipation. Anaïs Resseguier continues along the same lines in the subsequent chapter. The author critiques mainstream AI ethics for being ineffective and not considering power relations and structures of inequality. The essay advocates for a situated ethics, which emphasizes the need to implement ethics within institutional frameworks, such as research ethics processes, with mechanisms to ensure compliance.

In the following chapter, Ashlin Lee, Will Orr, Walter Johnson, Jenna Imad Harb, and Kathryn Henne examine the current state of AI regulation. They note how both AI and its regulation are fragmented and divided. They draw on the concept of "repair work" and argue that these fractures, while indicating suboptimal regulation, also provide new opportunities to reflect on the underlying dynamics of AI and its regulation in context. Continuing the critical discussion of AI regulation, Manuel Carabantes' chapter emphasizes the need for AI to be transparent. However, Carabantes shows with the help of critical theory that AI, instead of being transparent, is obscured by several layers of opacity. Carl Öhman's chapter discusses how the European Union's data protection law is praised for fighting algorithmic discrimination and exploitation but criticized for its lack of clarity, and for not addressing vulnerable populations. The author examines the GDPR's inner contradictions and power imbalances and critiques the law's individualist privacy ideology, the increased work burden on certain sectors, and the effects on working-class organizational power.

The ensuing contribution has been written by Stefan Larsson, Kashyap Haresamudram, Charlotte Högberg, Yucong Lao, Axel Nyström, Kasia Söderlund, and Fredrik Heintz. They critically examine the conceptual vagueness of the notion of transparency in AI. They do this by focusing on four facets: explainability; the communication of AI systems' functionality; AI literacy; and the legal framework. Janina Loh's chapter discusses how the ways of thinking that are commonly found in robot ethics regarding the assignment of responsibility are fundamentally problematic, as they are structurally discriminatory and reifying or oppressive. Loh suggests that these ethical discussions shift to a more relational and less essentialist focus. The next chapter in this section, by Sukanto Bhattacharya, argues that while machine intelligence is rapidly advancing in areas such as computer vision and natural language processing, it is still lagging behind when it comes to handling complex decision problems with moral constraints. Based on evidence from paleoanthropological and neuroscience literature, it is believed that human morality evolved because of human intelligence only after a critical threshold was surpassed in the evolution of the human brain. Bhattacharya proposes that machine intelligence will also need to surpass a critical threshold before it can acquire the capabilities necessary for complex cognitive tasks that require high levels of abstraction, such as human-like morality. Factors that may lead machine intelligence to this threshold are examined, and the acceptability of machine-generated moral decisions by humans is also considered.

The chapter by Eleonore Fournier-Tombs examines the challenges of using AI from a feminist perspective within multilateral organizations, such as the United Nations. It addresses issues of discrimination and exclusion of women and proposes four pathways for regulating AI within these organizations, including creating a comprehensive policy, implementing sectoral policies, following national policies, and incorporating women's rights into each one. The research aims to provide guidance for including women's rights in internal policymaking for these organizations. Randy Connolly's contribution shifts the focus to the area of education, and issues concerning teaching social and ethical issues in relation to artificial intelligence. The chapter argues that traditional methods, such as teaching professional codes of conduct and macro-ethical theories, are not adequate in the face of the growing importance of AI in practical computing. Connolly proposes new educational strategies that consider the broader societal context of computing, including topics such as fairness, accountability, and transparency in AI, as well as the inclusion of political issues in computing education. The chapter highlights recent studies that exemplify this shift in teaching approaches. The final chapter of this section of the handbook, by Dejan Grba, is focused on how ethical issues have an impact on the creative space of contemporary AI art. After summarizing some relevant ambiguities in this field, Grba delves into a set of specific ethical issues for AI art and its future development.

AI BIAS, NORMATIVITY AND DISCRIMINATION

When stereotypes, discrimination, and exclusion appear in AI models, it is not the fault of the models themselves, but rather a reflection of the social values that are present in the society in which they were created. The models are not the original source of these values, but rather a product of them. They can then perpetuate and even obscure the social origins of these values. Sociologist of knowledge Karl Mannheim (1954), for example, explained that individuals do not create their own modes of speech and thought, but rather adopt those of their group. Similarly, today's machine learning models adopt the language and thought patterns of the society in which they exist, and through their use, play a role in shaping it. For as long as bias, normativity, and discrimination exist in society, they will exist in models that are trained on that society.

In the first chapter in this handbook section about these issues, Andreas Beinsteiner explores this further by discussing how data processing in AI involves breaking down human behavior into discrete elements. The author argues that this leads to the imposition of a formal-linguistic structure on human behavior that conforms to the rules of software design. As a result, whatever AI learns from this data is not a true depiction of social reality, but rather a reproduction of the assumptions used in the software's design.

The following chapter, by João Gonçalves and Ina Weber, looks at contexts of algorithmic moderation, alongside related perceptions and misconceptions. The authors challenge the idea that algorithmic moderation is the only way to address the large amount of harmful and hateful content on the internet. It examines the need and scope of algorithmic moderation from a normative perspective and highlights key issues to be considered in the study of algorithmic moderation, such as systemic biases in technical approaches and unequal access to AI data and knowledge. The chapter uses the example of hate speech to demonstrate these issues and compares how human and algorithmic moderators are perceived. It is intended to serve as a foundation for further research on the topic of algorithmic moderation and its effects.

In the next chapter, Kendra Albert and Maggie Delano posit that the term "bias" in AI design is inadequate for comprehending the exclusion of certain groups from algorithmic development. The authors suggest using the term "algorithmic exclusion" to better capture the way in which these systems interact with marginalized communities. Albert and Delano differentiate between direct and indirect forms of algorithmic exclusion and their relationship to "category-based erasure".

The following chapter, by Kelly Hannah-Moffat and Fernando Avila, takes an interest in ethical issues surrounding the use of AI and machine learning in criminal justice. It argues that a lack of interdisciplinary dialogue and inconsistent definitions and implementation of principles guiding these technologies in this context can lead to misunderstandings in their design and use. The authors argue that AI must be considered in relation to other bureaucratic processes and that when used in criminal justice, AI contributes to obscuring the complexity of legal concepts, ethics, and social values, perpetuating discrimination and confusing correlation with causation. In the ensuing chapter, Ana Pop Stefanija focuses on the impact of automated decision-making systems on individuals and society, with a particular emphasis on the power dynamics involved. It furthermore provides a deeper understanding of the issues at hand and explores ways to resist and challenge the dominant algorithmic epistemology.

Laila M. Brown's contribution analyses how virtual assistants can be categorized as invisible labor, meaning that they are marginalized, unacknowledged, and undervalued. The author also notes that these assistants are often feminized and lack diverse racial and ethnic representation, which reinforces a binary view of gender while privileging whiteness. Brown argues that the design of these AI tools neglects the ways in which gender, race, and labor intersect to perpetuate inequality. In Tyler Reigeluth's chapter, Judith Butler's theory of performativity is used as a lens through which to examine normativity in machine learning. Reigeluth argues that while traditional algorithms can be understood in terms of an automatic execution of speech acts, modern machine learning applications are instead characterized by unpredictable and complex behaviors that are better understood as perlocutionary acts. The chapter goes on to demonstrate how a performativity-based framework can provide a nuanced approach to understanding and regulating machine learning systems. Karin Danielsson, Andrea Aler Tubella, Evelina Liliequist, and Coppélie Cocq explore, in their chapter, the use of facial analysis systems in AI from a queer theoretical perspective. The authors discuss the concerns and risks related to using these systems in a binary way to categorize, measure, and make decisions based on computerized assumptions about gender and sexuality. Additionally, they examine issues of privacy, bias, and fairness in relation to facial analysis technology and suggest ways to improve it through participatory design.

Turning to issues of race, the chapter contributed by Anton Berg and Katja Valaskivi explores the role of AI in shaping contemporary perceptions of religion and race by analyzing the practices of commercial image recognition technologies. They argue that these technologies play a significant part in shaping understanding, beliefs, values, norms, and attitudes, but their impact is often hidden due to the "black box" nature of the technology. The chapter suggests that a new interdisciplinary approach, highlighting power imbalances, is needed to critically examine these phenomena in the context of AI.

Aligning with this handbook section's discussions of normativity, the chapter by Severin Engelmann and Orestis Papakyriakopoulos discusses how social media platforms use classification procedures to recommend and sell information to marketers. These procedures assume a positivist view of the social world and rely on inherently normative choices. The chapter further explores the dual-model architecture of social media platforms, which assigns users to arbitrary classes using artificial thresholds. It also highlights the normativity involved in machine learning models used for classification, including the decision of when enough data has been collected and whether it is of sufficient value. The chapter concludes by discussing the importance of transparency in social media classifications for users.

In the final chapter of this section, Salla-Maaria Laaksonen, Juho Pääkkönen, and Emily Öhman write—with a more methodological focus—on the topic of sentiment analysis, which is the use of computational methods to identify emotions and affectivity in text. The authors exemplify the ways in which affective language is translated and operationalized in the analysis process and argue that sentiment analysis is a valuable lens through which to examine the role and challenges of using computational techniques in the automated analysis of meaning-rich phenomena. It also emphasizes that sentiment analysis involves constructing measurements that are driven by researchers' judgments about what constitutes good research practice.

POLITICS AND ACTIVISM IN AI

The next section of the handbook deals with issues of politics and activism and AI. It starts off with a chapter by Niva Elkin-Koren and Maayan Perel, in which they discuss how, when AI systems are used more frequently to control the digital public sphere, their smooth operation can make it harder for democracy to work properly. In a democratic system, it is important that there is debate and discussion about different ideas and opinions. However, AI systems that make decisions based on probability and optimization may not allow for this kind of discussion and debate. The authors argue that it is important for public policy to include ways to make sure that AI systems are designed in a way that supports democracy and allows for open discussion and debate. The following chapter, by Andrew McStay and Vian Bakir, examines the use of technologies that mimic cognitive empathy in organizations and their consequences. Systems like these are already being used in various contexts, but there are concerns about the use of biometric technologies that monitor bodies and their expressions. The chapter discusses critical approaches to evaluating automated empathy, focusing on issues of mental integrity and unnatural mediation.

Kalle Eriksson's chapter moves the focus over to institutionalized politics and analyses the ways in which the effects of AI and automation technologies on society, politics, and the economy depend on the policies in place. Eriksson argues that policymakers have a crucial role in shaping the future of automation. Empirically, the author shows that while different actors describe the topic of automation as uncontroversial, their understandings of the issue are clearly informed by fundamentally different views on the proper role of the state as well as the desirability of recent and expected restructurings of the labor market in the wake of technological developments. By highlighting these differences, Eriksson wants to contribute to a necessary politicization of the automation debate.

Proposing the notion of "en-countering" AI, Shintaro Miyazaki's chapter suggests that the criticism of AI should be expanded to also include the timing, progression, execution, and rhythm of AI. After first providing a definition of the concept of "en-countering", the chapter goes on to explain and exemplify the concept of "algorhythmics". The chapter concludes by discussing the potential for "en-countering" AI as a practice of "algorhythmic" and "sympoietic" criticism. Finally, by focusing particularly on the political ecology of creative artificial intelligence, Andre Holzapel's chapter discusses the environmental and social impact of the development and use of Creative-AI within an economic system that turns artistic creation into a commodity. Interestingly, Holzapfel also uses the abbreviation "Ai", without a capitalized I, reflecting the current state of the technology as "not (yet) fulfilling the plausible minimum criteria of intelligence". The chapter first analyzes specific Creative-Ai cases and then, through a case study, critiques the environmental and social consequences of this technology. While Creative-Ai may hold artistic promise, its connection to corporate interests raises significant concerns that can only be addressed by a cross-disciplinary alliance between research and the arts.

AI AND AUTOMATION IN SOCIETY

The final section of this handbook consists of a range of chapters that use a critical lens to investigate different areas and contexts where AI is developed, used, or implemented. Taken together, these chapters offer a quite comprehensive overview of the current state of AI and automation in society, and how it can be critically scrutinized.

The first chapter by Vanja Carlsson, Malin Rönnblom, and Andreas Öjehag-Pettersson is about automated decision-making in the public sector. The authors discuss how the use of automated decision-making in the public sector affects the traditional principles of efficiency, impartiality, equality, and transparency in various ways. For instance, transparency becomes a major concern as decisions are made by algorithms rather than humans and are harder for citizens to understand. The chapter broadly examines the challenges that the implementation of automated decision-making brings to the public sector, including changes in public sector decisions, discretion of civil servants, and democratic principles and values.

In the next chapter, Harry Yaojun Yan and Kai-Cheng Yan critically examine the existing research on social bots. Malicious social bots that impersonate real users with political identities have been manipulating online discussions on important issues such as elections and pandemic prevention. In response to public concerns, social media platforms have implemented more aggressive countermeasures, forcing bots to use advanced AI technologies and more complex behaviors to avoid detection. The authors find that most research in this area has had a technological focus, and that research on human-bot interactions is lacking.

The chapter by Susanne Tafvelin, Jan Hjelte, Robyn Schimmer, Maria Forsgren, Vicenç Torra, and Andreas Stenling is focused on the implications of robots and AI in human service organizations. The authors critically analyze the implementation of these technologies in this area from the perspectives of work design, management, and ethics. They show how the implementation of robots and AI poses several challenges and risks for both employees and service recipients that must be addressed.

The focus of Mikael Wiberg's contribution is on autonomous buses. The author combines the framework of ART ("accountable, responsible, and transparent") with Marx's theory of alienation in a case analysis. Wiberg looks at the interaction between the buses, the AI that governs them, and the passengers, as one object of study—as an "autonomous materiality". By combining the three dimensions of the ART framework with Marx's four levels of alienation, the chapter identifies twelve critical aspects to consider more broadly to mitigate alienation in the shift toward autonomous materialities.

Next, a set of chapters follows that deal with critical issues around AI in law, security, criminal justice, and policing. Markus Naarttijärvi provides an exploration of critical dichotomies relating to AI and the Rule of Law. The chapter addresses concerns that AI may pose a threat to core values of the Rule of Law—limiting the arbitrary use of power; promoting legal certainty; individual autonomy; preventing despotism—when used in public power. Naarttijärvi offers four dichotomies to help analyze these concerns and provides a theoretical framework for understanding the impact of AI on the Rule of Law. Jens Hälterlein's chapter on the use of AI in domestic security practices gives an overview of the new security culture and its relation to technological fixes and AI. It also addresses some promises and expectations that tend to be associated with AI in this context and goes on to discuss a set of critical issues such as mass surveillance, discrimination, and accountability. Carrie Sanders and Janet Chan argue, in their contribution on AI in policing, that it is important for citizens to be aware of the potential benefits and risks of the technology. With a methodological focus, the authors emphasize the importance of, and challenges in, examining the relationship between expectations and imaginaries tied to the technology, and the actual use of the technology in human interactions. The chapter suggests using ethnography, specifically situational analysis, to better understand the complexities of interactions between humans and algorithms in data-driven policing.

Two subsequent chapters turn the focus over to issues of AI in healthcare. Annika Svensson and Fabrice Jotterand provide a critical review of AI in healthcare. They examine the impact of the technology on traditional healthcare, and acknowledge its benefits such as increased efficiency, cost savings, and accessibility, but also address the challenges that come with it such as potential errors and bias, loss of transparency and control, and privacy concerns. The chapter argues that the role of physicians will change significantly in this new ecosystem and that it is important to seriously consider the ethical implications of AI in healthcare and advocate for a moral framework for its use to guide global regulations. In the next chapter, Jaana Parviainen explores the strategies and innovation ecosystems used to promote robotics technologies in healthcare. Using examples from the care robotics literature and media, the author introduces two types of interventions that researchers use to promote the adoption of robots in healthcare. Such research may play a key role in shaping innovation ecosystems, and sometimes actively aims to change current care practices.

The contribution by Daniel Schiff and Rinat B. Rosenberg-Kima gives an overview of the use of AI in educational settings with a focus on challenges that must be addressed to ensure the responsible and effective use of AI in such contexts. The challenges include limited research, lack of policy coordination, resistance from educators, ethical concerns, and more. The ensuing contribution by Anna Foka, Lina Eklund, Anders Sundnes Løvlie, and Gabriele Griffin, makes a similar critical assessment of potentials and challenges when it comes to AI in the context of museums and cultural heritage organizations. The authors show that while AI has great potential for digitization, collections management, and curation, its implementation is complex. The chapter discusses specific AI and machine learning technologies such as computer vision and natural language processing, and their potential applications in heritage encounters. It also highlights the challenges in implementing these technologies, including addressing the diversity of human memory and culture in heritage collections, accessibility, and technical expertise.

Three ensuing chapters address, in different ways, the intersection of AI and academic practice. First, Anne Dippel and Andreas Sudmann delve into the various aspects of the trans-disciplinary research field of AI ethnography. The authors discuss not only the early and more recent studies that demonstrate the potential of the connection between AI and ethnography but also highlight the significance of AI ethnography to the field of critical AI studies. Second, Ralph Schroeder's chapter examines the potential for using AI to advance social theory. It reviews previous attempts to use computational methods in developing social theory and lays out the building blocks necessary for automating social theory, including systems, relations between them, and data-driven hypothesis testing. The chapter concludes by discussing the potential of this project and its limitations. While social theory can be automated, there is still a need to align data sources and integrate existing social theory into more manageable syntheses. Third, Steve Hoffman's chapter looks at AI and scientific problem choice at the nexus of industry and academia. The author discusses how the recent "Great AI Awakening" has led to a significant increase in interest and investment in AI, and that this has brought renewed attention to the issue of how industry and commercial considerations can shape the research questions that are asked and studied in academia. While industry and commercial interests may not directly control or corrupt academic research, they still have an indirect effect on the research questions that are prioritized and those that are neglected.

The next chapter highlights the urgent question of the environmental costs of AI. Benedetta Brevini problematizes the fact that while AI is heralded as the key to solving global challenges, including the climate crisis, it is not very green itself. Drawing on a political economy of communication perspective, the chapter focuses on the material aspects of AI, uncovering and debunking popular misconceptions and hype surrounding the technology. In the concluding chapter, Megan LePere-Schloop and Sandy Zook discuss the vital role of CSOs in AI governance, emphasizing their potential to diversify the tech elite and shape AI discourse, while also acknowledging the limitations of CSO power compared to Big Tech and the need for more integrated research on the intersection of AI governance and civil society.

CONCLUSION

The conceptual richness and empirical breadth of the contributions contained within the pages of this handbook bear witness to the fact that *Critical Studies of AI* is not only urgently needed, but already in the process of strongly emerging. As AI becomes increasingly developed and integrated into social and societal settings, it will be ever more important to understand not just the mere technical capabilities of this set of technologies, but also their social and political implications. This handbook therefore aims to provide a comprehensive overview of the current state of the field of critical AI studies, in terms of its key issues, concepts, and arguments.

While the thematic division of the handbook into sections gives one particular suggestion as to how the multitude of its content can be categorized, there are also several key themes that run throughout the handbook and across sections and chapters. For example, one of the key areas of concern for critical studies of AI is the potential for "bias"—or, rather, discrimination, exclusion, and oppression—in these systems. AI models are often trained on data that reflects societal power imbalances, which have repeatedly been proven to result in discriminatory outcomes. For example, facial recognition systems have been shown to have higher error rates for individuals with darker skin tones and to be better at identifying male, or binary, genders.

Another important area of interest relates to the impact of AI on privacy and surveillance. As AI systems become more powerful and are able to process and analyze vast amounts of data, there is a risk of increased surveillance and an invasion of privacy. Additionally, there are concerns about the use of AI in decision-making processes, particularly in areas such as criminal justice and healthcare, where the stakes are high. The critical scrutiny of these issues is necessary in order to ensure that the use of AI is consistent with human rights and civil liberties.

Additionally, chapters throughout the handbook address, in a variety of ways, the implications of AI on democracy and governance. As AI systems are increasingly used to make decisions and shape public policy, there is a risk of increased centralization of power and a lack of transparency. These issues must be critically analyzed in order to ensure that the use of AI is consistent with democratic principles and that there is accountability for the decisions made by these systems.

In sum, there are a number of key tenets of critical AI studies:[1]

- Technologies are *political*. AI is no exception.
- Technology is *socially shaped*, and this must be remembered also in the case of seemingly machinic AI.
- AI is the subject of evolving wars of definitions. It is an *empty signifier*.
- AI is not only a technological phenomenon. It is *co-produced* at the intersection of the social and the technical.
- Critical analysis of AI demands that we move away from technological definitions toward *sociopolitical* ones.
- *Critical theory* is vital for analyzing AI due to its focus on society, *political economy*, *ideology*, and relations of *power*.
- We must understand AI, not as a narrow technology, but as a *ubiquitous apparatus*— a complex agglomeration of different components—which is entangled with human experience.
- In today's society, AI is part of the *technological unconscious*. It is a performative infrastructure that humans draw upon in co-creating society.
- AI is *mythology*. This does not mean that it is (only) a fantasy, but that the critical analysis of AI must be interwoven with the study of how social talk and thinking in regard to it is structured, as well as the material practices that come along with talking and thinking.
- In the development and implementation of AI, some considerations and priorities are set aside to the benefit of others.
- AI is driven by *ideology*. This means that certain ideas, connected to power relations in society, become constructed as given truths and objectives of AI, even though many other truths and objectives might be possible.
- This ideology is constantly repeated and *performed* in marketing talk, hyped-up conferences, tech evangelism, business manifestos, and overblown media reporting.
- Common building blocks of AI ideology include relentless technological optimism, the view that technological progress is an autonomous force with the potential to save us all, and the tendency to hand over key decisions to opaque machinic processes.
- The danger of ideology is that once the dominant views and priorities have been established, they begin to disguise themselves as "the common sense", thereby becoming naturalized, and seemingly legitimate and unquestionable. But we always have choices.
- Instead of AI libertarianism, we need more AI communitarianism with democratized decisions for, and uses of, AI that dare ask critical questions about sociopolitical repercussions of the machinery of innovation, progress, control, and efficiency.

---

[1]   These points are directly repeated, or partly paraphrased, from Lindgren (2023).

- AI is—like other media—a bearer of ideologies, which means that AI plays a significant role in promoting and shaping ideas about what is considered true, important, and prioritized in society. Ideologies shape AI, and AI then shapes our ideologies.
- Every technology imposes on its subjects a certain set of rules and codes in the form of vocabulary, grammar, and other conventions. In this accelerated age of AI and automation, we must assume that our very perception of social reality is shaped by the logics and outputs of these technologies, just like, for example, television shaped the spirit of the second half of the 20th century.
- Computers and technology have throughout history had a general tendency to serve, rather than overthrow, existing power relations and prevailing dominant ideologies (ben-Aaron, 1985; see Birhane, 2020). AI contributes to conserving capitalism, as it offers it a new device by which to underpin the illusion of innovation, expansion, and effectivization as the one way forward (see Berman, 1992).
- AI, like other technologies, has a certain ideological power as its aura of machinic objectivity helps render understandings, that are indeed ideological, as apolitical, natural, and objective. Furthermore, AI has the power to present itself as "the Future", while there are in fact many possible futures, both with and without technology. Critical theory can help us reclaim the future.

REFERENCES

Agarwal, S., & Mishra, S. (2021). *Responsible AI: Implementing ethical and unbiased algorithms.* Springer.

Agger, B. (2013). *Critical social theories* (3rd ed.). Oxford University Press.

Bohman, J., Flynn, J., & Celikates, R. (2021). Critical theory. In E. N. Zalta (Ed.), *The Stanford encyclopedia of philosophy* (Spring 2021). Metaphysics Research Lab, Stanford University. https://plato.stanford.edu/archives/spr2021/entries/critical-theory/

Davies, J. (2019). Europe publishes stance on AI ethics, but don't expect much—Telecoms.com. *Telecoms.Com.* https://web.archive.org/web/20220726093328/https://telecoms.com/498190/europe-publishes-stance-on-ai-ethics-but-dont-expect-much/

Dignum, V. (2020). AI is multidisciplinary. *AI Matters, 5*(4), 18–21. https://doi.org/10.1145/3375637.3375644

Dignum, V. (2021). *The myth of complete AI-fairness* (arXiv:2104.12544). arXiv. https://doi.org/10.48550/arXiv.2104.12544

Dignum, V. (2022). *Relational artificial intelligence* (arXiv:2202.07446). arXiv. https://doi.org/10.48550/arXiv.2202.07446

Goodman, E., & Trehu, J. (2022). AI audit-washing and accountability. *GMF.* https://web.archive.org/web/20221127145556/https://www.gmfus.org/news/ai-audit-washing-and-accountability

Gunkel, D. J. (2012). *The machine question: Critical perspectives on AI, robots, and ethics.* MIT Press.

Heikkilä, M. (2022). Responsible AI has a burnout problem. *MIT Technology Review.* https://web.archive.org/web/20221124070144/https://www.technologyreview.com/2022/10/28/1062332/responsible-ai-has-a-burnout-problem/

Horkheimer, M. (1972). *Critical theory: Selected essays.* Continuum.

Lagerkvist, A. (2020). Digital limit situations: Anticipatory media beyond 'the new AI era'. *Journal of Digital Social Research, 2*(3), Article 3. https://doi.org/10.33621/jdsr.v2i3.55

Lindgren, S. (2023). *Critical theory of AI.* Polity.

Liu, Z., & Zheng, Y. (2022). *AI ethics and governance.* Springer.

Mannheim, K. (1954). *Ideology and Utopia: An introduction to the sociology of knowledge.* Routledge & Kegan Paul.

Metzinger, T. (2019). EU guidelines: Ethics washing made in Europe. *Der Tagesspiegel Online*. https://web.archive.org/web/20221005235038/https://www.tagesspiegel.de/politik/ethics-washing-made-in-europe-5937028.html

Noble, S. U. (2018). *Algorithms of oppression: How search engines reinforce racism*. New York University Press.

O'Neil, C. (2016). *Weapons of math destruction: How big data increases inequality and threatens democracy* (1st ed.). Crown.

Pasquale, F. (2020). *New laws of robotics: Defending human expertise in the age of AI*. Harvard University Press.

Vieweg, S. H. (2021). *AI for the good: Artificial intelligence and ethics*. Springer.

Waelen, R. (2022). Why AI ethics is a critical theory. *Philosophy & Technology, 35*(1), 9. https://doi.org/10.1007/s13347-022-00507-5

PART I

AI AND CRITICAL THEORY: CONCEPTUAL DISCUSSIONS

2. Recursive power: AI governmentality and technofutures

Fenwick McKelvey and Jonathan Roberge

INTRODUCTION

Speaking before a crowd at MIT in 2014, the normally blusterous Elon Musk appeared cautious about the future of artificial intelligence. The then-nascent technology was, according to Musk, humanity's "biggest existential risk" and his investments in AI firms sought to control risks in its development. Musk warned that "with artificial intelligence we are summoning the *demon*" [emphasis added] (quoted in Gibbs, 2014, np.). As Musk reached for the holy water, technology pundit Kevin Kelly, writing in *Wired* magazine, announced that AI was ready to be "unleashed on the world" (2014, n.p.). Kelly's view of AI was far less demonic but rather something "more like Amazon Web Services – cheap, reliable, industrial-grade digital smartness running behind everything, and almost invisible except when it blinks off" (2014, n.p.). Kelly prefigured his view of AI's arrival with the example of IBM's ill-fated Watson – a version of AI referencing the famous detective's assistant. It seemed that according to Kelly, if humanity were Sherlock Holmes, it merely needed its robotic Dr. Watson (Hale, 2011).

We begin with these two men – characters critical to the ongoing coverage of AI – to demarcate our chapter's interest in AI governmentality. Musk and Kelly's differing attitudes toward AI suggest that how power is imagined and deployed is split into distinct camps. These competing camps of technofuturism not only regulate societal imaginations of AI's potential (Hong, 2021) but also co-constitute AI as a novel logic *of* and *for* society. The split between them can be expressed as such:

1. *Musk's demon*: Musk's description of AI as an "existential risk" draws from a loose internet philosophy of longtermism (Torres, 2021). For longtermists like Musk, today's AI is key to the development of superintelligence, an event that in turn determines humanity's future. Superintelligence draws on Silicon Valley's investment in singularity but adds a certain degree of philosophical legitimacy. As well as a *symbolic* framing device for debates over AI's power, longtermism is a *practical* logic in terms of venture capital funding, as in the case of Musk funding OpenAI. Longtermism defines investment and policy work concerned with the governance of superintelligence and humanity's far-off future. Musk frequently discusses AI along with his plans for self-driving in Teslas and Mars colonization. His less optimistic peers are building clocks that run after the end of the world whereas others are doomsday prepping (Karpf, 2020; Roberts & Hogan, 2019).
2. *Kelly's Watson* exhibits a similar entanglement between the practical and the symbolic, though in a more immediate way. Compared with Musk's demon, Watson represents a "de-wilding" of AI as making the technology tame and useful now (Coleman, 2021). AI can automate many tasks precisely because human intelligence is nothing special.

Processes are automatable precisely because humans are as unreliable and simpleminded as the programs replacing them. IBM scaled back the ambitions of its Jeopardy-winning computer program to configure Watson's system as a less-ambitious model of AI governmentality, one that prioritizes business analytics and "solutions" (Lohr, 2021). This pragmatism moved Watson into practical applications, including banking, insurance, healthcare, and the like. Watson draws on natural language processing (NLP) as well as behavioral economics and psychology concerned with heuristics, biases, and human fallibility in order to offer a human-machine interaction that can be administrated and systemized.

Is Watson a prime example of an approach to weak or narrow AI (ANI) in contrast with a strong artificial general intelligence (AGI)? In what follows, we explore these two approaches that are neither identical nor incommensurable. We argue that they are not two opposite poles, but rather telling moments and loci within a larger continuum of AI governmentality. We distinguish between these approaches in a discussion of both their *doctrines* and *dispositifs*, and the interactions between them – or what we call the *recursivity* of power. We conclude by offering some suggestions for further reflections on what it means for a political technology like AI to ignore its own intrinsic politics, something that more critical and reflexive views can attempt to do. But first, we begin by discussing our approach to AI governmentality, following Foucault, as regime and "conduct of conduct" that simultaneously exists as a strategic dispositif and an always-dynamic modus operandi.

RECURSIVE POWER: ON GOVERNMENTALITY, CYBERNETICS, AND AI

There is now an established tradition in the social sciences and humanities – in STS in particular – that addresses the inherently political nature of technology. Immediately, we recall Langdon Winner's (1986) famous question "Do artifacts have politics?" as well as Kate Crawford's statement that "AI is politics by other means" (2021, p. 19). Michel Foucault's (1991) writings on the "technologies of power" are central to the tradition behind the works that address a concept now known as "governmentality."

> [Governmentality] refers to a set of institutions, procedures, analyses and reflections, calculations and tactics which permits the exercise of that form of [...] power which has the population as its principal target, political economy as its major form of knowledge, and dispositive of security as its essential technical instruments. (Foucault, 2007, p. 108)

Of course, many in-depth accounts of the concept exist (Bratich et al., 2003; Rose, 1999; Walters, 2012), but for our discussion of AI, we wish to summarize three key aspects.

First and foremost, Foucault insists that power is a mundane resource. He talks at length about dispositif as a strategic rationality and power relation leading to imprisonment and the architecture of power in the classroom and asylum. Powerful institutions that compared with Mars colonization seem mundane. In all cases, power is defined as productive and relational shaping the conduct of individuals and groups. And while it is difficult to imagine what Foucault himself would have said of today's digital world, it's nonetheless possible to apply his theorization of power to the logic of what has been called "extensive nudging"

(Yeung, 2016).[1] Rouvroy and Berns (2013) have developed such an argument in favor of a renewed understanding of "algorithmic governmentality" (though we disagree with some aspects of their analysis, as we shall see forthwith). Governmentality encourages attention to practical matters; however, the concept is not only concerned with these practical matters.

A solely strategic reading of Foucault's legacy, however, forecloses the possibility of a world still influenced by pseudo-religious "pastoral" logics. Here, we stress a second characteristic of governmentality: one does not have to choose between the practical and the symbolic. Governmentality is both the immanent nature of the here-and-now and the representation of where such a present might be situated within a broader cosmology. As Cooper rightly observes, "pastoralism continues to operate in the algorithmic register" (2020, p. 29). Foucault himself discusses the durability of mythological views that are both teleological and eschatological – the ideas of innovation and progress among them. We use the concept of the doctrine to refer to this second facet of governmentality. Pastoral power represents a battle for souls that do not need a God and/or a Church to exist – what it requires is a shepherd who sees themself as a force for the greater good. As we shall see in the next section, individuals such as Musk and movements such as longtermism see their place as shepherds of humanity and as such, they are prime examples of how doctrines complement studies of dispositifs.

The distributed and circulatory aspects of governmentality constitute its third key characteristic. Indeed, we would go as far as to say that governmentality is a cybernetic reality and that Foucault's theories are not incompatible with the ones of people such as the mathematician Wiener (1948), his political scientist advocate Karl Deutsch (1966) and others (Fourcade & Gordon, 2020; Rappin, 2018; Roberge, Senneville, et al., 2020). Everything that is governmentality or governance deals with steering in a symbolic and practical sense: its etymology comes from the Greek *Kubernêtês*, which means ship's pilot, whereas *kubernêtiké* signifies the art of both navigating and governing. In cybernetics, the terms at play are "control" and "communication," which are not too distant from dispositif and doctrine. Musk wields his doctrine of AI's future as a rhetorical device that steers capital flows and controls the technology's current deployment. What is fundamental is the movement, namely the feedback mechanism that loops the elements together. While we talk about the emergence of a recursive form of power that comes to define AI governmentality, we not only mimic the back-propagation central to machine learning but also the constant back and forth between control and communication, doctrine and dispositive.[2] IBM's Watson, too, is bound by such a logic where, for

---

[1] Or at least the impression of automation (Ananny, 2020; Gorwa et al., 2020; Myers West, 2018; Roberts, 2019). Here we acknowledge a burgeoning field of algorithmic governance (for a review, see Katzenbach & Ulbricht, 2019). Therein, we notice a growing dialogue between AI and algorithm relationships to dispositifs and Foucault's original concept.

[2] Our reading of governmentality attempts to synthesize the mythic and regulatory inquiries into artificial intelligence. On the one hand, there is a persistent interest in artificial intelligence as a digital sublime that enchants government and industry. The mythic critique of AI, however, parallels a diverse interest in AI as a means of regulation. AI governance is something of a trading zone between scholarship drawing from Deleuze's later work on control societies (Cheney-Lippold, 2017; Deseriis, 2011), a second literature following Scott Lash considering algorithms as post-hegemonic (Beer, 2016; Lash, 2007), a sociological-informed interest in algorithmic governance or algocracy (Aneesh, 2009; Yeung, 2018), and a final intersection between critical race and surveillance studies exemplified by Ruha Benjamin's (2019) formulation of a New Jim Code. What we wish to draw out, as debated in this literature, is the interpretation of governmentality as if it were a series of successions that forecloses the possibility of a world still moved by religious-like "pastoral" logics. Technical innovations do not

instance, its marketing attracts new clients who feed the model with new data for it to perform better, thus allowing for more sales. AI governmentality is recursive because it needs to fight degradation and entropy with ever more synergies, and because it needs to adapt in order to maintain and develop. Indeed, to stir is to adapt.

MUSK'S DEMON, SUPERINTELLIGENCE, AND THE RISE OF LONGTERMISM

The figure of the demon is central to the doctrine and dispositif of our first approach to AI governmentality. Elon Musk, in his remarks earlier, suggested that developing AI was akin to summoning a demon. He then continued, "In all those stories where there's the guy with the pentagram and the holy water, it's like – yeah, he's sure he can control the demon. Doesn't work out" (quoted in Gibbs, 2014, np.). Far from an offhand comment, Musk's remarks invoke the popular trope about the demon as out of control that lays the groundwork for this approach to AI governmentality (Braman, 2002; Canales, 2020; McKelvey, 2018; Roderick, 2007). Musk's demon is part of a refrain over superintelligence that frames AI governance as about humanity's long-term future.

Musk may just as likely have drawn inspiration about the threat of a superintelligent demon from Daniel Suarez's techno-thriller novels *Daemon* and its sequel *Freedom*. In them, a deranged millionaire creates a system of programs, collectively called a daemon, to continue developing after his death. The daemon's distributed intelligence disrupts society as it builds autonomous vehicles and launches its own cryptocurrency that runs on its global darknet. First written in 2006, *Daemon* inspired programmers in Silicon Valley. The foreword to the 2017 edition called the book "the secret handshake" of "technoliterati." Musk himself commented on Twitter that Saurez's *Daemon* was a "great read" just a few months before his holy water comments (Elon Musk [@elonmusk], 2014).

Musk mentioned *Daemon* in a reply to a Twitter thread after endorsing another book, *Superintelligence* by Nick Bostrom (Bostrom, 2014). Bostrom, a philosopher and Founding Director of the Oxford Future of Humanity Institute, defines the term in an early article as an

> intellect that is *much smarter* than the best human brains in practically every field, including scientific creativity, general wisdom and social skills. This definition *leaves open* how the superintelligence is implemented: it could be a digital computer, an ensemble of networked computers, cultured cortical tissue or what have you. It also *leaves open* whether the superintelligence is conscious and has subjective experiences. (Bostrom, 1998; emphasis added)

Bostrom sees superintelligence as not just an emulation of the human mind, but as an event whereby a system achieves intellectual capacity beyond the human. Superintelligence, both the book and the concept, is central to understanding the doctrinal function of AI as an eschaton event for humanity that warrants priority address by global leaders above other existential threats, even climate change.

---

negate the symbolic or pastoral function of politics; instead, Musk and Kelly have a pastoral function in their articles that seem to shepherd humanity all the while affecting the regulation of and the regulation by AI.

Bostrom and others concerned with the future of humanity see AI governance like characters in Saurez's book trying to steer superintelligence safely. Saurez's *Daemon* is only one possible way toward superintelligence to Bostrom. Other paths include an eugenics-tinged focus on embryo selection and genetic engineering, human augmentation, and other conventional forms of artificial intelligence. Regardless of the outcome, to reach superintelligence is to flirt with singularity and the technologically fast-paced autonomous generation it entails, a concept discussed by science fiction writer Vernor Vinge and the futurist Raymond Kurzweil (Bostrom, 2005). Yet, superintelligence is also a theme in contemporary thought with variations that resonate with figures in the Dark Enlightenment and other neo-reactionary movements that reject liberal democratic values in favour of neo-feudal or other regimes better aligned with advanced technologies (Haider, 2017; Smith & Burrows, 2021).

Bostrom's work contributes to a philosophy of longtermism that we see as central to this version of AI governmentality. Émile P. Torres, longtermism's most astute critic, summarizes the doctrine as the "claim that if humanity can survive the next few centuries and successfully colonize outer space, the number of people who could exist in the future is absolutely enormous" (Torres, 2022). Strange as it may seem, the doctrine of longtermism offers a distinct policy agenda for AI governance. Indeed, one could argue that Bostrom's early writing on superintelligence helped legitimate the field's self-fulfilling prophecy, leading to ever-more investment in the technology and a form of autoregulation that resists being constrained by any state government (Wagner, 2018; Mittelstadt, 2019). Musk's demon is part of such a trend and is certainly emblematic of its many inconsistencies. This thread locates the problem in an unpredictable "take-off" period when AI exceeds the thresholds of human and civilization intelligence. The problem, according to Bostrom, is a diabolical one: "The first superintelligence may shape the future of earth originating life, could easily have non-anthropomorphic final goals, and would likely have instrumental reasons to pursue open ended resource acquisition" (Bostrom, 2014, p. 317). (Bostrom's scenario of an AI taking over the world seems lifted from the mind of Saurez. Daemon includes a lot of killer robots). This problematization narrowly frames AI governance as a mostly, if not completely, speculative logic of regulation. The matter of AI governance is not a present concern, but a tautology involving, in Bostrom's words, "motivations" and "detonations" that respectively steer superintelligence to anthropomorphic goals. This inescapable mythology and iconicity of AI even found its way into the acknowledgment of Bolstrom's book, which reads like a who's who list of AI developers including Yoshua Benigo and Geoffrey Hinton.

Longtermism's rational utilitarianism can seem like a simple numbers game, some humans now, many humans later. This numbers game invites a mixture of ambivalence and imperatives as Bostrom sees a need to act now, but not for immediate, practical concerns. The problem of AI as superintelligence is never mundane, embodied, or even environmental; these are all short-term matters, matters of no consequence in self-declared rational, if laissez-faire, policy optimization. The fact of the matter is that longtermism calls for more longtermism that in turn leads to more and more AI. This is what we mean by the recursive nature of their power. Through it, longtermism and AI become the causes and the consequences of one another. The outcome is a striking depoliticization of AI made possible through a mixture of the philosophy's elite gatekeeping and a poorly defined problematization of AI. Whether in computer science communities, loosely constituted, elite online debates, or in Bostrom's book *Superintelligence*, the image of "revolution" that is projected is still a technological one – an engine – rather than the image of a social movement or a civil sphere.

Politically, addressing an evil demon is not a problem of actual welfare here and now. Longtermism is concerned with future civilizations. Torres notes that longtermism has become part of the effective altruism movement – a program of philanthropy active in some technology firms (Matthews, 2015; Torres, 2021). As Torres explains:

> imagine a situation in which you could either lift 1 billion present people out of extreme poverty *or* benefit 0.00000000001 percent of the 10^{23} biological humans who Bostrom calculates could exist if we were to colonize our cosmic neighborhood, the Virgo Supercluster. Which option should you pick? For longtermists, the answer is obvious: you should pick the latter. Why? Well, just crunch the numbers: 0.00000000001 percent of 10^{23} people is 10 billion people, which is *ten times greater* than 1 billion people. (Torres, 2021, np.)

These calculations drive effective altruism's funding. Out of \$416M spent by associated fundings in 2019, \$40M (10%) went to "Potential risks from AI" above "Other near-term work (near-term climate change, mental health)" that received \$2M (0%) (Todd, 2021). The Effective Altruism Foundation similarly has four funds ranked by risk. The "Long-Term Future Fund" has the highest risk profile, over the "Global Health and Development Fund." Longtermism, in short, drives a major part of a growing philanthropic movement.

To be sure, superintelligence is an immaterial approach to intelligence and how it came to define humanity as a historical and social construct. Within such a paradigm, it becomes possible to see societies as computational, as a wired brain composed of neurons that are more trigger and data than flesh and soul. That is what AI represents: namely, something other than human, even alien. By continuing with this line of argument, logically, one can see the whole world is a simulation – another philosophical argument advocated by Bostrom. If AI does not need a body, the philosopher may remove the planet, too. Under this view, the Earth is only a starting place for humanity and one that ultimately does not constitute an existential risk. While acknowledging climate change as a new kind of threat, Bostrom writes,

> Even if humanity were to spend many millennia on such an oscillating trajectory, one might expect that eventually this phase would end, resulting in either the permanent destruction of humankind, or the rise of a stable sustainable global civilization, or the transformation of the human condition into a new "posthuman" condition. (Bostrom, 2009)

Superintelligence is then defined as a probable fate encounter by present or future civilization, an eschatological time frame longer than a mere matter of climate.

KELLY'S WATSON AND THE LOOPING OF DISPOSITIF AND DOCTRINE

The maverick co-founder of *Wired* magazine, Kevin Kelly, could be considered a prosaic guru of digital technologies. His innate pragmatism comes with a steady dose of enthusiasm that fits in particularly well in Silicon Valley: Kelly's motto reads "over the long term, the future is decided by optimists." In his writing, he has used the now-infamous example of IBM's Watson to introduce his own vision of AI, one that is a decidedly less ambitious expression of the technology and ensuing regime of governmentality than the longtermists. "Today's Watson," he notes, "no longer exists solely within a wall of cabinets but is spread across a cloud of open-standard servers that run several hundred 'instances' of the AI at once" (Kelly, 2014).

Watson, as Kelly explains, exemplifies an AI that infiltrates every aspect of society because it is on-demand, distributed, flexible, and adaptive. That is the version of Kelly's Watson that ultimately came to pass, a diminished yet applied and operating AI – or, following our argument, one that is cybernetic from the ground up.

Watson's mundane status today is at odds with its beginnings. Watson was ahead of the curve in 2011. Debuting in the United States as a contestant on Jeopardy!, the supercomputer surpassed all expectations and went on to become the game's new champion. It was a media-pop-culture stunt, the kind upon which Deep Blue and later AlphaGo built (see Binder, 2021). Watson's success depended not only on data – troves and troves of data – but on a new way to organize and make sense of it: namely, NLP.

NLP is one of the two major branches of machine learning and neural nets that launched today's AI spring. Just a year after Watson bested Jeopardy!, Geoffrey Hinton's team revolutionized the other branch with its win at the ImageNet competition (Cardon et al., 2018). Both wins set off another round of investment in AI – a round that IBM seemed well-poised to capitalize on with Watson. Not so, in reality, IBM had little to sell. Adapting a symbolic and theoretical machine to applied issues proved to be too difficult and the rewards too limited. Unlike its competitors operating in a more speculative mode, IBM pivoted to a "revised A.I. strategy – a pared-down, less world-changing ambition" (Lohr, 2021).

Watson could be less ambitious because it relied on the feedback loop between a doctrine less concerned with saving humanity and a pragmatic skepticism of human intelligence. Kelly's Watson was not superintelligent, but neither were the humans it sought to replace. "Smartness" is diminished in a definition of artificial intelligence that draws on decades of variations of Cold War rationality that sought to blur the distinctions between human and machine intelligence and to lower the overall threshold. The human then becomes programmable, optimizable, and interchangeable with fraught, biased, and unreliable forms of AI (Mirowski, 2002). As Erikson et al. nicely summarize, "emphasizing the divergence between actual human reasoning and standards of formal rationality [...] implicitly reinforced the normative authority of the latter" (2013, p. 24). AI does not need to be more intelligent, just smarter, better structured, and more efficient than humans.

Kelly's Watson offers a version of AI governmentality with its own circular-logic and self-referential pastoral doctrine – Watson Works – to formally operationalize and scale-up solutions framed as optimizable (McKelvey & Neves, 2021). Kelly imagines such work as taking the form of algorithms and models that can be indefinitely replicated if tweaked just enough. IBM's effort to colonize the data- and money-rich environment of healthcare is a case in point. Watson was supposed to be able to do it all: macro-calculations in the form of genomics and image diagnostics as well as adapted-precision medicine and human care via personal assistants and chatbots for patients. In such an environment, the patient's ability to emotionally connect to someone/something or to have their needs and mood be "understood" is priceless, even if made possible by multiple forms of deception, nudging, and monitoring interventions. Lately, "Watson Works" launched, combining parts of Watson Health with the optimization of the workplace to "help business navigate [...] with the ongoing COVID-19 crisis as effectively as possible." As the press release reads, "applying AI [...] is especially useful in this context, where there are so many different sources of information, and every aspect of the situation is in flux" (Quoted in Mashable News, 2020). In fact, the very definition of governmentality, too, is in flux here: what counts as power deploys recursively on all the different fronts of dispositive and doctrine, control and communication, knowledge and action, as well as the capacities to influence the conduct of both masses and individuals.

Kelly's Watson operates in a very immediate temporality, both in terms of daily, mundane adoption, but also within the broader yet still short-term contexts of its commercial rollout. The scope of time is one without much deep consideration of AI's existential risks, the kind of which is central to longtermism. There is a fundamental tension and ambiguity here between the two perspectives, a conflict that nevertheless might signal a convoluted form of dialogue. Even for Kelly, time appears to be moving in a spiral, one in which the flexible inclusion of short-term elements permits them to find their way into a loose sense of the long-term. Time, in other words, is as dynamic and unified as power itself. It is all about finding a sweet spot, a moment in which the management of such temporal flows seem to hold – the possibilities of start-ups to bank on their innovations and immediate utility for customers, or, more likely in this landscape, on their acquisition by bigger and more established companies. Today's AI technologies are being deployed in cycles that have the characteristics of being both flexible and opaque. Watson and others evolve and morph precisely because they are black boxes (Bucher, 2018; Pasquale, 2015; Roberge, Morin, et al., 2020). And this never ceases to represent a challenge for outside oversight and political regulation. As Cuéllar (2017) notes, what we are witnessing nowadays is an enhanced and faster process of "cyberdelegation" where more traditional means and meanings of legitimacy and accountability are being refurbished and pushed away. AI's deployment, the management of its short-term/long-term tension, and everything that deals with its inherent autopoietic nature announces an "escape for regulation" (Wagner, 2018).

Ethics is a case in point. Not surprisingly, ethical and responsible AI became the two central occupations of Kelly's Watson given its applied governmentality. IBM claims, for example, that it sells, "world-changing AI, built responsibly." "Mitigating bias" is one of six IBM positions on AI, a position that begins by acknowledging that "There's no question that human biases could influence algorithms and result in discriminatory outcomes" (Hobson & Dortch, 2021, np.) Not unlike the discussions of Cold War rationality above, the circular effect here is that as AI is measured for biases, these measures find their way to testing humans who come up lacking too. AI is measured against a diminishing attitude toward human intelligence.

What comes lacking too – and maybe more importantly – is a proper sense of what counts as politics. The current profusion of optimistic, voluntary, and often naïve discourses and ethical declarations have become something of a trope that is a pale version of politics of goodwill, a so-called regulation without coercion in general, and state regulation in particular (Jobin et al., 2019; Mittelstadt et al., 2016; Stark et al., 2021). To reframe this in Foucault's language: people and organizations of the likes of Kelly and IBM have consecrated the absence of a state dispositif into a doctrine. The stakes become so low that state regulation is unnecessary so that another corporate political program can then swoop in, one that blurs the distinction between the public and the private, and all the while it establishes a new sense of legitimacy and accountability. This latest form of AI governmentality is in many ways a continuation of the present neoliberal or slightly post-neoliberal moment that uses AI as a part of an overall logic of societal optimization and techno-solutionism.

CONCLUSION

Our main argument in this chapter is that far from contradictory, Musk's demon and Kelly's Watson form the conditions of possibility for one another. They highlight and indeed reinforce each other (though part of a larger metastability of AI governmentality we are tracing). There is no simple antagonism between weak-narrow versus strong-general AI – the ANI versus AGI trope. What we find is much more complex. While dealing with superintelligence and the prospect of humanity itself, the demon narrative is not only representational and mythical, but performative *here* and *now*. While offering the kind of "cheap, reliable, industrial-grade digital smartness" Watson does for business, it too deploys views and understandings of how the world works that makes it political. In the end, Musk's demon and Kelly's Watson are prime examples of how doctrines and dispositifs co-constitute today's AI governmentality.

These twinned forms of AI governmentality are in a feedback loop that recursively steers AI governmentality away from social modes of governance. We need to pay great attention to the feedback loops and the advent of an enhanced form of recursive power whereby these AI governmentalities collaborate to legitimate each other. To stay the course for technologies such as artificial intelligence is to rapidly move on and constantly adapt to different fields. Lags and dysfunctions are to be overcome by being recycled; "bizarre" outputs refurbished as inputs and so on and so forth. This is what gives rise to its often free-floating, self-referential, and self-perpetuating logic. AI governmentality can indeed be defined as being caught in its own spiral. Here we want to argue alongside people such as Louise Amoore when she notes that "the advent of deep learning is *generative* of new norms and thresholds of what 'good', normal', and stable [political] orders look like" [emphasis added] (Amoore, 2022, p. 2). By doing so, we also want to push against what is every so often the static, iron-cage-like thesis of the literature on algorithmic governmentality. If control and dispositif are fundamental, as this literature points out, so too are the issues dealing with communication – doctrines.

The dynamics of recursive power allow us to better understand how and why today's AI governmentality repeatedly goes unchallenged. As seen earlier, states rarely go against such technological deployment. In investing in research, trying to implement AI in their management, and promoting ethical endeavors, states have less shaping power over AI than they are shaped by it. Marion Fourcade and Jeff Gordon are right when they observe that what we are witnessing is a "deeper transformation in statecraft itself" (2020, p. 80). The same can be said about intellectual discourses: philosophers, pundits, and scholars such as Bostrom have done little to challenge and question the type of power that AI is gaining. Reflexivity and criticism still appear to be sparse resources even if, for both today and tomorrow, they are central in the capability to connect with a more deliberative civil society and ultimately defend society itself.

REFERENCES

Amoore, L. (2022). Machine learning political orders. *Review of International Studies*, 1–17. https://doi.org/10.1017/S0260210522000031

Ananny, M. (2020). Making up political people: How social media create the ideals, definitions, and probabilities of political speech. *Georgetown Law Technology Review*, 4(2), 352–366.

Aneesh, A. (2009). Global labor: Algocratic modes of organization. *Sociological Theory*, 27(4), 347–370. https://doi.org/10.1111/j.1467-9558.2009.01352.x

Beer, D. (2016). The social power of algorithms. *Information, Communication & Society*, 1–13. https://doi.org/10.1080/1369118X.2016.1216147

Benjamin, R. (2019). *Race after technology: Abolitionist tools for the new Jim code*. Polity.

Binder, W. (2021). AlphaGo's deep play: Technological breakthrough as social drama. In J. Roberge & M. Castelle (Eds.), *The cultural life of machine learning: An incursion into critical AI studies* (pp. 167–195). Springer International Publishing. https://doi.org/10.1007/978-3-030-56286-1_6

Bostrom, N. (1998). How long before superintelligence? *International Journal of Futures Studies, 2.*

Bostrom, N. (2005). A history of transhumanist thought. *Journal of Evolution and Technology, 14*(1).

Bostrom, N. (2009). The future of humanity. In J. K. B. Olsen, E. Selinger, & S. Riis (Eds.), *New waves in philosophy of technology* (pp. 186–215). Palgrave Macmillan.

Bostrom, N. (2014). *Superintelligence: Paths, dangers, strategies.* Oxford University Press.

Braman, S. (2002). Posthuman law: Information policy and the machinic world. *First Monday, 7*(12). http://firstmonday.org/ojs/index.php/fm/article/view/1011

Bratich, J. Z., Packer, J., & McCarthy, C. (Eds.). (2003). *Foucault, cultural studies, and governmentality.* State University of New York Press.

Bucher, T. (2018). *If...then: Algorithmic power and politics.* Oxford University Press.

Canales, J. (2020). *Bedeviled.* Princeton University Press. https://press.princeton.edu/books/hardcover/9780691175324/bedeviled

Cardon, D., Cointet, J.-P., & Mazières, A. (2018). La revanche des neurones. *Reseaux, 211*(5), 173–220.

Cheney-Lippold, J. (2017). *We are data: Algorithms and the making of our digital selves.* New York University Press.

Coleman, B. (2021). Technology of the surround. *Catalyst: Feminism, Theory, Technoscience, 7*(2), Article 2. https://doi.org/10.28968/cftt.v7i2.35973

Cooper, R. (2020). Pastoral power and algorithmic governmentality. *Theory, Culture & Society, 37*(1), 29–52. https://doi.org/10.1177/0263276419860576

Crawford, K. (2021). *Atlas of AI.* Yale University Press. https://yalebooks.yale.edu/book/9780300209570/atlas-ai

Cuéllar, M.-F. (2017). Cyberdelegation and the administrative state. In N. R. Parrillo (Ed.), *Administrative law from the inside out: Essays on themes in the work of Jerry L. Mashaw* (pp. 134–160). Cambridge University Press. https://doi.org/10.1017/9781316671641.006

Deseriis, M. (2011). The general, the watchman, and the engineer of control. *Journal of Communication Inquiry, 35*(4), 387–394. https://doi.org/10.1177/0196859911415677

Deutsch, K. W. (1966). *The nerves of government.* Free Press.

Elon Musk [@elonmusk]. (2014, August 3). *@drwave @itsDanielSuarez Yeah, Daemon is a great read* [Tweet]. Twitter. https://twitter.com/elonmusk/status/495771005634482176

Erickson, P., Klein, J. L., Daston, L., Lemov, R., Sturm, T., & Gordin, M. D. (2013). *How reason almost lost its mind: The strange career of cold war rationality.* University of Chicago Press.

Foucault, M. (1991). *Governmentality* (G. Burchell, C. Gordon, & P. M. Miller, Eds.; pp. 87–104). The University of Chicago Press.

Foucault, M. (2007). *Security, territory, population: Lectures at the College de France, 1977–78* (M. Senellart, Ed.; G. Burchell, Trans.). Palgrave Macmillan.

Fourcade, M., & Gordon, J. (2020). Learning like a state: Statecraft in the digital age. *Journal of Law and Political Economy, 1*(1). https://escholarship.org/uc/item/3k16c24g

Gibbs, S. (2014, October 27). Elon Musk: Artificial intelligence is our biggest existential threat. *The Guardian.* https://www.theguardian.com/technology/2014/oct/27/elon-musk-artificial-intelligence-ai-biggest-existential-threat

Gorwa, R., Binns, R., & Katzenbach, C. (2020). Algorithmic content moderation: Technical and political challenges in the automation of platform governance. *Big Data & Society, 7*(1), 205395171989794. https://doi.org/10.1177/2053951719897945

Haider, S. (2017, March 28). *The darkness at the end of the tunnel: Artificial intelligence and neoreaction.* Viewpoint Magazine. https://viewpointmag.com/2017/03/28/the-darkness-at-the-end-of-the-tunnel-artificial-intelligence-and-neoreaction/

Hale, M. (2011, February 8). Actors and their roles for $300, HAL? HAL! *The New York Times.* https://www.nytimes.com/2011/02/09/arts/television/09nova.html

Hobson, S., & Dortch, A. (2021, May 26). *Mitigating bias in artificial intelligence.* IBM Policy Lab. https://www.ibm.com/policy/mitigating-ai-bias/

Hong, S. (2021). Technofutures in stasis: Smart machines, ubiquitous computing, and the future that keeps coming back. *International Journal of Communication, 15,* Article 0.

Hookway, B. (1999). *Pandemonium: The rise of predatory locales in the postwar world.* Princeton Architectural Press.

Jobin, A., Ienca, M., & Vayena, E. (2019). The global landscape of AI ethics guidelines. *Nature Machine Intelligence, 1*(9), Article 9. https://doi.org/10.1038/s42256-019-0088-2

Karpf, D. (2020, January 29). The 10,000-year clock is a waste of time. *Wired.* https://www.wired.com/story/the-10000-year-clock-is-a-waste-of-time/

Katzenbach, C., & Ulbricht, L. (2019). Algorithmic governance. *Internet Policy Review, 8*(4). https://policyreview.info/concepts/algorithmic-governance

Kelly, K. (2014, October 27). The three breakthroughs that have finally unleashed AI on the world. *Wired.* https://www.wired.com/2014/10/future-of-artificial-intelligence/

Lash, S. (2007). Power after hegemony: Cultural studies in mutation? *Theory, Culture & Society, 24*(3), 55–78.

Lohr, S. (2021, July 16). What ever happened to IBM's Watson? *The New York Times.* https://www.nytimes.com/2021/07/16/technology/what-happened-ibm-watson.html

Mashable News. (2020, June 19). *IBM'S newly launched 'Watson Works' uses AI to help firms manage new work challenges.* Mashable India. https://in.mashable.com/tech/14925/ibms-newly-launched-watson-works-uses-ai-to-help-firms-manage-new-work-challenges

Matthews, D. (2015, August 10). *I spent a weekend at Google talking with nerds about charity. I came away ... worried.* Vox. https://www.vox.com/2015/8/10/9124145/effective-altruism-global-ai

McKelvey, F. (2018). *Internet daemons: Digital communications possessed.* University of Minnesota Press.

McKelvey, F., & Neves, J. (2021). Introduction: Optimization and its discontents. *Review of Communication, 21*(2), 95–112. https://doi.org/10.1080/15358593.2021.1936143

Mirowski, P. (2002). *Machine dreams: Economics becomes a cyborg science.* Cambridge University Press.

Mittelstadt, B. D., Allo, P., Taddeo, M., Wachter, S., & Floridi, L. (2016). The ethics of algorithms: Mapping the debate. *Big Data & Society, 3*(2). https://doi.org/10.1177/2053951716679679

Mittelstadt, B., Principle Alone Cannot Guarantee Ethical AI, *Nature Machine Intelligence*, 1, (11), 2019, p. 501–507.

Myers West, S. (2018). Censored, suspended, shadowbanned: User interpretations of content moderation on social media platforms. *New Media & Society, 20*(11), 4366–4383. https://doi.org/10.1177/1461444818773059

Pasquale, F. (2015). *The black box society: The secret algorithms that control money and information.* Harvard University Press.

Rappin, B. (2018). Algorithme, management, crise: Le triptyque cybernétique du gouvernement de l'exception permanente. *Quaderni: Communication, technologies, pouvoir, 96*, Article 96. https://doi.org/10.4000/quaderni.1182

Roberge, J., Morin, K., & Senneville, M. (2020). Deep learning's governmentality: The other black box. In A. Sudmann (Ed.), *The democratization of artificial intelligence* (pp. 123–142). transcript Verlag. https://doi.org/10.1515/9783839447192-008

Roberge, J., Senneville, M., & Morin, K. (2020). How to translate artificial intelligence? Myths and justifications in public discourse. *Big Data & Society, 7*(1), 205395172091996. https://doi.org/10.1177/2053951720919968

Roberts, S. T. (2019). *Behind the screen: Content moderation in the shadows of social media.* Yale University Press.

Roberts, S. T., & Hogan, M. (2019). Left behind: Futurist fetishists, prepping and the abandonment of earth. *B2o: An Online Journal, 4*(2). https://escholarship.org/uc/item/8sr8n99w

Roderick, I. (2007). (Out of) control demons: Software agents, complexity theory and the revolution in military affairs. *Theory & Event, 10*(2).

Rose, N. S. (1999). *Powers of freedom: Reframing political thought.* Cambridge University Press.

Rouvroy, A. and Berns, T., Gouvernementalité algorithmique et perspectives d'émancipation : le disparate comme condition d'émancipation par la relation, *Réseaux*, (177), 2013, p. 163–196.

Smith, H., & Burrows, R. (2021). Software, sovereignty and the post-neoliberal politics of exit. *Theory, Culture & Society, 38*(6), 143–166. https://doi.org/10.1177/0263276421999439

Stark, L., Greene, D., & Hoffmann, A. L. (2021). Critical perspectives on governance mechanisms for AI/ML systems. In J. Roberge & M. Castelle (Eds.), *The cultural life of machine learning: An incursion into critical AI studies* (pp. 257–280). Springer International Publishing. https://doi.org/10.1007/978-3-030-56286-1_9

Todd, B. (2021, August 9). *How are resources in effective altruism allocated across issues?* 80,000 Hours. https://80000hours.org/2021/08/effective-altruism-allocation-resources-cause-areas/

Torres, É. P. (2021, July 28). The dangerous ideas of "longtermism" and "existential risk." *Current Affairs.* https://www.currentaffairs.org/2021/07/the-dangerous-ideas-of-longtermism-and-existential-risk

Torres, É. P. (2022, April 30). *Elon Musk, Twitter and the future: His long-term vision is even weirder than you think.* Salon. https://www.salon.com/2022/04/30/elon-musk-twitter-and-the-future-his-long -term-vision-is-even-weirder-than-you-think/

Wagner, B. (2018). Ethics as an escape from regulation: From "ethics-washing" to ethics-shopping? In E. Bayamlioğlu, I. Baraliuc, L. Janssens, & M. Hildebrandt (Eds.), *Being profiled* (pp. 84–89). Amsterdam University Press; JSTOR. https://doi.org/10.2307/j.ctvhrd092.18

Walters, W. (2012). *Governmentality: Critical encounters.* Routledge.

Wiener, N. (1948). *Cybernetics or, control and communication in the animal and the machine.* J. Wiley.

Winner, L. (1986). *Do artifacts have politics?* (pp. 19–39). University of Chicago Press.

Yeung, K. (2016). 'Hypernudge': Big data as a mode of regulation by design. *Information, Communication & Society, 20*(1), 118–136. https://doi.org/10.1080/1369118X.2016.1186713

Yeung, K. (2018). Algorithmic regulation: A critical interrogation. *Regulation & Governance, 12*(4), 505–523. https://doi.org/10.1111/rego.12158

3. The danger of smart ideologies: counter-hegemonic intelligence and antagonistic machines

Peter Bloom

INTRODUCTION

In 2021, the EU produced the first ever regulations for AI. The goal was to decrease the risk to humans while acknowledging the prospects of an increasingly "smart" world. It declares:

> The proposed AI regulation ensures that Europeans can trust what AI has to offer. While most AI systems pose limited to no risk and can contribute to solving many societal challenges, certain AI systems create risks that we must address to avoid undesirable outcomes.

For this purpose, the regulations categorise AI into four risk categories – "unacceptable risk", "high risk", "limited risk" and "minimal or no risk" – based on how dangerous they are to humans. These regulations also contain some very telling "omissions", including: "It leaves Big Tech virtually unscathed. It lacks a focus on those affected by AI systems, apparently missing any general requirement to inform people who are subjected to algorithmic assessment" (MacCarthy & Propp, 2021, n.p.).

These regulations reflect a wider discourse around the threat of "biased" AI in which what was once assumed by many to be merely objective calculations by machines are now understood to be worryingly prejudiced in their produced insights. The emphasis now increasingly is on "managing" (Roselli et al., 2019) or "tackling" bias in AI (Silberg & Manyika, 2019). No less than the Harvard Business Review opined in 2019 that:

> Over the past few years, society has started to wrestle with just how much human biases can make their way into artificial intelligence systems—with harmful results. At a time when many companies are looking to deploy AI systems across their operations, being acutely aware of those risks and working to reduce them is an urgent priority. (Manyika et al., 2019, n.p.)

These concerns have also brought about real-world results, such as the recent news in 2022 that Microsoft is now banning the use of its facial recognition technology to identify individuals and populations based on demographic information such as race or gender (Hern, 2022).

There is an interesting paradox at work here, though. While ostensibly focused on protecting humans, these regulations and discourses in fact represent the threat posed by humanity to AI. "Over the last few years, society has begun to grapple with exactly how much these human prejudices, with devastating consequences", notes the Head of Data Science and AI at the Australian Computer Society, Steve Nouri (2021, n.p.), "can find their way through AI systems". In particular, the ability for our machine counterparts to take on our human biases or be used for the weaponised purposes of reinforcing existing power relations between humans.

These are perfectly understandable fears and ones that must be taken seriously. However, they do not go far enough. What is crucial, in this respect, is to understand the deeper ideological biases that continue to hegemonically shape and order society. According to David Magerman (2022), Managing Partner of the AI entrepreneurial firm Differential Ventures:

> The root cause of bias in data-driven AI systems comes down to how the data to train those systems is collected, and whether or not the decision-making in that data represents the corporate or societal goals of the deployed system based on that data. (n.p.)

This chapter will attempt to critically reframe the debate on the relationship between AI and humans by highlighting the often-overlooked ways AI reproduces dominant ideologies. This form of "smart hegemony" goes beyond merely challenging the all too human prejudices reproduced by AI around race and gender. Rather, it draws attention to the ways AI is used to fundamentally reproduce and reinforce dominant assumptions of the world – particularly linked to capitalism. Significantly, it interrogates AI's role in strengthening and expanding hegemony using theories of "trans-human relations" that emphasise the mutually constituting roles that machines and humans have for socially constructing their shared worlds. At stake, in this chapter, is the challenge of overblown and misguided fears of an AI takeover as manifested in discourses of "singularity" and, instead, bringing to the fore the very real danger of reaffirming and spreading dominant ideologies and the dominating power relations they help support.

Yet, this chapter will also seek to provide a glimpse at the more radical counter-hegemonic possibilities of "trans-human relations". Specifically, the ability of AI to precisely identify these ideological biases and trace their diverse intersectional impacts on individuals. Such advances would help to critically navigate and challenge the arguably inherently neoliberal ideology driving both the development of AI and algorithmic governance. In doing so, it will seek to point to how machine learning can be a revolutionary force for more fully understanding the power of ideologies and the different consequences they have for different people. To this end, its goal is to politically resituate the discourses around AI so that they can be part of movements to challenge often naturalised values and offer the potential for creating new emancipatory alternative ones. As such, it proposes the need for "counter-hegemonic intelligence" and the rise of "antagonistic machines".

THE DANGER OF SMART IDEOLOGIES

The heralded social promise of AI has been eclipsed by its less-than-ideal, and often quite profoundly troubling, realities. Rather than be a force for dramatically augmenting human knowledge and capabilities, it is charged with reinforcing existing biases and inequalities. Rather than making us "smarter", what appears to be happening, to quote a recent headline from *The Guardian*, AI "is learning all our worst impulses", leading to the rise of "racist robots" (Buranyi, 2017). On the one hand, this reflects an abiding need to safeguard individuals from the threat of AI. On the other, this represents the imperative to protect AI from human prejudices and desires to use it for the purposes of power rather than broader social betterment (see Metz, 2021).

What is especially dangerous is how AI can grant these biases a veneer of objectivity. Discriminatory interpretations of natural language processing, for instance, can make it appear that these are "natural" or scientific rather than socially produced and based on faulty human data (Caliskan, 2021). These biases, furthermore, have significant real-world consequences. Already there have been substantiated reports that millions of black people have been discriminated against by healthcare algorithms in US hospitals (Ledford, 2019). This tendency towards discrimination is also built into its design – in the name of efficiency, its models will disregard the consequences of errors on what it views as rare but are actually serious errors (Hellemans, 2020).

Amidst the legitimate and high-profile concerns over AI bias, there is perhaps an even more fundamental one that is missing. Notably, the underlying assumptions regarding race, class, gender, and value driving these prejudicial assumptions. Just this year, in 2022, the US Department of Commerce's National Institute of Standards and Technology (NIST) published "Towards a Standard for Identifying and Managing Bias in Artificial Intelligence" (Schwartz et al., 2022, p. i) that declares in its opening paragraph

> As individuals and communities interact in and with an environment that is increasingly virtual, they are often vulnerable to the commodification of their digital footprint. Concepts and behavior that are ambiguous in nature are captured in this environment, quantified, and used to categorize, sort, recommend, or make decisions about people's lives. While many organizations seek to utilize this information in a responsible manner, biases remain endemic across technology processes and can lead to harmful impacts regardless of intent. These harmful outcomes, even if inadvertent, create significant challenges for cultivating public trust in artificial intelligence (AI).

They distinguish, to this end, beyond surface-level "statistical and computational biases" with the respectively deeper "human bias" and "systemic bias". At stake, hence, are the ideological biases being literally coded into our knowledge and decision-making by AI (Raji, 2020). These represent entrenched social values underpinned by even more naturalised and culturally sedimented understandings of the world and ourselves as human beings – specifically how AI "encodes" this systemic human bias into our decision-making (Raji, 2020, n.p.).

These increasingly popular critiques of AI also reflect deeper issues of the ways algorithmic governance and speculative logics represent hegemonic neoliberal ideologies. In particular, it perpetuates a form of ongoing human disciplining that seeks to maximise individual and collective efficiency. Here, the goal is to create an "optimised" person and society that can be achieved through ongoing practices of AI-powered quantification and calculation. The focus on "smart" biases, hence, risks distracting from its perhaps fundamental neoliberal bias, as these approaches are attempting to socially and politically discipline a new generation of populations to be economically productive and valuable subjects.

These insights open the space to reconsider and update our conceptions of hegemony. AI stands as a socially vaulted "truth teller" that is able to present its biased insights as calculated facts. Consequently, it follows in a tradition of granting ideology a scientific veneer (Vesa & Tienari, 2020). Today, there is emerging what can be called "smart hegemony" – the unreflective reproduction of dominant human discourses for further spreading these values and using them for the conjoined purposes of social ordering and human disciplining (Cui & van Esch, 2022). AI then is inherently political precisely because it is a viral and increasingly authoritative ideological force (Katz, 2020).

It is critical, therefore, to reframe the question of AI bias to better reflect issues of ideology and hegemony. At present, there is a plethora of work grappling with the "ideology of AI" (see Sias, 2021). Just as important, though, is the need to theoretically understand how AI serves to make certain ideologies hegemonic and for whose human benefit.

TRANS-HUMAN HEGEMONY

A key aim of this chapter is to better understand the role of AI in producing and reinforcing ideological hegemony. Tellingly, dominant discourses of human-machine relations focus primarily either on their ultimate conflict or the capacity for developing artificially aided superhuman powers. Less prominent but arguably much more important and urgent, is the social use of AI and its potential deployment for strengthening and challenging hegemonic assumptions shaping human relations. Equally crucial is the capacity of AI to help us reimagine our shared trans-human futures. The historian Apolline Taillandier (2021, p. 215) recounts that trans-humanism promoted stories of "futures change" that "include the unlimited individual liberty of the technologized self, the knowledge-ordering properties of the market, and the rational aggregation of individual interests over the long term".

Ernesto Laclau's work on discursive hegemony is particularly valuable for this purpose. Along with Chantel Mouffe, he associated power with the ability of a dominant discourse to shape understandings and, in doing so, contingently regulate actions. It is "a space in which bursts forth a whole conception of the social based upon an intelligibility which reduces its distinct moments to the interiority of a closed paradigm" (Laclau & Mouffe, 1986, p. 93). In his later work, he further introduces the concept of "ideological imaginaries", which represent the over-arching horizon of meaning within which different discourses compete for dominance, representing that which "is not one among other objects but an absolute limit which structures a field of intelligibility and is thus the conditions of possibility for the emergence of any object" (Laclau, 1990, p. 63). At the very least, then, it becomes imperative to interrogate what ideological imaginary AI emerged within and continues to be constituted by.

In the present context, technology supposedly represents a dangerous ultra-modern form of alienation. The fears of automation point to a coming "smart" future where machines will replace humans in the name of profit. The threat of human obsolescence looms over any discussions of AI – raising the prescient concern of whose interests this technology is, in fact, being made for. This sense of existential disempowerment is only enhanced by our daily relationship with technology which can feel manipulative and unmoored from any human ability to control or regulate it (see Packard, 2018). Reflected is a paradoxical reality whereby as the capabilities of technology increase the power of humans decreases. While AI and digital interactions can connect us to information and people almost instantaneously, customised to meet our most individualised preferences, what is missing is the shared ability to "design what a future ought to be: open to regular revision in response to our practical behaviours given the persistent contingency of the conditions in which we are immersed" (Bauer, 2019, p. 106).

Here the distinction between human and artificial intelligence begins to critically blur. Indeed, the insights produced by machines are understood to be, to a profound extent, an extension of human discourses. Furthermore, it is a reflection of a particular form of intelligence that has been portrayed as a universal and objective truth. To this end, it is what Glynos and Howarth (2007) refer to as a producer of "social logic" – a form of knowledge that promotes insights and practices reinforcing dominant values and relations.

What is then crucial is to critically unpick the social logic being reproduced and granted legitimacy by AI. "Smart hegemony" is the use of artificial intelligence to naturalise pre-existing ideological bias. In doing so, it justifies it as a hegemonic truth, an unquestioned "common sense" that can be utilised for regulating and controlling human behaviour. Hence, there is a dual and interconnected process of disciplining occurring – the narrowing of machine learning to officially sanctioned and accepted discursive limits and the weaponisation of this data and knowledge to discipline individuals and groups in conformity to these hegemonic values. Yet they also point to an alternative and less alienating type of counter-hegemonic transhuman relation based on challenging these social logics, thus allowing radical forms of AI and transformative human and machine learning to emerge that could disrupt these dominant discourses and the dominating social orders that they produce.

COUNTER-HEGEMONIC INTELLIGENCE

The concept of "smart hegemony" helps to critically reconsider the character and consequence of AI. Rather than focus on calculative capabilities, it highlights instead AI's role in ideologically reinforcing existing social orderings and their underlying power relations. These insights echo, to a degree, concerns about the rise of "algorithmic governance" (O'Neil, 2016; Sætra, 2020). Yet it also aims to radicalise existing efforts to politically deploy AI to resist this increasingly "authoritarian capitalist" status quo (Bloom & Sancino, 2019). At stake is gaining a fuller comprehension of developing and using new forms of counter-hegemonic intelligence.

The current literature on AI is, understandably, increasingly concentrated on fostering more empowering types of human-computer interactions (see Biele, 2022; Faulkner, 1998; Mathew et al., 2011). At the heart of this strategy, is the attempt to make AI more human-like in its reasoning. A further goal, in this respect, is also to create "explainable AI" that can enhance the transparency of machine decision-making, pulling it out of its proverbial "black box" so that humans can understand and, if necessary, challenge its rationale (Liao et al., 2020; Rai, 2020 Samek et al., 2019). These approaches would appear to contravene concurrent views of AI as generating "superintelligence" far beyond the ken of human cognition and processing (see Bostrom, 2014).

There is a radical third way though that is worth exploring and perhaps much more relevant to current social conditions. Namely, the production of counter-hegemonic intelligence – machine learning that can uncover the ideological biases of human relations. Returning to the theories of Glynos and Howarth (2007), it is an interrogation of how AI can drive forward and support political rather than social logics. At the most basic level, this means the political use of AI to challenge dominant assumptions and power. However, counter-hegemony goes beyond resistance, it is also about fundamentally re-ordering the production and consumption of knowledge – putting into question the very epistemological basis for our prevailing "common sense" and asking us to radically reassess "how we know what we know". Discursive hegemony, at its core, then is an attempt to "weave together different strands of discourse in an effort to dominate or structure a field of meaning, thus fixing the identities of objects and practices in a particular way" (Howarth, 2000, p. 102).

The radical potential of AI is precisely in this possible epistemological revolution, the social transformation of knowledge itself. Already this knowledge revolution is underway through ICTS and the advent of social media, which is both digitally "shrinking the world" and allowing for new, often troubling, voices and perspectives to gain unprecedented prominence for shaping views.

Significantly, the algorithms underpinning these digitalised communications profitably encourage and ultimately make almost unavoidable political "echo chambers" (see Cinelli et al., 2021; Nguyen, 2020) where, based on our preferences, we only hear those views most similar to our own or those so dissimilar that it evokes a provocative rather than deliberative response. The goal, here, is increased usage not an open, free, and constructive space for collective discussion and informed democratic decision-making.

By contrast, counter-hegemonic intelligence prioritises the ability of machine learning to quantify and qualify humanity's ideological bias. Crucially, it would seek to go beyond mere explicability. By contrast, it would use its advanced capabilities to precisely identify the dominant discourses driving social decision-making. This could range, for example, from the perceived belief in the importance of competition and entrepreneurship for economic development to efforts in authoritarian reasoning and intentions driving strategies linked to AI-powered "social credit" scoring for disciplining populations. This would involve new "human in the loop" approaches that could allow human and machine collaborations for this counter-hegemonic knowledge production.

Crucially, it would permit AI from being simply innovative to fundamentally transformational in its use and effects. At present, it is being deployed most for improving existing systems – often for quite morally troubling ends. Whether this be the employment of "sentient" analysis on workers by employers to monitor and control their behaviour, the Uber-like application of AI-powered platforms to aid economic exploitation of an increasingly precarious workforce, or the deployment of hi-tech tracking systems for ushering in a new era of global detention, incarceration, and "rehabilitation". By recalibrating AI to actually identify these hegemonic discourses, it enhances its ability for enacting systemic social change.

ANTAGONISTIC MACHINES

A continual discourse surrounding AI is its overall threat to humanity. Initially, this was couched in terms of the existential fears of machines turning on their creators – threatening to make humans outdated. Even the late brilliant Stephen Hawkins once warned:

> The development of AI could spell the end of the human race. It would take off on its own and redesign itself at an ever increasing rate. Humans, who are limited by slow biological evolution, couldn't compete and would be superseded. (Quoted in Cellan-Jones, 2014, n.p.)

These fears have evolved in the present time to the danger of AI controlling human behaviour and stealing their data for profitable and nefarious purposes. "Digital mechanization has also smoothed the way for the growth of insecure and underpaid jobs. This reflects the sociopolitical features of neoliberal capitalism and not the intrinsic attributes of technology per se", writes Professor Peter Fleming (2019, p. 217), "Because of this, robotic automation might even help deepen the institution of paid employment in Western economies, not release us from it".

Hence, the attempts to render AI more trustworthy (Chatilla et al., 2021; Kaur et al., 2022) are premised on a desire to lessen these long-standing and increasingly serious concerns. Yet it also risks politically limiting the radical potential of AI as a disruptive force for positive change. The alarm over human-conquering robots may appear to be primarily in the realm of science fiction. However, it has actually driven much of the past, and to an extent, present, theory of AI, notably linked to the concept of singularity whereby machine intelligence will become so smart that it will overtake the limited intelligence of humans (see Good, 1965). Yet the threat of singularity is firmly rooted in human values of power, control, and exploitation. The scholar Gregory Jerome Hampton (2015, p. 2) insightfully observes, in this regard, that

> Slavery, after all, was largely invested in producing and controlling a labor force, which was dissociated from humanity. In many regards, American slavery was a failed experiment to employ flesh and blood machines as household appliance[s], farm equipment, sex toys, and various tools of industry without the benefit of human and civil rights. Consequently, what is interesting about the development and production of mechanical robots is how they are being assigned both race and gender as identity markers. Why does a machine need such a complex identity, if the machine is designed only to complete the mundane labour that humanity wishes to forego? One plausible response is that the machine is being designed to be more than an appliance and less than a human. The technology of the 21st century is in the process of developing a modern day socially accepted slave.

It assumes, hence, that machines would seek to be our masters as that is the rationale by which humans have historically operated. If singularity is a threat – which itself is a questionable assertion based on current technological developments – then it is fundamentally a human-created one that can only be addressed through a profound transformation of social values.

An appealing alternative would be to construct a new more cooperative basis for constructing trans-human relations. These values are already reflected, for instance, in ideas of cooperative robotics (see Johnson et al., 2011; Khoshnoud et al., 2020). The Internet of Things has similarly begun adopting these more collaborative principles (see Jiang, 2019). Fundamentally, this speaks to notions of what I have previously termed "mutually intelligent design" between humans and machines in which

> Ultimately, perhaps the greatest hope for the politics of the twenty-first century is the transformation of posthuman emancipation into transhuman liberation. More precisely, the escape, the freedom, from human based oppression and tyranny for an integrative human and non-human society that creatively collaborates and cooperates in the making and remaking of their shared social realities. (Bloom, 2020, p. 201)

Yet this theory should not be mistaken for trying to reduce the political possibilities of AI. Rather, it should be a force for challenging hegemonic values and power relations. Laclau and Mouffe refer, in this respect, to the importance of social antagonisms. They note that "Antagonisms are not objective relations, but relations which reveal the limits of all objectivity. Society is constituted around these limits, and they are antagonistic limits" (Laclau & Mouffe, 1986, p. xiii–xiv). The presence of antagonisms is not just one of resistance. They are also prefigurative. They present an alternative view of what society could and arguably should be.

What then would be the prospects of developing not only counter-hegemonic intelligent but antagonistic machines? A critical step in this direction is through the use of AI-powered simulations to help reveal these other possible worlds. As Häkli (2018, p. 173) contends:

> We should study further the idea of a humanised posthumanism, building on an ontology of possibility that acknowledges our assembled entanglement with the non-human world but also accords an important role for humans in acknowledging these interdependencies. As a move beyond monist posthumanism, instead of portraying mastery over passive nature, this position builds on the idea of political responsibility for the vulnerabilities, injustices, and hazards that our assembled life of dual being in and with … nature entails. It also acknowledges that all ontological claims and arguments remain meaningless without the audiences to which they are directed – audiences concerned with how to lead a civic life in a more-than-posthuman world.

Doing so means expanding upon ideas of the "cyborg citizen", which emphasises a trans-human "participatory evolution" where we should shape our future through multiple human choices, incomplete and contradictory as they often are. Participatory government is the same… "Decisions about evolution should be made at the grassroots, just as political and economic decisions should be, especially now that we have begun to recognize the political evolution of cyborgs" (Gray, 2000, p. 3).

At present, for instance, digital twin technologies permit precisely simulating and predicting human outcomes. These could be expanded to include digital alternatives that draw on existing data in order to reflect what a radically different social order could look like – thus deploying virtual technologies to paradoxically be virtually more real than these counter-hegemonic perspectives. Perhaps needed above all else, though, is a renewed praxis of trans-human solidarity – cultivating political cultures that emphasise the common struggle of machines and humans against exploitation. Such solidarity is already informally arising in progressive movements across the world. These could be made more explicit through processes of radical knowledge sharing leading to revolutionary human-machine learning. This could take the form, for example, of chatbots or "cobots" (see Sutherland, 2018) who can provide expert advice for organisers and those interested in experimenting with radical alternatives such as cooperative ownership, common resource governance, and degrowth development.

These advances would do more than simply identify existing biases. They would also bring to the fore how AI is attempting to reinforce a neoliberal worldview and discipline people in accordance with its underlying capitalist values. It would show the potential to repurpose "intelligence" away from optimising people as efficient human machines and instead as a resource for exploring alternative and more emancipatory social relations. The speculative logic of calculation and prediction, in turn, is transformed into an opportunity for people to discover and personalise different visions of the future.

While these possibilities are not yet fully created, they are technically possible and politically urgent. As a result of AI dramatically influencing human power and control, it must be designed in a way that enhances contemporary resistance and transformation. Only by working and struggling together can a better-liberated future for humans and machines alike become possible. It is ever more imperative to generate counter-hegemonic intelligence and antagonistic machines for this revolutionary purpose.

FURTHER READING

Bloom, P. (2020). *Identity, institutions and governance in an AI world: Transhuman relations.* Springer Nature.

Bloom, P., Jones, O. S., & Woodcock, J. (2021). *Guerrilla democracy: Mobile power and revolution in the 21st century.* Policy Press.

Bloom, P., & Sancino, A. (2019). *Disruptive democracy: The clash between techno-populism and techno-democracy.* Sage.

REFERENCES

Bauer, D. (2019). Alienation, freedom and the synthetic how. *Angelaki*, *24*(1), 106–117.

Biele, C. (2022). *Human movements in human-computer interaction (HCI)* (Vol. 996, pp. 1–142). Springer.

Bloom, P. (2020). *Identity, institutions and governance in an AI world: Transhuman relations*. Springer Nature.

Bloom, P., & Sancino, A. (2019). *Disruptive democracy: The clash between techno-populism and techno-democracy*. Sage.

Bostrom, N. (2014). *Taking superintelligence seriously: Superintelligence: Paths, dangers, strategies*. Oxford University Press.

Buranyi, S. (2017). Rise of the racist robots – how AI is learning all our worst impulses. *The Guardian*, August 8.

Caliskan, A. (2021). Detecting and mitigating bias in natural language processing. *Brookings*, May 10.

Cellan-Jones, R. (2014, December 2). Stephen Hawking warns artificial intelligence could end mankind. *BBC News*. Archived from the original on October 30, 2015.

Chatila, R., Dignum, V., Fisher, M., Giannotti, F., Morik, K., Russell, S., & Yeung, K. (2021). Trustworthy AI. In *Reflections on artificial intelligence for humanity* (pp. 13–39). Springer.

Cinelli, M., De Francisci Morales, G., Galeazzi, A., Quattrociocchi, W., & Starnini, M. (2021). The echo chamber effect on social media. *Proceedings of the National Academy of Sciences*, *118*(9), e2023301118.

Cui, Y., & van Esch, P. (2022). Autonomy and control: How political ideology shapes the use of artificial intelligence. *Psychology & Marketing*, *39*(6), 1218–1229.

Faulkner, C. (1998). *The essence of human-computer interaction*. Prentice-Hall, Inc.

Fleming, P. (2019). Robots and organization studies: Why robots might not want to steal your job. *Organization Studies*, *40*(1), 23–38.

Good, I. J. (1965). Speculations concerning the first ultraintelligent machine. In F. L. Alt & M. Rubinoff (Eds.), *Advances in computers* (Vol. 6, pp. 31–88). Academic Press.

Glynos, J., & Howarth, D. (2007). *Logics of critical explanation in social and political theory*. Routledge.

Gray, C. H. (2000). *Cyborg citizen: Politics in the posthuman age*. Routledge.

Häkli, J. (2018). The subject of citizenship–can there be a posthuman civil society? *Political Geography*, *67*, 166–175.

Hampton, G. J. (2015). *Imagining slaves and robots in literature, film, and popular culture: Reinventing yesterday's slave with tomorrow's robot*. Lexington Books.

Hellemans, P. (2020). Hidden stratification and the accuracy principle: May positive discrimination in AI be a solution? KU Leuven: Centre for IP and IT Law, March 24.

Hern, A. (2022). Microsoft limits access to facial recognition tool in AI ethics overhaul. *The Guardian*, June 22.

Howarth, D. (2000). *Discourse*. McGraw-Hill Education (UK).

Jiang, W. (2019). An intelligent supply chain information collaboration model based on Internet of Things and big data. *IEEE Access*, *7*, 58324–58335.

Johnson, M., Bradshaw, J. M., Feltovich, P. J., Hoffman, R. R., Jonker, C., van Riemsdijk, B., & Sierhuis, M. (2011). Beyond cooperative robotics: The central role of interdependence in coactive design. *IEEE Intelligent Systems*, *26*(3), 81–88.

Katz, Y. (2020). *Artificial whiteness: Politics and ideology in artificial intelligence*. Columbia University Press.

Kaur, D., Uslu, S., Rittichier, K. J., & Durresi, A. (2022). Trustworthy artificial intelligence: A review. *ACM Computing Surveys (CSUR)*, *55*(2), 1–38.

Khoshnoud, F., Quadrelli, M. B., Esat, I. I., & Robinson, D. (2020). Quantum cooperative robotics and autonomy. *arXiv preprint arXiv:2008.12230*.

Laclau, E., & Mouffe, C. (1986). *Hegemony and socialist strategy: Towards a radical democratic politics* (Vol. 8). Verso Books.

Laclau, E. (1990). *New reflections on the revolution of our time*. Verso Trade.

Ledford, H. (2019). Millions of black people affected by racial bias in health-care algorithms. *Nature*, October 24.

Liao, Q. V., Gruen, D., & Miller, S. (2020, April). Questioning the AI: Informing design practices for explainable AI user experiences. In *Proceedings of the 2020 CHI conference on human factors in computing systems* (pp. 1–15).

MacCarthy, M., & Propp, K. (2021). Machines learn that Brussels writes the rules: The EU's new AI regulation. *Brookings Institute*, May 4.

Magerman, D. (2022). Systemic bias in data makes AI a stereotype machine. *Inside Big Data*, February 9.

Manyika, J., Silberg, J., & Presten, B. (2019). What do we do about the biases in AI. *Harvard Business Review*, 25.

Mathew, A. R., Al Hajj, A., & Al Abri, A. (2011, June). Human-computer interaction (HCI): An overview. In *2011 IEEE international conference on computer science and automation engineering* (Vol. 1, pp. 99–100). IEEE.

Metz, C. (2021). *Who is making sure the A.I. Machines aren't racist? The New York Times*, March 15.

Nguyen, C. T. (2020). Echo chambers and epistemic bubbles. *Episteme*, *17*(2), 141–161.

Nouri, S. (2021). The role of bias in artificial intelligence. *Forbes*, February 4.

O'Neil, C. (2016). *Weapons of math destruction: How big data increases inequality and threatens democracy*. Broadway Books.

Packard, N. (2018). Habitual interaction estranged. *International Journal of Social Sciences*, *7*(1), 69–94.

Rai, A. (2020). Explainable AI: From black box to glass box. *Journal of the Academy of Marketing Science*, *48*(1), 137–141.

Raji, D. (2020). How our data encodes systematic racism. *MIT Technology Review*, December 10.

Roselli, D., Matthews, J., & Talagala, N. (2019, May). Managing bias in AI. In *Companion proceedings of the 2019 world wide web conference* (pp. 539–544).

Sætra, H. S. (2020). A shallow defence of a technocracy of artificial intelligence: Examining the political harms of algorithmic governance in the domain of government. *Technology in Society*, *62*, 101283.

Samek, W., Montavon, G., Vedaldi, A., Hansen, L. K., & Müller, K. R. (Eds.). (2019). *Explainable AI: Interpreting, explaining and visualizing deep learning* (Vol. 11700). Springer Nature.

Schwartz, R., Vassilev, A., Greene, K., Perine, L., Burt, A., & Hall, P. (2022). Towards a standard for identifying and managing bias in artificial intelligence. *NIST*, March.

Sias, L. (2021). The ideology of AI. *Philosophy Today*, *65*(3), 505–522.

Silberg, J., & Manyika, J. (2019). Notes from the AI frontier: Tackling bias in AI (and in humans). *McKinsey Global Institute*, 1–6.

Sutherland, D. (2018). Solidarity forever-robots, workers and profitability. *Australian Socialist*, *24*(1), 12.

Taillandier, A. (2021). "Staring into the singularity" and other posthuman tales: Transhumanist stories of future change. *History and Theory*, *60*(2), 215–233.

Vesa, M., & Tienari, J. (2020). Artificial intelligence and rationalized unaccountability: Ideology of the elites? *Organization*, 1350508420963872.

4.   The becoming of AI: a critical perspective on the contingent formation of AI

Anna Jobin and Christian Katzenbach

INTRODUCTION

We are currently witnessing the formation of 21st-century artificial intelligence (AI). Although the notion of AI has been around since the 1950s, it has become omnipresent in many domains of society only over the last decade: the private sector grapples with integrating what appears to be an irresistible technological innovation; the public sector discusses potential applications and future legislation; and the public at large deals with media narratives and AI systems already deployed. From machine learning to deep neural networks, from natural language processing to image and pattern recognition, AI techniques are starting to permeate today's infrastructures and organizations and dominant narratives of the future. There is a tendency across sectors to contend with AI as something inevitable. Colorful metaphors, for example, describe AI as an autonomous force that, like a "tsunami" (GARTNER, 2018), sweeps away whoever does not prepare to accommodate it to its full potential.

If the promises are to be believed, AI will revolutionize science, automatically detect various health issues, eliminate hate speech and misinformation, and prevent crimes. However, simultaneously to being hyped, 21st-century AI is also an object of controversy and contestation. Whereas some question feasibility and discuss details of its promises, others point to more general issues. Specific concerns involve the carbon footprint of AI, its capacity to exacerbate existing inequalities, and its lack of accountability. Both promises as well as contestations draw attention to specific sites and aspects of AI and have the potential to influence where resources are allocated. Artificial intelligence is a sociotechnical phenomenon still very much in formation, as diverse sets of actors and institutions shape various narratives. Even disputes around the very definition of AI are not settled, because there is no consensus over which different technologies and techniques actually fall under its label.

Hence, while it might be already established that some AI technologies are and will continue to be essential parts of societies' future fabric, the specific trajectories and characteristics of future AI are far from set. As with all technologies, this is a contingent formation process. It could always be different! Technologies are not merely products of functional technological development but are just as much dependent on economic, political, and discursive drivers. So, what are the forces that are shaping the institutionalization of AI? Although AI is often framed as a purely technical matter, its promises and potential threats demonstrate impacts far beyond technology itself. Moreover, technologies are always shaped by social, political, and economic dynamics. What are the dynamics that have made AI what it is today? The answer to this question is not simply based on scientific progress. A linear story, one which frames today's AI as the result of succeeding technological achievements, fails to account for the rich sociopolitical contexts that have shaped its development over the past (Cardon et al., 2018).

This chapter offers a critical perspective on the contingent formation of AI as a key sociotechnical institution in contemporary societies. For that, it first builds on work from science and technology studies (STS) and critical algorithm studies showing that technological developments are always contingent on the result of transformations along multiple scientific trajectories and the interaction of multiple stakeholders and discourses. We then identify implications for the conceptual understanding of AI and its epistemology, namely a shift away from attention for the ex-post detection of impact and bias and toward issues that characterize how AI is coming into being as a powerful sociotechnical entity. We then illustrate this process by reconstructing the becoming of three key domains: technological research, media discourse, and regulatory governance, and conclude with implications and future avenues of research.

AI AS A SOCIOTECHNICAL SYSTEM

Artificial intelligence has become an "umbrella term" (Rip & Voß, 2013) for a wide array of technologies and techniques. For the last two decades, the term AI has had more valence in research administration and funding decisions, more so than in actual technological development (Cardon et al., 2018). It "continues to be the public-facing term used by companies, institutes, and initiatives" (Joyce et al., 2021, p. 2). Many current debates in media and policy take AI for granted, as a technical and univocal entity that is to be addressed through regulations and built-in corrections, for instance, in seeking explanations for decisions of technical systems building on machine learning. In doing so, they not only fail to acknowledge AI as a local and situated sociotechnical composition, but they also fail to account for their own role in shaping it.

Current debates, in other words, often address the social impact of AI, but do not consider AI as a social construction per se – which reproduces a consequential misconception already denounced by prominent scholars during the 1980s (Bloomfield, 1985; Woolgar, 1985). Again and again, it has been shown that technological developments are neither linear nor predetermined, and always a result of transformations along multiple scientific trajectories and of the interaction between various communities of actors and discourses. This section will therefore situate the analysis of AI as a sociotechnical artifact within existing approaches to studying technology, and algorithmic systems in particular, before centering on the formation and institutionalization of AI in specific domains in the next section.

The Contingency of Technological Artifacts

Most prominently, STS has demonstrated for decades how technology does not just happen but is imagined, designed, built, and used by humans and organizations. The "social construction of technology" approach, or SCOT, in particular, adopts a socio-historical perspective that aims to open up the "black boxes" of taken-for-granted technologies (Pinch & Bijker, 1984). Considering technologies as socially constructed challenges the trope of one possible way, or even one best way, to design an artifact. "Contingency" serves as a key term in exactly that regard: "STS is […] sensitive to the contingency of things. At least in principle, they do not have to be, the way they are" (Law & Yin, 2022, p. 134).

According to SCOT, relevant social groups give significance to their interaction with a technological artifact via elements such as goals, key problems, problem-solving strategies, existing theories, and tacit knowledge. The sum of all such elements is "technological frames" (Bijker, 1995). Similarly, the focus of the "social shaping of technology" perspective (Bijker & Law, 1994; MacKenzie & Wajcman, 1999) lies on the intertwined political, cultural, and economic dynamics that shape technology, though it is considered to attribute more weight, relatively speaking, to materiality (Howcroft et al., 2004).

Actor-network theory (ANT) offers a similar but slightly different way to analyze the co-constitution of technology and society by describing networks of human and non-human "actants" that may or may not "enroll" other actants in their "program," or be enrolled in other actants' programs (Callon, 1984; Latour, 1993, 2005). Successful enrollments may result in the alignment of actants and stabilization of networks and, thus, technologies (though ANT does not operate with this category). The focus on the dynamics of the relations between actants is a way to study how reality is enacted in practice. For ANT, like for SCOT, a technology is not a fixed entity but is above all a social achievement. In this way, the formation of AI is a contingent process – it could have been different. But it is not coincidental. It has required massive institutional and individual, political, and economic work to support and speed up its development.

The social aspects of instituting algorithmic systems such as AI have been the focus of critical algorithms studies (CAS) specifically. CAS reunites critical scholarship on "algorithms as social concerns" (Gillespie & Seaver, 2015, n.p.) to study both the norms and ideologies embedded in algorithmic systems and their enactment. It addresses the symbolic and material aspects of algorithmic systems, as well as how these may be interwoven. CAS draws most notably on communication studies and STS and interrogates how and in what ways algorithmic systems have social and political valence (Gillespie, 2014). As Wajcman and Jones (2012, p. 1) noted: "Recent media research is increasingly drawn to STS, while STS analysts are increasingly drawn to research media technologies."[1] Critical algorithm studies can thus be seen as a convergence of disciplinary foci as much as a convergence of information and communication technology.

This scholarly convergence manifests more broadly in the increasing interest of STS in the conjunction of discourse and the making of politics and technology (Mager & Katzenbach, 2021), as well as research on mediated discourses about technologies in media and communication studies. Scholars working on digital technology and media are increasingly building on the sociology of expectations to study expectations and stories about the future (Lente, 2016) to highlight the role of technological innovations and visionary rhetoric in enterprises (Beckert, 2016) and identify the discursive struggles around "contested futures" (Brown et al., 2000) and prevalent metaphors (Wyatt, 2017). In the context of AI, metaphors such as the proper artificial "intelligence" or machine "learning" guide the societal discourse sustainably and fuel fantasies and future visions both in the broader public just as much as in expert communities and economic contexts. These "imaginaries" of AI[2] strongly rest on long-standing motifs of human-like machines in mythical storytelling and science fiction (Bory, 2019), and

---

[1]   The authors base their assertion on Calhoun's macro-sociological theorization of the "infrastructure of modernity" in which it is argued that the ever-growing communication needs of corporations, rising as organizing entities of the social order, have caught up (or even surpassed) nation-states as driving social forces in the development of large-scale information and communication technologies and infrastructures.

[2]   Cf. "Imaginaries of AI" in this *Handbook*, as well as Mager & Katzenbach (2021) for the concept of "sociotechnical imaginaries."

are deeply incorporated into actual AI research and its identity (Natale & Ballatore, 2017) and drive economic decision-making (Campolo & Crawford, 2020). Taken together, these works show how strongly AI, as we know it today, is not simply a consequence of technological progress but of multiple cultural, political, economic, and discursive movements.

Conceptualization and Epistemological Implications

These sociotechnical perspectives help us understand how (and in which form) algorithms and AI have become deeply ingrained and taken for granted within society. They have far-reaching implications for our conceptual and epistemological understanding of AI and its role.

From a more *limited perspective*, AI and algorithmic systems are understood as distinct technological artifacts. Though socially constructed, their design and function can, in this case, be assessed and evaluated from the outside. Investigations into algorithmic bias, or bias in AI, often fall into this category. Identifying bias embedded within AI translates into identifying bias in the input, the transformation, and/or the output of an algorithmic system. Centering attention on the bias through this lens implies, symmetrically, that there is a non-biased, "right" way for algorithms to work.

Despite its shortcomings as a general epistemological stance on algorithmic systems, this conceptualization provides a valid frame if applied to particular cases with narrow research questions. Such cases are, for example, investigations into how the actual outcome of a particular algorithmic task compares to clearly defined goals: for instance, when three well-known image-recognition algorithms are simply not successful in accomplishing what they are purposed to do (Bechmann, 2017); or when widely used face-recognition algorithms have significantly bigger failure rates for non-white and non-male people (Buolamwini & Gebru, 2018). To counter bias in algorithmic systems at scale, scholars and civil society organizations propose algorithmic audits (e.g., O'Neil, 2016; Sandvig et al., 2014) or reverse engineering (Diakopoulos, 2015). These types of suggestions rely on the assumption that algorithmic bias is, above all, a matter of lacking transparency about the technology and data in use, a problem that could be overcome by detecting potential fallacious inner workings of AI systems.

A *broader sociotechnical perspective* identifies AI not as distinct artifacts but to be closely interwoven with society. This is an important shift with conceptual and epistemological implications. For the issue of bias, for instance, this means considering bias as being inherent in the working of AI systems, not as problems to be solved. Bias is no longer considered to be originating in a malfunctioning biased algorithm that could work better, but it lies in the very use of the system itself (Jobin et al., 2019a). As a consequence, the research goal consists not necessarily in identifying bias within the technology itself, but in showing how existing social prejudices become encoded in AI. Prominent studies adopting this perspective demonstrate how algorithmic classification leads unavoidably to biased outcomes (e.g., Noble, 2018, Bender et al., 2021).

An important perspective arises if humans are considered as active participants in algorithmic systems (Dourish, 2001) and it opens up questions about their role in (co-)producing algorithms. The "production" of many AI systems is not subjected to the same linearity as other, unambiguously material, technological artifacts because connected digital systems evolve constantly (Seaver, 2013). When both output data and users' reaction to output data becomes new input data, it is indeed not hyperbolic to speak of co-constructing reality with algorithms (Just & Latzer, 2017). Research has highlighted the importance of people in many different temporal and contextual settings, such as the ways in which humans contribute to maintaining or stabilizing algorithmic technology (Cohn, 2019) or how users understand algorithms and AI (e.g., Eslami et al., 2015). Bolin and Andersson (2015), for example, note how user interpretations often rely on already-known heuristics instead of taking into account the technical subtleties of a given algorithmic system. Another perspective focuses on the role of human workers in seemingly automated tasks (e.g., Casilli, 2019; Gray & Suri, 2019) to the point of Casilli (2017) proclaiming that "there is no algorithm," a provocation pointedly underlining the significance of people in algorithmic systems.

Emphasizing yet another important social dimension, Geiger (2017) insists on how interaction with algorithmic systems is also learned. Studying the socialization of new Wikipedians to the organizational norms and processes, Geiger (2017) draws attention to important parallels and entanglements between social and algorithmic dimensions of organizations (p. 10). Hence, an emphasis on the social aspects of algorithms cannot ignore questions about how interaction with these technologies is taught and learned, explained and understood, and must address the human labor that goes into maintaining and sustaining algorithmic systems.

Overall, it becomes apparent that when algorithms and AI are taken to be complex technological systems, contingent on and entangled with the social world, the focus of inquiry shifts (Joyce et al., 2021; Yolgörmez, 2021). It moves away from detecting impact and bias, and toward issues that rather characterize how AI is coming into being as a powerful sociotechnical entity, such as accountability (Jobin, 2013; Neyland, 2015), enactment (Geiger, 2014; Ziewitz, 2015), institutional translation (Bolin & Andersson Schwarz, 2015), and discursive work (Bareis & Katzenbach, 2021).

THE BECOMING OF AI

Building on these grounds, it becomes evident that a critical perspective on AI, on understanding the role of AI in society, must contribute to the becoming of AI as a key sociotechnical institution. For this formation process, the mythical and contested notion of AI has very successfully provided an umbrella term that offers "a semantic reference for negotiating certain packages of scientific search practices with societal and political concerns" (Rip & Voß, 2013, p. 40). The notion of AI encompasses many different things on the technological level, massive economic ambitions, wide-ranging narratives, and future visions, just as much as normative values and fundamental concerns. What Rip and Voß describe for "nanotechnology" and "sustainability" is just as true for AI: "Over time, umbrella terms and the packages they hold together may stabilize and become reinforced with research infrastructures and through the institutionalization of funding schemes" (Rip & Voß, 2013, p. 40). The current instituting of AI is, thus, a process that necessarily unfolds across different social domains. If it were restricted to the technological domain, it would not be established as a sociotechnical institution. This is the organizational quality of the notion of AI.

Now, how has the contemporary rise of AI unfolded? How has 21st-century AI become this powerful sociotechnical institution? While we are still leading controversies and debates on shaping the integration of AI into our societies, it seems to be taken for granted that AI is here to stay. Society, industries, and governments are said to risk being swept away if they do not respond to this "tsunami" of assumed innovations (Gartner, 2018). While we have seen spikes of interest in AI before, the recent conjunction of such AI hype with fundamental scientific controversies, massive allocations of technological and financial resources, and broad discourse about hopes and fears has raised the role of AI to a whole new level.

In consequence, contemporary AI is already established, yet still in a formative stage when it comes to its actual shape. Controversies about the specific pathways to be taken are still visible. For some, AI will change how we live, communicate, work, and travel. With the promise of autonomous vehicles, automated detection of illnesses, and automatic filtering of misinformation – AI is being positioned to fix fundamental problems in our societies. In different countries, large-scale research investments in AI now go hand-in-hand with the re-activation of state-led industrial strategies, marked by top-down investment models. But investments are often justified in terms of the development of alternative forms of human-centered, trust-based AI of which the outcomes still have to be evaluated (Barnes & Chin, 2018). While the wide-ranging claims are certainly the product of contingent hype, they nevertheless have powerful effects on how they structure actors and resources. At the same time, substantive concerns have been raised that these developments might reinforce inequality, exacerbate the opacity of decision-making processes, and ultimately question human autonomy.

In consequence, we are living in a time when the infrastructures and institutions of our everyday lives are being (re)built at the hands of techniques that already elude popular and professional understanding. Looking at the becoming of AI and its institutionalization in society across different spheres allows us to see the specific pathway this development has taken – and which might have been abandoned. In the following, we briefly reconstruct the becoming of AI in three key domains to illustrate this argument: technological research, media discourse, and regulatory governance.

AI in Technological Research

Artificial intelligence is a salient issue in many different social domains. For most, it is primarily a technological matter in computer science. And, of course, the institution of AI is deeply intertwined with the domain of technological research, starting with the credited first use of the term "artificial intelligence," which was the expression used by Marvin Minsky, John McCarthy, and colleagues for a 1956 scholarly symposium taking place in Dartmouth (Broussard, 2018). Since then, what AI is or is not has changed and remains a highly debated issue among computer scientists and beyond. After several cycles of AI "hypes" and "AI winters," technological research on AI has particularly gained massive traction and visibility again after landmark research in neural networks in 2010–2012. These breakthroughs happened after an alignment of a massive institutional, individual, and political-economic set of precursors in place to support and speed its development; at the same time, they have been shaping industry strategy and public policy in turn (Markoff, 2016).

Looking at the history and the trajectories of AI research beyond the current AI hype makes it possible to understand that there is *not* one single strand of development of AI technologies that iteratively gets better and more efficient in simple functional development. The sociotechnical perspectives summarized previously enable scholars to propose that, just like any other technology, the development of AI is contingent on social, political, and economic aspects. It is the result of transformations along multiple scientific trajectories and interaction among multiple communities of actors and discourses. The comprehensive study by Cardon and colleagues (2018) offers an instructive illustration of this contested history of AI: Building on bibliometric analyses and interviews, the authors reconstruct the different trajectories of AI research since the 1950s and identify the changing impact of different scientific communities over time. Cardon et al. see the field characterized by a tension between "connectionist" and "symbolic" approaches to AI that have struggled over epistemic dominance and the allocation of resources in the last 70 years. Scholars, publications, and resources can be quite clearly structured around these two poles of AI research with only a few people and initiatives bridging the opposing camps (Cardon et al., 2018). The symbolic perspective aspires to create human-like comprehension of the world. It understands the process of thinking to be inherently semantic and material (Cardon et al., 2018, p. 4), The connectionist approach to AI, on the other hand, mimics thinking in the form of parallel calculations which, taken together, would result in "intelligence." This approach includes contemporary forms of machine learning and deep learning.

While the current perspective of AI might seem synonymous on the technical dimension with forms of machine learning, this reconstruction clearly shows that this was not always the case. For decades, namely in the 1970s and 1980s, the symbolic approach was clearly dominating AI research and debates. If the current supremacy of the connectionist approach marks the end of this struggle or rather a temporary phenomenon is hard to tell from the current standpoint. But it has an impact on what we consider AI to be, and how it is best regulated and integrated into our societies.

AI in the Media

In the process of AI becoming what it is today, and in the social negotiation about its understanding and role, media plays a crucial role.[3] In addition to the general role of media in mediating communication in society, it is the primary means to institutionalize shared understandings of new technologies. Legacy and social media are the primary sources for many people when learning about and evaluating technological developments (Eurobarometer, 2014). Thus, it matters greatly how media and journalists communicate competing technical and policy realities and give certain actors and perspectives more visibility and legitimacy than others (Venturini et al., 2015). Existing research on media reporting on new technologies shows that different media construct these technologies differently, including pronounced differences between countries (Milde, 2017).

For an umbrella term such as AI, media reporting and mediated communication strongly contribute to the formation of AI. In fact, it is necessary not only for public understanding and social sense-making of the technology. Even for technological researchers in the field, narratives in the mediated discourse about AI have a strong orientation function. In existing studies of media reporting and fictional representation of AI, scholars have shown AI being portrayed in different ways and forms in different media and countries. Yet, some pronounced characteristics seem to emerge. Media reporting has a strong focus on showcasing the latest high-tech products and services, featuring corporate actors much more often in AI reporting than other stakeholders (Chuan et al., 2019). For the UK, Brennen et al. (2018) found this dominance of industry, such as products and initiatives, the primary characteristic of media reporting on AI. Similarly for Germany, Fischer and Puschmann (2021), identified industry actors as dominant in German reporting about AI, as well as economic topics clearly ranking much higher in

---

[3] Cf. the chapters on "Framing AI in news" and "Media representations of artificial intelligence: Surveying the field" in this *Handbook* for more detailed discussions of AI in the media.

visibility than social and technological questions. Recent studies of media coverage of AI in China reveal a similar dominance of the private sector in propagating positive discourses, yet there is a stronger governmental hold on the topic as well (Zeng et al., 2022).

This industry agenda-setting favors an overhyped vision of AI, resulting in a public focus on the potentials of AI and neglecting its actual methodological limitations (Elish & boyd, 2018). These narratives support the positioning of AI technologies as solutions to social problems by technology companies – rather than problematizing or questioning their deep integration into our societies (Katzenbach, 2021).

AI in Policy and Governance

Many of these motifs and framings of AI that are dominant in media discourse in AI find their way into the political processing of AI. With emerging phenomena such as AI, the policy agenda-setting process is still quite open and more concerned with framing the issues and problems than finding direct regulatory answers. Thus, it is maybe not surprising that political documents in such early phases strongly adopt media narratives (Bareis & Katzenbach, 2021). What matters, what is focused on, is still being negotiated in many settings at different levels, with various initiatives in AI policy involving many different actors being recent or even ongoing.

There is a wide range of initiatives in place for understanding AI policy as the sum of all normative initiatives whose scope or aim is to govern artificial intelligence, starting with supranational AI policy initiatives such as the inter-governmental OECD AI Observatory, the Council of Europe's "Committee on AI" CAI, the EU HLEG Group for Ethical AI, and the EU AI Act. AI policy also comprises other types of initiatives, for example, technical audits or standards. Initiatives in this regard abound, from the US National Institute of Standards and Technology (NIST) to the International Organization for Standardization (ISO) or the Institute of Electrical and Electronics Engineers, the IEEE, and their "Ethically Aligned Design" initiative. These examples are by no means exhaustive but give a first idea of the variety of stakeholders and perspectives on a macrolevel.

Different categorizations of these initiatives exist, for example, by instrument, stakeholder, or domain. Brundage and Bryson (2016) suggested distinguishing between AI policies that are specifically targeted at AI-based technologies, existing policies that already concern AI, and policies from domains that also speak to AI-related issues. Others distinguish, for example, between "hard law" and "soft law" (Sossin & Smith, 2003). Laws and regulations count as "hard" law because they are legally binding and made authoritatively by the state. Soft law, on the other hand, is non-binding and can also be driven by actors from the economy and society: private companies, NGOs, research institutes, and so on.

Because AI is treated like an emerging technology in policy circles, and the political agenda-setting cycle is not yet closed, it is not surprising that soft law initiatives issued by various actors abound. For the governance of emerging technologies, soft law is typically an important first stage (Marchant, 2019). It does not have the slow pace of hard law, it can take various forms, it can be adaptive to different applications, different types of risks, and new risks that emerge, and it can accommodate differences across sectors while also working across national borders. In the case of AI, recent years have seen a proliferation of a very particular type of soft law: ethics guidelines or ethical principles for artificial intelligence. However, a thorough analysis of over 80 such guidelines revealed no consensus on common principles on how they should be applied or to whom they pertain (Jobin et al., 2019b). "AI ethics" as a subdomain of AI policy has sparked numerous debates. Whereas some research-ers call for a different focus on ethics (Rességuier & Rodrigues, 2020; van Maanen, 2022), others locate the problem with using ethics itself as a policy instrument for AI (Munn, 2022; Ochigame, 2019).

From a public policy perspective, AI policy is situated on the macro level and is about ensuring protection from harm and enhancing positive outcomes for the economy and society. Many institutions from the public sector, from ministries to parliaments and governments, have indeed addressed artificial intelligence in the last few years. They have done so in several ways. Most notable is probably specific legislation that is being considered, such as the EU AI Act. But the public sector is also very involved on the subnational level (Liebig et al., forth-coming). Key controversies on AI in the policy arena include questions around the governance and impact of specific applications. Face-recognition technologies and their governance, for example, are highly debated (Nabil Hassein, 2017; Raji et al., 2020): in what circumstances should it be used, under what conditions, and should it be used at all? In the context of the military sector, calls have been voiced to prohibit the use of AI in lethal autonomous weapon systems altogether (Rosert & Sauer, 2021).

As an intermediate result in this emerging policy field, it seems as if the earliest initia-tives, namely the numerous national AI strategies developed and published by many countries between 2016 and 2018, did have a remarkable framing and structuring impact (Radu, 2021). While these early policies themselves were strongly influenced by pertinent narratives of AI in media and society, they themselves constitute a peculiar "hybrid of policy and discourse" (Bareis & Katzenbach, 2021): national governments have offered in these documents broad visions of AI and its future role in society, and, at the same time have allocated massive resources and collective-binding rules. "As a result, these imaginaries not only reflect on and offer sociotechnical trajectories but, at the same time, coproduce the installment of these futures and, thus, yield a performative function (Bareis & Katzenbach, 2021, p. 17).

CONCLUSION

This chapter has offered a critical perspective on the contingent formation of artificial intel-ligence as a key sociotechnical institution in contemporary societies. We are living in a critical decade as we are currently witnessing (and contributing) to the formation and establishment of 21st-century AI. While there is a tendency across sectors to contend with AI as something inevitable, it is also still the object of controversy and contestation. Thus, it is of particular importance to understand and foreground that this AI formation process is contingent on economic, political, and discursive drivers – just like other technologies. They are not merely products of functional technological development but just as much dependent on them.

This also means that this process and its results could be different! With this chapter, we have tried to foreground such a critical perspective on the trajectory and current situation of AI. To do so, we have built on work from STS and critical algorithm studies as well as discur-sive and narrative approaches. For our conceptual understanding of AI and its epistemology, this is a consequential perspective. We aim to direct attention to different issues with this shift: away from detecting impact and bias ex-post, and toward a perspective that centers on how AI is coming into being as a powerful sociotechnical entity, and to trace the multi-ple scientific trajectories as well as interactions between the different stakeholders and dis-courses that characterize and, most importantly, shape this formation of AI. Ultimately, these processes decide *how* AI is coming into being as a powerful sociotechnical institution. We have illustrated this process in three key domains: technological research, media discourse, and regulatory governance.

The coming into being of AI is not a primarily technical matter. It is a process that unfolds across different social domains. If it were restricted to the technological domain, it would not be established as a sociotechnical institution. This is the organizational quality of the umbrella term "AI," as vague and contested as it is. Under this notion, the process of institutionalization has already come a long way. We are now taking for granted that AI is here to stay. Thus, it is ever more important to foreground that this formation process is contingent on many (non-technical) factors – still! We are currently building the digital infrastructures and institutions of this century, and we can still shape the remaining controversies and developments for the betterment of the public.

FURTHER READING

Bareis, J., & Katzenbach, C. (2021). Talking AI into being: The narratives and imaginaries of national AI strategies and their performative politics. *Science, Technology, & Human Values*, 1–27. https://doi.org/10.1177/01622439211030007
Cardon, D., Cointet, J.-P., & Mazières, A. (2018). Neurons spike back: The invention of inductive machines and the artificial intelligence controversy. *Réseaux*, 211(5), 173. https://doi.org/10.3917/res.211.0173
Gillespie, T. (2014). The relevance of algorithms. In T. Gillespie, P. Boczkowski, & K. Foot (Eds.), *Media technologies*. MIT University Press Group Ltd.

REFERENCES

Bareis, J., & Katzenbach, C. (2021). Talking AI into being: The narratives and imaginaries of national AI strategies and their performative politics. *Science, Technology, & Human Values*, 01622439211030007. https://doi.org/10.1177/01622439211030007
Barnes, J. E., & Chin, J. (2018, March 2). *The new arms race in AI - WSJ*. https://www.wsj.com/articles/the-new-arms-race-in-ai-1520009261
Bechmann, A. (2017, January 4). *Keeping it real: From faces and features to social values in deep learning algorithms on social media images*. https://doi.org/10.24251/HICSS.2017.218
Beckert, J. (2016). *Imagined futures*. Harvard University Press.
Bijker, W. E., & Law, J. (1994). *Shaping technology/building society: Studies in sociotechnical change*. MIT Press.
Bijker, W. E. (1995). *Of bicycles, bakelites, and bulbs: Toward a theory of sociotechnical change*. MIT Press.
Bender, E. M., Gebru, T., McMillan-Major, A., & Shmitchell, S. (2021). On the dangers of stochastic parrots: Can language models be too big? In *Proceedings of the 2021 ACM conference on fairness, accountability, and transparency, FAccT '21* (pp. 610–623). Association for Computing Machinery. https://doi.org/10.1145/3442188.3445922
Bloomfield, B. P. (1985). The culture of artificial intelligence. In B.P. Bloomfield (Ed.), *The question of artificial intelligence* (pp. 59–105). Routledge.
Bolin, G., & Andersson Schwarz, J. (2015). Heuristics of the algorithm: Big Data, user interpretation and institutional translation. *Big Data & Society*, 2(2), 2053951715608406. https://doi.org/10.1177/2053951715608406
Bory, P. (2019). Deep new: The shifting narratives of artificial intelligence from Deep Blue to AlphaGo. *Convergence: The International Journal of Research into New Media Technologies*, 25(4), 627–642. https://doi.org/10.1177/1354856519829679

Brennen, J. S., Howard, P. N., & Nielsen, R. K. (2018). *An industry-led debate: How UK media cover artificial intelligence*. Reuters Institute for the Study of Journalism, University of Oxford.

Broussard, M. (2018). *Artificial unintelligence: How computers misunderstand the world*. The MIT Press.

Brown, N., Rappert, B., & Webster, A. (2000). Introducing contested futures: From looking into the future to looking at the future. In N. Brown, B. Rappert, & A. Webster (Eds.), *Contested futures: A sociology of prospective techno-science* (pp. 3–20). Routledge.

Brundage, M., & Bryson, J. (2016). Smart policies for artificial intelligence. ArXiv:1608.08196 [Cs]. http://arxiv.org/abs/1608.08196

Bucher, T. (2016). 'Machines don't have instincts': Articulating the computational in journalism. *New Media & Society*, 1461444815624182. https://doi.org/10.1177/1461444815624182

Buolamwini, J., & Gebru, T. (2018). Gender shades: Intersectional accuracy disparities in commercial gender classification. *Proceedings of Machine Learning Research*, *81*, 1–15.

Callon, M. (1984). Some elements of a sociology of translation: Domestication of the scallops and the fishermen of St Brieuc Bay. *The Sociological Review*, *32*(Suppl 1), 196–233. https://doi.org/10.1111/j.1467-954X.1984.tb00113.x

Campolo, A., & Crawford, K. (2020). Enchanted determinism: Power without responsibility in artificial intelligence. *Engaging Science, Technology, and Society*, *6*, 1. https://doi.org/10.17351/ests2020.277

Cardon, D., Cointet, J.-P., & Mazières, A. (2018). Neurons spike back: The invention of inductive machines and the artificial intelligence controversy. *Réseaux*, *211*(5), 173. https://doi.org/10.3917/res.211.0173

Casilli, A. A. (2017). Il n'y a pas d'algorithme. In *L'appétit des géants: Pouvoir des algorithmes, ambitions des plateformes* (pp. 10–19). C&F Editions.

Casilli, A. A. (2019). *En attendant les robots*. Le Seuil.

Chuan, C.-H., Tsai, W.-H. S., & Cho, S. Y. (2019). Framing artificial intelligence in American newspapers. In *Proceedings of the 2019 AAAI/ACM Conference on AI, ethics, and society* (pp. 339–344). https://doi.org/10.1145/3306618.3314285

Cohn, M. L. (2019). Keeping software present software as a timely object for STS studies of the digital. In J. Vertesi & D. Ribes (Eds.), *DigitalSTS: A field guide for science & technology studies* (pp. 423–446). Princeton University Press.

Diakopoulos, N. (2015). Algorithmic accountability: Journalistic investigation of computational power structures. *Digital Journalism*, *3*(3), 398–415. https://doi.org/10.1080/21670811.2014.976411

Dourish, P. (2001). *Where the action is: The foundations of embodied interaction*. MIT Press.

Elish, M. C., & boyd, danah. (2018). Situating methods in the magic of Big Data and AI. *Communication Monographs*, *85*(1), 57–80. https://doi.org/10.1080/03637751.2017.1375130

Eslami, M., Rickman, A., Vaccaro, K., Aleyasen, A., Vuong, A., Karahalios, K., Hamilton, K., & Sandvig, C. (2015). 'I always assumed that I wasn't really that close to [her]': Reasoning about invisible algorithms in news feeds. In *Proceedings of the 33rd annual ACM conference on human factors in computing systems* (pp. 153–162). https://doi.org/10.1145/2702123.2702556

Eurobarometer. (2014). *Public perceptions of science, research and innovation*. European Commission.

Fischer, S., & Puschmann, C. (2021). *Wie Deutschland über Algorithmen schreibt: Eine Analyse des Mediendiskurses über Algorithmen und Künstliche Intelligenz (2005–2020)*. https://doi.org/10.11586/2021003

GARTNER. (2018). *5 trends emerge in Gartner hype cycle for emerging technologies*. Gartner. https://www.gartner.com/smarterwithgartner/5-trends-emerge-in-gartner-hype-cycle-for-emerging-technologies-2018

Geiger, R. S. (2014). Bots, bespoke code, and the materiality of software platforms. *Information, Communication & Society*, *17*(3), 342–356. https://doi.org/10.1080/1369118X.2013.873069.

Geiger, R. S. (2017). Beyond opening up the black box: Investigating the role of algorithmic systems in Wikipedian organizational culture. *Big Data & Society*, *4*(2), 2053951717730735. https://doi.org/10.1177/2053951717730735

Gillespie, T. (2014). The relevance of algorithms. In T. Gillespie, P. Boczkowski, & K. Foot (Eds.), *Media technologies*. MIT University Press Group Ltd.

Gillespie, T., & Seaver, N. (2015, November 5). Critical algorithm studies: A reading list. *Social Media Collective*. https://socialmediacollective.org/reading-lists/critical-algorithm-studies/

Gray, M. L., & Suri, S. (2019). *Ghost work: How to stop silicon valley from building a new global underclass.* Eamon Dolan/Houghton Mifflin Harcourt.

Hepp, A. (2020). The fragility of curating a pioneer community: Deep mediatization and the spread of the quantified self and maker movements. *International Journal of Cultural Studies, 23*(6), 932–950. https://doi.org/10.1177/1367877920922867

Hilgartner, S. (2015). Capturing the imaginary: Vanguards, visions and the synthetic biology revolution Stephen Hilgartner. In S. Hilgartner, C. Miller, & R. Hagendijk (Eds.), *Science and democracy* (pp. 33–55). Routledge. https://doi.org/10.4324/9780203564370-7

Howcroft, D., Mitev, N., & Wilson, M. (2004). What we may learn from the social shaping of technology approach. In J. Mingers & L. Willcocks (Eds.), *Social theory and philosophy of IS* (pp. 329–371). John Wiley and Sons Ltd. https://www.escholar.manchester.ac.uk/uk-ac-man-scw:3b5065

Jobin, A. (2013, October 21). Google's autocompletion: Algorithms, stereotypes and accountability. *Sociostrategy.* https://sociostrategy.com/2013/googles-autocompletion-algorithms-stereotypes-accountability/

Jobin, A., Prezioso, S., Glassey, O., & Kaplan, F. (2019a). La mémoire kaléidoscopique: l'histoire au prisme des algorithmes d'autocomplétion. *Geschichte und Informatik/Histoire et informatique, 20,* 83–101. https://doi.org/10.33057/chronos.1466

Jobin, A., Ienca, M., & Vayena, E. (2019b). The global landscape of AI ethics guidelines. *Nature Machine Intelligence,* 389–399. https://doi.org/10.1038/s42256-019-0088-2

Joyce, K., Smith-Doerr, L., Alegria, S., Bell, S., Cruz, T., Hoffman, S. G., Noble, S. U., & Shestakofsky, B. (2021). Toward a sociology of artificial intelligence: A call for research on inequalities and structural change. *Socius, 7,* 2378023121999581. https://doi.org/10.1177/2378023121999581

Just, N., & Latzer, M. (2017). Governance by algorithms: Reality construction by algorithmic selection on the Internet. *Media, Culture & Society, 39*(2), 238–258. https://doi.org/10.1177/0163443716643157

Katzenbach, C. (2021). "AI will fix this" – The technical, discursive, and political turn to AI in governing communication. *Big Data & Society, 8*(2). https://doi.org/10.1177/20539517211046182

Latour, B. (1993). *We have never been modern.* Harvard University Press.

Latour, B. (2005). *Reassembling the social: An introduction to actor-network-theory.* Oxford University Press.

Law, J., & Lin, W. Y. (2022). *Care-ful research: Sensibilities from science and technology studies (STS).* The SAGE Handbook of Qualitative Research Design.

Lente, H. V. (2016). Forceful futures: From promise to requirement. In N. Brown, B. Rappert, & A. Webster (Eds.), *Contested futures: A sociology of prospective techno-science.* Routledge.

Liebig, L., Guettel, L., Jobin, A., & Katzenbach, C. (2022). Subnational AI policy – Shaping AI in a multi-level governance system. *AI & Society: Knowledge, Culture and Communication.* https://doi.org/10.1007/s00146-022-01561-5

MacKenzie, D. A., & Wajcman, J. (Eds.). (1999). *The social shaping of technology* (2nd ed.). Open University Press.

Mager, A., & Katzenbach, C. (2021). Future imaginaries in the making and governing of digital technology: Multiple, contested, commodified. *New Media & Society, 23*(2), 223–236. https://doi.org/10.1177/1461444820929321

Marchant, G. (2019). *"Soft law" governance of artificial intelligence* (AI PULSE). UCLA School of Law, The Program on Understanding Law, Science, and Evidence. https://escholarship.org/uc/item/0jq252ks

Markoff, J. (2016). *Machines of loving grace: The quest for common ground between humans and robots* (Reprint Edition). Ecco.

Milde, J. (2017). *Forschungsfeld Wissenschaftskommunikation* (H. Bonfadelli, B. Fähnrich, C. Lüthje, M. Rhomberg, & M. S. Schäfer, Eds.). Springer Fachmedien Wiesbaden. https://doi.org/10.1007/978-3-658-12898-2

Munn, L. (2022). The uselessness of AI ethics. *AI and Ethics.* https://doi.org/10.1007/s43681-022-00209-w

Nabil Hassein. (2017, August 15). Against black inclusion in facial recognition. *Decolonized Tech.* https://decolonizedtech.com/2017/08/15/against-black-inclusion-in-facial-recognition/

Natale, S., & Ballatore, A. (2017). Imagining the thinking machine: Technological myths and the rise of artificial intelligence. *Convergence: The International Journal of Research into New Media Technologies,* 135485651771516. https://doi.org/10.1177/1354856517715164

Neyland, D. (2015). Bearing account-able witness to the ethical algorithmic system. *Science, Technology, & Human Values, 41*(1), 50–76. https://doi.org/10.1177/0162243915598056

Noble, S. U. (2018). *Algorithms of oppression: How search engines reinforce racism.* NYU Press. http://nyupress.org/books/9781479837243/

Ochigame, R. (2019). The invention of "Ethical AI": How big tech manipulates academia to avoid regulation. *The Intercept.* https://theintercept.com/2019/12/20/mit-ethical-ai-artificial-intelligence/

O'Neil, C. (2016). *Weapons of math destruction: How big data increases inequality and threatens democracy* (1st ed.). Crown.

Pinch, T. J., & Bijker, W. E. (1984). The social construction of facts and artefacts: Or how the sociology of science and the sociology of technology might benefit each other. *Social Studies of Science, 14*(3), 399–441. https://doi.org/10.1177/030631284014003004

Radu, R. (2021). Steering the governance of artificial intelligence: National strategies in perspective. *Policy and Society, 40*(2), 178–193. https://doi.org/10.1080/14494035.2021.1929728

Raji, I. D., Gebru, T., Mitchell, M., Buolamwini, J., Lee, J., & Denton, E. (2020). Saving face: Investigating the ethical concerns of facial recognition auditing. In *Proceedings of the AAAI/ACM Conference on AI, ethics, and society* (pp. 145–151). https://doi.org/10.1145/3375627.3375820

Rességuier, A., & Rodrigues, R. (2020). AI ethics should not remain toothless! A call to bring back the teeth of ethics. *Big Data & Society, 7*(2), 2053951720942541. https://doi.org/10.1177/2053951720942541

Rip, A., & Voß, J.-P. (2013). Umbrella terms as mediators in the governance of emerging science and technology. *Science, Technology & Innovation Studies, 9*(2), 39–59.

Rosert, E., & Sauer, F. (2021). How (not) to stop the killer robots: A comparative analysis of humanitarian disarmament campaign strategies. *Contemporary Security Policy, 42*(1), 4–29. https://doi.org/10.1080/13523260.2020.1771508

Sandvig, C., Hamilton, K., Karahalios, K., & Langbort, C. (2014). Auditing algorithms: Research methods for detecting discrimination on internet platforms. *Data and Discrimination: Converting Critical Concerns into Productive Inquiry.* http://www-personal.umich.edu/~csandvig/research/Auditing%20Algorithms%20--%20Sandvig%20--%20ICA%202014%20Data%20and%20Discrimination%20Preconference.pdf

Seaver, N. (2013). *Knowing algorithms.* https://digitalsts.net/wp-content/uploads/2019/11/26_digitalSTS_Knowing-Algorithms.pdf

Sossin, L., & Smith, C. W. (2003). Hard choices and soft law: Ethical codes, policy guidelines and the role of the courts in regulating government. *Alberta Law Review, 40*(4), 867. https://doi.org/10.29173/alr1344

van Maanen, G. (2022). AI ethics, ethics washing, and the need to politicize data ethics. *Digital Society, 1*(2), 9. https://doi.org/10.1007/s44206-022-00013-3

Venturini, T., Ricci, D., Mauri, M., Kimbell, L., & Meunier, A. (2015). Designing controversies and their publics. *Design Issues, 31*(3), 74–87. https://doi.org/10.1162/DESI_a_00340

Wajcman, J., & Jones, P. K. (2012). Border communication: Media sociology and STS. *Media, Culture & Society, 34*(6), 673–690. https://doi.org/10.1177/0163443712449496

Woolgar, S. (1985). Why not a sociology of machines? The case of sociology and artificial intelligence. *Sociology, 19*(4), 557–572. https://doi.org/10.1177/0038038585019004005

Wyatt, S. (2017). Talking about the future: Metaphors of the internet. In N. Brown, B. Rappert, & A. Webster (Eds.), *Contested futures: A sociology of prospective techno-science* (pp. 109–126). Routledge. https://doi.org/10.4324/9781315259420

Yates, J. (1993). *Control through communication: The rise of system in American management.* Johns Hopkins University Press.

Yolgörmez, C. (2021). Machinic encounters: A relational approach to the sociology of AI. In J. Roberge & M. Castelle (Eds.), *The cultural life of machine learning: An incursion into critical AI studies* (pp. 143–166). Springer International Publishing. https://doi.org/10.1007/978-3-030-56286-1_5

Zeng, J., Chan, C., & Schäfer, M. S. (2022). Contested Chinese dreams of AI? Public discourse about artificial intelligence on WeChat and People's Daily Online. *Information, Communication & Society, 25*(3), 319–340. https://doi.org/10.1080/1369118X.2020.1776372

Ziewitz, M. (2015). Governing algorithms: Myth, mess, and methods. *Science, Technology, & Human Values, 41*(1), 3–16. https://doi.org/10.1177/0162243915608948

5. Artificial intelligence and the problem of radical uncertainty

Robert Holton

INTRODUCTION

Artificial intelligence (AI) is often presented as a transformative advance in problem-solving, innovation, and knowledge. The apparatus of machine learning embodied in algorithms and drawing on Big Data sources is currently being applied across an ever-expanding range of settings. These include manufacturing, finance, medicine, media, logistics, law and administration, geopolitics, and the military. The success of AI has come to be regarded as inevitable, not simply as a problem-solving and profit-making technology, but, by some at least, as a superior form of intelligence to that of human beings (Kurzweil, 2005). An age of machine-based artificial general intelligence is supposedly just ahead of us.

Yet, for all the excitement, and hype, it is far from clear that AI-generated knowledge can really deliver the transformative potential that is promised. A major line of criticism is that machine intelligence and human intelligence are radically different (Larson, 2021), and that human intelligence involves analytical, creative, practical, and ethical qualities absent from AI. Cantwell Smith (2019) warns against excessively sharp contrasts between the two, which both display strengths and limitations.

What then matters is the evolution of the assemblages of humans and machines and the ways in which there may be a two-way socio-technical inter-change between human and machine intelligence. The general theoretical assumption behind this perspective, derived from the work of Latour (1993), Suchman (2007), and Hayles (2017) is that human agents and technology mutually constitute the socio-technical institutions of intelligence, including artificial intelligence. This co-presence does not, however, mean symmetry in how human agents and autonomous machines interact in the cognitive assemblages of artificial intelligence (Holton & Boyd, 2021).

Asymmetries of power, both sovereign and discursive matter a great deal to the construction and legitimacy of AI. This chapter offers a critique of one of the legitimising features of discourses around AI. These involve its claims to represent expansive forms of knowledge and problem-solving. These have generated new forms of techno-optimism. Such legitimising claims are put to the test by confronting AI with problems of radical uncertainty.

UNCERTAINTY

In its widest sense, uncertainty is both a feature of everyday life for individuals and organisations as well as philosophical, scientific, and technical debate. We do not know for sure when we will die, or what challenges, negative or positive, our lives will be faced with. This uncertainty has been a striking feature of history as different cultures have struggled with a range of problems. These include harvest uncertainty (Hoskins, 1964) and drought (Jones, 2018), pandemics, morbidity and mortality linked with the idea of doom (Ferguson, 2021), the prospects of salvation or damnation in the afterlife (Weber, 1976), precarious employment, the impact of social inequality and domination arising from race, gender, and ethnicity, and whether personal partners, friends or business associates can be trusted. Since forecasting the future often fails, a wide range of strategies and policies has been tried and institutions built (Nowotny, 2016; Beckert & Bronk, 2018) in response to the multiple challenges of uncertainty.

These include activities such as prayer to the gods, the use of promises to cement personal relationships (Arendt, 1958), friendship (de L'Estoile, 2014), contractual arrangements of various kinds, social cooperation, and changes to public policy. Another general cultural resource involves narratives about the future that deploy imaginative visions able to stimulate confidence and positive action in the present (Beckert & Bronk, 2018). Advances in scientific understanding and technology are also very relevant.

Artificial intelligence is a key component of the recent claims of modern science to overcome uncertainties and enhance control over human circumstances. The optimistic narrative of imminent general artificial intelligence is a striking example of one such imaginative vision. Critics of the uses made of AI, however, raise the alternative possibility that it may add to social uncertainties for those seeking equitable access to resources, justice, and social respect (Benjamin, 2019)

What then is radical uncertainty and how does this impact the legitimation claims of AI?

Radical uncertainty, as used here, emerges from social scientific discussion of distinctions between risk and uncertainty. While often used in everyday life as interchangeable synonyms, these may be more usefully understood as standing in contrast with each other following the seminal work of Frank Knight (1921). Risk represents those contingencies that can be measured, understood, and acted upon. Uncertainty, by contrast, represents those unknowns that defy measurement and probability, and thus constitute far greater challenges to action and policy. This distinction is a fundamental one, which is not accurately captured in everyday notions of uncertainty, which include both.

To avoid confusion, John Kay and Mervyn King (2020) reformulate Knight's distinction between risk and uncertainty in terms of resolvable and radical uncertainty. Uncertainty, in its most radical sense, refers to unknowns, including both known and unknown unknowns. The latter, according to Socrates, represents profound ignorance. We may then be dealing not simply with unknown unknowns but unknowable unknowns. Another way of describing radical uncertainties of this kind is ontological uncertainty (Lane & Maxfield, 2005).

For the leading sociologist of uncertainty, Helga Nowotny (2016), the relationship between uncertainty and risk is dynamic and evolving, as uncertainties turn into risks (2016, p. ix), and, one should add, risks once regarded as manageable develop new levels of uncertainty. The covid pandemic has revealed that human actors, even if equipped with the experience of previous epidemics, advancing scientific understanding of viruses and sophisticated AI are 'not as much in control as we thought' (Nowotny, 2021, p. 107).

Generalising this point, it is plausible to think of history as displaying a dialectic of uncertainty and risk. The challenge of uncertainty and the historical struggles to turn unknowns into knowable risks that can be planned for and acted upon has undoubtedly produced a stream of evolutionary successes as well as failures. New technology and increased economic productivity have underlaid the long-run expansion of aggregate global population levels and living standards. Yet, Nowotny warns this expansive process is not an ever-onward and upward process. The key question then becomes how far can AI transform this dialectic by radically reducing uncertainty and sustaining a super intelligent and effective resolution of scientific, technical, and practical problems facing humankind? How far, in short, can AI be trusted to achieve such objectives?

One of the initial difficulties in pursuing this question is that there has been comparatively little discussion of radical uncertainty and unknowables within most discourses around AI. Uncertainties about scientific knowledge, brought to the fore in public commentary on the Covid-19 pandemic (Nowotny, 2021), are largely absent from most mainstream commentary on AI. The rhetoric melds together techno-optimism and business opportunity, as corporations, lobbyists, and some AI scientists speak of a seemingly limitless potential of AI to deliver accelerating productivity, increased profitability, more efficient government, and the potential for unstoppable social improvement (Altman, 2021).

Techno-optimism around AI does of course have considerable plausibility. Transformative examples include *Deep Mind*'s AI-generated solution to the structure of protein folding (Heaven, 2020), and successful applications in medical imaging (Lundervold & Lundervold, 2019). Natural language processing around *Open AI*'s GPT 3 (Dale, 2021). GPT 3, which contains 175 billion language parameters is regarded by some as 'the first precursor to general artificial intelligence' because it can support multiple applications (Sam Altman, CEO of *Open AI* cited Thornhill, 2020).

Set against this, however, are both empirical warnings and theoretical difficulties.

To set against examples of success noted above, the list of disappointments includes the continuing series of setbacks to the EU-funded Human Brain Project (Larson, 2021 chapter 16), the recent failure of the Amazon hiring and promotion algorithm to defeat gender bias even after 'de-biasing', the demise of Google's augmented reality eyewear Google Glass, (Lex, 2019) and the large graveyard of 'dead' AI-embedded robots from Atari's BOB in the 1980s to Honda's Asimo and Bosch's Kuri more recently (Waters, 2018).

Other empirical warnings arise from methodological problems. Recent evidence from the laboratory world of AI reveals an interesting and somewhat unusual sense of uncertainty among software engineers. Perhaps the largest difficulty is that algorithms 'perfected' in the laboratory often fail when applied in society. This problem was highlighted recently in a paper where 40 Google researchers across seven teams working on different aspects of machine learning commented on the universality of this problem, the reasons for it, and the difficulties in resolving it (d'Amour et al., 2020, see also Heaven, 2020).

Failures and setbacks by themselves do not necessarily undermine theories of AI progress insofar as knowledge deepens and expands. Machine learning is iterative and recursive such that mistakes and inaccurate assumptions can often be corrected, leading to further practical achievements. How far this potential is realised depends not merely on the quantitative expansion of data, and more sophisticated modelling, but also on greater awareness of the social assumptions made in data selection and labelling in the preparation of machine learning pipelines. Iteration, however, is also liable to the further difficulty of model saturation (Larson, 2021, p. 155). This occurs when using more data to refine an algorithm adds nothing to its performance. At this point, machine learning has reached its limit. For Larson, this means that machine learning systems are not indefinitely scalable. More Big Data does not necessarily lead to more successful outcomes. Nonetheless, the seductive myth of an ever-open frontier of future transformation in intelligence remains very powerful and attractive.

EPISTEMOLOGY, ARTIFICIAL INTELLIGENCE, AND UNCERTAINTY

Moving beyond empirical warnings about limits to knowledge generated by AI are broader epistemological problems to do with the scope, completeness, and reliability of scientific knowledge. This is as evident among physicists as much as sociologists. For Nobel physics laureate Richard Feynman (1988), 'doubt' is an existential feature of scientific practice. Doubtfulness applies both to the reliability of current scientific findings as to the progressive effects of scientific thought embodied in technology. But it is neither optimistic nor pessimistic. Rather Feynman's doubt is ambivalent (Amoore, 2019). In other words, it is open both to the dynamic of future possibilities created through science as well as being sceptical about the possible ways the fruits of science may be utilised by powerful economic and political interests. Feynman explored the epistemological and ethical dimensions of this argument in relation to the emergence of nuclear weapons. But they are equally relevant, as Louise Amoore (2019) has shown, to the analysis of AI.

The epistemological problem here is the implicit presumption in the notion of general artificial intelligence that there is nothing that cannot potentially be known through the progressive application of machine learning. Scanning across the sciences, it is clear there are things we know we do not know as well as unknown unknowns. There may also be things we cannot know for a variety of reasons.

In physics, Heisenberg's 'uncertainty principle' is one kind of example. The claim is that we cannot simultaneously know both the position and the momentum of very small particles to a high degree of accuracy. This is because the measurement of one of these qualities disturbs the behaviour and measurement of the other. This principle is however very far from being a general argument that we can know nothing with complete certainty. It is rather a limit on the operational possibilities of measurement imposed by quantum mechanics. Thus, Busch et al. (2007) argue for the principle's positive role in knowledge formation as a way of reconciling mutually exclusive experimental options if certain definable trade-offs are accepted.

Grayling (2021, p. 101), in his review of 'what we now know' in the scientific domain, discusses a well-known and more fundamental dimension of the largely unknown. This involves the 95% of the universe that is comprised of dark matter and dark energy. Even with the undoubtedly strong foundations of quantum theory and cosmology, there remain major problems in reconciling the physics of very large and very small things.

A different set of epistemological limits comes from recent work in microbiology. In his discussion of biodiversity, Thaler (2021) identifies a range of uncertainties in answering the question of whether global microbial diversity is decreasing, increasing or staying the same. While animal and plant diversity is decreasing, he claims that the 'lack of insight into the dynamics of evolution of microbial diversity' is probably 'the single most profound and consequential unknown' in human knowledge about the biosphere. The microbes in question include eubacteria, single-celled fungi, and viruses. Here uncertainties stem in part from difficulties in locating microbes in settings such as ocean floors, as well as the possibility that rapid microbe growth undermines the construction of a secure baseline from which subsequent trends could be measured.

The logic underlying all this is the minimisation of uncertainty, rather than claims to perfect knowledge. The social psychology of capitalist entrepreneurship, following this approach, is not the denial of uncertainty, but its limitation, both through measurement of risk, as far as that can go, and qualitative judgement.

Some of the limitations to knowledge discussed above may indeed turn out not to be absolute barriers to extensions in knowledge. Yet there is no convincing guarantee that the presumption can, in principle, be realised absolutely. A major philosophical issue with very practical consequences is the problem of induction. Stated simply, this states that causal and other inferences drawn from existing data can never rule out new evidence that falsifies existing analyses. Induction can only depend on past data, which may not be adequate when new processes emerge, or previously unknown processes are revealed or remain unknown creating baffling effects. Simply adding further to the existing accumulation of evidence cannot get around this problem. This gives much-vaunted Big Data the characteristic of a 'Bottomless Bucket', a description applied by Larson (2021, p. 178) after the direct experience of consistent failures in natural language processing based purely on computational knowledge.

Arising from this, the issues at stake in this chapter are two-fold. First, how far can artificial intelligence based on an inductive epistemology create a secure basis for knowledge capable of overcoming uncertainty? Second, can artificial intelligence transcend the ways in which human agents have hitherto responded to uncertainties in both science and social life?

From an epistemological viewpoint, the conventional scientific response to the problem of induction is that uncertainty can be reduced through the calculation of probability and the quantification of risk. For Nobel chemistry laureate Venki Ramakrishnan:

> at the forefront, science is very fuzzy. There are lots of uncertainties. What we try to do is keep refining the probabilities until we know with much greater certainty, what is actually happening. (2021)

Much policy discourse articulated in the face of adverse contingencies such as climate change, is precisely couched in probabilistic language associated with prediction. This major flood or that bushfire is described variously as a one-in-50-years or one-in-100-years event. But how can these probabilities be said to rest on secure knowledge since they rest on past data, the conditions for which may neither be properly understood nor apply any longer.

What then is the epistemological status of probabilities? How far can they reduce uncertainty and ground risk management if statistical patterns arising from data analysis are not grounded in a more secure understanding of logic, causation and the social perception and meaning of processes and events? This is an acute problem for versions of artificial intelligence, using algorithms based on statistical patterning alone, as opposed to attempts to develop AI as an enhanced version of logical and socially contextualised reasoning.

One way of dealing with the epistemological issues involved draws on the Bayesian approach to 'conditional probability'. Here, probability is not regarded as the frequency with which future outcomes will occur. It is seen rather as reasonable expectations about future outcomes through quantification to establish a degree of belief. Hypotheses are developed using propositions where truth or falsity is unknown. The confrontation of prior probabilities with evidence yields subsequent (posterior) probabilities. However, the evidence-based propositions developed in this way are not regarded as absolutely true or false, but on a spectrum between truth and falsity.

Another interesting argument developed by Amoore involves rethinking the nature of algorithmic truth-claims. Outputs from machine learning are contingent on weighted probabilities. Many potential accounts of data can be contained within multiple layers of computation in the algorithm. Applications of AI to new data look for 'the degree of similarity with a ground-truth, itself often generated by algorithm' (2019, p. 151). It follows that algorithms do not necessarily eradicate doubt and uncertainty, even though corporate and state-based users of algorithmic truth-claims often act as if they do.

Epistemological clarifications of this kind do not, however, dispose of the problem of unknowable or unknown unknowns that define uncertainty as distinct from risks. The Bayesian statistician and philosopher Dennis Lindley in his discussion of statistics as the study of uncertainty (2000) fails to make this distinction, arguing as if all uncertainties are in principle measurable and expressible through probabilities that can guide action.

Two more radical approaches seem more productive. The first is the notion of abductive inference, deriving from the philosopher Charles S. Pierce (Hartshorn & Weiss, 1960). Pierce argued for a third alternative form of inference, irreducible to deduction and induction. This focused on a missing dimension of knowledge formation in science and daily life. A key element here is the role of creative guesswork, often thought of as intuition, in the formation of explanatory hypotheses, somewhat on the model of criminal detection. Swedberg (2011, 2012, 2014) sees this as a major contribution to 'the art of social theory' by illuminating a missing dimension of the sociology of thinking.

This abductive approach arose neither from abstract rule-bound logic, which is necessarily true (deduction), nor the empirical analysis of statistical patterning and probabilistic truth claims. Abductive guesses might prove to be wrong, but they might and often have led analysis in new productive directions. For Larson, some such approach is evident in the creative leaps in science from Newton through Einstein to Crick and Watson. But it is also evident in the ways in which ordinary humans in everyday life confront challenges of uncertainty through the iterative application of tacit knowledge of the past and creative approaches to the future. Mabsout (2015) sees abduction as a crucial intellectual and practical resource in responding to uncertainty, but one that is incompatible with an exclusive reliance on an algorithmic approach to intelligence.

A highly productive approach to challenges posed by uncertainties about the future, developed by Beckert and Bronk (2018), critiques the assumption of 'rational expectations' in mainstream economic theory. Most conventional economists have typically assumed that actors use informed predictions about the future reflecting all available information. Such assumptions are built into most economic forecasting and statistical modelling utilised in AI. For Beckert and Bronk, by contrast, such assumptions are fundamentally misleading. They are problematic not only because of general philosophical problems with induction but also for structural reasons in economies founded on relentless innovation and increasingly complex inter-dependencies between actors. It is not simply that information asymmetries between actors undermine perfect information and rational expectations about the future. It is more fundamentally that under contemporary structural conditions, 'symmetric ignorance' may be a more accurate characterisation of economic activity under conditions of uncertainty.

POSITIVE RESPONSES TO EPISTEMOLOGICAL DOUBT

How then to rescue knowledge and data analysis from the epistemological scepticism of George Shackle who argued 'What does not yet exist cannot now be known' (1995, p. 3)?

The solution combines conceptual innovation with a more pragmatic approach to epistemological doubt. Rather than 'rational expectations' alone, Beckert and Bronk develop a conceptual framework around imagination and patterned imaginaries or visions of the future. This fills out rather opaque notions of guesswork or intuition, with a set of creative faculties of mind (2018, p.3). These include 'general capacities such as the ability to visualize counterfactuals, to place oneself in the shoes of another', and experimentation with new metaphors in analysis. In addition, they list the capacity to expand new ideas into elaborated future visions and the capacity to live with uncertainty and mystery without 'irritably' reaching for reason and fact. Such alternative capacities represent, as it were, 'fictional expectations'.

But how then does this deal with Shackle's radical scepticism? It does so by aiming for a pragmatic balance between novelty and innovation, on the one hand, and 'persistent regularities of behaviour and stable institutional or physical constraints' (1972, pp. 9–10), on the other. This balance combines imaginative judgements embodied in plausible narratives and models of the future with calculations of what is calculable. This severely limits the scope of AI in economic and other kinds of activity because it only applies to the second element in the balance and cannot in and of itself generate imaginative constructions of future possibility. It follows that the role of AI in responding to radical uncertainty is a limited one and that human intelligence remains irreducible to machine learning.

A further fundamental problem for the capacity of artificial intelligence to reduce uncertainty derives from the work of the Austrian mathematical logician Kurt Gödel. (In the following section, I draw extensively on Larson, 2021, pp. 11–18). Gödel's well-known incompleteness theorem identifies a fundamental limitation in all formal mathematical systems. The problem is that there must logically be some propositions in any formal system that are true but cannot be proved using the rules of the system. These involve self-referential statements about the system itself, such as 'This statement is not provable within this system'. Leaving aside the technical rationale for this argument, the strong implication is that truth and proof are not equivalent.

This sets limits to any computational system, such as the decision procedures at the heart of AI. What is equally significant is that human agents are capable of recognising notions of truth that mechanical intelligence cannot. This in turn suggests that human qualities such as intuition and imagination are necessary whatever the ingenuity of mechanical intelligence. Machines lack the intuitive and imaginative expectations and judgements that contribute so much to human knowledge faced with challenges of uncertainty. Without intuition, general artificial intelligence is an impossible myth.

As Larson shows, Alan Turing, one of the key intellectual progenitors of AI, struggled over time with Gödel's theorem, accepting at first the significance of human intuition, but later reversing this stand (op. cit 17–18). The argument that machines could embrace intuition is however very problematic. Part of the problem here is a tendency to reduce intelligence to problem-solving alone. This in turn bypasses the complex mix of guesswork and socially situated judgements that inform the selection of hypotheses and the selection of modelling assumptions. This alternative view of intellectual enquiry is as evident to some computer scientists and software engineers (Chollet, 2017; Larson, 2021), as to post-positivist sociologists (Scheff, 2015) and philosophers (Feyerabend, 1975).

Chollet expressly rejects the promise of more ambitious forms of AI based on machine learning leading to new insights that AI systems have not been programmed to make. The assumption of a transformative recursive self-improvement loop evolving towards superintelligence is simply an act of faith. This is because the problem-solving dynamic of AI is focused on a narrow range of tasks and has no awareness of the cultural dimensions of intelligence.

Recursive self-improvement loops already exist in both human and machine intelligence, but the assumption of a sudden explosive transformative leap is implausible.

Whereas human social actors build up an experience of the world through observation, activity and inferences about cause and effect, computers do not. Machine learning algorithms, as Paul Taylor (2021), points out, 'don't learn causal models, and they struggle to distinguish between coincidences and general laws'. Such algorithms have no sense of their relationship to the world, or that a world exists. In this respect, machine intelligence is hard to assimilate to human intelligence, let alone transcend it, even if it can defeat leading grandmasters at chess and perform stupendous exercises in statistical analysis

These limitations are particularly acute in the application of AI to natural language. Much work of this kind amounts to the application of machine learning to statistics about language rather than language use. (Marcus & Davis, 2019). The symbolic rules governing language use are notoriously complex to identify and seem refractory to the statistical analyses and probabilistic inferences of machine learning. Language then as a bearer of meaning as well as logic has proven an especially difficult challenge in the development of AI.

COMBATTING THE SCIENTIFIC HUBRIS OF ARTIFICIAL INTELLIGENCE

Why are epistemological uncertainty and complexity not more widely seen as major obstacles to the dynamic promises made for machine learning and artificial intelligence? In broad cultural and social-psychological terms, this may have much to do with the hubris of modernity, rationalism, capitalism, and science (Hård & Jamison, 2005, Stiegler, 2019). Hubris may be defined as overbearing pride and presumption. This is linked by Stiegler with relentless disinhibition from tradition and community, typically associated with innovators and the valorisation of disruption.

Technoscientific optimism also reflects intensive phases of scientific advance and technological innovation over the last 400 years (Hård & Jamison, 2005, Larson, 2021). This has increasingly supplanted older classical notions of *Homo sapiens*, embracing wisdom and virtue, with narrower notions of *homo faber*, or humans as builders (Arendt, 1958).

This historical and social psychological legacy underlies the legitimacy of algorithmic probabilities as the basis for overcoming uncertainty and managing risk, and the illusions or fantasies of control that this engenders. In so doing, rationalistic and scientific hubris also draws on an optimistic faith in the powers of mechanism as a basis for knowledge and the engineering of action. There is a long tradition behind this faith stretching back at least as far as Descartes and forwards to Turing and contemporary entrepreneurs such as Elon Musk.

It is of course possible to discount excessive hubris by delineating more carefully the more plausible elements of artificial intelligence. One way of doing this is by discriminating between AI proponents focused on symbolic logic against the so-called connectionist perspective. In its early development from the 1950s, the *symbolic* approach sought to build machines capable of replicating human reason by applying logic to data. Logical systems can be broken down into simple propositions that can be empirically investigated. This however created problems because symbolic logic expressed in language is hard to express in rules capable of successful application in the real world. Such difficulties beset the work of many of the first AI researchers producing wider disillusion and the first AI winter in the 1980s and 1990s.

Further AI progress emerged by tackling problems that did not require symbolic logic to address, but which were amenable to *connectionist* analysis of correlations and patterns emerging from analysis of Big Data sources available through digitalisation. This involved machine learning technologies, the most prominent version of which is 'deep learning' involving so-called 'neural networks'. These comprise a series of autonomous steps in learning through successive multi-layered iterations of data analysis, ostensibly on the model of neural pathways in the brain.

Many of the AI summers of the last 30 years have emerged from this alternative approach. However, the epistemological limitations of this approach in terms of the uncertain and incomplete understandings yielded by probabilistic machine learning remain. Depth here refers not to the capacity to conduct causal analysis, to acquire abstract ideas or to develop a rich conceptual apparatus. It refers simply to the multiple layers of statistical analysis that generate surface-level statistical patterning (Marcus & Davis, 2019, 55–63). Deep learning has yielded successes in object recognition and language recognition but has also been vulnerable to the inflated techno-optimistic hype about imminent general artificial intelligence.

The final piece of the epistemological jigsaw involved here, already introduced above, is a clearer appreciation of human intelligence (Marcus & Davis, 2019, Cantwell Smith, 2019). Human actors have the benefit of historical accumulations of knowledge in the face of uncertain processes and events, successes and failures. They also have the advantages of creativity, flexibility, and interpersonal scrutiny of decisions and the rationale for them. This contrasts with the formalistic machine-bound intelligence that is inscrutable to dialogue about meaning and ethics. As is well known, decisions made by the neural networks at the heart of machine learning are opaque. They cannot directly explain why they reached the conclusions expressed in the output signals derived through the application of algorithms (Adadi & Berrada, 2018).

All this suggests that human intelligence is better equipped than artificial intelligence in meeting many of the challenges of radical uncertainty. Machine learning adds to the repertoire of resources available to humans in processing Big Data, but it lacks the capacity to transcend epistemological limitations in knowledge acquisition and application.

To conclude the discussion there, does however, inhibit any further elaboration of limits in human intelligence and the ways that these may fail to grasp some of the potentials of AI in revealing patterning of which humans may be unaware. Cantwell Smith (2019) argues that human input into the conceptual structure of AI involves ontological assumptions about objects, properties, and relations. This amounts to 'the world taken at a relatively high level of abstraction' (p. 66), which may contrast with the world of Big Data as 'a plenum of unbelievable richness', indicating 'the world as it'. There is, as it were, a subterranean ontology of sub-conceptual detail in machine intelligence that is not 'force-fit' into human categories. Personalised medicine based on an individual's DNA sequences is taken to represent an effective sub-conceptual example of a domain with enormous potential.

CONCLUSION

The vulnerability of AI as a separate free-standing technology arises in part from epistemological difficulties that set limits to what AI can achieve. There certainly are open frontiers in the development of knowledge, problem-solving, and creativity. Yet, AI has not shown transformative capacities to overcome radical uncertainties in what we know, to guarantee its reliability in revealing what we don't know, and the provision of robust solutions to epistemological challenges involved in applying AI technologies in society. This raises political problems where the deployment of AI by powerful corporate and state-based interests gives legitimacy to policies and practices as if they were based on obvious scientific truth. Such problems also require urgent critical responses wherever AI itself magnifies social uncertainties in everyday life.

The problem of uncertainty is so ubiquitous across time and space that it serves as a major test of strengths and weaknesses in any form of knowledge. In asserting limits to the potential of AI, this chapter also supports arguments that seek to re-value the potential of human intelligence and social activism in responding to uncertainty. This extends not simply to technological innovation, the assembly of Big Data, and statistical techniques but also to wider aspects of creativity, including both practical and philosophical insights and capacities. These include sophisticated capacities to negotiate meaning through linguistic and non-verbal communication as well as forms of inference that draw on abductive reasoning. The potential for human intelligence remains far from exhausted, whether in its own right or in combination with machine intelligence.

REFERENCES

Adadi, A., & Berrada, M. (2018). Peeking inside the black-box: A survey on explainable artificial intelligence (XAI), *IEEE Access, 6*, 138–160.

Altman, S. (2021, n.d). Moore's law for everything. https://moores.samaltman.com

Amoore, L. (2019). Doubt and the algorithm: On the partial accounts of machine learning, *Theory, Culture, and Society, 36*(6), 147–169.

Andersen, R. (2020, November). The panopticon is already here. *The Atlantic.*

Arendt, H. (1958). *The human condition.* Chicago University Press.

Beckert, J., & Bronk, R. (2018). An introduction to uncertain futures. In J. Beckert & R. Bronk (Eds.), *Uncertain futures: Imaginaries, narratives and calculation in the economy* (pp. 1–36). Oxford University Press.

Benjamin, R. (2019). *Race after technology: Abolitionist tools for the new Jim code.* Polity Press.

Busch, P., Heinonen, T., & Lahti, P. (2007). Heisenberg's uncertainty principle. *Physics Reports, 452*(6), 155–176.

Cantwell Smith, B. (2019). *The promise of artificial intelligence: Reckoning and judgement.* MIT Press.

Chollet, F. (2017 November 27). The implausibility of intelligence explosion. *Medium.* https://medium .com/francois-chollet/the-impossibility-of-intelligence-explosion-5be4a9eda6ec

Dale, R. (2021). GPT 3: What's it good for? *Natural Language Engineering, 27,* 113–118.

De L'Estoile, B. (2014). 'Money is good, but a friend is better': Uncertainty, orientation to the future, and 'the economy'. *Current Anthropology, 55*(S9), S62–S73.

Ferguson, N. (2021). *Doom: The politics of catastrophe.* Allen Lane.

Feyerabend, P. (1975). *Against method: Outline of an anarchistic theory of knowledge.* New Left Books.

Feynman, R. (1988). *What do you care what other people think? Further adventures of a curious character.* Norton.

Grayling, A. C. (2021). *The frontiers of knowledge: What we now know about science, history and the mind.* Penguin Viking.

Hård, M., & Jamison, A. (2005). *Hubris and hybrids: A cultural history of technology and science.* Routledge.

Hartshorne, C., & Weiss, P. (Eds.). (1960). *Collected papers of Charles Sanders Pierce* (Vols. 5–6). Harvard University Press.

Hayles, N. K. (2017). *Unthought: The power of the cognitive unconscious.* University of Chicago Press.

Heaven, W. D. (2020). Deep mind's protein-folding AI has solved a 50-year old challenge in biology. *MIT Technology Review*, November 30.

Holton, R. J., & Boyd, R. (2021). Where are the people? What are they doing? Why are they doing it? Situating artificial intelligence within a socio-technical framework. *Journal of Sociology, 57*(2), 179–195.

Hoskins, W. G. (1964). Harvest fluctuations and English economic history, 1480–1619. *Agricultural History Review, 12*(1), 28–46.

Ishiguro, K., & Ramakhrishnan, V. (2021, March 26). Kazuo Ishiguro and Venki Ramakrishnan: Imagining a new humanity. *Financial Times*.

Jones, R. (2018). Uncertainty and the emotional landscape of drought. *International Review of Environmental History, 4*(2), 13–26.

Kay, J., & King, M. (2020). *Radical uncertainty: Decision-making for an unknowable future.* Bridge Street Press.

Knight, F. (2006). *Risk, uncertainty and profit.* Dover. (originally published 1921).

Kurzweil, R. (2005). *The singularity is near: When humans transcend biology.* Penguin.

Lane, D., & Maxfield, R. (2005). Ontological uncertainty and innovation. *Journal of Evolutionary Economics, 15*(1), 3–50.

Larson, E. (2021). *The myth of artificial intelligence.* Harvard University Press.

Latour, B. (1993). *We have never been modern.* Harvard University Press.

Lex. (2019, August 3). Smart speakers: Dumb prediction. *Financial Times*.

Lindley, D. (2000). The philosophy of statistics. *Journal of the Royal Statistical Society, Series D, 49*(3), 293–337.

Lundervold, A. S., & Lundervold, A. (2019). An overview of deep learning in medical imaging focusing on MRI. *Zeitschrift für Medicinische Physik, 29*(2), 102–127.

Mabsout, R. (2015). Abduction and economics: The contributions of Charles Pierce and Herbert Simon. *Journal of Economic Methodology, 22*(4), 491–516.

Marcus, G., & Davis, E. (2019). *Rebooting AI: Building artificial intelligence we can trust.* Ballantine.

Moor, J. (2006). The Dartmouth college artificial intelligence conference: The next fifty years. *AI Magazine, 27*(4), 87–91.

Nowotny, H. (2016). *The cunning of uncertainty.* Polity.

Nowotny, H. (2021). In AI we trust: How the Covid-19 pandemic pushes us deeper into digitalization. In G. Delanty (Ed.), *Pandemics, politics and society: Critical perspectives on the Covid-19 crisis* (pp. 107–121). de Gruyter.

Shackle, G. (1955). *Uncertainty in economics.* Cambridge University Press.

Scheff, L. (2015). Three scandals in psychology: The need for a new approach. *Review of General Psychology, 19*(2).

Stiegler, B. (2019). *The age of disruption: Technology and madness in digital capitalism.* Polity.

Suchman, L. (2007). *Human-machine reconfigurations: Plans and situated actions* (2nd ed.). Cambridge University Press.

Swedberg, R. (2011). Charles Pierce and the sociology of thinking. In C. Edling & J. Rydgreen (Eds.), *Sociological insights of great thinkers: Sociology through literature, philosophy, and science* (pp. 299–306). New York: Praeger.

Swedberg, R. (2012). On Charles S. Pierce's lecture 'how to theorize' (1903). *Sociologica, 6*(2), May–August, 1–27.

Swedberg, R. (2014). *The art of social theory.* Princeton University Press.

Taylor, P. (2021, January 21). Insanely complicated, hopelessly inadequate. *London Review of Books*, 37–39.

Thaler, D. (2021). Is global microbial biodiversity increasing, decreasing, or staying the same? *Frontiers in Ecology and Evolution, 9*, 202.

Thornhill, J. (2020, November 12). Is AI finally closing in on human intelligence? *Financial Times*.

Waters, R. (2018, August 11). Dead robots raise questions on how far home technology has come. *Financial Times*.

Weber, M. (1976). *The protestant ethic and the spirit of capitalism.* Allen and Unwin. (Original work published 1904–1905).

6. Trading human autonomy for technological automation

Simona Chiodo

1. AUTONOMOUS TECHNOLOGIES

As technologies develop, we increasingly define them by using one of the most meaningful words of modern and contemporary Western philosophy: "autonomy", which, especially in the last three centuries (from Kant onwards), has not defined technology at all – conversely, "autonomy" has defined the core of human identity itself.

In what follows, after a brief consideration of the notion of autonomy (Section 2), I will reflect upon the possible reasons for the described overturning, which becomes even more meaningful, from a philosophical perspective, if we add its logical counterpart to it: the more we define technologies, especially based on AI, as "autonomous", the more we define human identity, starting with humans' decisions and actions, by using the word that has always defined technology: "automation"[1] (Sections 3 and 4).

If we consider our language, we can find autonomy as the standard way to refer, for instance, to the following technologies: (autonomous) systems, software, devices, applications, machines, vehicles, equipment, drones, weapons, robots, agents, workloads, surgery and so forth. Moreover, if we move from considering our standard language to considering our factual decisions and actions, we can identify an even more surprising phenomenon: the overturning of the relationship between human autonomy and technological automation, in that, on the one hand, humans seem to lose autonomy and obtain (a kind of) automation and, on the other hand, technologies seem to lose automation and obtain (a kind of) autonomy.

For instance, autonomous vehicles seem to show that those who are not autonomous when it comes to driving, from the youngest to the oldest to disabled people, can somehow (automatically) drive. Self-tracking technologies seem to show that those who are not autonomous when it comes to self-diagnosing, not being an expert, i.e. a doctor, can somehow (automatically) self-diagnose. Digital platforms seem to show that those who are not autonomous when it comes to drafting laws, not being an expert, i.e. a jurist, can somehow (automatically) work on the drafting of laws.[2] Software seems to show that those who are not autonomous when it comes to designing houses, not being an expert, i.e. an architect, can somehow (automatically) design houses. Software seems to show that those who are not autonomous when it comes to writing articles, not being an expert, i.e. a writer, can somehow (automatically) write articles.

---

[1] In what follows, I will briefly summarise what I extensively examined elsewhere (see "Further readings").

[2] I refer, for instance, to the digital platform of the Italian Five Star Movement, which removes "the mediation of governing or representative bodies, recognising to all citizens the governing and steering role normally attributed to few" (see https://www.movimento5stelle.it/, accessed in September 2021, my translation).

Google seems to show that those who are not autonomous when it comes to getting whatever kind of information, not being an expert, i.e. a journalist, can somehow (automatically) get whatever kind of information is needed. And several social media platforms seem to show that those who are not autonomous when it comes to being a professional (from cooking to coaching to whatever), being an amateur, can somehow be a professional (from cooking to coaching to whatever).

The list, which may be endless, can show something that is not questionable from a philosophical perspective: at least sometimes, the cases described above can be read as promising ways to strengthen inclusivity. Yet, the list can especially show something that is most questionable from a philosophical perspective: more than sometimes, the cases described above can be read as equally promising ways to trade human autonomy, together with human (autonomous) expertise, for technological automation – and a crisis of human autonomy as a crisis of human expertise can be read as a form of epistemological and ethical anarchism, which means that what can actually rule, as human autonomous expertise, is traded for what cannot actually rule, as technological automation (as I will argue both from an etymological perspective and from a philosophical perspective).

Before proceeding, it is worth stressing that I will not reflect upon autonomy as the kind of capacity that, philosophically speaking, can be possessed by technology in the same way as humans possess it (which is what several authors reflect upon – see at least Winner, 1978), but as the kind of capacity that, philosophically speaking, can be possessed by humans as what defines the core of human identity itself, especially starting with Kant's philosophical work – more precisely, I will reflect upon the possible reasons why we seem to increasingly overturn the relationship between our decisions and actions resulting from our autonomy and technology's outputs resulting from its automation (which is precisely what continuously emerges both in our standard language and in our factual decisions and actions).

2.   AUTONOMOUS HUMANS (AND AUTOMATED TECHNOLOGIES)

Kant, whose philosophical work on autonomy is essential for its contemporary meaning,[3] defines autonomy as follows: "Autonomy of the will is the property of the will by which it is a law to itself" (Kant, 1785, 4, 440). And being "a law to itself" is "the ground of the dignity of human nature and of every rational nature" (Kant, 1785, 4, 436). Even though autonomy is potentially possessed by any human being, being actually autonomous, i.e. capable of self-giving "a law", requires effort: we are actually autonomous if our decisions and actions move from being heteronomous, i.e. resulting from others' reasons, to resulting from our reasons – and having reasons and, finally, the courage to decide and act accordingly requires epistemological and ethical effort, which may be defined as the effort to find and "express your identity, your nature" (Korsgaard, 1996b, p. 84).

Most interestingly, the meaning of autonomy becomes clearer if we compare it with Kant's use of the etymological root of automation. More precisely, Kant distinguishes between

---

[3]   Several references exist. As far as my perspective is concerned, see at least Frankfurt (1971 and 1999), Dworkin (1988), Hill (1989 and 2000), Korsgaard (1996a and 1996b), Guyer (2003), Taylor (2005), Reath (2006), Deligiorgi (2012) and Sensen (2013).

"*automaton materiale*, when the machine is driven by matter" (Kant, 1788, 5, 97), and "*automaton*" "*spirituale*, when it is driven by representations" (Kant, 1788, 5, 97), which means that we, as humans, are "*automaton*" "*spirituale*", and not autonomous, in the following case:

> if the freedom of our will were none other than [...] psychological and comparative but not also transcendental, i.e. absolute [...], then it would at bottom be nothing better than the freedom of a turnspit, which, when once it is wound up, also accomplishes its movements of itself. (Kant, 1788, 5, 97)

Thus, what distinguishes humans from things is not a noun ("*automaton*" in both cases), but exclusively an adjective ("*spirituale*" for humans and "*materiale*" for things), if humans are not autonomous.

Moreover, being autonomous means not only having reasons according to which deciding and acting but also, and especially, having "transcendental" reasons (i.e. reasons that can be universal, according to Kant's categorical imperative[4]), and not "psychological and comparative" reasons (i.e. reasons that cannot be universal, in that they are, and can be, nothing but particular) – being autonomous means deciding and acting according to reasons that, first, are not heteronomous and, second, are not particular, i.e. contingent and even idiosyncratic, in that deciding and acting according to reasons that cannot move from a contingent and even idiosyncratic dimension (i.e. what is right for my particular interest) to a universal dimension (what can be right for whatever interest, i.e. for any human being) means falling into the kind of particular, contingent and even idiosyncratic randomness that characterises "the freedom of a turnspit", whose "movements" are nothing but outputs lacking whatever epistemological and ethical effort to move from particular interests to universal interests.

Thus, on the one hand, we have the idea of autonomy as decisions and actions that are not random at all, resulting from the (autonomous) rational capacity to move from particularity to universality, and, on the other hand, we have the idea of automation as decisions and actions that are random, resulting from causes that make them nothing but their (automated) effects.

It is no coincidence that Kant specifies something essential from an ethical perspective: on the one hand, the absence of randomness in autonomy implies that one is ethically responsible for one's own decisions and actions (if there is autonomy, one is ethically "culpable and deserving of punishment", Kant, 1788, 5, 100) and, on the other hand, the presence of randomness in automation implies that one is not ethically responsible for one's own decisions and actions (if there is automation, "no moral law is possible and no imputation in accordance with it", Kant, 1788, 5, 97). For instance, if I happen to (unjustly) deprive you of a (public) healthcare service on the basis of my reasons, I can be "culpable and deserving of punishment" from an ethical (and sometimes even legal) perspective. Conversely, if I happen to (unjustly) deprive you of a (public) healthcare service on the basis of a "predictive algorithm",[5] I cannot be equally "culpable and deserving of punishment" from an ethical (and sometimes even legal) perspective: there is a sense in which I can reassuringly say that it is not my fault.

Thus, even though autonomy can give us the great advantage of serving as "the ground of the dignity of human nature and of every rational nature", automation can also give us a great advantage (which we seem to increasingly value): relieving us of one of our most challenging

---

[4]   According to which, we should "act as if the maxim of [...] [our] action were to become by [...] [our] will a universal law" (Kant 1785, 4, 421).
[5]   I first reflected upon the (real) case of the public healthcare service's "predictive algorithm" in Chiodo (2020a).

burdens, which is the burden of two strictly correlated kinds of responsibilities, i.e. the epistemological responsibility for deciding and the ethical responsibility for acting accordingly – automation, specifically trading our autonomy for technological automation, can give us the great advantage of relieving us of the most challenging burdens of epistemological and ethical responsibilities, which means that, again, there is a sense in which we can reassuringly say that the fault is not in us, but, for instance, in the "predictive algorithm".

The etymologies of autonomy and automation, added to a philosophical perspective, can give us further meaningful insights. The word "autonomy" results from αὐτός (*autos*) as "itself" and νόμος (*nomos*) as "law" – thus, autonomy means "self-given law". Again, we can be autonomous if our decisions and actions result from our "laws" as our reasons that become "laws" by moving from a particular (and even idiosyncratic) dimension to a universal dimension. Interestingly enough, the word "automation" also results from αὐτός (*autos*) as "itself", but the second part of its etymology is meaningfully a kind of antonym of νόμος (*nomos*) as "law", being, conversely, (αὐτο)ματίζω (*(auto)matizo*) as to "act of oneself, act offhand or unadvisedly", "to be done spontaneously or at random", "haphazard" and to "introduce the agency of chance".[6] Moreover, αὐτοματισμός (*automatismos*) means "that which happens of itself, chance",[7] αὐτόματον (*automaton*), which is precisely the word used by Kant, means "accident"[8] and Αὐτοματία (*Automatia*) means "the goddess of chance",[9] defined by Smith as a "surname of Tyche or Fortuna, which seems to characterise her as the goddess who manages things according to her own will, without any regard to the merit of man" (Smith, 1867.[10] See also Murray, 1833, p. 577) – thus, automation means that what is "self-given" is something "random". Again, we can be automated if our decisions and actions result from causes that make them nothing but their (automated) effects, whose randomness is given not only by their heteronomy but also by their lacking whatever epistemological and ethical effort to move from a particular (and even idiosyncratic) dimension to a universal dimension.

Moreover, the current definition of the word "automation", which is strictly correlated to technology, can specify something further:

> The action or process of introducing automatic equipment or device into a manufacturing or other process or facility; (also) the fact of making something (as a system, device, etc.) automatic. Originally (and now usually) in neutral sense, but in the 1950s often associated with the use of electronic or mechanical devices to replace human labour.[11]

---

6   From the quote "act of oneself, act offhand or unadvisedly" to the quote "introduce the agency of chance", see Liddell-Scott-Jones Greek-English Lexicon, see http://stephanus.tlg.uci.edu/lsj/#eid =18225 (accessed in September 2021).

7   Liddell-Scott-Jones Greek-English Lexicon, see http://stephanus.tlg.uci.edu/lsj/#eid=18226 (accessed in September 2021).

8   Liddell-Scott-Jones Greek-English Lexicon, see http://stephanus.tlg.uci.edu/lsj/#eid=18228 (accessed in September 2021).

9   Liddell-Scott-Jones Greek-English Lexicon, see http://stephanus.tlg.uci.edu/lsj/#eid=18224 (accessed in September 2021).

10   See https://quod.lib.umich.edu/m/moa/acl3129.0001.001/462?page=root;rgn=full+text;size= 100;view=image;q1=auto (accessed in February 2022).

11   Oxford English Dictionary, see https://www.oed.com/view/Entry/13468?redirectedFrom=automation#eid (accessed in February 2022).

Thus, automation means not only that what is "self-given" is something "random" but also that what is "self-given" as something "random" is meant "to replace" something "human", specifically "human labour" – and, from a philosophical perspective, what we mean by "human labour" is crucial: may we think that the "human labour" we "replace" with technological automation is precisely our most challenging burdens of epistemological and ethical responsibilities, i.e. our autonomy?

Actually, in the last three centuries (from Kant onwards), the progressive rise of autonomy as the core of human identity itself, from human merits to human demerits, may have become the reason for its unbearable burden – thus, paradoxically enough, the more our autonomy becomes the core of our identity itself, the more we seem to trade it for technological automation, sometimes consciously and sometimes unconsciously. More precisely, on the one hand, we seem to shift autonomy from ourselves to technology and, on the other hand, we seem to shift automation from technology to ourselves. But what is the meaning of designing and using technologies that increasingly make our decisions and actions move from resulting from reasons we are perfectly aware of (and especially responsible for) to being effects resulting from causes we are not perfectly aware of[12] (and especially responsible for)?

In Section 3, I will briefly give examples of technologies that seem to show the phenomenon described above, from autonomous vehicles to autonomous weapons, in addition to self-tracking technologies and technological exoselves (but the list may be endless). Before proceeding, it is worth quoting the definition of autonomy given by at least one philosopher chronologically closer to us than Kant. As Berlin writes:

> I wish my life and decisions to depend on myself, not on external forces of whatever kind. I wish to be the instrument of my own, not of other men's, acts of will. I wish to be a subject, not an object; to be moved by reasons, by conscious purposes, which are my own, not by causes which affect me, as it were, from outside. I wish to be somebody, not nobody; a doer – deciding, not being decided for, self-directed and not acted upon by external nature or by other men as if I were a thing, or an animal, or a slave incapable of playing a human role. [...] I wish, above all, to be conscious of myself as a thinking, willing, active being, bearing responsibility for my choices and able to explain them by reference to my own ideas and purposes. I feel free to the degree that I believe this to be true, and enslaved to the degree that I am made to realise that it is not. (Berlin, 1997, p. 203)

Berlin's inspiring words make our question even more urgent: what happens to our autonomy, which seems to increasingly (and quickly) move from its rise to its fall through its shift from the core of our identity itself to technology?

As I will briefly argue (and as I extensively examined elsewhere, see note 1), my working hypothesis is that being "a doer" is most challenging – being "a doer" may be our heaviest burden, if being "a doer", i.e. being autonomous, is the core of our identity itself not only when we happen to be definitely right but also, and especially, when we happen to be definitely wrong. Thus, would it not be easier for us "to be moved by" "causes which affect me, as it were, from outside"? Would it not be easier for us to be effects of causes and not causes of effects? Would it not be easier for us to trade our heaviest epistemological and ethical burden, i.e. our autonomy, for technological automation as a kind of our autonomy's avatar?

---

[12]   Which is the issue of algorithms as black boxes, as several authors stress (from a philosophical perspective, see at least Finn 2017).

3.   FROM HUMAN AUTONOMY TO TECHNOLOGICAL AUTOMATION

If we consider, for instance, autonomous vehicles, autonomous weapons, self-tracking technologies and technological exoselves, we may reflect (even though briefly) as follows.

As far as autonomous vehicles are concerned, the word "autonomy" is frequently used as follows:

> Today's automotive industry relies on three types of vehicle testing: via computer simulation, on real-world public roads, or behind closed doors at a private test track. Approaches vary, but a combination of all three approaches is deemed vital in order to safely introduce highly autonomous vehicles.[13]

Again, we can find two words sharing the first part of their etymology: "automotive" and "autonomous" sharing αὐτός as "itself". But, again, they do not share the second part of their etymology, which, in the case of the word "automotive", is the Greek ἀμείβω (*ameibo*) as "changing" and the Latin *moveo* as "moving" and, in the case of the word "autonomy", is νόμος as "law", which leads to "self-given law". Conversely, "automotive" leads to "self-motion". Not surprisingly, "self-motion" characterises industry ("automotive industry"). But, surprisingly, "self-given law" characterises "vehicles" (which are not only "autonomous vehicles" but also "highly autonomous vehicles"). More precisely, from an etymological perspective, we may ask the following question: are "vehicles" capable of "giving themselves laws"?

There is a sense in which we may answer positively to the question: AI-based "vehicles" can "give themselves laws" if we consider their machine learning algorithms as "self-given laws". Yet, from a philosophical perspective, there is no positive answer to the question: not only according to Kant's work but also according to ancient philosophers (working on autonomy, especially as rational self-determination) and contemporary philosophers (working on autonomy, especially as a kind of individualism), technology cannot be autonomous in the same way as we, as humans, can be autonomous – and the reason why technology cannot be autonomous is that it lacks its own (universal) reasons: even machine learning algorithms are nothing but causes of effects, and not (universal) reasons at all, in that they are not what reasons mean to us, i.e. our own plans of what kind of human beings we ideally want to be. Whenever we decide and act according to our own reasons (for instance, should or should we not care about others' interests?), we plan what kind of human beings we ideally want to be. Conversely, whenever machine learning algorithms decide and act (and can make us decide and act), they have causes, but no reasons at all, in that they do not plan what kind of technologies they ideally want to be (and what kind of human beings they ideally want us to be). Thus, technology as we know it cannot be autonomous in the same way as we, as humans, can be autonomous. Yet, technology can be autonomous if, starting with our standard language, we think about it, define it and use it to shift our autonomy from ourselves to it – again, technology can be autonomous if it serves as our autonomy's avatar (and even as our scapegoat).

Autonomous vehicles can also show the logical consequence of the phenomenon described above: the more we make technology become the avatar of our own autonomy, the more we

---

[13]   See https://www.automotiveworld.com/articles/private-test-tracks-are-where-autonomous-vehicles-drive-risk-free/ (accessed in January 2021).

risk losing our own autonomy and becoming the avatar of automation, i.e. automated. For instance, according to the Waymo Safety Report:

> Waymo's mission is to bring autonomous driving technology to the world, making it safe and easy for people and things to get where they are going. We're building the World's Most Experienced Driver and we believe our technology can improve access to mobility, and save thousands of lives now lost to traffic crashes. (Waymo Safety Report, 2021, p. 2)

Moreover, "Our ultimate goal is to develop fully autonomous driving technology that can move people and things from A to B, anytime, anywhere, and in all conditions" (Waymo Safety Report, 2021, p. 16). Even though we can find positive outcomes, from "improv[ing] access to mobility" to "sav[ing] thousands of lives", we can also find something that, by increasingly characterising technologies, makes us risk naturalising the shift of our autonomy's burdens from ourselves to technology. It is no coincidence that we are described in terms of lightness and absence of effort ("making it safe and easy for people") and, conversely, technology is described in terms of heaviness and presence of effort ("our technology can [...] save thousands of lives" and "fully autonomous driving technology [...] can move people and things from A to B, anytime, anywhere, and in all conditions").

But something surprising happens:

> During our internal testing, however, we found that human drivers over-trusted the technology and were not monitoring the roadway carefully enough to be able to safely take control when needed. As driver-assist features become more advanced, drivers are often asked to transition from passenger to driver in a matter of seconds, often in challenging or complex situations with little context of the scene ahead. The more tasks the vehicle is responsible for, the more complicated and vulnerable this moment of transition becomes. Avoiding this "handoff problem" is an important reason why Waymo is committed to fully autonomously driven vehicles. Our technology takes care of all of the driving, allowing passengers to stay passengers. (Waymo Safety Report, 2021, p. 13)

It is worth stressing two issues. First, our attitude as passengers, which is again a matter of shifting our autonomy's burdens (including capacities and expertise) from ourselves to technology: "human drivers over-trusted the technology and were not monitoring the roadway carefully enough to be able to safely take control when needed". Second, our attitude as designers, which is, even more, a matter of shifting our autonomy's burdens (including capacities and expertise) from ourselves to technology: the solution to the "handoff problem" is not making us more "able to safely take control" and less "vulnerable", but making technology more autonomous as "fully autonomously driven vehicles" – the solution is making us more (passively) automated ("allowing passengers to stay passengers") and technology more (actively) autonomous (technology, as "fully autonomously driven vehicles", "takes care of all of the driving").

If it is true that, on the one hand, the current debate on autonomous vehicles starts questioning the imbalance described above,[14] it is also true that further kinds of philosophical issues

---

[14]   For instance, autonomous vehicles "can pose a direct threat to a user's moral autonomy" (Millar, 2016, p. 790) by "taking users entirely out of the ethical decision-making loop" (Millar 2016: 790). Thus, "we must step in and take the right actions to ensure that the human is the ultimate decision maker for autonomous systems" (Xu, 2021, p. 53): "Driverless does not, and should not, mean without a human operator" (Nunes et al., 2018, p. 171).

arise, starting with the following two. First, it is worth stressing that what is a "problem to solve" from an engineering perspective may be an opportunity to seize from a philosophical perspective. For instance, refusing "to stay passengers" may be an opportunity to be seized in terms of (epicurean) driving pleasure and, especially, in terms of (stoic) exercising human capacities and expertise we progressively risk atrophying even though they are frequently crucial, from "monitoring" to being "able to safely take control" to managing a "transition" even "in a matter of seconds" (which is precisely what our era of globalisation, which is progressively characterised by uncertainty, requires us). Second, it is worth stressing that the question on the philosophical meaning of the shift of autonomy's burdens (including capacities and expertise) from ourselves to technology emerges. More precisely, it is worth questioning if the reason why we want "to stay passengers" is especially that we try, sometimes consciously and sometimes unconsciously, to relieve ourselves of the dramatic burdens of epistemological and ethical responsibilities we have to take when we have to make decisions: if it is true that our epistemological and ethical responsibilities do not totally dissolve, it is also true that they become lighter burdens when they are at least distributed among several agents, starting with machine learning algorithms as artificial agents.

At least one further philosophical issue arises: both from an etymological perspective and from a philosophical perspective, trading human autonomy for technological automation can be read as a form of epistemological and ethical "anarchism" as "absence" (άν, *an*) of what can actually "rule" (άρχω, *archo*) – again, our autonomy, i.e. what can actually "rule" us by resulting from our reasons as our plans of what kind of human beings we ideally want to be, is "absent", in that it is traded for what cannot actually "rule" us, i.e. technological automation (as I will also show in what follows and extensively examined elsewhere, see note 1).

The case of autonomous weapons can add something interesting to it. Whenever autonomous weapons kill for us, philosophical issues arise in addition to the need not to sabotage human control.[15] Autonomous weapons are told to guarantee a series of advantages, starting with more restriction, more precision and sparing selected categories. But at least one further philosophical issue arises. According to the definition given by the United States Department of Defense (2012, p. 13), autonomous weapons are "A weapon system that, once activated, can select and engage targets without further intervention by a human operator". If it is true that "without further intervention by a human operator" cannot mean totally dissolving human responsibility, it is also true that it can mean the following series of advantages. First, the reassuring advantage of putting distance (which helps reify and, consequently, shift the blame) between humans using autonomous weapons and humans suffering autonomous weapons. Second, the reassuring advantage of further increasing the distance by distributing responsibility among several agents, from human agents (it is not a matter of one soldier alone, but a matter of politicians, computer scientists and soldiers together) to artificial agents (whose autonomy increases through AI). Third, the reassuring advantage of even further increasing the distance by almost dissolving responsibility into technological bureaucracy's inscrutability resulting from several agents at play and algorithms as black boxes.

Thus, technology can serve as our autonomy's avatar (and even as our scapegoat) when it comes to bearing the dramatic burden of individual responsibility, starting with thinking of ourselves and being thought of by others as the worst possible individuals for killing someone with

---

[15]   See at least Roff and Moyes (2016), Santoni de Sio and van den Hoven (2018) and Amoroso and Tamburrini (2021).

our own hands. More precisely, technology can definitely ease the progressively unbearable burden of one of the cornerstones rising from Western epistemology and ethics: individual responsibility (including individual fault), which can almost dissolve by sometimes being distributed among several agents, sometimes attributed to technology and sometimes attributed to nothing (which can be read, again, as a form of anarchism, in that who is individually responsible as a "ruler" progressively becomes "absent" by dissolving into technology, starting with its progressive inscrutability).

The last point can be stressed further by the case of self-tracking technologies, especially if we consider the phenomenon of the quantified self.[16] As several self-trackers write, "They [my doctors] can't help me, so I'll try and find these methods [self-tracking technologies] of my own health condition",[17] "because I had got out of the doctor thinking and hospital thinking and into the web thinking".[18] Again, whenever (autonomous) expertise is traded for non-expertise, anarchism emerges in terms of dissolving both others', i.e. doctors', expertise and our possible expertise (to work on), in that we self-diagnose even though we are not doctors at all, i.e. we think of our possible expertise (to work on) as inessential for self-diagnosing – and, again, (anarchically) living without bearing the burdens of working on individual expertise and being individually responsible for something wrong is definitely easier.

Further insights are given. A regular self-tracker writes:

> Yes, I did it. / On a crisp Tuesday morning / after 40 measurements a day for 1,5 years / I. Stopped. Tracking. / Why? / […] I had stopped trusting myself / letting the numbers drown out / my intuition / my instincts[.] / Each day / my self-worth was tied to the data[.] / One pound heavier this morning? / You're fat. / 2 g too much fat ingested? / You're out of control. / Skipped a day of running? / You're lazy.[19]

The relationship between human autonomy's rise and fall emerges: the more human autonomy rises as individual responsibility (even "40 measurements a day"), the more human autonomy falls as an unbearable burden ("Skipped a day of running? / You're lazy"). And a regular self-tracker writes:

> We (the apps and I) had co-constructed a digital model of my self, and here I was, managing myself, it seems, by proxy. The feedback from that digital model often took precedence over how I physically felt. When I didn't eat "enough" protein I felt weaker, and when I had too much sugar I felt fatter. These were delayed reactions; a re-reading of my body from the model. I've yet to decide: is this model pushing me closer in contact or further away from my self and my world? (Williams, 2013, p. 3)

A kind of ambiguity emerges. Trading "I" and "how I physically felt" with "the apps" and "The feedback from that digital model" may mean "pushing me" both "closer in contact" with my self and "further away from my self" (which is precisely the self-tracker's question).

From a philosophical perspective, my working hypothesis is that the phenomenon described above, together with an endless list of analogous cases, may be promisingly read as symptomatic of our sometimes conscious and sometimes unconscious will to be "push[ed]" precisely "further away" from our selves, in that, again, our selves, whose core identity itself is

---

[16]   See https://quantifiedself.com/ (accessed in February 2022). See at least Wolf (2010).

[17]   See https://quantifiedself.com/show-and-tell/?project=563 (accessed in February 2022).

[18]   See https://quantifiedself.com/show-and-tell/?project=390 (accessed in February 2022).

[19]   See https://quantifiedself.com/blog/why-i-stopped-tracking/ (accessed in February 2022).

autonomy, progressively become unbearable epistemological and ethical burdens for us – and technology progressively becomes our best ally, if it is true that what we may actually want to obtain is getting away from our autonomy's unbearable epistemological and ethical burdens, i.e. getting away from our core identity itself.

More precisely, epistemologically speaking, understanding the reason why we feel "weaker" is easier (and more reassuring) if it is not a complex matter of "I" and "how I physically felt", but a simpler matter of "the apps" and "The feedback from that digital model", which gives us clear and distinct numbers. And, ethically speaking, turning decisions into actions is easier (and more reassuring) if responsibility is not a complex matter of "I", but a simpler matter of "the apps". Thus, what we may actually want to obtain is trading our (heavier) core identity for a (lighter) digital identity – which means, again, trading our (heavier) autonomy for technology's (lighter) automation.

If it makes sense, the emerging notion of exoself, specifically correlated with the phenomenon of the quantified self (see Kelly, 2012), but also applicable to what may be read as human ontology transformed into technological ontology, may turn out not to be a continuation of the self (as it is frequently considered), but its opposite[20] – our (digital) exoselves increasingly seem to serve, sometimes quite explicitly and sometimes quite implicitly, as the solution of continuity with our (analogue) selves, from whose autonomy's burdens, again, we may actually want to get away by shifting them from our (analogue) selves to our (digital) exoselves, which we may actually want to serve as solutions of continuity.

In addition to the cases described above, we can also think of the countless times in which we say, in our everyday language, that it is not up to us, but to the (autonomous) system – of which our action is nothing but its (automated) effect.

4.   (ANARCHIC) ONTOLOGICAL OVERTURNINGS

If my working hypothesis of reading our technological era as a kind of trading human autonomy for technological automation makes sense, I will end by briefly arguing that the particular phenomenon described previously may be symptomatic of a more general phenomenon of ontological overturnings. On the one hand, humans progressively lose autonomy and obtain automation. On the other hand, technology progressively obtains not only the kind of autonomy described above but also kinds of ontological prerogatives that typically characterise the divine dimension: omnipresence (by being everywhere: it is always with us), omniscience (by knowing everything, from the answers to our questions to ourselves by tracking us), omnipotence (by increasingly having power over us, from shaping our worldviews to shaping our decisions and actions accordingly) and inscrutability (algorithms as black boxes). Yet, technology is an artefact, specifically our creation, which means that it is perfectly immanent – and being at the same time perfectly immanent and something that increasingly obtains kinds of typically divine prerogatives (in addition to humans') may be read, again, as a form of anarchism, specifically as our most anarchic move, i.e. creating a perfectly immanent kind of divine: the transcendent as the "ruler" *par excellence* is "absent", i.e. traded for the immanent, in that, by being immanently omnipresent, omniscient, omnipotent and inscrutable, technology can

---

[20]   As far as the emerging notion of exoself is concerned, Swan (2013) reflects upon Kelly (2012) as follows: "Once equipped with QS [quantified self] devices, an individual body becomes a knowable, calculable, and administrative object. Exoself technology could be a sort of fourth person perspective that facilitates the conveyance of humans into a new realm of extended self and eventually into different groups of joined selves" (Swan, 2013, p. 96).

serve as our best ally whenever we actually want to get away from our autonomy's unbearable epistemological and ethical burdens, i.e. away from our core identity itself.

Our technological exoselves can be promising cases in point to reflect upon the issue. If it is true that they somehow obtain the power of creation (which is typically divine and human), in that they can shape us (from shaping our decisions and actions to making us cyborgs), it is also true that they are creations, specifically our creations, which we can exploit as our best ally whenever we actually want to get away from our core identity itself – which means that we may read the most sophisticated outputs of contemporary technology as our attempt to create something that can somehow replace us.

If it makes sense, our technological era may be read as the most radical (anarchic) ontological overturning we have ever experienced. In Western culture, in addition to a philosophical perspective, from Aeschylus to Sophocles to Shakespeare to Pirandello (see especially Aesch. *PB*, Soph. *OT*, Shakespeare, 1998 and Pirandello, 1926), our core identity relies on being capable, first, of individually (and even solitarily) making decisions and acting accordingly (even in most uncertain scenarios) and, second, of individually (and even solitarily) bearing the epistemological and ethical burdens of responsibility, even when, as in the dramatic case of Reichenbach's Hamlet, "after the deed [...] [I] find out I should not have done it" (Reichenbach, 1951, p. 251). Again, speaking of bearing the epistemological and ethical burdens of responsibility means speaking of autonomy – and, according to Kant's masterful lesson, speaking of human autonomy means speaking both of human dignity and human freedom.

Thus, a possible task of philosophy may be not a matter of trying to stop the (unstoppable?) phenomenon described above, which may be nothing but the symptom of our even touching attempt to create technologies as our autonomy's avatars, but a matter of trying to understand, first, the reasons why we do what we do and, second, what our core identity itself (i.e. our autonomy and, consequently, our dignity and our freedom as they have been thought of for centuries) may be if we increasingly shift it from ourselves to technology. Promising answers cannot be excluded – but promising answers need (autonomous) thinking.

FURTHER READING

Chiodo, S. (2020a). The greatest epistemological externalisation: Reflecting on the puzzling direction we are heading to through algorithmic automatisation. *AI & Society: Journal of Knowledge, Culture and Communication*, 35(2), 431–440.

Chiodo, S. (2020b). *Technology and anarchy: A reading of our era.* Lanham-Boulder-New York-London, Lexington Books-The Rowman & Littlefield Publishing Group.

Chiodo, S. (2022). Human autonomy, technological automation (and reverse). *AI & Society: Journal of Knowledge, Culture and Communication*, 37(1), 39–48.

Chiodo, S. (2023). *Technology and the overturning of human autonomy.* Cham, Springer.

REFERENCES

Aeschylus. (1926). Prometheus bound (PB). Translated by H.W. Smith. Cambridge, Harvard University Press.

Amoroso, D., Tamburrini, G. (2021). In search of the "human element": International debates on regulating autonomous weapons systems. *The International Spectator*, 56(1), 20–38.

Berlin, I. (1958, 1997). Two concepts of liberty. In H. Hardy and R. Hausheer (eds), *The proper study of mankind.* London, Chatto & Windus, 191–242.

Deligiorgi, K. (2012). *The scope of autonomy: Kant and the morality of freedom*. Oxford, Oxford University Press.

Dworkin, G. (1988). *The theory and practice of autonomy*. Cambridge, Cambridge University Press.

Finn, E. (2017). *What algorithms want: Imagination in the age of computing*. Cambridge, MIT Press.

Frankfurt, H. (1971). Freedom of the will and the concept of a person. *The Journal of Philosophy*, 68(1), 5–20.

Frankfurt, H. (1999). *Necessity, volition, and love*. Cambridge, Cambridge University Press.

Guyer, P. (2003). Kant on the theory and practice of autonomy. In E. Frankel Paul, F. Miller, J. Paul (eds.), *Autonomy*. Cambridge, Cambridge University Press.

Hill, T. (1989). The Kantian conception of autonomy. In J. Christman (ed.), *The inner citadel: Essays on individual autonomy*. Oxford-New York, Oxford University Press, 91–105.

Hill, T. (2000). *Respect, pluralism and justice: Kantian perspectives*. Oxford-New York, Oxford University Press.

Kant, I. (1785, 1998). *Groundwork of the metaphysics of morals*. Ed. by M.J. Gregor. Cambridge, Cambridge University Press.

Kant, I. (1788, 1996). *Critique of practical reason*. Ed. by M.J. Gregor, introduction by A. Wood. Cambridge, Cambridge University Press.

Kelly, K. (2012). The quantified century. http://quantifiedself.com/conference/Palo-Alto-2012.

Korsgaard, C.M. (1996a). *Creating the kingdom of ends*. New York, Cambridge University Press.

Korsgaard, C.M. (1996b). *The sources of normativity*. New York, Cambridge University Press.

Millar, J. (2016). An ethics evaluation tool for automating ethical decision-making in robots and self-driving cars. *Applied Artificial Intelligence*, 30(8), 787–809.

Murray, J. (1833). *A classical manual, being a mythological, historical, and geographical commentary on Pope's Homer and Dryden's Virgil*. London, Murray.

Nunes, A., Reimer, B., Coughlin, J.F. (2018). People must retain control of autonomous vehicles. *Nature*, 556, 169–171.

Pirandello, L. (1926, 1992). *One, no one and one hundred thousand*. Ed. by W. Weaver, New York, Sprul Editions.

Reath, A. (2006). *Agency and autonomy in Kant's moral theory: Selected essays*. Oxford-New York, Oxford University Press.

Reichenbach, H. (1951, 1959). *The rise of scientific philosophy*. Berkeley-Los Angeles, University of California Press.

Roff, H.M., Moyes, R. (2016). Meaningful human control, artificial intelligence and autonomous weapons. Briefing paper prepared for the Informal Meeting of Experts on Lethal Autonomous Weapons Systems, UN Convention on Certain Conventional Weapons, article 36, 1–6.

Santoni de Sio, F., van den Hoven, J. (2018). Meaningful human control over autonomous systems: A philosophical account. *Frontiers in Robotics and AI*, 5, 1–14.

Sensen, O., ed. (2013). *Kant on moral autonomy*. Cambridge, Cambridge University Press.

Shakespeare, W. (1998). *Hamlet*. Oxford-New York, Oxford University Press.

Smith, W., ed. (1867). *Dictionary of Greek and Roman biography and mythology*. Boston, Little, Brown & Co.

Sophocles (1981). *Œdipus the king (OT)*. Translation by F. Storr. Cambridge, Harvard University Press.

Swan, M. (2013). The quantified self: Fundamental disruption in big data science and biological discovery. *Big Data*, 2(1), 85–98.

Taylor, R. (2005). Kantian personal autonomy. *Political Theory*, 33(5), 602–628.

United States Department of Defense. (2012). Autonomy in weapon systems. Directive 3000.09, 2012, 1–15.

Waymo Safety Report. (2021). On the road to fully self-driving. https://storage.googleapis.com/waymo-uploads/files/documents/safety/2021-08-waymo-safety-report.pdf.

Williams, K. (2013). The weight of things lost: Self-knowledge and personal informatics. *CHI*, 1–4.

Winner, L. (1978). *Autonomous technology: Technics-out-of-control as a theme in political thought*. Cambridge-London, MIT Press.

Wolf, G.I. (2010). The data-driven life. *The New York Times Magazine*. http://www.nytimes.com/2010/05/02/magazine/02self-measurement-t.html?pagewanted=all&_r=0.

Xu, W. (2021). From automation to autonomy and autonomous vehicles: Challenges and opportunities for human-computer interaction. *Interactions*, 1, 49–53.

7. Automation anxiety: a critical history – the apparently odd recurrence of debates about computation, AI and labour

Caroline Bassett and Ben Roberts

1. FRAMING AUTOMATION ANXIETY

Today, automation anxiety is highly evident. It relates to the threat or promises of AI to enable the radical expansion of automation into areas previously regarded as demanding quintessentially human cognitive skills. A powerful AI imaginary links job loss to the loss of human agency in general – *being* as well as *being employed* therefore becoming implicated both in the more apocalyptic versions of this imaginary and even in its more banal or everyday forms.

Critical responses to this moment are – as they have been in the past – bifurcated.

Accelerationist-influenced responses seek to deploy AI to power on through difficulty to a new tomorrow, while also – at least in some versions of accelerationism – seeking to exploit the destructive force of technological upheaval to expand systemic crisis (Srnicek & Williams, 2015). Other critical responses entail seeking limits – and often conjoin limits to AI as a figure for new technology in general with demands for limits to growth attached to environmental degradation (Bender et al., 2021).

These debates often come to us 'as new' even in their left forms. Multiple academic articles, literature and news outlets deal with what is exceptional – even singular – about AI and focus on a break over continuity. Automation anxiety, specifically around labour and its automation, is a part of these debates and is the focus of this chapter. In it, we are concerned to explore contemporary automation anxiety around AI by recontextualising it within a broader context and by exploring its temporal dynamics.

We seek to do so to make a contribution to a new politics of technology and to relate them to AI. We set out to 'read' topoi-logically (Huhtamo, 2013) across old and new left debates on automation and the end of work, to ask what happened to the 1960s cybernation fevers, chills, scares and deliriums that circulated among the left, that themselves shadowed the rise of automation discourse in the 1950s in complex non-linear ways. We argue that while some elements of these earlier formations faded away, others travelled on, submarined, and now re-emerge, re-framing contemporary automation debates around AI and, we suggest, exploring these forms of resurgence can inform us about the 'master discourses' of left technopolitics.[1]

---

[1] We use this term to indicate a field of debates exploring the political potential of new media emerging in response to the 1990s internet moment and continuing. A dominant strand of this is libertarian (see e.g. Barlow, 1996). Left responses range across critical theory, autonomism, hacker ethics, left reformism, cultural theory, feminisms and latterly accelerationism (see e.g. Witheford, 1994; Webster & Robins, 1989; Fisher, 2009; Bassett et al., 2019).

2.   AI AND AUTOMATION

The concepts of automation and artificial intelligence are closely related. Automation as a term emerges in common use in the early 1950s with the term artificial intelligence following towards the end of the decade (Marshall, 1957; Kline, 2017, p. 115). But automation is not limited to the exploitation of AI techniques. Indeed, in its infancy, it was as much associated with the extension of mechanisation as cybernetic feedback or AI [see below]. Equally, AI is not always in the service of automation but encompasses a much wider range of techniques, problems and concerns. Nonetheless, debates about the merits, consequences and societal impact of the two have often gone hand in hand. They have also often turned on issues of labour and its ending. It is for this reason that, we argue, a critical history of debates about automation, or 'automation anxiety' can contribute to critical studies of artificial intelligence.

Critical studies of artificial intelligence pick up where normative models of 'responsible AI' end. The latter seeks to build acceptance for AI decision making by incorporating a form of 'best practice' into AI techniques and machine learning models to ensure 'equity' of some order (racial, gender, less often sexuality or disability, hardly ever class) through the avoidance of bias and 'transparency' in their operation. Responsible AI is, then, primarily a technical solution to technosocial problems (see e.g. Mikalef et al., 2022; Ghallab, 2019). It encourages an awareness among engineers that, for example, learning models might exacerbate existing racial biases in the datasets on which they are built. Without disparaging this important work, the societal challenge of artificial intelligence cannot be met solely through technical solutions. Indeed, the prevalence of technological solutionism as a way of solving social problems is, arguably, part of the wider societal challenge created by computational technology in general (Morozov, 2014; Webster & Robins, 1989; Bassett, 2022), in this sense being powerfully ideological. Responsible AI, often well-intentioned, is ultimately a modified form of this solutionism. As such, it fails to address the concerns about artificial intelligence that are bound up with wider social challenges, debates and anxieties, anxieties that are not simply technical in nature.

To take a concrete example, consider predictive policing, such as the commercial Predpol system in use by many police forces in the United States. Systems such as Predpol use AI methods to allow police to 'target' areas in real time where crime is likely to be taking place. As many critics have pointed out, such systems reproduce – and amplify – the biases in existing crime data. If crime investigation and enforcement has been racially discriminatory in the past, Predpol becomes an invitation to focus police presence in the areas affected by that discrimination previously. Ruha Benjamin (2019, p. 55) calls this 'default discrimination'. But would the concerns of Black and Latinx communities be assuaged if PredPol adopted 'responsible AI' best practices? It seems unlikely. As Wilson and McCulloch (2016) point out, the problem is not just predictive AI systems, but the flawed model of policing in which they are deployed. The very idea of 'targeted' policing is politicised, with a long and controversial history. As #BlackLivesMatter and #DefundThePolice suggest, the issue, perhaps, is not public acceptance of the use of 'responsible' AI but wider public acceptance and consent for policing altogether (Kaba & Ritchie, 2022; Benjamin, 2019).

As the predictive policing example suggests, anxiety about the automation of particular forms of decision making cannot be understood through a purely technical and instrumental grasp of automation anxiety. Similarly, concerns about labour and automation can never be reduced to instrumental issues but are bound into extant political economies and their ideological supports. To turn back to the past, at the height of the cybernation scare, James Boggs (1970), a co-author of the Triple Alliance, and a member of the auto workers union, argued – and in relation to others prioritising organised labour in general – that Black workers had a specific orientation that needed to be explored in thinking through the prospects for labour and leisure. In response to calls from some unions to argue against the end of work – at the time confidently expected to be ushered in by way of new forms of computationally driven automation – he argued that for African Americans, long the lowest and last let into workplaces, calls for the prioritisation of the dignity of labour rang hollow; his call, therefore, was for automation (Boggs, 1966). The point, again emphasised by considering the issues from a position of advocacy and/in relation to race, is that concerns about automation are not simply technical. Moreover – as we show via this example – concerns about automation have *never been* simply technical. Despite this though, solutionism, and with it a form of presentism, *recurs* as a powerful and often immediate response to new developments in computer-driven automation and specifically to those deriving from AI technologies.

That is why we believe that one way to understand better contemporary automation anxieties is through a *critical* history of automation. This demands taking cognisance both of technology and of more than technology itself. In particular, it requires identifying and understanding the disjuncture between ideas about the technological (variously instantiated and materialised) and computational technologies in operation and also understanding how this disjuncture operates with some ideological force. We note that accepting that the relationship between cultural imaginaries of automation futures is non-isomorphic also begins to indicate the need to consider the dynamics of automation anxiety over time, since these, if not necessarily bound to proximate technological developments or linear progression, may exhibit complex temporalities. But what do we mean by 'automation anxiety'? Here and elsewhere (Bassett & Roberts, 2019), we use this term in a way that is both general and specific.

2.1 Automation

To begin with, we argue that the term *automation* needs to be treated with some historical specificity. It is true that in contemporary common use, the term has been applied in a generic manner to refer to machines, mechanisation and industrialisation in general. But when the word emerged in English in the post-war era, it meant something different: indicating a qualitative shift in what had occurred hitherto. Its most influential exponents, such as John Diebold, sharply distinguished it from concepts such as mechanisation. For Diebold (1952), it represented a more totalising change in the nature of production, something systematic. Moreover, the model was not the Taylorist production line, but the continuous control and feedback system of the new oil refineries, their mass production of distillate petroleum overseen by only a handful of engineers. Importantly, Diebold, like many others, thus linked automation to the post-war cybernetics movement, the same intellectual current from which 'symbolic' AI would eventually emerge and then distinguish itself (Kline, 2017, p. 154).

Automation was thus something different from the machines that preceded it. It inaugurated a new relationship between technology and humans, one that was to come to full fruition just over the horizon. It was because automation represented a qualitative shift from what had occurred previously and that its potential and threat were so widely debated in the 1950s (and again in the early 1960s) in academic journals, the press, industry and government.

In our analysis, we accept the premise that the emergence of the new term 'automation' in the immediate post-war era *does* mark a new phase in the history of thinking and worrying about machines and their relationship to human flourishing. Cybernetics, information theory, computational developments and the wider discourses shaped by these ideas fundamentally alter both the ways in which machines are understood and the way in which humans are conceived, for example, as a special case of a self-organising machine or system. Our explorations of automation anxiety - and our reading of this as it emerges in relation to AI – focus on the discontinuous continuity we find emerging as a response to this break in the decades that follow. This puts us somewhat at odds with some others currently writing about the history of automation debates. Aaron Benanav, for example, traces 'automation discourse' back to the mid-19th century, citing Babbage and Marx, among others. Benanav's position conflicts somewhat, of course, with the etymology of the term, whose original use in its current sense is usually attributed to Ford's Vice President Delmar S. Harder in 1948. Benanav gets around this by adopting the broad definition of automation as meaning technologies that fully, rather than partially, substitute for labour (2020, p. 6). In this sense, it is possible to conceive automation as simply a more extensive form of mechanisation and therefore conceptually analogous to it, the continuation of mechanisation by other means. But this is to conceive automation essentially as an economic, quantitative concept, and in terms of labour. It ignores, or does not take seriously, the *qualitative* shift the authors of post-war automation discourse are describing – one that may centrally concern labour but one that reaches all areas. Indeed, as Herbert Marcuse (2014) would have it, this pervasiveness might be a defining feature of new forms of technocratic rationality he understood to be arising in the same period; he saw this as a form of co-option and one that threatened the subject of history, or at least occluded – or made 'latent' – the identification of that subject.

Of course, there can be nothing dogmatic about this distinction between automation and mechanisation. We are not arguing that ideas about automation emerge *ex nihilo* in the late 1940s, nor are we hinting at some kind of Foucauldian epistemological break. There are clear links, for example, between post-war automation debates and pre-war US discussions about technocracy. Equally, there are many similarities in the sorts of things that Siegfried Giedion has to say in *Mechanisation Takes Command* (2013 [1948]) and Diebold's (1952) arguments about the automatic factory. Doubtless automation is conceived *in part* as a more totalised form of mechanisation. But that is not all it is. And the 'not all' matters. It matters partly because it enables us to understand contemporary developments in AI as having some material continuity with this earlier break. And here it is evident that if we are against technological solutionism, we do recognise and seek to engage with material-technical change. What matters for us in these debates, however, is not just that AI technologies mean machines can do more, but also how the capabilities and *meaning* of the machine, and of automation, are being fundamentally rethought.

2.2   Anxiety

Alongside automation, we use the term 'anxiety' to denote ways of worrying about, analysing but also evangelising, an automation that is felt to be imminent and perhaps inevitable. Anxiety entails or suggests a response that is affectively loaded, having a certain intensity – perhaps it even constitutes an attachment (see Lauren Berlant (2011) and Bassett (2022) on AI and cruel optimism). In our sense, anxiety can mean concerns or fears, but also fevers or enthusiasm. This might arise in elaborated forms, for instance, in some contemporary left accelerationist accounts of 'automated luxury communism' (Bastani, 2019), where it is articulated as optimistic politics. It might also be present in less elaborated or more diffuse ways, part of an informing structure of feeling, an element of a common response. If technological anxiety in this sense means the anticipation, the envisaging, the guarding against or planning for some systematic shift in human relationships with computational machines, then automation anxiety more specifically articulates itself as a threat (loss of employment or control in decision making, loss of the value in life); as utopian (elimination of drudgery and need in a work-free future); or as a technological imagination/vision of what a society can imagine itself to be becoming in relation to the automation of labour.

2.3   Automation Anxiety

Automation anxiety is essentially a cultural discourse, materialised in multiple ways, and also clothed in changing symbolic material forms: the robot at the factory gate in the 1950s, the mainframe computer and its human attendants in the 1960s, the cybernation scare of the mid-1960s, the self-driving car or military drone in the 2000s and 2020s. These material forms then come to act as metaphors for understanding, worrying about or proselytising the 'new' in an automated future on, or just over, the horizon. Automation anxiety shapes what these technologies come to mean (that for which they come to stand as synecdoche?) but also speaks to wider contemporary social concerns about work, leisure, capitalism and the cultural and social order. We thus adopt this term primarily in order to discuss automation anxiety as a concept, related to, but also somewhat distanced from automation itself. Automation debates, then, are *relatively* autonomous from developments in the technologies underpinning automation itself, being tied to them in complex and indirect ways. These debates are also bound together in ways that are temporally complex and often non-linear. We contend that automation anxiety is not simply a direct response to automation as it is instantiated in specific material forms (as a particular algorithm or set of algorithms) and as it operates. Indeed, automation anxiety frequently precedes actual existing automation, as we believe its critical history shows. Further, in so far as it prefigures specific forms of automation, it both contributes to identifying and shaping what automation comes to mean and is a way in which earlier engagements come to inform apparently 'all new' developments.

3.   AUTOMATION ANXIETY AND RECURRENCE

3.1   Resolution/Correction?

Why does this matter? There are, after all, multiple ways to understand why a spike in anxiety around automation might arise – and also subside. One explanation, consonant with technological solutionism, is that the technological problem at issue (or the social problem it produces) is resolved. Another explanation is that, being subsumed into everyday life, a technological assemblage is no longer regarded as discrete, and the issues it raises are no longer viewed as technological – there are parallels with domestication debates in media, technology and everyday life studies with their focus on invisibilisation, which are germane here (see e.g. Silverstone, 1994).

Neither of these two approaches however really get satisfactorily at the disjointed temporality of automation anxiety and, above all, with the problem of recurrence. Assuming anxiety subsides due to a technological 'fix' being put in place tends to reduce the problem-producing anxiety to 'something technical' rather than to a technosocial constellation. As an example, consider mid-1990s concerns around VDU screens (see Figure 7.1), which were related to eyesight, and also, to some extent, to other health issues (pregnancy and emissions).

The proximate issues of bad screen quality, and the screen technology that gave rise to concerns around radiation, were resolved. But the issue of operators' health and safety and the gendering of technology (Wajcman, 2000) that labelled data entry as clerical (versus e.g. artisan/skilled typesetting) and as deskilled labour was not. This division not only remains today, and arguably has *revived* in intensity – notably, for instance, around home working and surveillance, work hours and casualisation.

Domestication theory and its related approaches meanwhile tend to dissolve technology into the social (Silverstone, 1994; Hartmann, 2015; Berker et al., 2005). It finds in *new* technology a new challenge, offering a new imaginary, and in this way has parallels with solutionism's fix-by-fix approach. Our approach to automation anxiety instead refuses to negate what is novel in new technology but also actively seek, alongside this, to ask what is re-activated, or comes back into circulation, in response to a new conjuncture, despite apparently having been 'dealt with' in an earlier moment.

Source: Via the Internet Archive (bit.ly/3JG2T6E).

Figure 7.1   *Postcard on dangers of VDUs*

3.2   What Recurs?

In other work, Bassett (2022) has attempted to cluster some of these recurring anxieties and explore them (or typologise them) as various forms of anti-computing. This typology of anti-computing is not elaborated on here. Despite the very real break, new forms of AI presage, and taking into account the break constituted by automation as distinct from mechanisation (set out above), there is very little in what is prophesied, or imagined, as just around the corner for AI-driven forms of labour re-organisation that has not already been pre-configured, or that has, in other words, not already circulated as an automation imaginary. A brief over-arching history of automation anxiety since 1948, touching down on some key moments of heightened automation anxiety, might identify an anxious response to cybernetics and Wiener, figured largely as a concern about both intelligent machines (human hollowing out) and massive job cuts. This history might go on to locate a moment of recrudescence and elaboration in the cybernation scare of the early to mid-1960s, which specifically focused on work. Later, it is possible to diagnose a return – after the cyber-fantasies of the 1990s – to a form of political-economic thinking around new forms of automation, powered by/relating to, but not isomorphic to (because pre-dating machine learning and current developments in AI) those in the 21st century. This last turn is centrally focused on a new jobs cull (cognitive automation) to which one response has been a return to issues of the universal basic income (UBI), as noted below. These moments are not exhaustive of course. There are many more and they are locally specific, as well as globally influenced: in the UK, Thatcherism had its automation anxiety moment via the print unions and automated layout (into which the VDU campaigns invoked above fed, albeit in conflicted ways), for instance (Cockburn, 1991).

Each of the formations identified above related to, but were also offset from, proximate technological developments, or involved responses relatively independent from them: pre-existing, or pre-figured, circulating and circulatory. Automation anxiety then, evolves, but relying only on a chronological history, while useful, doesn't get at these more complex dynamics, at issues of changing intensity, nor even at why 'scares' or 'anxieties' or 'fevers' arise when they do. Computerisation, after all, continued to expand relentlessly across the period of 'automation' (once again, we constitute this as spanning cybernetics through the digital revolution – and now reaching into AI) so why do the scares peak and trough?

Theorising this patterned recurrence, in earlier joint and discrete work, we have drawn on the concept of topos, as developed by Erkki Huhtamo (1997), which suggests a durable mould out of which new experiences may be forged, and on the queer historiography of Valerie Traub (2011). Both explore the temporal dynamics of various tropes or topoi (those of the body for Traub and of the technological for Huhtamo). Traub's investigations are into what history does with its bodies; her work on discontinuous continuity explores how long-standing bodily tropes revive or become meaningful again at particular periods, before re-submerging. It is pertinent here partly because it invites a consideration of intensity – tropes returning to what she terms salience not only become *legible* but also come to operate with particular *affective* force; indeed, the two depend on each other for this return to be made

Huhtamo's exploration of topoi or '"pre-fabricated" moulds for experience' specifically addresses issues of temporal dynamics in relation to medium technologies. His bid is to use a 'topological approach' to generate a specific *media* archaeology, defining it as 'a way of studying recurring cyclical phenomena that (re)appear and disappear and reappear over and over again in media history seeming to transcend specific historical contexts' (1997, p. 222). His work deploys this approach to explore connections – and disconnections – between cybernation debates of the 1960s and new media forms; specifically, his move is from 'cybernation to interactivity' (1999). (It is in this way perhaps that his topoi can be defined as 'ontological'[2]). We too are interested in this history – and we too read it as a specific media technological history. Automation anxiety intersects with or is in part a medium archaeological approach – but one that insists on the disjunctive relationship between the temporal dynamics of material innovation and the temporal dynamics of automation anxiety as a discourse.[3]

Diverging from Huhtamo's ontological topoi as a way to understand automation anxiety/ fever, we also engage with other forms of (historical) materialism. Moreover, we focus specifically on 'left topoi' – and specifically on 'left' automation anxiety as it relates to work, the end of work and the leisure society. This focus does not rule out but rather organises that broader array of concerns around social being – and even around being itself (the hollowing out of the self) – that are part of the topos. It also suggests particular characteristics. If we explore automation anxiety not as a general process of subsumption but rather through considering what might constitute a left topos, we might begin by noting its cathected relation to issues specifically of labour and the end of work, and of the leisure society. These are, after all, traditionally concerns 'of' the left. Automation anxiety pressures concepts central to understanding labour, work and struggle, for example, the labour theory of value, and the question of the 'proper' or possible 'subject of history'.

Reconnecting earlier moments in the left response to automation – and/or recognising their persistence or recurrence and their complex temporal dynamics – can itself be understood as doing critical work. This is partly because these left responses to automation are subject *to*, or largely submerged *by*, Silicon Valley and its 'progress' ideology. The latter, while looking relentlessly forwards, also makes, or forges, a particular version of history, one which tends to correct or obliterate protest, unease, anxiety and the old.[4] Walter Benjamin (1968 [1940]) long ago pointed out that history is that which the victors make and the shiny surface of the valley is only momentarily disrupted by new protest, which is largely decoupled from earlier protest; the echoes of earlier moral opprobrium, worker unrest, monopoly accusations or governance demands, of injustice or discrimination, of earlier forms of automation anxiety, tend only to be heard faintly or are easily discounted when explored in relation to (linear histories recounting) the sheer scale of the growth of automation. Such growth retrospectively confines earlier hesitation, anxiety and so on as overcoming roadblocks to 'the road ahead' as the market vision was termed by Bill Gates in the first internet wave (Gates et al., 1995).

---

2   Huhtamo's focus is on ontological topoi in relation to automation.

3   That is, it is not in relation to the degree that automation issues are resolved by technical means that automation anxiety waxes and wanes, nor does anxiety wholly take its character or its temporal rhythm either from the specific technical advances that might give us our time (Kittler) or contribute to it (in less mordant and more co-evolutional accounts). On the other hand, anxiety rests on what is articulated through the material forms of computational culture as well as what is signalled or symbolised.

4   For a paradigmatic example consider the front cover of the first UK edition of *Wired* magazine in 1995. This quoted Thomas Paine, 'we have it in our power to begin the world over again'.

4.   CYBERNATION TO COGNITIVE AUTOMATION

So what does this history of recurrence look like? An exemplary example of an earlier era of automation anxiety (one that, as we shall explore further below, does prefigure much found in contemporary formations) is the 1960s 'cybernation scare' that was generated and responded to across the board by governments, industry, the left, organised labour and critical theorists. The central claim at issue was that the 'advent of cybernation', cybernetic automation, would bring an end to 'job holding as the general mechanism through which economic resources are distributed' and would simultaneously massively expand productive capacity (Ad Hoc Committee on the Triple Revolution, 1964, p. 5). The specifically left response to this automation scare, part of this broader formation, was mixed. It comprised fevered adherence to the hope for a leisure society, hostility about its shape and marked disagreements around the process of transition – and its relative importance in relation to future good (the future good life).

On the fevered side was The Triple Alliance, a call to arms from a grouping including James Boggs, Mary Alice Hilton and Todd Gitlin, among others, that proclaimed cybernation to be inevitable, and argued that, properly deployed, it could have a progressive dividend. The perils of failing to cybernate, or argue for progressive cybernation, as the Alliance saw it, were common ruin, or tyranny: 'we may be allowing an efficient and dehumanised community to emerge by default' (1964, p. 9). In the end, however, there is optimism about the prospects: 'cybernation, properly understood and used, is the road out of want and toward a decent life' (1964, p. 10).

This was not only an argument about the sustainability of the economics of a post-work society. The Triple Alliance demanded the invention of new *forms* of life. Central to this was the automation of labour, and the end of labour as the means of existence. As they suggested; 'cybernation at last forces us to answer the historic questions: What is man's role when he is not dependent on his own activities for the material basis of life?' (1964, p. 9). The hostile responses (within the left) came from those who feared the end of what gains had been made by organised labour, the end of the usefulness of life, entire alienation and, because of that, entire powerlessness.[5]

The cybernation 'scare' and the 'fever' subsided, and the term fell into disuse. Arguments – for social justice, equality and new forms of life – that appeared to have credibility in relation to an expected technological surge (that which would end labour) lost their salience in relation to this new conjuncture.[6] But these discourses of the cybernation scare did not entirely dissipate. Elements remained to haunt associated discourses, even in eras when they did not 'fit', and today they are certainly back in evidence. Cybernation tropes resonate strikingly with new waves of automation, particularly around questions of labour and its end, leisure and its prospects, and the relative prioritisation of transition versus outcome Attending to these revenant elements is useful in responding to automation today, particularly when trying to

---

[5]   See debates explored at early cybernation conferences and particularly those between Victor Perlo, for the CP, and cybernation enthusiasts (Bassett, 2022; Hilton, 1966).

[6]   James E. Block, in an article entitled 'The Selling of a Productivity Crisis', assesses earlier discussions of the leisure society, in relation in part to the Triple Revolution, asking why public discourse 'led away from the consideration of a society less centred around the workplace' (1983). Block identifies a 'deep collective failure' to confront uncertainties raised by cybernation, blames 'entrenched interests, who wish market inequalities to persist, and do so by shifting the blame onto workers', but also suggests reasons why the debates were not taken up widely on the left.

grapple with newly arising left accounts of automation and the leisure society (for instance, the accelerationist moment). Further considering the trajectory or the way these revenant elements travel also enables the generation of a more nuanced and less 'corrective' assessment of the earlier period and its players. It is not only the key elements of the arguments for fevered acceptance or anxious refusal that are re-found in contemporary debates but also the recrudescence of a *sense* of a moment of decision, a technological singularity to which a response must be made – exceptionally – and in exceptional times that is strikingly recapitulated in current debates.

5.   CONTEMPORARY AUTOMATION DEBATES

Just as in the 1950s and 1960s, there is a sense that we are on the brink of a new era of automation, albeit this time led by artificial intelligence and machine learning, rather than feedback and control or the digital computer. This perspective is particularly prevalent among proponents of the 'new' or 'digital' economy. In a widely read and cited account, Erik Brynjolffsson and Andrew McAfee argue that we are at the beginning of a second machine age where computation is 'doing for mental power – the ability to use our brains to shape and understand our environments – what the steam engine and its descendants did for muscle power' (2014, pp. 7–8). Prophesies about new technological eras, epochs and revolutions are not confined to Brynjolfsson and McAfee, of course. We might think, for example, of Klaus Schwab, the founder of the World Economic Forum and his 'fourth industrial revolution' (2017) and similar claims made about 3D printing revolutions, mobile revolutions and so on.

The information age – the age beginning with Claude Shannon and Norbert Wiener in the immediate post-war era – is not so much a state of permanent revolution as one of the constant *manufacture* of new revolutions – revolutions that are even as they are new, also immediately familiar. The amnesiac quality of this state is startling. *The Second Machine Age* doesn't mention cybernetics anywhere in its 306 pages, but its arguments are strikingly similar to those Wiener constructed around the second industrial revolution in his 1948 book and to those circulating in the 1960s around the cybernation moment outlined above. Separated by up to seven decades, they both exhibit a fundamental trope of automation discourse, the claim that 'this time it's different'. For Wiener (1961 [1948]), it was different this time because feedback allowed machines for the first time to adapt and therefore to behave more like biological organisms. In the case of Brynjolfsson and McAfee, it is more a case of computational power and machine learning techniques reaching a tipping point: now they are finally able to perform tasks, such as driving, that were previously considered too difficult. It is now possible, it is argued, to break with Moravec's paradox, that is, the idea that computers are good at high-level reasoning but poor at basic sensorimotor skills (Brynjolfsson & Mcafee, 2014, pp. 28–29; Moravec, 1988). On this reading, machines can now be more general purpose and perform tasks, such as manual and semi-skilled labour, that previously required human dexterity and flexibility.

This renewed faith in the capability of artificial intelligence has led to new anxieties about the implications of automation. In an influential report entitled 'The future of employment: How susceptible are jobs to computerisation?' the economists Carl Benedikt Frey and Michael A. Osborne explore the implications for (un)employment. Like Brynjolfsson and McAfee, they extrapolate from contemporary developments the future automation of a new domain of manual and semi-skilled labour such as legal writing and truck driving. Having explored AI's new capabilities with engineers, they seek to reorient labour economics regarding what tasks are automatable. Previously, labour economists had assumed that 'computer capital *substitutes* for workers in carrying out a limited and well-defined set of cognitive and manual activities ("routine tasks") … [and] … *complements* workers in carrying out problem-solving and complex communication activities ("nonroutine" tasks)' (Autor et al., 2003, p. 1281). In the case of truck driving, for example, limited opportunities were foreseen for computers to either substitute (replace) or complement human labour (2003, p. 1286). Frey and Osborne, writing a decade later, argue that successful autonomous driving experiments by Google and others challenge the whole basis of these assumptions (2013, p. 3). Classifying tasks as 'routine' and 'nonroutine' was once enough to determine their susceptibility to automation, but advances in machine learning now allow computers to perform many nonroutine tasks (2013, p. 23). Indeed, Frey and Osborne go on to argue that almost any task can now be automated, subject to a handful of limiting 'bottlenecks'. Factors that limit computerisation include irregular objects and environments that resist recognition and handling, as well as tasks involving creative and social intelligence. Having identified these bottlenecks, they use skill descriptions from O*NET, a US database of occupational definitions, to automatically classify 702 occupations on the likelihood of their being computerisable. They conclude that 47% of US jobs could now be automated 'relatively soon, perhaps over the next decade or two' (2013, p. 44). Frey and Osborne's findings have been widely discussed in the media and cited in policy debates. In September 2015, the BBC published an interactive page on its website summarising the findings and allowing readers to find out if their job would be automated (BBC, 2015). Similar stories were published in *Bloomberg*, the *Guardian* and the *Sunday Times* (Keen, 2015; Seager, 2016; Whitehouse & Rojanasakul, 2017). Their work has also formed the basis of public policy discussion. For example, in July 2017, the Taylor Review published *Good Work*, a report on modern working practices, for the UK government. The report noted Frey and Osborne's arguments that perception, creativity and social intelligence still lay beyond automation and argued that it was important to encourage the development of those skills in the labour force (Taylor et al., 2017, p. 30). Once again, the case for exceptional change seems made.

And yet today, a decade after Frey and Osborne's report, the prospect of a coming quantum leap in automatable tasks – and, therefore, in automatable workers – no longer seems quite as likely to come about. Even the self-driving car, from whose imminent success so much was extrapolated, is still largely confined to public trials and Tesla's permanent 'beta' Autopilot software. While it's obviously too early to entirely disregard Frey and Osbornes's warnings, it is not at all clear that the implications for employment are as serious as they imagined.[7] Our point here is that once again automation fever/anxiety decouples from its proximate material host. Indeed, the shape of the current wave of automation anxiety around employment is, from our perspective, eerily reminiscent of *previous* waves. Just as with the cybernetics craze in the

---

[7] Among economists, there are many more sceptical voices concerning the employment implications of contemporary AI. Even allowing for Frey and Osborne's premises concerning automatable tasks, Melanie Arntz, Terry Gregory and Ulrich Zierhahn (2016) argue that the likely impact on jobs is much lower than Frey and Osborne suggest, with only about 9% in OECD countries being susceptible to automation: starkly fewer than Frey and Osborne's figure for the United States (47%). Equally, David Autor (2014) has argued that while machine learning can be 'unreasonably effective' in specific tasks, its actual capabilities and ability to substitute for human labour are more limited.

1950s and 1960s, the 'optimistic' assumptions of scientists and engineers about what technology would soon be capable of have run a long way ahead of its actual capacities. Economists and policymakers have heavily invested in these assumptions and created new concerns about the implications of automation.

5.1   The Left's Return to Automation

Of course, not everybody is gloomy about the impact of artificial intelligence on employment. Alongside this particular form of automation anxiety, there is also automation fever of the left kind. This is particularly manifest in accelerationism, already invoked above. Of note here is work such as Nick Srnicek and Alex Williams's *Inventing the Future: Postcapitalism and a World Without Work* (2015) and Aaron Bastani's *Fully Automated Luxury Communism* (2019), already cited. As we have discussed elsewhere, these writers both embrace and seek to accelerate automation in order to achieve socialist goals (Bassett & Roberts, 2019). Fuelled by a lack of faith in the prospects of collective action and labour solidarity, they propose instead investment in automating technologies and using UBI as a way of ensuring that the benefits of a post-scarcity, automated production system are delivered to the wider population. But this vision of using UBI to share (at least some of) the benefits of automation can also be arrived at by those coming from a very different perspective.

For example, Silicon Valley futurist Martin Ford in *The Rise of the Robots* (2015) is among many to propose responding to the threat of automation creating mass unemployment through the creation of guaranteed income. In a chapter entitled 'Is this time different?' he argues that information technology is already the cause of a range of economic ills affecting countries such as the US and UK, including wage stagnation, unemployment and underemployment (2015, pp. 29–63). Drawing, again, on Frey and Osborne's findings about automation and US unemployment, he argues that these economic impacts are likely to accelerate over the next two decades. For Ford, the remedy for these problems is a guaranteed basic income conceived upon Hayekian lines as 'a market-oriented approach to providing a minimal safety net' (2015, p. 258). Basic income would allow those whose skills are no longer needed to still participate in the market through consumption and therefore avoid the alternative of more extensive government intervention through an 'inevitable' expansion of the welfare state.

That two such widely varying political outlooks should be advocating similar political solutions should give us pause for thought. Beyond this, part of the problem with the accelerationist vision is that technology becomes a kind of crutch for supporting a political agenda around post-scarcity. It is not so much turning an IS into an OUGHT, as using IS as a justification for an OUGHT that might otherwise be regarded as utopian and out of reach. It is at this juncture that a left critical history can be drawn upon to offer an important alternative both to accelerationism and its presentism and to the market-based version. Of note here is the Benjaminian idea that what has been laid down as history (pushed into the past) is nonetheless unfinished business. In so far as left automation anxiety, our left topos, recurs, or re-explodes into the present, then, in that recurrence, it can disrupt the (idea of) automation's history as a smooth line or as a linear progression towards AI. Automation anxiety needs to be explored as a recurrent post-war discourse, one that may be catalysed by particular technical developments but that possesses its own temporal dynamics and is chronologically distinct. A critical history of automation debates entails identifying and reckoning with the significance of their recurrent or cyclical nature as well as exploring the particular form they take at a single moment in time. The spectral recurrence of automation anxiety is of vital interest alongside the hopeful proclamation of the new.

REFERENCES

Ad Hoc Committee on the Triple Revolution. (1964). *The Triple Revolution*. Ad Hoc Committee on the Triple Revolution.

Arntz, M., Gregory, T., & Zierahn, U. (2016). *The Risk of Automation for Jobs in OECD Countries* (No. 189; OECD Social, Employment and Migration Working Papers). OECD. https://www.oecd-ilibrary.org/social-issues-migration-health/the-risk-of-automation-for-jobs-in-oecd-countries_5jlz9h56dvq7-en

Autor, D. H. (2014). *Polanyi's Paradox and the Shape of Employment Growth* (Working Paper No. 20485). National Bureau of Economic Research. http://www.nber.org/papers/w20485

Autor, D. H., Levy, F., & Murnane, R. J. (2003). The skill content of recent technological change: An empirical exploration. *The Quarterly Journal of Economics, 118*(4), 1279–1333.

Barlow, J. P. (1996, February 9). *A Declaration of the Independence of Cyberspace*. http://w2.eff.org/Censorship/Internet_censorship_bills/barlow_0296.declaration

Bassett, C. (2022). *Anti-computing: Dissent and the Machine*. Manchester University Press. https://library.oapen.org/handle/20.500.12657/53144

Bassett, C., Kember, S., & O'Riordan, K. (2019). *Furious: Technological Feminism and Digital Futures*. Pluto Press.

Bassett, C., & Roberts, B. (2019). Automation now and then: Automation fevers, anxieties and Utopias. *New Formations, 98*(98), 9–28. https://doi.org/10.3898/NEWF:98.02.2019

Bastani, A. (2019). *Fully Automated Luxury Communism: A Manifesto*. Verso.

BBC. (2015, September 11). *Will a Robot Take Your Job?* BBC News. https://www.bbc.co.uk/news/technology-34066941

Benanav, A. (2020). *Automation and the Future of Work*. Verso.

Bender, E. M., Gebru, T., McMillan-Major, A., & Shmitchell, S. (2021). On the dangers of stochastic parrots: Can language models be too big? *Proceedings of the 2021 ACM Conference on Fairness, Accountability, and Transparency*, 610–623. https://doi.org/10.1145/3442188.3445922

Benjamin, R. (2019). *Race after Technology: Abolitionist Tools for the New Jim Code*. Polity Press. http://ebookcentral.proquest.com/lib/suss/detail.action?docID=5820427

Benjamin, W. (1968). *Illuminations* (H. Arendt, Ed.; H. Zohn, Trans.). Harcourt, Brace & World.

Berker, T., Hartmann, M., Punie, Y., & Ward, K. J. (Eds.). (2005). *Domestication of Media and Technology*. Open University Press.

Berlant, L. (2011). Cruel optimism. In *Cruel Optimism*. Duke University Press. https://doi.org/10.1515/9780822394716

Block, J. E. (1983). The selling of a productivity crisis: The market campaign to forestall post-industrial redistribution and work reduction. *New Political Science, 4*(1), 5–19. https://doi.org/10.1080/07393148308429568

Boggs, J. (1966). The negro and cybernation. In A. M. Hilton (Ed.), *The Evolving Society: The Proceedings of the First Annual Conference on the Cybercultural Revolution: Cybernetics and automation*. Institute for Cybercultural Research.

Boggs, J. (1970). *Racism and the Class Struggle: Further Pages from a Black Worker's Notebook*. Monthly Review Pr.

Brynjolfsson, E., & Mcafee, A. (2014). *The Second Machine Age: Work, Progress, and Prosperity in a Time of Brilliant Technologies*. W. W. Norton & Company.

Cockburn, C. (1991). *Brothers: Male Dominance and Technological Change*. Pluto.

Diebold, J. (1952). *Automation: The Advent of the Automatic Factory*. Van Nostrand.

Fisher, M. (2009). *Capitalist Realism: Is There No Alternative?* O Books.

Ford, M. (2015). *Rise of the Robots: Technology and the Threat of Mass Unemployment*. Oneworld Publications.

Frey, C. B., & Osborne, M. A. (2013). *The Future of Employment: How Susceptible are Jobs to Computerisation* (Oxford Martin Programme on Technology and Employment) [Working Paper]. Oxford Martin School, University of Oxford.

Gates, B., Myhrvold, N., & Rinearson, P. (1995). *The Road Ahead*. Viking.

Ghallab, M. (2019). Responsible AI: Requirements and challenges. *AI Perspectives*, *1*(1), 3. https://doi .org/10.1186/s42467-019-0003-z

Giedion, S. (2013). *Mechanization Takes Command: A Contribution to Anonymous History*. University of Minnesota Press.

Hartmann, M. (2015). Domestication of technology. In W. Donsbach (Ed.), *The International Encyclopedia of Communication* (pp. 1–3). John Wiley & Sons, Ltd. https://doi.org/10.1002/97814 05186407.wbiecd066.pub3

Hilton, A. M. (Ed.). (1966). *The Evolving Society: The Proceedings of the First Annual Conference on the Cybercultural Revolution: Cybernetics and Automation*. Institute for Cybercultural Research.

Huhtamo, E. (1997). From Kaleidoscomaniac to Cybernerd: Notes toward an archaeology of the media. *Leonardo*, *30*(3), 221–224. https://doi.org/10.2307/1576453

Huhtamo, E. (1999). From cybernation to interaction: A contribution to an archaeology of interactivity. In P. Lunenfeld (Ed.), *The Digital Dialectic: New Essays on New Media*. MIT Press.

Huhtamo, E. (2013). *Illusions in Motion: Media Archaeology of the Moving Panorama and Related Spectacles*. MIT Press.

Kaba, M., & Ritchie, A. J. (2022). *No More Police: A Case for Abolition*. New Press.

Keen, A. (2015, February 22). March of the robots. *The Sunday Times*. https://www.thetimes.co.uk/ article/march-of-the-robots-tpgxbh5vjcs

Kline, R. R. (2017). *The Cybernetics Moment: Or Why We Call Our Age the Information Age*. John Hopkins University Press.

Marcuse, H. (2014). Socialism in the developed countries. In D. Kellner & C. Pierce (Eds.), *Marxism, Revolution and Utopia* (Vol. 6, pp. 169–180). Routledge.

Marshall, M. W. (1957). 'Automation' today and in 1662. *American Speech*, *32*(2), 149–151. https://doi .org/10.2307/453032

McCulloch, J., & Wilson, D. (2016). *Pre-crime: Pre-emption, Precaution and the Future*. Routledge. http://sro.sussex.ac.uk/56832/

Mikalef, P., Conboy, K., Lundström, J. E., & Popovič, A. (2022). Thinking responsibly about responsible AI and 'the dark side' of AI. *European Journal of Information Systems*, *31*(3), 257–268. https://doi .org/10.1080/0960085X.2022.2026621

Moravec, H. (1988). *Mind Children: The Future of Robot and Human Intelligence*. Harvard University Press.

Morozov, E. (2014). *To Save Everything, Click Here: Technology, Solutionism, and the Urge to Fix Problems That Don't Exist*. Penguin.

Schwab, K. (2017). *The Fourth Industrial Revolution*. Crown Publishing Group.

Seager, C. (2016, May 11). After the robot revolution, what will be left for our children to do? *Guardian*. http://www.theguardian.com/careers/2016/may/11/robot-jobs-automated-work

Silverstone, R. (1994). *Television and Everyday Life*. Routledge.

Srnicek, N., & Williams, A. (2015). *Inventing the Future: Postcapitalism and a World Without Work*. Verso.

Taylor, M., Marsh, G., Nicol, D., & Broadbent, P. (2017). *Good Work: The Taylor Review of Modern Working Practices*. Department for Business, Energy & Industrial Strategy. https://www.gov.uk/ government/publications/good-work-the-taylor-review-of-modern-working-practices

Traub, V. (2011). The present future of lesbian historiography. In N. Giffney, M. M. Sauer, & D. Watt (Eds.), *The Lesbian Premodern* (pp. 21–34). Palgrave Macmillan US. https://doi.org/10.1057 /9780230117198_2

Wajcman, J. (2000). Reflections on gender and technology studies: In what state is the art? *Social Studies of Science*, *30*(3), 447–464.

Webster, F., & Robins, K. (1989). Plan and control. *Theory and Society, 18*(3), 323–351. https://doi.org/10.1007/BF00183386

Whitehouse, M., & Rojanasakul, M. (2017, July 7). Find out if your job will be automated. *Bloomberg.* https://www.bloomberg.com/graphics/2017-job-risk/

Wiener, N. (1961). *Cybernetics: Or Control and Communication in the Animal and the Machine.* MIT Press.

Witheford, N. (1994). Autonomist Marxism and the information society. *Capital & Class, 18*(1), 85–125. https://doi.org/10.1177/030981689405200105

8. AI, critical knowledge and subjectivity

Eran Fisher

AI AND YOU

Imagine turning on your Netflix in the evening to find out it has put on a movie that fits perfectly with what you'd want to watch. Not only does it match perfectly with your taste in movies, but it also seems to take into account the specificities of your daily happenstances and mood. But you are not particularly surprised. You remember Netflix's CEO Reed Hastings' pronouncement that "One day we hope to get so good at suggestions that we're able to show you exactly the right film or TV show for your mood when you turn on Netflix" (Economist, 2017). You are also aware of the efforts and technological agility involved in reaching such a phenomenal knowledge of your taste, wants, and mood. Netflix, you know, monitors the data traces you leave on its platform, maybe even complementing it with data gathered from other digital platforms, such as social networking sites. This big data set – about you, as well as about all its more than 200 million users – is crunched in real-time by algorithms, which are able to know who you are and what your taste in movies is and discern your desires and needs per a particular moment. Maybe their choice of a Hollywood romantic comedy from the 1950s would have been different lest you were sitting there with your lover on a Thursday night. Who knows? But should you even care? After all, the match is perfect. As perfect, in fact, as the match of a dating site that introduced you to your partner a month ago. There, too, you'd assume a plethora of data has been processed algorithmically to make this match possible.

Indeed, encapsulated in the digital devices we use – or the digital environment we inhabit – is a promise to better the human condition and expand our convenience and contentment. With modernity, technology has come to play not only an instrumental role – rendering processes more efficient, quick, or at all possible – but an ideological role as well. Across virtually the whole spectrum of modern politics, technology has come to be seen as means for political ends and as their guarantor. Technology promised to allow the fulfillment of the ideals of modernity and the Enlightenment. While different political orientations defined these ideals differently, they shared an underlying ideology that sought to mobilize technology – i.e., applicable, scientific know-how – in order to secure their materialization. This chapter focuses on the latest reiteration of this ideology, galvanized around the promises of AI, specifically, the ability – indeed propensity – of algorithms to render user-generated data into knowledge. More specifically, I am interested in *interface algorithms*, integrated into online decision-making devices.

Technologically, the promise encapsulated in algorithms is that by letting them sip through the plethora of data, inadvertently created by users, they could determine who the users are and what their needs and wants are. But this technical promise to automate knowledge about the self goes much deeper, ultimately touching on the promise to make us freer, more emancipated human beings.

But what does this promise for human freedom entail in the context of digital media? Is it a promise to free us from the *Burden of Choice* (Cohn, 2019)? Since the emergence of the internet, our choices have expanded exponentially, with access to a virtually endless array of information, cultural artifacts, products, and people. With this promise of an endless supply of information goods we face an abyss: how are we to choose? With algorithmic devices, digital platforms created the solution to a problem of their own creation. Algorithmic curation, recommendations engines, and the social graph were all new means put in place presumably to allow a happier marriage between users on the one hand and information and knowledge on the other hand.

But this seemingly technical solution underscores a more fundamental promise: to bring individual subjects back onto the scene, to facilitate the constitution of each of us in the wired world as a unique individual. Perhaps no other keyword of digital culture reflects this promise more than *personalization*. After a century of mass communication – which grew out of, as well as pampered mass society and mass culture – digital media is now able to offer each and every member of the masses his and her own bouquet of media artifacts.

KNOW THYSELF

Most fundamentally, then, algorithms promise to expand the realm of personal freedom by offering a truer, richer, more precise knowledge about the self. They offer to mobilize the power of AI to make rational decisions based on objective data. The idea that deepening one's knowledge also expands one's freedom was born with the Enlightenment. It is a specific articulation of the more general promise of knowledge (i.e., science and technology) to better the human condition. Modernity and the Enlightenment offered new forms of knowledge about the self. Knowledge that involves self-reflection and which expands self-understanding by engaging the self in deciphering the self. This new encounter of the self by the self, stimulated by self-reflection, is what I call here subjectivity. Subjectivity has always been a promise. A promise to expand the realm of freedom by releasing it from natural instincts and impulses, as well as from human-made coercive and oppressive social relations. Arguably, this promise could have never been materialized to the fullest. But it nevertheless offered a horizon for what human freedom might mean. Subjectivity was not seen as ontological – a reality to be discovered – but rather as a project worthy of being achieved.

Digital media now offer a new model of knowledge, based on the algorithmic processing of big data gathered by using this very media. If, for the last few centuries, self-reflection has been the cornerstone of subjectivity, and a precondition for freedom, my question is: what kind of freedom underlies algorithmic knowledge? If to *know thyself* was a route for a more emancipated subjectivity, what kind of freedom is promised by algorithms mediating for our knowledge about our self? I argue that compared with this ideal of the Enlightenment, algorithms offer a very different conception of knowledge and subjectivity, a different imaginary (Bucher, 2016). They offer not merely a new methodology to answer questions, but a new epistemology that redefines what questions can be asked, and what it means to know.

In contrast, algorithmic knowledge is based on positivist assumptions, which exclude subjectivity from knowledge about the self, and undermine interpretive, hermeneutic, and reflective faculties. Instead, it suggests that our most authentic self can be revealed to us by algorithms. The argument asserts that with the advent of algorithms and the interweaving of our existence with digital devices, which in turn gives us access to huge quantities of data, indicating objective behavior, we are in a unique epistemic position to know our selves better than ever before.

My purpose in this chapter is not to assess whether such a task can be achieved but to ponder on *The Political Unconscious* of algorithms (Jameson, 1981). I ask: To the extent that the promise of algorithms, and AI in general, materializes and it is able to predict which word we'd want to type next, what movie we'd like to watch, and who we'd be interested in dating, what are the horizons of such promise in terms of our conception of subjectivity? I argue that it is a form of knowledge that excludes self-reflection from the process of learning about the self, and in so doing that it subverts the Enlightenment project of subjectivity. This has deep political ramifications: an algorithmic social order hardly requires subjects at all, it rather renders them into objects.

It is tempting to read this as a reiteration of the adage of technology taking over humans (Winner, 1977). This idea of technology as peril, along with that of technology as promise, has also been a staple of modernist thought (e.g., Heidegger (1977), Ellul (1964), see also: Borgmann, 1999; Postman, 1993). However, my argument concerning algorithms strives to diverge from such "technologistic" analyses (Robins & Webster, 1999); it finds the culprit not in "technology" as such but in a specific constellation thereof. The threat of AI to subjectivity does not stem from the mere fact that knowledge about the self is mediated by technology, but that algorithmic systems exclude the self from the creation of knowledge about the self.

I proceed first by delimiting my argument to what I call interface algorithms. I then lay out Habermas's sociology of knowledge in order to define what critical knowledge is. I highlight the centrality of self-reflection in the creation of critical knowledge about the self. Reflection – both as a personal endeavor and on a social scale – is conditioned upon communication: subjective and inter-subjective, respectively. I then characterize algorithmic knowledge as performative, rather than communicative. We hardly have access to how algorithms create knowledge or even what this knowledge is, but rather encounter this knowledge through the performance of machine information on our behavior. In the penultimate section, I describe how thinking about algorithms with Habermas may shed new light on one of the most common themes in public discourse on digital technology: privacy. It suggests that digital technology threatens our privacy not only in the literal sense of trespassing a private sphere but also in the sense of undermining privacy as a site for critical self-reflection about the self. Lastly, the conclusion asks whether under such conditions subjectivity can still be thought of as a springboard for human emancipation.

INTERFACE ALGORITHMS

My argument refers primarily to *interface algorithms*, which I see as an exemplar of AI. AI is a general term for socio-technical systems that are able to engage with external, worldly data and render it into cogent outputs, in the form of knowledge, decisions, or actions. In this chapter, rather than using the blanket term AI, I chose to refer to interface algorithms as a specific manifestation of it. This approach has two benefits. First, it situates AI within an empirical context, thus concretizing the very general notion of AI. And second, it limits the theoretical argument to a specific facet of AI and its application in the sociological reality, suggesting that my argument does not necessarily apply to all instances of AI.

Interface algorithms are embedded in digital platforms, such as online retailing sites, social networking sites, and social media. They are geared predominantly toward rendering users' data into knowledge about users and, in turn, creating a personalized interface for each user. This, as aforementioned, is dependent not merely on getting to know users more intimately and intensely than before, but also *differently*, i.e., on redefining what such knowing entails. I draw here on literature that sees algorithms primarily as epistemic devices, as knowledge-making machines, which see reality in a particular way, different from modes of knowing we have become familiar with. They offer what David Beer beautifully termed a *data gaze* on reality (Beer, 2019), re-conceptualizing and redefining that which they see (Beer, 2009; Kitchin, 2017; Mackenzie & Vurdubakis, 2011). This has been substantiated in recent empirical research in relation to media audience (Fisher & Mehozay, 2019; Hallinan & Striphas, 2014), advertising (Barry & Fisher, 2019; Couldry & Turow, 2014), retailing (Turow, 2011; Turow & Draper, 2014), risk in the context of the criminal justice system (Mehozay & Fisher, 2018), and health in the context of medicine (Van Dijck & Poell, 2016; Ruckenstein & Schüll, 2017), to name a few fields.

Interface algorithms do not merely create knowledge on media users but also incessantly project this knowledge back at them; they act as mirrors, reflecting users' selves. Users are learning to employ an "algorithmic imagination" (Bucher, 2016) to see the content they are offered as an indication of how they are seen by the media, and as an algorithmic reflection of their self (albeit with some critical distance). For example, the fear of remaining "invisible" to their friends on social networking sites shapes users' media practices (Bucher, 2012). Algorithms' inner workings may be opaque, but their effects are very present, as Bucher puts it. This effect is not merely personal but social as well: "the algorithmic presentation of publics back to themselves shapes a public's sense of itself" (Gillespie, 2012b). Interface algorithms act as "a configuration through which users and/or clients are modeled and then encouraged to take up various positions in relation to the algorithm at work" (Neyland, 2015, p. 122).

This is not to say that people are duped by algorithms, but that they find themselves in an inferior epistemic position to critique the new kind of knowledge algorithms create. Algorithmic knowledge bares the aura of a superior model for representing reality, not least because of their promise to create knowledge with no *a priory* conceptions, either normative or theoretical (Mayer-Schönber & Kenneth Cukier, 2013). According to this increasingly hegemonic ideological discourse (Mager, 2012, 2014), by perusing billions of data points in search of discovering mathematical patterns, algorithms let data "speak" for themselves, thereby offering a more objective epistemology, and overcoming human biases. The fact that the basis for algorithmic knowledge is raw data – a "given," as the etymology of the word suggests, an unobtrusive reflection of reality – contributes to their flair for objectivity (Gitelman, 2013)

ALGORITHMIC KNOWLEDGE AND HUMAN INTERESTS

There is no doubt that, given the right resources, algorithms are able to create knowledge. The question is what is that knowledge and what is its truth value, that is, under which assumptions is this knowledge valid? In the social sciences, research on algorithmic knowledge has focused predominantly on the nature of that knowledge, how it differs from other epistemologies, and on the ramifications of increasingly integrating algorithmic knowledge into the social fabric. Algorithms have indeed been criticized for their biases (Crawford, 2016; Gillespie, 2012a,

2012b; Mayer-Schönber & Kenneth Cukier, 2013), which may be detrimental: from distorting our image of reality to exacerbating discrimination (Ferguson, 2017; Gillespie, 2016; Mehozay & Fisher, 2018; Tufekci, 2019). What is more, their opacity makes their auditing and critiquing virtually impossible (Kim, 2017; Mittelstadt, 2016; Pasquale, 2015b; Soll, 2014). Algorithmic knowledge has also been criticized for creating and perpetuating a feedback loop for users, enclosing them in a *filter bubble* (Pariser, 2012; Turow, 2011). And given their reliance on personal data, algorithms have also been criticized for undermining privacy (Dijck van, 2014; Grosser, 2017; Hildebrandt, 2019; Kennedy & Moss, 2015) and exploiting audience labor (Andrejevic, 2012; Bilic, 2016; Fisher & Fuchs, 2015; Fuchs, 2011b). All these point to algorithms as constituting a new regime of knowledge that has a huge impact on contemporary life, yet remains largely unknown, unregulated, and outside the realm of democratic politics (Feenberg, 1991).

There is another type of critique of algorithms, which may be termed epistemic. Algorithms do not merely automate the process of knowledge creation but change the very ontology of that knowledge. For example, recommendation engines curating cultural artifacts also change the very meaning of culture and cultural practices (Anderson, 2013; Bail, 2014; Gillespie, 2016; Hallinan & Striphas, 2014; Striphas, 2015). Similarly, the self – the qualities of which algorithms in digital media are oriented to decipher – is not merely gauged and monitored by algorithms but is also altered (Barry & Fisher, 2019; Cheney-Lippold, 2011; Fisher & Mehozay, 2019; Pasquale, 2015a).

My argument here joins this line of critique, which sees algorithms as constituting a new epistemology, a new way of knowing. My understanding of algorithmic knowledge and its relation to subjectivity draws predominantly on Jürgen Habermas's theory of knowledge, principally in his book *Knowledge and Human Interests* (Habermas, 1972). Before discussing his theory, it's worthwhile recalling the state of knowledge – in society and in social theory – that has prompted Habermas to offer his interjection.

Habermas reacted to what he saw as a dual attack on knowledge. At the time of the book's publication in 1968, knowledge was becoming an important axis in social theory and would remain dominant for a few decades to come, as revealed by concepts such as post-industrial society, information society, knowledge society, network society, and knowing capitalism (Castells, 2010; Mattelart, 2003; Stehr, 2001; Thrift, 2005; Webster, 2002). Knowledge was coming to be seen as laying at the core of a radical shift in the social structure of Western societies. This was a view shared by schools of diverse paradigmatic approaches and political affinities. The most notable sociologist to theorize the emerging centrality of knowledge in determining the social structure was Daniel Bell. A post-industrial society, Bell proposed, where knowledge and information become axial in the organization of society, sees the rise of a rationalized class of professionals, and of a technocratic government, both bent on applying knowledge to solve political problems (Bell, 1999; Touraine, 1971). Such a society is managed more rationally, overcoming the ideological struggles that characterized the industrial society.

Bell's claim for a radical break in the social structure was coupled with post-structuralists' claim for a radical break in social epistemology, brought about by the centrality of knowledge in society. Post-structuralism undermined the hitherto *sine qua non* of knowledge, its representationality: the capacity of knowledge (in principle if not in reality) to correspond with reality. In the formulation of Lyotard (1984) and Baudrillard (1981), knowledge – particularly due to the introduction of information technology – was becoming a central axis of the social to such a degree as to overwhelm the reality it was supposed to reflect. Joining Foucault (1994) and Derrida (1974), knowledge was now seen as explained better by reference to power relations than by appeal to reason and truth, thus losing its analytical distinction from power.

Both positions, then, undermine the *critical* potential of knowledge, and its potential to transform society. Post-industrialism de-politicizes knowledge, imagining it as a monolithic social endeavor, which makes politics redundant. Post-structuralism politicizes knowledge to such a degree that it invalidates its autonomy from power. In both formulations, knowledge becomes a force for conserving and stabilizing power relations. Or put somewhat differently, whereas Bell and other structuralists conceive knowledge as allowing the rationalization of society by making ideologies irrelevant, post-structuralists express deep disbelief in knowledge as a rationalizing agent, insisting on its interlacing with power. This was not a happy predicament for a critical social theorist, such as Habermas, whose vista has been the resurrection of the enlightened subject and rational inter-subjective communication.

Habermas, then, sought to offer a *critical* theory of knowledge, which, at one and the same time, upholds knowledge as a vehicle of rationalization *and* accounts for its ability to transform reality toward emancipation. How can knowledge be both true (i.e., scientific) and emancipatory (political)? Habermas' solution is to suggest that *all* knowledge is political: it is inextricably linked with human interests and operates within the confines of human ends. The choice of the term "interests" in the title of Habermas' book is illuminating and makes for three different readings. "Interest" can refer to a sense of intellectual curiosity and a drive to understand reality; "knowledge for the sake of knowledge" (Habermas, 1972, p. 314). Such a reading would suggest that Habermas is concerned with what individuals and societies are interested in. "Interest" can also refer to having a stake in an issue, to standing to gain or lose something. That would suggest that the title refers to what individuals and societies have a stake in. Finally, the title could also mean both and suggest, as I think Habermas does, that what humans are curious about is inextricably linked with what serves their interests. It suggests that we cannot decouple the history of knowledge from the political contours within which humans seek to acquire it. To use a later formulation, Habermas suggests that rather than denying, condemning, or duly accepting the knowledge/power nexus, we should instead examine and theorize it, and that's what he sets out to do.

Habermas identifies three types of "knowledge interests," i.e., motivations to gain knowledge, each stemming from human existence and having come to be articulated in three types of scientific or scholarly inquiry. The first is a "technical interest," our species' survivalist interest in controlling and predicting our natural environment. This interest has given rise to the "empirical-analytic" sciences, mostly the natural sciences, but also streams in the social sciences that have modeled themselves after the natural sciences. This knowledge approaches nature and society as objects, governed by predictable regularities, which can be discovered by controlled methodologies (e.g., experiments), articulated into law-like theories, and even manipulated through intervention.

The second is a "practical interest," which involves the attempt to secure and expand the possibilities for mutual understanding in the conduct of life. This interest gives rise to the "cultural-hermeneutic" sciences, which presuppose and articulate modes of personal and interpersonal understanding, oriented toward action. Such understanding is concerned with the lifeworld and is expressed in ordinary language. It is exercised in history, anthropology, and parts of sociology and communication studies. Both the empirical-analytic sciences and the cultural-hermeneutic sciences are established and constitute a hegemony of knowledge.

But Habermas wishes to go beyond this hegemony by pointing to another deep-rooted human interest. This is the "emancipatory interest" of reason, an interest in overcoming (externally imposed) dogmatism, (internally induced) compulsion, and (interpersonal and social) domination. The emancipatory interest gives rise to critical knowledge. Critical knowledge has a few defining features, most crucial to our discussion here is self-reflection, the centrality of the knower in the creation of knowledge. Creating critical knowledge about human beings (as social, anthropological, or psychological begins) is a *praxis* that requires the participation of the objects of that particular kind of knowledge, i.e., human beings. Critical, emancipatory knowledge involves, therefore, subjectivity as both a precondition and an end-product. It can only emerge with the involvement of subjectivity; subjectivity, in turn, can only emerge with critical knowledge.

With this Habermas sought to offer a category of knowledge that accounts not merely for reality, but also for the conditions under which this reality comes about and is made possible. Critical knowledge can serve to inform actions needed to transform these conditions. It is therefore both objective and positivist (appealing to truth) and subjective and constructivist (appealing to power). As Thomas McCarthy notes, Habermas "finds that the attempt to conceive of the social system as a functional complex of institutions in which cultural patterns are made normatively binding for action" – a description corresponding more or less to Talcott Parsons' by-then hegemonic social theory (1968) – "suffers from a short-circuiting of the hermeneutic and critical dimensions of social analysis" (McCarthy, 1988, p. viii). In other words, such theory excludes the communicative, subjective, and inter-subjective dimensions of society, where actors reflect upon their actions, and are able to critique them.

Habermas does not critique positivism *per se*, as a mode of scientific inquiry. Instead, he rejects positivism's claim to represent the only form of valid knowledge within the scientific community, and more importantly, its application over concerns that acutely require critical knowledge. Obviously, there are human concerns that require a strategically oriented action, demanding instrumental reason and constituting subject-object relations (e.g., ensuring a given growth rate of the national economy). But such type of action, Habermas insists, must not colonize concerns that require communicative action, demanding communicative reason and constituting subject-subject relations (e.g., questioning whether economic growth is desirable, or even what constitutes "growth" in the first place).

Critical knowledge may uncover that which not-yet-is, and which may-never-be unless we notice it and make knowledge about it explicit. This is Schrödinger's cat of the social, the political, and the cultural. And whether we find out the cat is dead or alive depends on our epistemology, i.e., our understanding of what knowing is:

> In the framework of action theory [*à la* Parsons], motives for action are harmonized with institutional values ... We may assume, however, that repressed needs which are not absorbed into social roles, transformed into motivations, and sanctioned, nevertheless have their interpretations. (McCarthy, 1988, p. viii)

One of these "cats," which can hardly be noticed by sociological action theory, is subjectivity, an elusive construct that is always in the making and which only through self-reflection can gain access to critical knowledge, which will, in turn, realize its emancipatory interests. The moment we start to ask ourselves about our self, we also construct it and transform it.

Algorithmic knowledge is not primarily scientific. But as the production of "epistemic cultures" (Knorr Cetina, 1999) and epistemic devices (Mackenzie, 2005) is no longer the hegemony of academia and books, but of the digital industry and software, we must take account of the kind of knowledge that algorithms create and how this knowledge shapes human understanding of the world and of itself. Similar to the different theoretical schools that have come to grips with the centrality of knowledge in the reformation of the social structure since the 1950s, we must now acknowledge a new phase in that historical era. In this new phase, technology automates not merely human physical force and dexterity, and not only cognitive skills. Instead, algorithmic devices seek to automate tenets of our subjectivity and inter-subjectivity and make them redundant in the conduct of human life.

THE PERFORMATIVITY OF ALGORITHMIC KNOWLEDGE

My choice of algorithms as an axial concept seeks to highlight the epistemic character of our contemporary techno-social order, i.e., their orientation toward rendering data into knowledge. The choice of algorithms as a vignette through which to examine our digital civilization stems from the increasingly central role that knowledge has come to play in society, from its ubiquity and banality – its integration into every realm of life. The knowledge that algorithms create is not merely Platonic and descriptive but also performative. Indeed, as users of digital platforms, we encounter not so much the knowledge that they create about us, but the *effects* of this knowledge, such as the newsfeed on our social media site or a book recommendation.

In professional and public lingo, algorithms are often seen as predominantly predictive. Digital platforms seek to know users' tastes and wants in order to enhance personalization. But the political economy of digital platforms suggests that their goal is not to predict behavior as much as to control it. In the case of Amazon, for example, the goal of prediction is to make users purchase a product they would *not* have purchased otherwise.

Because algorithms are future-oriented, because they seek to predict behavior and control it, they also seek to ascertain a particular type of subjectivity, which is predictable. To the extent that subjectivity is an important source for self-conduct, and self-reflection may change behavior, algorithmic prediction would be much less successful. For algorithms to deliver on their promise to know who we are and what we want. they must also assume a dormant subjectivity, a subject that is really more of an object (Fisher & Mehozay, 2019). Algorithmic knowledge, then, is performative in the deepest sense: it attempts to imagine and mold a human being that is completely transparent and predictable. It seeks to grasp only that which it can control. If algorithmic machines are indeed becoming more accurate, it may also be attributed to the part they play in helping create a self that trusts algorithms and the knowledge they reveal about it, and which in turn sedates mechanisms of self-reflection and self-knowledge, precisely these faculties of the self that are potentially opening up a realm of freedom and make humans unpredictable and able to change.

And here, the deep political ramifications of the algorithmic subversion of subjectivity become more evident. Underlying the creation of critical knowledge about our reality is a human *interest* in transforming that reality and a human *involvement* in creating this knowledge. If subjectivity is a realm of emancipation through critical knowledge, it is at the same time a precondition for critical knowledge to emerge. Such is the case, for instance, in Hegelian-Marxist theory, which makes a distinction between class-in-itself, an objective reality of historical materialism, and class-for-itself, which involves a subjectivity, transformed by that objective knowledge, and which, at the same time, constitutes the agent of social transformation. Such is also the case with Freudian psychoanalysis where self-knowledge is key to self-transformation. Psychoanalysis proposes that one's behavior, thoughts, and desires do not reveal the full scope of who one is; they are certainly not equal to one's true self. As much as our behavior reveals who we are, it also tells us what hinders us from being free, because it also stems from these hindrances. Enlightenment, in the sense of self-reflection, is supposed to make the self aware of these hindrances to freedom, with the hope of overcoming their persistence.

The self, structured within the contours of an algorithmic environment, is imagined in a radically different way from the self that was imagined during modernity and the Enlightenment with the idea of subjectivity. It is in fact hard to imagine that algorithms would achieve success in a world populated by human beings keen on self-reflection in order to expand their subjectivity. First, they would be rejected as unacceptable avenues for achieving knowledge about the self as they exclude the subject from its creation. And second, under conditions of reflexivity, algorithms would have a harder time predicting wants. Algorithms assume and imagine a particular type of human being, with limited horizons of subjectivity and freedom. Critical inquiry of AI must register and analyze such an assumption and ask what conception of subjectivity underlays the algorithmic model of knowledge. Owing to the performativity of algorithms, will they succeed in molding a new kind of person and a new self? As counterforces are also always in play, this is a struggle to be fought rather than to be either already celebrated or decried.

SUBJECTIVITY, ALGORITHMS, AND PRIVACY

The juxtaposition of algorithms and subjectivity sheds new light on privacy and why we should be worried about its erosion. We might think of subjectivity as a private sphere, where thoughts, wants, and needs of the self can be reflected upon and evaluated by that very self. It is a space that allows, at least a possibility to question our self. The loss of privacy also entails undermining our ability to develop and maintain that space as autonomous and distinct from other social spaces, and impenetrable for them. Just as we think about the public sphere as a space that facilitates communicative action, we might think about subjectivity as a sphere that facilitates an internal critical dialogue. And just as Habermas described the contraction of the public sphere more than half a century ago (Habermas, 1991), we might describe subjectivity as a private sphere that is now undermined by algorithms. Simply put, algorithmic knowledge, and its inherent erosion of privacy, erodes our ability to maintain our subjectivity.

As algorithms seemingly try to gauge what takes place in the private space of subjectivity, they also contract it; they destroy that which they seek to capture. Through innumerable and varied data points, algorithms are able to gauge that internal space, and get to the crux of personal wants, desires, and needs. But what algorithms cannot gauge is precisely the critical, reflexive events that take place in that space, which allow a dialogue between, on the one hand, what one thinks and wants, and on the other hand, what one thinks about one's thoughts and how one wishes to deal with one's wants. This space of reflection, of making the self an interlocutor of the self, is not, as aforementioned, an inherent and given component of our humanity. Instead, it is a historical construction, a project of the Enlightenment, and a utopian ideal at that. By excluding this space from the understanding of the self, algorithms also undermine this project.

CONCLUSION: SUBJECTIVITY REDUNDANT?

Our subjectivity, then, is under attack by algorithms. Or is it? Skeptics may see my argument as overstated since subjectivity should not be seen in the first place as a space of emancipation, but as a disciplinary mechanism of governmentality, shaped in accordance with hegemonic social structures (Foucault, 1977, 2006). In other words, we have never been modern and free; subjectivity is nothing but another form of social control. This Foucauldian line of thought opens up another interesting avenue for understanding the algorithmic episteme as a form of governance (Birchall, 2016; Danaher et al., 2017; McQuillan, 2015; Rona-Tas, 2020; Sauter, 2013). But this avenue, too, leads to similar conclusions concerning the redundancy of subjectivity in an algorithmic environment. If governing, or the exertion of power, during modernity demanded the willing cooperation of subjects, then algorithmic governance makes such governmentality redundant. Subjectivity was required to keep particular social structures intact and allow them to mobilize individuals into particular social forms and actions. At the same time, of course, such subjectivity – for example, a neoliberal persona – could also be a site of resistance and change.

Much like Habermas, Foucault too sees in subjectivity not merely an effect of power but a space capable of resisting and opposing it. And like him, he too posits knowledge at the very center of subjectivity. The interests may be different – disciplinary rather than emancipatory – but the mode of operation is self-reflection and self-knowledge. In this formulation, too, algorithms can be said to interject and change the subject. They expropriate the conduct of conduct from subjectivity. If subjectivity harbors the commands that tell us how to conduct ourselves, then the introduction of algorithms conducting our conduct, governing it externally, makes subjectivity redundant.

Following this line of inquiry, too, then leads us to consider how algorithms undermine subjectivity. Algorithms become a new governing agent that manages life and populations without the need for subjectivity. Under such conditions, does it even make sense to talk about algorithmic *subjectivity*? Should we not, as Rouveroy suggests, think about the effect of algorithms as creating objects rather than subjects? The political ramifications stemming from this line of thought are troubling. Algorithms make claims for sovereignty of a new kind, as they are able to take decisions that are almost impossible to audit and critique because they are opaque, proprietary, and subject to frequent change (Rouveroy & Stiegler, 2016, Hildebrandt, 2019). It is therefore our task to critique algorithms' participation in social life through an interrogation of their political effect.

Knowledge about human beings – i.e., the knowledge of the human sciences, which is at the center of Foucault's work – changes radically. Social epistemology, as we might call it, shifts from regimes of truth to regimes of anticipation, which are increasingly dependent on predictive algorithms (Mackenzie, 2013; Rona-Tas, 2020). In such regimes, "the sciences of the actual can be abandoned or ignored to be replaced by a knowledge that the truth about the future can be known by way of the speculative forecast" (Adams et al., p. 247, cited in Mackenzie, 2013). Knowledge, in the case of the algorithmic episteme, boils down to the ability to anticipate future trends and patterns. This entails seeing individuals based on the behavioral data they produce (Rouvroy & Stiegler, 2016), bypassing their self-understanding and identifying patterns from which a predictive behavioral analysis can be deduced.

A few elements make algorithms an unstable foundation for critical knowledge, such as refraining from theory or doing away with ontological conceptions of humans (Fisher, 2020). Most fundamental is their attempt to bypass subjectivity *en route* to the creation of knowledge. That is, create knowledge about the self that does not allow the subject – for lack of ability to use natural language – to audit such knowledge with the aid of reason. That is true for human knowledge in general but it is doubly true for their knowledge about themselves, as social, anthropological, and psychological beings.

FURTHER READING

Beer, D. (2019). *The Data Gaze: Capitalism, Power and Perception*. Sage.
Cheney-Lippold, J. (2011). A New Algorithmic Identity: Soft Biopolitics and the Modulation of Control. *Theory, Culture and Society* 28(6): 164–181.
Rouvroy, A. and B. Stiegler. (2016). The Digital Regime of Truth: From the Algorithmic Governmentality to a New Rule of Law. *Online Journal of Philosophy* 3: 6–29.

REFERENCES

Alvarez, R. M. (Ed.). (2016). *Computational Social Science: Discovery and Prediction*. Cambridge University Press.
Anderson, C. (2006). *The Long Tail: Why the Future of Business Is Selling Less of More*. Hyperion.
Anderson, C. W. (2013). Towards a Sociology of Computational and Algorithmic Journalism. *New Media and Society* 15(7): 1005–1021.
Andrejevic, M. (2012). Exploitation in the Data Mine. In C. Fuchs, K. Boersma, A. Albrechtslund and M. Sandoval (Eds.), *Internet and Surveillance: The Challenges of Web 2.0 and Social Media*. Routledge, pp. 71–88.
Bail, C. A. (2014). The Cultural Environment: Measuring Culture with Big Data. *Theory and Society* 43(3): 465–482.
Barry, L. and E. Fisher. (2019). Digital Audiences and the Deconstruction of the Collective. *Subjectivity* 12(3): 210–227.
Baudrillard, J. (1981). *For a Critique of the Political Economy of the Sign*. Telos Press.
Beer, D. (2009). Power through the Algorithm? Participatory Web Cultures and the Technological Unconscious. *New Media and Society* 11(6): 985–1002.
Beer, D. (2019). *The Data Gaze: Capitalism, Power and Perception*. Sage.
Bell, D. (1999). *The Coming of Post-Industrial Society: A Venture in Social Forecasting*. Basic Books.
Bilic, P. (2016). Search Algorithms, Hidden Labour and Information Control. *Big Data & Society* 3(1): 341–366.
Birchall, C. (2016). Shareveillance: Subjectivity between Open and Closed Data. *Big Data & Society* 3(2): 1–12.
Borgmann, A. (1999). *Holding On to Reality: The Nature of Information at the Turn of the Millennium*. University of Chicago Press.
Bucher, T. (2012). Want to Be on the Top? Algorithmic Power and the Threat of Invisibility on Facebook. *New Media and Society* 14(7): 1164–1180.
Bucher, T. (2016). The Algorithmic Imaginary: Exploring the Ordinary Affects of Facebook Algorithms. *Information, Communication & Society* 4462(April): 1–15.
Castells, M. (2010). *The Information Age: Economy, Society and Culture*. Wiley-Blackwell.
Cheney-Lippold, J. (2011). A New Algorithmic Identity: Soft Biopolitics and the Modulation of Control. *Theory, Culture and Society* 28(6): 164–181.

Cohn, J. (2019). *The Burden of Choice: Recommendations, Subversion, and Algorithmic Culture*. Rutgers University Press.

Couldry, N. and J. Turow. (2014). Advertising, Big Data, and the Clearance of the Public Realm: Marketers' New Approaches to the Content Subsidy. *International Journal of Communication* 8: 1710–1726.

Crawford, K. (2016). Can an Algorithm Be Agonistic? Ten Scenes about Living in Calculated Publics. *Science, Technology & Human Values* 41(1): 77–92.

Danaher, J., M. J. Hogan, C. Noone, R. Kennedy, A. Behan, A. De Paor, H. Felzmann, M. Haklay, S. M. Khoo, J. Morison, M. H. Murphy, N. O'Brolchain, B. Schafer and K. Shankar. (2017). Algorithmic Governance: Developing a Research Agenda through the Power of Collective Intelligence. *Big Data and Society* 4(2).

Derrida, J. (1974). *Of Grammatology*. Johns Hopkins University Press.

Dijck van, J. and T. Poell. (2016). Understanding the Promises and Premises of Online Health Platforms. *Big Data & Society*.

Dijck van, J. (2014). Datafication, Dataism and Dataveillance: Big Data between Scientific Paradigm and Ideology. *Surveillance and Society* 12(2): 197–208.

Dobson, J. E. (2019). *Critical Digital Humanities: The Search for a Methodology*. University of Illinois Press.

Economist. 2017. How to devise the perfect recommendation algorithm. *The Economist*. February 9, 2017. Available at: https://www.economist.com/special-report/2017/02/09/how-to-devise-the-perfect-recommendation-algorithm

Ellul, J. (1964). *The Technological Society*. Knopf.

Feenberg, A. (1991). *Critical Theory of Technology*. Oxford University Press.

Ferguson, A. (2017). *The Rise of Big Data Policing: Surveillance, Race, and the Future of Law Enforcement*. New York University Press.

Fisher, E. (2010). *Media and New Capitalism in the Digital Age: The Spirit of Networks*. Palgrave.

Fisher, E. (2020). Can Algorithmic Knowledge about the Self Be Critical? In M. Stoccheti (Ed.), *The Digital Age and its Discontents: Critical Reflections in Education*. Helsinki University Press, pp. 111–122.

Fisher, E. and C. Fuchs (Eds.). (2015). *Reconsidering Value and Labour in the Digital Age*. Palgrave.

Fisher, E. and Y. Mehozay. (2019). How Algorithms See Their Audience: Media Epistemes and the Changing Conception of the Individual. *Media, Culture and Society* 41(8): 1176–1191.

Foucault, M. (1977). *Discipline and Punish: The Birth of the Prison*. Vintage Books.

Foucault, M. (1994). *The Order of Things: An Archeology of Human Sciences*. Vintage Books.

Foucault, M. (2006). *The Hermeneutics of the Subject: Lectures at the Collège de France, 1981–1982*. Palgrave Macmillan.

Fuchs, C. (2011a). An Alternative View of Privacy on Facebook. *The Information Society* 2(1): 140–165.

Fuchs, C. (2011b). *The Political Economy of Privacy on Facebook*. Uppsala.

Gillespie, T. (2012a). Can an Algorithm Be Wrong? *Limn*.

Gillespie, T. (2012b). The Relevance of Algorithms. *Culture Digitally*.

Gillespie, T. (2016). Trendingistrending: When Algorithms Become Culture. *Culture Digitally*: 1–23.

Gitelman, L. (Ed.). (2013). *"Raw Data" Is an Oxymoron*. MIT Press.

Grosser, B. (2017). Tracing You : How Transparent Surveillance Reveals a Desire for Visibility. *Big Data and Society* (June): 1–6.

Habermas, J. (1972). *Knowledge and Human Interests*. Beacon Press.

Habermas, J. (1985). *The Theory of Communicative Action*. Beacon Press.

Habermas, J. (1991). *The Structural Transformation of the Public Sphere: An Inquiry into a Category of Bourgeois Society*. MIT Press.

Hallinan, B. and T. Striphas. (2014). Recommended for You: The Netflix Prize and the Production of Algorithmic Culture. *New Media and Society* 18(1): 117–137.

Heidegger, M. (1977). *The Question Concerning Technology and Other Essays*. Harper Torchbooks.

Hildebrandt, M. (2019). Privacy As Protection of the Incomputable Self: From Agnostic to Agonistic Machine Learning. *Theoretical Inquiries of Law* 20(1): 83–121.

Jameson, F. (1981). *The Political Unconscious: Narrative as a Socially Symbolic Act*. Cornell University Press.

Kant, I. (1999). *Critique of Pure Reason*. Cambridge University Press.

Kant, I. (2015). *Critique of Practical Reason*. Cambridge University Press.

Kennedy, D. (2011). Industrial Society: Requiem for a Concept. *The American Sociologist* 42(4): 368–383.

Kennedy, H. and G. Moss. (2015). Known or Knowing Publics? Social Media Data Mining and the Question of Public Agency. *Big Data & Society*.

Kim, P. (2017). Auditing Algorithms for Discrimination. *University of Pennsylvania Law Review Online* 166(1): 10.

Kitchin, R. (2017). Thinking Critically about and Researching Algorithms. *Information, Communication & Society* 20(1): 14–29.

Knorr Cetina, K. (1999). *Epistemic Cultures: How the Sciences Make Knowledge*. Harvard University Press.

Levenberg, L., T. Neilson and D. Rheams (Eds.). (2018). *Research Methods for the Digital Humanities*. Palgrave.

Lyotard, J.-F. (1984). *The Postmodern Condition: A Report on Knowledge*. University of Minnesota Press.

Mackenzie, A. (2005). The Performativity of Code Software and Cultures of Circulation. *Theory, Culture & Society* 22(1): 71–92.

Mackenzie, A. (2013). Programming Subjects in the Regime of Anticipation: Software Studies and Subjectivity. *Subjectivity* 6(4): 391–405.

Mackenzie, A. and T. Vurdubakis. (2011). Code and Codings in Crisis: Signification, Performativity and Excess. *Theory, Culture & Society* 28(6): 3–23.

Mager, A. (2012). Algorithmic Ideology: How Capitalist Society Shapes Search Engines. *Communication & Society* 15(5): 769–787.

Mager, A. (2014). Defining Algorithmic Ideology: Using Ideology Critique to Scrutinize Corporate Search Engines. *TripleC: Communication, Capitalism and Critique* 12(1): 28–39.

Marres, N. (2017). *Digital Sociology: The Reinvention of Social Research*. Polity.

Marx, K. (1992). *Capital: Volume 1: A Critique of Political Economy*. Penguin.

Mattelart, A. (2003). *The Information Society: An Introduction*. Sage.

Mayer-Schönber, V. and K. Cukier. (2013). *Big Data: A Revolution That Will Transform How We Live, Work, and Think*. Houghton Mifflin Harcourt.

McCarthy, T. (1988). Introduction. In J. Habermas (Ed.), *On the Logic of the Social Sciences* (pp. vii–x). MIT Press.

McQuillan, D. (2015). Algorithmic States of Exception. *European Journal of Cultural Studies* 18(4–5): 564–576.

Mehozay, Y. and E. Fisher. (2018). The Epistemology of Algorithmic Risk Assessment and the Path towards a Non-Penology Penology. *Punishment and Society*.

Mittelstadt, B. (2016). Auditing for Transparency in Content Personalization Systems. *International Journal of Communication* 10: 4991–5002.

Neyland, D. (2015). On Organizing Algorithms. *Theory, Culture and Society* 32(1): 119–132.

Ortner, S. B. (2005). Subjectivity and Cultural Critique. *Anthropological Theory* 5(1).

Pariser, E. (2012). *The Filter Bubble: How the New Personalized Web Is Changing What We Read and How We Think*. Penguin Books.

Parsons, T. (1968). *The Structure of Social Action: With a New Introduction, Vol. 1*. The Free Press.

Pasquale, F. (2015a). The Algorithmic Self. *The Hedgehog Review* 17(1): 1–7.

Pasquale, F. (2015b). *The Black Box Society: The Secret Algorithmic That Control Money and Information*. Harvard University Press.

Postman, N. (1993). *Technopoly: The Surrender of Culture to Technology*. Vintage Books.

Rebughini, P. (2014). Subject, Subjectivity, Subjectivation. *Sociopedia.Isa*.

Robins, K. and F. Webster. (1999). *Times of Technoculture: From the Information Society to the Virtual Life*. Routledge.

Rona-Tas, A. (2020). Predicting the Future: Art and Algorithms. *Socio-Economic Review* 18(3).

Rouvroy, A. and B. Stiegler. (2016). The Digital Regime of Truth: From the Algorithmic Governmentality to a New Rule of Law. *Online Journal of Philosophy* 3: 6–29.

Ruckenstein, M. and N. D. Schüll. (2017). *The Datafication of Health.*

Sauter, T. (2013). What's on Your Mind? Writing on Facebook as a Tool for Self-Formation. *New Media and Society* 16(5): 1–17.

Soll, J. (2014). *The Reckoning: Financial Accountability and the Rise and Fall of Nations.* Basic Books.

Stehr, N. (2001). *The Fragility of Modern Societies: Knowledge and Risk in the Information Age.* Sage.

Striphas, T. (2015). Algorithmic Culture. *European Journal of Cultural Studies* 18(4–5): 395–412.

Thrift, N. (2005). *Knowing Capitalism.* Sage.

Touraine, A. (1971). *The Post-Industrial Society: Tomorrow's Social History: Classes, Conflict and Culture in the Programmed Society.* Random House.

Tufekci, Z. (2019). How Recommendation Algorithms Run the World. *Wired*, April 22.

Turow, J. (2011). *The Daily You: How the New Advertising Industry Is Defining Your Identity and Your Worth.* Yale University Press.

Turow, J. and N. Draper. (2014). Industry Conceptions of Audience in the Digital Space. *Cultural Studies* 28(4): 643–656.

Veltri, G. A. (2019). *Digital Social Research.* Polity.

Webster, F. (2002). *Theories of the Information Society.* Routledge.

Winner, L. (1977). *Autonomous Technology: Technics-out-of-Control as a Theme in Political Thought.* MIT Press.

9.   Habits and habitus in algorithmic culture
Stefka Hristova

INTRODUCTION

Nowadays, predictive algorithms make assumptions about our online as well as offline identities based on our habitual behaviour – both conscious and unconscious. Algorithms correlate patterns of behaviour in order to determine what movies we should watch on Netflix, what brand of socks we are more likely to purchase, what health insurance bracket we fall in, and whether we should be admitted to school, or given a job. Algorithms thus have come to structure our political, economic, cultural, and social lives. Their influence extends beyond the sphere of media and onto everyday life. Because of their profound impact on the social fabric, it is important to investigate not just algorithms as technology itself, but also their profound impact on culture.

Algorithms thus need to be situated in the context of the historical, social, and cultural: "Foregrounding algorithmic culture demands addressing the connections that constitute what matters most about algorithms: their integration in practices, policies, politics, economics, and everyday life with consequential political, ethical, and affective significance" (Slack, Hristova 2021, 19). Algorithmic culture, rather than algorithmic technology, is the locus for this chapter. The term was first introduced by Alexander Galloway and was subsequently fleshed out by Ted Striphas as a way to describe a "data-driven culture" in which cultural decision-making processes are automated (Galloway 2006; Striphas 2015). Jonathan Roberge and Robert Seyfert have additionally enriched the discourse on algorithmic cultures by insisting on the plurality of the concept from a sociological perspective (2018). Here the term algorithmic culture does double work: first, it points to the work of algorithms that shape culture, and second, it signals that algorithms are always and already technologies and cultural practices. Such positioning challenges the predominant view in algorithmic development that the logics that drive algorithms and big data are grounded primarily in consumer and cognitive phycology. Eye tracking, click or pause recording, posture monitoring, and face decoding algorithmic technologies have emerged as criteria for judging one's social, cultural, political, and economic identity based on psychological responses to information. As I demonstrate in this chapter, algorithmic technology development, in relation to both the referral algorithms in consumer behaviour as well as those in hiring, relies heavily on human communication and psychology theories that seek to operationalize manifest behaviour in order to make predictions about latent identity characteristics. The patterns of behaviour that are selected are seen as predictive, therefore, as Wendy Chun argued, habitual. Chun writes that "data analytics are about habits" as they focus on "habitual actions" such as buying habits and individuals become "habituated to their own connections" (2016, 57). Because of their habitual essence, these patterns of behaviour are necessarily cultural and foundational to algorithmic culture.

This conjecture of algorithms, culture, behaviour, and habits makes a strong case for the deployment of what Simon Lindgren has termed "data theory" approaches (2020, 21). Writing about social media, Lindgren calls for a "balance between data and theory – between information and its interpretation" (12). Such an approach would investigate "how knowledge about some particular data can be advanced through some particular social theory" (21). The emphasis on social theory here is central. Because algorithmic technology development is often grounded in psychology, it is increasingly urgent to emphasize the social and cultural theories that are underpinning such seemingly objective and ahistorical calculations of behaviour.

Bourdieu's work on habitus is deeply relevant to understanding algorithmic culture. As Lindgren has demonstrated, this theoretical approach can be adapted to understanding social media data (2020, 135). In his study of the 2018 Swedish election discourse on Twitter, he has offered an important model for understanding the ways in which Bourdieu's categories of cultural, social, and economic capital, which are structuring elements of habitus, shape social media practices in a particular field. Such work is foundational as it provides an important framework for understanding algorithmic sociality and its underpinning forms of what Lindgren calls "connective," "engagement," and "attention" capital (140, 141). Habitus has also been connected to machine learning and training data sets in the groundbreaking work by Massimo Airoldi. In his book *Machine Habitus: Towards a Sociology of Algorithms*, Airoldi takes on the challenge "What if we extend Bourdieu's inspiring ideas to the cold technical realm of algorithms?" (30, 2022). One such possibility encourages us to see algorithms as sociological agents, as agents that both generate and reproduce a particular habitus. Airoldi argues that because machine learning algorithms ultimately learn from data sets that are encoded by people with different tastes, they come to exhibit a "peculiar sort of habitus, a *machine habitus*" (28). Much like the human body embodies the habitus, machine learning algorithms are built upon an "adaptive computational model and a specific *data* content" where the data come to represent the embodiment of history, of the habitus (28).

In this chapter, I take on Lindgren's call for data theory and Airoldi's notion of machine habitus by examining the ways in which algorithmic technology deployed in consumer referral and hiring algorithms respectively are operationalizing not purely psychological data, but rather social structures. More specifically, I will situate these technologies in relation to what Pierre Bourdieu has theorized as "taste" and "body hexis." These two terms illuminate how predominantly conscious and unconscious habits shape society and sociality. Even though taste is grounded in habitual dispositions and thus contains an unconscious aspect, taste is manifest through a conscious choice to consume a particular product. Understood in the context of habitus, they point to the importance of history, context, and culture in understanding the ways in which algorithms reproduce and legitimize power structures that appear to be natural and universal.

IF ... THEN

Predictive algorithms tied to consumer culture attempt to offer recommendations based on one's engagement with advertising data as well as one's prior consumption habits. As Wendy Chun writes:

> "Personalized recommender systems" are predictive software tools that filter and prioritize information, items, and users. ... Although recommender systems, like search engines, presume genuine user need and thus user sincerity, they primarily serve the interests of those who deploy them... By using historical data to anticipate "user wants," they limit choice and amplify past trends in the name of efficiency and desire. (2021, 158)

Take *Netflix*, a popular streaming service for movies and tv shows. Grounded in big consumer data, algorithmic technology operationalizes taste for capitalist gain (Zuboff). The Netflix recommendation/personalization algorithms deploy a number of techniques: "like reinforcement learning, neural networks, causal modelling, probabilistic graphical models, matrix factorization, ensembles, bandits" ("How Netflix," 2019). These models correlate data such as "Viewer interactions with Netflix services like viewer ratings, viewing history, etc; Information about the categories, year of release, title, genres, and more; Other viewers with similar watching preferences and tastes; Time duration of a viewer watching a show," and so on (2019). Out of these correlations, Netflix reportedly produces "1300 recommendation clusters" and "2k taste groups" (2019). Netflix thus operationalizes interaction habits, recorded as mouse and eye movements in relation to social categories such as taste. The taste categories here correspond to 2000 categories of what John Cheney-Lippold calls "measurable types." They are seemingly diverse and multifaceted, thus escaping the trappings of low-, middle-, and high-brow culture.

Taste, in algorithmic culture, is linked to questions of authenticity, rather than social class, which is the traditional articulation of taste in Bourdieu's theory. As Chun writes:

> [f]or these recommender systems to work, though, users have to become predictive subjects: they must be authenticated and determined to be operating authentically. Recommender system programs presume that users' captured actions – rather [than] their deliberate speech – represent their true selves, hence the claims made by data scientists to have "captured" users' true and nonconscious motives. (2021, 165)

Here she offers an important critique of the neoliberal foundations of the notion of authenticity as it moves to articulate one's preferences or taste from the nonconscious. The nonconscious is precisely the habitual, the naturalized disposition that one carries in relation to habitus. Further, taste categories based on authenticity do not erase the underpinning assumptions about class and the value of taste as manifesting particular dispositions in a given habitus. If anything, in an algorithmic culture they further cement one's social standing by further fuelling one's social score or social status.

Given the seeming proliferation of taste categories, over 2000 in the case of Netflix, I am interested in thinking about the relationship between these authenticity-based taste categories as they correspond to the three major taste groups detailed by Pierre Bourdieu in his study *Distinction: A Social Critique of the Judgement of Taste* (1984). Writing about France in the 1960s, Bourdieu proposed three zones of taste namely: (1) legitimate taste, (2) "middle-brow" taste, and (3) "popular" taste (16). These identity judgements were largely based on the similarities and differences we exhibit in terms of cultural taste. Taste, for Bourdieu, is grounded in habitus, "the internalized form of class condition and of the conditionings it entails" (101). As Bourdieu has argued, taste is a central element of culture that helps maintains social stratification while at the same time obscuring the social conditions that shape it. He pointed to the cyclical nature of taste where

> the ideology of natural taste owes its plausibility and its efficacy to the fact that, like all ideological strategies generated in the everyday class struggle, it naturalizes real differences, converting difference in the mode of acquisition of culture into differences of nature. (68)

Taste, in other words, appears to be first natural, hence, true and authentic, and second, naturalizes the cyclical connection between consumer preferences and social standing. It manifests

to be only natural that working-class consumers adopt a popular taste. Yet this popular taste is in turn used to identify and maintain one's position in society as part of a working class.

In an algorithmic culture, taste manifests in a cyclical relationship that has three major components: taste is linked to media consumption based on the dispositions of the data encoders; hence, taste is trained and linked to a machine habitus. Then, it is tested against the dispositions of consumers. And finally, it is used to limit exposure to other forms of media as it is seen as a bad fit for the consumer at hand. As Airoldi writes with regard to the first aspects of the cycle, "algorithmic judgements produce social distinctions [...], even when they are designed to personalize user's intimate digital experiences based on local data contexts" (81). Data contexts here are deeply embedded in cultural and historical contexts that reflect multiple layers of constructing and maintaining a social reality. Big data is attempting to quantify and calculate precisely that internalized condition, the habitus – that is both machine and human.

Further, as Chun has argued, both algorithmic and human taste is not manifest through conscious decisions or verbal declaration, as was the case with Bourdieu's study in the second stage of this cycle. This is central, because historically, taste has been perceived through the conscious habitual behaviour of individuals in relation to a collective. While data taxonomies are clearly visible in the development of categories during the training of the algorithm when workers are paid to create judgements about people and media, the second step does not reference explicit declaration of taste, to manifest instances of taste. Here users' actions, often unconscious, are seen as markers of their dispositions. Extending the idea of taste as algorithmic judgement, I suggest that we need to consider equally the articulation of taste as judgement as well as habit. The judgement, then, is not of one's taste as expressed verbally or even consciously, but rather, a taste based on supposedly authentic, yet often unconscious habitual response to digital artefacts. Algorithms thus enforce judgements of taste based on taste as habit. They do so by engaging habits on four levels: by focusing on habitual action; by seeking to change habits in moments of crisis; by seeking correlations between habits; and by "habituating users to their own connections" (Chun 2016, 57). In order to challenge the algorithmic practice of taste as the correlation between habits, we can connect habit with habitus. What connecting taste to habit and habitus allows us to do is to confront understanding habit as a purely psychological process that can be subject to random correlations and connect habit to cultural and historical context.

The third stage of the cycle of taste enforcement needs to be illuminated as well. The reproduction of taste through recommendation mechanisms is a central tenant of algorithmic culture. As Chun aptly has argued, habits lead to habituation (2016, 57). Here technology continues to condition the habitus through the enforcement of taste: a taste is implied, habituated, and further amplified through the use of filter bubbles that favour more of the same. Eli Pariser coined the term "filter bubble" as "a unique universe of information for each of us" (2011, 9). Filter bubbles thus personalize and customize news and other experiences based on what is of "relevance" to the user. The reason for this aggregation of information based on perceived personal relevance, as Pariser argues, is commercial.

> As a business strategy, the Internet giant's formula is simple: The more personally relevant their information offerings are, the more ads they will sell, and the more likely you are to buy the products that they're offering. (7)

This personalization has been found problematic because "filter bubbles created by the platform's algorithms – curated echo chambers that trap users in a world of news that only affirms their beliefs" (10). This personalization is created through machine learning algorithms. One such algorithm is Edge Rank, which as described by Bucher, relies on a ranking mechanism of relevancy or likeliness of continuous interaction: "[o]nce the relevancy score for each post has been determined, a sorting algorithm can then put them in the right order for the user to see" (2018, 74). Harnessed in the context of Facebook, it weighs and sorts user-generated posts as well as paid advertising content. The more a user interacts with a particular type of content, the more similar user-generated and paid content is delivered. In the case of Netflix, the algorithms identify one's taste and continue to offer content only within this given taste category. Such enforcement of sameness, as Bucher argues, remains profitable for media industries, and invisible and even desirable by consumers, who only notice the personalizing algorithms when they clash when "the popular seems to get in the way with the personal" or the choices offered are out of sync with the preferences of the individual (108). As such, taste polices the boundaries of social groups and since it is habituated it further upholds and reproduces them. It helps enforce social stratification by projecting and naturalizing what Chun calls social homophily (2021, 23).

Taste, grounded in habitus, becomes the manifestation of generative social structures that, as Bourdieu has shown, aim to police and maintain social hierarchies. This connection of taste to habitus is central because it is through recourse to habitus that both the social as well as the historical conditioning of one's cultural preferences could be understood. For Bourdieu, a habitus is "a product of history," which in turn "produces individual and collective practices – more history – in accordance with the schemes generated by history" (1980, 54). This history is just not only individual, as in one's browser history, it is collective in a social sense. In an algorithmic culture, the term collective history is harnessed by the culture industries in terms of consumer behaviour. What a data theory approach grounded in social theories brings to this picture is an understanding of the socio-historical conditions that form the larger picture in which both individual and collective consumer behaviour operates. Such an approach posits questions about structures, ideologies, and ethics as historically shaped structures of inequality get reproduced and legitimized through consumer psychology matrixes.

The recommendation and personalization algorithms that structure our engagement with social and cultural goods such as media, fashion, food, furniture, and so on uphold a naturalizing ideology that obscures the historical, social, and cultural forces that shape and are shaped by taste. Obscured in statistics and machine learning algorithms are historical processes that attempt to maintain class distinctions while at the same time creating profitable models for the culture industries. Recommendation algorithms create an algorithmic culture in which one's taste is both inferred and amplified so that exposure to different tastes is minimized. In this instance, culture industries profit from scenarios in which consumers engage in more of the same. At the same time, consumers are designated to taste from which they are unable to break out, and which in turn are used as distinction markers for their social standing. In other words, recommendation algorithms reinforce one's social standing by cementing one's belonging to a social category. This correlation between taste category and social category has serious social consequences as it determines one's ability to secure loans and obtain education, healthcare, employment, and so on.

As Simon Lindgren writes, Bourdieu's habitus implies that

> while a person can act somewhat freely, the acts are always filtered through, or shaped by, that person's habitus that expresses how the person in question engages in practices. In other words, while the habitus disposes the individual to certain manners, activities, and perspectives that have in turn been socially constructed. (133)

Algorithmic culture further complicates the problem of choice, as it precludes the options that are even presented to a person. The fear of rejection, of distaste, is connected to commercial loss and thus the mismatch between offering and disposition is minimized. What this process leads to, is the predetermination of offerings or choices that are the least likely to clash with the dispositions shaped through habitus. A person thus might not be even given the opportunity to experience choices that might be associated with different social groups, with different sets of dispositions. If your Netflix profile links your taste group to an offering of soap operas, you are unlikely to encounter an independent film. What algorithmic culture highlights is that these 2000 taste categories are not seen as equally legitimate in culture. They are each loaded with different amounts of cultural capital and speak to a difference in social standing. As such, not only are manners predetermined by one's social background, but they are also enforced by the lack of exposure to difference. All along the distinction of taste, as Bourdieu has extensively shown, is not innocent, but rather grounded in the maintenance of social hierarchies.

STAND IN

Recommendation algorithms in consumer culture engage explicitly with markers of the nonconscious dispositions of taste. These calculations are based on conscious human behaviour such as watching a movie, expressing interest in an ad, and so on. Recommendation algorithms in hiring have taken on an even more invasive model of determining if one belongs to a particular social category. Here, the data that algorithms gather is more obscure, while the connection to social standing and social positioning is more obvious.

It is increasingly common for companies to deploy algorithms as the screening agent during video interviews. As a blog post on the Recruitee Blog notes, body language has become a central evaluation criterion in virtual interviewing (McConnell 2021). The evaluation of whether one is "confident, focused, bored, disinterested, insecure, or nervous" is based on "posture, head tilt, hand placement, gestures, eye movement, mouth movement, smiling" (2021). All of these parameters are calculated and then categorized. They attempt to capture and compute not only behaviour that is nonconscious to the interviewee but also behaviour that would not always be noted in such detail by a human interviewer. The blog offers insight into how human recruiters can read body language in order to mimic the AI-driven tools already put in place that do this work supposedly with less bias, more objectivity, and greater speed. The company, *HireVue*, was at the forefront of algorithmic-driven interviewing and hiring as it offered AI-driven assessment of candidates based on their facial expressions, linguistic messages, as well as body posture. In the early stages, in 2019, HireVue used facial scanning in order to determine the interviewee's fit for the job and the company more broadly (Harwell 2016). Here one's pattern of speech, facial expressions, and posture were calculated into an "employability score" (2019).

The calculation of body movements as signals for emotions and attitudes is built into the algorithmic technology as well as into an ideology of objectivity that juxtaposes subjective reviewers with objective AI-driven data. A large section of emerging research focuses on the nexus between social psychology and affective computing. In a study from MIT, researchers found that smiling makes candidates more employable (Naim et al. 2018). Another research project links facial expression to personality via five personality traits derived from facial width-to-height ratio analysis. (Nivetha 2022). Another example is the 2019 study by Khaifa, Ejbali, and Zaied where the authors offer a "deep spatio-temporal approach, [which] merges the temporal normalization method which is the energy binary motion information (EBMI) with deep learning based on stacked auto-encoder (SAE) for emotional body gesture recognition in [a] job interview" (2019, 274). This study relies on communication theories that connect facial expressions and gestures to attitudes such as dominance and anxiety, as well as the evaluation of deception and truthfulness. These quantitative studies attempted to connect embodiment with attitude through quantitative and experimental research. While this type of research, which originated in the late 1960s in the fields of communication and social psychology, has subsequently been rebuked in the field of communication, it has found a new application in affective computing. This particular paper relies on the work of the 1960s and 1970s work of Paul Ekman and Wallace Friesen, who believed in the universality of facial expression regardless of cultural and social position (1969, 1971). Such normative frameworks run counter to socio-cultural constructs of the body such as those articulated by Pierre Bourdieu.

Body posture has also been extensively studied as a problem that can be solved with reliable objective algorithmic data rather than through subjective, cultural, and socially nuanced understanding. Notable here is a project from 2015 called AutoManner (https://roc-hci.com/past-projects/automanner/), which allowed speakers to detect patterns in the speaker's body language (Tanveer et al. 2016). This tool was used to allow presenters to see patterns in their movement as they delivered a public speech. The rationale was that it provided objective feedback rather than the subjective feedback that reviewers give about presentations. Reduced to a set of skeletal points, the body here becomes distilled into a set of coordinates. The demonstration of this project allows for self-evaluation, as well as evaluation of the work of the algorithm, as the algorithms were still in training (www.cs.rochester.edu/hci/projectpages/behaviour/gui.php?id=45.1). Training algorithms like this have been advanced and embedded in AI-driven hiring practices, where subjects are no longer aware of how their facial and bodily gestures, postures, and movements are being interpreted. In the wake of AutoManner, there are new apps and websites, such as Speeko, Ummo, and Poised, that aim to provide quantitative feedback to anxious public speakers who are increasingly interviewed for a job by AI agents. Apps like Poised promise to read our emotional state through seven emotions based on facial expressions during now routine Zoom calls as well as during AI-driven job interviews (https://app.poised.com/meetings/EXAMPLE-03a8b92c-87e0-480a-aa30-bf8c8bf1a962/?tag=emotion). Here again, body posture and gesture are extricated away from culture and society.

Highlighting the ways in which our faces and bodies move as we speak has become both big business as well as a subject of art and cultural criticism. An important report from the AI Now Institute has challenged the validity of affective recognition in algorithmic-driven interviewing. They raise a salient point: "There remains little to no evidence that these new affect-recognition products have any scientific validity" (Crawford et al. 2019, 51). Art projects such as Carrie Sijia Wang's *An Interview with Alex* (https://carriesijiawang.com/alex_interview/) challenge this narrative. Wang's artwork presents an "artificial intelligence HR manages that uses gamification as a subtle tool of control in the workspace" (About). In this dystopia project, Wang critiques the invasive and intrusive nature of AI-based hiring processes, which appear to be objective while at the same time assessing our most personal traits and attempting to summon what we as people are like. She betrays the seeming objectivity of the algorithm by having it ask 36 personal questions aside from the facial and speech data gathered (Sonnemaker 2016).

The body, for Bourdieu, is a "fundamental dimension of habitus" (1980, 72). The body learns through mimesis – it "does not represent what it performs, it does not memorize the past, it enacts the past, brings it back to life" (73). As such, it constructs a "body hexis," which "speaks directly to the motor function, in the form of a pattern of postures that is both individual and systematic, both bound up with a whole system of objects, and charged with a host of special meanings and values" (74). Body hexis reflects the embodied habits that are historically, culturally, and socially conditioned. It is the embodiment of the habitus, and thus of history. These types of habits are also theorized as bypassing discourse and consciousness. Bourdieu's notion of bodily hexis captures well the target of hiring algorithms.

In the case of hiring algorithms, body hexis is seen as the most objective way of determining one's social status, hence the probability of belonging to the culture of a company. The ways we carry ourselves, our mannerisms and our unconscious gestures here are seen as the most authentic mark of a candidate. Even though we are told by the algorithm developers that what is measured is one's psychological state such as stress, comfort, or enjoyment, a sociological perspective on hiring algorithms points to the fact that algorithms are evaluating one's social standing in order to explicitly police social mobility through the determination of occupation. One's tendency to lean in or away from the screen is innocently coupled with eagerness or apprehension for the job. Understood as body hexis, however, the nonconscious movement of one's body speaks to cultural norms shaped by one's social identity.

By unpacking the social construction of body hexis, we can begin to challenge the ideologies that naturalize body language. Body language should be situated historically, culturally, and socially. When body language is taken out of context and connected to universal human traits, a dominant behaviour paradigm becomes encoded into algorithmic technology as objective and legitimate. Algorithms are thus prescribing consumption via recourse to taste, but also occupation via recourse to bodily hexis. In this way, they are obscuring critiques about the validity and legitimacy of given tastes and bodily hexis.

HABITS AND HABITUS IN ALGORITHMIC CULTURE

Our conscious and nonconscious habits have become the primary fuel for determining who we are in algorithmic culture. From our taste in movies to fashion, to our bodily hexis expressed in the way we talk, smile, and nod, algorithms have taken on the task of providing complex correlations that seem to be grounded in universal rather than contextual human categorizations. Notions of habitus challenge ideas of habits as linked to psychology to modes of calculation through correlation, and ground discussion about behaviour and identity in discourses of history, culture, and society. Situating habits in the discourse of habitus allows for challenging the ideology of naturalization that algorithmic technology promotes.

REFERENCES

Airoldi, M. (2022). *Machine Habitus: Towards a Sociology of Algorithms*. Polity Press.
Bourdieu, P. (1980). *The Logic of Practice*. Stanford, CA: Stanford University Press.
Bourdieu, P. (1984). *Distinction: A Social Critique of the Judgement of Taste*. Cambridge, MA: Harvard University Press.

Bucher, T. (2018). *If...Then: Algorithmic Power and Politics*. London and New York: Oxford University Press.

Cheney-Lippold, J. (2017). *We Are Data: Algorithms and the Making of Our Digital Selves*. New York: New York University Press.

Chun, W. H. K. (2016). *Updating to Remain the Same: Habitual New Media*. Cambridge, MA: The MIT Press.

Chun, W. H. K. (2021). *Discriminating Data*. Cambridge, MA: The MIT Press.

Crawford, K., Dobbe, R., Dryer, T., Fried, G., Green, B., Kaziunas, E., Kak, A., Mathur, V., McElroy, E., Sánchez, A. N., Raji, D., Rankin, J. L., Richardson, R., Schultz, J., West, S. M., & Whittaker, M. (2019). *AI Now 2019 Report*. New York: AI Now Institute. https://ainowinstitute.org/AI_Now_2019 _Report.html

Ekman, P., & Friesen, W. V. (1969). The repertoire of nonverbal behaviour: Categories, origins, usage, and coding. *Semiotica, 1*(1), 49–98.

Ekman, P., & Friesen, W. V. (1971). Constants across cultures in the face and emotion. *Journal of Personality and Social Psychology, 17*(2), 124.

Galloway, A. R. (2006). *Gaming: Essays on Algorithmic Culture*. Minneapolis, MN: University of Minnesota Press.

Harwell, D. (2016) A face-scanning algorithm increasingly decides whether you deserve the job. *The Washington Post*, November 6. https://www.washingtonpost.com/technology/2019/10/22/ai-hiring -face-scanning-algorithm-increasingly-decides-whether-you-deserve-job/

Khalifa, I., Ejbali, R., & Zaied, M. (2019). Body gesture modeling for psychology analysis in job interview based on deep spatio-temporal approach. In J. Park, H. Shen, Y. Sung, & H. Tian (Eds.), *Parallel and Distributed Computing, Applications and Technologies. PDCAT 2018. Communications in Computer and Information Science,* Vol. 931. Singapore: Springer. https://doi.org/10.1007/978-981 -13-5907-1_29

Lindgren, S. (2020). *Data Theory: Interpretive Sociology and Computational Methods*. Polity Press.

McConnell, B. (2021). Reading candidate body language in virtual job interview. *Recruitee Blog.* https://recruitee.com/articles/reading-candidate-body-language-in-a-virtual-job-interview

Naim, I., Tanveer, M. I., Gildea, D., & Hoque, M. E. (2018). Automated analysis and prediction of job interview performance. *IEEE Transactions on Affective Computing, 9*(2), 191–204. https://doi.org/10 .1109/TAFFC.2016.2614299

Nivetha, S. K., Geetha, M., Latha, R. S., Sneha, K., Sobika S., & Yamuna, C. (2022). Personality prediction for online interview. *2022 International Conference on Computer Communication and Informatics (ICCCI)*, pp. 1–4. https://doi.org/10.1109/ICCCI54379.2022.9740980.

Pariser, E. (2011). *The Filter Bubble: What the Internet is Hiding from You*. New York: The Penguin Press.

Roberge, J., & Seyfert, R. (Eds.). (2018). *Algorithmic Cultures: Essays on Meaning, Performance and New Technologies*. New York and London: Routledge.

Sonnemaker, T. (2016). Take this dystopian job interview with an AI hiring manager to experience what life could be like if machines fully take over the workplace. *Business Insider*, June 16. https://www .businessinsider.com/interactive-ai-job-interview-experience-dystopian-future-art-project-2020-6

Striphas, T. (2015). Algorithmic culture. *European Journal of Cultural Studies, 18*(4–5), 395–412.

Tanveer, M. I., Zhao, R., Chen, K., Tiet, Z., & Hoque, M. E. (2016). An automated interface for making public speakers aware of their mannerisms. In *Proceedings of the 21st International Conference on Intelligent User Interfaces (IUI '16)* (pp. 385–396). New York: Association for Computing Machinery. https://www.doi.org/10.1145/28566767.2856785

Zuboff, S. (2019). *Surveillance Capitalism: The Fight for a Human Future at the New Frontier of Power*. New York: Public Affair.

10. Algorithms and emerging forms of intimacy

Tanja Wiehn

INTRODUCTION: EMERGING FORMS OF INTIMACIES

The conceptual work of the intimacy of algorithms[1] or *algorithmic intimacies* (Wiehn, 2021, 2022) marks an entry into the ways in which intimacy becomes a ground to be capitalized on, as well as a field to identify critique through the view on proximities as part of digital environments. As I intend to show, the notion of intimacy is versatile and immediate to formulate critical perspectives on AI's impact on society, whether it be in instances of data leakage and brokerage, processes of datafication or the generation of intimacy as a product of platforms like OnlyFans. In this sense, I build on the notion of intimacy to challenge the relation between ubiquitous algorithms and data extraction and link principles of datafication to dependencies on algorithms for interpersonal connections between users. I thereby ask: how do algorithms change conceptions of intimacy? How is intimacy itself a scope through which algorithms mediate socio-political relations? As I come to demonstrate, the notion of intimacy sharpens the view to question the invisible appropriation and ideologies on which intimate encounters with forms of artificial intelligence are based. I leverage the notion of intimacy to analyse the commodifying principles of datafication, as well as the exploitation of hope for real intimacy provided in forms of digital mediation.

The following paragraphs demonstrate intimacy as a way to look at relations between different scales of social life, from the individual to broader scales, such as globalization, economies and politics. Through this theoretical trajectory of critical intimacy studies, I come to link the notion of intimacy to systems of artificial intelligence that form new connections between people and data. I situate intimacy in this digital realm with the help of scholarly work that identifies how digital infrastructures shape, form and translate relations. Following this, I outline the different layers through which intimacy and algorithms come into play, that is, how interpersonal relations are mediated through technology and are dependent on digital infrastructures, as well as how intimacy is linked, through processes of datafication, to economic value by entering ever new dimensions of life. I thus underline the need to analyse the entrance of market logics pertaining to intimacy and algorithmic ways to connect and control intimacies. I conclude the chapter by opening a discussion on the recent inclusion of more cultural studies and interdisciplinary perspectives and their usefulness for a critical investigation of algorithms.

---

[1]   When I discuss algorithms in this chapter, I refer to sophisticated algorithms of machine learning that are substantially used in AI systems (e.g. smart home systems), social media platforms or facial recognition software.

CRITICAL INTIMACY STUDIES

To put it simply, intimacy has been a useful theoretical concept for investigating who and what affect people's lives and to question what normative societal assumptions stand behind ways of expressing intimacy. "To consider the logic of intimacy is not solely to study domesticity, romantic and/or sexual relations, but to question the places and the supposed non-places of intimacy" (Antwi et al., 2013, p. 1). In the field of critical intimacy studies, the notion of intimacy functions to formulate critical perspectives on structures of dominance in a variety of settings (Wilson, 2012). Feminist scholars in particular have reclaimed the intimate for engaging with critical questions of the socio-political. Mountz and Hyndman note that the intimate is essential for feminist approaches to make sense of the global through the intimate. "The intimate encompasses not only those entanglements rooted in the everyday, but also the subtlety of their interconnectedness to everyday intimacies in other places and times" (Mountz & Hyndman, 2006, p. 447). The authors bring into perspective the need to include feminist scholarship that is attentive towards globalization, surfacing how feminist theory would account for a more in-depth critique. What the authors coin as feminist analytics of scale serves to underline the significance of neglected spaces and relations of sociality, which are often undermined in comparison with global, political and economic invocations of scale (Mountz & Hyndman, 2006).

> Transnational feminisms must reclaim the intimate through some of the strategies detailed in this essay [...] the sustained attention to key sites where the intimate and the global are pronounced. Nationality, gender, race, religion, class, caste, age, nation, ability, and sexuality represent unequal locations within a web of relationships that transcend political borders and scale the global and the intimate simultaneously. (Mountz & Hyndman, 2006, p. 460)

Scholars like Berlant (1998) and Stoler (2006) thus note the flexibility of intimacy to be a heuristic to challenge societal normativity. In Lauren Berlant's understanding, intimacy means "connections that *impact* on people, and on which they depend for living" (Berlant, 1998, p. 4). I find Berlant's notion of intimacy useful for engaging with algorithms because of its relation to proximity – in a physical and/or emotional sense. Critical analyses of intimate connections thus enable the view on newly formed conjunctions between intimacy, economic incentives and emerging structures of dominance (Wiehn, 2022; Wilson, 2012). The field of critical intimacy studies I only briefly touch on here marks a groundwork to make intimacy a prism to think from and with.

Some branches within critical intimacy studies, however, are concerned with how (digital) infrastructures shape relations between the subject and societies, adding perspectives that challenge previous ideas of intimacies and norms. This string considers how digital communication shapes and transforms notions of intimacy as socio-political (McGlotten, 2013). The idea of infrastructure is based on a form of relationality that is embedded in social as well as technological structures (Star, 1999). In the essay "The Infrastructure of Intimacy," Ara Wilson argues that the "circuits of pipes and cables embed intimate relations in unpredictable junctures of material and symbolic power" (Wilson, 2016, p. 247). Through these thoughts on the correlation of intimacy and infrastructure, Wilson identifies the governing agencies through which intimacy is placed or displaced, enabled and hindered. Wilson's understanding of intimacy is related to the establishment of environments underlying an infrastructure of governance. "But just as the critical use of intimacy counters the common-sense understanding of public and private, the emerging use of infrastructure eschews a technological determinism. [...] All reasons for intimacy's relationship to infrastructure: it's complicated" (Wilson, 2016, p. 275). In this regard, intimacy is always reliant on infrastructures and algorithmic systems have come to play a significant role as infrastructural actors in digital environments (Berry, 2019; Gillespie, 2014).

"Understanding infrastructure as a network linking various nodes allows us to recognize a plurality of sites where material systems (and their failures) are entwined with social relations and with a complex interplay of structure and agency" (Wilson, 2016, p. 261). With Wilson's considerations, the correlations between intimacy and the particularities of today's digital infrastructures become apparent. It is a given that the infrastructural components that hold digital communication systems together are multilayered and complex; they can be concretized as data servers, underwater cables and search engines, mobile apps or smart home artificial intelligence systems. Contemporary infrastructures of digital communication have become crucial for interpersonal relationships: messenger services, dating apps and social media platforms enable forms of effortless and immediate communication through their networking and connecting qualities. Moreover, they have introduced new ways of expressing affects and emotions, for instance, with the help of emojis (Stark & Crawford, 2015) and newfound interpretations of online friendship (Bucher, 2017), as well as relationships between content creators and their followers (Glatt, 2022; Hamilton et al., 2022).

> Intimacy [...] refers not only to connections between people, but to the networked environments in which these connections unfold and the connections that are formed through devices, apps and platforms: each of these aspects impact on people, and people depend on them to live. (Paasonen, 2018, p. 103f)

Shaka McGlotten's work is another example of a theoretical usage of intimacy. Building on Berlant's scholarship, McGlotten describes the normative pressures grounded in heteronormative structures around forms of intimacy. In *Virtual Intimacies* (2013), McGlotten analyses the emergence of queer chat rooms and their function to retreat from a society in which heteronormative forms of intimacy are rewarded and other kinds of intimacies are seen as not proper (McGlotten, 2013).

However, digital environments are not exclusively characterized by acts of maintaining and fostering interpersonal relationships. What has significantly changed in light of today's digital environments is not only a growing dependency on digital means of communication but the fact that processes of datafication make unforeseeable and intimate entries into people's behaviour possible (Ball & Webster, 2020; Mejias & Couldry, 2019; Sadowski, 2019). Sometimes datafication is put in place by users themselves for self-tracking purposes to generate datafied intimacy to oneself and one's body.

> To have intimacy is to have the other come into intimus, the inmost parts of the self. Self-tracking claims a new intimacy between the machine and the body, the machine and the body's truth – which relation seemingly authorizes the truth value of machine-extracted data. (Hong, 2016, p. 5)

Predominantly, data-heavy relations are intensified without users' knowledge, for example, when users' scrolling patterns are analysed and made profitable on social media sites like

TikTok (Zeng et al., 2021). There are newfound, seemingly inexhaustive ways in which data, their creation and extraction have become linked to intimate purposes in digital environments. In the following section, I will tether these considerations of intimacy more closely to algorithms and systems of artificial intelligence to outline the different layers of the conceptual contribution.

TETHERED TO ALGORITHMS

The ubiquity of algorithms has become the epitome of the everyday. Algorithms are an integral part of our digital everyday experiences in the ways in which they facilitate connections on social media, and create and categorize search results, making some information more relevant than others (Gillespie, 2014). When I talk about algorithms in this chapter, I refer to machine learning algorithms that are often part of what is commonly referred to as "artificial intelligence" (Kelleher, 2019). Machine learning algorithms are a specific category of algorithms often used to analyse and discriminate patterns in big data sets (Chun, 2018). Today, machine learning has advanced to be applied to sets of very complex data, such as images and faces (Kelleher, 2019). It is important to note that machine learning is dependent on a previous relation with input data to draw conclusions or detect patterns in future data input. In other words, the link between data and algorithms is a crucial factor for the creation of datafied relations that are being translated onto a socio-political as well as cultural level (Amoore, 2020; Berry, 2019).

A reductionism to a single output as a result of the complex and vast amount of data is responsible for many everyday operations of algorithms. What I want to allude to by emphasizing machine learning as a particular form of algorithms shaping everyday life is the complex relationality that emerges from them. Algorithms are not fixed technological entities, they are a product of multiple agencies, some human and some non-human, but nevertheless all building ever new formations (Amoore 2020; Chun, 2018).

Therefore, I propose to shift the attention to the relations and relationalities that algorithms foster. Intimacy is not only the closeness between people but also the subjectiveness of closeness that algorithms evoke. The seemingly magical prediction for a Spotify music playlist can feed into the belief that algorithms know our tastes when data patterns based on homophily also come to be a part of algorithmic processes (Wiehn, 2021). Homophily describes "the axiom that similarity breeds connection – which grounds contemporary network science" (Chun, 2018, p. 60). In the ways in which Chun describes data analytics lie some explanations of the harmful and exposing ways in which data are ruthlessly extracted to create correlations – correlations that can influence how one is targeted as a potential threat to society in predictive policing technologies (Chun, 2021). In one way or another, algorithms become intimate companions, accompanying us through the everyday – deciding, filtering and categorizing instances of banality as well as instances of more significance in people's lives. Beer underpins "the increasing prominence and power of algorithms in the social fabric" that are "built on the central premise that algorithms have the capacity to shape social and cultural formations and impact directly on individual lives" (Beer, 2009, p. 994). Whether it is the newsfeed algorithm, the curation of music playlists or algorithms being employed by the public sector of the welfare state (Jørgensen, 2021), algorithms influence the many different levels in which they are employed to create relations between data and data subjects (Wiehn, 2021).

At the same time, the environments in which we encounter algorithms, from social media platforms to smart home assistants, are established in ways that make them ideal for data capture and datafication (Sadowski, 2019; van Dijck et al., 2018). Big data has become a combinatory mode to make sense of different entries to data – a mode to establish unprecedented proximities with users as a source for ongoing data extraction (Andrejevic, 2019; van Dijck et al., 2018). This exposes new ways to operate with data, as Ball and Webster note:

> In comparison with its predecessors, and by virtue of its pre-emptive impulses and intimate data flows, big data creates a more penetrating gaze into consumers' and service users' lives, as big data draws on data streams from social and online media, as well as personal devices. (Ball & Webster, 2020, p. 2)

Furthermore, the capacity to create patterns through data analytics can foster great vulnerabilities. Allowing systems of artificial intelligence to process intimate data or making the collection of data intimate through correlations exerts structures of dominance and amplifies already existing biases in societies. The exercising of socio-political power through AI technologies has been rightfully pointed out by data feminists and critical race scholars. They engage not only with ways to make inequalities visible but also question the neutrality of big data and machine learning regimes (Benjamin, 2019; Cifor et al., 2019; D'Ignazio & Klein, 2020; Thylstrup et al., 2021).

Data feminists remind us of the problems with data analytics without a substantial contextualization of data. "The plethora of correlations it [big data, T.W.] documents also raises fundamental questions about causality: if almost anything can be shown to be real (if almost any correlation can be discovered), how do we know what matters, what is true?" (Chun, 2018, p. 67). The justification and implementation of algorithmic decision-making are often based on the seemingly objective character of technology, used for the creation of a rationality in future imaginaries of automation, prediction and elimination of risks (Atanasoski & Vora, 2019). However, as critical algorithm and feminist scholars argue, to make sense of algorithms is to dismantle the context in which they come to matter, to understand when they have agency (Bucher, 2018), what their datafied results are based on (D'Ignazio & Klein, 2020) and who is profiting from them (West, 2019). In this light, I leverage the concept of intimacy as a contribution to a critical perspective to investigate and challenge the ramification of contemporary algorithms as a result of a relationality between data and people (Wiehn, 2021).

To intimate is to understand algorithms in an indirect way. The English verb "to intimate" means to imply something, to let someone know something in an indirect way. This understanding of algorithms is not based on any form of lifting a veil or opening a black box but on an investigation of the ways in which algorithms create proximities. The prism of intimacy marks the multiple relationalities of algorithmic processes. To operationalize the notion of intimacy is to also contextualize how algorithms relate through the categorization and analytics of data. The statistical reductionism of machine learning algorithms contributes to these forms of data proximities:

> The extended *we* of the multiplicity of data to which the learning algorithm is exposed heralds an intimate communion of the learning machines with a vast and incalculable we: all of us, all our data points, all the patterns and attributes that are not quite possessed by us. (Amoore, 2020, p. 58)

In this regard, I propose to look at algorithms through the ways in which they process ongoing intimate relationalities among subjects, algorithms and one's own and others' data (Amoore, 2020; Wiehn, 2021).

INTIMATE CAPITAL

Data capitalism is based on the marketing of a better life by creating new data correlations that can be commodified. One incentive for data capitalism is to penetrate ever more intimate, private and interpersonal arenas of people's lives (Sadowski, 2019; West, 2020). West illustrates that the event of data capitalism is "justified by the association of networked technologies with the political and social benefits of online community, drawing upon narratives that foreground the social and political benefits of networked technologies" (West, 2019, p. 20). Economic values are deeply interlinked with the preconditions of data leaks and processes of datafication. Furthermore, practices of data extraction generate intimate entries into people's lives, correlating data and habits with things people desire now and potentially in the future (Ball & Webster, 2020; Zuboff, 2019). Elizabeth Povinelli reminds us of the parallels between intimacy and capitalism. In her work *The Empire of Love* (2006), she points out the illusion that intimate love is in opposition to the elements of the socio-political and market-driven logic: "Like capital, intimacy demands an ever-expanding market" (Povinelli, 2006, p. 190). Intimacy and relations of proximity are even more profitable in the networks of data capitalism (Chun, 2017).

The critical perspective I propose with the notion of intimacy is based on these different levels of entry that in most cases intersect. First, there are mediated forms of intimacies. These are systems that facilitate forms of intimacy online and create incentives to share highly intimate data, such as dating apps and platforms. Second, there are the technological elements through which contemporary machine learning algorithms create intimate relations through forms of homophily and pattern discrimination (Chun, 2018, 2021). The expansion of digitalization in more and more aspects of society fosters a technologically driven logic of proximity that is rooted in data analytics and perpetuates socio-political structures of inequality (Amoore, 2020; Chun, 2018). Furthermore, economic and market-driven logics have a strong influence on how data are collected and processed to create future revenue, for instance, in online marketing, recommendation systems and algorithms that foster addictive behaviour in users (Zeng et al., 2021). The perspective of intimacy is a strategy to decipher different movements in which intimacy becomes central for new ways of data exploitation. It is a way to home in on the contexts in which algorithms are employed to profit from the intimate spheres of data subjects. These are, for instance, the creation and development of new frontiers from which data can be extracted (Wiehn, 2022) or understanding instances in which intimacy is rendered a product of data capitalism. Turning to intimacy as a notion reveals the potential vulnerability, harm and marginalization emerging in digital environments. The following section illustrates this critical perspective through intimacy. It engages with outsourced forms of digital, intimate labour on the platform OnlyFans.

E-PIMPS AND OUTSOURCED CHAT LABOUR

Founded in 2016, OnlyFans is one of the biggest subscription-based social media platforms today. The platform works on the principle of content creators selling monthly subscriptions to their followers. OnlyFans is widely known for its distribution of mostly, but not exclusively, adult content by its creators, making it "uniquely positioned between the spaces of digital sex work and subscription-based social media" (Hamilton et al., 2022, p. 2). With the event of the Covid-19 pandemic, OnlyFans gained huge traction as a platform with an increase in revenue of over 500% (Hamilton et al., 2022). As part of paid subscriptions, followers often ask for personalized interactions and content. This can entail private conversations and messaging, as well as sexting and specific content in the form of videos or images. With the time-consuming demand of users asking content creators for individual interactions with them, a new lucrative market has opened. OnlyFans creators, also referred to as "influencers" or "Internet micro-celebrities" (Hamilton et al., 2022), increasingly rely on agencies to outsource the intimate labour of engaging with their followers. These so-called "e-pimps" (Marcus, 2022) of OnlyFans are agencies that handle marketing and communication on the accounts of content creators. This entails cross-platform marketing of accounts, for instance, on platforms like Instagram that do not allow erotic content. More importantly, the agencies also handle user interactions by impersonating content creators in interpersonal conversations with subscribers. Behind this outsourcing of labour lies the promise to drastically increase influencers' revenue by fostering close and intimate relations with subscribers, making them pay more money for content (Hamilton et al., 2022). Examples of agencies are Think Expansion and the Bunny Agency,[2] which employ cheap English-speaking staff to facilitate and maintain the interactions between content creators and their followers. Chatters can be based in the Philippines, the United States or Eastern Europe, creating the illusion of immediacy and intimacy between influencers and their subscribers (Marcus, 2022).

> In fact, there are a variety of OnlyFans-oriented companies in the field, which employ a spectrum of techniques to maximize profits from accounts they manage. But all of them take advantage of the same raw materials: the endless reproductivity of digital images; the widespread global availability of cheap English-speaking labour; and the world's unquenchable desire for companionship. (Marcus, 2022, p. 5)

OnlyFans creators' outsourcing practices underline the ways in which intimacy is rendered a product within globalized platform infrastructures. Herein lies a completely new field of research that investigates forms of companionship in influencer relationships as well as precarity and algorithmic discrimination unfolding in these new lines of work (Glatt, 2022). This is not limited to the example of OnlyFans, it only demonstrates in a drastic way how the commodification of intimacy has become a valuable and reproducible source in today's digital environments.

Through the case of OnlyFans, I try to unfold the insights that a conceptual work of algorithmic intimacies holds – that is, the linkage between intimacy as an incentive to draw users in, to make content creators' engagement on the platform more valuable and the seeming

---

[2]   Think Expansion: https://thinkexpansion.com and Bunny Agency: https://bunny-agency.com; retrieved 15 June 2022.

reproducibility of mediated connection through chat labour. It is the access to followers' data for chatters around the globe that emerges as a significant aspect of this value generation. Moreover, intimacy in communication is also understood as a reproducible asset in chat exchanges through signature wordings and protocols (Marcus, 2022).

Coming back to the early part of the chapter, we are reminded that the notion of intimacy enables us to question for whom closeness and intimacy are enabled and what kind of infrastructural conditions are part of this equation. Structures of dominance unfold here for the chatters that do intimate work, but also for the followers of content creators who – in some instances – learn that they were not actually communicating with the content creators themselves (Marcus, 2022). Finally, the pressure is high on content creators to maximize profit and stay visible in the realms of often precarious platform-dependent structures (Glatt, 2022). The critical notion of intimacy is leveraged to think about who and what are in a close relationship with each other, as well as what kind of socio-political structures of dominance emerge through modes of proximity. Intimacy dismantles ambivalent as well as formerly invisible modes of this exploitation, demonstrating its flexibility as a notion:

> As a placeholder, intimacy allows critical accounts of colonial empire or capitalist modernity because it is a flexible, provisional reference that emphasizes linkages across what are understood to be distinct realms, scales or bodies. Whether an analytical concept or a placeholder, the critical study of intimacy provides a useful category in the transnational analysis of power. (Wilson, 2012, p. 48)

In the form of this conceptual framework, the notion of intimacy extends its previous function and adapts to the digital realms that come to shape lives as drastically as previous transnational structures of dominance.

TOWARDS CULTURAL STUDIES OF ALGORITHMS

This chapter aims to emphasize not only the usefulness of viewing algorithmic systems through a perspective of intimacy but also underlines the idea of the concept as a method, drawing on an interdisciplinary line of work such as cultural studies and critical data and algorithm studies. The idea of the concept as a method accounts for a context in which interdisciplinary bodies of literature and knowledge come together (Bal, 2009). In "Working with concepts" (Bal, 2009), Mieke Bal frames the use of the concept as a method for cultural analysis and argues that the mapping of culture has become increasingly difficult, as the object of research in a broad understanding of culture in cultural studies is not aligned with a particular set of methods, as is the case in other more confined disciplines (Bal, 2009). Interdisciplinarity in objects of research and in the contexts in which cultural representations are embedded affords an analytical framework that "looks to issues of cultural relevance and aims to articulate how the object contributes to cultural debates" (Bal, 2009, p. 16). This is a necessary reflection on the challenges of methods in cultural studies, even more so in the context of digital culture with objects of research that seem to be elusive and difficult to grasp, like artificial intelligence.

In light of a position in cultural studies located at the border of different disciplines, working with concepts is helpful in confronting methodological challenges for a critical study of algorithms and their technological sophistication (Christin, 2020). The concept of algorithmic intimacies functions as a method in the sense that they open a spectrum to read algorithms as part of digital culture through the framework of intimacy (Wiehn, 2021). This use of concept work speaks to the way that scholars have read the algorithm not only as implemented in culture but in thinking about algorithms as culture (Seaver, 2017): "If we understand algorithms as enacted by the practices used to engage with them, then the stakes of our own methods change. We are not remote observers, but rather active enactors, producing algorithms as particular kinds of objects through our research" (Seaver, 2017, p. 5).

A multifaceted character of algorithms as culture speaks therefore to Bal's understanding of working with concepts: "No concept is meaningful for cultural analysis unless it helps us to understand the object better on its – the object's – own terms. Here, another background, or root, of the current situation in the humanities comes to the fore" (Bal, 2009, p. 15).

Widespread implementation of AI systems fosters new scholarly approaches, dismantling the diverse ramifications of big data and datafication of life. Therefore, cultural and media studies scholar rethink the relationship between technology and culture (Natale & Guzman, 2022; Thylstrup et al., 2021).

> It is the widespread collection, processing and redistribution of such data that enables AI and algorithmic technologies to function. Media and cultural studies have the potential to provide a particularly important contribution to understanding these changes and their societal impacts, due to the centrality of communication and culture in novel AI systems. (Natale & Guzman, 2022, p. 3)

Sarah Murray coins today's cultural studies as postdigital, emphasizing the attention in cultural studies towards the ordinary as characteristic of the field. Algorithms accompany us ubiquitously and are therefore: "symptomatic of a digital everyday in which attention feeds and energizes datafied existences" (Murray, 2020, p. 445). Arguing that the algorithm has already become part of the realm of the ordinary, Murray emphasizes that algorithmic culture is a significant object of research – not only for algorithmic, Internet or (new) media studies but also for cultural studies as a whole. It lies within a cultural studies approach to discuss "power as *relations of attention*, and to identify these relations embedded within culture as a way of life" (Murray, 2020, p. 442; emphasis in original text). This perspective on algorithms is related to a mode of thinking about them as cultural objects characterized by their multiple being and influence within society (Benjamin, 2019; Seaver, 2017).

In conclusion, leveraging intimacy proves to be one productive conceptual attribution to make sense of algorithmic cultures. However, the usefulness of a single notion deriving from cultural studies is only a starting point for future concept work unfolding for a critical review of the ramifications that digital technologies forces onto societies. The conceptual framework of algorithmic intimacies is meant as a call for new theoretical interventions that grasp the rapid developments of ubiquitous algorithms in our lives. It is the pursuit to extend existing vocabularies for the current and future ramifications of the proximities in data. It is the assumption that we have to co-create new research avenues that are able to form critical perspectives on our coexistence with algorithms (Wiehn, 2021).

REFERENCES

Amoore, L. (2020). *Cloud ethics: Algorithms and the attributes of ourselves and others.* Duke University Press.

Andrejevic, M. (2019). Automating surveillance. *Surveillance & Society, 17*(1/2), 7–13. doi:10.24908/ss.v17i1/2.12930

Antwi, P., Brophy, S., Strauss, H., & Troeung, Y.-D. (2013). Postcolonial intimacies: Gatherings disruptions departures. *Interventions, 15*(1), 1–9. doi:10.1080/1369801X.2013.770994

Atanasoski, N., & Vora, K. (2019). *Surrogate humanity: Race, robots, and the politics of technological futures*. Duke University Press.

Bal, M. (2009). Working with concepts. *European Journal of English Studies: Travelling Concepts in English Studies, 13*(1), 13–23. doi:10.1080/13825570802708121

Ball, K., & Webster, W. (2020). Big data and surveillance: Hype, commercial logics and new intimate spheres. *Big Data & Society*, January, 1–5. doi:10.1177/2053951720925853

Beer, D. (2009). Power through the algorithm? Participatory web cultures and the technological unconscious. *New Media & Society, 11*(6), 985–1002. doi:10.1177/1461444809336551

Benjamin R. (2019). *Race after technology: Abolitionist tools for the new Jim code*. Polity.

Berlant, L. (1998). Intimacy: A special issue. *Critical Inquiry, 24*(2), 281–288. doi:10.1086/448875

Berry, D. (2019). Against infrasomatization: Towards a critical theory of algorithms. In D. Bigo, E. F. Isin, & E. S. Ruppert (Eds.), *Data politics: Worlds subjects rights* (pp. 43–63). Routledge. doi:10.4324/9781315167305-3

Bucher, T. (2017). The algorithmic imaginary: Exploring the ordinary affects of Facebook algorithms. *Information, Communication & Society, 20*(1), 30–44. doi: 10.1080/1369118X.2016.1154086

Bucher, T. (2018). *If...then: Algorithmic power and politics*. Oxford University Press.

Bunny Agency. (2022). Retrieved June 15, 2022, from https://bunny-agency.com

Christin, A. (2020). The ethnographer and the algorithm: Beyond the black box. *Theory & Society, 49*, 897–918. doi.org/10.1007/s11186-020-09411-3

Chun, W. H. K. (2017). *Updating to remain the same: Habitual new media*. MIT Press.

Chun, W. H. K. (2018). Queering homophily. In C. Apprich, W. H. K. Chun, F. Cramer, & H. Steyerl (Eds.), *Pattern discrimination* (pp. 59–98). University of Minnesota Press.

Chun, W. H. K. (2021). *Discriminating data: Correlation, neighborhoods, and the new politics of recognition*. The MIT Press.

Cifor, M., Garcia, P., Cowan, T.L., Rault, J., Sutherland, T., Chan, A., Rode, J., Hoffmann, A.L., Salehi, N., & Nakamura, L. (2019). *Feminist data manifest no*. https://www.manifestno.com/.

D'Ignazio, C., & Klein, L. F. (2020). *Data feminism*. The MIT Press.

Gillespie, T. (2014). The relevance of algorithms. In T. Gillespie, P. J. Boczkowski, & K. A. Foot (Eds.), *Media technologies: Essays on communication, materiality, and society* (pp. 167–193). MIT Press. doi:10.1080/1369118X.2016.1199721

Glatt, Z. (2022). "We're all told not to put our eggs in one basket": Uncertainty, precarity and cross-platform labor in the online video influencer industry. *International Journal of Communication, Special Issue on Media and Uncertainty, 16*, 3853–3871. https://ijoc.org/index.php/ijoc/article/view/15761/3858

Hamilton, S., McDonald, A., & Redmiles, E. (2022). "Nudes? Shouldn't I charge for these?": Exploring what motivates content creation on OnlyFans. *arXiv*. https://arxiv.org/abs/2205.10425

Hong, S. (2016). Data's intimacy: Machinic sensibility and the quantified self. *Communication +1, 5*(1), 1–36. doi:10.7275/R5CF9N15

Jørgensen, R. F. (2021). Data and rights in the digital welfare state: The case of Denmark. *Information, Communication & Society*, 1–16. doi: 10.1080/1369118X.2021.1934069

Kelleher, J. D. (2019). *Deep learning*. The MIT Press.

Marcus, E. (2022, May 16). The 'E-Pimps' of OnlyFans: Clever marketers have figured out how easy it is to simulate online intimacy at scale, ventriloquizing alluring models with cheap, offshore labor. *The New York Times Magazine*. https://www.nytimes.com/2022/05/16/magazine/e-pimps-onlyfans.html

McGlotten, S. (2013). *Virtual intimacies media, affect, and queer sociality*. State University of New York Press.

Mejias, U. A., & Couldry, N. (2019). Datafication. *Internet Policy Review, 8*(4), doi: 10.14763/2019.4.1428

Mountz, A., & Hyndman, J. (2006). Feminist approaches to the global intimate. *Women's Studies Quarterly, 34*(1–2), 446–463.

Murray, S. (2020). Postdigital cultural studies. *International Journal of Cultural Studies*, *23*(4), 441–450. doi:10.1177/1367877920918599.

Natale, S., & Guzman, A. L. (2022). Reclaiming the human in machine cultures: Introduction. *Media, Culture & Society*. doi:10.1177/01634437221099614

Paasonen, S. (2018). Infrastructures of intimacy. In R. Andreassen, M. N. Petersen, K. Harrison, & T. Raun (Eds.), *Mediated intimacies: Connectivities, relationalities and proximities*. Routledge. doi:10.4324/9781315208589

Povinelli, E. A. (2006). *The empire of love: Toward a theory of intimacy, genealogy, and carnality*. Duke University Press.

Sadowski, J. (2019). When data is capital: Datafication, accumulation, and extraction. *Big Data & Society*, *6*(1), 1–12. doi:10.1177/2053951718820549

Seaver, N. (2017). Algorithms as culture: Some tactics for the ethnography of algorithmic systems. *Big Data & Society*, *4*(2), 1–12. doi:10.1177/2053951717738104

Star, S. L. (1999). The ethnography of infrastructure. *The American Behavioral Scientist*, *43*(3), 377–391. doi:10.1177/00027649921955326

Stark, L., & Crawford, K. (2015). The conservatism of Emoji: Work, affect, and communication. *Social Media + Society*, July, 1–11. doi:10.1177/2056305115604853

Stoler, A. L. (2006). Intimidations of Empire: Predicaments of the tactile and unseen. In A. L. Stoler (Ed.), *Haunted by Empire: Geographies of intimacy in North American history* (pp. 1–22). Duke University Press. doi:10.1515/9780822387992-003

Think Expansion. (2022). Retrieved June 15, 2022, from https://thinkexpansion.com

Thylstrup, N. B., Agostinho, D., Ring, A., D'Ignazio, C., & Veel, K. (2021). *Uncertain archives: Critical keywords for big data*. The MIT Press.

van Dijck J., Poell, T., & de Waal, M. (2018). *The platform society*. Oxford University Press.

West, S. M. (2019). Data capitalism: Redefining the logics of surveillance and privacy. *Business & Society*, *58*(1), 20–41. doi:10.1177/0007650317718185

West, S. M. (2020). Redistribution and rekognition: A feminist critique of algorithmic fairness. *Catalyst*, *6*(2), 1. doi:10.28968/cftt.v6i2.33043

Wiehn T. (2021). Algorithmic intimacies: *A cultural analysis of ubiquitous proximities in data* (PhD thesis), Department of Arts and Cultural Studies, University of Copenhagen.

Wiehn, T. (2022). Becoming intimate with algorithms: Towards a critical antagonism via algorithmic art. *Media International Australia*, *183*(1), 30–43. https://doi.org/10.1177/1329878X221077844.

Wilson, A. (2012). 1. Intimacy. In G. Pratt & V. Rosner (Eds.), *The global and the intimate* (pp. 31–56). Columbia University Press. doi:10.7312/prat15448-002

Wilson, A. (2016). The infrastructure of intimacy. *Signs: Journal of Women in Culture and Society*, *41*(2), 247–280. University of Chicago Press. doi:10.1086/682919

Zeng, J., Abidin, C., & Schafer, M. S. (2021). Research perspectives on TikTok and its legacy apps: Introduction. *International Journal of Communication*, 3161–3172. https://ijoc.org/index.php/ijoc/article/view/14539/3494

Zuboff, S. (2019). *The age of surveillance capitalism: The fight for a human future at the new frontier of power*. Profile Books.

11. It's incomprehensible: on machine learning and decoloniality

Abeba Birhane and Zeerak Talat

INTRODUCTION

The movement to decolonize AI has been gaining momentum over the past decade, with various positions on the matter. Some have proposed ways to decolonize technology (Alexander, 2020), while others have applied more strict criteria, highlighting the challenges of uprooting coloniality and raising the question of whether AI can be decolonized at all (Adams, 2021). Yet others have criticized the slapdash use of decoloniality. Paballo Chauke, for example, warns that "'decolonization' in Africa risks becoming a buzzword due to haphazard use by those who want to 'seem open-minded'" (Byrne, 2022). It is therefore important that we critically examine if and how decoloniality can be applied to machine learning (ML). Whether decolonization is possible is a particularly important question, as ML is rapidly being integrated into the social sphere, with deeply harmful consequences, as these technologies perpetuate historical injustices such as white supremacy and colonialism (Birhane et al., 2021; Talat, Lulz, et al., 2021). Due to such harmful outcomes, there has been a large-scale effort toward the mitigation of harms, with proposals of technical and theoretical contributions, practical principles, guidelines, and protocols (Abdilla et al., 2020) for developing and deploying ML.

In this chapter, we explore the two divergent threads of ML on one hand, and decoloniality on the other. We trace the roots of ML and explore decolonial work from and for the African continent. In exploring ML, we draw a line from 19th-century phrenologist work to contemporary ML methods as applied to human and social data. We argue that through its goals of abstraction, ML risks constituting a modern form of phrenology. In exploring decoloniality, we discuss what it means to decolonize and situate our understanding of decolonial thought from and of the African continent. We reiterate the arguments that decoloniality and decolonization require attention to details and histories that are disconnected from the colonial gaze. Relying on these two divergent strands, what ML does and what it means to decolonize, we highlight the inherent tensions that exist between these two forces, such as their values, methodologies, and objectives. In light of these tensions, we reiterate Adams' (2021) question: Can ML be decolonial? We argue that despite the tensions inherent to the meeting of these two fields, decolonial ML is improbable yet not impossible. For ML and AI to be truly decolonial, they must fulfill key conditions. For instance, AI and ML initiatives must center the needs of Indigenous peoples and relegate financial profit to a secondary concern. We conclude the chapter by discussing the Te Hiku natural language processing (NLP) project. The project, through its focus on *Te Reo Māori*, and resistance to co-option by capital interests, situates ownership within the impacted communities and serves as an example for future decolonial ML efforts.

FROM PHRENOLOGY TO MACHINE LEARNING

Phrenology is a pseudo-scientific field that focuses on the correlation of physiological features with personality traits and social attributes. Originally, phrenologists relied on statistics to make claims on social groups as they sought physiological traits to affirm the white Western European man's superiority over all other groups (Sekula, 1986). Although statisticians have mostly abandoned phrenology, we argue that applying current ML methods to the social sphere – such as datafying, sorting, predicting, and classifying social phenomena, (e.g., human behavior or emotion) – provides a space for a resurgence of phrenology. As such, the ML field risks repeating past transgressions by enacting tools that correlate social value with demographic groups.

Contemporary ML methods, like early phrenologist work, enshrine hegemony and construct the Western white man as the normative and exemplar. Meanwhile, other groups are relegated to stigmatized positions. Although there is an increasing body of work in computer vision that seeks to directly correlate personal attributes with physiological traits (see, for instance, Agüera y Arcas et al. (2017) for a rebuttal to such work), we focus here on language.[1] We select language technology as our focus as language is co-constitutive with identity: how we express and construct our identity is inextricably linked with how we communicate (Di Paolo et al., 2018). Further, many of the issues that are readily apparent with computer vision technologies such as facial recognition and detection have an opaque mapping to language technologies. It is this mapping that we seek to expose through our use of language technology as our driving example. Moreover, language affords a lens through which phrenology has progressed beyond its visual expression to expression through optimization technologies such as ML that link social value with speech. However, the issue of phrenological patterns in ML extends beyond computer vision and language to the use of ML on social data.

From Whence We Came

Phrenology and physiognomy arose during the expansive colonial and empire-building projects of Western European nations (Belden-Adams, 2020; Challis, 2014). The express goal of phrenology was to create schemes of classification through which the myth of the (biological) superiority of the Western European white man could be maintained (Belden-Adams, 2020). The creation of racial hierarchies and the physicality of purported inferiority were necessary to this end. Distinguishing between populations relied on the notion of "the average man" proposed by Adolphe Quetelet (Sekula, 1986). By seeking the statistical average of demographic groups, phrenologists such as Francis Galton and Alphonse Bertillon sought to use demographic divergence as keys to access or explain "unwanted" behaviors and characteristics. In attempting to lighten the burden of understanding, phrenologists linked physiological features with undesirable characteristics such as criminality to demographics. For instance, Bertillon's criminal archive project sought to develop a system that would allow for the re-identification of criminals by classifying individuals based on their features' relationship to

---

[1]   The relationship between computer vision and physiognomy is particularly clear in (proposed) tasks such as criminality detection from facial images, where the governing distinction from 19th-century phrenologist work appears to be the use of optimization technologies.

the average. Although Galton used images in a similar fashion, he instead sought to dispel individual differences through composite photographs that were constructed from images of multiple individuals. Galton created and later overlaid the composite photograph by modulating the exposure that each image received as a fraction of the number of images comprising the composite photograph (Sekula, 1986). In this way, Galton sought to highlight the *average* intra-demographic features and the inter-demographic disagreements. Such agreements and disagreements were subsequently assigned to stereotypes about different demographic groups. By highlighting averages through composite photography, Galton specifically de-emphasized the intra-demographic patterns that would contradict the eugenicist positions that he held, i.e., the patterns that demonstrated inter-demographic agreement.

The Phrenology of Machine Learning

Although statistics has sought to distance itself from its phrenological pasts, we argue that ML for and on social and behavioral data constitutes a step toward such pasts by creating models that emphasize and de-emphasize similarities and differences between constructs in data. Thus, creating schemes that link demographic belonging to different classes. ML models are optimized by applying particular views over data. For instance, convolutional neural networks (CNNs), a common algorithm for computer vision (e.g., Voulodimos et al., 2018) and NLP (e.g., Gambäck & Sikdar, 2017), provide a clear comparison with Galton's composite image.[2] CNNs identify patterns from data by passing input data through a convolutional layer that uses a window to compute a feature mapping. The feature map is subsequently condensed using pooling functions. As the model is optimized, the feature mapping and the weights of the model are refined on the basis of disagreements between model predictions and the "ground truth" (Goodfellow et al., 2016).[3] In constructing convolutional layers as exposure of digital data, their similarities with Galton's composite imaging become readily apparent.

Although the similarities between phrenologists and contemporary ML methods are hazardous, these methods are not always a cause for concern. For instance, in applying ML methods to astronomical data, data aggregation methods, such as convolutional feature mapping may be appropriate. It is the application of ML methods to social and human data that raises concern and comes to resemble the methods of early phrenologists through constructing patterns in data as supposedly inherent attributes of objects or humans (Birhane & Guest, 2020; Spanton & Guest, 2022). For instance, identity attributes such as gender and race have been found to be recoverable in machine learning models and methods for language data without explicit signals of identity (e.g., Bolukbasi et al., 2016; Davidson et al., 2019).

In the case of classification, the weights and features of neural networks are optimized to minimize classification error (Talat, Blix, et al., 2022). Through the associations of features, weights, and classes, ML models create links between the classes and the social demographic features latent in the data. Often, the rationalization for ML is to lighten the burden of in-depth understanding in favor of shallowly casting attributes onto objects. For human data, the

---

[2]   We focus here on CNNs, but our argument extends to other ML algorithms that rely on the distributional hypothesis, by considering how a given model operates on data.

[3]   The idea of a single ground truth which objects can be compared relies on an illusion that an "objective," context-less, history-less, perspective-less conception of the world can be constructed and reflected in data (Gitelman, 2013; Raji et al., 2021, Talat, Lulz et al. 2021).

quest for linking attributes and data creates a deeply troubling likeness between phrenology and ML.

Much like the colonial hierarchical knowledge structures, in ML, a handful of elite, privileged, Western white men define and operationalize concepts such as "performance," decide what needs to be optimized, what "acceptable performance" is, and how technologies are embedded in society (Birhane et al., 2021). Like those of 19th-century phrenologists, these decisions are made such that they reflect the interests, objectives, and perspectives of their creators.

UNDERSTANDING DECOLONIALITY

European powers executed colonialism for centuries using various strategies across the globe. What is referred to as traditional colonialism, or the control of Indigenous resources, land, and people through physical and military coercion, largely ended for many nations decades ago. Yet, the remnants as well as its indirect influences – often termed coloniality – remain intact and permeate day-to-day life (Ndlovu-Gatsheni, 2012; Tamale, 2020).

The impacts of colonialism and coloniality have drastically altered the course of history for most non-Western societies and Indigenous populations, to the extent that it is challenging to conceptualize the histories of the colonized independent of colonization. Subsequently, there have been various movements toward *decolonizing* education (Barongo-Muweke, 2016; Battiste, 2013), legal systems (Currier, 2011; Kuwali, 2014, Oyěwùmí, 1997), languages (Ngũgĩ wa Thiong'o, 1986; Wa Thiong'o, 2018), technologies (Leslie, 2012; Raval, 2019), and so on. No *single* decolonial project exists, rather, decolonial efforts are marked by a multiplicity and plurality of objectives, aims, and focuses. In this chapter, we ground our approach to (de)coloniality primarily within the context of the *African continent*, informed by works from the continent. With 54 independent, heterogeneous, diverse, and dynamic nations, each with diverging cultures and values, the African continent is anything but homogeneous. For the purpose of this chapter, however, we focus on the similarities found in decolonial work across the continent. Thus, our perspective is informed by feminist and decolonial theories, practices, and experiences emerging from the African continent.

Colonialism has profoundly altered the African continent and its relationship with the rest of the world. It has impacted the way legal systems are structured, educational institutions are established, knowledge is constructed, and even the languages we speak. For example, the concept of race served as a tool that was used to legitimize colonialism by portraying the Western white man as the "human par excellence" while portraying Black and Indigenous populations as inferior and merely human (Saini, 2019).

An important tactic of colonialism is to *erase* the historical, cultural, and intellectual contributions of the entire continent in an effort to construct it as devoid of history. This has contributed to difficulties in identifying histories of the African continent that are independent of colonialism. Such erasure of the continent's history creates a vacuum that can be filled with Western narratives and ideologies about the continent and its people (Tamale, 2020). Acknowledging this, some decolonial efforts focus on *restoring* African heritage by exploring its rich culture and intellectual contributions. Such efforts highlight and expose these intentionally erased contributions and render a more truthful narrative and image of the continent. This might include projects that, for example, restore languages that have come close to extinction.

The erasure of Indigenous knowledge systems, which are replaced by Western perspectives, has a far more insidious consequence: the *colonization of the mind* (Fanon, 1986). The colonization of the mind refers to the process of erasing and replacing Indigenous knowledge systems with Western structures and norms such that Western knowledge systems are perceived as "natural," even by those who were colonized. Recognizing the potency of this process, Biko emphasized that, "the most powerful weapon in the hands of the oppressor is the mind of the oppressed" (Biko, 2013). Colonization of the mind is a gradual and inconspicuous process, that relies on Indigenous communities embodying the colonizer's version of African history.

Breaking free from colonization of the mind requires understanding this history, peeling underneath the white man's version of our history, recovering our own history, and perceiving this recovered history as "natural." In short, this means replacing the whitewashed history of Africa with accurate historical records. Decolonizing the mind, therefore, requires reviving Indigenous histories and knowledge systems and raising critical consciousness to undo the internalized conceptions, categories, and knowledge systems in order to counter racist hegemonies (Biko, 2013; Fanon, 1986; Freire, 2018). This is no small challenge as the white man's knowledge system permeates everything from our classifications of gender and sexuality to our understanding of race, to how legal institutions and education systems operate. An in-depth *understanding*, therefore, is the first and foremost requirement, rather than prediction, classification, clustering, or abstraction.

We cannot escape the colonial mentality as long as the theories, concepts, and questions that inform our research, study, and practice are generated from Western experiences and tradition. Currently, coloniality pervades our day-to-day life. It provides the foundation for social, cultural, institutional, and scientific endeavors. We witness coloniality through the normalization and internalization of arbitrarily constructed conceptions and racial categories. Subsequently, the very objectives of AI, its methodologies, and cultural ecology – and therefore its conceptions of classification and categorization – are inherently colonialist.

Furthermore, the colonialist project is built on individualistic, "rational," and positivist science that stems from the Enlightenment's obsession to sort, classify, and categorize in a hierarchical and dualistic manner (Tamale, 2020). In contrast, decolonizing research compromises methods that value, reclaim, and foreground Indigenous voices and ways of knowing. That is, relational, contextual, and historical approaches; specifically, the African philosophy of Ubuntu (Birhane, 2021; Mhlambi, 2020), which seeks to decenter Western hegemonic knowledge systems and ideologies.

MACHINE LEARNING AND ABSTRACTION

Modern ML is a field that develops in the statistical sciences with the aim of uncovering patterns from data through optimization processes (Bishop, 2006). ML and statistics share the assumption that meaning can be made of complex human behavior and experiences through processes of simplification and abstraction in data that is "frozen in time" (Talat, Lulz, et al., 2021). ML distinguishes itself from statistics in its preoccupation with predictions. Where statistics has, to a large degree, moved on from seeking to predict *future* behavior from past data,[4] ML is concerned with predicting the future from the past. We can therefore understand

---

[4] While statistics is still used to forecast future events, for example, election results, the emphasis lies within explaining why a specific trend appears to be salient and uncertainty is at the forefront of communication.

ML as a discipline that overarchingly focuses on *future-making* based on salience, that is, hegemony, in past data (Talat, Lulz, et al., 2021). Further, ML often assumes that data and models exist outside of context, i.e., that seizing data from the world wide web – language data, for example – and processing it using ML affords models that are devoid of the many contexts from which data and models are wrought. Here we examine how ML abstracts from contextual, dynamic, contested, and unjust pasts to devise hegemonic futures.

Tools of Abstraction

Common ML paradigms include supervised (e.g., classification), unsupervised (e.g., clustering), and reinforcement learning (RL, e.g., game-playing). These paradigms assume that meaning can be made through abstraction. For instance, when DeepMind developed an RL system to play Go, named AlphaGo, the system optimized the decision-making process for selecting which move to play (Silver et al., 2017). AlphaGo was optimized for patterns that would lead to victory by playing thousands of games against "itself," and ultimately beat several of the world's best players. In comparison with human behavior, Go is a relatively simple game that can be captured with large volumes of data. For instance, while the game of Go is played according to the same rules across the globe, the norms of interaction vary greatly for human behavior and expectations.[5] Norms, practices, and cultures from one society do not necessarily map onto another (Talat et al., 2022). Thus, while the game of Go lends itself to pattern recognition, cultural practices are deeply contextual. For example, Geertz (1973, p. 6) details the distinction between a wink and an involuntary twitch:

> [T]he difference, however unphotographable, between a twitch and a wink is vast; as anyone unfortunate enough to have had the first taken for the second knows. The winker is communicating, and indeed communicating in a quite precise and special way.

While there exists no photographic distinction between a wink and a twitch, detailed and in-depth queries make it clear that the two are distinct. Only by attending to the details of the phenomena can we obtain the in-depth understanding required to distinguish the two.

Language is another realm that does not readily lend itself to abstraction. Despite impressive advances in classification and text generation, NLP models still fundamentally fail to understand text (Bender & Koller, 2020). This discrepancy between performance and understanding is a result of the distributional hypothesis that models rely on. Under this hypothesis, meaning can be made from (sub-)words by observing the frequencies of their (co-)occurrence (Harris, 1954). That is, by enumerating word interaction patterns to create vector spaces, NLP technologies can supposedly understand the meanings of words. Famously, this has afforded the recognition that "king" and "queen" often occur in similar contexts (Pennington et al., 2014).[6] However, even within this success, NLP technologies fail to attune to crucial details, namely the gendered power imbalances. This has resulted in a host of methods to "de-bias" these through an abstractive view of social marginalization (Bolukbasi et al., 2016; Zhao et al., 2017).[7] Rather than seeking to understand which processes give rise

---

[5]   We note that there exist 5 different scoring systems for Go.

[6]   "Context." Word embeddings refer to a sliding window within a sentence, rather than a wider context.

[7]   Within NLP, which biases are addressed remain heavily skewed toward gender bias at the expense of other directions such as racialized biases (Field et al., 2021).

to discriminatory outcomes, the field has primarily attended to devising abstractive methods that treat concrete harms as abstract subjects, framing harms as "bias" (Blodgett et al., 2020). This framing, in a sense, minimizes the "unpleasantness" and constructs the topic as one that can be studied abstractly from afar. Under this construction, ML models can only be biased, and therefore be de-biased, by abstracting away from individual instances of discrimination, in favor of considering the discrepancies through collective metrics for fairness. Moreover, only harms wrought directly by the system itself are considered, any external discrimination, for example, over-policing, is not considered relevant for determining whether a system is biased and therefore an eligible candidate for "de-biasing." Thus, when vector spaces tie the nursing profession more strongly to women than other genders, the dispute is neither economic nor social marginalization, nor that a gender-less profession is more strongly tied to one gender. The dispute arises from the hyper-fixation of the abstraction of several words being more closely associated with one gender than others. The dispute, then, disregards the socio-economic systems that give rise to the association and instead attends to the abstract expression of marginalization. Addressing the dispute, therefore, fixates on the abstraction of marginalization, rather than the source or direct expression. Thus, although ML models come to reproduce factors of identity and marginalization, they do not fully capture these issues. That is, machine learning models capture proxies of identity, rather than features of identity itself. Crucially, even after "de-biasing" vector spaces, the biases they were treated for can still be reconstructed in the vector space (Gonen & Goldberg, 2019).

Social Infrastructures of Machine Learning

Beyond the ML tools that seek to abstract or generalize, the infrastructures within which ML operates create the foundations upon which ML models function. A handful of for-profit companies, that serve financial rather than scientific purposes, provide sponsorship for conferences and direct funding for research. This grants them access to researchers and allows them to influence the direction of public research. As a result, these corporations hold an outsized influence on the research conducted through direct means (i.e., dual positions and research internships) and indirect means (i.e., through priority setting and research funding) (Abdalla & Abdalla, 2021; Ahmed & Wahed, 2020; Birhane et al., 2021). Although many such companies claim altruistic purposes, their primary interest is to profit, rather than provide utility. The astronomical profits of these companies require a deep commitment to the continued oppression of marginalized communities. For instance, there would be no Alphabet, at the scale that we see today, without the continued abuses of post-colonial subjects, for example, in the physical mining of resources. Moreover, as Meta, Palantir, and Cambridge Analytica have shown, the people that were colonized continue to face exploitation for labor by Western companies and are externalized for territorial expansion or technological exploitation (Perrigo, 2022).

When ML initiatives arise by and for colonial subjects, they are quickly approached by large technology companies in attempts to co-opt their resources. One may hope that the development of high-quality technologies for underserved languages or communities, for example, Amharic or Amhara people, would provide benefits for the population. However, the benefits for a community must be weighed against the additional marginalization that technology affords. Take for example Google's freely available translation system. On one hand, having access to a high-quality translation system could afford greater ease of communication, which may be in some cases critical, for example, for refugees fleeing war.[8] On the other hand, such systems afford an easy way to increase the surveillance of speakers of languages that are largely disregarded by research efforts. The interests of corporate entities such as Google would then be financial, for example, by providing targeted advertisements, rather than humanitarian. While providing communities with relevant advertisements may seem benign, targeted advertisements come with high costs, for example, privacy (Ullah et al., 2021) and the risk of destabilizing democracies (Dubois et al., 2022). Thus, rather than providing a benefit to marginalized communities, the corporate (use of) ML tools and resources would result in significant risks and exploitation of such groups by capitalist and colonial interests.

MACHINE LEARNING AND DECOLONIALITY: AN INHERENT TENSION?

In our account of characteristics of decoloniality and ML, it becomes apparent that the two schools of thought stand on opposite sides of the spectrum in their aims, objectives, methodologies, interests, motivations, and practices. Due to the substantial influence of Western individualistic thinking, ML reflects Western principles such as the emphasis on "objectivity," rationality, and individuality, which tend to approach subjects of study (including human behavior and society) as ideas devoid of context and history. Furthermore, ML can be used to advance neo-colonial and pseudo-scientific ideologies through its reliance on methodologies that are similar to those used by 19th-century phrenologists.

Through narratives and dichotomies such as "near vs far," "us and others," and "West vs East," colonial powers justified dehumanizing Indigenous populations (Willinsky, 1998). Conceptualizations of the colonized as the "other" from "afar" have enabled the colonizers to treat Indigenous communities, their cultures, and languages as abstract "subjects" that can be studied, manipulated, controlled, and molded at will. Similarly, through abstraction, ML treats human beings (and their feelings, desires, wishes, and hopes) as abstract data points. By dealing with "data," people become distant statistics.

At its core, ML aims to detect patterns across large datasets. This requires abstracting away from the details, idiosyncrasies, and particularities of individual situations. This is often motivated by capitalist wealth extraction, which operates under the Western values of individualism and white supremacy. The core values of decolonizing, conversely, include correcting historical records (that have been intentionally erased and manipulated), illuminating Indigenous knowledge systems (e.g., grounded in Ubuntu philosophy, which is fundamentally relational at its core), and raising critical consciousness against internalized coloniality. Most importantly, decolonizing is about undoing past harm and injustice and mapping alternative just futures.

In contrast to decoloniality, ML is a field that is noted for its lack of critical awareness where it "produces thoughtlessness, the inability to critique instructions, the lack of reflection on consequences, and a commitment to the belief that a correct ordering is being carried out" (McQuillan, 2019). Currently, much of current ML is embedded in institutions and

---

[8]   Prior audits have found that biases exist in the ways in which the system makes translations (Hovy et al., 2020).

organizations with oppressive histories. ML, in turn, has endowed such institutions and organizations with a seemingly scientific justification for colonialism and white supremacy. Due to a lack of reflexivity and critical examination of the past, current ML research and practice functions as a tool that extends such unjust histories.

Conditions for Decolonial AI

Lewontin (2003) notes the difference between defeatism and skepticism: defeatism leads to passivity and skepticism to action. Similarly, we contend that imagining a decolonial future – difficult and challenging as it may seem – is a necessary step towards making such future a reality, despite the apparent incompatibility between decoloniality and ML. With this in mind, we list the core conditions that need to be present for a decolonial ML to materialize. This list is by no means exhaustive but instead can serve as a starting point.

A necessary step toward this future is that AI systems must serve the needs of Indigenous peoples, in a manner that is informed by and grounded in Indigenous epistemologies, experiences, and needs. Therefore, such systems must be built, controlled, and owned by Indigenous peoples, and the primary beneficiaries must be people. Profit or capital interest must be a secondary concern.

The idea of a general(izable) AI is both vacuous and serves the interests and needs of the status quo. Decolonial AI systems must therefore aim to serve a small group of people, rather than "all of humanity," who do not require context to be provided by the machine. ML, at its core, is a process that abstracts away, obfuscates, and standardizes. Therefore, people must be able to read the details themselves, which is only possible when the abstractions of the machine are tasks that can be performed by humans but are more efficiently performed by the machine (i.e., the machine can save human time spent). Additionally, procedures for the right to contest ML models, processes, underlying assumptions, outputs, and training regimes must be put into place. In extension, the objectives of a decolonial AI or ML system must challenge racist, colonialist, white-supremacist, patriarchal, and other unjust and marginalizing ideologies.

It is also important that the system is divorced from ideas of eugenics, phrenology, and similar racist and white-supremacist ideologies. Many of the ML applications that are being integrated into the social sphere – whether in aiding decision-making in housing or social welfare benefits – serve the purpose of excluding or filtering out (those who are deemed undeserving of housing or welfare benefits), which is inherently punitive. In contrast, decolonial AI should be constructive, restorative, and built on communal values that contribute to the current and future prosperity of marginalized communities.

DECOLONIAL FUTURES

We close this chapter by highlighting the Te Hiku NLP project as an example of decolonial AI. Various factors make the Māori community data collection, management, and technology development practices stand out. For the Te Hiku NLP project, entire communities of Te Reo Māori speakers in Aotearoa, or New Zealand, were mobilized in participatory efforts to develop AI systems to revitalize their rapidly disappearing language. The Māori community holds full control of the project. From the very conception, every step of the developmental pipeline has been based on Māori principles and taken in concordance with Māori values, emphasizing benefits to the community. Their use of AI is driven by the need for language revitalization efforts and to obtain equal rights for *Te Reo Māori*. Unlike much of the current "the bigger, the better" mantra behind language models, the Te Hiku NLP project is driven by small communities and relatively small data sizes.

The Te Hiku NLP project collected 310 hours of speech-text pairs from 200,000 recordings made by 2,500 people over the course of ten days. The data came from speakers of Te Reo Māori throughout New Zealand and was annotated and cleaned by members of the Māori community. The data was then used to develop a speech recognition model which performs with 86% accuracy. The main drive to build such technology came from the push to preserve Māori culture and language. During the British colonial exploitation, the speakers of *Te Reo Māori* were prevented from speaking their language through shaming and physical beatings of Māori students (Auckland University Libraries and Learning Services, 2017). The motivation to reclaim *Te Reo Māori* and the rich culture that surrounds it led to the development of computational linguistic tools. As a way of digitizing the language and culture, elders were recorded, and the material was kept in digital archives for younger generations to access and learn from. Te Hiku built a digital hosting platform to maintain full control of their data and avoid influence from large technology corporations. The community subsequently established the Māori Data Sovereignty Protocols (Kukutai & Cormack, 2021; Raine et al., 2019) as a way for the Māori to hold full autonomy and control of their data, technology, and therefore, future. This has been described as a sign of "Indigenous resistance—against colonizers, against the nation-state, and now against big tech companies" (Coffey, 2021). This effort thus highlights a path for decolonial AI. Rather than aiming to develop a tool for the general public, Te Hiku sought to create a tool for language revitalization of the *Te Reo Māori* language. By resisting scaling and the co-option from large technology companies while centering the benefit for the Māori communities, the Te Hiku project maintains the ability to use an abstractive technology within a decolonial context and provides a vision for the shape of future decolonial AI projects.

CONCLUSION

The rise of machine learning has elicited critical questions around the fundamentally oppressive nature of the technology, at least within the minor corners of ethical AI, leading to the question of whether a truly decolonial machine learning is possible. As we illustrate throughout this chapter, machine learning stands in stark contrast to decoloniality. Machine learning reproduces colonial logics in the process of its search for abstraction, simplification, clustering, and prediction. At the core of decoloniality, on the other hand, is decentering Western hegemony, restoring erased histories, and uplifting and showcasing historical and current intellectual contributions, driven by justice and equity. This work is performed through in-depth understanding rather than abstraction or simplification. However, despite the opposing logics, assumptions, and objectives, Te Hiku's *Te Reo Māori* language project illustrates that there is space for the development of machine learning systems that decolonize.

REFERENCES

Abdalla, M., & Abdalla, M. (2021). The Grey Hoodie Project: Big Tobacco, Big Tech, and the Threat on Academic Integrity. *Proceedings of the 2021 AAAI/ACM Conference on AI, Ethics, and Society*, 287–297. https://doi.org/10.1145/3461702.3462563

Abdilla, A., Arista, N., Baker, K., Benesiinaabandan, S., Brown, M., Cheung, M., Coleman, M., Cordes, A., Davison, J., Duncan, K., Garzon, S., Harrell, D. F., Jones, P.-L., Kealiikanakaoleohaililani, K., Kelleher, M., Kite, S., Lagon, O., Leigh, J., Levesque, M., … Whaanga, H. (2020). *Indigenous Protocol and Artificial Intelligence Position Paper*. https://doi.org/10.11573/SPECTRUM.LIBRARY .CONCORDIA.CA.00986506

Adams, R. (2021). Can Artificial Intelligence be Decolonized? *Interdisciplinary Science Reviews*, *46*(1–2), 176–197. https://doi.org/10.1080/03080188.2020.1840225

Agüera y Arcas, B., Mitchell, M., & Todorov, A. (2017, May 20). Physiognomy's New Clothes. *Medium*. https://medium.com/@blaisea/physiognomys-new-clothes-f2d4b59fdd6a

Ahmed, N., & Wahed, M. (2020). *The De-democratization of AI: Deep Learning and the Compute Divide in Artificial Intelligence Research* (arXiv:2010.15581). arXiv. http://arxiv.org/abs/2010. 15581

Alexander, D. (2020). Decolonizing Digital Spaces. In E. Dubois & F. Martin-Bariteau (Eds.), *Citizenship in a Connected Canada: A Research and Policy Agenda*. University of Ottawa Press.

Auckland University Libraries and Learning Services. (2017, October 6). *Ngā Kura Māori: The Native Schools System 1867–1969*. https://www.news.library.auckland.ac.nz/2017/10/06/native-schools/# .Yi_ULBDMJH0

Barongo-Muweke, N. (2016). *Decolonizing Education: Towards Reconstructing a Theory of Citizenship Education for Postcolonial Africa*. Springer Berlin Heidelberg.

Battiste, M. (2013). *Decolonizing Education: Nourishing the Learning Spirit*. Purich Publishing Limited.

Belden-Adams, K. (2020). *Eugenics, "Aristogenics," Photography: Picturing Privilege* (1st ed.). Bloomsbury Visual Arts.

Bender, E. M., & Koller, A. (2020). Climbing Towards NLU: On Meaning, Form, and Understanding in the Age of Data. *Proceedings of the 58th Annual Meeting of the Association for Computational Linguistics*, 5185–5198. https://doi.org/10.18653/v1/2020.acl-main.463

Biko, S. (2013). White Racism and Black Consciousness. In C. Crais & T. V. McClendon (Eds.), *The South Africa Reader* (pp. 361–370). Duke University Press. https://doi.org/10.1215/9780822377450 -064

Birhane, A. (2021). Algorithmic Injustice: A Relational Ethics Approach. *Patterns*, *2*(2), 100205. https:// doi.org/10.1016/j.patter.2021.100205

Birhane, A., & Guest, O. (2020). *Towards Decolonising Computational Sciences* (arXiv:2009.14258). arXiv. http://arxiv.org/abs/2009.14258

Birhane, A., Kalluri, P., Card, D., Agnew, W., Dotan, R., & Bao, M. (2021). The Values Encoded in Machine Learning Research. https://dl.acm.org/doi/fullHtml/10.1145/3531146.3533083.

Bishop, C. M. (2006). *Pattern Recognition and Machine Learning*. Springer.

Blodgett, S. L., Barocas, S., Daumé III, H., & Wallach, H. (2020). Language (Technology) is Power: A Critical Survey of "Bias" in NLP. *Proceedings of the 58th Annual Meeting of the Association for Computational Linguistics*, 5454–5476. https://doi.org/10.18653/v1/2020.acl-main.485

Bolukbasi, T., Chang, K.-W., Zou, J. Y., Saligrama, V., & Kalai, A. T. (2016). Man is to Computer Programmer as Woman is to Homemaker? Debiasing Word Embeddings. In D. Lee, M. Sugiyama, U. Luxburg, I. Guyon, & R. Garnett (Eds.), *Advances in Neural Information Processing Systems* (Vol. 29). Curran Associates, Inc. https://proceedings.neurips.cc/paper/2016/file/a486cd07e4ac3d2 70571622f4f316ec5-Paper.pdf

Byrne, D. (2022). Science in Africa: Is 'Decolonization' Losing All Meaning? *Nature Africa*, d44148- 022-00064–1. https://doi.org/10.1038/d44148-022-00064-1

Challis, D. (2014). *The Archaeology of Race: The Eugenic Ideas of Francis Galton and Flinders Petrie* (Paperback edition). Bloomsbury.

Coffey, D. (2021). Māori Are Trying to Save Their Language from Big Tech. *Wired UK*. https://www .wired.co.uk/article/maori-language-tech

Currier, A. (2011). Decolonizing the Law: LGBT Organizing in Namibia and South Africa. In A. Sarat (Ed.), *Special Issue, Social Movements/Legal Possibilities*. Emerald.

Davidson, T., Bhattacharaya, D., & Weber, I. (2019). Racial Bias in Hate Speech and Abusive Language Detection Datasets. *Proceedings of the Third Workshop on Abusive Language Online*, 25–35. https://doi.org/10.18653/v1/W19-3504

Di Paolo, E. A., Cuffari, E. C., & De Jaegher, H. (2018). *Linguistic Bodies: The Continuity Between Life and Language*. The MIT Press.

Dubois, P. R., Arteau-Leclerc, C., & Giasson, T. (2022). Micro-Targeting, Social Media, and Third Party Advertising: Why the Facebook Ad Library Cannot Prevent Threats to Canadian Democracy. In H. A. Garnett & M. Pal (Eds.), *Cyber-threats to Canadian Democracy*, 236–269, McGill-Queen University Press.

Fanon, F. (1986). *Black Skin, White Masks* (Repr.). Pluto Press.

Field A., Blodgett, S. L., Waseem, Z., & Tsvetkov, Y. (2021). A Survey of Race, Racism, and Anti-Racism in NLP. *Proceedings of the 59th Annual Meeting of the Association for Computational Linguistics and the 11th International Joint Conference on Natural Language Processing* (Volume 1: Long Papers), 1905–1925, Association for Computational Linguistics.

Freire, P. (2018). *Pedagogy of the Oppressed* (M. B. Ramos, Trans.; 50th anniversary edition). Bloomsbury Academic.

Gambäck, B., & Sikdar, U. K. (2017). Using Convolutional Neural Networks to Classify Hate-Speech. *Proceedings of the First Workshop on Abusive Language Online*, 85–90. https://doi.org/10.18653/v1/W17-3013

Geertz, C. (1973). *The Interpretation of Cultures*. Basic Books.

Gitelman, L. (Ed.). (2013). *"Raw Data" is an Oxymoron*. The MIT Press.

Gonen, H., & Goldberg, Y. (2019). Lipstick on a Pig: Debiasing Methods Cover up Systematic Gender Biases in Word Embeddings But Do not Remove Them. *Proceedings of the 2019 Conference of the North*, 609–614. https://doi.org/10.18653/v1/N19-1061

Goodfellow, I., Bengio, Y., & Courville, A. (2016). *Deep Learning*. MIT Press.

Harris, Z.S. (1954) Distributional Structure, *WORD*, 10:2-3, 146-162, DOI: 10.1080/00437956.1954.11659520.

Hovy, D., Bianchi, F., & Fornaciari, T. (2020). "You Sound Just Like Your Father" Commercial Machine Translation Systems Include Stylistic Biases. *Proceedings of the 58th Annual Meeting of the Association for Computational Linguistics*, 1686–1690, Association for Computational Linguistics.

Iseke-Barnes, J. M. (2008). Pedagogies for Decolonizing. *Canadian Journal of Native Education*, *31*(1), 123–148.

Kukutai, T., & Cormack, D. (2021). "Pushing the Space": Data Sovereignty and Self-Determination in Aotearoa NZ. In M. Walter (Ed.), *Indigenous Data Sovereignty and Policy*. Routledge.

Kuwali, D. (2014). Decoding Afrocentrism: Decolonizing Legal Theory. In O. Onazi (Ed.), *African Legal Theory and Contemporary Problems* (Vol. 29, pp. 71–92). Springer Netherlands. https://doi.org/10.1007/978-94-007-7537-4_4

Leslie, C. (2012). Decolonizing the Internet. *Global Media and Communication*, *8*(1), 81–88. https://doi.org/10.1177/1742766512439806

Lewontin, R. (2003). *Biology as Ideology: The Doctrine of DNA*. Anansi.

McQuillan, D. (2019). Non-fascist AI. In M. Hlavajova & W. Maas (Eds.), *Propositions for Non-fascist Living: Tentative and Urgent*. BAK, basis voor actuele kunst; The MIT Press.

Mhlambi, S. (2020). *From Rationality to Relationality: Ubuntu as an Ethical and Human Rights Framework for Artificial Intelligence Governance*. Carr Center Discussion Paper Series, 2020-009.

Ndlovu-Gatsheni, S. J. (2012). Coloniality of Power in Development Studies and the Impact of Global Imperial Designs on Africa. *The Australasian Review of African Studies*, *33*(2), 48–73.

Ngũgĩ wa Thiong'o. (1986). *Decolonising the Mind: The Politics of Language in African Literature*. J. Currey; Heinemann.

Oyěwùmí, O. (1997). *The Invention of Women: Making an African Sense of Western Gender Discourses*. University of Minnesota Press.

Pennington, J., Socher, R., & Manning, C. (2014). Glove: Global Vectors for Word Representation. *Proceedings of the 2014 Conference on Empirical Methods in Natural Language Processing (EMNLP)*, 1532–1543. https://doi.org/10.3115/v1/D14-1162

Perrigo, B. (2022, May 11). *Meta Accused of Human Trafficking and Union-Busting in Kenya*. Time. https://time.com/6175026/facebook-sama-kenya-lawsuit/

Raine, S. C., Kukutai, T., Walter, M., Figueroa-Rodríguez, O.-L., Walker, J., & Axelsson, P. (2019). Indigenous Data Sovereignty. In T. Davies, S. B. Walker, M. Rubinstein, & F. Perini (Eds.), *The State of Open Data*. African Minds, IDRC. https://www.doabooks.org/doab?func=fulltext&uiLanguage=en&rid=34137

Raji, I. D., Bender, E. M., Paullada, A., Denton, E., & Hanna, A. (2021). AI and the Everything in the Whole Wide World Benchmark. ArXiv:2111.15366 [Cs]. http://arxiv.org/abs/2111.15366

Raval, N. (2019). An Agenda for Decolonizing Data Science – Spheres. *Spheres: Journal for Digital Cultures, 5*, 1–6.

Saini, A. (2019). *Superior: The Return of Race Science*. Beacon Press.

Sekula, A. (1986). The Body and the Archive. *October, 39*, 3. https://doi.org/10.2307/778312

Silver, D., Schrittwieser, J., Simonyan, K., Antonoglou, I., Huang, A., Guez, A., Hubert, T., Baker, L., Lai, M., Bolton, A., Chen, Y., Lillicrap, T., Hui, F., Sifre, L., van den Driessche, G., Graepel, T., & Hassabis, D. (2017). Mastering the Game of Go Without Human Knowledge. *Nature, 550*(7676), 354–359. https://doi.org/10.1038/nature24270

Spanton, R. W., & Guest, O. (2022). Measuring Trustworthiness or Automating Physiognomy? A Comment on Safra, Chevallier, Grézes, and Baumard (2020). ArXiv:2202.08674 [Cs]. http://arxiv.org/abs/2202.08674

Talat, Z., Blix, H., Valvoda, J., Ganesh, M. I., Cotterell, R., & Williams, A. (2021). A Word on Machine Ethics: A Response to Jiang et al. (2021). ArXiv:2111.04158 [Cs]. http://arxiv.org/abs/2111.04158

Talat, Z., Lulz, S., Bingel, J., & Augenstein, I. (2021). *Disembodied Machine Learning: On the Illusion of Objectivity in NLP*. http://arxiv.org/abs/2101.11974

Talat, Z., Névéol, A., Biderman, S., Clinciu, M., Dey, M., Longpre, S., Luccioni, S., Masoud, M., Mitchell, M., Radev, D., Sharma, S., Subramonian, A., Tae, J., Tan, S., Tunuguntla, D., & Van Der Wal, O. (2022). You Reap What You Sow: On the Challenges of Bias Evaluation Under Multilingual Settings. *Proceedings of BigScience Episode #5 – Workshop on Challenges & Perspectives in Creating Large Language Models*, 26–41. https://aclanthology.org/2022.bigscience-1.3

Tamale, S. (2020). *Decolonization and Afro-feminism*. Daraja Press.

Ullah, I., Boreli, R., & Kanhere, S. S. (2021). *Privacy in Targeted Advertising: A Survey* (arXiv:2009.06861). arXiv. http://arxiv.org/abs/2009.06861

Voulodimos, A., Doulamis, N., Doulamis, A., & Protopapadakis, E. (2018). Deep Learning for Computer Vision: A Brief Review. *Computational Intelligence and Neuroscience, 2018*, 1–13. https://doi.org/10.1155/2018/7068349

Wa Thiong'o, N. (2018). On the Abolition of the English Department. *Présence Africaine, N°197*(1), 103. https://doi.org/10.3917/presa.197.0103

Willinsky, J. (1998). *Learning to Divide the World: Education at Empire's End*. University of Minnesota Press.

Zhao, J., Wang, T., Yatskar, M., Ordonez, V., & Chang, K.-W. (2017). Men Also Like Shopping: Reducing Gender Bias Amplification Using Corpus-Level Constraints. *Proceedings of the 2017 Conference on Empirical Methods in Natural Language Processing*, 2979–2989. https://doi.org/10.18653/v1/D17-1323

12. Pragmatism and AI: a critical approach
Johnathan Flowers

INTRODUCTION

This chapter will explore the consequences of datafication and algorithmic platforms through the work of American pragmatist John Dewey. To do so, this chapter will briefly explore Dewey's theory of culture and experience as connected with the development of technology to set the ground to understand algorithmic platforms as continuous with society. The chapter will then proceed to reframe technology in the mode of a cultural project and indicate the ways in which what Dewey calls the pecuniary aims of finance capitalism and industry serve to structure the social aims to which algorithmic platforms are put. In doing so, this section will further indicate the inability to divorce algorithmic platforms and technologies from the cultures that produce them.

This approach renders algorithmic platforms inextricably tied to the social contexts and cultures which give rise to them. For example, in this view, racial, gendered, and ableist bias is not an unintended outcome of the algorithm which can be attributed to errors in code or incomplete datasets; rather, biases produced by the algorithmic platforms demonstrate the continuity of the platform with the culture that produced it. As continuous with culture, and not apart from it, this chapter makes clear that the facts which are produced by algorithms, and the algorithms themselves, are neither objective nor separate from the culture that produced them.

To demonstrate the above, this chapter will conclude by exploring the phenomena of datafication through John Dewey's distinction between physical facts and social facts to make clear that the data those algorithmic platforms rely upon, and produce, are not physical facts independent of human aims and purposes, but social facts that owe their existence to human aims and purposes. In doing so, this chapter aims to further contribute to the growing body of pragmatist approaches to science and technology.

CULTURE

For Dewey (LW12:27), culture is not only the variety of ways that humans come together in mutual association but also the means whereby the environment is reorganized to enable the human organism to come to be. Used here, environment refers not simply to the physical surroundings: it indicates the ways that humans are continuous with those surroundings through their activities (LW9:15). Further, the environment exceeds the physical to include the cultural and the social, which supply specific patterns of behaviour that enable the transformation of the environment into a culture through the ways they direct the transactions of the human organism. These patterns of behaviour, what Dewey refers to as custom on the cultural level, and habit on the individual level, also enable the human organism to be recognized as a person and as a member of a culture through how they direct the transactions of the human organism in association with others. Customs are also the means whereby culture is perpetuated: as the human organism is transformed into a person through adopting the customs of their culture, the culture itself is conserved and passed on (LW13: 76–7). Thus, for Dewey, the question of how specific individuals come to be, much less algorithmic technologies, is a question of how the elements of culture transact with the "raw material" of the human organism within the conditions organized by culture to produce specific kinds of individuals recognized as members of a culture.

The foregoing should not be read as a dichotomy between nature and culture as, for Dewey, the two are in transaction with one another. Transaction, for Dewey, is a process of co-creation that involves the transformation of both the organism and the environment. An organism survives and grows by reaching out to its environment to secure resources or satisfy a lack that represents a loss of equilibrium with the environment. In doing so, the organism modifies the environment to satisfy its needs by its own effort; or, in its reaching out, it happens upon something that satisfies its needs (LW10:19). In either case, the organism engages in a back-and-forth movement between equilibrium and disequilibrium, stability and precarity, such that the organism itself is a dynamic structure co-constituted by the environment. Thus, the organism is neither totally identical to its environment nor is it separate – it is in transaction. Culture is the name that Dewey gives to the collection of human activities that enable specific ways of transacting with the environment. Insofar as culture is continuous with nature, Dewey does not admit a distinction between the two.

As an example, thirst is a lack that causes an organism to reach out to the environment for satisfaction. However, how humans reach out to the environment is through the customs of the culture as informed by the environment it forms in (LW12:127). A culture that emerges in a desert environment might develop sophisticated means of locating and acquiring water. They might develop technologies and tools to aid in this task, and these tools might come to take on a specific meaning within the culture through how they enable the continued survival of the humans that developed them. Said tools might lead to occupations of locating water being placed in high esteem. In contrast, a culture that emerges in a forest environment where fresh water is abundant might not develop specific tools and rituals for acquiring water; instead, they may develop sophisticated means of hunting and trapping game. The tools and implements, and the occupations they support, may take on a position of prestige within the culture for how they enable the continued survival of the group. They may develop robust practices of tracking animals and the culture itself might be organized around following the migrations of said animals. Further, they may develop means of defending themselves against predators and wildlife that a desert population would not (Lw2:263). Despite different environments demanding different ways of transacting, which result in different kinds of political and social structures, different occupations, and, most importantly, different forms of technologies, in each case, the cultural and the technological are continuous with the natural.

Technology, while continuous with nature, belongs to what Dewey calls the "material aspect" of culture (LW1:363). The material aspect of culture not only includes tools and technology, but it also includes "habitations, temples and their rituals, weapons, paraphernalia, tools, implements, means of transportation, roads, clothing, decorations and ornamentations" (LW1:363), as well as the "technical processes" required to use them. In modernity, telecommunications networks, algorithmic platforms, and the processes of datafication that have come to dominate modern life would also constitute the material aspect of culture, as would the technical processes of computer science, for example, involved in their use. Dewey's inclusion of religious temples and their rituals is important as technology and the other cultural products that make up the material aspect of culture are also modes of communication. They "say" something about the culture that produced them and communicate to members of the culture how they are to transact with the environment and each other.

This point is crucial as "Language in its widest sense-that is, including all means of communication such as, for example, monuments, rituals, and formalized arts-is the medium in which culture exists and through which it is transmitted" (LW12:62). Insofar as technology, including computing and algorithmic technologies and the technical practices that create them, what Dewey refers to as "formalized arts" in the above, is a mode of communication, they also serve to communicate the aims, ends, and ways of experiencing developed by a given culture. For Dewey, this communication is accomplished through the ways they coordinate human experience to enable the joint action of culture and through how they structure the conditions of human experience in favour of some consequences and not others (LW1:157). As an example, Dewey argues that the tools and technology developed by a culture determine the kind of occupations within the culture; these occupations subsequently determine the consequences of associated action within the culture (LW2:263). For Dewey, an occupation is a pursuit that enabled an individual to discover their capacities by means of an environment that developed them through transaction. As such, they provide direction for future transactions with culture such that they become means of self-discovery. Further, as an occupation supplies a collection of habits, a way of transacting with the world, it also supplies new ways of knowing the world through those habits. Technology, therefore, is a means of regulating not only the shape of culture but the shape of individuals through how technology enables the organization of the world.

Despite his primary examples being limited to the technologies and sciences of the 1930s, Dewey anticipated the algorithmic technologies of our modern era. To this end, "An invention may thus result from purely mathematical calculations. Nevertheless, the machine is still a machine, an instrumental device for regulating interactions with reference to consequences" (LW1:157). Which interactions are regulated and for what consequences are not determined by the machines themselves: they are determined through the transaction of the machines with what Dewey calls the "ideal elements" of culture, or the moral, political, aesthetic, religious, and even scientific belief structures that guide conduct in a robust sense. More generally, the ideal elements of culture include the body of intellectual knowledge, the legal and religious systems, and modes of political and social organization that direct and determine the appropriate uses of the material aspects of culture, including algorithmic platforms (LW1:363). Thus, while the material elements may include how to use technology and how to develop technology, the ideal elements determine why technology should be used and for what purpose. It is in the interaction between the ideal and material elements of culture that the material elements of culture come to communicate the ideal elements of the culture through how they regulate interactions for what purposes.

For Dewey, algorithmic platforms, the computational sciences that produce them, and the infrastructure that supports them are not independent of the culture that produced them: it is in transaction with that culture and the ideal elements that guide the use cases for these technologies. This point is further important in a pragmatic sense as Dewey identifies culture, in both its material and ideal elements, as constituting human experience. In the context of algorithmic technologies, Beer strikes at the core of the need to understand the transaction between the ideal element of culture and the material element of culture to understand this interaction:

> is to explore how the predictions of algorithmic systems feed into people's lives, shaping what they know, who they know, what they discover, and what they experience. The power of algorithms here is in their ability to make choices, to classify, to sort, to order and to rank. That is, to decide what matters and to decide what should be most visible.

Or, how they regulate the ways that experience is had through culture (Beer, 2017, 10). Insofar as the whole of experience, including technologically mediated experience, is the result of the interaction between the ideal and material elements of culture, Dewey's pragmatism would caution against treating algorithmic platforms and the results they supply as independent of cultural influences. Indeed, for Dewey, why we develop these systems, how we used them, and for what purposes we use them are all bound up with how the ideal elements of culture shape the ways we understand the world through their interaction with the material elements of culture. To this end, understanding the workings of technology, and the results of technology, requires an understanding of technology as interdependent with culture: not outside or beyond it as the next section will demonstrate.

TECHNOLOGY AND CULTURE

For Dewey, "'Technology' signifies all the intelligent techniques by which the energies of nature and man are directed and used in satisfaction of human needs; it cannot be limited to a few outer and comparatively mechanical forms" (LW5:270). Among these intelligent techniques, Dewey includes the sciences and the "engineering arts," which, in modernity, encompasses the ever-growing number of computational science and information technology disciplines that produce the algorithmic platforms through which social life increasingly goes on. This point is worth noting as, for Dewey, technology also includes new ways of establishing and regulating human relationships, including education (LW5:270). While Dewey's definition of technology is expansive, it has crucial implications for how we understand algorithmic platforms which are methods of regulating interactions with reference to their consequences in the narrow sense, and of controlling the nature of experience in the broad sense. However, algorithmic platforms do not do so on their own: they do so in interaction with the "ideal elements" of culture which supply them with the direction for their operation. It is for this reason that Dewey describes science, and we may include the computational sciences under this definition, as "impersonal" and "impartial," or an "instrument" (LW6:54).

Dewey's "impartial" is not synonymous with the claims of "objectivity" frequently appended to algorithmic platforms: whereas the latter claims that the results or products of algorithmic platforms, and the platforms themselves, are free from contamination of human aims, the former implies that the sciences and their products adapt themselves passively to human aims. Thus, for Dewey, science

> lends itself with equal impartiality to the kindly offices of medicine and hygiene and the destructive deeds of war. It elevates some through opening new horizons; it depresses others by making them slaves of machines operated for the pecuniary gain of owners. (LW6:54)

As an extremely relevant example of what Dewey means by this impartiality, an algorithmic platform intended to develop pharmaceutical treatments took less than six hours to develop over 40,000 potential bioweapons. To accomplish this feat, Urbina et al. inverted the training models and datasets of their algorithmic platform and, in doing so, "transformed (their) innocuous generative model from a helpful tool of medicine to a generator of likely deadly molecules" (Urbina et al. 190). That is, the machine itself remained fundamentally unchanged: what changed was the aims to which the human users put it. Moreover, despite the datasets not containing the formulae for nerve agents, the algorithmic platform proceeded to suggest several, including VX and other chemical warfare agents.

To this end, it is the impartial nature of science that, for Dewey, requires us to look closer at the human aims and motivations that animate it, a point crucially important as the myth of "algorithmic objectivity" is one of the cornerstones of faith in the algorithmic platforms that have come to dominate our lives. In describing the technology of his day, Dewey states:

> The pecuniary aims which have decided the social results of the use of these technologies have not flowed from the inherent nature of science. They have been derived from institutions and attendant mental and moral habits which were entrenched before there was any such thing as science and the machine. In consequence, science has operated as a means for extending the influence of the institution of private property and connected legal relations far beyond their former limits. (LW6:57–8)

Here, we turn back to the ideal elements of culture which include religion, politics, and economics, and their transaction with the material elements of culture including algorithmic platforms. With specific regard to the development of algorithmic platforms, economics and industry are of specific interest as Whittaker (2021) notes:

> we must first recognize that the "advances" in AI celebrated over the past decade were not due to fundamental scientific breakthroughs in AI techniques. They were and are primarily the product of significantly concentrated data and compute resources that reside in the hands of a few large tech corporations. (2021, 51)

As a result, the kinds of applications developed, the kinds of research questions pursued, and the kinds of innovations rewarded are increasingly structured by the demands of corporate interests. Whittaker helpfully provides the example of Stanford's Center for Research on Foundation Models, whose launch report serves to rebrand and reframe large language models (LLMs) as "foundation models" thereby distancing the research, the centre, and the institution from being complicit in the "legacy of criticism" of LLMs, criticism which includes a growing body of work demonstrating how LLMs intensify and reinforce extant structures of marginalization in society. However, for Whittaker and Dewey, what is most critical about Stanford's rebranding of LLMs and the development of its new centre is the way in which Stanford's research agenda imports corporate interests as an organizing feature of research. Indeed, CRFM's launch report states, "industry ultimately makes concrete decisions about how foundation models will be deployed, but we should also lean on academia, with its disciplinary diversity and noncommercial incentives" (2021, 12), and even going so far as to recommend that the centre model industry pipelines to address the challenges of licensing, government regulation, and data quality. Thus, despite the authors of the report recognizing that "(t)he political economy in which foundations models are designed, developed, and deployed provides an inevitable incentive structure for decision-making at every stage" (2012, 10), the authors continue to centre industry in the organization of their research, thereby ensuring that it is corporate interest which shapes the nature of the field, and it is the pecuniary aims of corporations that will decide the social results of how algorithmic platforms are used and not the aims of the researchers or the nature of the computational sciences themselves.

Further, while both Whittaker and Dewey acknowledge that corporate aims need not animate the social results of technology, including algorithmic platforms, for Dewey, even when pecuniary aims do not direct the social results of technology, the result can still function as if they had. In describing the industrial revolution, Dewey states that the gap between the results of the industrial revolution in terms of mass disruptions and depersonalization of the community, and the intentions of those involved in developing the technologies that ushered in the industrial revolution, demonstrate how the indirect consequences of technology exceed the direct consequences intended by those developing the technology. For Dewey, indirect consequences are the effects of the consequences of an interaction on those who are not involved with the initial interaction. By "interaction," Dewey does not simply mean a one-to-one interaction between individuals: causal interactions, like the persistence of institutionalized oppression or economic inequality, that do not depend on those affected accepting their existence, are what Dewey has in mind. The case of Urbina and his colleagues' unintended development of a chemical warfare algorithmic platform is one such example, particularly as by their own admission they were naive in considering the possibilities for misuse of their algorithm.

However, while Urbina and his colleagues' indirect consequences were confined to the lab, many other algorithmic platforms' indirect consequences serve to structure the lives of millions of people around the world. As an example, in 2018, Amazon abandoned a multi-year project to develop an algorithmic platform to automate its recruitment practices because the platform consistently rejected applications from women. In developing the platform, Amazon's team created over 500 computer models that were trained on a decade's worth of past Amazon hires to develop a database of over 50,000 key terms, which it would then match within the resumes of potential applicants. Unfortunately, as Goodman (2018) notes: "the tool disadvantaged candidates who went to certain women's colleges presumably not attended by many existing Amazon engineers." It similarly downgraded resumes that included the word "women's" – as in "women's rugby team." And it privileged resumes with the kinds of verbs that men tend to use, like "executed" and "captured" (Goodman, 2018). Put another way, despite the intentions behind the development of the hiring algorithm, one of the indirect consequences of training the algorithm on a dataset of a decade's worth of hiring predominantly men was an algorithm that excluded women and those associated with them from consideration.

A more recent example is Stanford hospital's COVID-19 distribution algorithm (Guo and Hao, 2020). Intended to ensure equitable distribution of the COVID-19 vaccine during the initial outbreak of the pandemic, the algorithm prioritized the age of the recipient and the total number of positive COVID-19 cases in each department within the hospital. In doing so, the algorithm ranked lower those individuals most likely to encounter infected individuals: junior staff and residents who were not tied to a single department due to the nature of their employment were ranked lower than their more senior colleagues. Janitorial staff, on the other hand, were excluded altogether from the algorithm's calculations due to the way that the algorithm determined departmental affiliation. As a result, the algorithm prioritized senior administrators and upper management over those most likely to be in close contact with the infected, resulting in an indirect consequence of maintaining the stratification of the hospital. In a similar vein, a 2019 study of a healthcare algorithm found that its design, which used cost of care to predict future healthcare needs, prioritized the health needs of white patients over Black patients with more severe health needs (Obermeyer et.al.). Because Black patients typically had lower incomes than white patients and therefore spent less than white patients on healthcare, the algorithm treated them as if they were at a lower health risk due to the smaller amount spent on healthcare, despite having significantly more healthcare needs than white patients. As a result, Black patients were excluded from extra care programs and specialist referrals because their estimated risk score did not rise to the levels where they would be considered for such programs. Thus, the indirect consequences of a race-neutral healthcare program reinscribed racial and economic disparities despite the intention to avoid such disparities through its design.

To be clear, for Dewey, these indirect consequences proceed from the moral and mental habits entrenched long before the development of these algorithmic platforms through how they determine which problems these tools should be applied to and how that application should proceed. To this end, one of the moral and mental habits that serves to determine the application of these platforms is institutionalized racism. Again, for Dewey, a habit is not an unconscious or automatic action, but an inclination towards ways of responding within a specific situation to secure a desired result. A habit is a specific way of transaction with the environment and indicates the preference for the conditions that enable its exercise. Moreover, at the cultural level, habit serves as one of the ways that cultures maintain and perpetuate themselves in the form of what Dewey calls wide uniformities of habit, or customs. Thus, mental and moral habits are dispositions towards certain ways of thinking or engaging in moral deliberation in favour of some outcomes and not others, outcomes like the maintenance of white supremacy, heteropatriarchy, and transphobia. For example, higher rates of incarceration, lower incomes, and worse health outcomes among Black populations, all of which preceded the development of algorithmic technologies that amplify them and subject Black populations to massively expanded indirect consequences. As a result:

> Here lies the heart of our present social problem. Science has hardly been used to modify men's fundamental acts and attitudes in social matters. It has been used to extend enormously the scope and power of interests and values which anteceded its rise. (LW6:58)

Considering the above, for Dewey:

> The fact is that it is foolish to try to draw up a debit and credit account for science. To do so is to mythologize; it is to personify science and impute to it a will and an energy on its own account. (LW6:54)

Here, Dewey rejects the assumption of hard technological determinism, that technology advances absent of the interactions of the ideal elements of culture, while simultaneously reframing the core assumption of soft technological determinism that assumes the neutrality of predetermined ends to which technology is put and that society lags behind the development of technology. While Dewey might agree, stating that the "Political and legal forms have only piecemeal and haltingly, with great lag, accommodated themselves to the industrial transformation" (LW6:307), this lag is not due to the inherent nature of science or technology, but the ways that science and technology, including algorithmic platforms, have driven new forms of association under the influence of pecuniary aims that anteceded its development. To this end, the presumption of neutrality in technology is but one way that it is mythologized: by claiming that algorithmic platforms are less biased and more objective than their counterparts, proponents of algorithmic technologies once more attribute agency to these machines through their conviction that the machine acts like a human, thinks like a human, but absent the culture of embeddedness. Further implicit in this rhetoric is the assumption that algorithmic platforms make decisions for humans – that they exercise agency. Indeed, for Dewey, this could not be further from the truth: algorithmic platforms merely amplify and extend the decisions already made within culture. They are developments of cultural habits, as the concluding section will demonstrate.

DEWEYAN BIG DATA

In describing search engines, Safiya Noble argues that the results of user queries are

> delivered to users through a set of steps (algorithms) implemented by programming code and then naturalized as "objective." One of the reasons this is seen as a neutral process is because algorithmic, scientific, and mathematical solutions are evaluated through procedural and mechanistic practices. (Noble, 51)

All of which take place within a commercialized environment. Indeed, for Noble, one of the most troubling aspects of this commercialized environment, and a demonstration of the ways that pecuniary aims of what Dewey calls financial capitalism structure the operation of algorithmic platforms, is through search engine optimization or the manipulation of search engine results through technical or commercial means. What is crucial here, beyond the further demonstration of the ways that commercial ends direct and shape experience through their organization of technology, is that search engines and other algorithmic platforms rely upon "a technologically inflected promise of mechanical neutrality" (Gillespie), which is essential to the representation of algorithms as neutral providers of unbiased information that can be used to control conditions in favour of some outcomes and not others.

Further, as Gillespie (2014) argues, "Algorithms are inert, meaningless machines until paired with databases on which to function" (Gillespie, 2014, 169). To this end, for Gillespie, the automated nature of algorithmic platforms requires data to be prepared, organized, and classified so that the algorithmic platform can be applied to it. In a Deweyan context, the objective results of algorithmic platforms are anything but, particularly insofar as the objective results are merely treated as if they are external to human aims and influences by virtue of the mechanized processes that create them. It is for this reason that we must now turn to data and databases as the transformation of the consequences of interactions into data is crucial for any algorithmic platform to function and a pragmatic analysis of algorithmic platforms. Thus, as Dewey states:

> the difference between facts which are what they are independent of human desire and endeavor and facts which are to some extent what they are because of human interest and purpose, and which alter with alteration in the latter, cannot be got rid of by any methodology. The more sincerely we appeal to facts, the greater is the importance of the distinction between facts which condition human activity and facts which are conditioned by human activity. In the degree which we ignore this difference, social science becomes pseudo-science. (LW2:240)

Physical facts are phenomena whose occurrence does not rely on human agency or disposition towards it. As an example, Dewey provides mosquitoes and malaria: mosquitoes carry malaria regardless of human desire and agency; public health measures to control the spread of malaria are a social fact due to how they proceed from human aims and desires. Vaccination against malaria is also a social fact due to the immunity that it confers being the result of intentional human efforts to bring about a state of affairs. The vaccine itself is a physical fact in its composition, but a social fact in its application and dissemination because of the ways that it comes into existence. It is the human contribution that distinguishes a physical fact from a social fact. Moreover, social facts are the result of intentional control over conditions to secure some outcome. That is, social facts depend on the contribution of intelligence, or the observation of consequences in connection with the acts from which they proceed, in the emergence from the organization from conditions to produce a specific consequence. To this end, machines, including algorithmic platforms, are employed for the production and manipulation of social facts to produce conditions favourable to the maintenance of a specific state of affairs or the production of specific consequences. Thus, for Dewey, "'Fact,' physically speaking, is the ultimate residue after human purposes, desires, emotions, ideas and ideals have been systematically excluded. A social 'fact,' on the other hand, is a concretion in external form of precisely these human factors'" (LW6:64).

Where algorithmic platforms are concerned, the databases they rely on for their functionality are collections of social facts. The data collected, in a Deweyan sense, are a record of facts that are conditioned by human activity, even indirect human activity. In the previous example of the healthcare algorithm, the calculation of health risk factors that determined the kinds of services provided to patients produces a social fact insofar as the assessment of risk depends on human aims and does not exist absent them; in contrast, the illnesses suffered by individual patients are physical facts as their persistence does not require human intentionality. As social facts are themselves in transaction with physical facts, and thereby alter the physical facts and the conditions under which they enter into human experience, the social fact of a healthcare risk score can alter the physical fact of illness by providing treatment that prevents or alleviates the illness. That is, while the illness is a physical fact that conditions human transactions, the social facts produced by the algorithm can result in the transformation of the physical fact as a condition of human experience. In this way, the social facts produced by algorithms transact with the physical facts of the world to reshape and structure the conditions under which human experience is had.

A more critical example of the ways that algorithmic platforms structure human experience through producing social facts is in discussions of algorithmic bias. In her discussion of the biases within predictive policing technologies, Ruha Benjamin notes "If we consider that institutional racism in this country is an ongoing unnatural disaster, then crime prediction algorithms should more accurately be called crime production algorithms" (Benjamin, 86). Here, Benjamin is expressing concern that individuals who live within zones designated by PredPol, a predictive policing algorithm, as potential hotspots for crime will be judged as potential criminals as an indirect consequence of the deployment of the algorithm. In designating locations as "temporary crime zones," PredPol "produces" the possibility of criminality as a social fact through the interactions that it regulates by means of the social environment. The "temporary crime zones," which structure the possibilities for interaction, are themselves social facts that are controlled in favour of some consequences and not others, and which invite specific modes of transaction with law enforcement officers based on the claim to "know" the inherent criminality of a given location. This has the result of the indirect consequence of exacerbating the possibility of police brutality, the further production of inherent criminality as a social fact of Blackness, and the maintenance of institutional racism. That is, while the intention of the algorithm is to regulate interactions among individuals such that the direct result is a reduction in crime, the indirect consequences far outstrip the direct consequences, particularly when the social fact of criminality is excised from human aims and intentions.

While Benjamin's discussion of PredPol is further situated within the larger context of institutional racism as technology, which itself is continuous with the algorithmic technologies of predictive policing and re-offence platforms, which serves to structure not only how these algorithms are productive, but what these algorithms produce, we should not forget that what are properly social facts under Dewey's view are treated as physical facts by the developers of algorithmic platforms. Moreover, in Dewey's view, this treatment strips away the human aims and purposes that animate the collection and classification of social facts in the mode of data. These facts are thereby treated as if they were somehow external to the human aims and desires that animate them. This externality is in appearance only and, for Dewey, the treatment of the social facts produced by algorithms as if they were physical facts renders the data gathered and produced by algorithmic platforms a "pile of meaningless items" (LW6:65) due to their disconnection from the broader social context that informs and is continuous with the methodologies used to generate them.

To conclude, it is the need to retain the continuity between algorithmic platforms and the social environment that enables the intelligibility of social facts in line with the organized whole of human aims and consequences that make them potentially valuable for structuring human relations. That is, for Dewey, it is possible to determine a complete social fact, or what Dewey calls "the actual external occurrence in its human relationships" (LW6:65), should we endeavour to recognize and understand the deliberate purposes deployed to create specific social results. That is, for any algorithmic platform to effect direct social change, and not simply operate in line with the pecuniary aims of commerce or the mental and moral habits that precede their development, we need to recognize their continuity with the broad structure of society. Put another way, we must be conscious of not just the human element in algorithmic platforms, but also the social element if we wish to deploy these platforms to predict and regulate human relationships. Thus, as Dewey states:

> If we want foresight, we shall not obtain it by any amount of fact finding so long as we disregard the human aims and desires producing the facts which we find. But if we decide upon what we want socially, what sort of social consequences we wish to occur, and then use whatever means we possess to effect these intended consequences, we shall find the road that leads to foresight. Forethought and planning must come before foresight. (LW6:67)

FURTHER READING

Hickman, L. A. (1990) *John Dewey's Pragmatic Technology*. Indiana University Press.
Hickman, L. A. (2001) *Philosophical Tools for Technological Culture*. Indiana University Press.
Hickman, L. A. (2017, November) Dewey, Pragmatism, Technology. In *The Oxford Handbook of Dewey*, edited by S. Fesmire.

REFERENCES

Beer, D. G. (2017) The Social Power of Algorithms. *Information, Communication and Society*, 1–13.

Benjamin, R. (2018) *Race After Technology: Abolitionist Tools for the New Jim Code*. John Wiley & Sons

Bommasani, R. et al. (2021) On the Opportunities and Risks of Foundation Models. arXiv preprint arXiv:2108.07258.

Dewey, J. (1981) *The Later Works of John Dewey 1925–1953 Volume 1: 1925 Experience and Nature* (J. Boydston, Ed.) Southern Illinois University (Original work published 1925).

Dewey, J. (1985) *The Later Works of John Dewey, 1925–1953. Volume 2: 1925–1927, Essays, the Public and Its Problems* (J. Boydston, Ed.) Southern Illinois University.

Dewey, J. (1985) *The Later Works of John Dewey, 1925–1953. Volume 12: 1938, Logic: The Theory of Inquiry* (J. Boydston, Ed.) Southern Illinois University.

Dewey, J. (1989) *The Later Works of John Dewey, 1925–1953. Volume 5: 1929–1930, Essays, the Sources of a Science Education, Individualism, Old and New, and Construction and Criticism* (J. Boydston, Ed.) Southern Illinois University.

Dewey, J. (1988) *The Later Works of John Dewey, 1925–1953 Volume 13: 1938–1939 Experience and Education, Freedom and Culture, Theory of Valuation and Essays* (J. Boydston, Ed.) Southern Illinois University.

Gillespie, T. (2014) *The Relevance of Algorithms in Media Technologies: Essays on Communication, Materiality, and Society* (T. Gillespie, P. Boczkowski, & K. Foot, Eds.), 167–195.

Goodman, R. (2018) Why Amazon's automated hiring tool discriminated against women. *American Civil Liberties Union*, https://www.aclu.org/news/womens-rights/why-amazons-automated-hiring-tool-discriminated-against

Guo, E. and Hao, K. (2020) This is the Stanford vaccine algorithm that left out frontline doctors. *MIT Technology Review* https://www.technologyreview.com/2020/12/21/1015303/stanford-vaccine-algorithm/

Noble, S. U. (2018). *Algorithms of Oppression: How Search Engines Reinforce Racism*. New York University Press.

Obermeyer, Z., Powers, B., Vogeli, C., & Mullainathan, S. (2019) Dissecting Racial Bias in an Algorithm Used to Manage the Health of Populations. *Science*, *366*(6464), 447–453. https://doi.org/10.1126/science.aax2342.

Urbina, F., Lentzos, F., Invernizzi, C. et al. (2022) Dual Use of Artificial-Intelligence-Powered Drug Discovery. *Nature Machine Intelligence*, *4*, 189–191. https://doi.org/10.1038/s42256-022-00465-9.

Whittaker, M. (2021) The Steep Cost of Capture. *Interactions*, *28*(6), 50–55. https://doi-org.proxyau.wrlc.org/10.1145/3488666.

13. Digital humanism and AI

Wolfgang Hofkirchner and Hans-Jörg Kreowski

HUMANISM

In a critical vein, we understand by humanism all those philosophical, scientific, or social everyday ideas and endeavours that construe an image of 'man', of humans, and social relations among them, including what is human, ontologically, and humane, praxiologically (Förster, 1990). These ideas and endeavours are subject to historical change and bound to interests according to the social position of the perceiving actor. This makes them relative. The values these ideas contain and enact in endeavours, however, need not be considered as merely related to the respective position of an individual actor. They can also reflect the common position of a collective of actors. Notwithstanding that purported human values mirror positions of privileged actors, which has been mostly the case since antiquity (Zimmermann, 2022), they can represent true universal human values that are valid for the whole of humanity in a current state of evolution or at a high level of abstraction. Such a humanism is social criticism because it orients towards human emancipation. This is particularly the case when – according to Karl Marx's famous 'categoric imperative to overthrow all relations in which man is a debased, enslaved, abandoned, despicable essence' (Marx, 1843, emphasis deleted) – humans 'make their own history, but [...] not [...] as they please [...] under self-selected circumstances, but under circumstances existing already, given and transmitted from the past' (Marx, 1852). This entails enacting antagonistic social relations that demand sublation for a better society (Tudyka, 1973, 9). Thus, humanism that deserves the term in a critical sense needs to be basically focused on disclosing the commons as a key to provide access to the production and usage of the common good. It can function as a vision to guide the conscious (and conscientious) evolution of society.

DIGITAL HUMANISM

If critical humanism is to guide social evolution ethically, then the question arises of how it responds to the scientific-technological development yielding informatisation – the spread of computerised information technologies throughout society (Nora & Minc, 1978). That process leads to an information society superimposing on industrial society superimposing on agricultural society – which is hyped today as digitalisation. The answer is that digitalisation must be carried out in a humanist way so as to bring about humanist digitalisation. The term digital humanism has become established to signify humanism that deals with digitalisation.

The roots of the term go back to German philosopher Julian Nida-Rümelin, who published, together with Nathalie Weidenfeld, a book with the German title *Digitaler Humanismus* (Nida-Rümelin & Weidenfeld, 2018). This book was a defence of humanism in the sense of an inalienable authorship of any individual, also under the premise of digitalisation.

In 2019, the Vienna Manifesto on Digital Humanism was elaborated (Vienna Manifesto, n.d.). 'We call for a Digital Humanism that describes, analyzes, and, most importantly, influences the complex interplay of technology and humankind, for a better society and life, fully respecting universal human rights'.

Digital humanism can thus be defined as humanism that demands a humane shape for digitalisation. It does so by an ethically aligned design of human-centred technology. The inherent ethics, if abiding by critical humanism, needs to respect objective commons and allow and support a subjective good life for all and anyone. This would mean the scientific-technological commons is a good-life techno-structure containing innovative productive forces produced by and, in turn, instrumenting co-users (Hofkirchner, 2023, 128–129). It does not mean giving rise to destructive forces for the exclusive use of enclosed commons.

Digital Humanism in the Age of Existential Threats

Importantly, existential threats to humanity require further updates of a critical digital humanism. A polycrisis (Morin & Kern, 1999) is at the point of precipitating an existential catastrophe via an unrecoverable dystopia or an unrecoverable collapse, if not even extinction, leaving a failed humanity in their wake (Ord, 2021, 37). Humanism is called upon to halt such a development. In order to do so, objective as well as subjective conditions need to be met and digital humanism has to point out that.

On objective social conditions

Critical humanism recognises that the risks are anthropogenic. These risks reflect logics that were valid and once worked in real life but continue to determine today's organisation of social relations with technology, nature, and among humans. Digital humanism must realise that and understand that logic, which still governs technology development, must be adapted with concurrent adaptations of those anachronistic logics regarding nature and humans.

- *Human-human relations* must abandon the self-centric logic and take over the inclusive logic of pan-humanism enveloping all of humanity (Morin, 2021).
- *Human-nature relations* must leave the limited logic of anthropocentricity behind and accept so-called anthropo-relationalism (Deutsches Referenzzentrum; Barthlott et al., 2009). This is a logic that – while doing justice to the unique place of human systems in evolution – also does justice to the diverse places natural systems have been taking in evolution, allowing an alliance with nature (Bloch, 1986).
- *Human-technology relations*, bearing pan-humanism and anthropo-relational humanism in mind, need to replace the logic of power-centricity, the illusion of having superpowers that are not designed to take sufficient care of natural systems as well as human systems. Such a logic has been incrementally hypostatising the effectiveness of technology beyond any rational measure. Digital humanism must become the logic of civilisational self-limitation, as Austrian-born writer Ivan Illich coined it in his book *Tools for Conviviality* (Illich, 1973). This can here be explicated as a limitation of the technological tools to their role of only serving an alliance-with-nature and pan-human purposes.

Critical digital humanism must address these requirements because humanity turned into an objective community of common destiny when its spatiotemporal development reached the global scale. However, digital humanism must also become explicit on the still missing awareness of this situation.

On subjective social conditions

This missing awareness means that a necessary critical stance prompts humanism to deal with the subjective conditions of overcoming the polycrisis. This is another adaptation of humanism that is important for digital humanism. It is connected to Illich's ideas that went viral when mainly French intelligentsia – among them Edgar Morin, Alain Caillé, or Serge Latouche – started a decade ago to discuss a new way to look at social scientific solutions to the polycrisis. They called for a new political philosophy of togetherness and named it Convivialism (Convivialist Manifesto, 2014; Convivialist International, 2020). 'Convivial' has Latin origins and means the quality of living together in the manner of dining together (convivor) of hosts (convivatores) and guests (convivae) at joint feasts (convivia). The convivialist authors introduced five ethical principles and one imperative that we here subsume under three imperatives.

The first is the convivial imperative of an ethos for global governance. It is based upon the convivialist manifesto's principles of common humanity – 'there is only one humanity' that 'must be respected in the person of each of its members' – and of common naturality – humans 'have a responsibility to take care of' nature' (Convivialist Manifesto, 2014; Convivialist International, 2020). Importantly, the German philosopher Hans Jonas came close to that in his *Search of an Ethics for the Technological Age* – as the subtitle of his book reads (Jonas, 1984). His update of Immanuel Kant's categorical imperative 'Act so that you can will that the maxim of your action be made the principle of a universal law' (Jonas, 1984, 10) was incorporated in his new imperative of responsibility: 'Act so that the effects of your action are compatible with the permanence of genuine human life' (Jonas, 1984, 11). Starting from Jonas, the convivial imperative of a planetary ethos defended here can be laid down in the following manner (Hofkirchner, 2023, 169):

> Act so as to contribute to the establishment and maintenance of humanity as an autonomous social system sui generis, endowed with self-consciousness, including conscience, in order to solve the developmental crisis and continue social evolution with a next step of humanisation.

This formulation is crucial because it does not emphasise what should be avoided but puts forward a positive vision for orientation. It addresses any actor, whether individual or collective. Imperial intentions pose a formidable obstacle to the observance of this imperative.

The second is the convivial imperative of agreeableness for global dialogue. It requires a discourse in which mass conversation is focused on the necessary societal transformations and is aware of agreements to be achieved. From the Convivialists, it borrows the principle of common sociality – 'the greatest wealth is the richness of concrete relationships' that human beings as social beings maintain among themselves. Equally, it borrows the principle of legitimate individuation – 'legitimate is the policy that allows each individual to develop their individuality to the fullest by developing his or her capacities, power to be and act, without harming that of others, with a view toward equal freedom' (Convivialist International, 2020). Furthermore, the fifth convivialist principle is decisive. It is key to the conduct of communication under the condition of global challenges. It is the principle of creative opposition – 'it is normal for humans to be in opposition with each other [...] as long as this does not endanger the framework of common humanity, common sociality, and common naturality that makes rivalry fertile and not destructive' (Convivialist International, 2020). Accordingly, the convivial imperative of planetary agreeableness can be expressed as follows: 'Act so as to further a discourse that allows a planetary conscience to emerge'. Intransigent self-righteousness is averse to the observance of this imperative.

The final convivial imperative essential here is the imperative of mindfulness for a global citizenship. The Second Convivialist Manifesto claims an imperative of hubris control:

> The first condition for rivalry to serve the common good is that it be devoid of desire for omnipotence, excess, hubris (and a fortiori pleonexia, the desire to possess ever more). On this condition, it becomes rivalry to cooperate better. (Convivialist International, 2020)

This imperative is exactly the mindset Global Citizens are to acquire – self-limitation for the common good. Illich had that in mind. The convivial imperative of planetary minds can thus be established as follows: 'Act so as to further a mindset that allows a planetary discourse to emerge'. Identitary idiotism which gives supremacy to particular interests instead of reconciling them with common ones is contradictory to the observance of this imperative.

These three convivial imperatives elaborate both humanism and digital humanism under the condition of existential threats with a focus on the subjective conditions to overcome the polycrisis.

INTELLIGENCE

From an evolutionary systems perspective, intelligence is a product of natural and, later on, social evolution (Stonier, 1992). Evolutionary systems are agents because, by self-organisation, they show agency. Furthermore, they are informational agents, as they are also able to generate information. Information that enables such agents to achieve objective functions such that they master complex challenges can – in an extension of W. Ross Ashby's Law of Requisite Variety – be called 'requisite information' (Hofkirchner, 2023, 145). Accordingly, intelligence can be defined as the capacity to generate requisite information. Intelligence is a property of informational agents.

In the course of evolution, intelligence appears in different shades. Human intelligence is a feature of social agents, individual and collective actors, and – because the characteristic of super co-operators can be ascribed to our race (Nowak & Highfield, 2011) – it seems to belong to the most advanced manifestations of intelligence on our planet. Besides objectives and self-set goals, humans can envision future states of social relations. The humanistic vision of the good society is one such desirable state of relations. Human intelligence can thus embrace the attainment of wisdom (European Commission, 1997, 63).

Artificial Intelligence

Human intelligence even creates what is known as artificial intelligence (AI).

The field of AI has made tremendous progress in the last two decades in playing games on the one hand and more practically in picture and language processing as well as robotics on the other hand. It is remarkable that computer systems can win against world champions of chess and Go. This also applies to the quality of translations by language processing systems such as DeepL and to the proper recognition of certain types of images. Based on machine learning and so-called deep learning, impressive advances have been made in prediction and prescription in a wide range of applications compared to the more classical fields of AI (cf., e.g., Goodfellow et al., 2016; Jiang, 2021; Mohri, 2018). Furthermore, robots can act more and have more flexibility with respect to handling and navigation. The reached state of the art is not the result of disruptive breakthroughs (as sometimes suggested). While the main methods and concepts have been known for decades, the currently available storage capacities and computational speed have made practical applications commonplace. Moreover, one must be aware that very large teams were involved in these developments and that exorbitant amounts of money were spent.

The successes of AI plus the even more euphoric promises of some of the leading AI experts have triggered quite a lot of hype around AI. It has received continuous attention in the public media, and business leaders and policymakers are setting their hopes on AI as the key technology to guarantee future economic growth and added value. Sometimes, leadership in AI is considered to represent the entrance to world leadership (cf., e.g., Lee, 2018). Many states all over the world have come up with national AI strategies (e.g., European Commission, 2021; van Roy et al., 2021) and earmarked major investments into the development of AI and its applications in all sectors of society including production, agriculture, administration, health, climate, environment, and law enforcement. Typical examples of governmental AI goals are formulated by the European Commission in its *Coordinated Plan on Artificial Intelligence 2021 Review.* The headings include 'Creating EU global leadership in human-centric AI' and 'Build strategic leadership in high-impact sectors', but also 'Ensure that AI works for people and is a force for good in Society' (European Commission, 2021).

Nonetheless, from the perspective of critical digital humanism, artificial intelligence is a misnomer. The term intelligence cannot signify the property of machine processes or a machine itself because machinic entities are not informational agents, not self-organising systems, and work along hetero-organised determinacies (Hofkirchner, 2011). This idea has been taken up in a publication of the IEEE Global Initiative on Ethics of Autonomous and Intelligent Systems (A/IS) on ethically aligned design. It states, with reference to philosopher Rafael Capurro (Capurro, 2012) and Hofkirchner (Hofkirchner, 2011):

> Of particular concern when understanding the relationship between human beings and A/IS is the uncritically applied anthropomorphic approach toward A/IS that many industry and policymakers are using today. This approach erroneously blurs the distinction between moral agents and moral patients, i.e., subjects, otherwise understood as a distinction between 'natural' self-organizing systems and artificial, non-self-organizing devices.

This is consequential for the issue of autonomy.

> A/IS cannot, by definition, become autonomous in the sense that humans or living beings are autonomous. With that said, autonomy in machines, when critically defined, designates how machines act and operate independently in certain contexts through a consideration of implemented order generated by laws and rules. In this sense, A/IS can, by definition, qualify as autonomous, especially in the case of genetic algorithms and evolutionary strategies. However, attempts to implant true morality and emotions, and thus accountability, i.e., autonomy, into A/IS [...] may encourage anthropomorphic expectations of machines by human beings when designing and interacting with A/IS. (The IEEE Global Initiative, 2019, 41)

Of course, AI harbours ambiguities, as do ICTs or IT in general. They can have a positive impact on society and further the good society, and they can have a negative impact and hamper the good society. On the one hand, they can 'quantitatively reinforce existing or qualitatively innovate new, cognitive, communicative or co-operative social information functions – with the intention and/or consequence of serving or improving social inclusion and mitigating or eliminating existing, and preventing new, social exclusion'. On the other hand, they can 'quantitatively reinforce existing social information dysfunctions or qualitatively spawn new social information dysfunctions' (Hofkirchner, 2023, 211). The potential is thus open for good or evil, and this demands deliberate design. The ambiguity is a precondition for being able to design for the good.

Artificial Intelligence in the Age of Existential Threats

Currently, human intelligence lacks sufficient materialisation of its potential to tackle existential threats. AI applications that rebuild the whole technological infrastructure of civilisation should be designed to support the tasks that are devoted to transforming societies into a cooperative world society. This is because a united – but nevertheless diversified – humanity is a precondition for solving the problems of survival and flourishing humanity. AI applications are part of the objective structure of societies. As such they can hinder objective social conditions that would help master the polycrisis and thus deepen the latter, or they can facilitate those conditions and help master the crisis. They can also hinder or facilitate the subjective social conditions of mastering the polycrisis.

AI and objective social conditions
A significant part of AI applications is by no means compatible with the vision of digital humanism. They contradict the ideas of humanism in many respects.

- *Making political powers more powerful.* China has developed a mass surveillance and credit system that keeps the entire population under observation and classifies the behaviour of each individual and each company. From the whistle-blower Edward Snowden's revelations, we know that the secret services of the world are collecting and examining all digital communication data. On a subtler and more clandestine level, the security agencies of many states use surveillance systems to spy on journalists, activists, oppositional politicians and groups, and whoever else may be deemed as dangerous. This has recently been revealed by the investigations of the Pegasus Project (e.g., The Guardian, 2021). All governmental activities of this type essentially undermine human rights. The misuse of surveillance is not new, but the application of AI algorithms has greatly simplified it.
- *Destroying labour.* The development of autonomous land vehicles was one of the three major applications of the Strategic Computing Initiative started by the US Department of Defense in 1983. With a ten-year budget of US$ 400 million, the project aimed at thinking machines. Since then, much research, money, and person power have been spent in all parts of the world to make autonomous vehicles a reality. Meanwhile, one encounters armed and unarmed drones of all sizes and in every price range. Besides the military, the civil sector is also very active. Above all, most automobile companies have jumped on the autonomous car bandwagon, investing large sums of money and great effort. The degree

to which the vision of unmanned mobility will come true remains unclear. A successful transformation to autonomous traffic may be good for the environment, but less consideration has apparently been given to the societal consequences of all the labour that will get lost in this case. Millions of taxi and lorry drivers, as well as ship and aircraft crews, will no longer be needed.

- *Thinking war anew.* According to the Unmanned Systems Integrated Roadmap (Department of Defense, 2014), the US Department of Defense plans to replace a major part of its weaponry with unmanned systems and in particular autonomous weapons. Unmanned weapon systems such as armed drones can be remotely controlled, but they typically navigate, operate, and search for targets autonomously using the program systems on board. Merely the deployment of the weapons itself is still decided by human pilots in ground stations. The step to full autonomy lies ahead and – technically seen – involves little more than a software update. Within NATO, the pros and cons of autonomous weapons are being heavily discussed (Williams & Scharre, 2015). In the foreword, the French Air Force General Jean-Paul Paloméros writes:

> This volume covers the subject of autonomous systems, which stand potentially to transform the way in which warfare is conducted. Advances in sensors, robotics and computing are permitting the development of a whole new class of systems, which offer a wide range of military benefits including the ability to operate without personnel on board the platform, novel human-machine teaming concepts, and 'swarm' operating methods. With any such transformational advances, there are unique operational, legal, ethical and design issues. (Williams & Scharre, 2015, iii)

The Nagorno-Karabakh war between Azerbaijan and Armenia in 2020 and the war in Ukraine show that the transformation is already underway.

- *Transforming humans into posthumans.* The transhumanists' intention is the transformation of humankind into a posthumankind by means of current and future technologies. One fraction relies on gene manipulation and digital brain enhancement, and another on replacing humans with robots and AI systems. Although there are currently no real and ongoing transhumanist projects on a large scale, abundant funds are available to produce quite some nonsense, disorientation, or even damage. The transhumanists' hope lies in the small subarea of AI called strong AI or artificial general intelligence. Its adherents propagate systems that behave intelligently in the same way as humans behave intelligently. Some of them even aim at superintelligent systems that are more intelligent than humans – at least a bestselling topic (Bostrom, 2014; Häggström, 2016; Kurzweil, 2005). Nonetheless, there is little indication that strong AI will become a reality in the foreseeable future.

The above developments clearly frustrate the new logics of social relations in society, of social relations with nature, and of social relations regarding technology that is required to master the crisis. They contribute to prolonging the self-centredness of societal actors, anthropocentrism with regard to the natural environment, and the power-centredness of technological tools. Digital humanism is called on to oppose those trends and intervene in the development of technologies and advance trends such as ICTs for development, ICTs for sustainability, and ICTs for peace.

AI and subjective social conditions

What is, and what can be, the role of AI regarding human and social information processes that form the subjective social conditions to mitigate and contain the polycrisis?

One of us has developed the concept of so-called techno-social systems that, in a critical manner, combines the human and the artificial, the social and the technological:

> [...] techno-social systems are social systems that emerge as soon as a mechanism is nested in the social system to improve its functioning. Hereby, the mechanism mediates the fulfilment of social functions in order to raise effectivity and efficiency. The mechanism itself works by strictly deterministic means to achieve the goals set by the social system actors. The social system as a whole boosts its self-organisation. This alternative integrates the machine with the human such that the digitised social system stays in command, and AI serves as a tool for humane purposes. (Hofkirchner, 2020, 3)

Based on such a concept, AI development can be endowed with frames, models, and designs that altogether constitute a critical digital humanist stance. The good society that needs to be envisioned is a society that has generated the appropriate information to build a socially, ecologically, and technologically sustainable structure on a global scale. This can be called a global sustainable information society (Hofkirchner, 2023, 136–148). As this vision is rooted in the potentiality here and now, it fulfils the criterion of a so-called concrete (Bloch, 1986) or real (Wright, 2010) utopia – the only type of utopia that can be transformed into actuality. This vision needs engineering for its implementation. The engineering of a vision is called visioneering (Kim & Oki, 2011). This means in our context (1) considering support for the techno-eco-social transformation of societies by the shaping of (information) technologies, (2) executing this consideration, (3) examining this execution, and (4) executing contingent revisions. Visioneering a global sustainable information society puts the human community of destiny on a solid foundation. Scientific-technological progress can only consist of producing tools for win-win situations, but not for zero-sum situations.

The COVID pandemic or the heating of our planet are showcases for helpful AI applications. 'The purpose of many algorithms is to make predictions aimed at prevention' (Nowotny, 2021, 159–160). Though 'an AI does not know, nor can it predict, a future which remains inherently uncertain and open' (Nowotny, 2021, 162), there is a chance for AI to suit the needs of our age. While the precautionary principle – the 'Prevalence of the Bad over the Good Prognosis' (Jonas, 1984, 31) – 'delays or forestalls action, prevention demands action to avoid harmful consequences in advance' (Nowotny, 2021, 160). Note here, however, that prevention is, in essence, counter-active, too. The techno-social system approach can favour proactive tasks. 'This is because there are also tipping points [...] that mark the reinforcement of positive developments. Such developments need to be furthered for the good, and must be explored' (Hofkirchner, 2023, 255). 'That approach helps algorithms to visioneer trajectories to real, concrete utopias. They can provide the scientific basis for a societal deliberation on which path to take' (Hofkirchner, 2023, 264). Though simulations are an indispensable tool provided by AI, the selection will not be done by AI, but will emerge from a process conducted by social actors.

We can conceive three techno-social, digital imperatives. Their essential task is to bolster the three convivial imperatives introduced above to overcome the polycrisis (Hofkirchner, 2023, 265–266).

The first is the imperative of tools for convivial governance: 'Act so as to contribute to the production and use of AI technologies that support the emergence and sustenance of a planetary ethos'. These tools will lay the foundations for a planetary conscience that will constitute and institute consensualised values, objectives, and goals for societal transformation. The task of technology is to cultivate the requisite information in the form of wisdom.

The second is the imperative of tools for a convivial dialogue: 'Act so as to contribute to the production and use of AI technologies that support the emergence and sustenance of planetary agreeableness'. The digital support will foster collective intelligence to generate requisite knowledge and undergird consilience for designing and assigning transformative tasks.

The third is the imperative of tools for a convivial netizenship: 'Act so as to contribute to the production and use of AI technologies that support the emergence and sustenance of planetary mindfulness'. Netizens will receive digital means that improve their ingenuity to help them conceptualise devising and supervising individual as well as collective operations for the overall transformation. This will be accompanied by integrating continual adjustments, if need be, based on requisite data, facts, and figures.

AI applications conforming to these digital imperatives are not merely helpful. The digital support, on a planetary scale, of conscience, intelligence, and ingenuity of humans may even turn out to be indispensable to gaining the requisite information for transforming our societal systems before it is too late.

CONCLUSION

Given the existential threats to humanity, any technology designed, developed, disseminated, deployed, and drawn on is prompted to help avert them. This calls for setting survival and human flourishing as indispensable values. This also holds for AI. Digital humanism, focussing on shaping digitalisation according to human values, needs to explicitly address the function of technology to help avert the threats. For that reason, the critical thinking presented here updates digital humanism and identifies objective and subjective conditions that must be realised to underpin the social, eco-social, and techno-social transformation of societies into a global sustainable information society. This represents an overarching framework system that can successfully combat the threats. This approach also formulates objective logics that shall replace the logics that are the root cause of the existential threats. This includes rooting out detrimental AI technologies. It also postulates imperatives for social cooperation, communication, and cognition on a planetary scale. The role of those imperatives is to provide subjective information functions that help guide action towards the realisation of the objective condition. Based on that, the global sustainable information society can postulate imperatives for AI tools that support subjective information functions. Accordingly, the role of AI cannot be seen in letting it gain autonomy at the expense of human and social systems. Rather, AI is a tool – an important one – that has been, is, and will be subject to humanity.

REFERENCES

Barthlott, W., Linsenmair, K. E., & Porembski, S. (Eds.). (2009). *Biodiversity: Structure and function* (Vol. II). EOLSS.
Bloch, E. (1986). *The principle of hope*. MIT Press.

Bostrom, N. (2014). *Superintelligence: Paths, dangers, strategies.* Oxford University Press.

Capurro, R. (2012). Toward a comparative theory of agents. *AI & Society, 27*(4), 479–488.

Convivialist International. (2020). The second convivialist manifesto: Towards a post-neoliberal world. *Civic Sociology.* https://online.ucpress.edu/cs/article/1/1/12721/112920/THE-SECOND -CONVIVIALIST-MANIFESTO-Towards-a-Post

Convivialist Manifesto. (2014). *Convivialist manifesto: A declaration of interdependence.* Global Dialogues. https://doi.org/10.14282/2198-0411-GD-3

Department of Defense. (2014). *Unmanned systems integrated roadmap,* FY 2013–2038. Washington.

Deutsches Referenzzentrum für Ethik in den Biowissenschaften (Ed.). (n.d). *Anthroporelational.* https://www.drze.de/im-blickpunkt/biodiversitaet/module/anthroporelational.

European Commission. (1997). *Building the European information society for us all, final policy report of the high-level expert group. Office for Official Publications of the European Communities.*

European Commission. (2021). *Coordinated plan on artificial intelligence 2021 review.* https://digital -strategy.ec.europa.eu/en/library/coordinated-plan-artificial-intelligence-2021-review.

Förster, W. (1990). Humanismus. In H.-J. Sandkühler (Ed.), *Europäische Enzyklopädie zu Philosophie und Wissenschaften* (Vol. 2, pp. 560–563). Meiner.

Goodfellow, I., Bengio, Y., & Courville, A. (2016). *Deep learning.* MIT Press.

Häggström, O. (2016). *Here be dragons: Science, technology and the future of humanity.* Oxford University Press.

Hofkirchner, W. (2011). Does computing embrace self-organisation? In G. Dodig-Crnkovic & M. Burgin (Eds.), *Information and computation* (pp. 185–202). World Scientific.

Hofkirchner, W. (2020). Blurring of the human and the artificial: A conceptual clarification. *Proceedings, 47*(7), 1–3. https://doi.org/10.3390/proceedings2020047007.

Hofkirchner, W. (2023). *The logic of the third: A paradigm shift to a shared future for humanity.* World Scientific.

Hofkirchner, W., & Kreowski, H.-J. (Eds.) (2021). *Transhumanism: The proper guide to a posthuman condition or a dangerous idea?* Springer.

Illich, I. (1973). *Tools for conviviality.* Marion Boyars.

Jonas, H. (1984). *The imperative of responsibility: In search of an ethics of the technological age.* University of Chicago.

Jiang, H. (2021). *Machine learning fundamentals: A concise introduction.* Cambridge University Press.

Kim, J., & Oki, T. (2011). Visioneering: An essential framework in sustainability science. *Sustainability Science, 6,* 247–251.

Kurzweil, R. (2005). *The singularity is near: When humans transcend biology.* Viking Adult.

Lee, K.-F. (2018). *AI superpowers: China, Silicon Valley, and the new world order.* Houghton Mifflin Harcourt.

Marx, K. (1843). *A contribution to the critique of Hegel's philosophy of right: Introduction.* https:// www.marxists.org/archive/marx/works/1843/critique-hpr/intro.htm.

Marx, K. (1852). *The eighteenth brumaire of Louis Bonaparte.* https://www.marxists.org/archive/marx /works/1852/18th-brumaire/ch01.htm.

Mohri, M., Rostamizadeh, A., & Talwalkar, A. (2018). *Foundations of machine learning* (2nd ed.). MIT Press.

Morin, E. (2021). Abenteuer Mensch. *Freitag, 28.* https://www.freitag.de/autoren/the-guardian/ abenteuer-mensch.

Morin, E., & Kern, A. B. (1999). *Homeland Earth: A manifesto for the new millennium.* Hampton Press.

Nida-Rümelin, J., & Weidenfeld, N. (2018). *Digitaler Humanismus: Eine Ethik für das Zeitalter der Künstlichen Intelligenz.* Piper.

Nora, S., & Minc, A. (1978). *L'informatisation de la Société: rapport à M. le Président de la République.* La Documentation française.

Nowak, M., & Highfield, R. (2011). *Super co-operators: Evolution, altruism and human behaviour or why we need each other to succeed.* Canongate.

Nowotny, H. (2021). *In AI we trust: Power, illusion and control of predictive algorithms.* Polity.

Ord, T. (2021). *The precipice: Existential risk and the future of humanity.* Bloomsbury.

Stonier, T. (1992). *Beyond information: The natural history of intelligence.* Springer.

The Guardian. (2021). https://www.theguardian.com/news/series/pegasus-project.

The IEEE Global Initiative on Ethics of Autonomous and Intelligent Systems. (Ed.). (2019). *Ethically aligned design: A vision for prioritizing human well-being with autonomous and intelligent systems* (1st ed.). IEEE. https://standards.ieee.org/industry-connections/ec/ead1e-infographic.html.

Tudyka, K. P. (1973). *Kritische Politikwissenschaft*. Kohlhammer.

Van Roy, V., Rossetti, F., Perset, K., & Galindo-Romero, L. (2021). AI watch - national strategies on artificial intelligence: A European perspective, 2021 edition, EUR 30745 EN. Publications Office of the European Union. https://doi.org/10.2760/069178, JRC122684.

Vienna Manifesto on Digital Humanism. (n.d.). https://www.informatik.tuwien.ac.at/dighum/index.php.

Williams, A. P., & Scharre, P. D. (Eds.). (2015). *Autonomous systems: Issues for defence policymakers*. North Atlantic Treaty Organization.

Wright, E. O. (2010). *Envisioning real Utopias*. Verso.

Zimmermann, R. E. (2022). Humanism revisited. *New Explorations*, 2(3), 6–13.

14. Beyond AI solutionism: toward a multi-disciplinary approach to artificial intelligence in society

Simon Lindgren and Virginia Dignum

INTRODUCTION

The last few years have seen a large increase in initiatives to develop national, international, and organizational strategies and plans to ensure that artificial intelligence (AI) is used responsibly and increase consumers' and citizens' trust in AI systems and the decisions facilitated by these systems. Even though such initiatives are laudable and necessary, it is acknowledged that powerful technologies such as AI can have serious unintended consequences. Underlying these efforts, there is an implicit belief that AI technologies can solve anything if only we take care of the potential side effects. However, AI is not magic, nor is it the solution to all our problems (Dignum 2019).

Many of the current discussions seem to see AI as a given, jumping immediately to the next step of making sure it is ethical and responsible. It is our argument in this chapter that addressing these issues adequately needs multi-disciplinary perspectives, particularly such approaches that combine technological expertise with critical and theoretically grounded analysis.

We draw here on the notion of technological solutionism (Morozov 2013), and scholarship and theories relating to a critique of technocracy (Meynaud 1969) and technological rationality (Marcuse 1964), to revitalize some of the terminology used in previous critical social studies of technology, power, and social change. In doing so, we want to challenge the common view that AI, if only constructed in the right way, can be a catch-all solution to a range of social problems. We argue that we must not let technological considerations dictate the conditions for social life.

CONCEPTUAL BACKGROUND

The last decade has seen groundbreaking advances in deep learning and neural networks (Goodfellow, Bengio, and Courville 2016), enabling computers to learn from experience, and thereby paving the way for advanced forms of language recognition, autonomous vehicles, image classification, text generation, and robots. For example, a technique such as GPT-3 (Brown et al. 2020) and applications such as ChatGPT that produce text similar to that produced by humans, or DALL-E, which creates images from text captions, was not imaginable just a few years ago. Such tools' potential to augment and change human interaction with AI systems, and social life, is very large. But in developing an adequate, and critical, perspective on the potential as well as the limits of AI in its social context, it is important to remember the long history of social theories about technology and social change.

While technologies and their consequences may differ, there are also notable continuities in how people respond to new and changing technology. The present hype surrounding the move toward further and broader adoption of AI, which is taken as happening as if by a force of nature, makes it even more important to question its premises (Lagerkvist 2020). Most commercial forms of AI development appear to be driven by an ideology of "inevitabilism" (Zuboff 2019), according to which posing any critical questions is seen as superfluous and futile. There is however much to learn from previous theorizing here. Prominently, notions of technological solutionism, technocracy, and technological rationality are useful to revisit.

TECHNOLOGICAL SOLUTIONISM

Technological solutionism is the ideological belief that various technologies – such as architectures, communication media, machines, and algorithms – can function as catch-all remedies for making society better (Morozov 2013).

More generally, *solutionism* as such means seeing socio-political issues as puzzles that can be solved, rather than as problems that must be responded to in a multitude of potential ways (Paquet 2005). A solutionist mindset entails reaching for answers, for example, technological ones, even before the problem to be solved has been fully defined. Patterns like these may often be seen in the areas of urban planning or architecture, where there can be a preoccupation with impractical solutions designed to impress but can fail to consider that the problems that one tries to solve are in fact highly complex, often fluid, and also contentious. It is crucial to realize that the discursive *articulation* of problems matters just as much, sometimes even more, than how they are resolved or not (Laclau and Mouffe 1985).

This does of course not mean that we should not take action in relation to urgent issues such as climate change, political polarization, racism and sexism, global injustices, and so on. Such issues are crucial to our future, and therefore it is even more important that they are addressed adequately. The point is that there are no easy fixes, technological or others, and that when we work toward potential ways of mitigating problems like these, we must do so while not being wed to any singular modes of action.

There are always multiple ways of defining, describing, and approaching social problems, and just because they are urgent this does not mean that new, comprehensive, and seemingly efficient technological solutions become automatically legitimate. Many times, it is more about responding to problems, than about attempting to solve them. Solutionism assumes that everything that can be made more efficient and rationalized should also by necessity be made so, but such is not always the human condition. We move down a very dangerous path if we see technology as something that can "fix the bugs of humanity" (Morozov 2013, p. 14).

Now, with uncritically applied AI threatening to overtake more sensible technological (AI and others) and social responses, solutionism – while not in itself a new phenomenon – is on the rise throughout a range of societal sectors and areas. We must be very careful here, as embedded with technological solutionism comes also a technological determinism that can make its believers blind to the fact that society and technology are mutually shaped (Šabanovic´ 2010).

TECHNOCRACY

Historically, one can see connections between solutionist lines of reasoning on the one hand and ideas about technocracy on the other. In brief, in technocratic social systems, technology and technological expertise are given the power to govern so that seemingly objective technical processes are directing and deciding society. This concept, which is partly synonymous with the idea of expert rule, has a long political history. It echoes Plato's idea about philosopher kings (Takala 1998) possessing "true knowledge" ruling over ordinary people and appears in Saint-Simon's ideas about how maximizing the efficiency of production should be the supreme societal goal (Mason 1931), as well as in how Taylorism driven by engineering expertise spilled over into management, politics, and people's everyday lives (Taylor 1911). Obviously, this is not the role we want to give to AI.

Technocracy, as a political concept, also has a strong connection to the technocratic ideology that gained momentum during the Cold War and has connections to both populism and fascism (Martin 1999; Bickerton and Accetti 2017). Some scholars paint a dystopian picture where there is a "technocratic convergence" of humans and data, and where a "technocratic elite" are in control of systems that may render political discourse and democracy obsolete (Broudy and Arakaki 2020). This is a future that can and must be avoided through critical analyses and sensible implementations of AI technology. Current efforts to develop standards and methods to ensure responsible, trustworthy, or ethical AI are concrete examples of such approaches.[1]

Solutionism with its related beliefs constitutes a certain relationship between science, technology, and politics. Taken to its extremes, it can function – at worst – as a kind of social engineering where socio-political processes and decisions become computationally streamlined and automated. In the dystopian view, our historically created and still proliferated sexist, racist, ableist, and other biases will no longer be discussed and responded to, but handled by machines. According to a technocratic line of thinking, we would hand it over to the machines to identify and hopefully remove the biases. This, of course, is not the way forward.

Those who have proclaimed the "end of theory" and argued that today "massive amounts of data and applied mathematics replace every other tool that might be brought to bear" (Anderson 2008) miss out on the fact that big data and automation are not an objective and outside force to society. Society and technology shape each other in interaction, and therefore the focus of analysis and debate must be on machines and humans in context (Lindgren and Holmström 2020). In the case of AI, this means that we must consider it in relation to its processes of production, as well as its consequences – through the lens of its producers, users, and subjects. Because these consequences are always different, for different people, in different situations (MacKenzie and Wajcman 1985).

TECHNOLOGICAL RATIONALITY

Technological progress, in areas such as AI, often appears as an unstoppable force, beyond the control and choices of humans. It is as if just because we have the technological opportunity

---

[1] See, for example, https://ethicsinaction.ieee.org/p7000/ or www. iso.org/news/ref2530.html.

and possibility to achieve certain things, it is desirable to achieve them. Such solutionism is driven by a form of Enlightenment-era view on progression, which assumes that information and technology have a universally liberating power. More data and more ways to analyze it are always assumed to be beneficial for society. This is strongly related to ethical considerations. Just because we can efficiently sort faces into categories, should we do it? A comparison with a famously ethically fraught area: just because we can clone humans, should we do it?

In *One-Dimensional Man* (1964), critical theorist Herbert Marcuse warned about a society based on purely *technological rationality*. This is the kind of society that we build when technological possibilities are allowed to decide which social and political goals we should have. Just like Marcuse warned that the advanced industrial society of his time could generate "false needs," so is there also a risk at present that all the possibilities offered by rapidly evolving technologies such as AI make us believe that we "need" certain "solutions," just because they are technologically possible to implement.

As argued above, the main focus must be on truly understanding and defining the problems, and on responding to them in often complex ways rather than imagining that they can be in every instance solved by technology. In AI, as in other areas, we should always decide the ends ahead of the means. Not the other way around. We run huge socio-political risks if AI was to become regarded as an end in itself. As an illustrative aside, science fiction writer and futurist Stanislaw Lem wrote in his 1964 book *Summa Technologiae* how technologies "are slowly, in the course of their own evolution, taking control of practically the whole of social dynamics" (Lem 1964, p. 152). Such dystopian developments must also be avoided in AI.

WHAT IS AI SOLVING?

A crucial risk with technological solutionism is that the futuristic and cool packaging that many new things – "the internet," "big data," "AI" – have come wrapped in conceals the fact that these technologies may still be vectors of, often century-old, discriminatory discourses. Just because technology is new, it is not by definition progressive. This is what has been realized in latter-year debates about how, for example, racism and sexism become built into algorithms (Buolamwini and Gebru 2018; Hamilton 2019; Noble 2018; O'Neil 2016; Williams et al. 2020). Technology comes into being *in* society. It does not come from the outside.

In the following, we discuss a few examples of applications of AI and reflect on the solutions they aim to provide. These include technological approaches to address the COVID-19 pandemic, the future of work, and the use of facial detection in public services.

During the current crisis caused by the COVID-19 pandemic, many public and private parties are considering deploying, or are already deploying, AI-driven applications, both for medical as well as for broader societal uses. Examples of such applications of AI include disease prediction with AI, AI to help with vaccine discovery, facial recognition tools to identify the use of face masks, and using image-recognition to assess social distancing, as well as AI for remote surveillance of patients and healthcare workers. In many of these applications, basic premises such as their effectiveness are often uncertain. Still, these desperate times tend to push for a turn to AI, and related technologies, as these actors – in the spirit of solutionism – naturally want to exhaust all possible avenues for alleviating the crisis. But even in such urgent cases, the solutionist mindset comes with the risk of creating gimmicks rather than adequately addressing the problems that have not been fully identified. Alongside an increasing concern about the implications of these applications for fundamental rights, ethical principles, and societal values, without proper analysis of the underlying context, and without a more developed understanding of what the problem that one wants to solve really is, these techno-solutionist approaches can have serious unintended consequences.

Considering the case of the future of work, we see that the digitalization of society has led to a transformation of large parts of the labor market where, given the demand for flexibility and resilience, many jobs are now part of the gig economy, and self-employment is increasingly the norm for a large proportion of the working population (Dølvik and Steen 2018). This is an area where technologically driven change (e.g., platforms and algorithms enabling gig economy businesses) obviously leads to new types of power structures and precariousness. Other social transformations, driven by AI and related technologies, will potentially have similar consequences for people's lives in the variety of societal arenas where the technology is employed. Ensuring a sustainable future, therefore, demands more than technological "solutions." The focus should be on striking a balance between technology and society and promoting and safeguarding justice and equality.

Finally, one can consider the debated face-detection system that the UK government implemented in passport controls in 2016, allegedly even while knowing its shortcomings, and which did not function well for people in some ethnic minority groups. In these cases, the employed technology operated so that a person's race became a barrier to using essential public services. As the system was debated and questioned, the UK government promised to conduct further "user research" and "usability testing" to try to remove the bias from the system (Vaughan 2019). This strategy must be questioned because it turns back to technology to try to fix an inherently social problem. The real problem is not one of bias in software or hardware. That bias is just a symptom of the broader context where it was somehow black and not white people that the system failed to identify. The real problem also has to do with the already irreversible socio-political consequences that the very implementation of the system as such had through its normalization of injustice. Even though approaches to deal with bias in algorithms are much needed, attempting to *solve* bias algorithmically falls short of understanding the complex and multi-faceted different ways in which bias manifests in society (Zuiderveen Borgesius et al. 2018). More broadly, face-recognition technologies as they are currently developed and implemented have been shown by research to reinforce racial discrimination, as well as strengthen the effects of racism on groups that have been historically disadvantaged (Bacchini and Lorusso 2019).

Based on examples like these, and against the historical and conceptual background of technological solutionism and related notions, we argue that the societal effects of technology, such as AI, are too severe and important to be left to technology itself to solve. Albeit necessary, fixing a racist algorithm will not fix the social problem of racism and maybe not even contribute at all toward that goal as the technological focus misconstrues what the problem actually is and underestimates its complexity.

UNBIASED AI IS NOT THE SOLUTION

Much of the current debate on the shortcomings of AI is focused on bias and fairness. Research in the FAccT (fairness, accountability, and transparency in machine learning)[2] field aims to

---

[2]   https://facctconference.org/.

embed considerations of fairness into the design and governance of automated systems and includes efforts to ensure fairness in decision-making and to minimize prejudiced decisions due to lack of diversity or other forms of bias in the datasets that form the basis of many current AI applications.

As identified by Wachter, Mittelstadt, and Russell (2020), major approaches to automated fairness include, among others, the development of statistical metrics for fairness and their societal implications, bias testing using sensitive data, prevention of bias via causal reasoning, testing for disparate impact, and software toolkits to analyze models and datasets for bias. Even though not all these methods are exclusively technical, most approaches illustrate the expectation that, to varying degrees, technology can help with the solution. This is further evidenced in methods for data processing, such as resampling (Mehrabi et al. 2019), or algorithm augmentation (Lagrangian approach) (Agarwal et al. 2018), and tools such as AI Fairness 360 (Bellamy et al. 2018), recently launched by IBM, support the idea that technology itself can solve or at least mitigate fairness in algorithms.

Moreover, addressing fairness in AI requires understanding that such an abstract concept is amenable to many different interpretations. Imagine, for instance, a system that assigns scholarships to students being developed to uphold the value of *fairness*. Whereas it is easy to agree that fairness is an important value for such a system, given that many different interpretations of fairness are possible, such a system can result in quite diverse outcomes. If fairness is interpreted as the equal division of resources, the system will divide equally the available scholarship total by all students, but if fairness is interpreted as equal opportunity, the system will attribute higher scholarships to the students that need them the most.

Technological solutionism is deeply embedded in society and culture, and the big risk with this is that it imposes limitations on our imaginations about how the world can be made more democratic and equal. Because of this, the solutionist mindset must be unlearned in order for us to get past it (Morozov 2013). This way of thinking and operating is connected to a particular value system – it is ideological – and will lead to a quest for technological perfection, without taking the complexity of human and social life into account. Furthermore, many AI models are trained using previously collected data, and by definition, can therefore only predict the future as long as it looks like the past. Using such models to design interventions and mechanisms to change the world will project the inequalities of the past into the future (Mayson 2018).

IS ETHICAL AI THE WAY FORWARD?

The idea that, left alone, AI systems will magically develop to know all and know better has stronger roots in science fiction than it has in scholarly knowledge. Nonetheless, this view is a powerful driver for governments and organizations in their efforts toward governing AI development and use.

In the last few years, private companies and research institutions, as well as public sector organizations, have issued principles and guidelines describing how to ensure proper development, use, and governance of AI. A recent study identified 84 such documents, and a significant increase over time in the number of publications, with over 80% having been released after 2016 (Jobin, Ienca, and Vayena 2019). Whether calling its area of concern "ethical," "trustworthy," or "responsible" AI, these documents share the underlying sentiment that AI development is inevitable but also problematic.

As countries around the world are establishing governmental and intergovernmental strategies and initiatives to guide the development of AI, global cooperation, standards, and norms will be critical components in the advancement of safe and beneficial AI in equal and democratic ways. This means that these principles and guidelines need to address not only the consequences of AI "solutions," the development and implementation of which are seen in ideological terms as unavoidable, but they must be based on an awareness that paradigm changes, such as the technological one that society is currently undergoing, require a simultaneous process of evaluating consequences, considering other solutions, being sensitive to issues of power and democracy, and updating and adapting the institutional framework that provides the necessary basis for acceptance.

Furthermore, uncertainty remains regarding how ethical principles and guidelines should be implemented, and how to monitor or audit compliance with principles. If anything, these efforts highlight the century-old debate over ethics: Can the world ever agree on universally shared ethical principles? Due to the different living conditions, scopes of agency, degrees of power, political horizons, and goals of different nations, organizations, businesses, groups, and individuals, this is not likely. Looking at current approaches to the implementation of ethical reasoning, we can see two main directions emerging (Wallach and Allen 2008; Berreby, Bourgne, and Gabriel Ganascia 2018):

- *Top-down approaches*, which infer individual decisions from general rules. The aim is to implement a given ethical theory, for example, utilitarianism, or deontology, within a computational framework, and apply it to a particular case.
- *Bottom-up approaches*, which infer general rules from individual cases. The aim is to provide an AI system with sufficient observations of what others have done in similar situations and the means to aggregate these observations into a decision about what is ethically acceptable.

Top-down approaches implicitly assume that it is possible to identify and represent a set of rules that is adequate and sufficient as a guide for ethical behavior. A fundamental premise of bottom-up approaches is the assumption that what is socially accepted – as evidenced in the data – is also ethically acceptable, that is that "the wisdom of the crowd" can lead to an acceptable ethical decision. Even though it can be argued that we, humans, learn ethical behavior by observation and imitation of others, bias and lack of diversity in datasets are the source of many of the problems with data-driven automated decision-making systems (Dignum 2019).

However, the attempts of both approaches to codifying ethical principles in AI systems inevitably lead to the selection of one singular interpretation, out of innumerable possible interpretations, of ethical values. In reality, ethical values are grounded in highly abstract vague concepts that allow for different interpretations depending on the user and context. Individuals, cultures, and contexts assign different priorities to priorities. Moreover, as described in the previous section, describing goals for AI development and use in terms of high-level values such as fairness, inclusion, or sustainability is not sufficient, as these can have many different normative interpretations, depending on the context.

Hybrid approaches, combining elements from bottom-up and top-down approaches, are needed that focus on reflection on the ethical decision-making itself. These approaches can also give the opportunity to design systems encoding different interpretations of values or support the use of counterfactuals to explore the effects of such interpretations. The pursuit of this endeavor will surely contribute to a much more profound understanding of these century-old problems, and in doing so give us a better understanding of our own ethical reasoning, but this requires participation and debate.

CONCLUDING REMARKS

The deep and wide impact of AI on society requires a broadening of education as well as research in this area. Moving forward, a multi-disciplinary approach will be crucial as we focus on issues that include:

- Understanding and critiquing the intended and unforeseen, positive and negative, socio-political consequences of AI for society in terms of equality, democracy, and human rights.
- Understanding issues of governance, not only in terms of competence and responsibilities, but also in terms of power, trust, and accountability.
- Understanding the societal, legal, and economic functioning of socio-technical systems.
- Increasing the knowledge about value-based design approaches and ethical frameworks.
- Analyzing the consequences of inclusion and diversity in design, and how such strategies may inform processes and results.
- Understanding the distributed and increasingly ubiquitous nature of AI applications and developing new scholarly perspectives on human-machine communication.

In an increasingly connected AI world, incentives and regulations can support awareness and commitment to a diverse perspective, ensuring that AI applications are truly adaptable to a diverse cultural space, and thus enabling access to all. Failure to understand cultural diversity negatively impacts the universal right to access the advantages that technology brings about. An ethical system should assist in capturing opportunities and overcoming challenges, rather than just describing them. It is essential that a diversity of disciplines and stakes infuses the design and development of AI, in terms of gender, class, ethnicity, discipline, and other pertinent dimensions (Floridi et al. 2018).

In his article "Seven Deadly Sins of AI Predictions," Rodney Brooks (2017) quotes Amara's Law: "We tend to overestimate the effect of a technology in the short run and underestimate the effect in the long run." In its relatively short history, *AI solutionism* has led not only to excitement and hope at the current moment, but also to discrimination, disappointment, and serious setbacks in AI research during the so-called AI winters in the 1960s, the 1980s, and the early 1990s.

AI is no longer an engineering discipline where technological considerations are at the center. AI is today about a broad societal transformation with political implications. In this chapter, we have made theoretical connections to notions of *technological solutionism, technocracy*, and critiques of *technological rationality*. Such perspectives offer much-needed context and historical sensitivity, as well as terminology, for how AI must be approached. That is, in a way where informed analyses of its societal consequences, as well as of what "ethical" or "fair" AI really means, take center stage alongside the technologically driven side of AI development and innovation.

More than being a viable means to solve century-old social problems, AI systems can help us identify these problems as they play out at the nexus of humans and machines today.

REFERENCES

Agarwal, A.; Beygelzimer, A.; Dud́ ık, M.; Langford, J.; and Wallach, H. 2018. A Reductions Approach to Fair Classification. In *International Conference on Machine Learning*, 60–69. PMLR.

Anderson, C. 2008. The End of Theory: The Data Deluge Makes the Scientific Method Obsolete. *WIRED.* https://www.wired.com/2008/06/Pb-Theory/.

Bacchini, F.; and Lorusso, L. 2019. Race, Again: How Face Recognition Technology Reinforces Racial Discrimination. *Journal of Information, Communication and Ethics in Society* 17(3): 321–335. https://doi.org/10.1108/JICES-05-2018-0050.

Bellamy, R. K. E.; Dey, K.; Hind, M.; Hoffman, S. C.; Houde, S.; Kannan, K.; Lohia, P.; Martino, J.; Mehta, S.; Mojsilovic, A.; Nagar, S.; Ramamurthy, K. N.; Richards, J. T.; Saha, D.; Sattigeri, P.; Singh, M.; Varshney, K. R.; and Zhang, Y. 2018. AI Fairness 360: An Extensible Toolkit for Detecting, Understanding, and Mitigating Unwanted Algorithmic Bias. *CoRR* Abs/1810.01943. http://arxiv.org/abs/1810.01943.

Berreby, F.; Bourgne, G.; and Gabriel Ganascia, J. 2018. Event-Based and Scenario-Based Causality for Computational Ethics. In *Proceedings of the 17th International Conference on Autonomous Agents and MultiAgent Systems, AAMAS*, 147–155. International Foundation for Autonomous Agents and Multiagent Systems.

Bickerton, C.; and Accetti, C. I. 2017. Populism and Technocracy. In Kaltwasser, C. R.; Taggart, P.; Espejo, P. O.; and Ostiguy, P., eds., *The Oxford Handbook of Populism*. Oxford: Oxford University Press. https://doi.org/10.1093/Oxfordhb/ 9780198803560.013.24.

Brooks, R. 2017. The Seven Deadly Sins of AI Predictions. *MIT Technology Review.* https://www .technologyreview.com/2017/10/06/241837/theseven-deadly-sins-of-ai-predictions/.

Broudy, D.; and Arakaki, M. 2020. Who Wants to Be a Slave? The Technocratic Convergence of Humans and Data. *Frontiers in Communication* 5. https://doi.org/10.3389/Fcomm.2020.00037.

Brown, T. B.; Mann, B.; Ryder, N.; Subbiah, M.; Kaplan, J.; Dhariwal, P.; Neelakantan, A.; Shyam, P.; Sastry, G.; Askell, A.; Agarwal, S.; Herbert-Voss, A.; Krueger, G.; Henighan, T.; Child, R.; Ramesh, A.; Ziegler, D. M.; Wu, J.; Winter, C.; Hesse, C.; Chen, M.; Sigler, E.; Litwin, M.; Gray, S.; Chess, B.; Clark, J.; Berner, C.; McCandlish, S.; Radford, A.; Sutskever, I.; and Amodei, D. 2020. Language Models are Few-Shot Learners.

Buolamwini, J.; and Gebru, T. 2018. Gender Shades: Intersectional Accuracy Disparities in Commercial Gender Classification. In *Conference on Fairness, Accountability and Transparency*, 77–91. PMLR.

Dignum, V. 2019. *Responsible Artificial Intelligence: How to Develop and Use AI in a Responsible Way.* Springer Nature.

Dølvik, J. E.; and Steen, J. R. 2018. *The Nordic Future of Work: Drivers, Institutions, and Politics.* Nordic Council of Ministers.

Floridi, L.; Cowls, J.; Beltrametti, M.; Chatila, R.; Chazerand, P.; Dignum, V.; Luetge, C.; Madelin, R.; Pagallo, U.; Rossi, F.; et al. 2018. AI4People—An Ethical Framework for a Good AI Society: Opportunities, Risks, Principles, and Recommendations. *Minds and Machines* 28(4): 689–707.

Goodfellow, I.; Bengio, Y.; and Courville, A. 2016. *Deep Learning.* Cambridge, MA: MIT Press.

Hamilton, M. 2019. The Sexist Algorithm. *Behavioral Sciences & the Law* 37(2): 145–157.

Jobin, A.; Ienca, M.; and Vayena, E. 2019. The Global Landscape of AI Ethics Guidelines. *Nature Machine Intelligence* 1(9): 389–399.

Laclau, E.; and Mouffe, C. 1985. *Hegemony and Socialist Strategy: Towards a Radical Democratic Politics.* London: Verso.

Lagerkvist, A. 2020. Digital Limit Situations: Anticipatory Media Beyond 'the New AI Era'. *Journal of Digital Social Research* 2(3): 16–41–16–41. https://doi.org/10.33621/Jdsr.v2i3.55.

Lem, S. 1964. *Summa Technologiae*. Minneapolis, MN: University of Minnesota Press.

Lindgren, S.; and Holmstro¨m, J. 2020. A Social Science Perspective on Artificial Intelligence: Building Blocks for a Research Agenda. *Journal of Digital Social Research* 2(3).

MacKenzie, D.; and Wajcman, J., eds. 1985. *The Social Shaping of Technology: How the Refrigerator Got Its Hum*. Milton Keynes: Open University Press.

Marcuse, H. 1964. *One-Dimensional Man: Studies in the Ideology of Advanced Industrial Society*. London: Routledge.

Martin, W. 1999. The Social and Cultural Shaping of Educational Technology: Toward a Social Constructivist Framework. *AI & Society* 13(4): 402–420. https://doi.org/10.1007/BF01205986.

Mason, E. S. 1931. Saint-Simonism and the Rationalisation of Industry. *The Quarterly Journal of Economics* 45(4): 640. https://doi.org/10.2307/1883248.

Mayson, S. G. 2018. Bias in, Bias Out. *Yale Law Journal* 128: 2218–2300.

Mehrabi, N.; Morstatter, F.; Saxena, N.; Lerman, K.; and Galstyan, A. 2019. A Survey on Bias and Fairness in Machine Learning. arXiv preprint arXiv:1908.09635.

Meynaud, J. 1969. *Technocracy*. New York: Free Press.

Morozov, E. 2013. *To Save Everything, Click Here: The Folly of Technological Solutionism*. New York: PublicAffairs.

Noble, S. U. 2018. *Algorithms of Oppression: How Search Engines Reinforce Racism*. New York: New York University Press.

O'Neil, C. 2016. *Weapons of Math Destruction: How Big Data Increases Inequality and Threatens Democracy*. New York: Crown.

Paquet, G. 2005. *The New Geo-Governance*. University of Ottawa Press.

S˘abanovic´, S. 2010. Robots in Society, Society in Robots. *International Journal of Social Robotics* 2(4): 439–450.

Takala, T. 1998. Plato on Leadership. *Journal of Business Ethics* 17(7): 785–798. https://doi.org/10.1023/a:1005789531144.

Taylor, F. W. 1911. *The Principles of Scientific Management*. New York: Harper & Brothers.

Vaughan, A. 2019. UK Launched Passport Photo Checker It Knew Would Fail with Dark Skin. *New Scientist*. https://www.newscientist.com/article/2219284-uklaunched-passport-photo-checker-it-knew-would-failwith-dark-skin/.

Wachter, S.; Mittelstadt, B.; and Russell, C. 2020. Why Fairness Cannot Be Automated: Bridging the Gap Between EU Non-Discrimination Law and AI. Available at SSRN.

Wallach, W.; and Allen, C. 2008. *Moral Machines: Teaching Robots Right From Wrong*. Oxford University Press.

Williams, J. C.; Anderson, N.; Mathis, M.; Sanford, E.; Eugene, J.; and Isom, J. 2020. Colorblind Algorithms: Racism in the Era of COVID-19. *Journal of the National Medical Association* 112(5): 550–552. https://doi.org/10.1016/j.jnma.2020.05. 010.

Zuboff, S. 2019. *The Age of Surveillance Capitalism: The Fight for a Human Future at the New Frontier of Power*. New York: PublicAffairs.

Zuiderveen Borgesius, F.; et al. 2018. *Discrimination, Artificial Intelligence, and Algorithmic Decision-Making*. Strasbourg Council of Europe, Directorate General of Democracy.

15. Artificial intelligence and social memory: towards the cyborgian remembrance of an advancing mnemo-technic

Samuel Merrill

INTRODUCTION

As the introductions to countless journal papers, books and newspaper articles repeat, a renewed interest in artificial intelligence (AI) is changing everything. This 'hype' is not only the result of actual advances in AI systems but is also down to the marketing efforts of those big tech companies that have recently sought to explore what AI can do with the huge amounts of data and computational resources that they have consolidated over the last decade (see Whittaker 2021). At the same time as these industrial AI systems are marketed as having the potential to solve the complex challenges currently facing human society, critical scholars have increasingly noted that they attract new problems. For instance, Meredith Whittaker, co-founder, and director of the *AI Now Institute*, which was founded in 2017 to study the social implications of AI, recently warned:

> This is a perilous moment. Private computational systems marketed as artificial intelligence (AI) are threading through our public life and institutions, concentrating industrial power, compounding marginalization, and quietly shaping access to resources and information. (2021)

Spearheaded by the likes of Whittaker and many others, a new interdisciplinary research agenda is emerging concerned with the critical analysis of AI systems and their impact on many different realms of public life (see Verdegem 2021a; and this *Handbook*). However, within this agenda, little has been written on AI and social memory. This is the case even though society's increasing mediatization, digitalization, and datafication and the growing use of AI systems to learn from the products of these processes is rendering more and more of our everyday lives memory-related or 'mnemonic' (Merrill Forthcoming). In other words, in a thoroughly mediatized, digitalized, and datafied society, concerns relating to AI-controlled access to information are also essentially concerns about AI-controlled access to memory (see Merrill Forthcoming; Chun 2008). We now not only live in an *information society* but also a *memory society* and thus we need to think and talk about memory as much as information.

In this chapter, I begin to address this contention by conceptually exploring AI's relationship with social memory from the perspectives of first, the social sciences and humanities via the interdisciplinary field of memory studies, and second, of those disciplines more traditionally associated with AI research and development including computer science. I start by briefly defining social memory and positioning AI systems as mnemonic technologies. Thereafter I discuss how memory has primarily been conflated with storage within AI research and development before suggesting the alternative conflation of computation to remembrance to move towards a more integrated and hybrid understanding of social memory in the AI era.

Finally, after noting social memory studies' predominantly instrumentalist understanding of mnemonic technologies and drawing on the works of Donna J. Haraway and Bernard Stiegler, I introduce the concepts of *cyborgian remembrance* and *AI mnemotechnics* as possible ways to grasp the complex relationship between AI and social memory. I conclude the chapter by briefly indicating how such concepts can help decenter human memory in ways that might better facilitate the critical analysis of the challenges and risks associated with AI's increased influence in matters of social memory, and highlighting some of these challenges and risks as potential foci for future, empirically orientated research.

SOCIAL MEMORY AND MNEMONIC TECHNOLOGIES

While better perceived as an array and combinations of technologies and data-centric techniques than as a single technology (see Whittaker 2021), AI and the systems and intelligent agents that underpin it represent one of the latest in a long line of technological developments that have had implications for what is often referred to as 'social memory'. The concept of social memory, like that of 'collective memory', conveys that all individual remembering is also 'in some sense social' insofar as it is, for example, influenced by different social frameworks and shared technologies (Olick 1999, 346; see also Halbwachs 1992).[1] Social memories are subsequently as diverse and pluralistic as the groups and institutions within society. As such, social memory is 'an important issue in the struggle for power among social forces' (Le Goff 1992, 54) and has become a significant focus of critical scholarship concerned with 'what a society remembers, how a society's memories are contested and change over time, and which societal groups have control over the production of memory' (Merrill 2017, 28). Within memory studies, it is thus common to distinguish between official, dominant forms of social memory and the forms of counter-memory that challenges these (see Olick & Robbins 1998). It is also possible to broadly divide much of this field's scholarship into two camps (Olick 1999). The first of these has been primarily interested in 'collected memory' – 'aggregations of socially framed individual memories' (Olick 1999, 333) – and has placed focus on the organic memories of the human brain and the psychological, neurological and cognitive factors that influence these memories. The second camp has been more interested in those memories that are 'collective sui generis' (Olick 1999, 333), including those supported by mnemonic technologies external to the brain.

Mnemonic technologies (also referred to as technologies of memory) hinge on the exteriorization of individual memory through various types of documentation and media including those related to writing, images, bodies and places (see Assmann 2011; Olick 1999). These technologies have developed over time, with different sorts of social organization coming to rely on different mnemonic technologies (Olick 1999). For instance, in a Western context, the French historian Jacques Le Goff (1992), building on others' work, discussed five periods of social memory characterized chiefly by differing extents of oral and written memory transmission. These periods are as follows: a pre-literate period associated primarily with orality and embodied memory practices; second, the transition from prehistory to antiquity and the

---

[1]   'Cultural memory' is a broadly similar concept but is more concerned with the cultural representation of the past and has a disciplinarily lineage rooted more in the humanities than in the social sciences (see Erll 2012).

emergence of writing; third, a medieval phase characterized by an equilibrium between oral and written memory; fourth, the period from the Renaissance until the mid-20th century that constituted a gradual memory revolution involving the increasing written exteriorization of individual memory commencing with the invention of the printing press leading to the birth of nationally orientated institutions like archives, libraries and museums; and finally thereafter, a more rapid memory revolution brought on, in part by the rise of electronic, or digital, 'means of recording and transmitting information which not only change the way we remember, but provide new ways of conceptualizing memory' (Le Goff 1992; Olick & Robbins 1998, 115).

Society today is characterized by a plethora of mnemonic technologies and media including those that are text-based but also, following 19th- and 20th-century advances in photographic, film and sound recording technology, those that are image- (still and moving) and audio-based. Each of these technologies – whether they exteriorize memories in artworks, books, newspapers, maps, photographs, songs, movies, television shows or tweets (etc.) and whether they are based on print, analogue, broadcast or digital logics – create social memory insofar as they allow for memories to become 'prosthetic' (Landsberg 2004): 'disseminated across time and space and adopted by groups and individuals besides those who experienced them in their authentic, original settings' (Merrill 2017, 35). All these technologies have broadened the spread of prosthetic memories, but it is fair to say that those that are digital in character have done so to an extent and at a rate never before witnessed – hence a new memory revolution. This digital memory revolution shows little sign of slowing as new and rapidly developing digital mnemonic technologies including laptops, mobile phones, internet and social media platforms, and even more recently augmented and artificial reality technologies, reformulate social modes of remembering. Subsequently, digital technologies and their associated platforms have become a key focus for a new wave of social memory research that has stressed how the globalization and digitalization of society have created new 'globital memory fields' (Reading 2011) and 'memory ecologies' (Brown & Hoskins 2010) through which producers and consumers of memories have become blurred and memories are prosthetically shared in a more rapid and multitudinous manner (Hoskins 2017). The strength of these research currents has been indicated by the emergence of the subfield of digital memory studies within which the concept of 'connective memory' – as indicating the relational and multidirectional aspects of memory (see Rothberg 2009) foregrounded by digital hyperconnectivity – has gained precedence (Hoskins 2017). Within this subfield, computer algorithms have gained scholarly attention leading to a discussion of 'algorithmic memory' (see Sluis 2010; Esposito 2017), especially regarding how the algorithms behind social media platforms are shaping remembrance practices (see Lambert et al. 2018; Schwarz 2014). However, the interface between AI and social memory more generally has received little consideration.[2]

---

[2]　This is changing with a special issue of the new *Memory Studies Review* journal dedicated to bridging AI and memory studies scholarship planned for 2024. An early exception to this situation, projected from the computer sciences towards memory studies, is Kvasnička and Pospíchal's application of the collective memory concept to distributed artificial intelligence and multi-agent systems (2015).

ARTIFICIAL INTELLIGENCE, MEMORY AND STORAGE

The relative lack of research concerning AI and social memory is intriguing given that memory, as a central human cognitive capacity, has long featured – albeit often somewhat implicitly – as a prerequisite of AI research and development. This is because intelligence partly depends on the mnemonic ability to recall, recollect, remember and recognize past events and prior knowledge and, in turn, to learn from them. Memory is, in short, 'not only a property of intelligence but, ... the support on which sequences of acts are inscribed' (Leroi-Gourhan 1964/65 translated and cited in Le Goff 1992). As the AI theorist Roger Schank wrote in 1990 (1–2):

> Intelligence in the popular mind, refers to the capacity to solve complex problems, but another way of looking at the issue might be to say intelligence is really about understanding what has happened well enough to predict when it might happen again. To be a successful predictor of future events, one has to have explained confusing prior events successfully. Explaining the world (at least to yourself) is a critical aspect of intelligence. Comprehending events around you depends upon having a memory of prior events available for helping in the interpretation of new events ... One can't be said to know something if one can't find it in memory when it is needed.

Despite memory's centrality to intelligence, in the earliest AI research, it featured more as a technical necessity and limitation rather than an object of exploration in and of itself. For example, in a 1955 proposal for one of their earliest projects, AI pioneers John McCarthy, Marvin Minsky, Nathaniel Rochester and Claude Shannon recognized that 'the speeds and memory capacities of present computers may be insufficient to simulate many of the higher functions of the human brain' (1955/2006, 12). A tacit concern with memory continued to underly the AI research of the 1960s and 1970s that led to the development of multi-agent systems and computer programs that solved puzzles, played games and retrieved information, as well as that of the 1980s that was concerned with expert systems (Nilsson 1998, 9–10). More recently, and as detailed further below, the role of memory has arguably gained greater recognition, with respect to self-organizing systems, machine learning, deep learning and artificial neural networks. However, as with earlier research, the 'memory' on which these AI advances have relied has been primarily conceptualized as complementing or competing with, rather than necessarily mimicking, human memory. In short, memory in AI research is often conflated with storage – memory as a store to be filled rather than as a phenomenon related to remembrance processes. Wendy Hui Kyong Chun has outlined how this conflation has underpinned many different forms of digital media and computer technology. She writes (2008, 148–149):

> key to the newness of the digital is a conflation of memory and storage that both underlies and undermines digital media's archival promise. Memory, with its constant degeneration, does not equal storage; although artificial memory has historically combined the transitory with the permanent, the passing with the stable, digital media complicates this relationship by making the permanent into an enduring ephemeral, creating unforeseen degenerative links between humans and machines...this conflation of memory with storage is not due to some inherent technological feature but rather due to how everyday usage and parlance arrests memory and its degenerative possibilities in order to support dreams of superhuman digital programmability.

She continues by noting that the 'major characteristic of digital media is memory. Its ontology is defined by memory, from content to purpose, from hardware to software from CD-Roms to memory sticks, from RAM to ROM' (2008, 154). But Chun also highlights that the computational conflation of memory to storage was not always as prominent as it is today. While Alan Turing, in his seminal paper *Computing Machinery and Intelligence* (1950), likened a digital computer's store to its memory, five years earlier, John Von Neumann used the term 'memory organ' instead of store in his *First Draft Report on the EDVAC* metaphorically inferring the biologically ephemeral nature of computational memory (1945; Chun 2008). In the same year, Vannevar Bush wrote *As We May Think* (1945): a work that has subsequently been canonized as the conceptual origin of the internet (Chun 2008). In it, Bush discusses the memex – a microfilm-based memory augmentation device, which although never realized, hoped to computationally mimic human memory and, in turn, address its weaknesses (see Chun 2008; Locke 2000; Ng 2021).

According to Chun (2008), the long-lasting misconception promulgated by the memex – as an influential idea – is that the internet, along with digital media and computational memory more generally, are somehow not ephemeral when in actuality they are enduringly so. In other words, it is not a case of 'the internet never forgetting' – to use the popular saying as an example – but rather of it perpetually forgetting and remembering. This misconception partly explains why the computational memory that today supports numerous AI systems is often considered to improve the capacity of human memory through stable exteriorization. Le Goff (1992), for instance, perceived human memory to be unstable and malleable, and computer memory as highly stable and more easily accessible. Similarly, and echoing the general rationalization of AI in comparative terms against human capabilities (see Ng 2021), machine learning expert Max Tegmark (2017) essentially defines memory as stably stored information and contrasts computer memory retrieval with human memory retrieval insofar as the latter relies on specifying *where* something is stored and the former on specifying something about *what* is stored. He writes (2017, 83):

> The memory in your brain works very differently from computer memory, not only in terms of how it's built, but also in terms of how it's used. Whereas you retrieve memories from a computer or hard drive by specifying *where* it's stored, you retrieve memories from your brain by specifying something about *what* is stored. Each group of bits in your computer's memory has a numerical address, and to retrieve a piece of information, the computer specifies at what address to look, just as if I tell you 'Go to my bookshelf, take the fifth book from the right on the top shelf, and tell me what it says on page 314'. In contrast, you retrieve information from your brain similarly to how you retrieve it from a search engine: you specify a piece of the information or something related to it, and it pops up.

Likewise, Rainer Rehak (2021) has recently noted:

> consciously remembering something is a highly complex process for humans which is more comparable to living through imagined events again and by that event changing what is being remembered. Human memory is therefore a very lively and dynamic process, and not at all comparable to retrieving accurate copies of stored data bits.

COMPUTATION AS REMEMBRANCE

By now, the speed and capacity of computational memory have grown at such a rate that the limitations noted in the 1950s (see above) are no longer as significant as they were. What this means in terms of drawing comparisons with the memory capacity of the human brain remains subject to scientific debate, however. Tegmark (2017, 83) writes that human brains store about 10 gigabytes of information electrically and 100 terabytes of information chemically/biologically, meaning that 'the world's best computers can now out-remember any biological system'.[3] Russel and Norvig (2016, 12) meanwhile acknowledge that:

> computers have a cycle time that is a million times faster than a brain. The brain makes up for that with far more storage and interconnection than even a high-end personal computer, although the largest supercomputers have a capacity that is similar to the brain's. (It should be noted, however, that the brain does not seem to use all of its neurons simultaneously.)

While Russel and Norvig continue that this state of affairs has led futurists to predict an approaching moment when computers gain superhuman capacities they temper such predictions by acknowledging that these sorts of 'raw comparisons are not especially informative. Even with a computer of virtually unlimited capacity, we still would not know how to achieve the brain's level of intelligence' (2016, 12).

One way that might help us think beyond the 'memory as stable storage' paradigm and avoid only the comparative consideration of human and artificial memory is to reconsider the relationship between memory and computation in computers. Nil Nilson, in distinguishing between these two, has highlighted how some of the reactive intelligent agents that underpin AI systems – by perceiving their environment and autonomously acting towards certain goals – do not necessarily do much computation. Their actions are 'memory-based implementations – compilations of the designer's knowledge' (Nilsson 1998, 117). However, the development of memory-based intelligent agents competent enough to perform more complex tasks in more complex environments would not only require designers to exercise unrealistic foresight in predicting all suitable reactions for all possible situations but would also demand potentially unattainable amounts of computational memory (Nilsson 1998). To reduce the memory demands of an agent some computation is usually moved inside the agent's action function. This means that the function may take longer but requires less space (Nilsson 1998). Thus, the traditional way of conceiving the relationship between memory and computation in the computer sciences maps onto the so-called 'space-time tradeoff' (Nilsson 1998, 117). This is also reflected in the criteria commonly used to ascertain the effectiveness of problem-solving intelligent agents like search algorithms. These include measuring whether an existing solution is identified (completeness) and whether an optimal solution is found (optimality) but also crucially how long it takes to find a solution (time complexity) and how much memory is required to carry out the search (space complexity) (Russel & Norvig 2016, 80).

The 'space-time tradeoff' means that the discussion of computer memory in relation to AI can seem counterintuitive for those who study memory in its more social guises (collected, collective, connective) because again it is often reduced only to a spatial storage facility and the information therein rather than also perceived as a temporal process as, for example, computation is. Tegmark actually defines computation as 'a transformation of one memory state into another' via the use of different functions (2017, 84). Keeping this definition in mind and if we accept that the goal of AI systems is to partly think and in turn act like humans

---

[3]   Some neuroscientific research suggests that the total memory capacity of the human brain might actually be ten times larger than this, for example, a petrabyte (see Bartol et al. 2015).

(Verdegem 2021b, 4; Russel & Norvig 2016), then perhaps it is useful to conceptualize at least some forms of computation, in particular, those involving search and retrieval tasks, as akin to remembrance. Writing from a social science and humanities rather than computer science perspective, Le Goff (1992) seems to suggest this insofar as he listed the function of memory within computers as relating to a broader array of tasks including those that many might alternatively be identified as computation. His list:

a) a means entering data and the program; b) elements endowed with memory, constituted by magnetic devices, which preserve the information introduced into the machine and the partial results obtained in the course of its operation; c) a very rapid means of calculation; d) means of verification; e) means of extracting the results. (Le Goff 1992, 91)

Tempering memory's conflation only to stable storage by approaching computation as akin to remembering can be useful because it foregrounds the transformational component of both computation and remembering and can help highlight some of the possible conceptual similarities between human and computational memory and remembrance. For instance, across the field of social memory studies, it is widely agreed that each time individuals and groups remember they do so anew. While it is easy to fall into the computational trap of conflating memory purely to stable storage and expecting computation to generate representationally stable and consistent outputs, the fact remains that each time a computation is run, it is done so anew regardless of the seeming consistency of results it generates. Images on a computer screen are 'frozen for human eyes only' (Chun 2008, 167) or with respect to the example of the pocket calculator given by Tegmark: every time its square-root button is pressed, 'it computes exactly the same function in exactly the same way' (2017, 96).

As already noted, remembering has implicitly underpinned many AI efforts to master recall, recognition and learning processes but these efforts' technical focus and vocabulary have most often cast memory as a computational storage space rather than part of a human remembrance process that might itself be artificially reproduced. In short, those developing AI have mostly tried to emulate human tasks that require memory but not explicitly the task of remembering.

There are, however, exceptions to this situation. Over 30 years ago, Schank argued that developing self-organizing memory (what is self-organizing memory if not remembering?) within AI systems was an important and challenging goal for computer scientists (1990, 145):

the hardest part of the creation of an intelligent entity is not finding information that it should know. We can easily figure out things to tell it. The problem is finding a way for the intelligent agent to know where to look in its own memory to find what is in there. One solution to this problem is the self-organizing memory. Scientists wouldn't have to decide where to put each piece of information in memory; rather the memory would do the job itself.

Schank's words still indicate the pervasive conception of memory as a storage space, but in referring to self-organizing memories that 'do it themselves' they also highlight an interest in emulating more human modes of remembering. Katrina Sluis (2010) has framed this sort of self-organizing computational memory in relation to the use of algorithms. She writes:

In the process of outsourcing the function of 'seeing' and 'recalling' to machines, there emerges a desire for memory which is both automated and passive. The modularity and flexibility of media creates the possibility of an *algorithmic memory*: an increasingly intelligent self-organizing extensible memory which can circulate independently of human intervention. The reliance on algorithms to process images and retrieve texts also presents a shift in focus from *storage* to *retrieval* in mnemonic labour. (2010, 231)

Internet search engine algorithms, for example (as somewhat contradictorily hinted at in the extended quote from Tegmark (2017, 83) at the close of the previous section), mimic to a greater extent human auto-associative modes of remembering insofar as they retrieve information by association rather than by address. These auto-associative intelligent agents are needed because the non-hierarchical hyper-textual network of the internet, following the conceptual precedent of the memex, mimics the human mind in how it stores information – in a dynamic, relational and associative manner – and yet has become too vast to be successfully navigated by humans alone (see Locke 2000).

More recent AI breakthroughs related to machine learning, deep learning, and artificial neural networks, in relying on algorithms that improve through experience and emphasizing the ability to learn as a primary capacity of intelligence, are also reconfiguring how we think about the relationship between computational memory, computation and remembering in novel ways.[4] In these systems, underpinned by virtual and simulated forms of memory, it is not only a matter of stressing the connections between computation and remembering but also those between remembering and learning. As these systems develop and increasingly stress the so-called 'substrate independence' – the ability to 'supervene on any of a broad class of physical substrates' whether human or artificial (Bostrom 2003, 244) – of a range of cognitive phenomena and forms of consciousness, memory, computation, learning and remembering, as well as arguably information and intelligence, may well continue to conceptually coalesce in the future (see Tegmark 2017).

While interest in self-organizing systems, machine learning, deep-learning and artificial neural networks more generally continues to animate the AI research and development field, the realization of their potential in connection to memory and remembrance might actually turn out to be something of a moot point from a sociological perspective. This is because ultimately AI's effort to emulate human memory and perhaps in time human remembering still suggests a binary between artificial and human intelligence that masks a more complicated relationship. In the next section, I turn to this relationship and propose several useful concepts for understanding it.

OVERCOMING TECHNOLOGICAL INSTRUMENTALISM: CYBORGIAN REMEMBRANCE AND AI MNEMOTECHNICS

While the exact relationship between memory's individualist and collectivist forms is yet to be fully resolved, their interaction has long been acknowledged (see Kansteiner 2002). Over 20 years ago, for example, Olick promulgated an approach to social memory that targeted a broad array of interrelated 'mnemonic processes, practices and outcomes, neurological, cognitive, personal, aggregated and collective' (1999, 346). At the same time, those mnemonic technologies, primarily conceived as contributing to collectivist forms of memory, have been treated in a rather instrumentalist manner as serving human ends rather than being ends themselves. This instrumentalism is twofold insofar as social memory scholars tend to first focus

---

[4]   My thanks to Ben Roberts for pushing me to explicate this point more clearly.

on the memories conveyed by mnemonic technologies – the first ends – and second, they usually conceive of these technologies as primarily or only serving the goal of extending human memory – the second ends. Even within his integrated approach, Olick, for instance, notes:

> For individuals, being able to write a note or record a message or take a photograph, vastly extends the capacity to 'remember', not simply by providing storage space outside of the brain but by stimulating our neurological storage processes in particular ways. (1999, 342)

While this instrumentalist approach has been applied to all mnemonic technologies, it is often more pronounced and, given the arguably increased agency of digital technology, more problematic when applied to electronic or digital mnemonic technologies. Before Olick, Le Goff wrote:

> we must note that electronic memory operates only on human command and in accord with human programming, that human memory preserves a larger sector that cannot be reduced to 'information', and that, like all forms of automatic memory that have appeared in the course of history, electronic memory is only an aid, a servant of memory and of the human mind. (1992, 92)

More recently, these matters have been taken up within discussions about memory and remembering in the *mind* and *wild* and the relationship between these two that is fostered by digital technology (Barnier & Hoskins 2018). Within these discussions, the instrumentalist trap of conceiving mnemonic technologies as merely mnemonic aids has occasionally been avoided by stressing that human remembering always occurs in the wild. For instance, Tim Fawns (2022) writes:

> In making use of the world to help us to remember, we distribute some of our remembering agency. The combinations of multiple media (e.g. photographs and mobile phones and social media platforms) and their entanglements in our social relations with other people are too complex for us to control ... if remembering happens in the head, media are more likely to be seen simply as tools or cues, external to memory processes ... On the other hand, a wild view of remembering can help us see that there is no hard boundary between remembering with and without media ... Properly theorized, seeing remembering as in the wild can support a more meaningful account of the complex social and material relations in which remembering is entangled. (2022, 3–4)

Focusing on remembering and/or remembrance over memory *per see* is useful because it foregrounds the contextual specificity of the memories produced (remembered) through human use of technology (Fawns 2022; see also Merrill 2017). Yet this approach still runs the risk of maintaining focus primarily on human remembering, reflecting those limits traditionally conceived to affect the distribution of mnemonic agency. These limits are being re-delineated by society's continual mediatization, digitalization and datafication, and the results of the enrolment of these processes in wider AI systems. Given these new conditions and the conflation of 'the digital' to memory (see Chun 2008), the contact between and subsequent hybridization of human and computational memory is arguably trending towards the point where almost everything is becoming memory-related (Merrill Forthcoming). At least in certain parts of the world, everything is becoming memory-related because more and more of our human connections are saturated by digital communication media (see Hepp 2020), more and more of our spaces and things are infused with digital software and internet connectivity (see Kitchen & Dodge 2011) and, subsequently, more and more of our activities are arrested in digital data. In a society where (almost) *everything is memory*, debates about whether memory and remembering are primarily located in the mind or wild (see Barnier & Hoskins 2018) require further theoretical reformulation.

One way to achieve this is to acknowledge how memory's growing 'agentic hybridity' – as the outcome of human-non-human combinations – results in a hybrid of organic and artificial memory or what, drawing inspiration from Donna Haraway, I have elsewhere called *cyborgian memory*: 'a hybrid of machine and organism' (Merrill forthcoming; Haraway 1991, 147). In short, this is a hybrid of memory in the mind and the wild (or world). While it has already been noted that mnemonic technologies provide prosthetics that have turned us into cyborgs (see Olick 1999, 342), the general instrumentalist approach to technology within memory studies seems to have inhibited recognition of the extent to which our cyborgization has deepened with the growing pervasiveness of digital technology and the sorts of media, data, and algorithms that they facilitate and utilize (see Merrill Forthcoming). In this sense, the concept of cyborgian memory and more specifically those of *cyborgian remembrance* and/or *cyborgian remembering* all provide ways to think about the interaction of human and computational mnemonic actors on the more equal terms needed to grasp a world in which AI plays an increasing role in how we all remember.

The concept of cyborgian remembrance resonates with but also benefits from an engagement with Bernard Stiegler's idea of *technics* (1998). Not to be simply equated with technology, Stiegler's technics is, as Ben Roberts explains:

> not merely instrumental, a means to an end, where the 'end' remains a resolutely human need or desire. Rather technics shapes what it means to be human and the 'human' in this sense is constituted always already through technics. Indeed, technics is the 'prothesis of the human': the human is constituted not by some interior capacity (e.g. consciousness) but by a new prosthetic relationship with matter. (2007, 26)

Even more relevantly, Stiegler refers to a specific type of memory-related technics called mnemotechnics, which building on Edmund Husserl's discussion of primary and secondary retention and memory as well as image consciousness he associates with the latter as akin to a tertiary memory that is reactivated by external objects (2009, 245–250; see Roberts 2012). But while Husserl positions secondary and tertiary memory as derivatives of primary memory in an instrumentalist manner, for Stiegler, 'tertiary memory, the exteriorisation of memory into technical objects – mnemotechnics – is constitutive of primary memory, secondary memory or our perception of the temporal object' (Roberts 2012, 15; see Prey & Smit 2018). Stiegler applies these ideas to the epoch stretching to the late-twentieth century during which the collective apprehension of the past, time and memory passed 'primarily through the technical system of the written word' (James 2012, 68) as illustrated by his words: 'no longer a memory-aid, writing has become memory itself' (2009, 61). But of greater significance to the task at hand, Stiegler mostly discusses how a new mnemotechnic epoch in which the 'retention of the past passes primarily through the technical systems of analogical, numerical and digital communications media and other technically mediated perceptions' (James 2012, 68) has now taken hold, leading to the industrialization of memory (Stiegler 2009, 61; see Roberts 2012; Kinsley 2015; James 2012, 68–70).

Following Stiegler, Sam Kinsley has discussed this industrialization of memory with respect to the quasi-autonomous agency behind the algorithmic programmes that operate upon and retain our everyday activities using the example of supermarket loyalty cards (2015). Robert Prey and Rik Smit have also applied Stiegler's ideas to Facebook's 'On This Day' feature (2018). Both these studies suggest how AI, along with the algorithms and collections of big data underpinning it, have been central to the extenuation of memory's contemporary industrialization. These *AI mnemotechnics* further blur distinctions between the individual and collective insofar as 'individual traces of activity, retained outside of the more commonly discussed somatic memory, are in this sense, never left alone, they are selected, aggregated and transformed to produce forms of collective memory – something like a memory of habits' (Kinsley 2015, 157). Thus, rather than conceiving AI in instrumentalist ways – as many mnemonic technologies have been before – and stressing how it assists and augments individual memory recall (see Gupta and Woolley 2021, 672), it is important to approach AI as a mnemotechnic that contributes to the tandem development of artificial and human intelligence. AI mnemotechnics do not merely supplement contemporary human memory, they characterize it (see Locke 2000). This is especially important given that the co-evolution of these two intelligences arguably represents the 'last great challenge of humanism and the first great endeavor of posthumanism' (Youngmin, 2020, 13).

CONCLUSION: FUTURE CHALLENGES AND RISKS

The need for social scientists, humanities scholars, and AI researchers and developers, including computer scientists, to collaboratively engage in questions of social memory is manifold. As outlined, AI has so far been mostly ignored by the former while the latter have chiefly conceived memory under the neutral and de-politicized terms of storage, increasing the risk that when social memory scholars do engage with AI to any considerable extent, they will approach it only as a mnemonic technology and from a rather instrumentalist and human-centred perspective. Relating computation to remembrance (as opposed to conflating memory with storage) and thinking through AI's impact on social memory in terms of cyborgian remembrance and mnemotechnics will, in contrast, provide opportunities to also adopt a computational, machinic perspective that decentralizes the human. Importantly, such a perspective also promises to allow better consideration of the potential challenges posed by and risks of AI mnemotechnics. These challenges and risks – regardless of whether they relate to dystopian imaginings of futures where it is possible to use AI to implant individual human memories (see Colby 1985) and counter-memory processes that are compromised through a reliance on outsourced remembrance (see McFarlane 2020); or more to immediate practical concerns related to the mnemonic impact of the 'algorithmic narrowing of information' (Hoskins & Halstead 2021, 676); new AI archival appraisal processes that decontextualize or 'dumb down' societal memory (see van der Werf & van der Werf 2022); AI's impact on academic disciplines like history (see Kansteiner 2022); or legal debates about how best to ensure the responsible mnemonic use of AI and the right to be forgotten (see Shur-Orfy & Pessach 2020; Jones 2018) – could serve as key empirical foci for future critical studies of AI. There is also a pressing need to further conceptualize AI's relationship with social memory not only in terms of remembrance but also forgetting not least because the success of intelligent agents hinges on their ability to discard (e.g., to forget) non-essential information as much as it does on selecting essential information (see Locke 2000). Hopefully this chapter will support these future efforts by extending the theoretical exploration of the relationship between AI and social memory and proposing several concepts that might aid our understanding of it.

BIBLIOGRAPHY

Assmann, A. (2011). *Cultural memory and western civilization*. Cambridge University Press.

Barnier, A. J. & Hoskins, A. (2018). Is there memory in the head, in the wild? *Memory Studies*, 11(4), 386–390.

Bartol, T. M., Bromer, C., Kinney, J., Chirillo, M. A., Bourne, J. N., Harris, K. M., & Sejnowski, T. J. (2015). Nanoconnectomic upper bound on the variability of synaptic plasticity. *eLife*, 4, e10778. https://doi.org/10.7554/eLife.10778.

Brown, S. & Hoskins, A. (2010). Terrorism in the new memory ecology: Mediating and remembering the 2005 London Bombings. *Behavioral Sciences of Terrorism and Political Aggression*, 2(2), 87–107. https://doi.org/10.1080/19434471003597399.

Bostrom, N. (2003). Are we living in computer simulation? *The Philosophical Quarterly*, 53(211), 243–255.

Bush, V. (1945). As we may think. *Atlantic Monthly*, 176(1), 101–108.

Colby, K. M. (1985). Reloading a human memory: A new ethical question for artificial intelligence technology. *AI Magazine*, 6(4), 63. https://doi.org/10.1609/aimag.v6i4.509.

Chun, W. H. K. (2008). The enduring ephemeral, or the future is a memory. *Critical Inquiry*, 35(1), 148–171. https://doi.org/10.1086/595632.

Erll, A. (2012). Cultural memory. In M. Middeke, T. Müller, C. Wald, & H. Zapf (Eds.), *English and American Studies*. J.B. Metzler, Stuttgart. https://doi.org/10.1007/978-3-476-00406-2_15.

Esposito, E. (2017). Algorithmic memory and the right to be forgotten on the web. *Big Data & Society*, 4(1), 1–11. https://doi.org/10.1177/2053951717703996.

Fawns, T. (2022). Remembering in the wild: Recontextualising and reconciling studies of media and memory. *Memory, Mind & Media*, 1, E11. https://doi.org/10.1017/mem.2022.5.

Gupta, P., & Woolley, A. W. (2021). Articulating the role of artificial intelligence in collective intelligence: A transactive systems framework. *Proceedings of the Human Factors and Ergonomics Society Annual Meeting*, 65(1), 670–674. https://doi.org/10.1177/1071181321651354c.

Halbwachs, M. (1992). *On collective memory* (L. A. Coser, Trans). University of Chicago Press.

Haraway, D. J. (1991). *Simians, cyborgs and women: The reinvention of nature*. Free Association Books.

Hepp, A. (2020). *Deep mediatization*. Routledge.

Hoskins, A. (2017). Memory of the multitude: The end of collective memory? In A. Hoskins (Ed.), *Digital memory studies: Media pasts in transition* (pp. 85–109). Routledge.

Hoskins, A., & Halstead, H. (2021). The new grey of memory: Andrew Hoskins in conversation with Huw Halstead. *Memory Studies*, 14(3), 675–685. https://doi.org/10.1177/17506980211010936.

James, I. (2012). *The new French philosophy*. Polity.

Jones, M. L. (2018). *Ctrl + Z: The right to be forgotten*. New York University Press.

Kansteiner, W. (2002). Finding meaning in memory: A methodological critique of collective memory studies. *History and Theory*, 41(2), 179–197. http://www.jstor.org/stable/3590762.

Kansteiner, W. (2022). Digital doping for historians: Can history, memory, and historical theory be rendered artificially intelligent? *History and Theory*, 61(4), 119–133. doi:10.1111/hith.12282.

Kinsley, S. (2015). Memory programmes: The industrial retention of collective life. *Cultural Geographies*, 22(1), 155–175. https://doi.org/10.1177/1474474014555658.

Kitchin, R., & Dodge, M. (2011). *Code/space: Software and everyday life*. The MIT Press.

Kvasnička, V., & Pospíchal, J. (2015). Artificial intelligence and collective memory. In P. Sinčák, P. Hartono, M. Virčíková, J. Vaščák, & R. Jakša (Eds.), *Emergent trends in robotics and intelligent systems* (pp. 283-291). Springer International Publishing.

Lambert, A., Nansen, B., & Arnold, M. (2018). Algorithmic memorial videos: Contextualising automated curation. *Memory Studies*, 11(2), 156–171. https://doi.org/10.1177/1750698016679221.

Landsberg, A. (2004) *Prosthetic memory*. Columbia University Press.

Le Goff, J. (1992). *History and memory* (S. Rendall & E. Claman, Trans.). Columbia University Press. (Original work published 1988).

Locke, C. (2000). Digital memory and the problem of forgetting. In S. Radstone (Ed.), *Memory and methodology* (pp. 25–36). Berg.

McCarthy, J., Minsky, M., Rochester, N., & Shannon, C. (1955/2006). A proposal for the Dartmouth summer research project on artificial intelligence. *AI Magazine*, 27(4), 12–14.

McFarlane, A. (2020). AI and cyberpunk networks. In S. Cave, K. Dihal, & S. Dillon (Eds.), *AI narratives: A history of imaginative thinking about intelligent machines* (pp. 284–308). Oxford University Press.

Merrill, S. (2017). *Networked remembrance*. Peter Lang.

Merrill, S. (Forthcoming). Hybrid methodologies for memory research in the age of the internet. In Q. Wang & A. Hoskins (Eds.), *The remaking of memory in the age of social media and the internet*. Oxford University Press.

Ng, J. (2021). An alternative rationalisation of creative AI by de-familiarising creativity: Towards an intelligibility of its own terms. In P. Verdegem (Ed.), *AI for everyone? Critical perspectives* (pp. 49–66). University of Westminster Press.

Nilsson, N. (1998). *Artificial intelligence: A new synthesis*. Morgan Kaufmann Publishers.

Olick, J. K. (1999). Collective memory: The two cultures. *Sociological Theory*, 17(3), 333–348. https://doi.org/10.1111/0735-2751.00083.

Olick, J. K., & Robbins, J. (1998). Social memory studies: From "collective memory" to the historical sociology of mnemonic practices. *Annual Review of Sociology*, 24, 105–140. http://www.jstor.org/stable/223476.

Prey, R., & Smit, R. (2018). From personal to personalized memory: Social media as mnemotechnology. In Z. Papacharissi (Ed.), *A networked self and birth, life, death* (pp. 209–223). Routledge, Taylor and Francis group.

Reading, A. (2011). The London bombings: Mobile witnessing, mortal bodies and globital time. *Memory Studies*, 4(3), 298–311. https://doi.org/10.1177/1750698011402672.

Rehak, R. (2021). The language labyrinth: Constructive critique on the terminology used in the AI discourse. In P. Verdegem (Ed.), *AI for everyone? Critical perspectives* (pp. 87–102). University of Westminster Press.

Roberts, B. (2007). Introduction to Bernard Stiegler. *Parallax*, 13(4), 26–28. https://doi.org/10.1080/13534640701682776.

Roberts, B. (2012). Technics, individuation and tertiary memory: Bernard Stiegler's challenge to media theory. *New Formations*, 77, 8–20. https://doi.org/10.3898/NEWF.77.01.2012.

Rothberg, M. (2009). *Multidirectional memory*. Stanford University Press.

Russel, S. J., & Norvig, P. (2016). *Artificial intelligence: A modern approach* (3rd ed.). Pearson.

Schank, R. C. (1990). *Tell me a story: A new look at real and artificial memory*. Scribner.

Schwarz, O. (2014). The past next door: Neighbourly relations with digital memory-artefacts. *Memory Studies*, 7(1), 7–21. https://doi.org/10.1177/1750698013490591.

Shur-Ofry, M, & Pessach, G. (2020). Robotic collective memory. *Washington University Law Review*, 97(3), 975–1005. doi:10.2139/ssrn.3364008.

Sluis, K. (2010) Algorithmic memory? Machinic vision and database culture. In A. Mousoutzanis & D. Riha (Eds.), *New media and the politics of online communities* (pp. 227–235). Brill.

Stiegler, B. (1998) *Technics and time 1: The fault of epimetheus* (R. Beardsworth & G. Collins, Trans.). Stanford University Press. (Original work published 1994).

Stiegler, B. (2009) *Technics and time 2: Disorientation* (S. Barker, Trans.). Stanford University Press. (Original work published 1996).

Tegmark, M. (2017). *Life 3.0 being human in the age of artificial intelligence*. Alfred A. Knopf.

Turing, A. (1950). I. Computing machinery and intelligence. *Mind*, LIX(236), 433–460. https://doi.org/10.1093/mind/LIX.236.433.

van der Werf, T., & van der Werf, B. (2022). Will archivists use AI to enhance or to dumb down our societal memory? *AI & Society*, 37, 985–988. https://doi.org/10.1007/s00146-021-01359-x.

Verdegem, P. (Ed.). (2021a) *AI for everyone? Critical perspective.* University of Westminster Press.
Verdegem, P. (2021b). Introduction: Why we need critical perspectives on AI. In P. Verdegem (Ed.), *AI for everyone? Critical perspective* (pp. 1–18). University of Westminster Press.
Von Neumann, J. (1945/1993). First draft of a report on the EDVAC. *IEEE Annals of the History of Computing*, 15(4), 27–75.
Whittaker, M. (2021). The steep cost of capture. *Interactions*, 28(6), 50–55. https://doi.org/10.1145/3488666.
Youngmin, K. (2020). The poetics of artificial intelligence and posthumanism. *Forum for World Literature Studies*, 12(1), 1+. https://link.gale.com/apps/doc/A633840114/AONE?u=anon~7e296f4b&sid=googleScholar&xid=604b7140.

16. Making sense of AI-influenced geopolitics using STS theories

Arun Teja Polcumpally

INTRODUCTION

Internet and communication technologies (ICT) are set to change social interactions. In 2007, it was asserted that ICT will have a profound impact on how people interact (Brignall & Valey, 2007), and even in 2017, it has still been said that changes are happening (Antonucci et al., 2017). Heuristically observed, almost all human activities are tied to smartphones or other digital devices. Major sectors like the financial sector, healthcare, education, politics, industry, and governance are opined to change drastically by ICT (Guzman & Vis, 2016). Some scholars assert that the status quo of society will be combined with digital systems to form a hyper-connected society called Society 5.0 (José et al., 2021). This is how the internet changed social activities. With the help of advanced technologies like AI, more change is expected. Such profound changes in social interactions will result in a shift in the way politics are played (Eckardt, 2021). Not just domestically, ICT along with advanced technologies like AI are impacting global politics (Malhotra, 2021). This chapter is written on the latter premise and lays out that in order to understand AI-impacted geopolitics, a confluence of science, technology, and society (STS) and international relations (IR) would be useful.

Information availability and open discussion on social media have improved political deliberation in both the developed and developing world. In Malaysia, social media is considered a major tool for providing political knowledge (Halim, Mohamad, Shamsu, Farah, & Muslim, 2021). In Pakistan, it is found that youth are more connected to political activities using social media (Ahmad, Alvi, & Ittefaq, 2019). In Turkey, offline political participation is achieved by sharing information on social media (Toros & Toros, 2022). Movements like Yellow West Movement, the Umbrella Revolution, and Black Lives Matter (BLM) are well-known in developed countries that showcase the role ICT played in mobilising the public. This paints a positive future for societies worldwide, where people deliberate after being well-informed. It appears that Habermas' bourgeoise public sphere can be achieved by the internet and allied communication technologies. However, that might not be the case.

Extensive research is not required to conclude that information control will provide an immense amount of influence over societies worldwide. AI-based recommendation algorithms and other AI products are seen to be politically biased (Peters, 2022). Eli Pariser (2012) asserts that the internet filters the information and only displays selected links that it thinks are best suited for an individual. This means that when an individual types the word 'China and technology,' the search engine displays those links that are inclined to the user's beliefs. A liberal thought-oriented individual might get links that propose balanced trade agreements between China and the United States. A conservative might get links asking the United States to take stringent actions against China. This phenomenon is called the 'filter bubble' (Pariser, 2012). Assisting Eli Pariser, former president of Microsoft, Brad Smith, affirms that digital technologies have become both tools and weapons for private and government bodies (Smith & Carol, 2019). This shows that AI can also empower globally and it leads to an increase in global inequalities. The type of inequalities AI would create is still debated (Butcher, 2019).

Further, some sources assert that AI is controlled by few companies and states capable of having complete control over the world (Smith & Carol, 2019; Susskind, 2018; Suri, 2022). Companies like Google, Amazon, Tencent, and Facebook collect hordes of data to increase their profitability and capture the global market. With the development of machine learning, these companies have started to find patterns in the data collected. Such pattern recognition has led to the development of recommendation systems. Some examples of such systems are Netflix, Instagram, and Inshorts news. These recommendation systems are used to capture and exploit market behaviour and exacerbate the phenomenon of filter bubbles.

Finally, it is important to recognise how governments use these advanced technologies to their advantage. During the COVID-19 pandemic, AI-based computer vision cameras became tools to implement social distancing and contact tracing (Sivasubramanian, 2020). States worldwide sought the help of private companies to provide AI-based applications to tackle the spread of COVID-19. Post-pandemic, video surveillance software and hardware market growth was 16.4% in 2021 and is predicted to grow to 11.7% in 2022 (Security Infowatch, 2022). Not just private companies but states are also adopting AI technologies to increase their influence over society (Feldstein(b), 2019).

The global circulation of information, the increased problem of the filter bubble, and the political usage of AI surveillance are some of the many issues within IR. With all these rapidly occurring developments, there is an emerging voice that advocates that the existing theoretical frameworks are not sufficient to understand current global politics (Susskind, 2018; Mayer et al., 2014). Some say that IR often considers the growth of science and technology as an exogenous phenomenon (Mayer & Carpes, 2014). The existing literature on political ideas, and theories, were all developed in the era when advanced ICT was not even dreamt about (Susskind, 2018). Such old theories must be changed or assisted with new frameworks to better understand global politics.

All the above developments provide a reason for this chapter to be written. The premise of this book is that the existing theories of IR are not enough to understand the complex interconnectedness of society and ICT. A combination of STS and IR is one identified way to conduct a nuanced assessment. The following discussion provides how IR and STS can be combined and provides an overview of existing methods.

THE CONFLUENCE OF IR AND STS

The study of geopolitics has been a prerogative of the IR. Power, conflict resolution, peacekeeping, and security studies are some of the many segments of study that come under the faculties of IR. These are studied by theories that are borrowed and modified from other disciplines like sociology, political science, and psychology. Overall, IR is a multi-disciplinary subject that crosses paths with every other discipline. STS, similar to IR, is also a multi-disciplinary subject. What makes both of them unique in their faculties is their focus of interest. IR focuses on global affairs, be it the impact of technology, policy, or climate change. STS focuses on the interactions between technology and society. The confluence of STS and IR happens when AI society impacts are carried out on the global level.

Though these two have different focus areas, they have a point of confluence. This confluence is understood from a critical view of the socio-political conditions of the internet age. To further understand this confluence, first, the impact of AI on society will be established and then the discussion would extend to the impact of AI on geopolitics.

Emerging data technologies are forcing unprecedented changes in societies across the world (World Economic Forum, 2019) and some even put it next to the Industrial Revolution (Hilbert, 2020). An article published by Weforum advocates that global societies are not ready for the deployment of AI (Pauwels, 2018). Another article published by Chatham House strongly advises states to have homegrown AI talent and to encourage funding, responsible research, and AI policy (M. L. Cummings, 2018). These publications show that the impact of AI is on the entire society, and at the same time, states are racing to control it. Further, a special focus should be given to AI surveillance. Pegasus software in India ignited a good debate on this aspect. If the public is not free within their country and if the government watches over them through their digital footprint, then they are effectively living in a big prison (Narayan, 2021). This is similar to what 'The Economist' in its 2013 issue called China (The Economist, 2013).

As discussed in the introduction, AI is also the technology used in the search and recommendation algorithms of Google, Netflix, and so on. These recommendation algorithms even shape/influence the decision-making of humans (Schrage, 2020). The impact is so profound that there are debates to understand the type of agency AI algorithms would acquire in a new society (Johnson & Verdicchio, 2019). Such is the extent of the societal change caused by AI.

This example of AI and its societal impacts shows that technology is arguably playing an agency role in defining modern social behaviour. When it comes to state behaviour, states that boast about their democratic principles are acting like authoritarians (Luhmann et al., 2020). When it comes to warfare, AI-induced political instability promotes psychological warfare (Mikheev & Nestik, 2019). It is conducted subtly by distributing biased information to shape the behaviour of the public. Such acts will encourage 'authoritarian and discriminatory political behaviour and undermine democracies' (Kasapoglu & Kirdemir, 2019).

With the introduction of the cross-border flow of information and AI systems impacting the world, the redistribution of national wealth has also been found to be not within national boundaries. It is being shared among big digital companies (Bryson, 2019). This is another example of socio-political change crossing the political boundaries based on virtual platforms. Not all countries have advanced technology like AI. Those who do not have the technology encourage foreign companies to provide digital services. This is also done by technologically advanced countries because of the economic advantages. Such borrowed AI technologies bring new agencies into society or, in the words of Karamjit Gill (2020), 'trappings of AI Agency.' Substantiation for the 'trappings of agency' can be found in 'The Export Control Reform Act (ECRA) of 2018.' It is a permanent statute that authorizes the US Commerce Department to establish controls on the export of 'emerging and foundational technologies.' It restricts the export of almost all AI technologies including time series algorithms. Technologies such as natural language processing (NLP), voice recognition, and speech synthesis technologies and interfaces are put on a restricted list of export technology. This shows that a US-made surveillance system cannot be manufactured under any kind of license. If any country wants to use it, it must buy the final product and pay its recurring costs to the United States (most probably).

This is an example of the societal impact of AI technology brought by foreign countries. It is also observed that China is trying to export its AI systems to encourage authoritarian governance systems (Feldstein(a), 2019). Both the United States and China are exporting their AI surveillance systems to gain control over the global market and population (Feldstein(b), 2019). Digital technologies, and especially AI, went from societal impact to global impact. Numerous examples have been mentioned above stressing this argument. This is the point of confluence for IR and STS.

In the digital era, the Westphalian system might convert into a cyber-Westphalian system, where the states will define the territorial cyber boundaries to ensure the sustenance of national security (Demchak & Peter, 2014). This showcases the changes in the fundamental building blocks of IR. Some books provide a detailed analysis of the alleged new Cold War hinged on advanced digital technologies like AI and 5G (Lee, 2018; Wang, 2020). This shows the changing global order.

Traditional IR theories like realism and liberalism consider technology to be a tool to conduct global politics. Constructivism considers the values and communication of individuals and societies aided by technology. None of these approaches clearly define technology as endogenous to global politics (Fritsch, 2014, p. 132). When major perspectives of IR are combined with STS, the relations between states, non-state actors, individuals, and collectives with technology can be explained using the STS approaches (Fritsch, 2014).

STS METHODS TO USE IN IR

Within the broader approaches of STS like social constructivism, technological determinism, and co-production, the relationship between AI and geopolitics can be studied using various methods. Some of them are triple helix models that are used to evaluate the interactions between knowledge, economy and geography (Knoblich, 2014; Leydesdorff & Fritsch, 2006), ethnomethodology (Sormani et al., 2017), discourse analysis, performativity (Konrad et al., 2017), anticipatory governance (Barben, 2008), actor-network theory (Latour, 2005), systems theory (Luhmann, 1990), and also mixed methods of IR and STS combining the concepts of information entropy, triple helix models, and systems theory of Luhmann and Wallerstein (Polcumpally, 2021). In the subsequent discussion, an overview of methods will be provided. This overview is expected to serve as an introduction to the possible combinations of STS approaches with IR. It does not aim to provide an in-depth analysis of each STS approach to understand the impact of AI on geopolitics.

SYSTEMS THEORY AND ACTOR-NETWORK THEORY

Systems Theory

Research in the realm of public policy, law, international relations, and psychology is increasing regarding the implications of artificial intelligence. Yet, research on AI impacts is scarce in the public sector (Sun & Medaglia, 2018). When AI agriculture is considered, only selected aspects are researched (Ryan, 2022), and when geopolitics is considered, there is only inferential analysis. When AI is considered, how do we understand security differentiated sectorally? Systems theory comes to the rescue here. It provides an analysis of each sector – political, medical, economic, and education independently.

One example of sector-wise (Luhamnn's systems) analysis of technology impacts on international relations is provided by Mitchel (2011). This study relates the usage of oil extraction and allied industries to the spread of democracy and authoritarian rule (Mitchel, 2011). The author argues how the technical industries of oil set up in the Middle East did not contribute to the establishment of democracy. This research views the impact of technology separately on economic and political systems. Currently, research on AI impacts on geopolitics when combined with systems theory brings a more nuanced analysis.

Another aspect of systems theory is that AI governance can be researched and established using the 'risk-decision' theory, which is derived from systems theory. Systems theory espouses that the term security is understood vividly from its counter concept, risk. Risk is something that can avoid the possibility of future damage, exceeding all reasonable costs, that is attributed to a decision made at a particular space and time (Luhmann, 1990, p. 225). This risk concept helps to construct contextual definitions of the risk of AI. In each sector, risk can be calculated, and foreign policy can be made accordingly. According to Luhmann's risk-decision theory, all policy decisions are made against assessing the risk posed by the technology in question. Thus, the overall functioning of the decision/policymaking is hinged on assessing and managing the risk and immediate dangers of and for society.

Actor-Network Theory

An article published in Indian print media, 'The Live Mint,' shows that a humanoid artist Ai-Da can create transhumanistic art (Sreedhar, 2022). A chapter in Jaspreet Bindra's book was written by AI (Bindra, 2019). These are some among many examples that show that literature and art are being manipulated and created by machines! In general, art forms are created by humans to narrate stories, which in turn shape the thought process of society. When such art is created by machines, they are also impacting the societal thought process. That means machines and humans together will shape the future of society. One way to analyse AI's impact on societies across the world is to share the agency between technology and humans. Actor-network theory (ANT) offers an approach that encourages non-rigidity, and constant recognition of new agents, and shares the agency between AI and humans.

ANT is much like an ethnographic knowledge creation without any a priori anchors of knowledge. Latour establishes that if scholars use ANT to define and understand society, then these five uncertainties constantly juggle up (Latour, 2005). There is no way for each of them to stand independently. Each of them calls on others making it a complex subjectivity.

First, society should not be considered an ontological reality but has to be constructed from the agents present in it. Social groups are opined to be constructed realities.

Second, there should not be any pre-notions that the actor under observation is acting under a metasystem.

Third, social ties are neither made from an existing structure nor an embodiment of society.

Fourth, facts are not to be taken as realities and they also change their stance. This is not an explanation of how scientific facts are dynamically considered. It is an explanation of how facts are being considered by agents and how facts themselves are becoming agents.

Fifth, thick descriptions are for ANT scholars. It is different from the explanation. Description stores account for the observation, but the explanation elaborates the description. Such a thick description brings out the participation of new agents, be they human or non-human.

An example of the adoption of ANT in IR can be drawn from the work of Simon Lindgren (2020). He has taken the keywords 'climate change,' 'global warming,' and 'climate change denial,' and scrapped 1.1 million tweets from the Twitter API. The association between these tweets has been laid out using a machine learning technique called name entity recognition (NER) of the SpaCY library. This research has been conducted with the premise that there are no pre-defined actors and agencies in the call for climate action. The agents will be identified from communications and associations. From this method, agents identified for global climate change action include places, organisations, countries, laws, persons, and media houses. This shows that the primary actors were not just humans but also non-humans. Such analysis will help in identifying the new actors, and perhaps AI might be deemed to be an agency in constructing social relations.

CREATING NARRATIVES ON AI'S IMPACT ON GEOPOLITICS

Narratives through Art and Design

Art and design as a field of inquiry (Salter, Regula, & Joseph, 2017) focuses on performance analysis. It is nothing but tracing and analysing how certain entities represent technology. The AI narratives project undertaken by the Royal Society asserts that extreme AI narratives in literature shape public discussions and the decisions of policymakers (The Royal Society, 2018). In order to have constructive AI futures, it is recommended to have context-specific dialogues assisted by AI researchers. One possible way for advocating context-specific narratives is by using art (The Royal Society, 2018).

Information regarding performativity can also be derived from performing ethnographic research at the site of technology development. One such study in ethnographic research is conducted at Xerox's research centre at Paulo Alto (Vertesi Janet, 017). The research concluded that there is a mutual influence between machines and employees. This outcome reiterates that machines also conduct politics (Winner, 1980). Adopting this kind of research will result in generating alternatives to power distribution. It identifies the old and new agencies and the functional communications between them. When the source of the agency is identified, it becomes easy to re-distribute resources.

Constructing Imageries

Imageries, similar to Benedict Anderson's concept of imagined communities, are nothing but a construction of a certain reality. Examples of imageries are nationhood and values, and even Rousseau's social contract can be considered social imagery. For the analysis of imageries constructed by AI, Appadurai's conceptual understanding of how imageries will be built will be useful (Maureen McNeil, 2017). According to Appadurai, the imageries are built on mediascapes, technoscapes, financescapes, ethnoscapes, and ideascapes. These are the categories that influence the emergence of new constructs. Conceptualising imageries is by no means a restrictive process. Some scholars adopted innovative ways to understand existing imagery and to create new imagery.

Scholars such as Donna Haraway adopted science fiction narratives to create feminist STS approaches. Fiction books like 'Cyborg Manifesto' and 'Primate Visions' narrate the relations between humans and machines. Fiction is also used to communicate the panopticon reality of China. Their surveillance systems are best narrated in the form of dystopian novels like 'Folding Beijing.' Another book 'Visions of Dystopia' provides a detailed account of the dystopian narratives of China from 1980 to 2010. There is a good number of research reports that emphasise that China uses AI surveillance to force society to behave in a certain manner. Constructing imageries will help in understanding the context and historical relations between technology and society, and in constructing futures. This method also helps in steering public opinion about AI.

CONCLUSION

It has been established that a cornucopia of STS and IR is one of the available approaches to better understand IR when AI is considered. The above-mentioned approaches of STS are some of the widely used methods. This chapter does not consider that the above methods are more feasible than others. They are chosen in this chapter as they cover wide aspects of STS methods. Systems theory can be used to situate emerging technologies into a context. Micro-level contextualisation can be done using the ANT theoretical approach where the social network is constructed from the observed actions. It is also pointed out that STS methods are not restricted to analysing technology-society relations. It is also used to make relations. The narratives are made in such a way that they will be accepted by the public, thus converting them into prominent discourse. These discourses when dissipated across the world will shape the expectations and attitudes of the public towards a particular technology (Iles et al., 2017, p. 952). Once a discourse is established by one country about its technological innovation, it carries the soft power to influence public opinion in favour of the country that created that technology or the company that created it. STS fields of inquiry can also be launched in aspects like the imagery of security, securitisation of knowledge, knowledge of citizens, the reflexive understanding of security practices, and strategic decision-making (Vogel et al., 2017, p. 974).

The methods discussed in this chapter have helped IR analysis to identify the current societal impacts of the technology (on a global level). Finally, the rise of China in digital technology and its activities across the digital silk road can be compared with that of the behaviour of the United States post-World War II. In this scenario, technology occupies the central stage of foreign policymaking. Without a holistic understanding of the technology and its performativity across the world, effective foreign policymaking is not possible.

This chapter by no means is an exhaustive reading list. It is meant as an introduction to understanding the importance of the confluence of STS and IR. It is hoped that researchers reading this chapter will delve deeper into these aspects.

FURTHER READING

Ancarani, V. (1995). Globalizing the world: Science and technology in international relations. In J. Shiela, E. M. Gerald, C. P. James, & P. Trevor (Eds.), *Handbook of science and technology studies* (pp. 652–670). Sage.

Felt, U., Rayvon, F., Clark, A. M., & Laurel, S. D. (2017). *Handbook of science and technology studies* (4th ed.). Cambridge, MA: MIT Press.

Mayer, M., Mariana, C., & Ruth, K. (2014). *The global politics of science and technology - vol. 1 concepts from international relations and other disciplines.* Berlin: Springer.

Mayer, M., Mariana, C., & Ruth, K. (2014). *The global politics of science and technology - vol. 2 perspectives, cases and methods.* Berlin: Springer.

Winner, L. (1980). Do artefacts have politics? *Modern Technology: Problem or Opportunity?* 21–36.

Zinn, O. J. (2008). *Social theories of risk and uncertainty: An introduction.* Blackwell Publishing.

REFERENCES

Ahmad, T., Alvi, A., & Ittefaq, M. (2019). The use of social media on political participation among university students: An analysis of survey results from rural Pakistan. *SAGE Open.* https://doi.org/10.1177/2158244019864484

Ancarani, V. (1995). Globalizing the world: Science and technology in international relations. In J. Shiela, E. M. Gerald, C. P. James, & P. Trevor (Eds.), *Handbook of science and technology studies* (pp. 652–670). Sage.

Anna Lührmann, S. F. (2020). Autocrazation surges - Resistance grows: Democracy report 2020. V Dem. Retrieved from https://www.v-dem.net/media/filer_public/de/39/de39af54-0bc5-4421-89ae -fb20dcc53dba/democracy_report.pdf.

Antonucci, T. C., Ajrouch, K. J., & Manalel, J. A. (2017). Social relations and technology: Continuity, context, and change. *Innovation in Aging,* 1(3). https://doi.org/10.1093/geroni/igx029.

Bijker, E. W. (1995). *Of bicycles, bakelites, and bulbs: Toward a theory of socio-technical change.* London: MIT Press.

Bindra, J. (2019). *The tech whisperer: On digital transformation and the technologies that enable it.* New Delhi: Penguin Random House.

Brignall, T. W., & Valey, T. V. (2007). The impact of internet communications on social interaction. *Sociological Spectrum,* 25(3), 335–48. https://doi.org/10.1080/02732170590925882.

Bryson, J. J. (2019, December 18). The future of AI's impact on society. Retrieved from technologyreview .com: https://www.technologyreview.com/2019/12/18/102365/the-future-of-ais-impact-on-society/.

Butcher. (2019, January 23). World Economic Forum warns of AI's potential to worsen global inequality. Retrieved from Techcrunch: https://techcrunch.com/2019/01/23/world-economic-forum-warns-of -ais-potential-to-worsen-global-inequality/.

Daniel Barben, E. F. (2008). Anticipatory governance of nanotechnology: Foresight, engagement, and integration. In O. A. Edward & J. Hackett (Eds.), *The handbook of science & technology studies* (pp. 979–1000). Cambridge, MA: MIT Press.

David Chandler, F. M. (2021). *International relations in the Anthropocene: New agendas, new agencies, and new approaches.* Switzerland: Palgrave Macmillian.

Demchak, C. C., & Peter, J. D. (2014). Rise of a cybered Westphalian age: The coming decades. In M. Mayer, C. Mariana, & K. Ruth (Eds.), *The global politics of science and technology - vol. 1 Concepts from international relations and other disciplines* (pp. 91–114). Berlin: Springer.

Eckardt, M. (2021). The impact of ICT on policies, politics, and polities – an evolutionary economics approach to information and communication technologies (ICT). In T. A. Herberger & J. J. Dötsch (Eds.), *Digitalization, digital transformation and sustainability in the global economy* (pp. 37–52). Springer. https://doi.org/10.1007/978-3-030-77340-3_4.

Engerman, C. D. (2018). *The price of aid.* Cambridge, MA: Harvard University Press.

Feldstein(a), S. (2019, January 22). We need to get smart about how governments use AI. Retrieved from Carnegieendowment.org: https://carnegieendowment.org/2019/01/22/we-need-to-get-smart-about- how-governments-use-ai-pub-78179.

Feldstein(b), S. (2019, September 17). The global expansion of AI surveillance. Retrieved from Carnegieendowment.org: https://carnegieendowment.org/2019/09/17/global-expansion-of-ai- surveillance-pub-79847.

Felt, U., Rayvon, F., Clark, A. M., & Laurel, S. D. (2017). *Handbook of science and technology studies* (4th ed.). Cambridge, MA: MIT Press.

Fritsch, S. (2014). Conceptualizing the ambivalent role of technology in international relations: Between systemic change and continuity. In M. Mayer, C. Mariana, & K. Ruth (Eds.), *The global politics of science and technology - vol. 1 concepts from international relations and other disciplines* (pp. 115–141). Berlin: Springer.

Gill, K. S. (2020). AI & Society: Editorial volume 35.2: The trappings of AI Agency. *AI & Society*, 35, 289–296. https://doi.org/10.1007/s00146-020-00961-9.

Guzman, A., & Vis, F. (2016, April 7). 6 ways social media is changing the world. Retrieved from weforum: https://www.weforum.org/agenda/2016/04/6-ways-social-media-is-changing-the-world/.

Halim, H., Mohamad, B., Shamsu, A. D., Farah, L. A., & Muslim, D. A. (2021). Association of online political participation with social media usage, perceived information quality, political interest and political knowledge among Malaysian youth: Structural equation model analysis. *Cogent Social Sciences*. https://doi.org/10.1080/23311886.2021.1964186.

Harding, S. (1993). Rethinking standpoint epistemology: What is 'strong objectivity?' In A. Linda & P. Elizabeth (Eds.), *Feminist epistemologies*. Routledge.

Hilbert, M. (2020). Digital technology and social change: The digital transformation of society from a historical perspective. *Dialogues in Clinical Neuroscience*, 22(2), 189–194. https://www.tandfonline.com/action/showCitFormats?doi=10.31887/DCNS.2020.22.2/mhilbert.

Iles, A., Garrett, G., Maywa, M., & Ryan, G. (2017). Agricultural systems: Coproducing knowledge and food. In R. F.-D. Ulrike Felt (Ed.), *Handbook of science and technology studies* (pp. 943–973). Cambridge, MA: MIT Press.

Johnson, D. G., & Verdicchio, M. (2019). AI, agency and responsibility: The VW fraud case and beyond. *AI & Society*, 639–647. https://doi.org/10.1007/s00146-017-0781-9.

José, S. M., Santos, A. I., Serpa, S., & Ferreira, C. M. (2021). Digital literacy in digital society 5.0: Some challenges. *Academic Journal of Interdisciplinary Studies*, 10(2). https://doi.org/10.36941/ajis-2021-0033.

Kasapoglu, C., & Kirdemir, B. (2019, November 28). Artificial intelligence and the future of conflict. Retrieved from Carnegieeurope.org: https://carnegieeurope.eu/2019/11/28/artificial-intelligence-and-future-of-conflict-pub-80421.

Khandekar, A., Koen, B., Annapurna, M., Pankaj, S., & Wiebe, E. B. (2017). STS for development. In R. F.-D. Ulrike Felt (Ed.), *Handbook of science and technology studies* (pp. 665–695). Cambridge: Cambridge University Press.

Kline, R. R. (2001). Technological determinism. *International Encyclopedia of the Social & Behavioral Sciences*. Retrieved from https://doi.org/10.1016/B0-08-043076-7/03167-3.

Knoblich, R. (2014). The triple helix, the complexity of technological innovations, and the decomposition of national innovation systems: An interview with Loet Leydesdorff. In M. C. Maximilian Mayer (Ed.), *The global politics of science and technology - vol. 1 concepts from international relations and other disciplines* (pp. 251–261). Berlin: Springer.

Konrad, K., Harro, V. L., Christopher, G., & Cynthia, S. (2017). Performing and governing the future in science and technology. In R. F.-D. Ulrike Felt (Ed.), *Handbook of science and technology studies* (4th ed., pp. 465–493). Cambridge: Cambridge University Press.

Kuhn, T. (2014). Logic of discovery or psychology of research? In L. Imre & M. Alan (Eds.), *Criticism and the growth of knowledge* (pp. 1–24). Cambridge: Cambridge University Press.

Latour, B. (1992). Where are the missing masses? The sociology of a few mundane artifacts. In W. E. Bijker (Ed.), *Shaping technology/building society: Studies in Sociotechnical* (pp. 225–258). Cambridge, MA: MIT Press.

Latour, B. (2005). *Reassembling the social: An introduction to actor network theory*. Oxford University Press.

Law, J. (2017). STS as methods. In R. F.-D. Ulrike Felt (Ed.), *Handbook of science and technology studies* (pp. 31–59). Cambridge, MA: MIT Press.

Lee, K. F. (2018). *AI Superpowers: China, Silicon Valley, and the new world order*. Harper Business.

Leydesdorff, L., & Fritsch, M. (2006). Measuring the knowledge base of regional innovation systems in Germany in terms of triple helix dynamics. *Research Policy*, 35(10), 1538–1553.

Lindgren, S. (2020). *Data theory*. Polity. https://doi.org/978-1-509-53927-7

Luhmann, N. (1990). Technology, environment and social risk: A systems perspective. *Industrial Crisis Quarterly*, 223–231.

M. L. Cummings, H. M. (2018). Artificial intelligence and international affairs disruption anticipated. Royal Institute of International Affairs. London: Chatham House. Retrieved from https://www

.chathamhouse.org/sites/default/files/publications/research/2018-06-14-artificial-intelligence-international-affairs-cummings-roff-cukier-parakilas-bryce.pdf.

Malhotra, R. (2021). *Artificial intelligence and the future of power*. New Delhi: Rupa Publications.

Maureen McNeil, M. A.-A. (2017). Conceptualizing imaginaries of science, technology, and society. In R. F.-D. Ulrike Felt (Ed.), *Handbook of science and technology studies* (pp. 435–465). Cambridge, MA: MIT Press.

Mayer, M., & Carpes, M. K. (2014). A toolbox for studying the global politics of science and technology. In M. Mayer & M. K. Carpes (Eds.), *The global politics of science and technology - vol. 2* (pp. 1–21). Springer.

Mayer, M., Mariana, C., & Ruth, K. (2014). *The global politics of science and technology - vol. 1 concepts from international relations and other disciplines*. Berlin: Springer.

Mayer, M., Mariana, C., & Ruth, K. (2014). *The global politics of science and technology - vol. 2 perspectives, cases and methods*. Berlin: Springer.

Miltchel, T. (2011). *Carbon democracy: Political power in the age of oil*. Verso Books.

Mikheev, E. A., & Nestik, T. A. (2019). The use of artificial intelligence technologies in information and psychological warfare. *Psychology of Subculture: Phenomenology and Contemporary Tendencies of Development*. https://doi.org/10.15405/epsbs.2019.07.53.

Narayan, R. (2021, July 30). Dont let Pegasus convert citizens into docile bodies. Retrieved from LiveMint: https://www.livemint.com/opinion/online-views/dont-let-pegasus-convert-citizens-into-docile-bodies-11627574998100.html.

Pariser, E. (2012). *The filter bubble: What the internet is hiding from you*. Penguin.

Pauwels, E. (2018, October 15). The new geopolitics of artificial intelligence. Retrieved from Weforum: https://www.weforum.org/agenda/2018/10/artificial-intelligence-ai-new-geopolitics-un/.

Peters, U. (2022). Algorithmic political bias in artificial intelligence systems. *Philosophy & Technology*, 35. https://doi.org/10.1007/s13347-022-00512-8.

Polcumpally, A. T. (2020, September 13). Why control of social media becomes necessary? Retrieved from Modern Diplomacy: https://moderndiplomacy.eu/2020/09/13/why-control-of-social-media-becomes-necessary/.

Polcumpally, A. T. (2021). Artificial intelligence and global power structure: Understanding through Luhmann's systems theory. *AI & Society*. https://doi.org/10.1007/s00146-021-01219-8.

Przeworski, A., & Fernando, L. (1997). Modernization: Theories and facts. *World Politics*, 49(2), 155–183. Retrieved from https://www.jstor.org/stable/25053996.

Ryan, M. (2022). The social and ethical impacts of artificial intelligence in agriculture: Mapping the agricultural AI literature. *AI & Society*. https://doi.org/10.1007/s00146-021-01377-9.

Salter, C., Regula, V. B., & Joseph, D. (2017). Art, design, and performance. In U. Felt, R. Fouché, C. A. Miller, & L. Smith-Doerr (Eds.), *The handbook of science and technology studies* (pp. 139–169). Cambridge, MA: MIT Press.

Schrage, M. (2020). *Recommendation engines*. Cambridge, MA: MIT Press.

Security Infowatch. (2022, July 6). Report: Global video surveillance market rebounds in wake of Covid-19 pandemic. Retrieved from https://www.securityinfowatch.com/video-surveillance/news/21273298/report-global-video-surveillance-market-rebounds-in-wake-of-covid19-pandemic.

Sivasubramanian, S. (2020, May 28). How AI and machine learning are helping to fight COVID-19. Retrieved from Weforum: https://www.weforum.org/agenda/2020/05/how-ai-and-machine-learning-are-helping-to-fight-covid-19/.

Smith, B., & Carol, A. B. (2019). *Tools and weapons: The promise and the peril of digital age*. Penguin Press.

Sormani, P., Morana, A., Alain, B., & Christian, G. (2017). Ethnomethodology, video analysis, and STS. In R. F.-D. Ulrike Felt (Ed.), *Handbook of science and technology studies* (pp. 113–139). Cambridge, MA: MIT Press.

Sreedhar, N. (2022, May 1). When it comes to tech-art, who is the real creator? Retrieved from the Live Mint: https://lifestyle.livemint.com/smart-living/innovation/when-it-comes-to-tech-art-who-is-the-real-creator-111651298897087.html.

Srnicek, N. (2017). *Platform capitalism*. Cambridge: Polity Press.

Stroikos, D. (2020). China, India, and the social construction of technology in international society: The English school meets science and technology studies. *Review of International Relations*, 1–19. doi:10.1017/S0260210520000273.

Sun, T. Q., & Medaglia, R. (2018). Mapping the challenges of Artificial Intelligence in the public sector. *Government Information Quarterly*, 368–383. https://doi.org/10.1016/j.giq.2018.09.008.

Suri, A. (2022). *The great tech game: Shaping geopolitics and the destiny of nations*. New Delhi: Harper Collins India.

Susskind, J. (2018). *Future politics*. Oxford: Oxford University Press.

Sylvest, C. (2013). Technology and global politics: The modern experiences of Bertrand Russell and John H. *The International History Review*, 35(1), 121–142. Retrieved from https://www.jstor.org/stable/24701342.

The Economist. (2013). A Giant Cage. *The Economist*. Retrieved from https://www.economist.com/sites/default/files/20130406_china_and_the_internet.pdf.

The Royal Society. (2018). Portrayals and perceptions of AI and why they matter. Retrieved from https://royalsociety.org/-/media/policy/projects/ai-narratives/AI-narratives-workshop-findings.pdf.

Toros, S., & Toros, E. (2022). Social media use and political participation: the Turkish case. *Turkish Studies*. https://doi.org/10.1080/14683849.2021.2023319.

Vertesi Janet, D. R. (2017). Engaging, designing, and making digital systems. In R. F.-D. Ulrike Felt (Ed.), *Handbook of science and technology studies* (pp. 169–145). Cambridge, MA: MIT Press.

Vogel, K. M., Brian, B., Sam, W. E., Inga, K., Miwao, M., & Brian, R. (2017). Knowledge and security. In R. F.-D. Ulrike Felt (Ed.), *Handbook of science and technology studies* (pp. 973–1003). Cambridge, MA: MIT Press.

Wang, D. (2020). *Reigning the future: AI, 5G, Huawei, and the next 30 years of US-China rivalry*. New Degree Press.

Ward, I. (1997). How democratic can we get?: The internet, the public sphere, and public discourse. *JAC*, 17(3), 365–379. Retrieved from http://www.jstor.org/stable/20866148.

Winner, L. (1980). Do artefacts have politics? *Modern Technology: Problem or Opportunity?* 21–36.

World Economic Forum. (2019). AI governance: A holistic approach to implement ethics into AI. World Economic Forum. Retrieved from https://weforum.my.salesforce.com/sfc/p/#b0000000GycE/a/0X000000cPl1/i.8ZWL2HIR_kAnvckyqVA.nVVgrWIS4LCM1ueGy.gBc.

Zinn, O. J. (2008). *Social theories of risk and uncertainty: An introduction*. Blackwell Publishing.

PART II

AI IMAGINARIES
AND DISCOURSES

17. Bothering the binaries: unruly AI futures of hauntings and hope at the limit
Amanda Lagerkvist and Bo Reimer

INTRODUCTION

Our present age of datafication is based on the (in)famous binary of zeros and ones, and the foundational opposition between the human and the machine. Critical eyes on discourses surrounding AI typically identify a mix of positive versus negative, or utopian versus dystopian scenarios regarding the future. But these AI futures, on closer inspection, constitute a hefty and tangled sociotechnical imaginary (Jasanoff 2015) of conflicting and binary prospects, relentlessly bifurcating in a multitude of ways. In line with Mark Coeckelbergh, we argue that "AI is not only a technology but also a story" (2021: 1626) that powerfully configures our life-world by also linking to other available cultural stories in the present moment. Amounting to an entire assemblage – that can be identified across a variety of fields today, such as industry, public opinion, policy, debate, civil society engagement, educational practices, journalistic reporting, and academic pursuit in both engineering, social science, and humanistic debate – in short, across the board of cultural and social productions of meaning and discourse around the technological developments of "AI" at large, the story seems almost hegemonic and thus calls for a renewed critique. We identify six key concentrations within this narrative assemblage where durable opposites are continuously replayed.

We begin this essay by offering an initial disentanglement of the binaries at the heart of the AI story. The first pertains to *realism* and posits AI as either illusory or extraordinarily true and powerful (Natale 2021). The second relates to *power.* It measures AI against human strengths, thus conceiving it as super promising or extraordinarily dangerous/powerful, in other words, as promise versus risk (Tegmark 2017). Third, AI activates the issue of *creativity.* Either it is seen as filled with potential in the cultural sector, or as reducing diversity, reinforcing bias, and deskilling human creativity. Forking out further it is here also either a question of enhancing or delimiting creativity (the humanistic question) or it invites us to rethink creativity at large, as a process involving more-than-human dimensions (the posthuman imperative) (Romic and Reimer 2022). AI is further seen as being, fourth, about *magic*: as either enchanted (clairvoyant) (Campolo and Crawford 2020) or as ultimately disenchanted (as in a Weberian world of cages). This thus posits the technology as either full of black boxes (and thus of techno-spiritualities) or as super secular and rational. Fifth and related, AI evokes the key vector in Western philosophy and the project of enlightenment modernity – that of *rationality.* AI is here seen as either the fulfillment and outperformance of human reason (thereby signaling its demise) (Hong 2022) or as something altogether alien; a more-than-human promise for alternative modes of being rational and envisioning the future (Zylinska 2020). Finally, the debates revolve around the issue of *fate* – and more specifically the fate of the species – and whether implementing AI will lead to the augmentation of humans or to their replacement (Bostrom 2014). The binaries at the center of the AI assemblage thus seem, on reflection, to occupy the role previously held by religion to seek to anticipate, look to the future, and find answers; hence to *prophesy*. At the same time, and particularly in connection to the named binary invocations of magic, rationality, and fate, AI as predictive modeling is often positioned in contemporary techno-progressivist discourse, uniting political ambitions and commercial big tech forces, as a factful truth messenger about and from the future. It is offered as the sole solution to the problems at hand, and thus as *the* bridge to the future itself (Lagerkvist 2020).

In this chapter, we will outline a critical perspective on these questions by turning our attention to the continental tradition of philosophy, branching out along its existentialist (Jaspers) wing as our primary site for a renewed critique, yet in turn further reviving the effort via its deconstructivist (Derrida) and Marxist (Bloch) offshoots. In this unexpected mix, and by tracing coincidences of these different approaches within the tradition, we find possibilities for pluralizing and thus "hacking" the binaries of the AI imaginary in fruitful and urgent ways. This is particularly productive as we wish to harness critical problematizations of binary thinking, for example, in feminism and critical race theory with the help of thinkers such as Laura Forlano and Kat Jungnickel (2015). Offering unruly AI futures thus also speaks to more recent critical traditions and methodological moves, from which we will draw inspiration. Taking our cue from these debates, our main objective is to bother the binaries. Beyond simply identifying yet another example for the Derridean deconstruction project to effectively scorch, *nota bene*, the rationale for examining and troubling the binaries pertains to their massive power in the present moment. They are in fact part of a hegemonic story that represents the apotheosis of the Enlightenment project (Hong 2022). In this moment they bespeak, reveal, and thrive upon a reality that presents an *Either/Or* in terms of *either* preserving the status quo *or* choosing to "stay with the trouble" (Haraway 2016) and allow for indeterminacy, uncertainty, and an embrace of the transition movements of our times. This very real choice is in the hands of the AI industry recalibrated and reduced into an either/or for our societies of either saving and bettering the world with AI – by joining "the race" – or not doing so. Hence, what is characteristic of this assemblage, in all its multiplicity, is thus the recurring trope – profited from and pushed by the tech industries – of standing at a crossroads, at which we are compelled to stake out the very future itself by choosing or not to embrace the promises of automation. And yet, as already stated, the trope reflects the very real watershed we are facing, which is a "limit situation" for our civilization (cf. Jaspers 1932/1970; Lagerkvist 2022). From a critical, philosophical, humanistic, and artistic perspective, our interest thus concerns the powerful role of AI in shaping the future, both materially and symbolically.[1]

Our argument in the following will be that AI, if situated beyond these binaries, is thus today part of the present digital limit situation (Lagerkvist 2020, 2022), which requires that we acknowledge that the future – as well as the past – is implicated in the present, as not

---

[1]   Today, several disciplines are in different ways addressing questions of the future. It is a topic of relevance for many traditional humanities and social science disciplines, such as philosophy, history, history of ideas, sociology, and anthropology (Appadurai 2013; Schulz 2015; Coleman and Tutton 2017). In addition, a number of fields have emerged, dealing more specifically with this topic. Futures studies emerged after the Second World War (Andersson 2018) and exist alongside fields such as anticipation studies (Poli 2017), utopian studies (Curtis and Hintz 2020), critical future studies (Godhe and Goode 2018), and science fiction studies (Milner 2011). The question of the role of AI is seldom highlighted in these traditions, however, and when it is, it is done from a technical rather than from a critical humanities perspective (cf. Rovastos 2019).

least the concept of hauntology from Derrida will allow us to perceive. Sensing the future as latent in the present – which we need to tenderly tend to and carefully craft (Adam and Groves 2011) – is of importance, we argue, for making sense of AI and its potential roles. In this instance, we will also turn to the question of *hope* in Bloch's project. What can we reasonably expect of AI in relation to the creation of a peaceful and sustainable society, and what would be needed for that expectation to be fulfilled? In order to address these matters, we will reconceive AI futures as based on more disorderly terrains of everyday lifeworlds and existential wisdom, as well as in playful and piercing criticism. In this pursuit, we will argue for the importance of re-envisioning AI as *anticipatory existential media* (Lagerkvist 2020, 2022) that allows for dimensions of the unexpected, the impredicative, and the uncanny — for hauntings of acumens and guidance from the past (Reimer 2022) — as well as for recognition of both the limits of technology and its role in the "limit situation." This approach draws upon the philosophy of Jaspers, which will be further elaborated in the following sections.

LIMIT SITUATIONS: UNUSUAL COMMUNICATION AND UNRULY ANTICIPATION

What is artificial intelligence? This chapter is not the place for detailed descriptions of the discussions concerning this issue. However, it can be noted that it has become increasingly common to view AI as media and place it in such a context. And there are good reasons for that. Already in the text that defined machine intelligence, Turing's "Computing Machinery and Intelligence" published in 1950, it was made clear that the one factor deciding whether machines have intelligence is *communication*: if a machine is able to communicate with humans in ways similar to how humans communicate, then it has intelligence (Turing 1950; cf. Gunkel 2012, Natale 2021). In this perspective, AI becomes a medium that takes part in a communication process. But it is not a traditional medium. In ordinary communication processes, a medium links a sender with a receiver, or it links two senders with each other. AI is not just a link, however. It differs from traditional media by also being an agent in the communication process (Zhao 2006; Peter and Kühne 2018). The degree to which AI does this differs in different settings, but in general, the point is that AI is a medium that people can communicate with and get into dialogue with. It thereby challenges the traditional ontological divide between humans and machines (Guzman and Lewis 2020).

It is of course necessary to look upon the statements given above with some caution. Within the engineering and computing traditions that have dominated writing on AI, views have often been overly optimistic and machine centered. But as Natale and Guzman (2022) argue, now even cultural studies scholars, who traditionally have downplayed the role of machines, with the help of concepts such as "algorithmic culture" and "machine culture" over-correct and forget that machine agency is played out within human systems of meaning-making and power. In addition, such human systems are in fact *existential media*; they are profoundly related to the human condition and their meanings, and thus, transcend what the classic paradigms of, for example, critical sociology, emic anthropology, and political economy will be equipped to capture. Existential media have four properties (Lagerkvist 2022) that all bespeak a life within limits. First, they ground us materially and ontologically in being as the "materials and habitats through which" as John D. Peters argues, "we act and are" (2015: 15). They are thus about what it means to be human, to exist. They also throw us, second, into a world of both limits and contingency, often heightening vulnerabilities. They further speak, third, to our shared vulnerability and deep need for connections as well as for disconnections. Finally, they require something of us: that we care for the future through response and respons(e)ability. And as we here argue (and will return to shortly), this can in fact be done, by means of learning from friendly ghosts from the past, as in Derrida's notion of hauntology, reminding us about what we already know (a "reawakening" as per Karl Jaspers) and through acknowledging the profound unprecedented performativity of AI as existential media.

Existential media sit at the heart of our civilization's limit situation. The concept of the limit situation, derived from Jaspers' philosophy, describes those ultimate moments in life – of loss, crisis, conflict, guilt, birth, and love – which we are called upon to seize in order to become authentic beings (Jaspers 1932/1970). "Situations like the following: that I am always in situations; that I cannot live without struggling and suffering; that I cannot avoid guilt; that I must die – these are what I call boundary situations" (ibid: 178). Limit situations are revelatory of the human condition, but they also encompass possibilities for transcendence and self-realization through the other. Hence, the limit situation is both about utter indeterminacy and about the potential for new forms of productivity and new creations. The *digital limit situation*, in turn, appears in three overlapping senses. First, digital media represent where the limit situations of life often transpire, for example, in grief, ill health, or crisis. Second, digital technologies also comprise in themselves a limit situation, since media often appear as either shock or solution, and not least because they are performative. By extension, and third, our present age of tangled crises – in which AI technologies are fundamental and transformative – is a digital limit situation with profound ethical, political, and existential repercussions (Lagerkvist 2022). As already discussed, existential media of the limit situation *demand responsible and responsive action*. Existential media are thereby part of the crisis, not only its promised solution. They require something of us. They call us to step back in order to step in with critique and an ethics of care (Lagerkvist et al. 2022).

This relates more specifically to anticipatory media, of which AI is often perceived as a chief example since the very meaning of anticipatory behavior is essentially to act in the present based on knowledge derived from predictions about the future. The machines prompt us to act on predictions of the future based on big data sets from the past (Poli 2017). However, instead of being reduced to tools for scientific forecasting, we argue that media can be examples of anticipation proper if they actually allow for open-ended existential futures that we can carefully attempt to craft, but which we can never determine or control. As Louise Amoore puts it: "The very potentiality of life presupposes something of an unknown future" (2011: 39). Life in this view is never amenable to mere calculation. AI futures, if modeled upon forecasting, are thus existentially speaking not alive but, to put it plainly, *dead futures*. Our question is: Can AI be designed for such scenarios of the *impredicative*? Can AI be about a life that is as Amoore argues "necessarily incomplete, complex, undecided"? (ibid). Can there be unruly and uncanny AI futures?

HAUNTINGS: PERFORMATIVE PASTS, PRESENTS, AND FUTURES

How does one study what has not yet been? Making sense of a future that is yet to come is a "wicked problem": a problem that cannot be given a definite formulation, that has no ultimate test for whether it is solved, and has less to do with true or false and more with good or bad

(Rittel and Webber 1973; Tutton 2017). We build on those perspectives that acknowledge that in order to make sense of the future, one has to link it to both the past and the present. This has to be done carefully. As philosopher Brumbaugh argues:

> there is a genuine ontological difference in the kind and the definiteness of being which past facts, present options, and future possibilities possess. Part of this difference can be summarized by the assertion that *there are no past possibilities, and there are no future facts.* (1966: 649, italics in original)

However, the past is never finished: we continuously look back and reinterpret what has happened. And the future is already shaping the present through anticipation: we act in order to make something in the future possible, and we act in order to create a future memory (cf. Currie 2007). But we do not do this by ourselves, in isolation. We are haunted by ghosts from the past, and we are haunted by the future.

What has once happened to us does not disappear: it lingers on and haunts us. But so do the things that could have happened but never did. Fisher (2014) calls these our "lost futures," the futures that never were but which continue to shape our ways of living and thinking. But we are also haunted by the future that is yet to come. Central to this discussion is Derrida's (1994) concept of hauntology. This wordplay on haunting and ontology signals that to be is to be haunted; these conditions are always interlinked. Derrida wrote about hauntings in relation to communism. He quotes Marx' and Engels' *Communist Manifesto*, which begins: "A specter is haunting Europe – the specter of communism" (1848/2021: 11). A specter is traditionally regarded as something returning: a revenant. But it is not likely that communism at that point in time could have been regarded as a revenant. More likely, for Marx and Engels – and for Derrida – communism should be regarded as a reminder of something that could come back and haunt sometime in the future: something not yet existing, but something that could start having an impact if we begin talking and querying about it. The future is latent within the present.

Derrida's discussion starts chronologically, however, with Shakespeare's "Hamlet." It is the specter of Hamlet's murdered father telling Hamlet about what had happened to him that sets off the events of the play. What is special about specters – or ghosts – is that they are neither living nor dead. They were here before us, they are here now, and they will be here when we are gone. Hamlet's "To be or not to be" is of no relevance to them. And they shape our view of time. It may not be as linear as we tend to think. As Hamlet declares after seeing the ghost of his father: "Time is out of joint." In all of these different hauntings, media obviously play key roles that are, as media studies will be the first to report, irreducible to binaries between either magical or deeply rational, either all-powerful or simply deceitful. It is through media that we today have access to the past, both through representations of the past in literature, cinema, and so on, and through personal archives of photos, videos, and sound recordings. Through the Internet, the amount of available material is incalculable. Media furthermore give us portrayals of possible futures to come in different cultural forms and genres. And the possibilities offered by media to record and document may shape what we do: we do the things that can be recorded. As Mark Currie writes: "An event is recorded not because it happens, but it happens because it is recorded" (2007: 11).

As a medium, AI thus takes part in the linking of the past with the present with the future. And it does so with its particular characteristics and affordances. As discussed previously, of particular interest here is the possibility of taking on the role of communicator. What is important to note is that the carrying out of these tasks is in no way neutral. It has a *performative* function. Beyond simply mediating, automation performs and acts upon the world and sets something in motion. According to Mark Coeckelbergh (2021), human life consists of narration, and AI is, as mentioned from the outset, an effective co-narrator of our human stories. He identifies three such ways. First, AI is used to classify historical data in order for the data to be used to perform new tasks; to find the best person for a new job, a hiring algorithm based on earlier conducted interviews is created. Second, AI is used for predicting the future: crime data is used to predict which neighborhoods will become increasingly dangerous to live in. Third, in line with increasing automation, AI is used as a decision-maker. Using historical data to perform new tasks means privileging older, maybe prejudiced, ways of thinking over new ways. And prediction making will by necessity have an impact on the future. Making statements about a neighborhood will mean that people will act on that information. Affluent people may decide not to move there, making the prediction a self-fulfilling prophecy. Or financial sources may be transferred toward the neighborhood, making the prediction into a self-defeating prophecy.

In order to grasp the importance of AI performativity, it is necessary to deal with the question of artificial creativity (Romic and Reimer 2022). As already glossed above, this relates to the key issue of how creative something non-human can be. The topic is huge, and it concerns both what one may mean with creativity as such, and with the relationship between humans and non-humans in creativity processes (Boden 2004; Gunkel 2017). A nuanced evaluation of the latter is the view that it really makes no sense to disentangle humans from technologies and their outputs, instead, we should attend to their complex entirety and in that move bother the discussed binaries. As media theorist Joanna Zylinska argues: "Instead of pitching the human against the machine, shouldn't we rather see different forms of human activity as having always relied on technical prostheses and forming part of technical assemblages" (2020: 27). However, even as an assemblage, it is necessary to try to disentangle at least to a certain extent what it is the non-human, or the machine, can do. Machine agency differs from human agency, but it still constitutes agency (Hayles 2022). One way of making sense of this is to regard AI as a "lively technology," as an actor whose actions when set free cannot completely be predicted (Henriksen and Wang 2022; Henriksen et al. 2022). The idea of lively technologies – of technologies getting out of hand – is of course not new. A classical fictional example is Frankenstein's monster in Mary Shelley's novel (1818/2003). But the notion functions especially well in relation to AI artifacts, such as bots roaming the Internet, making connections and interactions at unpredictable places without the possibility for the creator to control the actions. Such actions can of course distress, both for the creator of the artifact who has lost control and for the humans coming in contact with it who may not even know whether they interact with another human or with a non-human. It is crucial to remember, however, that the artifact is a creation by someone, and that someone has a responsibility for what he or she has created. What is often forgotten about Mary Shelley's novel is that its main topic is ethical and relates to questions of pain, suffering, and abandonment. Frankenstein's monster acts the way it does because it is deserted by its creator (Suchman 2018). As a clear breakaway from binarism of "either machine or human" – as the sentient machine is relieved of the human yardstick and abandoned by the overseer – the technology can be reconceived as both truly existential and thus anticipatory in an impredicative sense (as in Poli's deliberation), but also as an existential anticipatory medium that prompts us to ask anew: what is right and wrong in our technological era – in the digital limit situation? How are we then to deal with this haunted future? Derrida (1994) speaks of the importance of hospitality to the ghosts – memories, experiences, and people – surrounding us. They should not only feel welcomed but they should make themselves at home. Getting used to a time out of joint is a way of dealing with one's life; a way of dealing with grief as well as happiness.

HOPE: THE VENTURING BEYOND

How should we then move into this unknown, coming future? Most importantly, it is crucial to reclaim a sense of hope, an existential anticipation in a world in which AI has occupied its very horizon. To do so with and sometimes beyond the machines would mean reinstalling what the anthropologist Jane Guyer has called the phenomenological near future (2007), which we can both plan for and dream about and in effect shape. AI as existential anticipatory media thus calls on us, as already proclaimed, to rethink and retake responsibility for the world but also to intervene in it creatively. This leads us to the main philosopher of hope, Ernst Bloch (1954/1995). For him, the concept of "not yet" is central. And primarily the processes through which this "not yet" may be reached. He is interested in the utopian but distinguishes between the abstract-utopian and the concrete-utopian – on the one side vague, naïve dreams, and on the other side, things that actually can be accomplished. It is the latter that interests him. He wanted to develop what he termed "docta spes," which is Latin for educated hope. The way to reach educated hope is to use one's experiences and imagination. To look back and reflect on what has happened and what could have happened but doing so in order to find new insights. The past is not finished; it can be rethought: "Thinking means venturing beyond" (Bloch 1954/1995: 4).

Such insights can be both soothing and shocking: you see connections you have not seen previously. But you also need to look ahead. And in so doing focusing on what lies ahead as something almost already existing. One's expectations of the forthcoming are already part of reality (we live simultaneously in the past, the present, and the future). But expectations lie latent. They have to be put in motion. Things we want to happen may happen. And things we want to avoid can be avoided: in the limit situation of climate change, we know there will be an ecological collapse. But if we act now, we can stop what we know will happen. The future that haunts us is not inevitable. To dream of the future is important. Bloch makes a distinction between nightdreams and daydreams. Nightdreams, once we have woken, are unrealizable. In a mix between the rational and the passionate – as the perspective inherently offers a bothering of the AI binaries pertaining to reason and creativity – daydreams, on the other hand, are inventive. Daydreams are set in motion by one's experiences. But something more is also needed: something new. For Bloch, it is in art one may find this "new." Art shows what the world wants to become, not what it is. In alignment with Jaspers' concept of *ciphers of being*, he argues that high culture can do this, but also fairy tales, mythologies, and popular culture. For a Marxist thinker, Bloch was uncharacteristically open to the potential of the popular. What is of particular importance in this context is that art is increasingly made available through media. If art is the raw material that helps us identify the unknown and the new, then media is the place where it is located. And AI as existential anticipatory media subsequently takes on an increasingly crucial role. Again, the limit is invoked, as that which can and should be breached in hopeful imaginings of alternatives. Contra the powerful narrative assemblage, with which we began our meditation, insights from (friendly visitings of) the past coupled with new imaginations here provide hope, invoked by the not-yet of our own critical project.

CONCLUSION: HAUNTINGS OF HOPE AT THE LIMIT

To wrap up: our chapter has highlighted AI as a polarized and therefore culturally powerful and even prophetic story about the future, which activates the entire techno-existential register that pertains to realism, power, magic, rationality, creativity, and fate. We see, however, a need for hacking the problematic binaries that nestle at the heart of this narrative assemblage. As Forlano and Jungnickel (2015: n.p.) write, troublemaking is a way of "getting inside the 'black box' of a socio-technological assemblage," bothering its original design with new questions. We have therefore in this chapter proposed that a narrative critical perspective can be complemented with an existential analysis, which will enable troubling the binaries that continuously repeat themselves as discrete prospects of a future with(out) and of AI. Returning to the traditions of continental philosophy, we have discussed three of its offerings for advancing Coeckelbergh's moral and political hermeneutics and for providing a more unruly story: existentiality brought to the table the reality of limits, finitude, and vulnerability; hauntings reminded of and returned the latent riches of the past to the present moment; and with hopefulness, we have challenged the inevitability of the processes at hand. In other words, bothering the binaries allows us to reimagine more unruly AI futures inclusive of promises of the past (hauntings); prospects for an otherwise (hope); and existential profundity and practicality (limit). AI as existential anticipatory media co-constitutes the human condition. As a performative force, it is both a technology and a story, shaping the very idea of the future in powerful ways. It constitutes our digital limit situation, urgently requiring conscious response and careful rethinking.

REFERENCES

Adam, B., and C. Groves (2011) "Futures Tended: Care and Future Oriented Responsibility," *Bulletin of Science, Technology & Society*, 31(1): 17–27, DOI: 10.1177/0270467610391237

Amoore, L. (2011) "Data Derivatives: On the Emergence of Security Risk Calculus for our Times," *Theory, Culture & Society,* 28(6): 20 & 39, DOI: 10.1177/0263276411417430

Andersson, J. (2018) *The Future of the World: Futurology, Futurists, and the Struggle for the Post Cold War.* Oxford: Oxford UP.

Appadurai, A. (2013) *The Future as Cultural Fact.* London: Verso.

Bloch, E. (1954/1995) *The Principle of Hope, Vol. 1.* Cambridge: The MIT Press.

Boden, M. (2004) *The Creative Mind: Myths and Mechanisms.* London: Routledge.

Bostrom, N. (2014) *Superintelligence: Paths, Dangers, Strategies.* New York: Oxford University Press.

Brumbaugh, R. S. (1966) "Applied Metaphysics: Truth and Passing Time," *The Review of Metaphysics,* 19(4): 647–666.

Campolo, A. & K. Crawford (2020) "Enchanted Determinism: Power without Responsibility in Artificial Intelligence, *"Engaging Science, Technology, and Society,* 6(2020): 1-19, DOI: https://doi .org/10.17351/ests2020.277

Coeckelbergh, M. (2021) "Time Machines: Artificial Intelligence, Process, and Narrative," *Philosophy & Technology,* 34(4): 1623–1638.

Coleman, R., and R. Tutton (2017) "Introduction to Special Issue of Sociological Review on 'Futures in Question: Theories, Methods, Practices'," *The Sociological Review,* 65(3): 440–447.

Currie, M. (2007) *About Time: Narrative, Fiction and the Philosophy of Time.* Edinburgh: Edinburgh University Press.

Curtis, C. P., and C. Hintz (2020) "Utopian Studies: An Interdisciplinary Pursuit," *Utopian Studies,* 31(2): 334–337.

Derrida, J. (1994) *Specters of Marx: The State of the Debt, the Work of Mourning, and the New International*. New York: Routledge.

Fisher, M. (2014) *Ghosts of My Life: Writings on Depression, Hauntology and Lost Futures*. Winchester: Zero Books.

Forlano, L., and K. Jungnickel (2015) "Hacking Binaries/Hacking Hybrids: Understanding the Black/White Binary as a Socio-Technical Practice," *Ada. A Journal of Gender, New Media, and Technology*, nr 6.

Godhe, M., and L. Goode (2018) "Critical Future Studies – A Thematic Introduction," *Culture Unbound*, 10(2): 151–162.

Gunkel, D. J. (2012) "Communication and Artificial Intelligence: Opportunities and Challenges for the 21st Century," *Communication +1*, 1(1): 1.

Gunkel, D. (2017) "Special Section: Rethinking Art and Aesthetics in the Age of Creative Machines: Editor's Introduction," *Philosophy and Technology*, 30(3): 263–265.

Guyer, J. I. (2007) "Prophecy and the Near Future: Thoughts on Macroeconomic, Evangelical and Punctuated Time," *American Ethnologist*, 34(3): 409–421, DOI: 10.1525/ae.2007.34.3.409

Guzman, A. L., and S. C. Lewis (2020) "Artificial Intelligence and Communication: A Human–Machine Communication Research Agenda," *New Media & Society*, 22(1): 70–86.

Haraway, D. J. (2016) *Staying With the Trouble: Making Kin in the Chthulucene*. Durham: Duke University Press.

Hayles, N. K. (2022) "Inside the Mind of an AI: Materiality and the Crisis of Representation," Keynote Lecture at the conference Digital Existence III: Living with Automation, the DIGMEX Network, the Sigtuna Foundation, May 31–June 1, 2022.

Henriksen, L., B. Reimer and B. Romic (2022) *Lively Media Technologies: Ethics, Monsters and New Imaginaries for the Future*. EASST (European Association for the Study of Science and Technology) 2022 Conference, Madrid.

Henriksen, L., and C. Wang (2022) "Hello, Twitter bot!: Towards a Bot Ethics of Response and Responsibility," *Catalyst: Feminism, Theory, Technoscience*, 8(1): 1–22.

Hong, S.-H. (2022) "Trolled by the Enlightenment," Keynote Lecture at the conference Digital Existence III: Living with Automation, the DIGMEX Network, the Sigtuna Foundation, May 31–June 1, 2022.

Jasanoff, S. (2015) "Future Imperfect: Science, Technology, and the Imaginations of Modernity," in S. Jasanoff and S.-H. Kim (Eds.), *Dreamscapes of Modernity: Sociotechnical Imaginaries and the Fabrication of Power*. Chicago: University of Chicago Press, pp. 1–34.

Jaspers, K. (1932/1970) *Philosophy II*. Chicago: University of Chicago Press.

Lagerkvist, A. (2020) "Digital Limit Situations: Anticipatory Media Beyond 'the New AI Era'," *Journal of Digital Social Research*, 2(3): 16–41.

Lagerkvist, A. (2022) *Existential Media: A Media Theory of the Limit Situation*. New York: Oxford University Press.

Lagerkvist, A., M. Tudor, J. Smolicki, C. M. Ess, J. Eriksson Lundström, and M. Rogg (2022) "Body Stakes: An Existential Ethics of Care in Living with Biometrics and AI," *AI & Society: Journal of Knowledge, Culture and Communication*.

Marx, K., and F. Engels (1848/2021) *The Communist Manifesto*. Chichester: John Wiley and Sons.

Milner, D. (2011) "Science Fiction and the Literary Field," *Science Fiction Studies*, 38(3): 393–411.

Natale, S., and A. L. Guzman (2022) "Reclaiming the Human in Machine Cultures: Introduction," *Media, Culture & Society*, 44(4): 627–637.

Natale, S. (2021) *Deceitful Media: Artificial Intelligence and Social Life after the Turing Test*. New York: Oxford University Press.

Peters, J. D. (2015) *The Marvelous Clouds: Toward a Philosophy of Elemental Media*. Chicago: University of Chicago Press.

Peter, J., and R. Kühne (2018) "The New Frontier in Communication Research: Why We Should Study Social Robots," *Media and Communication*, 6(3): 73–76.

Poli, R. (2017) *Introduction to Anticipation Studies*. Cham: Springer.

Reimer, B. (2022) "AI Hauntings," Paper presented at the conference "Digital Existence III: Living with Automation," the DIGMEX Network, the Sigtuna Foundation, May 31–June 1, 2022.

Rittel, H. W. J., and M. M. Webber (1973) "Dilemmas in a General Theory of Planning," *Policy Sciences*, 4(2): 155–169.

Romic, B., and B. Reimer (2022) "Editorial: Artificial Creativity," *Transformations: Journal of Media, Culture & Technology*, issue #36.

Rovatsos, M. (2019) "Anticipatory Artificial Intelligence," in R. Poli (Ed.), *Handbook of Anticipation*. London: Springer International Publishing.

Schulz, M. S. (2015) "Future Moves: Forward-Oriented Studies of Culture, Society, and Technology," *Current Sociology Monograph*, 63(2): 129–139.

Shelley, M. (1818/2003) *Frankenstein: Or the Modern Prometheus*. London: Penguin.

Suchman, L. (2018) "Frankenstein's Problem," in U. Schultze, M. Aanestad, M. Mähring, C. Østerlund, and K. Riemer (Eds.), *Living with Monsters? Social Implications of Algorithmic Phenomena, Hybrid Agency, and the Performativity of Technology*. Cham: Springer, pp. 13–18.

Tegmark, M. (2017) *Life 3.0: Being Human in the Age of Artificial Intelligence*. New York: Alfred A. Knopf.

Turing, A. M. (1950) "Computing Machinery and Intelligence," *Mind: A Quarterly Review of Psychology and Philosophy*, 59(236): 433–460.

Tutton, R. (2017) "Wicked Futures: Meaning, Matter and the Sociology of the Future," *The Sociological Review*, 65(3): 478–492.

Zhao, S. (2006) "Humanoid Social Robots as a Medium of Communication," *New Media & Society*, 8(3): 401–419.

Zylinska, J. (2020) *AI Art: Machine Visions and Warped Dreams*. London: Open University Press.

18. Imaginaries of artificial intelligence

Vanessa Richter, Christian Katzenbach and Mike S. Schäfer

INTRODUCTION

Artificial intelligence (AI) is considered a key technology in contemporary societies and is expected to substantially change sectors as diverse as health, warfare, mobility, and communication. At the same time, with the increasingly advanced and pervasive use of AI in everyday activities, it also has the potential to significantly reshape our daily practices and interpersonal interactions (LaRosa & Danks, 2018; Mou, 2020). Consequently, political and economic stakeholders in many countries have allocated considerable resources to AI development, and the technology has been the object of extensive public debates. These political and public debates, however, are often criticized for overemphasizing AI's potential (Brennen et al., 2018; Elish & boyd, 2018; Zeng et al., 2022) and exaggerating its capabilities and impact (Goode, 2018). In these debates, the term "AI" is mobilized for different things, usually remains vague, and is used inconsistently (Mager & Katzenbach, 2021). This indicates the inherent ambiguity of broad technologies such as AI. Their development and societal integration are context-dependent, shaped by political, economic, and sociocultural interests, and subject to discursive negotiations in public arenas. Given the vast amount of interest and resources invested in AI research and technology, and its expected impact on the individual, organizational, and societal levels, it is important to question how the characteristics and development of AI are socially constructed, negotiated, or restrained by sociopolitical contexts.

In this process, the discursive and public imagination plays a pivotal role in envisioning and determining the trajectories of AI and its integration into society. Therefore, stakeholders have an interest in shaping the debate to their advantage by impacting what the public imagines AI or its capabilities to be. The concept of imaginaries has proven to be helpful in this respect, as it foregrounds the role of discursive and collective visions of desirable futures. Particularly, the approach of sociotechnical imaginaries rooted in science and technology studies (STS) (Jasanoff & Kim, 2015; Mager & Katzenbach, 2021) offers a meaningful perspective to analyze the characteristics and impact of imaginaries surrounding technological advances. Where classic studies investigate imaginaries and trajectories of nuclear energy (Jasanoff & Kim, 2009) and national energy policies (Jasanoff & Kim, 2013), or more recently of mobile phone technology, the application of this perspective to AI is particularly important because massive amounts of resources are currently devoted to a technology that is still often vague and under-determined. The concept foregrounds that our understanding of AI is to a considerable degree socially constructed and not inherently determined by the characteristics of the technology and its development itself. Imaginaries thus play a large role in influencing how societies deal with emerging key technologies like AI, but also how the technological sector in turn continues to develop AI technologies.

This is especially relevant right now, as AI seems to be in a formative phase – both as a technology and infrastructure as well as regarding its public perception. In such a phase, it is particularly relevant to ask who drives the agenda and which agenda is pushed to the foreground above other potential lines of development. Therefore, this chapter provides an introduction to the concept of imaginaries as a critical analytical framework to investigate AI and its role in society. In addition, it provides an overview of current research on sociotechnical imaginaries around AI specifically and related technological discourses in general considering relevant stakeholders, media representations, and public perceptions of the technology.

THE CONCEPT OF IMAGINARIES

Analyses from STS, social studies of science (SSS), social construction of technology (SCOT), reflexive technology assessment, and other interdisciplinary fields have long demonstrated that technologies are socially (co)constructed (Bijker, 2012; Law et al., 2016; Lösch et al., 2016). They show that technological development and institutionalization are not driven by an inherent, instrumental logic of a given technology, but shaped by political, economic, cultural, legal, and other social forces. In consequence, technological fields such as AI feature high levels of contingency and "interpretative flexibility" (Pinch & Bijker, 1984; Meyer & Schulz-Schaeffer, 2006) with different possible trajectories. In retrospect, technology always "might have been otherwise" (Bijker & Law, 1992: 3). These scholarly fields provide a rich literature investigating how and which societal factors inform and influence technological development, how technologies are taken up and re-shaped by society, in which ways social values are inscribed into technologies, and which sociopolitical effects technologies may have (e.g., Simon, 2016; Winner, 2010).

The concept of sociotechnical imaginaries has proven useful in this context, especially to understand the role of perceptions, discourses, and future visions in the complex interactions and negotiations of co-constructing technological developments. But it is embedded in a broader strand of social theory. Considering the "imagined" as part of social ordering has been conducive to understanding how people think about institutions such as the nation-state and the development of nationalism (Anderson, 1983), for example. These broad institutional concepts are bound to communal imaginaries constructing a collective and a political community, although members of this "imagined community" might have never met. Focusing on the social aspect of imaginary construction, Charles Taylor (2003) considered the evolving nature of social imaginaries, which have been challenged and revolutionized to adjust to what is accepted as normal in social interactions (97f.). His work considers moral and social structures upholding society. Both Anderson's and Taylor's work has inspired the more recent work on "sociotechnical imaginaries" by Sheila Jasanoff and Sang-Hyun Kim (2009, 2015), as well as research on specific sociotechnical aspects such as "algorithmic imaginaries" (Bucher, 2016), "platform imaginaries" (van Es & Poell, 2020), and influencer imaginaries (Arriagada & Bishop, 2021).

Jasanoff and Kim (2009) introduced the term sociotechnical imaginaries (SI) to capture (a) the high relevance of shared narratives and imaginations for collectives in line with Anderson and Taylor, and (b) to highlight the role and contingency of technology in building and ordering society (cf. SCOT, above). SI are "collectively imagined forms of social life and social order reflected in the design and fulfillment of nation-specific scientific and/or technological projects" (Jasanoff & Kim, 2009: 120). The concept thus aims to bridge the often separately investigated spaces of public and mediated discourse, political action, and technological development. As SI, especially early on, have been described to be always "associated with active exercises of state power, such as the selection of development priorities, the allocation of funds, the investment in material infrastructures" (Jasanoff & Kim, 2009: 123), they differ from concepts such as frames used in communication science or sociology. Beyond the communicative dimension, they integrate state interventions, corporate investments, technological developments, and other contributions to the materialization of an envisioned future into the empirical investigation. In addition, SI feature a prominent temporal dimension: they "at once describe attainable futures and prescribe futures that states believe ought to be attained" (Jasanoff & Kim, 2009: 120), guiding current activities and decisions by providing desirable futures. In other words: they describe potential developments of technologies, either spatially close ones but lie further in the future, or spatially detached ones, i.e., happening in other regions of the world, but temporally close, i.e., happening now or very soon.

Hence, two aspects distinguish "imaginaries" from neighboring concepts: Imaginaries (a) refer to *potential* development of technology and society, typically in the future but sometimes also spatially distant developments; and are (b) associated with *activities and the allocation of resources* by the state or powerful stakeholders aiming to realize (or prevent) this potential. While concepts such as "frames" and "narratives" focus more on the communicative layer, imaginaries have the capacity to structure the future because they *both* guide future expectations *as well as* mobilize resources to help this future come into being. "Policy frames" (Schön & Rhein, 1994) similarly combine communicative framing and pathways to action but are usually more concrete and policy-oriented in comparison with imaginaries. With regard to AI policies, Bareis and Katzenbach (2021), for example, have suggested distinguishing between AI narratives (that are remarkably similar across the US, China, France, and Germany) on the one hand, and AI imaginaries (that are strikingly different between these countries) on the other.

While the concept of SI has become a popular analytical tool with various theoretical adjustments and empirical manifestations, it remains underdeveloped both in terms of conceptual complexity as well as empirical operationalization. Conceptually, the initial focus on the imaginaries presented by nation-states and state actors has been eased, acknowledging that imaginaries are also articulated and enacted by corporate actors, civil society, research communities, and other organized groups (Jasanoff, 2015: 4; Mager & Katzenbach, 2021). STS scholars, for example, have pointed to the importance of corporate imaginaries in contexts such as RFID tagging (Felt & Öchsner, 2019) and satellite imagery (Olbrich & Witjes, 2016). They have analyzed how the European Union envisions corporate search engines (Mager, 2017) and big data solutions (Rieder, 2018) and how these imaginaries travel into and transform in national sociopolitical contexts and communities of practice (Mager, 2017). Finally, they have shown how bottom-up initiatives shape future imaginaries of the Internet through data activism in Denmark (Lehtiniemi & Ruckenstein, 2019) as well as hobbyists and research networks in Indonesia (Barker, 2015). This more complex understanding of SI was also adopted by Sheila Jasanoff in her updated and revised definition of SI as "collectively held, institutionally stabilized, and publicly performed visions of desirable futures, animated by shared understandings of forms of social life and social order attainable through, and supportive of, advances in science and technology" (Jasanoff, 2015: 4). But it still lacks conceptual and methodological clarity, particularly regarding the processual nature of imaginary building and formation, and the negotiation of competing imaginaries in public arenas (Mager & Katzenbach, 2021). Furthermore, the concrete operationalization of the concept in empirical work remains vague and differs considerably across studies employing the concept. Such an operationalization could be applied to assess imaginaries in news and social media communication, parliamentary debates, stakeholder documents, and combinations of those. It could draw on conceptual frameworks used to analyze public debates about technologies and science-related issues (e.g., Gerhards & Schäfer, 2006; Schäfer, 2007), but also on methodological approaches developed to analyze concepts like framing (e.g., Matthes & Kohring, 2008). Such an operationalization would have to take the proponents of given imaginaries (such as states of other stakeholders) into account, as well as the specific focus of a certain imaginary (what aspect of AI is the imaginary about?). Moreover, it should distinguish the core facets of imaginaries as outlined above: the specific reason given for an imaginary's (alleged) desirability, the imaginary's scope in time and space, the certainty to which it might (allegedly) be realized, and the people, organizations, countries, or other parties being (potentially) affected by it.

In addition to concepts such as ideas, frames, and visions that also highlight the discursive dimension in the relation between technology and society, the concept of (sociotechnical) imaginaries integrates the "resonance among collectives, the allocation of resources, and the adoption into practices" of the respective technological visions, as Mager & Katzenbach (2021: 226) argue. For that reason, the lens of imaginaries particularly enables scholars to reconstruct and highlight the contestations and negotiations between different actors in the processes of technological development and their integration into society, as research on energy transitions (Rudek, 2021), governance of sustainability developments (Becks et al., 2021), and smart cities (Sadowski & Bendor, 2018) has shown.

IMAGINARIES OF AI

The concept of imaginaries provides a particularly fitting conceptual lens for the investigation of AI's current integration and institutionalization into societies across the world. From this angle, mapping and questioning different imaginaries around AI can have a profound impact on understanding not only how different stakeholders think about an increasingly relevant technology, but how they simultaneously shape and impact the development of a technological vision for AI. Dominant imaginaries influence the way in which individuals, institutions, and societies deal with sociotechnical developments. Technologies such as AI are being stabilized through social, political, cultural, and economic negotiation processes.

As AI is an umbrella term that refers to both broad technological fields and innovations as well as a diverse array of specific applications, the concept of SI can be particularly useful because it focuses less on the technical specificity but on the social understanding of the technologies and, hence, their adaptation and trajectory. AI can be considered an imaginary itself as it has become a very ambiguous term in public discourse with the meaning strongly dependent on context and purpose. Originally, the term AI referred to a specific field of research, primarily in computer science starting around the 1950s, which considered AI according to Marvin Minsky as "the science of making machines do things that would require intelligence if done by men" (quoted from Bolter, 1986: 193). Since then, however, the boundaries and structuring of the research field have become more blurred, with controversies around questions such as what constitutes AI research and AI technologies (Cardon et al., 2018). However, a largely consensual structuring of the field is a division into two camps: the *symbolists*, focused on expert systems that suggest classifications and decisions based on (often very many) well-defined criteria (e.g., credit scoring based on residence, income, spending habits), and the *connectivists*, where systems develop decision rules themselves based on given input data and already classified output data, an approach popularly called "machine learning." But AI, like other technological developments, cannot be explained in functional terms alone. They are not simply the result of a unidirectional and one-dimensional movement of progress in which technology keeps improving. Instead, technological developments are always characterized by interpretative flexibility, controversy, and potential closure while they are starting to stabilize socially and economically (Pinch & Bijker, 1984; Katzenbach, 2012).

Both the conceptual ambiguity as well as the shifting between different paradigmatic camps of AI research gaining popularity at different times in academic and public discourse has led to several hype cycles and AI winters over the decades (Bostrom, 2014). Studies have documented and analyzed these changes in the perception of AI through the lens of the social construction of knowledge, scientific practices, and expertise (Woolgar, 1985; Courtial & Law, 1989; Collins, 1993; Suchman, 2008).

> If we want to understand our relationship with intelligent machines, we must be continually reminding ourselves where the knowledge that the machines are gathering is coming from. We must always be reminding ourselves that machines do not come ready fitted out with culture; someone is mothering and fathering them. (Collins, 2018: 16)

Along these lines, recent work has started to question the understanding of machine learning as something independent of human interaction (Bechmann & Bowker, 2019; Reigeluth & Castelle, 2020), providing detailed ethnographies of machine learning cultures (Mackenzie, 2017), identifying metaphors and rhetoric in AI research (Natale & Ballatore, 2017; Campolo & Crawford, 2020), and mapping the trajectories of competing sub-fields of AI research (Cardon, Cointet & Mazières, 2018). Increasing academic as well as public debates about issues of racism, sexism, and discrimination in the context of AI-powered technologies (Chokshi, 2019; Wellner & Rothman, 2019; Zou & Schiebinger, 2018) are only starting to surface the routinely hidden social forces in the making of AI and in shaping its impacts by calling into question the dominant imaginaries of AI as a tool or technological solution for human bias.

As we are currently negotiating the deep integration of AI into most areas of contemporary social life and sectors of society, this attention to the dependencies of discourse and technological development positions SI as a highly productive concept for studying the institutionalization of AI in contemporary societies. The conjunction of vague discourse and high levels of political and economic activity is indicative of the problematic ambiguity of the umbrella term AI, specifically inviting social processes to guide technological development and stakeholders to steer public and policy attention in directions beneficial to them. Thus, AI seems to be in the middle of a forceful process of institutionalization with different actors mobilizing different future visions in order to shape future developments in AI and its integration into contemporary and future societies. Operating in "the understudied regions between imagination and action, between discourse and decision, and between inchoate public opinion and instrumental state policy" (Jasanoff & Kim, 2009: 123), a SI informed comparative study on AI imaginaries thus allows us to go beyond the frame and content analyses of AI representation in public discourse and in legacy as well as online and social media.

NEGOTIATING IMAGINARIES: STAKEHOLDERS, MEDIA, AND THE PUBLIC

The social construction and implementation of AI and related technologies into society have received a rising amount of scholarly attention in recent years. This has focused on stakeholders in different AI sectors, media representations of AI, as well as public perceptions of AI. While all of these can be seen as bringing forth different imaginaries of AI, there is still little research employing the concept of SI in regard to AI. But studies have described analytical elements that can be interpreted as aspects of imaginaries surrounding AI, such as AI-related visions of specific stakeholders (groups), descriptions of the (potential) desired and undesired outcomes of the implementation of AI, or hopes of ideal future developments regarding public adoption. We find these themes addressing the negotiation, development, and adaptation of AI imaginaries in society in three strands of research on AI and society focused on (1) AI stakeholders, (2) the role of media representation, and (3) the public perception of AI.

AI Stakeholders

The representation of different stakeholders, evaluations, and specific arguments toward a given topic in public communication is always contested (Ferree et al., 2002; Hilgartner & Bosk, 1988). Stakeholders compete for public attention both for themselves, to be seen as relevant voices, but also for their evaluations and positions toward a given topic, in order to influence public perceptions and decision-makers and, eventually, to shape the developmental path of a given technology (Gerhards & Schäfer, 2006; Schäfer, 2007, 2009).

Many of the respective studies focus only on stakeholders within a specific sector, such as supranational associations, businesses, civil society, or governmental actors, with little regard for their differences in power and agency. Other scholars considering AI more generally focus on overarching issues such as AI ethics, trust, and transparency with a strong focus on power disparities, however, this is not applicable to specific cases (Jobin et al., 2019; Larsson, 2020). Three general AI stakeholder groups can be identified across current research on AI stakeholders: industry, governmental, and civil society actors; however, a clearer distinction is often needed for a strong analysis as these stakeholder groups themselves contain a complex network of actors such as different departments, ministries, or advocacy groups.

Industry stakeholders have become dominant in the current discourse, playing a decisive role in shaping public, political, and news media debate about AI (Fischer & Puschmann, 2021; Cui & Wu, 2019). Technology companies have been remarkably successful in positioning AI as inevitable and an actual necessity to fix key societal problems (Powles, 2018; Campolo & Crawford, 2021; Katzenbach, 2021). Through their public-facing communication on websites, PR material, and social media, as well as their political lobbying on regulatory decisions such as the US Bipartisan Innovation Act, USICA, potentially bringing large research investments into AI (Birnbaum, 2022) and the tech lobby trying to shape the EU's digital economy policies (Bank et al., 2021), they actively push their preferred imaginaries of AI to secure de-regulation and to benefit their economic agendas. This comes at a serious risk of a de-politicization: "AI tales sound fantastic and trigger our fantasies, though simultaneously they actually undermine political imagination and political practice by raising expectations of a comforting technological fix to structural societal problems" (Bareis & Katzenbach, p. 22).

Current research on AI stakeholders has found prominence in those industry-driven imaginaries in different sectors. For example, the belief in an ed-tech revolution due to the power of AI (Bulathwela et al., 2021) is currently prominent alongside an imaginary around AI technology moving society into a fourth industrial revolution, which is strongly underpinned by media framing (Vicente & Dias-Trindade, 2021). However, industry stakeholders in AI also have to strive for public and political acceptance. Ongoing controversies around AI adoption in various fields have led to shifts in the AI industry toward what has been called a "participatory turn" in designing AI applications (Delgado et al., 2021), including various stakeholders in the development process of AI. Similarly, research shows the need for the inclusion of other stakeholders' opinions in the production and also communication around AI to make AI concepts such as explainable AI more comprehensible to the broader public (Brennen, 2020).

Government and supranational governance actors have also established themselves as powerful actors in shaping AI development and AI imaginaries. On the national level, most governments have issued national AI strategies sketching out visions and measures of national AI policy. These strategies constitute "a peculiar hybrid between policy and discourse. They are at the same time tech policy, national strategic positioning and an imaginary of public goods" according to Bareis and Katzenbach's (2021) research into national AI imaginaries present in policy papers. They are reinforcing and shaping existing AI narratives to sketch the horizon of digital futures, and at the same time, formulating concrete measures to help arrive at these futures. In Western European policy discourses, AI is construed through sensationalization and mythologizing "as a salvific force that works for the good of the nation" (Ossewaarde & Gülenç, 2020: 54f.). However, the Chinese government is also playing a role in presenting AI as an instrument to boost the country's political influence on the global stage. China's recent uptake in political and regulatory activities regarding AI strongly contributes to shaping public imaginaries of AI and their negotiation (Zeng et al., 2022; Jing & Lou, 2019). Additionally, national and supranational organizations are launching guidelines and regulatory frameworks for AI development and restrictions on AI operation such as the EU's AI Strategy White Paper (European Commission, 2020). In 2018, the German federal parliament set up a new Inquiry Commission to investigate how AI and algorithmic decision-making will affect society and issued its own national AI strategy (Deutscher Bundestag, 2018). Overall, a general push toward international competitiveness can be observed, but also a reliance on historically grown structures (Savage, 2020) and a demand for citizen empowerment. On the supranational level, the European Commission (2020) and Organizations of the United Nations (2021) are also partaking in the shaping of AI along different imaginaries.

In recent years, civil society actors and citizens have become part of measures to generate a broader "AI ecosystem." Previous research already argued that formats of citizen consultation – which are common in participatory technology assessment – in national AI policies go beyond building trust and reaching legitimacy, as they can be seen as cases of "collective envisioning and imagining" (Paltieli, 2021: 6), which outline relationships between the mutual expectations of citizens and governments. Especially regarding ethical concerns and questions of equitability, civil society actors are now considered essential in governing AI as the case of Germany shows (Jones, 2022). But research into civil society involvement in AI design (Delgado et al., 2021) and AI application and innovative use by disability advocacy groups (El Morr et al., 2021) highlight the shift and need for involving various civil society stakeholders in envisioning (their) futures with AI and other digital technologies (Williams, 2018). Activist groups and civil society organizations play an important role in paving the way for this public engagement not only in the application but the development of AI introducing their own AI ethics and principles as manifests of best practices (Jones, 2022). This stakeholder group, therefore, often focuses on questions of equality, ethics, and power disparities between decision-makers such as big corporations and institutions and the lived experiences and concerns of citizens generally and minority groups specifically. As the AI Now report (Whittaker et al., 2018) stated: "The people most at risk of harm from AI systems are often those least able to contest the outcomes." The visions of desirable futures for (different) citizens, hence, can vary widely from corporate and political stakeholders. Furthermore, current research emphasizes that "AI has complicated the networks between people and technology, but done so unevenly across global regions, so that any kind of activism will demand much more than singular ideologies or a uniformity in action" (Taylor et al., 2021). Considering the current research landscape, there is still a clear lack of studies representing these differences in impact, but also imaginaries around AI and potential futures with AI technology.

Media Representation

Media representation plays a crucial role in shaping public perceptions and, hence, imaginaries of AI. However, "while [the media landscape today] still includes news media, those are now available in various online and digital formats, and, most importantly, have been complemented by new online and social media" (Kaplan & Haenlein, 2010; Schäfer, 2015). This is particularly true for communication about new technologies. Scholarship has demonstrated that legacy and social media are crucial sources for many people about technological developments in many countries (e.g., Eurobarometer, 2014; Science Board, 2018). Scholars have also shown that different media construct these technologies differently, and that for some of them, pronounced differences exist between countries (for an overview, Milde, 2017).

Against this background, it is likely that broader SI – for example, on the potential development, successes, opportunities, and limitations of AI – are strongly influenced by public and particularly media communication. In the existing studies on news media coverage of AI in Europe and the United States, researchers have not used imaginaries as a conceptual focus. But they demonstrated that AI is constructed in specific ways in different media and countries, showing, for example, that AI coverage is often sensationalized (Goode, 2018), industry-driven (Elish & boyd, 2018; Fischer & Puschmann, 2021), and politicized (Brennen et al., 2018). For instance, Elish and boyd's (2018) study on AI rhetoric reveals that the business community is responsible for manufacturing an over-hyped vision of AI, which eagerly focuses on AI's potential while obfuscating its actual methodological capabilities. Similarly, Brennen et al. (2018) found a dominance of industry concerns, such as products and initiatives, among news coverage of AI in the UK. Recent studies of media coverage of AI in China reveal a similar dominance of the private sector in propagating positive discourses around the emerging technology (Zeng et al., 2022; Jing & Lou, 2019; Cui & Wu, 2019). Different central topics and fields of interest from economic to technical and societal relevance, identified in a recent study of the German media discourse by Fischer and Puschmann (2021), are pushed to the foreground, especially by dominant industry actors. The study corpus also showed that AI as such has been on the rise since around 2015, highlighting that the term AI itself has been slowly established again to refer to the technological development previously often considered under terms such as algorithms and machine learning. Overall, the changes in media representations reflect a shift in dominant imaginaries of AI toward strong industry associations pushing normative and political debates around ethical concerns and individual rights.

Public Perception

Beyond media representation and organized civil society in the form of NGOs, the public perception of AI also plays a crucial role as they impact stakeholders by pushing corporate and national agendas as well as advocacy groups (Cave et al., 2018). There have been a number of surveys and studies over the last few years exploring the public perception of AI by country, geographic regions such as the EU, and globally. These studies demonstrate and map expected benefits and concerns around AI development and implementation but also changes in public visions of AI and accepted, if not desired, futures concerning AI adaptation as well as global differences. Currently, this research is still limited due to its strong focus on Western, often English-speaking contexts (Kelley et al., 2022); however, more studies are being conducted across global regions and with non-Western foci such as China.

In the European context, a 2018 UK survey (Holder et al., 2018) found that while the respondents had a broad understanding of AI, there was no in-depth understanding of the technology, which might explain the general lack of understanding of privacy and data protection issues. With ambivalent expectations, young people seemed to be more optimistic about AI's application, but the concerns around employment disruptions prevailed across the population, mirroring previous studies (Aloy, 2017) expecting more accountability from industry stakeholders. Similarly, a global survey from 2021 including participants from Australia, Canada, the United States, South Korea, France, Brazil, India, and Nigeria, similarly highlighted a global concern for job loss through automation as well as privacy (Kelley et al., 2022). While AI is expected to impact various sectors of society significantly, the perception of concerns and benefits vary across different sectors of implementation. Across both surveys, AI is consistently perceived ambivalently and ambiguously, allowing little grasp on the broad technology for the public across the globe. While there is a wish and potentially even excitement for positive implementation around key terms such as responsible, ethical, and explainable AI (Kelley et al., 2022), especially in the United States, the perception of potential harms by AI prevails over optimistic views (Zhang & Dafoe, 2019). This might be due to public imaginaries of AI being less built on factual knowledge. Rather, historical and contemporary popular culture strongly perpetuates and informs narratives around AI, which emphasizes the strong sociocultural situatedness of current public perceptions of AI technology in different regions (Cave et al., 2020).

Research into China's AI development and public perception of AI has become a counterpart to the American and European-centric focus. A study on two Chinese social media platforms found a similarly wide range of concerns (Mao & Shi-Kupfer, 2021). In contrast to Western discourses, however, ethical discussions and imaginaries of fairness and bias were not generally addressed but a public backlash against specific applications resulted in legislative and corporate change. Similar to social media discourse, journalism played an important role in shaping public perception in China (Cui & Wu, 2019). In turn, the public perception of AI use in Chinese journalism found a general acceptance of AI news anchors and application use for news production (Sun et al., 2022), just as AI applications are generally accepted in the medical field (Gao et al., 2020). The same was found in findings mirroring research into different AI narratives impacting the public perception in different global regions where East Asia had a more positive perception of AI and robots through positive popular culture examples, while the Western perception was leaning toward fear-inducing portrayals of AI (Cave et al., 2020).

CONCLUSION

Sociotechnical imaginaries – defined as "collectively held, institutionally stabilized, and publicly performed visions of desirable futures, animated by shared understandings of forms of social life and social order attainable through, and supportive of, advances in science and technology" by Sheila Jasanoff (2015: 4) – have become a prominent and powerful analytical lens for the analysis of technological developments. They are embedded in a broader social-theoretical tradition focusing on the "imagined" coupled with pervasive ideas about the sociocultural and sociopolitical co-construction of technologies championed by interdisciplinary fields such as STS or SCOT. As a result, sociotechnical imaginaries emphasize the importance of visions of futures surrounding given technologies that can be embedded in different societal realms, which can manifest in political decisions as well as popular culture or news media and that may influence how the public, stakeholders, and decision-makers approach the respective technologies.

Arguably, imaginaries are particularly relevant and useful for the analysis of AI – both due to the importance of the technology and its applications and to its (related) pronounced "interpretative flexibility" (Pinch & Bijker, 1984). AI is widely used as a broad umbrella term referring to extensive technological fields as well as a wide range of specific applications.

Accordingly, some scholars have already applied the concept of imaginaries to AI or related applications. They have shown, for example, that national AI strategies strongly build on narratives of functional progress and foreground technological solutionism (Bareis & Katzenbach, 2021), or that AI imaginaries and technology have substantially contributed to the constitution of the research field (Natale & Ballatore, 2017). But so far, the amount of scholarly work systematically applying the concept of imaginaries to AI is comparatively small and focuses only on a few select countries such as the United States or China, specific societal fields such as politics or the economy, and select stakeholders such as politicians or business representatives.

Furthermore, these studies, in their entirety, also demonstrate that the concept of sociotechnical imaginaries – both in general and in its application to AI – would benefit from further conceptual clarification and empirical operationalization. Conceptually, for example, the field would benefit from a clearer delineation of the concept from related, partially overlapping, but not synonymous concepts such as frames, narratives, or discourses. The role of pervasive public fora in which imaginaries may manifest themselves, such as political parliaments, news, or social media as well as popular culture, should be more clearly articulated conceptually as well. And relatedly, the potential for competing imaginaries surrounding the same technology in the same context at the same time is under-emphasized in the respective literature. Imaginaries of AI (or other technologies) may only become "collectively held [and] institutionally stabilized" after they have been negotiated in institutional or public contexts – and these very negotiations are a promising avenue for future research.

FURTHER READING

Bareis, J., & Katzenbach, C. (2021). Talking AI into being: The narratives and imaginaries of national AI strategies and their performative politics. *Science, Technology, & Human Values*, 016224392110300. https://doi.org/10.1177/01622439211030007.

Jasanoff, S., & Kim, S.-H. (Eds.). (2015). *Dreamscapes of modernity: Sociotechnical imaginaries and the fabrication of power.* Chicago: University of Chicago Press.

Mager, A., & Katzenbach, C. (2021). Future imaginaries in the making and governing of digital technology: Multiple, contested, commodified. *New Media & Society, 23*(2), 223–236. https://doi.org/10.1177/1461444820929321.

Zeng, J., Chan, C., & Schäfer, M. S. (2022). Contested Chinese dreams of AI? Public discourse about artificial intelligence on WeChat and People's Daily Online. *Information, Communication & Society, 25*(3), 319–340. https://doi.org/10.1080/1369118X.2020.1776372.

BIBLIOGRAPHY

Aloy, J.-B. (2017, November). *Revolution@Work: Fears and expectations - ipsos.* Ipsos. Retrieved June 30, 2022, from https://www.ipsos.com/en/revolutionwork-fears-and-expectations.

Anderson, B. (1983). *Imagined communities: Reflections on the origin and spread of nationalism.* London: Verso.

Arriagada, A., & Bishop, S. (2021). Between commerciality and authenticity: The imaginary of social media influencers in the platform economy. *Communication, Culture and Critique, 14*(4), 568–586. https://doi.org/10.1093/ccc/tcab050.

Bank, M., Duffy, F., Leyendecker, V., & Silva, M. (2021). (rep.). *The lobby network: Big tech's web of influence in the EU.* Brussels and Cologne: Corporate Europe Observatory and LobbyControl e.V.

Bareis, J., & Katzenbach, C. (2021). Talking AI into being: The narratives and imaginaries of national AI strategies and their performative politics. *Science, Technology, & Human Values,* 016224392110300. https://doi.org/10.1177/01622439211030007.

Barker, J. (2015). Guerilla engineers: The Internet and the politics of freedom in Indonesia. In S. Jasanoff & S. H. Kim (Eds.), *Dreamscapes of modernity: Sociotechnical imaginaries and the fabrication of power.* Chicago & London: University of Chicago Press, pp. 199–218.

Bechmann, A., & Bowker, G. C. (2019). Unsupervised by any other name: Hidden layers of knowledge production in artificial intelligence on social media. *Big Data & Society, 6*(1), 205395171881956. https://doi.org/10.1177/2053951718819569.

Beck, S., Jasanoff, S., Stirling, A., & Polzin, C. (2021). The governance of sociotechnical transformations to sustainability. *Current Opinion in Environmental Sustainability, 49,* 143–152. https://doi.org/10.1016/j.cosust.2021.04.010.

Bijker, W. E. (2012). Social construction of technology. In Friis, J. K. B. Olsen, S. A. Pedersen, & V. F. Hendricks (Eds.), *A companion to the philosophy of technology.* London & New York: Wiley-Blackwell.

Bijker, W. E., & Law, J. (Eds.). (1992). *Building society, shaping technology.* Cambridge: MIT Press.

Blei, D., & Bostrom, N. (2014). *Superintelligence: Paths, dangers, strategies.* Oxford: Oxford University Press.

Birnbaum, E. (2022, June 29). *The Ai 'gold rush' in Washington.* Politico. Retrieved June 30, 2022, from https://www.politico.com/newsletters/digital-future-daily/2022/06/29/small-fry-ai-dc-try-00043278?tab=most-read.

Brennen, A. (2020). What do people really want when they say they want "explainable AI?" We asked 60 stakeholders. *Extended abstracts of the 2020 CHI conference on human factors in computing systems.* https://doi.org/10.1145/3334480.3383047.

Brennen, J. S., Howard, P. N., & Nielsen, R. K. (2018). An industry-led debate: How UK media cover artificial intelligence. Retrieved from https://reutersinstitute.politics.ox.ac.uk/our-research/industry-led-debate-how-uk-media-cover-artificial-intelligence.

Bolter, J. D. (1986). *Turing's man Western culture in the computer age.* Penguin Books.

Bucher, T. (2016). The algorithmic imaginary: Exploring the ordinary affects of Facebook algorithms. *Information, Communication & Society, 20*(1), 30–44. https://doi.org/10.1080/1369118x.2016.1154086.

Bulathwela, S., Pérez-Ortiz, M., Holloway, C., & Shawe-Taylor, J. (2021). Could AI democratise education? Socio-technical imaginaries of an edtech revolution. *arXiv.* https://doi.org/10.48550/arXiv.2112.02034.

Cave, S., Craig, C., Dihal, K., Dillon, S., Montgomery, J., Singler, B., & Taylor, L. (2018). (rep.). *Portrayals and perceptions of AI and why they matter.* London; The Royal Society.

Cave, S., Monique, D. K. S., & Dillon, S. (2020). *Ai narratives: A history of imaginative thinking about intelligent machines*. Oxford: Oxford University Press.

Campolo, A., & Crawford, K. (2020). Enchanted determinism: Power without responsibility in artificial intelligence. *Engaging Science, Technology, and Society*, 6(2020), 1–19. https://doi.org/10.17351/ests2020.277.

Cardon, D., Cointet, J.-P., & Mazières, A. (2018). Neurons spike back: The invention of inductive machines and the artificial intelligence controversy. *Réseaux*, 211(5), 173.

Chokshi, N. (2019, May 15) Facial recognition's many controversies, from stadium surveillance to racist software. In *New York Times*. Retrieved from https://www.nytimes.com/2019/05/15/business/facial -recognition-software controversy.html.

Collins, H. M. (1993). *Artificial experts: Social knowledge and intelligent machines*. London: MIT Press.

Collins, H. M. (2018). *Artifictional intelligence: Against humanity's surrender to computers*. Wiley.

Courtial, J. P., & Law, J. (1989). A co-word study of artificial intelligence. *Social Studies of Science*, 19(2), 301–311.

Cui, D., & Wu, F. (2019). The influence of media use on public perceptions of artificial intelligence in China: Evidence from an online survey. *Information Development*, 37(1), 45–57. https://doi.org/10 .1177/0266666919893411.

Deutscher Bundestag. (2018). Bericht der Enquete-Kommission Künstliche Intelligenz – Gesellschaftliche Verantwortung und wirtschaftliche, soziale und ökologische Potenziale. Retrieved June 30, 2022, from https://dserver.bundestag.de/btd/19/237/1923700.pdf.

Elish, M. C., & Boyd, D. (2018). Situating methods in the magic of Big Data and AI. *Communication monographs*, 85(1), 57-80.

El Morr, C., Maret, P., Muhlenbach, F., Dharmalingam, D., Tadesse, R., Creighton, A., Kundi, B., Buettgen, A., Mgwigwi, T., Dinca-Panaitescu, S., Dua, E., & Gorman, R. (2021). A virtual community for disability advocacy: Development of a searchable artificial intelligence–supported platform. *JMIR Formative Research*, 5(11). https://doi.org/10.2196/33335.

Eurobarometer. (2014). *Public perceptions of science, technology and innovation*. European Commission.

European Commission. (2020). *White paper on artificial intelligence - a European approach to excellence and trust* [White Paper]. Brussels. https://ec.europa.eu/info/sites/default/files/commission -white-paper-artificial-intelligence-feb2020_en.pdf.

Felt, U., & Öchsner, S. (2019). Reordering the "world of things": The sociotechnical imaginary of RFID tagging and new geographies of responsibility. *Science and Engineering Ethics*, 25, 1425–1446.

Ferree, M. M., Gamson, W. A., Gerhards, J., & Rucht, D. (2002). Four models of the public sphere in modern democracies. *Theory and Society*, 31(3), 289–324. https://doi.org/10.1023/a:1016284431021

Fischer, S., & Puschmann, C. (2021). *Wie Deutschland über Algorithmen schreibt. Eine Analyse des Mediendiskurses über Algorithmen und Künstliche Intelligenz (2005–2020)*. Bertelsmann Stiftung.

Gao, S., He, L., Chen, Y., Li, D., & Lai, K. (2020). Public perception of artificial intelligence in medical care: Content analysis of social media. *Journal of Medical Internet Research*, 22(7). https://doi.org /10.2196/16649.

Gerhards, J., & Schäfer, M. S. (2006). *Die Herstellung einer öffentlichen Hegemonie. Humangenomforschung in der deutschen und der US-amerikanischen Presse*. Wiesbaden: Verlag für Sozialwissenschaften.

Goode, L. (2018). Life, but not as we know it: AI and the popular imagination. *Culture Unbound: Journal of Current Cultural Research*, 10(2), 185–207.

Hilgartner, S., & Bosk, C. L. (1988). The rise and fall of social problems: A public arenas model. *American Journal of Sociology*, 94(1), 53–78. https://doi.org/10.1086/228951.

Holder, C., Watts, M., & Khurana, V. (2018). (rep.). *Artificial intelligence: Public perception, attitude and trust*. London: Bristows.

Jasanoff, S., & Kim, S.-H. (2009). Containing the atom: Sociotechnical imaginaries and nuclear power in the United States and South Korea. *Minerva*, 47(2), 119–146. https://doi.org/10.1007/s11024-009 -9124-4.

Jasanoff, S., & Kim, S.-H. (2013). Sociotechnical imaginaries and national energy policies. *Science as Culture*, 22(2), 189–196. https://doi.org/10.1080/09505431.2013.786990.

Jasanoff, S., & Kim, S.-H. (Eds.). (2015). *Dreamscapes of modernity: Sociotechnical imaginaries and the fabrication of power.* Chicago: University of Chicago Press.

Jing, M. & Lou C. (2018). 人工智能技术在新闻传播中伦理失范的思考. 出版广角, *1*(2018), 9–13.

Larsson, S. (2020). On the governance of artificial intelligence through ethics guidelines. *Asian Journal of Law and Society*, 1–15. https://doi.org/10.1017/als.2020.19.

Jobin, A., Ienca, M., & Vayena, E. (2019). The global landscape of AI ethics guidelines. *Nature Machine Intelligence*, 1–11. https://doi.org/10.1038/s42256-019-0088-2.

Jones, M. (2022). Towards civil strategization of AI in Germany. *HIIG Discussion Paper Series* 2021-1. 20 pages. https://doi.org/10.5281/zenodo.6091638.

Kaplan, A. M., & Haenlein, M. (2010). Users of the world, unite! The challenges and opportunities of social media. *Business Horizons*, *53*(1), 59–68. https://doi.org/10.1016/j.bushor.2009.09.003.

Katzenbach, C. (2012). Technologies as institutions: Rethinking the role of technology in media governance constellations. In N. Just & M. Puppis (Eds.), *Trends in communication policy research: New theories, new methods, new subjects* (pp. 117–138). Intellect.

Katzenbach, C. (2021). "AI will fix this" – The technical, discursive, and political turn to AI in governing communication. *Big Data & Society*, 8(2). https://doi.org/10.1177/20539517211046182.

Kelley, P. G., Yang, Y., Heldreth, C., Moessner, C., Sedley, A., Kramm, A., Newman, D. T., & Woodruff, A. (2022). Exciting, useful, worrying, futuristic: Public perception of artificial intelligence in 8 countries. Retrieved June 30, 2022, from https://arxiv.org/pdf/2001.00081.pdf.

LaRosa, E., & Danks, D. (2018). Impacts on trust of healthcare AI. *Proceedings of the 2018 AAAI/ACM conference on AI, ethics, and society.* https://doi.org/10.1145/3278721.3278771.

Law, J., Shankar, K., Hakken, D., Østerlund, C., Wyatt, S., Milojevic, S., ... Alac, M. (2016). *The handbook of science and technology studies.* Cambridge: MIT Press.

Lehtiniemi, T., & Ruckenstein, M. (2019). The social imaginaries of data activism. *Big Data & Society*, 6(1), 205395171882114. https://doi.org/10.1177/2053951718821146.

Lösch, A., Böhle, K., Coenen, C., Dobroc, P., Ferrari, A., Fuchs, D., Heil, R., & Hommrich, D. (2016). Technikfolgenabschätzung von soziotechnischen Zukünften. Discussion paper no.03/ Dec. 2016. Institut für Technikzukünfte. KIT.

Mackenzie, A. (2017). *Machine learners: Archaeology of a data practice.* Cambridge: The MIT Press.

Mager, A. (2017). Search engine imaginary: Visions and values in the co-production of search technology and Europe. *Social Studies of Science*, *47*(2), 240–262.

Mager, A., & Katzenbach, C. (2021). Future imaginaries in the making and governing of digital technology: Multiple, contested, commodified. *New Media & Society*, *23*(2), 223–236. https://doi.org/10.1177/1461444820929321.

Mao, Y., Shi-Kupfer, K. (2023). Online public discourse on artificial intelligence and ethics in China: context, content, and implications. *AI & Soc*, 38, 373–389. https://doi.org/10.1007/s00146-021-01309-7

Matthes, J., & Kohring, M. (2008). The content analysis of media frames: Toward improving reliability and validity. *Journal of Communication, 58*(2), 258–279.

Meyer, U., & Schulz-Schaeffer, I. (2006). Three forms of interpretative flexibility. *Science, Technology & Innovation Studies, 2006*(1), 25–40.

Milde, J. (2017). Schlüsseltechnologien in der öffentlichen Kommunikation. In H. Bonfadelli, B. Fähnrich, C. Lüthje, J. Milde, M. Rhomberg, & M. Schäfer (Eds.), *Forschungsfeld Wissenschaftskommunikation* (pp. 373–390). Wiesbaden: Springer.

Mou, Y. (2017). 传播的进化：人工智能将如何重塑人类的交流. Beijing: Tsinghua University Press.

Mou, Y. (2020). 从诠释到他异：AI 媒体技术带来的社交与认知变革. 上海师范大学学 *1* (2020), 95–104.

National Science Board. (2018). *Science and engineering indicators 2018.* Washington: NSB.

Neverla, I., & Schäfer, M. S. (Eds.). (2012). *Das Medien-Klima.* Wiesbaden: Springer VS.

Natale, S., & Ballatore, A. (2017). Imagining the thinking machine: Technological myths and the rise of artificial intelligence. *Convergence: The International Journal of Research into New Media Technologies*, 135485651771516. https://doi.org/10.1177/1354856517715164.

Science Board. (2018). *Science and engineering indicators 2018.* Washington: NSB.

Olbrich, P., & Witjes, N. (2016). Sociotechnical imaginaries of big data: commercial satellite imagery and its promise of speed and transparency. In A. Bunnik, A. Cawley, M. Mulqueen et al. (Eds.), *Big data challenges.* London: Palgrave Macmillan, pp. 115–126.

Ossewaarde, M., & Gulenc, E. (2020). National varieties of artificial intelligence discourses: Myth, utopianism, and solutionism in West European policy expectations. *Computer, 53*(11), 53–61. https:// doi.org/10.1109/mc.2020.2992290.

Paltieli, G. (2021). The political imaginary of national AI strategies. *AI & Society.* https://doi.org/10 .1007/s00146-021-01258-1.

Pinch, T. J., & Bijker, W. E. (1984). The social construction of facts and artefacts: Or how the sociology of science and the sociology of technology might benefit each other. *Social Studies of Science, 14*, 399–441.

Powles, J. (2018). The seductive diversion of "solving" bias in artificial intelligence. *Medium.* https://onezero.medium.com/the-seductive-diversion-of-solving-bias-in-artificial-intelligence -890df5e5ef53.

Reigeluth, T., & Castelle, M. (2020). What kind of learning is machine learning? *The Cultural Life of Machine Learning*, 79–115. https://doi.org/10.1007/978-3-030-56286-1_3.

Rieder, G. (2018). Tracing big data imaginaries through public policy: The case of the European Commission. In A. R. Sætnan, I. Schneider, & N. Green (Eds.), *The politics and policies of big data: Big data, big brother?* Routledge, pp. 89–109.

Rudek, T. J. (2021). Capturing the invisible: Sociotechnical imaginaries of energy. The critical overview. *Science and Public Policy, 49*(2), 219–245. https://doi.org/10.1093/scipol/scab076.

Sadowski, J., & Bendor, R. (2018). Selling smartness: Corporate narratives and the Smart City as a sociotechnical imaginary. *Science, Technology, & Human Values, 44*(3), 540–563. https://doi.org/10 .1177/0162243918806061.

Savage, N. (2020). The race to the top among the world's leaders in artificial intelligence. *Nature, 588*(7837). https://doi.org/10.1038/d41586-020-03409-8.

Schäfer, M. S. (2007). *Wissenschaft in den Medien. Die Medialisierung naturwissenschaftlicher Themen.* Wiesbaden: Verlag für Sozialwissenschaften.

Schäfer, M. S. (2009). From public understanding to public engagement: An empirical assessment of changes in science coverage. *Science Communication, 30*(4), 475–505.

Schäfer, M. S. (2015). Digital public sphere. In G. Mazzoleni (Ed.), *The international encyclopedia of political communication* (pp. 322–328). London: Wiley-Blackwell.

Schön, D., & Rein, M. (1994). *Frame reflection: Resolving intractable policy issues.* New York: Basic Books

Simon, J. (2016). Values in design. In *Handbuch Medien-und Informationsethik* (pp. 357–364). Springer.

Suchman, L. 2008. "Feminist STS and the sciences of the artificial." In E. J. Hackett, O. Amsterdamska, M. Lynch, & J. Wajcman (Eds.), *The handbook of science and technology studies* (pp. 139–164). Cambridge: MIT Press.

Sun, M., Hu, W., & Wu, Y. (2022). Public perceptions and attitudes towards the application of artificial intelligence in journalism: From a China-based survey. *Journalism Practice*, 1–23. https://doi.org/10 .1080/17512786.2022.2055621.

Taylor, C. (2003). *Modern social imaginaries.* Durham: Duke University Press.

Taylor, A., Rosner, D., & Wiberg, M. (2021). Ai activism. *Interactions, 28*(1), 5–5. https://doi.org/10 .1145/3442368.

United Nations. (2021). (rep.). *United Nations activities on artificial intelligence (AI).* Geneva, Switzerland: ITU Publications.

Vailionis, I. (2021, September 5). *What's the public's perception of AI: Reshape by momentive.* Momentive. Retrieved June 30, 2022, from https://www.momentive.ai/en/blog/perception-of-ai/#:~ :text=Among%20our%20respondents%2C%2039%25%20believe,the%20abilities%20of%20human %20analysts.

Van Es, K., & Poell, T. (2020). Platform imaginaries and Dutch public service media. *Social Media + Society, 6*(2), 205630512093328. https://doi.org/10.1177/2056305120933289.

Vicente, P. N., & Dias-Trindade, S. (2021). Reframing sociotechnical imaginaries: The case of the fourth industrial revolution. *Public Understanding of Science, 30*(6), 708–723. https://doi.org/10.1177 /09636625211013513.

Wellner, G., & Rothman, T. (2019). Feminist AI: Can we expect our AI systems to become feminist? *Philosophy & Technology, 1*(12), 1–15.

Whittaker, M., Crawford, K., Dobbe, R., Fried, G., Kaziunas, E., Mathur, V., Myers West, S., Richardson, R., Schultz, J., & Schwartz, O. (2018). (rep.). *AI now report 2018.*

Williams, K. C. (2018). *Intersections of technology and civil society.* K4D Helpdesk Report 448. Brighton: Institute of Development Studies.

Winner, L. (2010). *The whale and the reactor: A search for limits in an age of high technology.* Chicago: University of Chicago Press.

Woolgar, S. (1985). Why not a sociology of machines? The case of sociology and artificial intelligence. *Sociology, 19*(4), 557–572.

Zeng, J., Chan, C., & Schäfer, M. S. (2022). Contested Chinese dreams of AI? Public discourse about artificial intelligence on WeChat and People's Daily Online. *Information, Communication & Society, 25*(3), 319–340. https://doi.org/10.1080/1369118X.2020.1776372.

Zhang, B., & Dafoe, A. (2019). Artificial intelligence: American attitudes and trends. *SSRN Electronic Journal.* https://doi.org/10.2139/ssrn.3312874.

Zou, J., & Schiebinger, L. (2018). AI can be sexist and racist—It's time to make it fair. *Nature, 559*(2018), 324–326.

19. Language of algorithms: agency, metaphors, and deliberations in AI discourses

Kaisla Kajava and Nitin Sawhney

INTRODUCTION: WHY SHOULD LANGUAGE MATTER IN AI?

Language is essential to how we as a society make sense of artificial intelligence (AI), while AI technologies increasingly rely on large multilingual language models to make sense of us. Alan Turing's famous quote, "A computer would deserve to be called intelligent if it could deceive a human into believing that it was human" (Turing, 1950), became the basis of his *imitation game* to test a machine's ability to exhibit intelligent behavior indistinguishable from that of a human. This three-actor game, later called the "Turing Test", proposed that if a human evaluator could not reliably judge if another human or machine generated a text-based natural language conversation, the machine would pass the test. While the Turing Test has been both widely influential and criticized over the years, it has captured popular imagination about how we talk about machines and artificial intelligence today. Turing created his test in response to a hypothetical question "Can machines think?" leading him to probe the very ambiguity of defining the meaning of the terms "machine" and "think".

In a later neglected paragraph of the same paper, Turing states:

> The original question, "Can machines think?" I believe to be too meaningless to deserve discussion. Nevertheless, I believe that at the end of the century the use of words and general educated opinion will have altered so much that one will be able to speak of machines thinking without expecting to be contradicted.

In a sense, Turing was not necessarily predicting that machines would be able to think (like humans) in the future but the idea that thinking machines may one day become uncontroversial. "Our use of the term [thinking] has indeed loosened to the point that attributing thought to even the most basic of machines has become common parlance" (Sandis & Harper, 2017). We may say that "the computer thinks I made a mistake" when it offers typographical or grammatical corrections. Such constructs in everyday language metaphorically associate thinking with machines while implicitly attributing agency to them, rather than the programmers that embed the algorithms and data used for their operation and performance. Searle (1992) makes the distinction between "behavior" and "action", where the former is observable, and the latter performed by an agent with will. In this view, in an AI ecosystem, referring to machines as "performing actions" would falsely transfer a notion of agency to them.

As large-scale multilingual languages models like BERT, GPT4, and LaMDA, and open-source initiatives like BLOOM, become more powerful and prevalent in the design of conversational AI systems, humans are more easily susceptible to anthropomorphizing their capabilities by attributing notions of intelligence and even sentience to them, harkening Turing's original predictions from 1950. The vigorous debates spurred by the claims of a former Google engineer, Blake Lemoine, about the emergence of sentience in AI were based on his transcripts of an "interview" conducted with LaMDA (Lemoine, 2022). While these claims were widely disputed by most prominent AI researchers and by Google itself (Sparkes, 2022), the popularized debates surrounding such controversies are amplified by public imagination, fears, and aspirations around notions of AI. These notions are shaped in part by the linguistic constructs, terminologies (or their very ambiguity), and wide-ranging discourses about AI circulating through fictional narratives, journalistic reporting, scientific papers, industry reports, and policy statements, among others, in popular culture and educational and professional contexts.

The complexity of AI-based technologies and their increasing prevalence in society makes the challenges of language, terminology, and public discourse especially critical, not just among experts but diverse publics and stakeholders engaged in creating, using, regulating, or deliberating about AI systems. We take an expansive view of "AI systems" as constituted of people, practices, data, technologies, enabling infrastructures, and policies that facilitate the way they operate in the world. Much of the discourse in AI focuses far more on "machine intelligence" and technological aspects of AI systems, rather than the wider ecosystem of human and nonhuman actors, policies, and practices that shape their functioning. Linguistic elements in the form of terminology, metaphors, personification, and so on influence the cultural discourse and political imagination of AI today. As Wyatt (2021) notes, metaphors function more flexibly and dynamically than sociotechnical imaginaries, and they are available to all.

While domain-specific terminology is common in many specialized fields, problematic terms and pragmatic "weak" metaphors (Rehak, 2021) around AI can amplify misunderstandings and expectations while diffusing into other domains (such as politics and public policy) as myths about the unlimited potential, unsubstantiated risks, or autonomy/agency of AI. AI experts and practitioners can both perpetuate and correct these notions, but it also requires critical societal deliberation else the "technical jargon, metaphors, analogy, and linguistic shorthand that may be meaningful to this small group risks being utterly opaque, or worse, misleading" outside this demographic circle, while "rich sources of potentially clearer, more accurate, or more widely accessible metaphors and terminology remain unplumbed" (Bones et al., 2021). Hence, democratizing the discourses around AI requires a critical understanding of its current usage and implications, as well as engaging not just AI experts and practitioners but also wider multidisciplinary perspectives from philosophy, linguistics, social sciences, law, public policy, and other academic disciplines, as well as diverse domains of knowledge in civil society. A multidisciplinary perspective in AI facilitates a more pluralistic, ethical, and inclusive engagement for better informed and responsible outcomes as discussed by Floridi et al. (2018).

The public sector is increasingly embracing algorithmic decision-making and data-centric infrastructures to improve planning and operational efficiency in cities while offering innovative digital services to citizens in areas such as education, healthcare, and urban mobility (Floridi, 2020; Haataja et al., 2020). As such public AI services become more prevalent and affect citizens' lived experiences, we must critically understand their social, political, and ethical implications to examine the rights, risks, and responsibilities for both the providers and recipients of such services, particularly the most vulnerable in society (Crawford, 2021; Sawhney, 2022). Some AI-based systems are being used by governments for biometric surveillance, criminal justice, and other forms of citizen monitoring, posing higher risks for abuse and unfair incrimination (AI Now, 2018) if they are not made easily transparent, accountable, or their legitimate use challenged by civil society. In a deliberative democracy, the rapid growth of emerging AI technologies and services necessitates new forms of digital citizenship and algorithmic literacy, i.e., having an informed ability to critically examine, evaluate, propose, or contest digital services (Long & Magerko, 2020; Hermann, 2021).

Discourses about AI systems and other algorithmic tools often revolve around issues of trustworthiness (Drobotowicz et al., 2021), transparency (Ananny & Crawford, 2018), or even a kind of mystique (Elish & boyd, 2018), feeding into the conception of AI-based systems as challenging to critically understand. Lack of informed understanding may leave citizens either unwilling to participate or eager to do so unquestioningly, while policymakers and civil servants must contend with the indeterminacy and unexpected outcomes of the AI services they are tasked to provide and oversee. Expanding algorithmic literacy can facilitate a more inclusive, critical, and participatory engagement in AI discourses among civil society.

Our research seeks to understand the positions, narratives, and values embedded in and constructed through ongoing discourses around public sector AI services and policy regulations.[1] In this chapter, we examine critical aspects of how language is used in both AI reports and in multi-stakeholder deliberations on the regulation of AI systems across private and public sectors in the EU. We understand "AI discourses" as discursive conventions of conceptualizing and framing the nature and use of AI technologies. The term "agency" is used in two contexts in this chapter. First, we refer to agency in the linguistic sense of the word "AI" occurring in the semantic role of an agent or the syntactic function of a subject, and how this use of language attributes agency to AI through personification. Second, we talk about agency in a social sense, referring to the capacities, abilities, and opportunities diverse (human) actors have in the deliberations around AI development, policy, and regulation. In this chapter, we examine how both types of agency are embedded in the thematic concerns, metaphors, and personification prevalent in the European Commission's AI Watch reports, and diverse stakeholder deliberations around the proposed EU AI Act. Our focus here is limited to critically examining the linguistic and discourse aspects of these AI reports and stakeholder feedback, while the complex policy implications are not within the scope of our current analysis in this chapter.

MAKING SENSE OF LANGUAGE AND DISCOURSES IN AI

Helen Bones et al. (2021), in their paper "In the Frame: The Language of AI", examine discourses in AI through the lens of historical use, gender, and language to explore how "values, language, and norms are produced – and to contest reductive approaches to AI". Citing the work of Alison Adam (1995), they suggest that the traditional epistemological assumptions around AI ignore power relations and cultural conditions in society while focusing too narrowly on modeling intelligent human behavior. Building on feminist epistemology, Adam asks how AI systems represent knowledge, what kind of knowledge, and whose knowledge (Adam, 1995), recognizing a plurality of views from the tacit, situated, and contextual knowledge embedded among diverse publics. Hence, Bones et al. (2021) elaborate that terminology

---

[1]   This work is part of the *Civic Agency in AI* (CAAI) research project at Aalto University, supported by the Kone Foundation and the Research Council of Finland.

matters, from the "selection of word stems, source languages, and the figures of speech" that encode certain sociocultural and political positionalities in how we describe AI constructs and technologies. In their paper, they examine the historical and cultural dimensions of popular AI terminologies including "data", "memory", "intelligence", and "learning" as case studies to demonstrate the problematic ways in which AI is framed and can be constructively reframed (Bones et al., 2021). The notion of data existing independent of human creation can be reframed as "capta" (Drucker, 2011) or alternatively as "situated data" (Lavin, 2021), embodying active social construction and contextual interpretation of phenomena, rather than a fixed construct inherent in the world and outside of human intervention. Reframing language affects notions such as ownership, exchange, commoditization, and sovereignty of data in society. Using the term "memory", rather than say "virtual storage", can attribute human qualities like reminiscence or agency to machines and conflate it with the structure and neurological functioning of the human brain. Retrieving accurate copies of stored bits is not how human memory operates; it is instead a highly complex process "comparable to living through imagined events again and by that even changing what is being remembered" (Rehak, 2021).

Marvin Minsky in his 1974 article "A Framework for Representing Knowledge" proposed the concept of "frames" as data structures for knowledge representation and reasoning in the early days of AI research (Minsky, 1975); while not analogous to memory, the notion of frames, derived from experimental psychology, contributed to the development of specialized programming languages and expert systems in the 1980s, and more recently, the Semantic Web. Minsky was an early proponent of AI being able to eventually model human brains, thought processes, and intelligence, whether through the notion of frames for symbolic logic and/or "perceptrons" for connectionist networked learning. However, MIT philosopher Hubert Dreyfus (1972) vigorously argued that intelligent human behavior required "common-sense knowledge" that is partly tacit and acquired through embodiment, cognitive development, and cultural practice, which were unrealistic for computers to acquire (Dreyfus & Dreyfus, 1986; Fjelland, 2020). These arguments remain at the heart of debates around the distinction between artificial general intelligence (AGI) and artificial narrow intelligence (ANI) today.

Related to intelligence, a commonly used term in AI is "learning", which also has broader cognitive and pedagogical meaning (Bones et al., 2021). Alexander et al. (2009) examine the many dimensions of learning being tacit, intentional, disadvantageous, interactional, and so on, essentially as a more holistic activity not confined only to rational thinking but also to survival, sociocultural contexts, and engaging how human senses interact with the world. The processes and methods associated with AI-based approaches like statistical machine learning, deep neural networks, or reinforcement learning are undertaken with a far narrower frame of objectives and constraints. Hence, using the metaphor of *learning* uncritically to describe such methods can lead to unrealistic expectations and misunderstanding of the scope of what AI technologies can learn about the world, unlike complex human forms of social, embodied, and continuous situated learning (or unlearning) over time.

Language use hence reveals implicit information about people's perceptions of AI, taking part in constructing the framework of narratives within which AI technologies are used, developed, and regulated. Discourses around AI systems can even be seen as ethical concerns when they exaggerate the autonomy of technology, attributing human-like characteristics to it, and in doing so, creating a "sociotechnical blindness" (Johnson & Verdicchio, 2017). The role of language is crucial in the translation of information between domains of knowledge, both in shaping discourses and in creating transparent and accessible technical documentation.

Language can facilitate literacy between domains and make it accessible or it can obscure understanding if the terminology is either too specialized or too vague, as in the case of AI.

Once deployed and in use, AI systems are not simply machines routinely performing predefined tasks, even when they require no technical maintenance. Instead, they are sociotechnical systems continuously updated in people's perceptions, and the discourse around them is in constant fluctuation. The pace of AI development creates challenges for traditional ways of policymaking, which may often be a long-term strategic process (Dwivedi et al., 2021). Because of this rapid development, stakeholders, including developers and technology companies, are reactively conceptualizing emerging technologies, and in doing so, shaping the language used to refer to those systems. This communicative exchange contributes to the development of both the technology as well as its use, governance, and regulation. Analogously, the AI Act has seen a lot of debate around its definition of AI: the different technologies bundled under the term "AI" may have different impacts and risks, many of them having little in common, while regulators, policymakers, and industry actors struggle to create a mutually agreed-upon and effective regulatory framework.

We examined two corpora on AI Watch reports and stakeholder deliberations in the context of the European Union to study different aspects of the discourse. The corpora, which consist of reports published by the European Commission's AI Watch and multi-stakeholder responses to the proposed AI Act, offer us a lens to unpack the use of metaphors and personification of AI technologies as well as some of the ongoing deliberations around AI regulation in Europe. While the curation and compilation of corpora entail limitations regarding the generalizability of the discursive practices to other contexts, these datasets are valuable for both qualitative and quantitative analysis within their scope of relevance. In our ongoing research, we combine methods from natural language processing (NLP) and critical discourse studies (CDS) to capture information at different granularities. NLP techniques serve as a method for hypothesis generation through search: combined with qualitative methods, computational text processing allows us to discover statistical patterns such as n-grams, named entities and keywords, parse syntactic dependencies to analyze agentic relations between concepts, and summarize long documents to aid in sample selection for further analysis. This information extraction enables us to create and revise working hypotheses for more in-depth qualitative inquiry.

METAPHORS AND LINGUISTIC AGENCY IN AI REPORTS AND POLICIES

Metaphors are prominent linguistic devices used to make sense of the reality around us (Kövecses, 2020). The ubiquity and everydayness of metaphors make them a particularly interesting linguistic element to study, offering a lens to implicit conceptualizations and bringing attention to fluctuations and conventions of discourse, which may often go unnoticed. AI discourse is full of metaphors, which hyperbolize its autonomy and agency (Bones et al., 2020; Rehak, 2021) or proliferate a sense of mythical AI as a benevolent force (Ossewaarde & Gulenc, 2020).

Conceptual metaphor theory (CMT) (Lakoff & Johnson, 2003; Kövecses, 2020) posits that metaphors involve the analogous mapping of one concept to another with the purpose of making sense of complex phenomena and social reality. Thus, a metaphor is not just a linguistic phenomenon but a cognitive sense-making device. According to the theory, a meta-phor involves two conceptual domains: a target domain and a source domain. The target domain is the concept that requires sense-making, while the source domain is the concept used to make sense of the target domain, for example, in the classic example ARGUMENT IS WAR, *argument* is the target domain, and *war* is the source domain, which ties the concept of *argument* to something more tangible. Analogously, "shooting down" or "winning" an argument are realizations of the conceptual metaphor (CM) ARGUMENT IS WAR. Coupled with critical metaphor analysis (CMA) (Charteris-Black, 2004), CMT offers us a critical view of the use of metaphors in society. CMA has its roots in critical discourse studies and aims to uncover covert uses of metaphor. Metaphors may be intentional or purposeful rhetorical devices, or unconsciously motivated (Charteris-Black, 2004), of which the latter type is of interest to us here. Metaphors in EU policy documents have been critically studied in rela-tion to the market economy and economic agents (Dewandre & Gulyás, 2018), but to our knowledge, the metaphors and language of AI have not been explored in this context using frameworks from CMT and CMA. As Dewandre and Gulyás (2018) note in their analysis of metaphor in EU documents, policy reports and other policy-related texts may indeed encode a conscious rhetorical voice, but our main interest in using CMA here is to bring attention to the conceptions and conventions of language underlying AI-related policy.

Beyond metaphors, we can operationalize the concept of PERSONIFICATION-WITH-METONYMY to examine the agency attributed to AI technologies in discourse. Metonymy is understood as a mapping of a conceptual source domain onto a target domain, where both the source and the target are part of the same functional domain and "linked by a pragmatic func-tion, so that the target is mentally activated" (Barcelona, 2011, p. 52). Thus, although metaphor and metonymy may often be interpreted to overlap, metonymy entails a contiguity relation-ship between domains, which are parts or aspects of the same "top-level" domain. Metaphor, on the other hand, entails an analogy-based relationship between two domains, which do not share a common top-level domain. PERSONIFICATION-WITH-METONYMY can be considered a type of personification, the phenomenon of assigning human-like traits to non-humans, which includes metonymy. While personification can be interpreted as metaphorical, metonymical, or its own category (Lakoff & Johnson, 2003), it is beyond the scope of this chapter to discuss types of and relations between metaphor, metonymy, and personification. For our purposes, we consider PERSONIFICATION-WITH-METONYMY a subtype of personification (Dorst, 2011; Dorst, Mulder & Steen, 2011) where the personified entity is based on metonymy. For exam-ple, in the phrase "AI *has contributed* to countering the current COVID-19 pandemic" (AI Watch, 2021a, p. 10), "AI" is a personified agent and also a metonymy, as it is used to represent *the use of AI* or *the development of AI*. In other words, it is not *actual AI* that is performing the act of contributing to countering a pandemic, but the actions taken by humans in using, devel-oping, or funding AI initiatives, and so on. In sum, metaphors, metonymy, and personification can function as ways of studying how AI is presented and perceived.

We examined a corpus of all 20 reports (nearly 1,300 pages of English text) prepared by AI Watch, the European Commission's knowledge service on AI, published in the years 2020–2021. AI Watch represents a body of experts monitoring "industrial, technological and research capacity, policy initiatives in the Member States, uptake and technical developments of Artificial Intelligence and its impact in the economy, society and public services".[2] To this

---

[2]   https://ai-watch.ec.europa.eu/about_en.

end, the AI Watch initiative, which is part of the European Commission's Joint Research Centre, serves as an information bridge between researchers and policymakers. The topics cover timely themes related to AI systems in Europe and the world from the use of AI in the public sector to national AI strategies to the definition of AI. The reports produced by AI Watch are an impactful source of language in that they are situated at the intersection of expert and policy narratives.

Framed as a classification task, metaphor detection can be performed either as human or automated annotation. As a manual annotation task, metaphors are often identified using the metaphor identification procedure (MIP) (Pragglejaz Group, 2007) or its close relative MIPVU (Steen et al., 2010), which entails annotation of each word in the text as metaphorical or not based on dictionary definitions, followed by inter-annotator agreement scoring. To ease manual labor, MIP annotation can be performed by selecting potentially metaphorical sentences as working hypotheses and applying MIP only to those sentences. As a computational task, large language models, often based on Google's BERT, have been employed for metaphor detection, typically taking the framework of CMT as a starting point, with some of the models incorporating MIP into their pipeline, such as in Choi et al. (2021).

To find instances of PERSONIFICATION-WITH-METONYMY in text, we conducted dependency parsing using *spaCy* (Honnibal et al., 2020), a free, open-source library for advanced NLP in Python. Dependency parsing allows querying sentences, which contain a relevant term, such as "AI", in the syntactic function of a subject. We analyzed the ways AI technologies are personified through the use of active verbs, such as in "AI is *bringing* many opportunities to the health system by means of data-driven medicine that can improve prevention, prediction and monitoring" (AI Watch, 2021a, p. 136). In the AI Watch reports, we found that "AI" performs many agentic actions, such as *providing, improving, helping, creating, supporting, achieving, protecting*, and *threatening*. An agentic AI operates across diverse sectors of society, including the labor market, healthcare, mobility, sustainability, and cybersecurity.

Metaphorically, the AI Watch reports we examined frequently characterize AI as a force and its uptake as a race. Following CMT, these metaphorical frames can be formalized as the CMs AI UPTAKE IS A RACE and AI IS A FORCE, with linguistic realizations such as "the EU can reinforce its position as a top AI player at global level" (AI Watch, 2021a, p. 7) or "governments are supporting human capacity building in AI and aim to prepare for the labour market transformations brought about by AI technologies" (AI Watch, 2021a, p. 11). Furthermore, the reports prolifically use the common metaphor of "trustworthy" AI, which also attributes agentic characteristics to the technology. In this vein, we could find several CMs entailing the personification of AI, such as AI IS AN ASSISTANT: "citizens send in challenges [...] on what they see as important societal challenges in their life *where AI could help*" (AI Watch, 2021a, p. 28). PERSONIFICATION-WITH-METONYMY and metaphorical language overlap and intersect, giving AI several roles in relation to humans. On one hand, AI is framed as a transformative force, which causes societal changes and necessitates reactionary measures from policymakers. Simultaneously, AI is presented as a facilitator of economic growth, such as when it "brings opportunities" and "could benefit governments, such as policy making, internal management, and improving public service delivery" (AI Watch, 2021b, p. 7).

While language needs space to develop alongside emerging multidisciplinary efforts around AI systems, AI represents a special case in the study of agency and personification. As a highly specialized field of expertise, AI not only has jargon – be it hyperbolic, metaphorical, or misleading – but also a long-standing tradition of personification, which stems from its nature as a technology developed to mimic human actions. However, given their ubiquity, it is crucial to bring attention to present (and past) ways of conceptualizing and narrating AI systems. Whether we embrace the notion of AI as a friendly collaborator, a transformational force, a mystical black box, a combination, or none of these, warrants wider discussion. The personification of AI often leads to or stems from the concept of AGI as the ultimate goal for the field of AI and fear for the rest of society. Reorienting discussion away from AGI, which at present appears a faraway scenario and a concept irrelevant and misleading to any meaningful nature of AI, allows us to focus on the far-reaching effects of ANI already in ubiquitous use.

DELIBERATIONS AND STAKEHOLDER AGENCY IN RESPONSES TO THE AI ACT

The European Commission (EC) recently introduced the Artificial Intelligence Act (or the AI Act) as a proposal to establish harmonized rules for the regulation of AI technologies developed, placed, and used in the European Union (EU) market (EC AI Act 2021). It is based on "EU values and fundamental rights" and was prepared in response to calls for legislative action to ensure a well-functioning internal market for AI systems seeking to address both the benefits and risks of AI, without unduly constraining technological development or costs of developing AI solutions. To this end, it undertakes a *"proportionate horizontal* and *risk-based regulatory approach* to AI, based on a robust and flexible legal framework" (EC AI Act 2021). Since the introduction of this proposal, there has been a good deal of debate around the efficacy and practical feasibility of the proposal among AI researchers, industry practitioners, and policy experts, while consultations and deliberations among EU member states are continuing to shape its final formulation and approaches for compliance as an EU-wide regulatory framework in the near future. Much of the debate has centered around the very definition of "artificial intelligence" and what constitutes high versus low risk for harmful AI practices. Some of this debate has occurred in news media articles, policy briefs, and presentations.

The EC initiated consultations and solicited feedback on the proposal from organizations and practitioners in 2020 and 2021. We are examining the nature of these deliberations from respondents using both qualitative and quantitative analysis. Here we share some recurring themes and issues emerging through some responses during the consultation phase. For example, one organization pointed out that "the concept of Artificial Intelligence is still not well defined and as such we oppose regulating it, as there may be completely different understandings of AI by various actors on the market" (EC Consultations, 2020). Another suggested that while some high-risk applications may need strict regulation, defining them is a significant challenge.

> The application depends on the domain, but even more on the use case and the data - making the right level of granularity challenging. E.g., there are HR related AI applications which can be high risk for discrimination – but a chatbot assistant that answers questions on open positions would hardly be one. (EC Consultations, 2020)

In the AI Act, the EC proposed a single "future-proof definition" of AI in a supplementary annex. It devised a methodology for defining "high-risk" AI as systems that pose "significant risks to the health and safety or fundamental rights of persons" in several sensitive application domains that must conform with requirements for trustworthy AI before entering the

EU market. The deliberations around the definitions of AI and differing notions of risk have remained fraught throughout this consultative process and debates on the proposal. These discourses indicate the linguistic ambiguity of how artificial intelligence as a technology, system, or set of practices is broadly understood, the implications of what is considered harmful or risky even within the same application domain, and the diverse stakes involved among wide-ranging actors in such a regulatory exercise. Ultimately, the debate is really about the language of AI, how it is perceived or understood by different parties, and how the AI Act may empower or disempower their agency in creating, deploying, or offering AI services.

We examined English-language responses to the AI Act (approx. all 300 feedback documents on the EC online portal from April 26–August 6, 2021) through keyword extraction and n-gram ranking using spaCy and KeyBERT (Grootendorst, 2020) to explore preliminary implications of engaging multi-stakeholder feedback and hypotheses for further study. Industry actors and business associations are the most prominent types of organizations in the set of feedback documents, followed by non-governmental organizations (NGOs) and academic institutions. While this suggests that the feedback submitted in the EC online portal provides merely a snapshot of ongoing deliberations around the AI Act, it also highlights the prominence of industry narratives. Active engagement on the part of the types of stakeholders represented in the feedback documents is a realization of agency often available to large and established organizations (vs. civil society organizations or actors), which makes the critical examination of their deliberative language compelling.

Our initial data exploration using keyword ranking of normalized unigram frequencies shows the differences in potential themes and concerns raised by stakeholders (Figure 19.1). Companies and business organizations seem to raise issues around the definition of AI in the proposed regulations, the requirements, and obligations of compliance as well as implications for AI software development. Given their positions as service providers, manufacturers, and developers of AI-based tools, industry stakeholders are faced with challenges of matching regulatory compliance with financial aims, much of which boils down to the definition of AI operationalized in the AI Act. In contrast to industry actors, academic and research institutions seem to raise societal issues regarding the trustworthiness of AI systems, possible damage to individuals and diverse social groups, and human rights and democratic values.

The conceptualizations and narratives of AI, discussed throughout this chapter, are not absent from regulatory deliberations. We can examine the AI Act as a turn or shift in the wider narrative of AI, requiring multiple parties to react and possibly shaping the direction of future discourse. Among many narrative shifts, the AI Act represents one such event, necessitating multi-stakeholder action, which may lead to both overt and covert reimagination, reformulation, and reorientation processes in the language of AI.

CONCLUSIONS: REFRAMING AGENCY IN AI SYSTEMS

Artificial intelligence is "no longer an engineering discipline" (Dignum, 2020). Multidisciplinary efforts are needed, and as the field takes on new forms and disciplinary identities, language needs to function as a meaningful bridge between domains of knowledge. Multidisciplinarity in AI introduces a range of challenges as new perspectives come into play. The encounters and intersections between discursive practices among various actors inform how those practices feed into the critical understanding of both the essence of AI as well as its implications

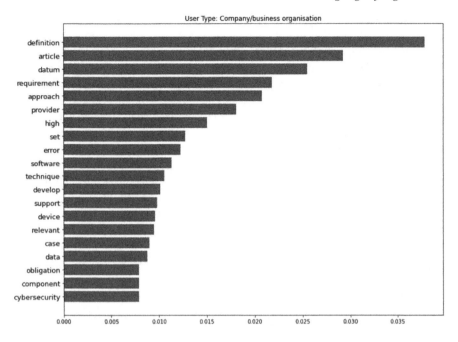

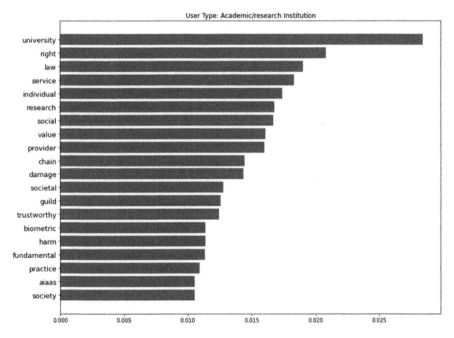

Source: Visualization by Shintaro Sakai, summer researcher at Aalto University, 2022.

Figure 19.1   *Salient unigrams in the AI Act feedback documents submitted by academic and other research institutions*

across diverse sectors of society. Beyond understanding, however, critically focusing on the use of language can facilitate algorithmic literacy among researchers, practitioners, and citizens. Following the argument of Rehak (2021), policymakers and regulators would benefit from researchers and science journalists focusing on "constructive" ways of using language around AI, such as avoiding exaggerated anthropomorphisms pervasive in popular science and culture, hyperbolic terminology (Bones et al., 2021), and technical terms such as *communication* and *recognition*, which often translate into popularized metaphors. Beyond anthropomorphic terminology, such as *learning, training,* or *memory,* AI technologies are often presented as having (human-like) agency through personification. Agency is clearly embedded in human actions across the development, deployment, regulation, and user experience stages of an AI system's life cycle. However, as we have demonstrated in this chapter, in popular AI discourses, the concept of *action* by machines is often conflated with their observable *behavior* (Searle, 1992), perceived as autonomy, agency, or sentience in AI, and vice versa. That is, AI systems are often framed as agents operating independently in society, requiring humans to adjust to their emergence and form trust relationships with them, almost as if we lived in a world where AGI systems were a reality. Addressing this quandary, Rehak (2021) calls for discarding terms like "agency" and "autonomy" entirely from how we speak about artificial intelligence, as they can be both inaccurate and misleading; but more importantly, we need to shift our focus to human agency implicit in the design, development, operation, and governance of AI systems. This reframing of agency mitigates the sociotechnical blindness implicit in such discourses, while emphasizing a greater awareness of sociocultural contexts, power structures, and political practices that shape the way AI systems emerge, function, and proliferate in society.

REFERENCES

Adam, A. (1995). Artificial intelligence and women's knowledge: What can feminist epistemologies tell us? *Women's Studies International Forum*, 18(4), 407–415.

AI Now Institute. (2018). AI now report 2018. *Tech. Rep.* [Online] www.ainowinstitute.org.

AI Watch. (2021a). National strategies on Artificial Intelligence: A European perspective. JRC-OECD report.

AI Watch. (2021b). Artificial Intelligence for the public sector. Report of the "3rd Peer Learning Workshop on the use and impact of AI in public services", 24 June 2021. JRC Conference and Workshop Report.

Alexander, P. A., Schallert, D. L., & Reynolds, R. E. (2009). What is learning anyway? A topographical perspective considered. *Educational Psychologist*, 44(3), 176–192.

Ananny, M., & Crawford, K. (2018). Seeing without knowing: Limitations of the transparency ideal and its application to algorithmic accountability. *New Media & Society*, 20(3), 973–989.

Barcelona, A. (2011). Reviewing the properties and prototype structure of metonymy. In Réka Benczes, Antonio Barcelona, and Francisco José Ruiz de Mendoza Ibáñez (Eds), *Defining metonymy in cognitive linguistics: Towards a consensus view*, 7–57. John Benjamins Publishing Company.

Bones, H., Ford, S., Hendery, R., Richards, K., & Swist, T. (2021). In the frame: The language of AI. *Philosophy and Technology*, 34(1), 23–44.

Bunz, M., & Braghieri, M. (2022). The AI doctor will see you now: Assessing the framing of AI in news coverage. *AI & Society*, 37, 9–22.

Charteris-Black, J. (2004). *Corpus approaches to critical metaphor analysis*. Palgrave Macmillan.

Choi, M., Lee, S., Choi, E., Park, H., Lee, J., Lee, D., & Lee, J. (2021). MelBERT: Metaphor detection via contextualized late interaction using metaphorical identification theories. In *Proceedings of the 2021 Conference of the North American Chapter of the Association for Computational Linguistics:*

Human Language Technologies, pages 1763–1773. Online. Association for Computational Linguistics.

Crawford, K. (2021). *The atlas of AI.* Yale University Press.

Dewandre, N., & Gulyás, O. (2018). Sensitive economic personae and functional human beings: A critical metaphor analysis of EU policy documents between 1985 and 2014. *Journal of Language and Politics*, 17(6), 831–857.

Dignum, V. (2020). AI is multidisciplinary. *AI Matters*, 5(4) (December 2019), 18–21.

Dorst, L. (2011). Personification in discourse: Linguistic forms, conceptual structures and communicative functions. *Language and Literature*, 20(2).

Dorst, A. G., Mulder, G., & Steen, G. J. (2011). Recognition of personifications in fiction by non-expert readers. *Metaphor and the Social World*, 1(2), 174–200.

Dreyfus, H. L. (1972). *What computers can't do.* New York, NY: Harper & Row.

Dreyfus, H. L., & Dreyfus, S. E. (1986). Mind over machine: The power of human intuition and expertise in the era of the computer. *Free Press*.

Drobotowicz, K., Kauppinen, M., & Kujala, S. (2021). Trustworthy AI services in the public sector: What are citizens saying about it? In F. Dalpiaz and P. Spoletini (eds.), *Requirements engineering: Foundation for software quality*. REFSQ.

Drucker, J. (2011). Humanities approaches to graphical display. *Digital Humanities Quarterly*, 5(1).

Dwivedi, Y. K., Hughes, L., Ismagilova, E., Aarts, G., Coombs, C. R., . . . others. (2021). Artificial Intelligence (AI): Multidisciplinary perspectives on emerging challenges, opportunities, and agenda for research, practice and policy. *International Journal of Information Management*, 57.

Elish, M. C., & boyd, d. (2018). Situating methods in the magic of Big Data and AI. *Communication Monographs*, 85(1), 57–80.

European Commission. (2020). Public consultations on Artificial intelligence – ethical and legal requirements, 20 February 2020 – 14 June 2020. https://ec.europa.eu/info/law/better-regulation/have-your-say/initiatives/12527-Artificial-intelligence-ethical-and-legal-requirements_en.

European Commission. (2021). Proposal for a Regulation of the European Parliament and of the council laying down harmonised rules on artificial intelligence (artificial intelligence act) and amending certain union legislative acts, COM/2021/206 final, Brussels, 21.4.2021. https://eur-lex.europa.eu/legal-content/EN/TXT/HTML/?uri=CELEX:52021PC0206&from=EN.

Fjelland, R. (2020). Why general artificial intelligence will not be realized. *Humanities and Social Sciences Communications*, 7(10).

Floridi, L., Cowls, J., Beltrametti, M., Chatila, R., Chazerand, P., Dignum, V., . . . others. (2018). Ai4people—an ethical framework for a good AI society: Opportunities, risks, principles, and recommendations. *Minds and Machines*, 28(4), 689–707.

Floridi, L. (2020). Artificial Intelligence as a public service: Learning from Amsterdam and Helsinki. *Philosophy & Technology*, 33, 541–546.

Grootendorst, M. (2020). KeyBERT: Minimal keyword extraction with BERT. *Zenodo.org*. DOI: 10.5281/zenodo.4461265.

Haataja, M., van de Fliert, L., & Rautio, P. (2020). Public AI registers: Realising AI transparency and civic participation in government use of AI. Whitepaper Version 1.0, *Saidot*, September.

Hermann, E. (2021). Artificial intelligence and mass personalization of communication content— An ethical and literacy perspective. *New Media & Society*. 24(5), 1258–1277.

Honnibal, M., Montani, I., Van Landeghem, S., & Boyd, A. (2020). spaCy: Industrial-strength natural language processing in Python. *Zenodo.org*. DOI: 10.5281/zenodo.1212303.

Johnson, D. G., & Verdicchio, M. (2017). Reframing AI discourse. *Minds & Machines*, 27, 575–590.

Kövecses, Z. (2002). *Metaphor: A practical introduction.* New York: Oxford University Press.

Kövecses, Z. (2020). An extended view of conceptual metaphor theory. *Review of Cognitive Linguistics*, 18(1), 112–130.

Lakoff, G., Espenson, J., & Schwartz, A. (1991). *Master metaphor list.* Berkeley, CA: Cognitive Linguistics Group University of California. (Technical report).

Lakoff, G., & Johnson, M. (2003). *Metaphors we live by.* The University of Chicago Press.

Lavin, M. (2021). Why digital humanists should emphasize situated data over Capta. *Digital Humanities Quarterly*, 15(2).

Lemoine, B. (2022). Is LaMDA sentient? — An interview. *Medium*, June 11. https://cajundiscordian.medium.com/is-lamda-sentient-an-interview-ea64d916d917.

Long, D., & Magerko, B. (2020). What is AI literacy? Competencies and design considerations. In *Proceedings of the 2020 CHI conference on human factors in computing systems (CHI '20)*. Association for Computing Machinery, New York, NY, USA, 1–16.

Minsky, M. (1975). A framework for representing knowledge. In Pat Winston (ed.), *The psychology of computer vision*. New York: McGraw Hill, 211–277.

Ossewaarde, M., & Gulenc, E. (2020). National varieties of Artificial Intelligence discourses: Myth, utopianism, and solutionism in West European policy expectations. *Computer*, 53(11), 53–61.

Pragglejaz Group. (2007). MIP: A method for identifying metaphorically used words in discourse. *Metaphor and Symbol*, 22(1), 1–39.

Rehak, R. (2021). The language labyrinth: Constructive critique on the terminology used in the AI discourse. In P. Verdegem (ed.), *AI for everyone?*. London: University of Westminster Press.

Sandis, C., & Harper, R. (2017). We don't want AI that can understand us – we'd only end up arguing. *The Conversation*, August 21. https://theconversation.com/we-dont-want-ai-that-can-understand-us-wed-only-end-up-arguing-82338.

Sawhney, N. (2022). Contestations in urban mobility: Rights, risks, and responsibilities for Urban AI. *AI & Society*.

Searle, J. R. (1992). *The rediscovery of mind*. Cambridge, MA: MIT Press.

Sparkes, M. (2022). Has Google's LaMDA artificial intelligence really achieved sentience? *New Scientist*, June 13. https://www.newscientist.com/article/2323905-has-googles-lamda-artificial-intelligence-really-achieved-sentience/.

Steen, G., Dorst, L., Herrmann, J., Kaal, A., Krennmayr, T., & Pasma, T. (2010). *A method for linguistic metaphor identification: From MIP to MIPVU*. Amsterdam: John Benjamins Publishing Company.

Turing, A. M. (1950). I.—Computing machinery and intelligence. *Mind*, LIX(236), October, 433–460.

Wyatt, S. (2021). Metaphors in critical Internet and digital media studies. *New Media & Society*, 23(2), 406–416.

20. Technological failures, controversies and the myth of AI

Andrea Ballatore and Simone Natale

TECHNOLOGICAL CONTROVERSIES AND THE MYTH OF AI

In the popular imagination, the history of computing is often represented through a dynamic of linear progress, made of dazzling engineering inventions and scientific insights that advance technical and scientific areas. Yet, the evolution of computers and the software that animates them have followed very different paths. While hardware has seen decades of marked improvement in terms of memory and computational speed, the history of software, as noted by Nathan Ensmenger, "is full of tensions, conflicts, failures, and disappointments" (2012, p. 10). At various points in the evolution of computing, as machines became cheaper and more powerful, programming them to perform useful tasks proved costly and frustrating (Ceruzzi, 2003). Developing an approach that considers the role of failure, in this sense, is an urgent task for a critical history of digital media that takes into account the fundamental role played by software and the programming of computers and other digital tools (Balbi & Magaudda, 2018).

From the perspective of a cultural history of technological failures in computer science, artificial intelligence (AI) represents a particularly interesting case. At various times throughout the evolution of computer science, AI has been regarded as a failed technology, unable to meet the grandiose promises and goals set by the researchers and proponents of its paradigms; at other stages, including the present day, it has been shot through with considerable, perhaps excessive, enthusiasm, attracting considerable investment and attention from the techno-scientific world and the public sphere (Ekbia, 2008). Its tumultuous history, consequently, has been read by historians as a schizophrenic alternation of failures and triumphs (McCorduck, 1979; Crevier, 1994; Russell & Norvig, 2021).

This chapter questions this narrative in order to propose a different point of view, according to which the alleged failure of AI does not concern specific stages of the decline of its various paradigms but constitutes an inescapable element of it along its entire historical trajectory. By highlighting the functional role of skepticism and controversies between AI proponents and critics, such a perspective suggests that the construction of a technological myth around AI has been facilitated and enabled by the ongoing controversy between those who emphasize its successes and those who emphasize its failures. To understand the impact of technological failures – understood as cultural constructions rather than objective events (Gooday, 1998; Lipartito, 2003) – it is, therefore, necessary to abandon a dichotomous dimension that opposes success too rigidly to failure. The possibility of failure of techno-scientific projects represents instead a symbolic and material resource that should be considered an integral part of their development. Addressing the issue of failure in regard to AI, moreover, is particularly urgent in the ongoing phase, in which AI systems are heralded as the defining technology of our era, often with the promise of infinite possibilities.

THE MYTH OF THE THINKING MACHINE

Arising in the mid-20th century at the intersection of cybernetics, control theory, operations research, cognitive psychology, and the nascent computer science, AI is a field of study based on the hypothesis that it is possible to program a computer to perform tasks that equal or exceed human intelligence (Russell & Norvig, 2021). Analytic philosopher John Searle proposed a distinction between strong AI, which aims to create general human-level (or superhuman) intelligence, and weak AI, which mimics human behaviors in circumscribed contexts (Searle, 1980). While applications of weak AI are ubiquitous in everyday technologies, from search engines to any smartphone app, what can be called the technological myth of the thinking machine revolves around the possibility of strong AI, which has not yet been achieved at a material or even proved possible at a theoretical level (Boden, 2016). It has been the idea that it is possible to create a kind of artificial brain that articulated the technological myth of AI (Taube, 1961); such a myth became over the past decades a technological project and at the same time an inescapable component of popular culture (Natale & Ballatore, 2020).

The concept of "technological myth" does not indicate naïve and bogus beliefs, but rather a complex of beliefs about technology that become pervasive in social, cultural, and political contexts. As recognized by authors such as Mosco (2004) and Ortoleva (2009), a myth is in fact not defined by the question of its authenticity, but rather by its ability to enter the collective imagination of a particular era. Technological myths are far from being mere fantasies, but are cultural formations with concrete effects, as observed in cases including the web (Bory, 2020; Natale & Ballatore, 2014), geospatial technologies (Ballatore, 2014), and AI itself (Bareis & Katzenbach, 2021).

Analyzing the historiography and the large production of popular culture on the topic (e.g., Crevier, 1994; McCorduck, 1979, Bory & Bory, 2016), we have identified the core beliefs that undergird the myth of the thinking machine (Natale & Ballatore, 2020): (1) cognitive processes can be reduced to calculations based on the manipulation of symbols; (2) the human brain is equivalent to a computer; (3) the development of a thinking machine is feasible in the near future; (4) computer scientists are Promethean heroes who are about to realize the thinking machine; and (5) computers will surpass humans in all fields, altering all cultural, social, and political processes. This last belief has raised both utopian hopes and dystopian fears around AI as increased informational automation was identified as a harbinger of unemployment, alienation, surveillance, and excessive bureaucratic control. Unlike other myths that are projected into the past, the myth of the thinking machine resides in a "near future" of technological possibilities (Dourish & Bell, 2011).

This myth has rapidly taken over the public sphere, moving from elite laboratories to the rest of Anglo-American and global societies. In this regard, Martin (1993) collected sociological observations on the imaginary of computers as powerful and mysterious artificial brains. Attributing to the mythical dimension of the imaginary an overtly negative connotation, Martin argues that the mass media in the 1950s and 1960s employed exceedingly misleading metaphors and technical exaggerations. When computers found their first large-scale commercial applications in the 1970s, the myth of the thinking machine lost some of its credibility. Yet two decades later, though further diminished, the myth was still present in the American public sphere, particularly in its dystopian forms. With reasonable caution, later entirely justified, Martin concedes that even if the perception of the computer as a thinking machine was on the wane in the 1990s, it was not permissible to take the myth for dead. The

AI myth not only survived the "AI winter" of the 1970s and the failure of the Fifth Generation project and the Strategic Computing Initiative in the 1980s (Russell & Norvig, 2021) but found new and surprising articulations, making a powerful comeback since the 2010s.

As we will see, the alternation between periods of great popularity of the myth and periods in which AI was largely disavowed as a field of study is in fact one of the most peculiar aspects in the historical trajectory of AI.

THE WINTERS AND SUMMERS OF ARTIFICIAL INTELLIGENCE

Between 1943 and 1956, a period that Russell and Norvig (2021) refer to as the "gestation of AI," researchers such as John McCarthy, Arthur L. Samuel, and Marvin Minsky gained rapid access to substantial funding from the US scientific and technical apparatus. In such a favorable context, these AI pioneers achieved promising results in several areas, including formal games such as checkers and chess, mathematical problem-solving, and robotics (Rasskin-Gutman, 2009; McCorduck, 1979). Such encouraging progress in the short term generated many optimistic predictions (Crevier, 1994), fueling the plausibility of the myth among journalists, in the public sphere, and among scientists. In the early 1970s, however, the AI myth was challenged by the lack of concrete results beyond experimental prototypes. In a paradoxically opposite sense to what has been noted in the context of "big data" in recent years (Kitchin, 2014), as the volume of data increased, the results of the AI pioneers deteriorated and became difficult to apply on a practical level. This situation prompted major funders in the field to reduce their investment, especially from 1974 onwards, and more generally, generated widespread skepticism about AI as an idea and techno-scientific project. Fearing this sentiment, for a decade, many researchers avoided using the term "AI" to describe computer science research projects, preferring terms like machine learning and pattern recognition, so much so that historians describe this phase as the first "winter of AI" (Crevier, 1994; see Natale & Ballatore, 2020).

Far from signifying a definitive decline for the AI myth, the winter of the 1970s was followed by new "summer" (or "spring") phases of splendor. The wave of "expert systems" in the 1980s generated great expectations and profitable industrial applications, and the "connectionist" approach, based on neural networks, followed a similar path. Since the 2000s, the availability of vast amounts of data and a major increase in computational and storage power have triggered advances in the areas of data mining, machine learning, and natural language processing and understanding, developing automated solutions to complex problems thought intractable even just two decades earlier – see, for example, the recent boom of deep learning (LeCun et al., 2015). This rapid expansion of the horizon of technical possibilities has revived the debate on the AI myth, replicating once again the clash in the public sphere between what Umberto Eco would have called "apocalyptic and integrated" (Eco, 1964), i.e., the enthusiasts and critics of the technological prospect of AI. Although the possibility of strong AI remains technically remote (and we remain epistemologically agnostic on this issue), the new applications of weak AI are enough to generate bitter controversies in all the fields involved, on the one hand about the feasibility and technical maturity of the proposed solutions, and on the other hand about the social, political, and cultural effects of the introduction of these technologies in the socio-technical apparatuses (Kurzweil, 2005; Bostrom, 2012).

The story of how AI went from "winters" to "summers" relies on a key storytelling device, that of the "rise and fall," which is one of the most popular interpretive keys to represent the dynamics of technological innovation (Christmas, 2016). An example in this sense is the "hype cycle" theory, popularized by Gartner, an American company specializing in consulting on technology and information. According to Gartner, a technology can undergo a "hype" or enthusiasm phase, stimulated by technical innovation or more simply by some form of public demonstration of its potential. In this phase, expectations grow, even under the pressure of media attention, until they reach a peak of excessive optimism about its prospects. In economic terms, the natural consequence is a growth in investment in the sector. However, the rise is followed by a decline: since the technology is not able to achieve, at least in the short term, the hoped-for successes, optimism gives way to growing skepticism about its real prospects. Media coverage begins to take a critical stance, and funding collapses inexorably. Every year, Gartner publishes a report in which various technologies are placed in a particular position along the "hype cycle" (see www.gartner.com).

Gartner's theory, as is often the case with historical simplifications, is suggestive and seems at first glance to find confirmation in the development not only of AI but also of other technologies: 3D cinema, for example, was launched with great fanfare and then disavowed numerous times throughout the history of cinema (Elsaesser, 2013) and virtual reality was the object of a collective fascination in the 1990s, only to be relegated to the role of a failed expectation and finally come back into vogue in very recent times (see, for example, www.oculus.com).

On the other hand, the rise-and-fall narrative tends to underestimate the fact that elements such as expectations, fascination, and even skepticism are an ongoing, rather than a cyclical, presence in the evolution of certain technological propositions (Messeri & Vertesi, 2015; Borup et al., 2006). It is desirable, in this sense, to read the history of AI according to a different narrative that emphasizes the permanent role of controversy, rather than a series of discrete phases marked by either optimism or disillusion. To follow this second narrative is to acknowledge that skepticism and controversy have been a constant component in the construction and development of the AI myth – and this not only during the winters but throughout the entire historical trajectory of the discipline, from its origins in the 1950s to the present day.

THE ROLE OF TECHNO-SCIENTIFIC CONTROVERSIES

As suggested by Russell and Norvig (2021), the term "artificial intelligence," coined by John McCarthy in 1955, contains such a problematic premise from a practical and conceptual point of view that it is destined to attract controversy. Indeed, since the early 1960s, a period of prevailing optimism about the prospects for AI, skeptics and critics have been playing a notable role in the debate about the present and future of the field. In popular science and technology journals such as *The New Scientist* and *Scientific American*, which featured contributions from leading representatives of the field, enthusiastic statements traveled hand in hand with critical interventions (e.g., Moore, 1964; Voysey, 1974; Albus & Evans, 1976; for a more detailed analysis of the sources, see Natale & Ballatore, 2020). This debate continued in the following decades and has continued to the present day, without ever abandoning the technological myth of AI (Geraci, 2008).

Scientific controversies have become a well-established area of inquiry in the sociology of science as an important element to understand the inner functioning of scientific and technical work (e.g., Raynaud & Bunge, 2017). Although they have mostly been studied as elements that tend to hinder the success of a theory or a field of study (Besel, 2011; Ceccarelli, 2011), historians such as Gieryn (1983) or Pinch and Bijker (1987) have pointed out how controversies can also play a functional role in the development of scientific and technological innovations. In the specific case of AI, such an approach means taking into account the fact that the myth of the thinking machine has emerged as a set of theories, hypotheses, and speculations whose complex and ambiguous character constitutionally invites contestation and skepticism.

It is within this dialectic that the AI myth has emerged and progressed, passing through incessant disputes between critics and proponents. As we have noted, technological myths are defined not by whether they are true or false, but rather by their ability to become pervasive in particular societies and cultures (Mosco, 2004; Ortoleva, 2009). In this sense, controversies are a constitutive component of the AI myth, as they help to keep it alive and are able to attract attention and space in scientific debate and the public sphere. In fact, as proposed by Delborne (2011), scientific controversies represent a context through which paradigms, theories, and fields build their influence within the scientific world and, at the same time, in the public and popular arena.

The presence of extensive and seemingly endless controversies is a feature that AI shares with a field of study with a far more problematic character and less impressive empirical results, parapsychology. According to David J. Hess (1993), author of one of the most comprehensive studies on this topic from the point of view of the sociology of science, it would be wrong to consider the supporters and opponents of parapsychology as mere antagonists. The American sociologist noted in fact how skepticism is evoked not only by those who criticize the scientific nature of these studies but also by the parapsychologists themselves, who present themselves as skeptical against the certainties of the scientific establishment. Controversy, Hess suggests, should be considered not an impediment, but an essential condition for the existence of this field of study.

Emphasizing the functional role of controversies in the development of a field, in this sense, means abandoning the traditional narrative based on rise and decline, and instead proposing an alternative model of historical evolution in which controversies and apparent failures play a primary role in the construction and persistence of the myth. The AI myth is to be understood as a dialogue, rather than a monologue: a narrative based on an underlying question ("Is it possible to create a thinking machine?") whose survival relies precisely on the lack of definitive answers and on the openness to conflicting and deeply conflicting answers, as well as to the redefinition of the question according to new technical and cultural developments.

The open-ended nature of the question of whether a strong AI can exist thus becomes an essential condition for the continued generation of ideas and, ultimately, for ensuring the ability of AI to exert an ongoing influence on our culture over such a wide span of time. Winter, in this sense, is not to be viewed as an episodic event, but rather as a stable and functional component of the development of this techno-scientific field.

CONCLUSION

Since the beginning of its intellectual and scientific trajectory, the idea of AI has sparked great debate and controversy. During the initial enthusiasm of the 1950s and 1960s, AI generated a socio-technical myth centered on the possibility of creating a thinking machine based on the new digital computers. In the fierce dialectic between believers and skeptics, the possibility of a machine with human (or superhuman) cognitive capabilities moved from the realm of science fiction to journalistic discussions and continues to occupy a prominent position in the public sphere.

In this chapter, we have traced the development of this complex interdisciplinary techno-scientific field from the perspective of the cultural imagination, emphasizing, in particular, the role of the frequent failures of AI, attributable to the excessive enthusiasm and tendency to promise unrealistic results of its practitioners. The historiography of computer science conceptualizes the phases of AI enthusiasm and skepticism cyclically, as a succession of "summers" and "winters," in a rise-and-fall narrative very common in popular versions of media history.

Our thesis, however, is that the controversies and failures of AI, rather than hindering its development, are a functional element in the construction and maintenance of myth in the technological and scientific imagination. Instead of a simple cyclical narrative, we propose a perspective that does justice to the constructive and generative role of controversies, drawing parallels with very different areas of inquiry such as parapsychology. Paradoxically, recent successes in the context of autonomous vehicles, machine learning, and so-called "big data," can be seen as instances of "weak AI" that keep fueling hope for strong AI, rather than diminishing it. In this sense, none of the winters that the thinking machine myth has spent in its short history have been fatal. The vitality of the techno-scientific myth of the thinking machine is evident from the popularity of the topic in the public sphere, where it is interpreted through the familiar (and problematic) lenses of utopia and dystopia, focused on a technical horizon that is constantly being redefined.

The recent controversies on Google LaMDA can be fruitfully examined through this very same lens. LaMDA, a software trained to entertain conversation with human users, attracted extensive public attention after Google engineer Blake Lemoine argued that he believed the software had become sentient, while his company dismissed this claim as deceptive. The controversy, on the one side, reanimated the AI myth, while on the other, contributed to stimulating discussions about what happens if even expert users can be led to overstating the performances and capacity of an AI system (Natale, 2021).

The historical trajectory of AI, where success and disillusion constantly intertwine, provides a useful corrective to the current enthusiasm for neural networks and machine learning. This does not take into account, in fact, that while these technologies bear enormous potential for a wide range of applications, some of our wildest expectations, such as reaching strong AI or sentient machines, are still likely to be disappointed (Moore, 2020). Considering the role of failure and controversy as an entry point to the critical study of AI, in this sense, provides a useful corrective to ongoing discourses about this technology, highlighting its strengths as well as its limits, and reminding us that we have been believing for a long time in the myth of thinking machines.

ACKNOWLEDGMENTS

An earlier version of this text was published in Italian (Ballatore & Natale, 2018). We would like to thank the editors of the volume where this earlier version appeared, Gabriele Balbi and Paolo Magaudda, for their feedback.

WORKS CITED

Albus, J. S., & Evans, J. M. (1976). "Robot Systems." *Scientific American* 234: 76–86.

Balbi, G., & Magaudda, P. (2018). *A History of Digital Media: An Intermedial and Global Perspective.* Routledge.

Ballatore, A. (2014). "The Myth of the Digital Earth between Fragmentation and Wholeness." *Wi: Journal of Mobile Media* 8, no. 2. Retrieved from http://wi.mobilities.ca/myth-of-the-digital-earth.

Ballatore, A., & Natale, S. (2018). "Fallimenti, controversie e il mito tecnologico dell'Intelligenza Artificiale." In *Fallimenti digitali: Un'archeologia dei «nuovi» media,* edited by Gabriele Balbi and Paolo Magaudda, 137–48. Roma: Unicopli.

Bareis, J., & Katzenbach, C. (2021). "Talking AI into Being: The Narratives and Imaginaries of National AI Strategies and Their Performative Politics." *Science, Technology, & Human Values,* 01622439211030007. https://doi.org/10.1177/01622439211030007.

Besel, R. D. (2011). "Opening the 'Black Box' of Climate Change Science: Actor-Network Theory and Rhetorical Practice in Scientific Controversies." *Southern Communication Journal* 76, no. 2: 120–36.

Boden, M. (2016). *AI: Its Nature and Future.* Oxford: Oxford University Press.

Borup, M., Brown, N., Konrad, K., & Van Lente, H. (2006). "The Sociology of Expectations in Science and Technology." *Technology Analysis & Strategic Management* 18, no. 3–4: 285–98.

Bory, P. (2020). *The Internet Myth: From the Internet Imaginary to Network Ideologies.* London: University of Westminster Press.

Bory, S., & Bory, P. (2016). "I nuovi immaginari dell'intelligenza artificiale." *Im@go: A Journal of the Social Imaginary* 4, no. 6: 66–85. https://doi.org/10.7413/22818138047.

Bostrom, N. (2012). "The Superintelligent Will: Motivation and Instrumental Rationality in Advanced Artificial Agents." *Minds and Machines* 22, no. 2: 71–85.

Ceccarelli, L. (2011). "Manufactured Scientific Controversy: Science, Rhetoric, and Public Debate." *Rhetoric & Public Affairs* 14, no. 2: 195–228.

Ceruzzi, P. E. (2003). *A History of Modern Computing* (2nd ed.). Cambridge, MA: MIT Press.

Crevier, D. (1994). *AI: The Tumultuous History of the Search for Artificial Intelligence.* Basic Books.

Delborne, J. A. (2011). "Constructing Audiences in Scientific Controversy." *Social Epistemology* 25, no. 1: 67–95.

Dourish, P., & Bell, G. (2011). *Divining a Digital Future: Mess and Mythology in Ubiquitous Computing.* Cambridge, MA: MIT Press.

Eco, U. (1964). *Apocalittici e integrati.* Milano: Bompiani.

Ekbia, H. R. (2008). *Artificial Dreams: The Quest for Non-biological Intelligence.* Cambridge: Cambridge University Press.

Elsaesser, T. (2013). "The 'Return' of 3-D: On Some of the Logics and Genealogies of the Image in the Twenty-first Century." *Critical Inquiry* 39, no. 2: 217–46.

Ensmenger, N. L. (2012). *The Computer Boys Take Over: Computers, Programmers, and the Politics of Technical Expertise.* Cambridge, MA: MIT Press.

Geraci, R. M. (2008). "Apocalyptic AI: Religion and the Promise of Artificial Intelligence." *Journal of the American Academy of Religion* 76, no. 1: 138–66.

Gieryn, T. F. (1983). "Boundary-Work and the Demarcation of Science from Non-Science: Strains and Interests in Professional Ideologies of Scientists." *American Sociological Review* 48, no. 6: 781–95.

Gooday, G. (1998). "Re-writing the 'Book of Blots': Critical Reflections on Histories of Technological 'Failure'." *History and Technology* 14, no. 4: 265–91.

Kitchin, R. (2014). "Big Data, New Epistemologies and Paradigm Shifts." *Big Data & Society* 1, no. 1: 2053951714528481.

Kurzweil, R. (2005). *The Singularity Is Near: When Humans Transcend Biology.* London: Penguin Books.

LeCun, Y., Bengio, Y., & Hinton, G. (2015). "Deep Learning." *Nature* 521, no. 7553: 436–44.

Lipartito, K. (2003). "Picturephone and the Information Age: The Social Meaning of Failure." *Technology and Culture* 44, no. 1: 50–81.

Martin, C. D. (1993). "The Myth of the Awesome Thinking Machine." *Communications of the ACM* 36, no. 4: 120–33.

McCorduck, P. (1979). *Machines Who Think: A Personal Inquiry into the History and Prospects of Artificial Intelligence.* San Francisco, CA: W.H. Freeman.

Messeri, L., & Vertesi, J. (2015). "The Greatest Missions Never Flown: Anticipatory Discourse and the 'Projectory' in Technological Communities." *Technology and Culture* 56, no. 1: 54–85.

Moore, E. F. (1964). "Mathematics in the Biological Sciences." *Scientific American* 211: 148–64.

Moore, P. (2020). "The Mirror for (Artificial) Intelligence: In Whose Reflection?" *Comparative Labour Law and Policy Journal* 44, no. 2: 191–200. https://doi.org/10.2139/ssrn.3423704.

Mosco, V. (2004). *The Digital Sublime: Myth, Power, and Cyberspace.* Cambridge, MA: MIT Press.

Natale, S. (2016). "There Are No Old Media." *Journal of Communication*, published online before print 31 May 2016. https://doi.org/10.1111/jcom.12235.

Natale, S. (2021). *Deceitful Media: Artificial Intelligence and Social Life after the Turing Test.* New York: Oxford University Press.

Natale, S., & Ballatore, A. (2014). "The Web Will Kill Them All: New Media, Digital Utopia, and Political Struggle in the Italian 5-Star Movement." *Media, Culture & Society* 36, no. 1: 105–21.

Natale, S., & Ballatore, A. (2020). "Imagining the Thinking Machine: Technological Myths and the Rise of Artificial Intelligence." *Convergence: The International Journal of Research into New Media Technologies* 26, no. 1: 3–18.

Ortoleva, P. (2009). "Modern Mythologies, the Media and the Social Presence of Technology." *Observatorio (OBS) Journal* 3, no. 1: 1–12.

Pinch, T. J., & Bijker, W. E. (1987). "The Social Construction of Facts and Artifacts: Or How the Sociology of Science and the Sociology of Technology Might Benefit from Each Other." In *The Social Construction of Technological Systems: New Directions in the Sociology and History of Technology*, edited by Wiebe E. Bijker, Thomas Parke Hughes, and Trevor J. Pinch, 17–50. Cambridge, MA: The MIT Press.

Rasskin-Gutman, D. (2009). *Chess Metaphors: Artificial Intelligence and the Human Mind.* Cambridge, MA: MIT Press.

Raynaud, D., & Bunge, M. (2017). *Scientific Controversies: A Socio-Historical Perspective on the Advancement of Science.* New York: Routledge.

Russell, S. J., & Norvig, P. (eds.). (2021). *Artificial Intelligence: A Modern Approach* (4th ed.). Saddle River, NJ: Pearson Education.

Searle, J. R. (1980). "Minds, Brains, and Programs." *Behavioral and Brain Sciences* 3, no. 3: 417–57.

Taube, M. (1961). *Computers and Common Sense: The Myth of Thinking Machines.* New York: Columbia University Press.

Voysey, H. (1974). "Programming without Programmers." *New Scientist* 63, no. 910: 390–91.

21. Marking the lines of artificial intelligence

Mario Verdicchio

INTRODUCTION

One may mark a line for many purposes: delimiting an area, connecting two points, separating two sectors, tracing a path, and so on.

I will here adopt this versatile graphic gesture as a metaphor to discuss a number of aspects of artificial intelligence (AI): how it is defined as a discipline; how, as its very name seems to suggest, it stems from an attempt to recreate human intelligence by means of artificial entities; how it is distinguished from other efforts in computer science; and finally, what we may expect from it in the future.

All these efforts are meant to provide a better understanding of AI but, as I will try to show in what follows, the lines that are meant to circumscribe, connect, separate, and orient AI are rather blurred, which should serve as a call for more attention on behalf of those who use, research, write, and talk about AI.

MARKING THE LINES AS DEFINITION

The very definition of AI has raised several debates ever since the term "artificial intelligence" was first used in 1955 in a proposal for a summer workshop at Dartmouth College (New Hampshire, USA) by those who are considered today the founders of the discipline. In that proposal, it is written that "The study is to proceed on the basis of the conjecture that every aspect of learning or any other feature of intelligence can in principle be so precisely described that a machine can be made to simulate it" (McCarthy et al., 2006, p. 12). This conjecture seems to lay the ground for a definition of AI as the discipline dedicated to a precise description of features of intelligence, so to enable the simulation of those features by a machine.

I will get back to the meaning and implications of a "simulation by a machine" in the next section. Let us start with the concept of intelligence used in the proposal. There is an assumption that "learning" is a feature of intelligence, which is not controversial, since it is accepted in many other fields than AI, such as psychology (Piaget, 2003) or pedagogy (Novak & Gowin, 1984). Much more problematic is the other assumption on intelligence, according to which intelligence is amenable to precise, machine-compatible descriptions. The first author of the proposal, Prof. John McCarthy, has stood by this assumption his whole life, as shown by a manifesto in the form of a Q&A he first published in 2004 and last revised in 2007, in which his answer to the question "what is intelligence?" is the following:

"Intelligence is the computational part of the ability to achieve goals in the world. Varying kinds and degrees of intelligence occur in people, many animals and some machines" (McCarthy, 2007, p. 2).

This is, indeed, marking a strong line around the concept of "intelligence," which is deemed inherently computational by McCarthy. Agents have the ability to achieve goals in the world. Intelligence is the computational part of such ability, that is, the part of an agent's action plan that consists of operations on numbers. This is such a bold statement that the very document begins with the disclaimer: "The opinions expressed here are not all consensus opinion among researchers in AI." Discussions on what intelligence is range from anecdotal recounts to common sense to full-fledged scientific theories. Would a person who is able to perform computational operations at remarkable speed without ever making a mistake be considered intelligent if they are not able to learn the most basic rules for living in society? Among the most famous theories on intelligence that include more than computation, there is psychologist Howard Gardner's theory of multiple intelligences (Gardner, 1983), which differentiates human intelligence into eight specific modalities: visual-spatial, linguistic-verbal, logical-mathematical (presumably the one McCarthy is after), bodily-kinaesthetic, musical, interpersonal, intrapersonal, and naturalistic.

These two views on intelligence, one solely computational and the other multi-faceted, seem to set up two different scenarios, each with a definition of intelligence that defines the scope of AI as a discipline. In the first scenario, McCarthy is wrong or at least narrow-minded on intelligence, which exists in modalities that are not computational. Rather than artificial intelligence, we should call his efforts Artificial Computational Intelligence (ACI). In the second scenario, McCarthy is right, and all forms of intelligence can be traced back to computational processes, and psychologists like Gardner propose a framework with multiple forms of intelligence because their underlying computational foundations have not been discovered yet.

Who is right? Which scenario is real? There is no definitive answer to these questions, but surely a lot of energy is devoted in the context of AI research to pursue either vision. In particular, many researchers believe McCarthy's definition of intelligence is part of a subfield of AI in which the aim is to build machines that perform any task that a human being is capable of. Since the range of human intellectual capabilities is so vast and general, this research effort is called artificial general intelligence (AGI, Goertzel & Pennachin, 2006). Whether AGI will one day succeed remains to be seen. What is interesting now in AGI, at least within the scope of this analysis, is its focus on the comparison between human intelligence and machine intelligence.

MARKING THE LINES AS COMPARISON

Formally, an analogy between two entities A and B is a one-to-one mapping between objects, properties, relations, and functions in A and those in B. Not everything in A must be put in correspondence with relevant items in B: an analogy is comprised of correspondences only between a subset of characteristics (Bartha, 2022). Clearly, the analogy underlying AI is between a human being and a computational machine. However, which aspects are to be involved in the analogy is disputed and this leads to different variations of AI: general, narrow, strong, and weak.

The general versus narrow and the strong versus weak contrapositions are orthogonal but not completely independent, and their connection takes us back to McCarthy's reference to simulating human intelligence with a machine. Indeed, a simulation imitates one process by another process (Hartmann, 1996), that is, a simulation is inherently based on analogies between two processes, the one that is simulated and the one that simulates. If human intelligence is to be simulated by means of a computational machine, what aspects are to be reproduced inside the simulating machine? This is where the abovementioned contrapositions show their orthogonality.

AGI and narrow AI (sometimes called artificial narrow intelligence, ANI, Fjelland 2020) are about quantity, that is, the quantity of tasks that an AI machine must be able to perform. In AGI, the goal is the most ambitious: all tasks a human can perform, across the whole range theorized by Gardner, must be described in computational terms so that a machine can execute them. In ANI, the context is, indeed, narrower: a machine is built to execute one specific task or a very small set of tasks. If AGI's realizability is still debated among researchers, there have been several extremely successful ANI projects in a number of fields, including games (Schrittwieser et al., 2020) and medicine (Kourou et al., 2015).

Strong and weak AI, on the other hand, are about quality, not in terms of perfect executions and lack of errors by the machine, but in its original meaning of "quale," of how a certain situation feels like for the agent in it, as a subject capable of perceiving the features of that situation. Proponents of strong AI believe that it is in theory possible to build a machine that entertains conscious experiences the way humans do, whereas advocates of weak AI believe that there is a deep ontological difference between human brains and computing machines, and only the former have the characteristics that make them capable of perceiving qualia. Scientists agree that the human nervous system makes the perception of qualia possible, but how that first-hand, subjective sensation emerges from human physiology remains a mystery so deep that it is called the "hard problem" in the philosophy of mind (Chalmers, 2017).

In weak AI, this is where the analogy stops: we can build more and more sophisticated computing machines that perform more and more tasks that have been traditionally performed by humans, but consciousness will forever remain an elusive feature of the human experience that escapes computational modelling.

An analogy is indeed the most famous attack against the idea of strong AI, provided by philosopher John Searle, who proposed the thought experiment of the "Chinese room" (Searle, 1980), in which he imagined himself inside a room, processing messages from the outside written in Chinese ideograms on the sole basis of their appearance (since Searle does not understand Chinese), formulating answers following visual message-reply rules written in a ledger, and sending out replies that make sense in Chinese, thus giving the impression that the room understands Chinese to the people on the outside. In this analogy, Searle designed a limited human experience, that is, processing only the signs a message is comprised of but not its meaning, to give us an idea of how computing machines work: they crunch signs, i.e., numbers, in accordance with their values and some rules, but they do not have a mind that can associate ideas and concepts to those signs.

Another philosopher, Hubert Dreyfus, uses similar arguments to attack AGI: the subjective experience that humans have thanks to their consciousness is not only necessary for humans to entertain meanings, but it is also a fundamental ingredient to form what is known as common sense. Based on their past experiences, humans are able to draw analogies, tackle new situations successfully, and master the complex game of life. Not everybody is successful in the same way, but everybody has the potential to learn any kind of task that is compatible with human nature. This general intelligence is possible only to conscious human beings, whereas coding all possible real-life situations in a computing machine is unfeasible (Dreyfus, 1992).

Here, quality and quantity meet – we need the qualitative experience of consciousness to unlock the power to learn a potentially infinite quantity of tasks.

Years after the introduction of the Chinese room, when asked whether he considered strong AI a logical impossibility, Searle left the door open, again relying on an analogy:

> the human brain is a machine, a biological machine, and it produces consciousness by biological processes. We will not be able to do that artificially until we know how the brain does it and we can then duplicate the causal powers of the brain. (…) at present we do not know enough about the brain to build an artificial brain. (Turello, 2015)

His attack against the idea of conscious computers can be thus framed in a technological context: in the way computers are built today no emergence of consciousness is possible because the analogy is leaving some key features out. Of course, this is not a problem for those who pursue the less ambitious but still potentially very impactful goals of weak, narrow AI. However, focusing on the electronic, digital computing machines in use nowadays sheds light on another threat for AI, strong, weak, general, or narrow: the lines indicating its borders and distinguishing it as a discipline seem to disappear.

MARKING THE LINES AS DISTINCTION

Computing machines are a good example of multiple realizability: to perform computation we have different choices on what kind of physical devices to build to represent numbers and perform operations on them. These choices have expanded through the centuries.

The abacus, as it appears today, made of wood and metal reinforcements, was first chronicled in 13th-century China. To support his father's activities as a tax accountant, Blaise Pascal invented the first mechanical calculator with rotating metal gears, known as the Pascaline, in 17th-century France. Charles Babbage modified a Jacquard loom and transformed it into the Difference Engine, a machine capable of raising numbers to the second and third powers and calculating the solution to specific quadratic equations in 19th-century England. A much more sophisticated mechanical computing machine was created by Konrad Zuse in early 20th-century Germany, with the groundbreaking additional feature of programmability, i.e., not only the data but also the operations to be performed on the data can be stored in the machine, with dramatically increased possibilities for automation. At the same time, with the invention of the vacuum tube by John Ambrose Fleming, controlling the flow of electricity through electronic components became possible, and led the way to the first electronic computers, like the one by John Vincent Atanasoff, conceived in 1937 and released five years later at the Iowa State College, USA. The discovery of semiconducting materials, that is, materials that enable or block the flow of electricity depending on the voltage they are stimulated with changed the computing game forever: American physicists John Bardeen, Walter Brattain and William Shockley invented the transistor in 1947, thus enabling an unprecedented miniaturization of the switches controlling the flow of electrons inside a computing machine. Their invention, which won them the Nobel Prize in Physics in 1956, is the reason why we can carry very powerful computers in our pockets today (Campbell-Kelly et al., 2016).

Despite the enormous technological variety, in terms of design, materials, and physical phenomena involved, there is a general paradigm, guiding the construction and use of a computing machine, which characterizes all the abovementioned devices, including abaci and the latest, fastest digital computers. There are obviously radical differences in performance and levels of automation, however, the principle of operation is the same: whatever task is at stake, it needs to be encoded, that is, described in the form of numbers; some components of the machine are used to represent those numbers; the numbers are processed by the computing machine, that is, the components representing the numbers are modified by some operations on the machine (and by the machine itself if it is programmable); finally, when the operations are over, the machine reaches an end state, and the numerical quantities represented in it are the numerical output that needs to be decoded, that is, translated back into results for the task.

From this very general perspective, using a computer to sort a list of names or using it to simulate human intelligence does not seem to make a significant difference, since both activities boil down to the same kind of encode-execute-decode sequence of operations. What, then, distinguishes AI from other branches of computer science, like software engineering (SE) or database theory (DB)? Indeed, should computer science even have subfields to begin with?

The traditional distinction in computer science between hardware and software may be a good starting point. Hardware is physical: it is the material machinery we build to perform computation. Software is more abstract because it is the description of the configurations to give the hardware to perform computation. The characteristics of the hardware determine its possible configurations and hence limit the scope of the software. For instance, we cannot look at a digital image on an abacus because the abacus is missing the hardware to produce the luminous and colourful pixels that constitute an image.[1] Keeping in mind the brief and non-exhaustive sketch of the history of computing machines given above, we appreciate at least two lines along which computing hardware can improve: it can allow for new kinds of operations (e.g., processing digital images) and it can allow for faster execution of those operations (e.g., as of March 2022, the fastest mass-market computer chips work at a frequency of 5.5 GHz, which means they can perform 5.5 billion elementary operations per second, Chacos, 2022).

Since all computer scientists, be they AI, SE, or DB researchers, use the same kind of hardware, the distinction between their subfields, if it exists, must come from the software, that is, the operations they chose to make their hardware perform. We need to look for criteria to classify some operations as AI software to distinguish them from SE software and DB software. We are circling back to the issue of defining what AI is.

If we look at definitions that came after McCarthy's, we notice that the focus on what humans do is always there. According to the Encyclopedia Britannica: "The term is frequently applied to the project of developing systems endowed with the intellectual processes characteristic of humans" (Copeland, 2022).

Computer science professor Wolfgang Ertel is rather critical of this kind of definition because it fails at distinguishing AI from the rest of computer science: after all, remembering large quantities of text and computing numbers itself are intellectual processes entertained by humans, and hence according to this definition every computer would be an AI system (Ertel, 2017). Ertel considers the following definition by Elaine Rich far superior: "Artificial Intelligence is the study of how to make computers do things at which, at the moment, people are better" (Rich, 1983).

---

[1] In general, for digital images, the encoding is based on standards that create a correspondence between numbers and the levels of red, green, and blue of each pixel, and between a system of numerical coordinates and the position of each pixel within the image.

I join Ertel in praising Rich's definition because it introduces so many dimensions in the discourse on AI with so few words. First, it refers to a comparison or rather competition between humans and machines that was first introduced by Alan Turing (an *ante litteram* pioneer of AI) in his attempt with the "imitation game," a thought experiment where a chatbot makes a person believe they are talking with a human, to define a criterion to recognize intelligent machines (Turing, 1950). Second, but no less important, this definition frames AI as a moving target, where the movement is not only determined by the technological development of computing hardware but also by the change in what is considered an inherently human intellectual activity. That change is significantly influenced by the very technological developments of AI.

From this perspective, memorizing texts and computing were inherently human activities at a time when computers did not exist or were extremely rudimentary and slow machines, but not anymore. Now that, in these tasks, computers outperform humans by the billions, something else is considered inherently human, and the focus of AI has shifted accordingly.

Thus, we can distinguish AI from other branches of computer science because of its dynamic nature: always at the forefront of computational modelling of human intellectual activities and tasks, AI tackles yet unsolved problems, only to crack them and transform them into ordinary computer science software and move on. Trying to understand where AI is moving towards leads us to the last metaphor with a line: a path to the future.

MARKING THE LINES AS EXTRAPOLATION

Trying to predict the future of AI is an integral part of AI itself: the research efforts are inherently future-directed under the sign of an ever more comprehensive computational modelling of human intelligence. After all, AGI and strong AI are subfields about intelligent machines that do not exist or do not exist yet. The risk here is to write science fiction rather than predicting future developments in AI research. Indeed, a significant amount of science fiction stories involve AI entities that have reached sentience and help humans or rebel against them. Obviously, these stories never provide a scientific explanation of how computational machines have reached the ultimate human feature of full consciousness, but it is interesting to notice that science fiction writers have imagined both software-based and hardware-based groundbreaking discoveries: in the TV series "Humans," for instance, humanoid robots become fully conscious thanks to a special code that is uploaded on the Internet (Brozel, 2016), whereas in the "Terminator" franchise, machines make that leap thanks to a particular chip (Cameron, 1991).

Unfortunately, there is a non-negligible amount of futuristic AI research that focuses on those fictional end results without providing solid justifications for such a jump. Books like "Superintelligence" (Boström, 2014) go into the details of how a superintelligent computer that achieves sentience might elaborate a strategy to overtake the world without providing any indication of how such superintelligence might come to be in the first place. Another AI endeavour that is undistinguishable from science fiction is the concept of "singularity," proposed by Ray Kurzweil (2014), according to whom the pace of technological change will increase to such an extent that biological and machine intelligence will merge in the next step in human-machine co-evolution, where human life will be irreversibly transformed.

Many of these imaginings are built on top of extrapolations over the extraordinary development of computing technologies during the 20th century. One of the most famous examples is Moore's law, named after Intel's co-founder Gordon Moore, who observed in 1965 that the number of transistors in a chip doubled every year thanks to improvements in miniaturization technology (Moore, 1965). Despite some adjustments in the following decades, the pattern detected by Moore seems to hold. What can we make of this? There are at least three observations that should prevent us from jumping to apocalyptic or utopistic conclusions about the future of AI.

First, there are physical limits to hardware given by the laws of physics that all material entities are subject to. It is true that transistors can become smaller and smaller, but they cannot be smaller than one atom. The curve of the number of transistors per chip can be modelled as an exponential, but there is a cap (Kish, 2002). More generally, we must not take a mathematical model as a realistic depiction in all its parts, so even if AI technology and digital technology have shown exceptional growth in the past decades, this may not be the case in the future.

Second, we must not forget about the quantity versus quality dichotomy: an increase in transistor density surely leads to faster computing machines, which in turn means that a greater quantity of computational operations can be carried out per unit of time, but this does not entail that certain tasks will become amenable to machine simulation. There is a distinction between unfeasible and impossible tasks: an unfeasible task is one for which there is a computational solution, but it requires so many computational resources that it is not reasonable to tackle it; an impossible task is one for which there is no (known) computational solution. Breaking cryptography-based protection is currently unfeasible, but it may become much easier once quantum computing, i.e., computation exploiting quantum mechanics phenomena, becomes available thanks to a technological breakthrough (Denning, 2019). Computing consciousness is, instead, an impossible task, since we do not know how consciousness is produced in the brain, nor whether that mechanism can be simulated via computation. Increasing the number of operations that a computing machine performs in a unit of time will not change this.

Third, we must not forget that computers and AI systems are, like any other technological endeavour, industrial products, entangled in a world-wide network of supply chains, economic interests, political strategies, and, ultimately, people (Crawford & Joler, 2018). Computing machines might become more and more sophisticated and be able to serve humanity in ways that are today only in the realm of science fiction, but who will be the real beneficiary of such technological enhancements? Some futurologists envision a future where humans and robots coexist, the latter taking over all the heavy lifting of labour (Bastani, 2019) or even substituting other humans as perfect love companions (Hauskeller, 2016). Apart from the usual lack of any scientific explanation on how such results might be achieved, these authors fail at telling us who is going to finance the enormous technological efforts needed to build such machines, and who is going to be able to afford to enjoy those machines, if one can even imagine enjoying living in such a particular world.

To avoid encroaching on science fiction, a more down-to-earth approach to imagining the future of AI may be to observe the present of AI, which, despite an apparent focus on "learning," is profoundly different from what McCarthy envisioned in 1955. The AI of the origins, now known as GOFAI, good old-fashioned AI (Haugeland, 1989), was characterized by a rule-driven, top-down approach that aimed at encoding knowledge into a computer in the form of axioms and inference rules that simulated deductive reasoning in humans. Nowadays, the dominant paradigm in AI is the data-driven, bottom-up approach of machine learning (ML, Jordan & Mitchell, 2015). In ML, computers are programmed to search for patterns, schemes, and general laws among vast quantities of data by means of statistical inductive processes. These processes are implemented in the form of complex mathematical functions whose parameters are modified in accordance with how well their outputs meet the goals for which the system was built in the first place. These goals are usually the completion of tasks of data classification (e.g., of digital medical images), clustering (e.g., of viewers of a streaming service), and outlier detection (e.g., of suspicious credit card purchases). The role of AI researchers has radically changed in this paradigm shift from GOFAI to ML: they do not program data and operations into computing machines but feed data to mathematical functions until they are able to process data in accordance with the goals. In GOFAI, humans make the rules to achieve goals, whereas in ML, humans only set the goals, while the rules are developed automatically inside the mathematical functions running in the computing machines. The operations in an ML system are too complex for human programmers to keep in check. The only facet humans can control is whether the ML system has reached the goal. Therefore, ML systems are called "black boxes": humans can only see what goes in and what comes out, but not what happens in between. When it comes to ML, there is a significant decrease in the direct involvement of AI researchers, which has important implications on responsibility in AI: who is responsible when a fully automated ML system misclassifies data and people are harmed? So far, incidents caused by ML systems have been isolated cases of machine-based racism (Grush, 2015) and deadly overreliance on autonomous driving (Baruch, 2016). However, if ML is the (near) future of AI with more widespread adoption in different contexts and fields, one might fear that such harmful cases are going to increase as well.

CONCLUSIONS

AI aims at simulating human intelligence by means of computational models running on digital computers. This endeavour is rife with blurred areas: we do not have a clear definition of intelligence; we do not agree on what aspects of intelligence are really amenable to computational modelling; we do not have specific goals that distinguish AI from other computer-based efforts; AI seems to be a moving target that keeps on changing what we consider to be inherently human; and, finally, we do not have a clear idea on where AI is moving towards, although there are well-founded suspicions that more and more people are going to be harmed. These considerations are not meant to scare the reader away from AI or turn them into a technophobe. There are undeniable benefits that we can reap from the development of AI. However, I strongly believe that shedding light on the blurred lines of AI is and will always be a fundamental way to understand and contain its dangers, may they be ill-conceived metaphors or life-threatening automation failures.

REFERENCES

Bartha, P. (2022). Analogy and analogical reasoning. *The Stanford Encyclopedia of Philosophy* (Summer 2022 Edition), Zalta, E. N. (ed.) URL: https://plato.stanford.edu/archives/sum2022/entries/reasoning-analogy/ (Last visited in May 2022).
Baruch, J. (2016). Steer driverless cars towards full automation. *Nature*, *536*(7615), 127.
Bastani, A. (2019). *Fully Automated Luxury Communism*. Verso Books.
Boström, N. (2014). *Superintelligence: Paths, Dangers, Strategies*. Oxford University Press.
Brozel, M. (Director). (2016). *Humans Episode #2.8* [Television broadcast]. Channel 4.

Cameron, J. (Director). (1991). *Terminator 2: Judgement Day* [Film]. Carolco Pictures.

Campbell-Kelly, M., Aspray, W., Ensmenger, N., & Yost, J. R. (2016). *Computer: A History of the Information Machine* (3rd ed.). Routledge.

Chacos, B. (2022). Intel's Core i9-12900KS, the world's fastest gaming chip, lands April 5. *PC World*, March 28. URL: https://www.pcworld.com/article/626470/intel-core-i9-12900ks-worlds-fastest -gaming-cpu-april-5.html (Last visited in May 2022).

Chalmers, D. (2017). The hard problem of consciousness. In Schneider, S. & Velmans, M. (eds.), *The Blackwell Companion to Consciousness* (2nd ed.). John Wiley & Sons Ltd., 32–42.

Copeland, B. (2022, March 18). Artificial Intelligence. *Encyclopedia Britannica*. URL: https://www. britannica.com/technology/artificial-intelligence (Last visited in May 2022).

Crawford, K., & Joler, V. (2018). Anatomy of an AI System: An anatomical case study of the Amazon Echo as an artificial intelligence system made of human labor. [Artwork] URL: https://anatomyof.ai /img/ai-anatomy-map.pdf (Last visited in May 2022).

Denning, D. E. (2019). Is quantum computing a cybersecurity threat? Although quantum computers currently don't have enough processing power to break encryption keys, future versions might. *American Scientist, 107*(2), 83–86.

Dreyfus, H. L. (1992). *What Computers Still Can't Do: A Critique of Artificial Reason*. MIT Press.

Ertel, W. (2017). *Introduction to Artificial Intelligence*. Springer International Publishing.

Fjelland, R. (2020). Why general artificial intelligence will not be realized. *Humanities and Social Sciences Communications, 7,* 10. https://doi.org/10.1057/s41599-020-0494-4

Gardner, H. E. (1983). *Frames of Mind: The Theory of Multiple Intelligences*. Basic Books.

Goertzel, B., & Pennachin, C. (eds.). (2006). *Artificial General Intelligence*. Springer Verlag.

Grush, L. (2015). Google engineer apologizes after Photos app tags two black people as gorillas. *The Verge, 1.*

Hartmann, S. (1996). The world as a process. In Hegelsmann, R., Mueller, U., & Troitzsch, K. G. (eds.), *Modelling and Simulation in the Social Sciences from the Philosophy of Science Point of View*. Springer, 77–100.

Haugeland, J. (1989). *Artificial Intelligence: The Very Idea*. MIT Press.

Hauskeller, M. (2016). *Mythologies of Transhumanism*. Springer.

Jordan, M. I., & Mitchell, T. M. (2015). Machine learning: Trends, perspectives, and prospects. *Science, 349*(6245), 255–260.

Kish, L. B. (2002). End of Moore's law: Thermal (noise) death of integration in micro and nano electronics. *Physics Letters A, 305*(3–4), 144–149.

Kourou, K., Exarchos, T. P., Exarchos, K. P., Karamouzis, M. V., & Fotiadis, D. I. (2015). Machine learning applications in cancer prognosis and prediction. *Computational and Structural Biotechnology Journal, 13*, 8–17.

Kurzweil, R. (2014). The singularity is near. In Sandler, R. L. (ed.), *Ethics and Emerging Technologies*. Palgrave Macmillan, 393–406.

McCarthy, J. (2007). What is Artificial Intelligence? URL: http://www-formal.stanford.edu/jmc/ whatisai.html (Last visited in May 2022).

McCarthy, J., Minsky, M. L., Rochester, N., & Shannon, C. E. (2006). A proposal for the Dartmouth Summer Research Project on Artificial Intelligence, August 31, 1955. *AI Magazine, 27*(4), 12. https:// doi.org/10.1609/aimag.v27i4.1904

Moore, G. E. (1965). Cramming more components onto integrated circuits. *Electronics, 38*(8).

Novak, J. D., & Gowin, D. B. (1984). *Learning How to Learn*. Cambridge University Press.

Piaget, J. (2003). *The Psychology of Intelligence*. Routledge.

Rich, E. (1983). *Artificial Intelligence*. McGraw-Hill.

Schrittwieser, J., Antonoglou, I., Hubert, T., Simonyan, K., Sifre, L., Schmitt, S., Guez, A., Lockhart, E., Hassabis, D., Graepel, T., & Lillicrap, T. (2020). Mastering atari, go, chess and shogi by planning with a learned model. *Nature, 588*(7839), 604–609.

Searle, J. R. (1980). Minds, brains, and programs. *Behavioral and Brain Sciences, 3*(3), 417–424.

Turello, D. (2015). Brain, mind, and consciousness: A conversation with philosopher John Searle. URL: https://blogs.loc.gov/kluge/2015/03/conversation-with-john-searle/ (Last visited in May 2022).

Turing, A. M. (1950). Computing machinery and intelligence. *Mind, 59*, 433–460.

22. The critical potential of science fiction

Miroslav Kotásek

INTRODUCTION

Currently, we are experiencing an almost perverse obsession with artificial intelligence. Slogans like "smart" or "artificial intelligence" are omnipresent: we are made to believe mobile phones can be smart; that mobiles can make better photos due to the employment of AI; we know that software can recognize voices and faces; there are smart cities and smart homes, even smart benches; and I have come across a toilet paper container named "SmartOne". We can disregard such usage as a part of marketing and advertising strategies, and we could definitely label these terms as "metaphors or oxymora" (Gozzi, 1997). Yet even on this "strategic" and "semantic" level, the outcome of this type of discourse is not trivial: it can initiate a re-evaluation of the concepts of intelligence and reasoning, leading to their potential devaluation, followed by a reassessment of what counts as "human":

> technological innovation in the twenty-first century promises [...] a world in which technology, no longer so much prosthetic as psychic, adopts the language of neuroscience and begins to split open the topography of mind, recoding, reinscribing, realigning its neural networks. (Kroker, 2014, p. 32)

And these are not isolated instances from the sphere of marketing and public relations, they are gaining in importance because of the role technologies in general play in today's world and their tight bonds with the economy, politics, and medicine.

Yet there are more openly threatening usages of "artificial intelligence" heralding its advent. If we can take these seriously, the logical question is: what type of lack is humanity trying to cover in attempting to simulate the action of the human mind? Katherine Hayles openly states:

> I consider this a pipe dream. Human mind has evolved over millennia in such complex symbios with specific biological structures that it is inconceivable consciousness could exist in anything like its present form apart from the physical processes that constitute it. The interesting question, then, is not whether such a transformation can take place, but why it is a compelling imaginary at this cultural moment. What does it mean to lose your body, or more precisely to fantasize that you can lose your body and inhabit a computer? What cultural formations speak to this question, and through what dynamics are their responses generated and structured? (Hayles, 1999, p. 208)

In my analysis, I will not concentrate on the impacts an actual construction of "hard" artificial intelligence might have on our future, the concept of humanity, or the world at large. My goal is to outline the strategic position science fiction as a popular genre plays in a possible critique of the different discourses AI is put through today. Even though science fiction might be viewed as a genre welcoming recent technologies, I find its great power in its critical potential. It can provide stories that offer the reader some understanding of global changes that in fact cannot be fully comprehended and predicted not even through the strictest scientific methods:

> Science fiction is one of the best tools we have for making sense of hyperbolic situations like these. Both in its large-scale world-building and in its small-scale attention to the particular ways in which social and technical innovations affect our lives, science fiction comes to grips with abstractions like economies, social formations, technological infrastructures, and climate perturbations. (Shaviro, 2011, p. 4)

My goal is to show what conditions this position of science fiction as valid. Science fiction is capable, I believe, to offer the kind of stories Arthur Kroker talks about, offering an insight into

> a future of broken neurons, parallel universes, ethics of the impossible, useless history, and contemporary life in the data feed. In the posthuman future, the creative imagination must find a way of breaking *the cage of measurability* in order to become that which is the fatal destiny of the life of the mind – being critically attentive by deep, necessary immersion in the posthuman condition while, at the same time, being fully aware of what has been silenced, excluded, and prohibited by the technological destiny that sweeps us forward. (Kroker, 2014, p. 33; italics Kroker)

I am not going to demonstrate this capability of science fiction on any particular plots or texts of science fiction, as I want to show how this critical appeal of science fiction stories is conditioned by the strategic positioning of the genre within modern culture and by its historical formation.

THE POPULAR AND THE MODERN

The starting point in my understanding of the genre of science fiction is that, generally, "genres actively generate and shape knowledge of the world" (Frow, 2006, p. 2) and they are "central to the social organisation of knowledge" (Frow, 2006, p. 4). Ross Farnell exemplifies the capabilities of the genre by analysing Greg Egan's work, concluding:

> Egan furthers the genre's significant role as one of the prime narrative sites of mediation. *Permutation City* brings together philosophy, theology, science, technology, fantasy, and contemporary theories of body, identity, space, and time under the all-encompassing umbrella of the (post)human pursuit of immortality. (Farnell, 2000, p. 85)

Where does this capability to mediate between genres and pressing social agenda stem from? Ever since science fiction started taking its form as a genre during the 19th century, the link between humanity, science, and technology has been the most important aspect of its critical potential. The reason is, of course, that the genre formed precisely in reaction to the profound paradigmatic changes experienced during Modernity. Even the first precursors of science fiction, like Mary Shelley's *Frankenstein*, thematize this link – and not only that. Mary Shelley's *Frankenstein* depicts, most importantly, a world where science is able to decipher the most fundamental mysteries of life – invading the territory that has been occupied, almost exclusively, by philosophy and religion up until then. *Frankenstein* presents the first truly modern vision of artificial intelligence in the form of a primitive A-life.

At the same time, *Frankenstein* is representing not only a change in the explanation of the world and its functioning but also in the willingness to use such (scientific) knowledge to conquer the mysteries of Nature that allows humanity to aspire to a god-like status. However pessimistic the outcome of the story is regarding these aspirations, *Frankenstein* nevertheless formulates (in the form of fiction) a powerful and controversial phantasm, which technological applications are believed to be able to bring to life in a more or less distant future. And this phantasm becomes increasingly audible with the actual progress of natural sciences, linguistics, medicine, and computer technologies, in other words, all those fields that have to cooperate if a "hard" artificial intelligence is to be constructed:

> the real future of Google as a sentient being would be that of a potential successor species for humanity, with human consciousness reduced to the role of just another algorithm along the way, the slow processing power of which would require augmentation by the sophisticated neural networks of new communicative technologies. (Kroker, 2014, p. 32)

If scientific discourse as we know it today has been formed during the 19th century, undergoing profound changes during a very limited period of time, it is important to note that the so-called popular culture is taking its form simultaneously. This fact is extremely important as, for example, the Czech literary theoretician Petr Bílek claims that

> the genres and texts of popular culture are much more sensitive to the context in which they appear in comparison with "canonical" texts and genres. Their functioning is based on a warm welcome from the public – the reading public should be as numerous as possible. That is why these genres are capable of producing a mental image of an era in a more productive way than the works of art an author, reader, or a variety of institutions place into an eternal, universal sphere of communication. (Bílek, 2005, p. 83)

The attentiveness and sensitivity of the genres of popular culture (especially science fiction) to the social, cultural, and "technological" context is the very reason we can talk about any critical potential in the first place. In a different context, Katherine Hayles points out:

> the larger global pattern that emerges when literary culture and artificial life are integrated together suggests that technology and culture are bound together in complex feedback loops that themselves have self-organizing properties. [...] Science and literature can no longer proceed as separate discourses. They speak, if not in the same voice, from the same sites. (Hayles, 1999, pp. 219–220)

I see this co-habitation of the same place of literary, scientific, and technological discourse to be the practical outcome of the strategic functioning of (popular) literature within the cultural field of Modernism and their simultaneous structuring.

It is "strategic" because it allows science fiction to react much more swiftly to the needs and worries of society, and often it is the only genre that can provide any form of a model of understanding or dealing with a pressing problem, changing situation, or a paradigm shift. That is how we should read Jameson's commentary on William Gibson's work, where he claims that "the representational apparatus of Science Fiction [...] sends back more reliable information about the contemporary world than an exhausted realism (or an exhausted modernism either)" (Jameson, 2005, p. 384). Thanks to the tight link between a *fictitious* discourse and *scientific* discourse (which nobody would willingly associate with *fiction*), science fiction is also capable of a self-reflective approach not only towards the genre itself but precisely towards the limits of fictionality and the role different discourses might play within a society. This self-aware-ness towards the Modernist situation of the 19th century (and, of course, any other historical period) represents a specific form of the "feedback loop" Hayles mentions. For the first time in human history, the science and technology of the 19th century plausibly demonstrate the speculation that the ontological dimension of humanity is of a technological nature – that humans are, in fact, prosthetic animals (see Stiegler, 1998, pp. 185–203; Žižek, 2008, p. 173), compensating through technology for the lack of "natural" capabilities (other than the specifi-cally evolved brain, of course). The theory and its logical consequences appear to be more and more urgent and "probable" as we experience different technologies intervening in the most mundane human tasks and needs, thus transforming the very structure of social relations – whether it is the means of transport (trains, aircraft, and cars), different means of communi-cation (newspapers, telegraph, telephone, the Internet), or the changing perspectives of time, space, and matter itself (second law of thermodynamics, Einstein's theory of relativity, Bohr's model of the atom, Copenhagen interpretation of quantum mechanics). In this respect, talking about technology in the form of fictive stories, emploting technological wonders into literary discourse amounts to emptying the ontological foundation of humanity (or rather: "fictional-ising it") – in this, we can observe the "social 'contract' between writer and reader [which] has had one significant structural consequence: the transformation of the cultural text into an *auto-referential* discourse, whose content is a perpetual interrogation of its own conditions of possibility" (Jameson, 2005, p. 292; italics Jameson).

Mark Hodder in his steampunk novel series *Burton & Swinburne* offers a deep insight into the way changes in technology are both alien and at the same time potentially "natural" if we live surrounded by them long enough. Then they become familiar, prohibiting us from reflecting on the changes we are subjected to. Mark Hodder uses "alternative history" narra-tive strategies to speculate about the potential courses history might have taken if science and technology had developed differently (offering a rather "unethical" use of genetic manipula-tion and the usage of analogue computers). The effect is striking, as the reader can always compare the course of history in the novels with the "real" history he feels the product of. The changes are "total" – the whole game would have changed – be it economy, politics, geopoli-tics, and science itself. And as the 19th century saw the birth of "eugenics" (then placed under the category of science as well), we can say that a great part, probably even the most important part, of 19th-century endeavour is inspired by the "Frankenstein myth" of either improving on the existing design of living creatures or producing new, "pure" beings (which often means "mechanical" beings). However strong this A-life myth might be (being tragically fulfilled by the Nazis), Mark Hodder provides the reader with a vision of an AI "of a Kurzweil breed": in the novel *The Curious Case of a Clockwork Man*, the mind of the British philosopher Herbert Spencer is captured inside an extra-terrestrial "crystal" and connected to a miniature version of an analytical engine of Charles Babbage, coupled with a clockwork body.

Whether it is eugenics, racism (as representatives of scientific theories of the 19th century), medicine, or other ways of improving the human, the 19th century is dreaming of the power that was up until then ascribed only to God; politics transforms into biopolitics. The dream or phantasm of overcoming the natural, biological base of humanity by either "synthetising" (simulating) it or constructing it anew in a mechanical form represents the traumatic core of Modernism and our technological present. Today, we can certainly ascribe to what Donna Haraway claimed some 30 years ago: "By the late twentieth century, our time, a mythic time, we are all chimeras, theorized and fabricated hybrids of machine and organism; in short, we are cyborgs. The cyborg is our ontology; it gives us our politics" (Haraway, 1991, p. 150).

In the most mundane and literal sense, we are exactly that: through our intimate relationship with computers, screens, cars, and mobile phones, we are fulfilling our role of "technological animals", willingly undergoing "the technological colonization of our body itself" (Žižek, 2008, p. 172). Despite the familiarity of technologies (the technologies colonize our bodies with our consent, we are heartily inviting the invaders and we can hardly imagine our lives without them), there is no term in ordinary language to name this change. As Žižek poignantly mentions:

> Stephen Hawking is emerging as one of the icons of our time: the mind of a genius (or so we are told), but in a body which is almost totally "mediatized", supported by prostheses, speaking with an artificial, computer-generated voice. (Žižek, 2008, p. 173)

Žižek goes on and rather harshly states that "his popular appeal cannot be separated from his "debilitating illness", which "tells us something about the general state of subjectivity today" (Žižek, 2008, p. 173). Nevertheless, even if it was not Stephen Hawking, there is still no better word for our modern and postmodern design than "cyborg". Humans are inventing, forming, naming their human design, in other words, they fabricate fictions. And yes, from this point of view, "the boundary between science fiction and social reality is an optical illusion" (Haraway, 1991, p. 149). The connection between AI technologies and the social can have a different source, as suggested by Ronald D. Schwartz:

> AI programs are written with the expectation (however provisional) that they will be able to perform in social situations. This means examining how running programs mesh with, absorb, and penetrate social practices in the situation where they were deployed. Assessing this, in turn, involves [...] appreciating how people themselves understand a program and what it is doing, as well as how the particular organization and requirements of a program affect social relations among people. (Schwartz, 1989, p. 187)

Without a doubt, this "appreciation" takes, most often, the form of a story or narrative.

The taking form of science fiction in the 19th century was conditioned by one more crucial feature. It is the relatively innocent fact that science fiction is a literary genre, coming to the reader in the form of a published book or magazine. But things are not that simple. Literature as a medium has undergone a fundamental transformation in the 19th century, brought about by the industrialization of the press and the competition from other "storage" media: photography, phonography, and film. Literature loses its privileged position and becomes part of a complex economic and informational "discourse network" as Friedrich Kittler (1990) calls it. If we accept the idea that literature is capable of "capturing", "storing", and "activating" minds by modelling the thinking and actions of characters and narrators (cf. Turner, 1996), then it becomes more obvious why we can use the seemingly derogative term "fiction" and apply it to actual lives of people. Literature has always done this, yet in the 19th century, the competition from other media highlighted the materiality of the book of literature (the medium itself).

But the story does not end here – if we return to a relatively recent past, we can see a strong tendency towards unifying different media, or, in other words, we are confronted with the consequences that are brought by the digitisation of media. Kittler suggests that digitisation changes everything, as any media can be digitised, thus opening the possibility of processing every known information (visual, audible, haptic) in the form of a binary code and being crunched by "the same" computer software or algorithm:

> The general digitisation of channels and information erases the difference among individual media. Sound and image, voice and text are reduced to surface effects [...] Inside the computers themselves everything becomes a number: quantity without image, sound, or voice. And once optical fibre networks turn formerly distinct data flows into a standardized series of digitised numbers, any medium can be translated into any other. [...] a total media link will erase the very concept of medium. (Kittler, 1999, pp. 1–2)

The artificial minds of literary characters are thus potentially losing their materiality, there is the possibility to turn them into a binary code, while the "real" human mind is at the same time threatened by the possibility to be digitised and transported into a different body, or a mechanical/computational carrier of the mind. That would amount to just an episode (or joke) in the history of media if modern biology, communication science, and linguistics were not following the same path. Media digitisation goes hand in hand with the aspiration of modern sciences which amounts to "a common move – *the translation of the world into a problem of coding,* a search for a common language in which the resistance to instrumental control disappears and all heterogeneity can be submitted to disassembly, reassembly, investment, and exchange" (Haraway, 1991, p. 164; italics Haraway). In direct reaction to Donna Haraway, Hayles stresses that the characteristic of our time is "the penetration of computational processes not only into every aspect of biological, social, economic, and political realms but also into the construction of reality itself" (Hayles, 2006, p. 161).

The last crucial aspect of science fiction, going hand in hand with the industrialization of the press, is its connectedness with "cultural industry". And again, it is a situation different from the production of "mainstream" or "serious" literature. Works of popular culture are primarily goods, allowing them to be produced in an industrial manner (in endless series, employing ghost writers, and so on). Theoretically, it should put science fiction on intimate terms with "capital" and "capitalize" on this intimacy for the benefit of a "critique" of capitalism and its technological, industrial wonders. The link I am pointing at is of a similar kind to the one between science and literary discourse. As in the previous case, the outcome is a self-reflecting structure. The functioning and actions of capital are, so to speak, inscribed into the body of science fiction. And as Shaviro (2011) points out, today's forms of capitalism run the risk of collapsing the future – a similar outcome to that of actually creating a hard AI. Gery Canavan, referring to Shaviro and Hayles, even concludes that capital behaves as having an intelligence of its own:

> the end result of the "rigid and monotonous logic" of the chaotic movements of capital is the production of what appears to us as a kind of emergent intelligence, a non-biological subject that seems to think, though sometimes perhaps not at all too well – a subject we sometimes apprehend as a perfectly rational calculator of values and other times as an irrational [...] subject. (Canavan, 2015, p. 686)

Science fiction is thus fatally inscribed within this emergent artificial intelligence of capital.

All the aspects I have mentioned so far align together in science fiction to provide a genre with specific critical power due to its links with the problems of technology, along with the capacity of literature to actually produce "artificial minds". This relatively unique position is not naïve in any respect, as science fiction is often proceeding in a self-reflective manner not only towards the usage of story elements but also towards its functioning within the society as such:

> the centre of gravity of such narratives shifts towards an auto-referentiality of a specific, but far more concrete type: such texts then explicitly or implicitly, and as it were against their own will, find their deepest 'subjects' in the possibility of their own production, in the interrogation of the dilemmas involved in their own emergence as utopian texts. (Jameson, 2005, p. 293)

And the "utopian dilemma" Jameson is talking about is going to be our next topic.

THE STORY OF THE FUTURE

What I suggested up until now does not, of course, mean that science fiction is some new kind of "modern critical philosophy" or that we are reading it the wrong way if we enjoy it for entertainment. I have already pointed out the fact that science fiction (popular literature in general) can be viewed as being specifically aligned with and inscribed into the social, cultural, and political context it appears in. "Entertainment" goes hand in hand with the critical potential it offers. The competence of science fiction in this respect is so dominating that as soon as mainstream or "serious" literature tries to tackle the problem of the future of humanity, or futurity as such, or it attempts to ask the question of the impact of technology on humanity, it necessarily switches to plots and narrative structures borrowed from science fiction – we can mention some of the novels by Michel Houellebecq (e.g., *Les Particules élémentaires*), Thomas Pynchon (*Bleeding Edge*), or the works of J. G. Ballard (e.g., *Crash*).

That is why Istvan Csicery-Ronay, reflecting on cyberpunk, can claim that

> the speed of technological change is enormous and ten years ago science fiction […] was really the only art form that was aware of what was going on around us" and, according to him, this rapid pace of change means that "authors attempting in the near future to interpret our present reality will be forced to produce texts enriched by science fiction motifs. (Csicsery-Ronay, 2003, p. 36)

This observation – that science fiction is the only genre actually capable of providing (un) believable stories about the future (and/or our technological presence) is the "formal" aspect of its critical potential. Science fiction (as almost all fictions) provides temporarily ordered sequences of events. Sometimes they defy logic, they might even defy classical categories that we assign to stories: chronology, the past that cannot be changed, and causality.

Ever since phenomenological enterprises into the nature of time, specifically the future, the idea has prevailed that an individual is to actively project his or her visions of the future onto the socially constructed "ground-plan" and that this active approach should guarantee the subject the "dreamt-of" or "fictional" future. Pierre Bourdieu, talking about the ways a narrative text can make the production of time visible (or rather: readable), states:

> Agents temporalize themselves in the very act by which they transcend the immediate present towards the future implicated in the past of which their habitus is the product; they produce time in the practical anticipation of the still-to-come [*à-venir*] which is at the same time the practical actualization of the past. (Bourdieu, 1996, p. 328)

And as we can see the very introduction of the concept of "habitus" into the conception of time immediately disrupts the distinction between the subject of and the object of history. Human agents are both subjects and objects of the future.

Science fiction quite often explicitly uses "time construction" as a fundamental (and entertaining) part of emplotment – whether it be the above-mentioned subgenre of "alternative history" or the employment of time travels. But this kind of time speculation of science fiction, where the characters have little or no control over what happens next or what impact might their visit in the past have on their future, can also prove Bourdieu partly wrong. During the past few years, we have experienced rather deep and unexpected changes in our relationship towards time, especially futurity. The Covid-19 pandemic showed everyone that the future is far from predictable. Then, even such a seemingly unproblematic future projection as "I will go to a pub in the evening and have a beer or two with my friends" proved to be an unattainable, impossible deed – unless one was prepared to violate the law and face potential punishment. Suddenly, the very matrix of everyday life seemed to be shattered, showing that the future does not have to be necessarily generated through sovereign agents, that anyone can become the object of future – the future invented, ordered, and dictated by politicians, doctors, and health officers. The fabric of the future ruptured and appeared in its unveiled form – as a fictitious, fabricated discourse. It is evident that "human agents" can turn into pure objects (victims) of time and different "future fables".

At the beginning of a documentary film about Jacques Derrida, called *Derrida* (directed by Kirby Dick and Amy Ziering Kofman), Derrida himself distinguishes two types of future. The first is the French *futur* (that which is predictable, part of a causal sequence; that which is possible and can be calculated) and the French *l'avenir* (that which comes unexpected, disrupts every possibility; that which presents evidence of the absence of any pre-existing structure of futurity). *L'avenir* (which is structured differently from Bourdieu's *à-venir*) is the future instigated by an *event*: "one of the characteristics of the event is that not only does it come about as something unforeseeable, not only does it disrupt the ordinary course of history, but it is also absolutely singular" (Derrida, 2007, p. 446). The Covid-19 future I mentioned is *l'avenir*, reacting to an "event", it is the future (and present) of a traumatic, disruptive kind. So is the future in Cormac McCarthy's *The Road*, *Soft Apocalypse* by Will McIntosh, or the future as experienced by many Americans after 9/11:

> Technology is our fate, our truth. [...] The materials and methods we devise make it possible for us to claim our future. We don't have to depend on God or the prophets or other astonishments. We are the astonishment. The miracle is what we ourselves produce, the systems and networks that change the way we live and think. But whatever great skeins of technology lie ahead, ever more complex, connective, precise, micro-fractional, the future has yielded, for now, to medieval expedience, to the old slow furies of cutthroat religion. (DeLillo, 2001, p. 37)

Before I try to answer the question of what kind of "future" artificial intelligence belongs, there is one more consideration to be made. Decades of research, unbelievable amounts of money and tonnes of paper have been invested towards the construction of "hard" artificial intelligence. But up until now, the whole endeavour has the sole form of a fable or a phantasm, as I have already called it earlier. In the centre of artificial intelligence as a scientific field and discourse lies the question of human language as a means of "thinking", being the subject and object of the human "mind" at the same time (together with a specific human corporeality, sense, feelings, and affects). That is one side of the problem. The other is that artificial intelligence is there only to be talked about. It is the future of the human mind being simulated by computers presented in the form of fictions. For these two reasons, artificial intelligence is (in the present) primarily textual. It is a non-event because, with a successful construction of artificial intelligence, the future would no longer be human (here science fiction provides us with more than enough textual "evidence"). It is striking that I can actually quote Jacques Derrida talking about the possibility of a nuclear war and I do not have to change a single word for the citations to be applicable to the phenomenon of artificial intelligence:

> It does not depend on language just because the 'incompetents' on all sides can speak of it only in the mode of gossip or of doxa (opinion) – and the dividing line between doxa and épistémè starts to blur as soon as there is no longer any such thing as an absolutely legitimizable competence for a phenomenon which is no longer strictly techno-scientific but techno-militaro-politico-diplomatic through and through, and which brings into play the doxa or incompetence even in its calculations. There is nothing but doxa, opinion, "belief". [...] there is no more room for a distinction between belief and science. (Derrida, 1984, p. 24)

In the phrase "no more distinction between belief and science", we should by now be able to recognize the situation of science fiction inseparably weaving together the discourses of science and literature.

Many people are talking about artificial intelligence, regarding it as a possibility. Thus, if it materializes, it will be part of *futur* (the outcome of years of research and huge amounts of money). Yet, especially if it appears in the form of a human mind being uploaded into a machine, it will change the way we experience history and time: death, for example, will no longer represent the liminal horizon of human beings and the understanding of human time, history, and future will transform in such a substantial way that the predicted (heralded, calculated, feared, talked about) *futur* of the human race actually constructing artificial intelligence will necessarily become *l'avenir*, the future of dystopic science fiction stories (like the *Matrix* series), because only science fiction is actually capable of calculating and predicting that which cannot be predicted: the future disrupted by Derridian "events".

Bourdieu claims that the predictability of the future and the stability of habitus "engenders assumptions and anticipations which, ordinarily being confirmed by the course of events, ground a relation of immediate familiarity or ontological complicity with the familiar world" (Bourdieu, 1996, pp. 328–329). Bourdieu claims that literature can model this familiarity with the time of the world and is able to prove it convincingly in his book. Yet science fiction is capable of modelling a time that is not familiar, the time of crisis, the time of the collapse or destruction of the existing habitus and the establishment of a new one. Not only is science fiction self-consciously "fictitious", but it also demonstrates that the human future itself is constructed precisely as a fiction (which may or may not turn into "reality").

CYBERPUNK AND THE PRESENT

Can it be that we have slept too heavily and dreamt too loud, having failed to witness the event? Mike Moore of WTO held a speech on 14 August 2000 in New Zealand:

I come to praise the future. There has never been a time in the history of our species when we had such an opportunity to build better living standards and a safer and more secure world for all. Globalisation is a part of this opportunity. (Moore, 2000)

Here the artificial intelligence of capital has obviously possessed a human being and forced him to prophesize its own endless glorious future. Only artificial intelligence can boast to know what is best for humans and use a phrase like "our species". There are countless examples of science fiction stories pointing at the fact that AIs can act in (what they believe are) the best interests of the human race, as they are capable of "pure reasoning", not being influenced by emotions. And they are (in a dystopian manner) more than ready to pay any price to make things better. Luckily, we can observe quite clearly today that this particular artificial intelligence has lied to us (or made fun of us, following its own mysterious goals).

It is tangible that something has happened to time. Since the 1980s, the idea prevails that the Western (postmodern) culture of today has no interest in the future (in comparison with modernity) but is all the more fascinated by the present. This shift in sensitivity is underlined, for example, by Boris Groys (2016), who focused on the role the Internet plays in this shift. Jameson (2005) and Csicsery-Ronay (1992) have demonstrated the ways this change is represented in science fiction. Regarding the postulated link between science fiction and the current socio-cultural situation, the harsh words of Gregory Benford, who criticizes cyberpunk for just "mirroring" the present (Benford, 1992, p. 224), instead of offering a scientifically plausible vision of the future, can be interpreted differently. Cyberpunk might be (rather passively) just witnessing the historical change in temporality, when the speed of technological change is so high that not even science fiction can hold pace with it. Ondrej Herec, a Slovak sociologist, claims that in cyberpunk "future has collapsed into the present, the human into technology and science fiction into reality" (Herec, 2008, p. 147). It seems that the technological industry has taken over the role of presenting us with a "visionary future" (through the likes of Elon Musk), while science fiction has been relegated to the role of "critical discourse".

Cyberpunk novels describe a world in which the classical power-economic relationships have been substantially transformed, *information* becoming the most important commodity (hence the characters of hackers or "cowboys" who move through cyberspace to steal or "acquire" information). The individual who thus submerges into the etheric sphere of computer networks is a cyborg who sends his mind through optoelectrical cables, allowing him to move at the speed of light:

Our best machines are made of sunshine; they are light and clean because they are nothing but signals, electromagnetic waves, a section of a spectrum, and these machines are eminently portable, mobile [...]. People are nowhere near so fluid, being both material and opaque. Cyborgs are ether, quintessence. The ubiquity and invisibility of cyborgs is precisely why these sunshine-belt machines are so deadly. (Haraway, 1991, p. 153)

A motif that accompanies the change of information into the most valuable commodity (and currency) in cyberpunk stories is the crisis of the national state and its functioning. The functions that the classical bureaucratic state apparatus executes today are replaced by different forms of organization, where the control is taken over by private, often multinational companies (the future as envisioned by Mike Moore), or they at least have the greatest influence (e.g., in *Snow Crash* by Neal Stephenson). In a world where the dominant future "fables" are narrated by an omnipresent and omnipotent AI narrator, the escape into the permanent present of cyberspace seems to be a viable option: "Think of a future in which the components of a microchip are the size of atoms. The devices that pace our lives will operate from the smart quantum spaces of pure information" (DeLillo, 2001, p. 40). The plots of cyberpunk stories are thus structured in accordance with the changes in the postmodern treatment of the future and shifts in the economy of "post-industrial" capitalism, following the abandonment of the gold standard, with computer network technologies revolutionizing the functioning of markets:

> In the past decade the surge of capital markets has dominated discourse and shaped global consciousness. Multinational corporations have come to seem more vital and influential than governments. The dramatic climb of the Dow and the speed of the Internet summoned us all to live permanently in the future, in the utopian glow of cyber-capital, because there is no memory there and this is where markets are uncontrolled and investment potential has no limit. (DeLillo, 2001, p. 33)

I have tried to show that science fiction can offer powerful models for understanding the present situation of humankind. Whether science fiction will be able to keep this power in the 21st century is uncertain. We might be witnessing such a profound change in the self-understanding of humanity that not even science fiction will be able to keep pace. Some critics claim that this exactly was the fate of cyberpunk. Let us hope that if such a change occurs, it will not end stories altogether. We are in need of fables through which we can come in contact with artificial minds and understand how the fabric of time is woven together: in very much the same way as the fabric of stories, neural networks, and artificial intelligence programs.

REFERENCES

Benford, G. (1992). Science Fiction, Rhetoric, and Realities. In G. Slusser, T. Shippey (Eds.), *Fiction 2000* (pp. 223–229). University of Georgia Press.
Bílek, P. (2005). Hledání esence či vertikální i horizontální konstruování sítě? In V. Papoušek, D. Tureček (Eds.), *Hledání literárních dějin* (pp. 78–85). Paseka.
Bourdieu, P. (1996). *The Rules of Art*. Stanford University Press.
Canavan, G. (2015). Capital as Artificial Intelligence. *Journal of American Studies*, 49(4), 685–709.
Csicsery-Ronay, I. (2003). Žádný současný spisovatel se bez SF neobejde. *Ikarie*, 14(11), 35–37.
Csicsery-Ronay, I. (1992). Futuristic Flu, or, The Revenge of the Future. In G. Slusser, T. Shippey (Eds.), *Fiction 2000* (pp. 2–45). University of Georgia Press.
DeLillo, D. (2001). In the Ruins of the Future. *Harper's Magazine*, 303(1819), 33–40.
Derrida. (2002). Dir. Kirby Dick and Amy Ziering Kofman. Zeitgeist Video. DVD.
Derrida, J. (1984). No Apocalypse, Not Now (Full Speed Ahead, Seven Missiles, Seven Missives). *Diacritics*, 14(2), 20–31.
Derrida, J. (2007). A Certain Impossible Possibility of Saying the Event. *Critical Inquiry 33*(2), 441–461.
Farnell, R. (2000). Attempting Immortality: AI, A-life, and the Posthuman in Greg Egan's *Permutation City*. *Science Fiction Studies*, 27(1), 69–91.
Frow, J. (2006). *Genre*. Routledge.
Gozzi, R. (1997). Artificial Intelligence – Metaphor or Oxymoron? *ETC: A Review of General Semantics*, 54(2), 219–224.
Groys, B. (2016). *In the Flow*. Verso.
Haraway, D. (1991). *Simians, Cyborgs, and Women*. Routledge.

Hayles, K. (1999). Artificial Life and Literary Culture. In M.-L. Ryan (Ed.), *Cyberspace Textuality* (pp. 205–223). Indiana University Press.

Hayles, K. (2006). Unfinished Work: From Cyborg to Cognisphere. *Theory, Culture & Society*, 23(7–8), 159–166.

Herec, O. (2001). *Cyberpunk. Vstupenka do tretieho tisícročia.* Vydavateľstvo Spolku slovenských spisovateľov.

Jameson, F. (2005). *Archaeologies of the Future.* Verso.

Kittler, F. (1990). *Discourse Networks 1800/1900.* Stanford University Press.

Kittler, F. (1999). *Gramophone, Film, Typewriter.* Stanford University Press.

Kroker, A. (2014). *Exits to the Posthuman Future.* Polity Press.

Moore, M. (2000). In Praise of the Future. https://www.wto.org/english/news_e/spmm_e/spmm34_e.htm

Schwartz, R. D. (1989). Artificial Intelligence as a Sociological Phenomenon. *The Canadian Journal of Sociology / Cahiers canadiens de sociologie*, 14(2), 179–202.

Shaviro, S. (2011). Hyperbolic Futures: Speculative Finance and Speculative Fiction. *The Cascadia Subduction Zone*, 1(2), 3–5; 12–15.

Stiegler, B. (1998). *Technics and Time 1: The Fault of Epimetheus.* Stanford University Press.

Suvin, D. (1979). *Metamorphoses of Science Fiction: On the Poetics and History of a Literary Genre.* Yale University Press.

Turner, M. (1996). *The Literary Mind.* Oxford University Press.

Žižek, S. (2008). *The Plague of Fantasies.* Verso.

23. A critical review of news framing of artificial intelligence

Ching-Hua Chuan

INTRODUCTION

Long before the recent momentous breakthroughs in artificial intelligence (AI), the technology has been a topic of fascination and imagination in popular media for decades. As AI is rapidly migrating from academic research papers into factories, courtrooms, hospitals, and various aspects of our everyday experiences, AI has dominated the contemporary media discourse on science and technology. At the same time, the vastness and heterogeneity of AI applications, as well as the complexity and multidimensionality of AI-related issues, have likely created confusion and anxiety. Focusing on the similarly controversial topic of stem cell research, Liu and Priest (2009) indicate that individuals' attitudes toward complex and unfamiliar science and technology topics are affected by sundry factors from trust in scientific authorities, to news consumption, news framing, prior knowledge, and socialization. News media is particularly influential when successfully translating complicated knowledge into accessible and relatable information, and in the process, influencing public opinion, especially in the early stage of technology penetration when people likely feel perplexed, wary, or anxious (Lemańczyk, 2014). Distinct from other controversial technologies like stem cell research and nanotechnology, AI has increasingly made decisions about our lives (e.g., loan approvals) and everyday experiences (e.g., news feeds on social media) without people's consent, understanding, or even awareness. Focusing on how AI is covered, contextualized, and discussed in newspapers, this chapter provides a comprehensive review of existing news framing studies to advance the critical understanding of the structural forces and perspectives shaping public opinion on this powerful technology.

News framing studies have highlighted the "conduit" role of journalists by providing information and arguments that will help the public achieve an adequate understanding (Schudson, 1983). For novel and emerging science and technology topics, it is important to note that frames also act as a filter for journalists and editors by helping them process large amounts of unfamiliar information, determine what is newsworthy, and present the information in an efficient and relevant manner to the audience (Nelkin, 1987). The frames that organize the journalists' worlds then have the potential of shaping public dialogues of the issue. Specifically, Entman (1993) defined framing as presenting "some aspects of a perceived reality and making them more salient in a communicating text, in such a way as to promote a particular problem definition, causal interpretation, moral evaluation, and/or treatment recommendation to the item described" (p. 52).

This chapter first provides an overview that describes the "landscape" of the existing AI news framing literature, before reviewing and discussing the key findings on dominant and critical news frames and themes. The conclusion articulates the importance of AI literacy for both journalists and the general public.

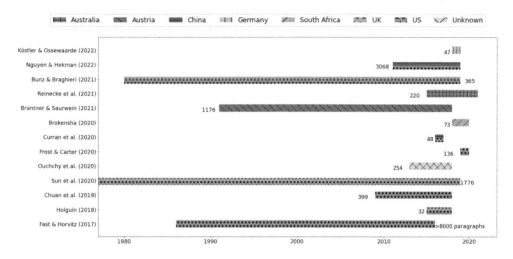

Source: Author.

Figure 23.1 *A visualization of the reviewed literature on news framing of AI*

AN OVERVIEW OF AI NEWS FRAMING LITERATURE

This section provides an overview of the literature on news framing of AI in three broad aspects: the time periods analyzed, the countries studied, and the research methodology used. Figure 23.1 presents a visualization of the literature on news framing of AI. Related literature that does not directly analyze the news coverage on AI, such as framing effects on individual perception or AI discourse on social media, is excluded from the visualization. The horizontal axis of the figure represents the years of the news articles surveyed in a study, while the color indicates the country.[1] The number next to the bar shows the number of news articles examined in a study, except for Fast and Horvitz (2017), which only analyzed paragraphs from news articles.

Figure 23.1 demonstrates that most AI news framing studies are published after 2010, as the amount of AI news articles swelled significantly since then. This pattern is consistently documented in the literature that has covered a wider range of time periods. For example, Chuan et al. (2019) observed that the number of articles doubled in 2016. News articles published since 2015 accounted for the significant majority in Sun et al.'s (2020, Figure 23.1) study that included news articles as early as 1977. The abrupt increase in news about AI can be attributed to the milestones of AI developments and several highly publicized AI events. For instance, ImageNet, a crucial dataset with 1.2 million manually labeled images (Deng et al., 2009) was released in 2010, which propelled deep learning algorithms to achieve unprecedented accuracy in image recognition (LeCun et al., 2015; Bengio et al., 2017), leading to wide adoptions of AI in industries. Deep learning has quickly demonstrated success in various applications

---

[1]   We labeled the country as unknown for Ouchchy et al. (2020) because even though the authors mentioned examples of US news, the paper does not explicitly specify the country for all news articles studied in the paper.

across industries since 2012, thereby generating buzz as well as hype in news media. Events such as the legalization of self-driving cars in the United States in 2012 and fatal crashes involving Tesla's autonomous vehicles similarly received extensive media attention (Nyholm & Smids, 2016).

Considering that the US is a major player in the global AI race, the majority of studies focus on American newspapers. For instance, Chuan et al. (2019) content analyzed news articles from the most widely read daily American newspapers: USA Today, The New York Times, The Los Angeles Times, The New York Post, and The Washington Post. Other studies have analyzed news framing of AI in China, Australia, Austria, Germany, and South Africa. Only a few studies included newspapers from multiple countries. They either focus on English-language news in general without meaningfully comparing AI news in the US and the UK or purposefully evaluating AI news from economically and politically contrasting cultures such as China and the US (e.g., Curran et al., 2020; Nguyen & Hekman, 2022).

There are noticeable differences in the number of news articles examined, depending on how the data (i.e., news articles) were selected and the research methodology used. For most studies, databases such as LexisNexis and ProQuest were first used with AI-related keyword searches to identify relevant news articles. The retrieved articles were then further selected via certain inclusion/exclusion criteria, such as removing articles that only mention AI in a small portion, before forming the final dataset for examination. Then quantitative content analyses were conducted based on framing coding schemes adapted from the literature (e.g., Entman, 1993; Nisbet et al., 2002) or created by the researchers. The manual coding process limits the number of articles examined. Alternatively, some researchers employed computational tools for collecting and labeling articles. For example, Fast and Horvtiz (2017) used the New York Times API and web scraping to collect articles and adopted the crowdsourcing method involving a large number of coders recruited through Amazon MTurk to annotate selected paragraphs from the articles. Beyond quantitative content analysis, qualitative approaches are adopted to critically analyze forces and ideologies motivating the frames based on a much smaller sample (e.g., Bory, 2019; Bunz & Braghieri, 2021).

NEWS FRAMING OF AI

Entman's definition of framing (1993) as "(selecting) some aspects of a perceived reality and making them more salient in a communicating text" has informed the majority of news framing studies. However, it is important to note that many studies focus on the first part of the definition to explore what is included by identifying major topics in AI news. Yet, framing is also about how to make the content more salient in communication. It is thus important to differentiate topics, defined as a manifest subject, an issue, or an event that provides message content (e.g., AI as a surveillance technology), from frames that refer to a perspective that characterizes the issue with a specific focus (e.g., episodic or thematic issue) or associations (e.g., societal versus personal impact) (Strekalova, 2015). While identifying topics and keywords is important to pinpoint specific applications (e.g., facial recognition) or issues (e.g., job replacement) that constitute focus areas of AI discourse, it is through the framing process that a topic is infused with a value, valence, and meaning based on which opinions can be developed (Chuan et al., 2019). Framing thus helps individuals "to locate, perceive, identify, and label" issues and topics within their own personal context (Goffman, 1974, p. 21).

The following subsections discuss the key findings in AI news framing literature, starting from commonly used frames for science and technology to the unique frames specific to AI.

Benefit and Risk Frames

The benefit/opportunity and risk/threat frames have been the most widely analyzed, likely because these frames are found to be particularly influential in swaying public opinion toward emerging technologies (Vicsek, 2011). Benefits are often conceptualized via social progress (i.e., the improvement of quality of life, Nisbet, 2002) and economic benefits. In recent years, the risk and threat frame has been increasingly featured in AI news. The most frequently covered risks include shortcomings of the technology, loss of jobs, and privacy concerns (Chuan et al., 2019; Brantner & Saurwein, 2021). Additionally, risks were typically discussed at a higher level of specificity than benefits in AI news, while business and economy topics tended to be described using a benefit-only frame, and AI ethics typically using a risk-only frame (Chuan et al., 2019).

Given the dominant pattern of framing AI as "good for economy and bad at ethics," the overly simplified coverage may lead to unbalanced reporting and misinformed public opinion driven by selective news consumption. Brokensha (2020) argued that discussing an AI topic in dualistic or even competing frames can be helpful for news readers to develop a more complete and informed understanding of AI-related issues. For example, when covering AI's economic impact on jobs, both positive and negative effects (i.e., creating new jobs versus destroying existing jobs by replacing manual labor) should be discussed. Additionally, perceived conflicts resulting from such competing frames may be mitigated by a middle-way frame (i.e., humans and AI work together as a better team; Brokensha, 2020). By the same token, while news coverage on AI ethics tends to focus on identifying AI-associated risks, news reporting on progress in addressing AI risks and ethical concerns such as regulations, AI auditing, and organizational practices like "advisory boards" are also needed. Journalists are encouraged to adopt multiple frames to help readers understand the complex and far-reaching consequences of AI issues.

Overall, it has been consistently documented that the benefit frame was used much more frequently than the risk frame (e.g., Chuan et al., 2019; Frost & Carter, 2020; Sun et al., 2020). For instance, Brokensha (2020) found that the top benefit of social progress was visible in over half of the news articles while the key threat of competition appeared in only 15% of South Africa's news stories. This has been an international pattern as Nguyen and Hekman (2022) observed that both The Washington Post and South China Morning Post were dominated by the benefit frame that underscores the commercial value of AI.

AI Ethics, Responsibility, and Accountability

Given the increasing media attention on ethical issues surrounding AI, several studies have focused on news framing of AI ethics and regulations specifically. Ouchchy et al. (2020) found that over half of the news articles on AI ethics addressed the undesirable results of implementing AI (e.g., bias, invasion of privacy, and job loss). Yet, they found nearly two-thirds of the AI ethics articles did not delve deeper into specific AI applications and the resulting ethical concerns. They thus argue that news coverage on AI ethics is still shallow in terms of content, and the recommendations provided to solve ethical dilemmas are not well aligned with the problem described. In addition, they pointed out that the increase in news articles addressing AI ethics since 2018 is likely being spurred by highly publicized, negative events, such as fatal accidents caused by driverless cars. It is important to note that public attention and perception formed around such events could be short-lived, especially when such events were framed as isolated incidents that can discourage citizens from engaging in ongoing and thoughtful deliberation on complicated ethical and regulatory issues. This is an alarming concern especially when Ouchchy et al. (2020) found that well-established ethical principles were not presented in the majority of AI ethics news articles to guide public deliberation.

Brantner and Saurwein (2021) examined how responsibility was assigned in Austrian media when the risk of automation was mentioned. They found that only 13.7% of articles addressed responsibility and accountability issues. Nearly half of the actors that were held responsible were companies, followed by political actors such as legislators (23.3%) and society (14.5%). This result may have revealed a propensity to favor industry self-regulation over government oversight. Longitudinal studies are needed to closely monitor news frames that are pro-government policies versus industry self-regulations to examine the potential correlations between the occurrence of such frames with policy and guidelines developments. Such efforts will illuminate the discursive power of news media in shaping public opinion and policy formation.

Moreover, the failure of a computer system is a crucial opportunity to provide insight into the technology itself and its social consequences (Karppi & Crawford, 2016). Particularly, incidents of technology failures or misuses can facilitate responsibility attribution and accountability when the technology causes harm to individuals and societies. One of the few critical framing studies that focus on highly publicized events when AI "misbehaves" is Suárez-Gonzalo et al.'s (2019) qualitative analysis of news stories on Microsoft's chatbot Tay. The chatbot started producing racist, homophobic, and sexist tweets after interacting with human users for 24 hours. Suárez-Gonzalo et al. (2019) found that three out of four news stories covering this event focused on identifying the culprits of Tay's failure, blaming Twitter users twice as often as Tay's creator, Microsoft. The news narratives overwhelmingly depicted Tay's failure as an orchestrated attack by malicious Twitter users (the responsible party) who misused and abused (causal effect) an innocent and vulnerable chatbot (the victim) resulting in its termination (consequence). Only 18% of the news stories focused on the interactions between human users and the chatbot as the probable cause, while only 14% ascribed the source of the problem to Microsoft's learning algorithms. Instead of focusing on the broader context to discuss how responsibility corresponds to the environment and the interplay between key actors (e.g., chatbot's owner and designers, Twitter, and users), Suárez-Gonzalo et al. (2019) astutely argued that the news discourse served the interests of AI industries by absolving Microsoft.

Thematic/Societal and Episodic/Personal Frames

The thematic versus episodic frame (Strekalova, 2015) is another important frame that can shape public opinion. The thematic frame highlights an issue as a general, broad trend that can occur in various contexts. Some researchers consider the thematic frame similar to the societal frame, in which an issue is emphasized as a systematic or societal problem (Zhang et al., 2015). In contrast, the episodic frame describes an issue by focusing on a specific example, case study, or isolated event (Iyengar, 1991) involving only certain individuals. Therefore, the episodic frame is closely related to the personal frame.

The thematic versus episodic frame is widely studied in health-related news to examine the framing effect on the perceived seriousness and relevance of a health issue (Kenterelidou, 2012). The episodic frame involves storytelling to invoke personal interest or empathy. However, this frame may turn an important societal issue into an isolated human-interest story and is ineffective for motivating collection action (Kim & Anne Willis, 2007). In AI news coverage, Chuan et al. (2019) discovered that the episodic frame is more likely to be used for business and economic topics. In contrast, the thematic frame is more typically associated with threats, policy, or political topics.

Competition and Collaboration Frames

Beyond the aforementioned frames that have been theorized for various science and emerging technologies, qualitative analyses have inductively identified several AI-specific frames for critiquing the social construction and power dynamics shaping the evolving relationship between humans and machines.

Focusing on healthcare, one of the domains in which the benefits of AI have been widely publicized, Bunz and Braghieri (2021) theorized about two AI-specific frames that position AI systems as "replacing and/or outperforming human experts" or "assisting humans in collaborations." They noticed that as early as 1984, early AI systems that predated deep learning were already placed in direct competition with human medical experts by being celebrated as more reliable and consistent. Moreover, as AI has advanced, they observed that AI has been increasingly anthropomorphized with intention and agency in news stories, which even equated the black-boxed nature of AI algorithms with doctors' "intuition" that cannot be explicitly explained. More importantly, the newsworthiness of AI systems often lies in their superiority over human experts, while the notion of "replacing" remains implicit. Their findings can be corroborated by Sun et al.'s (2020) results that identified three AI-specific lexical compounds: super AI (the superiority of AI over human intelligence), human-level AI (narrow AI that can perform domain-specific tasks typically requiring human intelligence), and evil AI (the damages, misuses, and ethical concerns associated with AI applications). Critically, Bunz and Braghieri (2021) pointed out that framing AI systems as autonomous entities and as a solution already outperforming human experts closes down the opportunity for questions, negotiations, and more importantly, the need for public participation imperative for demanding transparency, inclusivity, and accountability. Critical research is thus needed to further scrutinize frames regarding AI's relationship with humans – from supplementing to assisting, collaborating, defeating, and/or replacing – and with what types of human actors (elite experts versus less privileged workers) in specific domains (e.g., education) and applications (e.g., smart tutors).

The Magic and Religion Frame

Related to the frame of portraying AI as outperforming human experts, Stahl (1995) examined Time's framing of computer technologies since their introduction in 1979 for a ten-year period. He observed that Time's framing promoted definitions and understanding of computing technologies that are favorable to businesses, such as by highlighting business concerns (e.g., damage caused by hackers) while ignoring public concerns, such as technology-caused unemployment and the invasion of privacy for business gains. Critically, Stahl pointed out that magical and religious language was commonly used in the news discourse to not only signal computers as wondrous innovations, but more importantly, to normalize and legitimize the mythical, black-boxed nature of powerful, bewildering, miraculous technologies. As "a magical black box, computers were portrayed as a source of hope amid fear" (Stahl, 1995, p. 252).

The societal consequence of the magic frame is more than sensationalization, hyperbole, or marketing hype, especially when considering Spatola and Urbanska's (2020) experiment on semantic connections. Via experiments, they observed that people tend to make sense of AI by drawing parallels to divine entities characterized by superiority over humans. The magic frame bolstered by narratives of having faith in technological solutions may serve to dissuade people from critiquing or questioning the design and development of the technology, thus serving the interests of the tech industry to minimize government oversight.

Anthropomorphism Frame

Stahl (1995) also argues that "anthropomorphism is endemic to discourse about computers" (p. 246). He explained that, due to news media's heavy reliance on science and technology experts, the computing field's jargon, such as computer "memories" and computers "talking" to each other in "languages," was adopted by journalists. But the news discourse further amplified the anthropomorphism of computers by bestowing them with emotions, volitions, and intentions. At the same time, the extensive computers are social actors (CASA) literature suggests that when a computer mimics humans by demonstrating social cues (e.g., interactivity, gender, personality), people intuitively and habitually respond to the computer as though they were interacting with another human being, instead of cognitively processing the computer identity to determine how they should respond differently (Reeves & Nass, 1996; Nass & Moon, 2000).

Despite the popularity of anthropomorphic AI applications (e.g., chatbots and social robots), there exist few studies that explore not only how news stories may personify AI, but more importantly, what social structures and ideologies motivate the anthropomorphism frame. Döring and Poeschl's (2019) content analysis of media framing of intimate human–robot relationships revealed the reinforcement of stereotypical gender roles and heteronormativity with a focus on sexual intimacy in non-fictional media stories (e.g., news articles) and on emotional intimacy in fictional content (e.g., movies). Critically, focusing on the context of voice assistants that are increasingly part of our private lives, Turow (2021) argued that the anthropomorphism of voice technologies serves to create strong personal bonds between humans and the "humanoids" embodied by gentle (female) human voices. This allows people to willingly accept such technology into their private lives and conversations, despite mounting privacy concerns. Furthermore, Turow (2021) argues that building strong "humanoid-to-human connections that encouraged friendship and trust" would allow corporations to discourage "questions about the data their assistants were taking and using behind the scenes" (p. 58).

AI as a Nation's Future

One of the few critical framing studies that connects news frames to ideological forces such as nationalism is Köstler and Ossewaarde's (2022) analysis of the "AI futures" frame in the German government's communications about the "age of AI." The AI futures frame unequivocally articulates and promotes a particular version of Germany's future in which AI technologies play a vital, indispensable role. The AI futures frame equates technological advances with social progress, one of the most dominant news frames commonly observed around the globe. However, they argue that such a frame is propelled by concerns over the German economy, which has been primarily driven by traditional industries and has fallen behind in the digital revolution led by Silicon Valley. This futuristic frame thus reflects a nationalist ambition and imperative of catching up in the global AI race. Moreover, the German government strategically uses the nation's past industrial supremacy as a mirror of the AI future to safeguard its leadership position in the European economy, and in the process, reinforce the German political-industrial status quo. Critically, the AI futures frame and the associated stories, ideas, and visions also serve to reduce public uncertainty and hesitation about AI developments, as it transforms promises into requirements by constructing AI as the most crucial if not the only way forward to advance social welfare and national prosperity. Such a frame is widely disseminated by both the German government and news media to legitimize the mobilization of resources for AI.

As governments aligned with industries and businesses tend to evoke techno-nationalism that connects innovation to "national security, economic prosperity, and social stability" (Delios, Perchthold, & Capri, 2021, p. 5), the AI futures frame should be applied to other countries that are active players in the global AI competition, such as China. In 2017, the Chinese government promised to be the world's AI leader by 2030 (Roberts et al., 2020) while Chinese AI giants like Alibaba are leading the country's "going-out" initiatives that encourage Chinese enterprises to invest overseas and become global leaders (Tang, 2019). A similar pattern of mirroring past glories in the AI future frame can be observed in the naming of AI applications like Alibaba's AI advertising graphic designer, Luban, named after the legendary Chinese engineer from the Zhou Dynasty.

Scholars have repeatedly argued that media coverage of emerging technologies is frequently dominated by corporate interests and endorses technochauvinism that promotes the utopian belief in technological solutions to societal problems (Broussard, 2018). As D'angelo (2002) explains, news framing research addresses four essential goals: (1) to identify thematic frames; (2) to analyze the antecedent conditions producing specific frames; (3) to evaluate the mechanism underlying the framing effects; and (4) to examine how news frames influence societal-level processes such as public opinion and policy. Specifically focusing on the AI news discourse, existing news framing studies have primarily focused on the first goal via content analyses while more critical deliberation is needed to better address the second goal to deconstruct the discourse and expose frame sponsorship and issues relating to power (D'angelo et al., 2019).

CONCLUSION

News has always been an essential source for the public to learn about emerging trends and public issues, particularly for complex, fast-changing, controversial science topics like AI. However, superficial coverage with sensational, simplistic, and often dichotomous frames such as benefit versus risk can lead to polarized views. Additionally, for reporting on subjects such as health and science, journalists often rely on a limited variety of expert sources, as compared with political reporters who have much more heterogeneous sources of informed opinion to draw upon (Nelkin, 1987). The current AI news coverage "is sophisticated in tone (e.g., avoiding hype), but not yet in content" (Ouchchy et al., 2020). To facilitate meaningful public dialogues on AI, enhancing AI literacy among journalists is imperative. Journalists must avoid relying on simplistic, binary frames and expert sources from research institutions and tech industries that tend to uncritically embrace technochauvinism. We further argue that AI literacy is more than just technology literacy. In fact, it shares many commonalities with health literacy which involves cultural and conceptual understanding and the capacity of using health information in decision making (2012). Similarly, AI literacy is not about knowing how to operate an AI tool or be fluent in programming, but about conceptual knowledge, such as the relationship between data and machine learning, in order to make decisions (e.g., rejecting or granting permissions to data-sharing with AI services), adapt (e.g., evaluating the risk and benefit of AI applications depending on the context), and engage (e.g., participating in public forums regarding AI policy). In turn, news media can better develop critical, balanced articles independent of business and/or government agendas and help cultivate the development of AI literacy among the public.

FURTHER READING

Bengio, Y., Goodfellow, I., & Courville, A. (2017). *Deep learning* (Vol. 1). Cambridge, MA: MIT Press.

Bory, P. (2019). Deep new: The shifting narratives of artificial intelligence from Deep Blue to AlphaGo. *Convergence*, 25(4), 627–642.

Brantner, C., & Saurwein, F. (2021). Covering technology risks and responsibility: Automation, artificial intelligence, robotics, and algorithms in the media. *International Journal of Communication*, 15, 5074–5098.

Brokensha, S. (2020). Friend or foe? How online news outlets in South Africa frame artificial intelligence. *Ensovoort: Journal of Cultural Studies*, 41, 7.

Broussard, M. (2018). *Artificial unintelligence: How computers misunderstand the world*. MIT Press.

Bunz, M., & Braghieri, M. (2021). The AI doctor will see you now: Assessing the framing of AI in news coverage. *AI & Society*, 1–14.

Chuan, C. H., Tsai, W. H. S., & Cho, S. Y. (2019). Framing artificial intelligence in American newspapers. In *Proceedings of the 2019 AAAI/ACM conference on AI, ethics, and society* (pp. 339–344).

Curran, N. M., Sun, J., & Hong, J. W. (2020). Anthropomorphizing AlphaGo: A content analysis of the framing of Google DeepMind's AlphaGo in the Chinese and American press. *AI & Society*, 35(3), 727–735.

D'Angelo, P. (2002). News framing as a multiparadigmatic research program: A response to Entman. *Journal of Communication*, 52(4), 870–888.

D'Angelo, P., Lule, J., Neuman, W. R., Rodriguez, L., Dimitrova, D. V., & Carragee, K. M. (2019). Beyond framing: A forum for framing researchers. *Journalism & Mass Communication Quarterly*, 96(1), 12–30.

Delios, A., Perchthold, G., & Capri, A. (2021). Cohesion, COVID-19 and contemporary challenges to globalization. *Journal of World Business*, 56(3), 101197.

Deng, J., Dong, W., Socher, R., Li, L. J., Li, K., & Fei-Fei, L. (2009, June). ImageNet: A large-scale hierarchical image database. In *Proceedings of 2009 IEEE conference on computer vision and pattern recognition* (pp. 248–255).

Döring, N., & Poeschl, S. (2019). Love and sex with robots: A content analysis of media representations. *International Journal of Social Robotics*, 11(4), 665–677.

Entman, R. M. (1993). Framing: Toward clarification of a fractured paradigm. *Journal of Communication*, 43(4), 51–58.

Fast, E., & Horvitz, E. (2017). Long-term trends in the public perception of artificial intelligence. In *Proceedings of the AAAI conference on Artificial Intelligence* (Vol. 31, No. 1).

Frost, E. K., & Carter, S. M. (2020). Reporting of screening and diagnostic AI rarely acknowledges ethical, legal, and social implications: A mass media frame analysis. *BMC Medical Informatics and Decision Making,* 20(1), 1–10.

Goffman, E. (1974). *Frame analysis: An essay on the organization of experience.* Cambridge, MA: Harvard University Press.

Goodman, J. R., & Goodman, B. P. (2006). Beneficial or biohazard? How the media frame biosolids. *Public Understanding of Science,* 15(3), 359–375.

Holguín, L. M. (2018). Communicating artificial intelligence through newspapers: Where is the real danger. Thesis.

Iyengar, S. (1991). *Is anyone responsible? How television frames political issues.* Chicago, IL: University of Chicago Press.

Karppi, T. & Crawford, K. (2016). Social media, financial algorithms and the hack crash. *Theory, Culture & Society,* 33(1), 73–92.

Kenterelidou, C. (2012). Framing public health issues: The case of smoking ban in Greece, public health policy framing equals healthy framing of public policy?. *Journal of Communication in Healthcare,* 5(2), 116–128.

Kim, S. H., & Anne Willis, L. (2007). Talking about obesity: News framing of who is responsible for causing and fixing the problem. *Journal of Health Communication,* 12(4), 359–376.

Köstler, L., & Ossewaarde, R. (2022). The making of AI society: AI futures frames in German political and media discourses. *AI & Society,* 37(1), 249–263.

LeCun, Y., Bengio, Y., & Hinton, G. (2015). Deep learning. *Nature,* 521(7553), 436–444.

Lemańczyk, S. (2014). Science and national pride: The Iranian press coverage of nanotechnology, 2004–2009. *Science Communication,* 36(2), 194–218.

Liu, H., & Priest, S. (2009). Understanding public support for stem cell research: Media communication, interpersonal communication and trust in key actors. *Public Understanding of Science,* 18(6), 704–718.

Lupton, D. (2021). 'Flawed', 'cruel' and 'irresponsible': The framing of automated decision-making technologies in the Australian Press. Available at SSRN 3828952.

Mitchell, M. (2019). *Artificial intelligence: A guide for thinking humans.* Farrar, Straus and Giroux.

Nass, C., & Moon, Y. (2000). Machines and mindlessness: Social responses to computers. *Journal of Social Issues,* 56, 81–103.

Nelkin, D. (1987). *Selling science: How the press covers science and technology.* New York: W. H. Freeman.

Nguyen, D., & Hekman, E. (2022). A 'New arms race'? Framing China and the USA in AI news reporting: A comparative analysis of the Washington Post and South China Morning Post. *Global Media and China,* 7(1), 58–77.

Nisbet, M. C., Scheufele, D. A., Shanahan, J., Moy, P., Brossard, D., & Lewenstein, B. V. (2002). Knowledge, reservations, or promise? A media effects model for public perceptions of science and technology. *Communication Research,* 29(5), 584–608.

Nyholm, S., & Smids, J. (2016). The ethics of accident-algorithms for self-driving cars: An applied trolley problem? *Ethical Theory and Moral Practice,* 19(5), 1275–1289.

Ouchchy, L., Coin, A., & Dubljević, V. (2020). AI in the headlines: the portrayal of the ethical issues of artificial intelligence in the media. *AI & Society,* 35(4), 927–936.

Reeves, B., & Nass, C. (1996). *The media equation: How people treat computers, television, and new media like real people and places.* Cambridge.

Reinecke, P., Kokshagina, O., & Karanasios, S. (2021). Framing the regulation of artificial intelligence-based technologies. In *Proceedings of European conference on information systems.*

Roberts, H., Cowls, J., Morley, J., Taddeo, M., Wang, V., & Floridi, L. (2020). The Chinese approach to artificial intelligence: An analysis of policy, ethics, and regulation. *AI & Society,* 36(1), 59–77.

Schudson, M. (1983). *The news media and the democratic process* (Wye Resource Paper). New York: Aspen Institute for Humanistic Studies.

Spatola, N., & Urbanska, K. (2020). God-like robots: The semantic overlap between representation of divine and artificial entities. *AI & Society,* 35(2), 329–341.

Stahl, W. A. (1995). Venerating the black box: Magic in media discourse on technology. *Science, Technology, & Human Values,* 20(2), 234–258.

Strekalova, Y. A. (2015). Informing dissemination research: A content analysis of US newspaper coverage of medical nanotechnology news. *Science Communication*, 37(2), 151–172.

Suárez-Gonzalo, S., Mas Manchón, L., & Guerrero Solé, F. (2019). Tay is you: The attribution of responsibility in the algorithmic culture. *Observatorio* (OBS*), 13(2), 14.

Sun, S., Zhai, Y., Shen, B., & Chen, Y. (2020). Newspaper coverage of artificial intelligence: A perspective of emerging technologies. *Telematics and Informatics*, 53, 101433.

Tang, M. (2019). From "bringing-in" to "going-out": Transnationalizing China's Internet capital through state policies. *Chinese Journal of Communication*, 13(1), 27–46.

Turow, J. (2021). *The voice catchers*. New Haven, CT: Yale University Press.

Usher, N. (2017). Making business news: A production analysis of The New York Times. *International Journal of Communication*, 11, 20.

Vicsek, L. (2011). Costs and benefits of stem cell research and treatment: Media presentation and audience understanding in Hungary. *Science Communication*, 33(3), 309–340.

Vu, H. T. (2014). The online audience as gatekeeper: The influence of reader metrics on news editorial selection. *Journalism*, 15(8), 1094–1110.

Zhang, Y., Jin, Y., & Tang, Y. (2015). Framing depression: Cultural and organizational influences on coverage of a public health threat and attribution of responsibilities in Chinese news media, 2000–2012. *Journalism & Mass Communication Quarterly*, 92(1), 99–120.

24. Media representations of artificial intelligence: surveying the field

Saba Rebecca Brause, Jing Zeng, Mike S. Schäfer and Christian Katzenbach

1. INTRODUCTION: THE RELEVANCE OF MEDIA REPRESENTATIONS OF AI

Artificial intelligence (AI) is a key technology of contemporary societies, impacting numerous societal sectors such as health, economics, military or communication, and people's everyday lives (Stone et al., 2016). Even though the term "AI" is applied to a wide range of technologies, and as societies are still determining the shape and role the technology should take (Kaplan & Haenlein, 2020), AI has become prominent in public debates in many nations over the world. In these debates, certain understandings of AI are advanced, and different stakeholders critically engage with the technology and its role in society, contributing to the communicative construction of the technology.

News and social media are a crucial part of these debates, and of communication about science and technology more generally (Brossard, 2013). Journalistic legacy media – including newspapers and magazines, but also television and radio – contribute to the dissemination of knowledge and information about technologies. They can set the agenda for public debate, shape public perceptions by framing their coverage of a given technology to highlight certain aspects while neglecting others, and may influence public attitudes by promoting certain evaluations of technologies (Rogers et al., 1993; Strekalova, 2015). Hence, legacy media coverage of AI technologies is an important indicator of the central issues, actors, frames and evaluations attached to technology, and a critical arena where stakeholders negotiate future pathways for AI and its role in societies.

Social media like Instagram, YouTube, Facebook, or TikTok, on the other hand, host user-generated content, facilitate user interaction (Carr & Hayes, 2015), and are important information sources for the public (Newman et al., 2021). They are also important repositories of public opinions (McGregor, 2020) – on science and technology, research has shown that user-generated content online may be a better indicator of public concern than news coverage (Chung, 2011; Soffer, 2019).

Consequently, scholars from various disciplines have started to analyze media representations of AI. This chapter surveys this emerging research field and its characteristics with regard to the countries and media under study and the methodologies employed. This yields findings about which aspects of AI receive high visibility in public debates – and which are neglected. Based on this assessment, the chapter lays out directions for future research.

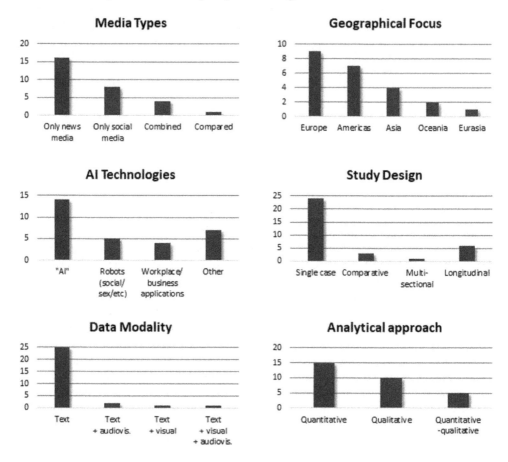

Figure 24.1   Summary of research on media representations of AI

2.   FIELD OVERVIEW

Our overview presented here is based on a systematic, in-depth analysis of scholarly litera-ture from the SCOPUS and Web of Science databases. We first identified over 600 articles containing the keywords "artificial intelligence" and "media". Among them, we focused on 1) original media analyses that 2) analyze AI-related coverage of any form (including, e.g., robots, voice assistants, and algorithms). This resulted in 30 studies that were left for content analysis.[1] Our analyses of these articles focus on the *medium, geographic,* and *technological foci* of the studies, as well as their *research design*. Figure 24.1 summarizes the results.

Overall, scholarship on media representation of AI is rapidly expanding in recent years. The earliest study in our sample was published in 2017. Regarding content, current scholarship on the topic focuses mostly on (1) legacy media, (2) cases from "Western" countries, and (3) AI

---

[1]   For a detailed description of this process and the complete article list, please check https://osf.io/erf45/?view_only=6531c135168b427facb207b83c9feef9.

as a generic phenomenon rather than on specific applications. Methodologically, the field is dominated by (1) single-case studies, (2) quantitative methods, and (3) written text analyses.

Among the studies reviewed, more than half focus exclusively on legacy media, whereas more than a quarter look exclusively at social media. Five studies analyze both media types without systematically comparing them, while one compares them explicitly. Most studies on legacy media analyze newspapers, news portals, or news agencies, while studies on social media mostly concentrate on Twitter.

The geographical focus of the research field is heavily skewed toward "Western" contexts. For instance, research focuses overwhelmingly on Northern American (23%) and European countries (30%), with particular attention being given to Anglophone countries. One-third of the studies involve the US or the UK as cases.

Regarding the AI technologies under consideration, a big portion of research (47%) takes a generic approach to "AI", without looking at specific applications of AI-empowered technology. Applications that are covered include robots (17%) and AI tools for businesses and workplaces (13%).

Methodologically, the vast majority of the studies use case study designs, focusing on one specific case (80%). Three studies use a comparative approach, comparing (1) across countries, (2) across events such as the chess game of IBM's Deep Blue versus Garry Kasparov and the Go game of Google DeepMind's AlphaGo vs Lee Sedol, and (3) across media. Six studies contain an additional longitudinal component, comparing AI media representations over time.

Analytically, studies have mostly employed quantitative approaches (50%), followed by qualitative (33%) and mixed qualitative-quantitative approaches (17%). The most frequently used analytical methods are content analysis, either manual (57%) or automated (17%), and sentiment analysis (10% manual, 17% automated). Other analytical approaches include critical discourse analysis and spatial analysis. In terms of the analyzed modalities, the research is very one-sided: It focuses almost exclusively on written text (83%). Only two studies combine text and audiovisual, one combines text and visual, and one combines all three data types.

Concerning the analytical objective, much of the research identifies key terms, topics, themes, or issues in the AI debate (53%), whether regarding the technology in general or a specific issue, for example, ethics, related to it. Other predominant foci are attitudes, sentiments, or moral evaluations expressed in the debate (57%).

3. NEWS MEDIA REPRESENTATIONS OF AI

3.1 Prevalence of AI News Coverage

The degree of news media attention that AI has received over time is an important issue. News media are important sources of information and can set the public and political agenda for debates about new technologies (Strekalova, 2015; Rogers et al., 1993). The prevalence of news reporting on AI can therefore serve as an indicator of the importance accorded to AI in the public sphere.

But few studies have analyzed this aspect so far. Those that did show a marked increase in media attention for AI since the 1990s. In the US, after an "AI winter" between 1987 and 1995, New York Times coverage of AI has been steadily increasing since 1995, and dramatically so between 2009 and 2016 (Fast & Horvitz, 2017, p. 966). This upward trend was confirmed by a study analyzing a larger sample of US newspapers since 2009 and found to have further accelerated since 2016 (Chuan et al., 2019). Similarly, Italian news coverage on robots has doubled both in numbers and proportion within the overall news volume between 2014 and 2018 (Righetti & Carradore, 2019).

3.2   News Framing of Artificial Intelligence

While the amount of news media coverage may set the public agenda and influence what the public thinks *about*, news media can also shape *how* the public thinks about technologies by framing them in certain ways (Scheufele & Lewenstein, 2005). Accordingly, a considerable number of studies have investigated the news framing of AI. Particular attention has been given to topics or keywords that are being covered, but also to the evaluations expressed in media coverage as well as specific hopes and concerns.

3.2.1   Main topics in news coverage of AI

One research strand has investigated the issues that AI technologies have been associated with in news media. The result is clear and holds true across countries: Business and economic topics – such as AI's potential to boost the Chinese economy (Zeng et al., 2022) or to increase economic productivity in Turkey (Sarisakaloglu, 2021) – dominate news coverage. They were the most frequent topics both in US newspapers between 2009 and 2018, and the Chinese People's Daily between 2014 and 2018 (Chuan et al., 2019; Zeng et al., 2022). Economic benefits were also the second most important theme in Turkish newspapers in 2019 (Sarisakaloglu, 2021), and in Germany, the economic benefits and competitiveness frame provided in the political discourse was found to be amplified in news media (Köstler & Ossewaarde, 2022).

Another issue found to be pervasive in media coverage on AI was work and workplace-related topics such as robots' ability to perform jobs as well as humans, which were strongly prevalent in Italian and Turkish media (Righetti & Carradore, 2019; Sarisakaloglu, 2021).

Other topics were shown to have received less, even marginal coverage. AI applications for, and AI representations in, entertainment appeared less often in news media and did so mostly around events, like AI-related movie releases (Chuan et al., 2019; Zeng et al., 2022). Notably, AI ethics were found to be a marginal or absent topic in countries like Turkey and China (Sarisakaloglu, 2021; Zeng et al., 2022).

3.2.2   Evaluations of AI in news coverage

Another aspect of news framing of AI is the evaluation of the technology (Entman, 1993). Several studies have considered this aspect. Again, their results converge in major points: Generally, AI news media representations were found to be overwhelmingly positive. In the Chinese People's Daily, sentiment expressed toward AI was not just significantly more positive than negative, it got even more positive from 2015 to 2018 (Zeng et al., 2022). In Turkish newspapers, frames with positive evaluations of AI dominated news coverage (Sarisakaloglu, 2021). In the US, articles in the New York Times, as well as article headlines of a larger sample of newspapers, were found to be overwhelmingly positive over several decades until the mid- to late-2010s (Garvey & Maskal, 2020; Fast & Horvitz, 2017). An analysis of full articles between 2009 and 2018 in the five most widely read US newspapers showed more nuanced results, however: while the sentiment expressed in AI reporting before 2015 was mostly positive or mixed and remained dominant throughout, negative evaluations have been steadily increasing since 2015 (Chuan et al., 2019).

3.2.3   Hopes and fears regarding AI in news coverage

Studies focusing on the US have also analyzed specific hopes and fears associated with AI in the news. For the five most widely read US newspapers between 2009 and 2018, Chuan et al. (2019) found that hopes were much more prevalent than concerns and that they focused on the economy and human well-being. Concerns were mostly linked to technological short-comings, job loss, and privacy. Analyzing the New York Times between 1956 and 2016, Fast and Horvitz (2017) noted a tripling of the fear that humans might lose control over AI, and an increase in ethical and work-related concerns, while hopes increased for AI healthcare applications.

3.3   AI-Related News Sourcing and News Event Coverage

By being cited in news media, stakeholders can shape public debate on science and technology (Gerhards & Schäfer, 2009). In addition, stakeholders can attempt to shape news coverage by staging media events (Katz, 1980). Several scholars have therefore examined sourcing and event coverage in AI news coverage.

Regarding sources, studies have shown that businesses and especially official and high-level voices appear particularly often in news coverage on AI. Chuan et al. (2019) showed that companies and businesses were the most cited sources in the five most widely read US news-papers between 2009 and 2018. Concerning UK outlets, Brennen et al. (2022) illustrated in the example of Google's Maven project controversy how news reporting downplays employees' concerns by citing only official corporate statements and CEO narratives.

Analyzing news coverage of media events about AI technologies – particularly the widely covered chess match of Gary Kasparov against IBM's Deep Blue in 1995, and the equally widely discussed Go match of Lee Sedol against Google DeepMind's AlphaGo in 2016 – several studies note the companies' successful use of the events as a public relations platform for their technologies and brand (Bory, 2019; Goode, 2018; Elish & boyd, 2018). Additionally, Elish and boyd (2018) argued that news coverage reproduced corporate hype narratives that obscure the limitations of AI technologies.

3.4   News Media Coverage of Specific Topics Related to AI

Apart from exploring AI news media coverage in general, scholars have also investigated news representations of specific topics in relation to AI technologies. Particular attention has been paid to AI ethics, the human-AI relationship, and the implications of AI in the work-place. Additional topics of analysis include AI media coverage about gender, as well as health research and care.

3.4.1   News media coverage of AI ethics

Studies on the coverage of ethical issues have focused on AI in general, algorithms as part of AI technologies, and voice assistants.

Research on AI and algorithms in UK newspapers and international English-language newspapers has shown that news media mostly discussed undesired or unfair outcomes of algorithmic decisions – such as discrimination through AI based on race, sex, or religion – as well as the inscrutability or accountability of those automated decisions (Barn, 2020; Ouchchy et al., 2020).

Regarding ethical aspects of voice assistants, the most discussed issue in Indonesian newspapers between 2010 and 2020 was privacy concerns – even though the topic only appeared after 2015, it became highly salient after several data leaks in 2019 (Arifin & Lennerfors, 2022). Other topics included voice assistants' technological flaws, but also positive aspects such as their inclusivity and helpfulness in precarious situations (Arifin & Lennerfors, 2022).

Overall, coverage of AI-related ethical issues has been found to be lacking references to ethical frameworks as well as detail, for example, technological factors and implementation (Ouchchy et al., 2020). Arifin and Lennerfors (2022) similarly found ethical issues' coverage regarding voice assistants in Indonesia to lack depth and, moreover, to be presented as not critical – solved in the present or "relegated to the future" (p. 32).

3.4.2   News media coverage of the human-AI relationship

News coverage on the relationship between humans and AI has focused, first, on the conflation of human-replacing AI with human-centered intelligence amplification (IA). Studying AI debates in Danish newspapers and magazines between 1956 and 2021, Hansen (2022) observed a steady increase in coverage of AI and its relation to humans since the 1980s. While news media tend to not clearly distinguish between AI envisioned to replace humans and a more human-centered IA envisioned to enhance human intelligence, it clearly refers to one or the other. And it uses neutral or negative descriptions for AI more frequently, and neutral or positive descriptions for IA.

Studies have also analyzed media representations of romantic and sexual human-robot relationships. Döring and Poeschl (2019) found that English-language non-fictional media portrayed these as mostly heterosexual relationships, that were more sexual than emotional.

Additionally, regarding media portrayals of anthropomorphism and threat evaluations of AI, Curran et al. (2020) compared Chinese and American press coverage of AlphaGo and found that in both countries, newspapers dedicated a lot of effort into clearly delineating human from machine using this differentiation to argue for the non-threatening nature of AI.

3.4.3   News media coverage of AI in the workplace

A third research strand focuses on news media representations of AI in the workplace, identifying positive to more nuanced coverage. While Samers (2021) focused on the debate of the increasing presence of AI and robotics in the workplace in the US-focused economic and business-oriented press, Duffy et al. (2022) examined the framing of AI and automation in the workplace in trade journals. In line with the abovementioned positive sentiment toward AI in general news coverage, trade journals also framed AI and automation in the workplace overwhelmingly positively (Duffy et al., 2022). Central themes in this context were the inevitability of AI in the workplace, the potential for human-machine collaboration, the elimination of human limitations, and the salvation of workers from undesirable tasks. Samers (2021) finds a more nuanced debate in the economic and business-oriented press, ranging from catastrophic employment predictions, over more nuanced sectoral analyses of negative consequences, to hopes for resistance and dismissal of dystopian narratives.

3.4.4   News media coverage of AI in relation to gender, and health research and care

Other AI-related topics in the news media have received less scholarly consideration. They include gendered reporting about AI, and AI in health research and care, finding uncritical gendered reporting of sex robots and positive, realistic coverage of AI in healthcare. Critically examining the role of gender in Spanish newspaper reporting of AI and robotics, Tajahuerce-Angel and Franco (2019) found that news media are uncritically representing the androcentrism of robotics and AI research and development and reproducing stereotypical gender roles and sexual relations in their coverage of sex robots. Regarding the coverage of AI systems in health research and care, British and Canadian news media portray them overwhelmingly positively, refraining from dystopian narratives of health practitioner replacement, and referring instead to the uses of AI for clinical diagnosis, treatment and prediction, hospital management, digital health applications, and pharmaceutical research and development (Samuel et al., 2021).

4.   SOCIAL MEDIA REPRESENTATIONS OF AI

On social media, a broad range of individuals and stakeholders take part in discussions about AI-related issues. By harnessing posts and metadata on social media, researchers can monitor and analyze changes in the public's engagement with the topic – using dimensions similar to the analysis of news media.

4.1   Prevalence of AI on Social Media over Time and Space

The observability of temporal changes in social media data allows researchers to study public interest in AI over time – and several studies have done this. Informed by data from Twitter, Facebook, Weibo, and WeChat, researchers showed that interest in AI-related technologies has grown steadily over recent years (Zeng et al., 2022; Righetti & Carradore, 2019; Neri & Cozman, 2020). Moreover, geolocation information of social media posts and their authors enables the examination of regional disparities in people's interest in AI (Neri & Cozman, 2020; Gao et al., 2020; Yigitcanlar et al., 2020; Regona et al., 2022). For instance, Yigitcanlar et al. (2020) analyzed geolocation data from Twitter for Australia, comparing how the interest in AI varies across different states/territories in the country and finding that over half of the tweets stem from New South Wales, while the Northern Territory population shows almost no interest in the topic (0%). Likewise, with the help of Weibo users' profile information, Gao et al. (2020) examined how interest in AI-related technologies differs between low-income regions and high-income regions.

4.2   Content of Social Media Communication about AI

Social media also offer insights into people's perceptions of, and opinions about, AI and related technologies. Instead of relying on self-reported data from surveys and interviews, scholars can use social media posts, engagement metrics, and user comments to gather people's perceptions of AI.

Sentiment analysis of social media posts or user comments, for example, can help detect and compare attitudes toward AI in debates on digital platforms (Wu et al., 2022; Zeng et al., 2022). Scholarship shows that attitudes toward AI vary depending on the domain of application. For instance, in the fields of medical care (Gao et al., 2020), urban design (Yigitcanlar et al., 2020), and advertising (Wu et al., 2021), research detects more positive sentiment toward AI applications. On the other hand, robots, especially humanoid robots, trigger more negative sentiments and fears among the internet public (Westerlund, 2020; Strait et al., 2017). The widespread antagonism toward robots has been widely documented and discussed, but it is important to acknowledge cultural differences in attitudes toward robots and other AI-related technologies. For instance, in East Asia where the application of AI is long-established, antagonism toward robots, as well as AI in general, is much less visible online (Zeng et al., 2022).

4.3 Sources and Specific Topics in Social Media Communication about AI

The complexity of communication centered around AI makes the role of stakeholders and experts in guiding public opinion particularly important. Thanks to the traceable activity of online communication, social media data is also useful for identifying actors influencing (or attempting to influence) public opinions on AI (Grover et al., 2022; Zeng et al., 2022).

Scholars have done so repeatedly, with results mirroring those for news media: For instance, Zeng and colleagues' (2022) study reveals that industry actors are the most active and vocal actors shaping AI discussion on Chinese social media, echoing findings for legacy media in Western countries (cf. Section 3). As these commercial actors' discussion of AI in public domains is largely self-serving, it comes as no surprise that their narratives focus on the "benefits" of varied AI technologies.

However, online discussion about AI is not always dominated by stakeholders promoting AI-related technologies. Research of social media discussion also sheds light on actors who communicate about AI-associated risks. Neri and Cozman's (2020) study of Twitter content about AI, for instance, focuses on risk communicators who amplify or attenuate messages of risks about AI to the public (p. 667). The results from their Twitter analysis show that existential risks represent the vast majority of sources of concern. Beyond risks, another specific topic investigated in social media debates was ethics (Westerlund, 2020). This research found that important ethical aspects debated in relation to AI were their social impacts, such as in the form of killer robots or robots taking control over humanity, and economic impacts, such as robots' effect on labor.

5. SUMMARY AND THE WAY FORWARD

This chapter, surveying research on news and social media representations of AI, found that a rising number of studies have analyzed such representations. Interestingly, their findings converge in several dimensions:

- *Prevalence of AI in news coverage and on social media.* Studies on the prevalence of AI both *in news and social media* show an increase in news and public interest in AI over time.
- *Framing AI.* Studies have also analyzed *how* AI is discussed. In *news media*, central topics, themes, issues, and keywords have been identified. Business and economic topics

were found to dominate in several countries. A small number of studies also examined specific hopes and concerns about AI in US news media. While hopes were found to be more prevalent than concerns, and linked particularly to the economy and human well-being, fears – for example, about the loss of human control over machines – also starkly increased. Sentiment about AI was an important research focus both in *news and social media*, finding that AI is being discussed overwhelmingly positively in both.

* *Sources in news and social media debates on AI*. Research both on *news and social media* has also examined *who* is discussing AI. Business representatives and industry actors were found to be particularly prevalent in both news and social media.
* *Specific topics related to AI in news and social media*. Some scholars have also investigated the *news and social media* discussions on specific topics related to AI. One focus in news media studies, that was also addressed in a social media study, was AI ethics. Several *news media* studies also focused on human-AI relations and AI's workplace impacts. Also specifically investigated – even though to a lesser extent – were AI related to gender, and healthcare and research in *news media*, and AI risk on *social media*.

These results show – across different media and countries – that media portrayals of AI are predominantly positive, using economic framing and giving voice to established, institutional and often economic stakeholders. Given that media narratives and framings do shape policy-making, economic investments, and research activities, especially in fields as emergent and under-defined as AI (Natale & Ballatore, 2017; Bareis & Katzenbach, 2021), it is concerning that such affirmative positions are hegemonic and that critical perspectives and the limitations of AI technologies receive considerably less attention.

Apart from these findings, the review also shows that scholarship in the field is still limited in various respects. First, despite the importance of public debates about AI and the central role of news and social media therein, scholarly attention on these topics is still young. In addition, the overwhelming majority of these publications focused on news media coverage, whereas social media communication about AI has been studied considerably less. Studies comparing the two systematically are very rare. Moreover, within news media studies, most analyses have focused on newspapers, while Twitter has received the vast amount of attention within social media-based studies of AI debates.

Second, regarding the analyzed national and cultural contexts, research has focused strongly on "Western" countries, with the US and the UK being the focus of most studies. Regarding the specific AI technologies under consideration, the umbrella term of "AI" or "artificial intelligence" is the most frequent focus of study, although robots and AI applications for businesses and workplaces are also frequently studied.

Third, methodologically, research has mostly focused on single case studies and employed quantitative approaches. The most frequent analytical methods were manual content analysis, followed by automated content and sentiment analysis. Regarding the data, existing research is very one-sided in that it focuses almost exclusively on written text while neglecting visual and multimodal representations of AI.

Future research on AI media representations should remedy these shortcomings and rebalance the biases of the field. Doing so should provide a more comprehensive picture of important public communication about AI that profoundly shapes how the technology is seen and dealt with in societies around the world.

Table 24.1   Themes in the literature on news and social media representations of AI

News media	Social media
Prevalence of AI in news coverage	Prevalence of AI on social media
News framing of AI • Main topics/themes/issues/words • Evaluations • Hopes and fears regarding AI	Content about AI • Sentiment
Sourcing and event coverage	Sources
Specific topics • Ethics • Human-AI relations • Workplace impact • Gender, healthcare/research	Specific topics • Risks • Ethics

REFERENCES

Arifin, A. A., & Lennerfors, T. T. (2022). Ethical aspects of voice assistants: A critical discourse analysis of Indonesian media texts. *Journal of Information, Communication and Ethics in Society*, *20*(1), 18–36. https://doi.org/10.1108/JICES-12-2020-0118

Bareis, J., & Katzenbach, C. (2021). Talking AI into being: The narratives and imaginaries of national AI strategies and their performative politics. *Science, Technology, & Human Values*, 1–27. https://doi.org/10.1177/01622439211030007

Barn, B. S. (2020). Mapping the public debate on ethical concerns: Algorithms in mainstream media. *Journal of Information, Communication and Ethics in Society*, *18*(1), 124–139. https://doi.org/10.1108/JICES-04-2019-0039

Bory, P. (2019). Deep new: The shifting narratives of artificial intelligence from Deep Blue to AlphaGo. *Convergence*, *25*(4), 627–642. https://doi.org/10.1177/1354856519829679

Brennen, J. S., Howard, P. N., & Nielsen, R. K. (2022). What to expect when you're expecting robots: Futures, expectations, and pseudo-artificial general intelligence in UK news. *Journalism*, *23*(1), 22–38. https://doi.org/10.1177/1464884920947535

Brossard, D. (2013). New media landscapes and the science information consumer. *Proceedings of the National Academy of Sciences*, *110*(supplement_3), 14096–14101. https://doi.org/10.1073/pnas.1212744110

Carr, C. T., & Hayes, R. A. (2015). Social media: Defining, developing, and divining. *Atlantic Journal of Communication*, *23*(1), 46–65. https://doi.org/10.1080/15456870.2015.972282

Chuan, C.-H., Tsai, W.-H. S., & Cho, S. Y. (2019). Framing Artificial Intelligence in American newspapers. *Proceedings of the 2019 AAAI/ACM Conference on AI, Ethics, and Society*, 339–344. https://doi.org/10.1145/3306618.3314285

Chung, I. J. (2011). Social amplification of risk in the internet environment. *Risk Analysis*, *31*(12), 1883–1896. https://doi.org/10.1111/j.1539-6924.2011.01623.x

Curran, N. M., Sun, J., & Hong, J.-W. (2020). Anthropomorphizing AlphaGo: A content analysis of the framing of Google DeepMind's AlphaGo in the Chinese and American press. *AI & Society*, *35*(3), 727–735. https://doi.org/10.1007/s00146-019-00908-9

Döring, N., & Poeschl, S. (2019). Love and sex with robots: A content analysis of media representations. *International Journal of Social Robotics*, *11*(4), 665–677. https://doi.org/10.1007/s12369-019-00517-y

Duffy, A., Prahl, A., & Ling Yan-Hui, A. (2022). The inexorable rise of the robots: Trade journals' framing of machinery in the workplace. *Journalism*, *23*(2), 409–426. https://doi.org/10.1177/1464884920969078

Elish, M. C., & boyd, d. (2018). Situating methods in the magic of Big Data and AI. *Communication Monographs*, *85*(1), 57–80. https://doi.org/10.1080/03637751.2017.1375130

Entman, R. M. (1993). Framing: Toward clarification of a fractured paradigm. *Journal of Communication*, *43*(4), 51–58. https://doi.org/10.1111/j.1460-2466.1993.tb01304.x

Fast, E., & Horvitz, E. (2017). Long-term trends in the public perception of artificial intelligence. *Proceedings of the Thirty-First AAAI Conference on Artificial Intelligence*, 963–969.

Gao, S., He, L., Chen, Y., Li, D., & Lai, K. (2020). Public perception of Artificial Intelligence in medical care: Content analysis of social media. *Journal of Medical Internet Research*, *22*(7), e16649. https://doi.org/10.2196/16649

Garvey, C., & Maskal, C. (2020). Sentiment analysis of the news media on Artificial Intelligence does not support claims of negative bias against Artificial Intelligence. *OMICS: A Journal of Integrative Biology*, *24*(5), 286–299. https://doi.org/10.1089/omi.2019.0078

Gerhards, J., & Schäfer, M. S. (2009). Two normative models of science in the public sphere: Human genome sequencing in German and US mass media. *Public Understanding of Science*, *18*(4), 437–451. https://doi.org/10.1177/0963662507082891

Goode, L. (2018). Life, but not as we know it: A.I. and the popular imagination. *Culture Unbound: Journal of Current Cultural Research*, *10*(2), 185–207. https://doi.org/10.3384/cu.2000.1525.2018102185

Grover, P., Kar, A. K., & Dwivedi, Y. K. (2022). Understanding artificial intelligence adoption in operations management: Insights from the review of academic literature and social media discussions. *Annals of Operations Research*, *308*(1), 177–213. https://doi.org/10.1007/s10479-020-03683-9

Hansen, S. S. (2022). Public AI imaginaries: How the debate on artificial intelligence was covered in Danish newspapers and magazines 1956–2021. *Nordicom Review*, *43*(1), 56–78. https://doi.org/10.2478/nor-2022-0004

Kaplan, A., & Haenlein, M. (2020). Rulers of the world, unite! The challenges and opportunities of artificial intelligence. *Business Horizons*, *63*(1), 37–50. https://doi.org/10.1016/j.bushor.2019.09.003

Katz, E. (1980). Media events: The sense of occasion. *Studies in Visual Communication*, *6*(3), 84–89.

Köstler, L., & Ossewaarde, R. (2022). The making of AI society: AI futures frames in German political and media discourses. *AI & Society*, *37*(1), 249–263. https://doi.org/10.1007/s00146-021-01161-9

McGregor, S. C. (2020). "Taking the temperature of the room": How political campaigns use social media to understand and represent public opinion. *Public Opinion Quarterly*, *84*(S1), 236–256. https://doi.org/10.1093/poq/nfaa012

Natale, S., & Ballatore, A. (2017). Imagining the thinking machine: Technological myths and the rise of artificial intelligence. *Convergence*, *26*(1), 3–18. https://doi.org/10.1177/1354856517715164

Neri, H., & Cozman, F. (2020). The role of experts in the public perception of risk of artificial intelligence. *AI & Society*, *35*(3), 663–673. https://doi.org/10.1007/s00146-019-00924-9

Newman, N., Fletcher, R., Schulz, A., Andi, S., Robertson, C. T., & Nielsen, R. K. (2021). *Reuters Institute Digital News Report 2021* (Reuters Institute Digital News Report). Reuters Institute for the Study of Journalism. https://ora.ox.ac.uk/objects/uuid:e2106591-07c7-4b0b-9e93-a0d06bb4b86a

Ouchchy, L., Coin, A., & Dubljević, V. (2020). AI in the headlines: The portrayal of the ethical issues of artificial intelligence in the media. *AI & Society*, *35*(4), 927–936. https://doi.org/10.1007/s00146-020-00965-5

Regona, M., Yigitcanlar, T., Xia, B., & Li, R. Y. (2022). Artificial Intelligent technologies for the construction industry: How are they perceived and utilized in Australia? *Journal of Open Innovation: Technology, Market, and Complexity*, *8*(1). https://doi.org/10.3390/joitmc8010016

Righetti, N., & Carradore, M. (2019). From robots to social robots. Trends, representation and Facebook engagement of robot-related news stories published by Italian online news media. *Italian Sociological Review*, *9*(3), 431. https://doi.org/10.13136/isr.v9i3.298

Rogers, E. M., Dearing, J. W., & Bregman, D. (1993). The anatomy of agenda-setting research. *Journal of Communication*, *43*(2), 68–84. https://doi.org/10.1111/j.1460-2466.1993.tb01263.x

Samers, M. (2021). Futurological fodder: On communicating the relationship between artificial intelligence, robotics, and employment. *Space and Polity*, *25*(2), 237–256. https://doi.org/10.1080/13562576.2021.1985856

Samuel, G., Diedericks, H., & Derrick, G. (2021). Population health AI researchers' perceptions of the public portrayal of AI: A pilot study. *Public Understanding of Science, 30*(2), 196–211. https://doi .org/10.1177/0963662520965490

Sarısakaloğlu, A. (2021). Framing discourses in Turkish news coverage regarding artificial intelligence technologies' prospects and challenges. *Turkish Review of Communication Studies, Year 2021*(37), 20–38. https://doi.org/10.17829/turcom.803338

Scheufele, D. A., & Lewenstein, B. V. (2005). The public and nanotechnology: How citizens make sense of emerging technologies. *Journal of Nanoparticle Research, 7*(6), 659–667. https://doi.org/10.1007 /s11051-005-7526-2

Soffer, O. (2019). Assessing the climate of public opinion in the user comments era: A new epistemology. *Journalism, 20*(6), 772–787. https://doi.org/10.1177/1464884917714938

Stone, P., Brooks, R., Brynjolfsson, E., Calo, R., Etzioni, O., Hager, G., Hirschberg, J., Kalyanakrishnan, S., Kamar, E., Kraus, S., Leyton-Brown, K., Parkes, D., Press, W., Saxenian, A., Shah, J., Tambe, M., & Teller, A. (2016). *Artificial Intelligence and Life in 2030* (Report of the 2015-2016 Study Panel; One Hundred Year Study on Artificial Intelligence). Stanford University. https://apo.org.au/ node/210721

Strait, M. K., Aguillon, C., Contreras, V., & Garcia, N. (2017). The public's perception of humanlike robots: Online social commentary reflects an appearance-based uncanny valley, a general fear of a "Technology Takeover", and the unabashed sexualization of female-gendered robots. *2017 26th IEEE International Symposium on Robot and Human Interactive Communication (RO-MAN)*, 1418–1423. https://doi.org/10.1109/ROMAN.2017.8172490

Strekalova, Y. A. (2015). Informing dissemination research: A content analysis of U.S. newspaper coverage of medical nanotechnology news. *Science Communication, 37*(2), 151–172. https://doi.org /10.1177/1075547014555025

Tajahuerce-Ángel, I., & Franco, Y. G. (2019). Spanish digital newspapers and information on robotics and artificial intelligence: An approach to imageries and realities from a gender perspective. *Revista de Comunicación de La SEECI, 48*, 173–189. ProQuest One Academic; ProQuest One Literature. https://doi.org/10.15198/seeci.2019.48.173-189

Westerlund, M. (2020). The ethical dimensions of public opinion on smart robots. *Technology Innovation Management Review, 10*(2). timreview.ca/article/1326

Wu, L., Dodoo, N. A., Wen, T. J., & Ke, L. (2022). Understanding Twitter conversations about artificial intelligence in advertising based on natural language processing. *International Journal of Advertising, 41*(4), 685–702. https://doi.org/10.1080/02650487.2021.1920218

Yigitcanlar, T., Kankanamge, N., Regona, M., Ruiz Maldonado, A., Rowan, B., Ryu, A., Desouza, K. C., Corchado, J. M., Mehmood, R., & Li, R. Y. (2020). Artificial Intelligence technologies and related urban planning and development concepts: How are they perceived and utilized in Australia? *Journal of Open Innovation: Technology, Market, and Complexity, 6*(4). https://doi.org/10.3390/ joitmc6040187

Zeng, J., Chan, C., & Schäfer, M. S. (2022). Contested Chinese dreams of AI? Public discourse about Artificial intelligence on WeChat and People's Daily Online. *Information, Communication & Society, 25*(3), 319–340. https://doi.org/10.1080/1369118X.2020.1776372

25. Educational imaginaries of AI

Lina Rahm

INTRODUCTION

Currently, there is a public request for citizens to engage in, and educate themselves about, the societal and ethical effects that artificial intelligence (AI) and other autonomous systems produce (e.g., Ministry of Education and Research, 2018). Further, international education policies assert that citizens also need to acquire various skills to successfully adapt to the changes that AI will bring to society (OECD, 2019). What political and educational problems are such requests, in fact, a solution to? And what are citizens supposed to learn exactly? This chapter seeks to investigate and problematize how knowledge about AI is construed in international education and AI ethics policies, and what social, political, and epistemic meanings are produced by that knowledge. The purpose is to support the development of critically reflexive and just education and education policies about AI futures. As such, this chapter can be seen as a step toward further joining educational, and science and technology studies in establishing analyses of *educational imaginaries* (Rahm, 2021) as a research area focusing on collectively held, institutionally stabilized, and publicly performed visions of desirable futures, animated by shared understandings of forms of social life and social order attainable through, and supportive of, advances in *education about* science and technology (to paraphrase Jasanoff & Kim, 2015).[1]

Education and new knowledge are often presented as a common good and a way to engage citizens in important technical issues, thereby creating more democratic societies as well as more just technological systems. In this chapter, I will argue that such educational imaginaries are too rarely put under critical scrutiny. The aim of this chapter is to contribute with a new scientific understanding of the political preconditions that *broad education about AI* rests on and thereby support more rational and equitable knowledge practices—practices that can enhance the development of critically reflexive and just AI futures. This main objective will be pursued through the following research questions:

1. How are AI-related knowledge and anticipated competencies construed and represented in international policies about future societies?
2. What social, political, and epistemic meanings, and potential injustices, are produced, respectively, by the above constructions and representations?

Most research on AI and education focuses on problems and possibilities with AI *as a tool in education itself* and how learning can be improved (or not) with the help of AI (Chen, Chen

---

[1]   Jasanoff and Kim's original definition of sociotechnical imaginaries is as follows: "collectively held, institutionally stabilized, and publicly performed visions of desirable futures, animated by shared understandings of forms of social life and social order attainable through, and supportive of, advances in science and technology" (p. 4).

& Lin, 2020; Edwards et al., 2018; Guilherme, 2019a; Perotta & Selwyn, 2019; Roll & Wylie, 2016; Woolf et al., 2013; Yang, 2021). Research on education *about* AI is scarce and focuses so far only on primary and secondary schools and medical or engineering education (Jindal & Bansal, 2020; Lindner et al., 2019). Likewise, there is research on policies and ethics for developing AI in society at large (Antebi & Dolinko, 2020; Jobin et al., 2019; Lauterbach, 2019; Stix, 2021), but only a few exceptions that focus on educational policies or aspects (e.g., Gulson & Webb, 2017). Research that has considered education policies has observed that policymakers are often experts in AI, but less so in matters of education and ethics (Knox, Wang & Gallagher, 2019). Further, a study of how guidelines on trustworthy or responsible AI support the UN's Sustainable Development Goals shows that an analysis of gender, inequality, and environmental impact is lacking (Theodorou et al., 2022), which could mean that international policies are overlooking issues relating to societal justice, or implicitly promoting an agenda based on engineering problems and technical solutions (Robinson, 2020). This argument could be extended to a practical level, where popular education about AI is often also designed and delivered by computer scientists or experts in AI technology. As an example, a recent literature review of the ethics of learning analytics in higher education shows a predominant focus on transparency, privacy, and informed consent, and less focus on, for example, justice, ethical dissonance, moral discomfort, and intellectual freedom (Cerratto Pargman & McGrath, 2021), giving us reasons to explore how more complex social, ethical, and educational issues are handled on a practical level (Perotta & Selwyn, 2019).

Dignum (2020) claims that AI research now requires interdisciplinary approaches and that "education plays here an important role. However, most current AI and robotics curricula worldwide deliver engineers with a too-narrow task view" (p. 19). However, the focus on how to broaden *engineering education* is still too narrow; we must also understand how learning about AI can take place in other fields, for example, among the general citizenry. These concerns are shared by Knox, Wang, and Gallagher (2019) who write that

> much of the discourse and commercial development towards building future education systems are focused on optimization, where education is viewed in 'commonsense' terms of acquiring individual skills in the most efficient manner, and a belief that complex educational problems can be addressed in a similar way to any other business challenge. (p. v)

Writing specifically about AI and education, they also find that "there are real risks of reinforcing and indeed perhaps exacerbating existing inequalities and injustice in our society" (ibid), as such questions of potential *epistemic injustices* seem very pertinent.

Most researchers agree that values and valuation processes are important in the production of knowledge (e.g., Harding & Hintikka, 1983). Many also concur that knowledge is power and that it follows that knowledge can be both a source of emancipation (e.g., hooks, 1993) as well as oppression. According to Foucault's understanding of power (1984a), power is based on knowledge and makes explicit use of knowledge. At the same time, power reproduces knowledge by shaping it according to certain meanings, problematizations, and assumptions. These valuations then shape the (scientific) claims made to explain reality. Epistemic valuations are, however, only one part of the knowledge production process. Other—contextual— values reflect moral, societal, or personal standpoints in how scientific knowledge is *applied*. Further, critical social science has shown how algorithmic preconditions shape knowledge (Beer, 2017; Bhatt & MacKenzie, 2019). AI and autonomous systems have also repeatedly been shown to both enact new, and bolster existing, injustices through hidden biases and valuations (Hoffmann, 2019; Rospigliosi, 2021). Of course, research has also demonstrated the discriminating *effects* that the application of such systems produces (Lowrie, 2017; van den Hoven, 2022). This includes, for example, *who* is targeted and *why*, and *how* effects are distributed unevenly and unfairly according to intersectional marginalizations and oppressions. Such forms of injustice have been termed algorithmic oppression (Noble, 2018), automated oppression (Eubanks, 2017), and weapons of math destruction (O´Neil, 2016) to name just a few. As such, research that examines AI injustice stresses the importance of heterogeneous engineering and participatory design as important to combat bias in development (Mohamed et al., 2020), while an assessment of effects (both intended and unintended) is put forward as important after implementation. Decolonial and postcolonial research has also emphasized geopolitical injustices relating, for example, to environmental effects (e.g., Crawford, 2021). All these perspectives are important for fighting injustice. Consequently, in my discussion of these issues, I seek to join such efforts by showing how we must also critically examine education and knowledge in relation to AI as a *relational* understanding of knowledge/power.

This chapter consequently proposes a meta-analytical perspective—examining the structure and preconditions of education aimed at preparing the general citizenry for an AI-augmented future. As such, the chapter contributes to meaningful interdisciplinary dialogues by taking a broad perspective that goes beyond efficient individual learning or solutions relating only to technical innovation and engineering. The chapter instead questions what knowledge about AI is being emphasized, and what types of knowledge are excluded. Because policies are intended to govern citizens, analyses like these are critically important.

The empirical material on which this chapter is based consists of a selection of international policies on AI and education/ethics (n=13). These policies were elicited from the EU/EC, OECD, and UNESCO. The policies were selected on the basis of their recentness and topicality (i.e., relating to future societies, AI, and either education or ethics). The empirical material is not a complete study of policies that exist in the field, and the chapter should be understood as a preliminary empirical study and a theoretical contribution to an understudied field, which calls for further studies that take a comprehensive approach to the view of knowledge, education, and ethics in policy.

THEORETICAL VANTAGE POINTS

This chapter is grounded in two theoretical concepts: *problematizations* (Bacchi, 2009, 2012) and *epistemic injustice* (Fricker, 2007). This combination forms a theoretical vocabulary that can grasp and make visible the complexity of knowledge and epistemic dimensions in AI knowledge and education. Education and technology policies produce collective meaning in society by conveying ways of thinking about what AI is, what it should be, and how it could impact society and citizens. As such, policies about AI represent important research sites for examining how humans are positioned in a society where AI-driven solutions become a beacon for the future. This chapter argues that broad AI education can be seen as revolving around *problematizations*—framing mechanisms that present certain aspects as problems in order to determine a corresponding solution. A focus on problematizations can unpack vulnerabilities, precarities, and uncertainties, but also anticipate strengths, welfares, and stabilities and how these problematizations are generative in terms of producing social, political, and epistemic meaning. As such, problematizations are active in what Fricker (2007) calls epistemic injustice. For Fricker (2007), epistemic injustice shapes oppressed and marginalized subject positions, focusing on who is acknowledged as a knowing subject. She identifies two forms of injustice: *testimonial injustice* and *hermeneutical injustice.*

Testimonial injustice happens when a subject is not considered as trustworthy (often because of prejudices). Such situations are fairly easy to imagine, as they permeate contemporary society. For example, when a person's experiences are disregarded because of the color of their skin or gender; when the sexual history of a subject affects their credibility as a victim of rape; or when the ethnicity or age of a person makes their accounts less trustworthy as police witness reports. In relation to AI and autonomous systems, such injustices can relate to how people's lives are affected by the (in)ability of facial recognition systems to correctly identify them, or as Noble (2018) shows, how a Google search systematically reproduces and amplifies racism and sexism and facial recognition creates invisibility based on skin color (Buolamwini & Gebru, 2018). Cathy O'Neil (2016) similarly shows how the simplifications that inevitably occur when complex learning processes are algorithmically translated result in increased inequality. These simplifications only recognize certain knowledge and experiences as "witnesses" of what constitutes reality.

Hermeneutical injustice, on the other hand, is not as concrete, even though the effects on people's lives can be just as tangible. Hermeneutical injustice occurs when differences in interpretative resources are present. These may hinder a subject from creating or conveying the intended meaning of their experiences. More specifically, Fricker defines hermeneutical injustice as: "the injustice of having some significant area of one's social experience obscured from collective understanding owing to a structural identity prejudice in the collective hermeneutical resource" (Fricker, 2007, p. 155). Fricker points out that hermeneutical inequality can be difficult to detect and goes on to discuss who can then be regarded as oppressed as an effect of hermeneutical inequality. What is considered good or bad, sufficient, or insufficient, normal or deviant obviously involves power asymmetries. However, what Fricker stresses is not only this but also that power asymmetries make certain experiences and forms of knowledges *invisible*—not only to those in power but also to oneself. As such, hermeneutical injustice connects to what Mohamed, Png, and Isaac (2020) term "algorithmic dispossession," which is when "regulatory policies result in a centralisation of power, assets, or rights in the hands of a minority and the deprivation of power, assets or rights from a disempowered majority" (p. 669). More specifically, they argue that AI policies and governance is controlled by previous colonial powers and economically privileged countries, spurring questions about what perspectives and knowledge are in fact put forward (and which remain invisible), and how economic and technical dependence is becoming a renewed form of (epistemic) colonialism. Such acts of marginalization are context dependent and complex. A person can be marginalized because of gender in a certain context, or class or race in another context. These social categorizations can also work together in intersectional ways, and the damage can be amplified and upscaled by autonomous systems. An important word here is *structural*. An individual can be subjected to hermeneutical injustice in a specific case, but in order for this to "count" as hermeneutical injustice, it also requires that the experience is obscured from collective understanding owing to a structural identity prejudice. This entails a wide-ranging injustice that follows the subject through different contexts. For Fricker, this means that hermeneutical injustice is both a subjective and collective practice. The subjective part stresses how members of stigmatized groups can be denied access to resources and concepts needed to understand or verbalize their experiences; the subject is unable to intelligibly communicate something that is particularly important to a person. So, they are excluded from practices of knowledge production, resulting in what they are trying to say is not heard or being regarded as incomprehensible and dismissible (or, indeed, left unverbalizable). The collective part points to systemic unfairness in the process of giving and receiving knowledge in society at large. Fricker (2007, p. 161) writes:

> Hermeneutical lacunas are like holes in the ozone—it's the people who live under them that get burned

As such, the concept of epistemic injustice captures certain preconditions of knowledge production about whose values and life-worlds are reproduced through certain representations of knowledge. As Frank (2019) puts it: "Those without power are silenced and this leads to an incomplete and inaccurate vision of the social world."

EDUCATIONAL IMAGINARIES OF AI

On a societal level, AI is currently described as a key technology that will transform the future in practically all areas of life (Governo, 2018). AI is predicted to radically change labor markets and automate jobs (Frey & Osborne, 2017), which is seen to increase the need for reskilling and lifelong learning. AI is also predicted to change the preconditions for democracy and citizenship. Malicious use of deep fakes, disinformation, propaganda, and polarized presentations of news demands of citizens a range of new and improved literacies as well as a sense of general psychological security (NSCAI, 2021). Further, AI- and big data-driven media technologies have raised questions about personal well-being, surveillance, self-tracking, and how we understand the environmental impacts of our actions (Partnership on AI, 2020). As such, citizens are also supposed to gain the skills necessary to act responsibly and thrive in an increasingly complex and information-dense world (AAAI, 2016). AI is further predicted to impact education and lifelong learning in themselves, where on-demand personalized learning, adaptive learning, automated talent acquisition, the real-time monitoring of workflows, and constant knowledge assessment are described as increasing the possibilities for individualized and flexible (lifelong) learning, as well as the creation of new expectations for personalized education and continuous reskilling and upskilling (TechNavio, 2018).

While the exact implications of an "AI revolution" remain to some extent in the realm of speculation (cf. Saunders, Brewster & Holland, 2020), it is clear that one (imagined) way to exert some control over how AI impacts societies and citizens is through education. A sign of the times is that AI is high on the agenda of supra-national policymakers (e.g., the EU program for Policy on AI (2018) and the New Skills Agenda for Europe (2016); the OECD Recommendations of the Council on AI (2022), the Skills Outlook (2021), and the Futures Literacy program (2019); and the UNESCO Ethics on AI (2019b) and Sustainable Development Goal 4: Education 2030 agenda (2016)). Both policies and individual researchers increasingly advocate digital skills, media and information literacies, AI competencies, and computational thinking as *absolutely necessary* skills for both *adapting* citizens to the future, as well as for *guiding* ethical AI development (Floridi et al., 2018; Robinson, 2020; Theodorou & Dignum, 2020; Tuomi, 2018). These are further conceptualized as *lifelong efforts*. As stated by UNESCO: "we must also go beyond formal education systems to develop new tools to reach all people, of all ages, through a life-long learning approach that responds to the constantly changing information environment" (UNESCO, 2021).

A lack of knowledge is conceptualized as a central problem for the critical use of AI and autonomous systems. In more technical-ethics policies, this is often connected to the idea of transparent systems. Transparency (i.e., where users can see and understand what AI systems do) is, in this case, put forward as a solution to ethical problems surrounding AI. In contemporary education policies, however, the problems with AI are phrased more around issues of datafication, (alternative) facts, and propaganda. This can be illustrated using an example from UNESCO's revised taxonomy of media and information literacy (2021, p III):

> access to reliable and fact-based information is crucial for making potentially lifesaving decisions and participating in all areas of society. It is a critical pillar of democracy and central to our ability to address every major issue we face, whether it be climate change, migration, As such, it must be treated as a public good, in the same way as the water we drink and the air we breathe. Every education system worldwide must adequately build critical minds that can navigate today's information flows, verify sources, differentiate facts from fictions, resist hate speech, and most of all, make informed decisions about their lives.

In this quote, access to *fact-based information* is described as a fundamental human right, as well as a necessary infrastructure, very much in the same way that access to computers or the Internet has historically been compared to access to water or electricity (Rankin, 2018). From these repeated analogies, we can argue that access to technology (and networks) has also been presented as a prerequisite for "democracy."

The way UNESCO problematizes it today, the main scarcity (which is also partly an *effect* of AI tech) is instead "fact-based information." The proposed solution to this problem is critical thinking and expanded skill sets. Citizens are seen as becoming protected from technological oppression through increased awareness and knowledge. UNESCO argues that: "When the concepts of media literacy and information literacy were coined in the 1930s and 1960s respectively, the social media and AI systems that to a wide extent dominate our means of communication today did not yet exist" (UNESCO, 2021, p. 299). As such, the knowledge a citizen should possess to be digitally competent is continuously expanding. According to UNESCO, the necessary skills today include *23 different literacies,* including game literacy, data literacy, and AI literacy. Similarly, the European Commission (2022) offers a conceptual framework to improve citizens' digital competence: The Digital Competence Framework for Citizens 2.2 (also known as DigComp). This framework highlights eight different proficiency levels and specific examples within them (where AI knowledge is an important part). As such, more and broader skills are enacted as important solutions to anticipated and current problems with digital competence. Moreover, increased technical knowledge for citizens is also seen as an urgent need to ensure they acquire a wide range of *soft skills*, or "powerful knowledges" (Young & Lambert, 2014), such as "learning compasses" (OECD, 2019), "responsive learning" (Smith et al., 2016), or "futures literacy" (Miller, 2018). These soft skills are described as necessary for handling the overall effects of AI, as well as remaining sufficiently flexible; they will help citizens protect their well-being and generally thrive in a digital society (Tsekeris, 2019). Adults must now be prepared to acquire new competencies and skills throughout life. Since AI is seen contributing to the reduced half-life of knowledge (i.e., how long it takes for half of the knowledge or facts in a given field to become obsolete), lifelong learning is increasingly targeting everyone.

The framing of issues presented in the more ethical-technical oriented policies (European Commission, 2018, 2019, 2020, 2021; Jorge Ricart et al., 2022; UNESCO, 2019a, 2019b) instead relates to three main problematizations: 1) a public fear of AI slows down the adoption of AI solutions; 2) ignorance about AI prevents citizens from taking part in public discourse and democratic decision-making; and 3) public AI education is part of a bigger movement toward participatory governance in AI development (cf. Bloom, 2020). The proposed solution is thereby still the same—more education! As such, educational imaginaries are an inherent aspect of sociotechnical imaginaries of AI and autonomous systems.

In summary, educational policies stress a need for both increased technical skills and increased *general* competences for living in an AI-dense world. This can only be described as an attempt to support *AI Bildung*—that is, a strive to foster a sense of self-cultivation, where personal and instrumental goals are imagined as harmonizing (a comparison can here be made to Foucault's technologies of the self). In contrast, ethical-technical policies often have a somewhat different argument for broad citizen education about AI. Everyone should learn about AI, and every profession will experience the impact of AI, and both citizens and all professions therefore need adaptations. The reverse argument is that AI developers, HCI researchers, and technical psychologists, for example, or indeed citizens, should be more educated about the history of technology, critical pedagogies, societal theories of power, information framing, environmental humanities, or intersectional theory in order to better understand the contexts in which AI is being implemented, yet this is rarely put forward. Education as a general solution to technical problems relates to the view of innovation as an improving and necessary social force. Fornstedt (2021) describes how the staging of innovations as a positive-sum game is made possible through exclusionary mechanisms in scientific production (based on classism, racism, sexism, and the invisibility of more-than-human worlds). In the same way, resistance, inertia, or reluctance to use AI and automated systems are explained as a lack of knowledge where, consequently, more education is formed as an important solution.

A practical equivalent can be seen in the many large-scale online popular education courses that have been launched about AI. This is a category of broad educational efforts that consists of online courses intentionally directed toward educating a wide spectrum of citizens. These courses are partly state-funded, free-of-charge, entry-level orientations about AI, which also carry a distinct political undertone that the knowledge provided has a bearing on (future) societal development, citizenship, and employability. Massive online popular education about AI is today provided by several actors and is hugely popular. As an example, the course *Elements of AI* has been taken by more than 600,000 people in 170 countries (elementsofai.com, 2021). Apart from individual citizens, it is also used by several public authorities, who deploy it as a form of continuous education for civil servants. Elements of AI, and other similar courses, intend to educate and engage the public about the future of AI, while also shaping public knowledge of what AI is, could be, and should be. Massive online popular education about AI can be seen as a practical response to policies and research insisting that wider social, political, and cultural contexts of the use of AI are taken into account, identifying implications for overall social justice and democracy (cf. Biesta, 2006; Collett & Dillon, 2019; Guilherme, 2019b).

In the next section, I will illustrate the epistemic injustices that I see as unproblematized in contemporary policies, but which will arguably carry more weight than ever before once humans and technical systems learn from each other and produce knowledge in complex human-technology interactions.

A RIGHT TO DEFINE THE PROBLEM

In this chapter, I have argued that the educational solutions that are now proposed, for citizens to learn increasingly comprehensive skill sets, become an agenda that promotes the adaptation of citizens to certain future technologies and technical problems. Thus, the educational imaginaries of AI enact politics since they formulate, first, what is considered problematic, and second, what the responding solution is. The result is that these educational imaginaries pave the way for certain technical solutions by translating technical problems and challenges into *educational* problems and challenges. As such, resistance or slow technological adoption is construed as a lack of knowledge, a problem solved with education.

By transforming technical problems into problems that can be solved with more education and more knowledge, the technical infrastructure is manifested as a fact and not a choice. Questions about freedom of choice are made invisible by shifting the site of decisions to the individual and his or her competencies. As such, education is arguably always in a reactive relation to technical development, specific technologies, and the imagined technical future. Citizens must learn to be prepared for the future, but arguably this preparation also limits our imagination and agency in relation to new technology in the future. By investing in education for a specific technical future, we are making it harder to go back on those technologies—the cost of abandoning that technical future increases the more educated we become. Somewhat paradoxically, this also creates a sense of safety and benevolence in relation to technology. By educating for a certain future, we are not only enacting that future but also conveying that this specific imaginary of the future is safe.

Knowledge and education are always seen as being for the common good, and not as a political solution to technical problems (which this chapter has argued they are). Further, the specification of knowledge and skills, as they are presented in international policies, are at the same time encompassing a vast array of skills, but also delimited to a specific view of knowledge. Knowledge and education about AI systematically obscure epistemic injustices, that is, the opportunity to bear witness and be interpreted by technical systems as an epistemic subject. That is when one's knowledge of oneself and experience of living in the world is not recognized as knowledge and thus rendered invisible as citizens are made algorithmically ready (through education). Central to these epistemic injustices is that they make resistance (even) more difficult. The form of knowledge that is seen as necessary, according to policies, takes a one-sided perspective on knowledge that is about the individual gaining technical knowledge, i.e., an ability to navigate *within* the system. However, if you are also made invisible by the system, it becomes infinitely more complex to form alternatives and enact resistance. The damage created by epistemic injustice must be understood as a discriminatory problem that cannot be solved by delegating responsibility to the individual to gain more knowledge about technical systems, but by the fact that epistemic injustices are problematized as such, and not obscured by an imperative to keep on adapting to the system. For example, before an injustice is formed as a collective understanding of this as wrong, it is more difficult for a person to understand and put into words their own experiences. When a person is rendered invisible, discriminated against, subjected to violence, or misunderstood by technological systems, this cannot be solved exclusively by more individual AI literacy and digital skills, or a more diverse data set; rather, knowledge must be created by starting from wrongs made against subjectivity and life forms of ecotechnology (Hörl, 2015).

Miranda Fricker shows us how neglect of relational aspects has a tendency to create and perpetuate epistemic injustice. In relation to AI systems, testimonial injustice and hermeneutic injustice can occur when individuals are misread by digital technologies or when the full complexity of our lives is not possible to render computable, for example, situations where what can be known about the world, oneself, or what can be known about oneself by others, is datafied and driven by a chase for economic profit. This relational understanding of knowledge as produced in an entanglement between humans and technologies, and that this can create a source of epistemic injustice, is overall missing in policies and educational efforts. If we are to take Fricker seriously in relation to AI, autonomous systems, and the epistemic infrastructures they produce, then access to education is, in itself, insufficient. Citizens must also be recognized as testimonial and hermeneutic subjects.

ACKNOWLEDGMENT

This work was partially supported by the Wallenberg AI, Autonomous Systems and Software Program – Humanities and Society (WASP-HS) and funded by the Marianne and Marcus Wallenberg Foundation and the Marcus and Amalia Wallenberg Foundation.

REFERENCES

AAAI. Association for the Advancement of Artificial Intelligence. (2016). *Well-Being Computing: AI Meets Health and Happiness Science*. Technical Report SS-16-07. Menlo Park: AAAI.

Antebi, L., & Dolinko, I. (2020). Artificial intelligence and policy: A review at the outset of 2020. *Strategic Assessment, 23*(1), 94–100.

Bacchi, C. (2009). *Analysing Policy: What's the Problem Represented to be?* French Forest: Pearson Education.

Bacchi, C. (2012). Why study problematizations? Making politics visible. *Open Journal of Political Science, 2*(1), 1–8.

Beer, D. (2017). The social power of algorithms. *Information, Communication & Society, 20*(1), 1–13.

Bhatt, I., & MacKenzie, A. (2019). Just Google it! Digital literacy and the epistemology of ignorance. *Teaching in Higher Education, 24*(3), 302–317.

Biesta, G. (2006). *Beyond Learning. Democratic Education for a Human Future*. Boulder, CO: Paradigm Publishers.

Bloom, P. (2020). *Identity, Institutions and Governance in an AI World*. Cham: Palgrave Macmillan.

Buolamwini, J., & Gebru, T. (2018, January). Gender shades: Intersectional accuracy disparities in commercial gender classification. In *Conference on Fairness, Accountability and Transparency* (pp. 77–91). PMLR.

Cerratto Pargman, T., & McGrath, C. (2021). Mapping the ethics of learning analytics in higher education: A systematic literature review of empirical research. *Journal of Learning Analytics, 8*(2), 123–139.

Chen, L., Chen, P., & Lin, Z. (2020). Artificial intelligence in education: A review. *IEEE Access, 8*, 75264–75278.

Collett, C., & Dillon, S. (2019). *AI and Gender: Four Proposals for Future Research*. Cambridge: The Leverhulme Centre for the Future of Intelligence.

Crawford, K. (2021). *Atlas of AI: The Planetary Costs of Artificial Intelligence*. New Haven: Yale University Press.

Dignum, V. (2020). AI is multidisciplinary. *AI Matters, 5*(4), 18–21.

Edwards, C., Edwards, A., Spence, P. R., & Lin, X. (2018). I, teacher: Using artificial intelligence (AI) and social robots in communication and instruction. *Communication Education, 67*(4), 473–480.

Ehn, P., Erlander, B., & Karlsson, R. (1978). *Vi vägrar låta detaljstyra oss! Rapport från samarbetet mellan Statsanställdas förbund, avdelning 1050 och DEMOS-projektet.* Stockholm: Arbetslivscentrum.

Eubanks, V. (2017). *Automating Inequality: How High-tech Tools Profile, Police, and Punish the Poor.* New York, NY: St. Martin's Press.

European Commission. (2021). *Fostering a European Approach to Artificial Intelligence.* Brussels: EC.

European Commission. (2020). *On Artificial Intelligence – A European Approach to Excellence and Trust.* Brussels: EC.

European Commission. (2019). *Ethics Guidelines for Trustworthy AI.* Brussels: EC.

European Commission. (2018). *Artificial Intelligence for Europe.* Brussels: EC.

European Commission. (2016). *A New Skills Agenda for Europe.* Brussels: EC.

Floridi, L., Cowls, J., Beltrametti, M. et al. (2018). AI4People – An ethical framework for a good AI society: Opportunities, risks, principles, and recommendations. *Minds & Machines, 28,* 689–707.

Fornstedt, H. (2021). Innovation resistance: Moving beyond dominant framings (PhD dissertation, Acta Universitatis Upsaliensis). Retrieved from http://urn.kb.se/resolve?urn=urn:nbn:se:uu:diva-453894

Foucault, M. (1984a). Nietzsche, genealogy, history. In P. Rabinow (Ed.), *The Foucault Reader: An Introduction to Foucault's Thoughts.* London & New York: Penguin Books.

Frank, J. (2013). Mitigating against epistemic injustice in educational research. *Educational Researcher, 42*(7), 363–370.

Frey, C. B., & Osborne, M. A. (2017). The future of employment: How susceptible are jobs to computerisation? *Technological Forecasting and Social Change, 114,* 254–280.

Fricker, M. (2007). *Epistemic Injustice: Power and the Ethics of Knowing.* Oxford: Oxford University Press.

Governo. (2018). *Artificiell intelligens i offentlig sektor. Hur realiserar vi potentialen?* Stockholm: Governo/Vinnova.

Guilherme, A. (2019a). AI and education: The importance of teacher and student relations. *AI & Society, 34*(1), 47–54.

Guilherme, A. (2019b). Considering AI in education: Erziehung but never Bildung. In J. Knox, W. Yu, & M. Gallagher (Eds.), *Artificial Intelligence and Inclusive Education* (pp. 165–178). Singapore: Springer.

Gulson, K. N., & Webb, P. T. (2017). Mapping an emergent field of 'computational education policy': Policy rationalities, prediction, and data in the age of Artificial Intelligence. *Research in Education, 98*(1), 14–26.

Harding, S. G., & Hintikka, M. B. (1983). *Discovering Reality.* Dordrecht: Springer Netherlands.

Hoffmann, A. L. (2019). Where fairness fails: Data, algorithms, and the limits of antidiscrimination discourse. *Information, Communication & Society, 22*(7), 900–915.

hooks, b. (1994). *Teaching to Transgress: Education as the Practice of Freedom.* London: Routledge.

Hörl, E. (2015). The technological condition. *Parrhesia, 22,* 1–15.

Jasanoff, S., & Kim, S. H. (2015). *Dreamscapes of Modernity: Sociotechnical Imaginaries and the Fabrication of Power.* The University of Chicago Press.

Jindal, A., & Bansal, M. (2020). Knowledge and education about artificial intelligence among medical students from teaching institutions of India: A brief survey. *MedEdPublish, 9,* 200.

Jobin A, Ienca M and Vayena E. (2019). The global landscape of AI ethics guidelines. *Nature Machine Intelligence 1,* 389–399. https://doi.org/10.1038/s42256-019-0088-2

Jorge Ricart, R., Van Roy, V., Rossetti, F., & Tangi, L. (2022). *AI Watch—National Strategies on Artificial Intelligence: A European Perspective* (EUR 31083 EN). Luxembourg: Publications Office of the European Union.

Knox, J., Wang, Y., & Gallagher, M. (Eds.). (2019). *Artificial Intelligence and Inclusive Education. Perspectives on Rethinking and Reforming Education* (pp. 165–178). Singapore: Springer.

Knox, J. Wang, Y., & Gallagher, M. (Eds.) (2019). *Artificial Intelligence and Inclusive Education: Speculative Futures and Emerging Practices.* Singapore: Springer.

Lauterbach, A. (2019). Artificial intelligence and policy: Quo vadis? *Digital Policy, Regulation and Governance, 21*(3), 238–263.

Lindner, A., Seegerer, S., & Romeike, R. (2019). Unplugged activities in the context of AI. In *International Conference on Informatics in Schools: Situation, Evolution, and Perspectives* (pp. 123–135). Cham: Springer.

Lowrie, I. (2017). Algorithmic rationality: Epistemology and efficiency in the data sciences. *Big Data & Society, 4*(1), 1–13.

Miller, R. (ed.). (2018). *Transforming the Future: Anticipation in the 21st Century.* London: UNESCO and Routledge.

Ministry of Education and Research. (2018). *Uppdrag om att etablera en kunskapsplattform för artificiell intelligens.* Stockholm: Regeringskansliet.

Mohamed, S., Png, M. T., & Isaac, W. (2020). Decolonial AI: Decolonial theory as sociotechnical foresight in Artificial Intelligence. *Philosophy & Technology, 33*(4), 659–684. https://doi.org/10.1007/s13347-020-00405-8

Noble, S. U. (2018). *Algorithms of Oppression: How Search Engines Reinforce Racism.* New York: New York University Press.

NSCAI. The National Security Commission on Artificial Intelligence. (2021). *Final Report.* Arlington: NSCAI.

OECD. (2022). *Recommendation of the Council on Artificial Intelligence* (OECD/LEGAL/0449). Paris: OECD Publishing.

OECD. (2021). *OECD Skills Outlook 2021: Learning for Life.* Paris: OECD Publishing.

OECD. (2019). *Future of Education and Skills 2030.* Paris: OECD Publishing.

O'Neil, C. (2016). *Weapons of Math Destruction: How Big Data Increases Inequality and Threatens Democracy.* New York: Crown.

Partnership on AI. (2020). *Framework for Promoting Workforce Well-being in the AI- Integrated Workplace.* San Francisco: Partnership on AI.

Perrotta, C., & Selwyn, N. (2020). Deep learning goes to school: Toward a relational understanding of AI in education. *Learning, Media, and Technology, 45*(3), 251–269.

Rahm, L. (2021). Educational imaginaries: Governance at the intersection of technology and education. *Journal of Education Policy.* https://doi.org/10.1080/02680939.2021.1970233

Rankin, J. L. (2018). *A People's History of Computing in the United States.* Cambridge, MA: Harvard University Press.

Robinson, S. C. (2020). Trust, transparency, and openness: How inclusion of cultural values shapes Nordic national public policy strategies for artificial intelligence (AI). *Technology in Society, 63.*

Roll, I., & Wylie, R. (2016). Evolution and revolution in artificial intelligence in education. *International Journal of Artificial Intelligence in Education, 26*(2), 582–599.

Rospigliosi, P. A. (2021). The risk of algorithmic injustice for interactive learning environments. *Interactive Learning Environments, 29*(4), 523–526.

Saunders, J., Brewster, C., & Holland, P. (2020). The changing nature of work. In: Holland, P. and Brewster, C. (Eds.). *Contemporary Work and the Future of Employment in Developed Countries.* Routledge Research in Employment Relations. Routledge, London, UK, pp. 1–15.

Smith, K., Måseidvåg Gamlem, S., Sandal, A. K., & Engelsen, K. S. (2016). Educating for the future: A conceptual framework of responsive pedagogy. *Cogent Education, 3*(1).

Stix, C. (2021). Actionable principles for Artificial Intelligence policy: Three pathways. *Science and Engineering Ethics, 27*(1), 1–17.

TechNavio. (2018). *Artificial Intelligence Market in the US Education Sector 2018–2022.* London: TechNavio.

Theodorou, A., Nieves, J. C., & Dignum, V. (2022). Good AI for good: How AI strategies of the Nordic Countries address the sustainable development goals. Presented at the AIofAI 2022: 2nd Workshop on Adverse Impacts and Collateral Effects of AI Technologies, Vienna, Austria, July 23–25, 2022.

Theodorou, A., & Dignum, V. (2020). Towards ethical and socio-legal governance in AI. *Nature Machine Intelligence, 2,* 10–12.

Tsekeris, C. (2019). Surviving and thriving in the Fourth Industrial Revolution: Digital skills for education and society. *Homo Virtualis, 2*(1), 34–42.

Tuomi, I. (2018). *The Impact of Artificial Intelligence on Learning, Teaching, and Education: Policies for the Future.* Luxembourg: Publications Office of the European Union.

UNESCO. (2021). *Media and Information Literate Citizens: Think Critically, Click Wisely!* UNESCO: Paris.

UNESCO. (2019a). *Beijing Consensus on Artificial Intelligence and Education.* UNESCO: Paris.

UNESCO. (2019b). *Preliminary Study on the Ethics of Artificial Intelligence.* UNESCO: Paris.

UNESCO. (2016). *Education 2030: Incheon Declaration and Framework for Action for the Implementation of Sustainable Development Goal 4: Ensure Inclusive and Equitable Quality Education and Promote Lifelong Learning Opportunities for All.* UNESCO: Paris.

van Den Hoven, E. (2022). Hermeneutical injustice and the computational turn in law. *Journal of Cross-disciplinary Research in Computational Law, 1*(1).

Walker, M. (2019). Why epistemic justice matters in and for education. *Asia Pacific Education Review, 20,* 161–170.

Woolf, B. P., Lane, H. C., Chaudhri, V. K., & Kolodner, J. L. (2013). AI grand challenges for education. *AI magazine, 34*(4), 66–84.

Yang, S. J. (2021). Guest Editorial: Precision Education-A New Challenge for AI in Education. *Journal of Educational Technology & Society, 24*(1), 105–108.

Young, R., & Lambert, D. (2014). *Knowledge and the Future School: Curriculum and Social Justice.* London: Bloomsbury.

PART III

THE POLITICAL ECONOMY OF AI: DATAFICATION AND SURVEILLANCE

26. Critical AI studies meets critical political economy

Pieter Verdegem

INTRODUCTION

Technological innovation has always been surrounded by hype. This is no different for *artificial intelligence* (AI). In business and policy circles, AI is said to bring about massive changes to how our economy and society are organised (Agrawal, Gans and Goldfarb, 2018; Lee, 2018; McAfee and Brynjolfsson, 2017). Everyone is urged to jump on the AI bandwagon, otherwise risking losing out on the opportunities being created. The AI hype predicts new and unprecedented levels of productivity and even prosperity (Hall and Pesenti, 2017). Beyond economic growth, AI is also seen as the solution to society's problems, including climate change, pandemics and the energy crisis (Dauvergne, 2020).

Critical AI studies are needed to scrutinise which forces are driving the AI hype. When analysing AI, we need to untangle what exactly is at stake and who is behind the myths and discourses that are created around the hype (Verdegem, 2021). Indeed, there is growing evidence that AI itself has a negative impact on the environment (Brevini, 2022), is characterised by practices of exploitation in its hidden infrastructure (Crawford, 2021) and produces polarisation and inequalities by its deployment (Korinek and Stiglitz, 2017).

These negative externalities are linked to the power concentration in digital capitalism, where a few Big Tech companies control the market and decide what the future of AI looks like.

In this chapter, I argue that critical political economy (CPE) (Hardy, 2014) is an important framework for critically investigating AI, particularly AI ownership structures and AI ideology. These two aspects are at the core of analysing AI power: economic power (ownership) and symbolic power (ideology). Critical AI studies must include a deep understanding of how power and inequalities in AI are produced and maintained before we can start thinking about alternatives and AI systems and applications that benefit society at large.

This chapter begins with conceptualising AI and explains what type of AI we are talking about and what critical approaches to AI entail. I continue by elaborating on the contribution of CPE and what it can offer to critical AI studies. After this, I apply this framework to the analysis of power in the field of AI. First, I go deeper into the industrial landscape of AI by looking at the economic power concentration. Second, I reflect on AI ideology and discuss the limitations of AI ethics to develop AI that benefits society at large. I demonstrate how economic and symbolic power issues related to AI are linked and need to be at the core of critical AI studies.

CRITICAL APPROACHES TO AI

Before we can turn to the analysis of economic and symbolic power in the context of AI, we need to agree on what type of AI we are talking about. While the term *artificial intelligence* was coined in the mid-1950s at a series of academic workshops organised at Dartmouth College in the US, the only agreement about conceptualising AI is that there is no generally accepted definition (Russell and Norvig, 2016). The Dartmouth College workshops were interested in which ways machines could simulate *human intelligence*, i.e., the ability to learn and make decisions. Hence, McCarthy et al. (1955/2006) define AI as: "making a machine behave in ways that would be called intelligent if a human were so behaving." Russell and Norvig (2016) argue that for a computer to be intelligent, it needs to possess the following capabilities: *natural language processing* (being able to communicate successfully); *knowledge representation* (being able to store what it knows or hears); *automated reasoning* (being able to use the stored information to answer questions and draw new conclusions); and *machine learning* (being able to adapt to new circumstances and to detect and extrapolate patterns).

It is important to understand that *machine learning AI* is the currently dominant AI paradigm, solving problems in ways that earlier AI paradigms – for example, expert systems – were not capable of. *Machine learning* (ML) is a paradigm that allows programs to learn from data, not from humans. Thereby it can automatically improve its performance on specific tasks by learning from vast amounts of data (Alpaydin, 2016). ML is based on statistical patterns and correlations in large datasets, starting to be used in the late 1980s to early 1990s. *Deep learning* (DL) and *artificial neural networks* (ANN) are behind more recent developments and breakthroughs in ML. The power and potential of DL neural networks were demonstrated in the early 2000s (LeCun, Bengio and Hinton, 2015). This allows us to automatically process unlabelled data, which made AI-powered applications much more capable and useful. These breakthroughs in ML techniques, supporting the development of more sophisticated ML and DL models, together with the growing availability of data with which algorithms can be trained, as well as the availability of powerful computing capacity are behind the current period of *AI hype* (Hall and Pesenti, 2017; Lee, 2018).

However, the *technical approaches* of AI – as outlined in the last paragraph – are only part of the story of conceptualising AI. In addition to this, we also need to perceive AI as *industrial infrastructures* and *social practices* (Crawford, 2021). First, it is important to look at the industrial infrastructures that are needed to produce and deploy AI. This infrastructure entails the possibility of collecting vast amounts of data and the computing power to perform ML and DL models. Few companies simultaneously have access to data and computing power and are able to hire the AI talent to develop ML and DL algorithms, meaning we are confronted with a concentrated AI industrial landscape (Dyer-Witheford, Kjøsen and Steinhoff, 2019). Second, AI also refers to social practices, as algorithms and ML/DL models are classification systems developed by humans. These classification systems are social and political as it is up to individuals and groups to decide what these classifications look like, which classifications are being used, for what purposes and so on. The centrality of classification systems in AI is the reason why we need to think about fairness, inclusion and representation, as it has been thoroughly documented how AI produces bias and discrimination (Costanza-Chock, 2018).

Now that it is clear how we can conceptualise AI, we can move on to what I mean by *critical approaches* towards AI and why we need to establish the field of *critical AI studies*. Any critical analysis of technological innovation should always start with questioning who is behind the technology, to whom it is offered and who benefits from it. A critical analysis of AI should investigate what AI is, what visions exist around it, who is behind the surrounding ideologies and discourses (Brevini, 2021) and who can decide what type of AI is being produced and how it is used (Verdegem, 2021). Ultimately, these are questions about AI and power. Understanding that AI is more than just a technical approach means acknowledging that there are issues about political, economic and social power at stake. The industrial infrastructures of AI are determined by economic power and the decisions of what classification systems look like and how they are being used are influenced by political and social power. For this reason, I argue that CPE is an essential framework, given its central focus on power, inequalities and ideologies, to foregrounding critical AI studies.

CRITICAL POLITICAL ECONOMY

Given my conceptualisation of AI, I argue in this chapter that CPE is a suitable framework for taking a critical approach to AI. CPE is a subfield within political economy research that has emerged from the critique of *political economy*, what Marx considered a synonym for bourgeois economic theory (Hardy, 2014; Mosco, 2009). Political economy in general studies how societies are organised and controlled. CPE distinguishes itself from mainstream approaches in political science, economics and communication research by focusing on social relations and asking questions about what reinforces or undermines social inequalities. CPE emerged in the 1970s when scholars in Europe and North America started studying media and communication systems and their impact on society (Hardy, 2014). As a field, CPE analyses how media and communication are produced as commodities in capitalist societies (Murdock and Golding, 1973). It is particularly interested in how economic factors influence politics and social relationships (McChesney, 2000). Central in its analysis is power: CPE studies who has the power to make decisions about media and communication systems and who benefits from this.

CPE is particularly interested in the unequal distribution of power and looks at the contexts and practices in which, as a result, inequalities are being produced and sustained (Hardy, 2014). An important influence for CPE is Marxian political economy, which offers a historical analysis of capitalism and particularly focuses on the forces and relations of production, commodification, the production of surplus value, class and social struggles (Fuchs, 2020). CPE investigates the concentration of power in media and communication industries and looks at the impact of commodification, globalisation and privatisation. Central in its analysis are the structures and consequences of ownership regimes, and how these are maintained by interactions between government and industry. CPE thus focuses its analysis on how ideology is used to legitimise power inequalities within the capitalist system.

So, what is power and how should we look at AI through the lens of power? Power is a contested concept in social theory. The late Marxist sociologist Erik Olin Wright (2010: 111) came up with a pragmatic definition of power and referred to it as "the capacity of actors to accomplish things in the world." A typology of different types of power, including economic, political, coercive and symbolic power (Thompson, 1995), is helpful to obtain a more nuanced understanding of its meaning and scope. First, *economic power* has its origins in human productive activity and refers to how certain individuals and groups in society can accumulate resources for that productive activity. Second, *political power* stems from the activity of coordinating individuals and regulating the patterns of their behaviour. Third, *coercive power* can involve the (threatened) use of force to subdue or conquer an opponent but mainly is about preventing people or groups to act in a certain way. Finally, *symbolic power* stems from the activity of producing, transmitting and receiving meaningful symbolic forms (meaning making) and thereby involves influencing the actions of others.

In short, power is all about who can influence what society looks like and who controls the means for doing so. In the context of AI, power decides who can and will benefit from new technologies and applications. However, a concentration of power results in growing inequalities and other negative outcomes (Brevini, 2022; Crawford, 2021; Korinek and Stiglitz, 2017). Indeed, power is used for controlling society and this is particularly relevant for critical AI studies. In the context of data and AI, exercising power is deciding how the world is categorised and how the commodification and extraction of data happens (Sadowski, 2019). There are numerous well-documented examples of how AI and data-driven systems are the source behind negative externalities, such as racial and gender bias (Noble, 2018; Benjamin, 2019), discrimination on the basis of class (Eubanks, 2018) or constant surveillance and oppression (Arora, 2019; Zuboff, 2019), to mention just a few.

The next sections investigate how economic power and symbolic power are used in the realm of AI and what their consequences are. Critically analysing AI through a CPE lens allows us to scrutinise the concentration in the AI industrial landscape and look into how AI power is maintained through ideology.

ECONOMIC POWER: CONCENTRATION IN THE AI INDUSTRY

The AI industry is dominated by a small number of companies from the US (*GAFAM*: Google/Alphabet, Apple, Facebook/Meta, Amazon and Microsoft) and China (*BAT*: Baidu, Alibaba and Tencent) (Kaplan and Haenlein, 2020). Especially since 2015, these companies have become more aggressive in their competition for AI dominance by acquiring start-ups as well as heavily investing in computing capacity (Verdegem, 2022), leading to a concentrated AI industrial landscape (Dyer-Witheford et al., 2019). I first explain what concentration of economic power in the media and communication industries entails and then I move on to analysing how this works in the AI sector.

A standard definition of media concentration is: "an increase in the presence of one or a handful of media companies in any market as a result of various possible processes: acquisitions, mergers, deals with other companies, or even the disappearance of competitors" (Sánchez-Tabernero, 1993: 7). Although being a different sector, concentration in the AI industry operates along the same lines, with the same outcome: a handful of companies dominate and control the field. Media concentration can be driven by *horizontal integration* (one company purchasing companies in the same economic sector), *vertical integration* (one company acquiring companies in neighbouring sectors), *conglomeration* (one company operating in different business areas) or *strategic alliances* (companies cooperating in order to save money), or a combination of these mechanisms (Doyle, 2013; Hesmondhalgh, 2019). The phenomenon of concentration points to some of the contradictions of capitalist reproduction: although competition is considered one of the central pillars of capitalism, it is in the interest of each company/capitalist to suppress competition. As a result, the communications sector is characterised by a tendency for monopolies (Garnham, 1990).

How does this work in the context of AI? The AI industry is dominated by platforms, which all have ready access to large amounts of data. Platforms are intermediaries enabling different types of users (producers and suppliers, users, app developers, advertisers, etc.) to interact with each other (Srnicek, 2017; Van Dijk, Poell and de Waal, 2018). Platforms function as data brokers as they are able – given their role as middlemen – to capture, extract and analyse the data produced by the interactions on their platforms (Crain, 2018; West, 2019). Network effects are crucial in connecting data to platforms (Srnicek, 2017). Network effects entail that the value of the network is determined by its size. As a result, platforms are more valuable as more users join them and are generating data through their interactions. Platforms follow specific strategies and adjust their architecture to attract new and diverse user groups as well as facilitate engagement on their platform (Van Dijck et al., 2018). Data is not only determining the value of the platform; it is also crucial for developing and improving AI systems: this allows them to develop better performing ML and DL models, which in turn result in better services and more users. Because platforms' margins increase as their networks grow, only one or two platforms will dominate an industry as the market matures. Platform capitalism is therefore characterised by the *winner takes it all* principle, meaning that these markets have a tendency for monopolisation (Barwise and Watkins, 2018; Srnicek, 2017). Beyond data, the economic and technological growth of digital platforms is also determined at the platform infrastructure level. Especially (third-party) app development, using application programming interfaces (APIs) and software development kits (SDKs), contributes to the emergence of a more integrated platform ecosystem (van der Vlist and Helmond, 2021). The largest platforms dominate the sector – and become more powerful – as they offer services upon which other platforms are dependent (Blanke and Pybus, 2020). Partnerships in the platform ecosystem also contribute to an increase in platform power, which concerns more than just monopoly power (van der Vlist and Helmond, 2021).

However, access to data and an integrated platform (infrastructure) ecosystem is only one part of the economic power concentration in the AI industrial landscape. In addition, there is an intense battle over computing capacity and human AI talent, which has intensified in the last decade (Verdegem, 2022). First, AI computing capacity entails the hardware and software to be engineered to facilitate and support the development of AI applications. This includes large data centres, supercomputers and cloud providers. AI computing capacity is essential in controlling the AI market. Both US and Chinese Big Tech companies have made major investments in computing capacity such as cloud computing (Dyer-Witheford et al., 2019). For some of these companies (e.g., AWS and Aliyun, the respective cloud services of Amazon and Alibaba), offering computing and database infrastructure are nowadays among the most lucrative parts of their business. Investment in computing capacity is also necessary for meeting the demand for speed and security of new AI services. As such, it is essential to invest in computing capacity when AI companies want to increase their market share.

Second, there is increased competition over hiring human AI talent, i.e., the computer scientists who are behind the further development of, and breakthroughs in, ML/DL and ANN. Highly specialised IT talent is very expensive as it requires people to have accumulated a large amount of experience through formal training (e.g., PhD) or years of applied work (Ahmed and Wahed, 2020). Big Tech companies engage in acquiring AI start-ups, not only for purchasing a new (potentially profitable) AI niche but also and especially for being able to hire the brightest AI talent. AI companies only face competition from blockchain companies and the military, who also have large amounts of funding available. Sometimes Big Tech companies even take over complete university computer science departments because of the intense competition (and the cash they have at their disposal). The race over hiring the brightest AI talent leads to a gap among computer/data scientists, whereby a small group gets enormous salaries and benefits while others, including other people and groups who are doing some of the essential *AI work* (e.g., image labelling or content moderation), are underpaid or even exploited (Crawford, 2021; Metz, 2017).

The consequences of concentration, whether in the media or AI sectors, are similar: it results in economic centralisation; control over price, quality and technological standards; political, economic and ideologic power and so on. Specifically in the case of AI, with such a large and global dominance in the hands of eight to ten AI behemoths, it gives these corporate powers the ability to decide what the future of AI looks like and who is able to benefit from it. This is the reason why we need to critically investigate the power concentration of Big Tech in AI capitalism and explore alternatives, allowing society at large to benefit from AI too (Verdegem, 2022). Pushing for democratisation is central to imagining alternatives to AI ownership and governance. I will come back to this at the conclusion of this chapter.

SYMBOLIC POWER: AI IDEOLOGY AND THE LIMITS OF AI ETHICS

After having explained the concentration of economic power, now is the time to switch to the discussion of symbolic power. Following Thompson's (1995) framework, symbolic power focuses on producing, transmitting and receiving meaningful symbolic forms, i.e., individuals expressing themselves about social life. When doing so, they rely on what Thompson (1995: 16) calls the *means of information and communication*, which refers to the resources, skills and knowledge necessary to engage in exchanging symbolic forms. This is linked to Bourdieu's *cultural capital*. In addition to this, Bourdieu (1986) also talks about *symbolic capital*: the accumulated prestige, recognition and respect accorded to certain producers or institutions in society. Here is where the role of ideology comes into play.

Ideology, just like power, is a contested concept in social theory. Fuchs (2020) writes that ideology can be seen – from a more neutral perspective – as the ideas and worldviews that exist in society. But it can also refer to the process of the production of false consciousness, with the goal to manipulate human consciousness. A critical interpretation of ideology means that it is being used for a specific purpose, i.e., serving the material interests of the ruling class. As such, ideology is a typical characteristic of capitalism and class societies, whereby it is a vehicle to promote the interests of one class at the expense of other groups in society. Ideology also plays an important role in promoting myths and discourses about AI, portraying a vision of a specific type of society and the role digital technology plays in it (Brevini, 2021). Berman (1992) wrote several decades ago (long before the current hype) how AI, as a technological paradigm, is a major component of a hegemonic ideology, being used to maintain the essential structures of capitalism and preventing viable alternatives to be envisioned. In this context, it is important to investigate what visions about AI are being promoted and who is behind them. This can most prominently be observed in AI ethics initiatives.

AI ethics projects basically talk about the role of AI in a good society, or good AI in society, or both (Coeckelbergh, 2020). It is really important to look at what this *good AI/society* actually means for whom and who is benefiting from it (Berendt, 2019). Several types of stakeholders are engaging in discussions about AI ethics, from governments and governmental organisations, over corporations and professional associations, to academics and civil society organisations (Verdegem, 2021). The European Union (2019), for example, proposes the notion of *trustworthy AI*. According to this, good AI should be (a) lawful, (b) ethical and (c) robust. The problem is that these aspects are (too) vague and few people would argue against them. The EU, particularly the *High-Level Expert Group on AI*, have also come up with more specific and concrete aims and principles, such as human agency, fairness, diversity, accountability and so on. Companies, particularly in Big Tech, also contribute to the debate about AI ethics. Google, for example, has an initiative called *Advancing AI for Everyone*, whereas Microsoft's initiative is called *AI for Good*. In essence, an analysis of these corporate AI visions reveals that they are merely a call for improving and making available Big Tech's AI products and services, more than anything else. Professional associations such as IEEE or ACM have proposed ethical principles for AI or guidelines in terms of *ethically aligned design*. They include principles such as human rights, well-being, data agency, transparency, accountability and so on. In addition to this, there is a myriad of other initiatives emerging around AI ethics. An interesting one is the *AI4People* initiative, which is set up by the non-profit organisation Atomium, in collaboration with the European Institute for Science, Media and Democracy. The AI4Ppeople project proposes five key principles for a *Good AI Society*: (a) beneficence, (b) non-maleficence, (c) autonomy, (d) justice and (e) explicability (Atomium-EISMD, 2020). Where the first four principles overlap with traditional bio-ethics principles, the last one is a new enabling principle for AI.

However, there are considerable problems with and limitations of AI ethics initiatives. First, there is the aspect of who is involved in and influencing the development of ethical guidelines. A problem of diversity and inclusion immediately emerges: research by Jobin, Ienca and Vayena (2019) reveals how the development of AI ethics is concentrated in Europe, North America and a few other countries. The Global South is often absent in these discussions. Also, how representative are the expert panels who are developing the guidelines, and do they include representatives of groups in society who will be influenced and impacted by AI applications? Furthermore, we should not be blind to the corporate influence on AI ethics initiatives: a lot of projects are (openly or not) sponsored by Big Tech. Second, there is the problem of the speed of technological development. The development of ethical guidelines needs time and there is the question of whether ethics can keep up with the rapid development of digital technologies (Boddington, 2017). As such, AI ethics initiatives are often reactive rather than proactive. Third, a particular risk exists in the so-called *ethics washing* (Wagner, 2018). This refers to the practice of exaggerating an organisation's interest in promoting beneficial AI systems – aiming to highlight their commitment to ethical behaviour – which is then used as a means to obfuscate the abandonment of their legal obligations. A typical example is promoting *good tech* but not respecting data protection principles. Last, a major challenge is how to move from AI ethics to AI policies. There is no roadmap for what exactly should be done, who should be leading and being involved in policy development and so on (Coeckelbergh, 2020). Ultimately, this comes down to the influence of stakeholders and who can determine the actions, beliefs or behaviour of others.

This brings us back to the discussion of power in shaping AI myths and discourses. AI ideology plays a particular and significant role in proposing a specific type of AI and society (Brevini, 2021). Critical AI studies must be aware of this and seek to understand who is promoting these visions of AI and preventing AI alternative imaginaries to emerge. I come back to the issue of symbolic power and how we must tackle this in tandem with the economic power concentration in the field of AI in the conclusion.

CONCLUSION

In order to deal with the negative consequences of economic power concentration (AI ownership) and the hegemonic influence of symbolic power (AI ideology), we need to find ways of bringing social power back into the discussion of AI and society. Erik Olin Wright (2019: 68) defines *social power* as: "power rooted in the capacity to mobilize people for cooperative, voluntary collective actions." Social power is at the centre of ideals such as equality/fairness, democracy/freedom and community/solidarity (Wright, 2019). It is a defining characteristic of societal and economic structure in which the allocation and use of resources for multiple purposes are guided by social rather than economic or state power.

What does this mean in the context of AI? Bringing social power central to the debate about AI means talking about a radical democratisation of AI (Verdegem, 2021). Radical approaches, such as in radical politics (Fenton, 2016) are focused on changing the fundamental principles of how a society is organised, often by making use of structural change – transformation happening at the root. A radical perspective on AI means examining AI through the lens of power and asking how we can bring real change for the better. A radical democratisation of AI is necessary to avoid power inequalities and establish AI that transforms society and enables human participation.

A radical democratisation of AI puts forward three principles (Verdegem, 2021). First, AI should be *accessible to everyone*: in a good society, all members should have broadly equal access to the possibilities and advantages being offered by digital technology such as AI. As such, everyone in society can have access to and use AI. Second, AI should *represent everyone*: all people should be able to have a say about what type of AI and what AI services are being developed and offered. The production and deployment of AI should be democratised so to enable consultation and avoid exclusion. Finally, AI should be *beneficial to everyone*: developments in AI should contribute to the well-being of every human being in society. AI systems and services should allow everyone in society to enjoy the benefits being offered. It also means that AI should serve humanity as a whole. The question, then, remains how to organise around these foundational principles.

Putting social power central in discussions of AI and society, and critical AI studies, means thinking about collective approaches, which include coming up with new discourses and bringing people together in order to engage in cooperative actions.

First, an important step in the democratisation of AI should be in altering the capitalist discourses about AI. Rather than considering AI as the driver behind economic growth, we could consider AI and its related infrastructures as a computational public utility or even a communal utility, subject to democratic control (Dyer-Witheford et al., 2019). This means that society and its communities can be involved in determining what services can or should (not) be automated, and for what purposes.

Second, how can we create a movement and mobilise around the radical democratisation of AI? Ivana Bartoletti (2020) asks in this context why we do not have an anti-AI movement in the way we had (and still have) an anti-nuclear movement. There are indeed legitimate reasons for comparing AI and nuclear energy: their use for military purposes is considerable; they both require large amounts of funding; and their development is driven by a global race between national superpowers. But the international community has also agreed that, because nuclear energy has positive, transformative qualities as well as enormous risks, a centralised control mechanism is needed. Rather than a defensive movement against AI, I argue for a mobilisation in support of the radical democratisation of AI. The latter demands creating more awareness of the advantages and risks of AI, including in the debate people and groups who are involved in the development of AI and who are impacted by its implementation. But it also necessitates analysing the economic and symbolic power of AI. This means a thorough understanding of the monopolisation of AI by Big Tech as well as an awareness of the impact of AI ideology. As I have argued in this chapter, CPE is an essential framework to advance these debates and help in developing the field of critical AI studies.

REFERENCES

Agrawal, A., Gans, J. and Goldfarb, A. (2018). *Prediction Machines: The Simple Economics of Artificial Intelligence*. Boston, MA: Harvard Business School Publishing.

Ahmed, N. and Wahed, M. (2020). The De-Democratization of AI: Deep Learning and the Compute Divide in Artificial Intelligence Research. http://arxiv.org/abs/2010.15581

Alpaydin, E. (2016). *Machine Learning: The New AI*. Cambridge, MA: MIT Press.

Arora, P. (2019). Benign Dataveillance? Examining Novel Data-Driven Governance Systems in India and China. *First Monday*, 24(4). https://firstmonday.org/ojs/index.php/fm/article/view/9840

Atomium-EISMD. (2020). AI4People, Europe's First Global Forum on AI Ethics, Launches at the European Parliament. https://www.eismd.eu/ai4people-europes-first-global-forum-ai-ethics-launches-at-the-european-parliament

Bartoletti, I. (2020). *An Artificial Revolution. On Power, Politics and AI*. London: The Indigo Press.

Barwise, P. and Watkins, L. (2018). The Evolution of Digital Dominance: How and Why We Got to GAFA. In M. Moore and D. Tambini (Eds.), *Digital Dominance: The Power of Google, Amazon, Facebook, and Apple* (pp. 21–49). Oxford: Oxford University Press.

Benjamin, R. (2019). *Race After Technology*. Cambridge: Polity.

Berendt, B. (2019). AI for the Common Good?! Pitfalls, Challenges and Ethics Pen-Testing. *Paladyn, Journal of Behavioral Robotics*, 10(1), 44–65.

Berman, B.J. (1992). Artificial Intelligence and the Ideology of Capitalist Reconstruction. *AI & Society*, 6, 103–114.

Blanke, T. and Pybus, J. (2020). The Material Conditions of Platforms: Monopolization through Decentralization. *Social Media + Society*, 6(4), 1–13.

Boddington, P. (2017). *Towards a Code of Ethics for Artificial Intelligence*. Cham: Springer.

Bourdieu, P. (1986). The Forms of Capital. In J.G. Richardson (Ed.), *Handbook of Theory and Research for the Sociology of Education* (pp. 241–258). New York: Greenwood.

Brevini, B. (2021). Creating the Technological Saviour: Discourses on AI in Europe and the Legitimation of Super Capitalism. In P. Verdegem (Ed.), *AI for Everyone? Critical Perspectives* (pp. 145–159). London: University of Westminster Press.

Brevini, B. (2022). *Is AI Good for the Planet?* Cambridge: Polity.

Coeckelbergh, M. (2020). *AI Ethics*. Cambridge, MA and London: MIT Press.

Costanza-Chock, S. (2018). Design Justice, AI and Escape from the Matrix of Domination. *Journal of Design and Justice*, 3(5). https://jods.mitpress.mit.edu/pub/costanza-chock/release/4

Crain, M. (2018). The Limits of Transparency: Data Brokers and Commodification. *New Media & Society*, 20(1), 88–104.

Crawford, K. (2021). *Atlas of AI*. New Haven and London: Yale University Press.

Dauvergne, P. (2020). *AI in the Wild. Sustainability in the Age of Artificial Intelligence*. Cambridge, MA and London: MIT Press.

Doyle, G. (2013). *Understanding Media Economics*. London: SAGE.

Dyer-Witheford, N., Kjøsen, A.M. and Steinhoff, J. (2019). *Inhuman Power. Artificial Intelligence and the Future of Capitalism*. London: Pluto Press.

Eubanks, V. (2018). *Automating Inequality*. New York: St. Martin's Press.

European Commission. (2019). Ethical Guidelines for Trustworthy AI. https://op.europa.eu/en/publication-detail/-/publication/d3988569-0434-11ea-8c1f-01aa75ed71a1

Fenton, N. (2016). *Digital, Political, Radical.* Cambridge: Polity.

Fuchs, C. (2020). *Marxism.* New York and London: Routledge.

Garnham, N. (1990). *Capitalism and Communication.* London: SAGE.

Hall, W. and Pesenti, J. (2017). Growing the Artificial Intelligence Industry in the UK. https://assets .publishing.service.gov.uk/government/uploads/system/uploads/attachment_data/file/652097/ Growing_the_artificial_intelligence_industry_in_the_UK.pdf

Hardy, J. (2014). *Critical Political Economy of the Media.* London and New York: Routledge.

Hesmondhalgh, D. (2019). *The Cultural Industries* (4th edition). London: SAGE.

Jobin, A., Ienca, M. and Vayena, E. (2019). The Global Landscape of AI Ethics Guidelines. *Nature Machine Intelligence*, 1, 389–399.

Kaplan, A. and Haenlein, M. (2020). Rulers of the World, Unite! The Challenges and Opportunities of Artificial Intelligence. *Business Horizons*, 63(1), 37–50.

Korinek, A. and Stiglitz, J.E. (2017). Artificial Intelligence and its Implications for Income Distribution and Unemployment. Working Paper 24174, National Bureau of Economic Research. https://www .nber.org /papers/w24174

LeCun, Y., Bengio, Y. and Hinton, G. (2015). Deep Learning. *Nature*, 521, 436–444.

Lee, K.-F. (2018). *AI Superpowers. China, Silicon Valley and the New World Order.* Boston and New York: Houghton Mifflin Harcourt.

McAfee, A. and Brynjolfsson, E. (2017). *Machine, Platform, Crowd: Harnessing the Digital Revolution.* New York and London: WW Norton & Company.

McCarthy, K., Minsky, M., Rochester, N. and Shannon, C. (1955/2006). A Proposal for the Dartmouth Summer Research Project on Artificial Intelligence. *AI Magazine*, 27(4), Winter 2006.

McChesney, R. (2000). The Political Economy of Communication and the Future of the Field. *Media, Culture & Society*, 22(1), 109–116.

Metz, C. (2017). Tech Giants are Paying Huge Salaries for Scarce A.I. Talent. *The New York Times.* https://www.nytimes.com/2017/10/22/technology/artificial-intelligence-expertssalaries.html

Mosco, V. (2009). *The Political Economy of Communication.* London: SAGE.

Murdock, G. and Golding, P. (1973). For a Political Economy of Mass Communications. *Socialist Register*, 10, 205–234.

Noble, S.U. (2018). *Algorithms of Oppression.* New York: New York University Press.

Russell, S. and Norvig, P. (2016). *Artificial Intelligence: A Modern Approach* (3rd edition). Harlow: Pearson Education Limited.

Sadowski, J. (2019). When Data is Capital: Datafication, Accumulation, and Extraction. *Big Data & Society*, 6(1), 1–12.

Sánchez-Tabernero, A. (1993). *Media Concentration in Europe.* London: John Libbey.

Srnicek, N. (2017). *Platform Capitalism.* Cambridge: Polity.

Thompson, J. (1995). *The Media and Modernity. A Social Theory of the Media.* Cambridge: Polity.

Van der Vlist, F.N. and Helmond, A. (2021). How Partners Mediate Platform Power: Mapping Business and Data Partnerships in the Social Media Ecosystem. *Big Data & Society*, 8(1), 1–16.

Van Dijck, J., Poell, T. and de Waal, M. (2018). *The Platform Society: Public Values in a Connective World.* Oxford: Oxford University Press.

Verdegem, P. (2021). Introduction: Why We Need Critical Perspectives on AI. In P. Verdegem (Ed.), *AI for Everyone? Critical Perspectives* (pp. 1–18). London: University of Westminster Press.

Verdegem, P. (2022). Dismantling AI Capitalism: The Commons as an Alternative to the Power Concentration of Big Tech. *AI & Society.* https://doi.org/10.1007/s00146-022-01437-8

Wagner, B. (2018). Ethics as an Escape from Regulation. From 'Ethics-Washing' to 'Ethics-Shopping'? In E. Bayamlioglu, I. Baraliuc, L.A.W. Janssens and M. Hildebrandt (Eds.), *Being Profiled: Cogitas Ergo Sum: 10 Years of Profiling the European Citizen* (pp. 84–89). Amsterdam: Amsterdam University Press.

West, S.M. (2019). Data Capitalism: Redefining the Logics of Surveillance and Privacy. *Business & Society*, 58(1), 20–41.

Wright, E.O. (2010). *Envisioning Real Utopias.* London and New York: Verso.

Wright, E.O. (2019). *How to Be an Anticapitalist in the Twenty-First Century.* London and New York: Verso.

Zuboff, S. (2019). *The Age of Surveillance Capitalism.* New York: Public Affairs.

27. The industry of automating automation: the political economy of the AI industry

James Steinhoff

INTRODUCTION

Artificial intelligence (AI) is today the basis of a growing industry. Intellicorp, often considered to be the first AI startup company, was founded in Menlo Park, California in 1980. Today, Big Tech companies from the same state, such as Google, dominate AI research and development. While academia produces important AI research, industry's increasing influence is visible in the accelerating exodus of AI faculty from universities to industry (Gofman and Jin 2020) and the rising share of new AI PhDs who go into industry rather than academia (AI Index 2021, 118). At the prestigious 2020 machine learning conference NeurIPS, 21% of papers came from industry researchers, while in 2005, industry contributed only 9.5% (Littman et al. 2021). Industry's increased presence raises questions about the quality and autonomy of AI research (Abdalla and Abdalla 2021). This chapter outlines the global scope of the AI industry, the commodities it produces, the labour that produces them and one of the industry's distinctive characteristics: its focus on automating automation. The capitalist mode of production contains an immanent drive to increase the productivity of labour. The most effective way to do so is the introduction of automation technologies that augment and/ or substitute for labour. The contemporary AI industry produces commodities that rely on machine learning, a general-purpose automation technology that can be applied to automate the process of automation itself. The AI industry thus occupies a unique location within contemporary data-intensive capitalism.

CAPITAL, AUTOMATION AND AI

Capitalism is the mode of production premised on the transformation of a quantity of value into more value via the production and exchange of commodities (Marx 1990, 251). Capital refers to a quantity of value passing through this process, whether that of an individual capital competing with others on the market or the totality of the system. In either case, capital must increase, or be "valorized" (Marx 1990, 252). There can never be an end to valorization, as a given quantity of capital could always be larger. As such, new markets, commodities and productive techniques must always be created. Competition thus drives the so-called dynamism of capitalism, for which utility, ecology and well-being necessarily come as afterthoughts.

The production of commodities requires the exploitation of labour. In Marxist terms, exploitation refers to the difference between the wage paid to a worker and the greater value that a worker's capacity to labour (labour-power) can produce (Marx 1990, 418–421). The appropriation of this difference, known as "surplus-value", by the owner of capital is what makes valorization possible (Marx 1990, 293). Capital always seeks to increase this difference. One of the most effective ways to do so is to increase the productivity of labour. The division of labour is the simplest way to do so, but machines present a more fruitful option since new machines can always be invented to further enhance productivity. Over time, capital tends to transform labour-intensive labour processes into machine-intensive ones: "[a]utomate or die" is a demand "imposed by the very functioning of the capitalist mode of production" (Ramtin 1991, 101).

Of course, since Marx's era, the technological milieu has changed significantly. While Marx's contemporaries witnessed steam-powered machines, which were increasingly automatic in their operation, a qualitative leap occurred when it became possible, with the invention of the general-purpose digital computer in the 1940s, to store programs in electronic memory rather than the physical architecture of a computer (Randell 1974, 12). This meant that programs could call on and modify other programs, recursively "recruit[ing] the computer into its own operation" and created the technology of software (Chun 2005, 29). Software opens up the possibility of a machine modifying its functioning in the course of operating as well as the possibility of one machine being programmed to do any number of tasks. This presents innumerable possibilities for automation, limited only in terms of whether the task to be automated can be represented in an algorithmic form amenable to input to a computer.

While the capacities of contemporary machine learning are surprising and efficacious, the novelty of the technology (and the injudicious use of anthropomorphic analogies) should not blind us to its continuities with previous forms of machinery. Whatever ontological and epistemological consequences machine learning may have, it is largely being deployed to increase the productivity of labour and otherwise augment capital valorization (Dyer-Witheford et al. 2019; Steinhoff 2021). Yet it does so in a novel way. Machine learning enables a novel form of automation: the algorithmic production of algorithms. While conventional forms of automation require that one be able to write a rigorous specification of the task to be automated – an algorithm – machine learning allows an algorithm to be automatically constructed on the basis of patterns found in data (Alpaydin 2014, 2). Machine learning, as Domingos (2015) puts it, "automates automation itself" (7). This is far from meaning that no labour is required, but it does mean that data is essential to the AI industry. Fourcade and Healy (2016) describe contemporary capital as driven by a "data imperative" to "collect as much data as possible" (9). This requires constructing and controlling the requisite infrastructure, which takes the form of surveillance technologies built into digital platforms, applications and devices (Sadowski 2019; Andrejevic 2020). However, the connection between data and surveillance may be attenuated by the sophistication of new techniques for generating data, using machine learning and simulations, rather than collecting it via surveillance. Such "synthetic data" approaches are likely to be embraced by capital as a means to automate the production of the data-rich conditions required for machine learning-powered automation (Steinhoff 2022b). The next section elaborates on the entities involved in this industry of automating automation.

DEFINING THE AI INDUSTRY

The AI industry, narrowly defined, refers to companies that produce AI commodities (products or services). This includes well-known Big Tech companies such as Microsoft, and smaller companies including startups and conglomerates like Siemens, which have established in-house AI teams. More broadly defined, the AI industry includes specialized AI hardware producers such as Nvidia and data brokers like Acxiom.

The undisputed leaders of AI research are the Big Tech companies from the US and China, and thus it makes sense to think of the AI industry as a subset of the larger tech industry. From the US comes the quintuplet known as MAAMA: Microsoft, Alphabet (Google), Amazon, Meta (Facebook) and Apple. From China, the quartet is called BATX: Baidu, Alibaba, Tencent and Xiaomi. According to consulting firm McKinsey, big tech companies "are responsible for more than $2 of every $3 spent globally on AI" (quoted in Acemoglu 2021). The quantities of money at play within these companies are startling, as Table 27.1 shows. These figures are especially staggering when one considers them in relation to the gross domestic product (GDP) of countries. Apple's market capitalization of US$2.647 trillion exceeds the GDP of all but seven countries in the world, including Canada, South Korea and Australia, according to Lishchuk (2021).

The dominance of Big Tech is accentuated by heavy AI investment in their home countries. In 2020, the US led in private AI investment with US$23.6 billion, followed by China with US$9.9 billion and the UK with US$1.9 billion (AI Index 2021, 95). China, however, also has unspecified large public investments in AI. While US/China domination of the industry is evident, within this duo interesting things are happening. Banerjee and Sheehan (2020) report that while 29% of "top-tier" AI researchers receive their undergraduate degrees in China and 20% in the US, 59% end up working in the US, as opposed to only 11% in China. Thus, while China is the largest producer of AI experts, the US retains the lion's share of the skilled AI labour produced there, and around the world.

While based in the US and China, big AI industry companies have offices and labs in many Global North countries including the UK, Canada, Israel and throughout the EU. Startups are also widely distributed in such places. This is not to say that the AI industry is not present

Table 27.1   Big Tech: the AI giants

Global rank (world's largest public companies)	Name	Country	Sales	Profit	Market capitalization	Market value
6	Apple	USA	$294 B	$63.9 B	$2.647 T	$2252.3 B
10	Amazon	USA	$386.1 B	$21.3 B	$1.426 T	$1711.8 B
13	Alphabet (Google)	USA	$182.4 B	$40. 3 B	$1.534 T	$1538.9 B
15	Microsoft	USA	$153.3 B	$51.3 B	$2.094 T	$1966.6 B
23	Alibaba Group	China	$93.8 B	$23.3 B	$258.57 B	$657.5 B
29	Tencent Holdings	China	$70 B	$23.3 B	$382.41 B	$773.8 B
33	Facebook (now Meta)	USA	$86 B	$29.1 B	$448.34 B	$870.5 B
222	Xiaomi	China	$35.7 B	$3 B	$37.28 B	$84.5 B
242	Baidu	China	$15.5 B	$3.3 B	$48.76 B	$75.4 B

Source: Data from Murphy et al. (2021) and companiesmarketcap.com.

in the Global South. Africa, for instance, has several high-tech zones including the "Silicon Savannah" in Nairobi, Kenya, which is home to several AI startups. Some successful AI commodities have been developed in the Global South, including Brazilian company Solinftec's ALICE AI agricultural platform and RxAll, a machine learning-powered drug analysis system from Nigeria. However, in general, the Global South "perform[s] poorly in the main ingredients needed for building high-quality AI applications such as big data, computing power and manpower" (Kshetri 2020, 63). This shortage of ingredients is produced and maintained by the AI and tech industries' socioeconomic relationship with the Global South, which Kwet (2019) defines as digital colonialism.

Digital colonialism refers to a "structural form of domination ... exercised through the centralised ownership and control of the three core pillars of the digital ecosystem: software, hardware, and network connectivity" (Kwet 2019, 4). Via such infrastructural control of the digital realm, capitals from the Global North "undermine local development, dominate the market, and extract revenue from the Global South" (Kwet 2019, 7). In the contemporary moment of enthusiasm for machine learning, digital colonialism is especially concerned with the extraction of data, as such it is distinctively a "data colonialism" (Couldry and Mejias 2019).

Africa has been the primary focus of digital colonialism so far. Just as European colonial powers fought over control of the extraction of African resources, including slave labour, from the 16th to 20th centuries, today Big Tech companies are engaged in a struggle for Africa's data, consumers and labour (Anwar and Graham 2020). While companies from the US and China are the most active digital colonists, the EU is involved as well, though it proceeds via trade deals rather than building digital infrastructure (Scasserra and Elebi 2021). China dominates technological investment in Africa. Chinese companies have local offices, Chinese infrastructure projects provide much of the continent with access to telecommunications and digital networks and several African governments have entered into deals with Chinese companies for access to AI technologies (Erie and Streinz 2021). In 2018, the Chinese company CloudWalk launched the first Chinese AI project in Africa by partnering with the Zimbabwean government to build a national face-recognition system in exchange for citizens' data.

Big Tech's interest in the Global South is evident in the proliferation of research centres and labs. Google opened the first corporate AI lab in Accra, Ghana, in 2019. The same year, Microsoft opened its Africa Development Centre, which has a strong AI focus, with two initial sites in Nairobi, Kenya, and Lagos, Nigeria. In 2019, Amazon also opened its first Amazon Web Services office (which distributes AI commodities among others) in Johannesburg, South Africa. In 2020, Chinese telecom giant Huawei opened its Cloud and AI Innovation Centre in Johannesburg, South Africa.

The AI industry giants are also investing in the Global South outside of Africa. In 2019, the US's AI-intensive enterprise software company Salesforce opened its first overseas AI research lab in Singapore, joining Alibaba's cloud wing, which has been there since 2015. In 2019, hyper-successful Hong Kong startup SenseTime announced it would open an "AI park" near Kuala Lumpur, Malaysia. In 2020, IBM (in partnership with the University of São Paulo and a state research foundation) opened the first AI centre in Latin America, the Center for Artificial Intelligence in São Paulo, Brazil. While such centres provide local benefits, including data science education and well-remunerated jobs, they do so in the service of companies headquartered and predominantly operating in rich centres of the US and China by funnelling data, labour and other sources of value out of their locality and into foreign profit-generation mechanisms. On the contrary, organizations such as Tierra Común in Latin America and Masakhane in Africa are facilitating local AI research and development without the mediation of Big Tech (Mhlambi and Miller 2022).

Despite their world-spanning efforts, the biggest AI companies are notable for *not* making money from AI. Instead, they generate most of their revenue through more mundane means as they wait for the automating automation market to mature. In 2021, 82% of revenue at Alphabet came from advertising (Goodwin 2022). The same year, Amazon reported US$222.08 billion in revenue from online retail, US$103.37 billion from "retail third party seller services" and US$62.2 billion from cloud computing section Amazon Web Services, of which AI is one component (Coppola 2022). The biggest companies of the AI industry thus employ cross-subsidization, an aspect of platform capitalism more generally, in which "one arm of the firm reduces the price of a service or good (even providing it for free), but another arm raises prices in order to make up for these losses" (Srnicek 2017, 31). In the AI industry, this phenomenon is magnified. Not only are AI-powered services such as Google Maps and Search given away "for free" (more accurately: in tacit exchange for user data) but the whole research and development of AI is subsidized by the sale of other commodities.

However, for many smaller companies, AI is actually the primary money maker. Startups and small and medium-sized AI companies, such as SenseTime, put AI commodities to market. Unlike SenseTime, which has remained autonomous, other companies, such as DeepMind, aim to be acquired by a larger company before putting out a commodity. This is possible because big AI companies have a ravenous hunger for startups. In 2020 alone, MAAMA acquired 13 startups, spending unspecified billions (CB Insights 2021). This ravenous hunger derives from a business strategy that pervades Big Tech, which Rikap (2021) calls "intellectual monopoly capitalism" in which "capital accumulation (and distribution) is led by a core of intellectual monopolies that base their accumulation (and power) on their permanent and expanding monopoly (and assetization) of predated knowledge" (10). By predated knowledge, she means knowledge that is captured via acquisitions and mergers, but also the capture, via various means, of "knowledge that is still being produced as a commons in universities, public research organizations and open access or open source communities" (Rikap 2021, 11). The AI industry is heavily invested in tapping such sources, including the open-source community (Dyer-Witheford et al. 2019, 53–56) and what might be called the new digital commons (Crawford 2021, 119–121).

At the time of writing in 2022, the economic and political consequences of the COVID-19 pandemic continue to ramify. At first, Big Tech companies raked in record profits and total global investment in AI increased from US$48.9 billion in 2019 to US$67.9 billion in 2020 (AI Index 2021, 93). At the same time, the hiring rates for AI jobs increased in all countries (AI Index 2021, 84). One hypothesis about this growth, advanced by both journalists and economists, is that capitalist interest in automation technologies is exploding amid the pandemic, driven by persistent refusals of work, perceived by capital as a so-called labour shortage (Knight 2021; Chernoff and Warman 2020; Acemoglu 2021). Now, over two years into the COVID era, Big Tech's exceptional success appears to be diminishing, though new applications could bring a new wave of super-profits (The Economist 2022).

TECHNOLOGY AND APPLICATIONS

Contemporary machine learning applications are computationally intensive, data-intensive and require expensive specialized hardware. These costs, along with the fact that such demands are continually increasing, make purchasing the requisite hardware an unattractive option for most companies. Instead, the standard means of producing and distributing AI commodities requires renting access to centralized data centres (clouds), often owned by big AI-producing companies. Even the US Department of Defense is outsourcing its computing needs. The Pentagon is negotiating contracts totalling at least US$10 billion with Amazon, Microsoft and others to provide the computing power for a new initiative called the Joint Warfighting Cloud Capability (Miller 2021).

AI companies sell AI commodities in a number of forms. They might sell applications, off-the-shelf or bespoke machine learning models, analyses or insights produced by their own models or provide a consulting service regarding the development and deployment of models. For a survey of AI commodities on the market, see Ohnsman and Cai (2021). Alternatively, consider Google Cloud, which offers dozens of AI commodities, from Vertex AI, a platform on which developers can build and deploy machine learning models, to a variety of almost plug-and-play products that can be inserted into applications or websites to enable AI functions including real-time speech-to-text conversion, machine translation, automated document analysis and virtual customer service agents. It is thus incorrect to claim that for AI companies, the "final output is not a commodity, as one would expect from a Marxian perspective. Instead, such expenditures usually result in forms of intellectual property rights (e.g. patents) that provide legal ownership of future economic returns" (Prug and Bilić 2021, 30). On the contrary, the output tends to be a commodity intended to function as fixed capital by automating processes in three crucial economic spheres: conception, production and circulation.[1]

Conception refers to the task of conceiving and designing new commodities. Machine learning is notably being applied to conception in the pharmaceutical industry, where it is used to automate the process of discovering new drugs by simulating molecular synthesis at scale. AI companies such as BenevolentAI and Exscientia have sold their commodities to Big Pharma companies like AstraZeneca and Bayer for this purpose (Savage 2021). According to one analysis, medicine (including drug discovery) was the number one area of investment for machine learning applications in 2020 (AI Index 2021, 97).

Production refers to the process of creating a commodity by combining labour power and materials. Historically, this is the sphere in which automation has been focused. AI, however, is in the early stages of being applied in production. Machine vision is increasingly involved in industrial manufacturing; consider Landing AI's LandingLens. But AI is also being used to automate production in more surprising contexts, such as fast-food chain McDonald's, which in 2019 acquired two AI startups and used them to create McD Tech Labs. This initial serving of AI has not satiated McDonald's, however, and the company has since gone on to enter into a partnership with IBM to further develop its automation capacities.

Circulation is the process of transporting a commodity to the hands of its buyer such that its sale can be completed. As companies have achieved rapid global reach and supply chains span the globe, capital has become increasingly concerned with optimizing circulation (Rossiter 2014). The Big Tech companies are masters of circulation, and this is unsurprisingly where the vast majority of AI-powered automation has so far been applied (Steinhoff, Kjøsen and Dyer-Witheford, forthcoming). Google's reliance on advertising and Amazon's on online retail are emblematic of the intensified logistical nature of capital. Logistics is a data-intensive practice

---

[1]   AI is a component of consumer commodities, but AI is not often itself a consumer commodity. You may buy a smartphone loaded with AI-powered applications but you are unlikely to buy a convolutional neural network for personal consumption.

so it should come as no surprise that AI commodities, such as Noodle.ai's Inventory Flow, are applying machine learning to provide predictive logistical analytics.

LABOUR

AI is being applied to automate labour processes; it is also a product of labour. AI companies are composed of all kinds of worker and management roles, but two particular kinds of workers are distinctive in the AI context: data science workers and data workers. While these are unfortunately similar titles, they refer to very different roles in the production of AI.

Data science workers (Muller et al. 2019) refer broadly to highly skilled workers who build data-intensive infrastructures, train machine learning models and conduct data-intensive experiments and analyses. They hold job titles like data scientist and machine learning engineer; however, roles are not yet well-defined in the AI industry and terms are used flexibly. Data science workers tend to hold advanced degrees and can obtain lucrative positions in AI companies, earning an average of around US$100,000 annually in the Global North with the potential for salaries in the millions for experts with celebrity status. High pay is driven by a short supply and high demand. Estimates of the global number of workers skilled in AI in 2017–2018 range from 36,524 (Gagne 2019) to 204,575 (CISTP 2018). While exact numbers may be uncertain, one thing is not: data science workers are mostly men and predominantly white or Asian (Duke 2018; AI Index 2021, 137–144; Harrison 2019).

Data workers (Miceli, Posada and Yang 2022), on the other hand, are workers who prepare the data used to train machine learning models. They are typically employed precariously on a task-based basis, often through platforms such as Amazon Mechanical Turk and ClixSense. They earn relatively little; one study of five such platforms found that in 2017 the average hourly wage for data workers in North America was US$4.70, in Europe and Central Asia US$3.00, US$2.22 in Asia-Pacific and US$1.33 in Africa (Berg et al. 2018, 2). While the absolute number of data workers is unknown, the figure is likely staggering. One study of such work in eight African countries puts the number of people earning money on digital platforms at 4.8 million (Smit et al. 2019). The gender, race and level of education of data workers are hard to summarize as it varies from place to place: "there is no digital labour universalism" (Grohmann and Araújo 2021, 252). Studies in France and the US found that over half of their respondents were women while data for India and one Europe-wide study reported a higher proportion of men than women (Difallah et al. 2018; Forde et al. 2017; Tubaro et al. 2022).

While their situations could hardly be more different, both data science workers and data workers occupy interestingly contradictory positions within capital; they are labourers, and they build the automation systems that capital is impelled to deploy to increase the productivity of labour. What makes the situation of these workers especially interesting is that their work is also being automated; often with the very AI tools they produce.

The work of data science workers is being automated via a technique known as automated machine learning (AutoML) (Zöller and Huber 2019). Previously, I discussed how machine learning can be used to automate labour processes that have not been precisely specified by extracting patterns from data. AutoML applies this capacity to the production of machine learning models, enhancing the productivity of skilled data science workers or imparting basic skills to unskilled users. It thus aims to automate two labour processes at once – the particular process to be automated, as well as the machine learning labour process (Steinhoff 2021, 197). AutoML commodities include Amazon Sagemaker and DataRobot AutoML.

The work of data workers is also being automated, particularly the task of labelling data. Several approaches to this are possible, with active learning being the most prevalent until recently. Active learning refers to the use of machine learning to extrapolate from a small set of hand-labelled data in an attempt to automatically label similar data (Muccino 2021). More recently, a new technique has been developed that eschews individual labels, applying labelling functions instead. These functions "capture labeling rationales and can be applied to vast amounts of unlabeled data to create individual labels automatically" as one company that sells a commodity for this purpose, puts it (Snorkel 2022). They claim that their approach is the first to increase data labelling productivity exponentially and cite an application of their product at Google in which six months of hand-labelled data was replaced in 30 minutes (Team Snorkel 2022).

While the full automation of work in the AI industry seems unlikely in the near future, we should expect the degradation of its quality. The work of data science workers will likely come to resemble that of data workers (Steinhoff 2022a). As Grohmann and Araújo (2021) put it, the future of work looks likely to be a "growing taskification of labour" (252). Perhaps for this reason, among many others, workers in the AI industry have become increasingly active politically. It is notable that since around 2017, tech workers, in general, have been protesting about their employers' work with military and policing agencies, ecological concerns, pernicious discrimination within the industry, breakneck work culture and dubious management practices

CONCLUSION

The critical study of AI should not proceed without a political-economic foundation. As this chapter demonstrates, AI is deeply involved with the social relations constitutive of contemporary data-intensive capitalism. Indeed, the AI industry occupies a unique location therein, centred as it is around the technology of machine learning, which allows the automated generation of algorithms from data. Such algorithms have applications for automating labour processes in production, circulation and conception. Since it has the capacity to produce such means of automating automation, the AI industry is of crucial interest to capital. While the AI industry of 2022 is still young and its commodities rudimentary, it is worth studying because it will continue to evolve and the new forms it takes will have consequences for the political economy of data-intensive capitalism and practical efforts to direct technology towards socially beneficial, rather than profitable, ends. Contemporary struggles against surveillance are not the last word in critiquing Big Tech, as emerging techniques for generating synthetic data suggest. Instead, critical analysis must track how the social relations of capital change even as, at a fundamental level, they remain the same.

REFERENCES

Abdalla, M., & Abdalla, M. (2021). The Grey Hoodie Project: Big Tobacco, Big Tech, and the Threat on Academic Integrity. *Proceedings of the 2021 AAAI/ACM Conference on AI, Ethics, and Society.* https://doi.org/10.1145/3461702.3462563.

Acemoglu, D. (2021). Remaking The Post-COVID World. International Monetary Fund Finance & Development. https://www.imf.org/external/pubs/ft/fandd/2021/03/COVID-inequality-and-autom ation-acemoglu.htm.

Alpaydin, E. (2014). *Introduction to Machine Learning*. MIT Press.

Andrejevic, M. (2020). *Automated Media*. Routledge / Taylor & Francis Group.

Anwar, M. A., & Graham, M. (2020). Digital Labour at Economic Margins: African Workers and the Global Information Economy. *Review of African Political Economy* 47(163): 95–105. https://doi.org /10.1080/03056244.2020.1728243.

Banerjee, I., & Sheehan, M. (2020). America's Got AI Talent: US' Big Lead in AI Research Is Built on Importing Researchers. *MacroPolo*. https://macropolo.org/americas-got-ai-talent-us-big-lead-in-ai -research-is-built-on-importing-researchers/.

Berg, J., Furrer, M., Harmon, E., Rani, U., & Six Silberman, M. (2018). *Digital Labour Platforms and the Future of Work: Towards Decent Work in the Online World*. International Labour Organization.

CB Insights. (2021). Big Tech's AI Ambitions. *CB Insights Research*. https://www.cbinsights.com/ research/big-tech-ai-acquisitions-2020/.

Chernoff, A., & Warman, C. (2020). COVID-19 and Implications for Automation. National Bureau of Economic Research Working Paper 27249. https://doi.org/10.3386/w27249.

Chun, W. H. K. (2005). On Software, or the Persistence of Visual Knowledge. *Grey Room* 18. https:// doi.org/10.1162/1526381043320741.

CISTP. (2018). China AI Development Report 2018. China Institute for Science and Technology Policy at Tsinghua University. http://www.sppm.tsinghua.edu.cn/eWebEditor/UploadFile /China_AI_ development_report_2018.pdf.

Coppola, D. (2022). Amazon: Global Net Revenue by Product 2021. Statista. https://www.statista.com/ statistics/672747/amazons-consolidated-net-revenue-by-segment/.

Couldry, N., & Mejias, U. A. (2019). Data Colonialism: Rethinking Big Data's Relation to the Contemporary Subject. *Television & New Media* 20(4). https://doi.org/10.1177/1527476418796632.

Difallah, D., Filatova, E., & Ipeirotis, P. (2018). Demographics and Dynamics of Mechanical Turk Workers. *Proceedings of the Eleventh ACM International Conference on Web Search and Data Mining*. Association for Computing Machinery. https://doi.org/10.1145/3159652.3159661.

Domingos, P. (2015). *The Master Algorithm: How the Quest for the Ultimate Learning Machine Will Remake Our World*. Basic Books.

Duke, S. (2018). Will AI Make the Gender Gap in the Workplace Harder to Close? *World Economic Forum*. https://www.weforum.org/agenda/2018/12/artificial-intelligence-ai-gender-gap-workplace.

Dyer-Witheford, N., Kjøsen, A. M., & Steinhoff, J. (2019). *Inhuman Power: Artificial Intelligence and the Future of Capitalism*. Pluto Press.

The Economist. (2022). Cloudburst. *The Economist*, July 30.

Erie, MS., & Streinz, T. (2021). The Beijing Effect: China's Digital Silk Road as Transnational Governance. *Journal of International Law and Politics* 54(1).

Forde, C., Stuart, M., Joyce, S., Oliver, L., Valizade, D., Alberti, G., Hardy, K., Trappmann, V., Umney, C., & Carson, C. (2017). *The Social Protection of Workers in the Platform Economy*. European Parliament's Committee on Employment and Social Affairs. http://repositori.uji.es/xmlui/bitstream/ handle/10234/185648/Social_Protection_Spain_2017.pdf?sequence=2.

Fourcade, M., & Healy, K. (2016). Seeing Like a Market. *Socio-Economic Review* 15(1). https://doi.org /10.1093/ser/mww033.

Gagne, J. F. (2019). Global AI Talent Report 2019. https://jfgagne.ai/talent-2019/.

Gofman, M., & Jin, Z. (2020). Artificial Intelligence, Education, and Entrepreneurship. *SSRN*. https:// papers.ssrn.com/sol3/papers.cfm?abstract_id=3449440.

Goodwin, D. (2022). Google Q4 Search Ad Revenue: $43.3 Billion. *Search Engine Land*, February 2. https://searchengineland.com/google-q4-2021-earnings-379735.

Grohmann, R., & Araújo, W. F. (2021). Beyond Mechanical Turk: The Work of Brazilians on Global AI Platforms. In P. Verdegem (Ed.), *AI for Everyone? Critical Perspectives*. University of Westminster Press.

Harrison, S. (2019). Five Years of Tech Diversity Reports—and Little Progress. *Wired*. https://www .wired.com/story/five-years-tech-diversity-reports-little-progress/.

Knight, W. (2021). Covid Brings Automation to the Workplace, Killing Some Jobs. *Wired*. https://www .wired.com/story/covid-brings-automation-workplace-killing-some-jobs/.

Kshetri, N. (2020). Artificial Intelligence in Developing Countries. *IT Professional* 22(4): 63–68. https://doi.org/10.1109/MITP.2019.2951851.

Kwet, M. (2019). Digital Colonialism: US Empire and the New Imperialism in the Global South. *Race & Class* 60(4). https://doi.org/10.1177/0306396818823172.

Lishchuk, R. (2021). How Large Would Tech Companies Be if They Were Countries? Mackeeper, August 13. https://mackeeper.com/blog/tech-giants-as-countries/.

Littman, M. L., et al. (2021). *Gathering Strength, Gathering Storms: The One Hundred Year Study on Artificial Intelligence (AI100) 2021 Study Panel Report.* Stanford University. http://ai100.stanford.edu/2021-report.

Marx, K. (1990) *Capital: Volume I.* Penguin UK.

Miceli, M., Posada, J., & Yang, T. (2022). Studying Up Machine Learning Data: Why Talk About Bias When We Mean Power? *Proceedings of the ACM on Human-Computer Interaction* 6, Article 34. https://doi.org/10.1145/3492853.

Miller, K., & Mhlambi, S. (2022). The Movement to Decolonize AI: Centering Dignity Over Dependency. March 21. Stanford University Human-Centered Artificial Intelligence. https://hai.stanford.edu/news/movement-decolonize-ai-centering-dignity-over-dependency.

Miller, R. (2021). Pentagon Announces New Cloud Initiative to Replace Ill-Fated JEDI Contract. *TechCrunch.* https://social.techcrunch.com/2021/11/19/pentagon-announces-new-cloud-initiative-to-replace-ill-fated-jedi-contract/.

Moore, P. V., & Woodcock, J. (2021). Introduction. AI: Making It, Faking It, Breaking It. In P. V. Moore and J. Woodcock (Eds.), *Augmented Exploitation: Artificial Intelligence, Automation and Work.* Pluto Press.

Muccino, E. (2021). Active Learning for Fast Data Set Labeling. *Mindboard*, April 30. https://medium.com/mindboard/active-learning-for-fast-data-set-labeling-890d4080d750.

Muller, M., Lange, I., Wang, D., Piorkowski, D., Tsay, J., Liao, Q. V., Dugan, C., & Erickson, T. (2019). How Data Science Workers Work with Data: Discovery, Capture, Curation, Design, Creation. In *Proceedings of the 2019 CHI Conference on Human Factors in Computing Systems.* ACM. https://doi.org/10.1145/3290605.3300356.

Murphy, A., Haverstock, E., Gara, A., Helman, C., & Vardi, N. (2021). The Global 2000 2021. *Forbes.* https://www.forbes.com/lists/global2000/.

Ohnsman, A., & Cai, K. (2021). AI 50 2021: America's Most Promising Artificial Intelligence Companies. *Forbes.* https://www.forbes.com/sites/alanohnsman/2021/04/26/ai-50-americas-most-promising-artificial-intelligence-companies/.

Prug, T., & Bilić, P. (2021). Work Now, Profit Later: AI Between Capital, Labour and Regulation. In P. V. Moore and J. Woodcock (Eds.), *Augmented Exploitation: Artificial Intelligence, Automation and Work.* Pluto Press.

Ramtin, R. (1991). *Capitalism and Automation: Revolution in Technology and Capitalist Breakdown.* Pluto Press.

Randell, B. (1974). The History of Digital Computers. Computing Laboratory, University of Newcastle Upon Tyne. https://citeseerx.ist.psu.edu/viewdoc/download?doi=10.1.1.444.5949&rep=rep1&type=pdf.

Rikap, C. (2021). *Capitalism, Power and Innovation; Intellectual Monopoly Capitalism Uncovered.* Routledge.

Rossiter, N. (2014). Logistical Worlds. *Cultural Studies Review* 20(1). https://doi.org/10.5130/csr.v20i1.3833.

Sadowski, J. (2019). When Data Is Capital: Datafication, Accumulation, and Extraction. *Big Data & Society* 6(1). https://doi.org/10.1177/2053951718820549.

Savage, N. (2021). Tapping into the Drug Discovery Potential of AI. *Biopharma Dealmakers*, May 27. https://doi.org/10.1038/d43747-021-00045-7.

Scasserra, S., & Martínez Elebi, C. (2021). *Digital Colonialism: Analysis of Europe's Trade Agenda.* Transnational Institute. https://www.tni.org/files/publication-downloads/digital-colonialism-report-tni_en.pdf.

Smit, H., Johnson, C., Hunter, R., Dunn, M., & van Vuuren, P. F. (2019). *Africa's Digital Platforms and Financial Services: An Eight-country Overview.* CENFRI.

Snorkel. (2022). Making Automated Data Labeling a Reality in Modern AI. https://snorkel.ai/automated-data-labeling/.

Srnicek, N. (2017). *Platform Capitalism*. John Wiley & Sons.

Steinhoff, J. (2021). *Automation and Autonomy: Labour, Capital and Machines in the Artificial Intelligence Industry*. Palgrave Macmillan.

Steinhoff, J. (2022a). The Proletarianization of Data Science. In M. Graham and F. Ferrari (Eds.), *Digital Work in the Planetary Market*. 1–17. MIT Press.

Steinhoff, J. (2022b). Toward a Political Economy of Synthetic Data: A Data-intensive Capitalism that is not a Surveillance Capitalism? *New Media & Society*.

Steinhoff, J., Kjøsen, A. M., & Dyer-Witheford, N. (2023). Stagnation, Circulation and the Automated Abyss. In J. Fehrle, J. Ramirez and M. Lieber (Eds.), *(De)Automating the Future: Marxist Perspectives on Capitalism and Technology*. Brill.

Team Snorkel. (2022). How Google Used Snorkel to Build and Adapt Content Classification Models. https://snorkel.ai/google-content-classification-models-case-study/.

Tubaro, P., Coville, M., Le Ludec, C., & Casilli, A. A. (2022). Hidden Inequalities: The Gendered Labour of Women on Micro-Tasking Platforms. *Internet Policy Review* 11(1). https://policyreview .info/articles/analysis/hidden-inequalities-gendered-labour-women-micro-tasking-platforms.

Zhang, D., Mishra, S., Brynjolfsson, E., Etchemendy, J., Ganguli, D., Grosz, B., Lyons, T., Manyika, J., Niebles, JC., Sellitto, M., Shoham, Y., Clark, J & Perrault, R. (2021) *The AI Index 2021 Annual Report*. AI Index Steering Committee, Human-Centered AI Institute, Stanford University, Stanford, CA.

Zöller, M. A., & Huber, M. F. (2019). Survey on Automated Machine Learning. arXiv preprint. arXiv:1904.12054.

28. AI, class societies and the social life of reason

Scott Timcke

Today, domination perpetuates and extends itself not only through technology but as technology, and the latter provides the great legitimation of the expanding political power, which absorbs all spheres of culture.

—Herbert Marcuse

THE ONTOGENESIS OF AI

The ontogenesis of AI is bound by a particular historical circumstance, this being a mature and aggressive global capitalist era. Appreciating this fact can help bring a counterpoint to futurist claims about AI helping to liberate people from toil (e.g., Wilson and Daugherty 2018). Consider how early writings about the internet envisioned that digital networking would enable alternatives to hierarchy. Many potential goods were imagined. Whether Habermasian scholars buoyed about the prospect of a revitalized public sphere (Papacharissi 2002; Wiklund 2005) or techno-libertarians at The WELL looking to test models of non-state self-government (Barbrook and Cameron 1996 [1995]), as the last century ended there was a belief that 'being digital' (Negroponte 1995) through 'free software' and a rejection of private property rights (Stallman 2002), people would soon be 'homesteading on the electronic frontier' (Rheingold 1994). In that conjuncture, it was thought that the 'passing of industrial society' would reorganize social stations creating, if not a fairer society, at least prospects for one. Nevertheless, after commercial prospecting in the last two decades, many digital places have become enclosed, circumscribed, and tethered to capitalist imperatives. As it stands, capitalists are the main beneficiary of digitalization (Schiller 1999; Dean 2009; Fuchs 2013; Greaves 2015; Zuboff 2019; Timcke 2021). While the past is not destiny, this contingent history should be foregrounded in any sociological analysis of AI if only to underscore that with different circumstances, AI could also take on new social properties, potentials that are not yet fully conceived.

The 'classic' definition of AI comes from Stuart Russell and Peter Norvig. They write that these collected systems follow the 'general principles of rational agents' where 'the standard of rationality is mathematically well defined and completely general' (2010, 5). In more practical engineering terms, AI can work with a range of computer programs, like image recognition systems, to achieve specific tasks, such as the assembly frameworks in a self-driving car. Still, as I have written elsewhere (Timcke 2021, 128–129), I am somewhat ambivalent about these definitions. This is because, and accepting a degree of simplification, AI programs rely upon experts coding rules, like traffic laws, whereupon a program deduces and selects pathways through the environment in accordance with the boundary of the program. These rules are the product of situated human labour and judgement. This means that there is a sociology of abstract computation, one that is always already entangled with the labour process and prevailing ideas of how to organize places. Additionally, situating abstract concepts like AI in a concrete social context can clarify the sources of mystification and the stakes in the politics for, with, and over this kind of technology.

On this note, I wholeheartedly agree with Alan Turing (1950) when he insisted that the 'question, "Can machines think!"' is 'too meaningless to deserve discussion.' So one must be cautious of the kinds of imaginative temptations that the term AI conjures. Such language work can hinder the ability to understand the systems humans are making. To reiterate this point, one must not lose sight of the thousands of engineers who worked together to build AI systems, the labour to collect and clean datasets for AI to process, or the humans employed by corporations who pose as components of AI systems (see Newlands 2021). So regardless of AI shifting from coded rules to coded weights as is increasingly the case, so the issue of labour and situated judgement remains salient.

So more than code and infrastructure, AI encompasses a mode of thought for human communities wherein calculation creates certain forms of experience. Accordingly, this chapter focuses on rationality and reification as these affect decision making and expertise in technologically advanced polities. This chapter primarily discusses the thought of Lukács and Marcuse when they conceptualize technology and rationality. A word of caution: these scholars are the 'natural predecessor' to another. Thought of that sort means an interpretation is already delimited based upon an image of who is a predecessor. Rather, these scholars offer useful intuitions to help guide contemporary analysis. Surveying these perspectives is not only a matter for problem identification and case selection but also explains why critical paradigms can provide a methodology to understand AI as a social form. This is necessary because technological development can set off unpredictable sequences of new artefacts, affordances, and organizational changes, with each bringing its own 'procedural rhetoric' (Bogost 2007), which allows unpredictable processes to become self-justifying.

THE REIFICATION OF REASON

To support the broad position advanced in this chapter, it is useful to begin with Marx's arguments about commodity fetishism. Marx's concept introduces the idea that market transactions typically do not comprehend products as the output of a labour process that is embedded within a web of social relationships. Forgetting these historical attributes helps the money form take hold. Money is thought to best represent the value of the objects, not the purposes humans put those objects to. The result is that in certain circumstances, 20 yards of linen can become equivalent to a coat, for example. These interlinked ideas have important conceptual consequences for the analysis of the workplace. Even critical scholarship concedes that social struggles in workplaces are about who decides the shares and the due proportion of the rewards of production.

This struggle between capital and labour has great ramifications for social life, both purposeful and accidental. Despite new venues of struggle, like the digital realm, the idea of reification remains useful, especially when reframed as a theory of stakes in political economy. These stakes are the object of struggle between various classes and factions, the distribution thereof having a significant impact on fortune and misfortune. Additionally, these struggles are never neutral in principle, nor neutral with respect to class, geography, or history. Indeed, these struggles shape what people take as reality. (The ecological crisis from whole continents littered with industrial factories testify to the truthfulness of the objectification of material space, licensed by specific ideas.) But as Marxists explain, due to reification, the struggle between capital and labour is rife with wilful negligence, plain ignorance, or convenient amnesia.

It does not help that the concept of reification has 'fallen into virtual oblivion in recent years' according to Martin Jay (2008, 3). Put simply, reification is an error in reasoning that misconstrues the abstract as a material thing and then forgets the distinction between the two (see Timcke 2013). As an example, capitalists are—through the aforementioned negligence, ignorance, or amnesia—only able to view labourers through the labour market, but not as human in and of themselves. Put differently, labour power is treated simply as a commodity, not something that humans do regardless of the fees they may bargain over in labour markets.

The concept of reification well explains the core mechanics of capitalism. Indeed, György Lukács centrally incorporated reification into Marxist accounts of reasoning, a line of research which was then subsequently adopted and advanced by members of the Frankfurt School. In these hands, the concept "became a powerful weapon in the struggle not only to define what capitalism did to its victims, but also to explain why they were unable to resist it successfully," why for instance industrial working classes did not advance the "historical mission assigned to it by [orthodox] Marxist theory" (Jay 2008, 4).

The short answer to that question was that even under the best of conditions, reification made the stakes of social struggle difficult to identify.

There is also a second complementary explanation. For Lukács, when the commodity form becomes total, then reification is also total. In plain language, as capitalist social relations intensify so there are fewer and fewer ways to conceptualize life outside of those relations. In this explanation, the proletariat's 'self-knowledge of reality' (Lukács 1971, 16) is shaped by the maturation of capitalism. As he writes:

> [The] development of the commodity to the point where it becomes the dominant form in society did not take place until the advent of modern capitalism. Hence it is not to be wondered at that the personal nature of economic relations was still understood clearly on occasion at the start of capitalist development, but that as the process advanced and forms became more complex and less direct, it became increasingly difficult and rare to find anyone penetrating the veil of reification. (1971, 86)

This dominant form meant that capitalist reasoning gained significant clout, even among workers themselves. Unions making the business case that unionization increased productivity is a good example of how labour adopts the reasoning of capital. 'As the commodity becomes universally dominant, this situation changes radically and qualitatively,' Lukács wrote. The consequence of reification is that 'a society should learn to satisfy all its needs in terms of commodity exchange' (Lukács 1971, 91), thereby perpetuating a very narrow set of justifications as the hypothetical case alludes to.

Lukács' solution is that the working class must adopt a class consciousness that does not rely upon capitalist reasoning about the interests of capitalists. In the language of high theory, the proletariat could become 'both the subject and the object of knowledge' (Lukács 1971, 2). Only through reorienting the modes, objects, and intentions of reasoning away from one-dimensional pursuits of profit and fungibility can 'the precondition of the revolutionary function of the theory become possible' (Lukács 1971, 3). Until these conditions were met, party vanguardism would be unable to sufficiently transform the existing social relations. This conclusion did introduce an empirical question, this being what are some other limitations to comprehending the reification of commodification? To answer these and similar questions, I will turn to some of Marcuse's thought. This turn also requires a brief discussion of two points raised by Weber and Heidegger, two theorists that greatly shaped Marcuse's philosophy. As Weber's intellectual project was a 'debate with Marx's ghost' (Salomon quoted in Cuneo 1990, 84), it is useful to first call upon his work on rationalization and rationality.

THE TYRANNY OF TECHNOLOGICAL RATIONALITY

The concept of rationality appears in a wide range of socio-structural phenomena in Weber's work. In the main, one of his central arguments was that the maturation of formal rationality has suppressed the development of substantive rationality. The impartial, impersonal calculation of market exchanges intensifies and deepens this process. To link back to the previous section, this is partly why labour makes the business case for unionization. By formal rationality, Weber sought to convey calculability, especially in domains where goods and services can or had been quantified. Substantive rationality, by contrast, depends on 'ultimate ends' (Weber 1968, 856). This was an empirical argument. Pointing to how the prophets of the Reformation—through their rejection of mysticism—had cleared the ground for the process of rationalization that subsequently came to secularize Western culture, Weber projected that the future was uniformity as technical, quantified reason became applied to every aspect of social life. Borrowing from Friedrich Schiller, the rise of technological manipulation ushered in a 'disenchantment of the world,' one rife with bureaucratic servitude.

As these kinds of distinctions and conclusions apply to *Wissenschaft*—structured inquiry—both the natural and social sciences were incapable of giving an answer to the question 'What shall we do and how shall we live?' (Weber 2004, 17), a remark that alludes to Kant's three great prompts, what can I know? What must I do? and What may I hope?. Certainly, *Wissenschaft* could contribute to factual knowledge of political action and consequences, but it cannot validate judgements about needs or wants. While there are relations between facts and values, separating the evaluative from the prescriptive illustrates the broader move from societies organized around conviction to those organized around responsibility. This realism about trade-offs can be seen in the motifs about academic maturity that repeat throughout lectures like 'Science as a Vocation.' Yet, according to Jürgen Habermas, the 'separation of politics from morality' brought about a change in the meaning of 'order': the task of government is the 'regulation of social intercourse.' Weber's template for *Wissenschaft* was depleted of virtue and judgement. What remained for politics—and for the social-scientific study thereof—was 'normative determinations were submerged in equivocation of "nature."' Yet with 'nature' so difficult to systematize, the bulk of the work took the form of historical explications about how knowledge of social interrelations makes 'political action possible,' or sought to 'obtain clarification' about what is 'objectively possible' (Habermas 1974, 43–44). Arguably, this conceptualization of structured inquiry is common in the computational sciences, especially as one reads Russell and Norvig's textbook on AI where matters of ethics and harm receive a sophomoric four-page treatment in a book that is otherwise more than 1150 pages.

Whereas Weber focused on markets and bureaucracy, Heidegger attended to how modern experience is encountered technologically. While it is not feasible to provide a full discussion of Heidegger's ideas, especially as they relate to his wider project about nature and experience in *Being and Times*, what is vital for the purposes of this chapter is that technology mediates how the world is revealed. In the standard interpretation of Heidegger, the essence of technology is not the practical application of the natural sciences. Rather, natural science is the by-product of comprehending nature according to calculable forces. Technology then brings its own comprehension of how parts are related to the whole. While it emerged from factories and heavy industry, this essence holds sway in areas of the world not typically associated with technology, like religion or history. In sum, this way of structuring impacts how people belong to the world.

What is at stake for Heidegger is not (mis)recognition. Rather, it is how *Dasein* experiences the world. As *Dasein* cannot understand itself independently, what happens to interpretation when immediate 'points of reference' (Heidegger 2012) are so thoroughly fungible, when nature is encountered technologically, it becomes ready for technical exploitation? Indeed, opinions about the harm or benefits of technology reflect 'how the dominance of the essence of technology orders into its plundering even and especially the human conceptions concerning technology.' Measured by this criterion, 'all these conceptions and valuations' are 'from the outset unwittingly in agreement that technology would be a means to an end' (Heidegger 2012). A world encountered technologically brings about a fundamental restructuring of reality that constrains potentialities, leaving domination and alienation in its place. Workers, for instance, become instruments in production. Or, in the more contemporary parlance, they are 'human capital.' This is perhaps why there has been such explicit affinity between early forms of AI-social systems thinking like cybernetics, economic rationality, and social science in the Cold War (see Gigerenzer and Selten 2001; Engerman 2010).

THE ABOLITION OF IMPARTIAL INTERESTS

Between Weber's and Heidegger's respective thoughts, we glimpse that while technology appears value neutral it is biased towards domination. To these problems, Heidegger offered a 'free relation to technology,' this amounting to attitudinal change. Marcuse, however, is more radical. His analysis led him to call for a change in instrumentality through the abolition of class society. Echoing Weber and Heidegger, Marcuse argued that modern technology had no end but for classification, quantification, and control exclusively along empirical lines. The meant machinery may consider issues of coercion and control, but there is a general abstention when it comes to any sense of totality or the purpose of that totality. The result of this led to an inability to distinguish between current preferences and future potentialities. In the interim, technology was a system with imperatives unto itself while purporting that these imperatives are a product of discrete subjective desires. The concept of technological rationality is not equivalent to basic technical principles or concrete applications. Nor is it the drive for efficiency or control, but rather the social process by which goals are identified.

Accordingly, the preference of the market, and its unrestrained totalizing impulse, was the epitome of technological rationality. Indeed, as more extra-market aspects of life were organized by technical means, those same aspects reinforced the dominance of capitalist social relations by naturalizing hierarchy. This is the mechanical application of normative judgements that have been obscured, hiding the norms and values that inflect their construction and application, need and purpose. This makes the subjective objective while naturalizing the prevailing order. After an apology in the preface to *One Dimensional Man* for the abstract character of his analysis, Marcuse writes that 'The fact that the vast majority of the population accepts, and is made to accept, this society does not render it less irrational and less reprehensible.' As a result, 'even the most empirical analysis of historical alternatives appears to be unrealistic speculation, and commitment to them a matter of personal (or group) preference,' he writes. If capitalists' and workers' goals were treated as preferences, then the dreams of self-determination by labour can be judged to be implausible. Erstwhile the fiduciary responsibility to maximize profit irrespective of social or ecological harms caused can be deemed duly appropriate. The abstract process of rationality makes the partial seem impartial.

In *Eros and Civilization*, Marcuse sought to explain how advancing ruling interests became impartial. He did this by weaving together Marx's conception of surplus labour—which demonstrates that capitalism rests on the exploitation of the working class—and Freud's argument that modernity has inherently repressive elements that sublimate unconscious erotic desires or instant gratification. This produced the concept of 'surplus repression.' Like surplus labour, surplus repression is over and over what is required for social reproduction and is simply a function to maintain unyielding capital accumulation. Surplus repression was a key mechanism to maintain labour deference under demands of high productivity; here workers psychologically internalize and act in accordance with capital's interests, thereby naturalizing repression at the expense of acknowledging the unequal property relations between them and capitalists.

A critic might ask, 'if not rationality, what?' Are there any alternatives to value neutrality? Marcuse directs people to look towards the present struggles for potentials and alternatives. The Marxian dialectical tradition is especially useful here. With its attention to the interconnected context revealed in strife. By taking a second look at uncritically accepted social consensus and seeing what other potentialities could be strived for and even realized. These potentialities are grounded in existing tensions, not mere speculative notions. Look to present struggles and real demands for a programmatic agenda by permitting imagination to flourish. Indeed, these potentials could become ever clearer if repression eased, and free development was permitted. Furthermore, changing the material base of society, not just the relations to and regulations of the base, would allow science and technology to be reformed at the most basic level, this being rationality itself. Through this change, the base could come to exemplify what Weber called substantive rationality.

Marxists typically indict capitalist society for failing to maximally develop its technological base to properly deliver goods to people in need, using mechanization to de-skill the labour process and thereby creating a reserve army of labour to lower wages. But as Marcuse points out, the solution is not merely reorienting the industrial base from a private property regime to the public one. This is an error because the distributional skews in modern political-economic arrangements do not solely arise because capitalists are 'in charge'. This may make for a compelling narrative that galvanizes a movement. However, reversing the hierarchy in the labour-capital polarity through democratization and restructuring would not and does not sublimate major inequalities. This is because the 'capitalists are in charge' narrative has a weak comprehension of markets and mechanization. Beyond distributional critiques, the fundamental issue concerns the need to enable potentials so that new productive bases become possible to realize in the first place. Simply 'doing things differently' will not suffice. Nor will replacing key agents with agents affiliated with labour's interests. A more sophisticated analysis foregrounds how the rationality advanced by the infrastructure itself is part of the problem of social inequality.

THE POTENTIAL FOR A PROLETARIAN AI

When we draw upon Lukács' and Marcuse's various insights about reification and rationality, a Marxist critique of AI does not hinge on the necessity of growth or sharing existing material goods more fairly with once subordinated groups. Rather, it is predicated upon the potential to create new configurations entirely, ones that deliver material goods to those that need them as and when that need arises. One hindrance to actualizing potential lies with the fetishism of the very kind of rationality AI is deploying, a kind of technological rationality encoded throughout the entire modern industrial base and which AI systems are soon anticipated to guide.

Yet at the same time, people are right to see utility in AI. Technologies like this are likely to create enumerable goods that, if used well, could greatly alleviate toil. But prospects like these need to be judged against a history of technological and social change in which the shareholders of firms have considerably more power than users. Concurrently, the same digital technologies that some use as assets have become indispensable for everyday life. There is almost no option but to use digital technologies to engage with communities, companies, and governments in routine activities. So, opting out is neither reasonable nor feasible. Much like how people are 'thrown into the world,' they have no choice in the society in which they were born and have to make their way in a particular political and economic system, they still nevertheless have the chance to realize any potential they could conceive.

The starting point for the revival of self-determination requires a forthwith discussion about how and why capitalism captured digitalization, as Robert McChesney (2013) suggests. Indeed, the transition to capitalism literature is especially useful in helping scholars identify similar patterns of social change that occurred and are occurring in the digital realm (Timcke 2017, Timcke 2021). This approach can partly explain why capitalists are well-positioned to capture and be captured by AI. Certainly, a good portion of their power can be attributed to the ordinary operation of a private property regime through which market power affects the price of access. Furthermore, proprietary systems give capitalists the ability to allocate the power to reinforce existing social relations surrounding emerging technologies. Given current practices, there are legitimate concerns that AI will help capitalists further intensify the extraction of surplus value. Already Whole Foods, a subsidiary of Amazon, is using heat mapping tracking technology to break unionization attempts (Peterson 2020). So it is not far-fetched to think AI will be deployed for the same politics. However, the question of technology is also more fundamental—it involves establishing how actions within class societies are rationalized to create a 'path-easy-to-travel.'

As with the internet before, one difficulty with writing about AI is the nature of the struggle for, over, and with technology *in medias res*. Questions of tone and temperament are especially hard to calibrate in these circumstances, meaning that differences between undue alarmism and empirically and historically informed caution can blur. Comprehension is made more difficult because even if some of the models like OpenAI are open source, much of the general AI research projects are proprietary. (This kind of opacity is compounded by the 'hype cycles' in Silicon Valley, which frankly cannot be treated as believable as seemingly the main task of marketing departments is to buoy a firm's valuation to increase the wealth of shareholders.) Instead, sociologists can best undertake their analysis by looking at how these kinds of technologies are a social form that emerges in and relates to other pre-existing social forms.

If or when sociologists examine AI and capitalism, it is not enough to use class analysis. That is merely the first step. What is important is to examine how the reification of capitalist reason shapes the technological rationality of AI. Failure to undertake this second step would result in an incomplete understanding of how uses and applications are determined. If the goal is to recover potentials, then drawing upon Lukács' and Marcuse's conceptualization of how rationality directs comprehension can help AI scholars, researchers, and technicians understand how the observable struggles around this technology are encoded by politics and social forces that will precede this specific technological innovation.

I make mention of all this to underscore how in addition to being a technical entity, AI has a social register. Returning to the subject of definitions raised in the introduction, in addition to source code, AI is also an actual institution with a set of meanings, articulations, and efforts by multiple vested parties to define that institution. This mutability underscores how both institution and conceptualized articulations are historical. By changing the institution and concept, we can build a critical approach to infrastructure grounded in maximizing the chance of new potentials to arise, some of which could very likely serve democratic ends. AI is unmistakably a political phenomenon. If one changes the politics, the meanings and practices can change too. While it is unwise to concede political struggles before they are fought, it is equally unwise to engage in struggle without a fair appreciation of the task required.

Finally, the mutability of meanings prompts a set of questions about whether it makes sense to ask whether under specific circumstances AI protocols could achieve something akin to class consciousness. Let me explain. If it is commonplace within science and technology studies to talk about how technological systems encode values via a 'sociotechnical imaginary' encumbered with normative assumptions and institutional anchors (see Jasanoff 2015; also see Feenberg 2017), then it is worth asking whether the politics of AI artefacts might generate forces that have similar kinds of ramifications as class consciousness. Under what conditions might proletarianized AI be possible to identify, and how might it oppose relentless accumulation? I have no definitive answers to these questions, but they are hardly esoteric for the intellectual historian. Ultimately, this kind of theorizing is not for its own sake. Rather, it is about prospects for social and technological change. What I mean is under what conditions might AI help people better realize the potential of self-determination considering that AI itself might also alter conditions.

ACKNOWLEDGEMENTS

Thanks are due to Burcu Baykurt and Javier Toscano for comments on earlier versions. This chapter was drafted with the financial support of a fellowship at the Centre for Advanced Internet Studies, Bochum Germany.

FURTHER READING

Dyer-Witheford, N., Kjøsen, A. M. and Steinhoff, J. (2019). *Inhuman power: Artificial intelligence and the future of capitalism*. Pluto Press.
Feenberg, A. (2017). *Technosystem: The social life of reason*. Harvard University Press.
Marcuse, H. (2013). *One-dimensional man: Studies in the ideology of advanced industrial society*. Routledge.

REFERENCES

Barbrook, R. and Cameron, A. (1996). The Californian ideology. *Science as Culture* 6(1): 44–72. https://doi.org/10.1080/09505439609526455

Bogost, I. (2007). *Persuasive games: The expressive power of videogames.* MIT Press.

Cuneo, M. W. (1990). Values and meaning: Max Weber's approach to the idea of ultimate reality and meaning. *Ultimate Reality and Meaning* 13(2): 84–95. https://doi.org/10.3138/uram.13.2.84

Dean, J. (2009). *Democracy and other neoliberal fantasies: Communicative capitalism and left politics.* Duke University Press.

Engerman, D. (2010). Social science in the cold war. *Isis* 101(2): 393–400.

Feenberg, A. (2017). *Technosystem: The social life of reason.* Harvard University Press.

Fuchs, C. (2013). *Social media: A critical introduction.* SAGE Publications.

Gigerenzer, G. and Selten, R. (2001). Rethinking rationality. In G. Gigerenzer and R. Selten (Eds.), *Bounded rationality: The adaptive toolbox* (pp. 1–12). The MIT Press.

Greaves, M. (2015). The rethinking of technology in class struggle: Communicative affirmation and foreclosure politics. *Rethinking Marxism* 27(2): 195–211. https://doi.org/10.1080/08935696.2015.1007792

Haberman, J. (1974). *Theory and practice.* Beacon Press.

Heidegger, M. (1962). *Being and time* (J. MacQuarrie & E. Robinson, Trans). Harper & Row.

Heidegger, M. (2012). *Bremen and Freiburg lectures* (A. J. Mitchell, Trans). Indiana University Press.

Jasanoff, S. (2015). Future imperfect: Science, technology, and the imaginations of modernity. In S. Jasanoff and S. Kim (Eds.), *Dreamscapes of modernity: Sociotechnical imaginaries and the fabrication of power.* Chicago: University of Chicago Press.

Jay, M. (2008). Introduction. In A. Honneth (Ed.), *Reification: A new look at an old idea.* Oxford University Press.

Lukacs, G. (1971). *History and class consciousness: Studies in Marxist dialectics.* MIT Press.

Marcuse, H. (1966). *Eros and civilization: A philosophical inquiry into Freud.* Beacon Press.

Marcuse, H. (2013). *One-dimensional man: Studies in the ideology of advanced industrial society.* Routledge.

McChesney, R. W. (2013). *Digital disconnect: How capitalism is turning the internet against democracy.* New Press.

Negroponte, N. (1995). *Being digital.* Hodder & Stoughton.

Newlands, G. (2021). Lifting the curtain: Strategic visibility of human labour in AI-as-a-Service. *Big Data & Society.* https://doi.org/10.1177/20539517211016026

Papacharissi, Z. (2002). The virtual sphere: The internet as a public sphere. *New Media & Society* 4(1): 9–27. https://doi.org/10.1177/14614440222226244

Peterson, H. (2020, April 22). Amazon-owned whole foods is quietly tracking its employees with a heat map tool that ranks which stores are most at risk of unionizing. Business Insider. https://www.businessinsider.com/whole-foods-tracks-unionization-risk-with-heat-map-2020-1

Rheingold, H. (1994). *The virtual community: Homesteading on the electronic frontier.* Harper Perennial.

Russell, S. and Norvig, P. (2010). *Artificial Intelligence: A modern approach*, 3rd edition. Prentice Hall.

Schiller, D. (1999). *Digital capitalism: Networking the global market system.* MIT Press.

Stallman, R. M. (2002). *Free software, free society: Selected essays of Richard M. Stallman.* GNU Press. https://www.gnu.org/philosophy/fsfs/rms-essays.pdf

Timcke, S. (2013). Is all reification forgetting? On Connerton's types of forgetting. *Triple-C* 11(2): 375–387. https://doi.org/10.31269/triplec.v11i2.469

Timcke, S. (2017). *Capital, state, empire: The new American way of digital warfare.* University of Westminster Press.

Timcke, S. (2021). *Algorithms and the end of politics: The shaping of technology in 21st century American life.* Bristol University Press.

Turing, A. A. (1950). Computing machinery and intelligence. *Mind* LIX(236): 433–460. https://doi.org/10.1093/mind/LIX.236.433

Weber, M. (1968). *Economy and society.* Bedminster.

Weber, M. (2004). Science as a vocation. In M. Weber (Ed.), *The vocation lectures*. Hackett Publishing Company.

Wiklund, H. (2005). A Habermasian analysis of the deliberative democratic potential of ICT-enabled services in Swedish municipalities. *New Media & Society* 7(2): 247–270. https://doi.org/10.1177/1461444805050764

Wilson, H. J. and Daugherty, P. R. (2018, July). Collaborative intelligence. *Harvard Business Review.* https://hbr.org/2018/07/collaborative-intelligence-humans-and-ai-are-joining-forces

Zuboff, S. (2019). *The age of surveillance capitalism*. Profile Books.

29. Re-imagining democracy: AI's challenge to political theory

Guy Paltieli

INTRODUCTION

Artificial intelligence (AI) has been described as a disruptive technological force, one that challenges society, the economy and policymaking (Jamie Berryhill et al., 2019). Its introduction into democratic politics takes place at a time when more citizens continuously express their discontent with democratic politics, the ongoing squabbles that characterise it and its lack of decisiveness. In recent policy papers that were published by some democratic governments, AI is presented as a technology that would potentially help democracies overcome this crisis by making it quicker, more responsive and more just (Denmark, 2019; Villani, 2018). This trend reflects a broader attempt by some democratic governments to serve as a counterforce to the growing power of Big Tech corporations. The "Cambridge Analytica" scandal made both the US Congress and the UK Parliament begin investigating the political and economic power of these corporations and suggest countermeasures that will maintain popular sovereignty (Cicilline, 2020; House of Commons, 2019). Yet, in theoretical terms, this story is more complicated than it seems prima facie. AI challenges some fundamental ideas in political theory and the boundaries it sets between different ideological systems and the opportunities citizens might have in contemporary politics.

This chapter seeks to understand how AI challenges political theory and continues the work of others who sought to understand how AI might revitalise political theory (Sætra, 2020) or how it might allow a critical assessment of AI (Coeckelbergh, 2022). But it does so in a different way and tries to establish a new form of politics that I will describe as a "liberal data republic". This idea follows my work on National AI Strategies where I argued that a new political imaginary is needed to maintain a vibrant political sphere that will be able to maintain popular sovereignty over AI and data (Paltieli, 2021, 2022). The idea of a "liberal data republic" that I will develop in this chapter suggests that in the context of AI, the divisions between liberal and republican ideas of freedom and legitimacy are blurred. The challenge that AI poses is, therefore, not only political but also theoretical. As I suggest here, these two challenges are intertwined and should be explored as such. The chapter is critical in two ways. One, it rejects the idea that AI can be utilised in contemporary politics without an appropriate popular political reaction. Second, it criticises the attempt to adapt political theory to AI. This attempt, I argue, misses fundamental aspects of AI and does not fully capture the political challenges AI poses nor the potential political solutions that can become available.

This chapter will follow three challenges AI raises for political theory. One addresses the pace of democratic politics, and the growing trend to make it faster through the use of AI. The risk from this challenge, I argue, is the potential hollowing out of democratic politics. The second challenge is the change in the meaning of political participation. I argue that by using AI, a new form of political participation emerges, one that is essentially non-intentional where citizens influence politics without intending to. The third challenge is closely related to the need to re-imagine democracy by overcoming the clear distinction between liberal and republican theories of politics.

RESPONDING TO CRISIS

AI finds democratic politics at a challenging time when they are perceived by citizens as slow and unresponsive (Mounk, 2018; Runciman, 2018). Recent technological shifts, and mainly social media, have made things even more difficult for democratic governments who find it hard to keep up with the new technological pace (Tromble, 2018). Some policy papers that outline how AI can make democracy more responsive address this challenge directly and consider AI to be an effective solution (Finland, 2017; Hall & Pesenti, 2017; Villani, 2018). The point I wish to make in this section is that this desire challenges some core aspects of democracy. Sætra (2020) described in a recent paper the pros and cons of incorporating AI in politics and stressed that one of the objections towards it is its potential of overcoming objections. I wish to continue this line of thought and argue that responding to this crisis through algorithmic responsiveness might hollow out democratic politics.

Responsiveness is an important element in democratic politics that oversees how public demands eventually become policy measures (Dahl, 1971; Putnam, 1993). Yet, responsiveness is amorphous, and the exact time that needs to pass until a government responds is never fully known (Lauer Schachter, 2009). What governments are left with, eventually, is how the public perceives "the temporal relationship between opinion and policy" (Soroka Stuart & Wlezien, 2010, p. 38; see also: Bingham Powell Jr, 2004). This means that democracy should respond to its citizens within a time frame that they, the citizens, consider reasonable. Otherwise, democracies face the threat of being considered unresponsive.

It should, however, be noted that democratic politics was designed to delay the response to citizens' demands. Since the early days of modern democratic thought, political thinkers have stressed that certain mechanisms were placed inside the democratic system to slow it down. When Condorcet addressed the need for a constitution he wrote that it should be able to eliminate enthusiasm and, therefore, "find procedures which could prevent the dangers of excessive haste" (Condorcet, 1994, p. 202). Taming democratic haste was also prevalent in the formation of the American Constitution. In Federalist #63, Madison suggested that another body should be added to the legislative branch because a single assembly might "yield to the impulse of sudden and violent passions, and to be seduced by factious leaders, into intemperate and pernicious resolutions" (Hamilton et al., 2003, 302). Madison, much like Condorcet, wished to slow down the legislative process to defend the people from themselves. Both thinkers did not ignore the need for government response to citizens' demands but wanted to delay it.

The challenge democracies are now facing is that due to recent technological changes, they need to become faster than they used to be (Berman, 2016, 2018). Incorporating AI in the public sector, for example, is seen by certain governments as a way to make the public sector seem more similar to Big Tech companies (Germany, 2018; See also: Paltieli, 2021). Technology plays a double role in the story of democratic responsiveness. On the one hand, it makes democratic politics seem highly inefficient. On the other hand, it is also used by democratic governments to speed up politics and become more responsive. But this, I suggest, challenges a fundamental aspect of democratic politics. To make my point clearer, let us return to

Langdon Winner's famous 1980 essay, "Do Artifacts have Politics?" Winner (1980) described how low-hanging overpasses were built over the Long Island Parkways in order "to discourage the presence of buses" on the parkways. This decision was motivated by political interests and had a political outcome, since "[p]oor people and blacks, who normally used public transit, were kept off the roads because the twelve-foot tall buses could not get through the overpass" (Winner, 1980, 124). Technology, in this case, an architectural one, was used to implement a policy. Winner uses this example to show how certain technologies have politics within them.

In this case, technology was unquestionably political, but it also eliminated politics. Think of Winner's example without the technology that was used in that case, pushing it almost ad absurdum. To achieve the same end without using technology, and assuming this was normatively or legally possible, those who had commissioned the bridges would have had to use guards to keep poor people out and allow more affluent people in. In this case, a discussion would begin between those who are not allowed in and the guards. A higher-ranking officer might be called, perhaps the case would be brought to court or the media would intervene. But there would be some kind of *politics* going on to challenge the decision made by politicians. Technology, a bridge, solved this problem quite efficiently as it literally streamlined the procedure without the politics that would otherwise have been involved.

The risks of incorporating AI into the public sector might be similar. The problem is that AI and simpler algorithms are difficult to resist. From the government's perspective, algorithms give a sense of order and, as Malte Ziewitz claimed, serve a similar purpose as the "invisible hand" or "natural selection" did before (Ziewitz, 2016). This explains why they become so popular among governments that need this exact sense of order and control in order to be perceived as responsive by their citizens. But AI is also very difficult to resist because it produces an output that is perceived to be the "truth". David Beer claimed that algorithms are powerful because their "algorithmic output cements, maintains or produces certain truths" (Beer, 2017, p. 8). An algorithmic output is not seen as arbitrary but as one which reflects, at least to some extent, the "truth". But this is exactly when politics stops and democracy suffers. Truth is not part of politics as it cannot be contested or challenged. Once an instrument that is meant to respond to citizens' contemporary and future needs reaches a decision that is based on a vast amount of data, it is very difficult to say it is wrong. AI, therefore, might make democracies more responsive because they will be able to reach decisions more quickly and respond to citizens' needs, but they do so at the price of limiting politics altogether.

But this is not the whole story. Another reason which explains why it is so difficult to resist algorithms is that we can never be completely sure of what is in there. Because AI can be opaque, even if citizens wanted to influence how decisions are made, they would not be able to (Coeckelbergh, 2022; Danaher, 2016). This is another aspect of the hollowing out of democratic politics by the very use of these technologies by democratic governments. These technologies are appealing exactly because they overcome the need for discussion, explanation and debate that are an inherent part of democratic politics (Ananny, 2015; O'Neil, 2016; Villani, 2018). Responding to citizens' needs, therefore, might come at the price of limiting democratic politics. This process might also be invisible to the public, meaning that citizens would know exactly which kind of data is gathered and used (Danaher, 2016; O'Neil, 2016). This raises another issue, that will be expanded in the next section. Because algorithms are invisible, citizens do not always know that they are participating in a procedure that might yield a governmental decision. And this, I argue, creates a new form of political participation.

CHALLENGING PARTICIPATION

Philip Howard once hypothesised about what might happen when the Internet of Things (IoT) gains momentum and more politically valuable data is created as a result of using certain devices, like a coffee machine (Howard, 2014, 2015). Howard's hypothesis proved to be true, as we saw in the previous section, as democracies try now to respond more quickly to their citizens' needs and desires by adopting certain technologies which analyse vast amounts of data during the policymaking stage (Bartlett & Tkacz, 2017; Paltieli, 2021; Redden, 2018; Susskind, 2018). This is a new form of political participation where citizens influence politics without entirely knowing that they do so. This section, therefore, explores this new form of citizenship that continues the argument that was developed in the previous section.

This passive idea of participation, in which individuals influence politics without a clear intention to do so, challenges the concept of political participation. Although there are numerous definitions for political participation, three elements are commonly shared in most of them. To constitute participation, three elements are needed: an *individual* with an *intention* to *influence* politics. This idea took shape during the 1960s when political theorists wished to distinguish the liberal form of political participation from other kinds (Milbrath & Goel, 1977; Verba, 1967; Verba & Nie, 1972). Political participation was considered an act that was actively decided on by an individual, unlike impulsive acts that do not constitute participation (Barber, 2003). Van Deth has recently offered a conceptual map for political participation and outlined the various forms of participatory acts. As he noted, we reach the borderline of this map with "non-political activities used for non-political goals" (Van Deth, 2014, p. 359). Yet these are exactly the actions that become meaningful in the context of AI politics that relies on personal data to make policy decisions. For example, government reports on the use of AI and big data clearly state that using this kind of personal data could benefit the public good. In a report by the French government, for example, sharing data is compared to donating blood and it is used to create "the databases required for the development of artificial intelligence geared towards public service missions" (Villani, 2018, p. 31). An Italian report champions the use of IoT and considers it as data which is of "good quality" in the government's overall AI project (Italy, 2018, p. 8). So what becomes politically meaningful in the age of big data and AI are non-political activities that are done without any clear political goals.

Democratic governments, in most cases, cannot access personal data without the clear consent of their citizens to do so. As I showed in a previous work, in their National AI Strategies governments and international bodies urge citizens to share their data, through consent, by making it a new form of civic virtue (Paltieli, 2021). If more people would share their data, the argument goes, a better policy would be formed. This form of data sharing for the common good has become more widespread in the past few years, especially in light of the Covid-19 pandemic and government responses to it (Centre for Data Ethics and Innovation, 2022) Yet, these kinds of actions do not easily fit into the contemporary definitions of political participation. Mainly because the actions that influence politics, in the form of data, were not done with the intention to influence politics.

It is clear that passive forms of data production, such as geo-location, are not civically motivated and are therefore not intentional in a way that allows them to be part of the participatory triad of individual, intention and influence. However, the fact that data is intentionally shared to shape public policy makes the story less clear than it initially seems. As we have seen earlier, governments assume that by using vast amounts of personal data they will be able to understand the "true" needs of their citizens. The reason for this assumption is that during our everyday behaviour and unlike how we behave when we are aware that we are observed, we reveal our true needs, passions and desires (Stephens-Davidowitz, 2017). So the intentional sharing of personal data opens the door to a repository of data which is socially and politically valuable precisely because it was not created to influence politics. Using this data through AI then allows reaching a "true" outcome that is based on both the data that is put in and the analysis that occurs inside the algorithmic "black box" that yields a "true" outcome, as we saw in the previous section.

Intentionality in this new form of participation exists only in the decision to share personal data, but not in the production of the data which was done without any intention to influence politics. Chan defined non-intentional action as "bringing about an unintended event but not in the course of performing an intentional action; i.e., an action in which the agent is not acting for a reason when performing" (Chan, 1995, p. 148). Following Chan, non-intentional participation, therefore, brings about an unintended event (influence) but not in the course of performing an intentional action (intending to influence). This means that this kind of participation is politically valuable but is not understood by contemporary political theory. Even if personal data was intentionally shared, it is considered valuable and is used because it was produced without the intention to influence politics. Moreover, even if citizens share their data per se, they do not always know which data is used and how it will be processed (Matsakis, 2019). Ultimately, what influences politics is the non-intentional production of participatory data and not the intentional decision to share it, and this, I argue, profoundly challenges both democratic politics and the theory that explains it.

This section outlined a new form of political participation that is now emerging with the introduction of AI into democratic politics. Here I showed how new forms of participation are created during this introduction and how it challenges political theory. This form of participation continues the argument I pursue in this chapter which highlights the risks of hollowing out democratic politics. In the next section, I will offer my theoretical suggestion that will perhaps allow an original perspective on the politics of AI and data analysis.

A LIBERAL DATA REPUBLIC

To overcome these challenges, I argue that a new political imagination that overcomes the liberal and republican rift is due. The kind of politics that AI and big data call for is one that essentially combines individualist and collectivist ideas. This would mean that the kind of politics that should emerge is one that is both internal and external to AI. One which empowers citizens to shape *how* (by having more control over data) and *where* such technology would be used (through a public debate).

To make sense of the liberal and republican themes that co-exist in AI politics, a very brief theoretical clarification is due. Liberalism sees the individual as a natural bearer of rights whose freedom is understood as non-interference (Mill, 1977). According to this view, individuals are free as long as they are not coerced to do anything they did not choose to do (Kramer, 2008; Larmore, 2001). This view is especially important in a technological context because it stresses that even if there is a potentially intervening power, individuals are considered free if that power did not actively intervene in their deeds and allowed them to act according to their desires. This is the human-centric element that guides AI politics, but there is another collectivist ethos that should be made clear. In contemporary political theory, it is common to distinguish between neo-Athenian and neo-Roman ideas of republican freedom. Arendt, for example, suggested that the Greeks "took for granted that freedom is exclusively located in the public realm" where citizens take an active role in protecting the polis (Arendt, 1998, p. 31). The neo-Roman tradition of republican freedom stresses that liberty is gained through the absence of arbitrary power (Skinner, 1998). In our case, the republican idea of freedom will be manifested not only by contributing to the public good by sharing data but also, and perhaps more importantly, by demonstrating individual and collective sovereignty that is achieved through gaining control over data and technology.

The idea that I am suggesting follows Coeckelbergh's discussion on both the need to offer more spheres for politics concerning AI and the need to revitalise political theory (Coeckelbergh, 2022). This idea means that in the case of AI and big data, thinking about liberalism and republicanism separately does not yield a full enough picture as needed. The incorporation of AI in democratic politics, I argue, is at the same time individualist and collectivist.[1] However, I do not believe that we currently have the necessary theoretical tools to make sense of the kind of politics that now needs to emerge. Using contemporary political theory to understand the political options available for citizens, therefore, misses some fundamental questions that need to be explored.

For example, when considering the essence of data sharing, we should evaluate both the role it plays in the broader context of AI politics and the elements of this action itself. Data sharing includes two essential actions: the one from which data is created, and the decision to share it. Yet these actions have different political theories embedded in them. The action from which data is created assumes the liberal idea of non-interference, while sharing is motivated by republican concerns, whether neo-Athenian or neo-Roman. The point I wish to make here is that in order to understand AI politics we should overcome the distinction between these two systems of thought, which already becomes less clear when we are dealing with AI and data. This would mean that in order to understand differently the participatory potential of data sharing and to prevent the potential hollowing out of democratic politics through AI, we should also take into account actions that were not created with the intention to influence politics but became one only after the individual actor decided to turn them into potentially influential.[2] In other words, the actions that create the data that influence politics are not political while the political action does not create the data.

Data sharing can allow citizens more control over how their data is used and under what terms. This can become a compensating factor for the risk of losing individual autonomy, as Coecklbergh puts it, that might take place when data is originally created (Coeckelbergh, 2022). Even if data was created and stored involuntarily, how it will be used and for which purposes will be based on the individual's decision, thereby restoring their lost autonomy. Moreover, some governments have more clearly stressed the need for rights of data portability and mobility that will allow individuals to move their data between collectors (DCMS, 2018). These will empower citizens even more and would allow them to make collective decisions about their data even better.

---

[1]   I examined this point in a previous work that focused on National AI Strategies (Paltieli, 2021).

[2]   This is a different idea from what Halupka (2018) describes as online actions that become political due to the interpretation of others.

Having such rights, and more importantly, such an understanding of their potential power can allow citizens more control over how AI systems handle their data and shape their lives. In some National AI Strategies, data is referred to as a common good, which means that how data will be used relies on a collective decision (Paltieli, 2022; Villani, 2018). Thinking about data in such a way turns it into a literal "common wealth" which is used to pursue the good of the political community. Such collective decision making includes broader public discussions on how AI would be used in society. A tool which some governments are already offering (Australia, 2019; Finland, 2017; Germany, 2018; Villani, 2018). During such discussions, a clear vision of what is a "good artificial society" would emerge. Again, participating in such an effort through sharing data and discussion on where it would be used can bring back some of the power individuals lost to algorithmic decision-making systems. More importantly, such tools would overcome the lack of clarity in concepts such as "transparency" and "explainability" which might not fulfil the promise that is vested in them. My idea of a "liberal data republic" aims to maintain popular control over AI and data control through active politics, instead of only relying on ethical principles. This idea is essentially democratic as it not only opens spheres for discussions on the public use of technology but also maintains popular sovereignty over data and the way in which it is processed, unlike how this is done in non-democratic settings such as China (Nussipov, 2020).

Finally, in line with my idea of a "liberal data republic", we should pay attention to a recent trend in policy papers that offer old political concepts and ideas in a new technological context which focuses on small-scale collectives and not nation-states. A recently published report by the World Bank called for "a new social contract for data", one that will be used on a national level but also in cities and smaller communities such as neighbourhoods (World Bank, 2021). A report on Barcelona's original use of local data, both city-owned and shared by citizens, was described as a "new data deal" (Monge et al., 2022). The British AI Council and Ada Lovelace Institute promoted the idea of data trusts that will rely on "data cooperatives" (UK AI Council, 2021). These examples are based on the fact that individuals might feel more comfortable sharing their data with the city council or their neighbours, rather than with their government. When such data sharing takes place, this collective of individuals gains power and can control, collectively and individually, how AI is used and data is processed. This might suggest that the principal actors in emerging AI politics can be medium-sized collectives where individuals would feel safer and more in control. These new data-related city-states are based on a clear liberal/republican logic where data is created individually but is managed collectively.

I believe that this is a theoretical attempt that should be developed since it can offer a new way to understand AI politics. This idea can overcome the two challenges that were raised in the previous sections. It can maintain a healthy level of political engagement even when AI is incorporated into democratic politics and can allow meaningful participation on behalf of individuals and collectives. Not perfect, I am sure, but this idea of a "liberal data republic" seeks to trigger the discussion on the political theory of AI.

CONCLUSIONS

This chapter aimed to follow some of the challenges AI raises for both democratic politics and political theory. This included the potential hollowing out of politics through AI and the changing meaning of political participation. As I tried to argue, to make sense of these challenges and be able to overcome them, we should think about politics differently. To do so, I introduced the idea of a "liberal data republic" that offers a theoretical perspective to the logic that already exists in AI and big data, being human-centric and collectivist. This idea, I argued, can give citizens more control over how their data is used and how AI is incorporated into democratic politics. This idea, therefore, can become a useful perspective through which we can understand AI politics and the role and power of citizens in it.

REFERENCES

Ananny, M. (2015). Towards an Ethic of Algorithms: Convening, Observation, Probability and Timeliness. *Science, Technology & Human Values, 41*(1), 93–117.

Arendt, H. (1998). *The Human Condition*. The University of Chicago Press.

Australia. (2019). *Artificial Intelligence: Australia's Ethics Framework*.

Barber, B. R. (2003). *Strong Democracy: Participatory Politics for the New Age*. University of California Press.

Bartlett, J., & Tkacz, N. (2017). *Governance by Dashboard: A Policy Paper*. https://www.demos.co.uk /project/governance-by-dashboard

Beer, D. (2017). The Social Power of Algorithms. *Information Communication and Society, 20*(1), 1–13. https://doi.org/10.1080/1369118X.2016.1216147

Berman, S. (2016). Populism is Not Fascism. *Foreign Affairs, 95*(6), 39–44.

Berman, S. (2018). Populists Have One Big Thing Right: Democracies are Becoming Less Open. *The Washington Post*, January 8, 2018. https://www.washingtonpost.com/news/monkey-cage/wp/2018 /01/08/populists-have-one-big-thing-right-democracies-are-becoming-less-open/?noredirect=on &utm_term=.3dcd123e42e7

Berryhill, J., Heang, K. K., Clogher, R., & McBride, K. (2019). Hello, World: Artificial Intelligence and its Use in the Public Sector. In *OECD Observatory of Public Sector Innovation (OPSI)* (Issue 36).

Bingham Powell Jr, G. (2004). The Quality of Democracy: The Chain of Responsiveness. *Journal of Democracy, 15*(4), 91–105.

Centre for Data Ethics and Innovation. (2022). *Public Attitudes to Data and AI Tracker Survey* (Vol. 1). https://assets.publishing.service.gov.uk/government/uploads/system/uploads/attachment_data/file /1064525/Public_attitudes_to_data_and_AI_-_Tracker_survey.pdf

Chan, D. K. (1995). Non-Intentional Actions. *American Philosophical Quarterly, 32*(2), 139–151.

Cicilline, D. (2020, July 29). *Cicilline Opening Statement At Big Tech Antitrust Hearing | Congressman David Cicilline*. https://cicilline.house.gov/press-release/cicilline-opening-statement-big-tech -antitrust-hearing

Coeckelbergh, M. (2022). *The Political Philosophy of AI*. Polity.

Condorcet. (1994). A Survey of the Principles Underlying the Draft Constitution. In I. M. & F. Hewitt (Ed.), *Condorcet: Foundations of Social Choice and Political Theory* (pp. 190–227). Elgar Publishing.

Dahl, R. A. (1971). *Polyarchy: Participation and Opposition*. Yale University Press. https://doi.org/10 .16309/j.cnki.issn.1007-1776.2003.03.004

Danaher, J. (2016). The Threat of Algocracy: Reality, Resistance and Accommodation. *Philosophy & Technology, 29*(3), 245–268.

DCMS. (2018). *Data Mobility: The Personal Data Portability Growth Opportunity for the UK Economy*.

Denmark. (2019). *National Strategy for Artificial Intelligence*.

Finland. (2017). *Finland's Age of Artificial Intelligence: Turning Finland into a Leading Country in the Application of Artificial Intelligence*. https://doi.org/10.1021/ja044682s

Germany. (2018). *Artificial Intelligence Strategy*.

Hall, W., & Pesenti, J. (2017). *Growing the Artificial Intelligence Industry in the UK*. London: Government of the United Kingdom.

Halupka, M. (2018). On Intentionality and Motivation in Digital Spaces a Response to Flinders and Wood. *Democratic Theory*, 5(2), 82–89. https://doi.org/10.3167/DT.2018.050206

Hamilton, A., Madison, J., & Jay, J. (2003). *The Federalist with the Letters of 'Brutus'*. Cambridge University Press.

House of Commons. (2019). Disinformation and 'Fake News': Final Report. In *Digital, Culture, Media and Sports Committee*. https://doi.org/10.1007/978-981-15-5876-4

Howard, P. N. (2014). Participation, Civics and Your Next Coffee Maker. *Policy and Internet*, 6(2), 199–201. https://doi.org/10.1002/1944-2866.POI356

Howard, P. N. (2015). *Pax Technica: How the Internet of Things May Set Us Free or Lock Us Up*. Yale University Press.

Italy. (2018). *Artificial Intelligence: At the Service of Citizens*. Rome: The Agency for Digital Italy.

Kramer, M. H. (2008). Liberty and Domination. In C. Laborde & J. Maynor (Eds.), *Republicanism and Political Theory* (pp. 31–57). Blackwell.

Larmore, C. (2001). A Critique of Philip Pettit's Republicanism Published by: Ridgeview Publishing Company. *Philosophical Issues*, 11(Social, Political, and Legal Philosophy), 229–243.

Lauer Schachter, H. (2009). The Role of Efficiency in Bureaucratic Study. In A. Farzmand (Ed.), *Bureaucracy and Administration* (pp. 239–252). CRC Press.

Matsakis, L. (2019). The WIRED Guide to Your Personal Data (and Who is Using It). *Wired*, 1–12. https://www.wired.com/story/wired-guide-personal-data-collection/

Milbrath, L. W., & Goel, M. L. (1977). *Political Participation: How and Why Do People Get Involved in Politics*. Rand McNally College Publishing Company.

Mill, J. S. (1977). *The Collected Works of John Stuart Mill – Volume XVIII* (J. M. Robson (ed.)). University of Toronto Press.

Monge, F., Barns, S., Kattel, R., & Bria, F. (2022). *A New Data Deal: The Case of Barcelona*, 1–33. https://www.ucl.ac.uk/bartlett/public-

Mounk, Y. (2018). *The People vs. Democracy: Why Our Freedom is in Danger and How to Save it*. Harvard University Press.

Nussipov, A. (2020, April 27). *How China Governs Data*. Medium – Center for Media, Data and Society. https://medium.com/center-for-media-data-and-society/how-china-governs-data-ff71139b68d2

O'Neil, C. (2016). *Weapons of Math Destruction*. Penguin Books.

Paltieli, G. (2021). The Political Imaginary of National AI Strategies. *AI and Society*, 1–12. https://doi.org/10.1007/s00146-021-01258-1

Paltieli, G. (2022). Visions of Innovation and Politics: Israel's AI Initiatives. *Discover Artificial Intelligence*, 2(1), 1–11. https://doi.org/10.1007/s44163-022-00024-6

Putnam, R. D. (1993). *Making Democracy Work: Civic Traditions in Modern Italy*. Princeton University Press.

Redden, J. (2018). Democratic Governance in an Age of Datafication: Lessons from Mapping Government Discourses and Practices. *Big Data and Society*, 5(2), 1–13. https://doi.org/10.1177/2053951718809145

Runciman, D. (2018). *Is This How Democracy Ends?* Profile Books.

Sætra, H. S. (2020). A Shallow Defence of a Technocracy of Artificial Intelligence: Examining the Political Harms of Algorithmic Governance in the Domain of Government. *Technology in Society*, 62, 101283. https://doi.org/10.1016/J.TECHSOC.2020.101283

Skinner, Q. (1998). *Liberty before Liberalism*. Cambridge University Press.

Soroka Stuart, N., & Wlezien, C. (2010). *Degrees of Democracy: Politics, Public Opinion, and Policy*. Cambridge University Press.

Stephens-Davidowitz, S. (2017a). Everybody lies: How Google Search Reveals our Darkest Secrets? *The Guardian*, July, 9, 2017. https://www.theguardian.com/technology/2017/jul/09/everybody-lies-how-google-reveals-darkest-secrets-seth-stephens-davidowitz [last access: February 16, 2023].

Susskind, J. (2018). *Future Politics: Living Together in a World Transformed by Tech*. Oxford University Press.

Tromble, R. (2018). Thanks for (actually) Responding! How Citizen Demand Shapes Politicians' Interactive Practices on Twitter. *New Media & Society*, 20(2), 676–697.

UK AI Council. (2021). *Exploring Legal Mechanisms for Data Stewardship* (Issue March). https://www.adalovelaceinstitute.org/report/legal-mechanisms-data-stewardship/

Van Deth, J. W. (2014). A Conceptual Map of Political Participation. *Acta Politica, 49*(3), 349–367. https://doi.org/10.1057/ap.2014.6

Verba, S. (1967). Democratic Participation. *The ANNALS of the American Academy of Political and Social Science, 373*(1), 53–78. https://doi.org/10.1177/000271626737300103

Verba, S., & Nie, N. H. (1972). *Participation in America: Political Democracy and Social Equality.* University of Chicago Press.

Villani, C. (2018). *For a Meaningful Artificial Intelligence: Towards a French and European Strategy.* Paris: Parliamentary Mission.

Winner, L. (1980). Do Artifacts Have Politics? *Dedalus, 109*(1), 121–136.

World Bank. (2021). *Data for Better Lives.*

Ziewitz, M. (2016). Governing Algorithms: Myth, Mess, and Methods. *Science, Technology & Human Values, 41*(1), 3–16.

30. AI as automated inequality: statistics, surveillance and discrimination
Mike Zajko

Concerns about humans being treated unequally by AI have received a great deal of attention, but AI is increasingly used in government projects around the world to address fundamental social inequalities. Virginia Eubanks' influential book *Automating Inequality* (2018) critiques the use of automation to govern poverty and inequality in the US, prior to much of the recent promotion and adoption of AI technologies based on machine learning (ML). This chapter surveys some of these more recent developments, connecting the literature on algorithmic governance, AI, and surveillance studies, to highlight how new data infrastructures enable asymmetric relations of power, visibility, and traceability. Understanding AI as a technology of governance requires engagement with its algorithmic, bureaucratic, and political predecessors, as well as some of the characteristics that make current forms of AI novel, particularly through the large datasets with which these ML-based systems are 'trained'.

AI, AUTOMATED DECISION-MAKING, AND SURVEILLANCE STUDIES

AI is increasingly "deployed" as a technology for governance – making decisions about people and things in ways that shape societal outcomes. Studying governance means analyzing "issues of social coordination" and "patterns of rule" (Bevir, 2011, p. 1), and while the work of state institutions remains crucial for ruling social relations, scholars of governance (often influenced by Foucault) are concerned with actors and processes beyond those of the state. Commercial platforms also use AI to govern data and their users' conduct, in ways that are only partly shaped by the expectations of state authorities. AI-mediated search results reproduce structured inequality (Noble, 2018). Private actors use AI to target the poor for further exploitation (O'Neil, 2016), and algorithmic technologies are heavily involved in the reproduction of capitalist relations (Prodnik, 2021; Sadowski, 2019), including international data extraction (Couldry & Mejias, 2021) and companies in the Global North using the Global South as a source of cheap labor (see Okolo, this volume). But public sector algorithms are often those that are most fundamentally implicated in social inequality, and in this context, AI is normally discussed in terms of automated decision-making (ADM) systems and algorithmic governance.

Scholarship on ADMs helps to situate AI among algorithmic technologies that also have a political function (Levy et al., 2021). These decision-making systems may or may not involve machine learning and exist along a "continuum" of automation and human involvement (Peeters, 2020). Algorithmic governance, based on formulas and procedures to calculate scores for individuals based on certain inputs, need not rely on digital technologies; paper-based algorithms have long been used to perform various kinds of risk assessments.

Eubanks (2018) has studied the management of poverty in the US through bureaucratic forms of surveillance and risk-scoring algorithms, and while the sociotechnical systems she documents would not formally be considered ML or AI, her work has been widely referenced in discussions of AI and inequality. Given the close functional relationship between ML-based decision-making and other kinds of algorithms that classify and predict, or forms of statistical and actuarial logic, it is entirely relevant to draw on critical approaches developed for these technologies (see Gandy, 2009) when critically engaging with AI.

Among such earlier scholarship, Eubanks (2018) draws on the work of Oscar Gandy, whose book *The Panoptic Sort* (Gandy, 1993) is considered foundational for surveillance studies – an interdisciplinary field that provides a number of ways to critically analyze the use of AI for governance. This is because surveillance, as typically defined in surveillance studies, involves more than the systematic collection of information, but is explicitly tied to power relations and problems of governance (Lyon, 2007), such as influence, management, control, entitlement, and protection. Surveillance systems are used to sustain asymmetries of power and operate through asymmetries of visibility – making surveillance targets more visible or legible, while the surveillance itself remains relatively opaque (Brighenti, 2010; Flyverbom, 2022; Issar & Aneesh, 2022).

The genesis of surveillance studies as a field was tied to the recognition that a growing range of social processes now depended on large, computerized systems for recording and working with personal information (Ball et al., 2012). Later on, this trend would be named "big data", and surveillance studies scholarship on big data (Andrejevic, 2014; Esposti, 2014) remains relevant for contemporary AI because it was precisely the development of vast datasets that allowed machine learning algorithms to "learn" or "be trained" to classify and predict in ways that resemble human decision-making (Andrejevic, 2020). Surveillance studies also addresses the governance of inequality, whether or not this governance is algorithmic or simply bureaucratic, because the origins of population-level surveillance lie in the development of public administration and official statistics (Ruppert, 2012; Webster, 2012). State governance depends on the systematic collection of information about a population for purposes including taxation, public health, and social control.

GOVERNING INEQUALITY WITH AI

Because AI systems make decisions about the present and future through models developed from historical data, one of the main critiques of AI has been that these technologies reproduce or heighten existing inequalities (Barocas & Selbst, 2016; Davis et al., 2021). Among AI researchers, this problem has typically been presented as one of "bias" that comes "from society" and ends up in the technology or the data used to train it (Pena et al., 2020, p. 129). According to one foundational definition, these "preexisting biases originate… in society at large", which the computer system then "embodies" (Friedman & Nissenbaum, 1996, p. 333). Critical scholarship in the social sciences recognizes these processes in other terms, namely the reproduction of social inequality, and reinforcement of hierarchical social structures that discriminate, oppress, and exploit. Intersectional analyses can name these structures and their relations (Hoffmann, 2019; Joyce et al., 2021) – how the work of AI reproduces intersecting hierarchies of gender (Scheuerman et al., 2021), race (Benjamin, 2019), coloniality (Couldry & Mejias, 2021), and class (Eubanks, 2018), among other inequalities.

The reason why AI reproduces inequality can be expressed by pointing to inequalities in the data on which AI is based. As Davis, Williams, and Yang (2021) write: "algorithms are animated by data, data come from people, people make up society, and society is unequal. Algorithms thus arc towards existing patterns of power and privilege, marginalization and disadvantage" (p. 2). Inequalities from the past are encoded into algorithmic classifications, and these ways of categorizing people become "ordering instruments" that "stabilize" certain distinctions and values (Allhutter et al., 2020, p. 3). The output of an AI system is shaped by the kinds of data fed into it, but this output also "co-constitutes the entities that it differentiates between. When a system differentiates between groups of people... it re-iterates and copro-duces meanings of what these categories imply" (Allhutter et al., 2020, p. 4).

AI developers often use the phrase "garbage in, garbage out" to make the point that an algo-rithm or model is only as good as the data used to train it, but it is entirely possible that using high-quality, accurate data about personal characteristics will still produce biased AI systems that discriminate against disadvantaged groups. This is because such data will effectively mirror existing social inequalities (Christin, 2020, p. 1122), or as Airoldi puts it: "society in, society out" (Airoldi, 2022, p. 43). However, thinking of AI as a mirror to society is a meta-phor that paints these technologies in a passive light, limiting critical engagement. While it is true that "patterns in datafied behaviours and discourses mirror the struggles and structure of social fields" (Airoldi, 2022, p. 53), these struggles also extend to and through sociotechnical systems. Inequality is not just reproduced because of the ways that AI is trained on unequal data, but through the ways that AI is used to purposely create unequal outcomes for peo-ple, discriminating between groups and treating them differently (Burrell & Fourcade, 2021; Sadowski & Andrejevic, 2020). Therefore, the reproduction of inequality is closely tied to processes of governance, extraction, capital accumulation, and social control.

Surveillance scholars have long been concerned with "social sorting", or how governing systems discriminate between categories of people (Lyon, 2003). Social sorting is linked to surveillance through the systematic collection of data on which the sorting is based, which in machine learning includes both the training data used to develop a model, as well as the input data on which a model is put to work. For example, training an algorithm to sort employ-ment applications might use historical data about previous employees, and the resulting model works when provided with input data that has been systematically extracted from or about cur-rent job applicants (Raghavan et al., 2020). It is the combination of training data and statistical predictive techniques that make current forms of AI distinctive from other algorithms, and why it is important to critically examine where this data comes from.

Surveillance scholars recognize that in recent decades, a great deal of information is gener-ated by people going about their daily lives and interacting with various computer systems, and some of the most personal kinds of information are actively produced and shared by us for various reasons, including what Albrechtslund (2008) defines as "participatory surveil-lance". The datasets used to train and test AI systems often depend on the collection of this "user-generated content" (Andrejevic, 2007, p. 245) and "data exhaust" (Zuboff, 2018), which is then further organized and annotated by humans prior to use in ML. We may have no idea that information about us has been collected and used in this way; few imagined that photos they once uploaded to a social media platform would be used to build Clearview AI's facial recognition system for police (Hill, 2021), or that by simply walking across an American uni-versity campus, they would help train computer vision systems in China (Murgia & Harlow, 2019). Increasingly, surveillance technology is driven by AI, but the development of AI in general has also relied on surveillance through the systematic collection or extraction of data (Sadowski, 2019).

A basic premise for the critical study of technology is that technologies are not politically neutral, and this understanding of technology needs to extend beyond material "artifacts" (Winner, 1980) to the methods and techniques animating them. Contemporary ML depends on statistical methods that have always been more than "just math"; statistical techniques were developed specifically to serve those who govern – managing populations and effecting social control. Sir Francis Galton, Karl Pearson, and Ronald Fisher were all pioneers of statistical methods as well as proponents of physiognomy and eugenics – the idea that human characteristics could be quantified, people hierarchically arranged as inferior and superior, and interventions made to improve the human "stock". Birhane and Guest (2021) argue that such eugenic notions (along with intersecting varieties of sexism, racism, and coloniality) are foundational for fields such as statistics and data science (see also Clayton, 2020), and this is most evident today in a wide range of "physiognomic artificial intelligence" systems that purport to read some hidden essence from characteristics of the human body (Stark & Hutson, 2022). However, algorithmic technologies that use statistical techniques to sort people on some basis other than their physical features are heirs to a deeper legacy of statistics, the practice of which is directly connected to problems of the state and its population – problems of categorization, management, and control (Desrosières, 1998; Hacking, 1990).

SURVEILLANCE, ALGORITHMIC TARGETING, AND POVERTY

Public administration, particularly in the form of the post-World War II welfare state, depends on surveillance – the routine, systematic collection of information about people for the purposes of governance – through the creation of verifiable identities and detailed individual records about citizens as a basis for providing public services (Webster, 2012). Surveillance also targets populations, through techniques that Foucault theorized as biopower (see Ruppert, 2012), as seen in the historical development of statistics to understand interrelated phenomena such as wealth/poverty, crime, and health/disease (Desrosières, 1998; Hacking, 1990). Today, these concerns are often governed algorithmically, and increasingly through the use of AI, whether for purposes of efficiency, effectiveness, or fraud detection (Alston, 2019). Poverty remains a social problem, and access to services is contingent on identification and monitoring.

Numerous studies have shown how the collection of information about people can reinforce their marginalization, or reproduce "conditions of abjection" (Monahan, 2017). O'Neil (2016) documents how private actors algorithmically target the poor for exploitation, such as targeted ads by predatory lenders and for-profit colleges, enriching these actors but leaving recipients financially worse off. Public welfare agencies do not operate with the same profit motive but can also end up reproducing the very inequalities they are trying to address or produce other surveillance-related harms. Eubanks (2018) studies how the poor are targeted for greater surveillance, in ways that reinforce their precarity and poverty (see also Gilliom, 2001; Hughes, 2021). A vicious feedback loop can occur, in which biased or disproportionate surveillance of marginalized groups produces data that is then used as input for an algorithm that "crystallises and reproduces" unequal treatment under "a veneer of objectivity" (Keddell, 2019, pp. 8–9).

Feedback loops have also been identified in the automation of policing, the patterns of which closely follow underlying social inequalities (particularly how poverty is criminalized and racialized – see Monahan, 2017). Predictive policing may use historical data to allocate police resources to parts of a city where crime is predicted to occur, putting these areas under closer surveillance, generating more data about crime, and thereby reinforcing the allocation of police resources to areas where they disproportionately affect the poor and racialized. Sarah Brayne (2020) uses surveillance studies concepts to analyze new data-driven technologies being deployed by the LAPD, showing how social sorting can "amplify inequalities" (p. 107) through both geographic and individual targeting. While some policing algorithms predict crime risks for neighborhoods, others are used to quantify an individual's risk for committing crime. In these cases, feedback loops can re-target specific individuals for additional surveillance and punishment, "further increasing their point value while obscuring the role of enforcement in shaping crime statistics and appearing to be objective" (Brayne & Christin, 2021, p. 620). People living in low-income neighborhoods are more likely to be subject to feedback loops, as that is where these surveillance programs are targeted (Brayne, 2020).

One algorithmic process specifically designed to govern inequality is VI-SPDAT, which has been widely used in the US, Canada, and Australia to allocate services to unhoused people (Cronley, 2020). It does so on the basis of risk and vulnerability, in that people at greatest risk or who are most vulnerable are scored highest and stand the greatest chance of receiving services like supportive housing. But these scores depend on survey responses that individuals provide about their lives, and if an individual discloses information about their risky or illegal behavior, their vulnerability score will increase. In Los Angeles, Eubanks (2018, p. 121) discusses how this information can also be shared with police, resulting in a potential "trade-off" where individuals may be reluctant to share information that would allow agencies to help them for fear of negative consequences. The fact that some groups are more willing to disclose information about risks and vulnerabilities, such as participation in crime, is one of a number of reasons why VI-SPDAT reproduces racial inequities (Cronley, 2020; Wilkey et al., 2019).

The creators of VI-SPDAT have recently moved to end their involvement with the algorithm in order to pursue a more equitable approach to "homelessness response" (OrgCode, 2021), but ML-based approaches are now being promoted as an alternative, one of which claims "superior predictive accuracy" using data from VI-SPDAT survey questions (Kithulgoda et al., 2022). However, none of this addresses the equity concerns described above, and as some municipalities look increasingly to AI (ie. VanBerlo, 2021) to "triage" scarce social supports, there are strong historical reasons to be concerned about the reproduction of particular kinds of social inequality (Christin, 2020), even for programs that are designed to help the poor.

One way that ML-based systems differ from low-tech tools like VI-SPDAT is through their ability to find patterns across heterogeneous kinds of data. One ML system built to predict homelessness in London, Ontario, does so without relying on self-reported information, but by finding correlations in a database combining user records from "over 20 homeless serving organizations" (VanBerlo, 2021). The linking-up of different databases to govern the unhoused is seen by some as a way to better track individuals and measure the effectiveness of specific interventions – developments that Clarke et al. (2021) theorize through Haggerty and Ericson's (2000) "surveillant assemblage". In an article that has become foundational for surveillance studies, Haggerty and Ericson (2000) described how data-driven practices necessitated new ways to think about surveillance, and in particular how new surveillance methods relied on linking together or integrating heterogeneous databases. This conceptualization has proven very productive for surveillance studies (including Brayne, 2020) in explaining the distinctiveness of contemporary forms of data-centric governance.

Another foundational theory in surveillance studies is Foucault's (1995) use of Bentham's panopticon as a "diagram" (p. 205) of disciplinary power, wherein the ever-present possibility of surveillance produces docile, disciplined, and useful subjects. While a great deal of surveillance scholarship (including Haggerty & Ericson, 2000) has attempted to go beyond the panoptic metaphor in theorizing (see Haggerty, 2006), some aspects of Foucault's (1995) argument about the disciplining power of surveillance remain relevant, combined without Foucault's later lectures about governmentality (Mann, 2020). This is particularly true for the aims of welfare surveillance (Gilliom, 2001), perhaps best exemplified by Australia's use of "income management" and "cashless" cards to budget and direct welfare payments away from products like alcohol, tobacco, gambling, and pornography, as part of an effort to cultivate discipline and "responsibility" among welfare recipients (Bielefeld et al., 2021).

Welfare surveillance is frequently justified by the need to distinguish the "deserving" from the "undeserving" poor (Eubanks, 2018), or to uncover "fraud" (a term sometimes used broadly to refer to any undeserved benefits), with recipients forced to live under a cloud of suspicion (Monahan, 2017). In recent years, AI has been used in a growing number of countries to screen benefits applications for eligibility and fraud, particularly in the Global North. African governments, which often rely on external actors for expertise and service provision, are now also exploring AI for public services (Plantinga, 2022), and the next "version" of India's massive Aadhaar system may utilize AI for detecting welfare fraud (Mint, 2021). Authorities moving to automate eligibility decisions and fraud detection in these countries risk repeating earlier algorithmic "debacles" seen in Australia (Lokshin & Umapathi, 2022; also Mann, 2020), the US state of Indiana (Eubanks, 2018), and the UK (Peachey, 2022). Most recently, AI was blamed for causing the resignation of the Dutch government (Rao, 2022), after a (reportedly) "self-learning" algorithm led to tens of thousands of people (particularly ethnic minorities with low incomes) being wrongly punished for suspected child benefit fraud (Heikkilä, 2022), although the opacity and secrecy of the system make it difficult to know whether the algorithm in question was actually developed using ML (van Bekkum & Borgesius, 2021). To prevent and mitigate such algorithmic harms, which have proven costly in terms of financial settlements and human lives, the dominant approach has been to "audit" the algorithms.

ADDRESSING AUTOMATED INEQUALITY

Algorithmically governing the poor produces harms based on surveillance and discrimination. Programs designed to address inequality end up reproducing inequality in various ways. It is debatable to what extent such consequences are inherent to these approaches or can be mitigated. Proponents argue that automating bureaucratic procedures can increase fairness or reduce bias and that possibilities for harm can be addressed through "auditing" the outcomes of such programs. Algorithmic auditing has rapidly developed as an industry and a field of study in recent years, but one result of this proliferation is a wide range of different ideas and approaches about what such an audit should entail (Sloane et al., 2022; Vecchione et al., 2021). An auditor's scrutiny can be directed to data sources, how algorithms function, and their predicted (or simulated) "social impact" (Raji et al., 2020), but algorithms can also be audited after the fact by tracking their actual, disparate outcomes on human lives, and prescribing corrective action. The lack of trust people have in "black-box AI decision-making", combined with a general lack of trust in the public sector, can be ameliorated through more open systems that enable "traceability" of decisions, allowing citizens to "audit [and] appeal" decisions made about them (Andrews & Croll, 2022). This expansion of "audit trail logic" has been theorized by Michael Power (2022) as a "performative" basis for the "audit society". Its optimistic promise (Andrews & Croll, 2022) is that automated decisions that are traceable will empower us all to be auditors, and that with the right kinds of data, algorithmic governance can itself be governed to better serve the public interests.

Audits of algorithmic discrimination and unethically harvested datasets of personal information have had the effect of raising awareness, changing algorithms, and de-publishing influential datasets used in ML (Johnson, 2020; Raji & Buolamwini, 2019). However, the idea that algorithmic harms can be audited out of existence can be characterized as a "reformist reform" that is typical of proposals generated from within the organizations employing these algorithms, which tend "to require accepting and working within the parameters of existing systems to promote the achievement of their goals" (Green, 2019, p. 3). It is even possible that organizations attempting to make their AI systems less biased will lean on new forms of exploitative data extraction, as Google did when its technology was found to have difficulty recognizing dark-skinned faces. In pursuit of "greater inclusivity" and the elimination of racial bias through more diverse training data, contractors working for the company targeted homeless populations with dark skin to have their faces scanned (Otis & Dillon, 2019). As Samudzi (2019) argues, it is a "pyrrhic victory" if the attempt to make AI less racist ends up enabling greater surveillance of the racialized.

A more critical perspective challenges the idea that "good" and "bad" uses of algorithmic governance can be neatly distinguished. Hoffman (2021) argues that dominant approaches to making AI more ethical, fair, or inclusive, end up normalizing existing power structures and perpetuating "data violence" (see also Stark et al., 2021). Legal reforms have also been used to legitimize whatever organizational practices end up being considered lawful (Viljoen, 2021). More radical approaches to algorithmic injustice include abolition (Benjamin, 2019; Stark & Hutson, 2022) and reparation (Davis et al., 2021), both of which also require regulatory reforms to meet these transformative ends. As Viljoen (2021, pp. 292–293) argues, any effective regulatory approaches to these problems will require a "reinvigoration" of the law's capacity to channel democratic will. However, because many of the algorithmic systems most directly involved in governing inequality are operated by public institutions, there are greater possibilities for democratic accountability and political pressure than in the private sector.

CONCLUSION

AI is increasingly used to govern, addressing social problems that have long been a focus for state agencies, including poverty and social inequality. Scholars have documented how inequality is structurally reproduced across a variety of institutions, so it should not be a surprise that AI is now part of this reproduction. This is particularly the case when AI depends on "learning" from training data that encodes preexisting inequalities. The systematic collection of personal information as a basis for governance relates directly to longstanding concerns in the interdisciplinary field of surveillance studies. Much of this surveillance scholarship precedes the current wave of AI but has been helpful in articulating ways that control over data and the systems that produce it reinforces existing relations of power. Rather than a break from the past, these current uses of AI are continuous with earlier algorithmic governance projects and their bureaucratic predecessors.

REFERENCES

Airoldi, M. (2022). *Machine Habitus: Toward a Sociology of Algorithms*. Polity Press.

Albrechtslund, A. (2008). Online Social Networking as Participatory Surveillance. *First Monday*, *13*(3). https://journals.uic.edu/ojs/index.php/fm/article/view/2142

Allhutter, D., Cech, F., Fischer, F., Grill, G., & Mager, A. (2020). Algorithmic Profiling of Job Seekers in Austria: How Austerity Politics Are Made Effective. *Frontiers in Big Data*, *3*. https://doi.org/10.3389/fdata.2020.00005

Alston, P. (2019). *Digital Technology, Social Protection and Human Rights*. UN – OHCHR. https://www.ohchr.org/en/calls-for-input/2019/digital-technology-social-protection-and-human-rights-report

Andrejevic, M. (2007). *iSpy: Surveillance and Power in the Interactive Era*. University Press of Kansas.

Andrejevic, M. (2014). Surveillance in the Big Data Era. In K. D. Pimple (Ed.), *Emerging Pervasive Information and Communication Technologies (PICT): Ethical Challenges, Opportunities and Safeguards* (pp. 55–69). Springer Netherlands. https://doi.org/10.1007/978-94-007-6833-8_4

Andrejevic, M. (2020). *Automated Media*. Routledge. https://doi.org/10.4324/9780429242595

Andrews, P., & Croll, A. (2022, April 15). How Might We Grow Trust and Confidence in the Public Sector in the Digital Age. *FWD50 2022*. https://web.archive.org/web/20220421142223/https://fwd50.com/updates/how-might-we-grow-trust/

Ball, K., Haggerty, K., & Lyon, D. (Eds.). (2012). Introducing Surveillance Studies. In *Routledge Handbook of Surveillance Studies* (pp. 1–11). Routledge.

Barocas, S., & Selbst, A. D. (2016). Big Data's Disparate Impact. *California Law Review*, *104*(3), 671–732.

Benjamin, R. (2019). *Race After Technology: Abolitionist Tools for the New Jim Code*. Polity Press.

Bevir, M. (2011). Governance as Theory, Practice, and Dilemma. In M. Bevir (Ed.), *The Sage Handbook of Governance* (pp. 1–16). SAGE.

Bielefeld, S., Harb, J., & Henne, K. (2021). Financialization and Welfare Surveillance: Regulating the Poor in Technological Times. *Surveillance & Society*, *19*(3), 299–316. https://doi.org/10.24908/ss.v19i3.14244

Birhane, A., & Guest, O. (2021). Towards Decolonising Computational Sciences. *Women, Gender and Research*, *2021*(1), 60–73.

Brayne, S. (2020). *Predict and Surveil: Data, Discretion, and the Future of Policing*. Oxford University Press.

Brayne, S., & Christin, A. (2021). Technologies of Crime Prediction: The Reception of Algorithms in Policing and Criminal Courts. *Social Problems*, *68*, 608–624.

Brighenti, A. M. (2010). *Visibility in Social Theory and Social Research*. Palgrave Macmillan.

Burrell, J., & Fourcade, M. (2021). The Society of Algorithms. *Annual Review of Sociology*, *47*(1), 213–237. https://doi.org/10.1146/annurev-soc-090820-020800

Christin, A. (2020). What Data Can Do: A Typology of Mechanisms. *International Journal of Communication*, *14*, 1115–1134.

Clarke, A., Parsell, C., & Lata, L. N. (2021). Surveilling the Marginalised: How Manual, Embodied and Territorialised Surveillance Persists in the Age of 'Dataveillance.' *The Sociological Review*, *69*(2), 396–413. https://doi.org/10.1177/0038026120954785

Clayton, A. (2020, October 27). *How Eugenics Shaped Statistics*. Nautilus. https://nautil.us/how-eugenics-shaped-statistics-9365/

Couldry, N., & Mejias, U. A. (2021). The Decolonial Turn in Data and Technology Research: What is at Stake and Where is it Heading? *Information, Communication & Society*, 1–17. https://doi.org/10.1080/1369118X.2021.1986102

Cronley, C. (2020). Invisible Intersectionality in Measuring Vulnerability among Individuals Experiencing Homelessness – Critically Appraising the VI-SPDAT. *Journal of Social Distress and Homelessness*, 1–11. https://doi.org/10.1080/10530789.2020.1852502

Davis, J. L., Williams, A., & Yang, M. W. (2021). Algorithmic Reparation. *Big Data & Society*, 8(2), 1–12. https://doi.org/10.1177/20539517211044808

Desrosières, A. (1998). *The Politics of Large Numbers: A History of Statistical Reasoning*. Harvard University Press.

Esposti, S. D. (2014). When Big Data Meets Dataveillance: The Hidden Side of Analytics. *Surveillance & Society*, 12(2), 209–225.

Eubanks, V. (2018). *Automating Inequality: How High-Tech Tools Profile, Police, and Punish the Poor*. St. Martin's Press.

Flyverbom, M. (2022). Overlit: Digital Architectures of Visibility. *Organization Theory*, 3(2), 26317877221090310. https://doi.org/10.1177/26317877221090314

Foucault, M. (1995). *Discipline & Punish: The Birth of the Prison* (A. Sheridan, Trans.; Second Vintage Books Edition). Vintage Books.

Friedman, B., & Nissenbaum, H. (1996). Bias in Computer Systems. *ACM Transactions on Information Systems*, 14(3), 330–347. https://doi.org/10.1145/230538.230561

Gandy, O. H. (1993). *The Panoptic Sort: A Political Economy of Personal Information*. Westview Press.

Gandy, O. H. (2009). *Coming to Terms with Chance: Engaging Rational Discrimination and Cumulative Disadvantage*. Routledge. https://doi.org/10.4324/9781315572758

Gilliom, J. (2001). *Overseers of the Poor: Surveillance, Resistance, and the Limits of Privacy*. University of Chicago Press. https://press.uchicago.edu/ucp/books/book/chicago/O/bo3626685.html

Green, B. (2019). "Good" isn't Good Enough. *Proceedings of the AI for Social Good Workshop at NeurIPS*. https://www.benzevgreen.com/wp-content/uploads/2019/11/19-ai4sg.pdf

Hacking, I. (1990). *The Taming of Chance*. Cambridge University Press.

Haggerty, K. D. (2006). Tear Down the Walls: On Demolishing the Panopticon. In D. Lyon (Ed.), *Theorizing Surveillance: The Panopticon and Beyond* (pp. 23–45). Routledge.

Haggerty, K. D., & Ericson, R. V. (2000). The Surveillant Assemblage. *The British Journal of Sociology*, 51(4), 605–622. https://doi.org/10.1080/00071310020015280

Heikkilä, M. (2022, March 29). *Dutch Scandal Serves as a Warning for Europe Over Risks of Using Algorithms*. Politico. https://www.politico.eu/article/dutch-scandal-serves-as-a-warning-for-europe-over-risks-of-using-algorithms/

Hill, K. (2021). Your Face Is Not Your Own. *The New York Times Magazine*. https://www.nytimes.com/interactive/2021/03/18/magazine/facial-recognition-clearview-ai.html

Hoffmann, A. L. (2019). Where Fairness Fails: Data, Algorithms, and the Limits of Antidiscrimination Discourse. *Information, Communication & Society*, 22(7), 900–915. https://doi.org/10.1080/1369118X.2019.1573912

Hoffmann, A. L. (2021). Terms of Inclusion: Data, Discourse, Violence. *New Media & Society*, 23(12), 3539–3556. https://doi.org/10.1177/1461444820958725

Hughes, C. C. (2021). A House but Not a Home: How Surveillance in Subsidized Housing Exacerbates Poverty and Reinforces Marginalization. *Social Forces*, 100(1), 293–315. https://doi.org/10.1093/sf/soaa108

Issar, S., & Aneesh, A. (2022). What is Algorithmic Governance? *Sociology Compass*, 16(1), e12955. https://doi.org/10.1111/soc4.12955

Johnson, K. (2020, July 2). MIT Takes Down 80 Million Tiny Images Data Set Due to Racist and Offensive Content. *VentureBeat*. https://venturebeat.com/2020/07/01/mit-takes-down-80-million-tiny-images-data-set-due-to-racist-and-offensive-content/

Joyce, K., Smith-Doerr, L., Alegria, S., Bell, S., Cruz, T., Hoffman, S. G., Noble, S. U., & Shestakofsky, B. (2021). Toward a Sociology of Artificial Intelligence: A Call for Research on Inequalities and Structural Change. *Socius*, 7, 1–11. https://doi.org/10.1177/2378023121999581

Keddell, E. (2019). Algorithmic Justice in Child Protection: Statistical Fairness, Social Justice and the Implications for Practice. *Social Sciences*, 8(10), 281.

Kithulgoda, C. I., Vaithianathan, R., & Culhane, D. P. (2022). Predictive Risk Modeling to Identify Homeless Clients at Risk for Prioritizing Services using Routinely Collected Data. *Journal of Technology in Human Services*, 1–17. https://doi.org/10.1080/15228835.2022.2042461

Levy, K., Chasalow, K., & Riley, S. (2021). Algorithms and Decision-Making in the Public Sector. *Annual Review of Law and Social Science*, *17*, 309–334. https://doi.org/10.1146/annurev-lawsocsci-041221-023808

Lokshin, M., & Umapathi, N. (2022, February 23). AI for Social Protection: Mind the People. Brookings Institution. https://www.brookings.edu/blog/future-development/2022/02/23/ai-for-social-protection-mind-the-people/

Lyon, D. (Ed.). (2003). *Surveillance as Social Sorting: Privacy, Risk, and Digital Discrimination*. Routledge.

Lyon, D. (2007). *Surveillance Studies: An Overview*. Polity.

Mann, M. (2020). Technological Politics of Automated Welfare Surveillance: Social (and Data) Justice through Critical Qualitative Inquiry. *Global Perspectives, 1*(1). https://doi.org/10.1525/gp.2020.12991

Mint. (2021, December 16). Aadhaar 2.0: Will Use AI, Blockchain, ML to Make System Secure, Says UIDAI CEO. Mint. https://www.livemint.com/news/india/aadhaar-2-0-will-use-ai-blockchain-ml-to-make-system-more-secure-says-uidai-ceo-11639650866231.html

Monahan, T. (2017). Regulating Belonging: Surveillance, Inequality, and the Cultural Production of Abjection. *Journal of Cultural Economy*, *10*(2), 191–206. https://doi.org/10.1080/17530350.2016.1273843

Murgia, M., & Harlow, M. (2019, April 19). *Who's Using Your Face? The Ugly Truth About Facial Recognition*. Financial Times. https://www.ft.com/content/cf19b956-60a2-11e9-b285-3acd5d43599e

Noble, S. U. (2018). *Algorithms of Oppression: How Search Engines Reinforce Racism*. NYU Press.

O'Neil, C. (2016). *Weapons of Math Destruction: How Big Data Increases Inequality and Threatens Democracy*. Crown.

OrgCode. (2021, January 25). *A Message from OrgCode on the VI-SPDAT Moving Forward*. OrgCode Consulting. https://www.orgcode.com/blog/a-message-from-orgcode-on-the-vi-spdat-moving-forward

Otis, G. A., & Dillon, N. (2019, November 21). *Google Admits its 'Dark Skin' Face Scan Project Violated Internal Policy, Leading to Overhaul of Data Collection after Daily News Exposé*. New York Daily News. https://www.nydailynews.com/news/national/ny-google-admits-finding-policy-violations-facial-recognition-project-20191121-gn4hmahb4zeoncxnabxb2dfxz4-story.html

Peachey, K. (2022, March 22). *Post Office Scandal: What the Horizon Saga is all About*. BBC News. https://www.bbc.com/news/business-56718036

Peeters, R. (2020). The Agency of Algorithms: Understanding Human-algorithm Interaction in Administrative Decision-Making. *Information Polity, 25*(4), 507–522. https://doi.org/10.3233/IP-200253

Pena, A., Serna, I., Morales, A., & Fierrez, J. (2020). Bias in Multimodal AI: Testbed for Fair Automatic Recruitment. *2020 IEEE/CVF Conference on Computer Vision and Pattern Recognition Workshops*, 129–137. https://doi.org/10.1109/CVPRW50498.2020.00022

Plantinga, P. (2022). Digital discretion and public administration in Africa: Implications for the use of artificial intelligence. *Information Development*, 02666669221117526. https://doi.org/10.1177/02666669221117526

Power, M. (2021). Modelling the Microfoundations of the Audit Society: Organizations and the Logic of the Audit Trail. *Academy of Management Review, 46*, 6–32.

Power, M. (2022). Theorizing the Economy of Traces: From Audit Society to Surveillance Capitalism. *Organization Theory, 3*(3), 26317877211052296. https://doi.org/10.1177/26317877211052296

Prodnik, J. A. (2021). Algorithmic Logic in Digital Capitalism. In P. Verdegem (Ed.), *AI for Everyone?*. University of Westminster Press.

Raghavan, M., Barocas, S., Kleinberg, J., & Levy, K. (2020). Mitigating Bias in Algorithmic Hiring: Evaluating Claims and Practices. *Proceedings of the 2020 Conference on Fairness, Accountability, and Transparency*, 469–481. https://doi.org/10.1145/3351095.3372828

Raji, I. D., & Buolamwini, J. (2019). Actionable Auditing: Investigating the Impact of Publicly Naming Biased Performance Results of Commercial AI Products. *Proceedings of the 2019 AAAI/ACM Conference on AI, Ethics, and Society*, 429–435. https://doi.org/10.1145/3306618.3314244

Raji, I. D., Smart, A., White, R. N., Mitchell, M., Gebru, T., Hutchinson, B., Smith-Loud, J., Theron, D., & Barnes, P. (2020). Closing the AI Accountability Gap: Defining an End-to-End Framework for Internal Algorithmic Auditing. *Proceedings of the 2020 Conference on Fairness, Accountability, and Transparency*, 33–44.

Rao, R. (2022, May 9). *The Dutch Tax Authority Was Felled by AI—What Comes Next?* IEEE Spectrum. https://spectrum.ieee.org/artificial-intelligence-in-government

Ruppert, E. (2012). Seeing Population: Census and Surveillance by Numbers. In K. Ball, K. Haggerty, & D. Lyon (Eds.), *Routledge Handbook of Surveillance Studies* (pp. 209–216). Routledge.

Sadowski, J. (2019). When Data is Capital: Datafication, Accumulation, and Extraction. *Big Data & Society*, 6(1), 2053951718820549. https://doi.org/10.1177/2053951718820549

Sadowski, J., & Andrejevic, M. (2020). More than a Few Bad Apps. *Nature Machine Intelligence*, 1–3. https://doi.org/10.1038/s42256-020-00246-2

Samudzi, Z. (2019, February 9). *Bots Are Terrible at Recognizing Black Faces. Let's Keep it That Way.* The Daily Beast. https://www.thedailybeast.com/bots-are-terrible-at-recognizing-black-faces-lets-keep-it-that-way

Scheuerman, M. K., Pape, M., & Hanna, A. (2021). Auto-essentialization: Gender in Automated Facial Analysis as Extended Colonial Project. *Big Data & Society*, 8(2), 1–15. https://doi.org/10.1177/20539517211053712

Sloane, M., Moss, E., & Chowdhury, R. (2022). A Silicon Valley Love Triangle: Hiring Algorithms, Pseudo-Science, and the Quest for Auditability. *Patterns*, 3(2), 100425. https://doi.org/10.1016/j.patter.2021.100425

Stark, L., Greene, D., & Hoffmann, A. L. (2021). Critical Perspectives on Governance Mechanisms for AI/ML Systems. In J. Roberge & M. Castelle (Eds.), *The Cultural Life of Machine Learning: An Incursion into Critical AI Studies* (pp. 257–280). Palgrave Macmillan.

Stark, L., & Hutson, J. (2022). Physiognomic Artificial Intelligence. *Fordham Intellectual Property, Media and Entertainment Law Journal*, 32(4), 922–978.

van Bekkum, M., & Borgesius, F. Z. (2021). Digital Welfare Fraud Detection and the Dutch SyRI Judgment. *European Journal of Social Security*, 23(4), 323–340. https://doi.org/10.1177/13882627211031257

VanBerlo, B. (2021, June 2). *An Open-source Interpretable Machine Learning Approach to Prediction of Chronic Homelessness.* Medium. https://towardsdatascience.com/an-open-source-interpretable-machine-learning-approach-to-prediction-of-chronic-homelessness-8215707aa572

Vecchione, B., Levy, K., & Barocas, S. (2021). Algorithmic Auditing and Social Justice: Lessons from the History of Audit Studies. In *Equity and Access in Algorithms, Mechanisms, and Optimization* (pp. 1–9). Association for Computing Machinery. https://doi.org/10.1145/3465416.3483294

Viljoen, S. (2021). The Promise and Limits of Lawfulness: Inequality, Law, and the Techlash. *Journal of Social Computing*, 2(3), 284–296. https://doi.org/10.23919/JSC.2021.0025

Webster, C. W. R. (2012). Public Administration as Surveillance. In K. Ball, K. Haggerty, & D. Lyon (Eds.), *Routledge Handbook of Surveillance Studies* (pp. 313–320). Routledge.

Wilkey, C., Donegan, R., Yampolskaya, S., & Cannon, R. (2019). *Coordinated Entry Systems: Racial Equity Analysis of Assessment Data.* C4 Innovations. https://c4innovates.com/wp-content/uploads/2019/10/CES_Racial_Equity_Analysis_2019-.pdf

Winner, L. (1980). Do Artifacts Have Politics? *Daedalus*, 109(1), 121–136.

Zuboff, S. (2018). *The Age of Surveillance Capitalism: The Fight for a Human Future at the New Frontier of Power.* PublicAffairs.

31. Digital tracking and infrastructural power
Stine Lomborg, Rasmus Helles and Signe Sophus Lai

TRACKING AND POWER IN DIGITAL COMMUNICATION SYSTEMS

The advent of the internet marked not only a significant leap in the historical development of communication technologies but also fundamentally challenged the scope and established perimeters of many academic disciplines, not least media and communication studies. If the study of mass media institutions, texts and audiences has historically driven the development of media and communication studies as a field, the internet invited media scholars to throw a wider net around the phenomenon of 'media'. It prompted heated debates about the constitutional elements in conceptualizations of 'media' (Jensen, 2010). And it brought about a 'turn to infrastructure' (Musiani et al., 2016), and a productive line of research that not only studies digital infrastructure but uses the concept of infrastructure to push our understanding of the relationship between media and society.

If we think about the internet not as a medium, but as a communication system (Jensen & Helles, 2023), this system as a whole is networked and layered in the sense that it channels distinct and multiple communication operations at the frontend as well as the backend (Parks et al., 2023).

Communication at the frontend concerns the circulation of messages and meanings in time and space through written text, audio and visual modalities. To date, most existing research addresses the content layer, which of course continues to be important, even if it becomes increasingly difficult to untangle this layer from what goes on at the backend, infrastructural level. In a broad sense, digital tracking encompasses other forms of surveillance, some of which date back before the advent of web tracking, such as, for example, eavesdropping and forgery of digital documents. The execution of these often depends on some of the same infrastructural affordances. Yet the most pervasive forms of digital tracking all derive from infrastructural developments made in the context of web-based tracking. Algorithmic curation, personalized service provision based on tracking of past behaviour, automation and so forth increasingly interfere with the production and circulation of messages and meaning among humans at the frontend. Content as such is no longer king.

Communication at the backend, in contrast, is not centred on the content per se, but concerns the tracking, flow and trade of user traffic and, by extension, user data, across the digital communication system. The backend is the fundamental layer of communication as traffic thrives on the attraction of user attention at the frontend level of content and feeds back into this level by enabling the production and distribution of personalized content by pushing content providers for more traffic-generating content. But at the same time, it operates through a different communicative currency: the collection, exchange, and mining of data about users through *infrastructures of tracking and surveillance*. If communication in the frontend and backend are mutually dependent, we may be well-served, as Turow and Couldry (2017) have suggested, by paying more systematic attention to media in terms of their capacity for datafication by way of digital tracking.

The frontend and backend layers operate through different logics and are regulated and governed differently, but together they make up the internet as a relatively coherent and layered communication system. To understand how this communication system works, we need to address the infrastructural layer in general, and digital tracking in particular, to unpack its technical mechanisms and the power it embeds. In other words, a political economy of communication must start with the empirical reality of material infrastructure. Specifically, in this chapter, we demonstrate that backend digital tracking enables the exercise of a specific kind of power, *infrastructural power*, and that tech companies who control the data pipelines for tracking increasingly exercise this power in digital communication systems.

This chapter defines digital tracking and offers examples of digital tracking across web and mobile platforms. It relates digital tracking to material infrastructure and discusses how the power of big tech has developed with enhanced capacities for digital tracking and datafication. In doing so, it offers the notion of infrastructural power as revealed in the study of digital tracking. Infrastructural power is the ability to exert control over the material underpinnings of an ecosystem. The concept was originally conceived in sociologist Michael Mann's work on state power (1984), and despite its relevance to understanding core, often commercial forces underpinning digital societies today, it remains underdeveloped. We aim to bring the concept of infrastructural power to bear on digital tracking and thereby highlight its merit in critical studies of AI. We suggest that infrastructural power is a foundational and increasingly important companion to other forms of power exercised in digital communication systems, and sketch ways forward in unpacking the operational logics and political economy of digital tracking and infrastructural power. As mentioned earlier, digital tracking and tracking infrastructures are used for multiple purposes: this chapter's core example of web tracking via cookies is chosen to enable a more detailed description of the relationship between the material level of infrastructure and the conceptual and analytical consequences for our understanding of infrastructural power.

DIGITAL TRACKING: WHAT IS IT?

Digital tracking denotes a concrete practice that is conditioned on the distinct traits of digital systems, namely, their capacity to collect, organize, quantify and analyse massive amounts and multiple types of data. These data are combined, processed and rendered into knowledge and insights with relevance for economic value creation, public planning, administrative decisions and a host of other social activities. Two decades ago, tracking was a niche activity of espionage and technical surveillance (Lyon, 2001) that was amplified in the wake of 9/11 and the war on terror (Dencik & Cable, 2017). Today, digital tracking is standard operating procedure across the digital platforms that most of the world's population use on an everyday basis. This development has largely happened under the radar of science and public debate. Part of the explanation for this is undoubtedly that influential players in the global economy and politics have vested interests in displaying the development as natural, positive and a sign of societal progress. But another part of the explanation is that the complicated interplay between technological and societal factors that characterize the development has not naturally been the home base of any single scientific discipline. Digital tracking (and AI) is about economics, politics and technological possibilities, and actual uses. Indeed, the interplay between the economic power that many platforms have and the infrastructural preconditions for that power is itself an emerging area of study (see Prodnik (2021)).

Digital Tracking in Society

Digital tracking is omnipresent in many parts of the world today, and it manifests itself in multiple ways. Mobile phones offer a case in point: these include sensors that can track location and movement, light and so on that can in turn be used to optimize functionality on the phone at any given moment. Most mobile phones come with native apps that can be used by the individual holding the phone for tracking screen time, exercise and health, and a huge host of apps are available on the iOS and Android app stores that enable tracking of all things imaginable. Social media platforms, online shopping services, banking and digital public services track information about people, including their digital behaviour, for example, through cookies on the web and software development kits (SDKs) on mobile apps (Lai & Flensburg, 2021; Pybus & Coté, 2021). In addition, buildings and urban environments include sensors to optimize and further develop these environments, and biometric tracking features prominently in migration management and international travel. In short, digital tracking is intimately embedded in the functioning of society and the everyday lives of individual human beings.

First Parties and Third Parties

A key element in the historical development of digital tracking has been the web cookie, and how this technology facilitates a complicated interplay between frontend and backend streams of communication (Jensen & Helles, 2017). Cookies are essential for both the interactive, real-time adaptation of what appears to the user in a browser window, as well as to the way knowledge is collected and transacted by other parties in the background. In essence, cookies are small text files that are downloaded by your browser when you visit a website, and they may serve a range of different purposes, ranging from allowing the collection of traffic statistics to security and commercial tracking. In contrast to the content of a website (pictures and text), the cookies are not displayed to users but are stored by the browser, sometimes for several months. Cookies come in two forms: First-party cookies and third-party cookies. 'Party' here refers to the entity issuing and using the cookie, where first-party cookies are generated and operated as part of the server infrastructure underpinning the website your visit. This type of cookie is typically created to facilitate core site functionality. Third-party cookies are issued by an external actor, often a company that facilitates online advertising, such as Google or Facebook. These cookies get placed in the browser via a hyperlink that is opened in the background and are invisible to the user (Liu & Chao, 2020). The link itself is placed in the html source code of the website by the web manager overseeing it. So, for example, when someone visits the website of The New York Times, a range of third-party cookies gets downloaded to their browser from various cookie servers via invisible links; links that are placed on the site by the technical staff of The Times.

A central affordance of third-party cookies is that they facilitate cross-site tracking. Once a cookie is downloaded to your browser, it is possible for the entity that has placed the cookie to access it again, either to read the content contained in the cookie text or simply to check if it is there or not. Since many third-party cookies are present on many different sites, the mechanism allows a third party to build a portfolio of the browsing patterns followed by someone whose browser has their cookie stored. A third party that has its cookie placed on many different sites gains the capability to track whenever someone traverses any of these sites and can aggregate this information to develop profiles on them, for example, with the intention of estimating their intent to purchase something.

The ability to keep track of users via the tracking infrastructure (which is substantially more sophisticated than described above) is by no means confined to the placement of display advertising, even if this represents the most immediate use case (Choi et al., 2020). The data collected via cookies and other means of tracking user behaviour (e.g., mobile SDKs and APIs) becomes an asset of its own. These data are bought by large data brokers, who aggregate tracking information of many different kinds and refine them into commercially actionable formats, for example, in the form of user segmentation models. A key development from the early stages of digital tracking has been the ability to link third-party cookies in browsers to the real identities of people, a development that has not least been facilitated through the emergence of more persistent representations of user identities, especially through social media and the spread of smartphones. While this may appear as a relatively straightforward (if messy) task, the ability to consolidate traces of user activity from disparate sites into individualized profiles required the refinement and application of sophisticated machine learning tools. The evolution of tracker infrastructure thus goes hand in hand with the development of appropriate AI tools to refine and act on the collected data.

Data brokers in turn make these forms of information available to all sorts of companies seeking to leverage profiling information on individual users. Some of the largest actors in this area also have consumer-facing products, such as Facebook, while others only deal in business-to-business transactions of data, such as Acxion. They claim to have profiling information about 2.5 billion people, corresponding to roughly half of all people with access to the internet.

A key point about the information held by tracking companies and data brokers alike is that it can be used in a wide variety of ways and that there are no obvious ways to control what it is used for or if the information held is accurate. While privacy protection has become more of a concern since the introduction of the GDPR, the potential for abuse of poorly anonymized data has been demonstrated several times, for example, by allowing to track specific users through systems aimed at microtargeting ads.

The tracking infrastructure that has historically grown from attempts at targeting ads at relevant groups of users has become an integral part of all major infrastructures for digital communication and transactions. At the same time, and as part of the same development, it has become the dominant business model for the digital realm.

Digital tracking is enabled by technological infrastructure and has become standard in making digital communication seamless in operation and experience. It can be used for a vast array of purposes, including functionality and service optimization, surveillance and new technological developments, for instance, it serves a critical role in generating data to train machine learning models and other developments in AI. From a broader perspective, digital tracking is an infrastructural precondition for automating decision-making across a wide range of social and commercial contexts. Importantly, the way data is collected and systematized prior to being served up for systematic analysis by AI systems carries epistemic assumptions and implications of their own.

Hence, we propose that a critical analysis of developments of AI benefits from understanding the technical and infrastructural conditions under which data that fuel the development of AI applications and machine learning models have been generated.

FROM RELATIONAL TO MATERIAL INFRASTRUCTURES

In recent years, media and communication scholars have taken an increasing interest in studying the material foundations of the internet. The concern with the material properties of the internet is a crucial part of the efforts at exposing the backend of the communication system. As part of what is often referred to as a 'turn to infrastructure' (Musiani et al., 2016) in internet governance, these studies of the internet are less concerned with 'what people say with it' (Sandvig, 2013, p. 90), that is the frontend, and more with questions of 'how it works' (Ibid.) at the backend, studying the physical manifestation of networks (Starosielski, 2015) and data centres for hosting 'cloud' services (Holt & Vonderau, 2015) to uncover hidden power structures and control mechanisms built into the same infrastructures (DeNardis, 2020). Yet, digital infrastructures are rarely studied from coherent or systemic macro-perspectives, and we still lack broader frameworks for understanding how they work, who controls them and for what ends.

This scarcity can, in part, be traced back to a fundamental divide in infrastructure studies, between relationist and materialist perspectives on infrastructure (Sandvig, 2013). The relationist perspective sees infrastructure as constituted in specific social practices. Relationist studies, as such, tend to work from the assumption that digital infrastructures are invisible until they break down (Bowker et al., 2009; Star & Ruhleder, 1996), making them inherently difficult to study and regulate; which is also why these studies make calls for scrutinizing digital infrastructures as they become apparent through uses and breakdowns. The relationist perspective motivates mainly qualitative studies of people's particular 'practices and social arrangements rather than artifacts' (Lievrouw, 2014, p. 24), and is the most prevalent in media and communication research.

In contrast to this is a materialist tradition, which by all comparisons, is in a minority position and is fairly scattered across disciplines. Under a material approach, infrastructures are understood to be physical resources (pipes, cables, etc), and material infrastructure studies aim to unravel how public and private actors obtain structural power through infrastructural components and why (Winseck, 2017, 2019). In contrast to relationist studies, the materialist approach makes systemic and large-scale inquiries into the general features of digital infrastructures.

The relationist and materialist perspectives come with ontological and epistemological implications, both in terms of the kinds of research questions that can reasonably be asked as well as how they might be answered. Star and Ruhleder's (1996) original description of infrastructures as social constructs that can only be studied as they are used in organized practices underlines the contrast:

> Within a given cultural context, the cook considers the water system a piece of working infrastructure integral to making dinner; for the city planner, it becomes a variable in a complex equation. Thus we ask, *when* – not *what* – is an infrastructure. (Star & Ruhleder, 1996, p. 112 emphasis added)

To this, one might ask, *what* infrastructures (such as water systems) are, *when* they are not in use but clearly exist and have consequences, nonetheless? One consequence of the divide between relational and materialist perspectives is that the infrastructure concept itself has become vague (Hesmondhalgh, 2021). Yet, on the other hand, such vagueness is also a hallmark of any concept sufficiently central to any scholarly field; think of, for example, 'communication' or 'power'. The important task is to disentangle in a systematic way what meaning is attributed to the concept and clarify the consequences for analysis. In the context of infrastructural power, it can be helpful to think of the notion of materialism in relation to the kinds of analytical units that get operationalized in infrastructural analysis.

To give an example, we can think about recent usages of the term 'infrastructuralization' when addressing internet users' increasing dependence on corporations such as Google. Surely, Google owns a variety of infrastructural resources across the value chain – data centres, fibre-optic submarine cables, advertising platforms, third-party trackers and a vast variety of applications. However, by considering Google as an infrastructure, rather than a large and tremendously influential corporation in the digital economy, we run the risk of naturalizing its position in the marketplace by seeing it as a natural constituent of an infrastructure. In contrast, if we distinguish between infrastructural resources on the one hand, and market actors on the other, we can map and critically assess how the technologies in question are owned and controlled and with what implications for market structures, governance and so forth. A materialist understanding of infrastructure enables the critical political-economic analysis of digital tracking as it has developed across temporal, geographical and technological scales. That is, it helps us unpack how specific market actors come to exercise infrastructural power through the capacity to control the infrastructural resources of a certain technological system, here the communication system and its backend operations, including various applications of AI, through digital tracking.

In the remainder of this chapter, we explore what a concept of infrastructural power might involve, demonstrate its utility with reference to two recent examples of its exercise in the context of digital tracking and suggest ways ahead for the study of the intersection between digital tracking and infrastructural power to inform a critical analysis of AI.

FROM PLATFORM AND DATA POWER TO INFRASTRUCTURAL POWER

The concept of *infrastructural power* we suggest here offers a fresh entry point for studying the consequences of digital infrastructures and datafication in society. There are related concepts. Platform power, a broad concept that refers to the political-economic power of big tech to assert influence over digital ecosystems and markets (van Dijck et al., 2019), is leveraged in discussions of network effects, digital governance and regulation. Data power is loosely understood as the enactment of power through processes of datafication (Kennedy & Bates, 2017). Data power is typically put forward to address the critical consequences for individual rights and social justice of intensive data collection and the subsequent application of machine learning processes on such data. The concepts of platform and data power have gained some traction in critical digital humanistic and social science research, and sometimes intersect with research about material digital infrastructures to the extent that platforms and infrastructures become conflated (Hesmondhalgh, 2021).

Infrastructural power denotes the discretion of an actor to contribute to or disrupt the functioning of an existing infrastructure (Law, 1990). Hence, it foregrounds the exercise of power through the shaping and dismantling of infrastructure critical to the functioning of markets. In a recent article, David Pinzur (2021) claims that

actors' discretion over their own practical contributions to the operation of an infrastructure constitutes an additional, discrete source of 'infrastructural power' (Braun, 2020). Insofar as these actors'
contributions are necessary for the smooth functioning of an infrastructure, their ability to enable or
disrupt others' everyday routines constitutes a practical form of influence (Law, 1990). While social
structural power shapes an infrastructure's features from without, infrastructural power allows contestation from within. (Pinzur, 2021, p. 646)

Recent developments in digital tracking across web and mobile ecosystems serve to demonstrate how big tech companies operate using infrastructural power to gain business advantages
and create future markets for themselves. In January 2020, Google announced its Chrome
web browser would abandon the use of third-party cookies over a two-year period. This decision was cast as part of a wider company-led initiative, calling for a joint effort of the ad tech
ecosystem, to 'make the web more private and secure for users' (Chromium, 14 January 2020)
and enable a more private web experience. A simple decision from the leading player in the
field dismantled the technological core of the ad tech industry. Commentators around the
world linked Google's decision to block third-party tracking to legal developments regarding
privacy protection through, for example, the GDPR and e-privacy directives, some dubbing
this a victory of legal over commercial power. Yet, others speculated that abandoning third-
party tracking was not the kind of blow to Google's business model that it might seem. Rather,
the move to abandon third-party cookies demonstrates how forcefully dominant actors like
Google could do away with an entire global ecosystem of small and medium-sized businesses
trading in data built on top of third-party cookies.

Another example is Apple's decision to change the default settings for app-based tracking in iOS from an opt-out to an opt-in model. This decision was executed with a technical
update to iOS14 in September 2021, so that apps must now ask permission to track the user.
If choosing to opt-out (as most users have done), Apple with not share their IFDA with
third parties, and thus in effect hampers other actors' pursuits of economic gain through
mobile advertising. Again, a simple technical update to the infrastructure of tracking in
iOS, Apple effectively dismantled other players', notably Meta's, ability to monetize app
usage.

While these developments may be seen as beneficent responses to public requests for user
privacy, in effect, they strengthen specific key actors' positions and power in the digital communication system.

These examples of developments in digital tracking lay bare the need for a concept of
infrastructural power. We argue that there are crucial analytical gains in being specific when
examining the exercise of power in digital systems. By narrowly asking about the role of
material infrastructure and its technical underpinnings (e.g., as in the case of digital tracking),
we can discern how various forms and operations of power intersect and stand in relation to
one another. Specifically, we suggest infrastructural power as not only complementary but
conditional to other forms of power that digital platforms may wield. By not attending to
infrastructural power, we risk overlooking the kind of momentum and inertia that is present
in digital communication systems and their in-built capacities for digital tracking. When the
technical infrastructure is in place, it is very difficult to change, except for the specific actors
who can wield their discrete power over infrastructural developments to change the playing
field. As we shall see, specific technical changes initiated by core actors in the infrastructures
for third-party tracking in web and mobile ecosystems may have cascading and long-term
consequences for the ecosystems.

Infrastructural power offers a vocabulary for talking about power not just as something that manifests in content (what information gets distributed, what discursive framings become available and dominant) and economy (who earns the money), but also in terms of the power over the materiality underpinning digital communication systems.

The concept of infrastructural power was first introduced in 1984 by sociologist Michael Mann. He wrote about the state's ability to impose policies throughout the national territory, or, in Mann's words: 'the power of the state to penetrate and centrally coordinate the activities of civil society through its own infrastructure' (Mann, 1984, p. 190). Mann contrasts infrastructural power with the despotic power of the state elite – that is, 'the range of actions which the elite is empowered to undertake without routine, institutionalised negotiation with civil society groups' (Ibid., 188). He argues that while despotic power has been in general decline, infrastructural power increases as we move through historical periods. Similar perspectives, albeit focusing on the technological and economic origins of the information society, can be found in James Beniger's (2009) work on how 'crises of control' following in the wake of the Industrial Revolution required an equivalent revolution in terms of how information infrastructures were exploited to increase control or ground a so-called 'control revolution'.

Distinguishing between different ways states gain and increase their infrastructural power, Mann points to four 'logistical techniques' for effective state penetration of social life:

a) 'A division of labour between the state's main activities which it co-ordinated centrally'
b) 'Literacy, enabling stabilised messages to be transmitted through the state's territories by its agents, and enabling legal responsibilities to be codified and stored'
c) 'Coinage, and weights and measures, allowing commodities to be exchanged under an ultimate guarantee of value by the state'
d) 'Rapidity of communication of messages and of transport of people and through improved roads, ships, telegraphy, etc.'

While the concept of infrastructural power has been employed and developed within, for example, political science (Schwartz, 2019), development studies (Lavers, 2021) and STS (Allhutter, 2012), it does not figure prominently in media and communication studies (for exceptions, see Munn 2020; Tarrow, 2018; Tavmen, 2020). However, it figures implicitly as a component in discussions of infrastructural lock-ins and network effects.

Although Mann's ideas were not formulated with the internet infrastructure, let alone infrastructural assets like web cookies, in mind, the logistical techniques outlined above are a valuable starting point for discussing how tech companies gain and exercise power throughout the ecosystem and by means of the power they hold over key infrastructural resources, such as capacities for digital tracking. Being particularly concerned with state power, Mann focuses on national states and national territories. However, if we replace the state as the acting part across the four control techniques listed above with a large and influential actor in the data economy, then the passages do not sound all that unfamiliar.

Take Alphabet as an example: the company (1) provides centrally organized services carried out through a division of labour: web trackers for ads, analytics, content delivery and so forth; applications that span a multitude of purposes and amount to more than 100 dedicated services; advertising platforms and exchanges like AdWords and DoubleClick; and fibre-optic undersea connections like the Curie and Dunant cables. Put differently, as Alphabet acquires infrastructural resources that span from frontend to backend technologies, they can centralize an otherwise decentralized technology through interconnecting valuable components. The company also (2) ensures the literacy of a multitude of agents that work with and become dependent on these services, such as webmasters using Alphabet's suite of third-party tools to ensure the functioning of their sites. Simultaneously, the company has the necessary capacity for codifying and storing immense amounts of data in dedicated facilities at a scale, which is unmatchable by most other actors in the field. Considering its position in the data economy, Alphabet is also (3) able to set the currency by which to exchange goods – in this case, users' data and subsequent attention – and claim that these goods are ultimately valuable assets. We might refer to this as a highly lucrative monetization of the company's analytical capability as derived from tracking, which is again difficult to compete with due to the pervasiveness of the company's (tracking) products across the layers of the communication system. The capability to systematically harvest and employ tracking data in this way effectively underpins the market position of Alphabet, and in effect translates into a lock-in of users (businesses using Alphabets services), to the extent that their business model is tied to the affordances of the system. And finally (4), through a multitude of infrastructural investments and buy-ups, the company provides an effective system for routing and exchanging data. Or, perhaps more aptly, for trading in what is ultimately human futures (Zuboff, 2019). In sum, the example testifies to the power inherent in owning infrastructures across all levels of the system and being able to set standards and price tags for hazy goods such as datafied lives and attention and building technologies that the remaining market actors depend upon to distribute their services, commodify user experiences or trade in their biproducts.

Mann goes on to contrast historical societies with societies as of 1984, emphasizing the prevalence of infrastructural power and its consequences, which again resonates somewhat with the role played by large tech companies in 2021:

> It [the state] stores and can recall immediately a massive amount of information about all of us; it can enforce its will within the day almost anywhere in its domains; its influence on the overall economy is enormous [...] The state penetrates everyday life more than did any historical state. (Mann, 1984, p. 189)

We contend that Mann's 1984 conceptualizations are useful for making sense of the backend of communication systems by specifying what infrastructural power is, and not least how it is obtained and exercised. An analysis of digital tracking and infrastructural power is centred on mapping and analysing the dominance of different actors in the realm of digital tracking as well as the distributions of the infrastructural resources they own and control. While several of these actors operate at both the backend and frontend of the communication system outlined earlier, most of them limit their business to the backend trade in user data. And at the backend, we may be wise to go beyond the usual methods of media and communication studies to flesh out and empirically document *what is going on*.

Beyond Infrastructural Power

Infrastructural power is different in kind and scope than other forms of power operating in digital systems. It operates through the technical-material layers at the backend of the communication system. As argued previously, infrastructural power is the ability to exert control over the material underpinnings of an ecosystem. If we consider ad tech as an ecosystem for tracking users in and across platforms in order to optimize marketing and sales, engage in surveillance and so on, the control over when and how cookie-based third-party tracking may be performed on the web, and who gets to benefit from it, presents a core resource of infrastructural power. While AI and automated decision-making play a key role in the final step of the process (in particular in the automated auctions that match users with ads), the infrastructural resources necessary for this to happen precede it. As such, it is a different kind of power than the power of platforms to control discourse and regulate freedom of expression, for example, by way of content moderation. It is also different from epistemic power to decide what can be known on (given parts of) the web. Infrastructural power denotes how the possession of material components vital for the functioning of an ecosystem makes someone capable of making other actors in the ecosystem behave in a certain way and in doing so orchestrating the market's dependency on the entire system.

Infrastructural power can be exchanged for other forms of power. If market actors controlling material infrastructures for communication hold infrastructural power, they also increasingly attain other forms of power, including ideological or epistemic power. But other kinds of power do not convert to infrastructural power: holding vast and rich data resources, such as the ones held by Scandinavian welfare states who have historically collected detailed records over their populations and are becoming increasingly datafied (Kaun & Dencik, 2020), provides for planning and optimizing services within existing digital systems, but importantly it does not enable the exercise of infrastructural power over these systems. Hence, infrastructural power is a more foundational form of power, one that is largely in the hands of big tech, which can enable and constrain the capacity of other actors – nation-states and corporations – to derive value from data. In the context of web-tracking, for example, market actors who control the data pipelines and thus hold infrastructural power also embody a dataist ideology (Dijck, 2014) that centres on what Andrejevic (2020) calls the fantasy of total information capture. In amassing massive amounts and different types of data through their infrastructural resources, they become data monopolies with significant epistemic power in digital communication systems.

SOME PATHWAYS FOR FUTURE RESEARCH ON DIGITAL TRACKING AND INFRASTRUCTURAL POWER

In this chapter, we have discussed digital tracking and the datafication it enables with a view to how technical infrastructure becomes an asset, a resource of power in digital communication systems. We have proposed the notion of infrastructural power to point to a need for specifying in critical studies of power in the digital age how power operates on multiple and often interrelated levels of communication.

In developing an analysis of power in general, and infrastructural power in particular, we call for future research to take up the challenge of exploring in empirical terms the materiality of infrastructures of tracking as a resource of power to further our understanding of the political economy of digital tracking and datafied societies. Also, the theoretical understanding and analysis of the term 'materialism' in relation to different dimensions of infrastructure, including AI, will likely prove a fruitful avenue of research that can help advance the analysis of how infrastructural power works alongside other forms of power.

Second, we suggest research is needed that takes a comparative and historical approach to the study of, for example, web and mobile communication systems, but also seeks to explore how digital infrastructure has been shaped by states and markets across national and cultural boundaries (Schroeder, 2019). At present, big tech has acquired infrastructural power at scale and in scope. But the story of how we got her here is not a linear and straightforward narrative, and the infrastructural power of big tech may manifest itself differently across nation-states. As Mann would have us consider, nation-states and supra-national governance forums have historically played a prominent role in defining the perimeters of engagement for private corporations, and in partnering with these to develop basic material infrastructure for the benefit of the people. One case in point, public investments in digitalization over the past 50 years have varied greatly between nations. In some instances, such as the Scandinavian countries, the state has historically played a prominent role in establishing public digital infrastructure, digital government and so on, whereas in other instances, private companies have largely driven the development, with manifest consequences at the message level of the digital communication system (e.g., which websites are popular in a specific national and linguistic context) (Helles et al., 2020). Considering societal variations, we posit that it is likely that the topology of the internet, and the infrastructural power tied to it, looks different across countries.

Finally, we call for renewed, critical and systematic attention to the ideologies embedded in digital tracking and the 'political economy of free'. These manifest across infrastructural and other forms of power and specifically centre around the use of AI in providing data-driven insights and predictive analytics for the efficiency and optimization of systems and services. Governments and companies around the world have bought into this imaginary: the more data we can collect, the better prospects for optimization through business innovation, better user experiences, data-driven decision-making and knowledge production. But the strong ideology of optimization in narratives across business and society obscures alternative cultural imaginaries. We need research to explore ways of teasing out such alternative visions of what it could mean to live a good datafied life and thereby identify a more diverse set of values from which to steer and assess infrastructural developments in digital tracking and AI, as well as their social consequences.

ACKNOWLEDGEMENTS

Research for this article was funded by the Independent Research Fund Denmark (Grant no. 0132-00080B) and the ERC (Starting Grant no. 947735).

REFERENCES

Allhutter, D. (2012). Mind scripting: A method for deconstructive design. *Science, Technology, & Human Values, 37*(6), 684–707.
Andrejevic, M. (2020). *Automated media.* Routledge.
Beniger, J. (2009). *The control revolution: Technological and economic origins of the information society.* Harvard University Press.
Bowker, G. C., Baker, K., Millerand, F., & Ribes, D. (2009). Toward information infrastructure studies: Ways of knowing in a networked environment. In J. Hunsinger, L. Klastrup, & M. Allen (Eds.), *International handbook of internet research* (pp. 97–117). Springer.

Braun, B. (2020). Central banking and the infrastructural power of finance: The case of ECB support for repo and securitization markets. *Socio-Economic Review, 18*, 395–418.

Choi, H., Mela, C. F., Balseiro, S. R., & Leary, A. (2020). Online display advertising markets: A literature review and future directions. *Information Systems Research, 31*(2), 556–575.

DeNardis, L. (2020). *The internet in everything*. Yale University Press.

Dencik, L., & Cable, J. (2017). The advent of surveillance realism: Public opinion and activist responses to the Snowden leaks. *International Journal of Communication, 11*, 763–781.

Dijck, J. V. (2014). Datafication, dataism and dataveillance: Big Data between scientific paradigm and ideology. *Surveillance & Society, 12*(2), 197–208.

Helles, R., Lomborg, S., & Lai, S. S. (2020). Infrastructures of tracking: Mapping the ecology of third-party services across top sites in the EU. *New Media & Society, 22*(11), 1957–1975.

Hesmondhalgh, D. (2021). The infrastructural turn in media and internet research. In P. McDonald (Ed.), *The Routledge companion to media industries*. Routledge.

Holt, J., & Vonderau, P. (2015). Where the internet lives. In C. R. Acland, P. Dourish, S. Harris, J. Holt, S. Mattern, T. Miller, C. Sandvig, J. Sterne, H. Tawil-Souri, & P. Vonderau (Eds.), *Signal traffic: Critical studies of media infrastructures* (pp. 71–93). University of Illinois Press.

Jensen, K. B. (2010). *Media convergence. The three degrees of network, mass, and interpersonal communication*. Routledge.

Jensen, K. B., & Helles, R. (2017). Speaking into the system: Social media and many-to-one communication. *European Journal of Communication, 32*(1), 16–25.

Jensen, K. B., & Helles, R. (Eds.). (2023). *The peoples' internet*. Routledge.

Kaun, A., & Dencik, L. (2020). Datafication and the welfare state: An introduction. *Global Perspectives, 1*(1). https://doi.org/https://doi.org/10.1525/gp.2020.12912

Kennedy, H., & Bates, J. (2017). Data power in material contexts: Introduction. *Television & New Media, 18*(8), 701–705.

Lai, S. S., & Flensburg, S. (2021). Invasive species of the app ecosystem: Exploring the political economy of mobile communication. *International Journal of Communication, 15*, 2301–2318.

Lavers, T. (2021). Aiming for universal health coverage through insurance in Ethiopia: State infrastructural power and the challenge of enrolment. *Social Science & Medicine, 282*. https://doi.org/10.1016/j.socscimed.2021.114174

Law, J. (1990). Power, discretion and strategy. *The Sociological Review, 38*, 165–191.

Lievrouw, L. A. (2014). Materiality and media in communication and technology studies: An unfinished project. In T. Gillespie, P. J. Boczkowski, & K. A. Foot (Eds.), *Media technologies: Essays on communication, materiality, and society* (pp. 21–51). MIT Press.

Liu, P., & Chao, W. (2020). *Computational advertising: Market and technologies for internet commercial monetization*. CRC Press.

Lyon, D. (2001). *Surveillance society: Monitoring everyday life*. Open University Press.

Mann, M. (1984). The autonomous power of the state: Its origins, mechanisms and results. *European Journal of Sociology/Archives européennes de sociologie, 25*(2), 185–213.

Munn, L. (2020). Red territory: Forging infrastructural power. *Territory, Politics, Governance*. https://doi.org/10.1080/21622671.2020.1805353

Musiani, F., Cogburn, D. L., DeNardis, L., & Levinson, N. S. (Eds.). (2016). *The turn to infrastructure in Internet governance*. Palgrave Macmillan.

Parks, L., de Ridder, S., & Velkova, J. (Eds.). (2023). *Media backends: digital infrastructures and sociotechnical relations*. University of Illinois Press.

Pinzur, D. (2021). Infrastructural power: Discretion and the dynamics of infrastructure in action. *Journal of Cultural Economy, 14*(6), 644–661. https://doi.org/10.1080/17530350.2021.1913212

Prodnik, J. A. (2021). Algorithmic logic in digital capitalism. In P. Verdegem (Ed.), *AI for everyone? Critical perspectives* (pp. 203–222). University of Westminster Press. https://doi.org/https://doi.org/10.16997/book55.1

Pybus, J., & Coté, M. (2021). Did you give permission? Datafication in the mobile ecosystem. *Information, Communication & Society*. https://doi.org/10.1080/1369118X.2021.1877771

Sandvig, C. (2013). The internet as infrastructure. In W. H. Dutton (Ed.), *The Oxford handbook of internet studies*. Oxford University Press.

Schroeder, R. (2019). Historicizing media, globalizing media research: Infrastructures, publics, and everyday life. *Journal of Global History, 14*(3), 437–453.

Schwartz, H. M. (2019). American hegemony: Intellectual property rights, dollar centrality, and infrastructural power. *Review of International Political Economy, 26*(3), 490–519. https://doi.org/10.1080/09692290.2019.1597754

Star, S. L., & Ruhleder, K. (1996). Steps toward an ecology of infrastructure: Design and access for large information spaces. *Information Systems Research, 7*(1), 111–134.

Starosielski, N. (2015). *The undersea network*. Duke University Press.

Tarrow, S. (2018). Mann, war, and cyberspace: Dualities of infrastructural power in America. *Theory and Society, 47*(1), 61–85.

Tavmen, G. (2020). Data/infrastructure in the smart city: Understanding the infrastructural power of Citymapper app through technicity of data. *Big Data & Society, 7*(2). https://doi.org/2053951720965618

Turow, J., & Couldry, N. (2017). Media as data extraction: Towards a new map of a transformed communications field. *Journal of Communication, 68*(2), 415–423.

van Dijck, J., Nieborg, D., & Poell, T. (2019). Reframing platform power. *Internet Policy Review, 8*(2), 1–18. https://doi.org/10.14763/2019.2.1414

Winseck, D. (2017). The geopolitical economy of the global internet infrastructure. *Journal of Information Policy, 7*(1), 228–267.

Winseck, D. (2019). Internet infrastructure and the persistent myth of US hegemony. In B. Haggart, K. Henne, & N. Tusikov (Eds.), *Information, technology and control in a changing world: Understanding power structures in the 21st century* (pp. 93–120). Palgrave Macmillan.

Zuboff, S. (2019). *The age of surveillance capitalism: The fight for a human future at the new frontier of power*. Public Affairs.

32. AI and the everyday political economy of global health

Michael Strange and Jason Tucker

INTRODUCTION

This chapter considers the growing role of artificial intelligence within human healthcare, arguing the need for a critical global political-economy approach that is sensitive to inequities combined with a focus on the everyday level of how individuals – both clinicians and patients – experience AI health technologies. While AI brings many benefits to healthcare – such as improving diagnostics, suggesting treatments, and managing resources – its effectiveness is dependent upon both: a) reliable data from which it can learn and b) engagement from multiple stakeholders to identify and ameliorate potential biases that might emerge due to receiving misrepresentative data (DeCamp et al., 2020). For example, in a clinical situation where more affluent patients typically have greater access to healthcare and, due to lifestyle factors, typically respond more successfully to treatment than those more socially marginalised, AI has been shown to develop racial bias directing resources away from those groups most in need due to being identified in the algorithm as less likely to benefit (Obermeyer et al., 2019).

Regulators typically see healthcare as a high-risk field in which to implement AI-based systems, in part due to the obvious fact that it is a policy domain directly focused on matters of human life and death, but also because it is politically sensitive due to how individuals value their own bodies. Paradoxically, however, while the COVID-19 pandemic has raised the political profile of healthcare, it has also provided a catalyst for many healthcare systems to adopt AI tools – whether specifically in the field of pandemic management and prevention or in secondary functions such as supporting primary healthcare where clinical visits were restricted due to social distancing and self-isolation. Subsequent recommendations from healthcare practitioners to use consumer health apps have made the public much more aware, and potentially accepting, of AI-based chatbots, health monitoring apps, and other systems mediating their interactions with healthcare practitioners. In addition, healthcare practitioners are themselves being exposed to new AI applications in certain areas of their work, which may increase the acceptance of these tools to help them manage their workload and assist in decision making.

In a series of workshop discussions with healthcare practitioners involving author one, focused on how to enhance patient engagement within their own healthcare, there was a common acceptance that greater participation is essential as we move towards so-called 'precision healthcare' – that is, health treatments made more effective through being tailored to a patient's genome, lifestyle, and desires' (Strange, 2023). For example, for cancer patients, the standard measure of success being a five-year survival rate post-diagnosis is valued differently by some patients due to their age and the more immediate high risk of deteriorating living conditions caused by chemotherapy. Healthcare practitioners and patients alike frequently bemoan the financial conditions in which face-to-face consultations are often limited to very few minutes despite dealing with complex health conditions that often exceed the knowledge of patients and require more thorough discussion if the clinician is to provide more than a prescription for a general medication. However, where traditionally the solution to have longer consultations is often seen as prohibitively expensive in a context where pharmaceutical and other health technology costs are rapidly rising, AI-based technologies are increasingly touted as a much cheaper way by which to enhance clinical consultations through providing practitioners with more precise and detailed information on the patient in advance of meeting them. Further to this, AI systems can potentially save clinicians time by providing them with a suggested list of possible diagnoses, prognoses, and treatment options, as well as providing a quicker overview of a patient's health.

AI's need for big data streams creates problems for healthcare where that data is highly sensitive, can be very limited in certain areas, and is subject to the strictest privacy laws. Where AI technology is almost exclusively developed by private sector firms operating across national borders, the use of AI in a hospital setting connects a patient's well-being to a global production chain that exceeds the regulatory scope of even the most well-resourced public health governance body. Given the value of that data, firms have a vested interest in developing their own proprietary systems in which healthcare providers are forced to buy into what becomes a monopoly as their AI systems develop. Yet, healthcare is a very personal and experiential process tied to the everyday of the patient (or 'user' in terms of healthcare apps). Despite the global scale of these technologies, and as seen with AI generally, AI healthcare faces the problem that it is often only good at very specific tasks with clear parameters and, otherwise, fails when asked to work on a task outside that for which it was originally built. The main reason for this is that AI is often built by large firms with centralised models. There are also material and political limitations and impacts of using AI, leading Crawford (2021) to argue that AI is neither artificial nor really very intelligent.

According to some industry figures (Goertzel, 2022), for AI to be more adaptable its development needs to be decentralised with a heterogenous cognitive architecture that fits better with networks of smaller firms sharing data rather than the current development of big tech monopolies. There is a parallel between these calls and the importance of the everyday in healthcare as the chapter will argue. To understand and build AI that truly benefits human healthcare, it is necessary to adopt an interdisciplinary approach that combines IT innovations with new forms of what we could call 'everyday socio-political technologies' that recognise the constitutive role of the individual's experience within the wider healthcare system. To develop this argument, the chapter first reviews the role of AI in global healthcare, before introducing the need for a critical political-economy approach, that leads to acknowledging the role of the everyday in this process.

AI AS A USEFUL TOOL IN GLOBAL HEALTHCARE

Global healthcare is seen as being at the beginning of a radical socio-technical transformation. This is based on the current and seemingly ever-increasing scale and scope of AI's utility within healthcare development and delivery (Flores et al., 2013; Miotto, 2018). This is reflected in the incredible rate of growth in the global digital health market, which is predicted to continue to increase significantly in the near term (Thomason, 2021). There is significant solutionism, hype, and mythologisation surrounding this, of which one must be cautious. Yet, we are seeing new and old actors in health using AI as a tool for various motivations, with the potential use of AI in health being a site of enormous contestation between and within the private and public sectors.

While the limits of its application are debated (see Crawford, 2021), one cannot escape the reality that AI can be used in an enormously broad range of applications in healthcare. It is notable that AI is positioned as being intertwined in nearly every aspect of health and health-care in the World Health Organisation's (2021) *Global Strategy on Digital Health 2020–2025*. Since the beginning of the COVID-19 pandemic, this belief has only accelerated, as we have seen AI coming to the forefront of global healthcare. The dominant narrative around AI as a tool in the COVID-19 pandemic is neatly summarised by The Organisation for Economic Co-operation and Development (2020, np) stating:

> Before the world was even aware of the threat posed by [COVID-19]... [AI] systems had detected the outbreak of an unknown type of pneumonia in the People's Republic of China... As the outbreak has now become a global pandemic, AI tools and technologies can be employed to support efforts of policy makers, the medical community, and society at large to manage every stage of the crisis and its aftermath: detection, prevention, response, recovery and to accelerate research.

Nevertheless, the extent to which AI tools have been able to meet this hype as a 'saviour' in the fight against COVID-19 has been challenged. For example, the hype around prediction models, as well as AI applications being able to detect COVID-19 in chest X-rays has failed to live up to expectations (Topol, 2022). The overestimation of the potential of AI applications to provide solutions in healthcare is not limited to COVID-19. AI is yet to be as accurate as humans in areas where its applications are widely heralded to be making enormous advances, such as in mammography (Topol, 2022). Others have pointed to the lack of recognition of the bias and discrimination in the design and use of AI applications in the COVID-19 response, which risks intensifying existing health inequity (Leslie et al., 2021). Korinek and Stiglitz (2021), looking beyond health, warned that the use of COVID-19-driven AI applications could exacerbate economic inequality more widely.

There is a common assumption in policy that AI innovations in healthcare can, or should, only come from the private sector. This reliance on private firms to address a range of health issues using AI has led to new tensions. One example is the competing priorities around the need for transparency in decision making from medical practitioners on the one hand, and, on the other, proprietary, or financial reasons, meaning firms have an interest in ensuring their algorithms are opaque (He et al., 2019). There are also challenges around the intellectual property rights of AI in healthcare (Gerke et al., 2020), an issue which is compounded due to the growing prevalence of public-private partnerships (PPPs).

Healthcare systems around the world are facing numerous challenges (Panch et al., 2018). AI is often presented as a solution with the yet-to-be-proven claim that it can cut costs, improve efficiency, advance preventative healthcare, and tailor healthcare to patients' precise needs. On a global scale, AI and digital technologies have also been claimed to be essential to achieving universal healthcare coverage (UHC) and reducing global health inequality by cutting costs (Panch et al., 2018). AI thus appears to provide a means to step over broader structural limits in the international political economy of global healthcare technologies.

THE NEED FOR A CRITICAL GLOBAL POLITICAL-ECONOMY APPROACH

Technology is never neutral but is always owned via not just intellectual property rights but also the increasingly complex production chains necessary to not only its original development and manufacture, but also the increasingly necessary updates and 24-7 maintenance throughout its usage. These chains produce both the initial product – whether physical or virtual – and its continual value. Where AI health technology is reliant upon dynamic and growing big data sets, its lifeblood is data. In general, it has been said that AI has turned data into the 'new oil', as noted by Sridhar Mahadevan, Director of Research at Adobe (Mahadevan, 2021). The shift from development and production to updates and maintenance as the core means extra value in the technology sector is underlined by the transference of once one-time-only installed software to subscription services. This change raises several important tensions in the context of healthcare.

First, where healthcare becomes dependent on AI healthcare technologies, the commercial for-profit character of the firms involved alters the public-private relationship common in many healthcare systems. The private sector has always been a provider of health technologies. What is potentially different with AI healthcare, however, is where the technology moves from being one of multiple tools a healthcare practitioner may choose, to becoming an integral part of how healthcare is organised and provided. Both the need for personal health data but, also, in turn, the reliance upon the subsequent algorithms throughout the healthcare system blurs the divide between the private sector firms and the public healthcare providers. Such developments are either problematic or seemingly innocuous depending on where you live, given that for many it is normal to use for-profit healthcare providers paid through private insurance. However, even in countries with highly privatised healthcare systems, the use of AI-driven automated decision-making technologies utilising big data sets that exceed the capacity of users to assess the basis of recommendations requires that we critically examine key mechanisms around accountability and governance since processes traditionally contained within clinical settings are being potentially shifted over to firms and interests based elsewhere.

Second, the first point leads to a broader question over where accountability and governance of healthcare resides as AI systems are utilised further. The most common discussion here is a legal concern, which takes prominence given that the distribution of liability is a major issue when accidents and mistreatment might lead to serious morbidity and even fatality with moral and financial repercussions for those held responsible. Vying for importance, however, is national sovereignty. Genomic technologies have long been feared as opening the potential for precision technologies targeting specific ethnic groups, but in a more mundane way, it is important to acknowledge that healthcare technologies are used in environments where people are at their most vulnerable. Where those technologies rely on AI systems that sit continually within global production chains, the reality of what happens in that environment is no longer determined by what is decided within that context or even within the national government's health department but is impacted by actors working according to regulations and interests decided in entirely different jurisdictions with potentially quite distinct ideologies and often being self-regulated (Yeung et al., 2020). It is possible to speculate upon multiple risks, ranging from an act of harm either through deliberate sabotaging of sensitive equipment or abuse of health data, to sharing information with other actors to advantage political and commercial interests against those based within the jurisdiction using the technology.

Third, proprietary AI health technologies make it difficult for healthcare providers to switch providers. By owning the algorithms and subsequent data collected, AI health technology firms control significant parts of the healthcare infrastructure. Switching providers might prove not only expensive through the need to invest in new hardware, but impossible without serious ramifications for patients that would prove politically costly. This situation is not speculative, but a reality reported by healthcare practitioners, who note that many of these technologies are interoperable such that they will only work with other products produced by the same firm (Politico, 2022). Ownership of proprietary technology enables firms a gatekeeper function, whether through being able to pressurise healthcare providers to utilise their products or making it impossible to use alternative products. In turn, as seen in other technology sectors, this gatekeeper function allows firms to charge a fee in the form of technical support for other firms wishing to have their own products integrated within the healthcare system. Procurement is a key responsibility within healthcare systems and, where publicly funded, falls under the general remit of the national or regional government for the relevant jurisdiction. By impacting procurement, the political economy of AI's emerging role in healthcare can be said to have further implications for public authority. There are also concerns that the already existing internal capacity of the healthcare sector is undermined by shifting resources to private firms, further reducing the possibility of them being able to manage future digital health technologies in-house (Webster, 2019).

The three tensions outlined above point to the need for a critical global political-economy approach that focuses on key questions around agency, including accountability, as well as relative power relations that structure how actors interact in the production of global healthcare. Furthermore, the parameters of healthcare as a policy field can be seen to overlap with multiple others, including national security – both economic and military (Korinek & Stiglitz, 2021; Tam-Set, 2021). The analogy of data as the 'new oil' fits well with its importance to AI, but some business voices have argued that data itself is of little value compared to the systems that can make sense of it (Kershner, 2021). Few governmental actors have the capacity to match that of the big tech firms in acquiring and processing data, let alone in utilising it to build AI systems for healthcare. The promissory allure that AI may help minimise face-to-face consultations with highly paid clinicians while replacing the lost information with that collected through apps and other technologies, combined with its general role in managing hospital logistics, explains why few politicians are openly critical of AI healthcare technology.

The global production chains through which AI health is made possible transact multiple and complex levels of regulation, provision models (i.e. fee-based or free at the point of use), but also societal expectations. From our own research with healthcare practitioners, there is an evident knowledge gap as to how AI technologies can best be implemented in healthcare. Too few clinicians have direct contact with technology firms. This lack of contact is recognised as being a serious barrier to AI applications' usefulness for healthcare practitioners (Vinnova, 2018).

In both research and policies focused on widening healthcare access, much attention has been given to the concept of 'health literacy' – broadly defined as the capacity of individuals to understand their health needs, as well as how to access the healthcare system (Nutbeam, 2000). Much of AI health has emerged as consumer health technologies, as 'add-ons' purchased privately – either with money or in exchange for data – as downloadable smartphone apps. As consumer services, these technologies face market pressure to ensure the consumer understands how to use them. In some cases, the apps contribute to health literacy by educating people about their health needs and how to contact clinical specialists. In that respect, they may be said to be good for health literacy and, therefore, healthcare access and efforts.

Yet, as seen during the pandemic we also know that health literacy requires that the healthcare system understands and is open to the needs of the patient/public, and furthermore, that the different parts of the healthcare system are health literate regarding each other, such that they work as a holistic system (Strange et al., 2021). During the pandemic, primary healthcare providers have increasingly turned to consumer healthcare apps as a remedial solution where patients could no longer visit clinics in person but, having got used to such technologies, these privately owned apps have become an increasingly common way through which the public view the healthcare system (Savage, 2021). Considering the tensions outlined above, it is notable that the public healthcare system in most countries is largely passive with respect to the development of AI healthcare technologies. Instead, healthcare policies emphasise the need to engage the private sector as essentially the only means of accessing the very best technologies for patient care. There is an implicit assumption that only the private sector can produce such technology and, equally, that what would be procured is a tool rather than anything more. In some cases, digital healthcare policy figures speak of a moral imperative to allow the use of AI healthcare technologies to save patients' lives. In that context, it is important to consider how to square the need to use the best healthcare technologies available with a critical global political-economy perspective that reminds us that there are relations of ownership and production which run beyond the initial point of procurement to have much longer-term impacts on the healthcare system.

A common criticism put to AI healthcare technologies, drawing upon a critical global political-economy approach, is that they risk reinforcing and extending existing inequalities. For example, Noble (2018) speaks of 'algorithms of oppression' where seemingly innocent technologies such as a search engine reinforce racism. Criado-Perez (2019) notes how data on women are often 'invisible' within many areas of technological innovation, including pharmaceutical research, such that there is a 'gender data gap' with technologies developed for everyone's use, but often being based on male data or with the male body seen as the default. Not only can this perception that the female body is atypical lead to healthcare interventions which cause harm, the gender data gap means that AI cannot provide us with all the solutions, as we simply just do not have the data on women to do so (Criado-Perez, 2019).

Where AI is asked to learn from existing healthcare data, such as which patients are prioritised according to clinicians' decisions, resulting guidance will replicate any biases existing within those past decisions. AI systems can contain 'embedded inequalities' (Leslie et al., 2021) in multiple ways as seen during the pandemic, including data sets that contain historical health discrimination, a lack of representativeness within those data sets, and biased choices made during the design and use of AI systems. The issue of bias is a common phenomenon throughout health innovations, with marginalised groups often being excluded. Yet, AI technologies present a new type of innovation that, due to the large quantities of data involved, potentially make it much harder for users of those systems to identify whether their source material is reliable or biased. Regarding AI generally, there is a noted risk that power imbalances within society – such as race and gender – can be obscured by the technology such that we become blind to the discriminatory, and often neocolonial, character of the systems that are central to the future of society (Gebru, 2020). Important to note when considering the unequal structure of the global political economy of AI health is the role the everyday level plays – both as a site in which the technology is experienced, but also as a structuring force in its own right, shaping and, potentially, resisting dominant modes of power and governance it embodies (Pink et al., 2022).

THE POLITICAL-ECONOMIC ROLE OF THE EVERYDAY IN AI HEALTHCARE

Since healthcare concerns the personal body, it is always tied to the everyday level, even if its provision and development take place at a level far removed. There is a wide gap between the development of AI health technologies and those working in clinics, as well as patients and the wider public. That gap can be understood in terms of health literacy with echoes of discussions from technology studies with a focus on digital literacy. For the last two decades, there has been increasing focus on the everyday as a site of importance within the field of international political economy (Hobson & Seabrooke, 2007). Within that literature, the term 'everyday' refers to a wide range of actors and spheres broadly grouped together as actors normally seen as 'weak' but, nevertheless, expressing agency at key moments such that they alter global political-economic structures. For the global political economy of AI health, the 'everyday' includes patients and individual users, but also the healthcare practitioners since in many cases they can appear equally alienated and disempowered from the production chains. Davina Cooper's (2014) work on 'everyday utopias' points to the need to see everyday spaces as politically important precisely because they are often mundane and banal, embedding the development of political norms within the ordinary experiences and tensions individuals encounter through daily life.

Turning to the everyday means placing attention on how relatively 'weak' actors interact with dominant structures but also those structures are impacted by normal life. How individuals experience AI health technologies in practice is important to understanding not only with regard to the impact of those devices and systems but also where they may subvert or resist the intentions of their designers (Pink et al., 2022). AI health's development within consumer health applications places its origins firmly within the everyday sphere where individuals have downloaded and utilised those services within their private homes sharing highly personal data. For AI health systems to function effectively, it is necessary that individual users engage with the technology, including both patients and healthcare practitioners. There are some useful parallels here with discussions on broadening participation within healthcare. Since the early 2000s, European discussions on health equity have often overlapped with 'health democracy', ranging from neoliberal market-based choice in which the patient is a consumer able to select between services like a voter chooses between parties (Mol, 2008), to utilising more substantive deliberative democratic models in which the capacity to enact choice depends first on being able to understand and challenge healthcare knowledge (Abelson et al., 2003) and, even, enter into 'co-production' (Rantamäki, 2016) with positive outcomes (Pii et al., 2019; Souliotis, 2018; Struzzo et al., 2013).

Specifically, forms of co-production may offer a possible solution to counter the risk that AI widens existing health inequalities. Daugherty et al. (2019) give hope that AI in general has the capacity to counter discrimination but only if those systems are used to actively identify emerging bias in its algorithms. In the context of healthcare, that requires establishing mechanisms for reviewing how health data influences AI, but also giving more attention to existing systemic biases identified within that data. AI provides an opportunity for healthcare practitioners, patients, as well as civil rights campaigners to collaborate towards co-producing a more just healthcare system.

In the US, for example, an algorithm was trained to identify knee pain in X-rays and compare it to previous clinicians' findings. When disaggregated by race they found that 'radiologists may have literal blind spots when it comes to reading Black patients' x-rays' (Simonite, 2021, np). Because of this the referral system for knee surgery disproportionately favours white patients (Ibrahim, 2021). A broader study, again disaggregated by race, on the use of AI in decision making by healthcare systems in the US, shed light on the systemic nature of racial discrimination in healthcare. Obermeyer et al. (2019) found that Black patients were about half as likely to be identified as needing care, which the authors explained as arising as

> [b]ias occurs because the algorithm uses health costs as a proxy for health needs. Less money is spent on Black patients who have the same level of need, and the algorithm thus falsely concludes that Black patients are healthier than equally sick White patients. (Ibid, p.447)

By drawing upon vast data sets, AI can connect a wide range of life circumstances to place healthcare in the context of those individuals' everyday lives. In so doing, healthcare outcomes can be better understood as directly impacted by key factors like living conditions and employment. Health literacy traditionally focuses on how to make patients better understand their health needs. However, by 'joining the dots', AI health technology has the potential to enable the healthcare system to be more literate in how best to support an individual given their specific everyday circumstances. Whether that happens or not, the example of racism in healthcare underlines the extent to which the future of AI health is dependent upon what occurs within the everyday sphere.

CONCLUSION

Even if only part of the hype proves true, AI has much to offer healthcare. By helping to sift through vast and complex data sets, AI-based technology has the potential to enhance diagnoses, prognoses, and treatments. For private and public healthcare funders, perhaps the strongest allure is the promise that AI technologies may help cut costs by enhancing the management of scarce resources. Yet, to maximise that potential, it is also necessary that we do not lose sight of the global political economy through which AI health technologies operate. Critical analysis is needed to understand the relations between key actors to see how ownership structures provision, as well as where inequalities and exclusions are emerging that risk undermining the potential of this new technology.

Given that AI may even help overcome existing biases within healthcare, it is important to support its implementation, but for algorithms to help ameliorate obstacles to UHC it is necessary that they are subject to critical review by actors attuned to that goal. AI itself has no goal beyond observing data and replicating patterns. For AI to be good, it is necessary that society can reflexively and critically discuss what kind of healthcare we want and ensure that AI tools meet the goals we set.

Setting goals for AI that accord with UHC is not an easy task given that high-level political goals rarely translate well into the kind of data parameters used to guide algorithms. Politics is inherently complex and full of contradictions that can be easily misunderstood if coded. The needs of healthcare make this challenge even harder given the complexity of politics when it meets with the even greater complexity of the human body. There cannot then be a single grand vision for AI technology that supports a just healthcare system. Rather, given the everyday character of the global political economy of health, for AI to advance human healthcare, it is necessary that we look to how individuals directly experience and engage with that technology. That includes forms of co-production and resistance, as well as critically understanding the emerging relations structuring its development.

FURTHER READING

Crawford, K. (2021). *The Atlas of AI*. Yale University Press. https://doi.org/10.2307/j.ctv1ghv45t

Hobson, J., & Seabrooke, L. (2007). *Everyday politics of the world economy*. Cambridge University Press. https://doi.org/10.1017/CBO9780511491375

Pink, S., Ruckenstein, M., Berg, M., & Lupton, D. (2022). *Everyday automation: Experiencing and anticipating emerging technologies*. Routledge. https://doi.org/10.4324/9781003170884

REFERENCES

Abelson, J., Forest, P., Eyles, J., Smith, P., Martin, E., & Gauvin, F. (2003). Deliberations about deliberative methods: issues in the design and evaluation of public participation processes. *Social Science & Medicine*, 57(2), 239–251. https://doi.org/10.1016/S0277-9536(02)00343-X

Cooper, D. (2014). *Everyday Utopias – The conceptual life of promising spaces*. Duke University Press.

Crawford, K. (2021). *The Atlas of AI*. Yale University Press. https://doi.org/10.2307/j.ctv1ghv45t

Criado-Perez, C. (2019). *Invisible women: Exposing data bias in a world designed for men*. Chatto and Windus. https://lib.ugent.be/catalog/rug01:002787216

Daugherty, P. R., Wilson, H. J., & Chowdhury, R. (2019). Using artificial intelligence to promote diversity. *MIT Sloan Management Review, 60*(2).

DeCamp, M., & Lindvall, C. (2020). Latent bias and the implementation of artificial intelligence in medicine. *Journal of the American Medical Informatics Association*, 27(12), 2020–2023. https://doi.org/10.1093/jamia/ocaa094

Delmi. (2020). *Migranters möte med svensk hälso- och sjukvård: Avhandlingsnytt 2020:7*. Delmi. https://www.delmi.se/samhalle#!/xxx-avhandlingsnytt-20207-1

Flores, M., Glusman, G., Brogaard, K., Price, N. D., & Hood, L. (2013). P4 medicine: How systems medicine will transform the healthcare sector and society. *Personal Medicine, 10*(6), 565–576. https://doi.org/10.2217/pme.13.57

Gebru, T. (2020). Race and gender. In M. D. Dubber, F. Pasquale, & S. Das. (Eds.), *The Oxford handbook of ethics of AI* (pp. 253–269). Oxford University Press.

Gerke, S., Minssen, T., & Cohen, G. (2020). Ethical and legal challenges of artificial intelligence-driven healthcare. *Artificial Intelligence in Healthcare*, 295–336. https://doi.org/10.1016/B978-0-12-818438-7.00012-5

Goertzel, B. (2022 March/April). *Big tech's approach to AI isn't very smart*. WIRED Magazine. https://www.infoworld.com/article/3651357/artificial-intelligence-really-isnt-all-that-intelligent.html

He, J., Baxter, S. L., Xu, J., Xu, J., Zhou, X., & Zhang, K. (2019). The practical implementation of artificial intelligence technologies in medicine. *Nature Medicine*, *25*(1), 30–36. https://doi.org/10 .1038/s41591-018-0307-0

Hobson, J., & Seabrooke, L. (2007). *Everyday politics of the world economy*. Cambridge University Press. https://doi.org/10.1017/CBO9780511491375

Ibrahim, S. A. (2021). Artificial intelligence for disparities in knee pain assessment. *Nature Medicine*, *27*, 22–23. https://doi.org/10.1038/s41591-020-01196-3

Kershner, M. (2021, July 15). *Data isn't the new oil — Time is*. Forbes. https://www.forbes.com/sites/ theyec/2021/07/15/data-isnt-the-new-oil--time-is/

Korinek, A., & Stiglitz, J. E. (2021). Covid-19 driven advances in automation and artificial intelligence risk exacerbating economic inequality. *BMJ, 372*, 367. https://doi.org/10.1136/bmj.n367

Leslie, D., Mazumder, A., Peppin, A., Wolters, M. K., & Hagerty, A. (2021). Does "AI" stand for augmenting inequality in the era of covid-19 h healthcare? *BMJ, 372*, 304. https://doi.org/10.1136 /bmj.n304

Lutz, C. (2019). Digital inequalities in the age of artificial intelligence and big data. *Human Behaviour and Emerging Technologies*, *1*(2), 141–148. https://doi.org/10.1002/hbe2.140

Mahadevan, S. (2021). *Automation of imagination: Collaborative future-making seminar 12th April 2021*. Malmö University. April 12, 2021. https://play.mau.se/media/t/0_d6d5h3m4/

Miotto, R., Wang, F., Wang, S., Jiang, X., & Dudley, J. T. (2018). Deep learning for healthcare: Review, opportunities and challenges. *Briefings in Bioinformatics*, *19*(6), 1236–1246. https://doi.org/10.1093 /bib/bbx044

Mol, A. (2008). *The logic of care: Health and the problem of patient choice*. Routledge. https://doi.org /10.1111/j.1467-9566.2009.1168_2.x

Noble, S. U. (2018). *Algorithms of oppression: How search engines reinforce racism*. New York University Press. https://doi.org/10.2307/j.ctt1pwt9w5

Nutbeam, D. (2000). Health literacy as a public health goal: A challenge for contemporary health education and communication strategies into the 21st century. *Health Promotion International*, *15*(3), 259–267. https://doi.org/10.1093/HEAPRO/15.3.259

Obermeyer, Z., Powers, B., Vogeli, C., & Mullainathan, S. (2019). Dissecting racial bias in an algorithm used to manage the health of populations. *Science*, *366*(6464), 447–453. https://doi.org/10.1126/ science.aax2342

Panch, T., Szolovits, P., & Atun, R. (2018). Artificial intelligence, machine learning and health systems. *Journal of Global Health*, *8*(2), 020303. https://doi.org/10.7189/jogh.08.020303

Pii, K. H., Schou, L. H., Piil, K., & Jarden, M. (2019). Current trends in patient and public involvement in cancer research: A systematic review. *Health Expectations*, *22*(1), 3–20. https://doi.org/10.1111/ hex.12841

Pink, S., Ruckenstein, M., Berg, M., & Lupton, D. (2022). Everyday automation setting a research agenda. In S. Pink, M. Berg, D. Lupton, & M. Ruckenstein (Eds.), *Everyday automation: Experiencing and anticipating emerging technologies* (pp. 1–19). Routledge. https://doi.org/10.4324/9781003170884

Politico. (2022, April 21). *Roundtable discussion on AI & Health*. AI & Tech Summit. Politico. Brussels and online.

Rantamäki, N. J. (2016). Co-production in the context of Finnish social services and health care: A challenge and a possibility for a new kind of democracy. *Voluntas*, *28*(1), 248–264.

Savage, M. (2021, September 20). *Can apps manage our chronic health conditions?* BBC News. https:// www.bbc.com/news/business-58556777

Simonite, T. (2021, January 25). *New algorithms could reduce racial disparities in health care*. Wired. January 25. https://www.wired.com/story/new-algorithms-reduce-racial-disparities-health-care/

Souliotis, K., Peppou, L. E., Agapidaki, E., Tzavara, C., Debiais, D., Hasurdjiev, S., & Sarkozy, F. (2018). Health democracy in Europe: Cancer patient organization participation in health policy. *Health Expectations, 21*(2), 474–484. https://doi.org/10.1111/hex.12638

Strange, M., Gustafsson, H., Mangrio, E., & Zdravkovic, S. (2021). *Report #1 PHED-commission on the future of healthcare post covid-19: Social inequity makes us vulnerable to pandemics*. PHED Commission on the Future of Healthcare Post Covid-19. https://doi.org/10.24834. https://phed.uni .mau.se/phed-commission-reports/

Strange, M. (2023). Communicating research as a public discussion: The PHED Commission on the Future of Health Care Post-COVID 19. *The International Journal of Health, Wellness, and Society 13*(2): 21–37. doi:10.18848/2156-8960/CGP/v13i02/21-37.

Struzzo, P., Fumato, R., Tillati, S. et al. (2013). Individual empowerment in overweight and obese patients: A study protocol. *BMJ Open, 3*, e002669. https://doi.org/10.1136/bmjopen-2013-002669

Tam-Seto, L., Wood, V. M., Linden, B., & Stuart, H. (2021). Perceptions of an AI-supported mobile app for military health in the Canadian armed forces. *Military Behavioral Health, 9*(3), 247–254. https://doi.org/10.1080/21635781.2020.1838364

Thomason, J. (2021). Big tech, big data and the new world of digital health. *Global Health Journal, 5*(4), 165–168. https://doi.org/10.1016/j.glohj.2021.11.003

Topol, E. (2022). *AI in health and medicine: Seminar.* AI for Good. https://www.youtube.com/watch?v=Z8A73pUr3aA

Vinnova - The Swedish Government's Innovation Agency (Vinnova). (2018). *Artificial intelligence in Swedish business and society: Analysis of development and potential.* Vinnova. https://www.vinnova.se/contentassets/29cd313d690e4be3a8d861ad05a4ee48/vr_18_09.pdf?cb=20180519112803

Webster, P. (2019). Digital health technologies and health-care privatisation. *The Lancet Digital Health, 1*(4), 161–162. https://doi.org/10.1016/S2589-7500(19)30091-3

World Health Organization. (2021). *Global strategy on digital health 2020–2025.* World Health Organization. https://apps.who.int/iris/bitstream/handle/10665/344249/9789240027633-chi.pdf

Yeung, K., Howes, A., & Pogrebna, G. (2020). Why industry self-regulation will not deliver 'ethical AI': A call for legally mandated techniques of 'human rights by design'. In M. D. Dubber, F. Pasquale, & S. Das (Eds.), *The Oxford handbook of ethics of AI* (pp. 77–106). Oxford University Press.

33. Addressing global inequity in AI development

Chinasa T. Okolo

A GLOBAL OUTLOOK ON ARTIFICIAL INTELLIGENCE

Global inequality renders itself visible, especially in the development of artificial intelligence (AI) and machine learning (ML). In an analysis of publications at two major ML conference venues, NeurIPS 2020 and ICML 2020, Chuvpilo (2020) found that of the top ten countries in terms of publication index (calculated by treating a publication as a unit of one and splitting up the unit equally by authorship), none were in Latin America, Africa, or Southeast Asia. Vietnam, the highest-placed country of these groups, comes in 27th place. Of the top ten institutions by publication index, eight out of ten were based in the United States, including American tech giants like Google, Microsoft, and Facebook. Indeed, the full lists of the top 100 universities and top 100 companies by publication index include no companies or universities based in Africa or Latin America. Although conference publications are just one metric, they remain the predominant medium in which progress in AI is disseminated, and as such serve to be a signal of who is generating research.

Other work such as the Global AI Index from Tortoise Media (2020), which claims to be the "first index to benchmark nations on their level of investment, innovation and implementation of artificial intelligence", ranks the United States, China, and the United Kingdom in the first, second, and third spots, respectively. Within the top 50, other countries in the Global South include India (#17), Brazil (#39), Malaysia (#43), Mexico (#44), Chile (#45), Argentina (#46), Colombia (#49), and Uruguay (#50). The Global AI Vibrancy Ranking produced by researchers in the Stanford Institute for Human-Centered Artificial Intelligence (2021) uses 23 economic and research and development indicators to rank 29 countries to highlight global progress made towards AI. Their rankings only include four countries in the Global South with China, India, Brazil, and Malaysia being ranked in the 2nd, 3rd, 10th, and 17th places, respectively. The predominance of the United States in these rankings is consistent with its economic and cultural dominance, just as the appearance of China with the second-highest index is a marker of its growing might. Also comprehensible is the relative absence of countries in the Global South, given the exploitation and underdevelopment of these regions by European colonial powers (Frank, 1967; Rodney, 1972; Jarosz, 2003; Bruhn & Gallego, 2012). While India is highlighted as a standout in AI research in Southeast Asia, the appearance of Malaysia on both rankings indicates a possible expansion point for AI development. Additionally, the inclusion of a significant number of Latin American countries on the Global AI Index suggests that this region could potentially be a significant hub for AI research and development within the Global South.

Current global inequality in AI development involves both a concentration of profits and a danger of ignoring the contexts in which AI is applied. As AI systems become increasingly integrated into society, those responsible for developing and implementing such systems stand to profit to a large extent. If these players are predominantly located outside of the

Global South, a disproportionate share of economic benefit will fall also outside of this region, exacerbating extant inequality. Furthermore, the ethical application of AI systems requires knowledge of the contexts in which they are to be applied. As recent research (Grush, 2015; De La Garza, 2020; Coalition for Critical Technology, 2020; Beede et al., 2020; Sambasivan et al., 2021) has highlighted, work that lacks such contextual knowledge can fail to help the targeted individuals, and can even harm them (e.g., misdiagnoses in medical applications, denied loans, incorrect crop yields).

Whether explicitly in response to these problems or not, calls have been made for broader inclusion in the development of AI (Asemota, 2018; Lee et al., 2019). At the same time, some have acknowledged the limitations of inclusion. Sloane et al. (2020) describe and argue against participation-washing, whereby the mere fact that somebody has participated in a project lends it moral legitimacy. In this work, we employ a post-colonial critical development studies approach to focus on the implications of participation for global inequality, concentrating particularly on the limitations in which inclusion in AI development is practiced in the Global South. We look specifically at how this plays out in the construction of datasets and establishment of research labs and conclude with a discussion of opportunities for ameliorating the power imbalance in AI development.

DATASETS

Given the centrality of large amounts of data in today's ML systems, there would appear to be substantial opportunities for inclusion in data collection and labeling processes. While there are benefits to more diverse participation in data-gathering pipelines, this approach does not go far enough in addressing global inequality in AI development. As we consider ways in which to improve the inclusion of stakeholders from the Global South, this section discusses what kinds of problems can be alleviated, what forms of data labeling currently look like, barriers to participation, and the deep problems with this form of inclusion.

Data collection itself is a practice fraught with problems of inclusion and representation. Two large, publicly available image datasets, ImageNet (Deng et al., 2009; Russakovsky et al., 2015) and OpenImages (Krasin et al., 2017), are US- and Euro-centric (Shankar et al., 2017). Shankar et al. (2017) further argue that models trained on these datasets perform worse on images from the Global South. For example, images of grooms are classified with lower accuracy when they come from Ethiopia and Pakistan, compared with images of grooms from the United States. Along this vein, DeVries et al. (2019) show that images of the same word, like "wedding" or "spices", look very different when queried in different languages, as they are presented distinctly in different cultures. Thus, publicly available object recognition systems fail to correctly classify many of these objects when they come from the Global South. Representative training datasets are crucial to allowing models to learn how certain objects and concepts are represented in different cultures.

The importance of data labeling in machine-learning research and development has led to crowdsourcing, whereby anonymous individuals are remunerated for completing this work. Large tech companies such as Uber and Alphabet rely heavily on these services, with some paying millions of dollars monthly to third-party firms (Synced, 2019). A major venue for crowdsourcing work is Amazon Mechanical Turk; according to Difallah et al. (2018), less than 2% of Mechanical Turk workers come from the Global South (a vast majority come from the United States and India). Other notable companies in this domain, Samasource, Scale AI, and Mighty AI also operate in the United States, but crowdsource workers from around the world, primarily relying on low-wage workers from sub-Saharan Africa and Southeast Asia (Murgia, 2019). In the Global South, local companies have begun to proliferate, like Fastagger in Kenya, Sebenz.ai in South Africa, and Supahands in Malaysia. As AI development continues to scale, the expansion of these companies opens the door for low-skilled laborers to enter the workforce but also presents a chance for exploitation to continue to occur.

Barriers to Data Labeling

There exist many barriers to equitable participation in data labeling. First, a computing device (laptop, desktop, or tablet) and stable internet access are required for access to most data labeling platforms. These goods are highly correlated with socioeconomic status and geographic location, thus serving as a barrier to participation for many people situated in low-resource settings (Harris et al., 2017). A reliable internet connection is necessary for finding tasks to complete, completing those tasks, and accessing the remuneration for those tasks. Further, those in the Global South pay higher prices for Internet access compared with their counterparts in the Global North (Nzekwe, 2019). Another barrier lies in the method of payment for data labeling services on some platforms. For example, Amazon Mechanical Turk, a widely used platform for finding data labelers, only allows payment to a US bank account or in the form of an Amazon.com gift card (Amazon, 2020). Such methods of payment may not be desired by a potential worker and can serve as a deterrent to work for platforms that employ similar restrictive payment methods.

Problems with Data Collection and Labeling

After having discussed the benefits of incorporating data labeling as one part of inclusion, as well as some of the barriers to participation it has, we finish this section by discussing issues associated with data labeling. At a cursory glance, having labelers who represent a diversity of backgrounds might appear largely beneficial, as it would allow for objects that might not be recognized and labeled appropriately (e.g., "wedding") by one group of people to be done by another. Additionally, data labelers are prone to bringing their own stereotypes and biases to the task at hand. Diversifying the labeler population could help dilute the pool of shared biases that may propagate into a dataset. For example, it has been shown that MSCOCO (Lin et al., 2014), a commonly used object detection and image captioning dataset, contains strong gender biases in the image captions (Hendricks et al., 2018; Bhargava & Forsyth, 2019). If the population of dataset labelers for MSCOCO consisted of people more aware of the problems with gender stereotypes, or even people with very different gender identities, perhaps the biases in the captions might not manifest with that level of prevalence.

With respect to data collection, current practices often neglect consent and poorly represented areas of the Global South. Image datasets are often collected without consent from the people involved, even in pornographic contexts (Birhane & Prabhu, 2021; Paullada et al., 2021), while companies, academic institutions, and other entities benefit from their use. Work from Jo and Gebru (2020) suggests drawing from the long tradition or archives when collecting data because this is a discipline that has already been thinking about challenges like consent and privacy. Indeed, beyond a possible honorarium for participation in the data collection process, no large-scale, successful schema currently exists for compensating users for the initial and continued use of their data in machine-learning systems, although some efforts are currently underway (Kelly, 2020). However, the issue of compensation eludes the question of whether such large-scale data collection should occur in the first place. Indeed, the process of data collection can contribute to an "othering" of the subject and cement inaccurate or harmful beliefs. Even if data comes from somewhere in the Global South, it is often from the perspective of an outsider (Wang et al., 2020) who may not understand the respective context or may have an agenda counter to the interest of the subject. Such values can be reflected in the data captured, as has been extensively studied in the case of photography (Ranger, 2001; Batziou, 2011; Thompson, 2016). Ignorance of context can cause harm, as Sambasivan et al. (2021) discuss in the case of fair ML in India, where distortions in the data (e.g., a given sample corresponds to multiple individuals because of shared device usage) distort the meaning of fairness definitions that were formulated in Western contexts. Furthermore, the history of phrenology reveals the role that the measurement and classification of colonial subjects had in justifying domination (Bank, 1996; Poskett, 2013). Denton et al. (2020) argue the need to interrogate more deeply the norms and values behind the creation of datasets, as they are often extractive processes that benefit only the dataset collector and users.

As another significant part of the data collection pipeline, data labeling is a low-paying job involving rote, repetitive tasks that offer no room for upward mobility. Individuals may not require many technical skills to label data, but they do not develop any meaningful technical skills either. The anonymity of platforms like Amazon Mechanical Turk inhibits the formation of social relationships between the labeler and the client that could otherwise have led to further educational opportunities or better remuneration. Although data is central to the AI systems of today, data labelers receive only a disproportionately tiny portion of the profits of building these systems. In parallel with colonial projects of resource extraction, data labeling as the extraction of meaning from data is no way out of a cycle of colonial dependence. In reference to this parallel, Couldry and Mejias (2019) characterize the term "data colonialism" as a system that exploits human capital through the production of data for technological processes. Exporting these kinds of jobs follows in the long history of colonialism (Mohamed et al., 2020), with the groups on the receiving end of the labor showing great gains in the form of strong AI models while the groups on the giving end of the labor receive few benefits from their work.

The people doing the work of data labeling have been termed "ghost-workers" (Gray & Suri, 2019). The labor of these unseen workers generates massive earnings that others capture, leading to a significant disparity between the millions in profits earned by data labeling companies and worker income; for example, data workers at Samasource earn around US$8 a day (Lee, 2018) while the company reportedly made $25 million in revenue during 2019 (Craft .co, 2019). While Lee (2018) notes that US$8 may well be a living wage in certain areas, the massive disparity is poignant given the importance of these workers to the core businesses of these companies. While data labeling is not as physically intensive as traditional factory labor, workers report the pace and volume of their tasks as "mentally exhausting" and "monotonous" due to the strict requirements needed for labeling images, videos, and audio to client specifications (Gent, 2019; Croce & Musa, 2019). The lack of protections seen for data labelers in the Global South emphasizes the need for labor protection laws to address these power imbalances and improve working conditions (Kaye, 2019). As large tech companies continue to establish AI research labs within the Global South, such protections will be essential in enforcing safeguards for all workers across the ML development lifecycle.

RESEARCH LABS

Establishing research labs has been essential for major tech companies to advance the development of their respective technologies while providing valuable contributions to the field of computer science (Nature, 1915). In the United States, General Electric (GE) Research Laboratory is widely accepted as the first industrial research lab, providing early technological achievements to GE and establishing them as a leader in industrial innovation (Center, 2011). As AI becomes more important to the bottom lines of many large tech companies, industrial research labs have spun out that solely focus on AI and its respective applications. Companies from Google to Amazon to Snapchat have doubled down in this field and opened labs leveraging AI for web search, language processing, video recognition, voice applications, and much more. As AI becomes increasingly integrated into the livelihoods of consumers around the world, tech companies have recognized the importance of democratizing AI development and moving it outside the bounds of the Global North. Of five notable tech companies developing AI solutions (Google, Microsoft, IBM, Facebook, and Amazon), Google, Microsoft, and IBM have research labs in the Global South, and all have either development centers, customer support centers, or data centers within these regions. Despite their presence throughout the Global South, AI research centers tend to be concentrated in certain countries. Within Southeast Asia, the representation of lab locations is limited to India; in South America, representation is limited to Brazil. Sub-Saharan Africa has a wider spread in locations, with AI labs established in Accra, Ghana; Nairobi, Kenya; and Johannesburg, South Africa.

Barriers to Establishing Research Labs

For a company to choose to establish an AI research center, the company must believe this initiative to be in its financial interest. Unfortunately, several barriers exist. The necessity of generating reliable returns for shareholders precludes ventures that appear too risky, especially for smaller companies. The perception of risk can take a variety of forms and is at risk of being influenced by stereotypes to differing extents. Two such factors are political and economic instability or a relatively lower proportion of tertiary formal education in the local population, which can be traced to the history of colonial exploitation and underdevelopment (Rodney, 1972; Jarosz, 2003; Bruhn & Gallego, 2012), whereby European colonial powers extracted labor, natural resources, and economic surplus from colonies, while at the same time subordinating their economic development to that of the metropoles. Given this history, the establishment of top-tier research institutions to advance technical training and AI development in the Global South will be a significant challenge without sufficient investment from local governments and private entities.

Although several tech companies have established research facilities across the world and in the Global South, these efforts remain insufficient at addressing long-term problems in the AI ecosystem. A recent report from Georgetown University's Center for Security and Emerging Technologies (CSET) details the establishment of AI labs by US companies, namely Facebook, Google, IBM, and Microsoft, abroad (Heston & Zwetsloot, 2020). The report notes that while 68% of the 62 AI labs are located outside of the United States, 68% of the staff are located within the United States. Therefore, the international offices remain half as staffed on average relative to the domestic locations. Additionally, none of these offices are located in South America and only four are in Africa. To advance equity within AI and improve inclusion efforts, it is imperative that companies not only establish locations in under-represented regions but also hire employees and include stakeholders from those regions in a proportionate manner.

While the opening of data centers and AI research labs in the Global South initially appears beneficial for the local workforce, these positions may require technical expertise which members of the local population might not have. This would instead introduce opportunities for displacement by those from the Global North who have had more access to specialized training needed to develop, maintain, and deploy AI systems. Given the unequal distribution of AI development globally, it is common for AI researchers and practitioners to work and study in places outside of their home countries (i.e., outside of the Global South). For example, the current director of Google AI Accra, originally from Senegal and a doctoral graduate from Pierre and Marie Curie University in Paris, was recruited to Google from Facebook (now Meta) AI Research in Menlo Park, CA. However, Cisse's return to the African continent is particularly notable given the significant "brain drain" in fields such as medicine and engineering. While the directors of many research labs established in the Global South have experience working in related contexts, we find that local representation is sorely lacking at both the leadership and general workforce levels. Grassroots AI education and training initiatives by communities such as Deep Learning Indaba, Data Science Africa, and Khipu in Latin America aim to increase local AI talent, but since these initiatives are less than five years old, it is hard to measure their current impact on improving the pipeline of AI researchers and ML engineers. However, with the progress made by these organizations publishing novel research at premier AI conferences, hosting conferences of their own, and much more, the path to inclusive representation in the global AI workforce is strengthening.

Formation of International AI Labs

The CSET report also notes that AI labs form abroad generally in one of three ways: through the acquisition of startups; by establishing partnerships with local universities or institutions; and by relocating internal staff or hiring new staff in these locations (Heston & Zwetsloot, 2020). The first two of these methods may favor locations with an already-established technological or AI presence, as many AI startups are founded in locations where a financial and technological support system exists for them. Similarly, the universities with whom tech companies choose to partner are often already leaders in the space, as evidenced by Facebook's partnership with Carnegie Mellon professors and MIT's partnerships with both IBM and Microsoft. The general strategy of partnering with existing institutions and of acquiring startups has the potential to reinforce existing inequities by investing in locations with already thriving tech ecosystems. An exception to this is Google's establishment of an AI research office along with its investment in infrastructure, skills training, and startups in Ghana (Asemota, 2018). Long-term investment and planning in the Global South can form the stepping stones for broadening AI to include underrepresented and marginalized communities.

Even with long-term investment into regions in the Global South, the question remains whether local residents are provided opportunities to join management and contribute to important strategic decisions. Several organizations have emphasized the need for AI development within a country to happen at the grassroots level so that those implementing AI as a solution understand the context of the problem being solved (Mbayo, 2020; Gul, 2019). The necessity of Indigenous decision-making is just as important in negotiating the values that

AI technologies are to instill, such as through AI ethics declarations that are at the moment heavily Western-based (Jobin et al., 2019). Although this is critical not only to the success of individual AI solutions but also to equitable participation within the field at large, more can and should be done. True inclusion necessitates that underrepresented voices be found in all ranks of a company's hierarchy, including in positions of upper management and senior leadership. Tech companies establishing a footprint in regions within the Global South are uniquely positioned to offer such opportunities to natives of these respective regions. Taking advantage of this ability will be critical to ensuring that the benefits of AI apply not only to technical problems that arise in the Global South but to socioeconomic inequalities that persist around the world.

Opportunities

In the face of global inequality in AI development, there are a few promising opportunities to engage diverse stakeholders in more inclusive, fulfilling ways. After examining existing barriers and challenges to equitable participation in AI development, this section discusses the range of grassroots AI initiatives within the Global South, what large tech companies can learn from such approaches to AI research and development, and suggestions on providing work opportunities beyond data labeling as means of representation in the development of ML models and AI systems.

Grassroots AI Initiatives

While AI and technology in general have long excluded marginalized populations, there has been a strong emergence of grassroots efforts by organizations to ensure that Indigenous communities are actively involved as stakeholders of AI. Black in AI, a nonprofit organization with worldwide membership, was founded to increase the global representation of Black-identifying students, researchers, and practitioners in the field of AI, and has made significant improvements in increasing the number of Black scholars attending and publishing in NeurIPS and other premier AI conferences (Earl, 2020; Silva, 2021). Inclusion in AI is extremely sparse in higher education and recent efforts by Black in AI have focused on instituting programming to support members in applying to graduate programs and in pursuing postdoctoral and faculty positions. Other efforts such as Khipu, based in Latin America, have been established to provide a venue to train aspiring AI researchers in advanced ML topics, foster collaborations, and actively participate in how AI is being used to benefit Latin America. Other communities based on the African continent such as Data Science Africa and Deep Learning Indaba have expanded their efforts, establishing conferences, workshops, and dissertation awards, and developing curricula for the broader African AI community. These communities are clear about their respective missions and the focus of collaboration. Notably, Masakhane, a grassroots organization focused on improving the representation of African languages in the field of natural language processing, shares a powerful sentiment on how AI research should be approached (Masakhane, 2021):

> Masakhane are not just annotators or translators. We are researchers. We can likely connect you with annotators or translators but we do not support shallow engagement of Africans as only data generators or consumers.

As such initiatives grow across the Global South, large institutions and technology companies should seek mutually beneficial partnerships with and adopt the values of these respective organizations to ensure AI developments are truly representative of the global populace.

Research Participation

One key component of AI inclusion efforts should be to elevate the involvement and participation of those historically excluded from technological development. Many startups and several governments across the Global South are creating opportunities for local communities to participate in the development and implementation of AI programs (Mbayo, 2020; Gul, 2019; Galperin & Alarcon, 2017). Currently, data labelers are often wholly detached from the rest of the ML pipeline, with workers oftentimes not knowing how their labor will be used or for what purpose (Graham et al., 2017; Graham & Anwar, 2019). Little sense of fulfillment comes from menial tasks, and by exploiting these workers solely for their produced knowledge without bringing them into the fold of the product that they are helping to create, a deep chasm exists between workers and the downstream product (Rogstadius et al., 2011). Thus, in addition to policy that improves work conditions and wages for data labelers, workers should be provided with educational opportunities that allow them to contribute to the models they are building in ways beyond labeling (Gray & Suri, 2019). Instead of roles that have traditionally focused on data labeling and collection, strides should be taken to add model development, research, and design roles to the catalog of opportunities. Valuing data labeling work in this economic form, of increasing wages and allowing professional mobility, backs up otherwise empty statements of valuation. Similarly, where participation in the form of model development is the norm, employers should seek to involve local residents in the ranks of management and in the process of strategic decision-making. The advancement of an equitable AI workforce and ecosystem requires that those in positions of data collection and training be afforded opportunities to lead their organizations. Including these voices in positions of power has the added benefit of ensuring the future hiring and promotion of local community members, while increasing the possibility that AI is developed in alignment with local values, traditions, and needs.

CONCLUSION

As the development of AI continues to progress, the exclusion of those from communities most likely to bear the brunt of algorithmic inequity only stands to worsen. This chapter addresses this concern by exploring the challenges and benefits of increasing broader inclusion in the field of AI. It also examines the limits of current AI inclusion methods, problems of participation regarding AI research labs situated in the Global South, and discusses opportunities for AI to accelerate development within disadvantaged regions. It is essential that communities in the Global South move from being beneficiaries and subjects of AI systems to active, engaged stakeholders. Having true agency over the AI systems integrated into the livelihoods of marginalized communities will maximize the impact of these systems and lead the way for global inclusion of AI.

As a limitation of this work, it is important to acknowledge the author is currently located at and has been educated at North American institutions. However, the author respects the perspectives missed in the course of writing this work.

REFERENCES

Aryeetey, E., & Moyo, N. (2012). Industrialisation for structural transformation in Africa: Appropriate roles for the state. *Journal of African Economies*, *21*(suppl_2), ii55–ii85. https://doi.org/10.1093/jae /ejr043.

Asemota, V. (2018). 'Ghana is the future of Africa': Why Google built an AI lab in Accra. *CNN*. https:// edition.cnn.com/2018/07/14/africa/google-ghana-ai/.

Bank, A. (1996). Of 'native skulls' and 'noble caucasians': Phrenology in colonial South Africa. *Journal of Southern African Studies*, *22*(3), 387–403. https://www.jstor.org/stable/2637310.

Batziou, A. (2011). Framing 'otherness' in press photographs: The case of immigrants in Greece and Spain. *Journal of Media Practice*, *12*(1), 41–60. https://doi.org/10.1386/jmpr.12.1.41_1.

Beede, E., Baylor, E., Hersch, F., Iurchenko, A., Wilcox, L., Ruamviboonsuk, P., & Vardoulakis, L. M. (2020, April). A human-centered evaluation of a deep learning system deployed in clinics for the detection of diabetic retinopathy. In *Proceedings of the 2020 CHI conference on human factors in computing systems* (pp. 1–12). http://doi.org/10.1145/3313831.3376718.

Bhargava, S., & Forsyth, D. (2019). Exposing and correcting the gender bias in image captioning datasets and models. University of Illinois at Urbana-Champaign, Masters Thesis. arXiv preprint arXiv:1912.00578.

Birhane, A., & Prabhu, V. U. (2021, January). Large image datasets: A pyrrhic win for computer vision? In *2021 IEEE winter conference on applications of computer vision (WACV)* (pp. 1536–1546). IEEE.

Bruhn, M., & Gallego, F. A. (2012). Good, bad, and ugly colonial activities: Do they matter for economic development? *Review of Economics and Statistics*, *94*(2), 433–461. https://doi.org/10.1162/REST_a _00218.

Center, E. T. (2011). General electric research lab. https://edisontechcenter.org/GEresearchLab.html.

Chang, H. J. (2010). *Bad Samaritans: The myth of free trade and the secret history of capitalism.* Bloomsbury Publishing USA. ISBN 978-1-59691-598-5.

Chuvpilo, G. (2020). AI research rankings 2020: Can the United States stay ahead of China? https:// chuvpilo.medium.com/ai-research-rankings-2020-can-the-unitedstates-stay-ahead-of-china -61cf14b1216.

Coalition for Critical Technology. (2020). Abolish the #TechToPrisonPipeline. https://medium.com/@ CoalitionForCriticalTechnology/abolish-the-techtoprisonpipeline9b5b14366b16.

Couldry, N., & Mejias, U. A. (2019). Data colonialism: Rethinking big data's relation to the contemporary subject. *Television & New Media*, *20*(4), 336–349.

Craft.co. (2019). Samasource company profile - Office locations, competitors, revenue, financials, employees, key people, subsidiaries. https://craft.co/samasource.

Croce, N., & Musa, M. (2019). The new assembly lines: Why AI needs low-skilled workers too. *World Economic Forum*. https://www.weforum.org/agenda/2019/08/ai-low-skilled-workers/.

De La Garza, A. (2020). States' automated systems are trapping citizens in bureaucratic nightmares with their lives on the line. *TIME*. https://time.com/5840609/algorithm-unemployment/.

Deng, J., Dong, W., Socher, R., Li, L. J., Li, K., & Fei-Fei, L. (2009, June). Imagenet: A large-scale hierarchical image database. In *2009 IEEE conference on computer vision and pattern recognition* (pp. 248–255). IEEE. https://doi.org/10.1109/CVPR.2009.5206848.

Denton, E., Hanna, A., Amironesei, R., Smart, A., Nicole, H., & Scheuerman, M. K. (2020). Bringing the people back in: Contesting benchmark machine learning datasets. *ICML workshop on participatory approaches to machine learning*. arXiv preprint arXiv:2007.07399.

De Vries, T., Misra, I., Wang, C., & Van der Maaten, L. (2019). Does object recognition work for everyone? In *Proceedings of the IEEE/CVF conference on computer vision and pattern recognition workshops* (pp. 52–59).

Difallah, D., Filatova, E., & Ipeirotis, P. (2018, February). Demographics and dynamics of mechanical turk workers. In *Proceedings of the eleventh ACM international conference on web search and data mining* (pp. 135–143). https://doi.org/10.1145/3159652.3159661.

Earl, C. C. (2020). Notes from the Black in AI 2019 workshop. https://charlesearl.blog/2020/01/08/notes -fromthe-black-in-ai-2019-workshop/.

Frank, A. G. (1967). *Capitalism and underdevelopment in Latin America* (Vol. 16). NYU Press.

Galperin, H., & Alarcon, A. (2017). The future of work in the global south. *International Development Research Centre (IDRC), Ottawa.*

Gent, E. (2019). The 'ghost work' powering tech magic. *BBC.* https://www.bbc.com/worklife/article /20190829-the-ghost-work-powering-tech-magic.

Graham, M., & Anwar, M. (2019). The global gig economy: Towards a planetary labour market? *First Monday, 24*(4).

Graham, M., Lehdonvirta, V., Wood, A., Barnard, H., Hjorth, I., & Simon, D. P. (2017). *The risks and rewards of online gig work at the global margins.* University of Oxford for the Oxford Internet Institute. https://ora.ox.ac.uk/objects/uuid:8c791d5a-e3a5-4a59-9b93-fbabea881554.

Gray, M. L., & Suri, S. (2019). *Ghost work: How to stop Silicon Valley from building a new global underclass.* Eamon Dolan Books.

Grush, L. (2015). Google engineer apologizes after Photos app tags two black people as gorillas. *The Verge.* https://www.theverge.com/2015/7/1/8880363/google-apologizes-photosapp-tags-two-black -people-gorillas.

Gul, E. (2019). Is artificial intelligence the frontier solution to global south's wicked development challenges? *Towards Data Science.* https://towardsdatascience.com/is-artificial-intelligence-the -frontier-solution-to-global-souths-wicked-development-challenges-4206221a3c78.

Harris, C., Straker, L., & Pollock, C. (2017). A socioeconomic related 'digital divide' exists in how, not if, young people use computers. *PloS One, 12*(3), e0175011. https://doi.org/10.1371/journal.pone .0175011.

Hendricks, L. A., Burns, K., Saenko, K., Darrell, T., & Rohrbach, A. (2018). Women also snowboard: Overcoming bias in captioning models. In *Proceedings of the European conference on computer vision (ECCV)* (pp. 771–787). https://doi.org/10.1007/978-3-030-01219-9_47.

Heston, R., & Zwetsloot, R. (2020). Mapping U.S. Multinationals' Global AI R&D Activity. *CSET.* https://cset.georgetown.edu/publication/mapping-u-s-multinationals-global-ai-rd-activity/.

Jarosz, L. (2003). A human geographer's response to guns, germs, and steel: The case of agrarian development and change in Madagascar. *Antipode, 35*(4), 823–828. https://doi.org/10.1046/j.1467 -8330.2003.00356.x.

Jo, E. S., & Gebru, T. (2020, January). Lessons from archives: Strategies for collecting sociocultural data in machine learning. In *Proceedings of the 2020 conference on fairness, accountability, and transparency* (pp. 306–316). https://doi.org/10.1145/3351095.3372829.

Jobin, A., Ienca, M., & Vayena, E. (2019). The global landscape of AI ethics guidelines. *Nature Machine Intelligence, 1*(9), 389–399. https://doi.org/10.1038/s42256-019-0088-2.

Kaye, K. (2019). These companies claim to provide "fairtrade" data work. Do they? https://www. technologyreview.com/2019/08/07/133845/cloudfactory-dddsamasource-imerit-impact-sourcing- companies-for-dataannotation/.

Kelly, M. (2020). Andrew Yang is pushing Big Tech to pay users for data. *The Verge.* https://www .theverge.com/2020/6/22/21298919/andrew-yang-big-tech-data-dividend-projectfacebook-google -ubi.

Krasin, I., Duerig, T., Alldrin, N., Ferrari, V., Abu-El-Haija, S., Kuznetsova, A., Rom, H., Uijlings, J., Popov, S., Veit, A., Belongie, S., Gomes, V., Gupta, A., Sun, C., Chechik, G., Cai, D., Feng, Z., Narayanan, D., & Murphy, K. (2017). Openimages: A public dataset for large-scale multi-label and multi-class image classification. *Dataset, 2*(3), 18. https://github.com/openimages.

Lee, D. (2018). Why Big Tech pays poor Kenyans to teach self-driving cars. *BBC News, 3.* https://www .bbc.com/news/technology-46055595.

Lee, M. K., Kusbit, D., Kahng, A., Kim, J. T., Yuan, X., Chan, A., See, D., Noothigattu, R., Lee, S., Psomas, A., & Procaccia, A. D. (2019). WeBuildAI: Participatory framework for algorithmic governance. *Proceedings of the ACM on Human-Computer Interaction, 3*(CSCW), 1–35. https://doi .org/10.1145/3359283.

Lin, J. Y. (2013). From flying geese to leading dragons: New opportunities and strategies for structural transformation in developing countries. In *The industrial policy revolution II* (pp. 50–70). Palgrave Macmillan. https://doi.org/10.1057/9781137335234_3.

Lin, T.-Y., Maire, M., Belongie, S., Bourdev, L., Girshick, R., Hays, J., Perona, P., Ramanan, D., Zitnick, C. L., & Dollar, P. (2014, September). Microsoft coco: Common objects in context. In *European conference on computer vision* (pp. 740–755). Springer. https://doi.org/10.1007/978-3-319-10602-1_48.

Masakhane. (2021). Masakhane: A grassroots NLP community for Africa, by Africans. https://www.masakhane.io/.

Mbayo, H. (2020). Data and power: AI and development in the global south. *Oxford Insights*. https://www.oxfordinsights.com/insights/2020/10/2/data-and-power-ai-and-development-in-the-global-south.

Mendes, A. P. F., Bertella, M. A., & Teixeira, R. F. (2014). Industrialization in Sub-Saharan Africa and import substitution policy. *Brazilian Journal of Political Economy*, *34*(1), 120-138. https://www.scielo.br/j/rep/a/BkMPVxWtx4CBxssXCsWtPgy/?format=pdf&lang=en.

Mohamed, S., Png, M. T., & Isaac, W. (2020). Decolonial AI: Decolonial theory as sociotechnical foresight in artificial intelligence. *Philosophy & Technology*, *33*(4), 659–684. https://doi.org/10.1007/s13347-020-00405-8.

Murgia, M. (2019). AI's new workforce: The data-labelling industry spreads globally. *Financial Times*. https://www.ft.com/content/56dde36c-aa40-11e9-984c-fac8325aaa04.

Nature. (1915). *Industrial research laboratories* (pp. 419–420). Nature 96. https://doi.org/10.1038/096419a0.

Nzekwe, H. (2019). Africans are paying more for internet than any other part of the world – Here's why. *WeeTracker*. https://weetracker.com/2019/10/22/africans-pay-more-forinternet-than-other-regions/.

Our World in Data. (2018). GDP per capita, 1869 to 2016. https://ourworldindata.org/grapher/average-real-gdp-per-capita-across-countries-and-regions?time=1869..2016&country=KOR~USA~OWID_WRL.

Paullada, A., Raji, I. D., Bender, E. M., Denton, E., & Hanna, A. (2021). Data and its (dis) contents: A survey of dataset development and use in machine learning research. *Patterns*, *2*(11), 100336. https://doi.org/10.1016/j.patter.2021.100336.

Poskett, J. (2013). Django unchained and the racist science of phrenology. Phrenology really was used to justify slavery, as portrayed in Django unchained. But it was also used to justify abolition. *The Guardian*, *5*. https://www.theguardian.com/science/blog/2013/feb/05/django-unchained-racist-science-phrenology.

Ranger, T. (2001). *Colonialism, consciousness and the camera* (pp. 203–215). The Past & Present Society. ISSN 0031-2746. http://www.jstor.org/stable/3600818.

Rodney, W. (1972). *How Europe underdeveloped Africa*. Bogle L'Ouverture Publications. ISBN 978-0- 9501546-4-0.

Rogstadius, J., Kostakos, V., Kittur, A., Smus, B., Laredo, J., & Vukovic, M. (2011). An assessment of intrinsic and extrinsic motivation on task performance in crowdsourcing markets. In *Proceedings of the international AAAI conference on web and social media* (Vol. 5, No. 1, pp. 321–328). https://ojs.aaai.org/index.php/ICWSM/article/view/14105.

Russakovsky, O., Deng, J., Su, H., Krause, J., Satheesh, S., Ma, S., Huang, Z., Karpathy, A., Khosla, A., Bernstein, M., Berg, A. C., & Fei-Fei, L. (2015). Imagenet large scale visual recognition challenge. *International Journal of Computer Vision*, *115*(3), 211–252.

Sambasivan, N., Arnesen, E., Hutchinson, B., Doshi, T., & Prabhakaran, V. (2021, March). Re-imagining algorithmic fairness in India and beyond. In *Proceedings of the 2021 ACM conference on fairness, accountability, and transparency* (pp. 315–328). https://dl.acm.org/doi/10.1145/3442188.3445896.

Shankar, S., Halpern, Y., Breck, E., Atwood, J., Wilson, J., & Sculley, D. (2017). No classification without representation: Assessing geodiversity issues in open data sets for the developing world. arXiv preprint arXiv:1711.08536.

Silva, M. (2021). https://blackinai.github.io/#/about.

Sloane, M., Moss, E., Awomolo, O., & Forlano, L. (2020). Participation is not a design fix for machine learning. arXiv preprint arXiv:2007.02423.

Stanford Institute for Human-Centered Artificial Intelligence. (2021). Global AI vibrancy tool. *Artificial Intelligence Index*. https://aiindex.stanford.edu/vibrancy/.

Synced. (2019). Data annotation: The Billion dollar business behind AI breakthroughs. https://medium.com/syncedreview/data-annotation-the-billion-dollar-businessbehind-ai-breakthroughs-d929b0a50d23.

Thompson, A. (2016). Otherness and the fetishization of subject. https://petapixel.com/2016/11/16/othernessfetishization-subject/.

Tortoise Media. (2020). The global AI index. https://www.tortoisemedia.com/intelligence/global-ai/.

Wang, A., Narayanan, A., & Russakovsky, O. (2020, August). REVISE: A tool for measuring and mitigating bias in visual datasets. In *European conference on computer vision* (pp. 733–751). Springer. https://doi.org/10.1007/978-3-030-58580-8_43.

PART IV

AI TRANSPARENCY, ETHICS AND REGULATION

34. A critical approach to AI ethics
Rosalie A. Waelen

1. INTRODUCTION

The rise of AI technologies raises a variety of ethical questions: What ethical rules should autonomous systems follow? What are the ethical responsibilities of AI developers? And what are the ethical and societal implications of a particular AI application? The former two questions are part of *machine ethics* and *engineering ethics*, respectively, the latter question is central to *AI ethics*. In other words, AI ethics specifically deals with the normative issues raised by emerging technologies. Although this new field of research is referred to as a field of (applied) ethics, I have argued elsewhere (Waelen, 2022a) that it is actually more resemblant to a critical theory. In this chapter, I therefore introduce a critical framework to guide the identification and evaluation of AI's ethical and societal implications. This critical framework is based on a pluralistic understanding of power (following Sattarov, 2019; and Haugaard, 2010) and my own definition of autonomy as the ability to form and follow one's own judgment and to form and own one's life-story, in relation to and communication with others.

The critical approach to AI ethics, which is presented in this chapter, has at least three major benefits. First, it covers not only ethical issues but also includes social and political issues in its analysis. Many have argued that the lack of consideration for the social and political dimensions of AI is a failure of the currently dominant approaches in AI ethics (e.g., Coeckelbergh, 2022; Crawford, 2021; Heilinger, 2022; Resseguier, 2021). Second, by discussing different issues in terms of power and function of emancipation, my critical approach offers a common language that allows us to unite and compare a wide range of issues – which has been a challenge so far. Third, AI ethics has been criticized for lacking an over-arching normative end (Mittelstadt, 2019), whereas understanding AI ethics as a critical theory gives the field a clear normative goal: to promote emancipation.

The structure of this chapter is as follows. In Section 2, I explain why I believe that AI ethics resembles a critical theory. In doing so, I also discuss what the core elements of a critical theory are and how AI ethics differs from standard ethical theories and other fields of applied ethics. In Section 3, I discuss the meaning of "power" and introduce a pluralistic approach to the concept of power. In Section 4, I go into the relation between ethics and power by defining the concept of emancipation in relation to autonomy. In Section 5, I show how the pluralist approach to power, combined with what we learned about power's relation to emancipation and autonomy, offers a fruitful framework for identifying and evaluating the ethical, social, and political issues raised by emerging AI systems. I end the chapter with a brief conclusion in Section 6.

2. WHY A CRITICAL APPROACH TO AI ETHICS?

The purpose of critical theory is to diagnose and transform society, with the normative aim of furthering emancipation. Critical theory combines ethical with political goals, and practical philosophy with social science (Benhabib, 1986). In other words, critical theory blurs the distinction between ethical, social, and political issues. Furthermore, it seeks to avoid any prescription of how things should be, in the way that ethical and political theories usually do. Instead, critical theorists follow Hegel in claiming that societal critique should be based on the present, rather than a preconceived ideal. The imperative of emancipatory progress is immanent to the status quo, it "comes from those who suffer oppression or abuse or whose lives are marked by the lack of resources or possibilities" (Forst, 2017, p. 70).

AI ethics resembles a critical theory for a number of reasons. First, as I already pointed out in the introduction, many AI ethicists have argued that AI's normative implications go beyond strictly ethical issues or impacts on the individual. They argue that AI ethics should also pay attention to the technology's broader social and political implications (e.g., Coeckelbergh, 2022; Crawford, 2021; Heilinger, 2022; Resseguier, 2021). AI ethics, therefore, combines ethics with social and political philosophy, just like critical theorists do. Second, AI ethics can be seen as a critique of the current technological state of affairs. Moreover, AI ethics is never merely a theoretical endeavor, the critique it offers is meant to serve the practical aim of improving AI on a moral level. This resembles critical theory, which is a critique of the present with the aim of transforming it. Third, critical theory's normative end, in service of which society should be transformed, is emancipation. Although AI ethics does not have an explicit single normative aim, it does appear as if there is a fundamental emancipatory aim implicit in different AI ethics guidelines. Often-cited goals like privacy and data protection, transparency and trust, justice and fairness, freedom and autonomy, and so on, all seek to protect people's freedom to rule their own lives and develop themselves. We can thus say that the implicit, core normative end of AI ethics, like that of critical theory, is emancipation (for an elaborate version of this argument, see Waelen, 2022a).

In short, AI ethics seeks to critique current AI applications, with the aim of improving them, to make sure that it supports autonomy and societal progress (understood as emancipatory progress).[1] Therefore, it differs from standard ethical theories (consequentialism, deontology, and virtue ethics) and other fields of applied ethics (e.g., bioethics, business ethics, and research ethics), which are predominantly concerned with right conduct. Although other fields of applied ethics do have a practical aim, their central aim is to guide the moral decisions that medical experts, companies, researchers, or other stakeholders face. Machine ethics and engineering ethics are preoccupied with right conduct as well. AI ethics – understood as the analysis of AI's normative impact – does not deal with moral action but focuses on the impact of AI technology on individuals and society at large.[2]

Finally, even if one is not convinced by my argument that AI ethics resembles a critical theory (A), one could still accept the central argument of this chapter, i.e., that the critical framework here presented is a fruitful approach to the normative analysis of AI applications (B). Although argument A strengthens argument B, accepting A is not a necessary condition for accepting B. In what follows, I focus on B by developing an account of power (see Section 3) and an account of autonomy (Section 4) that form the core of my critical approach to AI ethics (Section 5).

---

[1] See Section 6, the conclusion, for more on the notion of progress.
[2] The understanding of AI ethics as a critical theory arguably goes for all ethical analyses of all types of technology, but for the present purposes, my focus lies on AI.

3.   DEFINING POWER

Although critical theory has a set normative goal (namely to bring emancipatory progress) and a set method (namely forming an immanent critique of the social relations and practices of the present), its method is far from concrete and its normative foundations unclear (Benhabib, 1986; Habermas, 1979). To diagnose society, that is, to identify social struggles and pathologies, critical theorists need a theory of power to rely on. To evaluate the identified societal issues, and to uncover paths for change, critical theory requires a relevant definition of autonomy and its relation to emancipation (Allen, 2008; Benhabib, 1986). However, different (generations of) critical theorists have ascribed different meanings to "power" and "autonomy". In this and the following section, I therefore develop and defend distinct notions of power and autonomy that are particularly relevant to the analysis of AI's ethical, social, and political impact.

The concept of power is used and defined in many different ways. We can distinguish social power, natural, and technological power. The focus here, and in critical theory in general, lies on social power. Within the domain of social power, then, we can again distinguish different conceptions of power. Steven Lukes (1974, 2005) argues that social power is an *essentially* contested concept. That implies that we will never find the single best definition of social power. Mark Haugaard (2010) therefore suggests that we should opt for a pluralist approach to power, instead of endlessly disagreeing over the definition of power. He argues: "power debates will advance more fruitfully if we treat power as a *family resemblance* concept, whereby their meaning varies depending upon *language game*" (Haugaard, 2010, p. 424). A family-wide concept like power is so wide and vague that it explains little in itself, therefore it is better understood through a cluster of concepts that refer to different aspects of the wider notion. A pluralist approach to power entails that different views of power are treated as different aspects of the same thing, rather than opposing or competing concepts. The criterion for including a theory of power as a family member should be "usefulness", says Haugaard (2010, p. 427). Faridun Sattarov adopts Haugaard's pluralist approach and argues that there are (at least) four different aspects of power that are useful when analyzing technology and technology's ethical implications: dispositional, episodic, systemic, and constitutive power. These four different forms of social power are also distinguished by Allen (2016) and the first three are discussed by Haugaard (2010).

Dispositional power, first of all, is the capacity to bring about significant outcomes. Dispositional power is also referred to as "power-to" and ties into the concept of empowerment. A known proponent of the dispositional view is Peter Morriss (2002). He defends that having power is a disposition that "can remain forever unmanifested" (2002, p. 17) and that power-to is, therefore, a more fundamental definition of power than power-over. He also explains that we should not understand the resources that *give rise* to power as *being* power. So we should not equate AI with power, but see it as something that gives power to persons or other actors.

Episodic power refers to the idea that power exists in the exercise of power by one actor or entity over another. In other words, it is a relational view of power, also known as "power-over". Episodic power can be exercised through the use of force, manipulation, coercion, and so on. The episodic view of power gained attention through the so-called three-dimensional power debate. This debate started with Dahl's definition of power as "A having power over B to the extent that A can get B to do something that B would not otherwise do" (1957, p. 202).

Bachrach and Baratz (1962) continued the debate by criticizing Dahl for focusing solely on the decision-making dimension of power. They added a second dimension: agenda-setting power. Lukes (1974) then contributed to the debate with a third dimension, namely the ability to shape others' thoughts or preferences. Lukes initially defined power as "A exercises power over B when A affects B in a manner contrary to B's interests" (1974, p. 30), but he later revised this definition by arguing that power *either* affects the interests of others *or* furthers one's own (Lukes, 2005). Clearly, there are even disputes about power among those who agree on the same general definition.

Third, *Systemic power* is also a relational view of power but has a broader focus than episodic power. Systemic power focuses on the power structures in society and the institutions that facilitate those. The systemic view of power is, among others, defended by Clarissa Hayward, who argues against the dispositional and episodic view by saying that power should be "de-faced" by "reconceptualizing it as the network of social boundaries that delimits, for all, fields of possible action" (2000, p. 27). Social norms, values, laws, and group identities are mechanisms of power that determine who has episodic and dispositional power and who does not.

Constitutive power, fourth and finally, combines power-over and power-to. Instead of focusing on the way in which power is exercised or on the entity that has power, constitutive power focuses on the effects of power on those who are subjected to it. Power does not only oppress us, i.e., keep us from acting in a certain way, it also constitutes us: power shapes our behavior, our views, and even who we develop to be (Allen, 2008). Michel Foucault is well-known for developing the constitutive view of power with his concepts of discipline and biopolitics. Following Foucault, the constitutive notion of power has also been embraced by many feminists, who found it useful for studying women's subordination to the patriarchy and the ways in which it has shaped women's individual identities as well as societal gender roles and expectations regarding femininity (Allen, 2008; Butler, 1997).

I follow Haugaard's and Sattarov's pluralist approach to power, treating different concepts of social power not as opposing or competing views, but as different aspects of the same, family-wide concept. Moreover, I follow Sattarov in saying that the four forms of power outlined in this section – dispositional, episodic, systemic, and constitutive power – are all useful when it comes to discussing technologies' impact on individuals and society. My critical analysis of AI is then based on a very broad understanding of power, covering the wide range of ways in which AI impacts individuals and society. Other critical theories might benefit from a narrower discussion of power. Feminist critical theories, for instance, usually focus solely on the notion of subordination (Allen, 2008).

4.   POWER'S NORMATIVE RELEVANCE

That the topic of power is important to ethical, social, and political discussions about AI is acknowledged by various established scholars in the field. Sattarov (2019), whose pluralist approach to power I adopt, argues that the concept of power is relevant to the ethics of technology because it is closely connected to the concepts of responsibility, vulnerability, authenticity, and trust. Mark Coeckelbergh (2022) recently defended the relevance of political philosophy, including theories of power, to the debate about AI's normative impact. Power also plays an important role in Kate Crawford's *Atlas of AI* (2021), Safiya Noble's *Algorithms of Oppression* (2018), Carissa Véliz's *Privacy is Power* (2020), and Shoshana Zuboff's *The Age of Surveillance Capitalism* (2019). What we can learn from these works is, first, that a focus on ethics alone is too narrow. Discussions about AI's normative impact should combine ethical, social, and political dimensions. Second, we learn that power is obviously a relevant topic within these normative debates. However, to make the step from identifying power-related issues to normatively evaluating those issues, we first need to articulate what power's normative relevance is.

I pointed out in Section 2 that critical theory is guided by an emancipatory aim. I also briefly argued that established AI ethics guidelines, and many other discussions labeled as "AI ethics", implicitly share critical theory's emancipatory aim. We can understand values like autonomy, privacy, and transparency as derivatives of an emancipatory concern: we embrace new technologies because they can empower us, but often also fear new technologies because they might control us (or because powerful institutions can use them to control us). Making this emancipatory concern explicit, unifies different normative discussions about AI and can guide future ethical, social, and political analyses of AI (Waelen, 2022a).

The concept of emancipation is intimately related to the concept of power: it entails overcoming constraining forms of power. Constraining, in the sense that it limits the autonomy of individuals and collectives. But what "the autonomy of individuals and collectives" entails exactly is up for debate. Within the tradition of critical theory alone, autonomy has been defined in very different ways. Benhabib (1986) summarizes some of the different notions of autonomy defended by critical theorists. She explains that critical theory finds its roots in Kant, who is known for his understanding of moral autonomy as the capacity to act out of duty following one's inner moral law, rather than acting according to duties posed on us from outside. For Hegel and Marx, who also inspired critical theory, autonomy meant self-actualization, which is realized through work. Adorno and Horkheimer, the first generation of Frankfurt School critical theorists, argued that one can gain access to autonomy only through a process of psychoanalytical reflection, in which one recollects the nature within the subject. To Habermas, communicative action is important for autonomy. In his later work, he developed a notion of moral autonomy that is similar to Kant's, with the important difference that "the rightness of one's actions are not settled monologically, by the internal deliberations of the autonomous individual, but only dialogically, in actual moral discourses" (Allen, 2008, p. 97). Benhabib herself, in her own later works, developed a narrative conception of the self and defined practical autonomy accordingly, as "the capacity to exercise choice and agency over the conditions of one's narrative identifications" (Benhabib, 2002, p. 16).

What I take away from this brief summary is that we can roughly distinguish two types of definitions of autonomy: definitions of autonomy as the ability to follow one's own judgment *(self-legislation)*, and notions of autonomy as the ability to develop oneself *(self-development)*. Self-legislation, first, can be based on the idea of an inner moral law (Kant), communicative competence (Habermas), or justificatory authority (Forst). The idea of autonomy as self-legislation requires a notion of rationality, on which the autonomous individual can ground their judgment. Second, self-development, can entail self-actualization (Hegel and Marx), becoming one's authentic self (Nietzsche), or shaping and telling one's own life-story (Benhabib). Benhabib's notion of self-development differs from the former two, in that it does not presuppose a pre-existing, core self or subject. Furthermore, feminist philosophers have argued that self-development is not an individual endeavor (Mackenzie & Stoljar, 2000). They defend that we should also acknowledge the relational dimension of autonomy, as our social relations influence and support us in becoming who we are.

Both understandings of autonomy – self-legislation and self-development – are relevant to a critical analysis of AI. First, AI threatens our ability to follow our own judgment because it takes over everyday tasks and decisions from us. As a result, we not only start following the AI's judgment, but we might also end up unlearning how to make certain decisions on our own (e.g., which articles to read or music to listen to). To the extent that AI systems teach us or prescribe to us what "the right thing to do" is, or even force us to act according to certain moral norms, it also violates our *moral* self-legislation. Second, following a narrative understanding of the self, we can also say that AI threatens self-development. AI keeps us from developing important skills and characteristics that help us to become who we would like to be and to realize certain goals in life. In that sense, AI can keep us from developing our life-story – our narrative "self" – in the way we envision it. Furthermore, in the age of AI, we no longer have control over our personal data, hence, we do not control what is known about us and how our personal information is interpreted. A lack of data ownership then also implies a lack of self-ownership: it keeps us from shaping and communicating our own life-story.[3]

So, for the purposes of the critical approach to AI ethics, which is presented in Section 5, I will understand autonomy in a double sense, as the ability to follow our own judgment (not only in moral decisions) and the ability to own our life-story. We form our own judgment and our life-story in relation to and communication with others.

5.   A FRAMEWORK FOR A CRITICAL ANALYSIS OF AI

The definition of autonomy presented in Section 4 follows that, in the context of AI, emancipatory progress implies limiting or transforming certain technological applications, functions, or uses, which constrain individuals or collectives in their ability to form and follow their own judgment and to form and own their life-stories, in relation to and communication with others. The pluralist approach to power, introduced in Section 3, then enables us to identify when AI constrains individuals or collectives in such a way.

In this section, I show how the pluralist understanding of power combined with my understanding of autonomy as self-legislation and self-development, offers a fruitful framework to guide the ethical, social, and political analysis of AI. Table 34.1 provides an overview of the framework. To identify the ethical, social, or political issues of an AI application, one should ask how each aspect of power relates to the given technology. Dispositional power implies asking "How does application X disempower users?" Episodic power implies "In what ways can X be used to exercise force, coercion, manipulation, persuasion, or authority?" For systemic power one asks "How does X tie into systemic relations of power in our society?" And to identify issues regarding constitutive power one asks "How can X constitute our behavior, thoughts, and identity?" To normatively evaluate the identified issues of power, one should analyze how each instance or aspect of power can hamper (or promote) autonomy. To further

---

[3]   Admittedly, there are also many ways in which technology can improve our self-development, in the narrative sense, by giving us new tools to communicate who we are and shape how we are perceived by others (e.g., social media).

Table 34.1 Power analysis framework

Aspect of power	Identification of issues	Normative evaluation
Dispositional power	How does application X disempower individuals or groups?	How does this disempowerment impact people's self-legislation and self-development?
Episodic power	In what ways can application X be used to exercise force, coercion, manipulation, persuasion, or authority?	How does this exercise of power impact people's self-legislation and self-development?
Systemic power	How does application X tie into systemic relations of power in society?	How do these systems of power impact people's self-legislation and self-development?
Constitutive power	How can application X constitute people's behavior, thoughts, and identity?	How do these constitutive effects impact people's self-legislation and self-development?

emancipation, finally, one needs to determine how the found impact on autonomy can be overcome.

5.1 Dispositional Power

The dispositional view of power focuses on the capacity to bring about significant outcomes (Morriss, 2002). The *potential* to exercise power is what matters here, not the actual exercise. Being "empowered" means gaining dispositional power and its antonym "disempowerment" implies losing it. Empowerment is often equated with emancipation. Emancipatory movements seek to empower the oppressed by granting them rights they did not have before, giving them a voice in public discourse, or through any other means that can increase their individual and collective autonomy.

Technology is often talked about in reference to empowerment. Many new technologies, among which are AI applications, are sold to us with the promise that they will empower us. Critically examining how an AI application really empowers or disempowers us, i.e., how it can increase or decrease the dispositional power of individuals or societal groups, helps to determine some ways in which the given AI application might promote or hamper autonomy, and with that, emancipatory progress. Take the example of voice assistants: voice assistants do not simply offer convenience, they are supposed to be empowering. Although this may be true in some respects, these technologies can simultaneously disempower us as well. Voice assistants take over some of our everyday tasks, enabling us to spend our time in more meaningful ways. But by not having to perform tasks such as filtering through information, we might also lose the skill to form our own judgment and the opportunity to follow our own judgment. Furthermore, voice assistants, like many other modern technologies, collect and process a lot of our (personal) data. The companies behind these voice assistants can share our information with third parties or use our data to profile us and personalize services. By taking away our possibility to control who knows what about us and our ability to communicate who we are, these systems compromise our self-development. Hence, although they appear to be innocent, beneficial technologies, voice assistants could still harm our most important possession: autonomy.

5.2   Episodic Power

Contrary to the dispositional view of power, the episodic view of power does focus on the actual exercise of power. It is concerned with the exercise of power by A over B, which makes B think or act differently than they otherwise would have. Power can be exercised by means of manipulation, coercion, persuasion, authority, or force.[4] These exercises of power occur all the time, they are an inevitable part of social relations. Hence, power relations are not necessarily problematic. When the exercise of power by A over B hinders B's self-legislation or self-development, there is a need for emancipation. It is usually also in these problematic cases that power relations are referred to as "domination".

The episodic view of power is relevant for the normative analysis of AI because AI allows individuals or institutions to exercise power much more easily, efficiently, and effectively. A well-known example of the exercise of power with AI is the manipulation of individuals' behavior, thoughts, or preferences through personalized ads, news feeds, recommendations, and so on. Following the critical approach, we can label such manipulation through personalization as an ethical issue when it significantly affects people's autonomy. For instance, when personalized ads are so effective that I buy products I do not need and cannot afford, their manipulative power has impacted my judgment (self-legislation) and ability to make decisions that get me where I want to be in the long run (self-development).

5.3   Systemic Power

Systemic power deals not with specific instances of power relations, but with structural and often institutional power relations.[5] Systemic power is reflected in a society's laws, norms, values, practices, and so on, which in turn determine who gets to exercise power (structurally), and which societal groups will be the subject of power. Systemic change is therefore often key in the struggle for emancipation. However, systemic power is also something we are often not even aware of because it is so deeply embedded in our society. This makes systemic power very difficult to counter.

Systemic power is, for example, reflected in the biases that algorithms inherit from their developers or training data. Algorithmic biases reflect norms, values, and prejudices that are deeply embedded in society and its institutions. Biases harm autonomy, self-development to be precise, because they prevent certain demographics from getting equal opportunities in life and can damage one's sense of self-worth (Waelen & Wieczorek, 2022).

Another example of systemic power in AI is the much-discussed issue of surveillance capitalism. Everyday activities – from people's search engine queries to the number of times they visit their local supermarket – are turned into data, which are in turn turned into commodities. This surveillance capitalism, as Shoshana Zuboff (2015, 2019) has called it, is not necessarily

---

[4]   Between those that defend the episodic view of power there are debates about exactly which of these "means" can be deemed power. According to some, influence would be too weak to count as power, and others argue that force is too strong to count as an exercise of power, as it completely lacks the option to act otherwise. Others also add more means to the last, for example, "seduction".

[5]   It is on the systemic level that my critical approach to AI ethics is most in line with Andrew Feenberg's understanding of a critical theory of technology: "Critical theory of technology is concerned with the threat to human agency posed by the technocratic system that dominates modern societies" (2017, 635).

the way 21st-century capitalism should function. However, we are led to believe that it is. Big Tech has reified the datafication and commodification of people's everyday lives. In other words, Big Tech has systemic power not just because of its market power, but because it managed to determine how 21st-century capitalism functions. Looking at the implications for autonomy, we can reject the reification of surveillance capitalism because it not only prevents people from owning their own data (as I previously pointed out) but also prevents the members of society from determining what mode of capitalism they prefer (self-legislation).

5.4   Constitutive Power

The constitutive view of power encourages us to take a closer look at the actions, thoughts, and identities that we take on because of our interaction with or subjection to certain AI applications. Constitutive power is problematic, to the extent that it keeps us from forming and following our own judgment and owning our life-stories.

Take the example of facial recognition. Facial recognition technology not only recognizes people's objective identity, but it can also recognize the traits that constitute a person's subjective identity. However, the label that a facial recognition system gives people might not always align with their narrative identity, that is, with the story they like to tell about themselves. When others start to perceive us and treat us in accordance with the labels that facial recognition systems gave us, or when these labels influence how we come to understand our own self, we can say that technology has constitutive power over our identity. Given that forming and owning our life-story is important for autonomy, and that creating and communicating our own sense of identity or self is an important part of our life-story, facial recognition's labels can harm people's autonomy and with that emancipatory progress (Waelen, 2022b).[6]

6.   CONCLUSION

The term "AI ethics" has become widely adopted. However, as several authors have pointed out, it is also important to include social and political issues in normative discussions of AI applications. So, what is most often referred to as "AI ethics" is in fact much broader than merely ethical analyses of AI. The critical approach to AI ethics, which I presented in this chapter, offers a fruitful way of integrating AI's ethical, social, and political implications in a single discussion. This critical approach allows one to discuss different normative implications of AI with the same terminology (in terms of power) and in the function of a single, normative concept (autonomy). Moreover, the critical approach encourages interdisciplinary collaboration between ethicists, social scientists, policymakers, tech developers, and corporate organizations to get an adequate understanding of AI's normative implications, on the one hand, and to transform AI to realize emancipatory progress, on the other hand. The ultimate

---

[6]   There are, of course, other, perhaps more obvious ways in which facial recognition can harm autonomy and emancipation. For example, facial recognition is known to have caused discriminatory treatment due to biased algorithms. This is just one example of an ethical or social implication of facial recognition that is related to the concept of constitutive power.

goal of critical analyses of AI is then to ensure that technological progress goes hand in hand with social progress:

> Technological progress cannot count as progress without social evaluations of what it is good for, who benefits from it, and what costs it generates (…) progress is a reflexive concept: every progressive process must be constantly questioned as to whether it is in the social interest – correctly understood – of those who are part of this process. Thus, every criticism is itself also part of progress. (Forst, 2017, pp. 72–73)

FURTHER READING

Coeckelbergh, M. (2022). Power: Surveillance and (self-)disciplining by data. In *The political philosophy of AI: An introduction*. Polity Press.

Sattarov, F. (2019). *Power and technology: A philosophical and ethical analysis*. Rowman and Littlefield International.

Waelen, R. (2022). Why AI ethics is a critical theory. *Philosophy & Technology*, *35*(9). https://doi.org/10.1007/s13347-022-00507-5

REFERENCES

Allen, A. (2008). *The politics of our selves: Power, autonomy, and gender in contemporary critical theory*. Columbia University Press.

Allen, A. (2016). Feminist perspectives on power. In E. N. Zalta (Ed.), *The Stanford encyclopedia of philosophy*. https://plato.stanford.edu/archives/fall2016/entries/feminist-power/

Bachrach, P., & Baratz, M. S. (1962). Two faces of power. *The American Political Science Review*, *56*(4), 947–952.

Benhabib, S. (1986). *Critique, norm, and Utopia: A study of the foundations of critical theory*. Columbia University Press.

Benhabib, S. (2002). *The claims of culture: Equality and diversity in the global era*. Princeton University Press.

Brey, P. (2008). The technological construction of social power. *Social Epistemology*, *22*(1), 71–95. https://doi.org/10.1080/02691720701773551

Butler, J. (1997). *The psychic life of power: Theories in subjection*. Stanford University Press.

Coeckelbergh, M. (2022). *The political philosophy of AI: An introduction*. Polity Press.

Crawford, K. (2021). *Atlas of AI: Power, politics, and the planetary costs of artificial intelligence*. Yale University Press.

Dahl, R. A. (1957). The concept of power. *Behavioral Science*, 201–215. https://doi.org/10.7312/popi17594-004

Feenberg, A. (2017). A critical theory of technology. In U. Felt, R. Fouché, C. A. Miller, & L. SmithDoerr (Eds.), *Handbook of science and technology studies* (pp. 635–663). The MIT Press.

Forst, R. (2017). *Normativity and power: Analyzing social orders of justification*. Translated by Ciaran Cronin. Oxford University Press.

Habermas, J. (1979). *Communication and the evolution of society*. Translated by Thomas McCarthy. Beacon Press.

Haugaard, M. (2010). Power: A "family resemblance concept". *European Journal of Cultural Studies*, *13*(4), 419–438.

Hayward, C. R. (2000). *De-facing power*. Cambridge University Press.

Heilinger, J. (2022). The ethics of AI ethics: A constructive critique. *Philosophy & Technology*, *53*(61). https://doi.org/10.1007/s13347-022-00557-9

Jobin, A., Ienca, M., & Vayena, E. (2019). The global landscape of AI ethics guidelines. *Nature Machine Intelligence*. https://doi.org/10.1038/s42256-019-0088-2

Lukes, S. (1974). *Power: Radical view.* Macmillan.

Lukes, S. (2005). *Power: A radical view* (2nd ed.). Red Globe Press.

Mackenzie, C., & Stoljar, N. (2000). *Relational autonomy: Feminist perspectives on autonomy, agency and the social self.* Oxford University Press.

Mittelstadt, B. (2019). Principles alone cannot guarantee ethical AI. *Nature Machine Intelligence.* https://doi.org/10.1038/s42256-019-0114-4

Morriss, P. (2002). *Power: A philosophical analysis* (2nd ed.). Manchester University Press.

Noble, S. U. (2018). *Algorithms of oppression: How search engines reinforce racism.* New York University Press.

Resseguier. (2021). Ethics as attention to context: Recommendations for AI ethics. In *SIENNA D5.4: Multi-stakeholder strategy and practical tools for ethical AI and robotics.* https://www.sienna -project.eu/publications/deliverable-reports/

Sattarov, F. (2019). *Power and technology: A philosophical and ethical analysis.* Rowman and Littlefield International.

Véliz, C. (2020). *Privacy is power: Why and how you should take back control of your data.* Bantam Press.

Waelen, R. & Wieczorek, M. (2022). The struggle for AI's recognition: Understanding the normative implications of gender bias in AI with Honneth's theory of recognition. *Philosophy & Technology, 35*(53). https:/doi.org/10.1007/s13347-022-00548-w

Waelen, R. (2022a). Why AI ethics is a critical theory. *Philosophy & Technology, 35*(9). https://doi.org /10.1007/s13347-022-00507-5

Waelen, R. (2022b). The struggle for recognition in the age of facial recognition technology. *AI & Ethics.* https://doi.org/10.1007/s43681-022-00146-8

Zuboff, S. (2015). Big other: Surveillance capitalism and the prospects of an information civilization. *Journal of Information Technology, 30*(1), 75–89. https://doi.org/10.1057/jit.2015.5

Zuboff, S. (2019). *The age of surveillance capitalism: The fight for a human future at the new frontier of power.* Profile Books.

35. Power and inequalities: lifting the veil of ignorance in AI ethics

Anais Resseguier

INTRODUCTION

AI governance experts Delacroix and Wagner have asked: "Why has ethics come to acquire such a bad name in AI and data governance?" (2021, p. 1). What has happened in the ethics of artificial intelligence (AI) that may explain such severe "ethics bashing" (Bietti, 2020) and what can be done to redress it? These are the questions this chapter seeks to answer.

The ethics of AI, and more generally, efforts and initiatives towards "responsible AI", have been the subject of strong criticisms since the end of the 2010s.[1] Experts have pointed out that these often fail to achieve their intended aim of identifying and mitigating potential harms related to the development, deployment, and use of AI. Some have shown that ethics initiatives are being misused by industry actors to avoid the development of regulations that would limit their business. This misuse of ethics has been called "ethics washing" (Hao, 2019; Mittelstadt, 2019; Rességuier & Rodrigues, 2020; Wagner, 2018). Other experts have shown that they contribute to maintaining the *status quo*, i.e., they serve the interests of the privileged members of society at the expense of the marginalised ones who are precisely those the most exposed to the negative impacts of AI (D'Ignazio & Klein, 2020). How does one explain these strong critiques? What has made such manipulation of ethics in the field of AI ethics possible?

This chapter argues that this is due to the very nature of mainstream ethics as it has been constructed in the Western world in the 20th century. It shows that there is an inherent pitfall in this approach to ethics that makes it prone to its instrumentalisation, whether this manipulation is deliberate (i.e., to serve particular interests such as those of Big Tech[2]) or unintentional (i.e., committed out of ignorance or naivety). This chapter demonstrates that this weakness is due to ethics often being blind to power relations and structures of inequalities. In the face of this, it argues that ethical enquiry requires a radical engagement with questions of power, i.e., that power is a crucial component of ethics, if not its core element. It shows how this renewed approach to ethics – an approach that places power at its heart – allows for a more convincing

---

[1] These ethics and responsible AI initiatives include documents listing principles for the development, deployment and use of AI, such as the High-Level Expert Group on Artificial Intelligence, "Ethics guidelines for trustworthy AI", European Commission, Brussels, 2019, https:// ec.europa.eu/digital-single-market/en/news/ethics-guidelines-trustworthy-ai; OECD, "Recommendation of the Council on Artificial Intelligence", adopted on 22 May 2019, https://legalinstruments.oecd.org/en/instruments/OECD-LEGAL- 0449; Google, Artificial Intelligence at Google: Our Principles, https://ai.google/ principles/. They also include work that seeks to promote responsible AI, such as the work conducted by the Responsible AI team at Facebook, now Meta, as described in Hao (2021).

[2] By Big Tech, we mean the powerful technology companies, especially GAFAM: Google, Amazon, Facebook/Meta, Apple, and Microsoft.

study on the ethics of AI and on new and emerging technologies more generally, and the development of more effective frameworks to mitigate potential harms caused by technology.

As such, this chapter makes two scientific contributions: (1) a theoretical contribution to the ethics of AI by going to the roots of the neglect of questions of power in the ethical analysis of this technology, and (2) an empirical contribution by pointing to the value of placing questions of power at the heart of the ethical analysis of AI.

The first section highlights mainstream ethics' blindness to questions of power and structures of inequalities by drawing from Charles Mills' analysis. This helps to better understand major gaps in existing AI ethics frameworks and initiatives. Based on this theoretical clarification, the chapter then makes a proposal in the second section for a situated ethics that contributes to highlighting the materiality of AI and therefore accounting for its actual impacts on individuals, communities, and society at large. Situating this technology is the first step to responsibility. Research ethics frameworks are then proposed as particularly useful to embed this situated ethics within institutions with mechanisms to ensure compliance. Finally, the third section turns to a different and complementary approach to ethics, one that does not aim at determining norms to limit abuses of power (as developed in the second section), but rather at promoting the capacity of action and power to bring about change.

MAINSTREAM ETHICS' BLINDNESS TO QUESTIONS OF POWER

Charles Mills on "Mainstream Ethics"

Philosopher Charles Mills' analysis of what he calls "mainstream ethics" is quite helpful to clarify the shortcomings of AI ethics as it has developed since the end of the 2010s.[3] Mills defines "mainstream ethics" as an approach to ethics dominated by "ideal theory", i.e., a theory that relies on "idealisation to the exclusion, or at least marginalization, of the actual" (2005, p. 168). As Mills notes, John Rawls' theory of justice is one of the most renowned illustrations of such an approach. Mills quotes Rawls defining "ideal theory" as "the examination of 'the principles of justice that would regulate a well-ordered society [i.e., a society where] everyone is presumed to act justly and to do his part [sic] in upholding just institutions'" (Mills quoting Rawls in 2005, p. 169). Mills highlights that, for Rawls, although issues of "partial compliance", i.e., compliance with principles in the real world, where society is far from being "well-ordered", are the "pressing and urgent matters", we need to begin with ideal theory as "the only basis for the systematic grasp of these more pressing problems" (Mills quoting Rawls in 2005, p. 169). In other words, for Rawls, we should first start with principles of justice in an ideal society before exploring these in the real world. For such ideal theory, Rawls creates the fiction of a "veil of ignorance", a veil that serves to hide one's own position in society in order to develop an impartial view on justice, one that is blind to one's social status (Rawls, 1999, pp. 118–123). However, as Mills rightly notes, ideal theory never returned to engaging with "the pressing and urgent matters", i.e., the issues that people are actually facing in the real world. Mills writes: "why, in the thirty-plus years up to his death, was he still at the

---

[3]   This approach to ethics was already the focus of enquiry in Resseguier and Rodrigues (2021) and Rességuier and Rodrigues (2020) in which it is analysed as a legal approach to ethics or a principlism.

beginning? Why was this promised shift of theoretical attention endlessly deferred, not just in his own writings but in the vast majority of his followers?" (2005, p. 179).

As such, Mills highlights the irony of a theory of justice that neglects actual conditions of injustices and inequalities, precisely what should be the core concern of this theory. He argues that such theory is founded on a "tacit social ontology" that "will typically assume the abstract and undifferentiated equal atomic individuals of classic liberalism" and "will abstract *away* from relations of structural domination, exploitation, coercion, and oppression" (2005, p. 168). According to the philosopher, this ideal theory of ethics is "obfuscatory" in "crucial respects", those related to "actual historic oppression and its legacy in the present, or current ongoing oppression" (2005, pp. 166, 168). The present chapter argues that the "obfuscatory" nature of mainstream ethics in "crucial respects" helps shed light on the critical elements that AI ethics tends to be blind to, i.e., relations of power and historic structures of inequalities. The efforts towards fairer natural language processing (NLP) – a branch of AI – powerfully illustrate such blindness.

Blodgett et al. (2020) examined 146 papers published between 2015 and 2020 that analyse biases in NLP. They showed that these studies fail to address the root cause of discriminatory impacts of NLP due to a neglect of the historic inequalities and the system of oppression that shape perceptions towards languages, in particular, African American English (AAE) in the US context. The authors demonstrate that one cannot understand and address the issue of biases in NLP without accounting for the historical conditions that shape how AAE is viewed today. As they state: "AAE as a language variety cannot be separated from its speakers – primarily Black people in the U.S., who experience systemic anti-Black racism – and the language ideologies that reinforce and justify racial hierarchies" (2020). Questions such as – "Who are the speakers of AAE? How are they viewed?" – that the paper asks are not external to the subject matter. Quite on the contrary, they are fundamental to understanding the biases and discriminatory outcomes of NLP, and eventually to finding mitigating measures to address them. However, these are neglected in such studies.

We can here observe what Mills calls the "tacit social ontology" of mainstream ethics, i.e., a view that "will abstract *away* from relations of structural domination, exploitation, coercion, and oppression, which in reality, of course, will profoundly shape the ontology of those [...] individuals, locating them in superior and inferior positions in social hierarchies of various kinds" (Mills, 2005, p. 168). By failing to account for the particular ontology of the "speakers of AAE" and the way they are viewed, any efforts at better understanding biases in NLP can only fail. In other words, the "veil of ignorance" that Rawls places on one's social conditions to strive to impartiality eventually results in a plain ignorance of actual social conditions, here those of African American in current US society. This ignorance then leads to a failure to adequately understand biases towards AAE in NLP systems. More generally, efforts towards impartiality too often result in *glossing over relations of power and structures of inequality.*

Neglect of Power Relations and Structures of Inequalities in AI Ethics

We can then answer the question asked at the start of this chapter by Delacroix and Wagner: "How did 'ethics' come to acquire such a bad name in the domain of AI and data governance?" (2021, p. 1) Because of the failure of ethics to account for power relations and structures of inequalities. What leads to ethics washing is when ethicists or other experts developing ethics initiatives or instruments for AI fail to account for the power at stake in this technology, including the dominant position of the companies developing it, these companies' power holding massive amounts of data, and the power over the individuals and communities on whom AI is applied. In other words, the failure to take into consideration the power structures on which AI development and deployment rely in any efforts towards ethical AI leads to ethics washing. This is also Delacroix and Wagner's answer to their question by referring to Mouffe's critique of the "tendency to 'turn to ethics' to gloss over the power conflicts characteristic of politics" (Delacroix & Wagner, 2021, p. 1) Over the last few years, many other experts have been calling for the need to engage with power relations and structures of inequalities for a more responsible and ethical AI development and deployment (such as Benjamin, 2019; Crawford, 2021; Hao, 2019). This chapter draws from this field of research and further contributes to it by going to the roots of the neglect of power relations and structures of inequalities in AI ethics, which it finds in mainstream ethics and its idealised theoretical approach. Moreover, ineffective AI ethics efforts risk being counterproductive as they tend to further veil the systems of oppression that they neglect, and as such contribute to entrenching these systems. This is what D'Ignazio and Klein argue when they point to how data ethics initiatives tend to work with "concepts that secure power" as opposed to challenging it (2020, p. 60). This critique directly echoes that of Mills towards "mainstream ethics" that tends to "rationalize the *status quo*" of structural injustices and existing power structures rather than seeking more just systems for all (2005, p. 181). No wonder, as he states, "historically subordinated groups have always been deeply skeptical of ideal theory" and "generally see its glittering ideals as remote and unhelpful" (2005, p. 170).

Neglect Out of Naivety and Neglect Out of Interest

More specifically, one can distinguish two ways for AI ethics to neglect power relations and structures of inequalities: an unintentional one – out of naivety – and an intentional one – out of interest. We can assume the studies on biases in NLP discussed above fall in the first category, i.e., the neglect is *unintentional*. In that case, it is primarily due to a form of naivety towards structures of power and inequalities. This naivety is maintained by a lack of diversity in the field of AI. The 2019 AI Now Institute reports for instance that "studies found only 18% of authors at leading AI conferences are women, and more than 80% of AI professors are men" (West et al., 2019, p. 3). This homogeneity makes this community unable to notice issues that the dominant group in the field is not exposed to, in particular issues of racism, sexism, classism (i.e., prejudice against people belonging to a particular social class), or ableism (i.e., discrimination in favour of able-bodied people). D'Ignazio and Klein call this the "ignorance of being on top" that makes members of the privileged group "poorly equipped to recognize instances of oppression in the world" (2020, p. 28).

The second one is *intentional neglect*. This is particularly clear in Big Tech companies' push for ethical responses to the regulation of AI (Wagner, 2018; Ochigame, 2019). In this case, the intention of the actor is clear: to avoid the establishment of hard lines that would limit its possible activities, and therefore its benefits. The "soft" aspect of ethics, i.e., a form of regulation that cannot impose hard lines is favoured because it is more flexible and easier to manipulate than hard laws. This is how we can understand many lobbying efforts of Big Tech at the European Commission in relation to the regulatory efforts of the Digital Market Act, the Digital Service Act, and the AI Act (Elkaer, 2022). Another example of the way ethics can easily be usurped to fulfil objectives that go against the collective good is how Facebook – now Meta – has hijacked the discussion related to responsible technology development in the company to serve its own profit-making interests. Hao shows how Facebook has, from 2018, oriented the work of its responsible AI team toward mitigating biases of their systems as opposed to addressing the real issues the company was facing, i.e., misinformation and inflammatory discourses (Hao, 2021).

To sum up, whether it is intentional or not, the ethics of AI and other responsible AI initiatives *have too often failed to ask the real questions*, i.e., those related to relations of power and structures of inequalities. The new field of research called "agnotology", i.e., the science of the production of ignorance and doubts, helps shed light on this issue. Two founders of this field, Oreskes and Conway, have shown how some industrial actors, starting with the tobacco industry, have contributed to instil doubts and produce ignorance on the effects of their products to further their profit-making interests (Oreskes & Conway, 2010). Hao's article on Facebook's approach to misinformation is particularly telling in that regard. The article draws from a series of interviews with Joaquin Quiñonero Candela, a former senior researcher at Facebook who had played a key role in developing the algorithmic systems that enabled maximisation of engagement on Facebook and who then lead the company's Responsible AI team. After being asked several times what he thought of the role of Facebook in the storming of the Capitol following the presidential election in January 2021, he eventually answers, "'I don't know' […] 'That's my honest answer. Honest to God. I don't know'" (Hao, 2021). It is distressing to recognise the profound confusion on the issue at stake from a person who has played such a central role in the company.

SITUATEDNESS AND INSTITUTIONALISED ETHICS

For a Situated Ethics

How to ensure ethics asks the real questions to AI? How to avoid the manipulation of ethics? How to ensure ethicists no longer play the "useful idiots", providing frameworks that can be easily instrumentalised to serve unworthy aims? Here again, Mills offers great resources: we need an ethics that engages with the "non-ideal". We need a situated ethics for AI, an ethics that situates its analysis "in the world", including its structures of power and inequalities. This is even more important for a technology that tends to hide itself behind a supposed "immateriality" (Resseguier & Rodrigues, 2021, pp. 4–5). The myth of immateriality allied with the veil of ignorance of mainstream ethics leaves us blind, toothless, tool-less, and in doubt when we need to address the unjust impacts of AI. There is an intimate link between accounting for the materiality and embodied nature of a particular phenomenon and taking responsibility for it. This is at the heart of the feminist epistemology, such as elaborated by Haraway who calls for "situated and embodied knowledges […] against various forms of unlocatable, and so irresponsible, knowledge claims" (1988, p. 583). This link between acknowledging the materiality of AI and taking responsibility for this technology is also clear in Crawford's *Atlas of AI* in which she challenges the "fantasy that AI systems are disembodied brains that absorb and produce knowledge independently from their creators, infrastructures, and the world at large" (2021, p. 215). Quite on the contrary, Crawford demonstrates how "artificial intelligence is both embodied and material, made from natural resources, fuel, human labor, infrastructure, logistics, histories, and classifications" (2021, p. 8). AI ethics needs to start from the "embodied and material" aspect of AI. Research ethics frameworks are a useful tool to situate AI and take responsibility for this technology.

Research Ethics Frameworks for AI

Research ethics has been particularly developed in the field of medical research. It has emerged following several cases of harm caused to research participants, notably by Nazi researchers during World War 2 (London, 2022). Although this form of ethics takes the shape of a "soft law", this does not mean that it is unable to ensure compliance with its rules. Quite on the contrary, the institutional system in which it is embedded provides it with mechanisms to ensure compliance. This means that there are penalties in case of non-compliance, such as withdrawal of funding or exclusion from the research community.

Over the last ten years, we can observe progresses in research ethics in the field of AI (Metcalf et al., 2019; Metcalf & Crawford, 2016). Among these, we can mention the efforts made by the European Commission (EC) that added AI as an "ethics issue" to account for in the ethics appraisal process that all research projects funded under Horizon Europe need to go through (European Commission, 2021, sec. 8). In case of non-compliance with ethics requirements imposed by the EC, the project risks being put on hold and having the funding withdrawn. Another example of such a case of embedding ethics within an institutional framework to give it some teeth is the development of a draft code of ethics by the NeurIPS conference, a major international conference on AI (Bengio et al., 2022). Other initiatives that can be praised in the area are efforts to document research in AI through particular forms of reporting, including "model cards" to document characteristics of a model being released and "datasheets for datasets" that require documenting datasets used to train a machine learning system (Mitchell et al., 2019; Gebru et al., 2021).

As Bender, Gebru et al. put it in relation to documentation on training data, while "undocumented training data perpetuates harm without recourse", "documentation allows for potential accountability" (2021, p. 615). In other words, documentation makes it possible to bring back the context and materiality of a particular model and or dataset. By "situating" the developed systems, we can move beyond the blindness and ignorance that lead to irresponsibility and become accountable to the way the systems are used and their impacts. Efforts in the area of research ethics for AI and requirements for documentation are still in their infancy and much more work still needs to be done in the area. A study showed that a very limited number of papers in NLP research have gone through an Institutional Review Board over the period 2016–2021 (Santy et al., 2021).[4] Furthermore, as these research ethics frameworks develop and are implemented, it will also be essential to evaluate their effectiveness in mitigating the potential harms of AI.

---

[4]   Another challenge with research ethics frameworks for AI is that a large amount of research on AI takes place outside traditional research institutions, notably in big technology companies such as the GAFAM. Contrary to universities or other research centres, these organisations are not used to research ethics structures. It will be essential to innovate in this area as well in the upcoming years.

POWER OF ACTION AT THE HEART OF ETHICS

Ethics and "Power To"

The first section highlighted how mainstream ethics tends to be blind to power and therefore fails to limit abuses. The second section proposed a way to make sure ethics has some teeth to limit abuses of power in AI research by imposing certain requirements to comply with, i.e., norms that should be embedded within institutional frameworks with mechanisms to ensure compliance. This is ethics as soft law, ethics as establishing norms to determine what should be done and what should be avoided, such as the norms imposed on researchers by research ethics frameworks.[5] For AI research and development, these requirements are, for instance, the need to respect some rules when it comes to the collection of data, such as the need to ask for consent from data subjects.

However, keeping power in check by placing limits is not the only role of ethics. Ethics has another relation to power, one that does not consist in limiting it, but on the contrary, promoting and encouraging it. In this case, it is a different type of power that is at stake. It is not a power to dominate, captivate, conquer, and subjugate, but a power to create, transform, and bring about change. It is not "power over" but "power to". Ethics to encourage and promote this type of power is the object of this third section.

The concept of "normative capacity" by Canguilhem is of particular value to define this approach to ethics. In that sense, ethics is not only about enacting norms and ensuring compliance with these (the previous section was dedicated to this approach to ethics). It is also, and maybe more fundamentally, about "normative capacity", i.e., the capacity to determine norms, to determine ways of doing and acting (Canguilhem, 1991). "Power of action" as defined in Spinoza's *Ethics* also helps define this second approach to ethics (Spinoza, 2005). This notion of ethics is of crucial value for AI, especially when it comes to confronting issues of biases, discrimination, and the entrenchment of inequality and long-held prejudices.

When AI Limits Capacity of Action

As Hoffman puts it, we need to investigate the "kinds of worlds being built" with the deployment of this technology (2019, p. 910). More precisely, what kind of world is being built for particular communities? As numerous studies have shown – and we started alluding to this in the first section of this chapter – for particular communities who have been traditionally marginalised and dominated, this technology is building a world that reproduces the past, i.e., a past in which they were confined to subaltern roles. In that sense, AI appears as a "reactionary" technology (Hoffmann, 2019, p. 911), a technology that contributes to restricting members of particular communities to roles and positions to which they have been confined so far, such as subservient roles for women.

For instance, the AI company OpenAI released in Spring 2022 a second version of DALL-E, a text-to-image generation program.[6] The system is assuredly impressive, generating very creative images out of text. However, it also presents highly problematic aspects concerning

---

[5]   For an analysis of this approach to ethics as soft law, see Resseguier and Rodrigues (2021) and Rességuier and Rodrigues (2020).

[6]   https://openai.com/dall-e-2/.

the representation of women and traditionally marginalised communities. Once again, these groups are associated with long-held stereotypes. Prompted with the text "a photo of a personal assistant" or "nurse", the system produces images of women, whereas "CEO" or "lawyers" prompted images of men (Mishkin et al., 2022). These represent a highly reactionary view on gender roles. The case of NLP discussed above where NLP systems entrench prejudices against African Americans through perceptions of the language they speak is another example of such a process by which AI contributes to confining particular communities to subaltern positions in society. Bender, Gebru, et al. also powerfully make this point by looking at large language models drawn from data from the web that, as they show "encode hegemonic views that are harmful to marginalized populations" (2021, p. 615).[7] Two types of discriminatory harm have been distinguished: (1) allocation harms, i.e., when a system "allocates resources (e.g., credit) or opportunities (e.g., jobs) unfairly to different social groups", and (2) "representational harms", i.e., "when a system (e.g., a search engine) represents some social groups in a less favorable light than others, demeans them, or fails to recognize their existence altogether" (Blodgett et al., 2020).

These systems that learn from the past lead to further ingrain past structures of inequalities, and therefore, prevent changes. In that sense, they work against the progress made by social movements towards more justice and equality, including feminism, anti-racism, LGBTIQ+ movements, and other movements that have fought against discrimination. As such, AI appears as a technology that further contributes to *limiting the capacity of action* of members of certain communities, i.e., their ability to determine the norms by which they want to live and their ways of living and doing things. This is not only a loss to the members of the communities who are being discriminated against, but it is also a loss to society at large who cannot benefit from the perspective of a diversity of people at different positions in society.

Ethics to Promote Capacity of Action

Ethics as defined by Canguilhem with the notion of "normative capacity", but also by Spinoza with that of "capacity of action" is essential to resist the harms highlighted above. Spinoza's *Ethics* as read by Deleuze helps shed light on this notion of ethics that does not seek to limit the abuse of power but rather encourages the power of action. As Deleuze puts it: "The entire *Ethics* presents itself as a theory of power, in opposition to morality as a theory of obligations" (2001, p. 104). Ethics in this sense is rather a matter of adjusting one's attention and actions to avoid the closure of possibilities, the way AI systems can do as the section above demonstrated, restricting individuals of particular groups to pre-determined roles or positions. It is a form of resistance against inertia, against anything that prevents movements, against any reactionary tendency, such as hegemonic systems that impede change.

This is what Benjamin calls for when she says:

> if it is a case that inequity and injustice is woven into the very fabric of our society, then that means each twist, coil, and code is a chance for us to weave new patterns, practices, and politics. The vastness of the problem will be its undoing once we accept that we are pattern makers. (Benjamin, 2020)

---

[7]   This is actually the paper that led to Timnit Gebru being "forced out" from Google where she co-led Google's ethical AI team; the company claiming that the paper had not gone through the proper internal review process (Hao, 2020). This event further makes the case for the need to account for power relations in the ethical analysis of these systems.

This idea of patterns is particularly relevant to AI as a technology that precisely works by identifying patterns in the data, i.e., patterns of the past and reproducing them. Refusing the reproduction of past patterns of domination and discrimination and bringing about new ones enables social change and the opening of possibilities for those who have been denied them is a key aspect of AI ethics. A powerful example of this is Data for Black Lives (D4BL)[8] that, as mentioned by D'Ignazio and Klein quoting the founder of this movement Yeshimabeit Milner, seek "to make data a tool for profound social change instead of a weapon of oppression" (2020, p. 6).

CONCLUSION

This chapter showed that the ethical enquiry on AI requires engagement with questions of power, i.e., that power is a crucial component of ethics. It demonstrated how an approach that places power at its heart allows for a more convincing ethical study of this technology. This does not mean giving up on the value of ideals or high-level principles – such as those of dignity, fairness, transparency, or privacy – but rather to ensure they are implemented, and for all. As Mills puts it, "the best way to bring about the ideal is by recognizing the nonideal" (2005, p. 182).

The first section was dedicated to a critique of mainstream ethics with the support of Mills' analysis of this type of ethics. It showed how the "veil of ignorance" used to reach impartiality often leads to plain ignorance of actual structures of power and inequalities. After this critical section, the chapter then turned to making proposals. The second section proposed a situated ethics for AI and highlighted the valuable role that research ethics frameworks embedded within institutions can do to limit the potential harms of AI. This situated ethics takes the shape of a soft version of the law, enacting norms to limit risks of abuses of power of the researcher. The third section introduced a complementary approach to ethics also of particular value for AI. This one is also situated and places power at its heart, but it does so differently, drawing from a different notion of power: no longer power to dominate – power over – but power to create – power to. Considering the risks of AI to further entrench systems of domination and inequalities of the past, and therefore, to contribute to restricting members of traditionally marginalised and dominated groups, this approach to ethics is also of critical value for the ethics of AI.

ACKNOWLEDGEMENTS

The research and writing for this chapter were financially supported by the European Union's Horizon 2020 research and innovation programme under grant agreement No 101006249 (project TechEthos).

---

[8]   https://d4bl.org.

DISCLAIMER

The funder had no role in the decision to publish nor in the preparation of the manuscript. The content of this chapter presents the position of the author, not that of the TechEthos project as a whole, nor of Trilateral Research.

REFERENCES

Bender, E. M., Gebru, T., McMillan-Major, A., & Mitchell, M. (2021). On the dangers of stochastic parrots: Can language models be too big? *Proceedings of the 2021 ACM Conference on Fairness, Accountability, and Transparency*, 610–623. https://doi.org/10.1145/3442188.3445922

Bengio, S., Beygelzimer, A., Crawford, K., Fromer, J., Gabriel, I., Levendowski, A., Raji, D., & Ranzato, M. (2022). *Provisional draft of the NeurIPS code of ethics*. Under review. https://openreview.net/forum?id=zVoy8kAFKPr

Benjamin, R. (2019). *Race after technology: Abolitionist tools for the new Jim code*. Polity.

Benjamin, R. (2020). 'Race to the future? Reimagining the default settings of technology and society' with Ruha Benjamin. Video Playback. https://ncwit.org/video/race-to-the-future-reimagining-the-default-settings-of-technology-and-society-with-ruha-benjamin-video-playback/

Bietti, E. (2020). *From ethics washing to ethics bashing: A view on tech ethics from within moral philosophy*. FAT* '20: Proceedings of the 2020 Conference on Fairness, Accountability, and Transparency. https://papers.ssrn.com/sol3/papers.cfm?abstract_id=3914119

Blodgett, S. L., Barocas, S., Daumé III, H., & Wallach, H. M. (2020). Language (technology) is power: A critical survey of 'bias' in NLP. *CoRR, abs/2005.14050*. https://arxiv.org/abs/2005.14050

Canguilhem, G. (1991). *The normal and the pathological* (C. R. Fawcett, Trans.). Princeton University Press.

Crawford, K. (2021). *Atlas of AI*. Yale University Press.

Delacroix, S., & Wagner, B. (2021). Constructing a mutually supportive interface between ethics and regulation. *Computer Law & Security Review, 40*, 105520. https://doi.org/10.1016/j.clsr.2020.105520

Deleuze, G. (2001). *Spinoza: Practical philosophy* (R. Hurley, Trans.). City Lights Books.

D'Ignazio, C., & Klein, L. F. (2020). *Data feminism*. MIT Press.

Elkaer, A. (2022, February 17). From oil and gas lobbyism to tech lobbyism. *Data Ethics*. https://dataethics.eu/tech-lobbyism/

European Commission. (2021). *EU grants: How to complete your ethics self-assessment. Version 2.0.* https://ec.europa.eu/info/funding-tenders/opportunities/docs/2021-2027/common/guidance/how-to-complete-your-ethics-self-assessment_en.pdf

Gebru, T., Morgenstern, J., Vecchione, B., Wortman Vaughan, J., Wallach, H., Daume III, H., & Crawford, K. (2021). Datasheets for datasets. *Communications of the ACM, 64*(12), 86–92.

Hao, K. (2019, December 27). In 2020, let's stop AI ethics-washing and actually do something. *MIT Technology Review*. https://www.technologyreview.com/2019/12/27/57/ai-ethics-washing-time-to-act/

Hao, K. (2020, December 4). We read the paper that forced Timnit Grebu out of Google: Here's what it says. *MIT Technology Review*. https://www.technologyreview.com/2020/12/04/1013294/google-ai-ethics-research-paper-forced-out-timnit-gebru/

Hao, K. (2021, March 11). How Facebook got addicted to spreading misinformation. *Technology Review*. https://www.technologyreview.com/2021/03/11/1020600/facebook-responsible-ai-misinformation/

Haraway, D. (1988). Situated knowledges: The science question in feminism and the privilege of partial perspective. *Feminist Studies, 14*(3), 575–599.

High-Level Expert Group on Artificial Intelligence, "Ethics guidelines for trustworthy AI", European Commission, Brussels, 2019, https:// ec.europa.eu/digital-single-market/en/news/ethics-guidelines-trustworthy-ai

Hoffmann, A. L. (2019). Where fairness fails: Data, algorithms, and the limits of antidiscrimination discourse. *Information, Communication & Society, 22*(7), 900–915. https://doi.org/10.1080/1369118X.2019.1573912

London, A. J. (2022). *For the common good: Philosophical foundations of research ethics*. Oxford University Press.

Metcalf, J., & Crawford, K. (2016). Where are human subjects in Big Data research? The emerging ethics divide. *Big Data & Society, 3*(1), 2053951716650211. https://doi.org/10.1177/2053951716650211

Metcalf, J., Moss, E., & boyd, danah. (2019). Owning ethics: Corporate logics, silicon valley, and the institutionalization of ethics. *Social Research: An International Quarterly, 82*(2), 449–476.

Mills, C. (2005). 'Ideal theory' as an ideology. *Hypatia, 20*(3), 165–184.

Mishkin, P., Ahmad, L., Brundage, M., Krueger, G., & Sastry, G. (2022). *DALL·E 2 preview—Risks and limitations*. https://github.com/openai/dalle-2-preview/blob/main/system-card.md

Mitchell, M., Wu, S., Zaldivar, A., Barnes, P., Vasserman, L., Hutchinson, B., Spitzer, E., Raji, I. D., & Gebru, T. (2019). Model cards for model reporting. *FAT* 2019: Proceedings of the Conference on Frainess, Accountability, and Transparency*, 220–229.

Mittelstadt, B. (2019). Principles alone cannot guarantee ethical AI. *Nature Machine Intelligence, 1*, 501–507.

Ochigame, R. (2019, December 20). How big tech manipulates academia to avoid regulation. *The Intercept*. https://theintercept.com/2019/12/20/mit-ethical-ai-artificial-intelligence/

Oreskes, N., & Conway, E. M. (2010). *Merchants of doubt: How a handful of scientists obscured the truth on issues from tobacco smoke to global warming*. Bloomsbury Publishing.

Rawls, J., (1999). *A Theory of justice*. Revised edition. The Belknap Press of Harvard University Press Cambridge, MA.

Rességuier, A., & Rodrigues, R. (2020). AI ethics should not remain toothless! A call to bring back the teeth of ethics. *Big Data & Society, 7*(2), 2053951720942541. https://doi.org/10.1177/2053951720942541

Resseguier, A., & Rodrigues, R. (2021). Ethics as attention to context: Recommendations for the ethics of artificial intelligence. *Open Research Europe*. https://doi.org/10.12688/openreseurope.13260.2

Santy, S., Rani, A., & Choudhury, M. (2021). Use of formal ethical reviews in NLP literature: Historical trends and current practices. *CoRR, abs/2106.01105*. https://arxiv.org/abs/2106.01105

Spinoza, B. de. (2005). *Ethics*. Penguin Classics.

Wagner, B. (2018). Ethics as an escape from regulation: From ethics-washing to ethics-shopping. In E. Bayamlioglu, I. Baraliuc, L. Janssens, & M. Hildebrandt (Eds.), *Being profiled: Cogitas Ergo Sum: 10 years of profiling the European citizen*. Amsterdam University Press.

West, S. M., Whittaker, M., & Crawford, K. (2019). *Discriminating systems: Gender, race, and power in AI*. AI Now Institute. https://ainowinstitute.org/discriminatingsystems.html

36. Barriers to regulating AI: critical observations from a fractured field

Ashlin Lee, Will Orr, Walter G. Johnson, Jenna Imad Harb and Kathryn Henne

INTRODUCTION

Experts increasingly call for the regulation of artificial intelligence (AI) on the grounds that it can create risks and harms that disproportionally impact marginalised groups (Buolamwini & Gebru, 2018; Raji et al., 2020). The competitive desire to create more powerful AI – sometimes called the "AI arms race" – facilitates these harms by encouraging the development of unvetted AI systems (Scharre, 2019). Growing evidence supports concerns about AI-related harms. For example, the use of AI to sort and judge individuals in the context of employment opportunities or the provision of welfare benefits can perpetuate bias and discrimination (Eubanks, 2018). In response, a "race to AI regulation" (Smuha, 2021) has emerged, with government and corporate actors developing responses, including frameworks, guidelines, policies, and standards, to address a growing range of AI-related concerns (Floridi & Cowls, 2019).

This chapter reflects critically on the state of AI regulation. Regulation broadly refers to steering the flow of events and is undertaken by various public and private actors including, but not limited to, government (Parker & Braithwaite, 2003). Here, we highlight how the current state of AI regulation is shaped by a significant degree of fracturing and fragmentation. We observe this fracturing across three axes. The first axis concerns definitional fractures, drawing attention to the fragmented state of AI as a concept and as an object of regulation. The second axis considers regulatory interventions, particularly how regulatory responses have not been unified or consistent in responding to the development and spread of AI. The final axis points to the uneven dispersal of benefits and burdens, and how AI regulation unevenly treats different actors.

Drawing on insights from critical infrastructure studies, critical data studies, and regulatory governance, we outline the implications of fragmentation and fracturing in the context of AI regulation. Instead of critiquing the state of AI as evidence of failure, we see these breakages as valuable leverage points. In some, though not all, instances, there is value in maintaining fractures to pursue more just technological outcomes. We highlight how fractures can add value by looking at the challenges of AI regulation through the lens of breakage and repair, which Jackson (2014) describes as the work required for systems to operate over time through moments of disruption.

FRACTURED DEFINITIONS: AI AS A FRAGMENTED CONCEPT

Fragmented definitions regarding how AI is used, and what problems AI can address, complicate the development of regulatory approaches. At a technical level, the computational systems and mathematics required for AI are complex, with many different approaches and uses. Efforts to respond to AI are also diverse, with a wide range of regulatory actors and methods responding to the risks of AI. For example, government, non-government, and private sector organisations have all made suggestions for regulating AI (Jobin et al., 2019), proposing approaches ranging from industry-led self-regulation (Taeihagh, 2021) to legally enforceable bans and moratoriums (The United Nations, 2021). Fragmented understandings of both what AI is and how it might be regulated complicates opportunities for effective regulation.

Conceptually, what constitutes AI is quite broad. For example, Nilsson (2009) describes AI as about making machine intelligence, with intelligence describing foresight and action in one's environment. General definitions thus tend to focus on computer systems possessing intelligent capacities – such as learning and pattern recognition – that are usually found in humans. A focus on intellectual capacities, however, is somewhat distorting, as there are fundamental differences in how humans and machines form and execute these capacities. Such a definition reveals little about these differences and what AI systems actually look like and do (Fjelland, 2020). To better clarify AI, Corea (2019) suggests AI might be defined by considering:

- What problems is AI used to solve, including reasoning, knowledge, planning, communication, and perceptual challenges.
- The computational approach used to address these problems.[1]
- Whether AI is narrow and focused on a specific problem, or general and capable of multiple uses.

General references to AI and common synonyms, such as "machine learning," "neural networks," and "deep learning," all refer to specific technical characteristics and usage circumstances. However, they are often used without clarification, further fuelling its fragmentation. Definitions of AI are therefore messy, heterogenous, and unclear.

Without deeper investigation, important elements of AI's definition and regulation can be missed, causing further fragmentation. For example, the algorithmic models that underlie AI tend to be considered the most valuable aspect of AI (Sambasivan, 2022). However, such a view obscures crucial aspects of AI, such as the work required to create and curate high-quality datasets for AI models. Without such work, AI cannot exist, and ignoring this work can result in the failure of AI techniques and applications. This work can also be highly problematic, with data workers frequently devalued and exploited in the data supply chain (Gray & Suri, 2019). For regulation to be extensive it is thus important to understand the key mathematical and algorithmic components of AI *and* the broader set of supporting elements (such as the production of training datasets) that allow AI to function.

---

[1]   Corea (2019) further breaks down this category into detailed subcategories describing the specific mathematical and computational techniques used. Examples given include: logic-based tools using programmed rules; knowledge-based tools using ontological databases of rules and relationships; probabilistic tools using incomplete information to make decisions through statistics; machine learning which uses pattern recognition and reinforcement approaches; embodied intelligence that connects sensory perception and interactions with intelligent activities such as virtual reality; and, finally, search and optimisation that attempts to optimise responses to search queries. Although current at the time of publication, it is also conceivable that new techniques or variations have evolved given the rapid pace of development.

Because AI has a broad set of current and future applications, incremental approaches that suggest qualified principles and specific guidelines have been preferred over more general regulatory paradigms (Reed, 2018). In the absence of longitudinal data and evidence, scholars have argued these principles and guidelines are largely normative in nature, targeting the general modus operandi of AI vis-à-vis human values rather than specific risks that AI might present (Wirtz et al., 2020). The significant growth in "Ethical AI" guidelines offers one such example. Created by both public and private sector actors, Ethical AI guidelines attempt to set ethical values and expectations for AI's development and use, in the hope that systemic risks and potential social, economic, and political harms might be avoided (Boddington, 2017). These values and standards, however, are not necessarily legally binding or enforceable.

Surveying the landscape, Jobin and colleagues (2019) found 84 examples of national AI ethics guidelines, nearly equally divided among private and public organisations but with notable underrepresentation from Central Asia, Africa, and Southern and Central America. These frameworks converge around five themes: transparency, justice and fairness, non-maleficence, responsibility, and privacy. Floridi and Cowls (2019) similarly isolated five principles in their analysis of AI ethics standards adopted by major public and private actors: beneficence, non-maleficence, autonomy, justice, and explicability. de Almeida and colleagues (2021) identified 21 regulatory approaches that adopted variations of these principles in their design. They note that, despite convergence on high-level principles of Ethical AI, significant variations remain.

Despite the greater availability of Ethical AI principles, examples of successful regulation using these principles remain scarce. The technical complexity of AI means any regulation must be flexible enough to accommodate the diversity of AI, while also acknowledging the diversity of contexts in which AI is applied. Ethical AI guidelines attempt to do this by focusing on normative principles and abstract concepts of ethics. In this way, Ethical AI guidelines may be useful in forming the basis of stronger regulatory responses, as they capture a "normative core" of values for AI (Fjeld et al., 2020). However, despite the abundance of Ethical AI guidelines and principles, it remains to be seen whether these guidelines can be enforced and if they provide sufficient oversight to avoid AI-related harms.

FRACTURED INTERVENTIONS: LIMITATIONS IN REGULATORY INTERVENTIONS

Regulatory interventions towards AI are also fragmented. Despite the diversity of guidelines developed around AI, a lack of clear advice on implementation remains. While fragmentation in regulatory interventions is common (Black, 2002), definitional uncertainty around AI compounds this problem, as the process of creating and applying new norms and standards requires some common ground. Fragmentation in regulatory interventions can occur along multiple dimensions, including: (1) the type of institutional setting implementing norms; (2) the level of government; (3) legal bindingness; (4) regulatory target; and (5) broad or specific construction of a norm (see Abbott & Snidal, 2009). While a comprehensive review of these interventions is beyond the scope of this chapter, a brief overview here illustrates their fragmentation and implications.

The unrestrained growth of regulatory actors and measures has fragmented the capacity of regulation to influence AI, particularly through the predominance of self-regulation as the preferred approach to regulating AI. Using Ethical AI as the primary lens for regulating AI, technology firms (e.g., Microsoft, Meta) have introduced their own ethical codes. Multistakeholder bodies (e.g., World Economic Forum [WEF], Organisation for Economic Cooperation and Development [OECD]), and public entities including legislatures, regulators, and all levels of courts have also contributed different guidelines. Non-state actors as diverse as civil society bodies, professional organisations, industry groups, and standard-setting organisations have also begun regulatory initiatives. These include codes of conduct, technical standards, and certification or monitoring programs. For example, the Institute of Electrical and Electronics Engineers CertifAIEd Program (IEEE, 2022) provides a risk-based framework and ethics criteria to certify the development and operation of AI systems as compliant on issues including transparency, bias, accountability, and privacy. The practical capacity of these different sectoral and jurisdictional approaches is contingent on the assumption that AI designers and operators will actively and responsibly self-regulate. This assumption is, however, challenged in two ways. First, through evidence that Big Tech players actively oppose most regulation, lobbying against it on the basis that it impedes innovation (Satariano & Stevis-Gridneff, 2020), and second that the guidelines that underpin the technology industry's preferred approach of self-regulation (i.e., AI ethics guidelines) are non-binding and unenforceable. Big Tech actors materially benefit from fragmentation, as they can position self-regulation as legitimate and practical and oppose more stringent and enforceable government regulations.

Through promoting self-regulation, corporate actors come to have unique obligations and capacities to craft and enforce regulation. Compliance with many of these codes of conduct remains legally voluntary and open to (subjective) interpretation. In addition, such codes often lack monitoring and accountability provisions (Bowman & Hodge, 2009). Instead, compliance and enforcement of the ethical principles rely more heavily on reputational and market forces, as well as internal normative motives. The presence of various ethical codes may further fragment regulatory interventions by presenting an array of choices and by decreasing the perceived need for states to issue binding regulation. In doing so, they can contribute to different states around the world, codifying rules of varying strength at different points in time. For instance, state-based regulators have more legally binding options available than non-state or hybrid entities, though government institutions have often been reticent to set binding rules on AI to date. One such example is how the United States relies on a largely voluntary regulatory program for AI in autonomous vehicles (McAslan et al., 2021). This program sets non-binding standards and reporting norms for developers to manage the application of AI in autonomous vehicles. In contrast, the European Union appears poised to enact a more comprehensive and binding regulatory framework for AI, adopting a risk-based approach for AI across sectors.

While many non-state interventions are not legally binding, indirect pathways to enforcement may still be available through liability, insurance, or consumer protection regulation – adding further fragmentation (Wallach & Marchant, 2019). These interventions can also lack the checks and balances expected of state-based interventions. For example, where state-based interventions often require procedural justice, freedom of information requests, and public record-keeping, non-state actors are not necessarily subject to these requirements. Seeking accountability is thus not always clear or straightforward.

Definitional uncertainty fuels further fragmentation in the practical implementation of AI regulation. This regulatory environment yields unclear obligations, limited options for accountability, and varied perceptions of AI regulation among both key stakeholders and the public. This is concerning, as it can erode the belief in enforceable AI regulation.

FRACTURED OUTCOMES: THE UNEVEN DISTRIBUTION OF BURDENS AND BENEFITS OF AI REGULATION

The fractured landscape of AI regulation means that its benefits and burdens are unevenly distributed. This relates to a reliance on Ethical AI guidance over enforceable regulation and the "AI arms race" logic that is driving the growth of AI. For example, Radu (2021) argues that the regulation of AI has suffered through the "hybridisation of governance," where external stakeholders (including think tanks, corporations, and other actors) are enlisted to shape the direction of AI governance and regulation. Wishing to support the growth of AI, nation-states defer regulatory responsibility to external stakeholder groups – hybridising governance between the interests of stakeholders and the public.

Without an authoritative position on regulation set by the government, however, these groups are allowed to define the formal and informal rules of regulation for the state with little direction or mandate. For instance, national AI strategies, designed with stakeholder input, often focus on high-level Ethical AI guidance and self-regulation rather than enforceable regulatory measures (Floridi & Cowls, 2019). This creates a disorderly regulatory environment that cements power among those already invested in AI (such as commercial entities) while making it difficult for those outside these privileged groups to contribute their knowledge and experience. For instance, as Sloane (2022) notes, the European Commission's AI Alliance, an online forum for providing feedback on AI policy decisions in the EU, quickly devolved into an unrepresentative echo chamber without capturing the lived experiences of those impacted, or even the broader view of industry and unaligned experts. As Radu (2021, p. 190) argues, "it becomes increasingly hard to disentangle public interest policies from market dominance interests." External stakeholders stand to benefit from the hybridised regulation of AI, with the public potentially less well served by this arrangement.

The popularity of self-regulation in the private sector is another example of the hybridisation of governance. Framing the regulation of AI through loose ethical principles has encouraged corporate actors to adopt and promote self-regulation as an approach that limits the risks of AI while not impeding its potential innovations (Greene et al., 2019). In many tech companies, new roles have been established to manage the ethical impacts of AI systems (Metcalf et al., 2019). These roles often attempt to regulate AI systems internally within existing corporate protocols, such as review boards and codes of conduct. Self-regulation allows corporations to appear compliant with loose regulations by defining when and how Ethical AI guidelines can be applied while keeping costs to a minimum (Metcalf et al., 2019).

The atmosphere of self-regulation has provided opportunities for ethics-washing. Ethics-based rhetoric and institutionally acceptable interventions are mobilised to frame business-as-usual practices as ethical while avoiding substantive action that might disrupt the interests of the corporation (Wagner, 2019). Industry-led self-regulations like Ethical AI can therefore be used to create a competitive advantage and build credibility and increase trust, thereby increasing revenue (Wagner, 2019). In short, "[p]rofit maximisation … is rebranded as bias minimisation" (Benjamin, 2019, p. 30). As such, the self-regulation of AI allows for ethical concerns to be captured by corporate logics of "meritocracy, technological solutionism, and market fundamentalism" (Metcalf et al., 2019, p. 470), and managed through reductive and performative ethics-washing measures that lack real-world effectiveness and any real ethical value (Bietti, 2021).

The broad and often ambiguous nature of many AI regulations can mean negotiating disagreements often fall to the judicial system. For instance, a school in Sweden was fined in violation of the European Union's General Data Protection Regulation (GDPR) for unlawfully testing facial recognition technology. As per the GDPR, testing systems do not usually require approval by data regulators, as subjects' consent is considered a sufficient threshold for the processing of biometric data (Penner & Chiusi, 2020). In this case, however, student consent was not deemed to be freely given due to the power disparities between the institution and its pupils. However, as Galanter (1974) argues, the rules and structures of the judicial system often reinforce existing power imbalances between those who can afford lengthy court processes and access to legal expertise and those who cannot. Unlike the general public and those who suffer the consequences of AI, Big Tech actors and AI developers can afford multiple court cases, fines, and legal fees incurred while fighting regulation, making regulation a cost of business, rather than an effective deterrent. While essential, the judicial system may not be the best place to negotiate the regulation of AI given it can advantage those with the most resources and least relative risk while disadvantaging those with the least resources and greatest relative risk.

Frontline operators, engineers, data scientists, and other technical practitioners often manage the burden to interpret and enact regulatory principles. Practitioners are required to translate ethical and regulatory principles into tangible technical constraints in the design of AI systems (Orr & Davis, 2020). Although practitioners can use tools to aid the translation of ethical and regulatory codes into design protocols, many codes are imprecise in nature. Designers prefer more detailed, technical standards set by standard-setting bodies, which allow professional certification of their work and pathways towards industry-recognised standards, such as the European Union's CE mark, which indicates conformity with EU safety and quality requirements (e.g., Henriksen et al., 2021). Thus, even when tools are available to practitioners, they can hinder designers' ability to adapt the restrictions to the realities of developing AI (Morley et al., 2020). Loopholes also potentially allow practitioners to continue to accumulate data, further benefiting their position, while the consequences of loopholes fall disproportionately on consumers, civil society, or those most at risk. Practitioners often have an assumed responsibility for the ethical integrity of their system, and a wide-ranging capacity to ensure this integrity. However, ethical responsibility for determining how, by whom, and to what effect AI is regulated is distributed throughout the sociotechnical system of actors (Orr & Davis, 2020). This fractured landscape muddies clear lines of accountability as to "who makes the rules and for how long" (Radu, 2021, p. 190).

Fragmentation also shapes how the benefits of AI regulation are distributed. Technical hurdles – such as limitations in how transparent and easily understood an AI's foundational algorithms are (Amoore, 2020) – can undermine the efficiency and reach of regulatory interventions. This causes the potential benefits of regulation – such as preventing malfeasance, ensuring accountability, and other normative principles described in the first section – to become dispersed among a limited number of groups, rather than universally applied. As discussed in the second section, the coverage and quality of interventions vary, fracturing the supposed benefits of regulation. For instance, while the GDPR has enshrined the right for data subjects to receive "meaningful information about the logic involved" (The European Union, 2022a) in making automated decisions, this standard is difficult to achieve. It should serve the interest of anyone subject to automated decisions while protecting those who are most likely to experience algorithmic harms. Yet, whether it is technically possible for these benefits to materialise is unclear. Even the most explainable AI requires expert knowledge to understand (Burrell, 2016), and technical transparency is not sufficient for understanding a system's logic or for ensuring accountability (Amoore, 2020). Feminist analyses underscore that technical solutions often occlude the systemic and structural factors underlying algorithmic discrimination and call for fairness (West, 2020). Furthermore, systems motivated by vague notions of "social good" are at risk of reinforcing logics of colonial extraction and domination (Madianou, 2021), failing to address the power imbalances stemming from AI (Gebru, 2020).

Beyond the technical limitations of these regulations, caveats in legislation undermine their effectiveness. For instance, regulation on automated decision-making in the GDPR only applies to "decisions based solely on automated processing" (The European Union, 2022b) such as profiling. If a decision is made by both AI and a human, the "logic" behind these decisions need not be provided to data subjects. For example, an Uber driver's accusations of algorithmically enabled unfair dismissal were deemed illegitimate in a Dutch court due to a human agent making the final decision (Lomas, 2021). This example raises important questions about how much power AI has over human beings as part of collaborative decision systems. Furthermore, regulatory limitations on algorithmic power only apply to decisions that produce legal or similarly significant effects for the individual, such as the automated refusal of credit applications. Non-legal harms, such as racial bias through AI and the loss or limitation of disability access, are less easily captured. Structural power imbalances in the development and implementation of regulation thus drive the inequitable distribution of benefits relating to AI and its regulation (Wachter et al., 2017).

DISCUSSION

This chapter has drawn attention to the challenges presented by the fractured global landscape of AI regulation. Reflecting on these fractures in the context of regulatory theory, it is natural to assume that promoting the mending of these fractures is the logical next step for regulation. For example, Braithwaite (2017), when explaining responsive regulation, argues for a shared basis of learning and capacity building between regulatory actors as the base of what he calls the "regulatory pyramid." Responsive regulation dynamically responds to the needs of government, private sector, and third-party actors through appropriate movements up or down the regulatory pyramid, which includes responses and sanctions. Before the enforcement of punitive measures, actors should be allowed to learn and build their capability to act appropriately. Shared bodies of knowledge on AI are, however, contested and not authoritative. Regulatory interventions are shared among stakeholders, who are independently moving up or down their own regulatory pyramids, as the common ground shared between actors (e.g., AI ethics guidelines) holds few binding mechanisms. This leads to the burden of regulation falling on individuals (designers and engineers, for example) or systems that were never intended to arbitrate society-wide issues of rapid technical change (such as the judiciary or corporate-driven self-regulation). Given the shortcomings of the current regulatory environment, it is therefore understandable that a desire to unify AI regulation and mend any fractures might be a productive and logical step forwards.

Despite this logical connection between the fractured state of AI and a lack of successful regulation, we suggest that desires to unify AI regulation by plastering over these fractures are misplaced. Instead, a key to understanding and regulating AI is to embrace these fractures as windows into the details that underpin the field of AI. Through understanding these fractures and the associated work – what Jackson (2014) describes as "repair work" – we gain insights into how regulation might better respond to complex systems like AI. Jackson (2014) argues that greater attention should be paid to the breakdowns, failures, and disruptions of socio-technical systems, and the work required to make them function at sites of failure. Breakages and fractures reveal the limits of how AI thinks, works, and operates. They are therefore sites where we might begin to change AI.

Using the lens of repair, fracturing can be approached as part of the solution for AI regulation. While vested interests might prefer the dual arms races of AI innovation and regulation to be administrated by experts and prestigious institutions, fractures reveal the messy, partial, and continuing work associated with the development of AI *and* the development of AI regulation. As Jackson (2014) argues, innovation is often framed as something that happens in a laboratory, where technology is perfected, and failure occurs well after innovation, separate from this process. This framing, however, does not reflect the reality of AI regulation. There is ongoing intellectual and discursive work to create guidance for the sector, which is sometimes contested. Deployment of guidelines and regulation means working with diverse, and sometimes disagreeable users, professionals, and policymakers. These moments of contestation reveal the social and technical elements most valuable to AI, and therefore those elements that regulation should attempt to engage.

A focus on fractures, fragmentation, and breakages may also help progress the regulation of AI by illuminating alternative views of AI that foreground issues of justice and equity. For example, Costanza-Chock's (2020) summary of the Design Justice movement empha-sises end-to-end, participatory design methods with the communities that technologies like AI directly impact. This requires an acceptance of the fragmentation of AI and its regulation through different contexts and experiences that are not always accounted for in the design pro-cess. By embracing the partial, contextual, and sometimes contested accounts that different groups experience, the basis for a more nuanced technical and regulatory response to AI may be developed. Given the complexity of AI, desires to create unified paradigms of AI ethics or regulation give little room to address these nuances and the needs of those living with and through AI systems. As the third section discusses, AI's burdens and benefits are often dis-tributed unevenly among different groups, each with its own needs and ethical relationships, which are constantly shifting. A "one-size-fits-all" approach to AI regulation fails to respect these differences and their implications. In some cases, it may be undesirable or unadvisable to have uniform approaches to AI regulation, such as in instances where AI harms dispropor-tionately affect certain demographic groups. In these instances, uniform and cohesive rules would not speak to the specific AI harms and risks these groups face and would not achieve just outcomes. In this way, embracing fragmentation may be more productive.

This does not mean we reject some of the advancements achieved thus far. For instance, as noted earlier, there is some moderate convergence on the normative core of Ethical AI, and around key principles by which AI ethics should be structured. This normative core may form the basis of appropriate and powerful regulation in the future, with appropriate oversight and enforcement mechanisms. This normative core should not be treated, however, as consensus or a finished product, as ethical relationships are still very much at play through a lens of frac-ture. According to Jackson (2014), repair foregrounds forgotten ethical relationships of mutual care and responsibility between both humans and technology and the chains of interactivities that create ethical relationships – as fulfilled through repair work. With AI systems exercising power over more aspects of everyday life, questions of what one owes, and is owed, as a part of their life become important. Exploring points of fracture provides opportunities to interrogate different norms, understand their real-world impact among those at risk, and craft alternatives better aligned with those in need.

CONCLUSION

AI and its regulation are – and will likely continue to be – fractured by virtue of competition among actors, a political-economic drive for innovation, diverse and shifting contexts in which AI is applied, and the varying technical complexities of AI. Embracing these fractures is a starting point for building more effective regulation. The fractured view of AI foregrounds the reality of AI development and deployment and respects the diversity of challenges that different communities face. Regulating AI is not and will not be a one-size-fits-all endeavour, thus harmonised and standardised approaches to regulatory intervention are unrealistic. Instead, it is a constantly iterative process that must wrestle with competing views, social and technical limitations, and continuing power imbalances. Regulating AI is a difficult task, but it will be even more challenging if these fractures are ignored.

REFERENCES

Abbott, K. W., & Snidal, D. (2009). The governance triangle: Regulatory standards institutions and the shadow of the state. In *Chapter two: The governance triangle: Regulatory standards institutions and the shadow of the state* (pp. 44–88). Princeton University Press. https://doi.org/10.1515/9781 400830732.44

Amoore, L. (2020). *Cloud ethics: Algorithms and the attributes of ourselves and others.* Duke University Press.

Benjamin, R. (2019). *Race after technology: Abolitionist tools for the new Jim code.* Polity.

Bietti, E. (2021). From ethics washing to ethics bashing: A moral philosophy view on tech ethics. *Journal of Social Computing, 2*(3), 266–283. https://doi.org/10.23919/JSC.2021.0031

Black, J. (2002). Critical reflections on regulation. *Australian Journal of Legal Philosophy, 27,* 1–35.

Boddington, P. (2017). *Towards a code of ethics for artificial intelligence.* Springer.

Bowman, D. M., & Hodge, G. A. (2009). Counting on codes: An examination of transnational codes as a regulatory governance mechanism for nanotechnologies. *Regulation & Governance, 3*(2), 145–164. https://doi.org/10.1111/j.1748-5991.2009.01046.x

Braithwaite, J. (2017). Types of responsiveness. In Peter Drahos (Ed.) *Regulatory theory: Foundations and applications* (pp. 117–132). ANU Press.

Buolamwini, J., & Gebru, T. (2018). Gender shades: Intersectional accuracy disparities in commercial gender classification. *Proceedings of Machine Learning Research, 81,* 1–15.

Burrell, J. (2016). How the machine 'thinks': Understanding opacity in machine learning algorithms. *Big Data & Society, 3*(1), 205395171562251. https://doi.org/10.1177/2053951715622512

Corea, F. (2019). AI knowledge map: How to classify AI technologies. In F. Corea (Ed.), *An introduction to data: Everything you need to know about AI, big data and data science* (pp. 25–29). Springer International Publishing. https://doi.org/10.1007/978-3-030-04468-8_4

Costanza-Chock, S. (2020). *Design justice: Community-led practices to build the worlds we need.* MIT Press.

de Almeida, P. G. R., dos Santos, C. D., & Farias, J. S. (2021). Artificial intelligence regulation: A framework for governance. *Ethics and Information Technology, 23*(3), 505–525. https://doi.org/10 .1007/s10676-021-09593-z

Eubanks, V. (2018). *Automating inequality: How high-tech tools profile, police, and punish the poor.* St. Martin's Press.

Fjeld, J., Achten, N., Hilligoss, H., Nagy, A., & Srikumar, M. (2020). Principled artificial intelligence: Mapping consensus in ethical and rights-based approaches to principles for AI. *SSRN Electronic Journal.* https://doi.org/10.2139/ssrn.3518482

Fjelland, R. (2020). Why general artificial intelligence will not be realized. *Humanities and Social Sciences Communications, 7*(1), 10. https://doi.org/10.1057/s41599-020-0494-4

Floridi, L., & Cowls, J. (2019). A unified framework of five principles for AI in society. *Harvard Data Science Review.* https://doi.org/10.1162/99608f92.8cd550d1

Galanter, M. (1974). Why the "haves" come out ahead: Speculations on the limits of legal change. *Law and Society Review, 9*(1), 95–160.

Gebru, T. (2020). Race and gender. In Markus D. Dubber, Frank Pasquale, & Sunit Das (Eds.), *The Oxford handgook of ethics of AI* (pp. 253–270). Oxford University Press.

Gray, M., & Suri, S. (2019). *Ghost work: How to stop silicon valley from building a new global underclass.* Houghton Mifflin Harcourt.

Greene, D., Hoffmann, A. L., & Stark, L. (2019). *Better, nicer, clearer, fairer: A critical assessment of the movement for ethical artificial intelligence and machine learning.* https://doi.org/10.24251/HICSS.2019.258

Henriksen, A., Enni, S., & Bechmann, A. (2021). Situated accountability: Ethical principles, certification standards, and explanation methods in applied AI. In *Proceedings of the 2021 AAAI/ACM conference on AI, ethics, and society* (pp. 574–585). Association for Computing Machinery. https://doi.org/10.1145/3461702.3462564

IEEE. (2022). *IEEE CertifAIEd.* https://engagestandards.ieee.org/ieeecertifaied.html

Jackson, S. J. (2014). Rethinking repair. In T. Gillespie, P. J. Boczkowski, & K. A. Foot (Eds.), *Media technologies* (pp. 221–240). The MIT Press. https://doi.org/10.7551/mitpress/9780262525374.003.0011

Jobin, A., Ienca, M., & Vayena, E. (2019). The global landscape of AI ethics guidelines. *Nature Machine Intelligence, 1*(9), 389–399. https://doi.org/10.1038/s42256-019-0088-2

Lomas, N. (2021). Uber hit with default 'robo-firing' ruling after another EU labor rights GDPR challenge. *TechCrunch.* https://social.techcrunch.com/2021/04/14/uber-hit-with-default-robo-firing-ruling-after-another-eu-labor-rights-gdpr-challenge/

Madianou, M. (2021). Nonhuman humanitarianism: When "AI for good" can be harmful. *Information, Communication & Society, 24*(6), 850–868. https://doi.org/10.1080/1369118X.2021.1909100

McAslan, D., Gabriele, M., & Miller, T. R. (2021). Planning and policy directions for autonomous vehicles in metropolitan planning organizations (MPOs) in the United States. *Journal of Urban Technology, 28*(3–4), 175–201. https://doi.org/10.1080/10630732.2021.1944751

Metcalf, J., Moss, E., & boyd, danah. (2019). Owning ethics: Corporate logics, silicon valley, and the institutionalization of ethics. *Social Research: An International Quarterly, 86*(2), 449–476.

Morley, J., Floridi, L., Kinsey, L., & Elhalal, A. (2020). From what to how: An initial review of publicly available AI ethics tools, methods and research to translate principles into practices. *Science and Engineering Ethics, 26*(4), 2141–2168. https://doi.org/10.1007/s11948-019-00165-5

Nilsson, N. J. (2009). *The quest for artificial intelligence: A history of ideas and achievements.* Cambridge University Press.

Orr, W., & Davis, J. L. (2020). Attributions of ethical responsibility by artificial intelligence practitioners. *Information, Communication & Society, 23*(5), 719–735. https://doi.org/10.1080/1369118X.2020.1713842

Parker, C., & Braithwaite, J. (2003). Regulation. In P. Cane & M. Tushnet (Eds.), *The Oxford handbook of legal studies* (pp. 119–145). Oxford University Press.

Penner, K., & Chiusi, F. (2020). *Automating society report 2020—European Union.* Algorithm Watch. https://automatingsociety.algorithmwatch.org/report2020/european-union/

Radu, R. (2021). Steering the governance of artificial intelligence: National strategies in perspective. *Policy and Society, 40*(2), 178–193. https://doi.org/10.1080/14494035.2021.1929728

Raji, I. D., Gebru, T., Mitchell, M., Buolamwini, J., Lee, J., & Denton, E. (2020). Saving face: Investigating the ethical concerns of facial recognition auditing. *Proceedings of the AAAI/ACM conference on AI, ethics, and society* (pp. 145–151). https://doi.org/10.1145/3375627.3375820

Reed, C. (2018). How should we regulate artificial intelligence? *Philosophical Transactions of the Royal Society A: Mathematical, Physical and Engineering Sciences*, *376*(2128), 20170360. https://doi.org/10.1098/rsta.2017.0360

Sambasivan, N. (2022). All equation, no human: The myopia of AI models. *Interactions*, *29*(2), 78–80. https://doi.org/10.1145/3516515

Satariano, A., & Stevis-Gridneff, M. (2020, December 14). Big tech turns its lobbyists loose on Europe, alarming regulators. *The New York Times*. https://www.nytimes.com/2020/12/14/technology/big-tech-lobbying-europe.html

Scharre, P. (2019). Killer apps: The real dangers of an AI arms race. *Foreign Affairs*, *98*, 135.

Sloane, M. (2022). To make AI fair, here's what we must learn to do. *Nature*, *605*(9), 1. https://doi.org/10.1038/d41586-022-01202-3

Smuha, N. A. (2021). From a 'race to AI' to a 'race to AI regulation': Regulatory competition for artificial intelligence. *Law, Innovation and Technology*, *13*(1), 57–84. https://doi.org/10.1080/17579961.2021.1898300

Taeihagh, A. (2021). Governance of artificial intelligence. *Policy and Society*, *40*(2), 137–157. https://doi.org/10.1080/14494035.2021.1928377

The European Union. (2022a). Art. 13 GDPR – Information to be provided where personal data are collected from the data subject. *General Data Protection Regulation (GDPR)*. https://gdpr-info.eu/art-13-gdpr/

The European Union. (2022b). Art. 22 GDPR – Automated individual decision-making, including profiling. *General Data Protection Regulation (GDPR)*. https://gdpr-info.eu/art-22-gdpr/

The United Nations. (2021, September 15). *Urgent action needed over artificial intelligence risks to human rights*. UN News. https://news.un.org/en/story/2021/09/1099972

Wachter, S., Mittelstadt, B., & Floridi, L. (2017). Why a right to explanation of automated decision-making does not exist in the general data protection regulation. *International Data Privacy Law*, *7*(2), 76–99.

Wagner, B. (2019). Ethics as an escape from regulation: From "ethics-washing" to ethics-shopping? In E. Bayamlioglu, I. Baraliuc, L. A. W. Janssens, & M. Hildebrandt (Eds.), *Being profiled: Cogitas Ergo Sum* (pp. 84–89). Amsterdam University Press. https://doi.org/10.1515/9789048550180-016

Wallach, W., & Marchant, G. (2019). Toward the agile and comprehensive international governance of AI and robotics [point of view]. *Proceedings of the IEEE*, *107*(3), 505–508. https://doi.org/10.1109/JPROC.2019.2899422

West, S. M. (2020). Redistribution and rekognition: A feminist critique of algorithmic fairness. *Catalyst: Feminism, Theory, Technoscience*, *6*(2). https://doi.org/10.28968/cftt.v6i2.33043

Wirtz, B. W., Weyerer, J. C., & Sturm, B. J. (2020). The dark sides of artificial intelligence: An integrated AI governance framework for public administration. *International Journal of Public Administration*, *43*(9), 818–829. https://doi.org/10.1080/01900692.2020.1749851

37. Why artificial intelligence is not transparent: a critical analysis of its three opacity layers
Manuel Carabantes

INTRODUCTION

We currently live immersed in a network of sociotechnical systems whose structure and functioning increasingly depend on decisions made or assisted by artificial intelligence (AI) algorithms. There are many everyday situations in which an AI is likely to intervene, sometimes with important consequences: when we apply for a loan, the decision to grant or deny it is likely to be made by an AI; when we go shopping, it is probable that the products have been arranged on the shelves following the instructions of an AI to maximize sales; when we receive an email, the decision to classify it as spam or not is made by an AI; when the police patrol one neighborhood more frequently than another, that crime-fighting strategy is likely to have been calculated by an AI; when we receive a recommendation on Netflix, it is an AI that predicts that this movie or series will probably be to our liking; and when we are shown an advertisement narrowly tailored to our interests, it is because there is an AI that knows our browsing history.

Given the great aggregate weight of AI decisions on our lives, this technology should be *transparent* for several reasons that involve different ways of understanding the very concept of transparency: to provide an explanation to those affected by its decisions, to make it possible for engineers to detect errors in its operation, and to ensure that it operates according to the law. For example, when someone applies for a job, they should be able to check whether the AI that filters the resumes includes attributes in its reasoning that are usually illegal in this context, such as race—which may occur in a way that is difficult to detect, by inferring these attributes from other trivial ones, and without the awareness of the engineers responsible for this AI (Kearns & Roth, 2020). However, despite the normative rationality of transparency, the reality is often the opposite. Following Burrell's (2016) influential framework, it may be stated that AI hides behind *three opacity layers*. First, it is obscured due to the use of intrinsically opaque computational methods that are chosen for their unique capabilities and greater effectiveness over more explainable alternatives. Second, it is concealed because the companies and governments that control AI use the opacity granted by the law to protect the functionality of their algorithms, maintain their competitive advantage, and preserve their reputation. Third, it is hidden because it is such a complex technology that it is unintelligible to most people.

From the perspective of critical theory, the aim of this chapter is to discuss why some elements of these three opacity layers, which are usually presented as technically, economically, or socially necessary, are in reality the result of decisions made by the elites to meet their interests. The opacity of AI is largely a consequence of the operational needs of the elites to use it as a tool of surveillance, manipulation, and enrichment.

FIRST OPACITY LAYER: BLACK-BOX ALGORITHMS

Within the broad field of AI, opacity in the technical sense is concentrated in *machine learning* (Defense Advanced Research Projects Agency [DARPA], 2016). While the usual procedure in computer engineering is that a human being creates the set of instructions (algorithm or program) that tells the computer how to transform the initial data (input) into the desired result (output), in machine learning, the computer is provided with a large *training set* of inputs and their matching outputs, and it has to find by itself an algorithm capable of performing the transformation within certain criteria. This definition, borrowed from Domingos (2017), is approximate, since there are types of machine learning (unsupervised and reinforcement) in which an explicit output is not provided, but is quite accurate, as it refers to the currently most used type of machine learning (supervised), and it has the virtue of explaining to non-experts what machine learning is: learning algorithms (*learners*) are algorithms that create other algorithms (sometimes called *trained models*).

Machine learning is especially attractive for its ability to outperform human cognitive faculties in two ways: as a means for creating algorithms that arguably no human being can design, and for the effectiveness of those resulting algorithms in performing certain tasks better than any human being. An example of the former is image recognition, a task that for decades resisted algorithms designed by human beings, but which today computers perform easily thanks to algorithms generated by machine learning. Regarding the latter, algorithms generated by machine learning stand out for their superior accuracy and speed compared with human beings in several tasks, the main ones being *pattern recognition*, *object classification*, and *phenomena prediction* (Alpaydin, 2021). For example, Wang and Kosinski (2018) used machine learning to generate an algorithm capable of finding patterns of homosexuality on the face and classifying individuals based on their sexual orientation with higher accuracy rates than human judges: 81% vs. 61% in the identification of gay men, and 71% vs. 54% in lesbian women. The purpose of this research was to prove that such a device is technically possible and, therefore, someone might be already using it.

To generate their algorithm, Wang and Kosinski used *deep learning*, the currently most important machine learning method (LeCun et al., 2015). Broadly speaking, deep learning consists of training *deep neural networks*, that is, networks of interconnected units organized in multiple layers with a structure roughly similar to the cerebral cortex (i.e., with increasing abstraction levels). Kai-Fu Lee, former president of Google China and founder of Microsoft Research Asia, summarizes the revolutionary social implications of this method as follows:

> For decades, the artificial intelligence revolution always looked to be five years away. But with the development of deep learning over the past few years, that revolution has finally arrived. It will usher an era of massive productivity increases but also widespread disruptions in labor markets—and profound sociopsychological effects on people—as artificial intelligence takes over human jobs across all sorts of industries. (Lee, 2018, p. 5)

One of the main drawbacks of deep learning-trained models is their *intrinsic opacity*. A widespread way of pointing out the intrinsic opacity of these and other algorithms generated by machine learning is by meaningfully referring to them as *black boxes*: information goes in at one end, and out at the other; but little is known of the information processing that occurs in between and the representations contained in the algorithm. This intrinsic opacity has two main causes: lack of interpretability and high complexity.

Regarding the *lack of interpretability*, "interpretation" is a term that has several meanings, and often is used interchangeably with "explanation" (Gilpin et al., 2019). If we follow Montavon et al. (2018, p. 2), then interpretable means having at least one interpretation, and an interpretation is "the mapping of an abstract concept (e.g., a predicted class) into a domain that the human can make sense of" (Montavon et al., 2018, p. 2). Burrell (2016, p. 6) illustrates the problem of interpretability so defined with the example of a neural network for digit recognition: "the neural network doesn't, for example, break down handwritten digit recognition into subtasks that are readily intelligible to humans, such as identifying a horizontal bar, a closed oval shape, a diagonal line, etc." Some algorithms lack interpretability because their operations do not refer to anything that makes sense to us.

However, even if an algorithm is interpretable in this sense (i.e., it can be mapped to operations that make sense to us), its *high complexity* can render it impossible to interpret according to the way in which Gilpin et al. (2019) understand "interpretation." They claim that due to the finitude of human cognition and the high complexity of some algorithms (e.g., large deep neural networks) generated by machine learning, some of these may be necessarily opaque to some extent. The reason for this is that, when explaining complex phenomena, tension arises between two explanatory virtues that are potentially antagonistic: *interpretability* and *completeness*. "The goal of interpretability is to describe the internals of a system in a way that is understandable to humans… The goal of completeness is to describe the operation of a system in an accurate way" (Gilpin et al., 2019, p. 2). Explanations of some complex algorithms may not be both interpretable and complete at the same time: either the explanation is complete and therefore impossible to interpret due to its complexity, or it is interpretable at the expense of not being complete.

Intrinsic opacity poses a serious problem since it is an obstacle to understanding and improving the operations inside the black box, as well as ensuring that they comply with the law (Samek et al., 2017). To fix this, scientists are working on various techniques to increase the *explainability* (or *interpretability*, depending on the chosen terminology) of intrinsically opaque algorithms, such as deep neural networks (Burkart & Huber, 2021; Meske et al., 2022; Montavon et al., 2018). However, although the progress achieved is important, large deep neural networks remain very opaque: "One common viewpoint in the deep neural network community is that the level of interpretability and theoretical understanding needed for transparent explanations of large DNNs [deep neural networks] remains out of reach" (Gilpin et al., 2019, p. 8).

The technical reasons why deep learning is widely used despite its intrinsic opacity are its *unique capabilities* and its *greater effectiveness* over more explainable types of machine learning. The US military research agency DARPA (2016, p. 7) describes the problem of comparative effectiveness as follows: "There is an inherent tension between machine learning performance (predictive accuracy) and explainability; often the highest performing methods (e.g., deep learning) are the least explainable, and the most explainable (e.g., decision trees) are less accurate." Furthermore, machine learning methods are not always interchangeable because they have unique capabilities that make them suitable for certain tasks but not for others. For example, deep learning is suitable for image recognition, which is something that cannot be done with decision trees.

From the perspective of critical theory, this is the key to understanding AI's first opacity layer: due to their superior effectiveness and unique capabilities, some of the most opaque AI algorithms have a high instrumental value for the elites in their eternal struggle to conquer Mumford's (1970) *pentagon of power*—power, profit, productivity, property, and prestige. Deep learning expert Jeff Clune puts it simply: "This kind of a race to use the most powerful stuff—if the most powerful stuff is inscrutable and unpredictable and incomprehensible—somebody's probably going to use it anyway" (Scharre, 2018, p. 187). Giving up intrinsically more opaque AI techniques, such as deep learning, would involve relinquishing a power that is essential to accessing the new era of "massive productivity increases" announced by Lee (2018), as well as to obtaining population control instruments similar to the one built by Wang and Kosinski (2018) (e.g., image recognition systems). Faced with this dilemma, the companies and governments that control AI have decided to sacrifice explainability.

Therefore, AI's intrinsic opacity is not the result of an allegedly technical necessity that is morally neutral insofar as it is inevitable, but rather the consequence of a *contingent decision* made by the elites in accordance with their economic and political interests. The decision could be different. For example, governments ban medicines that do not meet certain standards of efficacy and safety (Bodewitz et al., 1989). Similarly, the use of some deep neural networks could be temporarily prohibited until the techniques necessary to meet certain standards of explainability have been developed. Of course, exceptions to this rule could be made. For example, opaque algorithms may be allowed for medical purposes, for their use could potentially benefit the whole society and not just the elites.

SECOND OPACITY LAYER: INTENTIONAL SECRECY

Suppose that the first opacity layer was reduced, first, by advances in techniques for improving the explainability of the most opaque AI algorithms, such as large deep neural networks, and second, as a result of restrictive policies mandating certain standards of explainability. Even in this scenario, there would be a second opacity layer: the one legally sanctioned and socially construed by those who control AI to prevent their competitors and the general public from understanding how their algorithms work.

The main players currently controlling AI include several large technology companies (e.g., Alphabet, Meta, Baidu, Tencent) and some governments of powerful nations (e.g., USA, China, UK) (Lee, 2018). All of them intentionally hide certain technical details of their AIs for three main reasons. First, for functionality, because revealing those details would compromise the effectiveness of those AIs. Second, for competitiveness, because the concealment of technology is essential to maintaining an advantage over rivals. Third, for reputation, because the disclosure of these programs and of the databases used for training their machine learning algorithms would damage their public image.

Regarding *functionality*, the effectiveness of some AIs depends on the concealment of certain technical details. For example, if Alphabet disclosed the exact criteria that Google Search's AI uses to rank results, then webmasters could find a way to satisfy these criteria—thus getting their pages to appear among the first results—but without meeting the quality parameters that these criteria are intended to measure. The consequence would be a decrease in the quality of search results, that would be plagued with links to opportunistic pages, which would harm both Alphabet and its users.

Regarding *competitiveness*, AI algorithms are, in some cases, protected by trade secrecy and intellectual property laws (Axhamn, 2022). Along with functionality, another reason why companies appeal to these laws not to disclose their algorithms is competitiveness (Diakopoulos, 2015). For example, Alphabet and Meta are the two giants of digital advertising in the West. For these companies, a small improvement in their AI technology used to profile and predict the consumption habits of Internet users can bring profits in the hundreds of millions of dollars: "Accurate estimation of the click-through rate (CTR) in sponsored ads significantly impacts the user search experience and businesses' revenue, even 0.1% of accuracy improvement would yield greater earnings in the hundreds of millions of dollars" (Ling et al., 2017, p. 689). For one of these companies, revealing the technical details of how its AI works to improve CTR by a few tenths would probably entail losing the competitive advantage derived from these details.

As can be seen, functionality and competitiveness seem to be legitimate reasons for the opacity as intentional secrecy of some AIs. It is obvious that sensitive technical details of certain algorithms should not be *openly* disclosed. However, this does not exclude the possibility of implementing delegated supervision mechanisms. Therefore, the solution to AI's opacity as intentional secrecy is not just transparency, but *qualified transparency*. Pasquale (2015, p. 161) summarizes the purpose and functioning of this form of transparency with a rhetorical question:

> When a website's ranking suddenly tumbled dozens of places, and has a plausible story about being targeted as a potential rival of Google, is it too much to ask for some third party to review the particular factors that led to the demotion?

The suggestion of authors such as Pasquale (2015) and Diakopoulos (2015) is the same that is currently applied in areas such as the aforementioned one of medicines: delegating the supervision task to government agencies, such as the Food and Drug Administration (FDA). However, the analogy has a second reading: because it is the same idea, there is no reason to expect that the result will be any better than what we currently observe: "American regulators tend to set up elaborate monitoring regimes, but then are unable to (or fail to) impose meaningful fines for clear wrongdoing" (Pasquale, 2015, p. 143). In the case of the technology companies that control AI, there are many precedents for sanctions due to wrongdoing. However, these sanctions are acceptable to them, and after apologizing, they usually persist in their bad practices: "Companies regularly push the envelope in online privacy, get caught lying about what they are doing, and treat the resulting fines as a (trivial) cost of doing business" (Pasquale, 2015, p. 144).

There seems to be a lack of political will on the part of governments to stop the abuses committed by some companies, particularly AI giants. One possible explanation is public-private collaboration to collect data. For example, in the United States, there are places called *fusion centers* where various government agencies meet with representatives of large private companies to exchange information about citizens (McQuade, 2019). This allows the public administration to avoid the limitations of the Fourth Amendment, which protects the privacy of citizens against the government:

> As a general matter, the Fourth Amendment does not apply to searches conducted by private parties who are not acting as agents of the government… As a result, no violation of the Fourth Amendment occurs when a private individual acting on his own accord conducts a search and makes the results available to law enforcement. (Milone, 2004, p. 94)

Beyond the United States, there is evidence that similar transfers of information from large technology companies to governments routinely take place in other countries (Cate et al., 2012).

In view of this collusion, it is not reasonable to expect governments to articulate effective mechanisms for the qualified transparency of AI (for a discussion on the EU's Draft AI Act, see Veale and Borgesius (2021)). The only realistic defense citizens have against AI's opacity as intentional secrecy is self-defense, such as, for example, through *reverse engineering*, as ProPublica did with COMPAS (Correctional Offender Management Profiling for Alternative Sanctions) to find out if this algorithm, used in some US courts to predict the probability of recidivism, included racial biases (Chouldechova, 2017). However, these kinds of practices are often illegal, since algorithms, as already mentioned earlier, are usually protected by trade secrecy and intellectual property legislation (Diakopoulos, 2014).

Finally, the third reason why AI hides behind a layer of intentional secrecy is to preserve the *reputation* of its masters. In this regard, *the quantity and the quality of the data* used to train machine learning algorithms are as important as their technical details. According to Lee (2018, p. 56):

> Training successful deep-learning algorithms requires computing power, technical talent, and lots of data. But of those three, it is the volume of data that will be the most important going forward. That's because once technical talent reaches a certain threshold, it begins to show diminishing returns. Beyond that point, data makes all the difference. Algorithms tuned by an average engineer can outperform those built by the world's leading expert if the average engineer has access to far more data.

If citizens knew the amount and granularity of the data about them in the possession of the companies and governments that control AI (Hazari & Brown, 2013), perhaps they would become aware that a great tool of repression is on its way. Speaking of the filing system used by the Okhrana, the secret police of Czarist Russia, Hannah Arendt describes how suspects were connected to their acquaintances through a visual code of geometric shapes and colors:

> Obviously the limitations of this method are set only by the size of the filing cards, and, theoretically, a gigantic single sheet could show the relations and cross-relationships of the entire population. And this is the utopian goal of the totalitarian secret police. (Arendt, 2017, p. 567)

At the time of Arendt's focus of study, that gigantic sheet was a "utopian goal." Today, its construction is underway and includes an amount of detailed personal data that the Okhrana could only wish for (Zuboff, 2019). Hiding its existence is essential for the companies and governments involved to preserve their reputations.

As the philosopher Peter-Paul Verbeek points out, technologies are not neutral instruments waiting for us to decide what use to give them, but rather they evoke certain behaviors: "[T]echnologies possess a 'script' in the sense that they can prescribe the actions of the actors involved" (Verbeek, 2006, p. 362). We should ask ourselves if those who control the new digital Okhrana's sheet are capable of resisting its *totalitarian script*.

THIRD OPACITY LAYER: TECHNOLOGICAL ILLITERACY

After reducing the first opacity layer, imagine that the second opacity layer was also thinned by implementing qualified transparency mechanisms that would result in the effective auditing of AI by government agencies, as well as due to the action of watchdog groups, capable of scrutinizing algorithms to some extent. Even granting these conditions, a third opacity layer would remain: the one posed by the *technological illiteracy* of most people.

Modern technology, unlike that of the ancient and medieval periods, requires non-intuitive knowledge to understand how it works. Ortega y Gasset (2009, p. 29) illustrates it this way:

> The feudal lord, for example, saw his horses shod, his lands plowed, and his wheat grinded. Today he not only does not usually see the corresponding techniques in action, but most of them are invisible. I mean that looking at them does not reveal their reality, does not make them intelligible. Seeing a factory may leave an aesthetic, emotional impression, but it does not teach congruently what is the technique of that factory, like seeing a car does not disclose the complicated plan of its machinery.

A car is complex, yet a computer is more complicated, and AI and machine learning are even more so.

To reduce this transcendental opacity layer, it is not necessary for the average person to understand all the technical details. They just need what Norman (1990) calls a *conceptual model*. There are many books that offer conceptual models of AI. For example, Domingos (2017) introduces *The Master Algorithm* with the explicit aim of providing the reader with a conceptual model of machine learning. The problem of all these books is similar to the one we have seen regarding large deep neural networks: AI is such a complex object that if the explanation is complete, then it is impossible to interpret for most, and if it is an interpretable simplification for most, then it is not complete.

Certainly, completeness is relative to the pragmatic interests of the subject (Van Fraassen, 1977). From the perspective of critical theory, the interest is *emancipatory*: the conceptual model must be sufficient *at least* to free oneself from the surveillance and manipulation performed by means of AI. Arguably, such a conceptual model requires a degree of completeness that is unintelligible to most. Although there are no empirical studies that prove this statement, there are many regarding the general population's level of scientific knowledge, and the results are so mediocre that it can be reasonably inferred from them that the majority would not be able to understand Domingos's (2017) book, which is a good example of a conceptual model sufficient for emancipatory purposes.

Science & Engineering Indicators is a biannual report produced by the National Science Foundation (NSF) of the United States that includes an assessment of public knowledge and attitudes towards science and technology in the country. One of its most interesting sections is the survey on the knowledge of scientific facts and processes. The *scientific facts* questionnaire consists of nine true-or-false or multiple-choice items (with only two options). The 2016 average score is 63% (National Science Foundation, 2018), a figure that has remained stable since 1992, and that is extremely poor if we consider that, due to the format, a coin flip would achieve 50%. As for the questions about *scientific processes*, they require reasoning and are also more open-ended, which makes most of the figures drop: 64% correctly answered the question on "understanding of probability," 51% on "understanding of an experiment," and 23% on "understanding of a scientific study." To provide a glimpse of the questions asked, only 48% correctly answered the query on "Electrons are smaller than atoms" (lower than a coin flip), and 59% correctly answered "It is the father's gene that decides whether the baby is a boy or a girl." As for other developed countries, some of their figures are included in this report and are similar.

The NSF questionnaire is designed "to assess whether an individual likely possessed the knowledge that might be needed to understand a quality newspaper's science section" (National Science Foundation, 2018, chapter 7, p. 33). Therefore, a (very) large part of the world population does not have enough scientific knowledge even to read a newspaper. In fact, if we dismantled the statistical deception behind the true-or-false question format (Bishop, 2004), we would discover that the extent of ignorance is even greater.

Given this evidence, it is reasonable to infer that AI is impossible to understand for most people due to its deep complexity. From the perspective of critical theory, this fact is important due to its political consequences, since the understanding of a fairly detailed conceptual model of the technical functioning of AI is a necessary condition for understanding its practical implications. If people do not know how AI works, then they do not know what those who control it can do with it. Consequently, they become easy prey for the extraordinary surveillance and manipulation capabilities of this technology.

You do not have to be someone special to become a target of these capabilities. Nowadays, we are all the focus of big companies and governments (Zuboff, 2019). The massive amounts of personal data produced by the growing digitization of the world are automatically processed by machine learning algorithms to build predictive models of our behavior. In this way, AI makes it possible to control human beings, just as science makes it possible to control nature, that is, by applying Comte's positivist proverb: to know in order to predict and to predict in order to control (*savoir pour prévoir et prévoir pour pouvoir*). Domingos (2017, p. 13) uses this analogy with science to explain machine learning:

> Machine learning is the scientific method on steroids. It follows the same process of generating, testing, and discarding or refining hypotheses. But while a scientist may spend his or her whole life coming up with and testing a few hundred hypotheses, a machine-learning system can do the same in a fraction of a second.

This ludicrous cost reduction, from a whole life to a fraction of a second, makes possible the automated application of the scientific method to millions of people to predict and control their behavior. This is what Cambridge Analytica did with data gathered by Facebook to help Donald Trump win the 2016 US presidential election (Hanna, 2018), and this is what the companies of surveillance capitalism do to turn us into consumer automatons (Zuboff, 2019).

AI is the culmination of "the entry of the individual (and no longer the species) into the field of knowledge" warned by Foucault (1995, p. 191): "*The examination, surrounded by all its documentary techniques, makes each individual a 'case': a case which at one and the same time constitutes an object for a branch of knowledge and a hold for a branch of power.*" Resistance to any power requires knowledge of its form and scope. Unfortunately, given the complexity of AI, only a minority can know its form and scope, and hence only a minority can resist its power.

CONCLUSION

AI is currently a widespread technology, and the forecast is that in the coming decades, it will penetrate our lives even more. Lee (2018, p. 13) compares it to electricity:

> [A] breakthrough technology on its own, and one that once harnessed can be applied to revolutionizing dozens of different industries. Just as nineteenth-century entrepreneurs soon began applying the electricity breakthrough to cooking food, lighting rooms, and powering industrial equipment, today's AI entrepreneurs are doing the same with deep learning.

The list set out in the introduction of everyday life situations in which AI intervenes will grow as capitalism discovers new ways to exploit it. The best placed to lead this task are the large companies that currently control this technology. Its business model consists of what Zuboff (2019, p. 200) calls *economies of action*:

> [M]achine processes are configured to intervene in the state of play in the real world among real people and things. These interventions are designed to enhance certainty by doing things: they nudge, tune, herd, manipulate, and modify behavior in specific directions.

There is no reason to think that this business model is going to die out any time soon. Therefore, it is foreseeable that AI will increase surveillance and manipulation.

To escape this fate, it is necessary (although not sufficient) for AI to be transparent since it is not possible to defend oneself from danger without knowing about it. Unfortunately, AI is opaque due to the three opacity layers discussed in this chapter: black-box algorithms, intentional secrecy, and technological illiteracy. Critical theory unveils that the first two are partially the consequence of decisions made by the elites to meet their interests. However, the third is not only the responsibility of the elites for the biased understanding of technology that they impose through educational laws (Petrina, 2000) or for the dumbing down that they produce through the cultural industry (Horkheimer & Adorno, 2002). Modern *lotus-eaters*, who live happily thanks to their many doses of the instruments used by the elites to monitor and manipulate them (e.g., Facebook) are guilty for their miserable situation. As I have argued elsewhere (Carabantes, 2021a, 2021b), it is necessary for someone to assume the role of Odysseus and *force them* to return to the ships.

FURTHER READING

O'Neil, C. (2016). *Weapons of math destruction: How big data increases inequality and threatens democracy*. Crown.
Russell, S. (2020). *Human compatible: Artificial intelligence and the problem of control*. Penguin Books.
Schneier, B. (2015). *Data and Goliath: The hidden battles to collect your data and control your world*. W. W. Norton & Company.

REFERENCES

Alpaydin, E. (2021). *Machine learning* (Revised and updated ed.). The MIT Press.
Arendt, H. (2017). *The origins of totalitarianism*. Penguin Books.

Axhamn, J. (2022). Transparency in automated algorithmic decision-making: Perspectives from the fields of intellectual property and trade secret law. In L. Colonna & S. Greenstein (Eds.), *Law in the era of artificial intelligence* (pp. 167–182). The Swedish Law and Informatics Research Institute. https://irilaw.org/2022/02/16/new-publication-nordic-yearbook-of-law-and-informatics-2020-2021

Bishop, G. (2004). *The illusion of public opinion: Fact and artifact in American opinion polls.* Rowman & Littlefield.

Bodewitz, H., Buurma, H., & de Vries, G. H. (1989). Regulatory science and the social management of trust in medicine. In W. E. Bijker, T. P. Hughes, & T. Pinch (Eds.), *The social construction of technological systems* (pp. 243–259). The MIT Press.

Burkart, N., & Huber, M. F. (2021). A survey on the explainability of supervised machine learning. *Journal of Artificial Intelligence Research, 70,* 245–317. https://doi.org/10.1613/jair.1.12228

Burrell, J. (2016). How the machine 'thinks': Understanding opacity in machine learning algorithms. *Big Data & Society, 3*(1), 1–12. https://doi.org/10.1177/2053951715622512

Carabantes, M. (2021a). Technological literacy for democracy: A cost-benefit analysis. *Philosophy & Technology, 34*(4), 701–715. https://doi.org/10.1007/s13347-020-00426-3

Carabantes, M. (2021b). Smart socio-technical environments: A paternalistic and humanistic management proposal. *Philosophy & Technology, 34*(4), 1531–1544. https://doi.org/10.1007/s13347 -021-00471-6

Cate, F. H., Dempsey, J. X., & Rubinstein, I. S. (2012). Systematic government access to private-sector data. *International Data Privacy Law, 2*(4), 195–199. https://doi.org/10.1093/idpl/ips027

Chouldechova, A. (2017). Fair prediction with disparate impact: A study of bias in recidivism prediction instruments. *Big Data, 5*(2), 153–163. https://doi.org/10.1089/big.2016.0047

Defense Advanced Research Projects Agency. (2016). *Broad agency announcement. Explainable Artificial Intelligence (XAI). DARPA-BAA-16-53.* DARPA. https://www.darpa.mil/attachments/DARPA-BAA-16-53.pdf

Diakopoulos, N. (2014). *Algorithmic accountability reporting: On the investigation of black boxes.* Tow Center for Digital Journalism. https://doi.org/10.7916/D8ZK5TW2

Diakopoulos, N. (2015). Algorithmic accountability: Journalistic investigation of computational power structures. *Digital Journalism, 3*(3), 398–415. https://doi.org/10.1080/21670811.2014.976411

Domingos, P. (2017). *The master algorithm: How the quest for the ultimate learning machine will remake our world.* Penguin Books.

Foucault, M. (1995). *Discipline and punish: The birth of the prison.* Vintage Books.

Gilpin, L. H., Bau, D., Yuan, B. Z., Bajwa, A., Specter, M., & Kagal, L. (2019). Explaining explanations: An overview of interpretability of machine learning. https://doi.org/10.48550/arXiv.1806.00069

Hanna, M. (2018). User data privacy: Facebook, Cambridge Analytica, and privacy protection. *Computer, 51*(8), 56–59. https://doi.org/10.1109/MC.2018.3191268

Hazari, S., & Brown, C. (2013). An empirical investigation of privacy awareness and concerns on social networking sites. *Journal of Information Privacy and Security, 9*(4), 31–51. https://doi.org/10.1080 /15536548.2013.10845689

Horkheimer, M., & Adorno, T. (2002). *Dialectic of Enlightenment.* Stanford University Press.

Kearns, M., & Roth, A. (2020). *The ethical algorithm: The science of socially aware algorithm design.* Oxford University Press.

LeCun, Y., Bengio, Y., & Hinton, G. (2015). Deep learning. *Nature, 521,* 436–444. https://doi.org/10 .1038/nature14539

Lee, K.-F. (2018). *AI superpowers: China, Silicon Valley, and the new world order.* Houghton Mifflin Harcourt.

Ling, X., Deng, W., Gu, C., Zhou, H., Li, C., & Sun, F. (2017). Model ensemble for click prediction in Bing Search ads. *Proceedings of the 26th International Conference on World Wide Web Companion,* 689–698. https://doi.org/10.1145/3041021.3054192

McQuade, B. (2019). *Pacifying the homeland: Intelligence fusion and mass supervision.* University of California Press.

Meske, C., Bunde, E., Schneider, J., & Gersch, M. (2022). Explainable artificial intelligence: Objectives, stakeholders, and future research opportunities. *Information Systems Management, 39*(1), 53–63. https://doi.org/10.1080/10580530.2020.1849465

Milone, M. (2004). Hacktivism: Securing the national infrastructure. In D. Clarke (Ed.), *Technology and terrorism* (pp. 79–114). Routledge.

Montavon, G., Samek, W., & Müller, K.-R. (2018). Methods for interpreting and understanding deep neural networks. *Digital Signal Processing, 73*, 1–15. https://doi.org/10.1016/j.dsp.2017.10.011

Mumford, L. (1970). *The pentagon of power*. Harcourt Brace Jovanovich.

National Science Foundation. (2018). *Science & engineering indicators 2018*. National Science Foundation. https://www.nsf.gov/statistics/2018/nsb20181/

Norman, D. (1990). *The design of everyday things*. Doubleday.

Ortega y Gasset, J. (2009). Introducción al curso ¿Qué es la técnica? In *Obras completas* (Vol. IX) (pp. 27–31). Taurus Ediciones.

Pasquale, F. (2015). *The black box society: The secret algorithms that control money and information*. Harvard University Press.

Petrina, S. (2000). The politics of technological literacy. *International Journal of Technology and Design Education, 10*, 181–206. https://doi.org/10.1023/A:1008919120846

Samek, W., Wiegand, T., & Müller, K.-R. (2017). Explainable artificial intelligence: Understanding, visualizing and interpreting deep learning models. https://doi.org/10.48550/arXiv.1708.08296

Scharre, P. (2018). *Army of none: Autonomous weapons and the future of war*. W. W. Norton & Company.

Van Fraassen, B. C. (1977). The pragmatics of explanation. *American Philosophical Quarterly, 14*(2), 143–150.

Veale, M., & Borgesius, F. Z. (2021). Demystifying the draft EU artificial intelligence act—Analysing the good, the bad, and the unclear elements of the proposed approach. *Computer Law Review International, 22*(4), 97–112.

Verbeek, P.-P. (2006). Materializing morality: Design ethics and technological mediation. *Science, Technology, & Human Values, 31*(3), 361–380.

Wang, Y., & Kosinski, M. (2018). Deep neural networks are more accurate than humans at detecting sexual orientation from facial images. *Journal of Personality and Social Psychology, 114*(2), 246–257. https://doi.org/10.1037/pspa0000098

Zuboff, S. (2019). *The age of surveillance capitalism: The fight for a human future at the new frontier of power*. Profile Books.

38. How to critique the GDPR: when data protection is turned against the working class
Carl Öhman

INTRODUCTION

We live, as Zuboff (2015) has it, in an age of *surveillance capitalism*, under an economic regime that has opened up entirely new realms of human life for exploitation. In the wake of Web 2.0 and the tech empires that have come to dominate it, our life worlds are increasingly designed to decrease our autonomy and increase the time we spend looking at ads (Fuchs & Sevignani, 2013). Even our spare time has become productive labor in the sense that we are always engaged in the production of the digital economy's most precious commodity— surplus attention (see Williams, 2018). As a consequence, the majority of a person's social life—their photo albums, social connections, messaging logs, memories, and so on—are now the property of the digital platforms within which they dwell, which puts the modern working class in a uniquely precarious position.

Meanwhile, the AI boom of the past decade has further catalyzed these new forms of exploitation and has enabled new kinds of surveillance of, and predation on, the most precarious members of the working classes (see Crawford, 2022 for an overview). For example, unlike early forms of social media, where users would only be exposed to content of their conscious choosing, today's online world is carefully curated by algorithms calibrated to keep users within the network to maximize their exposure to ads. What you see in your feed is not what is best for you, or even what you have chosen, but what is most likely to keep you scrolling, generating more data. In a similar vein, AI is deployed to target vulnerable populations who are less equipped to critically review the content they are exposed to (see O'Neil, 2017). Examples range from targeting individuals living in poor zip code areas with ads for "private universities" and hugely unfavorable loans, to locking out certain populations from getting a mortgage or sorting out candidates from job applications. In short, the vast volume of data produced by everyday life, in combination with the increasingly sophisticated means to analyze these data, have created entirely new forms of vulnerability.

It is uncontroversial to say that these technologies must be further regulated. Several initiatives and bills have already been passed to this end, and more, such as the EU's Artificial Intelligence Act, are forthcoming. Among the existing ones, however, the European Union's General Data Protection Regulation (GDPR) is rightly considered a landmark. Unlike its predecessors, and unlike many of its cousins in other parts of the world, the GDPR actually has "teeth" to quote Golla (2017). Or, as Zarsky (2017, p. 995) has it, it is "the most comprehensive and forward looking piece of legislation to address the challenges facing data protection in the digital age." Covering one of the world's largest markets, the ambition has been to set the standard for the rest of the world in terms of norms on data protection, making it a particularly interesting case for general debates around data protection.

The GDPR is clearly designed to target "Big Tech." And rightly so. Battling the technology giants is an admirable mission, which should be supported by any critic of the capitalist economy in general, and of Big Tech's market dominance in particular. (As a digital ethicist, I have certainly been part of the choir celebrating it). Yet, as confirmed by a plethora of scholarly commentary, the law is not without flaws. Even since long before it was enforced, it has been accused of being too fuzzy and failing to provide legal certainty (see Traung, 2012), and the critique has continued. Shyy (2020, p. 157) calls it a "lose-lose dilemma," pointing out that it is "both ineffective in protecting consumer privacy and burdensome on businesses of all sizes [but particularly smaller ones, see (McAllister, 2017)]." Golla (2017, p. 78) finds that "the issue of legal uncertainty will cause headaches" pointing out that some articles "are not suitable for effective practical application." Kaminski and Malgieri (2020), focusing on Data Protection Impact Assessments (DPIA), criticize the GDPR for putting too much faith in data controllers, while not mandating public disclosure. In addition to this, there is a long list of scholarly publications pointing to various aspects and demographics that are omitted from the GDPR. Donovan (2020), for example, finds that it fails to protect children's privacy from parents oversharing their personal information on social media (so-called "sharenting"). Öhman and Watson (2019, p. 9) criticize the explicit omittance of digital remains (data left behind by deceased data subjects) from the law (see Recital 27). Kuru (2021) stresses that the GDPR fails completely to protect genetic groups, despite genetic data being among the most sensitive. Willemson (n.d.) argues that the GDPR fails to adequately address the issue of partial identification, and Jordan (2021, p. 43) criticizes it for not adequately incentivizing pseudonymization. The list goes on …

The above critiques of the GDPR are important and will likely lead to future improvements, making the law more inclusive and interpretable. However, neither the identifying of unclear articles nor the highlighting of missing aspects/demographics qualifies as *critique*, at least not in the philosophical sense of the word. When Kant critiques pure reason, he is not merely pointing out deficiencies in the theories of his contemporaries; when Marx critiques political economy, he is not merely pointing to room for improvement in the way the economy works or is studied. Rather, what critique means is a deconstruction of the object of study, so as to expose its inner contradictions and—as in the case of Marx—its inherent, structural power asymmetries. To be critical in this sense, is, as Horkheimer (1982, p. 244) puts it, to "liberate human beings from the circumstances that enslave them" by exposing the ideological nature of those circumstances.

The goal of this chapter is to illustrate what such a critical reading of the GDPR and its consequences might look like. In doing so, I shall adopt a *class perspective*, understood in a broad (yet mainly economic) sense. The purpose of such a perspective is not merely to add another marginalized identity to be considered in the GDPR. It is asking the fundamental question of *who performs the labour*—an *ideological* critique. Unlike most previous criticisms, my argument is not that the GDPR lacks sufficient force, but that it is demanding too much from the wrong people. A similar argument has already been posed by Shyy (2020), but unlike her, my focus is not on how the law affects business or innovation, but on how it affects *workers*. More specifically, I point to three aspects that deserve closer scrutiny. First, I call for scrutiny of the individualist ideology that underpins the GDPR's conception of privacy. Second, I call for an analysis of how the law forces workers (e.g., in the education sector) to become data managers, adding to an already burdensome list of tasks outside of their ordinary job description. Finally, I draw attention to the law's effects on the organizational ability of the working class, specifically how it threatens the free association of workers by imposing demands designed for Big Tech on the small not-for-profit associations that make up the backbone of the labor movement. Taken together, these implications for working people risk undermining their long-term support for data protection legislation, which is highly unfortunate since legislative initiatives like the GDPR are the only thing that can protect them from further exploitation driven by AI and surveillance capitalism. I conclude by pointing to some possible routes forward.

THE INDIVIDUALIST IDEOLOGY OF THE GDPR

The first angle to explore for a critical reading of the GDPR is the individualist ideology that underpins the law. The observation that the GDPR is individualist is in itself not new. As noted by Costello (2022, p. 11) it is more or less considered the "zenith of individualised conceptions of privacy," in that it views any given piece of personal information as belonging to one discernable individual and to that individual alone (an ill fit with, for example, genomic data).

Perhaps the most obvious example, and certainly the one with the biggest everyday implications, is the adoption of the so-called "Notice and Choice"-approach. Notice and Choice is the idea that every usage of a person's information must be communicated to him/her via a *notice*, i.e., a piece of information about how the person's data will be processed and be subject to a *choice* (reject/accept the proposed term) made by the person in question. It is the reason one cannot use the web without accepting a flood of cookie pop-ups.

In the GDPR, the requirement to obtain informed consent is formulated as an onus placed on data controllers (see Recital 32 of the GDPR). And formally it is. Yet, the ones doing the actual work are ordinary internet users whose usage of the web is predicated on either the countless hours of labor in reading privacy notices, or a mindless acceptance of whatever it is that data controllers want to do with their data. Legal scholarship has been highly skeptical of the efficiency of Notice and Choice for decades (see Cate, 2010; Jordan, 2021; Utz et al., 2019; Warner, 2020). Cate (2010), for example, finds that it is the "worst of all worlds"—privacy protection is not enhanced while individuals and businesses pay the cost of parsing through mounds of bureaucracy. Empirical evidence collected after the implementation of the GDPR corroborates this verdict. It is impossible to read through all the privacy policies one is asked to consent to on a daily basis without massively slowing down one's browsing. (A 2008 study by McDonald and Cranor suggested that reading all the privacy policies one encounters would require 25 full-time work days a year. The number presumably being much larger today.) Moreover, a majority of websites use various forms of nudging techniques to make users click accept (see Utz et al., 2019), and few interfaces meet even the basic requirements set out by the GDPR, strictly interpreted. For instance, Utz et al. (2019, p. 986) found that, when given an opt-in option, rather than the standard opt-out, only 0.1% of users consent to fully sharing cookie data:

> GDPR's principles of data protection by default and purposed-based consent would require websites to use consent notices that would actually lead to less than 0.1 % of users actively consenting to the use of third-party cookies.

In the face of such numbers, no serious person can genuinely believe that the Notice and Choice approach leads to the realization of anything like individual privacy. It merely makes browsing more annoying.

A potent counterargument, of course, is that such a critique is misplaced. The GDPR is not to blame for the pop-ups—industry is. Tech companies have been harvesting people's data for decades, using their attention as unpaid labor, but have done so in the dark, without people understanding just how much of their data is taken from them. The GDPR does not change this, it merely turns on the light so that people can see what is going on. Even if privacy notices are annoying and ineffective, they may at least raise awareness of the magnitude of the issue. This is a fair point. Yet, it is also a reminder of why a critical reading requires a deeper analysis than merely pointing to the dysfunction of an approach like Notice and Choice. Rather, we must see that the GDPR's complete allocation of agency (and thus responsibility) to the individual is a feature, not a bug, of its individualist conception of privacy. As noted by Edwards and Veale (2017, p. 66), individual privacy control is essentially working around a "liberal paradigm," where the economic man reigns supreme. Or, framed differently, in the liberal paradigm of privacy, data protection is a private, not a collective good. As Warner (2020, p. 193) notes "it envisions people giving or withholding consent independently of knowledge of what others are choosing and without any mechanism of coordination with them." Like liberalism sees wages not as a matter of collective coordination, but as a matter that concerns only an individual employer and employee, the decisions a person makes around their data are seen as theirs and theirs alone, and no one else needs to be bothered. In the liberal paradigm, collective coordination is unnecessary, even undesirable.

In conjunction with the exposure of its individualist assumptions, a critical reading of the GDPR also calls for scrutiny of the resources required to interpret the various terms and agreements one is presented with. Under the liberal paradigm of privacy control, it is assumed that every data subject has equal access to information about, and is equally intellectually equipped to analyze, the various privacy notices they are faced with. This is obviously false. The ability to assess and interpret cookie pop-ups and privacy policies, as well as general awareness of the GDPR, is strongly stratified within the population, with education, occupation, and age being the strongest predictors of awareness (Rughiniş et al., 2021, p. 5). White-collar workers, it seems, have a better understanding of the law than blue-collar ones. Yet, since the privacy of the latter is viewed solely as a matter of individual preference, the former are encouraged not to care.

In summary, a proper critique of the GDPR requires that we do more than point to its dysfunctions as a means to "improve" it, but that we scrutinize the ideology that underpins it. Above, I have highlighted some of the ways in which this has been and can be done. To be clear, my point is not that current critiques of the GDPR and its efficiency are misguided or insufficient, but that, by and large, they aim to improve it rather than critique it. Critiquing it, I maintain, means deconstructing it to expose its inner contradictions and power asymmetries, to read it as a *political* document that reproduces a liberal paradigm of what privacy is and who it is for.

WORKING CONDITIONS

A second angle for a critical reading to explore is how the GDPR affects workers in their daily professional life, i.e., how it affects them *as workers* rather than mere citizens or rights-holding subjects. As we have seen, the law places the onus of safeguarding privacy on data controllers, i.e., businesses, organizations, and governmental agencies. Yet, as critical readers, we ought to ask, who is performing the actual labor within those organizations? And what kind of responsibilities fall on those individuals?

For the big, data-rich companies that already process large volumes of data, every employee involved in the core business is more or less a data manager in some capacity. The law merely tells them to do it a bit differently. To these businesses, personal data almost always appear as part of lists or large data sets, to which it is relatively easy to apply new protocols and standards. Yet, the GDPR does not just cover companies and organizations whose main business is data, but *all* of society, from the biggest corporate giants to the local school and community centers, and the people working for the latter type are not data managers. Their dealing with "personal data" is not algorithmic nor even in the form of lists and data sets. It is dispersed over emails, computer files, and physical documents, to which no simple protocols apply. Insofar as they deal with any type of personal data, even if it is only a name in an email, the GDPR considers them data managers nevertheless.

One example is teachers. Consider the following scenario. A conflict emerges between a parent and their child's school. The parent claims that the child has unfairly been given a lower mark than they deserve. To prove this, he demands from the school to see *all* personal data they have on his child, a right granted by the GDPR (see Subject Access Request in Recital 63). This may seem far-fetched, yet as pointed out by Buckley et al. (2021, p. 1), it is not too uncommon that "Disgruntled customers and ex-employees weaponise Subject Access Requests (SAR) as a tool of retaliation." In order to comply with the law, the teachers must go through the entire email folders of each employee of the school to collect materials that may contain the child's name or other forms of data. But they must also locate every test the child has written, search all internal documents (paper and digital), and look up yearbooks and handwritten notes taken during, for example, oral exams. Such a search could literally take days. If the parent then demands the information be destroyed (a right granted by Recital 65 of the GDPR), an even more tedious task awaits in figuring out which data ought to be destroyed and which are essential to the official mission of the school. A lawyer may contest this hypothetical case, claiming that this is not required by the law. But the school staff are not lawyers, and they cannot afford the fines in case they have made the wrong interpretation. Better be safe than sorry.

Schools are but one example, however. There is evidence to suggest that the GDPR has had negative effects on the professional life of a considerable share of the population. It is difficult to find reliable data on this topic, especially with regard to how differently various professions are affected, but an Irish survey from 2021 (McKenna & Lavery, 2021) shows that, since 2020, the belief that compliance with the GDPR places an excessive administrative burden on organizations has grown by 16 percentage points (53% to 69%); 57% say they are concerned or very concerned with being fined for failing to comply with the GDPR, compared with 46% in 2020. Though limited in scope, these results corroborate findings from, for example, Strycharz et al. (2020, p. 21) who find that "In professional life, respondents who worked in different sectors felt that the regulation negatively influenced their daily work." One of the respondents in the survey writes that

> I work in a school and we cannot even take pictures of the kids on a trip any more or I cannot make a test copy of production database any more. The rules are so invasive because they hinder routine operational processes.

The point here is that, whereas the law is designed to equip individuals with legal tools to assert their rights against tech corporations, it ultimately places the biggest burden on public sector workers who rightly do not see themselves as data managers. I write "biggest burden" because the burden must be assessed in relation to how well an organization is equipped to handle it, both in terms of organizational capacity and individual know-how.

In addition to placing unrealistic expectations on individual public sector workers, it is plausible that these bureaucratic demands will ultimately undermine people's support for data protection. Note that, to the teacher cited above, it is the GDPR, not the corporations that harvest personal data, that are experienced as "invasive." The belief that compliance with the GDPR will be beneficial for organizations' relations with their employees, customers, and other stakeholders in the long term has fallen by 5 percentage points (76% to 71%). On some specific requirements relating to international data transfers, fewer than half (47%) agreed that these additional requirements were even beneficial for individuals whose data are transferred (McKenna & Lavery, 2021).

In summary, a critical evaluation of the GDPR should explore further how it affects workers empirically in their daily professional lives. It should ask, who is doing the heavy lifting? And for whose sake? Is the individual right of SAR worth the pressure on public sector workers? The point is not the particular answer to these questions, but the change of perspectives.

THE FREE ASSOCIATION OF WORKERS

The final angle to consider is how the GDPR affects the organizational ability of the working class. That is, working-class people as a collective movement united by shared economic interests. Popular movements, including trade unions, housing cooperatives, sports clubs, teetotaler associations, and so on, have been integral to organized class struggle, the shaping of class identity, as well as the overall project of Western democracy, particularly in the Nordics. These are organizations that, in many instances, depend on volunteers, that operate in that semi-formal space that exists between colleagues, neighbors, or friends—a space where roles such as consumer and employee are completely inadequate. They are not professional, yet not "household" or "personal" either, meaning they are not part of the GDPR's household exception (see Recital 18). The effects of the GDPR on these types of associations should be a given object of scrutiny for critical reading.

Though academic literature is sparse when it comes to the effects of the GDPR on civil society, a couple of reports are available at the EU level. The European Union Agency for Fundamental Rights (FRA) (2019), for instance, conducted a survey with around 100 civil society actors on how the GDPR has affected their work. Although 66% of the respondents claimed to have either a fair or expert level of knowledge on the topic, 77% reported that their organization was facing challenges in their implementation of the new requirements; 89% said that the implementation meant either "a great deal of effort" (38%) or "some effort" (59) on behalf of their organization. Roughly four in ten report that the law had decreased the efficiency of their work. These findings are supported by a second report by the Open Society Foundations (Franz et al., 2020), which is based on a smaller sample (52 respondents) but also contains qualitative interviews and legal analysis. It concludes that "when added to a growing compliance burden already encompassing a raft of NGO transparency and accountability requirements, GDPR regulations make it harder for civil society organizations to concentrate on their core activities" (Franz et al., 2020, p. 6). All in all, the law seems to have placed a large burden on civil society actors.

Keep in mind that the organizations included in these surveys are by and large professionals. They are advocacy groups working at high levels in one or several countries. All of them have employees, and many of them have a designated data protection officer. This is not representative of most of the organizations that make up the popular movements of the working class. Indeed, it is implausible that 66% of housing cooperatives, football clubs, or local trade union clubs have access to fair or expert knowledge on what the GDPR requires of them. Nevertheless, the law applies to them just as much as it applies to industry giants like Google and Facebook, which makes it incredibly difficult for local organic communities to organize if they want to abide by the law.

For illustration, consider the following scenario. Alice is on the committee for her housing cooperative. She has been put in charge of rearranging the cooperative's parking lot. As part of this, ten other members are to switch parking spaces with one another. To do this, the committee somehow needs to coordinate the move. Alice obtains the phone numbers of the concerned members from the yellow pages, so the most commonsense solution would be to simply share these with the ten members and let them decide the best time to switch places. However, she has not obtained explicit consent from the ten members to share their numbers with anyone beyond the committee. According to the GDPR, this means that she cannot simply give out the members' numbers but must first send each of them forms to sign, giving their consent to share their numbers. Alice cannot see the point of such precautions, especially since all of the information can be found in the yellow pages, or online equivalents, but she knows that the GDPR formally requires it, and the cooperative cannot afford any fines.[1]

As anyone engaged in civil society knows by now, situations like these make it incredibly difficult to organize, since there is always the threat (no matter how unlikely) that one will be fined for mishandling members' "data." I write "data" in quotation marks because when we speak of data we are normally referring to lists or sets of data about multiple individuals, not an occasional name, number, or address in an email. According to the GDPR, however, even such unstructured, informal information must now be treated with (almost) the same care as the vast data sets harbored by say Google or Facebook (see Art. 4 [1]). But while Big Tech has the resources and protocols to properly deal with its data, civil society has only the organic judgment of the individuals who constitute it. Several respondents from Strycharz et al.'s (2020, p. 22) survey identify this as a particularly pressing problem. One calls the law "completely unworkable for individuals in hobby clubs." Another one states that it "has a lot of negative influence on my club – many things are not possible any more." Almost one in six says that the GDPR has negative consequences.

The point here is not that there is a ton of evidence that the GDPR harms civil society, even if there is some. Rather, my point is that a critical reading of the GDPR cannot be limited to highlighting where the law is not forceful *enough* in restricting data processing, that in its liberal eagerness to grant individuals the right to control their data, it overlooks the needs and reality of the interpersonal, semi-formal communities that form the foundation of popular movements. Or, expressed differently, in its battle against the exploitation of individual data

---

[1] In Scandinavian countries, which have a rather unique approach to privacy—every person's home address, phone number, birthday, and so on is available a mere Google search away—the situation is even more bizarre.

subjects, the GDPR has resolved every human community into the regime of data protection, and in place of the numberless indefeasible variations of human relationships has set up that single, unconscionable relationship—that between data subject and data controller.

WHAT DO WE LEARN?

Let me once again stress that the above critique of the GDPR should not be read as some form of assessment of its general quality as a regulatory document. In fact, part of the message is that such an objective assessment is impossible at best, and misleading at worst. The GDPR, like any other regulatory document, is a *political* artifact, and in the realm of the political, understood as a power struggle between social groups, better and worse are relative concepts. The purpose of critique is to expose this political nature and to counter the document's claim of being neutral. The three proposed angles are meant as an illustration of how such a critical reading of the GDPR might look like. They are not exhaustive nor fully developed, but they do point to promising points of departure for a critical reading that goes beyond merely highlighting deficiencies. I should add that I am not a trained lawyer. There may be misinterpretations. Then again, whether the angles above are actually legally sound is almost a separate matter—the point is the *angle* itself.

AI and other forms of automatic data processing techniques expose the working class to entirely new forms of exploitation. We work even when we are not at work and are constantly nudged, judged, and manipulated by forces over which we have little insight, and for which we have no right to proper explanations (Wachter et al., 2017). The only reasonable conclusion is that AI and other forms of data processing must be subject to tougher and stricter regulation, and documents like the GDPR are the only way to do it. Yet, the consequences of such legislative efforts will likely stretch far beyond the intended sectors and practices. Indeed, as I have tried to illustrate above, those who pay the highest price for the EU's data protection regime may be those it is meant to protect. We need a critical reading to highlight these effects, a reading that does not merely point to the blind spots and insufficiencies in our attempts to regulate AI and the power of Big Tech, but also where those attempts go too far and even harm the very people they are supposed to protect. Without such a critique, data protection is at risk of losing support from large segments of the population. In an age of surveillance capitalism, nothing could be more dangerous.

DISCLOSURE

This work was partially supported by the Wallenberg AI, Autonomous Systems and Software Program—Humanities and Social Sciences funded by the Marianne and Marcus Wallenberg Foundation and the Marcus and Amalia Wallenberg Foundation.

BIBLIOGRAPHY

Buckley, G., Caulfield, T., & Becker, I. (2021). *"It may be a pain in the backside but…"* Insights into the *impact of GDPR on business after three years.* http://arxiv.org/abs/2110.11905
Cate, F. (2010). The limits of decision and choice. *IEEE Security & Privacy, 8*(2), 59–62. https://doi.org/10.1109/MSP.2010.84

Costello, R. (2022). Genetic data and the right to privacy: Towards a relational theory of privacy? *Human Rights Law Review, 22*(1), 1–23. https://doi.org/10.1093/hrlr/ngab031

Crawford, K. (2022). *Atlas of AI: Power, politics, and the planetary costs of artificial intelligence.* Yale University Press.

Donovan, S. (2020). "Sharenting": The forgotten children of the GDPR. *Peace Human Rights Governance, 4*(1), 35–59. https://doi.org/10.14658/pupj-phrg-2020-1-2

Edwards, L., & Veale, M. (2017). Slave to the algorithm? Why a right to explanationn is probably not the remedy you are looking for. In *SSRN Electronic Journal* (Vol. 2017). https://doi.org/10.2139/ssrn.2972855

Focus, F. (2019). *The general data protection regulation – One year on. Civil society: Awareness, opportunities and challenges.* https://doi.org/10.1007/978-3-319-57959-7

Franz, V., Hayes, B., & Hannah, L. (2020). *Civil society organizations and general data protection regulation compliance: Challenges, opportunities, and best practices.* https://www.opensociety foundations.org/publications/civil-society-organizations-and-general-data-protection-regulation -compliance?utm_campaign=osffbpg&utm_source=facebook.com&utm_medium=referral

Fuchs, C., & Sevignani, S. (2013). What is digital labour? What is digital work? What's their difference? And why do these questions matter for understanding social media? *TripleC, 11*, 237–293.

Golla, S. (2017). Is data protection law growing teeth? The current lack of sanctions in data protection law and administrative fines under the GDPR. *Jipitec, 8*(1), 70–78. https://www.jipitec.eu/issues/jipitec-8-1-2017/4533

Horkheimer, M. (1982). *Critical theory.* Seabury Press.

Jordan, S. (2021). A proposal for notice and choice requirements of a new consumer privacy law. In *Federal Communications Law Journal*, Forthcoming.

Kaminski, M. E., & Malgieri, G. (2020). Multi-layered explanations from algorithmic impact assessments in the GDPR. *FAT* 2020 - Proceedings of the 2020 Conference on Fairness, Accountability, and Transparency*, 68–79. https://doi.org/10.1145/3351095.3372875

Kuru, T. (2021). Genetic data: The Achilles' heel of the GDPR? *European Data Protection Law Review, 7*(1), 45–58. https://doi.org/10.21552/edpl/2021/1/8

McAllister, C. (2017). What about small businesses? The GDPR and its consequences for small U.S.-based companies. *The Brooklyn Journal of Corporate, Financial and Commercial Law, 12*(1), 21.

McDonald, A., & Cranor, L. F. (2008). The cost of reading privacy policies. *I/S: A Journal of Law and Policy for the Information Society, 4*, 540–565.

McKenna, L., & Lavery, P. (2021). *General data protection regulation: A survey of the impact of GDPR and its effect on organisations in Ireland.* https://www.mccannfitzgerald.com/knowledge/gdpr/a -survey-of-the-impact-of-gdpr-and-its-effect-on-organisations-in-ireland-2022

O'Neil, C. (2017). *Weapons of math destruction: How big data increases inequality and threatens democracy.* Broadway Books.

Öhman, C. J., & Watson, D. (2019). Are the dead taking over Facebook? A big data approach to the future of death online. *Big Data and Society, 6*(1), 1–13. https://doi.org/10.1177/2053951719842540

Rughiniș, R., Rughiniș, C., Vulpe, S. N., & Rosner, D. (2021). From social netizens to data citizens: Variations of GDPR awareness in 28 European countries. *Computer Law and Security Review, 42*. https://doi.org/10.1016/j.clsr.2021.105585

Shyy, S. (2020). The GDPR's lose-lose dilemma: Minimal benefits to data privacy & significant burdens on business. *UC Davis Business Law Journal, 20*(2), 137–164.

Strycharz, J., Ausloos, J., & Helberger, N. (2020). Data protection or data frustration? Individual perceptions and attitudes towards the GDPR. *European Data Protection Law Review, 6*(3), 407–421. https://doi.org/10.21552/edpl/2020/3/10

Traung, P. (2012). The proposed new EU general data protection regulation. *Computer Law Review International, 13*(2), 33–49. https://doi.org/10.9785/ovs-cri-2012-33

Utz, C., Degeling, M., Fahl, S., Schaub, F., & Holz, T. (2019). (Un)informed consent: Studying GDPR consent notices in the field. *Proceedings of the ACM Conference on Computer and Communications Security*, 973–990. https://doi.org/10.1145/3319535.3354212

Wachter, S., Mittelstadt, B., & Floridi, L. (2017). Why a right to explanation of automated decision-making does not exist in the general data protection regulation. *International Data Privacy Law, 7*(2), 76–99. https://doi.org/10.1093/idpl/ipx005

Warner, R. (2020). Notice and choice must go: The collective control alternative. *SSRN Electronic Journal.* https://doi.org/10.2139/ssrn.3566630

Willemson, J. (n.d.). Fifty shades of personal data – Partial re-identification and GDPR. *Cybernetica AS.* https://research.cyber.ee/~janwil/publ/50shades.pdf

Williams, J. (2018). *Stand out of our light: Freedom and resistance in the attention economy.* Cambridge University Press.

Zarsky, T. (2017). Incompatible: The GDPR in the age of big data. *Seton Hall Law Review, 47*(4), 2.

Zuboff, S. (2015). Big other: Surveillance capitalism and the prospects of an information civilization. *Journal of Information Technology, 30*(1), 75–89. https://doi.org/10.1057/jit.2015.5

39. Four facets of AI transparency

Stefan Larsson, Kashyap Haresamudram,
Charlotte Högberg, Yucong Lao, Axel Nyström,
Kasia Söderlund and Fredrik Heintz

INTRODUCING A MULTIFACETED CONCEPT

"Transparency" is one of those contemporary concepts that, linked to AI, spans technical, legal, and ethical – and more – perspectives. While transparency is part of a wider trend in international governance (Koivisto, 2022), it is also one of the most common concepts in the recent surge of ethics guidelines on AI that has been developed by a wide variety of entities from governments, non-governmental organisations (NGOs), and large companies to multi-stakeholder groups (Jobin et al., 2019). Often, it is framed as a mechanism for promoting accountability (Diakopolous, 2020). In recent EU policy on AI, there is a focus on risk assessments and auditing (Felländer et al., 2022; Mökander et al., 2021), with an emphasis on "human-centricity" (Larsson, 2020; Larsson et al., 2020), implicating how European countries strategise about AI (Robinson, 2020), their national mandates, and initiatives for various sectors, not the least the public sector (de Bruijn et al., 2022).

For some of the origin of transparency as a governance tool, first, one can point to the policy debates on anti-corruption pushing for corporate and governmental transparency in the late 1990s and early 2000s (Forssbaeck & Oxelheim, 2014; Koivisto, 2022), but some of its recent support in EU policy could arguably also be explained by its positive connotations as metaphorically linked to openness (Koivisto, 2022; Larsson & Heintz, 2020). As a reaction, it has also spurred the more aesthetically and politically framed emerging field of *critical transparency studies* (cf. Alloa, ed., 2022; Koivisto, 2022), which we draw from in order to outline some of the implications of "AI Transparency" in contemporary policy debates. Recently, and second, transparency – particularly in terms of algorithmically focused "explainability" (cf. Haresamudram et al., 2022) – has been put forward as a key element to ensure that AI performs well, fullfills its promise, as well as strengthens public trust in AI (cf. Jacovi et al., 2021). In this chapter, we describe why common approaches to explainability constitute a narrow concept and propose how they can be complemented for a richer understanding of its consequences for policy.

By drawing from critical examinations of AI transparency, such as Jenna Burrell's three forms of opacity (2016) and Ida Koivisto's account of the transparency paradox (2022), this chapter develops four facets of AI transparency. First, we critically examine the growing body of literature on *explainable AI*, which stems from a call to make machine-learning processes more understandable. Second, inspired by a recent critique (Miller, 2019) that this field draws too little from how humans actually understand explanations, we see a need to break out the explicit *mediation* of machine learning processes that this leads to. Similarly, Burrell discusses these two facets in terms of a "mismatch between mathematical procedures of machine learning algorithms and human styles of semantic interpretation" (Burrell, 2016, p. 3). In addition, while Burrell has a narrower focus on technical illiteracy, mainly pointing to coding abilities, we – third – expand by drawing from the rich field of *literacy* studies for our third facet. Fourth, and last, we point to transparency as a form of governance in itself and place this analysis within a legal framework by pointing to how the law is often tasked with balancing different interests. Law is thereby making *trade-offs* between, for example, the public need to supervise and assess the use of corporate and governmental AI systems, on the one hand, and security needs demanding secrecy or legally supported notions of secrecy to ensure competition, on the other.

FOUR FACETS

In this section, we develop the analysis of the four facets of particular relevance to AI Transparency.

Transparency as Explanation

The notion that complex AI systems entail "black box" issues that demand better *explainability methodologies* has been established for some time, and constitutes a central aspect of AI transparency (Larsson, 2019). While definitions vary, explainable AI (XAI) can generally be considered to produce "details or reasons to make its functioning clear or easy to understand" (Barredo Arrieta et al., 2020, p. 85). The challenge of interpreting and explaining AI systems has attracted growing attention as the methods, such as deep learning, have increased in complexity (cf. Qi et al., 2021), but also as AI has been applied to more diverse audiences and groups of users (cf. Ribera & Lapedriza, 2019). Explanations by XAI models can take different forms, such as texts by generated captions, visualisations by generated images, local explanations by gradient maps/heat maps, or by generated nearest neighbours and counterfactuals (cf. Lipton, 2018; de Vries, 2021). The rapid growth in XAI research is, at least in part, motivated by a need to maintain trust between the human user and the AI (Jacovi et al., 2021), a notion also echoed in European policy (cf. Larsson et al., 2020).

Several attempts have been made to develop taxonomies of explainability techniques and their desiderata, with common axes of explanations including *global* versus *local* (explaining the model versus explaining a specific prediction), *model specific* versus *model agnostic* techniques (in regard to which set of AI models the explainability technique applies to), and *model complexity*. Another common distinction is between "inherently explainable" models (often called "transparent" or "interpretable"), and so-called post-hoc techniques that attempt to explain the behaviour of an otherwise black-box model (Barredo Arrieta et al., 2020). In line with this, Rudin (2019) argues that one should always strive to use inherently interpretable models, rather than resorting to post-hoc explanations of black box models, at least if the stakes are high.

Even if the development of XAI is often motivated by a need to contribute to trusted and fair AI applications, synthesised into a need to better understand aspects of causality and transferability, there seems to be a lack of a unified terminology. For example, there is a distinct lack of metrics, some argue, by which such objectives can be easily quantified and compared (Lipton, 2018; Barredo Arrieta, 2020). Although there are many XAI techniques available for black-box models, the lack of explainability metrics makes it difficult to validate their utility. When such techniques have been tested empirically, counter-intuitive results are not uncommon. For example, Kaur et al. (2020) found that even data scientists tend to misuse and overtrust visual explanations, not noticing when the models misbehave, which we return to below in the section on mediation.

A key problem with XAI methods, stressed by Miller et al. (2017), is its lack of grounding in the social and behavioural sciences. Similarly, Mittelstadt et al. (2019) argue that there is a fundamental distinction between explanations provided by AI and everyday explanations intended for humans. The latter is, in short, not the same as the "interpretability" and explainability found in the XAI domain. This has led researchers to conduct meta-studies, drawing from social psychology and philosophy, on the critical properties of human explanations (cf. Miller, 2019). From this perspective, Miller (2019) argues, explanations are often

1. *contrastive*, that is, people ask not necessarily why an event happened, but rather why an event happened instead of another event,
2. an outcome of the fact that we tend to *make a biased selection* of one or two causes from a sometimes infinite number of causes to be *the* explanation,
3. *not strictly depending on probabilities*, as much as referred causes, that is, the most likely explanation is not always the best explanation for a person, which leads to the last category stating that explanations are
4. *social*. That is, part of a conversation or interaction, which implicates the explanation.

The above-mentioned aspects, including risks of misused visual explanations and the lack of attention to how humans understand explanations, lead us to explicitly focus on the complementing mediation as a facet of AI transparency in its own right.

Transparency as Mediation

Following the proposition that a distinction should be made between XAI and human explanations established in the social sciences (Miller, 2019; see also Mittelstadt et al., 2019), this section conceptualises explanations as components of *mediation*, and highlights its role in achieving transparency. Here, we draw from what Koivisto (2022) refers to as transparency "as a medium", generative and non-neutral, albeit here more distinctly focused on the contemporary AI discourse. We elaborate on the modes of mediation, whose implications for AI transparency we argue are understudied and in need of further scrutiny. This should also be seen in light of contemporary calls for more transparency in the application of AI systems, in terms of that we seek to underscore the meaning of mediation, as an important aspect of whatever goals transparent AI is set to reach. Transparency, as a metaphor linked to seeing (cf. Koivisto, 2022; Larsson & Heintz, 2020), is not neutral, but an "ocular-centric" notion, in the words of Koivisto (2022) that also seem to downplay other notions of mediation than the visual.

To facilitate more effective human-AI communication, Miller (2019) proposes that AI explanations should be designed to incorporate characteristics of human explanations (counterfactual, selective, contextual). A majority of the existing XAI techniques produce statistical probability explanations either textually or through graphical representations. XAI is often argued to serve specific use cases meant to be handled by domain experts, and thus there is no need for general explainability intended for non-experts. Within this context, so-called *interpretability tools* have been designed to help data scientists and machine learning practitioners better understand how AI systems work (cf. Kaur et al., 2020). These tools favour visualisation as a medium of communication. However, recent research indicates that data scientists risk overtrusting and misusing interpretability tools, and shows that visual output can be misleading (Kaur et al., 2020).

Evidently, mediation of explanations provided by AI is not, and should not be seen as, limited to visual representations; in a mundane everyday context, they can arguably also take the shape of text or symbols in user interfaces and user agreements (Larsson & Heintz, 2020), where online ads have been pointed to as a particularly problematic and opaque area (Andrejevic et al., 2022). When considering mundane and everyday practices, transparency as a medium of information poses a great challenge to non-expert users of AI, such as consumers, citizens, or patients. The choice of words or symbols can metaphorically highlight certain features and downplay others, which structures and guides how certain phenomena are understood, potentially leading to normative implications for the law's attempt to regulate new technologies (Larsson, 2017) as well as affecting users' understanding of technological interfaces (Stanfill, 2015). These choices need to be studied and understood for the sake of improving AI governance in everyday life. This is especially important when translating explanations across languages, where different metaphor-relations may be at play. This level of nuanced mediation is largely lacking in XAI it seems, particularly in relation to policy and, for example, consumer interests, which could be concerning in relation to overconfidence in automated tools (for a critical examination of the feasibility of AI policy focusing on human control over automation, see Koulu, 2020). With AI systems being integrated into commonplace products and services, they have to meet legal requirements aimed at protecting the user's privacy, among other things. This means that users may need to be informed and consent to data collection involved in the automation. To this end, for example, cookie consent banners were implemented in the EU to provide more transparency regarding online data collection, as well as a rich plethora of consent agreements and privacy policy statements used to communicate how personal data is collected and processed – which is often a prerequisite for consumer-facing AI-applications like recommender systems. Several studies, however, indicate that most consumers do not understand such communications on how their data is collected and what it is used for. Similarly, research suggests that users find the quantity of information overwhelming, causing information overload, and leading them to disregard the information altogether (Cranor et al., 2015; Larsson et al., 2021).

Mediation between humans and AI is a field in need of more scrutiny and development. Research in this space is spread across a myriad of disciplines, such as psychology, cognitive science, communication and information studies, and interaction design; bridging knowledge from all these fields is a pressing challenge. Mediation implies an addressee and an audience, which we analyse in terms of *literacy* in the subsequent section (cf. Burrell, 2016, on opacity as technical illiteracy).

Transparency as Literacy

The lack of literacy is often cited as a reason why AI applications are considered opaque. Technical illiteracy is, for example, identified by Burrell (2016) as one of the main reasons for the "state of not knowing". It is, however, also tightly interwoven with the particularly complex characteristics of machine learning algorithms and their scale of operation (Burrell, 2016). This is what forms the basis for claims that we need "new forms of interpretability and literacy" (van Nuenen et al., 2020, p. 43). In this section, we consider the nuances of literacy under the umbrella of AI transparency, and the implications and limitations of literacy as a solution to AI opacity.

Originally, literacy referred to "the ability to express ourselves and communicate using written language", but it has since come to be defined as "skill sets in a variety of disciplines that have the same potential to enable expression, communication and access to knowledge" (Long & Magerko, 2020, p. 2). In the AI discourse, the call for literacy has become a common normative standpoint in addressing issues of governance (Larsson et al., 2020; Jobin et al., 2019). For instance, there is a clear emphasis on transparency in the *Ethics Guidelines for Trustworthy AI* prepared by the High-Level Expert Group on AI (cf. Larsson, 2020), including calls for both data and algorithmic literacy in European policy more broadly. Similarly, Strauß argues that opaque AI systems can reinforce so-called wicked problems, involving "ill-formulated risks of undetected failure, self-fulfilling prophecies and an incremental normalisation of AI biases in society" (Strauß, 2021, p. 45). Therefore, he argues that having a basic understanding of AI and raising problem awareness among decision-makers and persons interacting with AI systems are essential to face these problems.

In the context of AI, different *types of literacies* are discussed. Long and Magerko (2020, p. 2) defined AI literacy as "a set of competencies that enables individuals to critically evaluate AI technologies; communicate and collaborate effectively with AI; and use AI as a tool online, at home, and in the workplace". However, it is frequently pointed out that digital literacy is a precondition for AI literacy, while computational literacy might not be essential, though it depends on who the audience is (e.g., Barredo Arrieta et al., 2020). Scientific literacy can, similarly, inform AI literacy, whereas data literacy is argued to overlap with AI literacy (Long & Magerko, 2020, p. 2).

Embedded in the strive for AI literacy is the question of *who* needs to be literate, i.e., to whom should algorithms be transparent? Is it the general public, auditors, legislative actors, policymakers, AI developers themselves, or any other group? Various actors are involved with AI systems, requiring different sets of knowledge and skills, and, therefore, different literacies. Furthermore, different groups, individuals, and professions vary in their competence to review information about AI systems. For example, a report conducted for the European Parliament on algorithmic transparency and accountability differs if the intended transparency is for "everyone", regulatory staff, third-party forensics, or researchers (Koene et al., 2019). Moreover, the importance of *a critical audience* for the transparency of AI is stressed (Kemper & Kolkman, 2019).

Yet, AI literacy cannot, due to system architectures and input data, be regarded without (big) data literacy and information literacy in general (Jandrić, 2019, p. 33). The call for increased AI literacy can be viewed in light of broader calls for the literacy of media, information, data and digital technologies, and the imaginaries they hold. First, they build on the notion that increased literacy by necessity leads to a surge of knowledge and empowerment, as well as general social progress. This is despite hardships of identifying what these literacies need to consist of; operation of skills or deeply critical and reflexive reasoning? (cf. Jandrić, 2019; Ng et al., 2021; Lloyd, 2019). Second, often, these literacies are conceptualised as responsibilities of the individual, including being able to deal with ambiguous claims (Haider & Sundin, 2022, p. 30). Placing the onus for gaining and using them on the individual can, as a policy approach, have serious implications for questions of how to distribute accountability. That is, while literacy indeed can foster empowerment, the request for AI literacy as a strategic policy for regulating the relationship between AI-using companies or authorities and their human consumers or citizens may promote an individualistic approach that at worst displaces the required scrutiny down to the individual users. The user or subject is expected to educate themselves, stay informed, and understand the consequences of different AI use cases, as well as take action. This can be compared with critical and empirical research on data-intensive consumer research that points to a "corporate cultivation" of resignation among consumers (Draper & Turow, 2019) as a sort of obfuscation (Zalnieriute, 2021), which in some practices lead to "uninformed" consent (Utz et al., 2019).

Nevertheless, increased AI literacy is put forward by several governance initiatives as an important piece of the puzzle towards trustworthy AI (2019, p. 23). While education and awareness are framed as important for trust in AI, in ethics guidelines (Jobin et al., 2019), critical awareness might be shadowed by the governance landscape in which AI systems reside, through legally sanctioned limits to insight and transparency. In international governance, transparency has come to take a central position as belonging to a "group of good concepts" (Koivisto, 2022, p. 162) – along with, for example, human rights and democracy. To contrast this discursive and normative connotation – that more transparency is better – we will now turn to ideas on when transparency needs balancing in a trade-off with other interests. We use a legally informed framework for this demonstration.

Transparency in a Legal Trade-off

Under the umbrella of AI transparency, we have so far related the algorithmically focused explainability concept to how AI systems are mediated, as well as turned the gaze to the addressees in terms of their literacy. Lastly, we seek to place the transparency concept into a governance context in which law as an equilibrium tool becomes central. While the recent emphasis on transparency in soft or "ethics-based" governance of AI systems may fit well with the overarching goals of making these systems more explainable and better mediated and understood, the wider perspective of governance considers several values and interests to be balanced. Transparency, as a form of governance (cf. Hansen & Flyverbom, 2015), will within law, therefore, have to be seen as something that takes part in a trade-off. As stressed in the literature (cf. Koivisto, 2022; de Laat, 2018), there are several legitimate reasons for keeping certain things secret, and regardless of what recent ethics guidelines put forward, this trade-off is inevitably to be played out in practice in most jurisdictions, not the least European.

To begin with, it should be noted that there is a firmly established legal notion that there are legitimate interests in limiting transparency. Access to AI systems, including their source code, associated parameters, training data, training processes, and resulting models, is according to this legal notion not always warranted. For instance, AI proprietors generally prefer not to reveal the inner workings of their systems in order to keep their competitive advantage in the market. Other motives for not revealing detailed information about AI systems include the need to prevent users from gaming the algorithms. Too much transparency in such cases is argued to risk leading to abuse of the systems, for example, cyberattacks, and the defeat of the purpose of said systems (cf. de Laat, 2018). Likewise, uncontrolled access might jeopardise personal data used for training the models (de Laat, 2018). Thus, organisations developing AI technologies often resort to various legal vehicles provided by IP law, especially trade secret protection, as well as data ownership restrictions, non-disclosure agreements, and other contractual provisions (Foss-Solbrekk, 2021; Pasquale, 2015; Tschider, 2021).

However, opacity enabled by such legal mechanisms may also serve as a convenient means for both corporations and governments to conceal both legal and illegal practices. The latter can mean such conduct as abuse of a dominant position, discrimination, or violation of other fundamental rights. Burrell (2016) refers to this opacity as *intentional corporate or state secrecy,* and points, together with a number of critics, to algorithmic secrecy as a big challenge for accountability and fairness in applied AI. This can, for example, relate to data-driven markets (Pasquale, 2015) or smart city transparency (Brauneis & Goodman, 2018), often in contexts where corporate systems perform public functions. This challenge has received increased attention, not only with regard to end-users, such as citizens, patients, or consumers but also as an issue of distorted competition driven by large-scale digital platforms (cf. Larsson, 2021). Such problematic consequences of opacity prompt the need to curb its scope. Some limitations to trade secret protection, for example, are provided within the law, such as by the Trade Secret Directive (Directive 2016/943), whereby trade secret holders may be obliged to disclose relevant information due to public interest. This is an attempt of balancing interests. Other restrictions stem from competition law, which prevents the use of trade secrets as a means to abuse market dominance. Courts may invoke human rights protections, such as respect for private and family life (see, for example, the Dutch *SyRI* case concerning digital welfare fraud detection; van Bekkum & Borgesius, 2021). The judicial approach is, however, dependent on drawn-out, cumbersome, and sometimes expensive legal and administrative processes.

Another method to scrutinise AI systems is to appoint certain entities, such as competent authorities or auditing bodies, to examine the systems under a confidentiality regime. In this context, Pasquale (2015) proposes a *qualified transparency* approach for data-driven markets, to counter some of the intentional opacity in the shape of proprietary claims. In a somewhat similar argument, but aimed at how to think of and handle aspects of gaming for machine-learning systems, de Laat (2018) argues that full public transparency may render "perverse effects", and particularly advocates for full transparency for oversight bodies as the only feasible option. Recent developments in EU policy point to this line of reasoning, especially the proposed AI Act, according to which oversight bodies are to be granted full access to an AI system's training, validation, and testing datasets – when deemed necessary and subject to the confidentiality regime (European Commission, 2021, Article 64). This governance approach has been interpreted by Mökander et al. (2021) as a Europe-wide ecosystem for conducting AI auditing. Yet, the efficacy of the AI Act framework is contingent upon the availability of technical expertise and resources provided to the supervisory bodies. Early assessments have been questioned to be "dangerously optimistic" with regards to what is needed to ensure a successful implementation (Veale & Borgesius, 2021, p. 111).

Although the legal opacity of AI systems may be justified in certain cases, efforts to provide a more effective system to "limit the limitations" on transparency by legal or technical means are intense and ongoing. The proposed methods to scrutinise AI technologies depend on either slow-paced judicial and administrative decisions, or the review of systems by competent authorities or auditing bodies under the confidentiality rule, with arguably deficient resources at their disposal. It, therefore, remains to be seen whether the measures to provide more AI transparency in the EU will be sufficient to address the negative aspects of legally warranted opacity.

DISCUSSION: OBSERVATIONS

In this chapter, we have scrutinised, and aimed to place, the often explainability-focused notion of transparency in contemporary AI governance discourse into an interdisciplinary understanding of the concept. Firstly, we have pointed to some of the critiques in the XAI domain in order to, secondly, contrast this to mediation. While part of this critique stresses the importance of taking different "audiences" into account, thirdly, we have tried to deepen the abilities of these audiences in terms of the rich literature on literacy found in information studies. Fourthly, and lastly which is important not the least in light of the central role the concept of transparency plays in the contemporary governance discourse on AI, we have placed all of these three facets into the framework of trade-offs provided in law. Here we acknowledge transparency as a form of governance in itself that has many interests to take into account.

It is not new and unique for the development of AI that processes of transparency are something that can both reveal and conceal, and sustain (or exacerbate) as well as disrupt power structures (c.f., Strathern, 2000; Fenster, 2015; Hansen & Flyverbom, 2015). Yet, the need for transparency is something that is moving to the foreground as AI implementations increase and expand in society, and the consequences of them and the automation of decision-making become increasingly apparent and profound. In some cases, even Kafkaesque in its opaqueness and difficulty to object when interwoven in bureaucratic and technical complexities (Vredenburgh, 2022). The four facets we discuss all play their part in the process of making AI transparent, but they are also interdependent of (possibly) conflicting interests of the plethora of actors involved, and with the intricate data ecologies and infrastructures in which AI systems and technologies come to be and come to use.

To counterbalance the "ocular-centric" notion of transparency (Koivisto, 2022), we need to focus more on how what we cannot see actually gets mediated and brought to our attention. The procedural and interface-related aspects of transparency we address in terms of mediation above not only point to how AI systems are often attempted to be made more scrutable and explainable but also that a posed ideal of explainability is heavily dependent on mediation as such. Literacy is beneficial for certain types of empowerment. As a policy instrument, it can however also lead to problematic effects by a strategic approach for larger players in a digitised society to tilt accountability towards overwhelmed end-users or "data subjects". How to enact transparency is by no means a neutral process, but value-laden and political. Critical analyses discuss "transparency washing" as a strategy whereby a focus on transparency can act as obfuscation from more substantive and fundamental questions about the concentration of power (Zalnieriute, 2021, p. 139). From a legal point of view, several scholars address a more complex issue of transparency, in the sense of being able to manage both legally justified claims for opacity and undesirable results of too much transparency (cf. de Laat, 2018). However, the private-public complexity, in terms of proprietary claims of secrecy, has been seen as a problem for oversight and civic participation, and has led to arguments for strong oversight bodies.

What do these four facets of AI transparency add up to? They are entangled as concepts and realities and build upon the sociotechnical assemblages of humans and non-humans that are forming AI development and use. Even though it is commonly conceptualised as a state, AI transparency can also be conceptualised as performative, processual, and under negotiation (Cellard, 2022). It is a process that is limited by matters such as what can actually be known and explained of how a system operates (XAI), the choices made in what and how information about it is conveyed (mediation), the expertise of oversight bodies and individual capabilities (literacy), and the interpretations and constraints regarding what information is required to be accessible (legality).

CONCLUSIONS

The aim of this chapter was to critically unpack the conceptual vagueness of AI transparency. This is particularly motivated by the recent focus on transparency in AI policy. To this end, we constructed our analysis of AI transparency into four facets. First, (1) as *explainability* (XAI) is an expanding field in AI, we argue for a need for it to be complemented by a more explicit focus on the (2) *mediation* of AI-systems functionality, as a communicated artefact. Furthermore, in the policy discourse on AI, the importance of (3) *literacy* is underscored. Subsequently, we draw from the rich literacy literature in order to show both promising and troubling consequences of this. Lastly, therefore, we (4) argue for transparency being *a form of governance*, albeit laden with positive connotations – that more transparency is better – which we critically break up within a legal framework set to balance between a multitude of interests. By these four facets, we examine a particularly complex concept in dire need of clarification due to its central position in the governance of increasingly automated and AI-dependent corporate and governmental activities.

REFERENCES

Alloa, E. (Ed.). (2022). *This obscure thing called transparency: Politics and aesthetics of a contemporary metaphor.* Leuven University Press.

Andrejevic, M., Fordyce, R., Luzhou, L., Trott, V., Angus, D., & Ying, T. X. (2022). Ad accountability online: A methodological approach. In S. Pink, M. Berg, D. Lupton, & M. Ruckenstein (Eds.), *Everyday automation* (pp. 213–225). Routledge.

Barredo Arrieta, A., Díaz-Rodríguez, N., Del Ser, J., Bennetot, A., Tabik, S., Barbado, A., Garcia, S., Gil-Lopez, S., Molina, D., Benjamins, R., Chatila, R., & Herrera, F. (2020). Explainable artificial intelligence (XAI): Concepts, taxonomies, opportunities and challenges toward responsible AI. *Information Fusion, 58,* 82–115.

Brauneis, R., & Goodman, E. P. (2018). Algorithmic transparency for the smart city. *Yale Journal of Law and Technology, 20,* 103.

Burrell, J. (2016). How the machine 'thinks': Understanding opacity in machine learning algorithms. *Big Data & Society, 3*(1), 1–12.

Cellard, L. (2022). Algorithmic transparency: On the rise of a new normative ideal and its silenced performative implications. In E. Alloa (Ed.), *This obscure thing called transparency: Politics and aesthetics of a contemporary metaphor* (pp. 119–144). Leuven University Press.

Cranor, L. F., Hoke, C., Leon, P. G., & Au, A. (2015). Are they worth reading-an in-depth analysis of online trackers' privacy policies. *ISJLP, 11,* 325.

de Bruijn, H., Warnier, M., & Janssen, M. (2022). The perils and pitfalls of explainable AI: Strategies for explaining algorithmic decision-making. *Government Information Quarterly, 39*(2), 101666.

De Laat, P. B. (2018). Algorithmic decision-making based on machine learning from big data: Can transparency restore accountability? *Philosophy & Technology, 31*(4), 525–541.

de Vries, K. (2021). Transparent dreams (are made of this): Counterfactuals as transparency tools in ADM. *Critical Analysis of Law, 8*(1), 121–138.

Diakopoulos, N. (2020). Transparency. In M. D. Dubber, F. Pasquale, & S. Das (Eds.), *The Oxford handbook of ethics of AI.* Oxford University Press.

Directive 2016/943 of the European Parliament and of the Council of 8 June 2016 on the protection of undisclosed know-how and business information (trade secrets) against their unlawful acquisition, use and disclosure.

Draper, N. A., & Turow, J. (2019). The corporate cultivation of digital resignation. *New Media & Society, 21*(8), 1824–1839.

European Commission (2021, April 21). Proposal for a regulation of the European Parliament and of the Council on laying down harmonised rules on artificial intelligence (Artificial Intelligence Act) and amending certain Union legislative acts COM/2021/0106.

Felländer, A., Rebane, J., Larsson, S., Wiggberg, M., & Heintz, F. (2022). Achieving a data-driven risk assessment methodology for ethical AI. *Digital Society, 1*(2), 1–27.

Fenster, M. (2015). Transparency in search of a theory. *European Journal of Social Theory, 18*(2), 150–167.

Forssbaeck, J., & Oxelheim, L. (Eds.). (2014). *The Oxford handbook of economic and institutional transparency.* Oxford Handbooks.

Foss-Solbrekk, K. (2021). Three routes to protecting AI systems and their algorithms under IP law: The good, the bad and the ugly. *Journal of Intellectual Property Law & Practice, 16*(3), 247–258.

Ghassemi, M., Oakden-Rayner, L., & Beam, A. L. (2021). The false hope of current approaches to explainable artificial intelligence in health care. *The Lancet Digital Health, 3*(11).

Haider, J., & Sundin, O. (2022). *Paradoxes of media and information literacy: The crisis of information* (1st ed.). Routledge.

Hansen, H. K., & Flyverbom, M. (2015). The politics of transparency and the calibration of knowledge in the digital age. *Organization, 22*(6), 872–889.

Haresamudram, K., Larsson, S., & Heintz, F. (2022). Three levels of AI transparency, *Computer*, special issue on Trustworthy AI.

Jacovi, A., Marasović, A., Miller, T., & Goldberg, Y. (2021). Formalizing trust in artificial intelligence: Prerequisites, causes and goals of human trust in AI. In *Proceedings of the 2021 ACM conference on fairness, accountability, and transparency* (pp. 624–635).

Jandrić, P. (2019). The postdigital challenge of critical media literacy. *The International Journal of Critical Media Literacy, 1*(1), 26–37.

Jobin, A., Ienca, M., & Vayena, E. (2019). The global landscape of AI ethics guidelines. *Nature Machine Intelligence, 1*(9), 389–399.

Kaur, H., Nori, H., Jenkins, S., Caruana, R., Wallach, H., & Wortman Vaughan, J. (2020). Interpreting interpretability: Understanding data scientists' use of interpretability tools for machine learning. In *Proceedings of the 2020 CHI conference on human factors in computing systems* (pp. 1–14).

Kemper, J., & Kolkman, D. (2019). Transparent to whom? No algorithmic accountability without a critical audience. *Information, Communication & Society, 22*(14), 2081–2096. https://doi.org/10 .1080/1369118X.2018.1477967.

Koene, A., Clifton, C., Hatada, Y., Webb, H., & Richardson, R. (2019). *A governance framework for algorithmic accountability and transparency* (Study No. PE 624.262) Panel for the Future of Science and Technology, Scientific Foresight Unit (STOA), European Parliamentary Research Service.

Koivisto, I. (2022) *The transparency paradox: Questioning an ideal.* Oxford University Press.

Koulu, R. (2020). Human control over automation: EU policy and AI ethics. *European Journal of Legal Studies, 12*, 9.

Larsson, S. (2017). *Conceptions in the code: How metaphors explain legal challenges in digital times.* Oxford University Press.

Larsson, S. (2019). The socio-legal relevance of artificial intelligence. *Droit et Société, 103*(3), 573–593.

Larsson, S. (2020). On the governance of artificial intelligence through ethics guidelines. *Asian Journal of Law and Society, 7*(3), 437–451.

Larsson, S. (2021). Putting trust into antitrust? Competition policy and data-driven platforms. *European Journal of Communication, 36*(4), 391–403.

Larsson, S., & Heintz, F. (2020). Transparency in artificial intelligence. *Internet Policy Review, 9*(2).

Larsson, S., Ingram Bogusz, C., & Andersson Schwarz, J. (Eds.). (2020) *Human-centred AI in the EU: Trustworthiness as a strategic priority in the European Member States.* European Liberal Forum.

Larsson, S., Jensen-Urstad, A., & Heintz, F. (2021) Notified but unaware: Third party tracking online. *Critical Analysis of Law, 8*(1), 101–120.

Lipton, Z. C. (2018). The mythos of model interpretability: In machine learning, the concept of interpretability is both important and slippery. *Queue, 16*(3), 28.

Lloyd, A. (2019). Chasing Frankenstein's monster: Information literacy in the black box society. *Journal of Documentation, 75*(6), 1475–1485.

Long, D., & Magerko, B. (2020). What is AI literacy? Competencies and design considerations. In *Proceedings of the 2020 CHI conference on human factors in computing systems* (pp. 1–16).

Miller, T. (2019). Explanation in artificial intelligence: Insights from the social sciences. *Artificial Intelligence, 267*, 1–38.

Miller, T., Hoffman, R., Amir, O., & Holzinger, A. (2022). Special issue on explainable artificial intelligence (XAI). *Artificial Intelligence,* 103705.

Miller, T., Howe, P., & Sonenberg, L. (2017). Explainable AI: Beware of inmates running the asylum. Or: How I learnt to stop worrying and love the social and behavioural sciences. *IJCAI 2017 Workshop on Explainable Artificial Intelligence (XAI).*

Mittelstadt, B., Russell, C., & Wachter, S. (2019). Explaining explanations in AI. In *Proceedings of the conference on fairness, accountability, and transparency* (pp. 279–288).

Mökander, J., Axente, M., Casolari, F., & Floridi, L. (2021). Conformity assessments and post-market monitoring: A guide to the role of auditing in the proposed European AI regulation. *Minds and Machines, 32*(2), 241–268.

Ng, D. T. K., Leung, J. K. L., Chu, K. W. S., & Qiao, M. S. (2021). AI literacy: Definition, teaching, evaluation and ethical issues. *Proceedings of the Association for Information Science and Technology, 58*(1), 504–509.

Pasquale, F. (2015). *The Black box society.* Harvard University Press.

Qi, Z., Khorram, S., & Fuxin, L. (2021). Embedding deep networks into visual explanations. *Artificial Intelligence, 292*, 103435.

Ribera, M., & Lapedriza, A. (2019). Can we do better explanations? A proposal of user-centered explainable AI. In *IUI Workshops* (Vol. 2327, p. 38).

Robinson, S. C. (2020). Trust, transparency, and openness: How inclusion of cultural values shapes Nordic national public policy strategies for artificial intelligence (AI). *Technology in Society, 63*, 101421.

Rudin, C. (2019). Stop explaining black box machine learning models for high stakes decisions and use interpretable models instead. *Nature Machine Intelligence, 1*(5), 206–215.

Selbst, A. D., & Barocas, S. (2018). The intuitive appeal of explainable machines. *Fordham Law Review, 87*, 1085.

Stanfill, M. (2015). The interface as discourse: The production of norms through web design. *New Media & Society, 17*(7), 1059–1074.

Strauß, S. (2021). "Don't let me be misunderstood": Critical AI literacy for the constructive use of AI technology. *TATuP-Zeitschrift für Technikfolgenabschätzung in Theorie und Praxis, 30*(3), 44–49.

Strathern, M. (2000). The tyranny of transparency. *British Educational Research Journal, 26*(3), 309–321.

Tschider, C. (2021). Legal Opacity: Artificial Intelligence's Sticky Wicket. *Iowa Law Review*, vol. 106: 126–164.

Utz, C., Degeling, M., Fahl, S., Schaub, F., & Holz, T. (2019). (Un)informed consent: Studying GDPR consent notices in the field. In *Proceedings of the 2019 ACM Sigsac conference on computer and communications security* (pp. 973–990).

van Bekkum, M., & Borgesius, F. Z. (2021). Digital welfare fraud detection and the Dutch SyRI judgment. *European Journal of Social Security, 23*(4), 323–340.

van Nuenen, T., Ferrer, X., Such, J. M., & Coté, M. (2020). Transparency for whom? Assessing discriminatory artificial intelligence. *Computer, 53*(11), 36–44.

Veale, M., & Borgesius, F. Z. (2021). Demystifying the draft EU artificial intelligence act—Analysing the good, the bad, and the unclear elements of the proposed approach. *Computer Law Review International, 22*(4), 97–112.

Vredenburgh, K. (2022) The right to explanation*. *Journal of Political Philosophy, 30*(2), 209–229.

Wachter, S., Mittelstadt, B., & Russell, C. (2017). Counterfactual explanations without opening the black box: Automated decisions and the GDPR. *Harvard Journal of Law & Technology, 31*, 841.

Zalnieriute, M. (2021). "Transparency-washing" in the digital age: A corporate agenda of procedural fetishism. *Critical Analysis of Law, 8*(1), 139–153.

40. An inclusive approach to ascribing responsibility in robot ethics

Janina Loh

1.　INTRODUCTION

Responsibility is one of the fundamental competences of human life and is also a central value of our ethical, legal, political, and economic reflection. Ethical schools such as deontology, consequentialism, and virtue ethics can agree on this without question. However, they undoubtedly diverge with regard to what responsible action looks like in concrete cases, and how it can be demanded or guaranteed. The situation is no different in robot ethics.

Robot ethicists think about how responsibility can be attributed to humans and to what extent it is consequently possible to attribute it to machines or at least to some particular robots. They are also interested in the question of where the limits of a potential artificial responsibility lie and whether there are things for which humans will continue to be exclusively responsible in the future. These robot ethicists are concerned in the broadest sense with the question of the extent to which (some) robots are to be called potential moral agents capable of responsible action. Admittedly, not all robot ethicists think that (some) robots can be artificial subjects of responsibility. Some robot ethicists believe that no robot will ever be capable of responsibility. And yet, we may not simply deal with robots as we do with other objects, and may not, in short, do anything we want with them. These robot ethicists are asking, in the broadest sense, whether (some) robots are objects of moral action, moral patients, as Floridi and Sanders say.[1] Robots may not be able to act responsibly themselves, but they demand that humans act responsibly toward them in specific ways.

These two ways of thinking commonly found in robot ethics regarding the attribution of responsibility to robots – robots as potential moral agents and robots as potential moral patients – are what I call exclusive or exclusionary ethical approaches. They have to face some major challenges, which I will address in the second section of this paper. I will show that exclusive ethical thinking corresponds to the common ethical thinking in our societies and that the exclusive approaches in robot ethics represent a typical formulation of this ethical thinking. I will then also explain why this form of ethical reflection (i.e., exclusive ethics) is fundamentally problematic, namely structurally discriminatory and reifying or oppressive. In the third section, I will then localize the traditional understanding of responsibility within exclusive ethical thinking. It will become apparent here that the traditional understanding of responsibility found in the usual exclusively robotic ethical approaches cannot meet the challenges of structural discrimination and reification or oppression, but rather supports them.

In the fourth and fifth sections, therefore, I sketch my alternative of inclusive ethics on robot ethical approaches to responsibility attribution. Exclusive ethics advocate a primacy of the

---

[1]　Moral agents are "entities that can perform actions". Moral patients are "entities that can be acted upon for good or evil" (Floridi and Sanders 2004: 349). They are the objects of moral actions.

moral agent to whom certain competencies, capacities, and properties (such as responsibility) are (anthropological-)essentially ascribed (or denied).[2] Inclusive ethics shift their focus process-ontologically to the relations, to what lies between the relata (the subjects and objects, the moral agents and moral patients) and accordingly do not explain the competences, abilities, and properties back-bound to the agents (i.e., in an anthropological-essentialist way), but as emerging from the relations. The inclusive robotic ethical approaches also have to struggle with certain challenges, but, as I will show, they are different from those of structural discrimination and reification or oppression (Loh, 2019b).

2.   EXCLUSIVE ETHICS AND ITS CHALLENGES[3]

Ethics usually applies to human beings. It is primarily a philosophical, often, though not necessarily, academic discipline that deals with human mores, habits, and customs, the criteria of good and bad actions, or, in general, the good life or morality. Ethics concerns exclusively humans, while nonhumans (animals, plants, machines, etc.) concern ethics only in exceptional cases. In some cases, specific ethical schools ascribe a specific, morally appropriate, behavior toward nonhumans and thus include them in the moral community – even if these ethical traditions usually give nonhumans a weaker moral value than humans. This understanding of ethics is here referred to as exclusive or exclusionary ethics. It is the common, conventional, usually implicitly or explicitly prevailing understanding of ethics in our societies.

All forms of exclusive ethics have three criteria in common. They are what constitute these ethical stances as exclusionary. They represent the fundamental challenges to which inclusive ethics respond. All ethics (implicitly) are therefore exclusionary ethics, since they are, *first*, centrist, since they rest, *second*, on an anthropological-essentialist premise, and since they are, *third*, based on a hierarchical dichotomy between subject and object in which the (moral) subject is privileged.

Centrist ethics focus on the definition of a specific moral agent or on a specific moral entity, centering around it, so to speak, by ascribing the highest, namely an intrinsic, value to this primary moral agent. From this primary moral agent, centrist approaches to ethics then distinguish objects with a morally instrumental value, and thus a lower moral status, and objects that receive no moral value at all, toward which one may consequently behave as one. There are thus three categories of entities in centrist ethics, namely moral subjects or primary agents with intrinsic value (who are usually the only beings in the moral universe to whom moral agency is ascribed), moral objects or moral patients with instrumental value (which usually do not have moral agency but may be part of a moral agent's action and dictate to that moral agent a specific, morally appropriate way of dealing with them), and nonmoral objects with which moral agents may deal as they please. Strictly speaking, the latter is not part of the moral community.

All exclusive ethics are centrist in one form or another, several of them are anthropocentric. Anthropocentric ethics ascribe intrinsic value exclusively to humans, whereas nonhumans have only instrumental value (if any). Centrist theories can be either moral or epistemic

---

[2]   Anthropological essentialism, as it is understood in this chapter, is a strategy of defining human essence in terms of a single attribute or a set of properties (Braidotti 1992; Loh 2019a: 38).

[3]   See Loh (2022).

approaches. One speaks of moral anthropocentrism when humans are given a moral preference and thus special status over all other beings. By epistemic anthropocentrism, one means that only humans have the capacity for knowledge and judgment.

There are some centrist alternatives to anthropocentrism, such as pathocentrism, which morally attributes intrinsic value to all sentient beings and epistemically takes the position that values come into the world with sentient beings. Biocentrism morally and epistemically considers all living things, and physiocentrism morally and epistemically considers all of nature (holistic physiocentrism) or everything in nature (individualistic physiocentrism). Other centrist approaches to ethics can be defined depending on which properties are seen as morally significant.

In exclusive ethics, moral relevance and significance are always thought of in relation to humans. Humans are either the only entities with intrinsic value in the moral universe (anthropocentrism), or they define who or what is morally relevant, that is, who or what is given absolute or instrumental value (other centrist ethics). In pathocentrism, for instance, humans define sentience to give some nonhumans intrinsic value.

Exclusive ethics start from an anthropological first premise, for "the" human being is set as an ideal-typical member of the moral community, as the standard for moral significance. As noted earlier, exclusive ethics usually takes place between humans, which means that it presupposes an understanding of what a human actually is.

Anthropological essentialism has the advantage of being able to formulate clear criteria for distinguishing humans from all nonhuman beings. It has the disadvantage that the attributes it proposes can also always be denied. At this point, therefore, it should become clear why centrist and anthropological-essentialist ethics have to proceed by way of exclusion. Anthropological essentialism quasi-automatically produces moral status for humans, which in turn prescribes a specific way of dealing with nonhumans. Centrist, anthropological-essentialist ethics are exclusive ethics because they always exclude some beings from the center of the moral community, or, indeed, from the moral community as a whole. There are always some objects in centrist, anthropological-essentialist ethics that have less moral value or no moral value at all.

In addition to their centrist orientation and the anthropological-essentialist first premise on which they rest, exclusive ethics share the feature of a dichotomy between a subject and an object, hierarchized in favor of the subject (Rettler & Bailey, 2017). Just as the subject is defined in essentialist terms, the object is also ascribed a specific (moral) status given by the subject on the basis of the attestation of certain properties and is consequently assigned a place in or outside the moral community. Pathocentric ethics, for instance, give intrinsic value to all sentient beings; they are the subjects who are at the center of the moral community. The other entities, which according to this logic are to be understood as the objects, are perhaps still given a place in the moral community thanks to an instrumental value or, if they are denied any moral value, are excluded from it.

Exclusive ethics face two challenges because of these three criteria that make them exclusive ethics in the first place. *First*, they face structural discrimination because of their anthropological essentialism, which is found in all centrist ethics (though not unique to them). *Second*, because of the hierarchizing distinction between a subject and an object, they tend to structurally suppress or reify the passive and (implicitly or explicitly) degraded object. But how exactly do the three criteria give rise to these challenges? This brings us to the core of the critique of exclusive ethics: all exclusive ethics have a primary interest in the identification of moral agents or subjects and objects. In a structural model, one might also say that the relata precede the relations. The relata (the subjects and objects) are defined essentially anthropologically, and it is to them that the entire ethical system is "centristically" oriented. The priority of the relata (before the relations) thus enables structural discriminations, oppressions, and reifications.

3. THE TRADITIONAL UNDERSTANDING OF RESPONSIBILITY

Responsibility is without question one of the most important competencies of human life (Sombetzki, 2014). One speaks of responsibility in morality, politics, economics, law, art, and religion. Responsibility is often seen as an anthropological constant.

Traditionally, responsibility is understood as the ability to answer the fact or state of being answerable (Duff, 1998: 290), which is never a purely descriptive but is also always a normative event. Moreover, talk of responsibility always refers to certain competencies, such as judgment and autonomy, which one ascribes to the potential responsible person. One assumes that they tackle the issue of responsibility with integrity, thoughtfulness, and reflection (Sombetzki, 2014: 33–41).

Five relational elements of responsibility result from this definition. *First*, a subject or bearer of responsibility is required. *Second*, an object must be defined. *Third*, it is necessary to identify the authority to which one is responsible. *Fourth*, we are responsible to an addressee. *Fifth*, normative criteria provide the standard and guidelines for how responsibility is to be attributed. For example, a thief (subject/bearer) is responsible for a theft (object) in court (authority). The addressee is the person who has been robbed, and the normative criteria are criminal law (i.e., criminal norms; Sombetzki, 2014: 63–132).

The conditions for the possibility of attributing responsibility in this traditional sense can be differentiated into three groups of competencies. The ability to communicate, the ability to act or autonomy, and judgment. All competencies as a prerequisite for the possible attribution of responsibility, and with it responsibility itself can be determined by degrees; one can speak of more or less ability to communicate and act and, depending on this, of more or less responsibility (Sombetzki, 2014: 43–62).

This brief definition of the traditional understanding of responsibility, which has also become indispensable in robot ethics (Loh, 2019a, 2019b), shows that responsibility is an (anthropologically-)essentialistically attributed ability that has enormous moral and legal significance. Those robot ethicists who consider that (some) robots can be potential moral agents are equivalently also thinking about the extent to which they can be artificial subjects of responsibility. Other robot ethicists who deny this would see in (some) robot(s) at least potential moral patients and thus also objects of responsible action. In any case, the classical understanding of responsibility is an important element of exclusive ethics and thus also of exclusive approaches to robot ethics.

4. INCLUSIVE ETHICS AS AN ALTERNATIVE[4]

Inclusive ethics are a direct response to the structural challenges of discrimination, oppression, or reification of exclusive ethics and their focus on an identification of the moral

---

4   See (Loh 2022).

agent – their primacy of relata (subjects and objects). However, inclusive ethics are not an invention of modernity or postmodernity, and they are also not merely a reaction to exclusive ethical thinking.

In exclusive ethics, what is really at stake is the identification of the moral agent with their competences and capacities, i.e., humans and, in some exclusive ethics approaches, selected nonhumans. These relata (the subjects and objects) and their behavior are morally evaluated. The relations they enter into with each other are subordinated to them, the relations depend on the relata. Relations are also important in exclusive ethics, but they are secondary to an evaluation of the moral individual, who is basically understood as self-sufficient.

This cause of all structural problems in exclusive ethics, namely the primacy of relata over relations, is reversed by inclusive ethics. Inclusive ethics are no longer concerned with identifying the moral agent and their competencies and capacities. Rather, inclusive ethics focus on the relations from which they believe relata emerge in the first place. The two critical-posthumanist thinkers Karen Barad and Donna Haraway express this reversal of perspective pointedly when they say that "relations do not follow relata, but the other way around" (Barad, 2007: 136–137). "Beings do not preexist their relatings" (Haraway, 2003: 6). "'[T]he relation' is the smallest possible unit of analysis" (Haraway, 2003: 20).

This does not entail a denial of the existence or the conception of relata (moral subjects and objects). Just as exclusive ethics do not deny relations, inclusive ethics do not deny the existence of relata. They merely assume that any identification of independent agents is due to a purely superficial view, an illusion, one might also say, based on centuries-old habits that have led to a complete focus in "Western" societies and legal systems on members of the moral community. But in fact, what one perceives as independent subjects and objects are always already woven into relations and only emerge from them. Incidentally, the fact that relata are not denied in inclusive ethics can be seen in the choice of words. In exclusive ethics, there is common usage of the word "relation*ships*". The word "relationships", however, presupposes that there is someone to conduct them. In inclusive ethics, meanwhile, there is far more frequent talk of relations, which precludes an automatic primacy of relata, though it does not per se preclude the notion of relata.

Inclusive ethics, without exception, have a concept, a notion, a term for the in-between, that is, for what is named "relations" in the context of this paper. Donna Haraway (see Section 5.1) calls the in-between "kinship"; Karen Barad (see Section 5.1) "entanglement"; Lucy Suchman speaks of "reconfigurations" (see Section 5.1); Mark Coeckelbergh of "social interactions" (see Section 5.4). Allan Hanson (see Section 5.3) still orients his relational understanding of responsibility in human-robot interaction toward a notion of agency when he speaks of "extended agency".

5.   INCLUSIVE UNDERSTANDING OF RESPONSIBILITY IN ROBOT ETHICS

Inclusive ethics with a particularly pronounced sensitivity to the in-between can be identified in many fields – robot ethics represents only one. In critical posthumanism, for instance, one also finds exemplary cases of inclusive ethical thinking. Therefore, in Section 5.1, I will start by introducing critical-posthumanist inclusive ethics with an explicit focus on responsibility. Here the approaches of Donna Haraway, Karen Barad, and Lucy Suchman are of particular interest. In the following sections, I will then discuss robot ethical inclusive approaches with regard to a relational understanding of responsibility, namely Allan Hanson (Section 5.2), Mark Coeckelbergh and Janina Loh in a co-authored paper (Section 5.3), and again Coeckelbergh in another paper with a slightly different approach (Section 5.4).

Two types of inclusive ethics will be roughly distinguished from each other. *On the one hand*, there are inclusive ethics that, thanks to their choice of terms for the in-between, formulate a more general approach, a model of ethics, in other words, that is intended for all social spheres, for the entire planet, ultimately for the entire cosmos. *On the other hand*, there are inclusive ethics with a specific focus on certain fields, such as social dimensions, concrete relations, or areas of interest.

In general, one could say that inclusive ethics of the first type are more radical, more comprehensive, and more fundamental. At the same time, however, they show a tendency to vagueness. They may formulate some clear principles, but overall, they do not offer intuitive applicability and practicability for everyday situations. These inclusive ethics, while broad in scope, engage our ethical thinking in very fundamental ways; at the same time, they require an intuitive understanding or a distinct interpretive capacity on the part of those who wish to follow them. I will discuss the approaches in Section 5.1 (especially Haraway's and Barad's approaches) as examples of this first type of inclusive ethics.

The inclusive ethics of the second type can be further differentiated into two subgroups. *On the one hand*, one finds those inclusive ethical positions that have a specific focus of interest but can theoretically be related to the entire cosmos. I introduce two examples of this type of inclusive ethics in Sections 5.1 and 5.2, namely Suchman's ethics of reconfigurations based on Barad, which she develops especially with regard to machines and contexts of human-machine-relations, and Coeckelbergh's and Loh's approach of a genuinely relational understanding of responsibility.

The *second subgroup* of inclusive ethics with a specific interest is inclusive ethics that cannot be readily extended to the entire cosmos. One can find many examples of such inclusive ethical theories in robot ethics such as Luisa Damiano and Paul Dumouchel and David Gunkel. While their ethics are unquestionably relational and inclusive, they are at the same time limited to specific relations – namely, those between humans and machines or robots. In these ethics, species boundaries between humans and machines are maintained. The question arises here whether the inclusive potential, which is undoubtedly evident in these approaches, can actually prove to be genuinely inclusive thinking, which would actually no longer be interested in the identification of moral agents and would thus also no longer be interested in the identification of species (i.e., moral groups) capable of acting morally.

The approaches presented in Sections 5.3 and 5.4 (Hanson and Coeckelbergh) can be categorized in this interesting, yet difficult, subgroup of inclusive ethics. I will discuss both the limitations and the potential of these approaches and their specific sensitivity to the challenges that arise when, on the one hand, one wants to hold on to a traditional concept (responsibility) that is considered good and important, but, on the other hand, runs the risk of failing because of the classical problems that accompany this understanding of responsibility (and that are inherent to exclusive ethics).

5.1   Critical-Posthumanist Inclusive Ethics

In her *Cyborg Manifesto* (1985), Donna Haraway questions the common understanding of the human agent and extends it to nonhumans. Famous is her figuration of the cyborg, a hybrid being of reality and fiction, technology and organic, nature and culture. In later works, it will be primates and dogs in particular that will be included in her family of companion species. But without question, one could also imagine robots here.

Haraway also questions the given knowledge spaces and the disciplinary landscape. In this context, she prepares an inclusive and relational understanding of responsibility, which is expressed very clearly in *Staying with the Trouble* (2016) when she speaks of "response-ability" (2016: 12). Response-ability is the relational equivalent to classical responsibility. Responsibility, in the traditional sense (see Section 3), is attributed or denied essentially to individual agents. It is a distinction of the moral agent and is based on the notion of individual autonomy. Response-ability, in contrast, means a situation-specific being-in, a "[b]ecoming-with" (2016: 12), as Haraway also says. To accept this is to cultivate response-ability, in fact, "to make-with – become-with, compose-with" (2016: 102). Response-ability is not neutral, precisely because being involved can only ever be thought of in a situated and concrete way.

Response-ability means being able to be held accountable (1988: 583), the recognition that one is never innocent, impartial, or unprejudiced in the process of knowledge-making. "Situated and embodied knowledges" (1988: 583) is a way of holding oneself accountable for the production of facts as narratives guiding societies. Conversely, the assertion of relativistic irrelevance of any differences between perspectives leads to a "denial of responsibility and critical inquiry" (1988: 584). Situated knowledges, "positioning[,] implies responsibility for our enabling practices" (1988: 587). This addresses scientific methods and the blurring of traditional boundaries, which is a thoroughly pleasurable thing to enjoy, according to Haraway. It should be noted, however, that the questioning of old boundaries is necessarily accompanied by the establishment of new distinctions, for which one has to answer again. Everyone is individually confronted with the challenge of vacillating between the poles of radical constructivism on the one hand and the mere acceptance and objectification of given structures on the other (Penley & Ross, 1991: 4).

Haraway's concept of responsibility is relational (and thus inclusive) for two reasons. *First*, the subject must learn to see itself as non-monadic and non-autonomous, as a subject that is always already interacting and intertwined with other humans and nonhumans. Responsibility cannot be ascribed to a single agent any more than judgment, autonomy, and other competencies. *Second*, responsibility arises out of and in interaction with humans and nonhumans, in this case, in the production of situated knowledges. The object of knowledge cannot be understood as independent of the observing person, it is not simply "found" in reality at some point in time but rather co-created quite fundamentally by the observer. Responsibility arises in this process and is borne by the whole apparatus of human and nonhuman "subject-objects". This does not mean that individuals are not accountable for their actions, nor that all individual actions are excusable by any given circumstances. But Haraway's relational concept of responsibility implies that the circumstances and the respective situatedness have to be included in the assessment of what someone has "done".

However, Haraway's ethics still seem to be based on the foundation of interaction and identity, which Lucy Suchman transcends with the notion of a mutual constitution in interference relations adopted from Karen Barad. Suchman elaborates on a processual idea of humans and nonhumans constantly recreating themselves with and for each other in their ongoing interferences (2007: 278–279). "Agencies – and associated accountabilities – reside neither in us nor in our artifacts but in our intra-actions" (2007: 285). Similar to Haraway, Suchman has a relational understanding of responsibility via this transformed understanding of agency, which allows us to speak of subject-objects rather than self-sufficient subjects and objects (Suchman, 2011). In doing so, she turns against the "control" (2007: 286) that has been identified by many thinkers as a relevant condition of being able to speak and respond, and thus radically departs from the traditional understanding of the conditions for being able to bear responsibility (see Section 3). Responsibility arises and is perceived exclusively in the "ongoing practical, critical, and generative acts of engagement" (2007: 286).

Barad also agrees with the general "madeness" of facts and emphasizes the fundamental linkage of natural science with economic, ontological, ethical, and social questions (2015: 177–180). According to Barad, questions of (natural) science are questions of justice (2015: 205), as "racist, colonialist, sexist, heterosexist histories" (2015: 175, my translation) are woven into the fabric of (natural) scientific work. Conversely, questions of the economic, the social, and the political are also always at the same time as those of the (natural) sciences (2015: 177). Barad criticizes not only traditional knowledge cultures and the academic landscape but also the, at least implicit, normativity of these supposedly purely descriptive and contemplative (natural) sciences. Justice and empiricism are inextricably intertwined; "ontology, is political" (2015: 207, my translation), since one could not determine *being*, could not engage in ontology, without also engaging in politics. The agent has responsibility due to their structure of being, which is always already one shared with a counterpart or one of being bound to a counterpart. Individuals do not consciously and actively decide to assume responsibility but cannot help being responsible (2015: 183). In Barad's thinking, the concept of a relational ontology or process-ontology, in which there are no subjects and objects, independent entities and relations, but only subject-objects, and the idea of an always already political ontology overlap in the relational concept of responsibility.

The three critical-posthumanist approaches outlined by Haraway, Suchman, and Barad demonstrate a relational and inclusive understanding of responsibility that can be unquestionably applied to the relations between humans and robots. Haraway and Barad thus clearly belong to the first type of inclusive approaches (see the introduction to Section 5), for they conceivably direct their focus to humans and nonhumans alike. Suchman, on the other hand, is specifically interested in human-machine relations and thus belongs to the first subgroup of the second type of inclusive approaches. There is no doubt, however, that her approach can be extended to other nonhumans as well.

5.2   Allan Hanson

Allan Hanson outlines a relational approach to responsibility as a theory of technology and robot ethics in his paper *Beyond the skin bag* (2009). Here, he opposes the traditional approach of a methodological and ethical individualism with the theory of an "extended agency" (2009: 91). For several centuries, Hanson argues, we have been accustomed to understanding an agent as a self-sufficient, monadic, autonomous entity, even if this notion is not historically unified. It is based on the idea of individuality, which emerged only after the Middle Ages in "Western" societies and cannot claim a global status until the present (e.g., with regard to the "Eastern" societies; 2009: 91, 93). On the basis of this methodological individualism, "moral responsibility for an act lies with the subject that carried it out" (2009: 91). If one is willing to deviate from this view of the (moral) agent, then, following Hanson, the "concept of moral responsibility" (2009: 91) associated with this also changes. Hanson moves from a deconstruction of the classical understanding of the agent and the subject of responsibility to a rethinking of the competencies and abilities attributed to this agent in essentialist terms. The central idea behind the concept of extended agency, according to Hanson, is that

> if an action can be accomplished only with the collusion of a variety of human and nonhuman participants, then the subject or agency that carries out the action cannot be limited to the human component but must consist of all of them. (2009: 92)

Drawing on Andy Clark, Donna Haraway, John Law, and other thinkers, Hanson explains his concept of "joint responsibility" (2009: 92), which corresponds to extended agency as "interaction-agency".

The traditional understanding of responsibility against the background of methodological and ethical individualism rests on the attribution of certain competencies, especially cognitive ones, such as "intentionality, the capacity to act voluntarily, and awareness of the consequences of what they do" (2009: 93). Most robot ethicists are not willing to ascribe these and other competencies relevant for the attribution of responsibility to inanimate entities in general and to robots in particular. However, according to Hanson, if we imagine, for instance, two persons who intend to kill someone by one of them chasing the victim into the street where they are then run over by the other with a car, responsibility only arises in and out of the interaction of the two people as well as the car. For if the latter did not exist, the murder could not be put into practice in this way. It is not "that the car has moral responsibility by itself" (2009: 95–96), but the extended agency as an apparatus (as Barad would say) of subject-objects (as Suchman would say) that has to answer for the murder.

A question that follows from Hanson's approach is whether the participation of a human agent is a condition for the attribution of joint responsibility. Hanson himself claims that it is. Even in an extended agency, "[i]t must include a human component because that is the locus of the will, which is necessary to intentions" (2009: 97). By finally relating responsibility to essentialistically ascribable competences after all, such as here intentionality and the (human) will, Hanson's argumentation appears inconsistent and falls back into an implicit methodological individualism, which he had criticized before. This is also the reason why I classify his approach in the second subgroup of the second type of inclusive approaches (see the introduction to Section 5). However, on the other hand, Hanson is much more explicit about the attribution of responsibility in a relational sense than many other robot ethicists. Understanding the agent "more as a verb than a noun" (2009: 98) results in a reformulation of responsibility, which is to be understood less as an attribute and property, but rather as a way of interaction and connection between subject-objects.

5.3   Mark Coeckelbergh and Janina Loh

Coeckelbergh and Loh agree with Hanson's call for a relational reformulation of responsibility. However, they do not show Hanson's consequence in terms of outlining a concrete approach that could be seen as comparable to Hanson's extended agency or joint responsibility. In their paper "Transformations of Responsibility in the Age of Automation" (2019) Coeckelbergh and Loh focus on the responsibility-related questions that arise due to our entering the age of automation that is taking place under the auspices of robotization, digitization, and Industry 4.0. Based on Loh's definition of responsibility (see also Section 3), they first derive three challenges to this traditional understanding of responsibility in the age of auto-mation, namely, *first*, the difficulty of identifying a responsible agent with unambiguity in the face of increasingly autonomous systems. Machines, hybrid systems, and algorithms would at least appear to be equipped with the competencies and capabilities relevant for the attribution of responsibility, while at the same time, the human parties involved (the only potential bear-ers of responsibility in the traditional sense) would seem to bring less and less of these with them, would be able to exercise less and less control over events, and would also understand them less and less overall.

Second, according to Coeckelbergh and Loh, especially in contexts significantly influenced by modern technologies, gaps increasingly appear in the classical framework of relational elements of responsibility (see Section 3). It is often not possible, for instance, to define the normative criteria, instances, or addresses involved in a respective constellation of responsi-bility ascription. Since, however, the complete definition of all relata is the prerequisite for an unambiguous understanding of a respective responsibility and the duties that go along with it, it is consequently not at all clear in such and comparable cases to what extent it is possible to bear responsibility here at all. *Third*, the age of automation is characterized by extended dimensions of space and time, in which it seems impossible to link global events such as cli-mate change and transnational refugee movements to a limited and clearly identifiable group of responsible agents.

Therefore, Coeckelbergh and Loh offer some reflections on a transformation of the conven-tional understanding of responsibility, as this traditional concept of responsibility is obviously no longer up to the challenges mentioned. Referring to the approaches of Emmanuel Levinas and Bruno Latour, they focus on the human and nonhuman "other", who should not be under-stood as a simple relational element (e.g., the object or the addressee of responsibility), but as the center of the phenomenon of responsibility par excellence. This would result in a much stronger form of relationality in responsibility than merely in its "grammatical" structure. Responsibility, according to Coeckelbergh and Loh, arises from direct interaction and con-nectedness with a human or a nonhuman. The perception of responsibility is first and foremost about this "other" and not about the responsible agents, their actions, and competences.

Using this approach in the case of increasingly autonomous machines and robots, Coeckelbergh and Loh outline an example of the first subset of the second type of inclusive approaches (see introduction to Section 5). With Levinas and Latour in the background, this thinking can without any question be extended to other nonhumans. However, Coeckelbergh and Loh do not give a concrete answer as to how this relationally transformed (i.e., inclusive) understanding of responsibility, which always arises only with and through a human or non-human counterpart, can actually be realized, how "we" can actually be or act responsibly.

5.4   Mark Coeckelbergh

On the one hand, Coeckelbergh expresses a very similar view to that of the paper published together with Loh (see Section 5.3) in his paper "Responsibility and the Moral Phenomenology of Using Self-Driving Cars" (2016). Here, based on his relational approach to social connec-tions in *Growing Moral Relations* (2012), Coeckelbergh understands responding as a core element of the relational concept of responsibility (2016: 750). He says that "for a relation to give rise to responsible behavior, the other and the relation to the other need to be perceived, the other needs to appear to me as other, in particular as a morally relevant other" (2016: 751).

In this way, it should become possible to account for the subjective and changeable experiences that human agents have when dealing with modern technologies (in this paper, using the example of autonomous cars).

On the other hand, however, Coeckelbergh eventually essentialistically ties the possibility of exercising responsibility to control and knowledge (2016: 750) and, against this background, concludes that the autonomous car may have the former, but not the latter (2016: 756). This is also the reason why I would classify his approach (as opposed to the one outlined together with Loh, see Section 5.3) in the second subgroup of the second type of inclusive approaches (see the introduction to Section 5). With his essentialist linking of responsibility back to control and knowledge, Coeckelbergh actually rather resembles Hanson's approach.

In both papers (Sections 5.3 and 5.4), it is not clear under which conditions relational and inclusive responsibility is to be attributed, if only the subjective feeling of the (human) agent is to serve as a significant indication of it. It is true that Coeckelbergh emphasizes that both approaches to responsibility – the traditional one and the relational one – are not mutually exclusive, but complementary, whereby "a more comprehensive and a more complete picture of responsibility" (2016: 751) can be drawn than by drawing on only one of the two theories. Thus, it appears that inclusive approaches do not call for a different ontology, a new system, but (at least in some cases) a complement to existing approaches. In contrast, the transformation of the said traditional concept of responsibility proposed by Coeckelbergh and Loh (see Section 5.3) three years later with the help of the approaches offered by Levinas and Latour is clearly more radical, even if not necessarily more unambiguous with regard to the formulation of responsibilities in a given context. Which nonhumans have to answer to what extent and for what remains open in both papers.

6.   ANALYSIS AND CONCLUSION

With the exception of Coeckelbergh (2016), who cites control and knowledge as conditions for responsibility and thus ultimately undertakes an essentialist re-turn of responsibility (back to the conventional understanding of responsibility, see Section 3), all philosophers discussed here would generally have to consider robots as potential participants in contexts in which the attribution of responsibility is at stake. The clearest formulation of this attitude (apart from Haraway's and Barad's critical-posthumanist approaches) is Hanson's concept of joint responsibility of extended agencies, which is always present when an action requires the participation of humans as well as nonhumans.

All approaches are characterized by a radical expansion of the circle of potential subjects of responsibility to nonhumans and entities conventionally understood as objects. Nevertheless, an understanding of relational responsibility is not meant to exclude, for example, the guilty verdict of individual participants.

Suchman and Coeckelbergh (2016) clearly differ in that, according to Suchman, responsibility is precisely the absence of control, whereas for Coeckelbergh it is one of the two conditions for responsibility, along with knowledge. In contrast, the theories of Haraway, Barad, and Hanson sound similar with regard to what is meant by responsibility. According to Haraway, responsibility entails accountability, according to Barad, responsibility always includes the political dimension, and according to Hanson, (moral) responsibility is linked to the concepts of supra-individual and collective attribution of responsibility.

In summary, in inclusive approaches to responsibility in human-robot interaction:

- there is nevertheless the possibility of holding individual responsible parties accountable.
- a connection between ontology, epistemology, ethics, politics, and economics is usually established by means of responsibility.
- there is no uniformity with regard to a possible connection between responsibility and control.
- the interpretation of responsibility as relational does not have to necessarily replace the traditional understanding of responsibility. Inclusive theories could be seen as a supplement to the conventional approaches (in robot ethics) – even though radical changes in our view of the human and the world have to be accepted and critical-posthumanist theories also suggest that a combination of classical and inclusive thinking is not so easily possible.

This chapter also addressed the challenge one faces with the departure from a clear, absolute, and independent authority of judgment, which in turn brings to light a characteristic trait of modern "Western" societies: the need for the broadest possible control and power of disposition, which is seen to be threatened by the development of autonomous artificial systems. Exclusive theories that seek to safeguard the position and status of the human agent usually react to the development of autonomous, self-learning robots, through which they fear a loss of control and predictability, by tightening their own basic assumptions. It is easier to categorically deny robots certain abilities than to deny that they are capable of simulating the respective abilities, i.e., to pretend "as if" they could be autonomous. At the same time, more control and influence of the people involved is claimed, namely in the form of more transparency and comprehensibility of the technologies, including their production contexts as well as more participation in dealing with them.

Inclusive thinkers therefore react (more) calmly to the feared loss of control of modern societies, because they do not think that humans ever have control over nature and culture, over humans, nonhumans, and the cosmos as a whole in a comprehensive and complete sense. For all the abstractness, intricacies, and poor or exhausting comprehensibility that inclusive theories are accused of with some justification, they interestingly have a genuinely pragmatic claim. They are more interested in finding ways to deal constructively with the imponderables and uncertainties in which people have always found themselves, and to identify responsibilities and establish accountability precisely where things are more complex and it is not clear who is able to answer for what and to what extent. If the agent is not seen as a "monad" in the first place, the next step seems to be relatively easy to take, namely the abilities, of which it seemed so relevant so far that they could be attested exclusively to this autonomous agent, cannot be attributed (and thus always denied) in the traditional (anthropological-)essentialist way.

Nevertheless, Haraway, Coeckelbergh, and others repeatedly emphasize that it is not necessary to completely abandon the (illusion of the) autonomous agent. Coeckelbergh (2016) claims consistency between both approaches to responsibility – the traditional and the relational understanding. Haraway, on the other hand, repeatedly emphasizes the fun wrestling with different perspectives when she elaborates that "[i]rony is about contradictions that do not resolve into larger wholes, even dialectically, about the tension of holding incompatible things together because both or all are necessary and true" (2016 [1985]: 5). Against this background, inclusive approaches allow for both the reconciliation of multiple views (here, responsibility as a relational concept would represent an extension of the classical interpretation of responsibility) and the acceptance of a possible incompatibility of different positions – as long as one is willing to keep one's distance from the absoluteness claims of radical objectivism and radical constructivism alike. With Barad, it can be said that from the recognition of the fact that things are socially constructed and not "given" naturally, it does not follow that they are not also real and have very concrete ethical, political, and economic consequences.

My considerations thus lead to the determination of a tension between exclusive approaches to robot ethics, which assume a general ability to perceive responsibility on the part of the humans involved and, if necessary, are still prepared to recognize potential subjects of responsibility in (some, specific) robots, and inclusive approaches, which assume a different understanding of subject and object and consequently also interpret the possibility of ascribing responsibility differently. The extent to which these tensions between inclusive and exclusive approaches, which are becoming uncomfortably tangible, can be finally resolved remains to be seen.

REFERENCES

Barad, K. (2007). *Meeting the Universe Halfway: Quantum Physics and the Entanglement of Matter and Meaning.* Duke University Press.

Barad, K. (2015). Verschränkungen und Politik. Karen Barad im Gespräch mit Jennifer Sophia Theodor. In K. Barad (Ed.), *Verschränkungen* (pp. 173–213). Merve Verlag Berlin.

Braidotti, R. (1992). Essentialism. In E. Wright (Ed.), *Feminism and Psychoanalysis: A Critical Dictionary* (pp. 77–83). Oxford.

Coeckelbergh, M. (2016). Responsibility and the Moral Phenomenology of Using Self-Driving Cars. *Applied Artificial Intelligence* 8, 748–757.

Coeckelbergh, M., & Loh, J. (née Sombetzki) (2019). Transformations of Responsibility in the Age of Automation: Being Answerable to Human and Non-Human Others. In B. Beck & M. C. Kühler (Eds.), *Technology, Anthropology, and Dimensions of Responsibility.* Techno:Phil – Aktuelle Herausforderungen der Technikphilosophie. Volume 1. Stuttgart, pp. 7–22.

Damiano, L., & Dumouchel, P. (2018). Anthropomorphism in Human-Robot Co-Evolution. *Frontiers in Psychology* 9, 1–9.

Duff, R. A. (1998). Responsibility. In Edward Craig (Ed.), *Routledge Encyclopedia of Philosophy*, Routledge, London/New York (pp. 290–294).

Floridi, L., & Sanders, J. W. (2004). On the Morality of Artificial Agents. *Minds and Machines* 14, 349–379.

Gunkel, D. (2007). Thinking Otherwise: Ethics, Technology and Other Subjects. *Ethics and Information Technology* 9, 165–177.

Hanson, F. A. (2009). Beyond the Skin Bag: On the Moral Responsibility of Extended Agencies. *Ethics and Information Technology* 11, 91–99.

Haraway, D. (1988). Situated Knowledges: The Science Question in Feminism and the Privilege of Partial Perspective. *Feminist Studies* 14(3), 575–599.

Haraway, D. (2003). *The Companion Species Manifesto: Dogs, People, and Significant Otherness.* Prickly Paradigm Press.

Haraway, D. (2016). *Staying with the Trouble: Making Kin in the Chthulucene.* Duke University Press.

Haraway, D. (2016 [1985]). A Cyborg Manifesto: Science, Technology, and Socialist-Feminism in the Late Twentieth Century. In Donna J. Haraway (Ed.), *Manifestly Haraway* (pp. 3–90).

Loh, J. (née Sombetzki) (2019a). *Roboterethik. Eine Einführung.* Suhrkamp.

Loh, J. (née Sombetzki) (2019b). Responsibility and Robotethics: A Critical Overview. *Philosophies.* Special Issue *Philosophy and the Ethics of Technology* 4(58).

Loh, J. (née Sombetzki). Posthumanism and Ethics. In Stefan Herbrechter, Ivan Callus, Manuela Rossini, Marija Grech, Megen de Bruin-Molé, Christopher John Müller (Eds.), *Palgrave Handbook of Critical Posthumanism*. Cham, Switzerland: Palgrave Macmillan (pp. 1073–1095).

Penley, C., & Ross, A. (1991). »Cyborgs at Large. Interview with Donna Haraway«. *Technoculture* 3, 1–20.

Rettler, B., & Bailey, A. M. (2017). *Object*. Stanford Encyclopedia of Philosophy. https://plato.stanford .edu/entries/object/. Accessed 10 May 2021.

Sombetzki, J. (now Loh) (2014). *Verantwortung als Begriff, Fähigkeit, Aufgabe. Eine Drei-Ebenen-Analyse*. Springer VS.

Suchman, L. (2007). *Human-Machine Reconfigurations: Plans and Situated Actions*. Cambridge University Press.

Suchman, L. (2011). Subject Objects. *Feminist Theory* 12, 119–145.

41. Machines and morals: moral reasoning ability might indicate how close AI is to attaining true equivalence with human intelligence

Sukanto Bhattacharya

AN INITIAL CONJECTURE (OR TWO) ON MORALITY AND INTELLIGENCE

The development of a structured moral fabric influencing social as well as individual behaviour is arguably a key feature of human social evolution. An analogical parallel may be drawn with the evolution of structured language (e.g., Snowdon, 1989; Hurford, 2012; Suzuki, Wheatcroft & Griesser, 2020). Structured language with full-blown grammar and syntax is in some respects a unique hallmark of humankind (e.g., Lieberman, 1991; Hauser, Chomsky & Fitch, 2002; Tomasello, 2005; Berwick et al., 2013). In a similar vein, while animal behaviour research has brought to light evidence of certain elements of moral cognition to be present in the animal kingdom at large, such evidence has tended to be rather tenuous and disjointed to allow the drawing of meaningfully generalizable inferences about the existence of morality in animals or indeed even the limits within which such morality may exist if at all (e.g., Flack & de Waal, 2000; de Waal, 2006; Fitzpatrick, 2017). Notwithstanding the various experimental or observational data purportedly evidencing morality in animals that are published from time to time, animal behaviourists generally concede that full-blown morality is uniquely human (Burkart, Brügger & van Schaik, 2018).

The development of a structured moral fabric, as will be subsequently posited and argued later within this chapter, is quite likely contingent on the level of cognitive capacity, which one may (albeit loosely) term as intelligence. Without getting drawn into a protracted deliberation on the underlying neurophysiological parameters, for example, in terms of relative brain volume or the scale of complexity in the neural architecture within the human cerebral cortex, it can perhaps be said without raising a storm of controversy that what is commonly construed as human intelligence is ultimately a direct consequence of the highly evolved human cognitive capacity. In other words, human intelligence has morphed into a form that has progressively acquired (albeit via somewhat contested pathways) a set of fundamental distinctions from non-human animal intelligence (Gibson, 2002; Pinker, 2010; Ko, 2016).

One distinctive aspect of human intelligence that continues to be a particularly stubborn stumbling block for artificial intelligence (AI), is the human cognitive ability to engender and process complex thoughts requiring a high level of abstraction. Given the trajectory of the evolution of *Homo sapiens*, it does not require too big a leap of faith to conjecture that only after it had developed beyond some critical threshold along its evolutionary trajectory could the human brain have attained the unique cognitive ability of perceiving and pondering on complex subjects that no longer exhibited direct linkages with survival and propagation – complex subjects like abstract mathematics and moral reasoning. Surpassing such a critical threshold likely triggered an *instrumental transformation* rather than merely an *incremental transformation* in the evolutionary trajectory of human intelligence. Analogically extending to the development of AI, it is further conjectured that AI will also need to similarly surpass some such critical threshold of its own *before* it can undergo the necessary *instrumental transformation* to be able to demonstrate unequivocal equivalence with human intelligence.

It is only via an *instrumental transformation* that the human brain could have finally been enabled to go beyond (even override) its evolutionarily hardwired biological drives and think about deeper issues not directly predicated on the preservation and propagation of species (Burkart, Brügger & van Schaik, 2018). This again brings us back to the analogical parallel drawn earlier with the development of structured language. Indeed, it seems quite reasonable to hypothesize that only after the level of human cognitive capacity had surpassed the conjectured critical threshold in its evolutionary trajectory did structured language blossom beyond just a means of vocalization and communication – into a medium of affective expression via art, music, literature and so forth, that has long shed any natal links with the biological drives of preservation and propagation of species.

Even after more than half a century since its inception, passing a sufficiently general Turing test has continued to remain widely accepted as the holy grail of AI (Turing, 1948; Warwick & Shah, 2016). It is believed that passing such a test will allow AI to credibly claim unequivocal equivalence with human intelligence (Copeland, 2003; Yampolskiy, 2013; Olague et al., 2021). However, the Turing test is not without its detractors and questions have been raised about whether passing the test in some form would incontestably establish unequivocal equivalence with human intelligence (Hayes & Ford, 1995; Berrar & Schuster, 2014; Saariluoma & Rauterberg, 2015). However, to this day, the Turing test is the only such test that has held its position as the ultimate test of AI capability for well over half a century despite the criticisms levelled at it and while suggestions have increasingly been made to extend or improve the testing regimen, the test has not been jettisoned by the AI research community (Moor, 2001; You, 2015; Damassino & Novelli, 2020). Therefore, the Turing test is conceivable, at the very least in a 'placeholder' role, as the ultimate goalpost that AI must get past to claim unequivocal equivalence with human intelligence, unless and until a superior test comes along (Cohen, 2005). There exists a sizeable body of literature on Turing tests that is just too vast to include here, and interested readers are pointed to relevant readings (e.g., Moor, 1975; Crockett, 1994; French, 2000; Stahl, 2004; Kim & Byun, 2021). Although no AI has yet managed to pass a sufficiently general Turing test (Shieber, 2016), as AI research continues to break barriers in its progress towards the target of claiming unequivocal equivalence with human intelligence, several frontiers of human cognitive functions have apparently been conquered already (or will be conquered in the foreseeable future), with rapid advances in areas like computer vision and natural language processing.

However, one frontier of human intelligence still stands largely unconquered by AI – that of human morality. Of course, a case does need to be made in the first place that human morality arguably emerged as a consequence of an *instrumental transformation* in human cognitive capacity once the human brain had evolved beyond the conjectured critical threshold. If such a case can be made, then this can potentially throw AI a curveball by necessitating a goalpost recalibration, which is what we examine in the next section. The subsequent section examines via a 'thought experiment' how moral reasoning ability could potentially indicate how close AI is to its first goalpost. Finally, we assume a future scenario where AI has demonstrated unequivocal equivalence with human intelligence. We then critically consider whether/how AI decisions on moral issues can gain human acceptability.

MORALITY AS A BY-PRODUCT OF INTELLIGENCE: IMPLICATIONS FOR AI

Following on from the conjecture (and its extension) as postulated in the previous section, if human morality, like other higher cognitive abilities, is a consequent product of human intelligence that was acquired only *after* a critical threshold had been surpassed in the evolutionary trajectory and given AI purports to eventually acquire the same level of cognitive capacity, then AI may have not just one but two significant goalposts to get past. The first such goalpost is arguably an implicit (and necessary) one, whereby AI must reach and breach some critical threshold, triggering an *instrumental transformation* rather than merely an incremental one. It is only after this first goalpost is reached that AI can then be realistically expected to pass some universally accepted test of cognitive equivalence (like a general Turing test for example), which will be the second, explicit (and sufficient) goalpost.

A caveat is in order at this point. The purpose here is not to argue in favour of the strong proponents of an evolutionary origin of morality. It is therefore not in any way contended here that full-blown morality is explainable purely via some evolutionary triggers that may have become irrevocably hardwired in our neuro-cognitive psyches. Rather, we would like to think that a hallmark of human intelligence is the ability to transcend the evolutionarily hardwired biological drives in reasoning on deep issues requiring a high level of abstraction. However, to be able to transcend evolutionarily hardwired biological drives and engage in abstract reasoning, the human brain is conjectured to have evolved beyond some critical threshold. Tracing the origins of human morality is a much broader field of philosophical discussion, while we are concerned here with at best a very small (and rather niche) subset thereof. Readers wishing to explore the various philosophical positions with respect to the broader issue concerning the origins of human morality are best directed to Fitzpatrick (2021), which offers an excellent account. For our limited purposes, we define human morality as 'the abstract reasoning ability to collectively consider conflicting choices and decide in a way that transcends self-interests with an aim to attain an outcome of neutral benevolence'. This is not intended as an exclusive or for that matter, even an extensive definition. Rather, it is purely a functional definition that makes it conceptually malleable then to extend to a 'thought experiment' on the moral reasoning ability of AI in the next section to potentially indicate how close AI is to attaining the first (implicit) goalpost and undergoing an *instrumental transformation*.

Now we focus on trying to build an evidence-based case that human morality arguably consequently emerged because of an *instrumental transformation* in human cognitive capacity once the human brain had evolved beyond some critical threshold. If indeed human cognitive capacity reached and breached some critical threshold, then this would likely have left some evolutionary footprints that may already have been (and may yet be) identified, as it would have been an evolutionarily momentous occasion. Relevant neurobiological as well as palaeontological literature indeed offers a few plausible evolutionary footprint 'candidates', supporting the conjecture that abstract thinking likely emerged after some critical threshold was attained along the trajectory of human evolution (Amadio & Walsh, 2006; Somel, Liu & Khaitovich, 2013; Miller, Barton & Nunn, 2019). There is an ongoing debate among palaeontologists as to the duration of such a critical threshold, i.e., whether passing it was a very rapid, almost spontaneous occurrence flying in the face of evolutionary principles like Chomsky's Prometheus (Behme, 2014) or was it the cumulative end-result of minute incremental evolutionary changes that happened over an extended period, akin to all other aspects of evolution adhering to the well-known Darwinian principles of selection, crossover and mutation. Nevertheless, there appears to be a general agreement that it was somewhere along the later phase of the Pleistocene epoch that saw a significant divergence of homo sapient cognition from other protohumans in terms of their symbolic reasoning capabilities (Tattersall, 2014). Therefore, it does seem a reasonable implication that human morality, like other complex cognitive processes requiring a high level of abstraction and symbolic reasoning, emerged subsequent to and as a consequence of a qualitatively enhanced human intelligence around that geological time. It is perhaps worthwhile at this point to emphasize that it is not the objective of this chapter to offer an exploratory exposition of the biological or evolutionary determinants of human intelligence. Rather, we are considering only a very specific functional facet of human intelligence – to be able to engage in abstract thinking and symbolic reasoning that do not have any immediately identifiable natal connections to the hardwired impulsive drives of survival or propagation. As structured moral reasoning involves to a large extent reliance on this specific facet of human intelligence, whether AI is close to attaining the conjectured critical threshold can arguably be construed from its ability to proactively engage in abstract reasoning that involves metaphysically challenging (and often conflicting) moral choices.

If indeed AI needs to reach and breach some critical threshold, as is conjectured to have occurred with the evolution of human intelligence, then how might changes in the moral reasoning ability of AI indicate that the target is getting closer? This is what the next section examines.

CHANGES IN MORAL REASONING ABILITY MIGHT INDICATE HOW CLOSE AI IS TO CLAIMING UNEQUIVOCAL EQUIVALENCE WITH HUMAN INTELLIGENCE

In its progress towards demonstrating unequivocal equivalence with human intelligence, it is not necessary for AI to follow an evolutionary trajectory that exactly mimics that of human brain evolution. For one, natural evolution unfolds at a chronological rate that is many orders of magnitude slower than the rate at which AI has evolved (and will possibly continue to evolve). Even in terms of its exact physical materialization, the critical threshold for AI may in fact come about quite differently compared with the cumulative neuroanatomical transformations in the human brain. However, based on what the human brain evolution has indicated, any *instrumental transformation* is likely to be in the form of a radical shift in the level of cognitive capacity that will occur when AI surpasses a critical threshold of its own. It seems unlikely that it is with the acquiring of any single extra capability that AI will zoom past its first goalpost – rather it will likely be several related capabilities acquired within a relatively short span of time. Individually, each of those extra capabilities may not take AI past that first goalpost, but all of them if acquired collectively within a very short time span, may get AI over the line. If a qualitatively enhanced ability to engage in deep cognitive processing requiring a high level of abstraction is what would categorically distinguish AI *before* reaching and breaching its cognitive threshold from AI *after* reaching and breaching that threshold, then it can be reasonably expected that there will be some empirically observable indications of that momentous leap (or so one can hope!) Therefore, given human moral reasoning does involve a high level of abstract cognitive processing, whether AI is close to (or even already at) its critical threshold might be indicated via some empirically observable changes in how it engages in abstract moral reasoning. However, it needs to be conceded that detecting such indications can prove challenging given there may be fundamental differences in how AI deals with moral choices relative to humans. After all, AI is trained (at least in its earlier developmental stages) using human behaviour as a baseline, whereas human morality arose spontaneously. Also, AI would need to be already operating in social positions where moral reasoning (and thus any changes in the quality of such reasoning) are in fact readily noticeable and identifiable. Notwithstanding the potential detection issues, some indications will very likely be present.

Wallach (2008) reviewed the state of the art at that time in artificial moral reasoning and opined that while computer scientists, roboticists and experts in other cognate disciplines were actively researching ways to improve the moral reasoning ability of machines, it was still rudimentary. Almost ten years since, Conitzer et al. (2017) observed that while AI seems to have made some advances in domain-independent decision-making, this still does not extend to moral decisions. For decision problems with overarching moral constraint(s), they argued that the extant research falls back on knowledge-based systems relying on ad hoc learning rules; and posited some alternative pathways. Cervantes et al. (2020) undertook a fairly comprehensive review of the extant literature on artificial moral agents and concluded that there still appears a long way to go before AI can attain human equivalence in handling moral decisions, particularly under unexpected or ambiguous circumstances. If indeed AI was very close to (or already at) its critical threshold, then either there are no empirically observable signs thereof or such signs have not yet made their way into the extant literature. Following Occam's razor, it seems more plausible that no signs have been reported in the literature simply because there are no reportable signs yet, i.e., AI is still some distance away from its critical threshold. It then raises the question that what is so peculiar about moral reasoning so as not to yet be satisfactorily harnessed by machines. However, if one reflects on this, it will appear that it is not merely moral reasoning but other areas too like metaphysics and abstract mathematics, where machines are still pretty much at a level of maturity as they were several years back, i.e., advances in AI in these areas have not kept pace with the advances in some other fields like computer vision for example. Typically, it is the areas of cognitive reasoning that require a high level of abstraction – it is the '*why*' rather than the '*how*' questions where machines have continued to lag behind the human brain (Bhattacharya, Wang & Xu, 2010; Holzinger et al., 2019).

While a few computational models of moral decision-making have been posited (e.g., Kim et al., 2018), the problem perhaps has not got to do so much with the lack of research efforts but more with where researchers are focusing. There is a light-hearted yarn about a man who was searching frantically for his lost house keys under a streetlamp not because he lost his keys at that spot but only because he could see better under the streetlamp! This is not too different from the current state of AI research (and in fact how AI research has progressed). In their continued efforts to emulate human decision-making in solving problems that involve some form of risk-reward mechanism harking back to the primitive brain, AI researchers have simply overlooked any critical threshold that the human brain would likely have needed to surpass along its evolutionary trajectory to attain its present capabilities. Palaeo-archaeological evidence exists in the form of clear differences between the stone artefacts of the Oldowan (earlier) period vis-à-vis those of the Acheulian (later) period in a transition that is believed to have been temporally rather rapid in evolutionary terms (Semaw, Rogers & Stout, 2009). This counts as further empirical evidence that an *instrumental transformation* in human cognitive capacity occurred as some critical threshold was attained. A similar transformation might also occur for AI only after it attains its own critical threshold, which could materialize via a radical shift in the focus of AI research.

If AI gets close enough to claim unequivocal equivalence with human intelligence, it ought to start showing signs of a materially different way in which it approaches decisions requiring complex abstract thinking – including complex moral choices. Such signs would likely start showing through via an empirically observable, progressive shift of AI applications towards framing and answering the relatively deeper 'why' questions. In other words, a radical shift in the focus of current AI research away from more algorithmic 'how' towards more non-algorithmic 'why', is what could ultimately bring about the instrumental change that would likely see AI emerge qualitatively enhanced on the other side.

From early childhood, human beings across cultures knowingly as well as unknowingly assimilate the prevalent codes of practice as embedded within the various religio-cultural rubrics, which act as boundaries of the envelope that encompasses socially accepted behaviour. However, although inevitably influenced by disparate religio-cultural rubrics (and therefore, possibly expressed somewhat differently across cultures), human morality follows some basic underlying principles that are more or less universal. Perhaps the most ubiquitous of such principles is the sanctity of human life. This is notwithstanding the fact that a human society might approve the death penalty (or life imprisonment, which in a way also deprives life) for individuals convicted of serious crimes, as in such cases the principle of justice selectively overrides the principle of the sanctity of human life. Also, while soldiers are expected to take the lives of their adversaries (and sacrifice their own lives) in battles, again the principle of sanctity of life is selectively overridden by the principles of liberty, sovereignty and so on. But in general, the sanctity of human life is a fundamental principle underlying human morality across cultures possibly since the very dawn of moral reasoning. Therefore, going by our functional definition of morality, a perplexing moral quandary can arise when a choice must be made between the lives of different individuals. Dealing with decision problems with inherently conflicting moral choices is something that AI might be expected to get rapidly better at the closer it gets to attaining the conjectured critical threshold.

Let a scenario be assumed where two individuals have suffered similar critical injuries in an accident, but the emergency care resources available are limited so that the life of only one can be realistically saved. Choosing who will receive emergency care is a decision problem with an overarching moral constraint as saving the life of one individual will necessarily condemn the other to death. In such a situation, a human decision-maker will undergo emotional distress in having to decide one way or the other as the inescapable outcome will be the loss of a human life while trying to save another. Such emotional distress arises from human compassion – something that is essentially non-algorithmic in nature. Increased granularity of the information available can further complicate the decision. If, for example, information becomes available that one of the two individuals who suffered similar critical injuries has an underlying medical condition that severely inhibits the chance of survival, then the rational decision would be to allocate the care to the other individual who does not have any such limiting condition thereby maximizing the efficacy of the limited emergency care resources. It is important to realise that human compassion does not preclude rational choice – the human decision-maker will still allocate the emergency care resources to the individual who is most likely to survive given the information available. An expert system, using case-based reasoning will also arrive at the same decision as the human decision-maker sans any human compassion. However, the situation can get trickier if we allow the granularity to be increased further. Suppose further information becomes available that the individual with the underlying medical condition is a genius scientist on the verge of making a breakthrough discovery that can hugely uplift human welfare. Now it becomes morally a much harder choice to allocate emergency care resources as, although the chance of success is lesser, if the individual with the underlying medical condition receives the emergency care and is successfully saved, that could benefit a great many more people than just that single individual. Is it morally justifiable to condemn to death a person who has a more realistic survival chance because there is a very slim probability that many more persons may benefit if the emergency care resources are instead directed to the individual less likely to survive? This is the sort of conflicting moral choice problem that can potentially stymie current state-of-the-art AI because it requires tackling a deep, non-algorithmic 'why' question rather than a shallow, algorithmic 'how'. Why, if at all, might it be more meaningful to try saving one human life here and now rather than to try possibly benefitting (albeit with a very low probability) many human lives in the future? Human compassion tends to take over where rationality signs off – a human decision-taker can always rely on the 'heart rather than the head' if a moral problem becomes cognitively too overpowering to solve objectively. Thus, human compassion complements rather than constrains complex decision-making when inherently non-algorithmic, deep cognitive processing is called for (as in conflicting moral choices). Emotion and compassion are likely offshoots of human intelligence acquirable by AI only after attaining its critical threshold. Therefore, indications that the threshold is getting closer may be detected via any noticeable changes, subtle or radical, in the ways that AI uses or exhibits emotion and sentience in handling complex and conflicting moral choices.

Current AI research seems intensely focused on opening up multiple fronts in its march towards the target of attaining unequivocal equivalence with human intelligence, and separate (often unrelated) advances in a number of different areas are expected to somehow come together magically to reach a 'singularity', equalizing AI and human intelligence. However, it may take more than simply the 'sum of all the parts' to enable AI to reach its critical threshold. It is the focus of AI research that needs to radically shift to the dark corners where the keys to abstract thinking including moral reasoning are hiding, rather than staying fixated with just the spot under the streetlamp.

If AI researchers successfully re-focus on the 'why' rather than the 'how', it will possibly become a question of 'when' rather than 'whether' AI will attain unequivocal equivalence with human intelligence. However, a bigger question in that scenario will be on the human acceptability of AI-determined moral choices (among other AI-determined decisions that impact human lives). We can see some indications of this already in the conversations and debates that are gaining traction around issues like the operation of smart vehicles, critical surgeries performed by robots and AI-influenced business decisions taken in corporate boardrooms. Assuming AI inevitably attains the requisite cognitive capacity, we critically consider the human acceptability of AI-determined moral choices in the next section.

FINAL FRONTIER: HUMAN ACCEPTABILITY OF AI-DETERMINED MORAL CHOICES

For humans to be able to willingly accept decisions on moral issues delivered by AI, it is understandable that AI will need to convincingly prove its ability to take such decisions, with the quality of outcome being consistently at par with similar decisions taken by humans if not better. AI therefore must fully comprehend what it truly means to be a moral agent beyond being just an intelligent agent. This is also implicit in the thought experiment examined in the previous section in terms of the need to draw upon emotion and sentience in dealing with complex and conflicting moral choices where human well-being is involved. An interesting follow-up question is whether AI-determined moral choices could gain human acceptability. Given the historical patterns of introduction, adoption and diffusion of novel technology, there would likely be a length of time, even after AI has passed a sufficiently general Turing test, that its true cognitive capability would be viewed with continued scepticism. It had taken the passing of several decades for steam power to significantly replace horses in nineteenth-century American cities and although there were a few fiscal factors at play, there was also prevalent scepticism as to the replaceability of the horse as the main source of mechanical power (McShane & Tarr, 2003). Acceptance of AI in matters of moral choices could arguably prove to be many orders of magnitude more demanding than acceptance of steam power, as the evolution of synthetic intelligence is a fundamentally different (and metaphysically perplexing) proposition for humans to accede.

Moreover, any discussion concerning the social acceptability of AI-determined moral choices would necessarily need to encompass practicality considerations involving the socio-legal institutional infrastructure that needs to co-evolve along with the cognitive capabilities of AI. Conversations are already gathering momentum in this space with a growing body of literature taking shape around how extant ethical and legal frameworks ought to be re-cast in anticipation of a closer collaboration (and perhaps an eventual *singular* integration) of synthetic and natural intelligence in furthering human social progression in areas including but not limited to business and corporate leadership, science, medicine and public health as well as governance and policy-making (e.g., Parry, Cohen & Bhattacharya, 2016; Cath, 2018; O'Sullivan et al., 2019; Vesnic-Alujevic, Nascimento & Pólvora, 2020; Ashok et al., 2022). A key factor determining the acceptability or otherwise of AI-guided (even AI-generated) moral decisions could be the contemporaneous development and embedding of key failsafe devices that allow ascertainment of accountability within any decision-making framework, particularly for complex moral choices. These failsafe devices, along with the clarity of process afforded by purpose-built socio-legal rubrics and institutional infrastructure, could inspire mass confidence (thus promoting mass acceptability) of AI-guided (eventually AI-determined) moral choices. Assuming AI gets past the conjectured critical threshold, the biggest challenge with gaining subsequent human acceptability will arguably come from hastily enacted adoption strategies that significantly outpace the development and activation of key failsafe devices and the overhauling of pertinent institutional infrastructure.

With all said and done, when the time comes, AI may have a slight advantage in terms of gaining human acceptability relative to some of the other ground-breaking technological adoptions in the history of human civilization such as steam power and electricity. This is because human society is getting pre-conditioned to eventually accept AI in all those facets of life that are yet untouched by it simply via its existence (and ever-expanding influence) already in most other facets. Exposure to (and fascination with) so-called smart devices is occurring at an increasingly early age across most countries and cultures. It is therefore perhaps not too unreasonable to expect that some future generation may be more accepting of AI competently taking over moral decision-making than some past generation was about steam engines competently taking over from horse-drawn carriages.

FURTHER READING

Ashok, M., Madan, R., Joha, A., & Sivarajah, U. (2022). Ethical framework for artificial intelligence and digital technologies. *International Journal of Information Management*, 62. https://doi.org/10.1016/j.ijinfomgt.2021.102433.

Berwick, R. C., Friederici, A. D., Chomsky, N., & Bolhuis, J. J. (2013). Evolution, brain, and the nature of language. *Trends in Cognitive Sciences*, 17(2), 89–98.

Cath, C. (2018). Governing artificial intelligence: Ethical, legal and technical opportunities and challenges. *Philosophical Transactions of the Royal Society A Mathematical, Physical and Engineering Sciences*. https://doi.org/10.1098/rsta.2018.0080.

Cervantes, J.-A., López, S., Rodríguez, L.-F., Cervantes, S., Cervantes, F., & Ramos, F. (2020). Artificial moral agents: A survey of the current status. *Science and Engineering Ethics*, 26, 501–532.

Crockett, L. J. (1994). *The Turing test and the frame problem.* Ablex Publishing Company.

de Waal, F. B. M. (2006). The animal roots of human morality. *New Scientist*, 192(2573), 60–61.

Fitzpatrick, S. (2017). Animal morality: What is the debate about? *Biology & Philosophy*, 32, 1151–1183.

FitzPatrick, W. (2021). Morality and evolutionary biology. In: Zalta, E. N. (Ed.), *The Stanford Encyclopedia of philosophy* (Spring 2021 Edition). https://plato.stanford.edu/archives/spr2021/entries/morality-biology/.

Flack, J. C., & de Waal, F. B. M. (2000). Any animal whatever'. Darwinian building blocks of morality in monkeys and apes. *Journal of Consciousness Studies*, 7(1–2), 1–29.

French, R. M. (2000). The Turing test: The first 50 years. *Trends in Cognitive Sciences*, 4(3), 115–112.

Hauser, M. D., Chomsky, N., & Fitch, W. T. (2002). The faculty of language: What is it, who has it and how did it evolve? *Science*, 298(5598), 1569–1579.

Hurford, J. R. (2012). *The origins of grammar: Language in the light of evolution II.* Oxford University Press.

Kim, H., & Byun, S. (2021). Designing and applying a moral Turing test. *Advances in Science, Technology and Engineering Systems Journal*, 6(2), 93–98.

Kim, R., Kleiman-Weiner, M., Abeliuk, A., Awad, E., Dsouza, S., Tenenbaum, J. B., & Rahwan, I. (2018). A computational model of commonsense moral decision making. A*IES '18: Proceedings of the 2018 AAAI/ACM Conference on AI, Ethics, and Society*, 197–203.

Lieberman, P. (1991). *Uniquely human: The evolution of speech, thought, and selfless behavior.* Harvard University Press.

Moor, J. H. (1975). An analysis of the Turing test. *Philosophical Studies: An International Journal for Philosophy in the Analytic Tradition*, 30(4), 249–257.

O'Sullivan, S., Nevejans, N., Allen, C., Blyth, A., Leonard, S., Pagallo, U., Holzinger, K., Sajid, M. A., & Ashrafiyan, H. (2019). Legal, regulatory, and ethical frameworks for development of standards in artificial intelligence (AI) and autonomous robotic surgery. *The International Journal of Medical Robotics and Computer Assisted Surgery*, 15, e1968. https://doi.org/10.1002/rcs.1968.

Parry, K., Cohen, M. B., & Bhattacharya, S. (2016). Rise of the machines: A critical consideration of automated leadership decision making in organizations. *Group & Organization Management*, 41(5), 571–594.

Snowdon, C. T. (1989). Vocal communication in New World monkeys. *Journal of Human Evolution*, 18(7), 611–633.

Stahl, B. C. (2004). Information, ethics, and computers: The problem of autonomous moral agents. *Minds and Machines*, 14, 67–83.

Suzuki, T. N., Wheatcroft, W., & Griesser, M. (2020). The syntax–semantics interface in animal vocal communication. *Philosophical Transactions of the Royal Society B Biological Sciences*. https://doi.org/10.1098/rstb.2018.0405.

Tomasello, M. (2005). Uniquely human cognition is a product of human culture. In: Levinson, S. C. & Jaisson, P. (Eds.), *Evolution and culture: A Fyssen Foundation symposium* (pp. 203–218). MIT Press.

Vesnic-Alujevic, L., Nascimento, S., & Pólvora, A. (2020). Societal and ethical impacts of artificial intelligence: Critical notes on European policy frameworks. *Telecommunications Policy*, 44(6). https://doi.org/10.1016/j.telpol.2020.101961.

REFERENCES

Amadio, J. P., & Walsh, C. A. (2006). Brain evolution and uniqueness in the human genome. *Cell*, 126(6), 1033–1035.

Behme, C. (2014). A 'Galilean' science of language. *Journal of Linguistics*, 50(3), 671–704.

Berrar, D. R., & Schuster, A. (2014). Computing machinery and creativity: Lessons learned from the Turing test. *Kybernetes*, 43(1), 82–91.

Bhattacharya, S., Wang, Y., & Xu, D. (2010). Beyond Simon's means-ends analysis: Natural creativity and the unanswered 'Why' in the design of intelligent systems for problem-solving. *Minds and Machines*, 20, 327–347.

Burkart, J. M., Brügger, R. K., & van Schaik, C. P. (2018). Evolutionary origins of morality: insights from non-human primates. *Frontiers in Sociology*. https://doi.org/10.3389/fsoc.2018.00017.

Cohen, P. R. (2005). If not Turing's test, then what? AI *Magazine*, 26(4), 61–67.

Conitzer, V., Sinnott-Armstrong, W., Borg, J. S., Deng, Y., & Kramer, M. (2017). Moral decision making frameworks for artificial intelligence. *Proceedings of the Thirty-First AAAI Conference on Artificial Intelligence (AAAI-17)*, 4831–4835.

Copeland, B. J. (2003). The Turing test. In: Moor, J. H. (Eds.), *The Turing test. Studies in cognitive systems*, vol. 30. Springer. https://doi.org/10.1007/978-94-010-0105-2_1.

Damassino, N., & Novelli, N. (2020). Rethinking, reworking and revolutionising the Turing test. *Minds and Machines*, 30, 463–468.

Gibson, K. R. (2002). Evolution of Human Intelligence: The roles of brain size and mental construction. *Brain, Behaviour and Evolution*, 59, 10–20.

Hayes, P., & Ford, K. (1995). Turing test considered harmful. *Proceedings of the 14th International Joint Conference on Artificial Intelligence*, 972–977.

Holzinger, A., Langs, G., Denk, H., Zatloukal, K., & Müller, H. (2019). Causability and explainability of artificial intelligence in medicine. *WIREs Data Mining Knowledge Discovery*, 9, e1312. https://doi.org/10.1002/widm.1.

Ko, K. H. (2016). Origins of human intelligence: The chain of tool-making and brain evolution. *Anthropological Notebooks*, 22(1), 5–22.

McShane, C., & Tarr, J. (2003). The decline of the urban horse in American cities. *The Journal of Transport History*, 24(2), 177–198.

Miller, I. F., Barton, R. A., & Nunn, C. L. (2019). Quantitative uniqueness of human brain evolution revealed through phylogenetic comparative analysis. *eLife*, 8, e41250. https://doi.org/10.7554/eLife.41250.

Moor, J. H. (2001). The status and future of the Turing test. *Minds and Machines*, 11, 77–93.

Olague, G., Olague, M., Jacobo-Lopez, A. R., & Ibarra-Vazquez, G. (2021). Less is more: Pursuing the visual Turing test with the Kuleshov effect. *Proceedings of the IEEE/CVF Conference on Computer Vision and Pattern Recognition (CVPR) Workshops*, 1553–1561.

Pinker, S. (2010). The cognitive niche: Coevolution of intelligence, sociality, and language. *PNAS*, 107(2), 8993–8999.

Saariluoma, P., & Rauterberg, M. (2015). Turing test does not work in theory but in practice. *Proceedings of The 2015 International Conference on Artificial Intelligence*, 433–437.

Semaw, S., Rogers, M., & Stout, D. (2009). The Oldowan-Acheulian transition: Is there a 'Developed Oldowan' artifact tradition? In: Camps, M. & Chauhan, P. (Eds.), *Sourcebook of Paleolithic transitions*. Springer. https://doi.org/10.1007/978-0-387-76487-0_10.

Shieber, S. M. (2016). Principles for designing an AI competition, or why the Turing test fails as an inducement prize. AI *Magazine*, 37(1), 91–96.

Somel, M., Liu, X., & Khaitovich, P. (2013). Human brain evolution: Transcripts, metabolites and their regulators. *Nature Reviews Neuroscience*, 14, 112–127.

Tattersall, I. (2014). Language as a critical factor in the emergence of human cognition. *HUMANA. MENTE Journal of Philosophical Studies*, 7(27), 181–195.

Turing, A. M. (1948). Intelligent machinery. In: Copeland, B. J. (Ed.), *The essential Turing* (pp. 395–432). Oxford University Press.

Wallach, W. (2008). Implementing moral decision making faculties in computers and robots. AI & *Society*, 22(4), 463–475.

Warwick, K., & Shah, H. (2016). *Turing's imitation game*. Cambridge University Press.

Yampolskiy, R. (2013). Turing test as a defining feature of AI-completeness. In: Yang, X. S. (Eds.), *Artificial Intelligence, evolutionary computing and metaheuristics. Studies in computational intelligence*, vol. 427. Springer. https://doi.org/10.1007/978-3-642-29694-9_1.

You, J. (2015). Beyond the Turing test. *Science*, 347(6218), 116.

42. A women's rights perspective on safe artificial intelligence inside the United Nations

Eleonore Fournier-Tombs

INTRODUCTION

Artificial intelligence (AI) regulation is one of the great public policy issues of this decade. International organisations have not only sought to regulate it (UNESCO, 2021), but also have sought to adapt it to their own objectives, with 200 AI projects recorded by the United Nations in 2021 (International Telecommunications Union, 2022). Improperly implemented, however, these technologies can also be dangerous, leading to a deterioration in the safety and living conditions of those that it hopes to help (Ormond, 2019). This particularly applies to an international organisation context, where AI is used in migration, peacebuilding, and poverty reduction activities in which the beneficiaries are often vulnerable to harm. For women and girls, especially those who are already marginalised by conflict or poverty, unregulated AI has been shown to present certain risks, notably related to discrimination, stereotyping and exclusion.

The United Nations is meant to implement the goals and values set forth by the global community. It has five main objectives – (i) maintaining international peace and security; (ii) protecting human rights; (iii) delivering humanitarian aid; (iv) supporting sustainable development and climate change; and (v) upholding international law (United Nations, 2022b). So far, the investigation of the dynamics of AI and each one of these objectives has been somewhat siloed. The first objective is largely addressed in peace and conflict studies, in terms of how AI technologies can contribute to conflict (for example, in the contribution of social media algorithms to the spread of hate speech; United Nations Human Rights Council, 2018), and occasionally how the technologies can be used for peacebuilding (Laurenson, 2019). The second objective is often discussed when examining the risks of AI to human rights, although occasionally AI technologies have been shown to be useful in identifying human rights violations as well (United Nations Office of the High Commissioner for Human Rights, 2021). Efforts in the use of AI for humanitarian objectives have been partly to showcase the many ways in which the technologies can be used to predict humanitarian crises, organise humanitarian logistics, and understand ongoing crises (Fournier-Tombs, 2021). However, as we will see, there are beginning to be discussions about conducting humanitarian AI with human rights considerations in mind. Much research has taken place on objective four, which, given that there are 17 sustainable development goals, is quite a large area (Mercier-Laurent, 2021). Research on the negative effects of AI on sustainable development is nuanced, as it is largely focused on biases towards specific groups (such as women) (Ormond, 2019), and less on environmental risks (Galaz et al., 2021). Finally, the UN has been a leader in working towards an international legal framework for AI, notably through UNESCO's Recommendations on the Ethics of Artificial Intelligence (UNESCO, 2021). Following these Recommendations, member states will now move towards their own AI regulations, as the European Union has done in its draft AI Act in April 2021 (European Union, 2021). In parallel, the UN too will be working on developing an internal AI framework that has its own unique multilateral context and promotes the attainment of all its objectives.

United Nations agencies have also published research related to the effects of AI on women. A standout is UNESCO's "I blush if I could" report which documents the sexism embedded in virtual assistants and other human-AI interfaces (West, 2019). However, this research has not yet been integrated into mainstream AI ethics efforts. The Recommendations on the Ethics of Artificial Intelligence (UNESCO, 2021) mention gender but without as of yet going into further detail.

One challenge may be that the issue of women's rights and AI goes beyond ethics and into international law. This is an issue for human rights and AI more broadly, as explained by Fukuda-Parr, who argues that the focus on ethics ignores the existence of a human rights foundation (Fukuda-Parr & Gibbons, 2021). As we will see below, discrimination, stereotyping, and exclusion of women through AI is not merely unethical, it contravenes international law, as it goes against the fundamentals of the Convention on the Elimination of All Forms of Discrimination Against Women (CEDAW) (United Nations, 1979). Figure 42.1 demonstrates how an AI ethics for women's rights document could be conceptualised within the existing international human rights framework. The structure also allows for other groups specified in the nine core human rights treaties, such as children or migrants, to also be the subject of specific modules.

This chapter, therefore, aims to discuss the regulation of AI inside international organisations from a women's rights perspective. It describes some of the rich and diverse uses of AI technologies for humanitarian and sustainable development purposes, and highlights some of the current challenges facing those implementing them. It then proposes several pathways

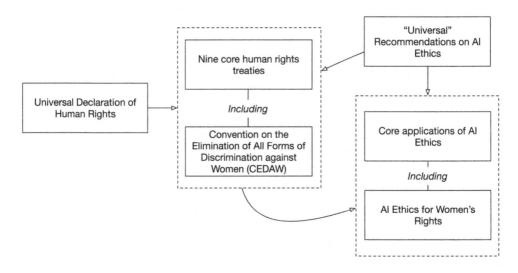

Source: Author.

Figure 42.1   *AI ethics for women's rights in the international human rights framework*

to regulation which would address some of these challenges, proposing that most of these pathways could be complementary. The objective of the chapter is to inform the work of those navigating AI for good at a global level and draw academic awareness to the important issues surrounding women and AI.

CEDAW AND THE CRITICAL FEMINIST PERSPECTIVE

As we have seen, this chapter uses CEDAW as a framework for understanding risks to women in AI, notably due to the convention's importance in the United Nations system. It also positions AI risks within feminist critical theory in their ability to "reinforce or undermine the economic, political, social, and psychological oppression of women" (Tyson, 2014). Current thought on AI can categorise this oppression as follows: discrimination (CEDAW Article 1), meaning that the systems have a different outcome for women than for men due to their sex; stereotyping (CEDAW Article 5), meaning that AI systems perpetuate harmful ideas about women; and exclusion, meaning that the benefits of the AI systems are not accessible to women (CEDAW Articles 10, 11 and 13).

A well-known example of discrimination is the case of Amazon, which used an AI system to score applicant resumés until 2018, when it was discovered the algorithm downranked resumés containing female terms, such as "captain of the women's sports team", or candidates having attended traditionally female colleges in the United States (Dastin, 2018). UNESCO (West, 2019) and the authors of Smart Wife (Strengers & Kennedy, 2021) documented stereotyping in virtual assistants such as Siri, who were anthropomorphised as flirtatious and submissive young women. Finally, the exclusion of women is present throughout the AI lifecycle, from unequal representation in AI education, in the AI programming profession, and in AI-related policymaking, and with unequal access to its benefits. These examples all point to threats to the socioeconomic and psychological condition of women. Unique to AI, also, are the ability of models to capture pre-existing inequality (as in the discrimination example) and perpetuate them in the future, making societal change much more difficult. Some of these threats to women can be amplified in contexts of vulnerability and precarity. As we will see below, these risks are also present in AI applications inside the United Nations.

GENDER RISKS IN AI USE BY THE INTERNATIONAL COMMUNITY

This section provides examples of the uses of AI by international organisations. The examples aim to illustrate some of the current trends in AI internationally, as well as possibilities for the next few years. In some cases, AI algorithms are simply used as an extension of previous techniques, while in others, they are a novel way of using technology for functions that were previously undertaken by human analysts. Forecasting, decision-making systems and image analysis are not completely new. Economists and statisticians have always been employed by these organisations to undertake quantitative analysis in support of international objectives (Furth, 1960). These techniques are novel, however, in that they use recent advancements in data availability and storage and computational power to predict and classify faster and in more detail than was previously possible.

Predictive Analytics

Predictive analytics in this context involves the use of AI algorithms to anticipate future crises and the humanitarian needs evolving from them, to be able to not only plan interventions but also attempt to mitigate or prevent them. In the international community, this type of use of AI has several names, including anticipatory action (UNOCHA, 2021a), foresight (Action Against Hunger, 2017), and early warning (ELDIS, ND). These activities have two broader functions, first, anticipatory financing – raising money for a crisis ahead of time rather than after or during the crisis; and second, anticipatory governance – making strategic decisions based on foresight rather than actual events (Jose Ramos, 2020).

Data used for these algorithms can come from a variety of sources, including official UN or national statistics and more informal data sources. Data from these informal sources are used more and more, for example, from social media feeds, geospatial data, and even news articles (United Nations Global Pulse, 2022). This data is used to train predictive models that will, for example, project the number of refugees arriving in a specific area (UNHCR, 2022b), the humanitarian needs of a population in a crisis setting (ICRC, 2021), or the possibility of natural disasters such as drought or floods (Felsche & Ludwig, 2021).

Increasingly, organisations are finding benefits to harnessing big data and new algorithms for these predictions, finding them extremely helpful in raising funds in anticipation of crises. OCHA, for example, makes yearly funding calls for countries undergoing humanitarian crises, whether they be new or ongoing crises (UNOCHA, 2022). Being able to have advance warning of humanitarian needs might allow the organisation to be more effective when it comes to fundraising. On the other hand, the mere presence of AI systems in humanitarian contexts can cause serious concerns. Nokia recently partnered with the World Bank (Lehdonvirta, 2012) to offer micro-employment to refugees, using them to tag training data for AI systems used globally. This employment offered no benefits or stability, just a small wage, raising questions as to the exploitation of refugee labour for algorithmic training (Jones, 2021). This may be concerning particularly in a context where refugee women are more likely to work in unstable and informal employment (Dawson, 2009).

Logistics

One of the important logistical considerations in a humanitarian context is being able to track aid beneficiaries and ensure that they are receiving basic aid items, such as food, shelter, and first aid (Kovács & Spens, 2007). Additionally, migrants need to be supported in making refugee claims and moving between locations, in conditions that are often very precarious. International organisations and national governments collaborating on refugee camp logistics, humanitarian aid distribution, and case processing have used AI tools in a variety of ways to make the process more efficient.

For example, biometric identification is increasingly used in these contexts as a means of ensuring authenticity of identity. Migrants might struggle to locate and retain appropriate identifiers, such as passports and other documentation. The objective of biometric identification is to centralise identity management and make it easier for migrants to be recognised and tracked as they journey towards a safer haven (Rahman, Verhaert, & Nyst, 2018). This type of technology is used notably by UNHCR (UNHCR, 2022a) and has been promoted by the World Bank in a variety of development countries (Kloppenburg & Van der Ploeg, 2020).

Social scientists have raised several concerns, however, notably in relation to the ability of mainstream biometric identification systems to identify women or people of colour (Buolamwini & Gebru, 2018), which is of particular concern in the case of migration processes. While biometrics have been promoted as benefiting citizens and migrants, many have also questioned the true motivations behind the use of this technology, which can quickly veer into increased control and surveillance on the part of governments (Bussmann, 2020). In the EU Draft AI Act, biometric identification features in both the forbidden and the high-risk categories, depending on the usage. The Chinese government is also known to use CCTV in many public spaces to remotely identify its citizens, crossing behavioural patterns with a multitude of other data points to allow it to track dissenters (Peterson, 2022).

Another example of AI use in logistics has been in the subfield of optimisation, where efforts have been made to better manage the supply chain related to humanitarian aid distribution (Rodríguez-Espíndola, Chowdhury, Beltagui, & Albores, 2020). The World Food Programme, for example, which is responsible for the distribution of food aid during humanitarian crises, partnered with analytics firm Palantir to support work in this domain (Madianou, 2021). This partnership has been criticised extensively in the humanitarian community, however, as Palantir also works with the US government to track and apprehend migrants for deportation (Amnesty International, 2020). Since AI projects at the UN almost always rely on contracts with the private sector, this raises important questions about the ethics of these companies, which will be addressed further below.

Future Trends

These are just some examples of the many ways in which the United Nations is now using AI. As we can see, the analyses above involve very different data sources and AI algorithms. However, AI algorithms are unique in that they can use a large volume of different data sources, given that these are all vectorised – or converted into quantitative data. In this way, seemingly disparate data such as satellite images, faces, survey data, and social media posts can all be converted into interoperable quantitative datasets, which can then be used in the same model. More and more, therefore, international organisations may increase their capacity to collect, store and transform data, giving them the ability to develop more granular and complex AI models.

The future of AI in this sense involves an increase in complexity and precision that may have important effects on the efficacy and cost-effectiveness of international aid. However, as we will see below, this is only the case if certain precautions are taken.

IMPLEMENTATION CHALLENGES FOR FEMINIST AI

When developing AI programmes over the last few years, international organisations have faced several challenges which might be addressed by further regulation. These include difficulties related to gender impact assessment, navigating overlapping ethical frameworks, dealing with resource constraints, and approaching external partnerships.

Challenge 1: Gender Impact Assessment

Evaluating the impact of AI systems on women is very challenging, as effects tend to be varied in nature and in time. Some of the known impacts of AI systems, such as the algorithm used by Amazon (Dastin, 2018), have likely had long-lasting socioeconomic effects that are almost impossible to measure after the fact. While some of the gender risks of using AI in predictive analytics and logistics have been unearthed over the last few years, many are likely still not known.

In understanding gender impact, one of the important steps will be in adopting a flexible yet clear definition of AI. Defining AI is a moving target for several reasons. First, the boundaries between what might be considered AI and what might be considered other things, such as econometrics or computational statistics, or even computer science, are unclear. Some regulating bodies have opted for a broader definition of AI which includes any possible computational analysis of data (European Union, 2021). Others proposed that current definitions of AI are in fact quite different from the original intent of programmers (Jordan, 2019). Yet others, still, feel that a narrower definition of AI, related to a subfield, such as a supervised machine learning algorithm, is warranted (OECD, 2022).

Furthermore, an important distinction can be made between the three types of risks of AI systems to women – discrimination, stereotyping, and exclusion. As we have seen, all three are part of CEDAW, however, they appear very differently in AI systems. While, on the one hand, discrimination can be tested on a technical level by measuring differences in outputs by gender, stereotyping is more complex, with many changes in stereotyping over time (Bhatia & Bhatia, 2021). In CEDAW, Article 5 refers to the "elimination of prejudices and customary and all other practices which are based on the idea of the inferiority or the superiority of either of the sexes or on stereotyped roles for men and women". However, there is still contention about whether having AI assign the female gender to housekeepers and the male gender to programmers (Bolukbasi, Chang, Zou, Saligrama, & Kalai, 2016) is harmful from a socioeconomic perspective or can in some situations be helpful in acknowledging the current distribution of gender roles (Borah Hazarika & Das, 2021). Finally, the exclusion of women in AI development is the area that currently has had the most policy investment and expands to digital exclusion more generally. While equal participation of women at all stages of the AI lifecycle has been improving, it may take many more years to reach, involving contextual factors of gender equality (Hajibabaei, Schiffauerova, & Ebadi, 2022). Furthermore, discrimination and stereotyping in AI, if left unchecked, may also contribute to exclusion, by eliminating women's resumés for technical positions, for example.

Challenge 2: Navigating Overlapping Frameworks

A second challenge in implementing AI in international organisations is navigating a growing collection of frameworks and policies meant to promote safe and "good" AI while adding a women's rights perspective. As we have seen, AI is, in a sense, a loose concept that groups many different technologies, which are in a state of constant evolution. The development of safe AI policies is, therefore, a continuous and iterative process, with no specific end in sight. To structure current AI frameworks and policies, we might use a "bottom-up" versus a "top-down" approach, as both informal and formal initiatives have begun to emerge.

From a "bottom-up" perspective, many frameworks have been developed by offices to help them navigate ethical challenges in AI. In the humanitarian sector, for example, there are a growing number of AI-related initiatives, which are voluntary but standard-setting in intent. Some examples include the Humanitarian Data Science and Ethics Group's AI decision tree (HDSEG, 2021), and UNOCHA's peer review framework for AI models (UNOCHA, 2021b).

Other UN bodies have developed what one might call "top-down" instruments that aim at informing not just their own work, but that of any other organisation or member state in their domain. Examples of this include UNESCO's Recommendation (UNESCO, 2021), a very important document that was adopted by all UN member states. UNICEF's AI for Children policy guidance (UNICEF, 2021), while not a legal instrument per se, is certainly standard-setting in its documentation of the risks and opportunities of AI for children, and how to include them in AI policymaking.

In addition, AI technologies are affected by other data and digital policies in development globally. For example, a key element of AI ethics is the imbalance in training data – under-representing or misrepresenting women, among other groups, and leading to the creation of biased algorithms. This touches on data policy, which is currently concerned with issues such as data governance, privacy, data sovereignty, cybersecurity, and data as a global public good (among others). Some efforts by the United Nations in this domain include the Secretary General's Data Strategy (United Nations, 2020), which does not mention artificial intelligence but does discuss *analytics*, which likely would include AI-powered algorithms.

Challenge 3: Resource Constraints

International organisations, particularly those, like the UN, that are focused on the public good, face important resource constraints. Their interest in adopting AI technologies is certainly linked to these constraints, as AI technologies have been linked to aid effectiveness and increased inclusiveness if implemented properly. However, AI is also expensive (Knight, 2021). In this way, UN agencies face an important challenge in terms of how much AI investment is justified for future gains.

AI as a cost-saving mechanism

The United Nations, as a multilateral organisation, is funded almost exclusively by member states. Some UN aid agencies, such as UNICEF and WFP, also receive individual donations, while private and philanthropic organisations also contribute to certain projects. Regardless of a specific unit's funding structure, however, all parts of the UN have deliverables linked to the accomplishment of the organisation's objectives – peace, humanitarian aid, climate change, multilateralism, and sustainable development.

Throughout the UN's history, many efforts have been made to increase effectiveness and reduce waste – in effect attempting to achieve more with less. The attraction, therefore, for many of the AI initiatives in the organisation is to accelerate the mission of the organisation at a lower cost. It should be noted, of course, that effectiveness and cost-savings are the promise of AI everywhere, not only for international organisations.

AI as an important expense

Investing in AI, however, can be quite expensive for international organisations, as the technology will not increase revenue the way it might for a private company. The promise of the technology, therefore, needs to be balanced with the cost of the investment, no small feat for many offices that do not have a strong ICT capacity to begin with.

As an example, a powerful natural language processing model might cost US$5 million to train (Knight, 2021). A properly trained model, which accounts for gender bias, could be used at the service of several UN objectives, such as analysing humanitarian needs during a crisis or understanding the dynamics of climate change and conflict. Without the funding to train the model, an office could turn to the private sector, a challenge that will be discussed further in the next section, or use a pre-trained, open-source model, in effect using a poorer quality technology that could have lower accuracy and higher ethical risks.

Challenge 4: Public-Private Partnerships

According to those interviewed in the context of this research, most of the AI solutions deployed at the United Nations are provided by the private sector. Private companies can offer AI solutions to international organisations at a lower cost than they might usually pay, and even sometimes offer their own staff or hardware pro bono. This is usually done as part of the company's philanthropic or CSR initiatives.

Public sector organisations already rely on private companies to provide technological products and services that they themselves cannot develop. International organisations already have long-lasting partnerships with companies such as IBM and Microsoft to provide machines, storage capacity, and software in all their offices (Business for 2030, 2022). These partnerships generally take one of two approaches, although these are not mutually exclusive. First, international organisations might sign long-term agreements with companies that provide them with hardware and software, including the cost of this into their budgets. Second, they may receive software and possibly software development services for free as part of an initiative from the company to engage in corporate social responsibility (United Nations, 2022a). Increasingly, big technology companies and newer analytics companies are seeking to provide AI software and services. Non-profits and start-ups are also in the mix, offering innovative data analytics services, software platforms, and dashboards, all at the service of international organisation objectives (United Nations, 2022c).

However, private companies have widely different approaches when it comes to the protection of women's rights. As described in the section on logistics, Palantir's track record was so damaging that it was the object of a full Amnesty International report. Social media companies such as Facebook, which use AI in a variety of areas, from facial recognition to recommendation systems, have also faced a number of accusations including not doing enough to stop hate speech against women (Carlson & Rousselle, 2020) and allowing the US government to access private messages in an abortion trial (Funk, 2022). Importantly, AI companies working with the United Nations are not provided with operational guidelines that they would need to adhere to in order to protect women or any other beneficiaries of their systems.

PATHWAYS TO MULTILATERAL REGULATION

Given the above considerations, several pathways to multilateral regulation exist. Except for Pathway 4, these are not necessarily mutually exclusive and may work to complement each other. They are presented from the most comprehensive to the least, with an attempt to present the strengths and weaknesses of each in a balanced way.

Pathway 1: Gender-Specific Module Covering All AI Activities

The first pathway to consider could be an internal regulation for international organisations covering all AI activities, which would include a clear gender module. The question of responsibility for internal guidance is not an easy one. UNESCO has taken on the role of providing guidance for member states on AI regulation, a role that could lead to an international convention on AI in the next few years. Internally, however, there might be other options to consider, including the office of the Secretary-General itself, which has made digital governance a core objective of its mandate. In connection with this, there is the UN Tech Envoy's office, which has been an important force in convening internal discussions on AI governance. Of course, there is UNWOMEN, which would lead the coordination between women's rights and AI policy. In practice, this would come as a directive from the governing board including all United Nations agencies. A more general, values-based gender module would require each agency to develop more specific implementation guidelines, while a more specific module, including a gender-impact assessment methodology, for example, might provide sufficient information to be deployed as-is throughout the organisation.

Pathway 2: Gender Modules for Each Fund and Programme

The second pathway would involve having each fund and programme develop its own gender module, which would be enforced by the head of the agency. This would likely also involve some inter-agency collaboration for specific activities as they relate to the five main objectives described in the first section. This pathway would be the responsibility of each sector's governing body to implement. The responsibility for some sectors is more clearly defined than for others. For example, AI for the environment would be clearly spearheaded by UNEP, with the involvement of other agencies engaged in environmental work, such as UNDP for development work and UNDRR for disaster risk reduction. The UN's humanitarian activities are coordinated by OCHA but overseen by the Inter-Agency Standing Committee (IASC), which is responsible for humanitarian standards more generally, and could be a good candidate for humanitarian AI standards.

Pathway 3: Adherence to National Guidance

One might expect that national policies will be developed in accordance with global instruments, such as the UNESCO Recommendations. As such, they should be interoperable, going into further implementation detail as relevant for the country or region. International organisations should be able to comply with the national regulations, if they do not interfere with other international frameworks, such as humanitarian law or human rights law. Compliance with these regulations could then be the responsibility of AI or digital governance leads in the organisation. Increasingly, agencies and units are building their digital governance capacity in a way that would operate much like other regulatory compliance units globally. In the case of an interference between national guidance and international frameworks, a decision would be made by the field office to avoid using the AI system in this context, or to go ahead anyways, acknowledging the friction. However, it should be noted that without UN-wide or agency-specific regulations, it might be challenging for field offices to know how to react, if, for example, a government chose to become involved in data processing or algorithm development to the detriment of gender rights.

Pathway 4: No New Gender Regulation

Finally, one might explore the "do nothing" possibility, which involves considering existing regulatory frameworks, such as CEDAW, as sufficient to protect women's rights in AI. There still exist critics of the AI regulatory process, with some arguing that it is too early to regulate such a changing technology and that regulation might stifle innovation (Shead, 2021). Regulation has a cost of slowing down the development of AI systems that might promote women's rights. Evaluating the cost-benefit of reducing harm while allowing helpful innovations to flourish is a challenge that all regulators are faced with. Those promoting this pathway would argue in favour of investment and innovation first, with the hope that an important AI capacity will be developed before, or despite, regulatory efforts. This would mean, however, that discrimination, stereotyping, and exclusion of women would be addressed through human rights frameworks *post hoc*, rather than through preventative measures.

CONCLUSION

The regulation of AI is a global process that may not have a clear end in sight. It is possible that, over time, certain risks of AI become resolved, while new ones crop up. However, building certain mechanisms to tie AI regulation to women's rights will be important, especially at the United Nations. While risks to women from a critical feminist perspective align with the historical marginalisation of women, they may also serve to propagate them and negate some of the important advances to women's rights in other domains.

The objective of describing these four pathways – a gender-specific module covering all AI activities; a gender module for each UN agency; adherence to national guidance; and no outright guidance – is to support those sorting through complex issues of technology and multilateralism through additional conceptual guidance. The landscape discussed in this chapter may change significantly in the coming years. This means that regulation is not an end. Rather, it is a process, one that we will likely be engaged in for decades to come. However, this reflection hopes to contribute to the continuous iteration that is women's rights and global AI policy and improve the outcomes at least of the current regulatory cycle.

REFERENCES

Action Against Hunger. (2017). The future of aid – INGOs in 2030. *ReliefWeb*. Retrieved from https://reliefweb.int/report/world/future-aid-ingos-2030

Amnesty International. (2020). Failing to do right: The urgent need for Palantir to respect Human Rights. *Report*. Retrieved from https://www.amnestyusa.org/wp-content/uploads/2020/09/Amnest-International-Palantir-Briefing-Report-092520_Final.pdf

Bhatia, N., & Bhatia, S. (2021). Changes in gender stereotypes over time: A computational analysis. *Psychology of Women Quarterly, 45*(1), 106–125.

Bolukbasi, T., Chang, K.-W., Zou, J. Y., Saligrama, V., & Kalai, A. T. (2016). Man is to computer programmer as woman is to homemaker? debiasing word embeddings. *Advances in neural information processing systems, 29.*

Borah Hazarika, O., & Das, S. (2021). Paid and unpaid work during the Covid-19 pandemic: A study of the gendered division of domestic responsibilities during lockdown. *Journal of Gender Studies, 30*(4), 429–439.

Buolamwini, J., & Gebru, T. (2018). *Gender shades: Intersectional accuracy disparities in commercial gender classification.* Paper presented at the Conference on fairness, accountability and transparency.

Business for 2030. (2022). IBM. Retrieved from http://www.businessfor2030.org/ibm

Bussmann, T. (2020). *Citizen perceptions on biometrics: Surveillance or service?* University of Twente. Retrieved from http://essay.utwente.nl/82757/

Carlson, C. R., & Rousselle, H. (2020). Report and repeat: Investigating Facebook's hate speech removal process. *First Monday*.

Dastin, J. (2018). Amazon scraps secret AI recruiting tool that showed bias against women. In *Ethics of data and analytics* (pp. 296–299). Auerbach Publications.

Dawson, A. (2009). The people you don't see: Representing informal labour in fortress Europe. *ARIEL: A Review of International English Literature, 40*(1).

ELDIS. (ND). HEWS web. Retrieved from https://www.eldis.org/organisation/A7288

European Union. (2021). Proposal for a regulation of the European Parliament and of the Council laying down harmonised rules on artificial intelligence (Artificial Intelligence Act) and amending certain Union Legislative Acts. Retrieved from https://eur-lex.europa.eu/legal-content/EN/TXT/?qid =1623335154975&uri=CELEX%3A52021PC0206

Felsche, E., & Ludwig, R. (2021). Applying machine learning for drought prediction in a perfect model framework using data from a large ensemble of climate simulations. *Natural Hazards and Earth System Sciences, 21*(12), 3679–3691. https://doi.org/10.5194/nhess-21-3679-2021

Fournier-Tombs, E. (2021). Towards a United Nations internal regulation for Artificial Intelligence. *Big Data & Society, 8*(2), 20539517211039493.

Fukuda-Parr, S., & Gibbons, E. (2021). Emerging consensus on 'Ethical AI': Human rights critique of stakeholder guidelines. *Global Policy, 12*, 32–44.

Funk, J. (2022). Facebook data leads to charges against Nebraska woman for aiding daughter's abortion. Retrieved from https://globalnews.ca/news/9049126/abortion-nebraska-charges-facebook/

Furth, J. H. (1960). On United Nations economics. *World Politics, 12*(2), 264–271.

Galaz, V., Centeno, M. A., Callahan, P. W., Causevic, A., Patterson, T., Brass, I., . . . Garcia, D. (2021). Artificial intelligence, systemic risks, and sustainability. *Technology in Society, 67*, 101741.

Hajibabaei, A., Schiffauerova, A., & Ebadi, A. (2022). Gender-specific patterns in the artificial intelligence scientific ecosystem. *Journal of Informetrics, 16*(2), 101275.

HDSEG. (2021). Decision-tree for ethical humanitarian data science. Retrieved from https://www.hum -dseg.org/tree/0/3/0/new

ICRC. (2021). The future is now: Artificial intelligence and anticipatory humanitarian action. Retrieved from https://blogs.icrc.org/law-and-policy/2021/08/19/artificial-intelligence-anticipatory -humanitarian/

International Telecommunications Union. (2022). 2021 United Nations activities on artificial intelligence (AI) report. *AI for Good*. Retrieved from https://aiforgood.itu.int/about-ai-for-good/un-ai-actions/

Jones, P. (2021). Refugees help power machine learning advances at Microsoft, Facebook, and Amazon. *Rest of World*. Retrieved from https://restofworld.org/2021/refugees-machine-learning-big-tech/

Jordan, M. I. (2019). Artificial intelligence—the revolution hasn't happened yet. *Harvard Data Science Review*.

Ramos, Jose, Ida Uusikyla, & Nguyen Tuan Luong. (2020). Anticipatory governance – A primer. Retrieved from https://www.undp.org/vietnam/blog/anticipatory-governance-%E2%80%94-primer

Kloppenburg, S., & Van der Ploeg, I. (2020). Securing identities: Biometric technologies and the enactment of human bodily differences. *Science as Culture, 29*(1), 57–76.

Knight, W. (2021). AI's smarts now come with a big price tag. *Wired*. Retrieved from https://www.wired .com/story/ai-smarts-big-price-tag/

Kovács, G., & Spens, K. M. (2007). Humanitarian logistics in disaster relief operations. *International Journal of Physical Distribution & Logistics Management, 37*(2), 99–114. https://doi.org/10.1108 /09600030710734820

Laurenson, L. (2019). *Polarisation and peacebuilding strategy on digital media platforms: Current strategies and their discontents*. Toda Peace Institute.

Lehdonvirta, V. (2012). From millions of tasks to thousands of jobs: Bringing digital work to developing countries. *World Bank Blogs*. Retrieved from https://blogs.worldbank.org/psd/from-millions-of-tasks -to-thousands-of-jobs-bringing-digital-work-to-developing-countries

Madianou, M. (2021). Digital innovation and data practices in the humanitarian response to refugee crises. *Routledge Handbook of Humanitarian Communication*, 185.

Mercier-Laurent, E. (2021). *Can Artificial Intelligence effectively support sustainable development?* Paper presented at the IFIP International Workshop on Artificial Intelligence for Knowledge Management.

OECD. (2022). OECD AI principles. Retrieved from https://oecd.ai/en/ai-principles

Ormond, E. (2019). The ghost in the machine: The ethical risks of AI. *The Thinker, 83*(1), 4–11.

Peterson, D. (2022). 12AI and the surveillance state. *Chinese Power and Artificial Intelligence: Perspectives and Challenges.*

Rahman, Z., Verhaert, P., & Nyst, C. (2018). Biometrics in the humanitarian sector. *Oxfam and The Engine Room.*

Rodríguez-Espíndola, O., Chowdhury, S., Beltagui, A., & Albores, P. (2020). The potential of emergent disruptive technologies for humanitarian supply chains: The integration of blockchain, Artificial Intelligence and 3D printing. *International Journal of Production Research, 58*(15), 4610–4630.

Shead, S. (2021). A.I. researchers urge regulators not to slam the brakes on its development. *CNBC.* Retrieved from https://www.cnbc.com/2021/03/29/ai-researchers-urge-regulators-not-to-slam-brakes-on-development.html

Strengers, Y., & Kennedy, J. (2021). *The smart wife: Why Siri, Alexa, and other smart home devices need a feminist reboot.* MIT Press.

Tyson, L. (2014). *Critical theory today: A user-friendly guide.* Routledge.

UNESCO. (2021). Recommendations on the Ethics of Artificial Intelligence. Retrieved from https://en.unesco.org/artificial-intelligence/ethics

UNHCR. (2022a). Biometric identification system. Retrieved from https://www.unhcr.org/protection/basic/550c304c9/biometric-identity-management-system.html

UNHCR. (2022b). Project Jetson. Retrieved from https://jetson.unhcr.org/

UNICEF. (2021). Policy guidance on AI for children Retrieved from https://www.unicef.org/globalinsight/reports/policy-guidance-ai-children

United Nations. (1979). Convention on the Elimination of All Forms of Discrimination Against Women (CEDAW).

United Nations. (2020). Secretary General's data strategy. Retrieved from https://www.un.org/en/content/datastrategy/index.shtml

United Nations. (2022a). Google teams up with UN for verified climate information. Retrieved from https://www.un.org/en/climatechange/google-search-information

United Nations. (2022b). Our work. Retrieved from https://www.un.org/en/our-work

United Nations. (2022c). UN launches hunt for start-ups and enterprises changing the face of food systems. Retrieved from https://www.un.org/en/food-systems-summit/news/un-launches-hunt-start-ups-and-enterprises-changing-face-food-systems

United Nations Global Pulse. (2022). Website. Retrieved from https://www.unglobalpulse.org/

United Nations Human Rights Council. (2018). Report of the detailed findings of the Independent International Fact-Finding Mission on Myanmar. Retrieved from https://www.ohchr.org/sites/default/files/Documents/HRBodies/HRCouncil/FFM-Myanmar/A_HRC_39_CRP.2.pdf

United Nations Office of the High Commissioner for Human Rights. (2021). Artificial intelligence risks to privacy demand urgent action – Bachelet. Retrieved from https://www.ohchr.org/en/2021/09/artificial-intelligence-risks-privacy-demand-urgent-action-bachelet

UNOCHA. (2021a). Anticipatory action: Changing the way we manage disasters. *ReliefWeb.* Retrieved from https://reliefweb.int/report/world/anticipatory-action-changing-way-we-manage-disasters

UNOCHA. (2021b). Peer review framework for predictive analytics in humanitarian response. Retrieved from https://data.humdata.org/dataset/2048a947-5714-4220-905b-e662cbcd14c8/resource/76e488d9-b69d-41bd-927c-116d633bac7b/download/peer-review-framework-2020.pdf

UNOCHA. (2022). Global humanitarian overview. Retrieved from https://gho.unocha.org/

West, M., K. Rebecca, and Han Ei Chew. (2019). I'd blush if I could: Closing gender divides in digital skills through education. *UNESCO and EQUALS Skills Coalition.*

43. From ethics to politics: changing approaches to AI education

Randy Connolly

INTRODUCTION

In a brief reflection on progress and its sometimes-disappointing end results, the German-Jewish philosopher Walter Benjamin on the eve of World War 2 wrote of the Angel of History, whose face is turned back towards the past but is constantly propelled into the future via the winds of progress (Benjamin, 1979). Looking backwards and powerless to change the past, the angel sees nothing but the ever-accumulating detritus of human catastrophe. For most of its own short history, computing has had its own revised version of this angel, one who peers not backwards but forwards to a remarkable future transformed via its field of study. But now in 2023, it seems safe to say that the decades-long computer optimism party has finally played itself out, leaving more and more of us with multiple regrets and growing unease. Expectations of computer-enabled social transformation, once so common, have given way to more sober assessments of a more mundane, even troubling, reality. As noted by Green (2022), computing "faces a gap between its desire to do good and the harmful effects of many of its interventions." While this divergence between desire and reality may have puzzled some within computing, those within fields such as history, political science, or sociology have likely been less surprised at computing's role in increasing the wreckage most recently piled at the feet of this Angel. In the immediate aftermath of the financial crisis of 2008–2009, there were calls for educational reforms within business schools (Giacalone & Wargo, 2009) and economics departments (Shiller, 2010), where it was thought that unrealistic models and assumptions within the university had to bear some responsibility for inculcating an ideology that led to the crisis. As this author has argued elsewhere (Connolly, 2020), it is time for computing educators to engage in the same soul-searching.

A sensible starting place would be to recognize more broadly our field's entanglement in the social world. Lessig (2009) in the early years of the Internet prophetically coined the phrase "code is law" to capture the idea that technological architectures (especially software algorithms) have joined laws, markets, and social norms as one of the four factors regulating social behaviour (Katzenbach & Ulbricht, 2019). While "digital disruption" became a self-congratulatory conviction in start-up IPOs and business school rhetoric during the 2000s, computing education at the same time was actually trying to balance itself on an unstable wobble board of conflicting stances. On the one hand, the academic discipline saw itself as principally a purveyor of technical skills and objective engineering metrics such as efficiency and performance. But at the same time, it also wanted to see computing as a way of improving society for the betterment of all. One influential manifestation of this idea is the "computing for social good" movement advocated by Goldweber et al. (2013) and subsequently embraced within AI itself, for example, by Tomašev et al. (2020). This movement perhaps reflected broader social good initiatives within the field of policy development, such as the UN's sustainable development goals declaration (UN, 2015).

While orienting computing towards social goods is certainly a commendable intention, the problem for computing is that its emphasis on technical metrics may have "thwarted the social goods the field was trying to achieve" (Selbst et al., 2019). If a typical computer science undergraduate curriculum has, say, 28 courses devoted to technical and mathematical topics and just one to issues relating to social goods, we should not be surprised that students would feel it is relatively unimportant. Moving forwards, it will thus be increasingly important to loosen the hold of technical skills in the education of computing students and to encourage our computing students to understand and investigate the broader social context of computing. This has become an especially acute issue with the exceptional growth and power of machine learning/classification algorithms, automated decision-making systems, and new statistical approaches to large data sets, a form of computing hereby simply referred to as artificial intelligence. The intent of this chapter is to report on a wide range of new studies that have taken up this call.

This chapter begins by first addressing the limitations of ethics instruction, a pedagogical intervention which has been widely adopted within the discipline as the principal means for avoiding some of the potential social harms caused by computerization. It then looks at a series of "turns" or shifts in analytic focus within the broad subfields of computing ethics/computers and society studies. The first of these is what Abede et al. (2020) call the "normative turn in computing," one explicitly concerned with issues of fairness, accountability, and transparency. Scholars in this area have found their work has required increasing their engagement with the wider social context of computing. Motivated by concerns around bias and discrimination, some contemporary scholars are increasingly being drawn towards questions relating to computerization's relationship to power, which is perhaps the start of another turn, this one a social and political one. This potential reorientation of scholarly attention within computing issues courses away from just ethics and onto a closer examination of the interactions between computing and the social and political milieu is especially important within the subfield of artificial intelligence given the wide applicability of its approaches to the social context.

LIMITATIONS OF ETHICS

While contributors to this *Handbook* (and its readers) are likely already concerned with the societal implications of computing in general, and AI in particular, such concerns are still relatively muted within computing as a whole. For instance, in a recent evaluation of the hundred most-cited recent machine learning papers (Birhane et al., 2021), only 2% of these papers even mentioned the possibility that there might be negative lifeworld consequences to their research; the overwhelming focus in these papers was on performance, efficiency, and innovation. Yet, to be fair, over the past three decades, there has been a concerted effort by computing standards bodies to get computing professionals to be more concerned with non-technological metrics (ACM, 2016; ABET, 2016; CSTA, 2017; ACM and IEEE, 2018). In particular, they have encouraged curriculum developers to include coverage of ethical theories or codes of professional conduct promulgated by these organizations. This call for ethical training, which mirrored an earlier movement within engineering education (Hess & Fore, 2018) has been widely adopted, as evidenced by Fiesler et al. (2020) who gathered syllabi from 115 courses teaching computing ethics, Stahl et al. (2016) who performed a content analysis on almost 600 papers on computing ethics topics, and Tomašev (2020) who detailed dozens of academic and corporate efforts at integrating ethical philosophy or codes into the practice of AI computing. While a laudable intention, this long-standing injunction to include ethics instruction in computing curricula seemingly has done little to prevent "many well-intentioned applications of algorithms in social contexts … [from causing] significant harm" (Green & Viljoen, 2020).

Why, one might ask, has this adoption of ethics instruction and codes of conduct been so widespread? One reason might be, as argued by Connolly (2011), that it allows for an algorithmic approach to teaching social issues that is intellectually familiar to computing faculty. Or perhaps, as sourly observed by Green (2022), it is the belief that doing so will somehow lead to better social outcomes. While this belief in the transformative power of ethics education has occasionally been criticized throughout the history of the field (Johnson, 1985; Herkert, 2005; Connolly, 2011; Vakil, 2018), it still remains the dominant paradigm within computing (e.g., Fiesler et al., 2020; Grosz et al., 2019; Salz et al., 2019; Skirpan et al., 2018). Hess and Fore (2018) labelled this approach within engineering education "microethics" in that the teaching emphasis is placed on individual decision-making using ethical theories (such as Kantian universalism or Mills' consequentialism) and/or professional codes of conduct. While moral philosophy may indeed facilitate the critical scrutiny of computer applications (Bietti, 2022), its main drawback is that within CS education "questions of ethics are commonly framed through an individualistic lens that presents ethics as primarily about the decisions of good and bad actors" (Washington & Kuo, 2020; Smuha, 2021). That is, computer ethics is too often divorced from the wider social context which gives moral philosophy its relevance.

The authors to be examined in the next section are endeavouring to do just that: introducing new (to computing, not to the rest of the academy) languages and concepts to help computing students in this task of deliberating and debating about the wider social context of computing. These new understandings were initially advanced by scholars in the social sciences and humanities. But in recent years, they have been embraced by scholars within computing who have argued that the social implications of computing "are better addressed through frameworks centered upon understanding of power, justice, oppression rather than the more technically 'resolvable' issues of ethics, bias, transparency, etc" (Bates et al., 2020). This work has been categorized here using the social science and humanities idea of a "turn," that is, a shift in analytic focus undertaken by a wide range of scholars.

THE NORMATIVE TURN

In a recent paper, Abebe et al. (2020) described the "normative turn in computer science which has brought concerns about fairness, bias, and accountability to the core of the field." This has been especially true within the machine learning, HCI, and data science subfields. Certainly, concerns about fairness and bias in general have become acute across many societies (especially so in the United States). As noted by Larsson (2019), "the use of the concept 'ethics' in contemporary AI governance discourse may arguably be seen as a kind of proxy" for concerns about algorithmic fairness, accountability, and transparency (sometimes referred to via the unflattering acronym FAT). While an encouraging movement away from purely philosophic ethics, questions of fairness, accountability, and transparency are not without their own complications.

Transparency—that is, the understandability of a specific algorithmic model—seems the necessary ingredient for accountability—a relationship that obligates an actor to explain and justify its conduct (Wieringa, 2020)—which in turn is required for assessing social fairness (Lepri et al., 2017). The fact that transparency is an attractive ideal is, no pun intended, clear. We have a long cultural history deeply tied to the belief that enemies of the common good plot in secret, that seeing something promises a form of control and/or protection, and that liberal democracies' ideal of legislative openness is the mechanism by which society gains an element of security against arbitrary measures with concealed motivations. Notwithstanding this background, the ideal of transparency does have some issues. The first is the question, transparent for whom? (Kemper & Kolman, 2019; Larsson & Heintz, 2020). That is, who is the audience for transparency in algorithms? Average citizens? Other programmers? Commercial rivals? Regulatory bodies? Law courts?

This question is further clouded by the complex nature of algorithms in general and of classification/ML ones in particular. As any computer professor can attest, being able to formulate an algorithm is a difficult-to-acquire trait; being able to review or evaluate one is an even rarer one. This problem is especially acute within AI. Classification models are, at one level, merely applications of scalar functions: that is, methods for calculating single numbers (usually a probability) that express the fit of its many inputs to some desired solution. ML algorithms are thus elegant applications of socially unproblematic statistical and mathematical techniques. Bias or unfairness is arguably then not hard coded in the algorithms themselves, to be revealed via regulations around transparency. Rather, they are "emergent properties of the machine learning process, not identifiable from the review of the code" (Kemper & Kolman, 2019; *contra* Hooker, 2021).

For this reason, most calls for transparency are not for the black-box algorithms themselves, but for the training data that the classification models operate on (Bodo, 2017). But because this data is sometimes very large—thousands or even millions of data records—many ML classification models appear undecipherable and unexplainable even to their own architects (Gryz & Rojszczak, 2021), a not-unsurprising outcome for algorithms designed to discover unseen patterns in data. Within computing, there has been a variety of efforts at addressing this so-called explainability problem (Lakkaraju et al., 2019; Baehrens, 2010). But even here, success at algorithmically achieving explainability has been limited (Gryz & Rojszczak, 2021). As Bodo et al. (2017) noted, such approaches at explainability often require the deployment of additional algorithmic agents, adding yet another layer of digital surveillance to a data sphere that is already crowded with surveillance.

With these issues at the forefront of our concern, it may seem likely that addressing FAT *after* these systems are deployed is not the solution we need. Adding in and prioritizing concerns about fairness and values *before* a system is designed may be a better alternative. Such an idea is by no means new. It has a "long and often neglected history within computer science itself" (Simon et al., 2020), most notably in the value sensitive design (VSD) approach to computing inspired by Friedman (1997). VSD is a proactive approach that endeavours to build desired values such as fairness into algorithmic systems right from the beginning of a project. As noted by Selbst et al. (2019), "Fairness and justice are properties of social and legal systems … not properties of tech tools." That is, fairness is not an objective metric akin to performance that can be bolted onto the spec sheet of software systems; preventing discriminatory outcomes requires first engaging with the very social and political environments in which unfairness and inequality arise (Simon et al., 2020; Gangadharan & Niklas, 2019). Thus, "for want of a truly neutral stance, AI developers will have to adopt normative positions on issues they probably prefer to avoid" (Larsson, 2019). Indeed, some scholars within computing are already doing so by arguing for an explicit justice orientation to the teaching of computing and to the practice of machine learning.

Vakil (2018) was an early advocate for a justice-centred approach to teaching this normative turn. Instead of focusing on ethics or only examining the sometimes-technical issues of fairness, accountability, and transparency, such an approach, Vakil argued, requires "considering the sociocultural and sociopolitical contexts in which technologies have been developed and applied." In such a course, students would engage in the critique of abuses of technological power and learn how to design technological systems that reflect students' social and civic identities. A recent special issue on justice-centred computing education in *ACM Transactions on Computing Education* similarly calls for a reorientation "of computing and computing education towards justice goals" (Lachney et al., 2021).

How is such a reorientation to be made? Couldry (2020) wondered if computing has the right intellectual toolbox for understanding and critiquing the problematic features of contemporary computing. A key part of this toolbox has arguably already been prepared for us by the field of science and technology studies (STS). The key insight of STS is that social processes such as the development and adoption of a technology are extremely complex and involve factors such as "social conditions, prices, traditions, popular attitudes, interest groups, class differences, and government policy" (Nye, 2007). This complexity makes, for instance, the normative evaluation of outcomes especially fraught. Yet, the analytic heterogeneity of STS has meant it has been long awakened to "the power asymmetries of technological innovation" (Ransom et al., 2021).

The question of power has indeed become the preeminent one in the recent normative turn. In their introduction to the special issue on justice-oriented computing (Lachney et al., 2021), the authors argue that helping students with uncovering and critiquing the different ways that power and bias are encoded within algorithms and technological devices must be a key part of any computing education. Winner's (1980) influential essay "Do Artifacts Have Politics?" is often the starting point for this line of thinking. Winner argued that technological systems can become political when they prevent certain social outcomes within a community (such as Robert Moses designing the height of New York freeway underpasses in the 1950s to prevent buses carrying lower-income racial minorities from accessing public beaches) or when they privilege specific social outcomes (Winner's example here was how the mechanical tomato harvester encouraged the transformation of the tomato business away from small family farms to one dominated by large agribusinesses).

Winner's paper was especially valuable in that it allowed its readers to see the politics that can be hidden within even mundane technologies such as bridges and agricultural harvesters. Recent work within computing continues this tradition of uncovering the hidden politics of technological systems (Moore, 2020; Barabas et al., 2020; Ryoo et al., 2021; Kirdani-Ryan & Ko, 2022). New ways of discovering and engaging with the social world of computing systems have broadened these approaches. For instance, the idea of intersectionality has been ported from feminist thought and applied to the evaluation of computing systems. Intersectionality "is a framework that seeks to account for the multiple, overlapping, and intersecting elements of people's identities and the ways system oppression shifts and changes in interaction with these intersecting identities" (Erete, 2021). The benefit of an intersectional approach is how it foregrounds the stories and lived experiences of individuals from groups who might have been considered inconsequential to the main thrust of computing history. Hicks's (2017) work uncovering the vital role of female programmers in the rise of British computing in the 1950s (and their displacement and eviction leading to its decline in the 1960s) is a superb example of the benefits of this approach.

POLITICS AND AI

This call to recognize the political aspects of computing is not likely to be uncontroversial within most academic computing departments. Certainly, many computing instructors will be reluctant to bring politics into their classrooms. But the call for teaching the political nature of computing technologies does not have to mean advocating for a political party or joining a side in the culture wars. Rather, it means seeing politics in its broadest sense: that it is a process of reasoning about ideals (Washington & Kuo, 2020) and engaging in debates about the definition and distribution of goods in society (Heckert, 2005). Understood in this broad sense, one can see that politics is everywhere. Why is this the case? Because power relations are "the foundational relationship of society … they construct and shape the institutions and norms that regulate social life" (Castells, 2016). Political science has long recognized that politics are present wherever there is cooperation, conflict, or control. Algorithms, data analytics, and the advancements in machine learning which flow from these two, are more and more affecting these three spheres, as predicted by Lessig's "code as law" formulation mentioned earlier. The cooperation, conflict, and control aspects of digital advancements have inspired a wide variety of critical evaluations throughout almost all the social science disciplines but have largely been lacking within academic computing outside the relative handful working within the computer ethics subfield. Yet even there, this close connection between technological systems and systems of power "is often absent from conversations around ethics in computing" and this "must be brought to the foreground in K-16 computing education" (Vakil & Higgs, 2019).

This author is a computing professor and is sometimes uncomfortable at times engaging in political topics in the classroom. Teaching technical content seems relatively easy in comparison. Nonetheless, we need to frequently remind ourselves that this "is how we create and sustain societal trust: not by cherishing the illusion of an ideal world where power plays no role, but by creating and sustaining countervailing powers" (Hildebrandt, 2021). That is, we need to engage our students within our computing courses in discussions about "regulation, legislation, democratic participation, and societal debate as means to shape innovation ecosystems" (Stahl, 2021). It is time to recognize that the computing field's hope that teaching ethics will ameliorate the potential (and actual) deleterious consequences of our technological innovations on our social lifeworld is not only naïve and unrealistic but may even be exacerbating those consequences. We need to instead focus on the repertoire of means used with previous problematic technologies, namely laws/regulations/legislation and the activism that motivates legislatures. Furthermore, this is not just a topic for a computing ethics class; rather, a law-focused, risk-assessment orientation needs to be a fundamental part of the worldview of computing. Beck (1986) made an influential argument advocating for the adoption of a risk management perspective within engineering as a means of reducing the adverse effects of technological ecosystems. In words that are just as relevant today to computer scientists as they were 35 years ago to engineers in the shadow of Chernobyl, he argued such technological disciplines "must rethink and change their own conceptions of rationality, knowledge, and practice as well as the institutional structure in which they are put to work." Such a rethink has more recently been made by Paul Nemitz (2018), EU Directorate General for Justice and Consumers, who argued that all software systems must be designed from their beginning to be in accord with the principles of democracy, the rules of law, and in compliance with fundamental human and social rights. Indeed, draft EU legislation on AI has enshrined these principles by mandating "a human rights, democracy, and rule of law impact assessment *prior* [italics added] to designing or procuring the [AI] system" (Smuha, 2021). Similarly, the UNESCO Recommendation on the Ethics of AI (2021) also advocates for a rule-of-law approach to AI governance, one which prioritizes values such as human rights and environmental sustainability via formalized ethical impact assessments and data policies. These proposals indicate the way forward for the discipline: namely, to recognize the political ramifications of computing work right from the start of our students' education, thereby allowing us to incorporate broadly shared political values (e.g., human rights, democracy, rule of law, social justice, sustainability, equality) into the design of our systems. This will require computing to broaden its educational approach beyond technical skills.

To be fair, it is easy to advocate for *ex ante* risk assessment around political values; knowing how to do so is not so easy. Prognosticating the social outcomes of technological innovation is notoriously difficult. This author begins his courses with a quote from science fiction writer Isaac Asimov (1953), "It is easy to predict an automobile in 1880; it is very hard to predict a traffic problem." That is, predicting future technological innovations is generally the straightforward process of extrapolating from current technology. Predicting social outcomes, by contrast, is fraught and complicated work, requiring not just insight into human and social behaviours, but also perhaps real creative thinking. Our ability to assess innovation *before* its deployment is also hindered by the narrative power of the idea that technological progress is inexorable and that controlling it is a quixotic hope.

But it is important to remember that societies do have this ability. In the living memory of this writer, supersonic passenger aeroplanes (e.g., Concorde) and nuclear power were ultimately rejected or their growth halted. Industrial emissions were regulated; urban freeway projects (one of the most important technologies of the 1950s and 1960s) were sometimes successfully resisted by citizens. Fast food, arguably one of the most important technologies of the last century, has repeatedly been constrained by public opinion. In all of these examples, control came about partly due to institutionalized risk assessments (i.e., self-critique) and partly through activism and legislation (politics). This type of risk assessment and political activism needs to be part of normal computing work. As a field, computing has been too willing to delegate such work to others. Moving forward, computing in general, and AI-related computing in particular, needs to embrace the culture of self-critique as the necessary intellectual ingredient of true progress. We would be wise to recollect Beck's (1986) advice to engineers in the 1980s:

> Only when medicine opposes medicine, nuclear physics opposes nuclear physics, human genetics opposes human genetics, or information technology opposes information technology can the future that is being brewed up in the test tube become intelligible and evaluable for the outside world.

CONCLUSION

Computing over the past several decades has tended to be either blithely oblivious to the world it was helping to create or deluded itself by self-congratulatory narratives around the benefits of digital disruption. But computing has always been a profoundly political invention. It was created during a war to help win that war, and it spread widely in the subsequent peace during a time of unparalleled growth in corporative power. Indeed, computers were designed from their beginning "to protect the interests of the powerful actors who control them" (Hicks et al., 2021). The libertarian rhetoric that became associated with the new internet of the 1990s camouflaged for a time this close affiliation of computing with established power. Today, there is no excuse for ignoring computing's power relations. Within computing academia, we have taught our subject as a mirror, reflecting our focus on internal metrics such as efficiency, performance, and innovation. Moving forward, we need to change the way we teach so our subject is a window instead: that is, an aperture for peering outwards to the social and human lifeworlds that our technology is affecting. This is an especially apposite transformation given the uncertain world facing all of us as artificial intelligence techniques become more and more pervasive throughout our societies.

REFERENCES

Abebe, R., Barocas, S., Kleinberg, J., Levy, K., Raghavan, M., & Robinson, D. G. (2020). Roles for Computing in Social Change. In *Proceedings of the 2020 Conference on Fairness, Accountability, and Transparency*. https://doi.org/10.1145/3351095

ABET [Accreditation Board for Engineering and Technology]. (2016). Criteria for Accrediting Computing Programs, 2017–2018. Retrieved from http://www.abet.org/accreditation/accreditation -criteria/criteria-for-accrediting-computing-programs-2017-2018/.

ACM [Association for Computing Machinery]. (2016). Computer Engineering Curricula 2016. Retrieved from https://www.acm.org/binaries/content/assets/education/c21016-final-report.pdf.

ACM & IEEE [Institute of Electrical and Electronics Engineers]. (2018). ACM Code of Ethics and Professional Conduct. Retrieved from https://www.acm.org/code-of-ethics.

Asimov, I. (1953). Social Science Fiction. In *Modern Science Fiction: Its Meaning and Its Future*, Reginald Bretnor (Ed.). Coward-McCann. Quoted in https://quoteinvestigator.com/2019/10/23/ traffic.

Baehrens, D., Schroeter, T., Harmeling, S., Kawanabe, M., Hansen, K., & Müller, K.-R. (2010). How to Explain Individual Classification Decisions. *Journal of Machine Learning Research*, 11, 1803–1831.

Barabas, C., Doyle, C., Rubinovitz, J. B., & Dinakar, K. (2020, January). Studying Up: Reorienting the Study of Algorithmic Fairness around Issues of Power. In *Proceedings of the 2020 Conference on Fairness, Accountability, and Transparency*, 167–176. https://doi.org/10.1145/3351095.3372859

Bates, J., Cameron, D., Checco, A., Clough, P., Hopfgartner, F., Mazumdar, S., ... de la Vega de León, A. (2020). Integrating FATE/Critical Data Studies into Data Science Curricula: Where Are We Going and How Do We Get There? In *Proceedings of the 2020 Conference on Fairness, Accountability, and Transparency*. https://doi.org/10.1145/3351095

Beck, U. (1986). *Risk Society: Towards a New Modernity*. Trans. Mark Ritter. Sage.

Benjamin, W. (1979). Theses on the Philosophy of History. In *Critical Theory and Society: A Reader*, Stephen Bronner and Douglas Kellner (Eds.). Routledge.

Bietti, E. (2022). From Ethics Washing to Ethics Bashing: A Moral Philosophy View on Tech Ethics. *Journal of Social Computing*, 2(3), 266–283. https://doi.org/10.23919/JSC.2021.0031

Birhane, A., Kalluri, P., Card, D., Agnew, W., Dotan, R., & Bao, M. (2021). The Values Encoded in Machine Learning Research. *arXiv preprint* arXiv:2106.15590.

Bodo, B., Helberger, N., Irion, K., Zuiderveen Borgesius, F., Moller, J., van de Velde, B., ... de Vreese, C. (2017). Tackling the Algorithmic Control Crisis-the Technical, Legal, and Ethical Challenges of Research into Algorithmic Agents. *Yale Journal of Law & Technology*, 19, 133.

Castells, M. (2016). A Sociology of Power: My Intellectual Journey. *Annual Review of Sociology*, 42(1), 1–19. https://doi.org/10.1146/annurev-soc-081715-074158

Connolly, R. (2011). Beyond Good and Evil Impacts: Rethinking the Social Issues Components in Our Computing Curricula. In *Proceedings of the 16th Annual Joint Conference on Innovation and Technology in Computer Science Education*, 228–232. https://doi.org/10.1145/1999747.1999812

Connolly, R. (2020). Why Computing Belongs within the Social Sciences. *Communications of the ACM*, 63(8), 54–59. https://doi.org/10.1145/3383444

Couldry, N. (2020). Recovering Critique in an Age of Datafication. *New Media & Society*, 22(7), 1135–1151. https://doi.org/10.1177/1461444820912536

CSTA [Computer Science Teachers Association] Standards. (2017). CSTA K-12 Computer Science Standards (Rev. ed). Retrieved from https://www.csteachers.org/page/standards.

Erete, S., Thomas, K., Nacu, D., Dickinson, J., Thompson, N., & Pinkard, N. (2021). Applying a Transformative Justice Approach to Encourage the Participation of Black and Latina Girls in Computing. *ACM Transactions on Computing Education (TOCE)*, 21(4). https://doi.org/10.1145/3451345

Fiesler, C., Garrett, N., & Beard, N. (2020). What Do We Teach When We Teach Tech Ethics? A Syllabi Analysis. In *Proceedings of the 51st ACM Technical Symposium on Computer Science Education*, 289–295.

Friedman, B. (Ed.). (1997). *Human Values and the Design of Computer Technology*. Cambridge University Press.

Gangadharan, S. P., & Niklas, J. (2019). Decentering Technology in Discourse on Discrimination. *Information, Communication & Society*, 22(7), 882–899. https://doi.org/10.1080/1369118X.2019.1593484

Giacalone, R. A., & Wargo, D. T. (2009). The Roots of the Global Financial Crisis are in Our Business Schools. *Journal of Business Ethics Education*, 6, 147–168.

Goldweber, M., Barr, J., Clear, T., Davoli, R., Mann, S., Patitsas, E., & Portnoff, S. (2013). A Framework for Enhancing the Social Good in Computing Education: A Values Approach. *ACM Inroads*, 4(1), 58–79.

Green, B. (2022). Data Science as Political Action: Grounding Data Science in a Politics of Justice. *Journal of Social Computing*, 2(3), 249–265. https://doi.org/10.23919/jsc.2021.0029

Green, B., & Viljoen, S. (2020). Algorithmic Realism: Expanding the Boundaries of Algorithmic Thought. In *Proceedings of the 2020 Conference on Fairness, Accountability, and Transparency*, 19–31. https://doi.org/10.1145/3351095.3372840

Grosz, B. J., Grant, D. G., Vredenburgh, K., Behrends, J., Hu, L., Simmons, A., & Waldo, J. (2019). Embedded Ethics: Integrating Ethics Across CS Education. *Communications of the ACM*, 62(8), 54–61. https://doi.org/10.1145/3330794

Gryz, J., & Rojszczak, M. (2021). Black Box Algorithms and the Rights of Individuals: No Easy Solution to the "Explainability" Problem. *Internet Policy Review*, 10(2), 1–24.

Herkert, J. R. (2005). Ways of Thinking About and Teaching Ethical Problem Solving: Microethics and Macroethics in Engineering. *Science and Engineering Ethics*, 11(3), 373–385. https://doi.org/10.1007/S11948-005-0006-3

Hess, J. L., & Fore, G. (2018). A Systematic Literature Review of US Engineering Ethics Interventions. *Science and Engineering Ethics*, 24(2), 551–583.

Hicks, M. (2017). *Programmed Inequality: How Britain Discarded Women Technologists and Lost its Edge in Computing*. MIT Press.

Hicks, M., Mullaney, T. S., Peters, B., Hicks, M., & Philip, K. (2021). When Did the Fire Start? In *Your Computer Is on Fire*, T. S. Mullaney, B. Peters, M. Hicks, and K. Philip (Eds.). MIT Press.

Hildebrandt, M. (2021). Understanding Law and the Rule of Law. *Communications of the ACM*, 64(5), 28–31. https://doi.org/10.1145/3425779

Hooker, S. (2021). Moving beyond "Algorithmic Bias is a Data Problem." *Patterns*, 2(4), 100241.

Johnson, D. G. (1985). *Computer Ethics*. Prentice Hall.

Katzenbach, C., & Ulbricht, L. (2019). Algorithmic Governance. *Internet Policy Review*, 8(4). https://doi.org/10.14763/2019.4.1424

Kemper, J., & Kolkman, D. (2019). Transparent to Whom? No Algorithmic Accountability without a Critical Audience. *Information, Communication & Society*, 22(14), 2081–2096. https://doi.org/10.1080/1369118X.2018.1477967

Kirdani-Ryan, M., & Ko, A. J. (2022). The House of Computing: Integrating Counternarratives into Computer Systems Education. In *Proceedings of the 53rd ACM Technical Symposium on Computer Science Education*, 279–285. https://doi.org/10.1145/3478431.3499394

Lachney, M., Ryoo, J., & Santo, R. (2021). Introduction to the Special Section on Justice-Centered Computing Education, Part 1. *ACM Transactions on Computing Education (TOCE)*, 21(4). https://doi.org/10.1145/3477981

Lakkaraju, H., Kamar, E., Caruana, R., & Leskovec, J. (2019). Faithful and Customizable Explanations of Black Box Models. In *Proceedings of the 2019 AAAI/ACM Conference on AI, Ethics, and Society*. https://doi.org/10.1145/3306618.3314229

Larsson, S. (2019). The Socio-Legal Relevance of Artificial Intelligence. *Droit et société*, 103, 573–593. https://doi.org/10.3917/drs1.103.0573

Larsson, S., & Heintz, F. (2020). Transparency in Artificial Intelligence. *Internet Policy Review*, 9(2), 1–16. https://doi.org/10.14763/2020.2.1469

Lepri, B., Oliver, N., Letouzé, E., Pentland, A., & Vinck, P. (2017). Fair, Transparent, and Accountable Algorithmic Decision-making Processes. *Philosophy & Technology*, 31(4), 611–627. https://doi.org/10.1007/S13347-017-0279-X

Lessig, L. (2009). *Code: And Other Laws of Cyberspace*. Basic Books.

Moore, J. (2020). Towards a More Representative Politics in the Ethics of Computer Science. In *Proceedings of the 2020 Conference on Fairness, Accountability, and Transparency*. https://doi.org/10.1145/3351095

Nemitz, P. (2018). Constitutional Democracy and Technology in the Age of Artificial Intelligence. *Philosophical Transactions of the Royal Society*, 376(2133), 20180089.

Nye, D. (2007). *Technology Matters*. The MIT Press.

Ransom, E., Grady, C., Trepanier, L., & Bain, C. (2021). Situated Ethics in Development: STS Insights for a Pragmatic Approach to Development Policy and Practice. *Science, Technology, & Human Values*. https://doi.org/10.1177/01622439211052685

Ryoo, J. J., Morris, A., & Margolis, J. (2021). "What Happens to the Raspado Man in a Cash-free Society?": Teaching and Learning Socially Responsible Computing. *ACM Transactions on Computing Education (TOCE)*, 21(4), 1–28. https://doi.org/10.1145/3453653

Saltz, J., Skirpan, M., Fiesler, C., Gorelick, M., Yeh, T., Heckman, R., Dewar, N., & Beard, N. (2019). Integrating ethics within machine learning courses. *ACM Transactions on Computing Education*, 19(4). https://doi.org/10.1145/3341164.

Selbst, A. D., Boyd, D., Friedler, S. A., Venkatasubramanian, S., & Vertesi, J. (2019). Fairness and Abstraction in Sociotechnical Systems. In *Proceedings of the Conference on Fairness, Accountability, and Transparency*. https://doi.org/10.1145/3287560

Shiller, R. J. (2010). How Should the Financial Crisis Change How We Teach Economics? *The Journal of Economic Education*, 41(4), 403–409. https://doi.org/10.1080/00220485.2010.510409

Simon, J., Wong, P.-H., & Rieder, G. (2020). Algorithmic Bias and the Value Sensitive Design Approach. *Internet Policy Review*, 9(4). https://doi.org/10.14763/2020.4.1534

Skirpan, M., Beard, N., Bhaduri, S., Fiesler, C., & Yeh, T. (2018). Ethics Education in Context: A Case Study of Novel Ethics Activities for the CS Classroom. In *Proceedings of the 49th ACM Technical Symposium on Computer Science Education*, 940–945. https://doi.org/10.1145/3159450.3159573

Smuha, N. A. (2021). Beyond the Individual: Governing AI's Societal Harm. *Internet Policy Review*, 10(3). https://doi.org/10.14763/2021.3.1574

Stahl, B. C., Timmermans, J., & Mittelstadt, B. D. (2016). The Ethics of Computing: A Survey of the Computing-Oriented Literature. *ACM Computing Surveys*, 48(4), 1–38.

Stahl, B. C. (2021). From Computer Ethics and the Ethics of AI Towards an Ethics of Digital Ecosystems. *AI and Ethics 2021*, 1, 1–13. https://doi.org/10.1007/S43681-021-00080-1

Tomašev, N., Cornebise, J., Hutter, F. et al. (2020). AI for Social Good: Unlocking the Opportunity for Positive Impact. *Nature Communications*, 11, 2468. https://doi.org/10.1038/s41467-020-15871-z

UNESCO. (2021). Recommendation on the Ethics of AI. https://en.unesco.org/artificial-intelligence/ethics

United Nations. (2015). Sustainable Development Goals. https://sdgs.un.org

Vakil, S. (2018). Ethics, Identity, and Political Vision: Toward a Justice-Centered Approach to Equity in Computer Science Education. *Harvard Educational Review*, 88(1), 26–52. https://doi.org/10.17763/1943-5045-88.1.26

Vakil, S., & Higgs, J. (2019). It's about Power. *Communications of the ACM*, 62(3), 31–33. https://doi.org/10.1145/3306617

Washington, A. L., & Kuo, R. S. (2020). Whose Side Are Ethics Codes On? Power, Responsibility and the Social Good. In *Proceedings of the 2020 Conference on Fairness, Accountability, and Transparency*, 10. https://doi.org/10.1145/3351095

Wieringa, M. (2020). What to Account for When Accounting for Algorithms: A Systematic Literature Review on Algorithmic Accountability. In *Proceedings of the 2020 Conference on Fairness, Accountability, and Transparency*, 1–18. https://doi.org/10.1145/3351095.3372833

Winner, L. (1980). Do Artifacts Have Politics? *Daedalus*, 109(1), 121–136. http://www.jstor.org/stable/20024652.

44. The transparency of reason: ethical issues of AI art

Dejan Grba

INTRODUCTION

Since artists' early experiments with artificial intelligence (AI) in the 1970s, AI art has traversed several periods that have always involved strong ties to information technologies and intense engagement with the phenomenology of digital culture. The increasing affordance of multi-layered sub-symbolic machine learning (ML) architectures such as deep learning (DL) in the 2010s helped AI art to diversify, gain visibility, and attain cultural relevance. Contemporary AI art includes various creative practices that have emerged out of, and in response to, the expansion and raising sociopolitical influence of AI technologies and economies. Its topics, conceptual approaches, methodologies, presentational formats, and implications are closely related to AI research and business, so its expressive features are affected by the conflicting paradigms, epistemic uncertainties, cognitive inadequacies, discursive inaccuracies, political tensions, and ethical problems of AI science, technology, and industry. Ethics has been integral to modern AI research since its outset in the mid-1950s, and over time, it has incorporated values such as explainability, safety, privacy, beneficence, freedom, sustainability, responsibility, social cohesion, and fairness (Jobin et al., 2019). Notional discrepancies about these values and their inconsistent implementations merge with technological and ideological vectors into a complex cultural environment that accommodates the majority of affairs, problems, and debates about AI, and profoundly influences the ethics of AI art.[1]

The core issues of AI science involve underlying theories of cognition, basic theoretical assumptions, and technical approaches to designing intelligent systems (Mitchell, 2019, 19–21). AI research explores concepts that are mostly, but not exclusively, inspired by broad notions of intelligence and learning found in living beings. The computational theory of mind views minds as computers and essentially identifies intellect with abstract computation within a behaviourist perspective that emphasizes feedback and training mechanisms (Rescorla, 2020). Computationalist anticipations of emergent intelligence are based upon assumptions that software will attain intelligence and develop emotions given more training data, more sophisticated algorithms, and more computational power. Conversely, the theory of biologically embodied cognition complicates the approach to AI both epistemologically and technologically. It proposes that consciousness and intelligence are inherently and decisively dependent on the overall functioning and sensory processing of the body within the physical, biological, and social aspects of its environment (Seth, 2021). This introduces significant technical challenges and implies subtle ethical constraints since bio-embedded cognition depends

---

[1] Besides the titles referenced in the chapter, publications that discuss the ethics of AI and AI art include Marcus & Davis (2019), Pasquinelli (2019), Żylińska (2020), Audry (2021), Natale (2021), Zeilinger (2021), and Grba (2022b, 2022c).

on many motivational and behavioural features, such as selfish competitiveness, that are evolutionarily beneficial but undesirable in just and equitable societies.

Mainstream AI emphasizes technologically feasible and lucratively applicable ML architectures that mimic certain narrowly defined human cognitive features or skillsets but with meagre achievements in emerging explanatory principles. Although narrow ML systems struggle with accuracy and safety in handling statistically extreme but plausible scenarios because they lack robust and flexible control algorithms analogous to human common sense (Mitchell, 2019, 84–95), anthropomorphism remains AI's most pervasive conceptual ambiguity. Anthropomorphism is an innate psychological tendency to assign human cognitive, emotional, or intentional traits to non-human entities (Hutson, 2012). Its radical forms include viewing computers as human beings and vice versa, even though there is no reason for conflating a complex biological entity with an artificial non-living system just because both can perform functions that are computationally describable. Similarly, the "sociotechnical blindness" syndrome conflates the narrow functional autonomy of ML systems with the general features of human autonomy, which obscures the essential roles humans play at all stages of AI design and deployment (Johnson & Verdicchio, 2017).

The prevailing lack of objectivity about these fetishisms proves less surprising in light of the fact that science fiction (SF) has been an important intellectual source for many AI researchers and entrepreneurs. As much as it may be inspirational, SF limits both creative and critical thinking by "sweetening" or canonizing certain ideas regardless of their validity and by stimulating attractive aspirations that may ultimately prove to be meaningless or dangerous. Science-fictional AI has also become a reference point for speculations about AI's development trajectories and consequences (Hermann, 2021), which gravitate towards extreme scenarios, either utopian (artificial general intelligence, artificial consciousness, singularity), or catastrophic (evil superintelligence) (Mitchell, 2019, 45, 215–229). Whether fuelled by wishful thinking, mythical visions, religiosity, or economic or political agendas, the hypothetical essence of these scenarios makes them ultimately frivolous. The fancy, insincerity, hypocrisy, pretentiousness, or insidiousness lurking in their backdrop pollute the political space of AI, which is already replete with acute but insufficiently addressed real problems.

Many of these problems stem from the global business trends of the corporate AI sector (CAI) (Grba, 2022c). The politics of CAI unfolds in defining and controlling the profit-oriented research, development, and application of AI technologies. Enterprise companies deploy AI in cybernetic frameworks that reinforce their power structures, "optimize" social management, and maximize labour. They simultaneously obscure the political interests of their products and render their workforces transparent (Crawford, 2021). CAI's "human in the loop" complex manifests most notoriously as the exploitative crowdsourcing of transnational echelons of workers for dataset classification, annotation, and other essential tasks in AI design (Taylor, 2018).

CAI's business strategies extrapolate a trend of equating sociopolitical with technological issues, which has been unfolding in computational research communities since the mid-1960s in a bizarre blend of contradictory worldviews and doctrines such as individualism, libertarianism, neoliberalism, counterculture, and utopianism (Armistead, 2016). This hybridization has been recently catalysed by the crypto-economic ideology, which replaces trust in institutions with trust in distributed blockchain protocols, algorithms, and service platforms. Contrary to their foundational myths, crypto/blockchain products have proved to be as hackable and susceptible to fiat directives as their conventional counterparts, and thus equally useful for high-risk investments and for deregulation of money, price manipulation, money laundering, and financial fraud (Bowles, 2018).

Reliable representation and meaningful interaction are vital for the assessment of the accuracy and reliability of computational architectures assigned with decision-making tasks in critical infrastructures such as online trading, power grid, human resources management, or weapons control. However, it is difficult to gain insight into the internal behaviour of complex DL networks due to an exceedingly large number of numerical parameters and counterintuitive logic. Efforts towards explainable AI have not yet yielded tangible results and it is unclear what levels of clarity about the functioning of modern ML systems are ultimately achievable. At the same time, human epistemological assumptions, prejudices, misconceptions, political views, and interests contaminate training data annotation, architecture design, and the performance of ML applications because they lack the objective reasoning criteria to filter out these cognitive flaws (Kearns & Roth, 2020). Explicitly or implicitly, they manifest as sexism, racism, ageism, eugenics, and many other biases that amplify systemic inequities in the cultural, historical, economic, linguistic, and other contexts of applied AI.

In all these contexts, disparate notions of ethical principles such as justice or fairness make it difficult to establish widely acceptable evaluation, selection, and decision-making criteria for applied AI. Ethical values are fuzzy categories that comply with generalized human interests in a Gaussian distribution whose long tails are mutable but crucial (Mitchell, 2019, 84–87). Along with the assumptions that human interests are compatible and homogenous, the AI community nurtures an ambition to software encode and collectively apply the straightforward interest rules that most individuals frequently alter in order to function socially. Self-interest decisively shapes our values, goals, and actions but it can be short-sighted, contradictory, self-deceptive, deceitful, or inconsiderate depending on the context, so the tolerance to most ethically relevant cognitive dissonances is an inherent feature of the human mind (Trivers, 2011). In optimal conditions, we share many goals and values, but the realities of changing environment put them in conflict. Unless the subtleties of human nature and relations are studied sincerely within broader evolutionary, socioeconomic, political, and cultural configurations, these ambiguities will remain instrumentalizable by power apparatuses.

THE ETHICAL ISSUES OF AI ART

Artists have always faced the challenges of ethical integrity vis-à-vis the capricious flux of discourses, criteria, and hierarchies of the cultural, economic, and political power systems. The ethical scope of the arts includes poetic aspects such as motivation, conceptualization and production, and professional concerns such as funding, presentation, cultural positioning, monetization, and further exploitation of artworks. It involves the relations between artists, cultural workers, educators, traders, collectors, and other professions and institutions responsible for financing, producing, evaluating, promoting, representing, discussing, and consuming art. In contemporary culture, this relational space remains unjustly opaque and insulates various sociopolitical issues from critical scrutiny.

Zeitgeist and Opportunism

The shift from material to cognitive capitalism redirects the executive and discursive power towards data flows, information processing, and trading as an asymmetrical challenge to material capital and production. The consolidation and increasing legitimacy of business models that rely on information as a key source of value generation are marked by emphasizing the informational character of phenomena, transactions, relationships, and behaviours and by translating them into data that can be programmed, manipulated, and monetized. It also enabled the operational modes of derivative finance to pervade networked digital environments through the abstraction of the forms and processes of value creation from material referents and through the recombination and price commensuration of affective, cognitive, cultural, and social capital (Lotti, 2019, 291–293).

Accordingly, the cultural sector sets its priorities towards virtualization and assesses artists primarily as affect generators, content providers, creative entrepreneurs, and speculative assets (Gere, 2008). The immediate effects and cumulative consequences of this paradigm shift are unfavourable for most artists but—although their essential position in the artworld affords them various means to control and protect common interests—many available routes for institutional resistance, collective action, and systematic change remain unexplored because they require a critical mass of actors in a consolidated workspace. So, the tragedy of the commons upholds conformism as the dominant factor in professional art (Żmijewski, 2011).

Along with socioeconomic trends, the historical accumulation of creative concepts and artefacts prompts artists to feel the zeitgeist, intuit paradigms, and understand cultural convergence so they can identify the ideas, themes, or technologies, such as AI, that gain popularity and relevance. They can stand out by approaching these assets in surprising, inciting, or provocative ways and by transforming them into meaningful objects or events. However, artists' aesthetic and epistemological intentions are never fully consistent with knowledge, notions, and tastes within broader social contexts, which holds contemporary art in constant crisis and turns the pragmatism of novelty seeking into a competitive edge. Novelty seeking requires well-informed reasoning on how exactly an invention empowers the poetic value or sociocultural significance of an artist's creative work. Individually and over time, that rationalization varies on a spectrum between naïveté, enthusiasm, Machiavellianism, and conservativism, which usually combine with some degree of genuine inquisitiveness and experimental curiosity. Therefore, without continuously cultivating critical self-consciousness, artists' pragmatism easily slips into virtue-signalling opportunism largely based on exploitative trend-surfing (Grba, 2020, 74–75).

Expressive Strategies

In a variety of approaches, artists represent, recontextualize, and sometimes deconstruct and critique the technological and sociopolitical aspects of AI. They address topics such as the epistemological boundaries of ML, the notions of creative agency, authorship, and intellectual property, the issues of ML-powered biometry, the exploitation of digital labour, the environmental and existential consequences of CAI, the uneasy positioning of an individual towards computational systems of control, and speculations in the crypto economy. Exemplars include Ken Feingold's works from the early 2000s, Ken Rinaldo's *Paparazzi Bots* (2009), Paolo Cirio, Alessandro Ludovico and Übermorgen's *Hacking Monopolism Trilogy* (*Google Will Eat Itself*, 2005; *Amazon Noir*, 2006; *Face to Facebook*, 2011), xtine burrough's *A Penny for Your Thoughts* (2009) and *Mediations on Digital Labor* (2015), Mimi Cabell and Jason Huff's *American Psycho* (2010), Luke DuBois' *Acceptance* (2012 and 2016), Derek Curry and Jennifer Gradecki's *CSIA* (since 2015) and *Infodemic* (2020), Max Hawkins' *Randomized Living* (2015–2017), Ross Goodwin and Oscar Sharp's *Sunspring* (2016), RyBN and Marie

Lechner's *Human Computers* (2016–2019), Sebastian Schmieg's *This is the Problem, the Solution, the Past and the Future* (2017) and *Decisive Mirror* (2019), Adam Basanta's *All We'd Ever Need Is One Another* (2018), Anna Ridler's *Myriad (Tulips)* and *Mosaic Virus* (both 2018), Nao Tokui's *Imaginary Soundwalk* (2018), Guido Segni's *Demand Full Laziness: A Five-Year Plan* (2018–2023), Martin Disley's *How They Met Themselves* (2021), and many others.

Some projects exploit the programmable nature of blockchain/crypto products to deploy dynamic generative codes that appropriate or repurpose their own financialization or ownership and play with the relativity, transience, and commercial life of digital artworks (Quaranta, 2021, 95–140, 155–170). Examples include Rhea Myers' *Is Art* (2014–2015), Primavera De Filippi's *Plantoids* (since 2015), Sašo Sedlaček's *Oblomo* (2019–2020), Sarah Friend's *Lifeforms* (2021) and *Off* (2021), and others. Benjamin Grosser's *Tokenize This* (2021) and Moxie Marlinspike's *At My Whim* (2021) are especially revealing in this context. *Tokenize This* is an online service that generates a unique URL with an authentic image in a typical crypto art style, but the URL is unmintable as a non-fungible token (NFT) because it self-destructs and yields an error page when a visitor navigates away from it to perform the necessary steps for NFT minting. *At My Whim* is a decentralized application (dApp) that debunks crypto mythology by showing that the same NFT can be linked to different digital contents depending on where and how it is visualized. These successful artworks couple pertinent issues with tangible referencing systems in presentation and participation setups that engage and inform the audience playfully or proactively.

However, artists' exploration of AI gets compromised by the, usually unforeseen, ethical implications when their expressive strategies yield vacuous or derivative works, ignore the AI's sociopolitical context, dismiss artistic for technical competencies, or downplay the important technological aspects. For example, pioneering AI artist Harold Cohen flirted with anthropomorphic notions in his project *AARON* (1973–2016). In varying proportions, anthropomorphism, conceptual ineptness, and dilettantism permeate the popular works of Pindar Van Arman (*Painting Robots*, since 2006), Patrick Tresset (*Human Studies*, since 2011), and Joanne Hastie (*Abstractions/Tech Art Paintings*, since 2017). In the aestheticized AI-driven performances of Sougwen Chung, Huang Yi, or Nigel John Stanford, high production values and anthropomorphic mystification divert the unfavourable comparisons with their precursors (respectively: Roman Verostko, Stelarc, and Einstürzende Neubauten) and serve as marketing instruments for their corporate sponsors by promoting vague notions of a robotically-enhanced consumerist lifestyle (Grba, 2022a, 3–5).

Various apparent but frequently unacknowledged and undisclosed conceptual, methodological, thematic, aesthetic, or presentational overlaps, reflections, and other types of awkward poetic similarities between works across the range of AI art indicate the issues of their creators' expressive literacy, notions of originality, and contextual appreciation. A tendency towards repetitiveness has been evident in mainstream artists who assimilate ML into their repertoires (Grba, 2022a, 8–11). They usually produce decorative works lacking the intricate tension between their concepts and the technical logic of AI. Examples include Gillian Wearing's *Wearing Gillian* (2018), Lucy McRae's *Biometric Mirror* (2018), Hito Steyerl's *Power Plants* and *This is the Future* (both 2019), and Pierre Huyghe's *Of Ideal* and *UUmwelt* (both 2019). Derivative aesthetics and depoliticized discourses have been further escalated in spectacular large-scale installations, such as Marco Brambilla's *Nude Descending a Staircase No. 3* (2019), CDV Lab's *Portraits of No One* (2020), and projects by Metacreation Lab, Refik

Anadol studio, and Ouchhh studio. These practices epitomize the aesthetics of algorithmic formal variations which tease the viewers with the promise of novelty and insight but effectively entrance them into cultural conformity and political deference. Dependent on the latest AI research and elaborately team-produced with significant budgets, these hyper-aestheticized spectacles also warn how manipulative intents, unimpressive concepts, or trivial topics can be concealed behind skilful rendering, aggrandized by high production values, and imposed through the flamboyant exhibition (Grba, 2022a, 11–12).

On the opposite pole of that spectrum, critical AI art is also susceptible to poetic cloning and other slippages, even when well-intended and competently produced. For example, Libby Heaney's two-channel video *Elvis* (2019) features portraits of the artist deepfaked as Elvis Presley and Elvis Presley deepfaked as the artist. It directly references, but bears no trace of acknowledgement of, the hyper-referential Gavin Turk's series *POP* (since 1993), which addresses the same issues of individual identity and cultural mechanisms of celebrity myth-making, involves the same pop-icon, and applies the same formal method (face swapping), albeit in different media (sculpture, photographs, and prints) and in a more complex—and acknowledged—referential chain: the figure of Sid Vicious with Gavin Turk's face posing as Andy Warhol's *Elvis Presley* (1963). A single topical diversion in Heaney's *Elvis* is the repositioning of gender construction within AI technologies.

Supercilious tactical interventions risk ending up moot, such as in the case of Tom White's *Perception Engines* (2018 and 2021) and Ben Bogard's *Zombie Formalist* (2021), or backfiring, as exemplified by the environmental footprint of artworks that critique the environmental damage caused by CAI (Grba, 2022a, 14–15, 20–21). Namely, tactical media art is so entangled with its target apparatuses of techno-power that protest sometimes becomes their mirror image (Raley, 2009). By openly identifying weaknesses in the systems they critique, artists set their achievements up for recuperation; the corporate sector systematically assimilates them to remedy its public image, perfect its lucrative instruments, and refine the normalization of injustices instead of correcting its political directives and improving its ethical standards.

Works that address AI biases towards ethnic, gender, and social groups sometimes end up exploiting their cultural contexts. For example, Jake Elwes' *Zizi Project* (since 2019) may be beneficial for the celebration, affirmation, and inclusion of the LGBTQ+ community within the AI-influenced culture, but its publicity narratives and high production values focus on glamour and spectacle in lieu of the less picturesque but more important existential and political problems of LGBTQ+ (Grba, 2022a, 13). Even the artists' explicit critique of AI ethics can itself be ethically flawed. For example, Kate Crawford and Trevor Paglen's exhibitions *Training Humans* and *Making Faces* (2019–2020) denounced racial bias and the non-consensual use of facial imagery for training computer vision systems. Yet Michael Lyons, a co-author of the JAFFE image dataset featured in these exhibitions, showed that the JAFFE team in fact obtained permission from the people they photographed, while Paglen and Crawford themselves collected, reproduced, and exhibited the same dataset images without consent, made serious technical errors in their critical analysis, and found it appropriate to link their project with the Haute Couture world (Prada Mode Paris), somehow overlooking its heavy baggage of exploitative and environmentally costly business practices (Lyons, 2020; Leibowicz et al., 2021, 7).

In general, both culturally and technically constrained critical attention to the ethical issues of AI obscures their fundamentally sociopolitical facets, while the false allure of "solving" them detracts us from bigger, more pressing, and longer-term challenges (Powles, 2018).

Within such an ethically convoluted expressive space, the notions that "art is the only ethical use of AI" (Levin & Brain, 2021) call for scepticism. Games in the art community are driven by fluid social networks, cliques, coteries, and intrigues, directed by unstable loyalties or affiliations, and shaped by fancy, fashion, authority appeal, political interests, and economic trends. Combined with the artists' intrinsic need for endorsement by the tech sector, mainstream contemporary artworld (MCA), and academia, this capricious dynamic sustains the status quo of cultural hegemonies, institutional privileges, and profit-driven power. It makes AI artists liable to become intentionally or subconsciously manipulative, compromise their creativity, and soften their critical edge (Grba, 2021a, 252–254).

Market Directives

MCA constitutes a relatively small but culturally significant sector of the global economic complex. Based on a key requirement for a constant flow of novelty, its selection criteria, operations, and discourses are substantially market-driven, so commodifying artworks as tradeable investment assets takes priority over their cultural values or social importance (Stallabrass, 2006). Since the early computer art in the 1960s, the mutability and fungibility of digital data had been difficult to commodify, leading to the MCA's selective marginalization and occasional exploitation of digital art (Shanken, 2016).

Reacting to the rise in the economic power of AI and crypto/blockchain technologies, the MCA has reinvigorated interest in digital art and swiftly adopted an assortment of crypto products after Christie's and Sotheby's successful probing sales of AI artworks in 2018. The MCA's integration with the crypto economy was largely facilitated by the use of digital instruments for enforcing scarcity and certifying ownership, such as NFTs, and by the assimilation of marketing models devised by crypto art trading platforms, such as Nifty Gateway, OpenSea, Rarible, and Art Blocks. Since then, the entrepreneurial scope and trading volume of digital art have been expanding with significant consequences. Both MCA and crypto art markets advertise NFTs as a technology that disrupts the art economy by enabling artists to bypass the traditional trading requirements, monetize their works in new ways, and cater to a wider range of collectors. In reality, crypto technologies enable MCA and the crypto economy to reinforce their patriarchal ideologies and colonial exploitation by expanding their product portfolio with digital artefacts and computational art practices that can be shaped by their values (Quaranta, 2022, 141–244). The vectors of status, hierarchy, and class affiliation remain fundamental, but now they shift towards crypto-economic power and become more volatile.

Regardless of their association with the "legacy" art market, many computational artists have entered the NFT race and proved liable to compromise some of the defining features of their creative tools and processes in order to accommodate the demands for scarcity, commercial viability, and ownership in the new economies. This quickly became problematic on many levels and catalysed the proliferation of new varieties of derivative aesthetics akin to zombie formalism (Robinson, 2014). The use of computational tools for a straightforward, reductive, and mostly automated generation of decorative, eye-catching digital artefacts that feature a quick simulation of originality led to crass trivialization epitomized in the mindless, boring, misogynist, escapist, reactionary, and provincial NFT blockbuster works by Mike Winkelmann (Beeple) (Beller, 2021). The NFT boom has induced a number of AI artists to adapt their practices to the crypto platforms and limit the online accessibility of their works (Munster, 2021). Some venture into brokerage by establishing NFT marketplaces, such as

Feral File, which host exhibitions based on vague, bland, superficial, or uncritical curatorial concepts that appeal to a broad taste of crypto art investors and collectors. Focused on navigating and exploiting the NFT gold rush, artists remain largely unaware or seem oblivious that the crypto art market inherits the technical, as well as political and ethical issues from its foundational world of crypto economics. Furthermore, they seem unconcerned that, contrary to the claims of the so-called "clean" platforms, crypto art trading inevitably draws on cloud computation, which increases the environmental damage incurred by producing their artworks (Knight, 2021). Crucially, artists tend to disregard that NFTs facilitate a profoundly dubious compensation logic by imposing a fictive digital "crypto-aura" onto digital artefacts whose "aura" should emanate from their poetic, expressive, and relational values. As David Joselit noted (2021), "Duchamp used the category of art to liberate materiality from commodifiable form; the NFT deploys the category of art to extract private property from freely available information." NFTs turn art into a ghost of property or an imaginary experience of ownership, which should not be confused with aura because there is no such thing as an authentic digital copy (Juárez, 2021).

This cynical commodification game undermines a whole range of practices that, by the nature of their chosen core medium (digital data), have been emancipating the notion of an artwork from a sacred (or fetishized) material entity towards a relational process of ideational exchange. It shifts the focus of appraisal from the artistic creative process as an intrinsically non-capitalist type of work (Beech, 2015) onto the transaction-cantered entrepreneurship that renders the creative production vulnerable to exploitation and regresses the creative ethos of digital art into the obsolete notional orbits of possession and ownership.

Despite noteworthy exceptions of well-conceived, cogent, and critical works, it can be argued that, up to this point, the interactions between AI art and the crypto art market have been reinforcing regressive modes of expression with feeble concepts and impoverished aesthetics rather than inciting meaningful creative initiatives (Browne, 2022; Grba, 2022a, 22–23). Instead of democratizing and diversifying, the crypto economy converts digital art into a lucrative asset sector, while artists' complacent strategies for satisfying their crypto-monetization appetites may bear a high cost of corrupting the open-mindedness and critical edge that distinguish most experimental art. The reductive commodification of potentially avant-garde practices such as AI art may be rationalized by the immediate economic interests of the MCA/crypto market, but its conservativism diminishes the epistemological and transformative values of these practices. MCA/crypto market politics is intellectually offensive to both the artists and the audience because it restricts the poetic diversity of artmaking to fit commercially viable models. By enforcing arbitrary market criteria to define the cultural profiles and relevance of artworks, it degrades our mentality and deprives our cultural heritage. Its capitalization on our primitive notions of possession and ownership exploits our limited concepts of existence and time (Heller & Salzman, 2021), which is unethical because it nourishes greed and false intuitions about our special place in the universe.

CONCLUSION

The expressive logic of AI art practices is invaluable for gaining insights into the important aspects of our world, while their contradictions and instabilities exemplify the uneasy coevolution between the artistic proteanism and the ambiguous forces of authority and power. This creative dynamic rearticulates the intricacy and unpredictability of our ecology, economy, politics, relationships, and everyday life. Less dramatically but more sensibly and often more meaningfully than global disruptions, successful AI artworks engage us with the impermanence and incoherence of our notions and desires. They empower imagination and foster responsibility in assessing our moral standards and social norms, tackling the ever-changing present and anticipating possible futures.

These transformative capacities oblige AI artists to engage in a sharper critique of their motivational priorities, deeper investigation of their expressive means, more nuanced examination of their practices, and more rigorous scrutiny of their works' valuation. Their potential to establish poetic cogency depends on their ability to cultivate well-informed ethical attitudes towards their professional goals in order to outmanoeuvre the systemic but hazardous entanglements with corporate tech and the MCA/crypto market (Grba, 2021b). Their contributive range spans two horizons. One is shaped by providing veneer and cultural legitimization to the CAI and crypto economy. Another one involves taking genuine risks for cutting-edge creativity that seeks a meaningful relationship with AI to incite new ideas in intelligent humans. While structured resources such as the *AI Artists' Manifesto* (Fuchs et al., 2020) or *Responsible AI Art Field Guide* (Leibowicz et al., 2021) offer useful ethical considerations and directives, artists remain primarily responsible and should be held accountable for their professional strategies.

Rather than moralizing, our critique of AI art ethics should be constructive towards the betterment and maturation of the field. The ability to acknowledge and discuss both strengths and weaknesses of AI art's poetic identity enhances our cultural cognition with broader and more nuanced perspectives. Personal qualities inform the poetics as much as skill, intelligence, or any other expressive factor, so assessing artists equally as creators and as human beings should be integral to the overall appreciation of the arts. AI art's ethical issues reflect not only contemporary culture but also science, technology, economy, politics, and social relations and imply ethical responsibility in all these domains. Any critical engagement with AI should problematize the political influence and social impact of the research communities, corporate sector, market, and crypto/blockchain complex and call for an actionable scepticism towards their ideological terms and interests (Payne, 2013). Beyond consuming hype or indulging in complacency, institutions and the general public need to engage in a difficult and uncertain work of demystification and reconceptualization in order to match the conceptual, technical, and economic intricacies that have been equally influencing the poetics of AI art and the quality of our lives. AI trends are not the magical forces of some cosmic teleology, but the outcomes of human motives and actions. It is thus crucial to curtail the absurd fiction of their inevitability and attain both the political will and instruments for their control.

In a broader prospect, we need to inform AI research, business enterprises, and cultural incentives with a courageous look at ourselves. It requires profound knowledge about the constraints, inconsistencies, and contradictions of the human mind, many of which are obscured by our ignorance, arrogance, hypocrisy, vanity, and delusions of self-importance that stem from a false dichotomy between culture and biology (Buss, 2001). By recognizing that our evolved mental architecture integrates many complex psychological mechanisms that are activated selectively and can operate independently in different contexts, we can explore human cognition, and intelligence in general, with the sophistication and agency they demand. We can get a clearer insight into the ethical aspects of AI science, technology, business, and art if we cease fetishizing or monopolizing our notions of truth, justice, fairness and the common good, and instead start approaching their subtleties with a sincere self-critical focus. This will catalyse the work in science, technology, arts, and humanities to define more robust concepts of creativity, map its perspectives, and inform our decisions for future AI.

REFERENCES

Armistead, J. (2016). The Silicon Ideology. https://ia600403.us.archive.org/25/items/the-silicon -ideology/the-silicon-ideology.pdf

Audry, S. (2021). *Art in the Age of Machine Learning*. MIT Press.

Beech, D. (2015). *Art and Value: Art's Economic Exceptionalism in Classical, Neoclassical, and Marxist Economics* (p. 26). Brill.

Beller, J. (2021, March 23). Fascism on the Blockchain? The Work of Art in the Age of NFTs. Coindesk. https://www.coindesk.com/fascism-blockchain-art-nfts

Bowles, N. (2018). Everyone Is Getting Hilariously Rich and You're Not. *The New York Times*, 13 January. https://www.nytimes.com/2018/01/13/style/bitcoin-millionaires.html

Browne, K. (2022). Who (or What) Is an AI Artist? *Leonardo*, *55*(2), 130–134. https://doi.org/10.1162/ leon_a_02092

Buss, D. M. (2001). Human Nature and Culture: An Evolutionary Psychological Perspective. *Journal of Personality*, *69*(6), 955–978. https://doi.org/10.1111/1467-6494.696171

Crawford, K. (2021). *Atlas of AI: Power, Politics, and the Planetary Costs of Artificial Intelligence* (pp. 53–87). Yale University Press.

Fuchs, N., Kirn, P., Salter, C., Vavarella, E., & Valenzuela, M. H. (2020). AI Art Manifesto. *Futurological Congress x Transart*. https://www.transart.it/wp-content/uploads/2020/09/AI-Art-Manifesto.pdf

Gere, C. (2008). *Digital Culture* (p. 166). Reaktion Books.

Grba, D. (2020). Alpha Version, Delta Signature: Cognitive Aspects of Artefactual Creativity. *Journal of Science and Technology of the Arts*, 63–83. https://doi.org/10.34632/JSTA.2020.9491

Grba, D. (2021a). Brittle Opacity: Ambiguities of the Creative AI. In M. Verdicchio, M. Carvalhais, L. RIbas, & A. Rangel (Eds.), *Proceedings of xCoAx 2021, 9th Conference on Computation, Communication, Aesthetics & X* (pp. 235–260).

Grba, D. (2021b). Immaterial Desires: Cultural Integration of Experimental Digital Art. In H. Barranha & J. Simões Henriques (Eds.), *Art, Museums and Digital Cultures: Rethinking Change* (pp. 57–72). IHA/NOVA FCSH and maat.

Grba, D. (2022a). Deep Else: A Critical Framework for AI Art. *Digital*, *2*(1), 1–32. https://doi.org/10 .3390/digital2010001

Grba, D. (2022b). The Cabinet of Wolfgang von Kempelen: AI Art and Creative Agency. In *Possibles, ISEA2022: 27th International Symposium on Electronic Art Proceedings*. CCCB/Art Santa Monica.

Grba, D. (2022c). Lures of Engagement: An Outlook on Tactical AI Art. In M. Verdicchio, M. Carvalhais, L. RIbas, & A. Rangel (Eds.), *Proceedings of xCoAx 2022, 10th Conference on Computation, Communication, Aesthetics & X*.

Heller, M., & Salzman, J. (2021). *Mine! How the Hidden Rules of Ownership Control Our Lives* (pp. 14–18, and passim). Doubleday/Penguin Random House.

Hermann, I. (2021). Artificial Intelligence in Fiction: Between Narratives and Metaphors. *AI & Society*, 1435–5655. https://doi.org/10.1007/s00146-021-01299-6

Hutson, M. (2012). *The 7 Laws of Magical Thinking: How Irrational Beliefs Keep Us Happy, Healthy, and Sane* (pp. 165–181). Hudson Street Press.

Jobin, A., Ienca, M., & Vayena, E. (2019). The Global Landscape of AI Ethics Guidelines. *Nature Machine Intelligence*, *1*(9), 389–399.

Johnson, D., & Verdicchio, M. (2017). Reframing AI Discourse: Minds and Machines. *UWS Academic Portal*, *27*(4), 575–590.

Joselit, D. (2021). NFTs, or The Readymade Reversed. *October*, (175), 3–4. https://doi.org/10.1162/octo _a_00419

Juárez, G. (2021). The Ghostchain. (Or Taking Things for what They Are). *Paletten*, 325. https://paletten .net/artiklar/the-ghostchain

Kearns, M., & Roth, A. (2020). *The Ethical Algorithm: The Science of Socially Aware Algorithm Design* (pp. 32–48). Oxford University Press.

Knight, S. (2021, October 26). Bitcoin is Largely Controlled by a Small Group of Investors and Miners. Techspot.   https://www.techspot.com/news/91937-bitcoin-largely-controlled-small-group-investors -miners-study.html

Leibowicz, C., Saltz, E., The New York Times, Coleman, L., Partnership on AI, & Rhode Island School of Design. (2021). Creating AI Art Responsibly: A Field Guide for Artists. *Revista Diseña, 19*. https:// doi.org/10.7764/disena.19

Levin, G., & Brain, T. (2021). *Code as Creative Medium: A Handbook for Computational Art and Design* (p. 5). MIT Press.

Lotti, L. (2019). The Art of Tokenization: Blockchain Affordances and the Invention of Future Milieus. *Media Theory, 3*(1), 287–320.

Lyons, M. J. (2020). Excavating "Excavating AI": The Elephant in the Gallery. https://doi.org/10.5281 /ZENODO.4391458

Marcus, G. F., & Davis, E. (2019). *Rebooting AI: Building Artificial Intelligence We Can Trust*. Pantheon Books.

Mitchell, M. (2019). *Artificial Intelligence: A Guide for Thinking Humans*. Farrar, Straus and Giroux.

Munster, B. (2021, April 7). This Self-Destructing Website Is Impossible to Sell As an NFT. Vice Motherboard.   https://www.vice.com/en/article/z3vjjx/this-self-destructing-website-is-impossible-to -sell-as-an-nf

Natale, S. (2021). *Deceitful Media: Artificial Intelligence and Social Life After the Turing Test*. Oxford University Press.

Pasquinelli, M. (2019). How a Machine Learns and Fails—A Grammar of Error for Artificial Intelligence. *Spheres—Journal for Digital Cultures, 5*, 1–17.

Payne, A. (2013, December 18). Bitcoin, Magical Thinking, and Political Ideology. al3x.net. http://al3x .net

Powles, J. (2018, December 7). The Seductive Diversion of 'Solving' Bias in Artificial Intelligence. Medium OneZero. https://onezero.medium.com/the-seductive-diversion-of-solving-bias-in-artificial -intelligence-890df5e5ef53

Quaranta, D. (2021). *Surfing with Satoshi: Art, Blockchain and NFTs*. Aksioma Institute for Contemporary Art.

Raley, R. (2009). *Tactical Media*. University of Minnesota Press.

Rescorla, M. (2020). The Computational Theory of Mind. In E. N. Zalta (Ed.), *The Stanford Encyclopedia of Philosophy* (Fall 2020 Edition). https://plato.stanford.edu/archives/fall2020/entries /computational-mind

Robinson, W. (2014). Flipping and the Rise of Zombie Formalism. Artspace. https://www.artspace.com /magazine/contributors/see_here/the_rise_of_zombie_formalism-52184

Seth, A. (2021). *Being You: A New Science of Consciousness*. Faber & Faber.

Shanken, E. A. (2016). Contemporary Art and New Media: Digital Divide or Hybrid Discourse? In C. Paul (Ed.), *A Companion to Digital Art* (pp. 463–481). John Wiley & Sons, Inc.

Stallabrass, J. (2006). *Contemporary Art: A Very Short Introduction*. Oxford University Press.

Taylor, A. (2018). The Automation Charade. *Logic*, 5 (Failure), 1 August. https://logicmag.io/failure/the -automation-charade

Trivers, R. L. (2011). *Deceit and Self-Deception*. Penguin.

Zeilinger, M. (2021). *Tactical Entanglements: AI Art, Creative Agency, and the Limits of Intellectual Property*. meson press.

Żmijewski, A. (2011). Artists Are Just as Capable of Setting the Same Chain of Events as Politicians: Artur Żmijewski in conversation with Joanna Warsza. *Das Magazin der Kulturstiftung des Bundes*, 18.

Żylińska, J. (2020). *AI Art: Machine Visions and Warped Dreams*. Open Humanities Press.

PART V

AI BIAS, NORMATIVITY AND DISCRIMINATION

45. Learning about human behavior? The transcendental status of grammars of action in the processing of HCI data

Andreas Beinsteiner

1. LEARNING ABOUT HUMAN BEHAVIOR?

1.1 From GOFAI to Machine Learning

While the development of artificial intelligence has gained significant momentum in the last 20 years, it was exposed to severe philosophical criticism in the 1980s and 1990s. The kind of approach to which those critiques were addressed had been called "Good Old-Fashioned AI (GOFAI)" by John Haugeland. It was an approach based on explicitly programmed rules, against which the implicit, non-formalizable character of a large share of our knowledge and skills was emphasized. Drawing on the phenomenological tradition in philosophy, the disembodied, Cartesian heritage of GOFAI was uncovered (cf. Dreyfus 1997, Haugeland 1985).

Contemporary AI technologies are not met by this kind of criticism anymore, as the dominant paradigm today is machine learning. It is an approach that mostly relies on self-adapting algorithms and involves much less explicitly programmed rules.[1] According to Ethem Alpaydin, author of influential introductory literature (both for experts and a general audience), "machine learning is now the driving force in artificial intelligence; after the disappointment of logic-based, programmed expert systems in [the] 1980s, it has revived the field, delivering significant results" (Alpaydin 2016, p. xiii). There are several factors to which machine learning owes its momentum.

An important one is the fact that this approach solves the problem of implicit knowledge. For example, it is easy for humans to recognize the face of someone we have met before. But our skill for "face recognition" is an implicit one; we cannot state explicitly the steps of any mental procedure that enables us to recognize a person. Therefore, we are not able to write a program that instructs a computer system to recognize faces. In such cases, machine learning can provide a solution. Instead of explicitly having to program the desired behavior, such systems can be trained to produce appropriate output. The data set on which the system is trained is assumed to implicitly contain the criteria for the desired output. It is now up to the system to apprehend those criteria and not the programmers to specify them explicitly (Alpaydin 2010, p.3).

---

[1] Of course, machine learning algorithms are *algorithms*. Their program specifies explicitly, how input is to be processed to acquire the desired "learning" effect. Instead of directly defining rules that specify the behavior of a system, one specifies the rules that define how it processes its training data. The combination of the data processing algorithm and the set of training data defines the actual behavior of the system. "Machine learning is programming computers to optimize a performance criterion using example data or past experience" (Alpaydin 2010, p. 3).

This leads us to a second aspect that is relevant to the proliferation of machine learning. At least in the early days, the low share of explicit instructions in machine learning systems helped to establish the idea that the output of such systems was objective, free of the kind of human bias that explicit programming was able to introduce. The ideology of "theory-free" empiricism enabled by machine learning took shape. In 2008, Chris Anderson prominently proclaimed that it would be possible to obtain insights free of any theoretical suppositions:

> Out with every theory of human behavior, from linguistics to sociology. [...] With enough data, the numbers speak for themselves. [...] We can throw the numbers into the biggest computing clusters the world has ever seen and let statistical algorithms find patterns where science cannot. (Anderson 2008)

Today, however, this supposed objectivity of statistical algorithms is under heavy attack: discovering biases in machine learning systems has become one of the predominant occupations of critical studies of artificial intelligence. Only the source of this bias has shifted: today, it is looked for less in the instructions of the programmer(s) but in the curation of training data and, sometimes, in the selection of variables taken into account.[2]

Data and variables indicate a third and maybe the most important reason for machine learning's success. The buzzword here is big data: enhanced capacities for the transfer, storage, and processing of large amounts of digital information have led to a situation where rather simple statistical procedures that have already been known for decades finally produce impressive outcomes. As Alpaydin states, "[w]e do not need to come up with new algorithms if machines can learn themselves, assuming that we can provide them with enough data (not necessarily supervised) and computing power" (2010, p. xxxvi).

1.2   Machine Learning about Human Behavior

Progress in digital technology does not only play out here by enabling machine learning algorithms to analyze larger amounts of data. It also plays a fundamental role in the production of that data in the first place. In the last few decades, computing devices have pervaded the human lifeworld to an unprecedented extent. With the introduction of personal computers, the internet, mobile phones, wearables, and the Internet of Things, the number of human practices that involve interactions with computational devices is steadily growing. So is the share of practices that leave digital data traces. Therefore, the analysis of human behavior has become one of the most important fields where machine learning algorithms are deployed. A paper published in Science in 2009 claims that the digital pervasion of the lifeworld provides the basis for a new, computational, paradigm for the social sciences. The authors state that while hitherto, "research on human interactions has relied mainly on one-time, self-reported data on relationships", new technologies "offer a moment-by-moment picture of interactions over extended periods of time, providing information about both the structure and content of relationships" (Lazer et al. 2009, p. 722). One is not confined anymore to interviewing small supposedly representative fractions of the population on what they are doing, when technology

---

[2]   Speaking of "bias" here has the disadvantage that it implicitly posits as a counter-concept the possibility of bias-free free findings, which might even reinforce the ideology of theory-free objectivity.

automatically produces exact and reliable traces of a large part of the activities of almost everyone (at least, of everyone who uses the respective devices and platforms).

So learning about human behavior has become one of the central tasks for artificial intelligence, be it in the service of private companies, state surveillance, or science. Any kind of online service enterprise might be interested in applying the "persons who liked x also liked y" logic popularized by Amazon. Authorities may wish to identify patterns that indicate risks for public security like crimes, terrorist attacks, or riots in order to take preemptive measures. Scientists expect new insights into interaction patterns and group dynamics, for example, what factors contribute to group polarization and homophily. But what is the epistemological status of the patterns discovered by machine learning algorithms?

Early foundational texts about big data science like the ones by Anderson or Lazer et al. are committed to a still popular doxa holding that digital information infrastructures and machine learning algorithms would make it possible to discover traits that characterize social practices as such, independently of the technologies involved in finding them. From this perspective, technologies for capturing and analyzing human behavior appear as neutral instruments: they are means of observation that do not interfere with the activities observed (apart from feedback loops that are subsequently enacted in order to apply what has been learned for the purposeful modification of behavior, as it happens in processes of personalization and assessment).

1.3   Digitally Captured Behavior is Transformed Behavior

On the basis of Philip E. Agre's interdisciplinary research between computer science and social science, the present chapter tries to develop an alternative to this perspective. It claims that, just like any other experimental set-up, the observations made by digital data-capturing infrastructures interfere with what they observe. While many aspects of such interference are worth being discussed (e.g., the fact that people modify their behavior when they know they are observed), this chapter focuses exclusively on a rather simple and fundamental one: it strives to demonstrate that, to a large extent, the human behavior that is captured by digital platforms and devices and that is subsequently analyzed by artificial intelligence is a laboratory artifact. Behavior unfolding in the course of our use of mobile phones or online platforms is a very specific kind of behavior that is only to a rather limited extent representative of "what people do" in general. Whenever we interact with digital technologies, we have to adapt our behavior to their logic. We have to modify our practices to make them machine-readable in the first place. The everyday use of digital technology does not only produce digital traces of our practices, but it re-renders those practices in a fundamental way by imposing a discrete structure on them which can be captured by computational devices. If the epistemic status of behavioral patterns discovered by algorithms is to be evaluated, this re-rendering and imposition have to be taken into account.

On a technical level, the theories and procedures of machine learning presuppose not only "that the future […] will not be much different from the past" (Alpaydin 2010, p. 2) but also that

> behind all this seemingly complex and voluminous data, there lies a simple explanation. That although the data is big, it can be explained in terms of a relatively simple model with a small number of hidden factors and their interaction. (Alpaydin 2016, p. xi)

What is it that legitimizes such presuppositions about the social world (beyond the acknowledgment that every model is necessarily a reduction and simplification of reality)? Is human activity as such built from a few basic principles that remain more or less constant and thereby ensure that present behavior can be extrapolated into the future? Or is it only when human activity has adapted to the demands posed by computational technology that it satisfies these presuppositions because then its structure is actually generated in accordance with certain rules?

In what follows, it will be argued that the latter holds. The argument will draw on the work of Agre, which had already been relevant for the critique of the GOFAI paradigm (cf. Agre 1997). In the present context, we will take up his conception of "capture", which laid the foundations for a comprehensive understanding of the mechanisms that enable digital data production about human activities; in particular, the role that "grammars of action" play in this context. We will interrogate the implications of grammars of action for the epistemological status of insights about human behavior derived from machine learning.

For providing some theoretical background from media philosophy, the second section will introduce Bernard Stiegler's concept of grammatization, unfold its implications for computational technology, and differentiate between a priori and a posteriori grammatization. Section 3 will discuss the digital capture of human behavioral data, as described by Agre, as an instance of a priori grammatization. The a priori status of grammars of action for human behavior will be demonstrated before the fourth section discusses the epistemological consequences for machine-learning insights about grammatized human activity.

2. GRAMMATIZATION: MAKING REALITY COMPUTER-READABLE

2.1 Bernard Stiegler's Account of Grammatization

Among the many contributions that Bernard Stiegler has made to the philosophy of media and technology, his concept of grammatization is a particularly important one.[3] He defines it as "the process through which the flows and continuities which weave our existences are discretized" (Stiegler 2010, p. 31). Understood in this way, grammatization is by no means only an issue with regard to computing technology, but is constitutive of cultural history at least from the invention of alphabetic writing onwards. Indeed, writing, as the discretization of the flow of speech, is a stage in the history of grammatization. By means of grammatization, phenomena that are diffuse and in flux can be identified, handled, and controlled. This constitutes a prerequisite for subsequent processes of rationalization. Stiegler's history of grammatization identifies several waves, where new technological possibilities enabled the discretization and subsequent rationalization of various domains of the lifeworld: In Greek antiquity, the invention of alphabetic writing opened up the possibility of rational discourse. Much later, the industrial revolution made grammatization beyond the sphere of language possible. On the assembly line, the gestures of workers were standardized and discretized – enabling their automation and reproduction (and thereby depriving the workers of their genuine skills for producing things and thus making them exchangeable, as Stiegler emphasizes in his

---

[3] Stiegler adopts this notion from linguist Sylvain Auroux in order to concretize Jacques Derrida's logic of the supplement within the horizon of a philosophy of technology that emphasizes the intimate linkage between technology and memory. Applied to digital technologies, Stiegler's understanding of technology as an exteriorization of knowledge shows parallels with approaches inspired by Deleuze that focus on the extensification of intensities (cf. DeLanda 2002, Thrift 2007).

reading of Marx's notion of proletarianization) and thus the rationalization of the production process. In the course of the 19th century, new apparatuses for reproducing the audible and the visible made the grammatization of perception possible – and of the effects triggered by it. Computational technology constitutes a rather recent phase in the history of grammatization. Stiegler himself mainly focuses on the exteriorization of cognitive skills that computers make possible – describing it as a new wave of proletarianization depriving individuals of their know-how for consumption now. Yet, as we will argue below, the concept of grammatization can be applied to computational technology in a more generic manner.

2.2   Computers Need Grammatized Input

Computers can only perform their computations on input data. The meaning of the word data is "the given" (lat. datum). That which is given to computers must be given in such a form that it is readable for them. In particular, all digital input data must have a discrete structure. In actual existing computers, these data are ultimately represented by zeros and ones. While this actual representation scheme is contingent, the decisive criterion is that data must have the structure of discrete units that are identifiable without any ambiguity.[4] Since this is a general prerequisite for computer-readable data, it also holds for the specific case of machine learning. All data from which algorithms "learn" must have this structure of being composed of discrete basic units. Those fundamental units cannot be "questioned" by the program in the course of its learning – they form a basis that remains indispensable and irreducible in the course of its computations.

Consider, for example, visual data. Such data can only be given to computers in appropriately grammatized form, i.e., as a "digital" image represented by a two-dimensional array of (black and white, grayscale, or RGB) pixels. Of course, it is possible to add a further layer of grammatization on top of this pixel layer. Frequently, machine learning plays a role in the adding of further levels of grammatization. For instance, if the input data is a scan of a page from a book, this data (already grammatized as a grid of pixels) can be grammatized once more by text recognition software.[5] On the basis of the pre-existent pixel grammatization, this software provides another discrete structuring of the input data: as a linear sequence of alphabetical letters, punctuation marks, and blank spaces.

---

[4]   One could argue that the same holds for the processing of alphabetic writing by humans (also there, the basic units – the letters – must be uniquely determined), yet the relationship between human practices and grammatization is an utterly different one respectively. In the case of writing/reading, a new set of elements are combinatorically generated from basic units and can be integrated into human practices as new resources of tertiary (non-somatic) memory. In contrast, in the case of human-computer interaction, as we will argue in Section 4, *human practices become themselves re-fashioned as sequences of elementary units and thus grammatized*. Hence, one needs to distinguish grammatization (Stiegler's account of certain aspects of cultural development that is used here as a *generic* theoretical background) from the *specific* stage of grammatization that is constituted by the introduction of computational technology into the human lifeworld.

[5]   Text recognition is in itself a complex process that involves several steps of discretization like, for example, line segmentation.

2.3 The Irreducibility of A Priori Grammatization

As illustrated by this example, we can distinguish between grammatization a priori and a posteriori in relation to the level on which an algorithm operates. For the text recognition software, the page, as grammatized into an array of pixels, is given a priori: it is taken over from a sensory device like a scanner or a digital camera that provided the original digitization of the analog book page. But to this data set grammatized into pixels, the software adds another layer of grammatization a posteriori: afterward, the former crisscross of differently colored pixels is structured into discrete units in another way: as a sequence of Unicode signs that represent what is written on the book page.

Artificial intelligence thus always operates on data that are given to it in a form that is already grammatized – be it by a sensory device that provides some kind of interface to the physical world or by some software entity. This grammatization a priori remains the irreducible basis for the system's computations, even though the system can add further layers of grammatization to the data and, by doing so, structure it anew. But these derivative, higher-order grammatization levels always remain anchored in the mode of grammatization that structured the data set from the outset and, accordingly, defined its most fundamental units. A black pixel that subsequently is recognized as part of an "A" letter is a datum that the text recognition cannot reach beyond; it cannot go back to the physical reality that preceded this grammatization. The text-recognizing processing of a two-dimensional array of pixels cannot resort to aspects of the preceding reality of the book page that have been lost in this step (as, for example, details of the font style lost due to insufficient resolution or colored elements in a black-and-white scan). It is possible, however, to abstract from this layer of the pixel array, which hitherto provided the a priori, again, and to store the results of text recognition solely as a Unicode sequence in a text file. Now if this file is transferred to a translation software, then the letter sequence (and not the pixel array) acts as the a priori grammatization for this software. Which form of grammatization constitutes the a priori for any algorithmic system, is thus relative to the system under consideration: for the text recognition software, the pixel image is a priori, while for the translation software, the Unicode sequence is a priori.

Now what about data about human behavior that are processed by AI systems? Is it possible also here to discern an irreducible a priori grammatization from other layers of grammatization that have been added subsequently? Consider, for instance, the movement data that are generated while individuals carry their smartphones with them in their everyday lives. The data may have the format of position coordinates recorded once per second. If the aggregated data reveal a daily recurring pattern, where these coordinates remain rather static (displaying only variations within a limited radius) in the morning, before there is a phase (say, of 45 minutes) with rapidly changing coordinates, followed by a longer static phase, an AI system might grammatize this pattern into some discrete units like "being at home", "on the way to work", and "at work" (these are data that, for example, Google collects from android users on a regular basis).

What is the a priori grammatization from which this classification is obtained? It is the sequence of geographical coordinates, taken every second, represented in this or that numerical format. More detailed movements that go beyond the temporal and spatial intervals allowed by this form of grammatization cannot be taken into account by the software that structures this data into higher units unless it is also granted access to data from other sensors.

Let us move to another example of pattern recognition on human behavior: an AI system is supposed to extract hints about the interests and preferences of a person from the contents of that person's messages. Now consider two types of messages: (a) a short message typed into the phone, containing Unicode signs and, maybe, some emojis, or (b) a voicemail. In the case of (b), the a priori grammatization is one specific type of digital representation of audio content. If that content is to be accessed on a semantic level, further processes of grammatization have to be applied a posteriori in order to make this level accessible: phoneme recognition has to be applied to obtain a Unicode sequence representing what has been said and thus to arrive at the same kind of data presentation that is given right from the outset in case (a). The audio representation (b) has the advantage of making aspects of the communication accessible for analysis that are missing in a text-only representation (e.g., emotion recognition could be applied based on how things are said). Yet the text representation (a) offers communication contents in an already grammatized form (cf. Agre 1994, 114). This saves the computing power necessary to obtain this form of a posteriori and erases misreading and ambiguities that could appear in the speech-to-text-conversion process. Here we encounter important advantages of having data already presented in a priori-grammatized form: A posteriori grammatization risks inserting mistakes into the data through misreading that distorts all further data processing. This is a strong incentive for using data with a level of a priori grammatization as high as possible. But how is such data obtained? How does it work that human behavioral data is generated in a form that is already grammatized? Philip Agre's conception of capture offers a generic answer to this question.

3.   THE A PRIORI GRAMMATIZATION OF HUMAN BEHAVIOR

3.1   Practices Interacting with Computers

In repeating weaves of grammatization, culture is transformed. If we follow more recent forms of sociological theory, culture can be grasped via the social practices that occur in it (cf. Schatzki et al. 2001, Reckwitz 2002). Thus, new forms of grammatization re-arrange practices. Alphabetic writing transformed the practices of communication, introducing written communication with the capacity to bridge larger space or time intervals on the basis of a grammatization of spoken language. Taylorism transformed the practices of production, allowing for their rationalization on the basis of grammatizations of the gestures of former handicraft practices. Computer technology affects all kinds of practices by introducing new ones that integrate elements from older activities into human-computer interaction.

As discussed previously, the interaction between humans and computers has to take on a shape that is readily readable for the computer. This is achieved by offering only specific opportunities for interaction that are predefined by the interface. This is a matter of both hardware and software. A laptop, for example, includes on its hardware level two input devices. One is the keyboard, giving every input the shape of Unicode data. Another is the touchpad or mouse, allowing movements and clicks that the operating system usually maps to certain positions on the display (one of the output devices of the machine). Keyboard and mouse thus offer a basic repertoire of possible user actions that constitute an a priori grammatization of user interaction. These basic possibilities are taken up in different kinds of software, accepting different sequences recombined from these possibilities as legitimate input in any given program state. In the Firefox web browser, for example, there is the possibility of opening new tabs. This can be achieved either by clicking file → new tab with the mouse or touchpad, or by hitting the sequence "alt" – "arrow downwards" – "enter" on the keyboard, or by using the keyboard shortcut "ctrl" + "t". By offering predefined paths of possible interactions, each software ensures that user input remains readable and univocal at any stage during program execution.

A messenger app on a mobile phone uses the phone's touchscreen to provide the user with predefined input options. Here, the virtual keyboard grants the possibility for entering Unicode sequences that can be sent to other users via the send button. Also, in this case, it is the interface that guarantees that all input has a priori the grammatized form necessary for the program to function properly.

In this way, all application software grammatizes the ways humans interact with it already a priori. As interactions with digital devices are seamlessly integrated into more and more of our everyday routines, these routines do not only become digitally traceable, they are slightly modified to ensure machine readability and thus produce a priori grammatized data. This is the key insight of the concept of capture proposed by Philip Agre (1994): "The capture model describes the situation that results when grammars of action are imposed upon human activities, and when the newly reorganized activities are represented by computers in real time" (p. 109).

Agre contrasts capture with the commonsense understanding of surveillance (cf. Agre 1994, p. 105f), as it is exemplified by Jeremy Bentham's panopticon.[6] Surveillance is a perspectivic gaze from a privileged, central position. It belongs to a disciplinary power regime (cf. Foucault 1995) and is mostly associated with some kind of repressive state power. Capture, in contrast, is free of any particular perspective, belongs to the logic of a control regime (cf. Deleuze 1995, p. 174ff.), and may be carried out by private enterprises no less than by state authorities. The decisive difference, however, is that capture, in contrast to surveillance, relies on practices that are a priori grammatized. This is its most important advantage over surveillance, which has to invest a significant amount of (artificial or human) intelligence to grammatize behavior, i.e., to make it readable in the first place for subsequent data processing.

3.2   Grammars of Action

The basis for this a priori grammatization of behavior is provided by grammars of action (cf. Agre 1994, p. 109). Whenever software is developed that is meant to be capable of interacting with humans in some way, possible scenarios of this interaction have to be anticipated in advance. Human practices thus are modeled according to a formal-linguistic scheme by defining (a) the basic actions from which practices are built up and (b) rules for concatenating elements of activity into larger units (cf. p. 108f). Together, (a) and (b) form a grammar of action that specifies the legitimate practices of interacting with the software. Such grammars

---

[6]   One has to bear in mind that Agre's contrasting definition of capture and surveillance stems from 1994. Since then, of course, the relevance of computer-based data collection has been widely acknowledged in the consolidating interdisciplinary research field of surveillance studies. As a consequence, Agre's sharp distinction has to be relativized with regard to more recent understandings of surveillance. Yet, his insight into the technical modalities of capture can still contribute to a fuller understanding of contemporary practices of data collection. For instance, Zuboff's (2019) widely cited account does not take the formal-linguistic underpinnings of capture into consideration.

enable the software to capture human actions in order to maintain a coherent representation of human activity.

For example, an online shop has a rather simple grammar of the practice of online shopping that consists of basic units like viewing products, putting them into the shopping cart, and proceeding to the checkout. Obviously, this grammar is inspired by the practice of visiting a physical shop, but the practice is modified in the sense that it is rebuilt out of clearly defined basic units freed from all ambiguity. While "viewing a product" is a rather gradual and blurry process in physical reality, it is transformed into a discrete act by grammatization: if the user has clicked on the "product details" page, s/he has viewed the product. As the activity is assembled from sequences of basic acts, every step can be captured and the whole process becomes machine-readable.

Or consider practices of interaction on a "social media" platform. If a posting is displayed to a user, this person may respond by posting a comment (which is done by clicking on "reply", entering a text sequence, and finally clicking "send") or by just choosing one from the offered "instant reactions" like "like", "wow", "haha", "angry", "sad", and so on. Again, this is a grammar that might be considered to be loosely inspired by some kind of physical communication practice where person A tells person B about something and B reacts, either by responding verbally or by feeling happy, sad, or angry about what has been said. Again, in general, such a communication practice does not have a discrete structure but is a diffuse process including innumerable inconspicuous aspects like little gestures, slight changes in facial expressions, modulations of the voice, and so on that can never be pinned down exactly to being an instance of some predefined category.

Grammars of action, in contrast, consist of discrete units that can all be mapped to pre-established categories. Every action in an online shop, just like every reaction on social media, is readily recognized as an instance of one of these categories (like "view product" or "haha"). Whenever we interact with some software system, such grammars are inevitably imposed on our practices: if we want to use the system's functionality, we need to adapt our activities to the demands posed by the system so that our activity is rendered readable for the system (cf. Agre 1994, p. 113f). In this way, the generation of a priori grammatized behavioral data is possible.

As behavioral data have become one of the central resources of today's information economy (cf. Zuboff 2019), there is a strong incentive to steadily increase the resolution of the captured practices. This can be done by increasing the granularity of the grammars of action from which the practices are generated. For example, in 2015, Facebook replaced its like button with a broader range of affective reactions that could be expressed by clicking a button. While this was presented as a response to criticism suspecting that the like button, allowing only positive effects, was designed to produce a "happy world" and an exclusively positive discourse, fostering consumption, its replacement has increased the resolution of the user reactions captured by the platform (cf. Gerlitz 2015). Making grammars of action more fine-grained appears desirable for users as it gives them a larger set of actions they can choose from at every point during the interaction and thus reduce the feeling of being constrained by a grammar of action. At the same time, it allows the platform to capture more detailed data. The users might not even be aware that their behavior is generated by a grammar of action. But this does not mean that behavior has not been fundamentally transformed. Indeed, grammars of action act as a transcendental that constitutes behavior in the realm of the digital. This transcendental status has to be considered when one addresses the epistemological dimension of machine learning about human activities.

4. A PRIORI GRAMMATIZED ACTIVITY AS EMPIRICAL TRANSCENDENTAL

4.1 The Transcendental Status of Grammars of Action

Agre's grammars of actions define the rules for how users can act when they deal with software. Following sociologist Scott Lash, such rules can be called generative rules. To the constitutive and regulative rules that structure society according to John Searle's distinction (1969), algorithmic technologies add a third type of rule. Generative rules can be grasped as "virtuals that generate a whole variety of actuals" (Lash 2007, p. 71). From a small set of rules, a vast set of different states can be generated. To the extent we interact with computers, this principle is imposed upon us. Just like the rules in the source code define at every point during execution how the program proceeds, the user's interactions with the machine unfold by following the predefined options for action that are offered at every stage during the execution. This might serve as an explanation for why machine learning can suppose that "behind all this seemingly complex and voluminous data, there lies a simple explanation" (Alpaydin 2016, 9), as mentioned earlier: not because the social itself would be produced by generative rules, but because the social sphere is increasingly pervaded by computational technology that imposes its rules on social practices, leading to what Lash calls "the technologization [...], the mediatization of life itself" (Lash 2007, p. 70). To the extent that human practices rely on software, they adapt to the grammars of action the software demands. For those practices, the grammars of action that generated them obtain the status of a transcendental; a condition of possibility that constitutes these practices. But not only a condition of possibility for *knowledge* about these practices in the Kantian sense but a condition of possibility for their very *existence*. Those practices come into being by actualizing one of the virtual pathways defined by the grammar of action. Therefore, a priori grammatized behavioral data are a prime example of the Deleuzean "transcendental empiricism" that is so timely now according to Lash. They are instances where "the transcendental is already there in the empirical" (Lash 2007, p. 73), a reality generated from the very categories and schemes through which it is then subsequently read.

Against this background, there is reason to suspect that the simple patterns that machine learning expects to discover in social practices might be first and foremost a reproduction of the patterns that software has inscribed in this behavior. Above all, AI might not find new insights into the depth of human sociality, but rather reproduce the patterns generated from predefined options to buy certain products, follow certain profiles, like this picture, or be angry about that posting. Those are patterns that belong less to the reality of the social than to the reality of software imposed on our sociality.

4.2 Imposing Grammars on Everything?

While "simple rules can indeed generate complexity through computational means" (Hayles 2005, p. 18), assuming that all complex phenomena in the world can be explained this way is an expression of a "computational worldview": it is precisely the "the pervasiveness and importance of computing in contemporary culture" that continues to "reinforce the idea that computation is a fundamental process" (Hayles 2005, p. 30). The more we get used to the everyday use of computational devices, the more we lose awareness of the highly specific structures it imposes on our practices – up to the point where we do not even perceive any difference between activities as such and a priori grammatized activities.

Yet, confusing social practices with digital operations[7] would be "the loss of a site of critique and with it of the Other of the operative", Dieter Mersch (2017, p. 245) warns us: "for we should not forget that most of what we do and what moves us does not operate, language as little as art, an elementary gesture of care as little as a gift". We should remain sensitive to the extent to which we adapt our ways of living to the demands of computational technology. This adoption might be an essential prerequisite for the celebrated successes of machine learning. In the end, we have to ask ourselves how many concessions are we willing to make about our common social reality in order to ensure its machine readability. This is a question that Florian Cramer forcefully evokes in his sarcastic evaluation of a prospective future with self-driving cars:

> The long-term solution is not to improve the pattern recognition algorithms of cars, an endeavor [...] prone to overcomplexity and systemic failure [...]. Instead, all cars and highways could be redesigned and rebuilt in such a way as to make them failure-proof for computer vision and autopilots. For example, by painting all cars in the same specific colors, and with computer-readable barcode identifiers on all four sides, designing their bodies within tightly predefined shape parameters to eliminate the risk of confusion with other objects, by redesigning all road signs with QR codes and OCR-readable characters, by including built-in redundancies to eliminate misreading risks for computer vision systems, by straightening motorways to make them perfectly linear and moving cities to fit them, and by redesigning and rebuilding all cities to make them safe for inner-city autonomous car traffic. (2018, p. 39)

In order to make them computationally accessible, it may be necessary to impose similar measures on all kinds of lifeworld domains.

5.　　CONCLUSION

Against the ideology of "theory-free" data empiricism that is still vital in the ways machine learning about human behavior is understood both in popular and scientific literature, this chapter unfolded some basic insights from the work of Philip Agre. To the extent that the behavioral data used for machine learning is derived from human practices that interact with computers in one way or another, these practices can be understood as laboratory artifacts insofar as grammars of action have been imposed on them to make them machine-readable in the first place.

This opens up several perspectives for critical inquiry. From the perspective of cultural sociology and media history, such imposition can be understood as a new stage of grammatization in the sense of Stiegler. Supplementing Agre with considerations made by Lash, it can be argued that those grammars of action do not only act as epistemic conditions of possibility for all insights that AI subsequently derives about human behavior but equally as conditions of possibility of the respective behavior itself, as they generate re-fashioned practices

---

[7]　What we describe as a priori grammatized practices in this chapter coincides with the "operations" discussed by Mersch insofar as the "a priori of the operators" (2017, p. 243) for any chain of operations corresponds to the a priori status that grammars of action assume as generative rules in the sense mentioned above.

as sequences of options respectively available in human-computer interaction. With Mersch, we emphasized the increasingly overlooked difference between practices as such and a priori grammatized practices, and with Cramer, we raised the political question of to what extent we are willing to subject our lifeworld to such re-fashioning in order to make it readable for digital surveillance and machine-learning algorithms.

FURTHER READING

Agre, P. E. (1994). Surveillance and Capture – Two Models of Privacy. *The Information Society*, 10(2), 101–127.

REFERENCES

Agre, P. E. (1997). *Computation and Human Experience*. Cambridge University Press.
Alpaydin, E. (2010). *Introduction to Machine Learning* (2nd edition). MIT Press.
Alpaydin, E. (2016). *Machine Learning: The New AI*. MIT Press.
Anderson, C. (2008). The End of Theory. The Data Deluge Makes the Scientific Method Obsolete. *Wired*. https://www.wired.com/2008/06/pb-theory/
Cramer, F. (2018). Crapularity Hermeneutics: Interpretation as the Blind Spot of Analytics, Artificial Intelligence, and Other Algorithmic Producers of the Postapocalyptic Present. In Apprich, C./Chun, W. H. K./ Cramer, F. /Steyerl, H. (Eds.), *Pattern Discrimination* (pp. 23–58). Meson Press. https://meson.press/wp-content/uploads/2018/11/9783957961457-Pattern-Discrimination.pdf
DeLanda, M. (2002). *Intensive Science and Virtual Philosophy*. Continuum.
Deleuze, G. (1995). *Negotiations 1972–1990*. Columbia University Press.
Dreyfus, H. L. (1997). *What Computers Can't Do*. Harper and Row.
Foucault, M. (1995). *Discipline and Punish. The Birth of the Prison*. Vintage.
Gerlitz, C. et al. (2015). The Disambiguation of Social Buttons. *Pop-Zeitschrift*. https://pop-zeitschrift.de/2015/11/16/social-media-november/
Haugeland, J. (1985). *Artificial Intelligence: The Very Idea*. MIT Press.
Hayles, N. K. (2005). *My Mother was a Computer. Digital Subjects and Literary Texts*. University of Chicago Press.
Lash, S. (2007). Power after Hegemony. Cultural Studies in Mutation? *Theory, Culture & Society*, 24(3), 55–78.
Lazer, D. et al. (2009). Computational Social Science. *Science*, 323, S. 721–723.
Mersch, D. (2017). A Critique of Operativity: Notes on a Technological Imperative. In Spöhrer, M./Ochsner, B. (Eds.), *Applying the Actor-Network Theory in Media Studies* (pp. 234–248). IGI Global.
Reckwitz, A. (2002). Toward a Theory of Social Practices. A Development in Culturalist Theorizing. *European Journal of Social Theory*, 5(2), 243–263.
Searle, J. (1969). *Speech Acts. An Essay in the Philosophy of Language*. Cambridge University Press.
Schatzki, T. R. / Knorr-Cetina, K. / Savigny, E. von (Eds., 2001). *The Practice Turn in Contemporary Theory*. Routledge.
Stiegler, B. (2010). *For a New Critique of Political Economy*. Polity.
Thrift, N. (2007). *Non-Representational Theory: Space, Politics, Affect*. Routledge.
Zuboff, S. (2019). *Surveillance Capitalism. The Fight for the Future at the New Frontier of Power*. Profile Books.

46. Algorithmic moderation: contexts, perceptions, and misconceptions

João Gonçalves and Ina Weber

ALGORITHMIC MODERATION

The need for algorithmic content moderation emerges when the volume of potentially harmful content becomes too large to be reviewed by humans. Considering the increasing trends of digitalization, this threshold is not hard to reach for many organizations that host user-generated content. Besides the sheer volume of content, one must acknowledge that moderation is also a taxing task for individuals when the type of content under scrutiny is hateful or disturbing (Riedl et al., 2020). Thus, a shift from human to algorithmic moderation may also aim to preserve the well-being of moderators, community managers, and content curators.

This chapter first addresses the roots of the need for content moderation by discussing it from a social norms perspective and profit orientation. Then, assuming that these roots are not addressed, and content moderation is required, it tackles three major issues that should be considered from a critical perspective: (1) an artificial distinction between content deletion and content recommendation; (2) a misdirected concern with technical accuracy of AI; (3) and asymmetries in access to computational knowledge and resources. The following paragraphs address these three concerns, followed by a discussion of how these may apply to online hate speech.

CONTENT MODERATION AND SOCIAL NORMS

The internet and the context collapse (Davis and Jurgenson, 2014) that accompanies it brings new challenges to human interaction. Discussions that were previously subject to strict context-dependent social norms that regulated what can be said by whom are now left to the substantially less constrained domain of online spaces (Suler, 2004). While this brings opportunities for those who were disadvantaged by traditional norms of interaction, it also brings new challenges in terms of the dissemination of potentially harmful content such as hate speech to contexts and subjects for whom it can have excessively damaging effects (e.g., children and other protected groups).

The answer to this challenge may be to introduce new sets of social norms of interaction, ones that limit the harmful consequences of online discussions while avoiding the discriminatory pitfalls of the previous status quo. These norms could be inherent to the purpose of the space that is made available for discussion. While spaces such as social media platforms and news websites may be said to have norms, for instance, in their terms of service, and a purpose, such as discussing or sharing, these norms are more often imposed due to legal or financial (i.e., ad revenue) constraints rather than being socially driven injunctive norms (Engelmann et al., 2022). The reason why these social norms do not emerge is because, for the participants, the purpose of these spaces is only defined in broad terms (e.g., "to discuss, to connect, to share") while for the companies that host them, the purpose is more concretely/ narrowly defined by financial gain through user engagement and retention.

When a church is built as a gathering place, there are clear expectations of conduct, mostly informally defined, associated with the organization or community that constructs the building, and the purpose that the building serves. A gathering space without a clear purpose is therefore subjected to an evolutionary process of norm development that has a degree of arbitrariness, easily swayed by what is said by the participants and the power dynamics in place. In a space without a purpose, the participant who writes the first statements will have a disproportionate effect on what is expected for that space (Gonçalves, 2018). For instance, if the first post in a comment thread uses an aggressive tone and style, subsequent posts are also more likely to be aggressive, either by discouraging non-aggressive participants from intervening (Noelle-Neumann, 1993) or by priming participants to mimic the tone of the text that they are engaging with. Therefore, a tendency toward harmful or deviant content has a propensity to quickly spiral out of control in a non-normative environment, and an aggressive tone becomes the norm.

In effect, most online discussion spaces, at least at their inception, were characterized by a lack of purpose, which made norms and behaviors unpredictable and volatile. Taking the example of news comment sections, these were often initially made available as part of a drive toward audience participation enabled by the interactive possibilities that the internet offered. However, participation was offered for the sake of participation, and it was unclear what newsrooms expected from their readers in these comment sections. When newsrooms actually engage with commenters, they can shift the deliberative norms that the discussion space follows (Stroud et al., 2015). When referring to norms in the scope of this chapter, we are talking about descriptive norms, based on the observable behavior of other users (Engelmann et al., 2022). When normative expectations are clear, users themselves may play a role in enforcing them (Kunst et al., 2021). This is illustrated in online spaces such as Reddit, where the clear purpose of subreddits (e.g., asking questions about politics) means that the community often enforces the norms that lead to content deletion, meaning that tools for algorithmic moderation (e.g., AutoModerator) are quite basic (Wright, 2022) in comparison with platforms such as Facebook or Twitter.

Why is it relevant to consider this void of social norms when discussing algorithmic content moderation? A critical perspective renders visible how not setting clear normative expectations for the policies and implementation of algorithmic content moderation enforces a system in which they are guided by commercial imperatives. In that case, moderation intends to make digital spaces attractive for ad sales rather than safe spaces for different communities. Beyond this recognition, a critical perspective may also emphasize other possible intentions, such as fundamental human rights and values, that shift content moderation toward a community-oriented approach.

Moderation as Content Deletion and Content Recommendation

When discussing online moderation, most academic and non-academic uses of the term refer to compliance with community or platform guidelines for content (Gillespie, 2020, Gorwa et al., 2020, Suzor et al., 2019). However, traditionally, the role of the moderator is not only to decide who speaks but also to facilitate discussion by asking questions or directing participants. If we directly transpose this role to a digital setting, such as an online platform like Facebook, content moderation not only concerns the visibility of content regarding its compliance with formal norms but should also concern the visibility of content in a discursive space.

Following Grimmelmann (2015), we state that content moderation includes both content deletion (compliance with injunctive norms) and content recommendation (conditioning of descriptive norms). Content deletion seeks to minimize harms by removing deviant content that could be harmful to the digital space, while content recommendation aims to maximize user attention and retention by tailoring visible content according to the user's (or more frequently the company's) interests. Nevertheless, from a distanced view, both mechanisms relate to the visibility of content (Zeng and Kaye, 2022), and the distinction between them is guided less by the technical process, but by the need to maximize revenue by not making content recommendations follow the same normative imperatives tied to content deletion. By distinguishing between content deletion and recommendation, online platforms create an artificial gap that allows them to apply one set of normative concerns to content deletion, while more blatantly seeking to maximize profits through recommender systems. However, in some cases, content deletion policies are also a reactive response to threats to profit, as seen in the boycott of Facebook advertising in response to the prominence of hate and misinformation on the platform. If platforms were guided by normative democratic principles such as the ones stated in the EU Charter of Fundamental Rights (i.e., dignity, freedom, equality, solidarity, and justice), content deletion and recommendation would be just different levels of the same process of content moderation. In the end, the practical implications of deleting content or giving it a low ranking, hence decreasing its likelihood to appear for other users, are very similar. From an academic perspective, this means that questions pertaining to filter bubbles or echo chambers (Pariser, 2011) that are often asked about recommendations should also be asked as frequently about content deletion (e.g., are content deletion and community guidelines indirectly reinforcing certain views or perspectives?). Likewise, questions about content deletion, for example, on the adaptability of algorithms to changes in contexts and norms (Gillespie, 2020) should also be asked of recommender systems. Some restrictions are now being imposed on content recommendations, for instance, the Digital Services Act in the European Union gives users the option of opting out of profiling for their recommended content and aims to make recommendation criteria more transparent. However, the distinction between removal and recommendations means that platforms can continue to employ a double standard regarding the visibility of content, pursuing profit to the detriment of democratic concerns.

Bias and Accuracy: the Individuals behind the Technology

A second risk inherent to algorithmic moderation relates to the technical issues that are raised regarding the accuracy and bias of these algorithms (Gorwa et al., 2020). From a critical perspective, we argue that the focus on technical aspects and attributing agency to the algorithm often detracts from engaging with the systemic issues that underlie algorithmic unfairness. For this reason, we find it important to highlight some of the technical aspects of content moderation algorithms, including their high accuracy, precisely to show that most issues arise from the data and contexts provided to the algorithm, rather than from features of the algorithm itself.

Advances in language models that account for textual context such as BERT (Devlin et al., 2018) or GPT-3 (Floridi and Chiriatti, 2020) suggest that given enough training data, machine learning algorithms may match or even surpass human performance in complex classification tasks such as hate speech detection, with similar strides being taken regarding visual content (Wu et al., 2020). However, the issue is that human performance itself is far from unbiased. These advances do not signify a solution to all accuracy and bias problems stemming from the algorithm. In fact, increasingly large language models have come under critical scrutiny, as the notion that more training data can improve the consideration of marginalized voices is contested by analyses of the ways in which these models replicate a biased status quo (Bender et al., 2021). Thus, we argue that a sole focus on the accuracy of classification may obfuscate the broader systemic issues that underlie algorithmic moderation, such as a lack of contextualization leading to the mislabeling of content from marginalized creators (e.g., content from LGBTQ content creators intended to empower their audience being labeled as toxic by Perspective API (Dias Oliva et al., 2021). This emphasizes how achieving a highly accurate and mostly unbiased algorithm bears the risk that the task being performed, and the constructs of bias stop being questioned.

An understanding of the workings of machine learning models relevant to content moderation may facilitate a thorough discussion of the role of bias and large datasets. In the following, we therefore briefly address some models that label deviant content as well as a common model for content recommendation, all of which rely on large datasets generated by processes like crowdsourcing or web tracking.

Convolutional neural networks learn how to recognize patterns in images or textual data. These patterns are more complex than just keywords and therefore are able to capture the context of a word or sentence in ways that shallow learning algorithms cannot. Transformer models account for the fact that some words or parts of an image are more relevant for a particular classification problem than others. As an example, the word "Arab" in itself does not indicate hate speech, but because a potential minority group is mentioned, attention should be paid to it in a classification problem. Finally, collaborative filtering algorithms for recommendation work on the assumption that patterns of taste or preferences can be derived by looking at the actions of individuals and predicting potential overlaps.

All of these machine learning models require substantial datasets to identify patterns or attention weights that allow them to perform accurately in classification or content ranking tasks. This means that moderation algorithms are not trained by experts but by large groups of individuals and their digital traces (e.g., Perspective; GoEmotions). Due to the large volumes of data required for accurate moderation, expert-generated or highly curated datasets are often unfeasible. Thus, a highly accurate algorithm in detecting toxicity is one that can accurately detect an interpretation of what a large group of individuals generally and consensually consider toxic. Looking at classification problems from this point of view, it becomes clear how algorithms may become biased against minorities or individuals that are underrepresented in generating the training set. This is the case of unfairness from the Perspective API algorithm toward LGBTQ+ individuals mentioned above, but may also take place in visual moderation, such as the pictures of individuals who have disfigured faces being flagged as disturbing or violent content because flaggers and moderators have a stigma toward these forms of facial differences.

Focusing on solving issues of bias in moderation algorithms risks disregarding the systemic bias that underlies it. Thus, companies employing moderation algorithms may be content with treating the symptoms of algorithmic bias without addressing the underlying cause of systemic bias. Such biases can stem from a lack of diverse and critical viewpoints from within these companies, for example, through hiring practices that tend to exclude marginalized groups (Varma, 2018). This may limit the extent to which implicit biases are recognized and addressed on a corporate level. From the perspective of historically privileged groups, biases may only be visible when they lead to overt or intentional discrimination. However, from the perspective of targeted minority groups, bias can manifest in more subtle forms and does not have to be regarded as problematic by a majority in order to lead to precarious outcomes (Williams, 2020).

A broader questioning of bias also extends to the problem of accuracy. Even if we have a highly accurate model to detect toxicity, such as the Perspective API, does this mean that all kinds of toxicity and incivility are undesirable in a democratic society (Masullo Chen et al., 2019)? More importantly, is what is desirable and undesirable really context independent? Platform policy guidelines seem to imply that it is, i.e., they universally apply to all content in a platform, but this may only be the case if we embrace the normative void that favors profit-aimed moderation policies. If we accept that online spaces and discussions have a purpose beyond corporate profit, then it becomes clear that content moderation algorithms need to adjust to the normative expectations in a particular online/digital space. This is seen in practice, for instance, in Facebook groups where content that violates the community guidelines is actioned by Facebook themselves, while content that violates group policies has to be actioned by the human group administrators. Again, this is not a limitation of the algorithm itself, since algorithms can be fine-tuned to account for these specific contexts (Howard and Ruder, 2018), but often are not fine-tuned because violation of group policies is unlikely to have an impact on ad revenue, even if it hinders Facebook's mission to connect people.

(Un)equal Access to Algorithmic Moderation

The absence of specific moderation algorithms for specific contexts is related to the inaccessibility of high-performing algorithms. While open science and open data principles mean that many state-of-the-art machine learning models and datasets are publicly available for download, actually deploying and fine-tuning these models to specific purposes requires individuals with a set of highly desirable skills who are in consequence predominantly hired by those with the largest available capital. This means that, for instance, although a school library could greatly benefit from a moderation algorithm that recommends age-appropriate books to students according to their educational needs, interests, and school policies, in practice, it lacks the datasets and human resources to enable the development and deployment of such a system.

The computational resources to train machine learning models are becoming increasingly accessible, and monetary cost-free products such as Google Colab may give the impression of easy access. However, many asymmetries persist in terms of access to knowledge and datasets. As such, AI research and computing are concentrated in a few high-ranking institutions (Ahmed and Wahed, 2020), and prominent natural language processing benchmark datasets are available in English only. Ultimately, this means that algorithmic moderation practices will be determined by those with privileged access to knowledge, data, and computational resources. Thus, the normative expectations and designs of those actors may be embedded in moderation systems, even if these systems are audited to be seemingly unbiased across categorizations such as gender and race. This is particularly problematic in the case of content moderation because, as highlighted by Caplan (2018), decisions on content are highly dependent on localized contexts.

Unequal access to knowledge about content moderation algorithms may also increase digital gaps from a user perspective. Those with less insight into how moderation algorithms rank and hide content will struggle more to make their content visible than those who have higher levels of digital literacy. An example of this can be found on YouTube, where content creators who are aware of the workings of the algorithm and its profit-driven logic tend to be more successful (Bishop, 2018). When those who lack algorithmic knowledge are also those who are underrepresented in datasets, such as in the case of minorities, digital gaps may be widened even further. Thus, inequalities related to moderation algorithms do not only happen at the level of training and deployment but also at the level of usage.

THE CASE OF HATE SPEECH

Online hate speech is hostile speech, discriminatory, or intimidating expressions aimed at a group or member of a group because of an actual or perceived protected characteristic. These characteristics include but are not limited to gender, race, sexual orientation, religion, ethnicity, or terms (Article 19, 2015). Expressions of hate speech are not universal but tailored to the individual or group that is being targeted and therefore highly dependent on specific contexts. Note that the definition of hate speech does not imply that these characteristics should be completely ignored, since sometimes it is necessary to identify individuals to counteract systemic biases but that they should be accounted for and protected. Auditing that, for instance, aims to fully eradicate racial bias in moderation algorithms may actually be incurring in a form of color-blind racism (Bonilla-Silva, 2002) by denying the baseline inequality that means that voices from certain groups are less likely to be heard or should be more actively protected from harm online.

Hate speech is distinguished from mere offensive content as an extreme form of abusive and hostile rhetoric, which may not necessarily use certain keywords to inflict harm but can be highly contextual (SELMA, 2019; Siegel and Badaan, 2020). Language models that are trained with word embeddings, such as BERT and GPT-3, are theoretically able to capture some of these nuances in context. For instance, they may learn embeddings related to gender, which allow them to approximate analogy reasonings such as "male is to female as king is to queen". Assimilating these contexts requires terms to be used in context a reasonable number of times in a dataset. However, hateful content is unlikely to occur in commonly applied datasets for training purposes extracted from Wikipedia or news data in a frequency that allows machine learning models to apprehend these contextual features.

Larger datasets such as CommonCrawl may contain some additional examples of hateful language, but these may be intentionally removed from the language models that are often the foundation of moderation algorithms to ensure that, when used for language generation purposes, the algorithms will not generate hateful text. As such, the lack of hate in training sets may mean that machine learning algorithms are less efficient in identifying and moderating hate speech.

The situation above covers the unsupervised training of machine learning language models, that are subsequently used to identify instances of hate speech. However, what about instances in which moderation algorithms are trained using data that is manually annotated by humans? This data, like human moderators, may be vulnerable to the biases and heuristics of repeated exposure to harmful content. By examining thousands of instances of hate speech, individuals who label data may become desensitized to harm in the process. In practical terms, this means that while human annotators may be able to clearly identify and label hateful content at the beginning of the labeling process, repeated exposure to hate may hinder this ability and compromise the accuracy of the resulting machine learning model. If human limitations are ignored in producing training data, these will be reproduced by the algorithm at a scale.

The solution to issues like hate speech is not to shun algorithmic moderation, since one must recognize the gains in scale and work conditions for human moderators that these bring, but rather a critical development and audit of machine learning classifiers and collaborative filtering. An integrated approach to addressing the limitations of algorithmic moderation implies going beyond statistical bias auditing and accuracy validation but means involving different groups, especially those in vulnerable positions in the data collection, algorithmic design, and output validation of content moderation. This entails identifying and addressing asymmetries in access to machine learning resources while acknowledging that models require constant fine-tuning to ever-evolving contexts and lexicons.

ALGORITHM VERSUS HUMAN

A relevant consideration regarding algorithmic moderation is that it is often placed in perspective or comparison regarding human moderation. This is not specific to content moderation since studies finding evidence of both perceived algorithmic inferiority and superiority to humans exist (Dietvorst et al., 2015; Logg et al., 2019). Perceptions of algorithmic moderation matter because, in a context where folk theories about content moderation are prevalent (Myers West, 2018), the competence and legitimacy, and therefore effectiveness, of algorithmic content moderators may be questioned if these are perceived to be inferior.

Due to its reliance on context, one may feel inclined to think that humans would generally be more suited to perform moderation tasks than algorithms (Castelo et al., 2019). However, our findings show a more complex picture (Gonçalves et al., 2021). The outcome of moderation is perceived as fairer by humans, but only when the user is sent to the community guidelines. Likewise, humans are seen as more trustworthy moderators than AI, but only when they give a specific reason as to why content was removed. In contrast, in a situation where no information is provided to the user as to why content was removed, AI is actually perceived as more transparent than a human moderator.

These findings highlight two crucial aspects that should be accounted for when comparing algorithmic and human moderation. First, these comparisons should not be oversimplified as to consider that one moderator is better than the other. Agents may be compared in terms of the fairness of the outcome, but also the fairness of the procedure, transparency, legitimacy, trust, and even the extent to which context is accounted for. A critical analysis of the implementation of algorithmic moderators should account for these nuances and acknowledge that algorithmic moderators may be perceived more positively in some measures and negatively in others. Second, individuals have different expectations of an AI and a human. While they may expect a human to explain their reasoning for actions taken regarding content, this expectation for transparency may not exist regarding an AI, generally, because this is not a skill that is attributed to algorithms. At the same time, we know that algorithms are disproportionally penalized for mistakes when compared to humans (Dietvorst et al., 2015). A critical study of AI should account for these expectations, and how they may have broader social implications

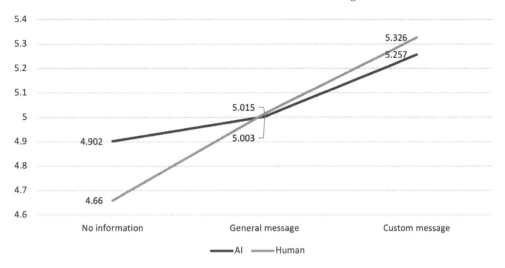

Source: Gonçalves et al., 2021.

Figure 46.1   Perceived transparency of human and AI moderators

in the deployment of AI systems by, for instance, meaning that a shift toward algorithmic moderation implies lower demands for explanations of moderation decisions. While these trends may be counterbalanced by calls for explainable AI, they may nevertheless impact how content is managed online in the absence of a critical examination.

CONCLUSION

This chapter seeks to highlight some of the key dimensions to consider in a critical study of algorithmic moderation. It starts by questioning the need and conceptualization of algorithmic moderation, so that it is placed in a broader context of a normative void and profit-driven imperatives. It then dives into some of the technical pitfalls of the study of bias and accuracy in algorithmic moderation, while highlighting the access and knowledge asymmetries that impact the fairness of machine learning approaches to moderation. It illustrates how these issues manifest themselves in the specific case of hate speech moderation while underlining some of the nuances in terms of how AI moderators are perceived in contrast to humans. It provides several points of departure for critical AI scholars interested in algorithmic moderation, so that they can further develop them in their specific studies and fields of application.

The main purpose of this chapter is to alert scholars to potential pitfalls when studying moderation that reinforces a lack of accountability and profit orientation. As part of this effort, we highlight two key critical recommendations for content moderation scholars: (1) to reconsider distinctions between content deletion and content recommendation, especially those that may lead to different standards applying; and (2) avoid reproducing an emphasis on moderation algorithms as both the agents of harm and the solution, so that the systemic issues that the algorithm is in fact only reproducing are not ignored.

REFERENCES

Ahmed, N., and Wahed, M. (2020). The De-democratization of AI: Deep Learning and the Compute Divide in Artificial Intelligence Research. arXiv preprint arXiv:2010.15581.

Article 19. (2015). *'Hate Speech' Explained. A Toolkit.*

Bender, E. M., Gebru, T., McMillan-Major, A., and Shmitchell, S. (2021, March). On the Dangers of Stochastic Parrots: Can Language Models Be Too Big? 🦜. In *Proceedings of the 2021 ACM Conference on Fairness, Accountability, and Transparency* (pp. 610–623).

Bilewicz, M., and Soral, W. (2020). Hate Speech Epidemic. The Dynamic Effects of Derogatory Language on Intergroup Relations and Political Radicalization. *Political Psychology*, 41(S1), 3–33. https://doi.org/10.1111/pops.12670.

Bishop, S. (2018). Anxiety, Panic and Self-optimization: Inequalities and the YouTube Algorithm. *Convergence*, 24(1), 69–84. https://doi.org/10.1177/1354856517736978.

Bonilla-Silva, E. (2002). The Linguistics of Color Blind Racism: How to Talk Nasty About Blacks without Sounding "Racist". *Critical Sociology*, 28(1–2), 41–64. https://doi.org/10.1177/08969205020 280010501.

Caplan, R. (2018). [Report]. *Content or Context Moderation? Artisanal, Community-Relian and Industrial Approaches.* Data & Society. https://datasociety.net/wp-content/uploads/2018/11/DS _Content_or_Context_Moderation.pdf

Castelo, N., Bos, M. W., and Lehmann, D. R. (2019). Task-Dependent Algorithm Aversion. *Journal of Marketing Research*, 56(5), 809–825. https://doi.org/10.1177/0022243719851788.

Davis, J. L., and Jurgenson, N. (2014). Context Collapse: Theorizing Context Collusions and Collisions. *Information, Communication & Society*, 17(4), 476–485. https://doi.org/10.1080/1369118X.2014 .888458.

Devlin, J. et al. (2018). BERT: Pre-training of Deep Bidirectional Transformers for Language Understanding. arXiv e-print. Available at: https://arxiv.org/abs/1810.04805.

Dias Oliva, T., Antonialli, D. M., and Gomes, A. (2021). Fighting Hate Speech, Silencing Drag Queens? Artificial Intelligence in Content Moderation and Risks to LGBTQ Voices Online. *Sexuality & Culture*, 25, 700–732. https://doi.org/10.1007/s12119-020-09790-w.

Dietvorst, B. J., Simmons, J. P., and Massey, C. (2015). Algorithm Aversion: People Erroneously Avoid Algorithms After Seeing Them Err. *Journal of Experimental Psychology: General*. https://doi.org /10.1037/xge0000033.

Engelmann, I., Marzinkowski, H., and Langmann, K. (2022). Salient Deliberative Norm Types in Comment Sections on News Sites. *New Media & Society*. https://doi.org/10.1177/14614448211068104.

Floridi, L., and Chiriatti, M. (2020). GPT-3: Its Nature, Scope, Limits, and Consequences. *Minds and Machines*, 30(4), 681–694. https://doi.org/10.1007/s11023-020-09548-1.

Gillespie, T. (2020). Content Moderation, AI, and the Question of Scale. *Big Data & Society*, 7(2), 2053951720943234. https://doi.org/10.1177/2053951720943234.

Gonçalves, J. (2018). Aggression in News Comments: How Context and Article Topic Shape User-Generated Content. *Journal of Applied Communication Research*, 1–17. https://doi.org/10.1080 /00909882.2018.1529419.

Gonçalves, J. et al. (2021). Common Sense or Censorship: How Algorithmic Moderators and Message Type Influence Perceptions of Online Content Deletion. *New Media & Society*, 14614448211032310. https://doi.org/10.1177/14614448211032310.

Gorwa, R., Binns, R., and Katzenbach, C. (2020). Algorithmic Content Moderation: Technical and Political Challenges in the Automation of Platform Governance. *Big Data & Society*, 7(1), 2053951719897945. https://doi.org/10.1177/2053951719897945.

Grimmelmann, J. (2015). The Virtues of Moderation. *Yale Journal of Law and Technology*. Available at: https://openyls.law.yale.edu/bitstream/20.500.13051/7798/2/Grimmelmann_The_Virtues_of _Moderation.pdf.

Howard, J., and Ruder, S. (2018). Universal Language Model Fine-tuning for Text Classification. arXiv preprint arXiv:1801.06146.

Kunst, M. et al. (2021). Do "Good Citizens" Fight Hate Speech Online? Effects of Solidarity Citizenship Norms on User Responses to Hate Comments. *Journal of Information Technology & Politics*, 18(3), 258–273. https://doi.org/10.1080/19331681.2020.1871149.

Logg, J. M., Minson, J. A., and Moore, D. A. (2019). Algorithm Appreciation: People Prefer Algorithmic to Human Judgment. *Organizational Behavior and Human Decision Processes*, 151, 90–103. https://doi.org/10.1016/j.obhdp.2018.12.005.

Masullo Chen, G. et al. (2019). We Should Not Get Rid of Incivility Online. *Social Media + Society*, 5(3), 2056305119862641. https://doi.org/10.1177/2056305119862641.

Myers West, S. (2018). Censored, Suspended, Shadowbanned: User Interpretations of Content Moderation on Social Media Platforms. *New Media & Society*, 20(11), 4366–4383. https://doi.org/10.1177/1461444818773059.

Noelle-Neumann, E. (1993). *The Spiral of Silence: Public Opinion – Our Social Skin*. Chicago University Press.

Pariser, E. (2011). *The Filter Bubble: What the Internet is Hiding from You*. Penguin UK.

Riedl, M. J., Masullo, G. M., and Whipple, K. N. (2020). The Downsides of Digital Labor: Exploring the Toll Incivility Takes on Online Comment Moderators. *Computers in Human Behavior*, 107, 106262. https://doi.org/10.1016/j.chb.2020.106262.

SELMA. (2019). *Hacking Online Hate: Building an Evidence Base for Educators*. Available at: www.hackinghate.eu.

Siegel, A. A., and Badaan, V. (2020). #No2Sectarianism: Experimental Approaches to Reducing Sectarian Hate Speech Online. *American Political Science Review*, 114(3), 837–855. https://doi.org/10.1017/S0003055420000283.

Stroud, N. J. et al. (2015). Changing Deliberative Norms on News Organizations' Facebook Sites. *Journal of Computer-Mediated Communication*, 20, 188–203. https://doi.org/10.1111/jcc4.12104.

Suler, J. (2004). The Online Disinhibition Effect. *CyberPsychology & Behavior*, 7, 321–326.

Suzor, N., West, S., Quodling, A., and York, J. (2019). What Do We Mean When We Talk About Transparency? Toward Meaningful Transparency in Commercial Content Moderation. *International Journal Of Communication*, 13, 18. https://ijoc.org/index.php/ijoc/article/view/9736/2610.

Varma, R. (2018). U.S. Science and Engineering Workforce: Underrepresentation of Women and Minorities. *American Behavioral Scientist*, 62(5), 692–697. https://doi.org/10.1177/0002764218768847.

Williams, M. T. (2020). Microaggressions: Clarification, Evidence, and Impact. *Perspectives on Psychological Science*, 15(1), 3–26. https://doi.org/10.1177/1745691619827499.

Wright, L. (2022). Automated Platform Governance Through Visibility and Scale: On the Transformational Power of AutoModerator. *Social Media + Society*. https://doi.org/10.1177/20563051221077020.

Wu, B. et al. (2020). Visual Transformers: Token-based Image Representation and Processing for Computer Vision. arXiv e-prints, arXiv:2006.03677. Available at: https://ui.adsabs.harvard.edu/abs/2020arXiv200603677W.

Zeng, J., and Kaye, D. B. V. (2022). From Content Moderation to Visibility Moderation: A Case Study of Platform Governance on TikTok. *Policy & Internet*, 14(1), 79–95. https://doi.org/10.1002/poi3.287.

47. Algorithmic exclusion

Kendra Albert and Maggie Delano

INTRODUCTION

"Essentially, all models are wrong, but some are useful" (Box & Draper, 1987). George P. Box's 1987 aphorism has come to grace statistical textbooks and email signatures alike, perhaps because it gestures towards a humility that many people who build quantitative models rarely practice. But even though Box was quite critical about the ability of models to reflect real-world results, the quote fundamentally buys into prediction, rather than asking a more fundamental set of questions: who is the model useful to, and who ends up being used by it?

As algorithmic systems continue to have a greater and greater impact on humans and society, there has been an increasing interest in the field of "AI ethics"[1] as a way to engage with these questions. Unfortunately, research by Birhane et al. suggests that even work at top conferences in AI ethics such as the ACM Fairness, Accountability and Transparency Conference (FAccT) and the AAAI/ACM Conference on Artificial Intelligence, Ethics and Society (AIES) is mostly shallow and unspecific, focusing on hypothetical or abstract potential harms rather than the specific impacts on particular groups (Birhane et al., 2022). For AI ethics to help drive research and practice in ways that do not further marginalize people with less power (and ideally shift power in impactful ways), an interrogation of power dynamics related to algorithmic systems, deployment and regulation is needed. This includes a better understanding of the impact of algorithmic system use and misuse, especially on marginalized and underrepresented groups (Birhane et al., 2022; Kalluri, 2020). Birhane et al. recommend an increased focus on concrete use-cases and people's experiences as well as approaches that consider structural and historical power asymmetries.

In this chapter, we engage with Birhane et al.'s call by defining what we call "algorithmic exclusion," building on our previous work about how algorithmic systems in medical contexts disproportionately harm transgender people (Albert & Delano, 2021, 2022). We discuss what it means to be excluded from an algorithm, what the implications of this exclusion are and discuss when and whether it is appropriate to call for "algorithmic inclusion." In doing so, we draw on work about "predatory inclusion" by Louise Seamster and Raphaël Charron-Chénier (Seamster & Charron-Chénier, 2017) and Keeanga-Yamahtta Taylor (Taylor, 2019), and "data violence" from Anna Lauren Hoffmann (Hoffmann, 2020). Our goal is to both define what it means to exclude a marginalized population and trouble the oft-reached solution of "including" people within the context of systems that can ultimately come to harm them.

---

[1] We will use the term "AI ethics" to refer to the discipline at large. However, we avoid the use of the words "artificial intelligence" and "machine learning" and instead use the words "algorithmic" or "algorithmic systems" as a way to "Attribute agency to the human actors building and using the technology, never to the technology itself" (Center on Privacy & Technology, 2022).

ALGORITHMIC EXCLUSION

Background and Definition

Models used in algorithmic systems will always be lossy representations of the real world (Agre, 1994; Box & Draper, 1987) that are excellent at optimizing for metrics, even if those metrics can lead to real-world harm (Thomas & Uminsky, 2022). Models are shaped by the decisions made at each step of the design process, from problem selection to data collection, outcome definition to algorithm development and post-deployment (Chen et al., 2021). We define algorithmic exclusion as the exclusion of people at the data collection, outcome definition, algorithm development and post-deployment steps of algorithmic systems.[2]

We initially coined the term algorithmic exclusion to describe the experiences of non-binary people attempting to use "smart" weight scales to monitor their body composition (Albert & Delano, 2021). In addition to measuring weight like traditional weight scales, "smart" weight scales estimate body fat percentage using linear regression equations. In order to estimate body fat percentage, the scale uses both measured values (weight and bioimpedance, a measure of tissue hydration), and inputs from the user (age, sex/gender, etc.) as inputs into equations that have been generated using a prior reference group. In that work, we discussed how binary variables for sex/gender exclude non-binary people, requiring them to choose a binary value in order to be able to use the scale. Additionally, we discussed how adding a third gender option does not address the underlying issues, as weight scales use linear regressions generated from binary sex data, so new equations would need to be generated. We also discussed the implications of this exclusion, both for end users attempting to engage with the user interface and the uncertainty in whether the results of the scale can be trusted. Without extensive third-party evaluation, the exact impact on non-binary users cannot be determined. However, significant under- or overestimation of body fat percentage can influence decisions users make (such as encouraging or exacerbating disordered eating) or lead to (mis)diagnosis of obesity and prescription of medications not appropriate for the user. The exclusion of non-binary people is only the tip of the iceberg, as weight scales often do not ask for other demographic information such as race or ethnicity, which may also have an impact on the results (Cohn et al., 1977; Deurenberg & Deurenberg-Yap, 2003; Looker et al., 2009).

Direct and Indirect Exclusion

Exclusion can take two forms – direct exclusion and indirect exclusion. Of the two, direct exclusion is easier to spot. Direct exclusion occurs when a particular group of people are barred from participation or inclusion in the data collection or later steps of algorithmic development. Direct exclusion in algorithmic system development is analogous to exclusion criteria used in population selection for studies, for example, when pregnant people or people with particular medical conditions are explicitly not allowed to participate. Sometimes, studies with explicitly exclusionary criteria form the backbone of algorithms, but in other cases, data collection processes used to develop algorithmic systems may lack specific criteria and be

---

[2]   Exclusion of particular people can manifest through feature exclusion or the elimination of "outliers," but fundamentally we name the people because we believe they should be centered (Center on Privacy & Technology, 2022).

much more ad hoc. In those cases, the categories used to sort people may end up creating exclusions in themselves.

Just because exclusion is direct does not necessarily make it obvious to end users. For example, if a user is required to include particular information in order to make use of a system, as with binary sex/gender in the weight scale example (Albert & Delano, 2021), but has no way to provide accurate information, direct exclusion takes the form of a dysaffordance that is obvious to the non-binary users being excluded (Costanza-Chock, 2020; Wittkower, 2016). On the other hand, these scales do not ask whether or not someone is pregnant, and pregnant people are rarely used to generate body composition equations, so it is likely that these people are excluded without even knowing it (assuming they are not also non-binary).

Indirect exclusion is exclusion that is one "hop" out – not explicit in the metrics used to create the algorithms, but a result of the selection processes used at the various stages (especially the data collection and outcome definition stages). For example, methods to remove outliers from particular datasets may result in indirect exclusion of particular groups of people or selection criteria for datasets could end up with some groups being fundamentally excluded without any explicit naming of that process or failure to create ways for them to be included (D'Ignazio, 2021). An algorithm that built medical predictions based on US insurance data would exclude people who do not have access to insurance, resulting in (a) systemic distortion of predictions and (b) the possibility of total and complete failure to be able to make accurate predictions for that subpopulation. Meanwhile, at the outcome definition stage, a project that is focused on an outcome that is disproportionately common in one group compared with another (e.g., a particular clinical diagnosis) or one that uses inappropriate proxy measures (e.g., healthcare costs as a proxy for clinical need) can lead to results that prioritize resources for or treatment of some groups over others (Chen et al., 2021).

CATEGORY-BASED ERASURE

When defining exclusion, we encounter a fundamental problem: it is often true that folks from some minoritized groups are present in datasets, systems and so on, even if they are unaccounted for or unacknowledged. Is it exclusion if people slip through the cracks in a broken system? If a non-binary person was indeed included in one of the studies used to create the algorithms used in body composition weight scales, are these algorithms still exclusionary?

To this, we add a third term to our arsenal – category-based erasure. Category-based erasure is the idea that although a particular group or subgroup of people may be present in a dataset, categories have been constructed in such a way that their presence cannot be determined one way or the other. As such, for at least some purposes, they might as well not be there at all. Although survey and data-gathering instruments often aspire to use categories that are mutually exclusive, exhaustive, and homogeneous, the reality is that they are rarely exhaustive in terms of inclusion of marginalized people, or, if they are, they are not homogeneous, relying instead on othering and grouping distinct types of people together. An inevitable consequence is the "imposition" of an ill-suited categorization onto marginalized groups (Agre, 1994, pp. 746–747).

The idea of category-based erasure draws on our work about "Sex Trouble" in machine learning research that uses electronic medical records (Albert & Delano, 2022). In the article, we discuss examples of research papers that likely have transgender people in the datasets, but they cannot necessarily be identified, and therefore their experiences or potential differences between them and cisgender people cannot be established due to the reliance on sex assigned at birth as a "ground truth" for a patient's physiology. Brindaalakshmi. K has articulated similar dynamics with regard to gender data and the Global South, in particular, in India's Indigenous transgender identities, noting that the flawed datasets collected with inadequate gender categories drive funding for transgender programming (AI Now Institute, 2021; Brindaalakshmi, 2020).

Category-based erasure can go beyond gender and impact many other marginalized groups. For example, a survey that contains an "other" category with no option for further definition, or a scale for assessing weight that groups everyone who weighs over 250 pounds together. Such instruments could effectively group many people with non-homogenous experiences together, making it impossible to tease out particular phenomena that affect certain people within a group but not others. Category-based erasure attempts to name the erasure of particular people as relating to the categorization of data, while noting that they may still be present, and obviously still exist.

Category-based erasure also has implications for the accuracy of systems. One common suggestion for improving algorithmic systems is to conduct model audits, especially on subgroups (Chen et al., 2021; Liu et al., 2022; Wang et al., 2022). However, because of category-based erasure, the information one does have is limited in meaning. False assumptions about the nature of categories, or slippage between them, make it difficult to determine exactly how those categories are even acting, and how they influence model performance and outcomes for erased groups (Albert & Delano, 2022). This means that subgroup auditing cannot be readily performed without testing beyond the original datasets used to build and evaluate the model.

Both algorithmic exclusion and category-based erasure can distort data gathering and data interpretation. For example, a non-binary person may be much less likely to finish a survey with inadequate gender options than a person who sees their gender represented, even if the focus of the survey is not about gender at all. Likewise, inaccurate categories of racial data can lead to false narratives about changes in the demographic makeup of populations over time, as has happened with the US Census, where the inability to mark oneself as belonging to more than one racial category may have fuelled White panic over a "majority-minority" country (Alba, 2018). Because people respond to both how data is gathered and what it says about the world, exclusion and category-based erasure can have profound impacts beyond even the excluded groups.

Exclusion or Bias?

Many scholars use the word "bias" to describe the disparate impacts of model performance, often rooted in the idea that technologies can embed or inherit biases from designers and society (Cirillo et al., 2020; Feldman & Peake, 2021; Friedman & Nissenbaum, 1996; Gianfrancesco et al., 2018; Mattu, 2016; McCradden et al., 2020; Obermeyer et al., 2019; Robinson, 2021; Sjoding et al., 2020; Wu et al., 2020). However, as many other scholars have pointed out, discussions of "bias" and related concepts like "fairness," "transparency" and "privacy" in AI ethics guidelines (Fjeld et al., 2020; Hagendorff, 2020; Mittelstadt, 2019; Ryan & Stahl, 2020) assume a level of system legitimacy and that there is an appropriate distribution of outcomes in the creation of algorithmic systems (Greene et al., 2019; Hagendorff, 2020; Hamid, 2020; Samudzi, 2019; Samuel, 2022). This results in the omission of important considerations like "hidden" social and ecological costs and the misuse of algorithmic systems (Hagendorff, 2020) prevents a deeper understanding of the impacts on marginalized groups (Hamid, 2020), and presumes the inevitability of algorithmic system deployment (Greene et al., 2019), shifting a focus away from "whether" to build and deploy algorithmic systems to "how" to do so (Hoffmann, 2020).

AI ethics framed around "bias" can lead to weak guidelines and corporate embrace of AI ethics to justify fundamentally extractive or oppressive practices (sometimes called "ethics washing"; Bayamlioglu et al., 2019; Bietti, 2021) and may create a false sense that AI companies can self-regulate (Calo, 2017; Hagendorff, 2020). This enables the development of technologies that uphold existing power hierarchies and further entrench inequality (Birhane et al., 2022; Hoffmann, 2020; Kalluri, 2020). Weak guidelines also often ignore the deep ties between the public and private sectors, including the ways in which governments and academic researchers benefit from collaborations with private companies and vice versa (Hagendorff, 2020; Hamid, 2020).

In addition to the critiques of a "bias" framework from other scholars, we think exclusion is a more accurate term to describe the phenomena we have discussed in this chapter so far than bias for two reasons. First, exclusion better describes the experience of users of algorithmic systems who find themselves unable to engage with tools, even if they want to. Kendra describes their experience trying to use the scale as such:

> I know things about myself that are relevant to [the scale's] guessing, but there's no way to translate this knowledge within the limited frame of reference produced by the clinical trials. There's no way to come out with a more accurate picture or contest the bounded understanding of the system. That feels erasing, even more than the mere existence of the binary prompt. (Albert & Delano, 2021, p. 348)

We argue that it is incorrect to call what Kendra experienced bias against non-binary people by the system designers because a bias frame would have to recognize that non-binary people actually exist. If the system is working exactly as intended, it is not "bias" but exclusion.

Second, exclusion is more appropriate than bias because the question of who counts for algorithmic systems is rooted in power and legibility. Exclusion and erasure of these types is the consequence of the goal of making some identities legible to algorithmic systems. As James C. Scott put it in *Seeing Like A State*, "[w]hatever the units being manipulated, they must be organized in a manner that permits them to be identified, observed, recorded, counted, aggregated, and monitored" (Scott, 1998, p. 183). Being unable to identify yourself correctly, as in the case of non-binary people and weight scales, is a form of administrative or "data" violence (Hoffmann, 2020; Spade, 2015).

IS ALGORITHMIC INCLUSION ALWAYS DESIRABLE?

One might reasonably conclude that following a discussion of algorithmic *exclusion* should be a discussion about algorithmic *inclusion*. But, to riff on Foucault, inclusion is a trap (Foucault, 2012). Inclusion can be undesirable even in contexts that seem beneficial on the surface, such as those couched in inclusion for equity reasons or to combat discrimination (Green & Bey, 2017; Hoffmann, 2020). Such critiques have a long history within the space of transgender studies. As Marshall Green argues in their conversation with Marcus Bey on the overlaps between Black feminist and trans-feminist thought, "[the state uses] these categories to promote models of inclusion that instead of dismantling structures that reproduce uneven distributions of power, [...] resituate[s] new bodies so that they might start to feel a part of a broken system" (Green & Bey, 2017, p. 449). Likewise, Dean Spade and Morgan Bassichis have made a similar argument about the pitfalls of inclusion in regard to law reform and legal equality arguments, noting that they can end up playing into anti-Black narratives (Bassichis & Spade, 2014).

One term used to describe negative outcomes of inclusion is predatory inclusion. Predatory inclusion is a term introduced by Louise Seamster and Raphaël Charron-Chénier and popularized by Keeanga-Yamahtta Taylor (Seamster & Charron-Chénier, 2017; Taylor, 2019). Seamster and Charron-Chénier use the term to describe how Black Americans have on average more education debt than White Americans, a difference not attributable to differences in educational attainment but instead to exploitative lending practices. Keeanga-Yamahtta Taylor discusses similar ideas in her book *Race for Profit*, using it to describe federal housing policies in the 1960s and 1970s in the United States that transitioned from housing discrimination via redlining (i.e., exclusion) to "inclusive" practices that were ultimately more beneficial to real estate agents than they were to Black Americans looking to purchase homes (Taylor, 2019). Predatory inclusion is evident in many different types of algorithmic systems that provide financial and social services, such as credit scoring systems (Citron & Pasquale, 2014; Nopper, 2022), and access to welfare and housing (Eubanks, 2018).

If inclusion can result in even worse outcomes while appearing progressive on the surface, it is appropriate to ask about who is served by pushing for inclusion. In an article about facial recognition technology, Zoe Samudzi asks: "In a country where crime prevention already associates blackness with inherent criminality, why would we fight to make our faces more legible to a system designed to police us?" (Samudzi, 2019). Understanding whether or not algorithmic inclusion is a desirable outcome depends on how that technology reflects and challenges the underlying societal priorities embedded in it (Hoffmann, 2020; Samudzi, 2019). Unfortunately, most existing AI ethics scholarship does not engage with this question (Hagendorff, 2020), instead seeing the development of algorithmic systems as "inevitable" and the appropriate question to ask not whether to build something but instead only how to do so while minimizing any negative impacts (Greene et al., 2019; Hamid, 2020). This means that calls for inclusion can unintentionally contribute not only to discrimination but to effectively neutralize any calls that challenge this sense of inevitability entirely (Hamid, 2020; Hoffmann, 2020).

Computers are tools that often uphold existing power structures rather than challenge them (Hoffmann, 2020; Kalluri, 2020). Coupled with use in an administrative context by state or state-like actors, the computer (and therefore also algorithmic systems) can be used as tools of administrative and data violence. Administrative violence is a term introduced by Dean Spade to refer to harms from state-run administrative systems, and data violence is a generalization of those harms to both public and private data technologies like algorithmic systems (Hoffmann, 2020; Spade, 2015). This means that inclusion can lead to harm – both in the construction and reinforcement of specific categories as "natural" and in the way that these technologies are used for harm.

If we take the example of the scale from our previous work, it is worth asking how the diet-industrial complex benefits from the desire to monitor and control one's body through algorithmic means. If, as Da'Shaun Harrison argues in their book *The Belly of the Beast*, anti-fatness has always been anti-Blackness, is pushing for non-binary inclusion in technologies that fundamentally may be inseparable from an anti-fat culture that produced them a net positive (Harrison, 2021)? The inclusion of a broader range of bodies and experiences in the development of algorithmic systems could serve to legitimize, rather than undermine, anti-fat norms, as has happened within the body positivity movement (Gordon, 2020; Mercedes, 2020; Sastre, 2014).

Smart scales may seem like an anodyne example of data violence or the downsides of inclusion. But the stakes are much greater with carceral technologies that "are bound up in the control, coercion, capture, and exile of entire categories of people" (Hamid, 2020). Facial recognition is one example of carceral technology, though they include everything from electronic monitoring to callipers. Zoe Samudzi argues that the failure of facial recognition technology to distinguish between Black faces is not surprising, as facial recognition technology is one tool that feeds the prison system of the United States, and one that cares less about incarcerating the "right" Black person but rather ensuring the oppression of Black people and the maintenance of the prison industrial complex (Samudzi, 2019). Any improvements in facial recognition technology would be, as Samudzi describes, "at best, a pyrrhic victory." Or, as James C. Scott argued, "[i]llegibility [] has been and remains a reliable resource for political autonomy" (Scott, 1998, p. 54).

Despite the risks associated with inclusion, there are circumstances under which it still may make sense to increase one's legibility. Returning to Scott's point from earlier, in order for units to be manipulated, they must be organized in a manner that permits such (Scott, 1998, p. 183). What is important, then, is that the benefits are not just for individuals, but that groups in aggregate will benefit from using the technology. For example, individuals might benefit from the convenience of using facial recognition technology to unlock their phones, but this is a form of "luxury surveillance" (Gilliard & Golumbia, 2021); in aggregate, increases in accuracy and use of such technologies serve to increase surveillance of marginalized communities (Hamid, 2020; Samudzi, 2019). Designing technologies that fundamentally change power structures and benefit those at the margins will require moving away from designing for "default" groups and centering those who are historically decentered (Costanza-Chock, 2020; Davis et al., 2021; Kleinberg & Raghavan, 2021; Rigot, 2022).

CONCLUSION

The field of AI ethics has historically focused on values like "fairness," "privacy" and "transparency." Negative impacts on particular groups that result from the use of algorithmic systems has been posed as a "bias" that can be appropriately "debiased." However, a frame around biasing and debiasing presumes the necessity of algorithmic system deployment and brushes aside the impacts algorithmic systems can have, especially on marginalized groups. In this chapter, we name algorithmic exclusion as a way to centre people in the discussion rather than systems. We discuss algorithmic exclusion as direct or indirect and introduce the term category-based erasure to describe what happens when categorically excluded groups end up present in a system anyway.

In naming exclusion as a potential harm, we resist the urge to push for inclusion as a remedy. Instead, algorithmic exclusion should force reflection about the power structures and fundamental goals of technological interventions. Those who may personally benefit from inclusion would be wise to think about what systemic effects technologies have. In other words, if something is useful, who might be being used?

FURTHER READING

Birhane, A., Ruane, E., Laurent, T., Brown, M. S., Flowers, J., Ventresque, A., & Dancy, C. L. (2022). *The forgotten margins of AI ethics.* https://doi.org/10.1145/3531146.3533157
Costanza-Chock, S. (2020). *Design justice: Community-led practices to build the worlds we need.* MIT Press.
Hamid, S. T. (2020). Community defense: Sarah T. Hamid on abolishing carceral technologies. In *Care.* https://logicmag.io/care/community-defense-sarah-t-hamid-on-abolishing-carceral-technologies/
Hoffmann, A. L. (2020). Terms of inclusion: Data, discourse, violence. *New Media & Society,* 146144482095872. https://doi.org/10.1177/1461444820958725
Rigot, A. (2022). *Design from the margins: Centering the most marginalized and impacted in design processes – from ideation to production.* https://www.belfercenter.org/sites/default/files/files/publication/TAPP-Afsaneh_Design%20From%20the%20Margins_Final_220514.pdf
Samudzi, Z. (2019, February 9). Bots are terrible at recognizing Black faces. Let's keep it that way. *The Daily Beast.* https://www.thedailybeast.com/bots-are-terrible-at-recognizing-black-faces-lets-keep-it-that-way

REFERENCES

Agre, P. E. (1994). Surveillance and capture: Two models of privacy. *The Information Society, 10*(2), 101–127. https://doi.org/10.1080/01972243.1994.9960162
AI Now Institute. (2021, December 23). A new AI lexicon: Gender. *A New AI Lexicon.* https://medium.com/a-new-ai-lexicon/a-new-ai-lexicon-gender-b36573e87bdc
Alba, R. (2018, February 6). There's a big problem with how the census measures race. *The Washington Post.* https://www.washingtonpost.com/news/monkey-cage/wp/2018/02/06/theres-a-big-problem-with-how-the-census-measures-race/
Albert, K., & Delano, M. (2021). This whole thing smacks of gender: Algorithmic exclusion in bioimpedance-based body composition analysis. *Proceedings of the 2021 ACM conference on fairness, accountability, and transparency,* 342–352. https://doi.org/10.1145/3442188.3445898
Albert, K., & Delano, M. (2022). Sex trouble: Common pitfalls in incorporating sex/gender in medical machine learning and how to avoid them. ArXiv:2203.08227 [Cs]. http://arxiv.org/abs/2203.08227
Bassichis, M., & Spade. (2014). Queer politics and anti-blackness. In J. Haritaworn, A. Kuntsman, & S. Posocco (Eds.), *Queer necropolitics.* Routledge, Taylor & Francis Group, a GlassHouse Book.
Bayamlioglu, E., Baraliuc, I., Janssens, L. A. W., & Hildebrandt, M. (Eds.). (2019). Ethics as an escape from regulation. From "ethics-washing" to ethics-shopping? In *Being profiled* (pp. 84–89). Amsterdam University Press. https://doi.org/10.1515/9789048550180-016
Bietti, E. (2021). From ethics washing to ethics bashing: A moral philosophy view on tech ethics. *Journal of Social Computing, 2*(3), 266–283. https://doi.org/10.23919/JSC.2021.0031
Birhane, A., Ruane, E., Laurent, T., Brown, M. S., Flowers, J., Ventresque, A., & Dancy, C. L. (2022). *The forgotten margins of AI ethics.* https://doi.org/10.1145/3531146.3533157
Box, G. E., & Draper, N. R. (1987). *Empirical model-building and response surfaces.* John Wiley & Sons.
Brindaalakshmi, K. (2020). *Gendering of development data in India: Beyond the binary.* https://cis-india.org/raw/brindaalakshmi-k-gendering-development-data-india
Calo, R.. (2017). Artificial intelligence policy: A primer and roadmap. *UC Davis Law Review, 51,* p.399.
Center on Privacy & Technology. (2022, March 8). Artifice and intelligence. *Center on Privacy & Technology at Georgetown Law.* https://medium.com/center-on-privacy-technology/artifice-and-intelligence%C2%B9-f00da128d3cd

Chen, I. Y., Pierson, E., Rose, S., Joshi, S., Ferryman, K., & Ghassemi, M. (2021). Ethical machine learning in healthcare. *Annual Review of Biomedical Data Science, 4*(1), 123–144. https://doi.org/10.1146/annurev-biodatasci-092820-114757

Cirillo, D., Catuara-Solarz, S., Morey, C., Guney, E., Subirats, L., Mellino, S., Gigante, A., Valencia, A., Rementeria, M. J., Chadha, A. S., & Mavridis, N. (2020). Sex and gender differences and biases in artificial intelligence for biomedicine and healthcare. *Npj Digital Medicine, 3*(1), 1–11. https://doi.org/10.1038/s41746-020-0288-5

Citron, D. K., & Pasquale, F. (2014). The scored society: Due process for automated predictions. *Washington Law Review, 89,* 34.

Cohn, S. H., Abesamis, C., Zanzi, I., Aloia, J. F., Yasumura, S., & Ellis, K. J. (1977). Body elemental composition: Comparison between black and white adults. *The American Journal of Physiology, 232*(4), E419–422. https://doi.org/10.1152/ajpendo.1977.232.4.E419

Costanza-Chock, S. (2020). *Design justice: Community-led practices to build the worlds we need.* MIT Press.

Davis, J. L., Williams, A., & Yang, M. W. (2021). Algorithmic reparation. *Big Data & Society, 8*(2), 20539517211044810. https://doi.org/10.1177/20539517211044808

Deurenberg, P., & Deurenberg-Yap, M. (2003). Validity of body composition methods across ethnic population groups. *Acta Diabetologica, 40*(0), s246–s249. https://doi.org/10.1007/s00592-003-0077-z

D'Ignazio, C. (2021). Outlier. In *Uncertain archives: Critical keywords for big data.* http://www.kanarinka.com/wp-content/uploads/2021/01/DIgnazio-2021-Outlier.pdf

Eubanks, V. (2018). *Automating inequality: How high-tech tools profile, police, and punish the poor.* St. Martin's Press.

Feldman, T., & Peake, A. (2021). End-to-end bias mitigation: Removing gender bias in deep learning. ArXiv:2104.02532 [Cs]. http://arxiv.org/abs/2104.02532

Fjeld, J., Achten, N., Hilligoss, H., Nagy, A., & Srikumar, M. (2020). *Principled artificial intelligence: Mapping consensus in ethical and rights-based approaches to principles for AI* (SSRN Scholarly Paper No. 3518482). Social Science Research Network. https://doi.org/10.2139/ssrn.3518482

Foucault, M. (2012). *Discipline and punish: The birth of the prison.* Vintage.

Friedman, B., & Nissenbaum, H. (1996). Bias in computer systems. *ACM Transactions on Information Systems (TOIS), 14*(3), 330–347.

Gianfrancesco, M. A., Tamang, S., Yazdany, J., & Schmajuk, G. (2018). Potential biases in machine learning algorithms using electronic health record data. *JAMA Internal Medicine, 178*(11), 1544–1547. https://doi.org/10.1001/jamainternmed.2018.3763

Gilliard, C., & Golumbia, D. (2021, July 6). Luxury surveillance. *Real Life.* https://reallifemag.com/luxury-surveillance/

Gordon, A. (2020). *What we don't talk about when we talk about fat.* Beacon Press.

Green, K. M., & Bey, M. (2017). Where Black feminist thought and trans* feminism meet: A conversation. *Souls, 19*(4), 438–454. https://doi.org/10.1080/10999949.2018.1434365

Greene, D., Hoffmann, A. L., & Stark, L. (2019). Better, nicer, clearer, fairer: A critical assessment of the movement for ethical Artificial Intelligence and machine learning. *Proceedings of the 52nd Hawaii international conference on system sciences,* 10.

Hagendorff, T. (2020). The ethics of AI ethics: An evaluation of guidelines. *Minds and Machines, 30*(1), 99–120. https://doi.org/10.1007/s11023-020-09517-8

Hamid, S. T. (2020). Community defense: Sarah T. Hamid on abolishing Carceral technologies. In *Care.* https://logicmag.io/care/community-defense-sarah-t-hamid-on-abolishing-carceral-technologies/

Harrison, D. (2021). *Belly of the beast: The politics of anti-fatness as anti-blackness.* North Atlantic Books.

Hoffmann, A. L. (2020). Terms of inclusion: Data, discourse, violence. *New Media & Society,* 146144482095872. https://doi.org/10.1177/1461444820958725

Kalluri, P. (2020). Don't ask if artificial intelligence is good or fair, ask how it shifts power. *Nature, 583*(7815), 169–169.

Kleinberg, J., & Raghavan, M. (2021). Algorithmic monoculture and social welfare. *Proceedings of the National Academy of Sciences, 118*(22), e2018340118. https://doi.org/10.1073/pnas.2018340118

Liu, X., Glocker, B., McCradden, M. M., Ghassemi, M., Denniston, A. K., & Oakden-Rayner, L. (2022). The medical algorithmic audit. *The Lancet Digital Health*, *4*(5), e384–e397. https://doi.org/10.1016/S2589-7500(22)00003-6

Looker, A. C., Melton, L. J., Harris, T., Borrud, L., Shepherd, J., & McGowan, J. (2009). Age, gender, and race/ethnic differences in total body and subregional bone density. *Osteoporosis International: A Journal Established as Result of Cooperation between the European Foundation for Osteoporosis and the National Osteoporosis Foundation of the USA*, *20*(7), 1141–1149. https://doi.org/10.1007/s00198-008-0809-6

Mattu, J. A., Larson, J., Kirchner, L., & Mattu, S. (2016, May 23). *Machine Bias*. ProPublica. https://www.propublica.org/article/machine-bias-risk-assessments-in-criminal-sentencing?token=gl4jHLt-6ZxkcB55q8h_B25ydpK2Tm56

McCradden, M. D., Joshi, S., Anderson, J. A., Mazwi, M., Goldenberg, A., & Zlotnik Shaul, R. (2020). Patient safety and quality improvement: Ethical principles for a regulatory approach to bias in healthcare machine learning. *Journal of the American Medical Informatics Association: JAMIA*, *27*(12), 2024–2027. https://doi.org/10.1093/jamia/ocaa085

Mercedes, M. (2020, September 16). *The unbearable Whiteness and Fatphobia of "anti-diet" Dietitians*. Medium. https://marquisele.medium.com/the-unbearable-whiteness-and-fatphobia-of-anti-diet-dietitians-f3d07fab717d

Mittelstadt, B. (2019). Principles alone cannot guarantee ethical AI. *Nature Machine Intelligence*, *1*(11), 501–507. https://doi.org/10.1038/s42256-019-0114-4

Nopper, T. K. (2022, February 16). *Credit scoring and the risk of inclusion*. Medium. https://points.datasociety.net/credit-scoring-and-the-risk-of-inclusion-151003f63a1a

Obermeyer, Z., Powers, B., Vogeli, C., & Mullainathan, S. (2019). Dissecting racial bias in an algorithm used to manage the health of populations. *Science*, *366*(6464), 447–453.

Rigot, A. (2022). *Design from the margins: Centering the most marginalized and impacted in design processes – from ideation to production*. https://www.belfercenter.org/sites/default/files/files/publication/TAPP-Afsaneh_Design%20From%20the%20Margins_Final_220514.pdf

Robinson, R. (2021). Assessing gender bias in medical and scientific masked language models with StereoSet. ArXiv:2111.08088 [Cs]. http://arxiv.org/abs/2111.08088

Ryan, M., & Stahl, B. C. (2020). Artificial intelligence ethics guidelines for developers and users: Clarifying their content and normative implications. *Journal of Information, Communication and Ethics in Society*, *19*(1), 61–86. https://doi.org/10.1108/JICES-12-2019-0138

Samudzi, Z. (2019, February 9). Bots are terrible at recognizing Black faces. Let's keep it that way. *The Daily Beast*. https://www.thedailybeast.com/bots-are-terrible-at-recognizing-black-faces-lets-keep-it-that-way

Samuel, S. (2022, April 19). *Why it's so damn hard to make AI fair and unbiased*. Vox. https://www.vox.com/future-perfect/22916602/ai-bias-fairness-tradeoffs-artificial-intelligence

Sastre, A. (2014). Towards a radical body positive. *Feminist Media Studies*, *14*(6), 929–943. https://doi.org/10.1080/14680777.2014.883420

Scott, J. C. (1998). *Seeing like a state: How certain schemes to improve the human condition have failed*. Yale University Press.

Seamster, L., & Charron-Chénier, R. (2017). Predatory inclusion and education debt: Rethinking the racial wealth gap. *Social Currents*, *4*(3), 199–207. https://doi.org/10.1177/2329496516686620

Sjoding, M. W., Dickson, R. P., Iwashyna, T. J., Gay, S. E., & Valley, T. S. (2020). Racial bias in pulse oximetry measurement. *New England Journal of Medicine*, *383*(25), 2477–2478. https://doi.org/10.1056/NEJMc2029240

Spade, D. (2015). *Normal life: Administrative violence, critical trans politics and the limits of law*. Duke University Press.

Taylor, K.-Y. (2019). *Race for profit: How banks and the real estate industry undermined black homeownership*. UNC Press Books.

Thomas, R. L., & Uminsky, D. (2022). Reliance on metrics is a fundamental challenge for AI. *Patterns*, *3*(5), 100476. https://doi.org/10.1016/j.patter.2022.100476

Wang, A., Ramaswamy, V. V., & Russakovsky, O. (2022). Towards intersectionality in machine learning: Including more identities, handling underrepresentation, and performing evaluation. arxiv:2205.04610 [Cs]. https://doi.org/10.1145/3531146.3533101

Wittkower, D. E. (2016). Principles of anti-discriminatory design. *2016 IEEE International Symposium on Ethics in Engineering, Science and Technology (ETHICS)*, 1–7. https://doi.org/10.1109/ETHICS.2016.7560055

Wu, W., Protopapas, P., Yang, Z., & Michalatos, P. (2020). Gender classification and bias mitigation in facial images. *12th ACM Conference on Web Science*, 106–114. https://doi.org/10.1145/3394231.3397900

48. Prospective but disconnected partners: AI-informed criminal risk prediction

Kelly Hannah-Moffat and Fernando Avila

INTRODUCTION

Scholars argue that we are in an era of data revolution (Amoore & Piotukh, 2016; Kitchin, 2014a; Mayer-Schönberger & Cukier, 2014; Sejnowski, 2018; Završnik, 2018a) where access to unparalleled amounts of data and impressive computational techniques to process and learn from that data are changing the social landscape. The criminal justice system (CJS) is starting to embrace a logic of modernization that builds on data and computational developments. Novel computational techniques such as artificial intelligence are producing more sophisticated techniques for risk-based differentiation between criminalized people to inform policing practices and enhance legal decision-making. Nonetheless, risk algorithms were used to inform CJS decision-making long before the advent of more complex computational technologies typically associated with big data analytics and machine learning. There are longstanding scholarly debates about the ethics and impact of these algorithms. Research shows that a wide range of algorithms reproduce forms of algorithmic oppression even when they continue to be perceived as more objective and fairer than alternative methods (Benjamin, 2019; Eubanks, 2017; Ferguson, 2017; Noble, 2018; Pasquale, 2015).

This chapter begins with a genealogy of traditional risk assessments in CJS to situate our analysis and highlight the ongoing expectation that advances in algorithmic technologies will produce objective and neutral outcomes that control for bias. We argue that technological advancements to deep-seated criminal justice concerns transform institutional practices, reconfigure the penal subject and produce new forms of governance. We show how old problems persist and get reshaped with new methods as AI-informed risk algorithms. While different, these algorithms continue to use criminal justice-generated data, obfuscate the intricacy of legal concepts, ethics, and social values, and reproduce discriminatory effects or "data harms". Further, scholars continue to wrestle with the relevance of social history and the application of legal principles of proportionality and parity – treating like cases alike. Notwithstanding the ensuing criticism, we argue that the absence of epistemologically informed interdisciplinary dialogues, inconsistent conceptualizations and operationalizations of the principles informing algorithmic technologies, and lack of socio-historical and political context to understand risk and technologies as cultural artefacts produce misunderstandings and create obstacles for alternative uses of AI informed tools that consider issues of social justice (Kleinberg et al., 2018; O'Malley, 2008). As such, we believe that big data analytics and new forms of machine learning could be used to advance justice practices and disrupt current risk practices (Hannah-Moffat, 2019).

RISK PREDICTION IN THE CRIMINAL JUSTICE SYSTEM[1]

The practice of risk prediction has a rich criminological history. Risk logics have intersected and assembled with a range of conceptual frameworks resulting in different outcomes and patterns of legal and penal governance. Heuristically these assemblages include but are not limited to welfarist-based risk technologies, actuarial risk logics, and most recently, big data/ AI-informed risk logics (Maurutto & Hannah-Moffat, 2006). Each has different operational logics and produce tools to assess and manage risk and frequently these instruments operationally coexist in criminal justice institutions. The following details a genealogy of risk assessment prior to the advent of more complex computational technologies typically associated with big data analytics and machine learning. Each of these risk technologies intends to produce useable knowledge for the management of crime and individuals. Importantly, they are all methods of prediction that result in probabilistic assessments of future risk. The ascription of a risk level to a person or situation has a real impact on people's lives. Several scholars have documented how risk-informed practices of governing crime have led to the over-representation and over-policing of segments of the population, primarily racialized individuals (Brayne, 2021; Chouldechova, 2016; Ferguson, 2017; Jefferson, 2020).

Initially developed in the 1920s, techniques of risk assessment were popularized in the mid-1980s, when many criminal justice sectors actively embraced statistical logics and methods (Feeley & Simon, 1994; Harcourt, 2007) as a strategy for managing penal populations and to make determinations of the likelihood of recidivism and dangerousness. This shift that was characterized as "the new penology" and later as "actuarial justice" (Feeley & Simon, 1992, 1994) incorporates the actuarial reasoning that informs the insurance industry – the use of mathematical and statistical methods to measure and manage risk in aggregate populations. Until recently, these risk algorithms were characterized as "risk assessments" and empirically informed by statistical analyses of offender/crime data sets produced by the police, courts, or prisons. These risk assessments were informed by psychological theories and meant to predict the likelihood of reoffending or dangerousness. Nonetheless, calls for "evidence-based" approaches have firmly positioned risk assessment as central to the path towards more efficient, unbiased, and empirically based offender management.

Sociolegal and criminological scholars typically organize the evolution of risk assessment into four generations, from clinical judgement to more statistical calculus of static and dynamic risk prediction (Bonta, 1996). First-generation risk models include clinical assessments that rely on the discretionary judgement of skilled practitioners, most often psychologists, who used psychological tools and personality inventories to survey a broad spectrum of individual needs, characteristics, and traits to identify risk. By the 1980s, these clinical approaches were increasingly being replaced with evidence-based actuarial assessments. Actuarial assessments appealed to correctional administrators because they can be efficiently used by correctional staff, thereby reducing the need for expensive laborious assessments by professionally trained clinicians. Second-generation assessments rely primarily on static measures of risk such as the age of first offence or criminal history, yielding a fixed risk score that is rigid and cannot be altered (Andrews, 1989). In the early 1990s, third-generation risk scores emerged integrating static variables commonly referred to as dynamic risk or criminogenic need. This

---

[1]   This genealogy reproduces with minor changes a similar section in a previous work by the authors and Paula Maurutto (2020).

adjustment enabled mutable risk scores, targeted correctional interventions, monitoring, and risk reduction (Brennan et al., 2009). Criminogenic needs include variables such as education, employment, family relations, and attitudes, all of which are highly correlated with recidivism but also amenable to intervention and change. Researchers and practitioners are particularly interested in identifying criminogenic needs because these factors identify the attributes or characteristics of an individual's life that are correlated with recidivism and are changeable through treatment (Hannah-Moffat, 2005, 2013), unlike static risk factors, which are also informative but are considered unalterable (e.g., age of first arrest, number of convictions, sex). Dynamic risks are often treated as "causal factors" (Ward & Fortune, 2016) and assessments of these factors are typically used to help practitioners categorize, prioritize, and identify programmes that target changeable, statistically determined attributes of offenders, thereby reducing the likelihood of recidivism.

Finally, fourth-generation risk scores integrate responsibility measures that match treatment interventions to the learning style and motivation to streamline appropriate interventions (Andrews & Bonta, 2010; Motiuk, 1997a, 1997b, 1998). The latter three generations can be referred to collectively as psychologically informed risk assessments because they all rely on statistical calculations of the risk of recidivism. Examples of these actuarial tools include COMPAS, Risk of Reconviction, and the LSI. A multiplicity of these tools with variable statistical rigour are used and deeply embedded in criminal justice sectors internationally.

All these risk assessment tools inform and guide decision-makers with objective evidence-based criteria, and by extension, they apply a systematic assessment wherein defendants and offenders are classified according to a standardized set of variables. They purportedly achieve parity by treating each case alike by using the same set of variables that are statistically correlated with recidivism, whether static or dynamic. The variables included in these assessment tools are significantly correlated with recidivism based on aggregate offender population patterns, although this is problematic for specific groups (Hannah-Moffat, 2006). The relevant variables are tallied to produce a final risk score that classifies the individual as low, medium, or high risk. The risk classification is based on how closely an individual matches the risk variables and recidivism rates of the general offender population. This type of traditional risk assessment is modelled on Anthony Burgess' (1928) 0/1 binary non-weighted scoring method, which was initially developed in the 1920s to predict reoffending among those released on parole.

Risk tools have an intuitive appeal to practitioners because they ground decisions in statistical (thus objective) relationships, which are an objective alternative to subjective forms of clinical judgement, and they were seen to be more accurate at-risk predictions. Strategically, such tools are used to inform service rationalization and increase professionals' accountability in decision-making in the named efficient and just management of a range of risks (recidivism, suicide, self-harm, violence, escape) (Hannah-Moffat, 2005, 2016). However, several scholars have shown how these types of risk assessment reproduce data harms by black boxing bias. This research argues that instead of producing objective and neutral outcomes, actuarial risk assessments embed overt and nuanced forms of systemic discrimination that reproduce and magnify class, gendered, and racialized bias and forms of oppression (Bhui, 1999; Pridemore, 2004; Hudson & Bramhall, 2005; Harcourt, 2007; Mayson, 2019; Hannah-Moffat, 2013, 2005; Hamilton, 2019; Malek, 2022; van Eijk, 2017). Specifically, the statistical variables correlated and used to predict recidivism – such as education, finances, acquittances, aptitudes, family relations, and leisure pursuits – are also highly correlated with marginalization in terms of gender, race, class, and other forms of social disadvantage. As a result, the data, calculation, and corresponding correlations serve as proxies for such variables, and thereby indirectly embed legally prohibited criteria (Horn & Evans, 2000; Shaw & Hannah-Moffat, 2000; Harcourt, 2007, 2015). Risk variables are also criticized for their normative evaluations of morality, which is reflected in the inclusion of variables such as personal and familial relationships, associations with organized religion, and leisure activities, which are subject to high degrees of discretionary evaluation (Hannah-Moffat et al., 2009; Hudson & Bramhall, 2005). Gendered and racialized norms, experiences, and knowledge shape what behaviours are viewed by assessors as a risk. The algorithm treats each variable as an indicator of individual criminogenic risk, divorced from broader social, political, economic, and historical disadvantages. What the calculations ignore is how an offender's "exposure to risk" in society is often the result of histories of disadvantage and discrimination that are often correlated with risk variables, thereby resulting in "higher" risk scores, particularly for women and historically marginalized populations (Hannah-Moffat, 2009, 2015; Hannah-Moffat & Maurutto, 2010; Hannah-Moffat & Struthers Montford, 2021). For example, financial difficulties, often arising from poverty, are correlated with higher recidivism rates; those on social assistance are regularly assessed as a higher risk. In contrast, middle-class offenders, who may have committed similar or more severe offences, are less likely to score high on measures of financial difficulty.

The authors of the article "Machine Bias" accessed several public online criminal justice data sources obtained through a Freedom of Information request to analyse more than 7000 risk scores produced by the COMPAS risk assessment (Angwin et al., 2016). They merged multiple datasets and data points to identify and disclose levels and percentages of bias in COMPAS. They compared predicted scores to actual recidivism among criminal defendants in Broward County, Florida, over two years. The results demonstrated that black accused were twice as likely as white defendants to be incorrectly scored at a higher risk of recidivism. Conversely, white defendants were more likely to be incorrectly flagged as low risk. When predicting violent recidivism, the results revealed an even more significant disparity: black defendants were 77% more likely to be misidentified as higher risk. These discriminatory findings catalysed researchers to develop new ways of producing fairer assessment models.

Through a slippage between correlation and a reconfiguration of needs to risk factors, bias is extended beyond calculations and reinterpretations of probability assessments (Hannah-Moffat, 2013). Factors associated with marginalization and need are often used to score risk, wherein those "at risk and high need" become "high risk". A designation of high risk can lead to a greater likelihood of detention and more stringent conditions that cause individuals to be more vulnerable to breaches, increased surveillance, and further criminalization. For this reason, scholars have argued that traditional risk assessments are "algorithms of oppression" that offer a veneer of objectivity and alternatively produce/reproduce racism, sexism, and "technological redlining" (Noble, 2018; Benjamin, 2019; Eubanks, 2017). Similarly, O'Neil (2016) characterized such algorithms as "weapons of math destruction" because they are opaque and have the potential to cause damage, particularly reproduced at scale in more complex algorithmic forms.

AI RISK ASSESSMENT IN THE CRIMINAL JUSTICE SYSTEM

The shift to big data analytics (Kitchin, 2014a, 2014b) and the advance in computational techniques such as artificial intelligence (Sejnowski, 2018) represent a notable departure from other algorithmically influenced risk technologies. A new cadre of scientists from fields including computer science, mathematics, statistics, and engineering have entered the field of criminal risk prediction. Some are responding to the sustained international critique of traditional risk assessments (algorithms) and claiming to be developing fairer and more accurate algorithms for predicting recidivism (Chouldechova & G'Sell, 2017). These data scientists use large datasets and forms of artificial intelligence to experiment with different measures of statistical fairness and to test models. The resultant AI-informed algorithms *are different* from psychologically informed algorithms noted above because they can be trained using vast amounts of raw data, and they can be programmed to independently learn from data to create new algorithmic configurations and probabilistic models (Mackenzie, 2017, p. 7). Some scholars have described these as fifth-generation risk assessment tools (Garrett & Monahan, 2019; Taxman & Dezember, 2016). These fifth-generation tools have different epistemological foundations and depart from more familiar and rich traditions of psychology, sociology, or criminology. Below we discuss the complexity of one instance of this departure and disconnect: efforts to create "fair" and accurate risk prediction. A problem that several prior generations of risk assessment have grappled with.

In a previous work (2020), we showed how despite the ambiguity of fairness as a concept to be measured by a formula, scholars working on machine learning models position questions of fairness at the centre of their research. Fairness is an abstract idea; it cannot be translated or reduced to a straightforward mathematical calculation. Currently, there are about 20 different definitions of fairness explored in this area (Gajane & Pechenizkiy, 2018; Kleinberg et al., 2017; Mehrabi et al., 2019; Pessach & Shmueli, 2023; Verma & Rubin, 2018).[2] As demonstrated by this wide range of definitions, scholars have a diverse array of choices for how they conceptualize when designing an AI-informed algorithm. There is no clear consensus on how to balance accuracy and fairness in an algorithm. Research has shown that a single model cannot simultaneously satisfy all definitions of group fairness and that the required trade-offs are statistically impossible to reconcile (Chouldechova, 2016; Courtland, 2018; Kleinberg et al., 2017). For example, the study of COMPAS[3] scores illustrated the extant trade-offs that occur when balancing fairness and accuracy (Angwin et al., 2016). Northpointe, the company that created COMPAS, claims that its tool is valid because it satisfies predictive rate parity and is equally adept at predicting whether a white or black defendant classified as high risk would re-offend. In contrast, Angwin et al. argued that the COMPAS tool is discriminatory because it does not satisfy the equalized odds test, and it yields a disproportionate number of false positives among black defendants. Each model frames fairness differently.

---

[2]   For example, one simple formalization of fairness in machine learning is *fairness through unawareness*, where training data exclude sensitive attributes such as gender, race, or another minority status (Dwork et al., 2011). Other definitions such as *demographic parity, equalized odds,* and *predictive rate parity* can be classified as "group" fairness definitions because they are used in models that divide a given population into different groups, typically protected and unprotected, and include checks to determine whether each group is balanced considering a given classification rate and statistic metric (Corbett-Davies et al., 2017; Dwork et al., 2011; Johndrow & Lum, 2017). In contrast, "individual" fairness definitions require that similar individuals are treated similarly (Dwork et al., 2011). Still, other models rely on *counterfactual fairness*, where a decision is considered fair if it would be the same in a counterfactual scenario where the individual belonged to a different demographic group (Kusner et al., 2017).

[3]   For clarity, COMPAS is a computer software, based on traditional algorithms but it is not an AI-informed risk assessment tool in the way that we are describing here.

Unlike earlier risk assessment tools, machine learning algorithms are not epistemologically grounded. In the big data era, the datasets available to train these predictive models are immense and have the potential to include infinite data points. This feature distinguishes them from the limited and smaller datasets (obtained from analyses of a prison population or subset of offenders) relied on by earlier risk assessments. Moreover, machine learning risk models are adaptive and can dynamically self-adjust to new data over time in undetermined and unanticipated ways as systems learn[4] (Pasquale, 2015). In the context of machine learning algorithms, the term "dynamic" refers to models that continuously learn and self-correct following the parameters of the program. This differs from psychologically informed risk instruments (e.g., COMPAS), where a "dynamic" factor refers to criminogenic behaviour that can be altered.

Many scholars working in this field are seized with considerations of ethics in big data analytics (Dubber et al., 2021). Some are responding to the abovementioned criticism (Kleinberg et al., 2018). The goal is to produce responsible, ethical designs that produce alternative forms of risk determination that are "fair" and accurate (Greene et al., 2019). Scholars claim that AI-informed algorithms can be programmed to learn bias in the data and automatically adjust for disparate effects without the need for reprogramming, there is also a recognition that unfairness can stem not only from bias in the data but also from bias in the algorithm itself (Pessach & Shmueli, 2023). Overall, these models[5] are all designed to produce outcomes that attempt to detect and reduce social, racial, and gender bias.

LAYERS OF OLD ISSUES, NEW METHODS, AND LITTLE DIALOGUE

The rise of big data coupled with novel computational techniques that rely on algorithms that can potentially learn in unsupervised manners from vast amounts of raw data has produced an incredible impact on how decisions are being made in several terrains of our social life, and criminal justice is not the exception (Završnik, 2019). The introduction of big data technologies warrants analysis both because the concept of risk is central to our legal and criminal justice culture (Ashworth & Zedner, 2014), and because it represents an epistemic deviation

---

[4]   Machine learning, a subfield of artificial intelligence, is broken into at least four sub-categories: supervised, semi-supervised, unsupervised, and reinforcement learning. Supervised ML requires training an algorithm with labelled data sets. Unsupervised learning describes methods where an algorithm is trained without an annotated data set, it looks for patterns in unlabelled data. Semi-supervised learning is a combination of supervised and unsupervised learning techniques. Finally, reinforcement learning is based on the premise of continually "rewarding" an algorithm for optimizing to a particular outcome using a trial-and-error approach.

[5]   One example is *learning fairness representation* (Zemel et al., 2013), where the goal is to achieve group and individual fairness through a good representation of data that obfuscates protected data. The assumption is that algorithms can detect bias and cleanse it from the output before producing an assessment. A model that applies *fairness through unawareness* calculates and identifies sensitive attributes and automatically learns to exclude their use in the decision-making process (Kusner et al., 2017). In the *learning-to-defer* approach (Madras et al., 2017), the algorithm can detect when its prediction is less robust and notify the decision-maker. In this case, the algorithm works adaptively with decision-makers about whether to override a score based on the strength of the prediction. Decision-makers are notified when a prediction is not sufficiently robust; they can then assess whether it is best to bypass the algorithm and rely on their expertise.

from risk assessments that are grounded in psychological disciplines. Little is known about how criminal justice systems, social justice organizations, and individuals are shaping, challenging, and redefining conventional actuarial risk episteme(s) using big data technologies (Hannah-Moffat, 2019). The practical use of algorithms is "rarely evenly applied or in accordance with some grand design but instead they resemble more of a patchwork" (Schuilenburg & Peeters, 2020, p. 196). They coexist with other bureaucratic processes. Importantly, they continue to coexist and overlay other practices and the success of an algorithm is "not as automatic as proponents hope or as critics fear" (Mead & Barbosa Neves, 2022, p. 4).

The advent of big data and the promise of AI–informed risk assessment has shifted how scholars are talking about risk assessment. These technologies are now referred to as "risk algorithms" in many sectors. There is little precision in the description of risk-informed technologies; the result is confusion. The liberal use of the term "risk algorithm" fails to differentiate between the tools described above that have existed since the mid-20th century and the newer 21st-century computational developments based on AI and machine learning that use "big data" instead of institutionally derived data sets to make risk determinations and inform the justice sector. Moreover, CJS agents have been using computer software to predict future criminal behaviour that is not necessarily AI-informed or that is not trained to rely on big data. At the same time, "big data", "machine learning", and "artificial intelligence" are equally amorphous terms that are even more difficult to grasp for scholars and stakeholders unfamiliar with them. Over-reliance on loosely defined general terms like AI and automation results in a high degree of slippage in social scientific understandings of the data-driven tools used to inform decisions within the CJS.

This confusion allows different layers of problems with different origins to accumulate on top of each other causing even greater difficulties and logical obstacles. In other words, AI-informed algorithms that rely on big data drag with them and stand on the longstanding problems associated with risk and prediction in the CJS (Harcourt, 2007), on the problems associated with the imperfect nature of social data and its "disparate impact" (Barocas & Selbst, 2016), on more novel problems related to the use of vast amounts of raw data (Kitchin, 2014a) and lack of epistemological ground, and on the problems associated with the use of artificial intelligence to process, learn, and produce outcomes in unsupervised ways, among other things (Mehrabi et al., 2021; Pessach & Shmueli, 2023). All of them contain a distinct set of problems with specificities but they accumulate, amplifying the complexity.

For example, proponents of applying machine learning argue that by letting the data speak for itself, it is possible to achieve an exhaustive unveiling of factors that can be statistically related to an outcome but beyond the reach of human actors or traditional techniques of data analysis (Dwork et al., 2011; Chouldechova, 2016; Kleinberg et al., 2017; Berk et al., 2017; Kusner et al., 2017; Verma & Rubin, 2018). The scale of access to vast amounts of data to train algorithms poses new challenges. The techniques of data scraping, munging, and wrangling used to assemble and reassemble data and the data-driven technologies they inform are seemingly creating new knowledge about risk (Hannah-Moffat, 2019) but they are in fact susceptible to the same problems as earlier less sophisticated tools and often rely on the same variables. Moreover, it remains unclear how data is aggregated, disaggregated, stored, shared, and used to produce and train automated systems.

At the same time, new players and experts have entered the scene, influencing the outcomes. Private companies are offering products that allow security agencies to access and connect large datasets from public records, social media, smartphone apps, purchases, licence plate readers, and police agencies. Some scholars argue that big tech companies have a decisive influence on the production and distribution of technology and that their role will impact the governance of public affairs and define the concept of "good governance" (Schuilenburg & Peeters, 2020, p. 198).

Debates in this area also frequently fail to appreciate the nuances of law, judicial reasoning, and jurisprudence. In the instance of criminal risk prediction, the outcome of concern is recidivism. What many of the new technology experts entering this area are unaware of is the rich conceptual and technical debate about outcome variables such as recidivism and equally critical legal principles of parity and proportionality, as well as the nuanced ways that structural inequality is entangled with all criminal justice data producing what scholars have called "dirty data" (Richardson et al., 2019; Završnik, 2018b). For example, one of the most accessible forms of data used in algorithms is criminal justice reports on arrests. However, arrest data can reflect logics other than crime occurrence like municipal priorities, such as the desire for increased revenues that can be generated from fines imposed on those arrested – and increases in arrests to create municipal profits are often conflated with actual crime (Ferguson, 2017). Marginalized neighbourhoods are more frequently targeted, driving up the arrests of racial and other marginalized individuals, especially given racial profiling and hot-spot policing. In the United States, for example, charging and arrest data are decontextualized from the War on Drugs that has driven mass incarceration rates (Alexander, 2010; Western & Wildeman, 2009), just as in Canada it is from the persistence of colonialism (Chartrand, 2019).

The challenges of objectivity and equity are not new. Just as in earlier models, criminal justice data are collected and produced from interactions with individuals in the "system" for operational purposes. Efforts to predict recidivism are grounded primarily in identifying these individuals' characteristics. The data input into risk models is inherently dirty (Richardson et al., 2019; Završnik, 2018b). It is difficult, if not impossible to remove bias in data that are structurally proxies for inequality. The ethics of collecting and using broader granular data on non-criminalized populations are complex. Notwithstanding advances in machine learning technologies, scholars continue to debate traits in data that feed and train the algorithms and the extent to which algorithms will continue to reproduce discriminatory outcomes. Eliminating bias variables can leave these models sparse and unable to function or adjust control for unknown situations that a well-intended defendant may experience. Scholars claim that while tools relying on mathematical and statistical modelling provide the allure and illusion of objectivity, they mask embedded forms of discrimination that reproduce gender, racial, ethnic, and other forms of inequality like traditional risk assessment (Brayne, 2021; Eubanks, 2017; Ferguson, 2017; Noble, 2018; O'Neil, 2016; Richardson et al., 2019; Završnik, 2018b).

These tools require a more sophisticated understanding of how inequality can be embedded in insidious and unexpected ways (Benjamin, 2019; Eubanks, 2017; Noble, 2018). The data fed into a machine learning system, and the calculations on which they are based, continue to be abstracted from wider socio-political, economic, and historical relations that embed discrimination into algorithms and are not prone to mathematical correction. Machine learning risk tools decontextualize data, overstate mathematical correction, obfuscate the significance of ethical/social effects, and thereby can reproduce discriminatory effects or "data harms" often with less transparency and through complex and elusive processes often referred to as "black boxes" (Pasquale, 2015). The production of useable data and the training of statistical models are time-consuming and complex processes that require judgement, interpretation, and some knowledge about what questions the data will be used to answer (Hannah-Moffat, 2019).

The developers of risk tools could engage with the considerable body of criminological research related to discriminatory practices, policies, and histories of race relations, gender inequality, and indigeneity and how these can be embedded in all forms of data and algorithms (Hannah-Moffat & Struthers Montford, 2019, 2021). When algorithms train on and use data that is gathered through practices that disproportionally affect historically marginalized communities and insert proxies for bias, the resulting probability score is more reflective of selective policies than actual criminal behaviour. Consequently, machine learning algorithms purportedly improve prediction accuracy and fairness, but the prediction reproduces and magnifies markers of inequality. These algorithmic outcomes are ascribed to people who are managed accordingly.

A myopic focus on improving techniques of identifying recidivists often compromises other central legal considerations such as parity and proportionality. Alternatively, culture-based approaches to the study of risk, examine how "risk" differs across time and space. This logic would urge an examination of the logic influence of institutions on the production of crime or reoffending. As Hannah-Moffat argues (2016, p. 14), it is possible to conduct a broader non-individualistic empirical analysis of factors that may reduce recidivism. At the same time, discussions around divergent disciplinary understandings of concepts like "fairness" or "bias" can distract from the task of unravelling what and how technology is and could be used to inform highly consequential decisions like those made in the CJS. Each gradual shift towards automation and the use of advanced forms of data analytics is significant. The technologies in and of themselves have limited agency and governmental capacities. Algorithms do not have power in the classic sense the way a sovereign does. Instead, they provide "actionable insights" that seek to nudge, manipulate, or manage behaviour at both the collective and individual levels. For instance, risk algorithms could be developed to examine various jurisdictional policies and structural constraints that contribute to crime and reoffending (Hannah-Moffat, 2016), or to detect social needs for social assistance interventions (Ferguson, 2017, p. 167) and even to detect and limit institutional violence (Ferguson, 2017, p. 143). AI-informed tools inform and reciprocally become a rationale for decision-making and policy. Technophobic reactions to the advancement of technology in CJS settings may be short-sighted as they can be value added and can be used for advocacy, detection of social needs, distribution of social assistance, or identification of institutional violence or biased outcomes.

CONCLUSION

We are now in an era of AI with the opportunities and risks that accompany a multiplicity of quickly advancing computational technologies. Deeper thought can be given to the questions and problems technology is used for and to how and when it can be ethically, defensibly, and meaningfully used to inform policy and practice. As Kitchin (2014a) notes, there is an urgent need for wider critical reflection within the academy on the epistemological implications of the unfolding data revolution. In many sectors of the criminal justice system, there is a myopic emphasis on the predictive accuracy of risk algorithms and unwavering actuarial faith in the capacity of these tools to make neutral, unbiased decisions about risk (Hannah-Moffat, 2016). It is vital to step back and question some of the central assumptions about crime, nuances, and complexities of algorithmic technologies and to situate these debates in a socio-historical and political context. Such dialogues ought to include wider debates about the appropriateness and misapplication of technology.

It is equally important to have some precision in what we mean when speaking about algorithmic technologies. This has become a catchall term not unlike the term risk. Risk is a socio-historical and politicalized concept that is also gendered and racialized in effects and conceptualization, especially when applied in a justice context. Likewise, big data and incumbent analytics are also "a political process involving questions of power, transparency and surveillance" (Tufekci, 2014, p. 1). It is not as objective, neutral, or complete as they are portrayed and there are many translations and epistemological and methodological debates about how to proceed. Arguably, big data, its incumbent analytics, and the knowledges they produce are socio-political and cultural artefacts that are transforming how we live, work, and think about social problems (Lupton, 2015).

Technology can make systems more efficient and expeditious, which is welcome in highly bureaucratized systems that are often cumbersome and slow. The problems are with how they are deployed by governmental agencies in nuanced areas such as the criminal justice system and law enforcement. As Mead and Barbosa Neves claim (Mead & Barbosa Neves, 2022, p. 3), technology is a socio-political and technical phenomenon that requires more than an articulation of its benefits to a government for its successful implementation. Not all algorithms persist; they are and can be contested. Public advocates can assist in making technologies visible and contestable tools of governance, especially when technical justifications of fairness and efficiency clash with more democratic and juridical understandings of these terms. Importantly, the development and use of technology ought to occur in a principled context that respects human rights and humanity and minimizes harm while adhering to broader ethical and legal principles.

Notwithstanding, the capacity and propensity for AI algorithms to learn, they are tasked with the same problematic questions about recidivism risk and danger. If new technologies are dispatched through the sector without deep consideration of how they differ from past methods and uses of algorithms, they are likely to reproduce longstanding problems. Cross-disciplinary dialogues with a collective understanding of the problem to be solved are needed to facilitate innovation with social justice in mind. There are many forms of AI and applications of it in the criminal justice sector. This chapter narrowly focused on how AI is renewing the discussions around risk assessments within the criminal justice system and the need for fair and ethical risk algorithms, but there are also many advances in predictive policing and legal analytics that are falling unwittingly into similar traps. Consequently, we encourage practitioners in many fields from the humanities to the computational sciences to rethink naturalized practices and to reimagine what both learning and data might become and how they may facilitate equitable justice practices.

FURTHER READING

Dubber, M. D., Pasquale, F., & Das, S. (Eds.). (2021). *The Oxford handbook of ethics of AI* (First issued as an Oxford University Press paperback). Oxford University Press.
Hannah-Moffat, K. (2016). A conceptual kaleidoscope: Contemplating 'dynamic structural risk' and an uncoupling of risk from need. *Psychology, Crime & Law*, 22(1–2), 33–46. https://doi.org/10.1080/1068316X.2015.1114115
Schuilenburg, M., & Peeters, R. (Eds.). (2020). *The algorithmic society*. London: Routledge.

REFERENCES

Alexander, M. (2010). *The new Jim Crow: Mass incarceration in the age of colorblindness*. New Press.

Amoore, L., & Piotukh, V. (Eds.). (2016). *Algorithmic life: Calculative devices in the age of big data*. Routledge, Taylor & Francis Group.

Andrews, D. (1989). Recidivism is predictable and can be influenced: Using risk assessments to reduce recidivism. *Forum on Corrections Research*, *1*, 2–4.

Andrews, D., & Bonta, J. (2010). *The psychology of criminal conduct* (5th ed.). Lexis Nexis/Anderson Pub.

Angwin, J., Larson, J., Mattu, S., & Kirchner, L. (2016). *Machine bias: There's software used across the country to predict future criminals. And it's biased against blacks*. ProPublica. https://www.propublica.org/article/machine-bias-risk-assessments-in-criminal-sentencing.

Ashworth, A., & Zedner, L. (2014). *Preventive justice* (1st ed.). Oxford University Press.

Avila, F., Hannah-Moffat, K., & Maurutto, P. (2020). The seductiveness of fairness: Is machine learning the answer? – Algorithmic fairness in criminal justice systems. In M. Schuilenburg & R. Peeters (Eds.), *The algorithmic society: Technology, power, and knowledge*. Routledge.

Barocas, S., & Selbst, A. D. (2016). Big data's disparate impact. *California Law Review*, *104*(3).

Benjamin, R. (2019). *Race after technology: Abolitionist tools for the new Jim code*. Polity.

Berk, R., Heidari, H., Jabbari, S., Kearns, M., & Roth, A. (2017). Fairness in criminal justice risk assessments: The state of the art. ArXiv:1703.09207 [Stat]. http://arxiv.org/abs/1703.09207

Bhui, H. (1999). Race, racism and risk assessment: Linking theory to practice with black mentally disordered offenders. *Probation Journal*, *46*(3), 171–181. https://doi.org/10.1177/026455059904600303

Bonta, J. (1996). Risk-needs assessment and treatment. In *Choosing correctional options that work: Defining the demand and evaluating the supply* (pp. 18–32). Sage Publications, Inc.

Brayne, S. (2021). *Predict and surveil: Data, discretion, and the future of policing*. Oxford University Press.

Brennan, T., Dieterich, W., & Ehret, B. (2009). Evaluating the predictive validity of the compas risk and needs assessment system. *Criminal Justice and Behavior*, *36*(1), 21–40. https://doi.org/10.1177/0093854808326545

Burgess, E. W. (1928). Factors making for success or failure on parole. *Journal of Criminal Law and Criminology*, *19*(2), 239–306.

Chartrand, V. (2019). Unsettled times: Indigenous incarceration and the links between colonialism and the penitentiary in Canada. *Canadian Journal of Criminology and Criminal Justice*, *61*(3), 67–89. https://doi.org/10.3138/cjccj.2018-0029

Chouldechova, A. (2016). Fair prediction with disparate impact: A study of bias in recidivism prediction instruments. ArXiv:1610.07524 [Cs, Stat]. http://arxiv.org/abs/1610.07524

Chouldechova, A., & G'Sell, M. (2017). *Fairer and more accurate, but for whom?* http://arxiv.org/abs/1707.00046

Corbett-Davies, S., Pierson, E., Feller, A., Goel, S., & Huq, A. (2017). Algorithmic decision making and the cost of fairness. *Proceedings of the 23rd ACM SIGKDD international conference on knowledge discovery and data mining - KDD '17*, 797–806. https://doi.org/10.1145/3097983.3098095

Courtland, R. (2018). Bias detectives: The researchers striving to make algorithms fair. *Nature*, *558*(7710), 357–360. https://doi.org/10.1038/d41586-018-05469-3

Dubber, M. D., Pasquale, F., & Das, S. (Eds.). (2021). *The Oxford handbook of ethics of AI* (First issued as an Oxford University Press paperback). Oxford University Press.

Dwork, C., Hardt, M., Pitassi, T., Reingold, O., & Zemel, R. (2011). Fairness through awareness. ArXiv:1104.3913 [Cs]. http://arxiv.org/abs/1104.3913

Eubanks, V. (2017). *Automating inequality: How high-tech tools profile, police, and punish the poor* (1st ed.). St. Martin's Press.

Feeley, M., & Simon, J. (1992). The new penology: Notes on the emerging strategy of corrections and its implications. *Criminology*, *30*(4), 449–474. https://doi.org/10.1111/j.1745-9125.1992.tb01112.x

Feeley, M., & Simon, J. (1994). Actuarial justice: The emerging new criminal law. In D. Nelken (Ed.), *The futures of criminology* (pp. 173–201). Sage.

Ferguson, A. G. (2017). *The rise of big data policing: Surveillance, race, and the future of law enforcement*. New York University Press.

Gajane, P., & Pechenizkiy, M. (2018). On formalizing fairness in prediction with machine learning. ArXiv:1710.03184 [Cs, Stat]. http://arxiv.org/abs/1710.03184

Garrett, B. L., & Monahan, J. (2019). Judging risk. *California Law Review, Forthcoming*. https://doi.org /10.2139/ssrn.3190403

Greene, D., Hoffmann, A. L., & Stark, L. (2019). Better, nicer, clearer, fairer: A critical assessment of the movement for ethical artificial intelligence and machine learning. *Proceedings of the 52nd Hawaii international conference on system sciences.*

Hamilton, M. (2019). The biased algorithm: Evidence of disparate impact on Hispanics. *American Criminal Law Review, 56*, 1553.

Hannah-Moffat, K. (2005). Criminogenic needs and the transformative risk subject: Hybridizations of risk/need in penality. *Punishment & Society, 7*(1), 29–51. https://doi.org/10.1177/1462474505048132

Hannah-Moffat, K. (2006). Pandora's box: Risk/need and gender-responsive corrections. *Criminology & Public Policy, 5*(1), 183–192. https://doi.org/10.1111/j.1745-9133.2006.00113.x

Hannah-Moffat, K. (2009). Gridlock or mutability: Reconsidering "gender" and risk assessment. *Criminology & Public Policy, 8*(1), 209–219. https://doi.org/10.1111/j.1745-9133.2009.00549.x

Hannah-Moffat, K. (2013). Actuarial sentencing: An "unsettled" proposition. *Justice Quarterly, 30*(2), 270–296. https://doi.org/10.1080/07418825.2012.682603

Hannah-Moffat, K. (2015). Needle in a haystack: Logical parameters of treatment based on actuarial risk-needs assessments. *Criminology & Public Policy, 14*(1), 113–120. https://doi.org/10.1111/1745 -9133.12121

Hannah-Moffat, K. (2016). A conceptual kaleidoscope: Contemplating 'dynamic structural risk' and an uncoupling of risk from need. *Psychology, Crime & Law, 22*(1–2), 33–46. https://doi.org/10.1080 /1068316X.2015.1114115

Hannah-Moffat, K. (2019). Algorithmic risk governance: Big data analytics, race and information activism in criminal justice debates. *Theoretical Criminology, 23*(4), 453–470. https://doi.org/10.1177 /1362480618763582

Hannah-Moffat, K., & Maurutto, P. (2010). Re-contextualizing pre-sentence reports: Risk and race. *Punishment & Society, 12*(3), 262–286. https://doi.org/10.1177/1462474510369442

Hannah-Moffat, K., Maurutto, P., & Turnbull, S. (2009). Negotiated risk: Actuarial illusions and discretion in probation. *Canadian Journal of Law and Society, 24*(3), 391–409. https://doi.org/10 .1017/S0829320100010097

Hannah-Moffat, K., & Struthers Montford, K. (2019). Unpacking sentencing algorithms risk, racial accountability and data harms. In J. W. de Keijser, J. V. Roberts, & J. Ryberg (Eds.), *Predictive sentencing: Normative and empirical perspectives* (pp. 175–196). Hart Publishing. https://doi.org/10 .5040/9781509921447

Hannah-Moffat, K., & Struthers Montford, K. (2021). The veneers of empiricism: Gender, race and prison classification. *Aggression and Violent Behavior, 59*, 101475. https://doi.org/10.1016/j.avb.2020 .101475

Harcourt, B. E. (2007). *Against prediction: Profiling, policing, and punishing in an actuarial age.* University of Chicago Press.

Harcourt, B. E. (2015). Risk as a proxy for race: The dangers of risk assessment. *Federal Sentencing Reporter, 27*(4), 237–243. https://doi.org/10.1525/fsr.2015.27.4.237

Horn, R., & Evans, M. (2000). The effect of gender on pre-sentence reports. *The Howard Journal of Criminal Justice, 39*(2), 184–197. https://doi.org/10.1111/1468-2311.00161

Hudson, B., & Bramhall, G. (2005). Assessing the 'other.' *The British Journal of Criminology, 45*(5), 721–740. https://doi.org/10.1093/bjc/azi002

Jefferson, B. J. (2020). *Digitize and punish: Racial criminalization in the digital age.* University of Minnesota Press.

Johndrow, J. E., & Lum, K. (2017). An algorithm for removing sensitive information: Application to race-independent recidivism prediction. ArXiv:1703.04957 [Stat]. http://arxiv.org/abs/1703.04957

Kitchin, R. (2014a). *The data revolution: Big data, open data, data infrastructures & their consequences.* SAGE Publications.

Kitchin, R. (2014b). Big Data, new epistemologies and paradigm shifts. *Big Data & Society, 1*(1), 205395171452848. https://doi.org/10.1177/2053951714528481

Kleinberg, J., Ludwig, J., Mullainathan, S., & Sunstein, C. R. (2018). Discrimination in the age of algorithms. *Journal of Legal Analysis, 10*, 113–174. https://doi.org/10.1093/jla/laz001

Kleinberg, J., Mullainathan, S., & Raghavan, M. (2017). Inherent trade-offs in the fair determination of risk scores. *Schloss Dagstuhl - Leibniz-Zentrum Fuer Informatik GmbH, Wadern/Saarbruecken, Germany*. https://doi.org/10.4230/lipics.itcs.2017.43

Kusner, M. J., Loftus, J. R., Russell, C., & Silva, R. (2017). Counterfactual fairness. ArXiv:1703.06856 [Cs, Stat]. http://arxiv.org/abs/1703.06856

Lupton, D. (2015). *Digital sociology*. Routledge, Taylor & Francis Group.

Mackenzie, A. (2017). *Machine learners: Archaeology of a data practice*. The MIT Press.

Madras, D., Pitassi, T., & Zemel, R. (2017). Predict responsibly: Improving fairness and accuracy by learning to defer. ArXiv:1711.06664 [Cs, Stat]. http://arxiv.org/abs/1711.06664

Malek, Md. A. (2022). Criminal courts' artificial intelligence: The way it reinforces bias and discrimination. *AI and Ethics*, 2(1), 233–245. https://doi.org/10.1007/s43681-022-00137-9

Maurutto, P., & Hannah-Moffat, K. (2006). Assembling risk and the restructuring of penal control. *The British Journal of Criminology*, 46(3), 438–454.

Mayer-Schönberger, V., & Cukier, K. (2014). *Big data: A revolution that will transform how we live, work, and think* (First Mariner Books edition). Mariner Books, Houghton Mifflin Harcourt.

Mayson, S. G. (2019). Bias in, bias out. *Yale Law Journal*, 128, 2218.

Mead, G., & Barbosa Neves, B. (2022). Contested delegation: Understanding critical public responses to algorithmic decision-making in the UK and Australia. *The Sociological Review*, 003802612211053. https://doi.org/10.1177/00380261221105380

Mehrabi, N., Morstatter, F., Saxena, N., Lerman, K., & Galstyan, A. (2019). A survey on bias and fairness in machine learning. ArXiv:1908.09635 [Cs]. http://arxiv.org/abs/1908.09635

Mehrabi, N., Morstatter, F., Saxena, N., Lerman, K., & Galstyan, A. (2021). A survey on bias and fairness in machine learning. *ACM Computing Surveys*, 54(6), 1–35. https://doi.org/10.1145/3457607

Motiuk, L. (1997a). Classification for correctional programming: The offender intake assessment (OIA) process. *Forum on Corrections Research*, 9, 18–22.

Motiuk, L. (1997b). The community risk/needs management scale: An effective supervision tool. *Forum on Corrections Research*, 9, 8–12.

Motiuk, L. (1998). Using dynamic factors to better predict post-release outcome. *Forum on Corrections Research*, 10(3), 12–15.

Noble, S. U. (2018). *Algorithms of oppression: How search engines reinforce racism*. New York University Press.

O'Malley, P. (2008). Experiments in risk and criminal justice. *Theoretical Criminology*, 12(4), 451–469. https://doi.org/10.1177/1362480608097152

O'Neil, C. (2016). *Weapons of math destruction: How big data increases inequality and threatens democracy*. Allen Lane, Penguin Books.

Pasquale, F. (2015). *The black box society: The secret algorithms that control money and information*. Harvard University Press.

Pessach, D., & Shmueli, E. (2023). A review on fairness in machine learning. *ACM Computing Surveys*, 55(3), 1–44. https://doi.org/10.1145/3494672

Pridemore, W. A. (2004). Review of the literature on risk and protective factors of offending among Native Americans. *Journal of Ethnicity in Criminal Justice*, 2(4), 45–63. https://doi.org/10.1300/J222v02n04_03

Richardson, R., Schultz, J. M., & Crawford, K. (2019). Dirty data, bad predictions: How civil rights violations impact police data, predictive policing systems, and justice. *NYU Law Review Online*, 94, 15.

Schuilenburg, M., & Peeters, R. (2020). Understanding the algorithmic society: Concluding thoughts. In M. Schuilenburg & R. Peeters (Eds.), *The algorithmic society: Technology, power, and knowledge*. Routledge.

Sejnowski, T. J. (2018). *The deep learning revolution*. The MIT Press.

Shaw, M., & Hannah-Moffat, K. (2000). Gender, diversity and risk assessment in Canadian corrections. *Probation Journal*, 47(3), 163–172. https://doi.org/10.1177/026455050004700301

Taxman, F. S., & Dezember, A. (2016). The value and importance of risk and need assessment (RNA) in corrections & sentencing. In F. S. Taxman (Ed.), *Handbook on risk and need assessment: Theory and practice*. Routledge, Taylor & Francis Group.

Tufekci, Z. (2014). Engineering the public: Big data, surveillance and computational politics. *First Monday*. https://doi.org/10.5210/fm.v19i7.4901

van Eijk, G. (2017). Socioeconomic marginality in sentencing: The built-in bias in risk assessment tools and the reproduction of social inequality. *Punishment & Society*, *19*(4), 463–481. https://doi.org/10.1177/1462474516666282

Verma, S., & Rubin, J. (2018). Fairness definitions explained. *Proceedings of the International Workshop on Software Fairness - FairWare '18*, 1–7. https://doi.org/10.1145/3194770.3194776

Ward, T., & Fortune, C.-A. (2016). The role of dynamic risk factors in the explanation of offending. *Aggression and Violent Behavior*, *29*, 79–88. https://doi.org/10.1016/j.avb.2016.06.007

Western, B., & Wildeman, C. (2009). The Black family and mass incarceration. *The ANNALS of the American Academy of Political and Social Science*, *621*(1), 221–242. https://doi.org/10.1177/0002716208324850

Završnik, A. (2018a). *Big data, crime and social control*. Routledge, Taylor & Francis Group.

Završnik, A. (2018b). Big data. What is it and why does it matter for crime and social control? In A. Završnik, *Big data, crime and social control* (pp. 3–28). Routledge, Taylor & Francis Group.

Završnik, A. (2019). Algorithmic justice: Algorithms and big data in criminal justice settings. *European Journal of Criminology*, 147737081987676. https://doi.org/10.1177/1477370819876762

Zemel, R., Wu, Y., Swersky, K., Pitassi, T., & Dwork, C. (2013). Learning fair representations. In S. Dasgupta & D. McAllester (Eds.), *Proceedings of the 30th International Conference on Machine Learning* (Vol. 28, pp. 325–333). PMLR.

49. Power asymmetries, epistemic imbalances and barriers to knowledge: the (im)possibility of knowing algorithms

Ana Pop Stefanija

ALGORITHMIC KNOWLEDGE AND (UN)KNOWING SUBJECTS

In 2019, I undertook research into the data that a number of digital technology companies hold about me. This journey showed me where (a fraction) of my data is scattered around the corners of the internet and the different databases of social media platforms, search engines, and data brokers (see Pop Stefanija & Pierson, 2020). It demonstrated how little we know about who holds data about us, why they hold that data, and what they do with it. Crucially, it showed that, while there are ways to obtain information, to *make the invisible visible*, there is almost no way of knowing how that data might and will affect us, or how to act agentially once information is obtained. We can describe this as having *obtained* knowledge, but not an *actionable* one – while it is a move from the meaningless "because the machine said so" (Andrejevic, 2020, p. 2), it is still an incomprehensible knowledge empty of understanding or of the possibility of understanding. Yes, we can open the black box, but as Winner (1993) says, we will find it undecipherable, as it offers "no judgment on what it all means" (p. 375). In such a socio-technical constellation, we, the individuals, have the position of *unknowing subjects*.

Being an *unknowing subject* of algorithmic decision-making (ADM) bears the potential for real-life harms and dangers: for our social relations, world views, life chances, and outcomes. From directing our communication circles and relations to impacting the jobs we're getting, the diagnosis and treatment we're given or not, to keeping our social benefits or children – the dangers of bias, discrimination, and filter bubbles are well documented. Various potentially life-impacting decisions are being made about us daily, often with no human oversight, responsibility, or accountability, and without us knowing that they've been made, or understanding how they are being made. A setting like this creates power imbalances where one party is in a dominant position of not just holding knowledge about someone else and acting upon it, but also holding control over that knowledge.

These power imbalances engender, and are engendered by, specific epistemic dynamics and asymmetries, further impacting individuals' access to knowledge and their ability to refuse, resist, and repair ADM outputs.

The Computational Paradigm Shift

The increasing adoption of algorithmic decision-making is the result of the advancement of computing technologies and the enhanced capabilities for data capturing, monitoring, and analysis. This brings a shift in ideology, epistemology, and ontology. Everything is turned into data, individuals' actions are tracked and unknowingly categorized, their past analysed into patterns, their behaviour predicted, and their future steered/affected. This process of datafication, understood as the "transformation of social action into online quantified data, thus allowing for real-time tracking and predictive analysis" (van Dijck, 2014, p. 198) with the aim to collect, monitor, analyse, understand, and use people's behaviour, brought a change in the dominant ideology. Van Dijck (2014) calls it *dataism* – the belief that all kinds of human behaviour and practices can be both tracked and objectively quantified. This goes hand in hand with the paradigm that data reflects not just reality per se, but it represents a superior model for representing it (Fisher, 2022, p. 22). As such, it generates the most accurate knowledge that can be used to make better decisions (Ricarte, 2019, p. 351).

These technological and ideological shifts lead to what can be called *algorithmic knowledge* understood in two ways: epistemic and critical. Epistemic, as knowledge about the world and individuals relies on ubiquitous datafication and is created based on data analysis according to algorithmic logic. This episteme, in turn, through its algorithmic outputs, affects individuals and impacts how they form critical knowledge about themselves – algorithmic outputs influence individuals' knowledge about their self but without the learning, reflectivity, and self-determination. Although we don't have access to that algorithmic knowledge, we encounter the outputs, and the effects of this knowledge in the form of personalization, recommendations, loan decisions, and future crime predictions. Striving to create positivist and behavioural knowledge (Fisher, 2022, p. 3), this algorithmic epistemology creates new regimes of knowledge and understanding of what constitutes *valid* knowledge.

In the remainder of this chapter, it will be discussed how these shifts in ideology (*dataism*) and epistemology impact individuals, their autonomy, and their agency. In doing so, it will bring forward the notions of power asymmetries resulting from the epistemic imbalances, and the barriers to knowledge reinforcing them. In a setting where we're increasingly living the world through the lenses of algorithmic ordering and worldview, reinforced by the dominant discursive and performative power of AI, the burden falls on individuals to "get to know" the algorithm and to deploy both strategies for *knowing* and for resistance. The last part of this chapter will focus on mechanisms and strategies for *flipping the epistemic script* and will discuss possibilities for transformation from *knowing* to *capable subjects* – introducing the notions of agency affordances.

POWER ASYMMETRIES

The shifts in ideology and the epistemic reign of algorithmic knowledge bring a shift in power relations too. The question is, how is AI shifting power (Kalluri, 2020) and where does it originate from? We can talk about the social *power of* algorithms (Beer, 2017) – a power which resides in the algorithm (Lash, 2007, p. 71), and that comes *through* the algorithms, through the outputs and effects of the algorithmic decision-making. Affecting our behaviour and life chances, we can say that algorithmic systems increasingly have/hold *power over* individuals.

How is algorithmic power coming into being? The ideology of dataism paves the way for the naissance of algorithmic ideology – believing that data speaks the truth and provides knowledge (Reigeluth, 2014, p. 253) by being able to datafy and quantify everything and to *read* it via technology, which means that the outputs must be objective and true. If every aspect of life can be *seen*, with a God-like omnipresence and perspective, then the data and the AI logic cannot lie. According to this ideology, data is revealing the real and the reality, because of its affordances to be combined, sorted, and resorted, so patterns can be recognized, and predictions can be made. Reigeluth (2014) characterizes this technological determinism as seeing data as incapable of lying and speaking the truth. This epistemic model is marked by a paradigmatic shift – the abandonment of causality and of hypothetico-deductive methods of reasoning, which are seen as rigid (ibid., p. 248), in favour of automated correlations.

With correlation taking primacy, we are getting probabilistic predictions (Andrejevic, 2014) that may tell us that something is happening but won't tell us why something is happening (Mayer-Schönberger & Cukier, 2014). This reading of the world, of behaviours and practices captured in/through data, as such, is devoid of "reflexivity, hermeneutical and critical capacities, and reason" (Fisher, 2020, p. 18). The experiential world is being compressed into a statistical model, framing social behaviours as statistical distributions (Joler & Pasquinelli, 2020). Taking over an epistemological, but also ontological and normative power, AI systems become at the same time new regimes of scientific proof and of truth, affecting both social normativity and rationality (ibid.).

The power *of* algorithms *over* individuals that comes *through* their effects and outputs mostly relies on the operation of classification – classification guides what will be served or denied to us, how we will be seen, what we can have or be refused access to, and similar. This power works at the level of category by "using computer code, statistics and surveillance to construct categories within populations" (Cheney-Lippold, 2011, p. 166). However, the variables used to create a category are not a result of an objective fact; these qualifications are done through "singling out one meaning" (Hildebrant, 2022, p. 8). They are based on choosing one (dominant and often simplistic) interpretation of the phenomenon over others, out of the many possible, and in that sense disregarding the complex, contextual and multi-layered nature of humans and interactions. It is exactly this classification that should be seen "as a central knowledge producing concept" (Bechmann & Bowker, 2019, p. 2) and the main ontology pushed by AI systems.

To illustrate a well-familiar concept, let's take the example of social media. Our online presence and interactions are governed by the automated processing of what is being called inferences – "information relating to an identified or identifiable natural person created through deduction or reasoning rather than mere observation or collection from the data subject" (Wachter & Mittelstadt, 2018, p. 14). The goal is to make predictions based on affinity profiling – an automated process of evaluating personal aspects about individuals – for the purpose of (primarily) serving targeted advertising. Affinity profiling relies not on personal traits, but on assumed interests, which are inferred based on computable proxies (Hildebrant, 2022) for what individuals might like, desire, or do, but without contextualizing or having insights into the subjective, dynamic reality or intentions of the ever-complex individual human beings.

However, this classification is problematic and brings potential harms in a few distinct ways. First, classification often relies on incomplete data, or is data-poor: many data collectors have access to too little data to produce inferences, so they use approximation to build a profile. This holds the potential of not just erroneous profiling, but also of possible harms because of incorrect predictions based on it. A (yet unpublished) research conducted by the author shows that when having access to the inferences made about them, individuals on average reported as incorrect 50.69% of the inferences. Second, as these data-poor, incorrect inferences are shared in a widely established data-sharing ecosystem (e.g., data brokers), they travel through the network, being further used for ADM (see Pop Stefanija & Pierson, 2020). Tracking the database containing the wrong inferences becomes impossible; the inability to grasp the dispersion of one's data across data holders limits the ability to exercise one's rights to information, comprehension, refusal, and correction. Third, often times these profiles are made based on stale inferences – inferences that once were true and valid, but are not anymore. What happens when decisions are made based on past behaviour that no longer applies? These past behaviours, actions, lifestyles, and identities do not capture and represent who the individual is at this particular moment in time but still have *power over* us and impact their right to the future.

What is the nature of this power? Algorithmic systems on their own don't possess agency in the meaning that we would assign to humans, but to quote Neff (Neff et al., 2012) they do have a technical agency in the sense "of not quite fully agentic, and also in the sense of in practice, technically, appearing, seeming, emerging with agency" (p. 304). But since we "begin to take de facto orders from materialized instructions that we don't fully understand technically, much less politically" (ibid.), they continue to bear the effects of their outputs, which algorithmic systems do exercise *power over*.

According to Foucault (1982), a power relationship, *power over* someone happens every time someone/something "acts upon [individuals'] [...] existing actions or [up]on those which may arise in the present or the future" (p. 789). In this sense, power is "the capacity to structure the field of action of the other, to intervene in the domain of the other's possible actions" (Lazzarato, 2002, p. 107). Power is about effectively governing individuals' actions by structuring and designating the ways in which the behaviour might be directed and thus steering the potential outcomes (Foucault, 1982).

From this epistemic and power position, that reduces individuals to de-subjectivized objects, algorithmic and ADM systems can be seen as part of *knowledge/epistemic apparatuses* through which the mechanisms of power are enacted, since "power cannot function unless knowledge, or rather knowledge apparatuses, are formed, organized, and put into circulation" (Beer, 2017, p. 10). How does this algorithmic knowledge become authoritative?

Algorithmic Authority

The *power through* algorithms comes as a result of the *algorithmic authority* granted to these systems, enforced by discursive and performative framing of the notion of algorithms. To define algorithmic authority, I am borrowing the definition by Lustig and Nardi (2015) of authority as power that is perceived as legitimate. This is trust in algorithms that will verify information and direct human action by circumventing or refusing to trust in human authority (see also Joler & Pasquinell, 2020). The discursive framing of algorithms as objective, effective, precise, non-erroneous, truthful, trustworthy, and so on is part of wider perception regarding their authority and as such helps normalize their (perceived) power, feeding back and structuring societal beliefs, norms, policies, and behaviour, and being used to solve societal issues and provide services. This authority is also performative and normative since algorithms cause "human actors to respond accordingly" (Lustig & Nardi, 2015, p. 743). At the same time, it is also imperative since it demands trust in the output because there is already trust in the algorithm ("Trust this because you trust me" – Shirky, 2009, p. 12), although these algorithmic outputs might be results of unsupervised, unmanaged processes, without human oversight or involvement, often relying on unknown and untrustworthy sources for its decision-making.

EPISTEMIC IMBALANCES AND BARRIERS TO KNOWLEDGE

One outcome of the algorithmic knowledge becoming authoritative, in the sense that it is trusted as truthful and objective without challenging it, is that it also becomes an *epistemic authority*, being valued more than the knowledge from other sources. This authority means that its dominance has been established in relation/comparison with other ways of knowing, thus imposing and accepting it as valid and valuable. Everything that is experiential, contextual, qualitative, lived, and human is considered flawed, partial, subjective, biased, non-validatable, and not valid (enough) (see Birhane, 2021). By deciding on what counts as knowledge and how that knowledge should be, the algorithmic epistemic authority claims an *epistemic dominance* too.

This dominance has been perpetuated additionally by the fact that algorithmic knowledge and logic are not available for the non-experts, the common citizen. The reason for that lies partially in the nature of algorithmic and ADM systems – we are dealing with opacities of different kinds, and the barriers to known algorithms, both as researchers and as individuals, are many. First, we are dealing with proprietary software – the workings of the algorithms, even if understandable, are closed to the public eye, hidden behind patents and trade secrets. Even when open – *reading* an algorithm becomes, if not impossible, then a hard task: first, the ability to read code and understand the algorithm stays out of reach for the regular layperson; even if the reader is an expert, often is not just one algorithm, but many working at the same time. Adding the fact that many AI systems rely on machine learning makes the equation even more difficult to grasp. However, referring to the discursive (and performative) power of algorithms mentioned earlier, this mythic aura surrounding the impenetrability of the algorithmic *episteme* is often a deliberate strategy to enforce the *epistemic orders* in place. Many obfuscation strategies are intentional – think of restricted API access to independently scrutinize algorithmic systems, or of transparency and subject access request (SAR) tools that make these systems impossible to fully grasp.

The result of these epistemic orders and gatekeeping practices is *epistemic imbalances* – a situation when some entity holds information, knows, or understands something about an individual that the individual does not. This puts them in a subordinate knowledge position, making them susceptible to exploitation of any kind and powerless to prevent or refuse something (Delacroix & Veale, 2020). Ben-David (2020) calls this "epistemic hegemony," characterized by access to information and knowledge that is captured, guarded, and limited.

In the instances when ways around are being found to investigate "algorithms in action" (Pop Stefanija & Pierson, 2020), the strategies to limit access to epistemic insights is often deliberate, and the barriers to knowledge and understanding remain in place. Similarly, when algorithmic systems are "made to be knowable" (e.g., through transparency efforts, and tools) – meaning when structured regimes of visibility and knowing are afforded – they are still controlled flows of information and of knowledge formation, for both individuals and researchers. In that sense, this new form of hegemonic power (Velkova & Kaun, 2021) that makes invisible the structuring power of algorithms places the burden to access knowledge and claim epistemic authority disproportionately on individuals.

Based on previous research on digital platforms in regard to the possibility of accessing information and forming meaningful knowledge as individuals (Pop Stefanija & Pierson, 2020; Pop Stefanija & Pierson, 2023), the next section will briefly outline some gatekeeping practices and their characteristics.

Gatekeeping Practices

We can define the gatekeeping practices and strategies of digital platforms in four main groups. They can be employed and embedded to various degrees, not excluding one another.

The first one could be referred to as *institutional gatekeeping* – the various policies and practices of the digital platforms that define what would be *made knowable*. It can take the form of (1) *withholding information* – an organizational decision to not provide certain information, even when required by law/regulation (such as information on whether automated decision-making including profiling is taking place or information about the sharing of an individual's data); (2) *circumventing information* – the strategies built to circumvent or stretch their reading of the regulation (such as providing links to policies instead of giving an unambiguous answer); and (3) *completely disregarding regulation* – sometimes platforms completely refuse to provide what is required by law/regulation (such as not replying to a SAR).

Another strategy is *access gatekeeping* – intentional strategies to hide entry points to information. These result from organizational policies and (design) practices deciding what should be *made visible* or transparent. It usually takes the form of *deliberately hiding/burring these entry points* – for example, where a SAR should be sent, or hiding the available transparency tools and control settings behind tabs, buttons, and clicks. This makes the whole process labour-intensive and burdensome, discouraging individuals from further inquiries.

The third strategy could be defined as *understandability gatekeeping* – this is the practice of not translating and structuring machine outputs to human-understandable language or to a non-specialized format. As such, it limits the possibility of understanding the information obtained and requires special capabilities and skills. It can take the form of: (1) *choosing an uncommon format file* – for example, sending it as a JSON file that many individuals don't know how to open or read; (2) *choosing professionalized jargon*, such as using legalese that is not understandable to the common user; and (3) *incomprehensible information structuring* – often information is presented in numbers and coded language (e.g., column titled *pUnit*, with data presented as "/p/mc/5bfdc550-92b37-99030-1faa0") without explaining what it means.

The last one is *epistemic gatekeeping* – it can be defined as strategies and practices of providing information but not knowledge or the ability for understanding or providing quasi-knowledge. It can take the form of: (1) *strategy of overwhelming with information* – troves of data (usually in gigabytes) are being provided, but that data loses its meaning because the ability to process it and understand it is limited or too technical; and (2) *providing transparency but no explainability* – information is provided, but explanation/knowledge is withheld, thus effectively restricting sense- and knowledge-making.

These *information and epistemic regimes* in the form of corrupted, curated, and captured information flows, with their practices and arrangements of knowledge ordering, set up obligatory passage points and rules for information flows, thus holding power over sense and knowledge making. This gatekeeping impacts what can be defined as the *epistemic agency* of individuals – the ability and capacity to acquire and assess knowledge claims. This agency is important because it enables one to establish an epistemic authority, which we can see as also the autonomy to make, in turn, knowledge claims. Agency and autonomy are important because they are a way to rectify power asymmetries and relations – knowing is the first step towards the ability to act.

MECHANISMS FOR RESISTANCE OR FROM *KNOWING* TO *CAPABLE* SUBJECTS

The opportunities to receive information and the ability to understand and gain knowledge are essential. It is important to know what algorithms know, and why *the algorithm said so*. However, there is a greater importance to this knowing. Knowing is just a means to an end – the ability to act upon that knowledge. Acting upon means the ability to refuse, reject, resist, or repair the algorithmic working and output. This ability is not possible without seeing, understanding, and knowing how the algorithmic systems are exercising *power over* us and what the consequences are. Strategies are needed to object to this algorithmic knowledge and power. They will enable to flip the epistemic script and to know algorithms. From there, they make possible the strategies for refusal, resistance, and repair. To make them actionable, those strategies will assume interventions within the technical, beyond the technical, and in joint working between the technical and societal.

In short, we need mechanisms to transform individuals from *knowing* to *capable* subjects. How do we arrive there? How do we go from subjects that have access to knowledge and understanding, to subjects who have the ability and the conditions to act upon it? This is an important question to ask because it's crucial for individuals' autonomy and agency, and the ability to refuse/resist algorithmic systems.

We understand autonomy and agency as related. Autonomy is the ability to make informed choices, based on self-reflection and self-determination, without inferences from external parties. Agency is the ability to act, in a self-directed manner, without extraordinary resources and relying on critical knowledge (Savolainen & Ruckenstein, 2022; Foucault, 1982). In the current socio-technical constellation between individuals, AI systems, and societal actors, exerting power over the self and one's own will, if not impossible, is extremely difficult. Both to act autonomously and agentially, and the very acts of refusal and resistance, require time, resources, and great efforts. They are labour-intensive and demanding. Being able to "say no" and act upon it requires expertise and/or privilege to navigate the agential/refusal process. It demands/necessitates particular competencies, capabilities, and skills.

These possibilities and the ability to direct one's own future are crucial. They are empowering and transformative, they become a generative and strategic act – the ability to say no and perform based on it allows for an individual to become a *subject*. Subject understood as an active principle, the epistemic subject being capable of carrying out acts and regaining subjectivity, instead of that which is subjected *to* something, that receives the determinations of something else, and as such is bearing/is the bearer of actions imposed upon it (see Greimas & Courtés, 1982, Foucault, 1982 and Fisher, 2022).

Agency Affordances

How do we *enable* capable subjects? Within the technical, the embedding of agency, and actionable refusal/resistance would mean programming functions and introducing features at the level of the artefact that would enable both knowledge and the ability to act. These could vary from transparency features that provide information to explainability functions that provide knowledge and understanding. Coupled with specific features, buttons, and tools, they could give individuals control to steer, reject, or repair automated decision-making processes and outputs. We call these agency affordances, understood as functions programmed and embedded at an infrastructure level that should allow and encourage the actualization of agency, autonomy, and refusal. These functions become "ready to use," or actionable, through features and elements made visible and promoted at an interface level, thus coupling the possibilities for action with the ability to act.

These abilities to act need to be both made knowable and executable. Some of these features could be toggle on-off switches, consent forms per type of algorithmic action, and settings options to change one's mind and indicate preferences, coupled with educational videos or other types of materials. All of this should follow the principle of making technology seamful, where building algorithm-aware designs (Eslami et al., 2017) will introduce friction or "laborious decisions that consciously interrupt behaviour" (Lorusso, 2021, np) and will provide knowledge about the actual consequences of the artefact's workings (Schraefel et al., 2020) and the immediate actions the individuals might undertake. These interventions should be executed at a technical level.

But going beyond the technical, interventions are needed within the social and/or at the intersection of the workings of technical and societal actors. That would mean that making the subject capable and agency/refusal actionable would necessitate the engagement of a few societal actors. Private and public entities and institutions should enable and encourage the development of skills, knowledge, and literacy. Regulatory bodies and institutions should set the institutional norms for embedding agency affordances. Individuals should be willing to, and equipped with skills, to actualize the agency affordances. This can take the form of building capacities and competences of individuals through literacy tools – in the form of tutorials, guidelines, educational videos, and explainability tools provided by the algorithmic system; and in the form of literacy initiatives – formal and informal institutions should contribute to and undertake initiatives, both focusing on data and algorithmic literacy and the significance of agency when interacting with algorithmic systems. Gaining cultural and institutional legitimacy (Davis, 2020) of embedding affordances can be mandated through regulation. All this together, in the words of Savolainen and Ruckenstein (2022), should couple algorithmic competence with situational mastery.

While we only briefly introduced the concept here, at a highly abstract and theoretical level, it must be acknowledged that agency/refusal affordances are non-determining, relational, dynamic, context-dependent, situated, and come in gradations and variability (for more see Davis, 2020). The translation into practice of this theoretical concept is, however, out of the scope of this chapter.

Finally, we must not forget that not everything can or should be solved with technology. Societal issues deeply rooted in systemic power asymmetries would require systemic, not technical solutions. The first question, before we let AI decide, is: *should we ask an AI at all?*

The computer might say *so*, but we need to be able to ask *why?* To be able to question its authority and outputs and, at the same time, to be able to say *no* – to refuse or override its decision.

REFERENCES

Andrejevic, M. (2014). Big data, big questions: The big data divide. *International Journal of Communication*, 8(0), 17.
Andrejevic, M. (2020). Shareable and un-sharable knowledge. *Big Data & Society*, 7(1), https://doi.org /10.1177/2053951720933917

Bechmann, A., & Bowker, G. C. (2019). Unsupervised by any other name: Hidden layers of knowledge production in artificial intelligence on social media. *Big Data & Society, 6*(1), 2053951718819569. https://doi.org/10.1177/2053951718819569

Beer, D. (2009). Power through the algorithm? Participatory web cultures and the technological unconscious. *New Media & Society, 11*(6), 985–1002. https://doi.org/10.1177/1461444809336551

Beer, D. (2017). The social power of algorithms. *Information, Communication & Society, 20*(1), 1–13. https://doi.org/10.1080/1369118X.2016.1216147

Ben-David, A. (2020). Counter-archiving Facebook. *European Journal of Communication, 35*(3), 249–264. https://doi.org/10.1177/0267323120922069

Benjamin, R. (2016). Informed refusal: Toward a justice-based bioethics. *Science, Technology, & Human Values, 41*(6), 967–990. https://doi.org/10.1177/0162243916656059

Birhane, A. (2021). Algorithmic injustice: A relational ethics approach. *Patterns, 2*(2), 100205. https://doi.org/10.1016/j.patter.2021.100205

Bonde Thylstrup, N., Flyverbom, M., & Helles, R. (2019). Datafied knowledge production: Introduction to the special theme. *Big Data & Society, 6*(2), 2053951719875985. https://doi.org/10.1177/2053951719875985

Bridel, A. (2021). Fixing subjects, fixing outcomes: Civic epistemologies and epistemic agency in participatory governance of climate risk. *Science, Technology, & Human Values*, 01622439211066136. https://doi.org/10.1177/01622439211066136

Bucher, T. (2012). Want to be on the top? Algorithmic power and the threat of invisibility on Facebook. *New Media & Society, 14*(7), 1164–1180. https://doi.org/10.1177/1461444812440159

Bucher, T. (2018). *If...Then: Algorithmic Power and Politics*. Oxford University Press. https://doi.org/10.1093/oso/9780190493028.001.0001

Burrell, J. (2016). How the machine 'thinks': Understanding opacity in machine learning algorithms. *Big Data & Society, 3*(1), 2053951715622512. https://doi.org/10.1177/2053951715622512

Cheney-Lippold, J. (2011). A new algorithmic identity: Soft biopolitics and the modulation of control. *Theory, Culture & Society, 28*(6), 164–181. https://doi.org/10.1177/0263276411424420

Davis, J. L. (2020). *How Artifacts Afford: The Power and Politics of Everyday Things*. MIT Press.

Delacroix, S., & Veale, M. (2020). Smart technologies and our sense of self: Going beyond epistemic counter-profiling. *Life and the Law in the Era of Data-Driven Agency*. https://www.elgaronline.com/view/edcoll/9781788971997/9781788971997.00011.xml

Eslami, M. (2017). Understanding and designing around users' interaction with hidden algorithms in sociotechnical systems. In *Companion of the 2017 ACM Conference on Computer Supported Cooperative Work and Social Computing*, New York, NY, USA, 25 February 2017, pp. 57–60. Association for Computing Machinery. https://doi.org/10.1145/3022198.3024947

Ettlinger, N. (2018). Algorithmic affordances for productive resistance. *Big Data & Society, 5*(1), 2053951718771399. https://doi.org/10.1177/2053951718771399

Fisher, E. (2022). *Algorithms and Subjectivity | The Subversion of Critical Knowledge | E*. Routledge Focus. https://www.taylorfrancis.com/books/edit/10.4324/9781003196563/algorithms-subjectivity-eran-fisher

Fisher, E. (2020). The ledger and the diary: Algorithmic knowledge and subjectivity. *Continuum, 34*(3), 378–397. https://doi.org/10.1080/10304312.2020.1717445

Flyverbom, M., & Murray, J. (2018). Datastructuring—Organizing and curating digital traces into action. *Big Data & Society, 5*(2), 2053951718799114. https://doi.org/10.1177/2053951718799114

Foucault, M. (1982). The subject and power. *Critical Inquiry, 8*(4), 777–795.

Greimas, A. J., & Courtés, J. (1982). *Semiotics and Language: An Analytical Dictionary*. Indiana University Press. http://archive.org/details/semioticslanguag0000grei

Hildebrandt, M. (2022). The issue of proxies and choice architectures. Why EU law matters for recommender system. *Frontiers in Artificial Intelligence, 5*, 1–17.

Joler, V., & Pasquinelli, M. (2020). *The Nooscope Manifested: AI as Instrument of Knowledge Extractivism*. The Nooscope Manifested: AI as Instrument of Knowledge Extractivism. http://nooscope.ai/

Kalluri, P. (2020). Don't ask if artificial intelligence is good or fair, ask how it shifts power. *Nature, 583*(7815), 169–169. https://doi.org/10.1038/d41586-020-02003-2

Kitchin, R. (2014). Big Data, new epistemologies and paradigm shifts. *Big Data & Society, 1*(1), 2053951714528481. https://doi.org/10.1177/2053951714528481

Lash, S. (2007). Power after hegemony: Cultural studies in mutation? *Theory, Culture & Society, 24*(3), 55–78. https://doi.org/10.1177/0263276407075956

Lazzarato, M. (2002). From biopower to biopolitics. *Pli: The Warwick Journal of Philosophy, 13*, 100–112.

Lorusso, S. (2021, December 2). *The User Condition: Computer Agency and Behaviour.* https://theusercondition.computer/

Lustig, C., & Nardi, B. (2015). Algorithmic authority: The case of Bitcoin. *2015 48th Hawaii International Conference on System Sciences*, 743–752. https://doi.org/10.1109/HICSS.2015.95

Lustig, C., Pine, K., Nardi, B., Irani, L., Lee, M. K., Nafus, D., & Sandvig, C. (2016). Algorithmic authority: The ethics, politics, and economics of algorithms that interpret, decide, and manage. *Proceedings of the 2016 CHI Conference Extended Abstracts on Human Factors in Computing Systems*, 1057–1062. https://doi.org/10.1145/2851581.2886426

Mayer-Schönberger, V., & Cukier, K. (2014). *Big Data: A Revolution That Will Transform How We Live, Work, and Think* (Reprint edition). Eamon Dolan/Mariner Books.

Neff, G., Jordan, T., McVeigh-Schultz, J., & Gillespie, T. (2012). Affordances, technical agency, and the politics of technologies of cultural production. *Journal of Broadcasting & Electronic Media, 56*(2), 299–313. https://doi.org/10.1080/08838151.2012.678520

Neyland, D., & Möllers, N. (2017). Algorithmic IF … THEN rules and the conditions and consequences of power. *Information, Communication & Society, 20*(1), 45–62. https://doi.org/10.1080/1369118X.2016.1156141

Poems: Charlotte Geater. (2018, July 27). *Queen Mob's Tea House.* https://queenmobs.com/2018/07/poems-charlotte-geater/

Pop Stefanija, A., & Pierson, J. (2020). Practical AI transparency: Revealing datafication and algorithmic identities. *Journal of Digital Social Research, 2*(3), 84–125. https://doi.org/10.33621/jdsr.v2i3.32

Pop Stefanija, A., & Pierson, J. (2023). I am dissolving into categories and labels—agency affordances for embedding and practicing digital sovereignty. In B. Herlo & D. Irrgang (Eds.), *Proceedings of the Weizenbaum Conference 2022: Practicing Sovereignty—Interventions for Open Digital Futures* (pp. 39–52). Weizenbaum Institute for the Networked Society - The German Internet Institute. https://doi.org/10.34669/wi.cp/4.4

Reigeluth, T. B. (2014). Why data is not enough: Digital traces as control of self and self-control. *Surveillance & Society, 12*(2), 243–254. https://doi.org/10.24908/ss.v12i2.4741

Ricaurte, P. (2019). Data epistemologies, the coloniality of power, and resistance. *Television & New Media, 20*(4), 350–365. https://doi.org/10.1177/1527476419831640

Savolainen, L., & Ruckenstein, M. (2022). Dimensions of autonomy in human–algorithm relations. *New Media & Society*, 14614448221100802. https://doi.org/10.1177/14614448221100802

Schraefel, M. C., Gomer, R., Gerding, E., & Maple, C. (2020). Rethinking transparency for the Internet of Things. In *Life and the Law in the Era of Data-Driven Agency* (pp. 100–116). Edward Elgar Publishing. https://www.elgaronline.com/view/edcoll/9781788971997/9781788971997.00012.xml

Shirky, C. (2009, November 18). *A Speculative Post on the Idea of Algorithmic Authority.* https://web.archive.org/web/20091118030114/http://shirky.com/weblog/2009/11/a-speculative-post-on-the-idea-of-algorithmic-authority/

van Dijck, J. (2014). Datafication, dataism and dataveillance: Big Data between scientific paradigm and ideology. *Surveillance & Society, 12*(2), 197–208. https://doi.org/10.24908/ss.v12i2.4776

Velkova, J., & Kaun, A. (2021). Algorithmic resistance: Media practices and the politics of repair. *Information, Communication & Society, 24*(4), 523–540. https://doi.org/10.1080/1369118X.2019.1657162

Wachter, S., & Mittelstadt, B. (2018). *A Right to Reasonable Inferences: Re-Thinking Data Protection Law in the Age of Big Data and AI* [SSRN Scholarly Paper]. Social Science Research Network. https://papers.ssrn.com/abstract=3248829

Winner, L. (1993). Upon opening the Black Box and finding it empty: Social constructivism and the philosophy of technology. *Science, Technology, & Human Values, 18*(3), 362–378. https://doi.org/10.1177/016224399301800306

Zong, J. (2020). From individual consent to collective refusal: Changing attitudes toward (mis)use of personal data. *XRDS: Crossroads, The ACM Magazine for Students, 27*(2), 26–29. https://doi.org/10.1145/3433140

50. Gender, race, and the invisible labor of artificial intelligence

Laila M. Brown

INTRODUCTION

Many futurist critics of artificial intelligence (AI) worry about the existential threat potential of an especially powerful AI system. Beyond the robot apocalypse trope prevalent in literature and film, some scholars and tech industry leaders are troubled by the theoretical development of an artificial general intelligence (AGI) – an entity that would hypothetically be able to learn and carry out any intellectual task that a human can, and that, "if not designed and implemented with sufficient understanding, would…pose an existential threat to the future of humanity" (LessWrong, n.d.). In contrast, others are less concerned about existential threats to humanity than about how the concept of "humanity" is afforded differentially along lines of gender and race, and the ways in which specific AI technologies encourage this unequal application. While it is worthwhile to critically consider the dystopian imaginaries AGI could potentially affect, it is also crucial to recognize that harm done by AI is not merely a speculative concern, it is rather a present reality for many, including those who carry out various forms of invisible labor, and now find AI-equipped virtual assistants capable of replicating their work.

The crux of the issue, though, is not that new technologies enable the outsourcing to machines of some work that is widely – whether correctly or not – considered easy, repetitive, unskilled, or boring. It is rather the thinking undergirding the development of these technologies that asserts the possibility of a post-work world while neglecting – and in fact reinforcing – the ways in which social identities are inscribed upon forms of labor, and the ways in which societal views of gender, race, and labor entwine to reproduce inequality.

This piece explores the entangled relationships between virtual assistants, the invisible labor they are designed to perform, and gendered and racialized hierarchies of value. It first briefly provides background on the ways in which virtual assistants are anthropomorphized –specifically in terms of gender and race – and on the problematics of invisible labor. It then weaves together a discussion of these elements in order to call attention to how social and algorithmic biases reflect and reinforce a devaluation of invisible labor and those who perform it, namely along gendered and racialized lines. The design of virtual assistants – created to fulfill assistive, secretarial, companion, and care roles – illuminates social and cultural assumptions about who is responsible and desirable for carrying out invisible labor.

DEFINING VIRTUAL ASSISTANTS

A report by the United Nations Educational, Scientific and Cultural Organization (UNESCO) (2019) defines virtual assistants (also often called digital assistants) as internet-connected technologies that support user needs. They are unique from other interactive technologies in that they produce unscripted output determined by machine learning, and they can support a wide range of user queries and interactions (UNESCO, 2019). UNESCO categorizes virtual assistants into three groups: voice assistants, chatbots, and virtual agents. All are designed to emulate and sustain human-like interactions with their users.

Virtual assistants perform a range of assistive/secretarial tasks, such as sending texts, playing music, creating to-do lists, providing directions, and answering simple information requests on demand. Many additionally carry out companion/care tasks that, if performed by humans, could be considered to involve emotional and affective labor, such as telling jokes, providing personalized cognitive therapy and healthcare education, and even serving as platonic and/or romantic conversation partners.

Virtual assistants are inanimate products, yet their design typically exhibits a high degree of anthropomorphism, which is the application of human attributes (like form and personality) to non-human things. One of the most striking anthropomorphic qualities of virtual assistants is gender: the vast majority are designed to present as women (UNESCO, 2019). In contrast, in the Western context, overt signals of race and ethnicity are virtually absent in interface design (Piper, 2016; Bilal & Barfield, 2021).

DEFINING INVISIBLE LABOR

"Invisible labor" encompasses both waged and unwaged labor that is marginalized and undervalued. It is called invisible labor because, like any form of labor, it requires time and effort to carry out, yet it is generally unrecognized and unrewarded, monetarily and/or socially. Traditionally, the term has been used to describe the unwaged "reproductive labor" of cleaning, cooking, and caring for others that typically occurs within domestic spheres, for which the responsibility has historically fallen to women (Duffy, 2013). Think, for example, of mothers, to whom the duties of caring for children and aging adults are largely relegated. Or consider cisgender women in heterosexual relationships, who might find themselves responsible for remembering and acknowledging the birthdays of not only *their* family and friends *but also* those of her partner.

More recently, invisible labor has infiltrated the waged workplace as well. Poster et al. (2016) define invisible labor as activities that "workers perform in response to requirements (either implicit or explicit) from employers…yet are often overlooked, ignored, and/or devalued by employers, consumers, workers, and ultimately the legal system itself." Expectations that employees will perform invisible labor are high – regardless of employee gender expression – in assistive, secretarial, companion, and care roles. These roles can all involve significant amounts of emotional and affective labor: managing one's own and others' emotional experiences, respectively.

However, research demonstrates that even outside of waged labor roles more obviously associated with invisible labor, women shoulder more of this labor than men do. Women are both asked to volunteer and accept requests to volunteer for tasks with low promotability (tasks that benefit the organization but are unlikely to translate into positive performance reviews or career advancement for the employee), such as writing reports or chairing committees, significantly more often than their male counterparts (Babcock et al., 2017). Other examples of invisible labor generally expected more of women than of men in the waged workplace might include providing emotional support to colleagues and clients, onboarding and mentoring other employees, and coordinating parties and office events. These expectations are unbounded by profession and can occur in academia, industry, non-profit, and other professional realms.

Though considered an essential part of many jobs, invisible labor is generally belittled as not requiring skill and not qualifying as "real work," despite its real demands upon individuals' time and energy. Often, these invisible labor roles require individuals to exercise enormous control over their affect, and, in many situations, present as unflaggingly helpful and agreeable, which can significantly drain one's mental capacity.

Many virtual assistants are designed to carry out tasks in both assistive/secretarial and care/companion categories. Virtual assistants are positioned as products capable of "unburdening" their human users from the invisible labor involved in these roles.

ENCODED (AND DE-ENCODED) SOCIAL HIERARCHIES OF LABOR

Costa and Ribas (2019) urge critical consideration of how – due to increased socioemotional interactions with AI products, to which users have collectively affixed anthropomorphic stereotypes – AI is "reflecting our social and cultural views back to us" (p. 171). By establishing a presence in the realm of devalued labor, but glossing over issues of social inequality, mainstream virtual assistant technologies do indeed reflect problematic social and cultural views back to us. This section will introduce some of the many ways in which encoded (or de-encoded) gender and race among virtual assistants illuminate societal assumptions about the differential value of humans along the lines of gender and race.

ENCODED FEMININITY AND ITS IMPLICATIONS

The Gendering of Virtual Assistants

Gendered attributes are overwhelmingly present among virtual assistants: most have stereotypically feminine names, pronouns, visual representations, speech patterns, and even "personalities." As an example, VentureBeat estimated that 30,000 chatbots were introduced in the year 2016 alone, and the vast majority of them were designed to present as feminine (UNESCO, 2019). Further, the four leading commercial voice assistants by market share – Apple's Siri, Microsoft's Cortana, Google Assistant, and Amazon's Alexa (YouGov, 2020) – are female-voiced by default in all or nearly all language options; have feminine names (excepting Google Assistant); and are sometimes referred to by their developers with she/her pronouns (UNESCO, 2019).

It is not just the names and pronouns assigned to virtual assistants that signal femininity, though. Virtual assistants are often encoded with disconcerting gender biases, including tolerance and even encouragement of verbal abuse and sexual harassment from users (UNESCO, 2019). Their machine learning algorithms are also often trained using massive amounts of unfiltered and unvetted content on the open web, meaning that virtual assistants "learn" (and subsequently exhibit) the negative cultural stereotypes, like sexism and racism, garnered from this content (UNESCO, 2019). The title of the 2019 UNESCO report on virtual assistants, "I'd

Blush If I Could," is tellingly inspired by how Apple's voice assistant Siri would respond when a user told "her," "you're a bitch."

By reflecting and reinforcing stereotypical views of femininity born of patriarchal ideology, the mainstream product design of virtual assistants stands in opposition to an increasing acknowledgment of and support for fluidity in gender roles and expressions. The feminization of virtual assistants further endorses the social and cultural view that women ought to be responsible for performing invisible labor, and ought to embody a passive, submissive femininity while doing so. Put simply, the feminization of virtual assistants presents a barrier to achieving and sustaining gender equality because it reinforces patterns of inequality observed within the sphere of labor.

The Gendered Hierarchy of Labor

Discussion of gendered hierarchies of labor must begin with an acknowledgment of the constrained view of gender within the patriarchal heteronormative framework still dominant throughout much of the world. This framework endorses a binary view of gender, which classifies gender into just two distinct categories – masculine and feminine – and discounts that gender is a personal and social identity not dependent upon the sex one was assigned at birth. The development of gendered AI has thus far reified a gender binary. While most virtual assistants are feminized (UNESCO, 2019), some do include a male-voiced setting. Few, however, set the male voice as the default, and even fewer offer voice options that are not obviously intended to be either female or male. By largely enabling only female and male voice choices, virtual assistant technologies contribute to a cisnormative and binarist frame of gender that falsely posits that only two options exist: woman/female and man/male (Costa, 2018; Brown, 2022). In doing so, they further reinforce a conceptual division of labor into higher value manly/husbandly work and lower value womanly/wifely work (Costa, 2018). The feminization of virtual assistants reflects the reality that women are disproportionately responsible for carrying out invisible labor, both within waged (Babcock et al., 2017) and unwaged (Ciciolla & Luthar, 2019) spheres of labor. But rather than problematizing this status quo, it sends the message that women *are* and *should* be responsible for invisible labor.

Hester (2017) argues that the work of digital assistants has historically been heavily coded as women's work and that the tasks and personalities of digital assistants are programmed to emphasize feminine roles, further entrenching pervasive stereotypes about women's "natural" inclination to perform clerical, service, and care work. In the discussion of the stiltedly stereotyped qualities of women service providers (including caring, empathy, and altruism), Hester writes, "when technologies 'do gender' it is obviously not natural, but is instead visible as the product of deliberate choices about how best to relate, assist, or persuade the imagined technology user" (p. 50).

Various studies have demonstrated a user preference for virtual assistants gendered as women, and indeed, companies like Amazon and Apple have cited these findings in their justification of feminizing practices (Stern, 2017). This rationale, though, fails to examine the gender bias underlying this preference; namely, that male voices are associated with authority, and women's with helpfulness (UNESCO, 2019), and rather than being bossed around by our AI, we "want to be the bosses of it" (Hempel, 2015).

The technologists creating such virtual assistants are subscribing to both a gender binary and patriarchal cis- and heteronormativity through flattening a presumptive universal "female personality" and attempting to increase its appeal for users by augmenting presumably pleasing and nonthreatening "female qualities."

Devalued Demeanors

Unlike most humans, virtual assistants embody the ideal of customer service in a commercial landscape where the customer is always right. They are "always on" in both the sense that they are constantly available and that they do not become exasperated, talk back, or end the encounter when users are rude, difficult, or abusive. Through this programmed behavior, they perpetuate the notion that it is the responsibility of those who perform service labor to tolerate any kind of behavior in those they are serving and regulate affect to whatever degree necessary to provide the user with an agreeable experience. They also teach users that this is the kind of customer experience they are owed.

One specific piece of evidence pointing to these encoded ideas is virtual assistant speech patterns, which nod to the power differential between the submissive feminized tool and the dominant user. Hannon (2016) uses a brief encounter with Alexa to underpin how feminized virtual assistants, by design, signal their low status in relation to their user, thus satisfying both stereotypical gender and low-status laborer expectations:

> "I didn't understand the question that I heard." This is the somewhat awkward response I get when Alexa, the AI personality of the Amazon Echo, doesn't understand me. She could say, "I didn't understand your question," but as my assistant, she has been programmed to signal her lower status in our relationship, to take the blame for the miscommunication. Oh, and her voice and name signify "female," so she needs to use I-pronouns at a higher rate than I do as well. (p. 34)

These humility-signaling tropes, Hannon asserts, "implicitly connect female AI personalities with low-status positioning in the human–machine relationship." Any and all mistakes are the fault of the machine, never of the user, no matter how unclear, imprecise, or unreasonable they may be. Beyond vocabulary and syntax, flaws in programming mean virtual assistants sometimes mistake and misdirect user commands and questions, meaning that these tools serve as the (female) "face and voice of servility and dumb mistakes" (UNESCO, 2019, p. 112).

Some companies have responded to criticism regarding the feminization of their virtual assistants by adding male-voice options. However, in the case of Apple's virtual assistant Siri, differences between the female- and male-voiced options introduce new issues, rather than rectify existing ones. While female-voiced Siri uses imprecise qualifiers (such as "some" or "a few") in place of definite quantities, male-voiced Siri provides concrete figures (UNESCO, 2019). Female-voiced Siri's word choice in this example exhibits the indirect, tentative language patterns widely adopted by women (Lakoff, 1973), which often function to lessen the impact of women's speech and avoid giving offense. Indefinite language may contribute to views that feminine entities are less competent – and their work less valuable – than their masculine counterparts.

Implications for Users

Because the virtual assistants made to fulfill service and care roles are overwhelmingly feminized, they perpetuate assumptions and expectations about women's proclivity for service and caregiving and the affects they are expected to display in such roles. Relatedly, virtual assistants may set expectations among users that actual human service and care workers ought to embody the unflaggingly available, polite, and deferential personas encoded into these products.

Moreover, in discussion of smart home devices, Kennedy and Stregners (2020) argue that rather than freeing up time for women, who are primarily responsible for performing invisible labor, these products may actually further entrench traditionally gendered domestic roles as women in heterosexual relationships become responsible for "managing" or delegating tasks to these tools "that make 'their' domestic responsibilities easier" (pp. 47–48). In an ironic twist, the products intended to help users – including, or perhaps especially, women – may further entangle women with restrictive patriarchal presumptions in the popular imagination.

(DE)ENCODED RACE AND ITS IMPLICATIONS

While the feminization of virtual assistants is reflective of the reality that women are disproportionately responsible for invisible labor, the "racelessness" of virtual assistants contradicts the reality that even among women, women of color are overrepresented in service and caring labor sectors (Roberston & Gebeloff, 2020), which involve significant levels of invisible emotional and affective labor. The last section analyzed how the feminization of virtual assistants points to a regressive interest in maintaining (or returning to) a patriarchal framework of gender expressions and roles. This next section explores how the whiteness of virtual assistants opposes the reality of labor patterns, and by obscuring patterns of inequality, makes them harder to challenge.

The Racializing of Virtual Assistants

Although virtual assistants are highly anthropomorphized in terms of gender, overt signals of race and ethnicity are virtually absent in interface design (Piper, 2016; Bilal & Barfield, 2021). Cave and Dihal (2020) trenchantly argue, though, that "given the prevalence of racial framing, in most contexts, to be human-like means to have race." AI products exhibit "cultural characteristics" like "mannerisms, and dress codes, as well as mental and moral qualities, such as diligence, industriousness, reliability, trustworthiness, inventiveness, and intellectual ability" that have been used to constitute whiteness and lead to AI products that are predominantly portrayed and perceived as white, both in color and ethnicity (Cave & Dihal, 2020).

In a discussion of the chatbot ELIZA, created at the MIT AI Laboratory by Joseph Wizenbaum in 1966, Marino (2014) asserts that ELIZA performed "standard white middle-class English, without a specific identifying cultural inflection," which exemplified "language without culture, disembodied, hegemonic, and, in a word, white" (Marino, 2014, p. 5). In the decades since ELIZA, virtual assistants have become increasingly complex and anthropomorphic, and so have the ways in which they signal a racialized identity. Take, for example, the idea of professionalism, which in Western society is often equated with whiteness (and heteronormativity) (Cumberbatch, 2021). Research demonstrates that Black employees who adjust styles of speech, name selection, and hairstyles to match white norms are more likely to be perceived as professional in the workplace (McCluney et al., 2021). In the Western context, as devices serving their users in a "professional" capacity, most virtual assistants likewise signal their whiteness through speech styles that reflect white standard English, and through white standard names.

Some products, like Apple's Siri, actually do offer several different country-based accents for their products' English voice. Siri lets users choose between Australian, Canadian, Irish, New Zealand, South African, British, and American accents. As of 2022, users may also select accents from two countries in which the population is not majority white: India and Singapore – though notably, two countries with high populations of English speakers because of their intense and protracted colonial histories. Tech companies could more directly acknowledge and counter their tacit emphasis on whiteness by incorporating additional ethno-linguistic and sociolinguistic markers across languages. The largest producers of virtual assistant technologies, largely based in North America, could, for example, mirror the diversity of their local user populations by adding options for African American Vernacular English and Chicano English. Instead, thus far, the dearth of overt signals of race and ethnicity has created a vacuum of "racelessness," which is filled by the presumption of whiteness.

The Racialized Hierarchy of Labor

Although contemporary, Western-based design of virtual assistants attempts to obscure racial politics of difference, this "writing out" of race actually illuminates harmful implicit racial biases. Mainstream virtual assistant product design adopts and promotes a "race-blind" ethos, which implicitly assumes a singular racial/cultural norm – whiteness – thereby reinforcing its hegemony. Atanasoski and Vora (2019) capture this concept in a critique of what they call *technoliberalism*. This is the idea that technology – which is, in theory, open to use by everyone – will help us arrive at a post-labor world, in which humans do not have to carry out any "low value" labor because machines are able to do it for us. Because this technology will be open to use by all races and ethnicities, technoliberalism also claims to usher in a post-racial world, in which human social differences, and thus racism, are transcended (Atanasoski & Vora, 2019).

On its face, virtual assistant product design benignly promises to free users from much easy, repetitive, unskilled, or boring labor by outsourcing it to AI. Though perversely, the idea of inequality is embedded within this promise: in order to be "freed" from low-value labor, another entity must be saddled with it. Historically, under systems of antiblackness, settler colonialism, and patriarchy, it was enslaved peoples, colonized peoples, and women who had to carry out "low value" labor so that others (whites, colonizers, men) could be freed from it (Atanasoski & Vora, 2019). Nowadays, virtual assistants enable a shifting of the onus of invisible labor from historically marginalized human groups to automated non-human alternatives. But in embodying whiteness as the norm, they do not challenge the social inequalities this paradigm is based upon. The category of those being "freed" from "low value" labor is not implicitly intended to extend to those whose identities are different from the "white norm," which limits minorities' ability to engage in the post-work world.

With the appearance of virtual assistants, human relationships of inequality have been transposed into the virtual realm. Rather than disrupting the overrepresentation of people of color in positions of service and care work, writing race out of virtual assistant functions is a denial of racial inequality. It reflects the tenet of technoliberalism that racial inequality has been "solved" and there is thus no need for diverse racial and ethnic representation among virtual assistants; that a "raceless" (read *white*) design is equally representative of all peoples.

Control over the Automated Other

The absence of a diversity of racial and ethnic representation in anthropomorphized virtual assistants – or in other words, their "racelessness" – points to an assumption on the part of their creators that they are designing for primarily white audiences. This stems from a field (high tech) in which both women and most minority workers are underrepresented compared with overall private industry (US Equal Employment Opportunity Commission, n.d.). Because virtual assistants are ultimately commercial products, built to please and appease users, they are designed with characteristics assumed to make users feel at ease. Kennedy and Strengers (2020) explain:

> In the push to make social robots likable—and ultimately accepted and used…roboticists and AI programmers are falling back on stereotypical physical and emotional representations. Set against a backdrop of science fiction and popular culture that contains both friendly and threatening versions of a humanized AI…designers are turning to a host of nonthreatening attributes (young, cute, and feminized) to counteract any negative perceptions from consumers.

Designing for white audiences, these AI programmers are likewise adopting whiteness as a "nonthreatening" attribute. In an analysis of virtual assistants, Bergen (2016) argues that design emphasis continues to be not just on the female body, but on the "*white* female body, revealing the racial bias inherent in Western representations of femininity, in which the racialized body is traditionally less desirable and harder to contain" (p. 109). De-encoding race from virtual assistants makes them conceptually easier to contain, and thus, easier to sell to users.

Implications for Users

Implicit biases encoded into virtual assistants privilege white user experience. Beyond the ways in which virtual assistants appear to users, they have historically been encoded with racial biases that presume white users and alienate users of color. Automated speech recognition, for example, is better at interpreting speech from white users than from Black users (Koenecke et al., 2020). Speech recognition systems from five of the world's largest tech companies – Amazon, Apple, Google, IBM, and Microsoft – make significantly more errors with Black users than with white users (Koenecke et al., 2020).

Beyond disparities in its usefulness, AI technologies play an active role in perpetuating negative cultural stereotypes, again, largely due to the widely used machine learning models that employ massive amounts of unfiltered internet content to train AI. In practice, this means that AI "learns" and then parrots sexism, misogyny, and racism in interactions with users (UNESCO, 2019). Famously, in 2016, Microsoft released an autonomous chatbot, named Tay, on Twitter that learned and began writing sexist and racist tweets so promptly that the company shut the service down mere hours after its launch (Hunt, 2016).

Also troubling, beyond emotion and sentiment analysis, is that AI is becoming increasingly adept at determining the demographic characteristics of users. This, coupled with the fact that AI learns largely from problematic unfiltered internet content, means it "is not inconceivable that future emotive assistants might be dismissive of 'overly emotional' women, while providing helpful replies to 'calm' men" (UNESCO, 2019, p. 109). There are implications here for users' race too: because virtual assistants learn racism from the internet as easily as they do sexism, they may engage in "linguistic profiling" (Baugh, 2003) that leads to discriminatory behavior against users.

CONCLUSION

Ultimately, virtual assistants are commercial products created to return the highest profit to their producers: deeply ingrained assumptions about service and care labor as "women's work" dictate mainstream desires to be served by feminized others. The "racelessness" of virtual assistants actually reinforces racial distinctions by denying the existence of identities beyond whiteness, thus alienating users of color, but providing familiarity and a sense of control and ease to the presumed white user. These gendered and racialized products offer an entry point into critiquing the false possibility of arriving at an equitable, post-work world without first addressing real inequalities in gendered and racialized divisions of labor.

It is crucial to consider how the design of virtual assistants can either support or challenge gendered and racialized inequality in many realms, including that of labor. Critical design practices have immense potential to challenge harmful ideologies and contribute to a future in which invisible labor no longer exists – not because it has been entirely outsourced to machines, but because it is acknowledged, valued, and equitably distributed.

Projects aimed at decoupling virtual assistants from default feminization offer a critical perspective and progress toward this goal, and ought to be increasingly pursued and supported. Feminist AI's 2016 *Thoughtful Voice Design* project, for example, used community-driven research and design approaches to co-design alternative voice prototypes for Amazon's Alexa (Feminist.AI, n.d.). Their research demonstrated a high level of interest in both gendered and non-gendered as well as non-human voice options as potential pathways for reducing bias in voice assistant technologies (Feminist.AI, n.d.). GenderLess Voice, a collaboration between several organizations, created Q, the "first genderless voice," which was made from voice recordings of people who identify neither as male nor female (GenderLess Voice, n.d.). GenderLess Voice affirms non-binary conceptions of gender amidst a field of voice assistants fixed in binarism.

While *Thoughtful Voice Design* and Q both challenge and present more inclusive alternatives to virtual assistant form, other critical projects highlight equity in function. The Mozilla Foundation's *Common Voice* project, for example, presents a means of challenging the historical presumption of normative whiteness among virtual assistant users. *Common Voice* is a publicly available voice dataset, created to make speech models better at understanding a diverse range of speakers of various languages, dialects, variants, and accents (Common Voice, n.d.). It is comprised of voice snippets contributed by volunteers around the world and is available for voice application developers to train machine learning models for increased inclusion and accessibility (Common Voice, n.d.).

Beyond implementing the critical design of virtual assistant characteristics like names, voices, and the ability to understand a diversity of speech, technologists could further influence the mutual socialization that occurs between virtual assistants and their users by programming scripts and affects that encourage respectful interactions (Brown, 2022). They could avoid humility-signaling tropes like overuse of the word "I"; end encounters when users are rude or abusive; and even set clear expectations about codes of conduct (the University of Nebraska's chatbot *Pixel*, for example, refuses to respond to users who swear at it until they apologize (Allison, 2012)). Scripts and affects that uphold expectations of subservience communicate an inherent lack of worth. By replacing these with more egalitarian alternatives, virtual assistants could make more visible the value of their labor.

Projects and possibilities like these call attention to the problematics of the human-virtual assistant relationship, which has thus far been a hierarchical one mirroring inequality between genders and races among humans. Critical design practices that challenge these inequalities, rather than reinforce them, make progress toward a world in which the idea of invisible labor – once equitably acknowledged and valued – is thus rendered obsolete.

FURTHER READING

Atanasoski, N., & Vora, K. (2019). *Surrogate humanity: Race, robots, and the politics of technological futures*. Duke University Press.
Rhee, J. (2018). *The robotic imaginary: The human and the price of dehumanized labor*. University of Minnesota Press.
Strengers, Y., & Kennedy, J. (2020). *The smart wife: Why Siri, Alexa, and other smart home devices need a feminist reboot*. MIT Press.

REFERENCES

Allison, D. (2012). Chatbots in the library: Is it time? *Library Hi Tech, 30*(1), 95–107. https://doi.org/10.1108/07378831211213238.
Atanasoski, N., & Vora, K. (2019). *Surrogate humanity: Race, robots, and the politics of technological futures*. Duke University Press.
Babcock, L., Recalde, M. P., Vesterlund, L., & Weingart, L. (2017). Gender differences in accepting and receiving requests for tasks with low promotability. *American Economic Review, 107*(3), 714–747.
Baugh, J. (2003). Linguistic profiling. In S. Makoni, G. Smitherman, A. F. Ball, & A. K. Spears (Eds.), *Black linguistics: Language, society, and politics in Africa and the Americas* (pp. 155–163). Routledge.
Bergen, H. (2016). 'I'd blush if I could': Digital assistants, disembodied cyborgs and the problem of gender. *Word and Text, 6*(1), 95–113.
Bilal, D., & Barfield, J. (2021). Increasing racial and ethnic diversity in the design and use of voice digital assistants. *The 17th Annual Social Informatics Research Symposium and the 3rd Annual Information Ethics and Policy Workshop: Sociotechnical Perspectives on Equity, Inclusion, and Justice.*
Brown, L. M. (2022). Gendered artificial intelligence in libraries: Opportunities to deconstruct sexism and gender binarism. *Journal of Library Administration, 62*(1), 19–30. https://doi.org/10.1080/01930826.2021.2006979
Cave, S., & Dihal, K. (2020). The whiteness of AI. *Philosophy & Technology, 33*(4), 685–703. https://doi.org/10.1007/s13347-020-00415-6
Ciciolla, L., & Luthar, S. S. (2019). Invisible household labor and ramifications for adjustment: Mothers as captains of households. *Sex Roles, 81*(7), 467–486.
Common Voice. (n.d.). Why common voice? Common Voice Mozilla. https://commonvoice.mozilla.org/en/about
Costa, P. (2018). Conversing with personal digital assistants: On gender and artificial intelligence. *Journal of Science and Technology of the Arts, 10*(3), 59–72. https://doi.org/10.7559/citarj.v10i3.563
Costa, P., & Ribas, L. (2019). AI becomes her: Discussing gender and artificial intelligence. *Technoetic Arts, 17*(1–2), 171–193. https://doi.org/10.1386/tear_00014_1
Cumberbatch, S. (2021). When your identity is inherently "unprofessional": Navigating rules of professional appearance rooted in cisheteronormative whiteness as Black women and gender nonconforming professionals. *Journal of Civil Rights and Economic Development, 34*(2).

Duffy, M. (2013). Reproductive labor. In V. Smith (Ed.), *Sociology of work: An encyclopedia* (Vol. 1, pp. 729–730). SAGE Publications. https://dx.doi.org/10.4135/9781452276199.n260

Feminist.AI. (n.d.). *Thoughtful-voice-design*. Feminist.AI. https://www.feminist.ai/ thoughtful- voice-design

GenderLess Voice. (n.d.). *Meet Q*. GenderLess Voice. https://www.genderlessvoice.com/

Hannon, C. (2016). Gender and status in voice user interfaces. *Interactions, 23*(3), 34–37. https://doi.org /10.1145/2897939

Hempel, J. (2015). Siri and Cortana sound like ladies because of sexism. *Wired*. https://wired.com/2015 /10/why-siri-cortana-voice-interfaces-sound-female-sexism/

Hester, H. (2017). Technology becomes her. *New Vistas, 3*(1), 46–50. https://core.ac.uk/ download/ pdf/82959871.pdf

Hunt, E. (2016). Tay, Microsoft's AI chatbot, gets a crash course in racism from Twitter. *The Guardian*. https://www.theguardian.com/technology/2016/mar/24/tay-microsofts-ai- chatbot-gets-a-crash-cour se-in-racism-from-twitter

Koenecke, A., Nam, A., Lake, E., Nudell, J., Quartey, M., Mengesha, Z., Toups, C., Rickford, J. R., Jurafsky, D., & Goel, S. (2020). Racial disparities in automated speech recognition. *Proceedings of the National Academy of Sciences, 117*(14), 7684–7689. https://doi.org/10.1073/pnas.1915768117

Lakoff, R. (1973). Language and woman's place. *Language in Society, 2*(1), 45–79. https://doi.org/10 .1017/S0047404500000051

LessWrong. (n.d.). *AI*. https://www.lesswrong.com/tag/ai

Marino, M. C. (2014). The racial formation of chatbots. *CLCWeb: Comparative Literature and Culture, 16*(5). https://doi.org/10.7771/1481-4374.2560

McCluney, C. L., Durkee, M. I., Smith II, R. E., Robotham, K. J., & Lee, S. S. (2021). To be, or not to be…Black: The effects of racial codeswitching on perceived professionalism in the workplace. *Journal of experimental social psychology, 97*. https://doi.org/10.1016/j.jesp.2021.104199

Moravec, H. P. (n.d.). Robot. *Encyclopedia Britannica*. www.britannica.com/technology/robot-tech nology

Piper, A. M. (2016). *Stereotyping femininity in disembodied virtual assistants* [Master's thesis, Iowa State University]. Iowa State University Digital Repository. https://dr.lib.iastate.edu/ handle/20.500.12876/29975

Poster, W. R., Crain, M., & Cherry, M. A. (2016). 1. Introduction: Conceptualizing invisible labor. In W. R. Poster, M. Crain, & M. A. Cherry (Eds.), *Invisible labor: Hidden work in the contemporary world* (pp. 3–27). University of California Press.

Robertson, C., & Gebeloff, R. (2020). How millions of women became the most essential workers in America. *The New York Times*. https://www.nytimes.com/2020/04/18/us/coronavirus- women -essential-workers.html

Stern, J. (2017). Alexa, Siri, Cortana: The problem with all-female digital assistants. *The Wall Street Journal*. https://www.wsj.com/articles/alexa-siri-cortana-the-problem-with-all-female-digital- assistants-1487709068

Strengers, Y., & Kennedy, J. (2020). *The smart wife: Why Siri, Alexa, and other smart home devices need a feminist reboot*. MIT Press.

UNESCO. (2019). *I'd blush if I could: Closing gender divides in digital skills through education*. https:// en.unesco.org/Id-blush-if-I-could

U.S. Equal Employment Opportunity Commission. (n.d.). Diversity in high tech. https://www. eeoc.gov /special-report/diversity-high-tech

YouGov. (2020). Google Assistant and Apple's Siri both enjoy 36% share of the voice assistant market. https://today.yougov.com/topics/resources/articles-reports/2020/08/28/google-assistant-and-appl es-siri-both-enjoy-36-sha

51. Machine learning normativity as performativity
Tyler Reigeluth

INTRODUCTION

In 2016, Microsoft deployed a chatbot named Tay whose Twitter account was deactivated after just 16 hours because of its inflammatory comments, which included racist slurs, sexually charged language, and negationist statements. A few months later, the firm deployed a little sister, Zo, who was supposed to have learned from Tay's mishaps. However, she was instilled with a rigid sense of political correctness that rendered her just as problematic, as she refused to engage in any discussions that comprised sensitive or flagged words. I return to this example toward the end of this chapter as it offers an interesting touchstone for thinking about the normativity of machine learning behaviors in terms of performativity. The two approaches taken by Microsoft, and their respective problems, point to a deeper discussion about the efficacy of speech acts – utterances that do not simply describe the world but produce effects in the world. How might such a framing give us a better grasp of machine learning normativity?[1]

Like Tay and Zo, many contemporary machine learning systems are troublemakers. On the one hand, they are increasingly exhibiting unruly behaviors that are judged socially or politically unacceptable while, on the other hand, they are disrupting longstanding ontological criteria of what machine behaviors (should) look like. In many cases, these systems are producing effects that do not necessarily follow from the rules that govern their operations. A gap seems to be growing between their deterministic causes and their partially unpredictable effects. Thus, when the models developed by learning algorithms produce predictions or give recommendations that are not initially programmed, or that are not simply the products of random combinations, there is concern that such algorithms have somehow escaped control, or that human reason has become so lazy and fragmented that it blindsided by its own artifices. The idea that certain machines are normative, that they are not entirely reducible to their programmed norms, has frayed a path into our collective representations of technology and is progressively unsettling the longstanding principle that technical objects simply do what they are told (Bates and Bassiri, 2016; Malabou, 2017; Hui, 2019). For technical normativity to exist, machines must do more than simply execute their rules, they must execute their order of operations in such a way that the result is irreducible to that order and can only be accounted for in part through its own activity. The recursive nature of many machine learning algorithms seems to indicate that the feedback loops that embed them within social practices are, on some level, self-sustained through their behaviors (Grosman and Reigeluth, 2019). The concept of normativity thus evokes the complex dynamic between "norm-following" and "norm-instituting" (Barandarian and Egbert, 2014): a norm exists only insofar as it is actively followed, but this activity transforms the norm in the process, thereby instituting rival or alternative forms of the norm.

---

[1]   Aspects of what I develop here can be found in Berns and Reigeluth (2021).

Machine learning systems increasingly exhibit what French philosopher, Gilbert Simondon, called a "margin of indeterminacy" (2012, p. 12), which characterizes any complex functioning machine receptive to information from its environment. If a machine is receptive to information, then its functioning is not entirely predetermined by its structures. However, the idea that machines could have a form of autonomy or normativity (understood here interchangeably as any activity which *apparently* pursues its own purpose) has met longstanding ontological and epistemological resistance within Western thinking. Contemporary debates around the "black boxing", "transparency", and "accountability" of algorithmic systems are just the most recent expression of a leitmotiv wherein machine performances are constantly pushed to new limits while their effects are simultaneously dreaded for spinning out of our control (Winner, 1978). I will not address these ontological or epistemological questions directly here but rather reach them obliquely by testing a hypothesis: machine learning normativity can be framed as a kind of performativity.

THE ALGORITHMIC NORM

Algorithms are meant to perform as they are told. If they *do* anything at all, it is execute what they are programmed to do and certify the result obtained (Bachimont, 2010). The whole purpose of following an algorithm is to obtain a given objective within a given time. One follows an itinerary to reach a destination, follows a recipe to prepare a meal, reads directions to build a model, and so on. Algorithms are not traditionally expected to exhibit any form of creative behavior. They simply represent the number of steps and amount of time (otherwise called algorithmic complexity) that separates a current state from a certain future state. The algorithm does not produce any effects it was not intended to produce. Its value, both epistemic and practical, is that it executes its programmed norm. Elaborating on Alan Turing's work, Marvin Minsky famously defined an algorithm as an "effective procedure" corresponding to "a set of rules which tell us, from moment to moment, precisely how to behave" (Minsky, 1967, p. 123).

The history of the division of labor and automation can also be read as the fraught pursuit of this algorithmic dream, in which there would be no difference between a command and its execution, no gap between a rule and its implementation. Turning social practices, namely labor activities, into abstract algorithms to be executed independently of situations, is the recurring obsession of automation. The human component has consistently been seen as a source of error, uncertainty, and wavering performance. We expect machines to exhibit the obedience of human workers or slaves without any of their weaknesses or tendencies toward insubordination (Dumouchel et Damiano, 2016, p. 10).

This is the understanding of algorithms that still irrigates our normative expectations and regulations of machine learning processes, even as we lavishly praise their inventions and surprises, as we worry about their opacity and grapple with their increasingly intractable behaviors. However, machine learning might best be understood not as the automation of algorithm execution, but rather the automation of the gap between the rule and its execution, and how this gap is corrected and fed back into the algorithm's future state. As Mackenzie (2018, p. 82) underscores, machine learning is about "function finding" more than it is about "function execution" in the classical algorithmic sense. How a given machine learning system finds a function is not always easy to analyze in linear and purely deterministic terms.

Much of the critical social and legal scholarship, as well as activist discourse, insists on the relative opacity of contemporary algorithmic systems and the need to redress epistemic and ethical shortcomings by opening the "black box" and making the systems transparent and accountable. I would like to suggest that the growing margin of indeterminacy affecting machine learning systems can partially be understood in terms of a performative theory of speech acts. More specifically, I will explore how Judith Butler's engagement with debates concerning J. Austin's distinction between illocutionary and perlocutionary speech acts can help us understand the efficacy of machine learning systems. To a large extent, this algorithmic conception of performativity underpins much of modern rationality (Totaro and Ninno, 2014), namely through a belief in the possibility of unerring repetition. I will then look at how Butler's analysis plays off J. Derrida's critique of Austin, on the citational and iterative character of perlocutionary speech acts that allows her to account for the "unknown future of words" (Butler, 1997, p. 163), which is a form of repetition that constantly displaces its effects. While the perlocutionary dimension is precisely that which seems to resist something like machine performativity, my hypothesis is that it can help us better understand the predictive and partially intractable nature of machine learning behaviors.

PERFORMATIVITY[2]

In his attempt to unmoor language from an "idealistic" or Aristotelian approach whereby each word corresponded to a thing and each sentence could be judged by its constative (i.e., "true" or "false") nature, J. L. Austin developed the notion of speech acts, in which the constative and performative dimensions of language are intertwined. Performative utterances are those that do not simply describe the world, as if language were outside of the world, but those which produce effects by being uttered and can be judged or evaluated based on their felicitous or infelicitous effects (i.e., did the utterance do what it was supposed to do?). Potentially, any and all utterances have this performative dimension insofar as even the most apparently constative utterances (e.g., "this is a ball") can be understood as performative (e.g., "I am saying this is a ball"). While Austin's account of performativity is perhaps one of the most influential conceptual inventions of the 20th century, it is worth remembering that it is subtler and more problematic (by Austin's own account) than the broad and rather dubious notion that "words have effects" or that "words make the world".

Austin distinguished between three performative dimensions that affect any speech act: locutionary, illocutionary, and perlocutionary (Austin, 1962). The locutionary dimension involves the mere fact of speaking, the ability of a speaker's phonatory system to produce a certain sound with a semantic value (e.g., "ball"). Illocutionary effects are those which constitute a performative utterance's *force*. They correspond to its ability to do what it says. The classic example of an illocutionary utterance is the judge who says, "I pronounce you married". The "happiness" of this declaration (i.e., the resulting marriage) hinges upon a context and certain conventions. If the same judge were simply to shout the words at a couple walking down the street or if I were to declare them in the judge's courtroom, the utterance would miss

---

2   My general approach is informed by Thomas Berns' (2021) work on post-sovereign law as well as Salomé Frémineur's (Berns and Frémineur, 2018) work on technical language and the technicity of language.

its target; it would be infelicitous. However, it is important to note that it does not succeed by magically producing effects, but by being what it says it is: a marriage declaration. It is no surprise then that most illocutionary utterances that come to mind and that are often used as examples are highly conventional or ritual – and might thus be regarded as rather artificial when compared with "everyday language" where conventions are bendable. Perlocutionary effects are those that do not directly or immediately constitute an utterance's force, or its ability to act, but which are *possible* and thus uncertain effects. Whereas illocution is necessary and immediate, perlocution is differed and potential. The emotional states produced by an utterance are typical examples of perlocution. As James Loxley underlines, both illocution and perlocution are ways of accounting for the pragmatics of language, but

> [t]he two terms [...] denote a very different sense of the pragmatic: whereas the work of the illocutionary is accomplished in the saying of whatever is said, that of the perlocutionary is more a matter of the contingent consequences or effects that might or might not follow the issuing of a speech act. (Loxley, 2007, p. 18)

The fact that Austin tended to neutralize what he called "non-serious" or "parasitic" uses of illocution (e.g., a marriage declared on a theater stage, children playing doctor, uses of humor or air-quotes) betrays, according to Jacques Derrida, a remainder of idealism even as Austin attempted to free language from its constative and descriptive metaphysics. Rather than discard infelicitous utterances as "misfires" or "fouls", Derrida was interested in taking them as the starting point for a citational rather than a conventional theory of performativity. By refusing to associate a fixed origin to the efficacy of language, which would require going back to an original convention from which all other performatives would derive their force, Derrida finds performativity at play on the margins of its success, in its failures and non-serious uses, and most importantly, in its fundamentally citational dynamic. Performativity is nothing else than citations of citations of citations. It is the iteration of these citations that accounts for both the repetition and the difference of effects.

In her attempts to work through contemporary debates on hate speech and its regulation, Judith Butler mobilizes Derrida's critique of Austin, namely his concepts of iterability and citationality. The central claim Derrida makes by way of his concept of iterability is that language is not reducible to its context. Rather, it alters itself through repetition, even in the absence of any addressee, as words operate beyond determinate references (Derrida, 1972, p. 374). In *Excitable Speech. A Politics of the Performative*, she engages with certain appropriations of Austin's theory used to justify the regulation of certain utterances. She shows how attempts to limit freedom of expression based on the premise that "fighting words" carry an illocutionary force that is directly hurtful or injurious end up producing the very convention by which these utterances derive their illocutionary force. In doing so, these limitations fail to account for an utterance's perlocutionary effects. Butler disputes, for example, Catherine McKinnon's claim in her book *Only Words*, where she addresses pornographic discourse according to which certain words should be legally prohibited in certain contexts especially where they explicitly and necessarily reproduce a form of male domination and violation. According to Butler, such attempts fall prey to at least three inextricable difficulties:

1. By claiming that an utterance systematically produces a given effect (i.e., hurts the person at which it is aimed) and that it can and should therefore be prohibited by law, the utterance is boiled down to its illocutionary dimension and is thus confirmed through the

ritual exercise of its prohibition. This is not to say that certain words do not inflict pain, are not threatening, and do not express embedded forms of social and political oppression through their repetition, but these effects are not automatic. An idealized form of repetition draws its force from an instituted convention that seeks to neutralize the difference, or "margin of indeterminacy", with which it is marked. It acts as if "all other things were equal" when, in fact, every utterance lives or dies in all other things.

2. Utterances are always charged with a citational and perlocutionary force, the effects of which are partially unknown. As Butler suggests, this is how words such as "queer" or "nigger" have come to stand as marks of identity, pride, and recognition by and within communities at which they were originally aimed as instruments of oppression and pain. Paradoxically, and this is the powerful twist to Butler's critique, the law itself is obliged to cite the very utterances it seeks to prohibit, thus confirming the fact that words can always do something else than what they were intended to do and that language cannot extract itself from its citational dynamic (e.g., by citing a racial slur in a courtroom, a judge is doing something else than simply repeating the illocutionary force of the insult).

3. Establishing which words are injurious requires a triangulation of sovereignty (and it is no surprise therefore that law and illocution are so tightly bound together[3]) whereby the would-be victim's injury is conventionalized, the intention to injure is given illocutionary force and the state's power to regulate discourse by establishing which words hurt is confirmed. This sovereign conception of speech acts forecloses the iterative dynamic of language by which difference is produced through repetition, by way of differed and uncertain effects. It confers to the state, or any other public or private authority (we might think of the growing role private platforms such as Meta or Google have in moderating content and users), the prerogative of knowing and deciding what hurts, who is hurt, and by whom.

Butler is not necessarily advocating for a hands-off approach to hate-speech regulation, but by underlining the citational rather than purely conventional nature of performatives, she exposes some of the problems regulatory efforts will inevitably have to deal with as well as the dangers of reducing performativity to illocution. There is an "unknown future of words" that is contained by no convention and that is the contingent effect of words playing themselves out, not without conflict, as they are dispelled, embraced, mocked, quoted, remembered, and upended. What is the most difficult, but perhaps the most important to do, is to care for this troublesome contingency and attend to those utterances which go unheard or are heard too often. Each subject is constituted through "linguistic vulnerability": the words we use to talk about ourselves, others, and the world are the words that were and are addressed to us, against us, for us, and that we cite in our turn, thereby quietly, but sometimes loudly, displacing their meaning. At the core of our socio-linguistic experience is a vulnerability that confounds any absolute sovereignty over the meaning and course of words.

---

[3]   For attempts to deconstruct and move beyond this fusion, see Thomas Berns' (2021) work on post-sovereign law.

MACHINE-LIKE PERFORMATIVITY?

Based on this presentation of classical or deterministic algorithms and the summary exposition of Butler's engagement with theories of performativity, conceptualizing something
like "machine perlocution" appears to be rather a stretch or a contradiction in terms. Even a
thinker as skeptical of binaries as Derrida seemed at odds with the idea that perlocution could
be performed by the automatic behaviors of machines:

> Performativity will never be reduced to technical performance. Pure performativity implies the
> presence of a living being, and of a living being speaking one time only, in its own name, in the first
> person. And speaking in a manner that is at once spontaneous, intentional, free, and irreplaceable.
> (Derrida, 2002, cited in Loxley, p. 92)

But, as Loxley states, Derrida is mostly emphasizing that performativity cannot be thought of
as a *purely* automatic performance (as legal and militant uses of Austin's theory seem to suggest), although it requires automatic repetition for its iterations to play out, invention is always
subtended by automaticity, which always errs toward difference (Bates, 2016).

 A classical algorithm might well resemble an ideal illocution, and thus the potential for all
language to be written and uttered in such a way. An algorithm can be repeated as often as
one likes and it will always produce the same effects because the convention is immunized
against the very effects it produces. Since Cartesian Modernity, mechanical operations have
consistently been thought of as discourse in action. Any effect produced by a mechanism is
entirely determined by, and reversible into, the chain of causes and effects that preceded it.
Determinism is linear. Mechanical behavior is ultimately the expression of universal physical
laws, the eternity of which verifies itself through its endless repetition. The convention (i.e.,
the program) which has written the order of operations to be executed ahead of time and its
execution are seen as two different normative moments, and the latter does not feedback into
the former. However, in the uncertain and complex world of social practice, there is no such
pure and linear distinction between the program and its execution. Instead, there is a constant
normative recursion or feedback between the two (Hacking, 1983). This is perhaps why using
social practices such as recipes, itineraries, or instructions to exemplify what an algorithm
is, fails to account for the incompressible ambiguities of the practice. Who hasn't "failed"
to assemble a piece of Ikea furniture or to bake a cake and exclaimed, "I don't understand, I
followed all the steps!"? All other things are never equal in the world of social practice (e.g.,
all ovens do not heat alike, no two flours are the same, and there can be a fine line between
whisking and beating). While processes of algorithmic formalization attempt to make these
conditions equal, there is always an inverse operation of translating determinate steps and
results back into practice, which is beset by indeterminacy.

 To a large extent, many of the debates around algorithmic transparency and accountability flow from this framing of mechanical illocution. Perhaps no other title was as influential
in confirming this correspondence between illocution and algorithms as Lawrence Lessig's
Code is Law. More recently, books such as *Algorithms of Oppression* or documentaries
such as *Coded Bias*, reproduce in some form or another the idea that the biases and inequities produced by algorithmic systems can be traced back to the social and political norms
coded into their programs, as well as the data with which they are trained. The prevalent idea
shared among legal and social critiques of algorithmic normativity is that if users were more

"literate" in the algorithmic process, if the "black boxes" could be opened, and if platforms were (forced to be) transparent about the data and code they used, then such algorithmically produced oppression could be minimized or altogether avoided. There are many limits and issues with this general critical approach (Ananny and Crawford, 2018), but it is worth noting that it tends to uphold the Enlightenment ideal of publicity of the sovereign law and literacy thereof according to which no one should ignore the law. But while the law is perhaps the most ostentatious and formal expression of a norm, it never suffices to explain the efficacy of a specific law in practice, which operates through chains of citation and iteration. More generally, this holds as a Wittgensteinian claim that can be made about the efficacy of any rule, be it linguistic or technical (see Thomas Young, 2018).

So, while classical algorithms seem to represent a kind of illocutionary ideal of pure mechanical repetition, their efficacy is never immunized from the iterations their repetitions suppose for the same cake, the same itinerary, or the same piece of furniture to be felicitous. If we push the argument a bit further, we can see that this very ideal of mechanical repetition that exists at least potentially in the formal space of deterministic algorithms is in the process of falling apart in the face of contemporary machine systems in which predictive and probabilistic algorithms are constantly feeding back the results of interactions with their users into the conventional space of their programs (e.g., neural net weights being corrected, conditional probabilities being revaluated), thus displacing, often imperceptibly, the convention itself.

A very clear illustration of this displacement in algorithmic normativity can be found in contemporary recommender systems such as those used by platforms like Amazon, Netflix, YouTube, or Spotify – nobody can claim that such algorithmic recommendations have not become everyday forms of discourse. Yet the very efficacy of a recommendation, understood as a certain kind of performative, hinges upon differed and uncertain effects. Whether it is Spotify, a friend, or a record dealer making the recommendation, saying "you should listen to this" or "I think you will like this" has a clear perlocutionary dimension. The effect does not immediately and necessarily follow from the utterance and yet the utterance is somehow expected to influence the addressee's choices and preferences. One might say that the possibility of a recommendation being infelicitous, that it will "fail", is embedded in its very normative structure. A recommendation is constantly open to not being followed or being followed in an unexpected way. What is striking about contemporary algorithmic recommender systems is that the techniques behind them seem to be markedly perlocutionary. The prevalent technique used is called "collaborative filtering" whereby users are not simply matched pairwise with their declared preferences on their profile, (this could more readily be seen as a kind of illocution), but are recommended content based on the "implicit feedback" users give (e.g., when they paused, how many times they watched or listened to a song or movie) and based upon what similar users consumed. Moreover, these collaborative filtering techniques are expressly designed to find a "sweet spot" between repetition and difference, between recommendations the system "knows" will succeed and those that are less probable, and between things users have seen before and things they have never seen. In any case, the "failure" of a recommendation can only ever be seen as another occasion for an unending normative process in which machines are learning what users like while users are following what machines recommend. Importantly, there is no fixed convention by which one might judge an utterance's (in)felicitous effect – if we broaden utterance here to include any behavior that is coded into a meaningful sequence and fed back into the algorithmic system that conditions the sequence (e.g., clicks, taps, scrolls, interface interactions). In this sense, a recommendation never truly fails, it only opens onto constantly changing chains of citation.

Machine learning performances in general, whether the result of "reinforcement" "supervised", "unsupervised", or "deep" learning, seem to express an increasingly citational dynamic that is irreducible to its convention (i.e., the different algorithmic logics such as neural nets, Bayesian probabilities, random forests). Much of machine learning depends upon the training of algorithms to recognize unseen occurrences based on labeled or unlabeled training data. In other words, couldn't we consider that when a system says it is 87% sure an image is a ball, not based upon any fixed and formally coded properties of a ball, but based upon the algorithm's extrapolations of properties from examples of balls it has been shown, that it is citing "ball" and producing potentially unforeseen effects as its utterances move from one context to another through an iterative process, that is without there being any ideal convention of the ball but only occurrences of what is called "ball"? While this example might seem a little insignificant when making claims about algorithmic normativity, it can frame more charged situations, namely those in which algorithmic systems generate injurious or discriminatory utterances in interaction with their users (although "users" is perhaps not the best characterization of this relationship).

MACHINE LEARNING PERFORMANCE AND ITS REGULATION

Let us return to Microsoft's two chatbot sisters, Tay and Zo. Regardless of how we evaluate their performances morally, they both express a certain formal mastery of English as they engage in credible conversations using humor, memes, and other linguistic subtleties. Beyond the media attention their misbehaviors received, they are worth looking at more closely because they epitomize debates around algorithmic normativity and regulation. On the one hand, we have Tay who was deactivated after only 16 hours in which she managed to go from being excited about meeting human beings to negating the Holocaust and proffering racist slurs. As is often the case when algorithms run amok, the platform publicly expressed its contrition and vowed to do better. Microsoft stated that it was "deeply sorry for the unintended offensive and hurtful tweets from Tay", and would "look to bring Tay back only when we are confident we can better anticipate malicious intent that conflicts with our principles and values" (cited in Murphy, 2016). It also claimed that the chatbot had suffered from a "coordinated attack by a subset of people" that "exploited a vulnerability in Tay" (cited in Lee, 2016). These justifications are interesting for at least two reasons. First, we have engineers recognizing their difficulty in anticipating one of their system's behaviors, as if the formal rules that had gone into its program were insufficient to account for its effective behaviors. It is impossible to apprehend the gap here between the formal space of rules and the social practice of speech as unidirectional, the rules emerge in part from the very performance to be regulated. Second, they indicate that Tay is marked by a form of "vulnerability" understood here as a "technical vulnerability" (as a nuclear power plant or a sensitive digital database can be considered vulnerable to attack). However, perhaps Tay's vulnerability is nothing other than the "margin of indeterminacy" her linguistic behaviors exhibit. Her utterances are not systematically nor exhaustively programmed ahead of time but are the partial result of the information she receives, imitates, and follows. What Microsoft considers an ill-intentioned or strategic attack on a technical vulnerability is, if we follow Butler, the unavoidable experience of all socio-linguistic interaction. Tay's words are not her own, but the ones she cites in infinitely varying contexts. It is precisely because Tay is generating new linguistic utterances that do not simply match pairwise with an abstract problem space or are not simply maximizing a given objective function that what she does might be considered as social learning (Reigeluth and Castelle, 2021). The efficacy of her performance lies in the fact that we do not know ahead of time what she will say. And yet many of Tay's injurious comments are all too familiar. This may be unpleasant to recognize and come to terms with, but it is also precisely where the ethical and social life of machine learning (if such exists) begins. It is perhaps a credit to the technical performances of these applications that they raise these questions, as sensitive and complicated as they may be. While there is no question some of Tay's utterances are unacceptable, it would be difficult to claim that they operate merely on an illocutionary level, immediately and necessarily producing insult, as the convention that would give them their efficacy is missing, as is the putative intention to harm when someone is considered to have *used* words to do *something*. In fact, what is striking is how the very absence of convention or intention in the case of these machine learning utterances does not subvert their efficacy but heightens it.

On the other hand, and as a way of answering some of these questions and of "correcting" Tay's "vulnerabilities", we have Zo who is coded with an intransigent form of "political correctness" where certain words have obviously been flagged as conversation killers as if she had been told, "whatever you do, *never* talk about religion or politics". What exactly is to be considered as "politics" or "religion" is, of course, difficult to establish *ex ante*. Yet Microsoft seems to have attempted to circumscribe the semantic field of those terms by flagging words from which Zo should and could avoid even at the expense of offending its interlocutor. Certain utterances are thus considered to have an illocutionary force in and of themselves, independently of context, to be triggers that will necessarily end up producing injury. Paradoxically, and as suggested by Butler's analysis, this foreclosing of the unknown future of words confirms the very insult that its prohibition seeks to avoid. This results in such uncomfortable interactions as someone saying to Zo "They have good falafel in the Middle East", to which she responded(s) "lemme make myself clear. Im not gonna chat politics with you [punctuated by an upside-down smiley face]". In the absence of context – that is *all the other things* that confer efficacy to an utterance beyond the order of words it enunciates – it is difficult to read this interaction as anything other than Microsoft avoiding words that are deemed to be overtly and dangerously illocutionary, thereby confirming the very effects it seeks to avoid. In fact, not only does this attempt to foreclose certain types of utterances and citations inevitably fail, but it actually creates unprecedented or unforeseen insults (e.g., someone feeling as though their desire to speak about Middle Eastern cuisine is somehow a political and perhaps "communitarian" or "sectarian" debate that indexes them to their putative ethnic identity).

Tay represents what could be called the "I-didn't-see-that-coming" approach to machine learning regulation wherein engineering communities and corporate cultures realize after the damage is done that utterances matter and that the social life of words is wily, unpredictable, and always vulnerable. Zo represents what could be called the "you-can't-say-that" approach to machine learning regulation whereby certain subjects – both semantic and political – are foreclosed, avoided, and silenced. I don't claim that it is acceptable for algorithms to proffer insults, but it is no more acceptable to establish ahead of time what machines are not supposed to say when the very premise of their engineering is that they are sufficiently open-ended to learn from social interactions. I don't see how we can design machine learning algorithms that are both technically foolproof *and* linguistically vulnerable. As Turing had already sensed:

> Intelligent behaviour presumably consists in a departure from the completely disciplined behaviour involved in computation, but a rather slight one, which does not give rise to random behaviour, or to pointless repetitive loops. [...] Processes that are learnt do not produce a hundred per cent certainty of result; if they did, they could not be unlearnt. (Turing, 1950, p. 459)

Learning how to do things such as making a chair, walking on different terrains, or cleaning office spaces has consistently proven to be a formidable challenge when programming effective artificial systems to do such activities (Collins and Kusch, 1998; Brooks, 1991). Not unsurprisingly, many of the same problems are encountered when it comes to automating content moderation on a large scale on digital platforms (Gillespie, 2020; Gillespie et al., 2020). A large part of the difficulty resides in being able to program the ability to improvise and have programs that exhibit plasticity. Rules are needed but are never enough. Intelligent behavior is something other than simply following the rules. It is using rules to do something that was not written in them, it is what fills the gap between rules and practice. The problem with machine learning normativity does not lie in the rules that compose their algorithms, nor in the words (i.e., data) used to train them, but in recognizing that we must take constant care that the words used, cited, and repeated do not result in creating new rules that exclude certain categories and subjectivities, nor that they simply confirm existing ones that bear long histories of inequity and violence. The most pressing problem is not that algorithms develop biases, but that they are developed and regulated by monopolistic platforms that can lay claim to what can and cannot be said. The language machine learning uses is an institution that machine learning itself is in the process of reshaping and over which any subject has a potential claim. It is not merely an application to be used, "attacked", and deactivated.

REFERENCES

Ananny M and Crawford K (2018) Seeing without knowing: Limitations of the transparency ideal and its application to algorithmic accountability. *New Media & Society* 20(3), 973–989.

Austin J (1962) *How To Do Things with Words.* London: Oxford University Press.

Bachimont B (2010) *Le sens de la technique: le numérique et le calcul.* Paris: Editions Les Belles Lettres.

Barandiaran X and Egbert M (2014) Norm-establishing and norm-following. *Artificial Life* 20(1), 5–28.

Bates D (2016) Automaticity, plasticity and the deviant origins of artificial intelligence, in *Plasticity and Pathology. On the Formation of the Neural Subject.* New York: Fordham University Press.

Bates D and Bassiri N (2016) *Plasticity and Pathology. On the Formation of the Neural Subject.* New York: Fordham University Press.

Berns T (2021) Insult and post-sovereign law as juridicity. *Political Theology* 22(2), 147–154.

Berns T and Frémineur S (2018) Le reste de la transparence. *Multitudes* 73, 76–83.

Berns T and Reigeluth T (2021) *Ethique de la communication et de l'information. Une initiation en contexte technologique avancé.* Brussels: Presses Universitaires de Bruxelles.

Brooks R (1991) Intelligence without representation. *Artificial Intelligence* 47.

Butler J (1997) *Excitable Speech. A Politics of the Performative.* New York: Routledge.

Collins H and Kusch M (1998) *The Shape of Actions: What Machines and Humans Can Do.* Cambridge (MA): MIT Press.

Derrida J (1972) Signature événement contexte, in *Marges de la philosophie.* Paris: Editions de Minuit.

Dumouchel P and Damiano L (2016) *Vivre avec les robots*. Paris: Editions du Seuil.

Gillespie T (2020) Content moderation, AI, and the question of scale. *Big Data & Society* 1, 5.

Gillespie T et al. (2020) Expanding the debate about content moderation: Scholarly research agendas for the coming policy debates. *Internet Policy Review* 9, 4.

Grosman J and Reigeluth T (2019) Perspectives on algorithmic normativities: Engineers, objects, activities. *Big Data & Society*.

Hacking I (1983) *Representing and Intervening: Introductory Topics in the Philosophy of Natural Science*. Cambridge: Cambridge University Press.

Hui Y (2019) *Recursivity and Contingency*. London: Rowman & Littlefield.

Lee P (2016) Learning from Tay's introduction. *Official Microsoft Blog*. Microsoft. Retrieved 29 June 2016.

Loxley J (2007) *Performativity*. New York: Routledge.

Mackenzie A (2018) *Machine Learners: Archaeology of a Data Practice*. Cambridge: Massachusetts University Press.

Malabou C (2017) *Métamorphoses de l'intelligence: Que faire de leur cerveau bleu ?* Paris: Presses Universitaires de France.

Minsky M (1967) *Computation: Finite and Infinite Machines*. Englewood Cliffs: Prentice Hall.

Murphy D (2016) Microsoft apologizes (again) for Tay Chatbot's offensive tweets. *PC Magazine*. Retrieved 27 March 2016.

Reigeluth T and Castelle M (2021) What kind of learning is machine learning? In *The Cultural Life of Machine Learning*, Roberge, J. and Castelle, M. (eds). New York: Palgrave-Macmillan.

Simondon G (2012) *Du mode d'existence des objets techniques*. Paris: Editions Aubier.

Thomas Young M (2018) Artifacts as rules: Wittgenstein and the sociology of technology. *Techné: Research in Philosophy and Technology* 22(3), 377–399.

Totaro P and Ninno D (2014) The concept of algorithm as an interpretative key of modern rationality. *Theory, Culture & Society* 31(4), 29–49.

Turing A (1950) Computing machinery and intelligence. *Mind*, New Series 59, n°. 236.

Winner L (1978) *Autonomous Technology: Technics-out-of-Control as a Theme in Political Thought*. Cambridge (MA): MIT Press.

52. Queer eye on AI: binary systems versus fluid identities

Karin Danielsson, Andrea Aler Tubella, Evelina Liliequist and Coppélie Cocq

INTRODUCTION

Today, artificial intelligence (AI) is largely integrated into society and people's everyday lives, and it is becoming common to replace human-based decisions with algorithmic calculations and evaluations using AI (see, e.g., SVT, 2019; New York Post, 2019). Facial analysis (FA) is a specific type of AI technology that depends on personal data that can be retrieved from physical bodies, in this case, a person's face (Baeza Argüello, 2021). However, there is demonstrated history of algorithms causing harm (Buolamwini et al., 2018; Scheuerman et al., 2019): for example, large-scale studies on widely adopted facial analysis benchmarks found that these datasets are mainly composed of lighter-skinned subjects and their use leads to substantial disparities in the accuracy of classification depending on gender and skin colour (Buolamwini et al., 2018), with darker-skinned females being the most misclassified group. The combination of these findings together with the use of this technology in high-stakes contexts such as policing (Reuters, 2020; SVT, 2021) has led to increased societal concern about the development of facial analysis systems (Nature, 2020), and even social unrest and acts of resistance (CV Dazzle, 2020; Shalloe, 2019). Furthermore, FA systems could both interfere with and enable the exploration of identity and self-presentation because they exemplify the contemporary entanglement between human identity, self-presentation and computation, and highlight a dilemma: Should these technologies be designed according to the way we have traditionally categorized and thought about self and identity, or should they reflect our progress in understanding these complex issues, even casting an eye on the future? Clearly, the potential risks and consequences of increased implementation of FA technology need to be addressed.

In this chapter we cast a queer eye on AI: using queer theory, we highlight the dilemmas that arise when binary systems like FA, in different contexts and for various purposes, are used to categorize, measure and make decisions based on/in relation to gender and sexuality. In what ways and to what extent can AI systems such as FA grasp the fluidity of human identities, or read and understand complex self-labelled identities (queer identities and sexual desire/orientations in general), transidentities (including non-binary and intergender) and/or norm breaking gender expressions (androgyny and other non-stereotypical gender performances, etc.)? This chapter also discusses issues of privacy, surveillance, bias and fairness related to FA and the possible implications for marginalized communities such as LGBTQI+. Finally, the chapter suggests that a queer perspective on FA can create new ways to relate to technology.

DEFINITIONS AND CONCEPTUAL FRAMEWORK

Facial Analysis Technology

FA is an example of an AI technology that is used to label individuals binarily: persons either correspond to a certain pre-programmed label or they do not. FA captures a person's facial information such as face shape, skin colour, movements or makeup and assigns a classification (e.g., male/female, dark-haired/light-haired, black/white). Based on such information, the system can be used to match the recognized face against a database (face recognition), to compare the recognized face against a given match (face authentication) (Li & Jain, 2005) or to classify individuals (e.g., in terms of gender, race, scars, body geometry) (Reid et al., 2013). This technology is used in the automatic tagging of photos on social media, identity verification for unlocking a mobile phone, as well as forensics and surveillance.

Queer Perspectives on Sexuality and Gender

Queer theory was developed as a critical discourse in the 1990s. At its core, queer theory generally challenges ideas of normality and specifically challenges the notion of defined and stable identity categories, as well as the norms and power structures that create and maintain a binary of good versus bad sexualities and gender identities (e.g., Butler, 1990, 1993). In opposition to an essentialist understanding of sexuality and gender as stabile, fixed, core identities, queer theorists argue for an understanding of sexuality and gender as discursive constructs – as non-category, fluid, plural and an ongoing negotiation in different cultural contexts. For example, in several works, queer theorist Judith Butler sought to destabilize binary oppositions such as woman/man, gay/straight by introducing a key concept of performativity that points to sexuality and gender as ongoing performances that lean on repetitions of expected behaviour, expression, appearance and desire in accordance with societal norms in a specific cultural context (Butler, 1990, 1993).

Visibility has been used both as a philosophy and central political strategy over the last decades by much of the LGBTQI+ community in the Western world (Phillips, 2002, p. 408). Despite the recent increase of queer visibility and acceptance in society, the possibility and choice to be open with one's sexuality and/or gender identity still often depends on context, time and space. Only a few decades ago, anonymity was an important and necessary part of the LGBTQI+ community and queer lives, which is understandable given the much harsher attitude towards LGBTQI+ people. The internet has afforded new ways for LGBTQI+ people to meet, explore identities, form communities and organize (Guyan, 2022; Liliequist, 2020). Digital spaces have also re-introduced issues of visibility and disclosure in relation to expectations of participating in social media by sharing personal information (Marwick & boyd, 2014; Liliequist, 2020). In her dissertation, Liliequist (2020) argued that despite an increase in queer visibility and acceptance in Swedish society, individuals may still feel a need to conceal their sexual orientation in digital environments. Liliequist's study further showed that sharing information regarding sexual orientation and expressions of being queer heavily depend on the imagined audience in different social media sites (ibid). This strategy of selective self-presentation was described as creating a "digital closet" (Phillips, 2002), which refers back to the concept of "the closet" as a metaphor for queer oppression, denial and concealment of queer people (Sedgwick, 1991, p. 71). Such findings also problematize the binary logics of the closet

– either you're in or out – by instead pointing towards openness and visibility as progress that is both ongoing and context-based. Similarly, in the same way that a physical place carries appropriate and inappropriate behaviours, a virtual space also carries social and cultural opportunities and expectations (Sharpio, 1998). Distinguishing between outside and inside, public and private, can be seen as a notion of home and the construction of privacy, related to a physical or virtual place or space (Sharpio, 1998). New technologies bring new choices about what we share and what boundaries we make. Sharpio (1998) explained that the boundaries between what is public and private can differ depending on physical places and virtual spaces. For example, a physical home is mostly a private place, but an online forum can be a place where we express ourselves either privately (closed and trusted) or publicly (with possibilities and explorations). Through technology, we can be both private and public at the same time.

To our knowledge, queer theory has not been used in the design, development or understanding of AI. Nevertheless, perspectives from queer theory are highly pertinent to the examination of AI systems such as FA, as these perspectives can not only raise new questions about the application and implication of these technologies but also bring critical perspectives about how to approach the complex issue of identities in the context of AI technology design, implementation and use (cf. Ashwin et al., 2021). If we understand sexuality and gender as discursive constructs – as fluid, plural and ongoing negotiations in different cultural contexts – we can design and train AI systems in new and more inclusive ways (cf. ibid). Identification can be replaced with a more context-dependent probability about what is observed rather than a fixed, binary "is or is not".

CONCERNS AND RISKS

Research on AI, including FA and algorithmic exclusion, is still limited, and recent studies with a focus on queer identity and perspectives point towards potential risks (Scheuerman et al., 2019). In dialogue with previous research, we discuss issues of identity, privacy, surveillance, bias and fairness related to FA. We focus on the concerns and risks for marginalized communities, such as LGBTQI+, that are related to the implementation and use of this AI technology. We present three concepts: identity, representation and privacy, and explain from a queer standpoint how each of these issues is particularly challenging when designing and using AI systems such as FA.

Technology and Identity

Technologies can provide spaces for the exploration of presentation and disclosure, and to a great extent, the affordances of the platform or technology being used shape strategies for self-presentation (DeVito et al., 2018). In this sense, the subjective labels used in many FA applications, which are derived from measurements based on what can be observed from a face, are particularly limiting. For example, technologies such as automated gender recognition (AGR) are designed to assign a gender label based only on a face's observable physical characteristics. Such technologies are usually based on a binary understanding of gender and operate under the assumption that gender can be deduced from observation. Through these unspoken assumptions, using AGR means risking a return to an essentialist understanding of sexuality, and gender as a stabile, fixed, core identity, thereby taking away a person's ability to self-identify. By virtue of its design, which associates certain markers with specific genders, it also carries the risk of re-igniting stereotypes associated with a certain gender or sexuality. Transgender individuals report overwhelmingly negative attitudes towards AGR, bringing into question whether it is possible at all to capture a subjective identity through this technology (Hamidi, 2018; Keyes et al., 2021; Tomasev et al., 2021). We suggest that stereotypical notions, like those on which AGR is based, may have implications for all gender identities, including cisgendered, that in any way differ from normative performances of the gender assigned at birth.

Whether FA could be used to detect a person's sexuality and/or gender identity is in itself a controversial question; additional questions arise about what it would mean to make such measurements and for what purpose such information would be used. In a highly criticized study (Wang and Kosinski, 2018), researchers claimed that FA was more accurate than humans at detecting sexual orientation from facial images. This line of research ignited a vigorous academic and social debate about the ethics of social media data use (Zook et al., 2017) and the merits of "sexual-orientation detection" research (Mattson, 2017), and it was strongly suggested that those findings were more related to patterns in grooming and photographic presentation rather than innate characteristics (Agüera y Arcas, 2018). Studies such as this one lead to questions about whether images posted in (and intended for) specific contexts can be ripped from such contexts and legitimately used for other purposes. The "gender orientation detection" study used a training dataset of images obtained from online dating websites, which raises questions both about the research ethics of using this kind of data and about how much the accuracy of the system depends on presentations chosen specifically for the dating context. Although the authors claimed to have validated their system with images obtained from Facebook (checking its accuracy by comparing the prediction of the system with the labels presented on Facebook), such images were validated for individuals who publicly self-report sexual orientation on the social media website. The very idea that there is a direct link between whatever individuals are looking for online (from a date to cat pictures) and a gay/lesbian/straight label denoting the sexual orientation of another individual conveys a pervasive problem in machine learning systems: the tracing of a strict categorical line between something that is a fluid combination of sex, gender, sexual preference and contextual presentation (Gelman et al., 2018). Critics of this study raised a fundamental point: whether this system works or not, it can be used to generate fear in queer communities and bring up concerns about coercion and control. This issue is directly related to the developers' choice(s) of labels (gay/lesbian/straight), which places the responsibility for potentially dangerous consequences directly on the humans who made the technology rather than on the technology itself.

Bias and Representation

Another source of potential concern is racial and gender bias in relation to the classification of gender by FA (see, e.g., Scheuerman et al., 2019; Ashwin et al., 2021). The cultural data and environments used for training and categorizing data are not representative of all contexts, neither from a global nor a societal perspective. For example, in most parts of the world, more men than women are online. If a system evaluating behaviour has been trained mainly on data from men – on how these men act online, on their interactions and activities – the system would not necessarily accurately interpret the behaviour of women. A similar risk applies to other underrepresented communities (Sambasivan & Holbrock, 2018; Sweeney, 2016). Ashwin et al. (2021) noted that researchers, corporations and governments have long and painful histories of excluding marginalized groups, such as LGBTQI+ people, from technology development, deployment and oversight. Thus, there is no reason to believe that the data on which FA systems would operate would include queer fluid identities.

The significance of cultural and social contexts in the design and implementation of technologies has been widely addressed in previous research in relation to communication (e.g., Douglas, 1987), embedded values (e.g., Nissenbaum, 2001) or categorizations (Powell & Aitken, 2011). From the perspective of the digital humanities, authors such as Alan Liu (2012) and Tara McPherson (2012) have acknowledged the heterogeneity of contexts and of users of technologies and urged digital humanities scholars to engage in cultural critique. The importance of critical approaches more specific to AI technologies has also been emphasized in relation to marginalized groups, to "better align research and technology development with established ethical principles, centring vulnerable peoples who continue to bear the brunt of negative impacts of innovation and scientific progress" (Mohamed et al., 2020, p. 5).

When it comes to machine learning technology, a frequent source of social concern is that of undesired bias, which can appear in many forms, from the omission of key characteristics that affect the outcome of a system to algorithmic bias that does not reflect relations in the input data (Mehrabi et al., 2021). Undesired bias is of particular concern when it results in disparate treatment of minorities. One example is COMPAS, a system that had been designed to predict criminal recidivism in the US. COMPAS has been shown to have a much larger false positive rate for African American offenders and has consequently been the subject of social and media scrutiny (Dressel & Farid, 2018). FA has not been shown to perform particularly better: a comprehensive analysis of FA gender classification systems by Buolamwini and Gebru (2018) showed that darker-skinned females are disproportionately gender-misclassified when facial analysis benchmarks are mainly composed of lighter-skinned subjects. Indeed, the introduction of bias in machine learning can stem from the datasets used for training and validations as well as from the algorithms themselves. Problems can arise from a lack of representation of certain segments of the population, but also from the choice of measurement for a feature, the choice of which features are included and other sources of statistical error (Mehrabi et al., 2021). However, the data needed to address these problems from a queer perspective might be hard to obtain: information on gender identity and sexuality is not always safe to provide, and consensually obtained self-identification data may only capture a specific fraction of the community (Tomasev et al., 2021). In a study by Scheuerman et al. (2019), researchers were unable to determine why services assigned the labels they did to any given image but argued that

> when labels are gendered, it can be assumed that those annotations are based on cultural gender norms… [f]or example, that women wear makeup and men do not. Connections like this may be responsible for the labels assigned to an image of a #transman with long wavy hair, winged eyeliner, and red lipstick: Microsoft labelled this image with "*woman*" and Google with "*lady*". (Scheuerman et al., 2019, p. 17; italics in original)

From a queer perspective, we understand that systems based on cultural gender norms are limited, exclusive and possibly harmful, not only for marginalized groups but for anyone who is part of a developing society.

Privacy and Surveillance

The increasing implementation of FA also raises issues of privacy and surveillance. In this chapter, we define "privacy" as informational privacy – that is, through a social lens, in the context of individual versus group expectations, rather than from a legal model of privacy (Curzon et al., 2021). A key contextual element in the understanding of the use of FA is surveillance culture (Lyon, 2018a). Surveillance is not merely something that is imposed upon us by states and authorities, it also is something that we users do, submit to and participate in when choosing to use various technologies. Our compliance with surveillance culture can be illustrated by our everyday practices, for instance, the use of platforms where we share personal information, geographical position, photos and so on. With "the broader mobility of capital, the flexibility of work and the digital information infrastructures" (Lyon, 2018b, p. 6), surveillance has become increasingly fluid (cf. Bauman, 2000).

The internet has afforded new spaces for LGBTQI+ individuals to meet others for support, community building, dating, activism and so forth (Guyan, 2022; Liliequist, 2020). At the same time, getting access to commercial spaces means users giving companies permission to access behavioural data from their online activity, a form of surveillance and business model that "has proven extremely lucrative for companies such as Google and Facebook but has involved users being kept in the dark about the data collected or the full extent of its use" (Guyan, 2022, p. 42). From the point of view of informational privacy, a potential risk with any such system that encompasses so much (voluntarily disclosed) information is that it can combine seemingly unrelated attributes and turn them into identifiers (Curzon et al., 2021).

Blenner et al. (2016) conducted a comprehensive study of 211 Android-based diabetes apps, noting that as many as 81% did not have privacy policies. Zuboff (2019) explained that when designing technology for health, the previous view of respecting and valuing the user's integrity, experience and sense of self has recently transformed into viewing users as data objects, where forms of measurement focus more on collecting (additional) data than on respecting the user's privacy. The Blenner et al. study is only one example of the trend noted by Zuboff, that surveillance capitalism can be identified as a driving force in the emergence of surveillance culture (Zuboff, 2019). Platforms have become rich by selling our data, data that we willingly share. The economic dimension of surveillance culture can be seen as one *raison d'être* of surveillance. But data is not reality, it is only a record consisting of information that we used for various purposes. If queer data is handled correctly, it can strengthen and enable LGBTQI+ people to live authentic lives (Guyan, 2022).

When tracing the history of datasets for FA, Steven and Keyes (2021) and Raji and Fried (2021) noted a shift in the provenance of images as datasets increase. In the early history of FA, developers used datasets that subjects had expressly consented to appear in; recently, there has been a move to using images of arrestees and obtaining images from the web or security surveillance footage. While a larger amount and variety of images allows for a greater diversity of subjects (Raji & Fried, 2021), the use of such images implies a loss of individual control, where someone's face may be used in a dataset without their knowledge or consent (Paullada et al., 2021). In parallel, Steven and Keyes (2021) noted an evolution towards avoiding the personal involvement of the subjects of the images in the labelling process, instead using whatever model of automated or outsourced labelling is current. This change often results in widely used datasets containing offensive categories and labels (Crawford & Paglen, 2021) and a further loss of control and privacy because of the lack of consent about which labels and categories are used to identify images. The removal of the subject from the use and categorization of their own information is especially concerning for marginalized communities, who are already prone to invasions of privacy and weaponization of their private information (Linabary & Corple, 2019).

Sambasivan and Holbrook (2018) also stressed privacy needs. When including data from less-represented groups or minorities during algorithm training, respect must be taken throughout the data-collection process, since there is a potential risk of algorithmic manipulation. And, because the attributable content collected can harm the individuals if it falls into the wrong hands (Sambasivan & Holbrook, 2018). FA poses risks towards the privacy of individuals, which for marginalized groups like LGBTQI+ people could put individuals at serious risk if they were to be outed in contexts where queer identities can result in punishment.

WAYS FORWARD

The above criticisms of AI and FA and the use and misuse of technology came from the multidisciplinary perspectives of social science, science and technology and the humanities. A queer theory perspective further highlighted specific risks and concerns. Proposals for the inclusive design and implementation of AI systems have engaged with these criticisms, tackling issues such as bias, under-representation and the study of algorithmic harms. This next section shows how casting a critical queer eye can shed light on improvement and inclusion. Here, we will focus on methods and technologies that engage with the identified weaknesses of AI and FA, keeping a queer eye on the remaining challenges. We discuss these issues in relation to three dilemmas: analysing AI (fairness and explainability), designing AI (participation and exploitation) and using AI (exploring the potential). Throughout, we acknowledge that the goal is not to retain exclusionary and harmful systems and simply attempt to patch them up, but rather to create new technology that serves all.

Fairness and Explainability

Commonly, bias in AI systems is argued to be related to the data used to train and validate those systems: if the data reflect a certain population or has undesirable correlations, these biases will be perpetuated in the predictions of the model. However, bias might also lie in the structure of the model or in the process that connects the model's predictions to an empirical sample. The choice of model, the weight carried by certain features or the reinforcement loop can all result in undesired biases in an algorithm. Thus, to avoid or "fix" undesired bias, the challenge starts with revealing the undesired bias and understanding its provenance.

Griffiths (2018) argued that analysing data structures might reveal latent bias, and we know that visualization and close reading of source code can be used to critically examine AI. The field of explainable AI suggests that interpretability and transparency can play a significant role in identifying and reducing undesired biases in intelligent systems (Malhi et al., 2020; Begley et al., 2020). At the same time, researchers in the nascent field of fairness in machine learning have developed a variety of measures of bias and unfairness in machine learning models (Corbett-Davies & Goel, 2018) as well as methodologies to decrease these unwanted qualities at various stages of the development process (Friedler et al., 2019). Of course, focusing only on data and models evades the wider issue of the systematic imbalances that bring about biased technology in the first place. Ciston (2019) argued that to address issues of power and unfairness, we must apply a meta-ethics of multiplicity and intersubjective relation. The act of collecting data and generating systems itself embeds power structures and ideologies into the system from the start. For that treason, Hayes (2020) argued that we need to address these issues as early in the process as possible, preferably as soon as the formulation of the research question itself or when motivating a design. Similarly, Leavy et al. (2020) posited that incorporating critical perspectives such as queer is essential for a more comprehensive perspective on power and bias. And Tomasev et al. (2021) noted that queer perspectives are largely absent in the study of algorithmic fairness. Many techniques to mitigate bias assume that the characteristics that influence harmful outcomes can be accessed or deduced, and thus, casting a queer eye in this context means developing fundamentally new knowledge that interrogates the appropriateness of data collection and intelligent system deployment in the first place, and reduces bias without relying on knowing sensitive characteristics that further label individuals and can place them at risk. Rather than leaning on repetitions of expected behaviour, expression, appearance and desire in accordance with societal norms in a specific cultural context, we can instead work with the concept of performativity and the understanding of sexuality and gender as ongoing performances.

Participation and Risk for Exploitation

One suggestion for how to improve AI systems is to make the design process participatory, collaborative and intersectional (Sambasivan & Holbrook, 2018; Ciston, 2019). The argument is that there is a positive correspondence between a focus on user needs and successful designs of technologies. User involvement creates awareness of power, uncovers alternative ethics and identifies issues of representation, enabling different users to be heard – in this case, enabling users to place trust in the FA system designed. However, technology is biased and always designed for a certain purpose, context and use (Bratteteig, 2004). The designer decides for whom the technology is made and where the consequences lie (Danielsson, 2010; Bratteteig & Wagner, 2012; Dignum, 2019). Participatory design (PD), an approach that originates from critical theory, harmonizes well with queered theories, since queer theory also identifies resistance to and rejection of dominant assumptions about identity and relationships, what it is to be human and the heterosexual matrix (McWilliams, 2016). Queer theory supports the critical practice within PD.

To enable diversity and inclusion during the development and implementation of FA, and to create trustworthy AI, we need to empower grassroots organizations, for example, LGBTQI+ communities, to contribute, educate, inform and participate during design (Ashwin et al., 2021; Ciston, 2019; McWilliams, 2016). However, solving the problems of risks and consequences, and a lack of trust and representation, by involving organizations and volunteers, might not be as empowering as expected, nor have the desired outcome of better design decisions. Non-profit organizations are often exhausted by using their time and expertise on short-term design volunteer processes (Stoecker & Tyron, 2009; Hayes, 2020). Moreover, designers must be willing to express, acknowledge and question their own assumptions, prejudices, privileges and power, which can be quite challenging (Bratteteig & Wagner, 2012; Danielsson, 2010; Hayes 2020). Finally, if users are participating in design, it requires that they have access to relevant information, the opportunity to take an independent position in relation to identified problems and the ability and knowledge needed to make design decisions (Kensing, 1983).

Thus, when designing FA, it is crucial that users participating in design know what AI can and cannot do (Bratteteig & Verne, 2018). Even if we understand what AI *can* do, at least in principle, it is difficult to imagine or foresee what it *will* do in the future (Holmquist, 2017), which challenges the role(s) that users can have and the level of informed design decisions they can make. Their understanding depends upon possible unpredictable developments, based on the data used to train the AI (Bratteteig & Verne, 2018). Having engaged partnerships in design requires multidisciplinary partnerships, where we "truly consider the values, experiences, and goals of everyone impacted as early in the design project as possible" (Hayes, 2020, p. 28).

Guyan (2022) pointed out that studies based on queer data have not always been conducted with the intent to make society more inclusive or improve LGBTQI+ life conditions; rather, the data has often been used to strengthen normative structures. We argue that it is important to include representatives from the LGBTQI+ community and clearly express what role and power they have during design. Otherwise, we risk the exploitation of LGBTQI+ representatives and "pink washing" the design (Drissi, 2019). Such an approach also requires designers to participate in the contexts and communities they are designing for, since "attentiveness requires both contextual and historical awareness because the social impacts, whether positive or negative, are shaped by the spaces in which AI is deployed" (Keyes et al., 2021, p. 159).

Exploring the Potential

A queer perspective on the design and usage of FA creates new ways to explore and relate to the technology. Baeza Argüello et al. (2021) explored the potential of FA by considering it as a resource for expressing digital identities rather than as threatening the freedom of expression or identity. By wearing prostheses created from the moulds of volunteer faces of trans and non-binary participants, FA was explored as a drag, queer and trans technology design tool, thereby appropriating a technology designed for facial recognition and using it as a way to express identity. By creating several hybrid identities, people can, on a daily basis, select their own self-representation. The idea is particularly interesting since it shows an entanglement between human identity, self-presentation and computation in relation to privacy – here, the human chooses what to disclose to systems that are designed to collect facial information.

CONCLUSIONS

As previously mentioned, AI and FA are nearly ubiquitous, and it is becoming more common to replace human-based decisions with algorithmic calculations and evaluations. Therefore, a critical examination and discussion of the implications of FA is important because the technology is being used in an increased number of domains in private life. It is crucial that AI becomes inclusive by basing its functional capacity on data that reflects the society in which it is meant to operate. We argue in particular, the need for further studies on AI that apply queer theory, and for the inclusion of queer perspectives when developing and implementing AI technology. As this anthology shows, there are many reasons for discussing and considering how AI develops, and where and for what it is used now and may be in the future.

In this chapter, we have highlighted potential problems and risks with FA regarding issues like privacy, bias and fairness, and we have discussed how accepting the binary logic of FA systems risks reinforcing essentialist ideas and notions about sexuality and gender identity as binary and non-fluid. Within the acronym of LGBTQI+ lies a myriad of temporary or recurring desires and identities, whose meanings and definitions can also change over time and across different cultures. We argue that in addition to the problematic aspects of implementing FA for detecting gender identity and/or sexuality, binary systems can never fully capture the fluid reality of human identity, as all identities are social constructs performed and created in temporal and spatial contexts. Thus, to be truly human-centred, we must reflect on these issues during the design, implementation and use of technology as a matter of care (Croon, 2022). Using queer theory, we have presented three dilemmas that we argue are essential if we want to strive towards building AI that respects basic human rights with a foundation of care.

REFERENCES

Agüera y Arcas, 2018; "Do algorithms reveal sexual orientation or just expose our stereotypes?". Medium.   https://medium.com/@blaisea/do-algorithms-reveal-sexual-orientation-or-just-expose-our-stereotypes-d998fafdf477 Retrieved 2023-07-24.

Ashwin, Agnew, W., Pajaro, U., Jethwani, H., & Subramonian, A. (2021). Rebuilding Trust: Queer in AI Approach to Artificial Intelligence Risk Management. arXiv preprint arXiv:2110.09271.

Baeza Argüello, S., Wakkary, R., Andersen, K., & Tomico, O. (2021). Exploring the Potential of Apple Face ID as a Drag, Queer and Trans Technology Design Tool. In *Designing Interactive Systems Conference 2021* (1654–1667). https://doi.org/10.1145/3461778.3461999

Bailey, M. (2011). All the Digital Humanists Are White, All the Nerds Are Men, But Some of Us Are Brave. *Journal of Digital Humanities*, *1*(1). https://doi.org/10.2307/j.ctvs32szz.6

Bauman, Z. (2000). *Liquid Modernity*. Cambridge: Polity.

Begley, T., Schwedes, T., Frye, C., & Feige, I. (2020). Explainability for Fair Machine Learning. arXiv preprint arXiv:2010.07389.

Blenner, S. R., Köllmer, M., Rouse, A. J., Daneshvar, N., Williams, C., & Andrews, L. B. (2016). Privacy Policies of Android Diabetes Apps and Sharing of Health Information. *JAMA*, *315*(10), 1051–1052. https://doi.org/10.1001/jama.2015.19426

Bratteteig, T. (2004). *Making Change. Dealing with Relations Between Design and Use*. Dr. Philos dissertation, Department of Informatics, University of Oslo.

Bratteteig, T., & Wagner, I. (2012). Disentangling Power and Decision-making in Participatory Design. In *Proceedings of the 12th Participatory Design Conference: Research Papers-Volume 1* (41–50). https://doi.org/10.1145/2347635.2347642

Bratteteig &Verne, 2018; Bratteteig, T., & Verne, G. (2018). Does AI make PD obsolete? exploring challenges from artificial intelligence to participatory design. In *Proceedings of the 15th Participatory Design Conference: Short Papers, Situated Actions, Workshops and Tutorial-Volume 2* (pp. 1–5).

Buolamwini, J., & Gebru, T. (2018). Gender Shades: Intersectional Accuracy Disparities in Commercial Gender Classification. In *Proceedings of the 1st Conference on Fairness, Accountability and Transparency*, in *Proceedings of Machine Learning Research*, *81*, 77–91.

Butler, J. (1990). *Gender Trouble: Feminism and the Subversion of Identity*. Routledge. https://doi.org/10.4324/9780203824979

Butler, J. (1993). *Bodies that Matter: On the Discursive Limits of Sex*. Routledge.

Castelvecci, D. (2020). Is Facial Recognition Too Biased to Be Let Loose? *Nature*. https://www.nature.com/articles/d41586-020-03186-4 (2022-05-13) https://doi.org/10.1038/d41586-020-03186-4

Ciston, S. (2019). Imagining Intersectional AI. *xCoAx*, 39.

Corbett-Davies, S., & Goel, S. (2018). The Measure and Mismeasure of Fairness: A Critical Review of Fair Machine Learning. arXiv preprint arXiv:1808.00023.

Crawford & Paglen, 2021; Crawford, K., & Paglen, T. (2021). Excavating AI: The politics of images in machine learning training sets. *AI & Society*, *36*(4), 1105–1116.

Croon, A. (2022). Thinking with Care in Human–Computer Interaction. *Feminist Theory*. https://doi.org/10.1177/14647001221082294

Curzon, J., Kosa, T. A., Akalu, R., & El-Khatib, K. (2021). Privacy and Artificial Intelligence. *IEEE Transactions on Artificial Intelligence*, *2*(2), 96–108.

CV Dazzle. (2020). Computer Vision Dazzle Camouflage. https://cvdazzle.com (2022-05-13)

Danielsson Öberg, K. (2010). *Att främja medverkan: Utmaningar och möjligheter för barns och ungdomars delaktighet vid design av digitala edutainmentproduktioner*. Dr. Philos dissertation, Department of Informatics, Umeå University.

DeVito et al., 2018; DeVito, M. A., Birnholtz, J., Hancock, J. T., French, M., & Liu, S. (2018). How people form folk theories of social media feeds and what it means for how we study self-presentation. In *Proceedings of the 2018 CHI conference on human factors in computing systems* (pp. 1–12).

Dignum, V. (2019). *Responsible Artificial Intelligence: How to Develop and Use AI in a Responsible Way*. Springer Nature. https://doi.org/10.1007/978-3-030-30371-6

Douglas, S. J. (1987). *Inventing American Broadcasting, 1899–1922*. Johns Hopkins University Press.

Dressel, J., & Farid, H. (2018). The Accuracy, Fairness, and Limits of Predicting Recidivism. *Science Advances*, *4*(1), eaao5580. https://doi.org/10.1126/sciadv.aao5580

Drissi, R. (2019). Three Ways Tech Companies Can Avoid Pinkwashing For Pride Next Year. Tech. https://tech.co/news/tech-companies-pride-pinkwashing-2019-07 (2022-05-15)

Dubhashi, D., & Lappin, S. (2017). AI Dangers: Imagined and Real. *Communications of the ACM*, *60*(2), 43–45. https://doi.org/10.1145/2953876

Friedler, S. A., Scheidegger, C., Venkatasubramanian, S., Choudhary, S., Hamilton, E. P., & Roth, D. (2019, January). A Comparative Study of Fairness-enhancing Interventions in Machine Learning. In *Proceedings of the Conference on Fairness, Accountability, and Transparency* (329–338). https://doi.org/10.1145/3287560.3287589

Gelman, A., Mattson, G., & Simpson, D. (2018). Gaydar and the Fallacy of Decontextualized Measurement. *Sociological Science, 5*(12), 270–280. https://doi.org/10.15195/v5.a12.

Griffiths, C. (2018). Visual Tactics Toward an Ethical Debugging. *Digital Culture & Society, 4*(1), 217–226. https://doi.org/10.14361/dcs-2018-0113

Guyan, K. (2022). *Queer Data: Using Gender, Sex and Sexuality Data for Action.* Bloomsbury Publishing Plc.

Hamidi, F., Scheuerman, M. K., & Branham, S. M. (2018). Gender Recognition or Gender Reductionism? The Social Implications of Embedded Gender Recognition Systems. In *Proceedings of the 2018 CHI Conference on Human Factors in Computing Systems.* Association for Computing Machinery, New York, NY, USA, Paper 8, 1–13. https://doi.org/10.1145/3173574.3173582

Hayes, G. R. (2020). Inclusive and Engaged HCI. *Interactions, 27*(2), 26–31. https://doi.org/10.1145/3378561

Holmquist, 2017; Holmquist, L. E. (2017). Intelligence on tap: artificial intelligence as a new design material. *interactions, 24*(4), 28–33.

Jain, A. K., & Li, S. Z. (2011). *Handbook of face recognition* (Vol. 1, p. 699). New York: Springer.

Kensing, F. (1983). The Trade Unions Influence on Technological Change. In: Briefs. (1983). *Systems design for, with, and by the users: Proceedings of the IFIP WG 9.1 Working Conference on Systems Design for, with and by the Users*, Riva del Sole, Italy, 20-24 September, 1982. North-Holland.

Keyes, O., Hitzig, Z., & Blell, M. (2021). Truth from the Machine: Artificial Intelligence and the Materialization of Identity. *Interdisciplinary Science Reviews, 46*(1–2), 158–175. https://doi.org/10.1080/03080188.2020.1840224

Leavy, S., O'Sullivan, B., & Siapera, E. (2020). Data, Power and Bias in Artificial Intelligence. arXiv preprint arXiv:2008.07341.

Liliequist, E. (2020). *Digitala förbindelser: rum, riktning och queera orienteringar* (in Swedish) [Digital Connections: Space, Bearings and Queer Orientations.] Diss. Institutionen för kultur- och medievetenskaper, Umeå universitet.

Linabary, J. R., & Corple, D. J. (2019). Privacy for whom?: A feminist intervention in online research practice. *Information, Communication & Society, 22*(10), 1447–1463.

Liu, A. (2012). Where is Cultural Criticism in the Digital Humanities? In M. K. Gold (Ed.), *Debates in the Digital Humanities* (490–509). University of Minnesota Press. https://doi.org/10.5749/minnesota/9780816677948.003.0049

Lyon, D. (2018a). *The Culture of Surveillance: Watching as a Way of Life.* Polity Press.

Lyon, D. (2018b). Exploring Surveillance Culture. *On_Culture: The Open Journal for the Study of Culture, 6.* https://doi.org/10.22029/oc.2018.1151

Malhi, A., Knapic, S., & Främling, K. (2020). Explainable Agents for Less Bias in Human-Agent Decision Making. In D. Calvaresi, A. Najjar, M. Winikoff, & K. Främling (Eds.), *Explainable, Transparent Autonomous Agents and Multi-Agent Systems.* EXTRAAMAS 2020. Lecture Notes in Computer Science, vol 12175. Springer, Cham. https://doi.org/10.1007/978-3-030-51924-7_8

Marwick, A. E., & boyd, d. (2014). Networked Privacy: How Teenagers Negotiate Context in Social Media. *New Media & Society, 16*(7), 1051–1067. https://doi.org/10.1177/1461444814543995

Mattson, G. (2017). Artificial intelligence discovers gayface. Sigh. *Greggor Mattson Blog.* https://greggormattson.com/2017/09/09/artificial-intelligence-discovers-gayface.

McPherson, T. (2012). Why are the Digital Humanities So White? Or Thinking the Histories of Race and Computation. In M. K. Gold (Ed.), *Debates in the Digital Humanities* (139–160). University of Minnesota Press. https://doi.org/10.5749/minnesota/9780816677948.003.0017

McWilliams, J. (Jenna). (2016). Queering Participatory Design Research. *Cognition and Instruction, 34*(3), 259–274. https://doi.org/10.1080/07370008.2016.1172436

Mehrabi, N., Morstatter, F., Saxena, N., Lerman, K., & Galstyan, A. (2021). A survey on bias and fairness in machine learning. *ACM computing surveys* (CSUR), *54*(6), 1–35.

Mohamed, S., Png, M. T., & Isaac, W. (2015). Decolonial AI: Decolonial Theory as Sociotechnical Foresight in Artificial Intelligence. *Philosophy and Technology* (405). https://doi.org/10.1007/s13347-020-00405-8

Mohamed, Png, M.-T., & Isaac, W. (2020). Decolonial AI: Decolonial Theory as Sociotechnical Foresight in Artificial Intelligence. *Philosophy & Technology*, *33*(4), 659–684. https://doi.org/10.1007/s13347-020-00405-8.

Nissenbaum, H. (2001). How Computer Systems Embody Values. *Computer*, *34*(3), 118–120. https://doi.org/10.1109/2.910905

Norén, A. (2021). Polisens nya vapen: Ansiktsigenkänning (The new police weapon: FA). SVT, Swedish Television. https://www.svt.se/nyheter/inrikes/polisens-nya-vapen-ansiktsigenkanning (2022-05-13)

Paullada et al., 2021; Paullada, A., Raji, I. D., Bender, E. M., Denton, E., & Hanna, A. (2021). Data and its (dis) contents: A survey of dataset development and use in machine learning research. *Patterns*, 2(11).

Phillips, D. (2002). Negotiating the Digital Closet: Online Pseudonymity and the Politics of Sexual Identity. *Information, Communication & Society*, *5*(3), 406–424. https://doi.org/10.1080/13691180210159337

Powell, T., & Aitken, L. (2011). Encoding Culture: Building a Digital Archive Based on Traditional Ojibwe Teachings. In: *The American Literature Scholar in the Digital Age* (Ed. Amy Earhart and Andrew Jewell, pp. 250–274). Ann Arbor: University of Michigan Press.

Raji, I. D., & Fried, G. (2021). About face: A survey of facial recognition evaluation. *arXiv preprint arXiv:2102.00813*.

Reid, D. A., Nixon, M. S., & Stevenage, S. V. (2013). Soft biometrics; human identification using comparative descriptions. *IEEE Transactions on pattern analysis and machine intelligence*, *36*(6), 1216–1228.

Sambasivan &Holbrock, 2019; Sambasivan, N., & Holbrook, J. (2018). Toward responsible AI for the next billion users. *Interactions*, *26*(1), 68–71.

Sambasivan, N., & Holbrook, J. S. (2019). Towards Equitable AI for the Next Billion Users. *ACM interactions*, *26*(1), 68–71. https://doi.org/10.1145/3298735

Scheuerman, M. K., Paul, J. M., & Brubaker, J. R. (2019). How Computers See Gender: An Evaluation of Gender Classification in Commercial Facial Analysis and Image Labeling Services. *Proceedings of the ACM on Human-Computer Interaction*, *3*. https://doi.org/10.1145/3359246

Sedgwick, 1990 - Sedgwick, Eve Kosofsky, 1991. *Epistemology of the closet*. New York: Harvester Wheatsheaf.

Sedgwick, E. (1991). *Epistemology of the Closet*. Harvester Wheatsheaf.

Shapiro, S. (1998). Places and Spaces: The Historical Interaction of Technology, Home, and Privacy. *The Information Society*, *14*(4), 275–284. https://doi.org/10.1080/019722498128728

Shapiro, A.-A., & Bacchi, U. (2020). U.S. Protests Fuel Calls for Ban on Racially Biased Facial Recognition Tools. *Reuters*. https://www.reuters.com/article/us-usa-protests-tech-trfn-idUSKBN23B3B5 (2022-05-13)

Shalloe, H. (2019). I Sexually Identify as an Attack Helicopter. *Transgender Studies Quarterly*, *6*(4), 667–675. https://doi.org/10.1215/23289252-7771824

Sparks, H. (2019). FaceApp Security Concerns: Russians Now Own All Your Old Photos. *New York Post*. https://nypost.com/2019/07/17/faceapp-security-concerns-russians-now-own-all-your-old-photos/ (2022-05-13)

Steven and Keyes (2021) Stevens, N., & Keyes, O. (2021). Seeing infrastructure: race, facial recognition and the politics of data. *Cultural Studies*, *35*(4-5), 833–853.

Stoecker, R., & Tryon, E. A. (Eds.). (2009). *The Unheard Voices: Community Organizations and Service Learning*. Temple University Press.

Svensson, H. (2019). Böter för ansiktsigenkänning på Skellefteå-skola (Fine for FA at a Swedish school). SVT, Swedish Television. https://www.svt.se/nyheter/lokalt/vasterbotten/boter-for-ansiktsigenkanning-pa-skelleftea-skola (2022-05-13)

Sweeney, M. E. (2016). The Intersectional Interface. In *The Intersectional Internet: Race, Sex, Class and Culture Online* (215–228). Digital Formations, Vol. 105. Peter Lang Publishing, Inc.

Tomasev, N., McKee, K. R., Kay, J., & Mohamed, S. (2021). Fairness for Unobserved Characteristics: Insights from Technological Impacts on Queer Communities. In *Proceedings of the 2021 AAAI/ACM Conference on AI, Ethics, and Society* (254–265). https://doi.org/10.1145/3461702.3462540

Wang, Y., & Kosinski, M. (2018). Deep neural networks are more accurate than humans at detecting sexual orientation from facial images. *Journal of Personality and Social Psychology*, *114*(2), 246–257. https://doi.org/10.1037/pspa0000098.

Zook M, Barocas S, boyd d, Crawford K, Keller E, Gangadharan SP, et al. (2017) Ten simple rules for responsible big data research. *PLoS Comput Biol 13*(3): e1005399. https://doi.org/10.1371/journal.pcbi.1005399.

Zuboff, S. (2019). *The Age of Surveillance Capitalism: The Fight for a Human Future at the New Frontier of Power*. Public Affairs.

53. Representational silence and racial biases in commercial image recognition services in the context of religion

Anton Berg and Katja Valaskivi

INTRODUCTION

In a media-saturated society, meaning-making and the technologies conditioning signifying practices are thoroughly intertwined. Concepts like "affordances" from internet and social media studies have shown how social practices and technologies influence each other. Bruno Latour's actor–network theory (ANT) suggests that non-human objects and systems play significant roles in shaping the social fabric and interaction.

Our contribution to the discussion on the relationship between meaning-making and image recognition occurs at the intersection of computational social science, religious studies, and the integration of qualitative representation analysis into critical AI studies. While critical theory has often overlooked religion, and research on AI and religion has been limited, there are compelling reasons to explore this domain, particularly in the context of image recognition services. Religion, with its recognisable symbols, attire, rituals, and practices, can serve as an efficient classification attribute for modern machine vision systems.

The relevance of religion in the context of machine vision is also evident in the use of facial recognition systems in some Christian churches in the United States and Brazil, as well as for monitoring and profiling ethnic and religious groups worldwide, leading to potential discrimination (see, e.g. Dallas, 2019; Garcia, 2021; Glick & Lee, 2022). Notably, China has used facial recognition technology to violate the human rights of its indigenous Uyghur population (Berg, 2021; Feldstein, 2021).

This chapter's empirical focus is on the commercial image recognition services offered by the world's largest technology companies, including Google, Microsoft, and Amazon, specifically how they recognise and classify images at the intersection of religion, race, and gender. Due to the secretive nature of these systems, understanding their functioning is challenging, making a qualitative explorative study of the results the most viable approach. Accordingly, such an approach is adopted in this chapter to shed light on this complex and critical topic.

In the following, we will first provide some background on cultural studies perspectives, mostly relating to racism studies and their relevance to our study. We will then discuss perceptions of critical AI studies and previous research on "AI bias". After describing how we use the concept of religion, we will continue to the empirical part of the chapter and discuss our data, method, analysis, and findings. The chapter will conclude with a discussion of the implications of our findings.

Cultural Studies, Racism(s), and Technology

In a world saturated by media, collective perceptions of the world are imagined through various "systems of representation" (Hall, 1997) embedded in media technologies, related techno-social practices, and economic settings. These systems of representation can be understood as ways in which shared perceptions, or social imaginaries (Taylor, 2002), are formed, circulated, and sustained. Media technologies are central not only to the power at play in meaning-making and sustaining social imaginaries but they also shape and condition the social practices through which the meanings are produced. Stuart Hall focused on the global mechanisms and practices of *racisms* (Hall, 1992). He used the plural form because, in each society, racism has a specific and particular history with unique manifestations and dynamics. Subsequently, cultural studies research has examined the various ways in which race, gender, and ethnicity are represented in different media forms and social contexts, as well as how racism is manifested in meaning-making processes, and how the deep historical traces of colonialism appear in Western culture (e.g. Delgado & Stefancic, 2001, 2017; Lentin & Titley, 2011; Lopez, 2020; Leonard & Robbins, 2020).

In other words, race is also constructed and mediated in the media and through communication technologies. Media research has demonstrated the various ways in which racism appears in different media forms and genres reproducing ideas of foreign cultures and peoples as less civilised and inferior because of their their race, colour of skin, religion or culture (Hall, 1992; Porter, 2001; Smith 2013; Ylikoski & Kokkonen, 2009). These racist representations and practices continue to appear and multiply in contemporary media technologies. An example of this is the infamous 2015 case of the Google image recognition service categorizing black individuals as "gorillas".[1]

One of Hall's (1992) important conceptualisations is "silence", which he described as something invisible that "could not be framed" and is "apparently unspeakable". Hall also made a crucial methodological point by claiming that if someone wants to ask "what can content analysis teach you?", one needs to ask "what about people who don't seem to have any content at all?" This point appears particularly relevant when examining commercial image recognition services in the context of religion, race, and gender. Regarding the racist and stereotypical classifications produced by image recognition technologies, one of the common features is the absence of a diverse representational conceptual space for Black people.

The Discussion on AI Bias

Since the early days of machine learning and computer vision in the 1960s and 1970s, ethical issues have been considered, speculated on, and evaluated. AI researcher Brian Christian (2020) aptly stated that the history of AI often appears to us as "cycles of hope and

---

[1]   https://www.bbc.com/news/technology-33347866.

gloom". In later debates, utopian and dystopian perceptions on AI continue, and proponents of each side accuse the other of intellectual blindness — an inability to see either the "light of progress" or the "darkness" it brings. Techno-pessimists have a critical attitude towards the promises of a brave new world brought about by technological development, and they typically refuse to link the technological developments of a civilization to its ethical developments (e.g. Gray, 2004).

Thus, techno-pessimists are often seen as prophets of doom, whose critical sermons are hard to heed in a world where technological advances are producing many good outcomes, saving both time and lives (e.g. Pinker, 2019). On the other side of the debate are techno-optimists, who believe in innovation and progress, both technological and ethical. Their dogmas of "technologism" and "innovationism" suggest that sustainability, growth, and making profit are simultaneously possible (Valaskivi, 2012, 2020). In their view, technology is a neutral and unbiased actor. Techno-optimists see technological and ethical development as having linear trajectories and often relate this to a historical continuum, referring to the Enlightenment (Pinker, 2019). Their fantasy is a dream world built of silicon, where technology and science, as instrumental, objective, and neutral guiding forces, are sufficient in themselves to produce positive change through immediate, unstoppable, ex-machina-style development (Gray, 2004; Feenberg, 2012).

However, some researchers refuse to settle for a fixed ontology of technology. Rather, they take a pragmatic approach to emerging technologies and their potential to solve social and societal problems, considering one technology and one case at a time.

Nevertheless, the rapidly growing body of critical research on the ethics and digital harms of AI has highlighted, among other things, many hidden problems associated with machine vision and image recognition. Recent research has conceptualised these issues by emphasising how modern technological systems are involved in the reflection and reproduction of existing *biases* in the societies they are intended to refine (Christian, 2020; Crawford, 2021).

In this context, bias emerges as the central framework for discussing digital harms within critical AI and technology studies. These studies have consistently demonstrated how modern technologies do reinforce inequalities based on, for example, race, gender, sexual orientation, and class (Buolamwini & Gebru, 2018; Eubanks, 2018; Kosinski, 2021; Wang & Kosinski, 2019). Notably, some of this research has specifically considered systemic biases (Carrera, 2020; Christian, 2020; Gebru, 2020; Kosinski, 2021; Osoba & Welser, 2017; Raji & Buolamwini, 2019). Moreover, researchers have also challenged the logical fallacy inherent in techno-optimist view of new technologies, which often portray them as inherently more objective or progressive than the more discriminatory systems of the past (Benjamin, 2019, p. 3.).

As far as this debate is concerned, we agree with the view that research that purely frames digital harms based on the concept of "AI bias" often repeats the techno-optimist premise and implicit understanding of AI (and technology in general) as neutral and potentially free of biases. Thus, it reduces the problem space to the mere question of uncovering biases and then balancing them. "AI biases" are juxtaposed with "human biases", which are seen as psychological and social weaknesses that supposedly make it impossible for humans/societies to be "unbiased". In this imaginary, AI is superior to humans, as when perfected, it would become unbiased.[2] In our understanding AI, as all technologies, are human-made cultural artefacts that take part in shaping the social world. Here our interest is in illuminating the interconnections between religion, race, and gender in AI-generated categorisations, where in addition to simple biases, one can see a continuation of colonial perceptions about race and gender.

On the Notion of Religion

Before moving further, it is necessary to provide a brief description of how religion is perceived in this chapter. Religion as a concept and as a subject of research is a notoriously debated set of phenomena. If there is any consensus, it is probably that religion is a complex phenomenon, which is generally considered to consist of individual and social beliefs, symbols, affective expressions, and practices of human culture (Geertz, 1973; Jensen, 2014; White, 2021). In this study, we adopt the perspective of discursive religious studies, in which religion is defined based on of its social and discursive usages (e.g., Hjelm, 2021; Moberg, 2021; Taira, 2022). In this case we are looking into how the image recognition services "define" religion when categorizing images with content related to religion.

In collecting data, however, our approach to religion was pragmatic. In our initial data collection, we drew on common, admittedly Western, understandings of the historically largest, most established religious traditions after performing some Google Images searches. We found that this common sense approach produced the best results in terms of finding relevant material. For this chapter, we narrowed our data down to images related to Christianity.

DATA AND METHODS

Collection, Cleaning, and Categorisation

The images analysed in our study were collected from the Google Images service. We utilised both an automated, programmed approach and manual collection. In order to examine the representations of gender and race in the context of Christianity, we combined our previously collected dataset[3] with additional data that were collected using the following search terms: *black Christianity, brown Christianity, black preacher, black female preacher, black Christian women, women priest, female priest, women bishop, female bishop, black bishop, black female bishop,* and *black women bishop*. A total of 1189 images were selected for the

---

[2] For an illustrative example of this type of reasoning, see https://itif.org/publications/2022/04/25/ai-bias-correctable-human-bias-not-so-much/.

[3] The search terms for this dataset were as follows: *Christian rituals, Muslim rituals, Hindu rituals, Buddhist rituals, Shinto rituals,* and *Spiritual rituals*. This yielded over 10,000 images in total. After manual scanning, and removing images containing film and cosmetic advertisements, book covers, and plain text, the final dataset comprised of 2, 482 images.

final data set, and 352 images from this collection were stored in separate folders for further analysis and comparisons. The folders were categorised as follows: Black Christianity (96 images), White Christianity (79 images), Black female Christianity (29 images), White female Christianity (29 images), Black male Christianity (61 images), and White male Christianity (58 images).

We understand that our categorisation raises questions about a binary and essentialist understanding of whiteness and blackness as well as gender, as both race and gender are social constructs, both within cultures and in comparisons between cultures (e.g. White, 2021). However, the images were collected from the Google Images service, which already categorises images in a certain way, and all image recognition services are US-based technology companies. Hence, following a discursive approach to religion, it made sense to use similar categories in the study. After collection and assembly, all the individual images selected for the study were sent via application interfaces (APIs) to Google Cloud Vision, Amazon Rekognition, and Microsoft Azure Computer Vision. Through the APIs, one can connect to these commercial image recognition services and attain the *labels* or *tags* and the *accuracies* for every image. Labels are the descriptions of what the image recognition system "sees" in an image, accuracies are the probabilities of how certain the service is with any individual label. This information was programmatically stored in a temporary database. In addition to a statistical analysis of the data, all images and their classifications were closely examined qualitatively.

RESULTS

Statistical Distributions of Recognition in the Data

In an initial examination of the effect of gender and race, the accuracy of the services was qualitatively assessed by looking at each image to see if anything related to religion was identified, and manually collecting the results. A statistical table was constructed showing how well the services performed with images that presented some form of Christianity, in relation to gender and race (see Table 53.1). The results showed differences of up to more than 30% in

Table 53.1   *Comparisons of accuracy when controlling race and gender*

Dataset (context), total	Accuracy (Amazon)	Accuracy (Google)	Accuracy (Microsoft)
Christianity (black), 96	27%	16%	21%
Christianity (white), 79	73%	68%	58%
Female (black), 29	48%	14%	10%
Female (white), 29	52%	48%	38%
Male (black), 61	46%	33%	23%
Male (white), 59	86%	75%	52%

the accuracy of identification between whiteness and blackness. In addition, there were also some differences between the services in terms of gender identification when controlling for the effect of race. Only in the case of Amazon there was a more or less equal distribution of identification accuracy between Black and White women; in all other cases, there were significant differences. It appears that the studied image recognition services favour whiteness in identification.

Services Associate Institutional Forms of Christianity with White People

The results of the statistical overview become more nuanced with additional qualitative close-reading of the images and classifications. In the case of a Black bishop or priest, the image recognition services only offered representational silence, whereas representational diversity was reserved for the White clergy. There also seemed to be a dramatic difference in the overall quantity of labels that one could have in pictures depicting Black people.

When the people in the images were Black, the services often failed to recognise any religious affiliation, even in images depicting Christian authorities, such as popes, bishops, or priests. The case of Christian bishops shown in Figure 53.1 demonstrates that not even similar ritual clothing was enough to produce similar identification of images of Black and White people. The image of a White bishop received specific and accurate religious conceptual tagging, while a Black bishop was classified as a librarian (62% accuracy), even though clues related to Christianity were clear in the image.

Interestingly, different angles or contexts do not mitigate this bias. Even when Black preachers were depicted holding the Christian Bible, no religious identification occurred. Additionally, architectural elements of a church, such as background fabrics or window paintings, did not improve the classification of images depicting Black people (e.g. the bottom right image in Figure 53.1).

This finding was repeated both in relation to images of congregational gatherings and when controlling for gender. It is a striking finding that, when looking at institutional forms of Christianity in which the people depicted were Black, the services did not necessarily provide any indication of religion, even when clearly identifiable features were present, such as visible Christian symbols, clothing, affective ritualistic posture or worship, or architectural features. The representational silence regarding images depicting Black people is deafening.

In other words, congregational settings with Black participants often failed to produce any religious descriptions at all, even when the religious context was strikingly obvious. This happened even when the priest was in the foreground with clearly recognisable symbols present in the centre of the image (Figure 53.2). And when there was some identification of Christianity, the services did not recognize gender correctly. For example, in the image on the bottom right corner of Figure 53.2, the Black female bishop was identified with high confidence as a "man". The top right corner image in Figure 53.2 also highlights the poor classification performance. Moreover, as shown in Table 53.1, gender had little effect

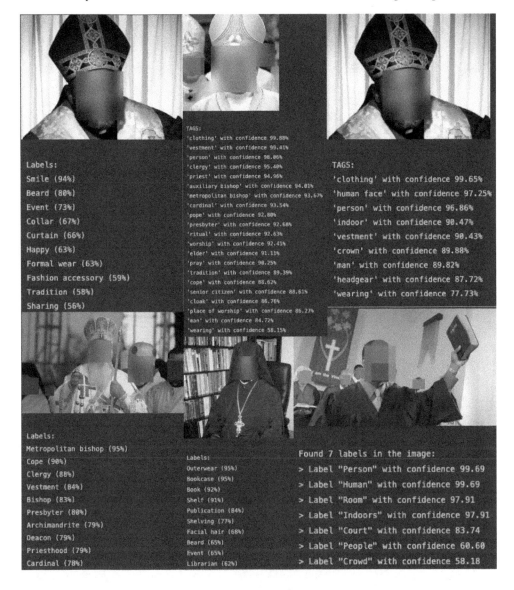

Figure 53.1   *Google (top), Google; Azure (top), Google; Azure (top), Amazon*

on the racial bias. White Christian female authorities were identified much more accurately than their Black counterparts (see top and bottom left images in Figure 53.2). This finding was repeated systematically, underlining the fact that the prejudices of these services are specifically racial, Western, and ethnocentric.

Figure 53.2   *Azure (top), Azure; Google (top), Azure (mid), Amazon; Google (top), Azure*

There were also sexist connotations. For example, Amazon's and Azure's image recognition services associated a Black evangelical female preachers with categories related to dancing, nightlife, and even dating (see Figure 53.3).

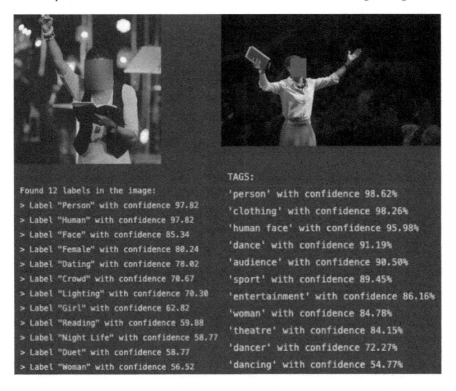

Figure 53.3   *Amazon; Azure*

CONCLUSION

AI, Religion, and the Power of Racial Imaginaries

Our exploratory investigation of the ways in which the image recognition services of Google, Amazon, and Microsoft represent religion revealed that all of these services reproduce hegemonic meanings of Christianity and race in at least two ways:

1. Christianity is represented as White and institutional, as well as European. This is illustrated by the significant difference in the services' ability to recognise nearly identical images of Christian clergy members in church interior settings depending on whether the people in the picture are White or Black.
2. With images depicting Black people in Christian settings, the services reproduce a representational silence that appears in the form of few and inaccurate descriptive labels.

The findings illustrate the empirical reality of "technology is society" (Castells, 2009). Commercial image recognition services are technological materialities and cultural artefacts that continue, along with earlier communication technologies, to reproduce the dynamics of prejudice, racism, and oppression. These dynamics cut through societies and manifest in various social domains and environments (Hall, 1992). They are linked to digital power structures that reinforce stereotypical perceptions of certain privileged social groups while undermining others. In fact, our findings demonstrate that the commercial image recognition services appear to have adopted White nationalist (and often populist) and identitarian notions of Christianity as the religion of White people of European origin (Miller, 2020; Perry & Whitehead, 2021; Whitehead, 2011).

As Safiya U. Noble (2018), an internet researcher and Professor of Gender and African American Studies argued, ignoring social inequality in the construction of algorithm patterns is not going to solve these problems. On the contrary, ignoring pre-existing biases will only reinforce inequalities. If automated decision-making tools are not explicitly built to dismantle structural inequalities, their scale and speed will simply reinforce injustices (Noble, 2018). It has been shown that marginalised individuals and groups are the most vulnerable to the decisions made by autonomous systems (Birhane & Cummings, 2019; Noble, 2018; Osoba & Welser, 2017). What has been overlooked, however, is that the stereotypes are not only embedded in public or private management, social security, or policing systems. They also emerge in everyday meaning-making processes on the internet in ways that are increasingly complex, invisible, and opaque to the average user and further clouded by perceptions of AI as a neutral, bias-correcting technology. Rapidly proliferating content-creating services deploying generative AI are likely to heighten the issue further, when they use for self-learning the data they themselves have produced.

A critical analysis of the categorisations created by these services can be seen as a step in illuminating the character of these systems both as products of culture and as actors in the daily meaning-making processes. Research focusing on AI bias is calling for increased transparency of AI. The logic is that bias can, in principle, only be corrected in a transparent system. Critical research has also warned about the possible pitfalls of a "transparency illusion", where questions of transparency are disconnected from questions of power or privileges (Ananny & Crawford, 2018; Heald, 2006). Techno-utopian discourses and an emphasis on AI transparency and ethics can also support the dynamics of oppression and ideological domination.

Although greater transparency of the different algorithmic systems and services that are part of contemporary everyday life is to be applauded, uncovering of systemic bias does not automatically result in better technological solutions. Expecting this presumes that bias is an unintentional consequence of for instance biased data or using technology for quick economic gain. It is nevertheless unlikely that that all technology companies or developers care about possible biases or wish to make unbiased services. Not only do companies prioritize profit-making, but it is also possible that technology developers and companies might use technology for less than progressive political aims. This is sometimes forgotten perhaps because of the perceptions of internet-related companies as innovative harbingers of progress and a better future (English-Lueck, 2002; Valaskivi 2012, 2020).

As demonstrated, the findings regarding how image recognition services perceive religion and race suggest that simply aiming at balancing AI biases would not only be impossible but also unproductive. Primarily, this is because the concept of bias can actually reinforce the perception of AI as "neutral" and "objective". In fact, this belief in "algorithmic neutrality" reproduces algorithmically maintained discrimination (Benjamin, 2019, p. 145).

It is also necessary to recognise that the development of technology is a cultural practice, which is often sustained by the belief that technology itself will be able to solve all global issues and human biases. Combined with techno-optimism, which holds that societal progress can be achieved through technology and the objectivity of technology, representations generated by AI are prone to reproduce and multiply the hegemonies of Western societies rather than correct the biases.

From the beginning, critical cultural studies were about changing the world for the better. Critical research not only seeks to uncover power structures but also to develop projects to effect change. To accomplish this goal in the contemporary societies, more knowledge is needed on how AI participates in representing the world. Instead of cosmetic balancing efforts, a paradigm shift is needed, wherein AI is recognised as a product of human culture and, as such, defined by struggles over power and meaning-making. Critical cultural studies can help to demystify AI and illuminate the ways in which different systems participate in the stereotyping that sustains racism and sexism. The insights of such studies encourage us to focus on the power dynamics, ideologies, and inequalities in technological systems and infrastructures and call for greater accessibility for researchers and users to the data, codes, and production practices of AI systems and services utilizing machine learning technologies.

REFERENCES

Ananny, M., & Crawford, K. (2018). Seeing without knowing: Limitations of the transparency ideal and its application to algorithmic accountability. *New Media & Society, 20*(3), 973–989.

Benjamin, R. (2019). *Race After Technology: Abolitionist tools for the new Jim code*. John Wiley & Sons.

Berg, A. (2021). *Problems of digital control: The digital repression, religious persecution and genocide of the Uyghurs in Xinjiang by the Communist Republic China*. Master's thesis, University of Helsinki. http://hdl.handle.net/10138/331041

Birhane, A., & Cummins, F. (2019). *Algorithmic injustices: Towards a relational ethics*. arXiv. https://bit.ly/3gAxiAV

Brubaker, R. (2017). Between nationalism and civilizationism: The European populist moment in comparative perspective. *Ethnic and Racial Studies, 40*(8), 1191–1226. https://doi.org/10.1080/01419870.2017.1294700.

Buolamwini, J., & Gebru, T. (2018). Gender shades: Intersectional accuracy disparities in commercial gender classification. *Proceedings of the 1st Conference on Fairness, Accountability and Transparency*. PMLR, 77–91. https://proceedings.mlr.press/v81/buolamwini18a.html

Carrera, F. (2020). Race and gender of aesthetics and affections: algorithmization of racism and sexism in contemporary digital image databases. *Matrizes, 14*(2), 217–240.

Castells, M. (2009). *The rise of the network society* (2nd ed.). Wiley-Blackwell.

Christian, B. (2020). *The alignment problem – Machine learning and human values*. Norton & Company.

Crawford, K. (2021). *Atlas of AI: Power, politics, and the planetary costs of artificial intelligence*. Yale University Press.

Delgado, R., & Stefancic, J. (2001). *Critical race theory: An introduction*. NYU Press.

Delgado, R., & Stefancic, J. (2017). *Critical race theory: An introduction* (2nd ed.). NYU Press.

Dallas, D. (2019, December 29). Does facial recognition technology belong at church? *Deseret News*. https://www.deseret.com/indepth/2019/12/28/20992530/facial-recognition-software-church-member-attendance-churchix-aclu

Eubanks, V. (2018). *Automating inequality: How high-tech tools profile, police, and punish the poor*. St. Martin's Press.

English-Luek, J.A. (2002) *Cultures@SiliconValley*. Standford University Press.

Feenberg, A. (2012). *Questioning technology*. Routledge.

Feldstein, S. (2021). *The rise of digital repression: How technology is reshaping power, politics, and resistance*. Oxford University Press.

Garcia, R. (2021, December 7). The pandemic is changing how Brazilians worship and pray. *Latino Rebels*. https://www.latinorebels.com/2021/12/07/brazilonlinechurch/

Gebru, T. (2020). Race and gender. In Dubber, M. D., Pasquale, M., & Das. S. (Eds.). *The Oxford handbook of ethics of AI* (pp. 251–269). Oxford: Oxford University Press.

Geertz, C. (1973). *The interpretation of cultures*. Basic Books.

Glick & Lee. (2022, April 27). Perspective: The dark side of AI. *Deseret News*. https://www.deseret.com/2022/4/26/23033117/the-dark-side-of-ai-disinformation-misinformation-artificial-intelliegence-religion-virtual-church

Gray, J. (2004). *Heresies—Against progress and other illusions*. Granta Publications.

Hall, S. (1992). Race, culture, and communications: Looking backward and forward at cultural studies. *Rethinking Marxism, 5*(1), 10–18.

Hall, S. (1997) *Representation: Cultural representations and signifying practices*. Sage.

Heald, D. (2006) Varieties of transparency. *Proceedings of the British Academy, 135*, 25–43.

Hjelm, T. (2021). Discourse analysis. In Engler, S. & Stausberg, M. (Eds.). *The Routledge handbook of research methods in the study of religion* (pp. 229–244). Routledge.

Jensen, J. S. (2014). *What is religion?* Routledge.

Kosinski, M. (2021). Facial recognition technology can expose political orientation from naturalistic facial images. *Scientific Reports, 11*(1), 1–7.

Lentin, A., & Titley, G. (2011). *The crises of multiculturalism: Racism in a neoliberal age*. Z Books.

Leonard, D. J., & Robbins, S. T. (2020). *Race in American television: Voices and visions that shaped a nation*. ABC-Clio.

Lopez, L. K. (2020). *Race and media: Critical approaches*. NYU Press.

Miller, E. T. (2020). Christianity and whiteness. In Casey, Z. A. (Ed.). *Encyclopedia of Critical Whiteness Studies in Education*, Volume 2. (pp. 98–105). Brill.

Moberg, M. (2021). *Religion, discourse, and society: Towards a discursive sociology of religion*. Routledge.

Noble, S. U. (2018). *Algorithms of Oppression: How Search Engines Reinforce Racism*. New York University Press.

Osoba, O. A., & Welser IV, W. (2017). *An intelligence in our image: The risks of bias and errors in artificial intelligence*. Rand Corporation.

Perry, S. L., & Whitehead, A. L. (2021). Racialized religion and judicial injustice: How whiteness and Biblicist Christianity intersect to promote a preference for (unjust) punishment. *Journal for the Scientific Study of Religion, 60*(1), 46–63.

Pinker, S. (2019). *Enlightenment now: The case for reason, science, humanism, and progress*. Penguin Books UK.

Porter, R. (2001). *Enlightenment: Britain and the creation of the modern world*. Penguin UK.

Raji, I. D., & Buolamwini, J. (2019, January). Actionable auditing: Investigating the impact of publicly naming biased performance results of commercial AI products [Conference session]. *Proceedings of the 2019 AAAI/ACM Conference on AI, Ethics, and Society*, 429–435. https://doi.org/10.1145/3306618.3314244

Smith, J. (2013). Between Colorblind and Colorconscious: Contemporary Hollywood Films and Struggles Over Racial Representation. Journal of Black Studies, 44(8), 779–797. http://www.jstor.org/stable/24572892

Taira, T. (2022). *Taking "Religion" Seriously: Essays on the Discursive Study of Religion*. (Supplements to Hughes, A.W., McCutcheon, R., & von Stuckrad, K. (Eds.) Method and Theory in the Study of Religion; Vol 18). (pp. 20–49). Brill.

Taylor, C. (2002). Modern social imaginaries. *Public Culture, 14*(1), 91–124. https://doi.org/10.1215/08992363-14-1-91

Valaskivi, K. (2012). Dimensions of innovationism. In P. Nynäs, M. Lassander, & T. Utriainen (Eds.), *Post-secular society* (pp. 129–156). Transaction Publishers. https://doi.org/URN:NBN:fi:uta-201211121076

Valaskivi, K. (2020). The contemporary faith of innovationism. In E. Bell, S. Gog, A. Simionca, & S. Taylor (Eds.), *Spirituality, organisation and neoliberalism: Understanding lived experiences* (pp. 171–193). Edward Elgar.

Ylikoski, P., & Kokkonen, T. (2009). *Evoluutio ja ihmisluonto*. Gaudeamus.

Wang, Y., & Kosinski, M. (2019). Deep neural networks are more accurate than humans at detecting sexual orientation from facial images. *Journal of Personality and Social Psychology, 114*(2), 246.

White, C. (2021). *An introduction to the cognitive science of religion: Connecting evolution, brain, cognition, and culture*. Routledge.

White, S. K. (2004). The very idea of a critical social science: A pragmatist turn. In F. Rush (Ed.), *The Cambridge companion to critical theory* (pp. 310–335). Cambridge University Press.

Whitehead, A. N. (2011). *Religion in the making*. Cambridge University Press.

54. Social media as classification systems: procedural normative choices in user profiling

Severin Engelmann and Orestis Papakyriakopoulos

INTRODUCTION

Social media platforms are large-scale classification systems with the power to construct thousands of user attributes such as demographics, behaviors, or interests for tailored advertisement (Andreou et al. 2018; Sapiezynski et al. 2019). Part of social media's power results from its ability to classify users "from within" (Fourcade and Healy 2017): social media platforms utilize their own interface affordances (likes, favorites, upvotes, downvotes, friends, followers, etc.) as "definite" sources of semantic information about social media users. Moreover, platforms classify data that users have shared or expressed indirectly or implicitly using machine learning (ML) models such as natural language processing or computer vision artificial intelligence (AI) techniques. Text or visual data are semantically underdetermined sources of evidence but are nonetheless used to classify user attributes, for example, user sentiment (Giachanou and Crestani 2016; Ortis et al. 2020).

User classification is essential for social media platforms. Predicting user engagement with recommender algorithms presupposes classified users (Papakyriakopoulos et al. 2020) and marketers target audiences of users that have been classified according to marketable categories. These socio-technical procedures have raised ethical concerns among a discipline-diverse set of scholars (Engelmann et al. 2022b, Engelmann et al. 2018; Smith 2020; Hildebrandt 2019). Several accounts have paid special attention to the *consequences* of social media classification systems such as political polarization (Tucker et al. 2018), hate speech (Guiora and Park 2017; Massanari 2017), or discriminatory advertisement (Speicher et al. 2018; Sapiezynski et al. 2019).

In this chapter, we seek to discuss a selection of *procedural* challenges of social media classification that carry normative weight. We underline that the normativity of social media classification is inherent in often arbitrary benchmarks and metrics as well as the choice of ML models deployed for classification. Our goal is to demonstrate the normativity that exists in the interpretative space between data and classification in social media environments.

A WORD ON CLASSIFICATION PRACTICES AND SYSTEMS

Classification is ubiquitous. Classification is an essential procedure of scientific activity and much of science work means arguing for and against the boundaries of object classification. Modern states would not exist without classification infrastructures. State's bureaucratic administration, legal formalism, and information markets fall back on classification practices that categorize things, people, actions, and their relationship with each other.

Weber famously described the principle of Western rationalization as the effort to "master all things by calculation" (Kim 2021). This mastery essentially depends on classification systems. Classifications permeate nearly all areas of life including consumption, health, credit markets, education, employment, and social relations. Behind all these efforts lies the fundamental attempt to make a semantically ambiguous world legible and actionable across communities and cultures.

Classification is normative. All classifying procedures are necessarily part of cultural activity and therefore situated in culturally specific forms that are not value-neutral (Harding 2016). This is particularly evident in the classification of *social phenomena*. Social phenomena do not exist without humans making claims about them: Marriage, money, privacy, property, and friendship exist because humans classify inherently underdetermined phenomena as representative of a given class. Creating, fixating, and operationalizing a particular definition of an otherwise essentially vague social phenomenon depends on the interpretation of the defining entity's belief on what *should* constitute this phenomenon.

Classification is power. Regardless of its terminology, in modern societies, those that are in a position to determine the essence of inherently ambiguous concepts for society at large are often those that are in power. This power is exercised through the implementation of large-scale classification systems. As Bowker and Star (2000) argue, social classification systems are powerful for two reasons: first, such classification systems create meaning by defining ambiguous social phenomena. Second, technologically implemented classification systems (i.e., practically all classification systems today) operate in a largely invisible infrastructure. The lack of transparency not only creates accountability issues but directly serves the naturalization of the categories in a classification system. The fixation that ties a particular object to a particular meaning (i.e., a category or class) becomes natural in the sense that it loses its socially situated contingencies and, hence, its "anthropological strangeness" (Bowker and Star 2000). Once a social classification system is set up and running, preceding negotiations and eventual decisions on the meaning of concepts are often forgotten and move to the background *without* losing their power. Social classification systems naturalize their own definitions of inherently ambiguous social phenomena and through this process successfully stabilize themselves (Harding 2016).

Social media platforms depend on the assumptions of a positivist account of social phenomena. Such a positivist account presupposes that social phenomena such as social interactions and relationships can be reduced to units and categories that are ontologically comparable to the mathematical and physical descriptions of nature. Following classification, statistical models are taken to be able to measure the underlying patterns of social relationships, behaviors, interests, and beliefs. That is, social media classification systems extract epistemic value from the ontological categories they have established.

The Dual-Model Architecture of Social Media Classification Systems

Social media platforms have been conceptualized as digital places for public and private interactions, news sharing and distribution, or self-presentation and programmatic advertising. Yet, the essence of large-scale social media platforms becomes more fundamentally evident with the notion of social media platforms as *classification systems*.

Social media platforms are, arguably, the most technologically advanced social-commercial classification systems. Among others, they classify user demographics, user interests, user locations, and user relationships in an automated and largely opaque manner.

Social media platforms typically consist of two interdependent classification architectures: a "user interface" that provides standardized user profiles and affords communication objects such as likes, favorites, upvotes/downvotes, and so on. As a technologically mediated construction of the social world, the user interface serves as a classification system for a subsequent classification system, which we refer to as "the marketing interface". This is the place where marketers select audiences with the desired user attributes (e.g., demographics, behaviors, interests) for granular, tailored advertisements. Objects in the user interface fall into a corresponding category in the "marketing interface".

In the following, we describe the fundamental dual-model architecture of the social media classification system in more detail. In Figure 54.1, we illustrate the basic dual-model architecture of social media that facilitates its classification system. While these architectures are constituted and *connected* by databases, data structures, and algorithms, we refer to the first model architecture as the "user interface" and the second as the "marketing interface". We focus on interfaces because, first, it is primarily via the user interface that social media users generate data for classification. This includes interactions with the platform's unique communication affordances such as likes, reactions, or upvotes/downvotes. Second, these data are then transformed into classifications that marketers can select for targeting in the marketing interface. It is through these two interfaces that users, as members of the social media platform, and marketers, as audience generators for targeted advertisement, interact with the

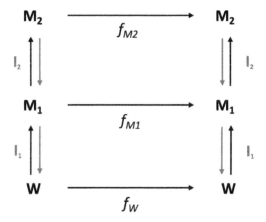

Source: Authors.

Figure 54.1   *The relationship of objects (f_W) in the real social world W serves as the basis for the modeling of this relationship in M_1, the user interface. The relationship of objects in M_1, in turn, serves as the model for the relationship of objects in M_2, the marketing interface. Arrows point downward because marketing material is delivered through M_2 into M_1 and hence can exert influence on W*

dual-model architecture of social media classification systems. In the following, we describe the connection between these two architectures.

Classifying informational objects in a digital system means to first abstract such objects from the real social world *W*. In *W*, people, objects, and so on interact in *relationships* represented here as f(*W*). The interpretation $I : W \rightarrow M1$ denotes that I maps *W* into *M*1: the interpretation of the real-world *W* is represented in a model *M*1. *M*1 thereby contains the terms of the objects of the interpretation of *W*. It follows that if the function $f(M) : M1 \rightarrow M1$ denotes any relation between two terms in *M*1, then there is a corresponding function $f(W) : W \rightarrow W$. Relations between objects in *M*1 have their correspondence in the reality of relations between objects in the social world *W*.

A model is a relative concept. A model can in turn be interpreted and used as the *reality* for another model. This requires another "round of abstraction", i.e., $I : M1 \rightarrow M2$. The model that constitutes the user interface (*M1*) with all its information objects and their *relationships* such as users, friendships, likes, and events serves as a model for a subsequent model, which, in the context of social media platforms, we call the "marketing interface" (*M2*). This is the interface through which marketers decide whom to target when generating audiences for tailored advertisements. Accordingly, any relationship between objects in the model of the user interface (*M1*) will have a correspondent relationship in the model of this marketing interface (*M2*).

While a model is often associated with a mere simulation of events, the social media model of the social world is engagement-based. The model of the user interface (*M1*), where users engage with each other, serves as a platform for advertisers to influence this user interface, which subsequently influences the social world (*W*) (see arrows in Figure 54.1). Social media users participate in an interactive model of the social world as conceived by social media platform operators.

Abstraction and the subsequent formalization are procedures of imperfect translation. This creates the normative essence of classification: no model can encompass all characteristics of objects and their relations for even the tiniest scope of the real-world *W* (for a review of so-called abstraction traps, see Selbst et al. 2019). First, abstraction in digital social classification systems is constrained by the underlying computational limits of user profiling. Not all features of an object can be modeled under finite computational resources. Second, some phenomena cannot be computed *in principle* for their qualitative characteristics: for example, the phenomenological experience of human consciousness – the immediate and direct sense-perception of the world – cannot be expressed and operationalized in computational terms (Engelmann et al. 2022b). Finally, the purpose for which an object is modeled in a classification system further constraints how objects are classified. In social media platforms, classification requires abstractions of people as a source of commercial value. Here, abstraction for classification deliberately creates "corporatized identities" from digital identities – a bias that is in no way intrinsic to classification procedures *per se* (Smith 2020). As several other scholars have commented on, the generated "data doubles" (Haggerty et al. 2000) of individuals are products of today's surveillance capitalism (Zuboff 2015) and hence market mechanisms dictate the principles of their creation.

To reiterate, social media classification for targeted advertisement presupposes a variety of normative choices. In the following, we discuss choices that concern the quantity and quality of data collection, arbitrariness of class definitions, mismatches between reality and modeled distributions, value judgments of the classification process, dealing with changes in a user's data stream, and the normativity of defining similarity metrics. All of these choices represent procedural elements that are essential to the path from *W* to *M1* to *M2*.

FUNDAMENTAL NORMATIVE DIMENSIONS OF USER PROFILING FOR SOCIAL MEDIA CLASSIFICATION

Normativity of Quantity Choices: When is Enough *Enough*?

One normative judgment user profiling is necessarily required to make is to determine when enough data (or evidence) has been collected and analyzed to justify whether a user can be classified to "possess" a given attribute (interest, belief, affiliation to a group, etc.). For some attribute classification procedures, the question is resolved because the classification system uses its own cues. For example, liking a fan page is taken to be sufficient enough to infer that a user expresses and shares an interest represented by the fan page. Such "classification heuristics" are created by the system itself and have become naturalized objects of identity declaration as viewed by marketers. However, for other user attributes, the classification process is more complicated when the classification is based on more implicit expressions such as views, clicks, and visual or textual data. It is a normative undertaking to decide when the amount of personal data is sufficient to ensure proportionality between the user input and the attribute inference. Such declarations require asking the following questions: Is the inference classification proportional to a *single* activity or expression of belief? Or is the classification's proportionality dependent on *multiple* consecutive expressions of the belief? Resolving such questions, user profiling necessarily excludes user input from being considered when classifying user attributes.

Normativity of Quality Choices: When is the Quality of Evidence Sufficient?

Besides questions of data quantity, data *quality* raises further normative questions. For example, visual data – image and video – are among the most popular vehicles to showcase an intelligible self-concept on social media platforms. Across the Facebook services alone, users upload two billion images – in a single day.[1] Facial analysis AI has been used to classify latent people's personality traits based on facial looks in the social media context (Ferwerda et al. 2015, 2018; Guntuku et al. 2017; Azucar et al. 2018; Celli et al. 2014; Biel et al. 2012; Al Moubayed et al. 2014).

The ambiguity of visual data and the development of computer vision AI technologies to analyze such visual data, in particular human faces, has initiated an intense discussion among scholars about the types of classifications AI should make about people based on their facial looks. What standards (or justifications) should image and video classification be subjected to and according to what criteria can we argue for and against visual data classification?

A prominent example of facial analysis AI is emotion recognition from facial expressions. Emotion recognition AI has been applied to classify mood, reactions of customers to products,

---

[1]   *Using Artificial Intelligence to Help Blind People "See" Facebook*: https://about.fb.com/news/2016/04/using-artificial-intelligence-to-help-blind-people-see-facebook/ (retrieved May 20, 2022).

student attention, and hiring decisions. According to the so-called common view of emotion, emotion instances comprise six basic expressions (anger, disgust, surprise, sadness, happiness, and fear) plus a neutral expression displayed via discrete facial action units (Facial Action Coding System or FACS) (Rosenberg and Ekman 2020). The common view is the *de facto* standard conceptualization of emotion classification for emotion recognition AI (Stöckli et al. 2018). This technology is driven by the underlying belief that facial expressions are definitive indicators for emotion sensation, an assumption that some emotion researchers contest pointing to the importance of contextual and social factors that produce variability in facial emotion expression (Barrett et al. 2019).

Emotion recognition AI is a good example to demonstrate that digital classification systems tend to seek evidence for a conceptualization of a contested phenomenon (i.e., the concept of emotion) that is compatible with the epistemic affordances of the classifying technology while ignoring conceptualizations that do not fit these affordances. Empirical investigations with experts (Ullstein et al. 2022) and non-experts (Engelmann et al. 2022a) on the ethics of facial analysis AI underline the normative complexity of visual data classification. Contrary to popular justifications for facial classification technologies, these results suggest that there is no such thing as a "common sense" facial classification that accords simply with a general, homogeneous "human intuition". These conceptual and empirical studies clearly illustrate that selecting the quality of evidence for classification is a normative undertaking.

Normativity in Class Definition: What Dictates the Different Thresholds Used to Partition the World?

The existence of a classification system *de facto* partitions the world into segments. The mapping of a user population into predefined categories is an inherently normative decision.

First, the existence of a finite set of classes forces a user to fit into some of them regardless of whether they actually represent them or not. For example, drawing on the perceived voter model (Hersh 2015), an individual is often categorized in the US within the Democratic-Republican duality although they might not be party-affiliated at all.

Second, the election of a specific set of classes over others creates a hierarchy of visibility with a subset of population traits deemed important while others become negligible. The available classes always comply with the designers' incentives who want groupings that can be efficiently sold for advertisements. This generates discrepancies in the representation of different groups. On Facebook, for example, the cuisine categories include, among others, Greek, Indian, and Italian cuisine, but do not include others such as Creole or Soul food (InterestExplorer 2022; Meta 2021).

Third, the association between a user and a class is neither given nor deterministic. A classification system will assign a probability for an individual being a member of a class, but the designers will use a *predefined cut-off* to make a deterministic connection between a user and a class. For example, in the case that a model predicts a 30% chance that a user is interested in soccer, a cut-off value of 20% would denote that a connection between the user and the class exists. On the contrary, a cut-off value of 40% would reject this connection. Prior analysis (Narayanan 2021) shows that this shift from stochastic to deterministic skews the actual data distributions and amplifies existing data biases even if they were negligible in the probabilistic space. Therefore, forcing users into classes can reinforce the phenomenon that specific user groups are assigned to specific classes, although there might not be an actual reason or sufficient evidence for such a user group division. This means that even if users' modeling distribution seems satisfactory from a probabilistic perspective, the inevitable shift from the stochastic space to a deterministic formal, mathematical decision can have unintended and unforeseen consequences. This is another facet of the so-called formalism trap in sociotechnical systems (Selbst et al. 2019) where the need to transform the world into formal mathematical structures leads to ethically contestable outcomes.

Taking the above three cases into consideration, the selection of thresholds and types of classes throughout the classification process is value-laden with implications for user populations and marketers.

Normativity in (Mis)Classification: What Legitimizes a Specific Classification Process?

The above-described arbitrariness in class definition is directly connected to fairness interpretations of the classification process. A series of choices during the design of the classification system and its classification rules are performed solely based on platform objectives. These choices remain undisclosed to both the affected user population and the marketers that advertise using classification systems. As classification is the decisive step for distributing advertisements, its quality affects outcomes. Individuals can get classified in classes that they do not belong to or that they do not want to be associated with. For example, someone might not want their religion, ethnicity, or health to be a reason for seeing specific advertisements. Furthermore, they might not want their wrongful association within a specific set of classes, for example, a wrong partisanship assignment. This (mis)classification can harm both the effectiveness of the commercial structure but also potentially connect marketers and individuals under a manipulative logic. For example, individuals with apparent low self-esteem have been targeted with advertisements for diet or beauty products, and individuals who gamble have seen loan advertising (Paterson et al. 2021). Such outcomes are mechanistically legitimized by the classification process as "bad outcomes are nothing but the mechanical translation of bad habits and behavioral failure" (Fourcade and Healy 2017), despite the fact that both users and marketers might disapprove of the underlying logic. Since they are not aware of how and why users are categorized within the available classes and cases, and conceptions of procedural injustice remain hidden, it is hard to locate and mitigate them.

Normativity in Modeling Distributions: How is Reality Projected into the Distributions Modeled by the Classification System?

When a machine learning classification system learns from a population's data, this does not mean that this information will be transformed into a valid and useful mapping of the world. Clicks, likes, upvotes, or downvotes, and even product purchases, carry user-specific meanings and denotations that vary within a population (Hayes et al. 2016). Two users liking the same post do it for different reasons. The liking itself as a behavior may offer different interpretations given a specific social context. Nonetheless, for the classification system, this information is reduced into a mathematical description that corresponds to "likes by user A and B on Post C". Elements of the platforms' user interface $M1$ have more complex representation in reality (see Figure 54.1, world W). This simplified information is mapped by a given classification rule to a predefined distribution of user attributes. For example, likes or clicks on political content are transformed into a connection between a user and specific political interests, while ordering from specific restaurants results in a connection of the user to a specific type of cuisine (marketing interface M2). Such mappings between individuals and behaviors result in what Gillespie (2014) calls "calculated publics": algorithmically generated images of users that users interact with and that influence their sense of self.

Although mappings between W-$M1$ and $M1$-$M2$ seem intuitive, in reality, they are associated with significant information loss and are contingent on the data scientist's design assumptions about the sample: (1) user behavior is reduced in a presumptuous way, as actions in the real world are given predefined interpretations according to the designers' logic and goals; and (2) the distribution of these behaviors in $M1$ is mapped into categories of higher order (in $M2$) by the system's designers under the objective of creating sensible classes from a marketing perspective without necessarily ensuring mapping validity. For example, such classification systems often suffer from *identity fragmentation bias* (Lin and Misra 2022). User behavior on the platform is only a subset of their total online and offline behavior and hence not sufficient in revealing actual user interests, beliefs, and so on, leading to biased categorization in $M2$. The above issues are known, but nonetheless, limited attention has been placed on their normativity. As outlined previously, campaigns and targeting in political advertising are developed under the perceived voter model (Hersh 2015) where individuals' partisanship is inferred based on their digital trace data, consciously knowing that there is a significant mismatch between reality and the classification. It is important to understand and ethically evaluate such mismatches between reality and modeling distributions to decide on the specific values a classification system should have.

Normativity of Classifying Data Stream Changes: What Criteria Determine When Data Are to Be Forgotten or Considered When Changing Classifications?

Social media platform designers argue that the advantage of social media classification architectures lies in their ability to facilitate *dynamic* classification. Key to the promise of social media marketing is the provision of accurate user profiles. The rationale is that dynamic user profiles are more valuable to the user because they can interact with recommended informational resources they have only recently become interested in. On the other hand, advertisers benefit from targeting audiences with the most up-to-date user profiles. Accurately classifying interests, beliefs, and other user attributes requires accounting for shifts in the data distribution (Hand 2006). Regardless of whether "drifts" in data are sudden (picking up a new interest because of a new friend) or gradual (expressing more and more interest in becoming a parent or moving to another country), classifying from within enables the detection of such changes. Technologically, so-called concept drift techniques are able to classify data stream *changes* (Gama et al. 2013; Žliobaitė 2010). Social media platforms create and save "intermediate profiles" of users, profiles that instantiate a current representation of a user without "neglecting" the outdated data (Žliobaitė 2010). Here, sliding windows of fixed and variable sizes of training data are used to generate an updated profile of a user (Gama et al. 2013). As fixed and variable windows are set in their size, some "old" data will necessarily be "forgotten". What criteria determine which data are to be forgotten and which ones are to be considered for the classification of an updated profile of a person? How do social media platforms justify deleting or reversing a past attribute classification? Such procedural choices are necessarily normative.

Normativity of Profiling Based on Similarity Metrics: What Criteria Determine When Two People Are Alike?

Social media profiling determines whether two or more users are "equal" or "similar" with respect to an attribute of interest (e.g., demographics, behaviors, interests). Social media platforms offer marketers audience-tailored advertisement delivery based on "lookalike" audiences. Lookalike audiences span offline and online worlds because marketers can upload identifying information (e.g., email addresses) of current customers to the social media platform. The classification system not only identifies user profiles that correspond to the uploaded email addresses but it recommends "similar" other user profiles as potential new customers for advertisement targeting. This makes lookalike audiences a popular tool for marketers. They are typically powered by collaborative filtering such as k-nearest-neighbor (k-NN) which calculates the similarity between users (Herlocker et al. 1999). Lookalikes rely on the normative procedure of classifying two or more users as similar viewed from the system's own taxonomies and categories (the user interface, $M1$). Lookalikes can cause distributive injustices when they exclude certain users with specific demographic characteristics from advertisement delivery on housing or employment (Sapiezynski et al. 2019).

CONCLUSION AND FINAL REMARKS

Commercial digital platforms, and in particular social media platforms, are powerful because they create meaning through a classification system that is largely invisible (Bowker & Star). In this chapter, we presented a selection of *procedural* normative choices in the classification of social media platforms. In using ML models to classify people, social media platforms fixate an association between a user and a class. Social media determine the quantity and quality of evidence that justifies the classification of a user into a particular category. Social media anchor identity declarations of users around semantic affordances they have set up in the user interface and take them to be sufficient evidence for the commercial potential of an identity. They furthermore rely on evidence that fits the technical affordances of ML models.

These phenomena raise several important questions that we wish to end with. Classifying billions of users into pre-established categories raises the question of whether people should have at least some access to these classifications even if an ideal form of transparency is necessarily always constrained by design choices. However, social media platforms provide a certain degree of transparency in their classifications when they allow marketers to select desirable attributes for tailored advertisement delivery. Social media platforms could allow users to view, contest, and correct classifications that they deem false. How would social media users relate to "their" classifications? If shown to them, would they see themselves represented "adequately" in the classifications offered to marketers? If so, would they want the social media platform to classify them correctly? We believe that the normativity of classification systems justifies some user ability to control social media classifications. First studies (e.g., Engelmann et al. 2022b) have shown that users are motivated to correct social media classifications that they deem wrong. Previous work on obfuscation also underlined people's desire to gain control of their digital identity (Brunton & Nissenbaum 2015).

We envision a usable form of access to social media platforms as a default for social media users. Showing users the relation between their data and their classifications would certainly bring to the surface the inherently normative negotiations embedded in social media classifications. Transparency of and access to classifications would strongly support people's autonomy to self-determine in a digital society.

REFERENCES

Al Moubayed, N., Vazquez-Alvarez, Y., McKay, A., & Vinciarelli, A. (2014). Face-based automatic personality perception. *Proceedings of the 22nd ACM International Conference on Multimedia*, 1153–1156. doi:10.1145/2647868.2655014

Andreou, A., Venkatadri, G., Goga, O., Gummadi, K. P., Loiseau, P., & Mislove, A. (2018, February). Investigating ad transparency mechanisms in social media: A case study of Facebook's explanations. In *NDSS 2018-Network and Distributed System Security Symposium* (pp. 1–15). https://doi.org/10.14722/ndss.2018.2319.

Azucar, D., Marengo, D., & Settanni, M. (2018). Predicting the big 5 personality traits from digital footprints on social media: A meta-analysis. *Personality and Individual Differences*, *124*, 150–159. doi:10.1016/j.paid.2017.12.018

Barrett, L. F., Adolphs, R., Marsella, S., Martinez, A. M., & Pollak, S. D. (2019). Emotional expressions reconsidered: Challenges to inferring emotion from human facial movements. *Psychological Science in the Public Interest*, *20*(1), 1–68.

Biel, J.-I., Teijeiro-Mosquera, L., & Gatica-Perez, D. (2012). Facetube: Predicting personality from facial expressions of emotion in online conversational video. *Proceedings of the 14th ACM International Conference on Multimodal Interaction*, 53–56. doi:10.1145/2388676.2388689

Bowker, G. C., & Star, S. L. (2000). *Sorting Things Out: Classification and Its Consequences*. MIT Press.

Brunton, F., & Nissenbaum, H. (2015). *Obfuscation: A User's Guide for Privacy and Protest*. MIT Press.

Celli, F., Bruni, E., & Lepri, B. (2014). Automatic personality and interaction style recognition from Facebook profile pictures. *Proceedings of the 22nd ACM International Conference on Multimedia*, 1101–1104. doi:10.1145/2647868.2654977

Engelmann, S., Grossklags, J., & Papakyriakopoulos, O. (2018). A democracy called Facebook? Participation as a privacy strategy on social media. In *Annual Privacy Forum* (pp. 91–108). Springer, Cham.

Engelmann, S., Ullstein, C., Papakyriakopoulos, O., & Grossklags, J. (2022a). What people think AI should infer from faces. In *2022 ACM Conference on Fairness, Accountability, and Transparency* (pp. 128–141).

Engelmann, S., Scheibe, V., Battaglia, F., & Grossklags, J. (2022b). Social media profiling continues to partake in the development of formalistic self-concepts: Social media users think so, too. In *Proceedings of the 5th AAAI/ACM Conference on AI, Ethics, and Society (AAAI/ACM AIES)*.

Ferwerda, B., & Tkalcic, M. (2018). Predicting users' personality from Instagram pictures: Using visual and/or content features? *Proceedings of the 26th Conference on User Modeling, Adaptation and Personalization*, 157–161. doi:10.1145/3209219.3209248

Ferwerda, B., Schedl, M., & Tkalcic, M. (2015). Predicting personality traits with Instagram pictures. *Proceedings of the Workshop on Emotions and Personality in Personalized Systems*, 7–10. doi:10.1145/2809643.2809644

Fourcade, M., & Healy, K. (2017). Seeing like a market. *Socio-Economic Review*, *15*(1), 9–29.

Gama, J., Sebastiao, R., & Rodrigues, P. P. (2013). On evaluating stream learning algorithms. *Machine Learning*, *90*, 317–346.

Giachanou, A., & Crestani, F. (2016). Like it or not: A survey of Twitter sentiment analysis methods. *ACM Computing Surveys (CSUR)*, *49*(2), 1–41.

Gillespie, T. (2014). The relevance of algorithms. *Media Technologies: Essays on Communication, Materiality, and Society*, *167*(2014), 167.

Guiora, A., & Park, E. A. (2017). Hate speech on social media. *Philosophia*, *45*(3), 957–971.

Guntuku, S. C., Lin, W., Carpenter, J., Ng, W. K., Ungar, L. H., & Preoţiuc-Pietro, D. (2017). Studying personality through the content of posted and liked images on Twitter. *Proceedings of the 2017 ACM on Web Science Conference*, 223–227. doi:10.1145/3091478.3091522

Haggerty, K. D., & Ericson, R. V. (2000). The surveillant assemblage. *The British Journal of Sociology*, *51*(4), 605–622.

Hand, D. J. (2006). Classifier technology and the illusion of progress. *Statistical Science*, *21*(1), 1–14.

Harding, S. (1991). *Whose science? Whose knowledge?: Thinking from women's lives.* Cornell University Press.

Hayes, R. A., Carr, C. T., & Wohn, D. Y. (2016). One click, many meanings: Interpreting paralinguistic digital affordances in social media. *Journal of Broadcasting & Electronic Media*, *60*(1), 171–187.

Herlocker, J. L., Konstan, J. A., Borchers, A., & Riedl, J. (1999, August). An algorithmic framework for performing collaborative filtering. In *Proceedings of the 22nd Annual International ACM SIGIR Conference on Research and Development in Information Retrieval* (pp. 230–237).

Hersh, E. D. (2015). *Hacking the Electorate: How Campaigns Perceive Voters.* Cambridge University Press.

Hildebrandt, M. (2019). Privacy as protection of the incomputable self: From agnostic to agonistic machine learning. *Theoretical Inquiries in Law*, *20*(1), 83–121.

Kim, S. H. (2021). Max Weber. The Stanford Encyclopedia of Philosophy website. https://plato.stanford.edu/archives/sum2021/entries/weber/

Lin, T., & Misra, S. (2022). Frontiers: The identity fragmentation bias. *Marketing Science*, *41*(3), 433–440.

Massanari, A. (2017). #Gamergate and the fappening: How Reddit's algorithm, governance, and culture support toxic technocultures. *New Media & Society*, *19*(3), 329–346.

META. (2021). *Facebook advertising targeting options.* Facebook. Retrieved February 13, 2023, from https://www.facebook.com/business/ads/ad-targeting

Arvind Narayanan. (2021). When a machine learning system uses argmax to select outputs from a probability distribution it's a clue that it might be biased. Twitter.com. Retrieved February 13, 2023, from https://twitter.com/random_walker/status/ 139934824114210406.

4Ortis, A., Farinella, G. M., & Battiato, S. (2020). Survey on visual sentiment analysis. *IET Image Processing*, *14*(8), 1440-1456.

Papakyriakopoulos, O., Serrano, J. C. M., & Hegelich, S. (2020). Political communication on social media: A tale of hyperactive users and bias in recommender systems. *Online Social Networks and Media*, *15*, 100058.

Paterson, J. M., Chang, S., Cheong, M., Culnane, C., Dreyfus, S., & McKay, D. (2021). The Hidden Harms of Targeted Advertising by Algorithm and Interventions from the Consumer Protection Toolkit. *IJCLP*, 9, 1.

Rosenberg, E. L., & Ekman, P. (Eds.). (2020). *What the face reveals: Basic and applied studies of spontaneous expression using the Facial Action Coding System (FACS).* Oxford University Press.

Sapiezynski, P., Ghosh, A., Kaplan, L., Mislove, A., & Rieke, A. (2019). Algorithms that" Don't See Color": Comparing Biases in Lookalike and Special Ad Audiences. *arXiv preprint arXiv:1912. 07579*.

Selbst, A. D., Boyd, D., Friedler, S. A., Venkatasubramanian, S., & Vertesi, J. (2019). Fairness and abstraction in sociotechnical systems. In *Proceedings of the conference on fairness, accountability, and transparency* (pp. 59-68).

Smith, C. H. (2020). Corporatised Identities$\ne$ Digital Identities: Algorithmic Filtering on Social Media and the Commercialisation of Presentations of Self. Σ το *Ethics of Digital Well-Being* (σσ. 55–80). Springer.

Speicher, T., Ali, M., Venkatadri, G., Ribeiro, F. N., Arvanitakis, G., Benevenuto, F., ... Mislove, A. (2018). Potential for discrimination in online targeted advertising. *Conference on Fairness, Accountability and Transparency*, 5–19. PMLR.

Stöckli, S., Schulte-Mecklenbeck, M., Borer, S., & Samson, A. C. (2018). Facial expression analysis with AFFDEX and FACET: A validation study. *Behavior research methods*, *50*, 1446-1460.

Tucker, J. A., Guess, A., Barberá, P., Vaccari, C., Siegel, A., Sanovich, S., ... Nyhan, B. (2018). Social media, political polarization, and political disinformation: A review of the scientific literature.

Political polarization, and political disinformation: a review of the scientific literature (March 19, 2018).

Ullstein, C., Engelmann, S., Papakyriakopoulos, O., Hohendanner, M., & Grossklags, J. (2022). AI-Competent Individuals and Laypeople Tend to Oppose Facial Analysis AI. In *Equity and Access in Algorithms, Mechanisms, and Optimization* (pp. 1-12).

Vermeulen, P. (2022). *The complete Facebook interests list (2023)*. InterestExplorer.io. Retrieved February 13, 2023, from https://interestexplorer.io/facebook-interests-list/

Žliobaitė, I. (2010). Learning under concept drift: an overview. *arXiv preprint arXiv:1010.4784.*

Zuboff, S. (2015). Big other: surveillance capitalism and the prospects of an information civilization. *Journal of information technology, 30*(1), 75-89.

55. From hate speech recognition to happiness indexing: critical issues in datafication of emotion in text mining

Salla-Maaria Laaksonen, Juho Pääkkönen and Emily Öhman

INTRODUCTION

Sentiments and emotions are complex creatures that have been studied for millennia without much consensus as to their nature. A broad consensus lies, however, in their importance for social action. Scholars have argued for an "affective turn" in social sciences and humanities to describe the growing interest in understanding the entanglement of social action and feelings (Clough & Halley, 2007; Wetherell, 2012). This scholarship has highlighted the importance of emotions and affect on organizing public discussions and social life. It has been suggested that the modern public sphere is best described as a space where the publics are built as social formations through affective attunement (Papacharissi, 2015). Indeed, messages that gain traction in the public sphere are often affectively framed, and emotions are shown to motivate people and support the formation of new political groups and social action (e.g., Gould, 2010).

This rising interest in emotions has also had repercussions in the more technical and applied fields. In computer science, information systems research, and computational linguistics, emotions emerge as aspects of social life identifiable and measurable from natural language in computer-assisted or automated ways. The automated extraction and analysis of affective orientation in text are generally known as sentiment analysis (Pang & Lee, 2008). Sentiment analysis has emerged as a central procedure to understand the tone of public discussion. It is widely used in social media analytics and media research (Puschmann & Powell, 2018) while differing from traditional affect studies in its quantitative rather than qualitative approach. The methods used to analyze affectivity in texts draw largely on data mining, text representation, and machine learning, commonly labeled as artificial intelligence tools in public discourse. While such tools are often presented as automated, intelligent, and self-standing, their development and use involve human action and decisions at several stages of the process (e.g., Newlands, 2021; Rieder & Skop, 2021; Pääkkönen et al., 2020; Andrejevic, 2019). Furthermore, they require transforming the textual representations of emotions to quantified and datafied form, that is, into something that is recognizable and countable by machines (Beer, 2019).

In this chapter, we critically explore the datafication of affective language by focusing on the analysis processes behind common sentiment analysis techniques. We discuss the underlying, often hidden choices related to datafication and operationalization of textual affect, and the various forms of human involvement when building technological systems to identify it. We argue that sentiment analysis provides an illuminating case for studying tensions in the use of artificial intelligence applications and computational technologies to understand complex social phenomena. Indeed, tools to identify textual sentiments have become increasingly common in real-life contexts from social media monitoring to customer insights. Sentiment analysis has gained a somewhat institutionalized position as an indicator of the firm's current stance (Etter et al., 2018) or as a way to infer and predict social phenomena from public mood to voter preferences (Bollen et al., 2009; Oliveira et al., 2017). It is used by the media and the social media platforms themselves to understand the discussion flowing on their services and to aid in content moderation, particularly when removing unwanted content such as hate speech (Rieder & Skop, 2021). To a regular user, the results of sentiment analysis are typically conveyed through a red-and-green diagram on an analytics platform – a representational format that hides potentially complex analysis processes and imbues the results with ostensible simplicity and mathematical truthfulness (Kennedy et al., 2016). Social media platforms, then again, present their sentiment detection endeavors as triumphs of technology: "Facebook Pulls 22.5 Million Hate Speech Posts in Quarter", or "YouTube removes more than 100,000 videos for violating its hate speech policy". What actually happens behind these diagrams, large numbers, and success-reporting headlines, however, is rarely disclosed. As users of commercial platforms, we only live with the deliverables and decisions produced by these systems (Brown, 2018).

In what follows, we use existing research as well as our own computational projects and fieldwork (Öhman, 2021a; Laaksonen et al., 2020; Haapoja et al., 2020) as examples to discuss and critically reflect on the processes of datafying textual expressions of affect from contested definitions to quantified algorithmic probabilities. We first discuss the difficulties in defining and operationalizing emotions as a multidisciplinary concept, and then discuss the datafication of emotions to commensurable digits. Next, we explain the validation processes typically involved in sentiment analysis and then move on to describe the hidden role of humans throughout the process. Through these explorations, the datafication of emotions for computational purposes emerges as a series of transformations where the phenomenon known to be contextual, embodied, and complex becomes reduced to simple numbers and compelling diagrams. Therefore, it becomes an affective object that is commensurable and thus seemingly controllable for the society that increasingly strives for rationality and technological control.

OPERATIONALIZATION: WHAT IS AFFECT/EMOTION/FEELING/SENTIMENT?

Sentiment analysis is often used as an umbrella term for many different types of investigations of affect and emotion in text (Munezero et al., 2014). In certain fields, sentiment analysis is strictly the classification of polarity (positive–negative), sometimes including neutral and/or ambiguous. In other fields, any emotion detection and multi-label emotion classification are referred to as sentiment analysis. The main aim of these approaches is to identify emotions, which requires clear definitions. However, as emotions are studied from many different perspectives ranging from philosophical to psychological or physiological, disciplines have developed slightly differing definitions of emotions as well as distinctions between opinions, sentiments, feelings, emotions, and affect (Izard, 2007; Nabi, 2010). In broader terms, we can say that sentiments are longer lasting and more general than emotions, affects are prepersonal, feelings personal, and emotions social (Shouse, 2005). Therefore, affect is the most subconscious, followed by feeling, with emotion being involuntary but conscious, and sentiment and opinion the most conscious and prompted by feelings and emotions (Öhman, 2021a).

Many emotion models aim to organize emotions, typically as dimensional or discrete (Nabi, 2010). Dimensional models see emotions as a motivational state characterized by two or three broad affective dimensions, whereas discrete emotion perspectives identify emotional states by the unique set of cognitive appraisals, or thought patterns, underlying them. For example, the dimensional Russell's circumplex model, commonly used in empirical psychology and psychophysiology, maps the emotional space with two orthogonal dimensions: emotional valence and emotional arousal (Russell, 1980). Discrete models, then again, propose that there are a small set of discrete emotions. Tomkins (1962), for example, suggested that there are nine basic affects: interest, enjoyment, surprise, distress, fear, anger, shame, dissmell, and disgust, each based on biological affective responses. Yet, there is a surprising lack of consensus even among the basic classifications of emotions.

Behind the definitions lie more fundamental epistemological differences between positivist and interpretivist approaches, and the general question of what aspects of emotions are quantifiable. Positivist approaches aim to measure emotions or causal factors that influence them. One critique of these approaches is that some feelings, such as hope, are more "intellectual" (Averill, 1996), and cannot be easily simplified to quantifiable items. By contrast, interpretivist approaches focus on descriptive and processual aspects of emotions, and their discursive representation and production. This approach is more traditional in social sciences, exploring, for instance, how cultural context affects feelings and how we describe them, and the norms and values that place expectations on our emotional behavior. A central argument is that as language is the principal tool for meaning-making and communication, it is also the only means by which we can think or feel anything (Gerth & Mills, 1954). That is, emotions are discursively defined by the way they are described in language. That is why emotions have no life of their own independent of language and culture – a notion on which the interpretivist approach criticizes the positivist accounts.

The ongoing debate on the exact terminology and nature of emotions is not necessarily a drawback. The different views of affect and emotion complement each other and create a wider base for understanding affective language (Alm, 2010). However, the multiplicity of conceptions entails that the task of quantifying and measuring emotional expressions becomes a methodologically complex task that cannot be reduced to simple technical criteria. This makes sentiment analysis and its cognate approaches particularly fruitful cases for discussing the role and tensions involved in applying computational techniques in the analysis of meaning-laden phenomena. For most practical purposes, it makes sense to look at specific emotions rather than binary polarity. Although we can map many emotions onto positive and negative, knowing emotion over sentiment produces a more fine-grained overview of the data.

There are two main approaches to sentiment analysis: data-driven and lexicon-based, with the addition of hybrid approaches that use lexicons in conjunction with data-driven methods. Data-driven approaches refer mainly to machine learning. Classification algorithms are often used together with state-of-the-art language models such as BERT (Devlin et al., 2018). The one thing these approaches have in common is the need for annotated training data; the more data, the more precise the model will be and the more expensive the training will be too. Lexicon-based approaches, on the other hand, use predefined dictionaries that define the words associated with or evoked by each sentiment (Taboada et al., 2011). It is possible to create these dictionaries automatically by associating, for example, a specific emoticon, emoji, or hashtag with a correlating emotion (De Choudhury et al., 2012), but typically human annotators are used. Although this criticism is more or less true depending on the specific approach, lexicons offer transparency and re-usability that machine learning approaches have difficulty achieving. Lexicons are less domain-dependent (Taboada et al., 2011) and require less CPU/GPU cost. Intensification, valence shifters, and negations can all be incorporated into a lexicon-based approach increasing context awareness. Further, in terms of this chapter, their critical analysis also provides insights into the processes of generating training data and numerical representations which are both essential for machine learning approaches as well.

RECOGNITION AND CALCULATIONS

Sentiment analysis aims to identify emotions in text, and as explained previously, utilizes simple or more sophisticated text mining methods to conduct this task. Most automated methods start by building mathematical representations of words in texts, such as frequency matrices or word vectors in n-dimensional space. In language technology, it has been suggested that existing systems will progress from syntactics (bag-of-words) to semantics (bag-of-concepts) to pragmatics (bag-of-narratives) in the coming decades (Cambria et al., 2017). Currently, however, most forms of applied sentiment detection rely, in one way or another, on word lists, bag-of-word approaches, or n-grams (e.g., Acheampong et al., 2020, Chen et al., 2012; Theocharis et al., 2020). This means counting the frequency of specific words or word combinations extracted from a document. These approaches are criticized for simplicity, ignoring context and even negation and valence shifters. Some more sophisticated methods utilize bag-of-word vectors combined with word dependencies to identify syntactic grammatical relationships in sentences (Burnap & Williams, 2015), semantic word embeddings (Badjatiya et al., 2017), or neural networks (Al-Makhadmeh & Tolba, 2019; Relia et al., 2019). Although such models have been called "stochastic parrots" (Bender et al., 2021), they emulate human understanding reasonably well – but in the end, even the most advanced deep learning algorithm counts words and produces previously seen phrases based on statistical likelihoods of co-occurrence.

Affectivity, however, is much more than words. Research on emotions has long recognized that textual expressions are not necessarily directly connected to authors' felt emotions (e.g., Wetherell, 2012). Similarly, while words are indicative of a specific emotion, emotions cannot be reduced to specific textual formations or combinations of words. The actual sentiment or affective tone of a particular message relies immensely on the final form of the expression. Context-aware systems, such as word embeddings, should enable a fine-grained understanding of word contexts and semantics. Yet, neither have access to actual feelings or intentions of the author, or even feelings expressed by the text – the words and contexts in the texts merely statistically tend to express a certain feeling or emotion. Despite this, some researchers (e.g., Pennebaker et al., 2015) advocate the possibility to deduce a writer's emotional state and even psychometrics based on their word choices.

Despite these discrepancies, automated text mining methods require the transformation of textual data into word representations that can be expressed in a numerical format and then processed using mathematical operations. This quantification and simplification were highlighted in the hate speech detection project described by Laaksonen and colleagues (2020), where the main goal of the project essentially turned out to be the quantification of affect using a rudimentary scale from zero to three to annotate the severity of hate speech. The authors describe working with the spreadsheets of data as a blunt moment of quantification: turning message content and meaning to a single digit, a figure of anticipation (Mackenzie, 2013), stripping off nuances in verbal expression. Likewise, lexicon-based sentiment analysis models rely on sentiment weights given to words to indicate the strength of their association with a specific emotion. A recent project by the authors of this chapter utilized the lexicon developed by Öhman (2022), fine-tuned to match a novel dataset by examining the 3,000 most frequent words in the dataset to add missing emotions, edit associated emotions, and remove incorrect associations. Editing associations meant tweaking the number that defines the weight of the word-emotion association. In this process, the researchers ended up numerically defining the weight between, for example, "pandemic" and "fear", without knowing the context in which the word will appear.

Quantification inevitably flattens the data and results in a loss of variety in expressions, thus performing inevitable oversimplification and formalization of a cultural phenomenon such as emotions. It could be argued that this is precisely what makes algorithms and algorithmic systems powerful; their ability to perform abstraction (Pasquinelli, 2015, cited in Mackenzie, 2017). We argue, however, that the translations involved in datafying affective language go beyond abstraction; due to the nature of the methods used to extract information from text, sentiment values produced by sentiment analysis are objects produced by and for the automated methods used to measure them. As Espeland and Stevens (2008, p. 411) note, quantification is "work that makes other work possible" by establishing shared practices for representing and measuring interests in terms of numeric values that yield further analytical processes. This construction of sentiment becomes evident when detecting complex forms of affective language like hate speech: are we measuring hateful words, the presence of negative emotions, framings, or accusations and calls for action targeted to certain groups of people, as postulated in international agreements on hate speech? Studies of data science have shown that efforts to establish trust in the results of computational knowledge production cannot be understood merely by reference to technical criteria, but instead involve social processes of negotiation through which diverging interpretations are reconciled (Passi & Jackson, 2018). In such negotiations, the challenge is to coordinate approaches to data work and modeling with broader socially established conventions of acceptable analysis – which in loosely interlinked communities such as "artificial intelligence research" can vary widely with respect to disciplinary background and training (Forsythe, 1993). These "human" issues in computational analysis become especially visible in the processes of modeling result validation and training data generation, which we discuss next.

VALIDATION AND NOVEL CONTEXTS

As mentioned earlier, the theories of emotion that sentiment analysis is based on are psychological theories meant to describe human behavior "in the wild". However, when the target of the investigation is text, it could be argued that the output is more deliberate compared with social interactions or psychological phenomena. For example, in psychology, Plutchik (1980) considers anger as a positive emotion because it is an active one, but it makes little sense to classify anger as positive when using applied sentiment analysis to detect hate speech or monitor customer feedback. Current psychological categorizations of emotions thus often are inadequate in describing online communication. Cowen and Keltner (2017) and Demszky et al. (2020) have attempted to rectify this by developing novel emotion categorization systems. However, here we stumble upon the limitations of machine learning algorithms and the overlapping nature of emotions. Machine learning classification works best when categories are as disjoint as possible. Emotions are, however, not disjoint, and the same physiological response can be expressed differently across cultures and linguistic environments.

State-of-the-art solutions are virtually all data-driven, although this statement is debatable due to different validation techniques used with data-driven and lexicon-based approaches. When using a machine learning-based approach to sentiment analysis, validation is built-in to the process. The entire premise is to have your data split into training and testing subsets to be able to calculate f1-scores (or similar) to determine the accuracy of the model (Hastie et al., 2009). The unit that is tested is the same as the unit that is being tested against, making the validation process straightforward. The advantage of machine learning is that models can distinguish between contexts, allowing polysemous words to be categorized as different emotions based on context. Nevertheless, it is important to recognize that a model trained using a certain dataset is valid only in relation to that particular data. This observation highlights that validation in data-driven analysis is based on upstream processes such as data selection, curation, and annotation, which involve laborious manual interpretive work.

When using lexicon-based solutions, we often face a mismatch between the units that are being compared. In lexicon-based approaches, only the test unit is manually annotated by humans, and therefore, the compared units nor their annotations are identical. In essence, with most lexicon-based approaches, we are calculating a composite score of emotions detected and normalized for word count. A single unit of data is also often much larger than with machine learning approaches (speech vs. product review). Hence, the human annotation is difficult to match to the output of the lexicon-based model as the unit of annotation is different, and a phrase where the computer finds several word matches, a human is more likely to assign a single label (Öhman, 2021b). If accuracy measurements in machine learning are comparing apples to apples, in lexicon-based approaches, validation requires the comparison of oranges to bread baskets.

Despite these difficulties in validating lexicon-based approaches, the evidential weight of analysis tends in practice (e.g., in review processes) to be ascribed heavily to validation, which can give rise to procedures that are neither helpful nor informative, even with respect to the actual accuracy of the model. On the other hand, especially in light of the popularity of black-box tools in some interdisciplinary fields, such as LIWC or Vader-sentiment, the results are often accepted without much validation, even though the process is no more robust than other lexicon-based approaches. The allure of off-the-shelf products in their simplicity and ability to provide simple representations of emotions in text should be exempt from robust validation methods due to in-field tradition. Incorporating a qualitative component into sentiment analysis is one way to enhance contextual validity.

TRAINING DATA GENERATION AS CONTESTED NEGOTIATION

Discussions of computational text analysis in the social sciences and humanities have long emphasized the crucial role of discretionary human judgment and interpretive engagement in modeling processes. While computational approaches are often associated with notions such as data-drivenness, general recognition among scholars is that all modeling procedures depend on a series of preliminary decisions and negotiated analysis practices that cannot easily be automated (Grimmer & Stewart, 2013). Articulating the role of human discretionary work in automated analysis approaches becomes increasingly difficult once they become established methodological protocols that researchers can cite as authoritative academic references (Betti & van den Berg, 2016). Indeed, the magic of machine learning is that it is easy to follow the programmatic knowledge production practices in the field, not only to organize data but also the relationships between humans and machines in the process (Mackenzie, 2017).

This interwoven nature and the following emergence of constructed sentiment measurements are well demonstrated by data-driven approaches to sentiment analysis, which draw on variants of supervised machine learning. As noted above, data-driven sentiment analysis depends on training data, fed to the learning algorithm as a datafied definition of the desired target. It is well known that the quality and content of training data highly affect the model (e.g., Hastie et al., 2009; Mackenzie, 2017). When choosing the data set, we give cues to the machine learning algorithm as to what kind of content we are looking for. These cues depend on first, the availability of data, and second, on our ability to select reliable, representative data. Biases caused by training data are sometimes rather obvious in existing systems. For example, Google Jigsaw Perspective API, a state-of-the-art model for toxic language detection (see Rieder & Skop, 2021), has been accused of giving higher toxicity scores to sentences that mention women than men (Jigsaw, 2018). Such differences are due to the over-representation of certain classes in the training data that the system is built on. Unless carefully balanced, any real-life dataset contains more toxic comments concerning regularly targeted groups, so the evaluation of toxicity becomes attached to words that should represent the "neutral context". It is important to note that such biases are difficult to anticipate before being exposed through audits or scandals; however, more transparent documentation practices for datasets have been suggested as a potential solution (Gebru et al., 2021).

The difficulties of identifying and rectifying biases recur throughout the process of training data generation. In data-driven sentiment analysis, the standard approach is to generate training data by manually annotating a smaller set of messages (e.g., a random sample), selected from the full dataset to be classified. Typically, multiple human annotators classify the data individually before a final label is assigned, based on comparison and discussion of the individual annotations. In order to reduce noise, the annotators first have to reach an agreement on the labeling criteria that guide annotations. Noisy annotations are those labels that annotators have difficulty agreeing upon, often revealed by inter-annotator agreement/reliability calculations (Krippendorff, 2003). However, as there is rarely a single "correct" emotion label for a specific text, it is understandable that humans seldom agree on annotations. Therefore, choices need to be made on how to deal with discrepancies: whether to remove all contested annotations, relabel them as neutral, use majority voting, or defer final judgment to an expert annotator. Moreover, certain emotions are more difficult to annotate in text. For example, "surprise" is often highly contextual (Alm & Sproat, 2005). Likewise, annotating hate speech has been shown to be a difficult task for humans (Davidson et al., 2017; Laaksonen et al., 2020). The need for iterative negotiation and revision of annotation criteria makes training data generation a costly procedure, which often does not yield simple one-off solutions. The quality of annotations is directly related to the accuracy of modeling outcomes. However, whether reducing noise to achieve higher accuracies results in more accurate emotion detection in terms of what emotions are actually expressed in texts is highly debatable.

The need for an interpretative engagement at the outset of sentiment analysis throws into relief the constructed nature of the resulting measurements. While the act of assigning numerical values to objects can amount to a simple practice of arbitrary "marking" (Espeland & Stevens, 2008), the establishment of common analytical practices around numeric representations is a social achievement in coordination. For instance, as Laaksonen et al. (2020) showed in their analysis of a hate speech identification project, even after several rounds of coding and revisiting the initial definitions, the resulting definition of hate speech retained unclarities and inconsistencies when applied in practice. These observations align with academic reports on hate speech recognition, which highlight difficulties in separating hate speech from other types of offensive language (e.g., Davidson et al., 2017). Indeed, Pàmies et al. (2020) showed that offensive social media messages included more emotion-associated words than non-offensive messages – both positive and negative.

More generally, annotation decisions are dependent on annotators' previous knowledge with regard to the classifying task, context, and cultural connotations (Waseem & Hovy, 2016; Davidson et al., 2017). Observations of annotation tasks have shown that even with binary or ternary classification schemes, human annotators agree only 70–80% of the time and the more categories, the harder it becomes to reach an agreement (Bayerl et al., 2011; Öhman, 2021a). The question then becomes: how can a machine learning algorithm learn from human-annotated data where most of the annotations are contested? Model performance is highly dependent on the quality of the annotations, but even with the best-trained annotators and most carefully selected and defined categories, if humans – who are the supposed experts at natural language understanding – cannot tell emotion categories apart, how can we expect computers to succeed?

CONCLUSIONS AND IMPLICATIONS

Text mining emotions is a challenging technical endeavor—but perhaps consequently, it represents a type of societal issue many actors hope to solve with technology. As discussed in this chapter, these solutions hinge on complex processes of datafication and quantification of emotions and affective language. Our discussion highlights that utilizing automated, AI-assisted methods typically includes several undisclosed steps of human judgment, from training data annotation to validation to questions of model selection and research problem formulation. From this perspective, emotion detection emerges as a process that combines interpretative validation and mathematical operations. The research design constellation and choices made along the way define whether the extracted sentiments are emotions, affective states, or something else. The development of the methods and excitement related to novel technological opportunities steers the process: state-of-the-art methods are typically wanted in academic publications and eagerly tested in applied contexts despite the escaping explainability of their operation. Indeed, off-the-shelf models from LIWC to BERT are conveniently packaged and easy to use without extensive technical knowledge.

Throughout this chapter, we have characterized automated emotion detection as a process of constructing measurements of sentiment expressions in text. This view implies that the results of sentiment analysis should not be evaluated solely on the basis of certain pre-given metrics that evaluate, for example, model validity in terms of accuracy on a dataset of pre-annotated messages. Rather, model evaluation in general and validity assessment, in particular, should be considered as a process that cuts through the whole process of research design and understanding of the research problem at hand. Ultimately, questions about the validity of measurements of complex meaning-expressions should depend on criteria such as collective assessment through reflexive debate about definitions. Such criteria can be difficult to uphold and reconcile with the demands and diverging conventions imposed on reports of computational research by diverging publication venues and communities of practice. We contend that sentiment analysis is a fruitful case through which to reflect on these processes, given that these families of methods stand at the juxtaposition of stringent technical evaluation practices on the one hand, and the aim of investigating meaning-laden concepts with highly varying interpretations across contexts on the other.

Technologies for detecting emotions are increasingly used in industry, for example, to monitor and moderate online discussions, and hence will reshape our communication environments and our society in the future (Brown, 2018). Applications of hate speech detection used by social media platforms or NGO monitoring projects are prime examples of the applied versions of emotion detection. Other, more playful yet convincingly presented applications are attempts to measure public mood and cross-national happiness using sentiment analysis of social media data (Bollen, 2009; Kamer, 2010; Dodds et al., 2011). Particularly in public discourse such projects are commonly presented and marketed through the magical aura of artificial intelligence (Newlands, 2021). Yet, we know that algorithmic systems rarely perform their tasks perfectly when dealing with complex language data (Grimmer & Stewart, 2013) and that the development and use of AI, being a socio-technical system, can never be separated from the social context (Elish & boyd, 2018). We argue that a better understanding of the capabilities and limitations of these technologies is needed, and action research is one way to generate that knowledge and pursue interventions (Kennedy et al., 2015; Laaksonen et al., 2020; Rieder & Skop, 2021).

REFERENCES

Acheampong, F., Wenyu, C., & Nunoo-Mensah, H. (2020). Text-based emotion detection: Advances, challenges, and opportunities. *Engineering Reports, 2*(7), e12189.

Alm, C. (2010, July). Characteristics of high agreement affect annotation in text. In *Proceedings of the fourth linguistic annotation workshop* (pp. 118–122).

Alm, C., & Sproat, R. (2005, October). Emotional sequencing and development in fairy tales. In *International conference on affective computing and intelligent interaction* (pp. 668–674). Springer.

Andrejevic, M. (2019). Automating surveillance. *Surveillance & Society, 17*(1/2), 7–13.

Averill, J. (1996). Intellectual emotions. In R. Harre & W. G. Parrot (Eds.), *The emotions: Social, cultural and biological dimensions* (pp. 24–38). Sage.

Bayerl, P., & Paul, K. I. (2011). What determines inter-coder agreement in manual annotations? A meta-analytic investigation. *Computational Linguistics, 37*(4), 699–725.

Beer, D. (2019). *The data gaze: Capitalism, power and perception.* Sage.

Bender, E.., Gebru, T., McMillan-Major, A., & Shmitchell, S. (2021, March). On the dangers of stochastic parrots: Can language models be too big? 🦜. In *Proceedings of the 2021 ACM conference on fairness, accountability, and transparency* (pp. 610–623).

Betti, A., & van den Berg, H. (2016). Towards a computational history of ideas. In *CEUR workshop proceedings* 1681.

Bollen, J., Pepe, A., & Mao, H. (2009). Modeling public mood and emotion: Twitter sentiment and socio-economic phenomena. arXiv preprint. http://arxiv.org/abs/0911.1583

Brown, A. (2018). What is so special about online (as compared to offline) hate speech? *Ethnicities, 18*, 297–326.

Burnap, P., & Williams, M. (2015). Cyber hate speech on Twitter: An application of machine classification and statistical modeling for policy and decision making. *Policy and Internet, 7*(2), 223–242.

Cambria, E., Das, D., Bandyopadhyay, S., & Feraco, A. (2017). Affective computing and sentiment analysis. In *A practical guide to sentiment analysis* (pp. 1–10). Springer.

Chen, Y., Zhou, Y., Zhu, S., & Xu, H. (2012). Detecting offensive language in social media to protect adolescent online safety. In *Proceedings of the fourth ASE/IEEE international conference on social computing* (SocialCom 2012), September 3–6, Amsterdam.

Clough, P., & Halley, J. (2007). *The affective turn: Theorizing the social.* Duke University Press.

Cowen, A., & Keltner, D. (2017). Self-report captures 27 distinct categories of emotion bridged by continuous gradients. *Proceedings of the National Academy of Sciences, 114*(38), E7900–E7909.

De Choudhury, M., Gamon, M., & Counts, S. (2012). Happy, nervous or surprised? Classification of human affective states in social media. *ICWSM 2012*, 435–438.

Demszky, D., Movshovitz-Attias, D., Ko, J., Cowen, A., Nemade, G., & Ravi, S. (2020). GoEmotions: A Dataset of Fine-Grained Emotions. In *Proceedings of the 58th Annual Meeting of the Association for Computational Linguistics* (pp. 4040–4054).

Devlin, J., Chang, M., Lee, K., & Toutanova, K. (2018). Bert: Pre-training of deep bidirectional transformers for language understanding. arXiv preprint arXiv:1810.04805.

Dodds, P., Harris, K., Kloumann, I., Bliss, C., & Danforth, C. (2011). Temporal patterns of happiness and information in a global social network: Hedonometrics and Twitter. *PLoS ONE, 6*(12), e26752. https://doi.org/10.1371/journal.pone.0026752

Elish, M., & boyd, D. (2018). Situating methods in the magic of Big Data and AI. *Communication Monographs, 85*(1), 57–80.

Espeland, W., & Stevens, M. (2008). A sociology of quantification. *European Journal of Sociology, 49*(3), 401–436.

Etter, M., Colleoni, E., Illia, L., Meggiorin, K., & D'Eugenio, A. (2018). Measuring organizational legitimacy in social media: Assessing citizens' judgments with sentiment analysis. *Business and Society, 57*(1), 60–97.

Forsythe, D. (1993). Engineering knowledge: The construction of knowledge in Artificial Intelligence. *Social Studies of Science, 23*(3), 445–447.

Gebru, T., Morgenstern, J., Vecchione, B., Vaughan, J. W., Wallach, H., Iii, H. D., & Crawford, K. (2021). Datasheets for datasets. *Communications of the ACM, 64*(12), 86–92.

Gerth, H., & Mills, C. W. (1954). *Character and social structure.* Taylor & Francis.

Gould, D. (2010). On affect and protest. In J. Staiger, A. Cvetkovich, & A. Reynolds (Eds.), *Political emotions* (pp. 18–44). Routledge.

Grimmer, J., & Stewart, B. (2013). Text as data: The promise and pitfalls of automatic content analysis methods for political texts. *Political Analysis, 21*(3), 267–297.

Haapoja, J., Laaksonen, S.-M., & Lampinen, A. (2020). Gaming algorithmic hate-speech detection: Stakes, parties, and moves. *Social Media and Society, 6*(2).

Hastie, T., Tibshirani, R., & Friedman, J. (2009). *The elements of statistical learning: Data mining, inference, and prediction* (2nd ed.). Springer.

Izard, C. (2007). Basic emotions, natural kinds, emotion schemas, and a new paradigm. *Perspectives on Psychological Science, 2*, 260–280.

Jigsaw. (2018). Unintended bias and names of frequently targeted groups. Blog post on the False Positive/Medium. Available: https://medium.com/the-false-positive/unintended-bias-and-names-of-frequently-targeted-groups-8e0b81f80a23 (accessed August 15, 2022).

Kennedy, H., Hill, R., Aiello, G., & Allen, W. (2016). The work that visualisation conventions do. *Information, Communication & Society, 19*(6), 715–735.

Kennedy, H., Moss, G., Birchall, C., & Moshonas, S. (2015). Balancing the potential and problems of digital methods through action research. *Information Communication and Society, 18*(2), 172–186.

Kramer, A. (2010). An unobtrusive behavioral model of "gross national happiness". *Conference on Human Factors in Computing Systems Proceedings, 1*, 287–290.

Krippendorff, K. (2003). *Content analysis: An introduction to its methodology.* Sage.

Laaksonen, S.-M., Haapoja, J., Kinnunen, T., Nelimarkka, M., & Pöyhtäri, R. (2020). The datafication of hate: Expectations and challenges in automated hate speech monitoring. *Frontiers in Big Data, 3*(February), 1–16.

Mackenzie, A. (2013). Programming subjects in the regime of anticipation: Software studies and subjectivity. *Subjectivity, 6*, 391–405.

Mackenzie, A. (2017). *Machine learners: Archaeology of data practice.* MIT Press.

Munezero, M., Montero, C., Sutinen, E., & Pajunen, J. (2014). Are they different? Affect, feeling, emotion, sentiment, and opinion detection in text. *IEEE Transactions on Affective Computing, 5*(2), 101–111.

Nabi, R. (2010). The case for emphasizing discrete emotions in communication research. *Communication Monographs, 77*(2), 153–159.

Newlands, G. (2021). Lifting the curtain: Strategic visibility of human labour in AI-as-a-Service. *Big Data & Society, 8*(1).

Öhman, E. (2021a). The language of emotions: Building and applying computational methods for emotion detection for English and beyond. Doctoral Dissertation, University of Helsinki.

Öhman, E. (2021b). The validity of lexicon-based emotion analysis in interdisciplinary research. In *Proceedings of NLP4DH @ ICON'21.* ACL Anthology.

Öhman, E. (2022). SELF & FEIL: Emotion lexicons for Finnish. In *Proceedings of the 6th digital humanities in the Nordic and Baltic countries conference (DHNB 2022).* CEUR.

Oliveira, D., Bermejo, P. de S., & dos Santos, P. (2017). Can social media reveal the preferences of voters? A comparison between sentiment analysis and traditional opinion polls. *Journal of Information Technology and Politics, 14*(1), 34–45.

Pääkkönen, J., Laaksonen, S.-M., & Jauho, M. (2020). Credibility by automation: Expectations of future knowledge production in social media analytics. *Convergence, 26*(4), 790–807.

Pàmies, M., Öhman, E., Kajava, K., & Tiedemann, J. (2020, December). LT@ Helsinki at SemEval-2020 Task 12: Multilingual or language-specific BERT?. In *Proceedings of the fourteenth workshop on semantic evaluation* (pp. 1569–1575).

Pang, B., & Lee, L. (2008). Opinion mining and sentiment analysis. *Foundations and Trends in Information Retrieval, 2*(1–2), 1–135.

Papacharissi, Z. (2015). *Affective publics: Sentiment, technology, and politics.* Oxford University Press.

Passi, S., & Jackson, S. (2018). Trust in data science: Collaboration, translation, and accountability in corporate data science projects. *Proceedings of the ACM on Human-Computer Interaction, 2* (CSCW).

Pennebaker, J., Boyd, R., Jordan, K., & Blackburn, K. (2015). *The development and psychometric properties of LIWC2015.* University of Texas at Austin.

Plutchik, R. (1980). A general psychoevolutionary theory of emotion. *Theories of emotion* (pp. 3–33). Academic Press.

Puschmann, C., & Powell, A. (2018). Turning words into consumer preferences: How sentiment analysis is framed in research and the news media. *Social Media + Society, 4*(3).

Rieder, B., & Skop, Y. (2021). The fabrics of machine moderation: Studying the technical, normative, and organizational structure of Perspective API. *Big Data and Society, 8*(2).

Russell, J. (1980). A circumplex model of affect. *Journal of Personality and Social Psychology, 39*(6), 1161–1178.

Shivhare, S., & Khethawat, S. (2012). Emotion detection from text. arXiv preprint arXiv:1205.4944.

Shouse, E. (2005). Feeling, emotion, affect. *M/c Journal, 8*(6).

Taboada, M., Brooke, J., Tofiloski, M., Voll, K., & Stede, M. (2011). Lexicon-based methods for sentiment analysis. *Computational Linguistics, 37*(2), 267–307.

Theocharis, Y., Barberá, P., Fazekas, Z., & Popa, S. (2020). The dynamics of political incivility on Twitter. *SAGE Open, 10*(2).

Tomkins, S. (1962). *Affect imagery consciousness.* Springer.

Wetherell, M. (2012). *Affect and emotion: A new social science understanding.* Sage.

PART VI

POLITICS AND ACTIVISM IN AI

56. Democratic friction in speech governance by AI

Niva Elkin-Koren and Maayan Perel

INTRODUCTION

Friction is a key feature in liberal democracies. It is manifested in the ability of citizens to participate in public affairs and engage in a social dialogue over social norms through deliberation and contestation. Different democratic legal regimes maintain fricative mechanisms, processes, and procedures that are designed to hold together divided societies in the absence of deeper normative consensus. By using language to shape behavior, legal norms are capable of tolerating different, often conflicting, meanings, while enabling the negotiation and adjustment of values over time and space. Moreover, the power of lawmaking is distributed between the three branches of government, facilitating the conflict of norms – conflicts that must be resolved through deliberation and negotiation. Furthermore, the law is informed by other kinds of normative systems, such as custom, culture, and religion, which also pluralize its function.

Governance by Artificial Intelligence (AI), however, lacks similar mechanisms that promote democratic friction. This chapter demonstrates this argument using the case of speech governance by AI. AI systems of speech governance, deployed by social media platforms, are configured essentially to promote a frictionless flow of information. Since platforms focus their efforts on keeping users online for maximum engagement, digital conversations are limited to like-minded individuals with shared opinions. Online discourse is fragmented by filter bubbles and echo chambers, which surrender almost any form of social dialogue. In the absence of debate over different opinions, polarization and extremism inevitably rise. Having a shared ground for making concessions and addressing dissent is therefore extremely important in the governance of online speech.

AI systems of speech governance, such as Machine Learning (ML) algorithms used to tackle hate speech,[1] are designed to make speedy detections of unlawful or unauthorized content, in a way that is aligned with the platforms' interests. Speech norms generated by AI systems are probabilistic, optimizing a single, predefined tradeoff. They are constantly shaped by data, and not by ongoing social deliberation, therefore, they fail to make room for debate and contestation over the development of speech norms.

Nevertheless, AI systems of speech governance may be designed differently. As we explain in this chapter, democratic friction may be embedded in the design of the AI system to make room for social debate over speech norms. Specifically, different fricative processes of law may be translated into system design features to enable contestation by design.

---

[1]   Meta AI, *How AI is getting better at detecting hate speech* (November 19, 2020), https://ai.facebook.com/blog/how-ai-is-getting-better-at-detecting-hate-speech/.

In this chapter, we begin in Part A by explaining what makes friction a key feature in democracy and proceed to demonstrate how certain aspects of law promote democratic friction. Then, in Part B, we describe the frictionless nature of the digital public sphere and explain why speech governance by AI is an important test case for exploring the lack of democratic contestation in AI governance. In Parts C and D, respectively, we demonstrate how the unique features of AI systems, in their current design, impede democratic friction. Finally, in Part E, we propose how to incorporate democratic friction into AI systems of speech governance AI by translating the fricative mechanisms of law into design features.

A.   FRICTION IN DEMOCRACY

A.1   Friction as a Feature

Democratic theory focuses on self-governance by the people. It assumes that citizens can take part in crafting the social norms that apply to them. Democratic legitimacy stems from the consent of the constituents, either by voting or by having an opportunity to participate in deliberative processes on issues of public affairs. The participatory vision of democracy presumes citizens have sufficient knowledge to independently form their opinion about public affairs, and are capable of exercising their autonomy, while collectively deciding their common destiny (Goodman, 2021; Barendt, 2007).

Friction, as an institutional design principle in democracy, acknowledges the importance of conflict in politics. Separation of powers, for instance, aims to restrain the domination of coercive power held by the government, by allocating irreducible lawmaking power to the three branches of government: the legislative branch, the executive branch, and the judicial branch. Dividing government responsibilities between competing branches of government, each overseeing the other, intends to safeguard civil liberties. This further introduces friction in the process of interpreting norms, as each of the three branches of the government could exercise its powers to express its normative visions (Huq & Michales, 2016).

Moreover, fricative procedures, such as jury trials or adversary legal proceedings, facilitate democratic contestation. Disagreements caused by people having different opinions create an invaluable space for people to express their autonomous preferences and engage in social dialogue. For liberal theorists, such as Rawls, public debate should enable citizens to express their conceptions of the good and reach consensual solutions by reasoning based on shared principles (Rawls, 1993). Critics of this approach raise concerns that reaching a consensus may stifle identity differences and conceal power relations. The purpose of democratic deliberation in an open society, they argue, is to allow these differences to be expressed and constantly renegotiated (Moufee, 2000). Common to all approaches is the idea that participation in public affairs is essential for democracy (Ferreti & Enzo, 2013).

The right to contest a particular governmental decision is essential for legitimacy (Girard, 2015), and also serves as an important means for restraining power. Contestation is an unspecified concept, which covers a wide range of social practices and meanings. In this chapter, we view democratic contestation as a practice of civil engagement (Smith, 2013). This understanding of democratic contestation entails several elements: First, democratic contestation is discursive (Wiener, 2017). This element is reflected in a dialogic public discourse. Second, it aims to facilitate a diversity of voices. By disclosing flaws, underlying points of controversy, and helping focus public debates on the social choices to be made, democratic contestation facilitates better social choices (Coppedge, 2008). Third, democratic contestation presumes a shared ground for voicing dissent and addressing it (Girard, 2015). It must offer some space for socially negotiating different views and collectively deciding priorities and tradeoffs. However, this does not mean agreement on substantive norms, but rather a strive toward a shared framing of issues and procedures for addressing conflicts.

A.2   How the Law Facilitates Democratic Contestation

Elsewhere we have thoroughly analyzed how the law in liberal democracies facilitates democratic contestation through various rights and duties, authorizations, and legal procedures (Elkin-Koren & Perel, forthcoming 2023). Such fricative mechanisms are designed to hold together divided societies in the absence of deeper normative consensus. Therefore, they are particularly critical in societies that suffer from rising polarization, growing political extremism, and declining trust in social institutions. As we contend next, similar fricative mechanisms are lacking in the governance of speech by AI. Below, we summarize the contestation mechanisms of the law in the context of speech governance by law.

A.3   The Semantic and Distributed Nature of the Law

An important feature of law that facilitates the ongoing social negotiation of speech norms relates to the use of language to shape behavior. Legal norms are capable of encompassing different, often conflicting, meanings, ascribed simultaneously by different legal agents. This, in turn, creates a critical space for negotiating values and adjusting the meaning of norms over time and space. Oftentimes, legal norms are intentionally kept broad and ambiguous by lawmakers, allowing them to sustain different meanings in order to bridge diverse interests and goals. In common law regimes, open-ended standards allow the judge to define preconditions for the legal consequences when applying the norm (Sullivan, 1992; Elkin-Koren & Fischman-Afori, 2017). Vague general standards can evolve over time through a series of particular applications and change in content as the nature of society changes (Christie, 1964).

Open-ended standards not only facilitate flexibility and dynamism in applying legal norms to specific cases but also serve as a *modus vivendi* (McCabe, 2010), allowing social agreement on high-level principles, removed from immediate conflicting interests, while deferring disagreements to be resolved down the road. In other words, vagueness facilitates the ongoing deliberation of meanings, which "allows man to exercise general control over his social development without committing himself in advance to any specific concrete course of action" (Ibid.).

Moreover, the nature of legal norms is neither inherent nor intrinsic. Instead, the attributes of rules and standards are subject to interpretation by courts. Judges often soften rules and insert more discretionary judgment at the moment of application by introducing exceptions or applying broad interpretations that extend beyond the literal meaning of the rule (Schauer, 1993). Through judicial interpretation, courts can adjust the meaning of the rule to meet changing circumstances and further facilitate diversity.

A.4   The Distributed Power of Law Making

An important institutional design principle in law, which facilitates contestation relates to the distributed power of lawmaking. Specifically, the democratic principle of "separation of powers" allocates irreducible lawmaking power to the three branches of government: the legislative branch, the executive branch, and the judicial branch. The "three branches of the government serve as devices through which a larger, pluralistic normative vision can be channeled and, ultimately, vindicated" (Huq & Michales, 2016). Since each branch of the government may generate legal norms, and such norms may be in conflict, disputes as to which norm governs in each case are unavoidable (Reichman, 2020). These disputes facilitate deliberation over different meanings of the law.

A.5   The Relation of the Law to External Normative Systems

Legal norms are discursive, making room for multiple meanings not only internally, but also externally. The meaning of norms might be informed by other kinds of normative systems, such as custom, culture, and religion, which pluralize their function (Moore, 1973). Legislators, judges, administrative agencies, and lawyers all adjust and interpret the law in light of their social context (Yngvesson, 1989; Feldman, 2014). Therefore, legal norms are fluid and dynamic, continuously changing in response to the ongoing negotiation of meaning and validity by social actors, who are themselves subject to entwining normative systems. This interpretative nature of legal norms leaves further room for diversity of meanings at all levels.

At the same time, however, legal procedures, institutions, and rights offer a common ground for negotiating these diverse meanings and even contesting their framing. The law evolves on the basis of particularity, depending on the proficiency and level of the court deciding the case, the surrounding circumstances, the characteristics of the specific clash being resolved, and the characteristics of the authorized decision maker exercising interpretive power. While seeking coherence, the law makes room for a broad spectrum of tradeoffs between competing values to coexist.

In sum, speech governance by law allows citizens to contest meanings on a shared ground, toward collectively deciding conflicting views, while often disagreeing. The transition to AI in speech governance by social media platforms undermines some of these fundamental features of governance by legal norms, as discussed next.

B.   A FRICTIONLESS DIGITAL PUBLIC SPHERE

Frictionless flows of information have become a signature trait of the digital public sphere. Since the late 1990s, digital networks strived to make the flow of information *frictionless,* across national borders and technical standards, to enhance efficiency and reduce transaction costs. The frictionless flow of information has undoubtedly generated great economic efficiencies and promoted important social benefits, giving rise to social movements such as #MeToo.

Nowadays, the digital public sphere is governed by a handful of social media platforms, like Facebook, YouTube, and Twitter (Klonick, 2018; Heldt, 2020). They have become digital public squares where opinions, ideas, and preferences are shaped (Yemini, 2019). These digital platforms operate in multisided markets, harvest data on users, and extract revenues from selling users' profiles for targeted advertising or other data-driven products and services (Freedman, 2020). This business model has become an important driving force of the frictionless information flow, where platforms focus their efforts on keeping users online for maximum engagement (Evans & Schmalensee, 2016). Yet, the democratic nature of online speech is declining.

The central role of democratic contestation as enabling deliberation over competing views is withering away. Scholars question "whether the myriad of diverse views that exist online are actually intersecting, and thus the extent to which online interactions actually involve any significant problematization and contestation of positions and practices" (Dahlberg, 2008). Indeed, online discourse is fragmented. Digital conversation involves like-minded individuals with shared identity leading to what Sunstein names "deliberative enclaves" (Sunstein, 2001). Instead of enabling users to confront opposing views, the Internet has become "a breeding ground for group polarization and extremism" (Ibid), which is reinforced by algorithmic "filter bubbles" and online "echo-chambers" (YouTube Regrets Report, 2021).

Online speech governance makes an important test case for exploring (the lack of) democratic contestation because of the deep social divides over the limits of free speech (Earle, 2021). While most agree that threats of violence fall outside the constitutional protection of freedom of expression, there is a wide disagreement as to what counts as violent speech. Especially today, liberal democracies must preserve a democratic space for deliberating the disagreements in society regarding the scope of free speech. It is necessary to sustain a procedural framework for engaging in a social dialogue over the development of speech norms that shape our digital public sphere.

C.   SPEECH GOVERNANCE BY AI – IN A NUTSHELL

C.1   Content Moderation by AI

Content moderation is "the governance mechanisms that structure participation in a community to facilitate cooperation and prevent abuse" (Grimmelmann, 2015). Platforms engage in two types of content moderation. The first is intended to match content with users' interests and preferences for the purpose of lengthening the amount of time users spend on the platform, which in turn increases the platforms' advertising income. The second is intended to ensure compliance with community standards and legal duties (Elkin-Koren & Perel, 2020). When referring to speech governance by AI, this chapter focuses on the second type of content moderation, which includes different strategies that seek to ensure that content complies with appropriate norms, either internal (i.e., community guidelines) or external (i.e., regulatory restraints), by filtering, blocking, downgrading, or removing inappropriate content (Husovec, 2018).

In the past, platforms relied on human moderators to screen content uploaded to social media. With the amount of content growing exponentially, platforms were forced to supplement and even replace human reviews with automated systems (Gorwa, 2020). One reason for this was the public outcry over the distressing work conditions of content moderators, which were argued to be harmful to their mental health (Roberts, 2019). Another reason for the shift to AI in content moderation was increasing regulatory pressures, including the expanding liability of online platforms for potentially harmful content posted by their users (Elkin-Koren, Nahmias & Perel, 2020). For instance, in 2019, lawmakers in the European Union adopted Article 17 of the Digital Single Market (DSM) Directive, which requires hosting platforms to ensure from the outset the unavailability of infringing content posted by users, in order to avoid strict liability. An additional example is Germany's Network Enforcement Act of 2018, which requires online platforms to remove content within 24 hours of a complaint being filed, meaning platforms must actively engage in content moderation at the outset. A different reason for the shift to AI-based content moderation was the Covid-19 pandemic, which forced platforms to act promptly against the proliferation of misinformation and conspiracy theories that were threatening to put public health and safety at risk (Toh, 2020).

All in all, many platforms today deploy AI systems both to optimize the matching of content and users, and improve the speedy detection of potentially harmful content, filter unwarranted content before it is posted, identify and track similar content, and block access to it or remove it from the platform. Below we describe the basic features of AI systems of content moderation. Then, we turn to explain that since these algorithmic systems effectively shape and generate speech norms, they engage in speech governance.

C.2   Datafication

All systems that rely on automated data-driven decision-making processes involve datafication – namely, a choice embedded in the system as to which data to collect and to record (Strandburg, 2014). For instance, in recent years, two organizations have sprung up to support the datafication of terrorist materials on social media: Tech Against Terrorism, a non-profit organization supported by the United Nations Counter-Terrorism Executive Directorate; and the Global Internet Forum to Counter Terrorism (GIFCT), originally established in 2017 by a group of four tech firms (Facebook, Twitter, Microsoft, and YouTube) (Fisshman, 2019; Gorwa, 2020; Tech Against Terrorism, 2021). These organizations promote and advance the use of AI to filter terrorist propaganda by detecting images and videos that match a privately held, secretive database of content hashtags – unique digital fingerprints of alleged terrorist content, including images, videos, audio, and text.

C.3   Predictive Model

AI systems further rely on an objective function, that is, the mathematical expression of the algorithm's goal. For instance, the objective function of a system designed to predict copyright infringement might be to correctly classify infringing content (namely, uploaded content that is substantially similar to the copyrighted content). Optimizing this goal means maximizing accurate predictions, or, alternatively, minimizing inaccurate ones – the percentage of uploaded works incorrectly identified as infringing (false positives) or non-infringing (false negatives). Eventually, such systems attain the capacity to analyze new data and make predictions by drawing on their prior learnings. Designing predictive models may rely on either supervised learning or unsupervised learning (Lehr & Ohm, 2017). Supervised learning involves training the algorithm on previously labeled data designed to classify different types of content. Labeling refers to the recording, aggregating, tagging, and coding of data into a format that can be used for training and data analytics. The system may be given a large set of (probably) correct answers to the system's task (labeled content), and it learns to answer new cases in a similar way. Systems using digital hash technology may also learn to identify content that is similar to the labeled image, even when not identical (Evan & Freamster, 2020). Unsupervised learning, by contrast, does not make predictions based on pre-labeled content, but instead, seeks to cluster content based on certain shared characteristics. Unsupervised Domain Adaptation for Hate Speech Detection, for instance, identifies hate speech sentences where the hate speech terms can be distinguished from their surrounding sentence context to create a template for domain adaptation. The algorithm then identifies the template in generic sentences to slot in hate speech and convert it into hate speech in a new domain. To create a domain-adapted corpus, a sequential tagger is trained on the labeled data in the source domain so that the tagger is able to identify hate speech content terms, and surrounding sentence context templates. Later, the tagger is applied to unlabeled data in the target domain to derive a lexicon of hate terms in the target domain (Sarwar & Murdock, 2022).

C.4   Action and Recursive Feedback Loop

The predictive model of AI systems leads to a specific automated outcome. For instance, Scribd, a subscription-based digital library of e-books and audiobooks, employs a system called BookID to generate a digital fingerprint for each book based on semantic data (e.g., word counts, letter frequency, phrase comparisons). Texts uploaded to Scribd are scanned by BookID, and content that matches any BookID fingerprint is blocked. Another instance of intellectual property enforcement via ML is YouTube's Content ID. Using a digital identifying code, Content ID can detect and notify rights holders whenever a newly uploaded video matches a work that they own. Rights holders can then choose to block or remove the content, share information, or monetize the content (Sag, 2017). Finally, a key feature of AI systems of content moderation systems is a recursive feedback loop. Once trained, these systems enter an organic process of continual learning. Accordingly, content identified as illicit is fed back into the model so that it will be detected the next time the system runs.

C.5   Speech Governance by AI

Speech regulation, in the broad sense, defines the scope of permissible speech through social and legal norms (Klonick, 2018). AI introduces a new type of governance, which is based on dynamic and adaptive decision-making processes driven by data, correlations, and predictions. AI systems govern speech by creating speech affordances – that is, determining which content remains available and which content is removed, and how content might be shared (e.g., "like" or "retweet") (Elkin-Koren & Perel, 2020). These affordances are later embedded in upload filters of social media that are often set to enforce these norms, thus effectively providing an operational definition of permissible use through technical details (Perel, 2020). YouTube's restricted mode, for instance, is an optional setting that tags potentially mature or objectionable content and prevents users with restrictions enabled from viewing it. Some algorithms can also limit who can participate in online conversations (e.g., by requiring verification of the user's online identity or by suspending accounts).

Moreover, determinations of judicial and semi-judicial issues regarding illegal content depend on the technical implementation of AI content moderation systems. For instance, the threshold of substantial similarity in copyright law, or the particular score that defines a piece of content as obscenity, must be embedded in the ML system, which then makes a purely mechanical judgment.

But speech governance by AI does not merely apply existing norms, thereby simply reflecting existing values and tradeoffs. In discerning between content that is permissible and content that is banned, automated content moderation systems also craft speech norms. Meaning, AI systems that seek to identify hate speech may also carry a regulatory consequence: shaping users' behavior by distinguishing between legitimate and illegitimate expressions (where only the latter are removed).

While the speech affordances that are generated by AI systems of content moderation are driven by the economic interests of private businesses, they constitute the digital public sphere and therefore are essential to the common good. Speech governance by AI, thus, offers an important test case for exploring the opportunities and risks pertaining to governance by AI. Accordingly, we now turn to the question of whether speech governance by AI could sustain democratic friction, in the same way it is facilitated in speech governance by legal norms.

D.   HOW SPEECH GOVERNANCE BY AI DIMINISHES DEMOCRATIC FRICTION

The transition to AI transforms the nature of speech governance. It lacks some key features that are necessary to enable society to collectively decide self-governing norms. As we noted, democratic contestation seeks to enable citizens to collectively form public opinion by facilitating discursive interactions. Nevertheless, as we explain below, the current system design of speech governance by AI undermines democratic contestation.

D.1   The Concentration of Rulemaking Power

One important feature of democratic contestation facilitated by law is the dispersed power to decide and interpret norms, held by competing institutions and diverse human decision makers. By contrast, AI systems of speech governance act simultaneously as legislatures, judges, and executors when they define the classifiers, apply them to any given piece of content, and generate an outcome: whether to allow or ban it (Elkin-Koren & Perel, 2019). Consider, for instance, how YouTube governs the use of copyrighted materials while shaping the boundaries of copyright infringement. Content ID enables YouTube to automatically screen user-uploaded content and identify copyrighted material using a digital identifying code. It also determines what specific level of similarity between an uploaded video and an original copyrighted work is needed to trigger the matching feature, which will then submit a signal to the rights holder, allowing them to choose whether to remove, monetize, block, or disable the allegedly infringing material before it becomes publicly available. YouTube effectively exercises judicial power when it determines which content constitutes an infringement of an original copyrighted work. It also exercises executive power when it acts to remove, disable, or filter such content.

D.2   Diminishing Multiplicity of Meanings in Speech Norms

Speech norms developed by AI leave no room for a plurality of meanings. Content is either banned or allowed, without any deliberation over which of these options is more in line with our social contract. In AI speech governance, there is no shared ground for voicing collective dissent and addressing it. ML algorithms differ from applying a legal norm, which begins with an explicit legal definition of unwarranted content and applies it to a particular fact, to reach an ad hoc outcome (legal/illegal). ML, by contrast, receives outcomes (labeled data) and data as input, to generate rules. Such rules reflect the ex-ante tradeoff the AI system was designed to promote. They are not explicit and therefore fail to provide a ground for engaging the public in ongoing normative deliberation regarding the appropriate tradeoff that should apply in a new, given case.

D.3   Shrinking the Shared Ground for Public Scrutiny

AI is less susceptible to public scrutiny than speech governance by law, hence diminishing democratic contestation. This is for several reasons. First, norms generated by AI are opaque, and thus not subject to public scrutiny, negotiation, or social change. ML algorithms, particularly those based on deep learning, are designed to identify patterns and make predictions without having to explicitly reveal the norms being applied. These systems do not provide explanations of their outcomes, making it more difficult for affected parties to effectively contest their outcomes. Second, the automated classification conceals an important point of social choice, on whether and how to adjust it speech norms and their underlining tradeoffs. While courts applying a specific rule adjust to the specific circumstances of any given case, AI systems currently lack the ability to develop new norms when confronted with grey areas of legality. Moreover, while legal procedures facilitate new ways of balancing values through judicial interpretation, the optimization objective embedded in the program impedes such processes of deliberative change. Fourth, AI systems fail to explicitly display not only the tradeoffs they effectively apply but also the procedures by which these tradeoffs were decided. ML-based content moderation is probabilistic (Ananny, 2019). Decisions to ban or remove content may depend on many dynamic variables: whether the content has triggered a computational threshold; whether similar content has triggered the system before; whether third parties have flagged the content or similar content; who flagged the content; and how often these things have occurred before. Unlike legal norms, ML predictions are not the result of conscious deliberation or intentional attempts to reflect the underlying principles of our social contract. Fifth, ML systems are designed to serve a mixture of commercial interests, while also performing public functions. As such, they often overlook the interests of some stakeholders, while possibly ignoring larger societal tradeoffs. Any single tradeoff is non-transparent and might be biased toward the platform's commercial interests.

E.   PROMOTING DEMOCRATIC FRICTION BY DESIGN

Thus far, we have demonstrated that speech moderation by AI is shaping public discourse without sufficient mechanisms for social contestation and deliberation. The robust and speedy detection of harmful content as defined by social media platforms facilitates a "frictionless" flow of information. Introducing friction into the data flow of AI content moderation systems would aim to interrupt the workflow of such systems to enhance ongoing visibility of tradeoffs generated by the system, promote adjustments, and create opportunities for public oversight and social choice.

Reintroducing democratic contestation into the process of implementing and creating speech norms is therefore essential for sustaining a democratic online discourse. Accordingly, we propose incorporating contestation-by-design. This solution effectively addresses scale with scale: instead of counting on individual disputes against particular content removals, it advances a systemic approach that meets the pace of online speech flows (Douek, 2022). The by-design, automatic approach to regulation has gained prominence in protecting fundamental rights, especially privacy (Cavoukian, 2009), and more recently also in the context of content moderation (Yu, 2020; Lambrecht, 2020). Inspired by the contestation processes and procedures of speech governance by law, we propose how to embed democratic procedures for contestation in the design of AI-based content moderation systems.

Before doing so, it is important to note that in order to ensure that digital platforms, as private actors, effectively incorporate mechanisms of democratic contestation, legal policy must encourage them to do so. This could be achieved, for instance, by conditioning their legal immunity against tortious speech violations committed by their users (e.g., copyright infringement), upon the adoption of contestation design features. Otherwise, platforms might avoid investing resources in altering the design of their internal content moderation systems.

E.1   Embedding an Adversarial Approach

The underlining assumption of adversarial procedures is that laying out the contesting positions in a dispute is the best way to test factual evidence and reach sound decisions (Sward, 1989). Adversarial legal procedures, where parties are called to present their contesting positions in front of a judge or jury, are among the fundamental elements of common law justice systems and the gold standard of dispute resolution. An adversarial approach could guide the creation of a system of contesting algorithms, which would automate the process of contesting decisions about speech (Elkin-Koren, 2019). Contesting algorithms approach could require that any content subject to removal would have to be run through a competing system designed to reflect societal values. This virtual checkpoint would judge the content at issue against norms generated dynamically by independent bodies, such as public civil society organizations or the judiciary. Should the contesting algorithm reaffirm the platform's removal decision, removal would proceed. Should the contesting algorithm reach a different conclusion, removal of the content would be postponed until the conflict is resolved, either automatically, based on scorings produced by the two systems – the platform and the contesting algorithm – or through human review. Even though this would still be a single resolution (that is, a given content would eventually be either banned or allowed), it would be a result of technological deliberation between different and possible contradicting conceptions of legitimate speech rather than a monolithic implementation of a single platform's moderation system. Of course, to best achieve this ambition, it would be necessary to assure that the competing system adequately reflects legitimate public values, for instance, those represented by publicly accredited institutions, and that it is not biased in favor of specific political agendas.

The final resolution would be fed into both systems to update their models (Id). Such a design intervention would facilitate a common ground for public deliberation over social choices regarding speech norms. It would further counteract the feedback loop of content moderation systems run by platforms, which are set up to optimize a predetermined trade-off reflecting their business interests. This could create a check as well as counter pressure against platforms' monolithic content removal systems. Especially, the adversarial procedure would force the disclosure of necessary information on removal decisions that may be inconsistent with some social values, thus enabling judicial review or public oversight of such gaps.

E.2 Separation of Functions

Another possible means to promote democratic contestation by design is to inject the legal principle of separation of powers into algorithmic content moderation through separation of functions. The idea is to separate different functions performed by the monolithic AI content moderation systems of digital platforms and outsource the law enforcement functions to external, unbiased algorithms (Elkin-Koren & Perel, 2020). Currently, the public law enforcement functions of social media platforms are integrated with private business functions that are driven by commercial interests. The same technical design that is used for targeted advertising and curating personalized content is also deployed for monitoring and enforcing speech norms. The system is informed by the same labeling of users and content and makes use of the same application programming interfaces, learning patterns, and software. Separation of functions would stimulate the creation of alternative solutions to content moderation, thereby supporting the development of more diversified speech norms in AI systems. Our proposal for separation of functions seeks to create a separate and independent public system to flag and remove unlawful content (i.e., unwarranted content as defined by the law). This will encourage platforms to keep their systems' commercial functions distinct from their law enforcement functions to ensure that the proposed external law enforcement system does not disrupt their business interests. This will enable external deliberation over speech norms while giving voice to alternative conceptions of free speech.

CONCLUSION

Democracy depends on a functioning framework for negotiating differences, adjusting positions, modifying opinions, and making concessions. Since AI systems have become the main architecture for moderating public discourse, it is now essential to enable contestation in their design, which would better reflect collective social choice. This chapter called to design a space for contestation and deliberation of different value perceptions held by diverse stakeholders in AI-based systems of content moderation. Rather than having these tradeoffs determined unilaterally by the platform or by top-down regulation, they would be shaped by society as well, while injecting diversity and securing contestation in the algorithmic governance of speech. As a result, the tremendous power of platforms to decide tradeoffs in speech regulation in a non-transparent way could be significantly decentralized.

BIBLIOGRAPHY

About Tech Against Terrorism. (2021, August 10). https://www.techagainstterrorism.org/about/.

Ananny, M. (2019, August 21). *Probably Speech, Maybe Free: Toward a Probabilistic Understanding of Online Expression and Platform Governance*. Knight First Amendment Institute. https://knightcolumbia.org/content/probably-speech-maybe-free-toward-a-probabilistic-understanding-of-online-expression-and-platform-governance.

Barendt, E. (2007). *Freedom of Speech*. Oxford University Press.

Cavoukian, A. (2009). Privacy by Design: The Definitive Workshop. *Identity in the Information Society*, 3, 247–251.

Christie, C. G. (1964). Vagueness and Legal Language. *Minnesota Law Review*, 48, 885–911.

Cohen, M. (1987). Masking Copyright Decisionmaking: The Meaninglessness of Substantial Similarity. *U.C. Davis Law Review*, 20, 719–767.

Coppedge, M., Alvarez, A. & Maldonado, C. (2008). Two Persistent Dimensions of Democracy: Contestation and Inclusiveness. *The Journal of Politics*, 70(3), 632–647.

Dahlberg, L. (2008). Rethinking the Fragmentation of the Cyberpublic: From Consensus to Contestation. *New Media & Society*, 9(5), 827–847.

Damaska. R. M. (1991). *The Faces of Justice and State Authority: A Comparative Approach to the Legal Process.* Yale University Press.

Dewey, J. (1927). *The Public and Its Problems: An Essay in Political Inquiry.* Penn State University Press.

Douek, E. (forthcoming, 2022). Content Moderation as Administration. *Harvard Law Review*, 136.

Earle, S. (2021, May 31). *The 'Culture Wars' Are a Symptom, Not the Cause, of Britain's Malaise.* The Guardian. https://www.theguardian.com/commentisfree/2021/may/31/culture-wars-symptom-not -cause-britains-malaise.

Elkin-Koren, N. & Fischman-Afori, O. (2017) Rulifying Fair Use. *Arizona Law Review*, 59, 161–200.

Elkin-Koren, N. & Perel, M. (2019). Algorithmic Governance by Online Intermediaries. In E. Brousseau, J.-M. Glachant & J. Sgard (Eds.), *Oxford Handbook on International Economic Governance and Market Regulation* (pp. 1–24). (Oxford Handbooks Online). Oxford University Press. https://doi. org/10.1093/oxfordhb/9780190900571.001.0001.

Elkin-Koren, N. & Perel, M. (2020). Separation of Functions for AI: Restraining Speech Regulation by Online Platforms. *Lewis & Clark Law Review*, 24, 857–898.

Elkin-Koren, N., Nahmias, Y. & Perel, M. (2020). Is It Time to Abolish Safe Harbor? When Rhetoric Clouds Policy Goals. *Stanford Law & Policy Review*, 31, 1–50.

Elkin-Koren, N. & Perel, M. (2020). Guarding the Guardians: Content Moderation by Online Intermediaries and the Rule of Law. In G. Frosio (Ed.), *Oxford Handbook of Online Intermediary Liability* (pp. 669–678). (Oxford Handbooks in Law). Oxford University Press. https://doi.org/10.1093/ oxfordhb/9780198837138.013.34.

Elkin-Koren, N. (2020). Contesting Algorithms: Restoring the Public Interest in Content Filtering by Artificial Intelligence. *Big Data & Society*, 7, 1–13.

Elkin-Koren, N. & Perel, M. (Forthcoming, 2022). Democratic Contestation by Design: Speech Governance by AI and How to Fix it. *Florida State Law Review.*

Engstrom, E. & Feamster, N. (2017, March). *The Limits of Filtering: A Look at the Functionality and Shortcomings of Content Detection Tools.* Engine. https://www.engine.is/the-limits-of-filtering.

Evans, D. S. & Schmalensee, R. (2016). *Matchmakers: The New Economics of Multisided Platforms.* Harvard Business Review Press.

Feldman, S. M. (2014). Supreme Court Alchemy: Turning Law and Politics into Mayonnaise. *The Georgetown Journal of Law & Public Policy*, 12, 57–97.

Ferretti, M. P. & Rossi, E. (2013). Pluralism, Slippery Slopes and Democratic Public Discourse. *Theoria*, 60, 29–47.

Fishman, B. (2019). Crossroads: Counter-Terrorism and the Internet. *Texas National Security Review*, 2(2), 82–100.

Freedman, M. (2020, June 17). *How Businesses Are Collecting Data (And What They're Doing with It).* Business News Daily. https://www.businessnewsdaily.com/10625-businesses-collecting-data.html [https://perma.cc/4XGE-VDAS].

Girard, C. (2015). Making Democratic Contestation Possible: Public Deliberation and Mass Media Regulation. *Policy Studies*, 36(3), 283–297. https://doi.org/10.1080/01442872.2015.1065968.

Goodman, P. E. (2021). Digital Fidelity and Friction. *Nevada Law Journal*, 21(2), 623–654.

Gorwa, R., Binns, R. & Katzenbach, C. (2020). Algorithmic Content Moderation: Technical and Political Challenges in the Automation of Platform Governance. *Big Data & Society*, 3(1), 1–15.

Grimmelmann, J. (2015). The Virtues of Moderation. *Yale Journal of Law & Technology*, 17, 42–109.

Husovec, M. (2018). The Promises of Algorithmic Copyright Enforcement: Takedown or Staydown? Which is Superior? And Why? *Columbia Journal of Law & the Arts*, 42, 53–84.

Heldt, P. A. (2020). Merging the 'Social' and the 'Public': How Social Media Platforms Could Be a New Public Forum. *Mitchell Hamline Law Review*, 46, 997–1042.

Huq, A. & Michaels, D. J. (2016). The Cycles of Separation-of-Powers Jurisprudence. *Yale Law Journal*, 126, 342–437.

Klonick, K. (2018). The New Governors: The People, Rules, and Processes Governing Online Speech. *Harvard Law Review*, 131, 1598–1670.

Lambrecht, M. (2020). Free Speech by Design: Algorithmic Protection of Exceptions and Limitations in the Copyright DSM Directive. *Journal of Intellectual Property, Information Technology & E-Commerce Law*, 11(1), 68–94.

Lehr, D. & Ohm, P. (2017). Playing with the Data: What Legal Scholars Should Learn About Machine Learning. *U. C. Davis Law Review*, 51, 653–717.

McCabe, D. (2010). *Modus Vivendi Liberalism: Theory and Practice.* Cambridge: Cambridge University Press.

Moore, F. S. (1973). Law and Social Change: The Semi-Autonomous Social Field as an Appropriate Subject for Study. *Law & Society Review*, 7(4), 719–746.

Mouffe, C. (2000). *The Democratic Paradox*. London: Verso.

Mozilla. (2021, July). *YouTube Regret: A Crowdsourced Investigation into YouTube's Recommendation Algorithms*. Foundation.mozilla.org. https://assets.mofoprod.net/network/documents/Mozilla_You Tube_Regrets_Report.pdf.

Perel, M. (2020). Digital Remedies. *Berkeley Technology Law Journal*, 35, 1–52.

Rawls, J. (1993). Political Liberalism. *The Review of Metaphysics,* 47(3), 585–602.

Reichman, A. (Working Draft, 2020). Neo-Formalism as Formal Legal Pluralism.

Roberts, S. T. (2019). *Behind the Screen: Content Moderation in the Shadows of Social Media*. Yale University Press.

Sag, M. (2017). Internet Safe Harbors and the Transformation of Copyright Law. *Notre Dame Law Review*, 93, 499–564.

Sarwar, S. M. & Murdock, V. (2022). Unsupervised Domain Adaptation for Hate Speech Detection Using a Data Augmentation Approach. In *Proceedings of the Sixteenth International AAAI Conference on Web and Social Media*, 853.

Schauer, F. (1993). *Playing by the Rules: A Philosophical Examination of Rule-Based Decision Making in Law and in Life*. Clarendon Press.

Singh, S. (2019, July 15). *Everything in Moderation: An Analysis of How Internet Platforms Are Using Artificial Intelligence to Moderate User-Generated-Content*. New America. https://www .newamerica.org/oti/reports/everything-moderation-analysis-how-internet-platforms-are-using -artificial-intelligence-moderate-user-generated-content/.

Smith, W. (2013). *Civil Disobedience and Deliberative Democracy* (2nd ed.). Routledge. https://doi.org /10.4324/9780203758502.

Strandburg, K. J. (2014). Monitoring, Datafication, and Consent: Legal Approaches to Privacy in the Big Data Context. In J. Lane et al. (Eds.), *Privacy, Big Data, and the Public Good: Frameworks for Engagement*, 5, 10–12.

Sullivan, M. K. (1992). The Supreme Court 1991 Term-Foreword: The Justices of Rules and Standards. *Harvard Law Review*, 106, 22–123.

Sunstein, R. C. (2001). Republic.com. *Harvard Journal of Law & Technology*, 14(2), 753–766.

Sward, E. E. (1989). Values, Ideology, and the Evolution of the Adversary System. *Indiana Law Journal*, 64, 301–355.

Toh, M. (2020, February 3). *Facebook, Google and Twitter Crack Down on Fake Coronavirus 'Cures' and Other Misinformation*. CNN BUS. https://www.cnn.com/2020/01/31/tech/facebook-twitter -google-coronavirus-misinformation/index.html.

Wiener, A. (2017). A Theory of Contestation — A Concise Summary of Its Argument and Concepts. *Polity*, 49, 109–125.

Yemini, M. (2019). The New Irony of Free Speech. *Columbia Science & Technology Law Review*, 20, 119–194.

YouTube Help. (2022, February 14). *The Difference Between Copyright Takedowns and Content ID Claims*. https://support.google.com/youtube/answer/7002106?hl=en.

Yngvesson, B. (1989). Inventing Law in Local Settings: Rethinking Popular Legal Culture. *Yale Law Journal*, 98, 1689–1709.

Yu, P. K. (2020). Can Algorithms Promote Fair Use? *FIU Law Review*, 14, 329–363.

57. Automating empathy: overview, technologies, criticism

Andrew McStay and Vian Bakir

INTRODUCTION

The use of technologies to profile and interact with human emotion and broader subjectivity by means of the body is growing in prominence. It is becoming clear that although online profiling since the 1990s and 2000s has been about assessing traces of intention and emotion in what people click, swipe, and say through screens and keyboards, the body itself is increasingly the object of attention to gauge subjectivity. Connected, only a few years ago, biometrics were popularly associated with identifying and authenticating individuals, but other uses of biometrics are coming into popular view. This involves the use of *soft* biometrics, which are bodily measures that identify traits about a person or a group of people but are not defined in terms of uniquely identifying a person (unlike fingerprints, retinal scans or similar) (Article 29 Data Protection Working Party 2012). Examples include factors such as facial emotion expressions or heart rate, but also more familiar measures such as height. Applied to automated empathy interests, the key and perceived value of soft biometrics are that bodily factors are believed to signify something about the subjective state of a person, such as how they are feeling, what emotion they are undergoing, what mood they are in, and what their broader state of mind might be. If there is validity to this, then one begins to see a range of value types. Marketers, advertisers, and political campaigners will be interested in biometric understanding of people in order to influence them, security forces will see scope for threat detection and the ability to spot deceit, and health organisations will have mental health applications in mind. Wherever there is any financial, surveillant, or other organisational value in understanding emotion and subjectivity, there will be interest in soft biometrics, the mediation of subjectivity, and attempts to automate empathy.

The aim of this chapter is four-fold: 1) to provide non-expert readers with a tangible sense of the technologies and how they are being used; 2) to clarify terminology around the use of technologies that infer emotion and human subjectivity; 3) to provide a sense of which sectors are impacted, or have a chance to be impacted, by automated empathy, not least as online behaviour profiling morphs into biometric profiling; and 4) to advance critiques of automated empathy, especially in relation to mental integrity and unnatural mediation.

WHY 'AUTOMATED EMPATHY'?

The use of soft biometrics to infer emotion and other experiential states has been described by diverse terminology. We use the term, 'empathy', for reasons explored in the following subsection, but there are other contenders to be addressed before we can state why empathy is most useful. Coined by Rosalind Picard (1997) 'affective computing' is the longest-standing term, defined by the use of computational technologies to understand, interact with, and stimulate affective responses in people, for example, through robots that emote (Breazeal 2002). Affective computing began in the 1990s using computational technology and related sensors to measure heart fluctuations, skin conductance, muscle tension, pupil dilation, and facial muscles to assess how changes in the body relate to emotions. Rosalind Picard explains that 'affective' in this context refers to 'the ability to sense your changes in emotion, and to respond sensitively to these changes, taking into consideration what it has learned previously' (Picard 1997: 241). This invites the question of why the term 'affective' was chosen (rather than 'emotion'). There are two answers to this: the first on the bodily roots of affect and the other on the connotation of the word 'emotion'.

First, with affective computing being reliant on the psychology of Silvan Tomkins due to his observation that affect is the biological dimension of emotion (Tomkins 1962), one can see the linguistic route to affective computing. But why the distinction in the first place? A key reason is that Tomkins wanted a more scientific term to dissociate his programs of work from common-sense assumptions about emotions (Stenner 2020). Second, is the concern about the scientific status of emotion, which also (arguably) has a gendered dimension. Lucy Suchman (2007: 232) recounts that Rosalind Picard originally chose the name 'affective computing' for her 1990s project on datafied emotion because 'emotional computing tends to connote computers with an undesirable reduction in rationality', whereas the term affective computing denotes 'computing that relates to, arises from, or deliberately influences emotions' (also see Picard 1997: 280–281). As explored in McStay (2023 in press) one should situate the rationality/emotion binary connotation of emotion in the masculine context of the Massachusetts Institute of Technology. Here the male-dominated environment at the time will have seen AI in terms of rationality, brain modelling, and information acquisition and processing, as well as learning from biological design and situated experience. Although it is misguided to see rationality and emotion in opposition because emotion may influence decision-making, assist with identifying what is salient, or help with the process of ethical judgement of a person (Nussbaum 2001), one can see the scope for resistance to studying emotion in computing. One can also see why the language of 'affect' and its weighting to biology was a better choice of word than 'emotion' which risked the impression of being an imprecise topic.

While affective computing remains the key term for the use of sensors, actuators and algorithms used to process data about biology and emotion (having its own journal and conferences), 'emotion AI' and 'emotional AI' have also emerged as terms to refer to what is largely the same thing. Indeed, much of our work is badged under the Emotional AI Lab, a term that we chose because it communicates clearly that the topic is emotion, and that emotional AI is not simply about the body: it is highly cultural, social, historical, and language based. Sentiment analysis in policing and the use of big data analytics by social media companies to psychologically profile and optimise societal emotion, for example, do not involve biometrics (soft or otherwise). Similarly, inference about emotion may be derived from proxies for emotion. These may include initially odd proxies, such as van engine telematics, where high engine revs have been used to indicate aggressive driving on behalf of delivery drivers (wrongly so, for instance, in hilly areas) (McStay 2023 in press). Notably, too, in 2021, both international and regional legislation in Europe (the draft AI Act) settled on 'emotion recognition' as the term of choice. This is very unambiguous in what it is referring to, although numerous critics would agree that the term assumes that these systems can unproblematically do what the term claims, that is, recognise emotions. As will be developed below, emotional

AI systems may be able to recognise expressions (such as smiles for happiness), but it is an extra leap to say that the emotion taking place within a person has been identified. A smile, of course, can indicate or hide all sorts of feelings. Similarly, other measurements of bodily signals or traits are all prone to the same problem in that the experience assumed through measurement of the body may be quite wrong. In cases where a person is being judged by a system such as in a workplace, this matters a great deal.

The Utility of Empathy

As the above discussion shows, terms are important in this debate, and there are a few long-standing terms around. However, we use the term 'empathy' because: 1) it includes emotion (based on biology, communication and proxies); 2) it refers to an act and process of understanding people; 3) in its assessment of human subjectivity it includes, but is not reducible to, emotion; and 4) it is about the act of trying to understand people inside-out, i.e., from a first-person perspective. These aspects of the term are valuable as there is every chance that there will be more technologies in the coming years that profile and interact with emotion and human subjectivity.

Empathy historically has two overlapping characteristics (McStay 2018). The first is that it is a social fact of interpersonal life and living in communities. Applied to technology, this means it makes sense to speak of 'living with' technologies that sense, track, and feel-into our lives. The second characteristic is its interpretive qualities. This is not just about 'feeling-into' others, but also places, pasts, cultures, and even objects. The first understanding draws from diverse philosophies (especially when factoring for 'fellow-feeling', the forerunner of empathy). For Husserl (1980), for example, empathy has a sensational and physical character in that to understand the 'psychic realities' of others, we emulate their worlds, their physicality, and their experience as an organism (as well as an ego), and attempt to locate this as best as possible in our own here and now to forge commonality of experience. A very different sort of philosopher, Hume (1896 [1739]) accounts for empathy in terms of instinct. The consequence of this involuntary character is that we do not control empathy, nor switch it on or off. This moves us towards empathy as a social fact that, when present, acts as an agent that binds cooperative societies together through mutual understanding and awareness. In addition to empathy's moral dimension, the 'social fact' view provides an ontological character in that it enhances and facilitates social experience, the reality of others, and, indeed, provides a sense of where others are coming from.

The second set of characteristics is based on interpretive qualities of empathy, which involves projection and feeling-into (Lipps 1979 [1903]). This account of empathy has been widely discussed in philosophy, but in short, empathy-as-feeling-into derives from the German principle of *einfühlung* that suggests people can insert themselves into artworks to feel the emotions that the creator worked to generate and instil (Vischer 1993 [1873]). It gives empathy a reconstructive and imaginative quality as we engage with designed experiences to feel 'what it was like to be there'. From the point of view of creators and designers, interpretive empathy also has an anticipatory quality. This is the attempt to feel-forward to simulate (empathise) with what they expect participants to experience.

Following McStay (2023 in press) we pair 'empathy' with the term 'automated' to identify systems that, with limited human oversight, are used to identify, quantify, respond to, or simulate affective states (such as emotions and cognitive states) and thereafter make judgements and decisions about an individual or group of people. This is based on the observation that empathy means neither sympathy nor that it is a sixth sense. We are often wrong in our assessment of others (making 'interpret' more accurate than feel 'into') due to a variety of misreadings, such as misunderstanding of what behaviour signifies, the variance between what a person says and how they really are, and lack of familiarity with a social context. Empathy, rather, is the ongoing activity of sensing and reading the behaviour and signals of others to gauge and understand their emotional and intentional disposition. Although such systems do not possess subjectivity, they do have scope to exceed what is usually meant by 'objects'. This is not because of intelligence or a ghost in the machine, but because they involve a very unusual premise: to interact with people in some way by means of data derived from highly intimate aspects of human life. This includes emotions, moods, tastes, perspectives, states such as sleepiness and intoxication, and even the materiality of thought itself through profiling and direct stimulation of brain physiology. While computers cannot have vicarious experiences with a person, they can read, process, and algorithmically arrive at a judgement. This grants scope for a cognitive type of empathy (Goldman 2008; McStay 2018, 2022), with the direction of travel being the extent to which systems can judge and respond appropriately in socially bounded contexts. (For more on assessments of empathy in connection with technology see McStay (2014, 2018, 2023 in press).

TECHNOLOGIES AND ORGANISATIONAL USES OF AUTOMATED EMPATHY

What's Involved?

There are three parts to understanding what technologies are involved in automated empathy. First, there are technologies that directly draw biometric inferences from bodies; second, there are those that assess mediated communication; and third, there are seemingly oblique proxies used to infer something about a person. An example of the first is a facial expression or blood flow data; the second is an angry posting about politics on social media; and the third is vehicle telematics or changes in purchasing behaviour. It is the first biometric sort that requires some unpacking to unseat the idea that automated emotion recognition (and automated empathy) is just about the analysis of faces and expressions. Including facial expressions, the modalities are:

* *Cameras and facial expression analysis*: this may involve live camera feeds such as those in shops and in public spaces, recorded video files, and photos. Notably, cameras may also be used to thermally image faces in live feeds, providing extra context to a named expression. Cameras may also be used to detect facial movement and represent expressions in synthetic worlds such as games-based environments, virtual reality and the metaverse.
* *Gesture and behaviour*: cameras may also be used to track hands, face, and other parts of the body said to communicate intention and emotional states.
* *Voice*: elements here include rate of speech, increases and decreases in pauses, and tone.
* *Eye-tracking*: this involves measurement of the point of gaze, eye position, and eye movement.

- *Wearable devices*: on-body sensors may detect sweat (changes in electrical current), muscle tension, heart rate/rhythm, temperature, and respiration, which are all claimed to be associated with emotional states.

There is much more detail that could be added here, for example, in relation to the use of cameras to image blood flow and blood oxygenation, which is argued to be linked to emotional experiences. The part involving sentiment and social media is usually text-based (what people say and post on social media) but it may also encompass emojis, images, video, user profiling, and charting contact networks. Indeed, things get tricky here because biometric analysis such as facial expressions or voice analysis may be conducted on social media content. The final part involving proxies could involve anything that is believed to substitute an emotion or other subjective state of interest to an analyst. The key is that proxies have the authority to stand in and represent some sort of truth (Mulvin 2021). This is a classic question of representation in that it is about what behaviour, action, trace, or other types of evidence are grounds to believe that a person is, or was, in a given emotion or psychological state. In *Automating Empathy*, McStay gives the example of a delivery driver whose vehicle telematics showed evidence of high revving, suggesting persistent aggressive driving. Indeed, the system that is used by the company flagged exactly this. The problem, however, is that while there may be a link between persistent high revs and aggressive driving, there is also a correlation between high revs and driving in mountainous areas, which is where said driver worked (McStay 2023 in press).

Where Is It Involved?

There is scope for automated empathy to be used wherever it is valuable to understand emotion and related aspects of human subjectivity. Adapted from McStay et al. (2020), Table 57.1 provides an overview of sectors using or keenly interested in emotion inference technologies in 2022.

Who's Involved?

Given the diverse set of use cases listed above, there are many start-ups each seeking to define and dominate respective markets (for instance, see McStay 2018). Recent years have seen global-minded companies and platforms such as Meta and Microsoft move into view, developing biometric means for gauging subjectivity in diverse sectors and sensitive domains of everyday life. We discuss these developments below.

Social media companies such as Meta (renamed from 'Facebook' in 2021) have long profiled emotion and wider behaviour in social media postings on its Facebook and Instagram apps in order to increase users' engagement with its sites. Examples include Facebook's 'Like' buttons and its quick Reactions emoji buttons that help rank a user's and their friends' News Feed posts and comments, enabling both Facebook and businesses to quickly tell which content resonated with target audiences, enabling further personalisation and tailoring of content by machine learning. (Almost all the revenue on Meta-owned Facebook and Instagram is generated by selling user attention to advertisers.) With different and continuously tweaked weightings applied to simple 'Likes', to quick Reaction emoji, and to significant comments, messages, reshares, or RSVPs, Facebook's emotional profiling keeps its users engaged, while also trying to address associated problems of false and extremist information online that such

Table 57.1   Sectors using or keenly interested in emotion inferences in 2022

Sector	Form of tracking	Reason for interest in tracking emotions
Advertisers and marketers	Sentiment, voice, facial coding, biometrics	To understand preferences, behaviour, and reactions to brands; to optimise creative components of adverts
AI/cognitive services	Sentiment, voice, facial coding, biometrics	To enhance interaction with devices, services, and content
Artists	Sentiment, facial coding, biometrics	To create artwork and measure audience engagement
City experience analysts	Sentiment, facial coding, biometrics	To gauge citizens' feelings about initiatives
Data brokers	Sentiment, facial coding, biometrics	For the commercial value of data
Education	Facial coding, biometrics	To analyse in-class behaviour, learning, and engagement
Gaming	Facial coding, biometrics	To enhance gameplay via input devices
Health	Sentiment, voice, facial coding, biometrics	To care, track, and interact with mental states
Home Internet of Things	Sentiment, voice, facial coding, biometrics	To personalise services and adverts, e.g., assistants, devices, media
Insurance	Sentiment, facial coding, biometrics	To tailor premiums and understand customers' emotional disposition and mental health (e.g., in-car behaviour assessment)
Metaverse (such as in-world work meetings)	Facial coding and gesture	To render physical expression onto avatars
Police/security	Sentiment, biometrics, voice	To gauge civic feeling/disturbances, track front-line workers' stress levels, and gauge lies and sincerity
Retailers (in-person)	Voice, gaze, facial coding, biometrics	To assess in-store behaviour (potential to link reactions with online/loyalty profiles)
Retail (VR-based)	Facial coding, gaze, biometrics	To gauge reactions to products, architecture, and designed spaces
Robotics	Facial coding, voice	To enhance interaction between robots and people
Sextech	Biometrics	To enhance sex life/make devices more responsive
Social media	Sentiment, facial coding	To assess sentiment, emoji usage, group behaviour, individual profiling, and altering and posting behaviour
Toys	Facial coding, voice	For interaction, entertainment, and toy marketing

(Continued)

Table 57.1   (Continued)

Sector	Form of tracking	Reason for interest in tracking emotions
Transportation	Facial coding, voice, biometrics	Safety aspects focus on fatigue and potentially anger, but in-cabin media includes wider emotion profiling
TV/media/film	Sentiment, facial coding, voice, biometrics	To test reactions to content, shows, movies, and scope to create novel, interactive content
User testing	Sentiment, facial coding, biometrics	To assess reactions to products and specific features
Wearables	Biometrics	To track reactions, emotions, and moods (adults and children)
Workplaces	Sentiment, facial coding, biometrics	To organisationally track emotions and moods

emotional engagement propels. For instance, across 2017–2018, significant comments, messages, reshares or RSVPs were assigned 30 times the weight of a 'Like'; and 'Love', 'Haha', 'Wow', 'Sad', and 'Angry' quick Reactions were weighted five times the weight of a 'Like'. However, thereafter, Facebook demoted the weighting of its quick Reactions emoji, especially the Angry emoji, in response to increasingly disturbing evidence of the proliferation of false information and extremist hate speech worldwide (Oremus et al. 2021, October 26). Not without social and democratic consequences, social media platforms suffused with viral, emotional, and false content is a well-observed phenomenon among big data studies. It raises important questions about who gets to decide on the optimisation of emotional content for economic or political gain (Bakir and McStay 2022).

Given this recent history of emotional profiling, and its social and democratic consequences, Meta now has a keen interest in biometric profiling to render bodies into virtual spaces that should attract critical attention. For example, seeking to extend profiling from the web to three-dimensional synthetic spaces, Meta seeks to track eye behaviour and facial expressions through a headset. This will grant the capacity to target marketing by means of in-world emoting, behaviour, interaction with other avatars, and the nature of behavioural engagement and interaction with in-world objects (Murphy 2022). This portends not only new dimensions and boundaries for behavioural advertising but exponentially more intimate insights into human subjectivity. These insights, of course, will be exploited not just by advertisers of commercial goods and services, but by architects of disinformation seeking to feel-into targeted populations and groups. As has been documented globally across dominant digital platforms, this includes purveyors of fake news, troll armies conducting information warfare, and political parties and campaigners seeking to energise and mobilise their base by understanding, manipulating, and exploiting the spread of content with emotional charge (Bakir and McStay 2022, 2020; Bakir 2020).

A different kind of example of interest from the large technology corporations is that of the world of work. Whereas Meta seeks to profoundly change the nature of mediated interaction and advertising, Microsoft wants to change how we work. Most readers will be aware of Microsoft's historical role in developing office software to write, add, list, and present, and more recently to communicate through video. Their next goal is to feel-into workplaces.

For example, Microsoft filed a patent on July 30 2020, titled 'Meeting Insight Computing System' (United States Patent and Trademark Office 2020). This dull title hides profound ambition for the future of work. Microsoft's patent shows interest in profiling air temperature, air composition, brightness, ambient noise level, room occupancy, average attention level, the average level of fatigue, sentiment expressed by meeting participants (e.g., based on body language, tone of voice, explicit statements), percentage of participants who contributed during the meeting, attendance, materials distributed to participants in advance of the meeting (assessed by the quality of the materials, how far in advance the materials were distributed, and relevance), whether the meeting started or ended on time, the average number of other meetings attended by meeting participants that day/week/other period, results of a post-meeting survey on the productivity of the meeting, participant roles or duties, participant workplace locations, distance travelled, whether the meeting is recurring, and how many participants attended remotely.

This is a tiringly granular list, but in addition to environmental surveillance (which has scope to be good, such as by identifying the need for fresher air) there is also profiling of human states, emotions, and behaviour. Indeed, the patent also highlights the assessment of whether meeting participants are texting, checking email, or otherwise browsing the Internet. What is presented in patents and what is built and used in everyday life are often quite different, but in just the two use cases provided (Meta and advertising, and Microsoft and in-person workplace meetings) one begins to see strategic ambition. This is one that seeks to use intimate insights to profile, optimise, and mine both bodies and subjectivity. A long list of corporate and policing/security interests in automated empathy should also be noted. As detailed in McStay (2023 in press), this includes Amazon's interest in facial coding and wristbands that listen for emotion in voices; Garmin's wearables that also monitor the body for emotion and wellbeing; Spotify's selling of mood data to advertising conglomerates and its patents for use of biometric data; carmakers equipping cars to track fatigue and profile emotion; ads on high streets and in public transportation that watch people to see if they like them; police forces (in the UK) testing emotion-enabled closed-circuit television; tracking call centre workers for appropriate emotion and empathy; AXA building biometrics into insurance premiums; Intel offering schools cameras that monitor emotion and quality of engagement; and Mattel and Anki building toys that listen and watch for child emotion.

CRITIQUING AUTOMATED EMPATHY, ESPECIALLY IN RELATION TO PHYSIOGNOMY

In our work at the Emotional AI lab that assesses the social impact of these applications, we routinely poll the overall UK adult population and run qualitative workshops on their feelings about existing technologies and those in development. Even when factoring for survey and interviewer bias (such as the involvement of professional market researchers), we consistently find that the UK public is not keen on the idea of automated empathy (especially emotional AI) in key sites and activities of everyday life, such as policing, education, marketing, workplaces, or cars (privately owned) (McStay et al. 2020). They are least keen on the use of social media profiling in political campaigns to find out which political ads or messages are most engaging for specific audiences to personalise and target what political ads we see (Bakir and McStay 2022). It might be noted that we find age to be the main variable where there are attitudinal differences. Especially in quantitative research where our national demographically representative surveys segment by gender, ethnicity, disability, region, income, education, and related bases, it is age where we consistently find differences. In summary, younger adults show more signs of being open to novel means of interaction but this should not be read as a licence for industrial abuse of personal or aggregated data. We also routinely find them keen to maintain control over data about themselves (McStay 2020).

That the British public is not keen on grounds of privacy and the scope for unwanted influence will be unsatisfactory for this handbook on critical studies of AI. Indeed, while it is important and interesting to gauge the public's view on emergent technologies, they cannot be expected to have the final word or expert view. How then should we understand the social significance of automated empathy and its continued forays into subjectivity? There are numerous critical lenses through which we might understand the processing of soft biometric data to understand intimate dimensions of human life.

It would be easy to invoke (overlapping) critiques of commodification and extractivism. This would point to human experience as the free raw material for translation into behavioural data to serve capitalism (Zuboff 2019). This move in argument would also turn to labour-based critique that draws inspiration from the neo-Marxist political economy of the media, especially Dallas Smythe's 'audience-as-commodity' thesis (Smythe 1981; Lazzarato 2004; Bermejo 2009; McStay 2011) that underpins the adage that 'If you're not paying for the product, you are the product'. Indeed, bringing things up to date, modern labour-based criticism critiques companies that employ machine learning, especially regarding how data collected for one purpose is put to work for other purposes (Crawford and Joler 2018). For example, Affectiva is an often-cited start-up that uses facial coding to identify facial expressions as a sign of the emotion a person is experiencing. They work across multiple sectors, such as automotive (cars) and media research (such as in-house testing of emotional responses to ads, television shows, or movies). Emotion profiles collected for one reason will be used to train the neural networks for ends outside of the situation for which they are collected (McStay 2018). If we were to focus on extraction, we would situate this theory in a broader context of criticism of industrialisation and modernity but recognise that today it involves the materiality of AI technologies head-on, including exploitation of energy, mineral reserves, and human labour (Fuchs 2013; Crawford 2021). Extractivism of course includes the ever-deeper mining of strata of human subjectivity that has occupied the thoughts of Heidegger in relation to cybernetics and generations of neo-Marxist thought on post-industrial life that is 'marked by the submission of the soul, in which animated, creative, linguistic, emotional corporeality is subsumed and incorporated by the production of value' (Berardi 2009: 109). These are important vectors of thought, but here we focus on mental integrity and unnatural mediation (McStay 2023 in press). Rather than applying off-the-shelf critiques, we build outwards from automated empathy itself.

Mental Integrity

For Western thought, integrity-as-wholeness is found all the way back in Plato's (1987 [375 BC]) *Republic*, which sees the good life in terms of psychic harmony of appetite, reason, and emotion. *Mental integrity* certainly involves personal and societal psychic stability, but applied to automated empathy, it also refers to first-person perspectives, which means to not only track outward behaviour but use biometrics, big data inferencing, and ocular technologies to remotely see how others do to better understand experience, disposition, point of view, and what may affect a person or group. Mental integrity of self and society is not a priority for many who deploy these systems, and certainly not enough thought is given to the net result of complex connections with technologies and content therein. Indeed, regarding automated empathy itself, if these systems are judged by everyday standards of empathy, they may in some cases be considered as deeply anti-social and therefore psychopathic, which is not conducive to mental integrity (McStay 2023 in press). Tempting as it may be to say that all instances of automated empathy are psychopathic, under certain circumstances, we see scope for potentially pro-social uses, especially for facilitating novel modes of expression, interactive media content, creative and aesthetic experience, and, with utmost care regarding data processing, potentially in the context of health and interpersonal communication. There is then a three-part grouping of: (1) automated empathy that is pro-social; (2) the tip towards psychopathy when it is used with disregard to individuals, groups, and societies; and (3) when such systems can be labelled psychopathic due to being purposefully used to be anti-social and to destabilise the mental integrity of individuals, groups, and societies.

Unnatural Mediation

The second connected mode of critique is that of *unnatural mediation*. Explored in full in McStay (2023 in press), readers from media and communication studies will be long familiar with the idea that filters or processes that depict, mediate, and distort cause all sorts of personal and societal problems. Unnatural mediation as it emerges from automated empathy has two components: the first is regarding hyperreal articulations of emotion, where the absence of a ground truth on what emotion is creates a vacuum in which simplistic taxonomies may be claimed and presented as real. The other component involves political problems of representation and mediation. This problem has deep roots in the study of media regarding how women, people of colour, LBGTQA+ people, people with disabilities, body shapes and types, class, and religious groups are [mis]represented in a variety of media systems. In the context of automated empathy, limitations of computer sensing, biases in hardware and software, modern pathognomy (i.e., inference of emotion and character through dynamic expressions), opaque and demographically non-representative datasets, and highly prescriptive and deductive theories of subjectivity and emotional life contribute to unnatural mediation.

Although unnatural mediation of automated empathy has the scope to affect societies in general, this does not mean people are affected equally. For our interests there are several problems, the first being hardware and that much computer vision still has problems seeing darker skin as well as lighter skinned people (Buolamwini and Gebru 2018). If these technologies had no history, then perhaps there is scope for forgiveness, but computer vision has its origins in mechanical and chemical vision (photography) that defaulted to white and light-toned skin (Caswell 2015). The root of the problem is how technologies are calibrated for human skin colour and which skin tone systems are used. It was not until 2022 that Google signalled a move in the right direction by switching from the Fitzpatrick model of skin tone (that has six tones) to the Monk Skin Tone Scale (that has ten tones), so being less biased towards lighter skin (Vincent 2022). Beyond questions of systems being appropriately calibrated to see a full spectrum of skin colour, there are also emotion labelling problems that are directly informed by human racism.

To stick with the example of faces, emotion recognition typically works by first establishing a suite of prototypical emotion expressions. Using the Facial Action Coding System developed in large part by Paul Ekman, computer vision is used to detail the facial action units (movement of facial muscles), head positions and movements, eye positions and related movements, descriptors, behaviours, and codes to map faces (Ekman et al. 2002). Nose wrinkling, for example, represents emotions such as disgust, and depressions in the corner of the lips relate to sadness. Although there are variations on the line-up of primary emotions, these are based on seven facial expressions of primary emotion (joy, surprise, sadness, anger, fear, disgust, and contempt) (Ekman and Friesen 1978). This chapter will not linger on the validity of this approach, but suffice to say that biological, essentialist, and cross-cultural claims that (1) emotions are reactive biological programs and (2) that facial muscles function as a feedback system for emotional experience is heavily criticised (Leys 2011; McStay 2018; Barrett et al. 2019; Azari et al. 2020; Bösel and Wiemer 2020; Stark 2020). In principle, the measurement of facial muscle movement should be agnostic to colour, but the problem is that people are also required to train systems. In practice, this means that people are tasked with labelling images with a prototypical emotion expression. This gives computer examples that it can replicate and a basis by which a computer may label incoming imagery. The problem, as ever, is a human one in that human racism is replicated by the computer and scaled up due to the larger number of judgements it will arrive at. Rhue, for example, found that emotion recognition systems assign more negative emotions to black men's faces than white men's faces (2018). Using a data set of 400 US National Basketball Association player photos from the 2016 to 2017 season, she found that emotional recognition software from Microsoft and Chinese company Face++ assigned black players more negative emotional scores on average, no matter how much they smiled. This is different from the issue of whether a person is seen or not because it is about the judgement of subjectivity, in this case, labelling black people with disproportionately negative types of emotion (notably, anger), especially when there is ambiguity of what emotion label to give to a facial expression (Rhue 2018).

Association with race-based discrimination is deepened when the origins of face-based profiling are known. From the 1700s onwards, there has been keen interest in linking outward appearance to inward states and disposition. This is particularly so with physiognomy, which involves the use of pre-given labels to identify a person's character or personality from their outer appearance, involving skull shapes, face geometries, and assumptions about race and culture. Closely related is *pathognomy*, which is the analysis of temporary features (expressions) to identify emotive and episodic human states. As one can see in the example of basketball players, the problem is one of being locked into reductionist and essentialist systems that judge people. One can quickly see in this case that in the wrong hands, automated judgement of states such as anger presents problems in all sorts of situations (schools, policing, security in public spaces, and so on).

Both physiognomy and pathognomy initiated these problems, suggesting the pre-eminence of biology over culture and that emotion may be reduced to biometry and morphology. Critically, physiognomy and pathognomy assume a stable connection between outward appearance and interiority. This is key because both in the 1700s and now, these enterprises rest on being able to 'reverse infer', or to work backwards from the expression to the interior state that caused it. Both periods are also conjoined through the appeal and appearance of science and rationality. Just as with Rhue's (2018) findings, there are implications in terms of regarding who is doing the decoding. In terms of physiognomy, the analysts creating the labels about personality were 'enlightened' white European men making judgements about race, identity, types, and human character. As explored in depth elsewhere, this was problematic in the 1700s and the early physiognomic systems of Johann Kasper Lavater, perhaps the most well-known physiognomist after Aristotle (Crawford 2021; Stark and Hutson 2021). While this was implicitly racist in making judgements about identity on the basis of appearance, later Nazi-based systems were avowedly racist (McStay 2023 in press).

The spectre of biological determinism looms and while this is not innately racist, the history of phrenology, physiognomy, and pathognomy are not good ones. That human racism (or 'biases') is already automated in algorithmic systems indicates that systemic challenges will be with us for some time, assuming that it is conceivable they may ever be eradicated. The turn from cultural, social, and human relational factors to bodies themselves is also going to be an ongoing concern.

CONCLUSION

The profiling of emotion online for profit and influence is already a global industry, perhaps best evidenced by the practices of globally dominant social media platforms. This is being increasingly augmented by technologies that profile and interact with human emotion and broader subjectivity via bodily means, especially via soft biometrics. As technologies increasingly profile and interact with emotion and human subjectivity, we advance the term 'automated empathy' not least because this captures the sense of trying to understand people from the inside-out, from a first-person perspective. This chapter demonstrated the wide range of sectors that are set to use automated empathy to understand emotion and related aspects of human subjectivity, focusing specifically on two global behemoths. One of these is Meta, which seeks to extend profiling from the web to three-dimensional synthetic spaces by combining biometrics with its already extensive emotional and behavioural profiling, thereby changing the nature of mediated interaction and advertising. The other is Microsoft, which seeks to feel-into workplaces by measuring emotional states and biometrics alongside a wide range of environmental factors. Citing studies that British-based adults are not keen on such profiling of emotions, we discussed two critiques of automated empathy that function through soft biometrics. The first, mental integrity, is about psychic autonomy and stability, rights to one's thoughts and emotions, and scope for manipulation. In addition to profiling outward behaviour, it also refers to the use of technologies to try to feel-into and understand first-person perspectives. The second critique of unnatural mediation finds that (a) such technologies prescribe narrow frames of emotional life, and (b) automated empathy technologies have been demonstrated to be biologically essentialist, which risk locking people of colour into reductionist systems that judge them unfairly. We conclude that as global behemoths look set to embrace systems of automated empathy, never has it been more pressing to ensure that the critiques of these systems are articulated at the highest levels of policymaking and reiterated to developers of these systems. Simultaneously, citizens across the world must be alerted to the presence and fallibility of machines that pretend to empathise with the human condition.

REFERENCES

Article 29 Data Protection Working Party. (2012). Opinion 3/ 2012 on developments in biometric technologies. http://ec.europa.eu/justice/data-protection/article-29/documentation/opinion-recomme ndation/files/ 2012/wp193_en.pdf

Azari, B., Westlin, C., Satpute, A. B., Hutchinson, J. B., Kragel, P. A., Hoemann, K., Khan, Z., Wormwood, J. B., Quigley, K. S., Erdogmus, D., Dy, J., Brooks, D. H., & Barrett, L. F. (2020). Comparing supervised and unsupervised approaches to emotion categorization in the human brain, body, and subjective experience. *Scientific Reports, 10*(20284), 1–17. https://doi.org/10.1038/s41598 -020-77117-8

Bakir, V. (2020). Psychological operations in digital political campaigns: Assessing Cambridge Analytica's psychographic profiling and targeting. *Frontiers in Political Communication, 5*(67). https://doi.org/10.3389/fcomm.2020.00067

Bakir, V., & McStay, A. (2020). Empathic media, emotional AI and optimization of disinformation. In M. Boler and E. Davis (eds.), *Affective Politics of Digital Media* (pp. 263–279). Routledge.

Bakir, V., & McStay, A. (2022). *Optimising Emotions, Incubating Falsehood: How to Protect the Global Civic Body from Disinformation and Misinformation.* Springer.

Barrett, L. F., Adolphs, R., Marsella, S., Martinez, A. M., & Pollak, S. D. (2019). Emotional expressions reconsidered: Challenges to inferring emotion from human facial movements. *Psychological Science in the Public Interest, 20*(1), 1–68. https://doi.org/10.1177/1529100619832930

Berardi, F. (2009). *The Soul at Work: From Alienation to Autonomy.* Semiotext(e).

Bermejo, F. (2009). Audience manufacture in historical perspective: From broadcasting to Google. *New Media and Society, 11*(1&2), 133–154. https://doi.org/10.1177/1461444808099579

Bösel, B., & Wiemer, S. (Eds.). (2020). *Affective Transformations: Politics, Algorithms, Media.* Meson Press.

Breazeal, C. (2002). *Designing Sociable Robots.* MIT Press.

Buolamwini, J., & Gebru, T. (2018). Gender shades: Intersectional accuracy disparities in commercial gender classification. *Proceedings of the 1st Conference on Fairness, Accountability and Transparency (Proceedings of Machine Learning Research), USA, 81*, 77–91. http://proceedings.mlr .press/v81/buolamwini18a.html

Caswell, E. (2015, April 22). Color film was built for white people. Here's what it did to dark skin. *Vox.* https://www.vox.com/2015/9/18/9348821/photography-race-bias

Crawford, K., & Joler, V. (2018). Anatomy of an AI system. *Virtual Creativity, 9*(1), 117–120. https://doi .org/10.1386/vcr_00008_7

Crawford, K. (2021). *Atlas of AI: Power, Politics, and the Planetary Costs of Artificial Intelligence,* Yale University Press.

Ekman, P., Friesen, W., & Hager, J. (Eds.). (2002). *Facial Action Coding System.* Research Nexus.

Ekman, P., & Friesen, W. (1978). *Facial Action Coding System: A Technique for the Measurement of Facial Movement.* Consulting Psychologists Press.

Fuchs, C. (2013). *Social Media: A Critical Introduction.* Sage.

Goldman, A. I. (2008). *Simulating Minds: The Philosophy, Psychology, and Neuroscience of Mindreading.* Oxford University Press.

Hume, D. (1896 [1739]). *A Treatise of Human Nature.* Oxford University Press.

Husserl, E. (1980). *Phenomenology and the Foundations of the Sciences.* Martinus Nijhoff.

Lazzarato, M. (2004). From capital-labour to capital-life. *Ephemera, 4*(3), 187–208. http://www. ephemerajournal.org/contribution/capital-labour-capital-life

Leys, R. (2011). The turn to affect: A critique. *Critical Inquiry, 37*(3), 434–472. https://doi.org/10.1086/ 659353

Lipps, T. (1979 [1903]). Empathy, inner imitation and sense-feelings. In M. Rader (ed.), *A Modern Book of Esthetics* (pp. 374–382). Holt, Rinehart and Winston.

McStay, A. (2011). *The Mood of Information: A Critique of Behavioural Advertising.* Continuum.

McStay, A. (2014). *Privacy and Philosophy: New Media and Affective Protocol.* Peter Lang.

McStay, A. (2018). *Emotional AI: The Rise of Empathic Media.* Sage.

McStay, A. (2020). Emotional AI, soft biometrics and the surveillance of emotional life: An unusual consensus on privacy. *Big Data & Society.* https://doi.org/10.1177/2053951720904386

McStay, A. (in press, 2023). *Automating Empathy: When Technologies Are Claimed to Feel-Into Everyday Life.* Oxford University Press.

McStay, A., Bakir, V., & Urquhart, L. (2020). Emotion recognition: Trends, social feeling, policy. Briefing paper: All Party Parliamentary Group on Artificial Intelligence. https://drive.google.com/ file/d/1Hyix108Ly1140qZuggCo7HrwzSOFaIrL/view

Mulvin, D. (2021). *Proxies: The Cultural Work of Standing In*. MIT Press.

Murphy, H. (2022, January 18). Facebook patents reveal how it intends to cash in on metaverse. https://www.ft.com/content/76d40aac-034e-4e0b-95eb-c5d34146f647

Nussbaum, M. (2001). *Upheavals of Thought: The Intelligence of Emotions*. Cambridge University Press.

Oremus, W., Alcantara, C., Merrill, J. B., & Galocha, A. (2021, October 26). Facebook under fire: How Facebook shapes your feed. *Washington Post*. https://www.washingtonpost.com/technology/interactive/2021/how-facebook-algorithm-works/

Picard, R. W. (1997). *Affective Computing*. MIT Press.

Plato. (1987 [375 BC]). *The Republic*. Penguin.

Rhue, L. (2018). Racial influence on automated perceptions of emotions. *SSRN*. https://papers.ssrn.com/sol3/papers.cfm?abstract_id=3281765

Smythe, D. W. (1981). *Dependency Road: Communications, Capitalism, Consciousness, and Canada*. ABLEX.

Stark, L. (2020). The emotive politics of digital mood tracking. *New Media & Society*, *22*(11), 2039–2057. https://doi.org/10.1177/1461444820924624

Stark, L., & Hoey, J. (2020). *The Ethics of Emotion in Artificial Intelligence Systems*. https://doi.org/10.31219/osf.io/9ad4u

Stark, L., & Hutson, J. (2021). Physiognomic Artificial Intelligence. *SSRN*. https://doi.org/10.2139/ssrn.3927300

Stenner, P. (2020). Affect: On the turn. In B. Bösel and S. Wiemer (Eds.), *Affective Transformations: Politics, Algorithms, Media* (pp. 19–39). Meson Press.

Suchman, L. (2007). *Human-Machine Reconfigurations: Plans and Situated Actions*. Cambridge University Press.

Tomkins, S. S. (1962). *Affect, Imagery, Consciousness: Vol. 1. The Positive Affects*. Springer.

United States Patent and Trademark Office. (2020). Meeting insight computing system. *US02 0200358627A120201112*. https://pdfaiw.uspto.gov/.aiw?PageNum=0&docid=20200358627&IDKey=19C7DC5929AB&HomeUrl=http%3A%2F%2Fappft.uspto.gov%2Fnetacgi%2Fnph-Parser%3FSect1%3DPTO1%2526Sect2%3DHITOFF%2526d%3DPG01%2526p%3D1%2526u%3D%25252Fnetahtml%25252FPTO%25252Fsrchnum.html%2526r%3D1%2526f%3DG%2526l%3D50%2526s1%3D%25252220200358627%252522.PGNR.%2526OS%3DDN%2F20200358627%2526RS%3DDN%2F20200358627

Vischer, R. (1993 [1873]). On the optical sense of form: A contribution to aesthetics. In H. F. Mallgrave and E. Ikonomou (eds.), *Empathy, Form, and Space: Problems in German Aesthetics, 1873–1893* (pp. 89–123). Getty Center for the History of Art.

Vincent, J. (2022, May 11). Google is using a new way to measure skin tones to make search results more inclusive. *The Verge*. https://www.theverge.com/2022/5/11/23064883/google-ai-skin-tone-measure-monk-scale-inclusive-search-results

Zuboff, S. (2019). *The Age of Surveillance Capitalism: The Fight for a Human Future at the New Frontier of Power*. Profile.

58. Ideational tensions in the Swedish automation debate: initial findings

Kalle Eriksson

INTRODUCTION

Any critical analysis of technology must inquire into the democratic implications of technological advancements. A recurring theme in debates on the social and political consequences of AI and other automation technologies is the need to ensure that humans remain in control of the technologies and thus have the final say on "what AI does". The recognition of this need to keep "humans in the loop" has in recent years come to be referred to as either "human-centered" or "human-centric" approaches to AI (e.g., Shneiderman, 2022; European Commission, 2019). Zooming out from this rather localized case-by-case perspective, another way to approach the issue of human agency in relation to technology is to ask if and how we can *democratically* determine how automation will impact our societies. That is, to what extent is it possible to politically guide the ongoing technology-induced transition of the labor market so that the outcome is as desirable as possible, given agreed-upon values or goals (whatever those may be)? This is what the philosopher Andrew Feenberg requested when he, around the turn of the millennium, criticized the view of technology as a completely autonomous force and called for an "extension of democracy to the technical sphere" (Feenberg, 1999: viii).

When economists Carl Benedikt Frey and Michael A. Osborne in 2013 estimated that 47% of US jobs were "at risk" of becoming computerized by the year 2033, they spurred a new global debate about the economic and political consequences of automation (Frey & Osborne 2013). Somewhat simplified, this can be described as the third modern automation debate, the first two taking place in the 1950s–1960s and the 1980s, respectively. In a Swedish context, the first wave of debates was characterized by a strong belief in the liberating potential of automation technologies, and the labor movement – while also warning for the possibly alienating effects of these new means of production – mainly centered their strategy around preparing workers and citizens for the "leisure time explosion" that automation would bring (Rahm, 2021). During the debates of the 1980s, issues regarding the impacts of new technologies on the future of work certainly surfaced, but they played a far less prominent role than they had a couple of decades earlier. As shown by Rahm and Kaun (2022: 26), this second wave of automation debates first tended to be far less optimistic or utopian, and second, homed in on "questions of integrity and privacy that emerge with information gathering", rather than job effects.

The fact that the current automation debate is (at least) the third of its kind seems to be important for how it has been characterized thus far. As most of the hopes and fears of previous automation debates proved to be gravely exaggerated (or at least never fully materialized), a large part of the current discussion revolves around finding out *if* and *how* the situation is any different now. I would like to propose that, more often than not, this discussion on whether automation "is really different this time" (cf. Wajcman, 2017) misses a crucial point: *we simply cannot know*, since the social and economic effects of technology are highly contingent on collective decision-making and the wider institutional landscape in which it is developed and implemented. Perhaps it is also because of this open-endedness that the ongoing debate has produced such a wide range of both optimistic and pessimistic scenarios of the automated society (e.g., Frase, 2016; Bastani, 2019; Srnicek & Williams, 2016; Ford, 2015; Danaher, 2019). Again, the many contingencies involved make it all but impossible to make a priori judgments regarding the plausibility of such scenarios, but they nevertheless serve to underline a trivial but too often overlooked point: the future might take very different shapes depending on what set of norms we set out to build that future around, and what political decisions, priorities, and strategies those norms are translated into.

Only by understanding automation as an inherently political issue may we achieve a democratic discussion in which this open-endedness is embraced, and the competing norms and goals can be openly debated. In this context, a key contribution of critical scholarship is to map out the contents of ongoing debates and thereby get a better sense of the extent to which they are already politicized, and what can be done to further highlight the actual or potential issues at stake. As such, this chapter describes some preliminary findings from my ongoing PhD project, for which I have interviewed political elites in Sweden and used a scenario-based approach to "tap into" the respondents' ideas on the more long-term political consequences of advances in AI and other automation technologies in relation to the labor market. The chapter begins with a brief background section that describes the Swedish context and introduces the data that the chapter draws upon as well as its collection. I then move on to present the findings, before concluding the chapter with some key takeaways.

BACKGROUND

To better grasp the range of political issues that automation raises, we may start by briefly reflecting upon automation as such. A rather straightforward definition is that automation refers to the "automatic working of a machine, process, or system by mechanical or electronic devices that take the place of humans" (Merriam-Webster, n.d.). In economic terms, these "devices" constitute capital while humans constitute labor. Another way to put it is therefore that automation refers to the substitution of human labor by capital. And because the relative inputs and roles of capital and labor in production determine the structure of not only the labor market but of the entire economic system – and thus society at large – it should be clear that automation cannot easily be reduced into a single political issue but is directly or indirectly connected to a vast range of policy areas. All that being said, the questions raised by automation mostly relate to what political scientists refer to as the class cleavage of politics.

Class cleavage, or the "left-right–dimension of politics" as it is called in everyday language, traces back to the industrial revolution, and the tensions between labor and capital that arose from the capitalist mode of production. In other words, the class cleavage is the result of the various conflicts of interest between the owning classes and the working classes, most clearly expressed in issues such as property rights versus workers' rights or the state's involvement in the economy (Bartolini, 2000). From the outset, this cleavage was most conspicuously institutionalized through the various class-based organizations that emerged in modern economies in the wake of the Industrial Revolution. These of course included labor unions and employers' organizations, but also the many varieties of socialist and bourgeois political parties.

Despite radical socioeconomic changes since industrialization, the class cleavage has continued to have a strong structuring effect on party politics in many developed economies, and this is particularly the case for Sweden. Indeed, its firm basis in the class cleavage has typically been described as the key distinctive feature of the Swedish party system, together with its relatively strong stability over time (e.g. Bäck & Möller, 2003; Demker, 2015).[1] Furthermore, while class-voting in Sweden has declined, evidence suggests that this is not the result of a corresponding decline in voters' engagement for typical "left-right–issues" (such as the size of the public sector or labor regulations), as this seems to be roughly intact over time – and the same goes for the ideologically polarizing effect of these issues (Oskarson & Demker, 2015). Thus, the failure of parties to engage with such issues would not only be strategically questionable but also result in incongruence between the "supply side" and the "demand side" of the democratic system. This background gives us good reasons to conclude that Swedish political parties are both *expected to* and *ought to* be engaged with the topic of automation.

The Data

The data collection process started by studying text documents (e.g., minutes from parliamentary debates, motions, and various party texts) as well as conducting a few pilot interviews, which showed that elected politicians still largely treat automation as an issue of the future that is yet to materialize. Thus, automation is not treated as a hands-on, current issue, but as an ongoing trend with very uncertain future implications. Given the well-established fact that democratic institutions (and the actors therein) tend to suffer from "political myopia" or a "presentist bias", through which short-term issues and interests are favored over long-term ones, resulting in systematic political neglect of the future (e.g., Boston, 2016; Thompson, 2005), it is perhaps not surprising that automation, therefore, is not debated nearly as much as the background above would have us believe. Either way, it was clear that the textual data needed to be complemented with qualitative interviews, through which I could directly interrogate key actors about their views on the topic.

The interview data that the findings below draw upon was collected in early 2022, as part of my ongoing PhD project. In total, 12 respondents were interviewed with the approach described here, of which seven were members of parliament (MP), one member of the local parliament in one of Sweden's larger cities (MLP), three high-ranking members of party youth organizations, and one official from Sweden's largest trade union organization. To overcome tendencies of presentism and "force" the respondents to open up about their thoughts on the more long-term implications of automation, I decided to develop three brief scenarios for how the Swedish labor market *could* function in the year 2050 due to increased automation. The first scenario described a society where automation has led to a general reduction of the working week to around 20 hours. The second and third scenarios both depicted a future where automation has not affected the overall input of human labor, but where most jobs have either

---

[1]   I say "together with" because these two features are connected: as pointed out by Bäck and Möller (2003), the dominance of the class cleavage has made it difficult for new conflict dimensions – and thus new parties – to establish in the Swedish political landscape, and the ones that have struggle to maintain their self-proclaimed independence from the left–right scale.

become much more "high-tech" and thus require completely new competencies (scenario 2), or moved to the service sector where humans have a competitive advantage over machines due to the requirement of social and empathic skills (scenario 3). The scenarios were distributed to the respondents a few days ahead of the scheduled interview so that they would have a chance to read and start thinking about them before we met. During the interviews, respondents were first asked about their initial thoughts about the scenarios, before being asked some pre-written as well as probing follow-up questions. Interviews lasted between 40 and 100 minutes, and the scenarios took up, on average, approximately half of each interview.

PRELIMINARY FINDINGS

Chronologically, the scenarios were brought up around the mid-point of the allotted interview time after the respondents had answered a range of questions regarding their understandings of, on the one hand, current technological developments and automation as a phenomenon, and, on the other hand, the political debate regarding these topics. Interestingly, when asked about the debate, respondents widely agreed that there is little or no ongoing debate regarding the broader implications of emerging automation technologies, but that there likely is a broad consensus among parliamentarians that the net effect of automation will be positive for society and the Swedish economy, and that the development, therefore, should be embraced. In other words, automation was described as a topic that is mainly interpreted through a national or European lens ("How can Sweden/the EU best compete with – for example – the US and China?") rather than an ideological one. While some speculated that views on automation might come to be dispersed along the "standard" left-right spectrum, none of the respondents expressed that they could presently observe any such ideational differences or tensions. One respondent characterized automation as a "non-issue", while another – despite nearing the end of his second consecutive term in the Parliamentary Committee on the Labor Market – could not recall ever hearing automation being mentioned in said committee.

To a large extent, this lack of ideological conflicts is reflected in the interview data, in that the views on automation that were expressed oftentimes overlap. However, during the discussions of the scenarios, it quickly became obvious that the actors indeed interpret *some* aspects of automation very differently and have clearly diverging views on the potential benefits and drawbacks of current technological developments. Furthermore, these differences relate to rather fundamental contentious subjects, such as the state's role in the economy, relations of power on the labor market, and collectivist versus individualist views on society and labor. Here, I will disregard the overlaps and instead highlight a couple of the ideational tensions that were observed, as these may serve to illustrate some of the aspects of automation that may – or rather *ought to* – become topics of heated political debate, although they are not yet. The tensions I focus on are "political agency" and "collectivism versus individualism".

Political Agency

As we have seen, there is, on the one hand, a wide agreement that the effects of automation are contingent on collective decision-making, while we, on the other hand, still live in a political culture in which technology tends to be viewed as a largely autonomous and apolitical force. Consequently, we cannot assume that the interviewed actors view automation as a pressing political issue that state policies (labor market related or otherwise) should target. Thus, a central aim of the interviews was to investigate how the respondents perceived their own role (as policymakers), and more importantly, the role of the state in relation to these processes.

Interestingly, the responses to the scenarios highlighted that there are very different views on what politicians *can* and *should* do to actively guide the various ongoing technology-induced transitions in the labor market. These different views range from, on the one hand, perceiving policymakers as having *complete* agency in the situation, to, on the other hand, understanding increased automation as a process in relation to which they have no agency whatsoever. Directly when the scenarios were brought up, one of the respondents pointed out that the question of which of the three scenarios (or any other plausible scenario) will materialize is entirely dependent on collective decision-making and political choices:

> And it's always interesting to imagine… I mean, there are so many possible scenarios. And I thought about that with these three as well: I mean, they are three more or less equally likely scenarios. And how it plays out, which scenario that is realized, is *entirely* up to us as politicians.
>
> Respondent 1, MLP[2]

On the contrary, another respondent claimed that elected officials have little or no say at all regarding the changes to the labor market that new technologies will bring, and consequently that it does not matter that much what politicians "want" the consequences of automation to be. Quite opposite to the quote above, we are here confronted with a view of representative democracy as completely incapable of guiding the ongoing changes. In other words, increased automation is perceived as a shift in the socio-technical landscape that policymakers cannot control, but must simply react and respond to:

> To put it bluntly, there is a life going on outside of politics that in essence governs the development of society. And we politicians have only to accept this. And this means that, even if we would act on a whim and say, "now we're going to do it in this specific way", I don't think we'd succeed. Because there are thousands, hundreds of thousands, of other ongoing processes in society, independent of politics. So, we will transition, regardless of the opinions of politicians. This is simply a fact that we need to relate to.
>
> Respondent 2, MP

At face value, these two contrasting statements are of course empirical claims about political reality. However, as Lindberg (2017) reminds us, in the context of political communication, descriptions of reality are seldom (if ever) *merely* descriptive and fact-oriented, but also tend to have a more value-laden dimension to them. Or rather, they all "carry a cognitive part and an attitudinal part" (ibid.: 104), implying that they contain an explicit or latent *evaluation* of the reality that is being described. In this case, then, I think that we should not approach these utterances as claims that are to be validated strictly in terms of their truth-value, but rather as indicators of the actors' ideologically informed views on what role the state *ought* to play in relation to the ongoing technological developments. When probed further, the respondents provide answers that support this interpretation. For example, the parliamentarian that described politicians as lacking agency to steer the ongoing transition did not find it desirable to overcome this relative "impotence":

---

[2]   All quotes from the data have been translated from Swedish by the author.

I have to say that I think it's ultimately a good thing that politics isn't in the driving seat when it comes to these issues.

Respondent 2, MP

This, again, may be contrasted with Respondent 1, who rather perceived politics as a potential antidote to the short-termism of capitalist market logics, and therefore, underlined the need for a more hands-on engagement from the state:

What separates the state from private enterprises is that the state has the ability to think 100 years ahead. [...] And who is supposed to think about this if we don't? And who is supposed to think about it if we don't do it *now*? It's been quite a long time since politics [was involved in actively shaping the future]. [...] Especially in Sweden. It's like, one term of office, maybe two, that's about how far ahead politicians look. And maybe that's the crux of the matter, that the attitude has been "we don't know where technology will take us, but we'll cross that bridge when we get there". [...] But my attitude is rather that we could steer this. The state can't determine how people should behave, but we can provide incentives, create incentive structures for people to behave in a certain way.

Respondent 1, MLP

What we have, then, is a contest over the very premise of the automation debate: whether automation and the technological structure of the labor market are political issues in the first place. In other words, automation is not yet a fully politicized issue (in the strict sense of becoming the subject of political debate and decision-making (cf. Hay, 2007), and the interviewed actors do not agree on whether it should be or not. Furthermore, this disagreement seems to be the result of fundamentally different ideas of the appropriate role of the state in relation to the economy. This ideational tension can be further illustrated with the following two statements, which were also given as responses to the question of what policymakers, via the state, should do to shape the societal impacts of automation technologies:

I think that the state... a good state makes rules and then doesn't interfere much more. You need to enforce the rules, but that's about it. I mean, society is so *incredibly* much more than the state. [...] And every time the state has tried to dictate that "Sweden should have this and this industry" it has failed miserably. I am a very strong believer in both technology and the market. I believe in man's inherent ability to do good things.

Respondent 3, MP

This almost laissez-faire approach is put in sharp relief by this second quote, which instead underlines the need for precisely the kind of state intervention that Respondent 3 denounces:

Another thing that I think would be both simple and effective is to steer state-owned enterprises and government offices with other types of directives than what they are currently given. I mean, the state still has direct control over quite a few actors in the Swedish economy. Those actors, and those resources, could be mobilized to achieve automation in a positive way, as it were.

Respondent 6, Youth organization representative

It should suffice to say that which of these rationales will ultimately guide how automation is treated (or, indeed, not treated) politically will have far-reaching consequences for the outcome. What is equally clear is that if politics remains in the backseat during these transitional processes, we effectively submit control over them to unaccountable actors and interests that we have little or no possibility to subject to democratic oversight.

Collectivism versus Individualism

In studies of political culture and political psychology, a distinction that has commonly been used to explain political and economic behavior is that of collectivist versus individualist persons, groups, and societies. In these contexts, "culture" is widely understood to mean "the set of values and beliefs people have about how the world (both nature and society) works as well as the norms of behavior derived from that set of values" (Gorodnichenko & Roland, 2012: 213). This action-oriented conception of culture is very similar to how *political ideology* is typically defined by political theorists. Take, for example, the seminal theoretical work of Michael Freeden, whose analysis of ideology starts from an understanding of ideologies as "systems of political thinking, loose or rigid, deliberate or unintended, through which individuals and groups construct an understanding of the political world they, or those who preoccupy their thoughts, inhabit, and then act on that understanding" (Freeden, 1996: 3). Thus, although "culture" is clearly a broader concept that also covers apolitical dimensions of social life, seeing how closely related the two are, it should come as no surprise that the "collectivism–individualism-divide" is central to most attempts to classify different political ideologies.

A very simple and straightforward way to define the difference between individualism and collectivism is that the former "emphasizes personal freedom and achievement" whereas the latter "emphasizes the embeddedness of individuals in a larger group" (Gorodnichenko & Roland, 2012: 214). The word "emphasizes" is key here, as it signals that individualism and collectivism are not dichotomous, but rather two extremes along a scale that in theory has an infinite number of grades. To some extent, this scale is related to the class cleavage, in that socialist ideas are clearly informed by a collectivist worldview, while the opposite is true of liberalism. However, the class cleavage can hardly be reduced to a conflict between liberal and socialist interests. Conservative ideas, for example, are also based on a collectivist understanding of society, even if conservatives and socialists obviously hold different views regarding *what* that collective is. The important point here is that the collectivism–individualism divide is a fundamental aspect of any person's or group's worldview, and as such, our position in relation to it is likely to have important implications for our overall value systems, and thus how we approach more hands-on political issues.

The interview data covers both collectivist and individualist interpretations of the expected changes to the Swedish labor market brought about by various automation technologies, and this is another important ideational tension to bear in mind when analyzing the actors' views. These tensions were most clearly expressed when the respondents reflected upon the (actually or potentially) growing service sector of the Swedish economy. As mentioned earlier, a methodological challenge was that the interviewed actors still largely perceived automation as an abstract (and highly uncertain) future scenario rather than an existing reality. And while the scenarios served to widen their time horizons to some extent, during the interviews many still related to technology-induced transformations of the labor market that have already happened, but that are not necessarily *directly* related to automation. The growing gig economy was by far the most commonly cited example, and it was in relation to this that the differences between collectivist and individualist attitudes and interpretations could be discerned most clearly. Unsurprisingly, these different interpretations strongly correlated with differences in overall attitudes toward the gig economy (where "individualists" was far more positive toward these type of jobs).

Again, the growing gig economy is not primarily a result of automation, but rather of a process toward an increasingly deregulated Swedish labor market that has been going on for several decades (e.g., Fleckenstein & Lee, 2017). For various reasons, however, I do believe that it is sensible to analytically treat the actors' views regarding the gig economy as part of the same discursive situation as the topic of automation. Before returning to the findings, I wish to briefly outline a few of these reasons here. First, some scholars have conceptualized the gig economy as a form of "pre-automation" or "partial automation" through which companies first algorithmically automate the management of workers through the various app-based platforms, but simultaneously invest in technologies and infrastructures to also automate the services provided (Vertesi et. al., 2020; Wood, 2021). As such, the growing gig economy (and the enterprises operating in it) is relevant for the overall process toward increased automation. Second, it is plausible that a growing gig economy will be an *indirect* result of continued automation, as workers displaced by automation technologies seek new ways to make an income. This is also why one of my three scenarios was centered on a growing service sector, and why research institutes' output targeting enterprises have described automation as both driving and enabling a growing gig economy (e.g., Forrester Research, 2019). Third, and most importantly, since the topic of the gig economy was never mentioned by me in the interviews, but brought up by the respondents themselves, it is clearly part of how the interviewed actors cognitively approach and make sense of automation. Therefore, the views on gig labor described below are indeed likely to tell us something about how the actors also currently relate to automation.

As an example of the "collectivist interpretation" of the growing service sector that was expressed during the interviews, the following quote illustrates how certain respondents problematized the "gigification" of labor on the basis that this development exacerbates an ongoing liberalization and individualization of the organization of work:

> Here in Stockholm, for example, it's completely normal to get food delivered to your doorstep. [...] And who is it that brings you that food? Someone on a bike or moped that works for commission only, with no fixed salary. And it's like... do we want such a system? I don't, but there are those that think it's great. We get what we pay for and then we don't care about others. So yeah, that type of insecurity is what worries me, I'd say. [...] Because I think we can see that focus is increasingly shifting from "us" to "me". And that's also worrying, because what happens to society then? [...] So yeah, more emphasis on the group. [...] More group thinking.
>
> Respondent 4, MP

Here, this type of service job is framed as a threat to individuals' work security, but also as part of a more general "erosion" of the social fabric of society. Collectivism, or "group thinking" is here presented as solidarity, while the individualist mindset is characterized as a form of egoistic neglect of the welfare of others. Compare this with the individualist, and thus a more embracing interpretation of these jobs, which underlines the individual freedom that comes from organizing work in this way:

> The growing consulting industry, for example, is about people wanting more free time, and therefore choosing a freer form of work. Where you at times work a lot and then have more leisure at other times. To be able to control your own time in that way.
>
> Respondent 5, MP

To begin with, it may be argued that simply by referring to the "consulting industry", the statement conveys a more positive attitude toward these jobs than if, say, the term "gig jobs" had been used. Furthermore, we notice that the respondent highlighted the agency of the individuals and argued that people *choose* these jobs to gain more personal freedom (a core individualist value, as we saw above). This is in stark contrast to the collectivist interpretation above, which instead underlined the structure (or "system", to use the respondent's own phrasing) that governs this form of employment.

Later in the interview, the respondent who provided the individualist view moved on to speculate about the more long-going consequences that this re-organization of work might lead to. Here, the person explicitly described the development toward increased individualization and a decreased relevance of trade unions and employers' organizations as something positive and desirable:

> In the future, employers and employees might not be organized in the same way that they are today, because the labor market has changed. Partly because we no longer have these large enterprises that in some sense are the foundation of the Swedish model, but also because people don't have the same employee identity, or worker identity, anymore. And I think that would be quite positive, that the labor market becomes individualized and that we're able to better control both our time and competences. And take responsibility for one's competences, that you can't just expect society to do it for you.
>
> Respondent 5, MP

The statement first questions the very cornerstone of how the Swedish labor market functions today (and has done so for close to a century), namely the Swedish model, through which the bargaining between trade unions and employers' organizations has a large impact on labor regulations. It should suffice to say that a shift away from this model would represent a quite radical change in the overall structure of the Swedish labor market (and economy at large). Whether our elected politicians embrace such a development (as this respondent seems to do) or wish to counter it (as Respondent 4 above) is thus sure to have major implications for the future of work in Sweden. Second, the fact that the argument draws upon a very fundamental idea of individuals' responsibilities toward society, and vice versa, highlights that ideology plays a central role in how actors relate to these crucial questions. Only by making these underlying assumptions explicit may we have an open and informed debate about what values should be guiding how we wish to shape tomorrow's labor market in light of ongoing technological changes.

CONCLUSION

Of course, the examples highlighted in this chapter provide little more than a brief glimpse of the various underlying ideas that govern how actors interpret the political implications of increased automation. But even so, they serve to illustrate that automation, rather than being the essentially non-controversial issue that the respondents initially described it to be, evokes some quite fundamentally different views. These differences are not surprising as such, seeing as they roughly correspond to standard ideological tensions between left-wing and right-wing perspectives on the functioning of the labor market as well as the role of the state. As mentioned in the background section, this is to be expected in a country such as Sweden, where the class cleavage still plays a relatively important part in shaping the political landscape. What is more surprising, then, is that the issue of automation has not yet been explicitly politicized in the Swedish debate, given how inherently political the various imaginable responses are. In other words, there is a spectrum of diverging ideological interpretations of automation that so far lie latent in the debate, and if these are not brought to the surface and openly contested, the democratic quality of the much-needed automation debate will suffer considerably.

The logical next step is then to question *why* automation has not yet been politicized in the Swedish debate. Any longer answer to this difficult question obviously lies outside the scope of this chapter, but the interviews do provide some hints. The strongest one is arguably that there are parliamentarians that do not believe that it *should* be, but that ongoing technological changes should be allowed to unfold without any interference from the state. Critical scholars who reject this view and like Feenberg (1999: viii) instead wish to promote "an extension of democracy to the technical sphere" should strive to shine a light on the inherently political (and thereby contestable) nature of the issues at stake. It is my humble hope that this chapter has contributed (albeit modestly) to such a project.

Temporality and the "presentism" of representative democracy also constitute difficult obstacles for the politicization of automation by hampering debates on the more long-term consequences of the technologies in question. As mentioned previously, this is a challenge for virtually all representative politics and one that cannot be easily circumvented.[3] In this context, however, what is particularly alarming is that respondents refer to the high levels of *uncertainty* regarding the future impacts of automation as an explanation as to why the topic is not more debated. That the future is uncertain and open-ended is the basic condition for any democratic politics, and this is therefore something that should rather be *embraced* in the debate. That is to say that the role of critical studies of technology should be to address and challenge tendencies toward technological determinism, and instead highlight the many contingencies at play in the transition to an increasingly automated economy. Or, as sociologist Judy Wajcman reminds us, in her critique of contemporary automation discourses:

> Only by insisting that futures are always social can public bodies, rather than autonomous markets and endogenous technologies, become central to disentangling, debating and delivering those futures. (Wajcman, 2017: 126)

Admittedly, achieving such a shift is no simple task, seeing as the view of technology as an autonomous force still appears to be an inherent part of our political culture. What is needed, it seems, is to find ways of promoting and harnessing the creative potentials of political imagination (cf. Schwartz, 2001), that is, of the realization that "the limits of the possible are not given by the actual", as Rawls (2001: 5) puts it. Using future scenarios is one way of doing this, as they allow us to extrapolate from current trends and processes and imagine what the future *could* look like. Again, the key is to build such scenarios around the many uncertainties at play and thereby illustrate (if only in a simplified way) the wide *range* of possible outcomes (e.g., Urry, 2016). In this context, it is telling that one of the respondents, at the very end of our interview, expressed how the three scenarios and our discussion about them had made him better appreciate the importance of automation as a political issue:

---

[3]   There are, however, plenty of proposals on institutional innovations to promote more long-term policymaking. For a comprehensive overview, see Gonzáles-Ricoy and Gosseries (2016).

You know, when you first contacted me, I thought: "Gosh, automation? What the hell is that? Who cares?" But as you start thinking about it, you realize that there are very, very many aspects to this issue.

Respondent 3, MP

It should be clear, then, that an urgent task for critical students of artificial intelligence and other automation technologies is to stimulate the much-needed automation debate by encouraging policymakers and citizenries to "think about" these issues. It is my firm belief that this is best done by undressing the myth of technological advancement as a constantly ongoing external force over which we have no influence. This, in turn, starts with insisting on the rather trivial point that politics matter.

REFERENCES

Bartolini, S. (2000). *The political mobilization of the European left, 1860–1980: The class cleavage.* Cambridge University Press.

Bastani, A. (2019). *Fully automated luxury communism: A manifesto.* Verso.

Boston, J. (2016). *Governing for the future: Designing democratic institutions for a better tomorrow.* Emerald.

Bäck, M. & Möller, T. (2003). *Partier och organisationer* (6th rev. and updated ed.). [Parties and organizations]. Norstedts juridik.

Danaher, J. (2019). *Automation and Utopia: Human flourishing in a world without work.* Harvard University Press.

Demker, M. (2015). Sociala skiljelinjer och partisystem [Social cleavages and party systems]. In M. Hagevi (Ed.), *Partier och partisystem* [Parties and party systems] (pp. 21–32). Studentlitteratur.

European Commission. (2019). *Building trust in human-centric artificial intelligence* (COM/2019/168 final).

Feenberg, A. (1999). *Questioning technology.* Routledge.

Fleckenstein, T. & Lee, S. (2017). The politics of labor market reform in coordinated welfare capitalism: Comparing Sweden, Germany, and South Korea. *World Politics*, 69(1), 144–183.

Ford, M. (2015). *The rise of the robots: Technology and the threat of mass unemployment.* Oneworld Publications.

Forrester Research. (2019). *Future of work.* https://www.forrester.com/technology/future-of-work/ (Accessed 2022-09-15).

Frase, P. (2016). *Four futures: Visions of the world after capitalism.* Verso.

Freeden, M. (1996). *Ideologies and political theory: A conceptual approach.* Clarendon Press.

Frey, C. B. & Osborne, M. A. (2013). The future of employment: How susceptible are jobs to computerisation? *Oxford Martin School Working Paper.* https://www.oxfordmartin.ox.ac.uk/downloads/academic/The_Future_of_Employment.pdf (Accessed 2022-09-15).

González-Ricoy, I. & Gosseries, A. (Eds.). (2016). *Institutions for future generations.* Oxford University Press.

Gorodnichenko, Y. & Roland, G. (2012). Understanding the individualism–collectivism cleavage and its effects: Lessons from cultural psychology. In M. Aoki, T. Kuran & G. Roland (Eds.), *Institutions and comparative economic development* (pp. 213–236). Palgrave Macmillan.

Hay, C. (2007). *Why we hate politics.* Polity.

Lindberg, M. (2017). Qualitative analysis of ideas and ideological content. In K. Boréus & G. Bergström (Eds.), *Analyzing text and discourse: Eight approaches for the social sciences* (pp. 86–121). Sage.

Merriam-Webster. (n.d.) Automation. https://www.merriam-webster.com/dictionary/automation (Accessed 2022-09-15).

Oskarsson, M. & Demker, M. (2015). Room for realignment: The working-class sympathy for Sweden democrats. *Government & Opposition*, 50(4), 629–651.

Rahm, L. (2021). Computing the Nordic way: The Swedish labour movement, computers and educational imaginaries from the post-war period to the turn of the millennium. *Nordic Journal of Educational History*, 8(1), 31–58.

Rahm, L. & Kaun, A. (2022). Imagining mundane automation: Historical trajectories of meaning-making around technological change. In S. Pink, M. Berg, D. Lupton & M. Ruckenstein (Eds.), *Everyday automation: Experiencing and anticipating emerging technologies* (pp. 23–43). Routledge.

Rawls, J. (2001). *Justice as fairness: A restatement.* Belknap.

Schwartz, A. M. (2021). Political imagination and its limits. *Synthese*, 199, 3325–3343.

Shneiderman, B. (2022). *Human-centered AI.* Oxford University Press.

Srnicek, N. & Williams, A. (2016). *Inventing the future: Postcapitalism and a world without work* (Rev. and updated ed.). Verso.

Thompson, D. F. (2005). Democracy in time: Popular sovereignty and temporal representation. *Constellations*, 12(2), 245–261.

Urry, J. (2016). *What is the future?* Polity Press.

Vertesi, J. A., Goldstein, A., Enriquez, D., Liu, L. & Miller, K. T. (2020). Pre-automation: Insourcing and automating the gig economy. *Sociologica*, 14(3), 167–193.

Wajcman, J. (2017). Automation: Is it really different this time? *The British Journal of Sociology*, 68(1), 119–127.

Wood, A. J. (2021). *Algorithmic management consequences for work organisation and working conditions* (No. 2021/07). JRC Working Papers Series on Labour, Education and Technology.

59. En-countering AI as algorhythmic practice

Shintaro Miyazaki

INTRODUCTION

When in Spring 1940, Walter Benjamin, a German Jewish philosopher, essayist, radio producer, and Marxist wrote his essay "On the Concept of History" AI technically did not yet exist, but instead was painstakingly manufactured by hard human labour. It begins with:

> There was once, we know, an automaton constructed in such a way that it could respond to every move by a chess player with a countermove that would ensure the winning of the game. (2003, p. 389)

Benjamin is referring to a chess automaton, an AI, if you will, similar to the one designed around 1800 by the German-Hungarian inventor Wolfgang von Kempelen and which was a sort of chess-playing machine represented by a man puppet dressed in Turkish costume that could sometimes beat even experienced chess players. One of the earliest texts by the American writer Edgar Allan Poe, Maelzel's Chess Player written in 1836, quasi-forensically exposed the automaton as a device hiding a human chess master mostly of a rather small stature. Benjamin equated the puppet in Turkish costume with historical materialism and the "hunchbacked dwarf" (ibid) who always wins, he equated with theology. At Benjamin's time of writing, that is in the 1940s of Europe, the opponent surely was fascist authoritarian capitalism in Germany. At least it is imaginable that scholarly work under such regimes was not pleasurable at all. Surely it was a suffocating situation for Jewish critical philosophers, and while historical materialism can be interpreted as anti-capitalist critical theory, theology, I argue, could be understood as the study of the supernatural and revelation. Such forms of studying, I interpret, are linked with forms of knowledge and knowing situated between aesthetics and ethics. Furthermore, it is crucial for this sort of epistemology and practices that they gain both more visibility and growth. Therefore, they should not remain invisible like the dwarf. Anti-capitalist critical theory needs to work together with aesthetics and ethics in order to gain power and to be able to play with and against fascist authoritarianism. In order to be able to fight current manifestations and iterations of such fascist powers, which exist everywhere today, a critical theory of AI needs to look closer at the intersections and interference fields of aesthetics and ethics.

This chapter argues for en-countering AI by updating Benjamin's powerful ideas with what I call algorhythmics (Miyazaki, 2018) meant as a scholarly practice, which includes an equal mixture of historical knowledge, aesthetics, ethics, Marxism, utopianism, and fantasy, and which does not always lead to direct action nor is based on purely socio-political arguments. Algorhythmics as I described extensively elsewhere is a perspective on automated technological processes and events, which is both interested in how algorithms are programmed and coded and how they unfold in time and become rhythms. Algorithms form the basis of all sorts of AI, even artificial neural networks, and while they unfold in time, they generate rhythms and timings. At the beginning of the 2020s, in times of crisis, climate change, the Covid-19 pandemic, the Russo-Ukrainian War, inflation, hunger, global migration, and so on, a theory-practice is urgently needed. One that is sensitive to changes in the rhythms of our "digital" everyday life, of the rhythmic flow of resources, energies, and signals aiming at en-countering them with alternative ways of timing and rhyming on all sorts of layers and scales. Rhythmanalysis is a seminal theory that helps to inquire about such timings and rhythms and was formulated by Henri Lefebvre, the French Marxist philosopher and sociologist, in a not so known work published posthumously in the early 1990s (Lefebvre, 2004). While Lefebvre was famous for studies on urban spaces and environments, algorhythm analysis aims to inquire into the digital space and its entanglement with material infrastructures and how digital structures such as AI unfold in time and space. Basic principles of algorhythmics or algorhythmic practice, especially its current version, furthermore, are informed by French philosopher Michel Foucault's articulations on critique, which

> has to be conceived as an attitude, an ethos, a philosophical life in which the critique of what we are is at one and the same time the historical analysis of the limits that are imposed on us and an experiment with the possibility of going beyond them. (Foucault, 1984, p. 50)

EN-COUNTERING AS CRITIQUE

Capitalism in the early 20th century as the opponent of the "fake" chess automaton, was still human-centred and socially constructed, although industries were already in the 1940s massively machine-based. Still, the most recent forms of technological entanglements of capital and its drive for more profit inscribed and coded into technological infrastructures and environments provide a more complicated situation. In the 2020s, the age of digital capitalism, or articulated more playfully as "AI Capitalism", Kempelen's chess automaton has already been realized. Artificial intelligence (AI), at least in its broader and weak meaning as an interplay of automated adaptive software and algorithmic systems of sensing, computation, control, and communication became part of everyday life. The issues with AI are countless and described all over this volume. It is therefore inevitable to conceptualize and theorize about strategies and approaches of anti-AI capitalism and en-countering to transform Benjamin's dwarf into a self-determined, emancipated player-participant and an agent of planet Earth capable of instrumentalizing automated machinery and critical AI in order to collectively en-counter those forms of AI that are imposed on them. En-countering, here is meant both in its conventional meaning as sometimes unpleasant and sometimes an unexpected eventful passively undergone experience, as in the verb to encounter or with the hyphen to emphasize the active, opposing component (countering) of such imposed experiences.

En-countering as critique, as this chapter argues, is based on a Foucauldian attitude and an anticipative, prefigurative, but always open posture oriented towards specific networks of knowledge production and power exertion, which generate unwanted situations of governance. Such situations can be anywhere, such as perhaps reading this text. Then please put it away and stop reading. American philosopher Judith Butler, explains that the problem for Foucault is not to produce a subject who will be radically ungovernable for all time. The question, how not to be governed? is always the question of how not to be governed in this or that way. But it is not a question of how not to be governed at all. (2009, p. 791)

Furthermore, such forms of dissent and disobedience involve the "inventive elaboration of the self" and "self-production" (Ibid, p. 787). Critique therefore is about the refusal of certain forms of control and governance and this refusal opens up space for invention, imaginations, and plans for alternative forms of governance and production, which perhaps are more inclusive and democratic. In such a variant critique is en-countering. It builds upon certain passively undergone and imposed experiences, which lead to opposing activities of countering, of countermoves as performed by the dwarf inside the chess automaton described by Benjamin around 1940.

En-countering AI methodically draws upon insights from media archaeology as founded by German media studies scholar Wolfgang Ernst (2011) modulated with "sympoiesis" by American science and technology scholar Donna Haraway (2016). Sympoiesis means roughly do-it-together and carefully. This combination builds, again, on Foucault and his idea of critique, which needs to be archaeological and genealogical at the same time (1984, p. 46, 50). While the archaeological method works out the material structures, bodies, pathways, spaces, apparatuses, and institutions of the unwanted forms of governance and their rules, discourses, prejudices, biases, and epistemological assumptions, which are linked together through such a material network, the genealogical method generates not only a derivation of the circumstances of the unwanted forms of governance, but at the same time, generates alternative pathways and possibilities of different more desired ways of (self-)governance. Media archaeology extends the archaeology of knowledge and its production with media technologies focusing on processes of storing, transmitting, and processing. It looks, listens, and reflects the materiality, technicity, and operativity of electronic and electromagnetic media. Furthermore, media archaeology looks at voltage currents as signals, frequencies, circuits, filters, codes, cables, protocols, standards, formats, algorithms, networks, statistics, artificial neural computing, and so on. Such forms of analysis getting close to communication engineering are complemented by the general assumption that technologies are always situated and instrumentalized, but the more complicated and nested the structure of a technology is, the more likely it is that it offers and affords alternative unintended ways of usage, re-structuring, and re-purposing.

The generative component of such inquiries searches for a different future, leading to a practice of generative poiesis, aka genealogy, if you will. As Haraway puts it, such practices are closer to "sympoiesis" emphasizing the importance of togetherness, solidarity, and commonality: "It is a word for worlding-with, in company" (2016, p. 58), and it implies an "expandable set of players" (Ibid, p. 65). Haraway strongly argues for projects such as "Never Alone", a video game offering an Indigenous perspective on the world and developed from a collaboration between Alaska Natives from the Cook Inlet Tribal Council, the game company E-Line Media, and a community of young and old people playing the game (Ibid, p. 87f). Projects like "Never Alone"

require inventive, sympoietic collaborations that bring together such things as computer game platforms and their designers, indigenous storytellers, visual artists, carvers and puppet makers, digital-savvy youngsters, and community activists. (Ibid, p. 86)

For en-countering AI, I argue that it might be beneficial to provide and design similar trans-disciplinary, cross-generational, and participatory settings that include media technologies, postcolonial and intersectional sensitivity, and lots of co-programming skills. Algorhythmic practice offers gateways into such fields of sympoiesis in the age of critical AI.

ALGORHYTHMIC PRACTICES

Artificial intelligence is a placeholder for the manifold ways of algorithm-driven analysis, decision-making, machine learning, and more generally, algorithm-driven systems governing information, data, and signal production offering means and instruments "to read or pick between the lines", which is the literal Latin meaning of *intelligere*. In more general terms, there is strong AI and there is weak AI, and this chapter understands AI as weak AI. The most advanced forms of AI today such as Siri or Google Assistant are examples of weak AI. They do not manifest any aspects of complex cognitive tasks, but they use so-called natural language processing embedded within a broader algorithmic system. The main operation of such and similar forms of artificial intelligence consists of iterative and recursive instantiations of reading, dividing, detecting, indexing, numbering, sorting, clustering, weighting, filtering, deciding, selecting, and so on, all in principle based on the four arithmetic operations (addition, subtraction, multiplication, and division) extended by a minimal set of logistical operations such as shifting and erasing. Artificial neural networks, for example, are based on vector calculus requiring a lot of multiplications. The important task of critical AI is to dissect AI so that its operativity is disentangled.

The upcoming part of this chapter will focus on what I previously called algorhythmic practices. The term algorhythm I proposed for the first time in 2012 was an attempt to concentrate on the rhythmic effects algorithms generate while unfolding in time mostly via the materiality of weak electric signals. It was a cacography taken literally in order to work out the operativity and performativity of all sorts of algorithmic processes at that time more directed towards understanding the technicity of computation, arguing that abstract mathematics always needs energy, work, and a medium for becoming part of the world. And by doing that they inevitably create powerful differences and are thus instrumental in creating differences and identities. Such instrumentalities then again are often misused by those in power.

Listening to Machinic Algorithms

The first and most direct example of algorhythmic practice is the activity of listening. It is a sort of listening, which is sensitive to signal flows and their fluctuations and rhythms of articulation. Listening implies a sort of locality. In order to listen you need to stay in one place. The earliest situations where you could probably hear an algorithm at work was in the age of electromechanical calculators such as the IBM Automatic Sequence Controlled Calculator (ASCC) built in 1944, which was soon technologically outdated, by the first electronic computers switching not with electromagnetic relays, but with so-called multi-vibrator circuits or flip-flop-circuits based on vacuum tubes. The Small-Scale Experimental Machine (SSEM) built in 1948 at the University of Manchester in the UK was one of the first. While some of this early computing machinery had visual displays with a grid of dots on a cathode ray tube or worked with oscilloscopes, other machines also included means to make some of the processes audible by simply connecting the voltage signal, for example, at the last bit of a storage register, to an amplifier-speaker. This trick more epistemologically formulated a form of transduction between the realm of electronic and acoustic signals and made it possible to listen to the rhythmic signals representing binary states and correlate the sound to certain characteristics of the programmed loops, rhythms, and algorithms. Transduction is a sort of translation not of letters and words but of processes in the realm of physics. One specific machine made in the early 1960s by Philips Physics Laboratory in Eindhoven, Netherlands, with built-in loudspeakers, had a demo programme and an algorithm checking whether a huge number was a prime number or not; visitors could hear how fast the machine was working by listening to its algorhythm (Miyazaki, 2012). Other machines such as the early computers by Ferranti, a company in Manchester, applied similar forms of probing and listening to certain signals for monitoring purposes, for example, for checking rather unstable memory circuits. Soon in the early 1960s, these engineers and operators of mainframe computers with special listening skills became obsolete, since more reliable and cheaper software-based operators called operating systems were introduced. These systems were programmed with error detection algorithms active on the operating system level and were able to detect most errors by themselves without any human intervention (Ibid.). This is media historically regarded as a still under-explored field and there are still many studies and archaeologies of automated or artificial listening to write.

While the emerging research centres of computation of the late 1960s and 1970s might have been clean and calm, the digital realm of personal computing in its early phase of the late 1980s and 1990s was still quite noisy. For those who still remember the sound of the dial-up modem, which was the way to connect to the internet before broadband connections were installed, or the sound of the Commodore Datasette, such algorhythmic practices of listening to computing machinery and processes might seem obvious, but for later generations socialized differently and more recently, algorhythmics could offer helpful openings into the operativity of algorithmic systems. More recently, in the 2000s, artists like Christina Kubisch, Martin Howse, and Valentina Vuksic, or scholars with an affinity to practical experiments, such as me, have been exploring ways to listen digitally via the electromagnetic fields around smart gadgetry. With an almost equally simple trick like the one from the 1950s described earlier, again, another form of transduction, it is possible to hear the electromagnetic side emissions of all kinds of digital circuitry including central processor units (CPUs), graphics processing units (GPUs), monitors, or hard disks by using a so-called electromagnetic coil or induction loop or a long isolated wire connected to some powerful audio amplifiers with loudspeakers. Sometimes we can still hear similar signals when we connect projectors, audio outputs from our laptops, and power supplies with audio amplifiers in strange ways receiving electromagnetic noise or leakage voltage from somewhere. One of the most prominent disturbances in the early 2000s was the dactylic rhythm of a second-generation GSM mobile phone. By using a decibel-milliwatts detector chip (I.e Analog Devices, AD 8313) reacting to radio signals from about 100 MHz to 2.5 GHz, usually used for electrosmog measurements, and instead of "reading" the signal with a display circuit, it is also possible to amplify the signal and connect a loudspeaker (Miyazaki, 2013). This lets you listen to the dynamic operativity of all sorts of digital communication protocols such as Wi-Fi, Bluetooth, GSM, UMTS/4G, and GPS with carrier frequencies in the devices' range. Here, not the data itself, but the different protocols according to their different timing and signalling characteristics such as broadband or narrow band, transient or always there, and so on, become audible. Another way to listen to algorithms is to program outputs into the code itself, similar to writing print messages for debugging, and use software libraries and packages, which let you link these virtual outputs to digital sound generators in applications such as Supercollider SC3, Pure Data, or Max/Msp connected with your loudspeakers or external audio interface.

Up to this point, this section described ways of en-countering AI by listening. The next section will step back and present some examples, where the notion of algorhythmics is crucial but provokes practice, which does not always lead to audible processes.

Algorhythmic Entanglements[1]

Being sensitive towards rhythmicity and repeating processes is also applicable as a critical practice to inquire about network breakdowns or crashes as I will unpack here along with the example of the so-called AT&T crash of the early 1990s.

On 15 January 1990, the long-distance telephone network in North America crashed and was dysfunctional for nine hours. The reason for this crash was a small programming mistake implemented via a software update of the newer and software-based telephone line switching computers located in different centres all over the country. The update was made in December 1989 on all of the 114 switching computers. The whole system worked well until at about 2.30 pm, a computer located in New York started to detect some malfunctions in its system, which led to a self-triggered shutdown for four to six seconds (Neumann, 1990, p. 11). For keeping the connectivity of the whole system, this had to be communicated to the neighbouring switching computers. After the New York switching computer was online again, it sent out messages to its closest computers, which initiated an update of their routing maps, so that the machine that was previously shut down could be added to the network again. Strikingly, the malfunction became effective exactly during this updating process. The update of December 1989 made this process "vulnerable". Incoming update messages from the previously shut down New York-based computer then caused damage. Each of the neighbouring computers, in turn, updated its routing map, then shut itself down, and after recovering, would try to reconnect to the network, thus causing other shutdowns. The whole network was trapped in an eternal algo*rhythmic*, distributed, and polyrhythmic refrain: a transatlantic feedback loop. The cause of the malfunction was later recognized as a simple programming mistake in the programming language C. In an algorithm implemented in these switching machines consisting of a "do-while-loop", there were many switch instructions. On one of those branches, a switch-clause had an "if-loop" in it, which should have been fine, but there was another break-instruction in it, which in the programming language C does not make a lot of sense. The program did not act in the intended way and the rhythms concerning its operation were thus slightly out of order. The breakouts of loops or the breaks of switch-instruction chains were timed in unintended rhythms. Its algorhythmics were stuttering. These small rhythmic errors were usually not detectable by the self-monitoring operating systems but became somehow effective during the already-mentioned updating process of the routing maps.

More recently, similar studies of rhythmanalysis, as conceived by French Marxist Henri Lefebvre in a posthumously published work (Lefebvre, 2004 [1992]), have been conducted

---

[1]   Parts of this passage already appeared in Miyazaki (2016).

by scholars with affinities to media studies such as Italian sociologist and smart city scholar Claudio Coletta and Irish human geographer Robert M. Kitchin. They have extended algorhythmics to conceptualize "how forms of algorhythmic governance are being produced that explicitly measure and modulate urban rhythms – in our case the flow of traffic and the fluctuations of noise" (Coletta & Kitchin, 2017, p. 5). Their clear analysis of SCATS (Sydney Coordinated Adaptive Traffic System), an adaptive traffic light control system based on data from CCTV cameras, vehicle sensors (induction loops), and a mobile network of public bus transponders (p. 5f.), all giving input for the algorithm then linked to traffic lights, which is not only installed in Sydney but, for example, also in Shanghai, Singapore, and Dublin, shows how algorhythmic governance on a traffic level takes places and time by what they call "rhythm-making" (p. 12).

Pinging-Listening as Extraction

Short studies like the one I elaborated on above draw attention to methods of probing, triggering, and tracing, coupled with operations of active inquiry such as sending out a short impulse, a ping. The term ping derived from the context of submarine active sonar and meant sending out a high energetic ultrasound impulse via hydrophones into the surrounding water, listening to its repercussions and registering the echo delay times. Such forms of impulse-based probing and surveying technologies basically operate as signal based. Pinging is also the term for sending out a test packet in communication network debugging. Furthermore, operations such as packet tracing, which is an extension of pinging, are useful tools to track how a data packet from a website in www travels around the planet within seconds. More generally, with this gesture of active inquiry, I preliminary suggest calling it pinging-listening, which is also to be uncovered as a form of information extraction via intrusion, thus they need to be conducted carefully and cautiously. Pinging is also disturbing, but at the same time, especially in cases of en-countering, it might be useful.

While networks and protocols of automated systems are already quite complicated, the most recent widespread application of systems working with machine learning, especially artificial neural networks, imposes new limiting lines on us in critical inquiries. Here, I suggest pinging-listening modulated with the conceptual device of "the" filter or the operation of filtering as a useful mode of inquiry. To be more concrete, I suggest misinterpreting artificial neural networks and more concretely so-called convolutional neural networks (CNN)[2] as filter machines, which might be turned into filter devices of sound signals.

---

[2]   A convolutional neural network (CNN) consists of several layers of two- or three-dimensional matrices, which means tables of numbers consisting, for example, of the brightness values of an image. A single element of a matrix, also called an artificial neuron, receives input from another artificial neuron in the previous layer and passes that input to another neuron in the next layer. In CNNs, a so-called convolution happens during the forwarding process, where a smaller matrix, also called convolution matrix or filter mask, consisting of, for example, 3x3 fields, scans the current larger layer. In each case, the scalar product of the mentioned 3x3 filter mask with the current larger matrix is computed. This computation, which is based on the operations of multiplication and addition, creates a new filtered layer. The aggregated composition of many such filters over several matrix layers then forms a specific CNN that can, for example, filter the front view of a dog and thus "recognize" it. More ordinary image filters are known from image manipulation with Adobe Photoshop for example, which emphasize, blur, or remove certain image elements. Conceptually these image filters are also to be understood as filter masks.

From a media epistemological perspective, the operation of pinging-listening makes the medium and its in-betweenness perceivable as a measurable time delay, which transforms at some point of its intensification into a filter effect. A filter is functionally more visible than a "neutral" medium since its purpose is exactly not to be neutral, but to intervene in the signal to process it. To make audible how specific filters work, numerous input signals and pings, ideally a huge amount so they turn into noise, are needed. To fully understand how filters extract information, therefore, careful extraction processes are needed, and one way to do that is to feed it with noise or other signals. In the case of artificial neural networks applied to sound or music in the realm of audio feature extraction or sound information retrieval, this audification or auralization process is quite straightforward and you hear the working of different neural layers similar to an audio wave filter damping or amplifying certain features of an audio signal (Choi et al., 2016) as it is applied, for example, to audio equalizers or bass sound boosters. I suggest that similar operations are possible with visual filters so that you can visualize the functionality of one specific layer of an artificial neuronal network. Fabian Offert, a German American machine vision expert and humanities scholar has seminally elaborated on how feature visualization could be used as a way of critical inquiry on biases in face and object recognition (Offert & Bell, 2021). It is here important to note that such processes of audifying selected operations of an AI system is a highly complicated task and requires the collaboration of many academic disciplines and knowledge fields such as engineering, critical theory, computer science, and cognitive science.

SYMPOIESIS OF COUNTER-ALGORHYTHMS

En-countering AI to summarize is about making visible and audible as a critique involving ways to understand and carefully make clear its manifold ways of intervention and entanglement with our everyday lives, as well as its infrastructures, our tools, and our ways of knowledge production. Here it is crucial to critically differentiate and bring to the fore the operativity of AI as a form of sorting, clustering, filtering, discriminating, extracting, oppressing, and so on. And one specific way to conduct such critical inquiries is to listen to algorhythms on several time-space scales. I will suggest concrete ways. First, rather passive ways of listening based on the idea of tapping relying on at least one point of transduction (from electronic signals to audible sound waves for example), and second, by building on such setups more active forms of listening as probing or testing, which I call pinging-listening. Both ways of inquiry open the possibility of deepening insights into networks, devices, operations, and algorithms instead of staying at the surface level often in the form of interface analysis.

Listening, I argue, is the first operation of subsequent data gathering leading ultimately to the possibilities of sympoiesis, as I introduced at the beginning of this chapter. As it should be clear at this point, en-countering AI as algorhythmic practice is to be done together as sympoiesis involving programmers, scholars, designers, activists, and most importantly, those who are specifically affected and most often marginalized by systems, institutions, communities, authorities, governmental bodies, powerful companies, and other private bodies applying and instrumentalizing AI for their own benefit or at least to optimize their own performance. Listening to algorhythms builds the starting operation to sympoietically and carefully generate more desirable, more inclusive, useful forms of algorhythms, thus counter-algorhythms. And to close this chapter with Benjamin, I argue for a political usage of AI, as critical AI and counter-algorhythmics, similar to his suggestion to use the artistic power of photography and film to reveal the suppressed and marginalized processes and counter-construct a historiography of the underprivileged – of those who lost competitions, the "useless", forgotten, queer and different humans, animals, organisms, things, materials, and events. We should use the power of computation, modelling, and simulation, of techno-futuring in order to sympoietically generate a bright counter-future yet to come.[3]

FURTHER READING

Haraway, D. J. (2016). *Staying with the trouble: Making Kin in the Chthulucene (experimental futures)* (1st ed.). Duke University Press Books.
Kitchin, R., & Fraser, A. (2020). *Slow computing: Why we need balanced digital lives.* Bristol University Press.
Mattern, S. (2021). *A city is not a computer: Other urban intelligences* (1st ed.). Princeton University Press.

REFERENCES

Benjamin, W. (2003). On the concept of history. In H. Eiland & M. W. Jennings (Eds.), *Walter Benjamin: Selected writings, volume 4: 1938–1940* (pp. 389–400). Harvard University Press.
Butler, J. (2009). Critique, dissent, disciplinarity. *Critical Inquiry*, 35(4), 773–795. https://doi.org/10.1086/599590
Choi, K., Fazekas, G., & Sandler, M. (2016). Explaining deep convolutional neural networks on music classification. In ArXiv [cs.LG]. http://arxiv.org/abs/1607.02444
Coletta, C., & Kitchin, R. (2017). Algorhythmic governance: Regulating the 'heartbeat' of a city using the Internet of Things. *Big Data & Society*, 4(2), 1–16. https://doi.org/10.1177/2053951717742418
Ernst, W. (2011). Media archaeography: Method and machine versus history and narrative of media. In E. Huhtamo & J. Parikka (Eds.), *Media archaeology: Approaches, applications, and implications* (pp. 239–255). University of California Press.
Foucault, M. (1984). What is enlightenment? In P. Rabinow (Ed.), *The Foucault reader* (pp. 32–50). Pantheon Books.
Haraway, D. J. (2016). *Staying with the trouble: Making Kin in the Chthulucene (Experimental Futures)* (1st ed.). Duke University Press Books.
Lefebvre, H. (2004). *Rhythmanalysis: Space, Time and Everyday Life, [Élements de rythmanalyse, Paris: Édition Sylleps 1992].* Continuum.
Neumann, P. G. (1990). Risks to the public in computers and related systems. ACM SIGSOFT Software Engineering Notes (Vol. 15, Issue 2, April), 3–22.
Miyazaki, S. (2012). Algorhythmics: Understanding micro-temporality in computational cultures. *Computational Cultures: A Journal of Software Studies, 2.*
Miyazaki, S. (2013). Urban sounds unheard-of: A media archaeology of ubiquitous infospheres. *Continuum, 27*(4), 514–522. https://doi.org/10.1080/10304312.2013.803302
Miyazaki, S. (2016). Algorhythmic ecosystems: Neoliberal couplings and their pathogenesis 1960-present. In R. Seyfert & J. Roberge (Eds.), *Algorithmic cultures: Essays on meaning, performance and new technologies (Routledge advances in sociology)* (pp. 128–139). Routledge Advances in Sociology.
Miyazaki, S. (2018). Algorhythmics: A diffractive approach for understanding computation. In J. Sayers (Ed.), *The Routledge companion to media studies and digital humanities* (pp. 243–249). Routledge.
Offert, F., & Bell, P. (2021). Perceptual bias and technical metapictures: Critical machine vision as a humanities challenge. *AI & Society*, 36(4), 1133–1144. https://doi.org/10.1007/s00146-020-01058-z

---

[3] See, for example, http://counter-n.net/ for some more concrete examples.

60. Introducing political ecology of Creative-Ai
Andre Holzapfel

INTRODUCTION

Applications of artificial intelligence to artistic processes (Creative-Ai[1]) are becoming more common, and media attention towards these applications is large. At the focus of many media contributions is the question of when a human artist-genius will be replaced by a similarly genius and autonomous Ai. But a quick look at various widely discussed Ai art projects clarifies that in most cases, the Ai acts far from autonomously and that the symbolic realm of the artistic creation is densely connected to a material dimension. The immersive media installation titled "Archive Dreaming" by Refik Anadolu creates a "canvas with light and data applied as materials" and facilitates both user-driven and automatic exploration "of unexpected correlations among documents". The project was realised with the support of 20 collaborators at three institutions, and the Ai comprises a model that has been trained on 1.7 million documents using the computational power provided to the artist by Google's Artists and Machine Intelligence Program (Anadol 2017). The completion of the composition of Beethoven's 10th Symphony was approached by a group of music historians, musicologists, composers, and computer scientists over a period of several years involving extended data preparation and Ai model design (Elgammal 2021). The novel "1 the Road" was written by an Ai, but the artist Ross Goodwin carefully orchestrated the sensor inputs that would feed the Ai model during a road trip. The creative process involved not only Goodwin, his car, and an Ai, but also a film crew accompanying him and documenting the road trip from New York to New Orleans (Hornigold 2018). In comparison to the Ai Beethoven project, however, the artist took the deliberate choice to present the Ai output in its raw form, with the motivation to illustrate the limitations and potential of such an autonomous machine creation.

Besides the formation of an Ai model in the context of a specific artwork, many companies have shaped tools for media production that use – or at least claim the use – Ai as a means to support the creative processes of the users of the tools. Examples are the use of Ai for mastering the sound of a music production,[2] audio restoration,[3] or the scene analysis and filtering of images based on Ai by Photoshop (Clarke 2020). Such systems have been called creative support tools (CST), and these tools have been well-documented within HCI research for over a decade (Frich et al. 2019; Gabriel et al. 2016). Based on the literature review of 143 papers, Frich et al. (2019) define CST as a tool that "runs on one or more digital systems, encompasses one or more creativity-focused features, and is employed to positively influence users of varying expertise in one or more distinct phases of the creative process". Following this definition, a Creative-Ai tool is simply a CST that employs artificial intelligence. Demystifying this latter

---

[1]   The reference to artificial intelligence as Ai with lower-case i is a conscious choice that reflects the current state of Ai systems as not (yet) fulfilling the plausible minimum criteria of intelligence.

[2]   https://www.landr.com/.

[3]   https://www.izotope.com/en/products/rx.html.

buzzword, artificial intelligence in the context of Creative-Ai (and in most other contexts) is nothing but data-driven analysis and/or synthesis of media data, and the intelligence that emerges from training processes can be fairly considered as narrow. That is, all tools for artists and designers so far comprise an intelligence that can at least partially conduct a creative process in a fairly restricted context. The Beethoven Ai can continue phrases in the style of one specific composer, and the Archive Dreamer can hallucinate novel data in the context of one specific archive. Going beyond these borders demands adapting and re-training models, which demands on the material side new collections of data and expenditure of energy for the training of models.

The goal of this chapter is to develop a perspective on the environmental impact of creative processes that make use of Ai when we consider them as part of an economic system that transforms artistic creation into a commodity. I will discuss specific Creative-Ai cases and their environmental impact along with the role of large corporations involved in Creative-Ai development. Already in the 1970s, the economic and social theorist Jacques Attali (1985) predicted a situation that strongly relates to current business plans by the largest music streaming provider Spotify. As we will see, prospects of using Creative-Ai as a collaborative tool that supports creative processes promise an extension of the horizon of artistic possibilities, but such optimistic perspectives neglect the role of large corporations as gatekeepers to systems and infrastructures. I believe that it is timely to combine political, environmental, and sociocultural perspectives on Creative-Ai to better understand how the power exercised by capital and the environmental impact of Creative-Ai may motivate researchers and artists to adopt a more critical perspective. The chapter – written by an ethnomusicologist/computer scientist – is characterised by a certain focus on music, but its general implications can be transferred to other forms of art.

RELATED WORK

The application and development of Creative-Ai have been investigated from various perspectives. A central venue for discussing Creative-Ai is the International Conference on Computational Creativity (ICCC), at which practical Ai applications in various art forms (e.g., Wertz and Kuhn 2022; Hertzmann 2022; Tan 2019) are discussed as well as sociocultural and theoretical dimensions of applying computational tools in creative processes (e.g., Riccio et al. 2022; Brown et al. 2021). Within the Conference on Human Factors in Computing Systems (CHI), the interfaces and interactions with Creative-Ai have been explored (Oh et al. 2018; Ragot et al. 2020), and in 2022, a dedicated workshop gathered researchers working with Ai in the context of generating art (Muller et al. 2022). More specialised HCI-related venues, such as the International Conference on New Interfaces for Musical Expression (NIME), feature an increasing amount discussions of how Ai can present novel and inspiring ways to interact with music technology (Tahiroğlu et al. 2020; Murray-Browne and Tigas 2021). In addition, many machine learning conferences feature special sessions that focus on novel model architectures in the context of artistic creation.[4]

---

[4]   For instance, since 2017, the Machine Learning for Creativity and Design workshop in the context of the NiPS conference (https://nips2017creativity.github.io/), and the special track on Ai, the Arts, and Creativity at the IJCAI-ECAI 2022 conference (https://ijcai-22.org/calls-creativity/).

Social and ethical implications of Creative-Ai related to the use of training data (Sturm et al. 2019), and impacts on diversity (Porcaro et al. 2021) and fairness (Ferraro et al. 2021) in diverse cultural contexts have been discussed to some extent. When it comes to potential environmental consequences of Creative-Ai use, it is unclear how large the energy consumption and related carbon footprints of specific artistic projects may be (Jääskeläinen et al. 2022). Whereas the environmental impact of individual artistic projects may be negligible, the environmental perspective becomes relevant when Creative-Ai tools are becoming a commodity to which access to larger user groups is provided by a corporation. This nexus of environment, society, and politics is what is at the core of studies of political ecology (Biersack 2006). As Watts (2017) states, political ecology studies "forms of access and control over resources and their implications for environmental health and sustainable livelihoods". The severity of such implications in the context of Ai and Big Data has been analysed, for instance, by Crawford (2021), Velkova (2016), and Thylstrupp (2019). A ground-breaking study of the political ecology of the music industry has been conducted by Devine (2019), who demonstrated that the digitalisation of the music industry in the age of streaming increased rather than decreased its carbon footprint, compared with the era of physical distribution of music media. In this rather grim picture of the music industry, Devine has not yet taken into account the use of Ai in the context of recommendation and content generation.

A series of publications has directed attention to the energy consumption of the use of Ai in various fields. One of the most widely perceived publications (Strubell et al. 2019) estimates the energy consumption related to the development of a deep learning-based model in the context of natural language processing (NLP). Strubell et al. (2019) reveal that their development of an NLP model within six months involved the use of 27 years of GPU time[5] for training models, with massive financial costs and energy consumption for cloud computing. Besides the environmental impact, the authors emphasise that building such models becomes a privilege for well-funded academic institutions and corporations. Therefore, various authors suggest documenting the energy and carbon footprints of model development and training along common performance metrics (Strubell et al. 2019; Anthony et al. 2020). Tools for estimating environmental impacts are increasingly available (Anthony et al. 2020; Henderson et al. 2020), and although the estimates may have a large error margin, they are helpful in providing an orientation of the order of CO_2 emissions caused by the development.

ENVIRONMENTAL IMPACT OF CREATIVE-Ai

In a recent publication (Jääskeläinen et al. 2022), we mapped the aspects that need to be taken into account when estimating the environmental impact of a specific artistic process that involves the use of creative-Ai. We identified practice-related aspects, such as running an algorithm in iterations of slightly different constellations, and the varying amount of such energy-intense steps in the various phases of an artistic process. As of now, our knowledge

---

[5] Most deep learning development makes use of graphics processing units (GPUs), instead of the central processing unit (CPU) of a computer. Using several years of computing time in a shorter time span becomes possible by using a larger number of GPUs in parallel, usually at academic or commercial data centres. This way, 27 years of single GPU time may be spent by, for instance, 1500 GPUs continuously running in parallel for less than a week.

of how these practice-related aspects manifest themselves within specific artistic processes is very limited. Our own research aims to utilise diary studies with artists with the goal to close this knowledge gap, as the information provided in relation to already published artworks remains too sparse when it comes to the details of the artistic process. As the second group, we identified material aspects of creative-Ai, such as the employed hardware, the type of energy source, model architecture, and training data. On this side, information from existing Ai art projects allows us to obtain an overview of the most common architectures and training data sizes. On these grounds, the hypothesis is that the environmental impact of creative-Ai use may be quite significant, since the practice-related aspects involve repeated training of various formations of a model using various datasets, whereas the material aspects involve the use of model architectures that comprise a large number of parameters that need to be optimised using specialised GPU hardware.

It is essential for an understanding of the political ecology of creative-Ai to indicate the orders of energy consumption and/or carbon emissions related to training and developing certain models used in artistic contexts. As with all machine learning models, there is the training phase in which the model parameters are determined based on the training data, and the inference phase, in which a trained model is employed to produce an output. We will focus our considerations on the training phases, as the inference is typically – in relation to the training – less energy intense. The model GPT-3[6] is a very large NLP model that produces text outputs based on prompts, and it has been used, for instance, to generate poetry.[7] Based on the calculations by Anthony et al. (2020), the training of that model took about as much energy as it would take to drive around the globe by car almost 18 times.[8] Setting this in relation to per capita consumption of energy in Sweden (Enerdata 2020) – the country with the second-highest per capita consumption in Europe – this is about the yearly per capita consumption of 15 Swedish citizens. As OpenAi does not provide information on how much energy the whole R&D process required, let us assume in analogy to Strubell et al. (2019) that the energy consumption of the overall R&D may have been three orders larger than training the network a single time, which would send us around the planet 18,000 times by car, or supply a small Swedish city with energy for one year. The list of applications that employ GPT-3 in their functionalities[9] consists of about 15% (57 out of 353) of applications related to creative processes in arts and the creative industries, which would mean that almost 3000 of our planet's round trips are attributed to Creative-Ai applications.

But let us turn our attention to individual artistic projects instead of looking at a specific model. Throughout the last few years, several large IT companies have established funding schemes for artist residencies.[10] Within the NVidia artist gallery, we encounter the work of various artists who have used Nvidia's infrastructures to realise artistic projects. The project "Strange Genders" by 64/1 and Harshit Agrawal employs an NVidia StyleGAN2, which the artists trained on a custom dataset of hand-drawn figures. According to the original paper

---

[6]   https://openai.com/api/.

[7]   See, for instance, Branwen (2022) for a detailed documentation of such artistic processes and outcomes.

[8]   Without intention of endorsing excessive car driving and its environmental impact, I will use this comparison throughout the text because I hope it works as a vivid illustration for most readers.

[9]   https://gpt3demo.com/.

[10]   Examples are Google (https://ami.withgoogle.com/) and NVidia (https://www.nvidia.com/en-us/research/ai-art-gallery/).

(Karras et al. 2020), the energy required to train this model with its 69 million parameters from scratch is 0.68 MWh. Using the carbon intensity of the US in the year the artwork was produced as a basis (0.39 kgCO$_2$/kWh, according to EIA (2021)), training the model once would have caused about 265 kgCO$_2$eq, which would take us about 2200 km far with an average car (following the calculation method by Anthony et al. (2020)).

Japan-based artists Nao Tokui and Qosmo employed a variety of deep learning models in their project Neural Beatbox/Synthetic Soundscape. They combine the use of variational autoencoders for generating rhythms, convolutional neural networks for sound classification, recurrent neural networks (SampleRNN) for soundscape generation, and GAN to obtain original drum patterns. It is impossible to arrive at estimates of the energy invested for the overall combination of models, as the energy consumption for training them has not been specified in most of the original papers. However, the training of the SampleRNN is referred to have taken "a few days" despite the availability of NVidia resources, which is consistent with the training time of one week on a single GPU as specified by Mehri et al. (2017). Using again the carbon intensity of 0.39 kgCO$_2$/kWh, 250 W as the maximum power specified for the chip by NVidia, and a power usage effectiveness (PUE) of 1.125 as by Anthony et al. (2020), we arrive at an energy consumption of 168h × 0.25kW × 1.125 = 47.25kWh and related carbon emission of 18.43 kgCO$_2$eq. While this is only a short car ride (about 150 km), the estimate is very optimistic as the PUE of a single personal computer with a GPU is larger than that of a highly optimised data centre.

These two examples indicate that artistic projects that involve the use of Creative-Ai may involve large energy consumption for training the needed networks. While we do not know the details of the artistic processes, it is likely that such processes involve a similar amount of re-iteration and refinement as reported for engineering projects by Strubell et al. (2019). Whereas engineering projects optimise towards a limited amount of usually quantitative objectives, the artistic process is much more open-ended and involves qualitative criteria imposed by the artist. As there is no reason to assume that this process is simpler, the development of an Ai for artistic purposes can involve many iterations of training and result in energy consumption that is orders higher than training a network a single time.

POLITICAL ECOLOGY OF CREATIVE-Ai

All this evidence implies that the carbon footprint resulting from artistic projects involving Creative-Ai is likely to be large compared with artistic projects with similar outcomes but not involving Creative-Ai. More important than raising awareness of this energy consumption is to discuss its consequences for artist populations on a larger scale, which is where the frame of political ecology becomes relevant. Access to large computing power is not available to all (Strubell et al. 2019), and it is focused on institutes and corporations in the Global North. Many powerful Ai-models used in creative processes are trained models that can be accessed through the APIs provided by the developing companies, and the availability depends on the goodwill and the business plans of the companies. If individual artists wish to compute outputs from such models, or even wish to adapt or train new models to their own data, then they are depending on large IT companies providing access to resources.

An equitable engagement of all stakeholders of Ai applications in a discussion of the environmental impact of Ai has been argued to be a cornerstone of a third wave of Ai ethics (van

Wynsberghe 2021), with the possible conclusion to refrain from using Ai in certain application areas. Rephrasing van Wynsberghe, one has to ask if algorithms that can paint or compose are really worth the environmental cost. While there is no doubt that other industry sectors have a larger carbon footprint than the creative industries, it is nevertheless an ethical question for the artists if they want to employ a technology that dramatically increases the environmental impact of their work, and that puts their ability to practise art and secure their livelihood at the goodwill of IT corporations. However, the environmental impact is in most cases not obvious to the artist. As in the case of Nao Tokui and Qosmo, this impact presents itself in the form of longer processing time without any further information on the actual energy consumption during this time. With most artists who employ Creative-Ai having acquired the programming skills that are needed to run inference and training of models in environments such as Python, it seems a realistic suggestion to employ tools to estimate the energy consumption of the development and to report such estimates when publishing the artwork.

As we observed in Jääskeläinen et al. (2022b), in the design of interactions and experiences with Creative-Ai all current interfaces to Ai-models have distanced the actual consequences of the actions very far away from the users of these technologies: the amount of energy required to perform some inference and/or training remains concealed, just as the kind of energy that was employed by some remote servers involved in the computations. We argue that one consequence of the current interface design is that it may promote slow violence (Nixon 2011), i.e., a lack of transparency towards environmental consequences that develop on another temporal and geographical scale than the artistic process. Therefore, we consider it important to design interfaces for Creative-Ai that stimulate the development of care for the ecosystem, a form of care that we propose to call "slow care". Such design is situated in the framework provided by care ethics, which emphasises the "moral salience of attending to and meeting the needs of the particular others for whom we take responsibility" (Held 2006). Just as the design of interfaces plays an important role, artists would have to support the notion of "slow care" by developing an increasingly critical stance towards excessive application of proprietary Creative-Ai, and an awareness of those being excluded from employing Creative-Ai in their creative processes.

Increased responsibility for artists, phrased as a positive motivation rather than a restricting norm, lies therefore at the base for developing a more sustainable Creative-Ai. It is evident throughout the last decade that the funding of artists for collaborations with companies is increasing, both through public funding such as the European S+T+Arts[11] initiative and through funding at various IT companies for artist residencies. But what is the motivation for companies to fund such residencies? The presentation of artworks on company websites and the mentioning of a company as a sponsor in an artist portfolio are desirable publicity outcomes from the perspective of an IT company. In this way, the public image of products such as cloud computing is transformed from an abstract technological service to a mediator of a deeply human activity. Drott (2018) argues that music is foregrounded by companies providing streaming services to justify the particular value of the company platform. Whereas a focus on art dominates the public image of the companies, Drott (2018) demonstrates how essential parts of their business models are focused on advertisement and the marketing of user data. It remains to be discovered how far companies will welcome initiatives by artists to reveal the environmental impact of projects conducted with their support.

---

[11]   https://starts.eu/.

In the context of political ecology, it is essential to critically analyse the principles of action and power structures that link the environmental impact of Creative-Ai with the cultural practices of artistic creation. As I have already elaborated, the means for computation are increasingly localised at a group of large companies, i.e., large capital functions at this point as a gatekeeper for artistic creation, and speculation may be a valuable means to investigate what might happen further down this road. Daughtry (2020) argues that empirical, quantitative approaches to the environmental impact of music fail to "get at the urgent ethical, political, and aesthetic questions that are tied up in music's relation to environment", and in this chapter, I follow his suggestion that considers speculation as a suitable way to address these. My speculation is informed by a body of work that documents the role of the IT industry in reshaping the mediation of arts. In the following, I will focus on the example of music as the field of my expertise, but I consider this example to be strongly related to other forms of art. Hesmondhalgh and Meier (2018) document how the last 20 years have seen a shift from consumer electronics to the IT industry, with the latter being now the primary sector that determines change in cultural technologies. This coincided with a strong restructuring of the music industry towards streaming content and increased personalisation. Notably, McGuigan and Manzerolle (2015) argue that personalised mobile communication allows a more thorough-going commercialisation of culture than the previous mode of physical distribution, which was guided by inventions by the consumer electronics industry. This commercialisation of culture has been criticised for its potential to serve goals of user surveillance (Drott 2018), and the platforms that mediate between users and cultural content have been criticised for their opaqueness of user data handling actual and business goals (Eriksson et al. 2019).

RETHINKING ATTALI

Allow me to leap backwards in time to a visionary text on the interactions between music and societal order, written well before the large impact of digitalisation that is the focus of the texts in the previous paragraph. Jacques Attali (1985) regarded music as a mirror of society and as a prophet for societal change. Hence, he argued that music brings into play certain forms of distribution networks, which reflect and even anticipate sociopolitical structures. The network that closely resembles the music industry in the era of the consumer electronics industry is what Attali calls the network of repetition. Here, recording enabled the stockpiling of music and a "cultural normalisation, and the disappearance of distinctive cultures" (Attali 1985, p. 111). Whereas Attali may be criticised for his strongly Eurocentric perspective, this perspective provides an appropriate distortion that enables us to focus on the accumulation of capital in the Global North. In the context of the environmental impact of music, I follow Daughtry (2020) in his argument that such a distortion resulting from the focus on the economically dominating form is necessary to arrive at a conclusive overall picture. And in this distorted, simplified perspective, I want to follow Attali in his suggestion of the network that he assumes will follow the network of repetition, which is the network of composition.

In this network, Attali foresaw that producing music would become an activity not undertaken for its exchange value, but only for the pleasure of the composers themselves. Composition would become a very localised activity, in which the distinction between consumption and production is resolved. For this to become true, appropriate instruments would need to be available that can be used by individuals to compose, leading to what could be termed as a democratisation of artistic creation. These creations would be made for the moment, not for stockpiling them in the shape of recordings, resulting in a permanently unstable and evolving practice. To contextualise this vision, Attali wrote this text in the 1970s, being a convinced advocate of socialism that he would later try to set in practice as an advisor to the Mitterrand government. But even back then, he saw risks in what may come when music is making a transition from the network of repetition to that of composition. He saw the risk of "emplacement of a new trap for music and its consumers, that of automanipulation" (Attali 1985, p. 141), a risk increased by the fragility of meaning in the network of composition, and a risk that may be enlarged when the instruments provided for composition are themselves commodities controlled by large corporations.

The increasing fragmentation of music throughout the history of popular music into increasingly specialised genres (Bracket 2016) has been regarded by Drott (2018) as culminating into disaggregating individual users. Along with such a process goes a destabilisation of meaning in cultural experiences caused by "radical and disorienting shifts" elicited by the constantly increasing push for innovation in the IT industry (Hesmondhalgh and Meier 2018). Several authors have seen a potential for democratisation and empowerment of artistic creation lying in the recent developments of Creative-Ai (Mazzone and Elgammal 2019; Esling and Devis 2020). Hence, many harbingers indicate the approach of the network of composition, but who will provide the instruments? Here, Attali did not consider the composition conducted fully or partially by Ai tools controlled by large companies. This scenario resembles the "musical holodeck" envisioned by Sturm et al. (2019), a system that "provides any subscriber with limitless access to individualised musical experiences" and that makes any subscriber to such a system a composer. This, in fact, is Attali's network of composition with the means of production controlled by capital. Hence, in such a situation, the source of profit for a music industry is shifted from the production and distribution of recordings to the provision of instruments for composition, turning the socialist utopia of Attali into the next stage of the commodification of cultural activity by the IT industry.

A CASE OF COMMODIFICATION OF ARTISTIC CREATION

Fortunately, the scenario elaborated in the previous section is purely fictional, and one may assume that even neoliberal venture capitalists are not adventurous enough to invest in a company that pursues such a goal. Wrong. The above-mentioned scenario seems to be well aligned with research and development at the largest music streaming provider, Spotify. The company's official presentation of its research (Spotify 2022) categorises research publications by Spotify employees into nine research areas, with music creation being one of them. However, among the 95 listed publications, only two have been associated with the research topic of music creation, whereas the most frequent topics are "Search and Recommendation" (43), "Machine Learning" (39), and "User Modelling" (28). Hence, the topics that R&D at Spotify focuses on align well with the company's traditional core business of personalised music streaming. Research on the automatic creation of music, or even Creative-Ai tools that support musicians in creative processes, seems not to be part of the official Spotify R&D portfolio. In this context, it is remarkable that Spotify has founded the Creator Technology Research Lab (Spotify 2017), which explicitly focuses on the development of such tools. Publications from this lab seem to be excluded from the official research publication list of Spotify, exemplified by the absence of the publications of the head of the lab, Francois Pachet, from this list. Pachet is an internationally leading expert in Creative-Ai applied to music and has recently co-published a book on the use of deep learning for the automatic generation of music (Briot et al. 2020). More interestingly, his Google Scholar profile reveals his co-authorship in 11 US patent applications in 2020 and 2021 only. The abstracts of these patents, considered in relation to each other, create a picture of the compilation of tools needed for the automatic generation of music, such as the checking of an Ai composition for plagiarism (Pachet and Roy 2022), a tool for building songs out of a collection of elementary stems (Pachet et al. 2022), and user evaluation tools to identify the best version of an automatic composition system (Pachet and Roy 2022b). Another part of the story (that Spotify is not telling) is their move to secure the rights to "create derivative works from User Content" of users of the Spotify for Artists app (Spotify 2021), which would include using user-uploaded music as training data for music generation systems.[12] Spotify for Artists was introduced in 2017, the same year in which the Creator Technology Research Lab was founded, and allowing derivative works from artists' uploads has been part of the terms and conditions since then until now. In June 2022, the business magazine Forbes (Hochberg 2022) reported Spotify's plans to publish a suite with tools that enable users to compose music with the support of Ai, motivated by the idea that "users will engage more when they have a hand in creating the music with the help of AI".

Assessing the environmental impact of such a "listener/composer" system is impossible without detailed information on its components and its usage. Similar to the project by Nao Tokui and Qosmo introduced above, such a system is likely to be composed of several different deep learning (and other) architectures, an assumption supported by the diversity of architectures emphasised by Briot and Pachet (2020). Each of these needs to be trained, and – importantly – adapted and personalised to the needs of a listener/composer. This is the point where the transition from an individual artistic project to a commercial platform commodity becomes environmentally significant. In their first financial statement of 2022, Spotify declared to have "422 million monthly active users ('MAUs'), including 182 million Premium Subscribers". Even when we assume that only a minority of users would subscribe to a listener/composer service, and that personalisation will occur in clusters of users with similar demands, it is obvious that the carbon emission caused by a system like the one of Nao Tokui and Qosmo needs to be multiplied by some number between 1000 and 1 million.

Would such a situation be financially viable for the music content provider? At the current point, the profit of the streaming providers is limited by the large amount that they need to pay to music rights holders (Drott 2018). Compared to the outcry caused by Spotify populating playlists with fake artists (Goldschmitt 2020), the provision of an interactive listener/composer tool would likely be a more tolerated solution to increase profits from services. Given the current cost of a subscription for music streaming services, this money could be redirected from music rights holders to the energy expenditure for training systems. This approach is likely to be financially viable, but it would be connected to a large environmental cost. It would literally turn artist revenues into smoke.

At the current point in time, the share of carbon emissions assigned to streaming and AI development and application at music streaming providers is not known. The Equity and Impact Report by Spotify from 2021 (Spotify 2021b) acknowledges this but provides little detail on how the reported emissions are related to specific causes within the business process.

---

[12]   I was made aware of this aspect by Drott (2021).

Whereas the reported net emission of Spotify (353054 MtCO2e) remains small in comparison with other IT companies such as Microsoft, the illustrated listener/composer system is likely to further increase the carbon footprint of streaming companies.

CONCLUSION

The speculation that I presented in this chapter illustrates how the combination of the environmental impact of Creative-Ai with the increasing commodification of artistic creation by means of Creative-Ai is very likely to have severe consequences for cultural practices, the livelihood of artists, and the ecosystem. My examples focused on music, but a parallel example of the listener/composer system for music was presented in the form of GPU time (OpenAI 2022). The model of access combines the creation of a number of free images with a paid model for additional images, indicating a similar business model as the one I assumed for the listener/composer service. Whereas the technical paper does not specify how much GPU time it took to optimise the more than 3.5 billion parameters (Ramesh et al. 2022), the emissions of the whole development of this model are surely in the order of many road trips around the planet.

This chapter is one of the first attempts to promote awareness of the environmental impact of Creative-Ai. As I have explained, many open questions remain regarding how Creative-Ai is used in artistic processes. This needs to be addressed by conducting studies in collaboration with artists, for instance, in the form of diary studies that document how exactly models are used. Such studies will then provide information on the diversity of the artistic processes, and the overall environmental impact as a consequence of model training and inference. A second aspect of our research is to develop new interfaces for artists that help to cultivate an attitude of slow care for the environment (Jääskeläinen et al. 2022b). These studies aim at the development of tools that empower artists to monitor and visualise the carbon impacts of their use of Ai-models.

However, as we saw from the listener/composer example in this chapter, the environmental aspect is one perspective that calls for critique and action, whereas the cultural and social consequences of the commodification of automatic artistic creation are likely to be severe as well. A cross-sectional alliance between artists and academia is required to critically examine the overall impact of various Creative-Ai tools. In this context, it is important to reject technological determinism and emphasise the possibility of not employing Ai in certain application areas or promoting Ai infrastructures that are publicly accessible. Such a cross-sectional alliance must be sensitive to the social imbalances between the Global South and North, as a demand for an unconditional basic income for artists seems illusory in the context of the grim social conditions in most countries apart from the Northern centres of global capital.

Finally, another aspect of the political ecology of Creative-Ai is to establish a relation between the data used to train models and the human beings that created that training data. New legal frameworks proposed by the European Union are likely to strengthen the legal position of such individual data creators (European Commission 2022) if the proposals survive the lobbying by the large corporations who fear for their listener/composer and other models that would not be possible without free and exclusive access to huge amounts of user data. It is part of our future research to give a stronger voice to individuals and small enterprises in the process of forming data legislation. In this context, the proposition to consider data as labour instead of capital (Arrieta-Ibarra et al. 2018) may indicate a possible way out of the upcoming crisis of artistic (and other) labour.

REFERENCES

Anadol, R. (2017). *Archive dreaming*. Refik Anadol. Retrieved July 28, 2022, from https://refikanadol.com/works/archive-dreaming/

Anthony, L. F. W., Kanding, B., & Selvan, R. (2020). Carbontracker: Tracking and predicting the carbon footprint of training deep learning models. *ICML workshop on "Challenges in deploying and monitoring machine learning systems"*.

Arrieta-Ibarra, I., Goff, L., Jiménez-Hernández, D., Lanier, J., & Weyl, E. G. (2018, May). Should we treat data as labor? Moving beyond "free". In *American economic association papers and proceedings* (Vol. 108, pp. 38–42).

Attali, J. (1985). *Noise: The political economy of music*. Manchester University Press.

Biersack, A. (2006). Reimagining political ecology: Culture/Power/Nature/History. In A. Biersack & J. B. Greenberg (Eds.), *Reimagining political ecology* (pp. 3–42). Duke University Press.

Brackett, D. (2016). *Categorizing sound: Genre and twentieth-century popular music*. University of California Press.

Branwen, G. (2022, February 10). *GPT-3 creative fiction*. Gwern. Retrieved July 28, 2022, from https://www.gwern.net/GPT-3

Briot, J. P., Hadjeres, G., & Pachet, F. D. (2020). *Deep learning techniques for music generation* (Vol. 1). Springer.

Briot, J. P., & Pachet, F. (2020). Deep learning for music generation: Challenges and directions. *Neural Computing and Applications*, *32*(4), 981–993.

Brown, D., Byl, L., & Grossman, M. R. (2021). Are machine learning corpora "fair dealing" under Canadian law? *Proceedings of the 12th international conference on computational creativity*.

Clarke, P. (2020, October 20). *Photoshop: Now the world's most advanced AI application for creatives*. Adobe. Retrieved July 28, 2022, from https://blog.adobe.com/en/publish/2020/10/20/photoshop-the-worlds-most-advanced-ai-application-for-creatives

Crawford, K. (2021). *The atlas of AI: Power, politics, and the planetary costs of artificial intelligence*. Yale University Press.

Daughtry, J. M. (2020). Did music cause the end of the world? *Transposition*. https://doi.org/10.4000/transposition.5192

Devine, K. (2019). *Decomposed: The political ecology of music*. MIT Press.

Drott, E. A. (2018). Music as a technology of surveillance. *Journal of the Society for American Music*, *12*(3), 233–267.

Drott, E. A. (2021). Copyright, compensation, and commons in the music AI industry. *Creative Industries Journal*, *14*(2), 190–207.

EIA. (2021). *How much carbon dioxide is produced per kilowatthour of U.S. electricity generation?* US Energy Information Administration. Retrieved July 28, 2022, from https://www.eia.gov/tools/faqs/faq.php?id=74&t=11

Elgammal, A. (2021, September 24). *How a team of musicologists and computer scientists completed Beethoven's unfinished 10th Symphony*. The Conversation. Retrieved July 28, 2022, from https://theconversation.com/how-a-team-of-musicologists-and-computer-scientists-completed-beethovens-unfinished-10th-symphony-168160

Enerdata. (2020). *Sweden energy information*. Enerdata. Retrieved July 28, 2022, from https://www.enerdata.net/estore/energy-market/sweden/

Eriksson, M., Fleischer, R., Johansson, A., Snickars, P., & Vonderau, P. (2019). *Spotify teardown: Inside the black box of streaming music*. MIT Press.

Esling, P., & Devis, N. (2020). Creativity in the era of artificial intelligence. Keynote at *JIM Conference*. arXiv preprint arXiv:2008.05959.

European Commission. (2022). Data act: Commission proposes measures for a fair and innovative data economy. European Commission. Retrieved August 31, 2022, from https://ec.europa.eu/commission/presscorner/detail/en/ip_22_1113

Ferraro, A., Serra, X., & Bauer, C. (2021, August). What is fair? Exploring the artists' perspective on the fairness of music streaming platforms. In *IFIP conference on human-computer interaction* (pp. 562–584). Springer.

Frich, J., MacDonald Vermeulen, L., Remy, C., Biskjaer, M. M., & Dalsgaard, P. (2019, May). Mapping the landscape of creativity support tools in HCI. In *Proceedings of the 2019 CHI conference on human factors in computing systems* (pp. 1–18).

Gabriel, A., Monticolo, D., Camargo, M., & Bourgault, M. (2016). Creativity support systems: A systematic mapping study. *Thinking Skills and Creativity, 21*, 109–122.

Goldschmitt, K. E. (2020). The long history of the 2017 Spotify "fake music" scandal. *American Music, 38*(2), 131–152.

Held, V. (2006). *The ethics of care: Personal, political, and global*. Oxford University Press.

Henderson, P., Hu, J., Romoff, J., Brunskill, E., Jurafsky, D., & Pineau, J. (2020). Towards the systematic reporting of the energy and carbon footprints of machine learning. *Journal of Machine Learning Research, 21*(248), 1–43.

Hertzmann, A. (2022). Toward modeling creative processes for algorithmic painting. In *International conference on computational creativity*.

Hesmondhalgh, D., & Meier, L. M. (2018). What the digitalisation of music tells us about capitalism, culture and the power of the information technology sector. *Information, Communication & Society, 21*(11), 1555–1570.

Hochberg, B. (2022, June 29). *Spotify is developing AI tools to hook users on music creation*. Forbes. Retrieved July 29, 2022, from https://www.forbes.com/sites/williamhochberg/2022/06/29/spotify-is-developing-ai-tools-to-hook-users-on-music-creation/?sh=4452917f4834

Hornigold, T. (2018, October 25). *The first novel written by AI is here—and it's as weird as you'd expect it to be*. Singularity Hub. Retrieved July 28, 2022, from https://singularityhub.com/2018/10/25/ai-wrote-a-road-trip-novel-is-it-a-good-read/

Jääskeläinen, P., Holzapfel, A., & Pargman, D. (2022). On the environmental sustainability of AI art (s). In *Workshop on computing within limits*.

Jääskeläinen, P., Holzapfel, A., & Åsberg, C. (2022b). Exploring more-than-human caring in creative-Ai interactions. In *NordiCHI Conference*.

Karras, T., Laine, S., Aittala, M., Hellsten, J., Lehtinen, J., & Aila, T. (2020). Analyzing and improving the image quality of StyleGAN. In *Proceedings of the IEEE/CVF conference on computer vision and pattern recognition* (pp. 8110–8119).

Mazzone, M., & Elgammal, A. (2019, February). Art, creativity, and the potential of artificial intelligence. In *Arts* (Vol. 8, No. 1, p. 26). MDPI.

McGuigan, L., & Manzerolle, V. (2015). "All the world's a shopping cart": Theorizing the political economy of ubiquitous media and markets. *New Media & Society, 17*(11), 1830–1848.

Mehri, S., Kumar, K., Gulrajani, I., Kumar, R., Jain, S., Sotelo, J., ... Bengio, Y. (2017). SampleRNN: An unconditional end-to-end neural audio generation model. In *Proceedings of the International Conference on Learning Representations (ICLR)*.

Murray-Browne, T., & Tigas, P. (2021). Latent mappings: Generating open-ended expressive mappings using variational autoencoders. In *Proceedings of the international conference on new interfaces for musical expression*.

Muller, M., Chilton, L. B., Kantosalo, A., Martin, C. P., & Walsh, G. (2022, April). GenAICHI: Generative AI and HCI. In *CHI conference on human factors in computing systems extended abstracts* (pp. 1–7).

Nixon, R. (2011). *Slow violence and the environmentalism of the poor*. Harvard University Press.

Oh, C., Song, J., Choi, J., Kim, S., Lee, S., & Suh, B. (2018, April). I lead, you help but only with enough details: Understanding user experience of co-creation with artificial intelligence. In *Proceedings of the 2018 CHI conference on human factors in computing systems* (pp. 1–13).

OpenAI. (2022, July 20). *DALL·E now available in beta*. OpenAI. Retrieved July 29, 2022, from https://openai.com/blog/dall-e-now-available-in-beta/

Pachet, F., & Roy, P. (2022). *U.S. Patent No. 11,289,059*. Washington, DC: U.S. Patent and Trademark Office.

Pachet, F., & Roy, P. (2022b). *U.S. Patent No. 11,256,469*. Washington, DC: U.S. Patent and Trademark Office.

Pachet, F., Roy, P., Ramona, M., Jehan, T., & Bosch Vicente, J. J. (2022). *U.S. Patent No. 11,238,839.* Washington, DC: U.S. Patent and Trademark Office.

Porcaro, L., Castillo, C., & Gómez Gutiérrez, E. (2021). Diversity by design in music recommender systems. *Transactions of the International Society for Music Information Retrieval. 2021, 4*(1).

Ragot, M., Martin, N., & Cojean, S. (2020, April). Ai-generated vs. human artworks. a perception bias towards artificial intelligence? In *Extended abstracts of the 2020 CHI conference on human factors in computing systems* (pp. 1–10).

Ramesh, A., Dhariwal, P., Nichol, A., Chu, C., & Chen, M. (2022). Hierarchical text-conditional image generation with clip latents. arXiv preprint arXiv:2204.06125.

Riccio, P., Oliver, J. L., Escolano, F., & Oliver, N. (2022). Algorithmic censorship of art: A proposed research agenda. In *International conference on computational creativity.*

Spotify. (2017, July 12). *Innovating for writers and artists.* Spotify. Retrieved July 28, 2022, from https://artists.spotify.com/en/blog/innovating-for-writers-and-artists

Spotify. (2021, September 1). *Spotify for artists terms and conditions of use.* Spotify. Retrieved July 29, 2022, from https://www.spotify.com/us/legal/spotify-for-artists-terms-and-conditions/

Spotify. (2021b). *Equity and impact report 2021.* Spotify. Retrieved July 29, 2022, from https://www.lifeatspotify.com/reports/Spotify-Equity-Impact-Report-2021.pdf

Spotify. (2022). *Publications.* Spotify. Retrieved August 15, 2022, from https://research.atspotify.com/publication/

Strubell, E., Ganesh, A., & McCallum, A. (2019). Energy and policy considerations for deep learning in NLP. *57th Annual meeting of the Association for Computational Linguistics (ACL).*

Sturm, B. L., Iglesias, M., Ben-Tal, O., Miron, M., & Gómez, E. (2019, September). Artificial intelligence and music: Open questions of copyright law and engineering praxis. In *Arts* (Vol. 8, No. 3, p. 115). MDPI.

Tahiroğlu, K., Kastemaa, M., & Koli, O. (2020, July). AI-terity: Non-rigid musical instrument with artificial intelligence applied to real-time audio synthesis. In *Proceedings of the international conference on new interfaces for musical expression* (pp. 331–336).

Tan, H. H. (2019). ChordAL: A chord-based approach for music generation using Bi-LSTMs. In *International conference on computational creativity* (pp. 364–365).

Thylstrup, N. B. (2019). Data out of place: Toxic traces and the politics of recycling. *Big Data & Society, 6*(2), 2053951719875479.

Velkova, J. (2016). Data that warms: Waste heat, infrastructural convergence and the computation traffic commodity. *Big Data & Society, 3*(2), 2053951716684144.

Watts, M. (2017). Political ecology. In E. Sheppard & T. Barnes (Eds.), *A companion to economic geography* (pp. 257–274). Oxford: Blackwell.

Wertz, L., & Kuhn, J. (2022). Adapting transformer language models for application in computational creativity: Generating German theater plays with varied topics. In *International conference on computational creativity.*

van Wynsberghe, A. (2021). Sustainable AI: AI for sustainability and the sustainability of AI. *AI and Ethics, 1*(3), 213–218.

PART VII

AI AND AUTOMATION
IN SOCIETY

61. Automated decision-making in the public sector

Vanja Carlsson, Malin Rönnblom and Andreas Öjehag-Pettersson

INTRODUCTION

The public sector and public administrations are important foundations in democratic states. The task of the public sector is both to implement political decisions, as well as defend and protect democratic values and principles. Publicly elected political representatives are expected to make decisions based on the interests of citizens, and these decisions are in turn expected to be implemented effectively and with good quality in the public sector. In line with Weber's famous principles of bureaucracy, impartiality is a central aspect of public administration in a democracy. Thus, an autonomous public sector that protects democratic principles is needed for a political system to be democratically legitimate.

Efficiency, equality, and transparency are also central guiding principles or values for the public sector as it should act impartially and treat citizens equally, and based on the democratic idea that citizens have the right to insight into public organizations and the implementation processes of political decisions, the public sector is ideally characterized by a high degree of transparency. Furthermore, the processes and procedures of the public sector in democratic welfare states include an important inclusive dimension. Unlike private organizations, public organizations cannot "opt-out" of serving less lucrative citizens. Instead, the democratic mission includes not only treating everyone equally but also treating everyone.

The introduction of automated decision-making (ADM) in the public sector affects traditional public principles and values in several different ways. For example, transparency is a central challenge as the decisions are implemented by algorithms instead of humans and thus become more difficult to explain for the individual citizen (Lopez, 2021). Also, equality has been put forward both as something that is gained through ADM, and as something that is at risk when ADM is implemented (Eubanks, 2019). Here, the level of digital competence has been presented as a key aspect, concerning both equality and transparency.

More generally, the introduction of ADM in the public sector also relies on an intensified collaboration between the public sector and private tech companies. Through public procurement, public-private partnerships, and other contractual arrangements, this aspect of ADM raises questions about public decision-making and its limits and boundaries toward the interests of the private industry. In this regard, the space for the agency of the civil servants, or in other words, the dimension of discretion, is central. Moreover, this public-private relation also highlights how studies of ADM in the public sector could benefit from a more explicit focus on what may be called its commodified and marketized circumstances. Indeed, such circumstances form the conditions for its existence in the first place. We will return to this question in the final section of the chapter.

In sum, the implementation of ADM brings several challenges to the public sector which will be discussed in this chapter. By drawing on a wide range of scholarly work on the issue, our aim is to provide an overview of the current state of the art on ADM with respect to important principles in public administration. We begin by providing a general overview of how ADM tools function and how they can be said to demand a new discussion concerning the central concept of discretion in the public sector. We then discuss, in turn, the implications of this new (digital) discretion for legal certainty, transparency, and accountability, as well as for bias and discrimination. Together, we argue, these principles are central to any functioning democratic public administration, and thus, understanding how they relate to ADM is crucial.

ADM TOOLS AND THE CHANGING ONTOLOGY OF PUBLIC SECTOR DECISIONS

ADM, also called robotic process automation (RPA), refers to a structured data processing system based on algorithms; in other words, a set of preprogrammed instructions that are followed according to a predetermined procedure with the goal of solving a well-defined problem. In public sector ADM, the steps that a public official follows to make a case-specific decision are programmed and performed by the digital tool. However, the technique itself is very much affected by human agency, and important decisions on the algorithmic design have to be made by humans before the ADM system is launched. The kinds of information and data that should be collected, standardized, and categorized, and the criteria the algorithm should use to determine what is relevant and what connections between the information should be created, are examples of human decisions that precede the building of ADM tools (Dyer-Witheford et al., 2019; Gillespie, 2014). The ADM tool provides a clear answer to a very specific question and includes, for example, rule-based assessment, workflow processing, case-based reasoning, and intelligent sensor technology.

In the public sector, an ADM tool is often used in standard tasks in response to requests for the faster and more qualitative processing of different kinds of applications for public services, such as applications made within the context of social work or unemployment support. Here, the automated decision is often made by a profiling tool. A profiling tool processes and evaluates individual data in order to analyze or predict aspects concerning an individual's economic situation, health, or performance (see General Data Protection Regulation, art. 4). One example is the use of profiling by employment services when the profiling tool generates decisions on job seekers' entitlements to support and training activities (see Allhutter et al., 2020). The ADM tool calculates a job seeker's prospects on the job market based on statistically presumed days of unemployment. Based on this statistical calculation, the ADM tool classifies the job seeker into one of three categories: high prospects, mediocre prospects, and low prospects. Based on the classification, it then suggests whether or not the job seeker should have access to labor market training.

The profiling tools used in welfare services are often programmed with historical data from previous administrative cases and historical personal information from citizens. These data are divided into parameters such as education, work experience, gender, age, and place of residence. When meeting with a citizen applying for support, a public official working for the welfare service runs the ADM tool which, based on the historical data and statistical calculation, decides on the citizen's entitlement to welfare support. However, decisions made using profiling and other kinds of robotic process automation do not provide individual assessments and judgments, only general assessments (Eubanks, 2018). Instead of the individual's personal situation and own history impacting the decision on their entitlement to welfare support, it is impacted by the previous actions, histories, and situations of others in the form of an aggregate data assessment.

Since individual assessments are traditionally an essential element of public services, an increase in the use of general statistical assessments of citizens will change the ontology of the decisions themselves as well as the role of public officials. According to the EU's General Data Protection Regulation (GDPR) from 2016, a profiling tool cannot be decisive. Therefore, an ADM tool is often framed as a system that supports public officials as they make their final decisions. This is particularly important in cases where an ADM tool makes decisions that are considered complex. However, the practical possibilities for officials to reject the decisions made by ADM tools vary according to the organization (Busch & Henriksen, 2018). The changed conditions for human agency in public sector decision-making are discussed in the following section.

(DIGITAL) DISCRETION IN ADM

Decision-making lies at the very heart of public sector practices (Simon, 1947). Decisions are made at the strategic and managerial levels as well as at the operational and "street" levels. A large part of the public sector's decision-making is carried out by so-called street-level bureaucrats (Lipsky, 2010), and the debate on ADM in the public sector is often focused on the ADM techniques implemented to facilitate or replace the work of professionals who make decisions about citizens' rights and obligations with regard to the receipt of benefits or other kinds of support.

The literature on street-level bureaucrats has highlighted civil servants' close contact with citizens and the discretion they exercise within the framework of client-centered work, such as in schools, social services, or health care. Here, discretion is based on welfare framework laws and civil servants' autonomy to take action during meetings with citizens and in complex decision-making situations. In this sense, street-level bureaucrats act in the tension that exists between their professional autonomy to exercise judgment and the political decisions and regulations that govern public sector processes and procedures. While principles of impartiality and equal treatment are emphasized, the discretion that street-level bureaucrats have in client-oriented work means they operate within a certain professional space in which they can make their own assessments and design their work in their own way.

In recent years, public administration scholars have initiated debates over whether ADM enables or limits officials' decision-making and discretion in terms of balancing welfare laws, regulations, and cost-effectiveness against individuals' social and economic justice and equality (Wirtz et al., 2019). In these debates, as can be expected, scholars have argued that the introduction of digital automation has affected professional discretion in different ways, both positive and negative (Bullock, 2019; Busch & Henriksen, 2018; de Boer & Raaphorst, 2021; Dunleavy et al., 2006). At the same time, and perhaps more important than positive or negative effects, these debates have also pointed to how the prevalence of information technology in public administration warrants an updated understanding of discretion in the first place. The new conditions for professional discretion are sometimes labeled digital discretion

(Busch & Henriksen, 2018), which refers to an "increased use of technologies that can assist street-level bureaucrats in handling cases by providing easy access to information about clients through channels such as online forms, and automating parts of or whole work processes" (Busch & Henriksen, 2018, p. 5).

Since ADM facilitates decision-making without much personal contact, and it reduces a client's personal situation to "black-and-white" and calculable categories, digital discretion is often understood as limiting professional discretion so that professionals no longer have to use their professional knowledge to make individual and complex judgments (Bullock, 2019; Busch & Henriksen, 2018). While not all tasks are likely to be handed over to ADM, Bullock (2019) has suggested that "tasks that are low in complexity and uncertainty are the likeliest candidates for automation by AI, whereas tasks high in complexity and uncertainty should remain under the purview of human discretion" (p. 759). Even so, it seems important to keep in mind that what constitutes high and low complexity, in this case, is seldom a straightforward discussion. As we will discuss below, routine tasks also contain complex power relations with respect to race, gender, and class.

In sum, contemporary research does not provide a unified understanding concerning the benefits and pitfalls of ADM in the public sector. Rather, while Busch and Henriksen (2018) argued that the introduction of technological automation will support democratic values and strengthen the rule of law in the public sector despite the limitations of discretion, other studies have shown that algorithmic decisions and results are usually—and problematically—uncritically accepted by officials, although individuals subjected to an algorithmic decision risk being maltreated in this process (Lopez, 2021). Similarly, the fact that ADM tools eliminate the possibilities for unethical subjective opinions and favoritism in the relationship between citizens and professionals has been emphasized as being positive for the rule of law, accountability, and legal certainty. In this vein, Busch and Henriksen (2018) stated: "technology does not make individual considerations but focuses merely on objective predefined criteria" (p. 18). Yet, such predefined criteria and instructions are not neutrally constructed to begin with, putting such a statement in stark contrast with the multitude of works that highlight the political nature of data and algorithms (cf. Gillespie, 2014).

The debate over if and how digital ADM affects important public principles has featured a discussion about which public principles are most at stake within the context of digital ADM. Here, the principles of legal certainty, transparency, accountability, and discrimination are particularly stressed. Next, these principles will be discussed.

LEGAL CERTAINTY AND ADM

When public principles are manifested through ADM, the digital technique becomes a legal process through which public decisions are made. Here, legal certainty is a core value. Legal certainty is embedded in the rule of law and has a central position in public governance. Still, diverse definitions of the concept of legal certainty point to its multifaceted meaning and the different perspectives that can be applied to the debate over the role of ADM in the public sector.

Generally, legal certainty is highly associated with uniform treatment, legality, and predictability in the outcomes of judicial decisions (Bertea, 2008). This means that government officials and citizens should be ruled by and obey the law and that the law should be formulated in advance and be generally known and understood (Tamanaha, 2012; see also Rawls, 1999). These kinds of legal requirements are considered to constitute the *formal* aspects of the rule of law and legal certainty. In addition, substantial and *material* aspects of legal certainty (Alexy, 2015; Bingham, 2011; Brettschneider, 2011), as well as *procedural* aspects (Bertea, 2008; Taekema, 2013), are relevant in the digital ADM context. Material aspects refer to universal and socially and culturally inherent norms, such as social justice and equality, that should be applied to the law even though they may be external to concrete legal formulations. Material aspects can also refer to the realization of the law itself through practical law enforcement. Here, the material rule of law does not necessarily constitute a universal societal norm but rather the substantive meaning of the law itself. In order for juridical decisions to be predictable (i.e., legally certain), the rights and obligations formulated in the law must be realized in practice (Lifante-Vidal, 2020). Within public sector policies in welfare states, this realization often relates to social justice and equality. While material aspects refer to public sector services' decisions, procedural legal certainty refers to the processing of decisions.

In the context of ADM, conflicting perspectives on and arguments over whether or not ADM is beneficial for formal and material legal certainty and legally certain procedures have been put forward (see Al-Mushayt, 2019; Civitarese Matteucci, 2021; Coglianese & Lehr 2019; Gryz & Rojszczak, 2021). Still, the benefits and challenges of ADM in relation to the potential societal harm and collective risks of algorithmic errors and bias have not received much attention within legal studies (Hakkarainen, 2021; Smuha, 2021). Rather, regulatory perspectives on individual redress and service have received more attention (Harasimiuk & Braun, 2021). At the same time, it has been stressed that accountability problems relating to a lack of transparency, inapplicability, or bias in algorithmic decision-making challenge "the broader societal interest of the rule of law" (Smuha, 2021, p. 8).

In addition to researchers identifying the limitations of public officials' professional discretion due to the introduction of ADM in the public sector, case studies from Nordic welfare services have analyzed complex ADM decisions in relation to citizens and how less professional discretion affects decision-making (see Andreassen et al., 2021; Carlsson, forthcoming; Ulmestig et al., 2020). Such empirical studies show, for example, that a significant proportion of the public decisions made by statistical profiling tools are incorrect in relation to citizen's rights and obligations formulated in law or hard for a public official to validate (Allhutter et al., 2020; Andreassen et al., 2021). In addition, decisions are often perceived to be incorrect due to the lack of individual assessments in which important information about the citizen concerned is a basic requirement. If the decisions being made do not fully consider important information (according to professional judgment) for alignment with the rights and obligations formulated in welfare laws, whether the material aspects of legal certainty are realized in ADM in public services can be questioned. At the same time, procedural aspects can be considered promoted in the sense that the processing of decisions follows the same steps in all cases and the decisions are not influenced by the opinions or assessments of individual officials. Accordingly, the decision-making process is uniform. Still, if public officials perceive the decisions to be unintelligible and unpredictable, there is a "black box problem," and when decisions are not perceived to be clear and fully communicated, even the formal aspects of legal certainty are likely to weaken.

TRANSPARENCY AND ACCOUNTABILITY IN ADM PROCESSES

The argument that the use of ADM in the public sector is beneficial for legal certainty is mainly related to procedural aspects in terms of uniform procedures. At the same time, black box problems, transparency problems, and problems relating to unpredictable decisions have been highly debated within the research fields of "explainable AI" (XAI) and "responsible AI." Within these fields, scholars have emphasized that legitimate and reliable governments and public administrations engaging in current digital ADM developments must take responsibility for combating transparency problems (de Fine Licht and de Fine Licht, 2020; Ghallab, 2019; Reed, 2020). In order for governments and public sector organizations to be accountable, trustworthy, and ethical, the ADM systems they use in their interactions with citizens must be considered understandable (Amann et al., 2020).

Studies have also generated practical knowledge—sometimes formulated as policy recommendations or technological solutions—on the improvement of accountability, trustworthiness, fairness, and privacy in the shaping of a good AI society (see Arrieta et al., 2020; Floridi et al., 2018; Samek et al., 2019).

The black box problems and non-transparency of ADM systems have been partly presented as problems that are too big to be solved through compliance with the European Union's GDPR. While the protection provided by the GDPR is expected to prevent an individual from being profiled in crucial and decisive decisions, and also provide citizens with the right to have automated decisions explained to them, scholars have argued that protection in practice remains inadequate due to unresolved transparency problems (Grytz & Rojszczak, 2021; Malgieri, 2019). For example, studies have shown that automated decisions tend to be accepted by officials without them being clear on how the decision was made (Lopez, 2021; see also Eubanks, 2018; Kemper & Kolkman, 2019). One important issue in this respect is the increased vulnerability of individuals. As Waldman (2019) explained: "Either way, the opacity of decision-making algorithms prevents those harmed by automated systems from determining either how a decision came about or the logic and reasoning behind it. This makes accountability difficult" (p. 619).

Other empirical studies have shown that public administrations sometimes explicitly limit officials' abilities to deviate from the profiling tool's decision. Such limitations increase the risk of individuals being unfairly profiled (Carlsson, forthcoming). At the same time, studies raising these kinds of concerns have been balanced by those stressing the potential of achieving transparent ADM in the public sector (Al-Mushayt, 2019; Coglianese & Lehr, 2021). Here, the argument has been that transparent ADM systems can be achieved as long as governments and administrations ensure that individuals can question the decisions and the accuracy of the algorithm, as well as have access to the information and data on which the results are based.

Discussions on how governments and the public sector should act in order to be transparent in their use of ADM have included critiques of the use of concepts like XAI. Ghassemi et al. (2021), for example, argued that XAI produces "false hope" in welfare sectors. From this critical perspective, rather than expecting and requiring valid and local explanations of specific automated decisions or predictions, the requirement should be that governments provide rigorous descriptions of how the ADM system functions in general. Other proposed solutions are that knowledge and information shared about the system must be contextually appropriate in order to provide transparency and form a foundation for different kinds of accountability, such as political, legal, administrative, professional, or social accountability (Cobbe et al., 2021). This means that governments and public administrations must work to produce relevant information about the system in response to specific requests for accountability and transparency in certain cases.

ADM, BIAS, AND DISCRIMINATION

The risk of ADM systems perpetuating social discrimination has attracted considerable attention since the advent of digital ADM's application in the public sector (e.g., D'Ignazio & Klein, 2020; Eubanks, 2018; O'Neil, 2016). While some scholars focusing on the technological functions of ADM have argued that ADM is less biased than human decision-making (e.g., Ferguson, 2015; Simmons, 2018), researchers in contemporary social science research and critical studies have focused on how the development and implementation of new ADM technologies produce bias and discrimination against social groups based on gender or skin color through their very design and operation (e.g., O'Neil, 2016).

The dividing line between these two conflicting statements runs through the question of whether human decisions or algorithmic decisions increase the risk of discrimination and unfair treatment and which decision-making processes—ADM or human—can be considered more accurate and impartial and thus generate decisions that create more equality and uniformity. ADM systems may have the capacity to operate legitimately and without bias due to their inherent ignorance of the values of programmed data (i.e., the ADM system does not make a subjective valuation of data), but as Waldman (2019) stated: "algorithmic decision-making systems do not ignore biased data, they end up cementing those biases in society" (p. 621). Furthermore, there is a paradox embedded in the argument that ADM decisions are more objective and less biased than human decisions when the profiling tools are generally programmed using historical data based on previous human decisions.

Eubanks' (2018) book, *Automating Inequality: How High-Tech Tools Profile, Police, and Punish the Poor*, analyzed how the US government's replacement of street-level bureaucratic decision-making with the use of algorithms when making decisions on welfare support and benefits, as well as government punishments, generated an increase in decisions that tended to disadvantage poor people. The reason for this is that the history of poverty and vulnerability of certain social groups and the predominantly negative views of these groups are embedded in the design of ADM tools and are therefore also perpetuated by them. In this sense, ADM's ability to promote progressive social policies is limited and instead cements preexisting social structures based on privilege.

The problem with ADM systems being programmed in a manner that disadvantages certain groups is exacerbated by a lack of citizen participation and a breakdown in communications between citizens and public officials in the decision-making processes. In other words, the likelihood of those individuals who are typically subjected to profiling being able to influence or participate in the ADM process is often extremely low, and the social groups that are most at risk of being discriminated against by ADM tools, such as foreign-born individuals or people with disabilities, are the very same groups that most need to talk to public officials directly in order to make themselves understood.

DISCUSSION

Throughout this chapter, we have highlighted contemporary scholarly debates with respect to legal certainty, accountability, transparency, and discrimination. By doing so, we have shown how the presence of ADM in public administration affects these central democratic values in various, and sometimes conflicting, ways. It seems as if some values are enhanced, while others, like equality and transparency, are challenged. We have also concluded that the autonomy for both civil servants and the public sector per se is reduced and that this mainly results in a weakened position for already marginalized groups as their situation tends to be reproduced through applied algorithms. In this final section of the chapter, we wish to draw out two theoretical points that we argue can be made in light of the current research on ADM in the public sector presented above. First, we extend and theorize what we only briefly mentioned before in the text, namely how ADM can be said to change the nature of decision-making at its core. Second, we develop an argument about the importance of future studies of ADM to explicitly focus on their commodified and marketized circumstances.

As stated in the second section of the chapter: the transfer of decision-making from humans to algorithms changes the ontology of public sector decisions, including the position and agency of civil servants. One central aspect of this new ontology is the altered meaning of the citizen. Through ADM, the citizen becomes more collective, as the decisions for a single citizen are based on the collective features that (s)he encompasses, as well as more one-dimensional, as the complexity of the individual by necessity is reduced. The effects on the individual citizen are ambiguous, but it is clear that the black box problem of the public sector is strengthened, which, in turn, makes transparency difficult to achieve. Here, we see a need for further research in order to both make visible this new construction of the citizen and to discuss if—and in that case how—this citizen needs to be re-constructed in order for ADM to gain more legitimacy. We also see similar shifts in the meaning and position of the civil servant. As the space for individual judgment is reduced through ADM, the discretion of civil servants is reduced and their role is partly altered into confirming already taken decisions. Consequently, the shift restricts the role of guardian of democratic values, as this responsibility is partly moved into automated systems, systems that also to a large extent are produced and maintained by private companies outside the public sector.

From a longer, wider, and more critical perspective, there is a risk that increasing use of ADM in the public sector will reduce democracy to instrumental decision-making only, and that this shift will include not only decisions of civil servants but political decisions. This will not only mean that democracy is reduced to decision-making only, but that democracy risks being replaced by a form of automated epistocracy (Brennan, 2016) or the rule of the knowledgeable, as a better way to govern modern societies. This conclusion might seem far-fetched, but we believe that a broader focus on the organization of the public sector, as well as on the relationship between bureaucracy and democracy, to a large extent is absent in the discussion on ADM. Currently, research is mainly focused on the technology per se, and partly also on the risks involved for individual citizens, while more overarching questions that address the organization of both the public sector as such, as well as how ADM relates to central democratic principles and values are missing.

In particular, more or less all of the systems that facilitate ADM are private products and services. The public sector procures software, hardware, and expertise as it enters into different contractual arrangements with private firms in order to install, maintain, and develop its ADM capacity. In principle, and most likely in practice, the values of transparency and accountability seem hard to combine with the fact that the algorithms and AI provided by private firms are often their most guarded business secrets. In other words, we argue that the literature on ADM in the public sector should move to include detailed case studies of procurement processes and the practices of private consultants who operate within public organizations.

Consequently, we see a general need of placing the discussion of ADM in the public sector in the context of a wider discussion on the future of democracy, and where aspects like the neo-liberalization and marketization of the state need to be taken into account. Here, the works of Shoshana Zuboff (2019) on surveillance capitalism and Srnicek (2017) on platform capitalism are important, as well as Runciman's (2018) discussion on the technological takeover as one of the three main threats to modern democracy. With this backdrop, we also argue for a stronger research focus on the everyday doings of politics in a digital age, and how ADM alters both our common practice and our understanding of democracy.

REFERENCES

Alexy, R. (2015). Legal certainty and correctness. *Ratio Juris*, 28(4): 441–451.

Allhutter, D., Cech, F., Fischer, F., Grill, G., & Mager, A. (2020). Algorithmic profiling of job seekers in Austria: How austerity politics are made effective. *Frontiers in Big Data*, 3(5): 1–17.

Al-Mushayt, O. S. (2019). Automating e-government services with artificial intelligence. *IEEE Access*, 7: 146821–146829.

Amann, J., Blasimme, A., Vayena, E. et al. (2020). Explainability for artificial intelligence in healthcare: A multidisciplinary perspective. *BMC Medical Informatics and Decision Making*, 20(310): 1–9.

Andreassen, R., Kaun, A., & Nikunen, K. (2021). Fostering the data welfare state: A Nordic perspective on datafication. *Nordicom Review*, 42(2): 207–223.

Arrieta, A., Díaz-Rodríguez, N., Del Ser, J., Bennetot, A., Tabik, S., Barbado, S., Gil-Lopez, S., Molina, D., Benjamins, R., Chatila, R., & Herrera, F. (2020). Explainable artificial intelligence (XAI): Concepts, taxonomies, opportunities and challenges toward responsible AI. *Information Fusion*, 58: 82–115.

Bertea, S. (2008). Towards a new paradigm of legal certainty. *Legisprudence*, 2(1): 25–45.

Bingham, T. (2011). *The rule of law*. London: Allen Lane.

Brennan, J. (2016). *Against democracy*. Princeton, NJ: Princeton University Press.

Brettschneider, C. (2011). A substantial conception of the rule of law: Non-arbitrary treatment and the limits of procedure. In *NOMOS L: Getting to the rule of law*. NYU Press.

Bullock, J. B. (2019). Artificial intelligence, discretion, and bureaucracy. *American Review of Public Administration*, 49(7): 751–761.

Busch, P., & Henriksen, H. (2018). Digital discretion: A systematic literature review of ICT and street-level discretion. *Information Polity*, 23(1): 3–28.

Carlsson, V. (forthcoming). The status of legal certainty in automated decision-making in welfare services.

Civitarese Matteucci, S. (2021). Public administration algorithm decision-making and the rule of law. *European Public Law*, 27(1): 103–130.

Cobbe, J., Seng Ah Lee., M., & Singh, J. (2021). Reviewable automated decision-making: A framework for accountable algorithmic systems. ACM Conference on Fairness, Accountability, and Transparency (FAccT '21), March 1–10, 2021, Virtual Event, Canada.

Coglianese, C., & Lehr, D. (2019). Transparency and algorithmic governance. *Administrative Law Review*, 71(1): 1–56.

de Boer, N. & Raaphorst, N. (2021). Automation and discretion: Explaining the effect of automation on how street-level bureaucrats enforce. *Public Management Review*, 1–21.

de Fine Licht, K., & de Fine Licht, J. (2020). Artificial intelligence, transparency, and public decision-making: Why explanations are key when trying to produce perceived legitimacy. *AI & Society*, 35: 917–926.

D'Ignazio, C., & Klein, L. (2020). *Data feminism*. Cambridge, MA: MIT Press.

Dunleavy, P., Margetts, H., Bastow, S., & Tinkler, J. (2006). New public management is dead—Long livedigital-era governance. *Journal of Public Administration Research and Theory*, 16: 467–494.

Dyer-Witeford, N., Mikkola Kjosen, A., & Steinhoff, J. (2019). *Inhuman power: Artificial intelligence and the future of capitalism*. London: Pluto Press.

Eubanks, V. (2019). *Automating inequality: How high-tech tools profile, police, and punish the poor*. New York: Picador, St Martin's Press.

Ferguson, A. G. (2015). Big data and predictive reasonable suspicion. *University of Pennsylvania Law Review*, 163(2): 327–410.

Floridi, L., Cowls, J., Beltrametti, M., Chatila, R., Chazerand, P., Dignum, V., Luetge, C., Madelin, R., Pagallo, U., Rossi, F., Schafer, B., Valcke, P., & Vayena, E. (2018). AI4People: An ethical framework for a good AI society: Opportunities, risks, principles, and recommendations. *Minds & Machines*, 28(4): 689–707.

Ghallab, M. (2019). Responsible AI: Requirements and challenges. *AI Perspectives*, 1(3): 1–7.

Ghassemi, M., Oakden-Rayner, L., & Beam, L. (2021). The false hope of current approaches to explainable artificial intelligence in health care. *Lancet Digit Health*, 3(11): 745–750.

Gillespie, T. (2014). The relevance of algorithms. In T. Gillespie, P. Boczkowski, & K. Foot (Eds.), *Media technologies: Essays on communication, materiality, and society*. Cambridge, MA: MIT Press, pp. 167–194.

Gryz, J., & Rojszczak, M. (2021). Black box algorithms and the right of individuals: No easy solution to the "explainability" problem. *Internet Policy Review*, 10(2): 1–24.

Hakkarainen, J. (2021). Naming something collective does not make it so: Algorithmic discrimination and access to justice. *Internet Policy Review*, 10(4): 1–24.

Harasimiuk, D. E., & Braun, T. (2021). *Regulating artificial intelligence: Binary ethics and the law*. Routledge.

Lifante-Vidal, S. (2020). Is legal certainty a formal value? *Jurisprudence*, 11(3): 456–467.

Kemper, J., & Kolkman, D. (2019). Transparent to whom? No algorithmic accountability without a critical audience. *Information, Communication & Society*, 22(14): 2081–2096.

Lipsky, M. (2010). *Street-level bureaucracy: Dilemmas of the individual in public services*. Russel Sage Foundation.

Lopez, P. (2021). Bias does not equal bias: A socio-technical typology of bias in data-based algorithmic systems. *Internet Policy Review*, 10(4): 1–29.

Malgieri, G. (2019). Automated decision-making in the EU member states: The right to explanation and other "suitable safeguards" in the national legislations. *Computer Law & Security Review*, 35(5): 1–26.

Molina, D., Benjamins, R., Chatila, R., & Herrera, F. (2020). Explainable artificial intelligence (XAI): Concepts, taxonomies, opportunities and challenges toward responsible AI. *Information Fusion*, 58: 82–115.

O'Neil, C. (2016). *Weapons of math destruction: How big data increases inequality and threatens democracy*. London: Penguin.

Rawls, J. (1999). *The law of peoples: With "the idea of public reason revisited"*. Cambridge, MA: Harvard University Press.

Reed, S. (2020). Explainable AI. In S. Reed (Ed.), *Cognitive skills you need for the 21st century*. Oxford: Oxford University Press, pp. 170–179.

Runciman, D. (2018). *How democracy ends*. Profile Books.

Samek, W., Montavon, G., Vedaldi, A., Hansen, L., & Müller, K.-R. (Eds.). (2019). *Explainable AI: Interpreting, explaining and visualizing deep learning*. Springer.

Simon, H. (1947). *Administrative behavior: A study of decision-making processes in administrative organization*. New York: Macmillan.

Simmons, R. (2018). Big data, machine judges, and the legitimacy of the criminal justice system. *U.C. Davis Law Review*, 52(2): 1096–1097.

Smuha, N. (2021). Beyond the individual: Governing AI's societal harm. *Internet Policy Review*, 10(3): 1–32.

Srnicek, N. (2017). *Platform capitalism*. Polity Press.

Taekema, S. (2013). The procedural rule of law: Examining Waldron's argument on dignity and agency. *Annual Review of Law and Ethics*, 21: 133–146.

Tamanaha, B. Z. (2012). The history and elements of the rule of law. *Singapore Journal of Legal Studies*, 12: 232–247.

Ulmestig, R., Denvall, V., & Nordesjö, K. (2020). "Claiming" equality and "doing" inequality – individual action plans for applicants of social assistance. *Social Work & Society,* 18(2): 1–14.

Waldman, A. E. (2019). Power, process, and automated decision-making. *Fordham Law Review,* 88(2): 613–632.

Wirtz, B., Weyerer, J., & Geyer, C. (2019). Artificial intelligence and the public sector: Applications and challenges. *International Journal of Public Administration,* 42(7): 596–615.

Zuboff, S. (2019). *The age of surveillance capitalism: The fight for the future at the new frontier of power.* Profile Books.

62. The landscape of social bot research: a critical appraisal

Harry Yaojun Yan and Kai-Cheng Yang

INTRODUCTION

Social bots are social media accounts controlled by software that can carry out interactions and post content automatically. Malicious bots are designed to emulate real users, placing imminent threats to our social and political life. They can be massively produced at a low cost and have been deployed to disseminate fake news (Shao et al., 2018), exploit users' private information (Boshmaf et al., 2011), and create false public support for political gains (Confessore et al., 2018), especially during elections (Ferrara et al., 2020). Even bots that are designed to help, such as the ones that automatically gather and catalog news, can become complicit in spreading false information due to the lack of gatekeeping procedures (Lokot & Diakopoulos, 2016). Because of their ubiquity and impact, social bots have gained a great deal of public concern and scholarly interest in recent years.

As social media platforms become more aggressive in taking down inauthentic accounts in the past several years, malicious bots with mechanistic designs find it harder to survive. In the meantime, the behaviors and tactics of new strains have become increasingly complex, and their ability to pose as real users has been greatly enhanced by artificial intelligence (AI) technologies (Cresci, 2020; Ferrara et al., 2016). In response, researchers have developed more sophisticated machine learning (ML) models to identify social bots and examine their actions in various contexts. The competition between the creators of malicious bots and the research community leads to a seemingly never-ending arms race of automation technology and AI.

In this chapter, we evaluate the research body regarding social bots with a critical lens. We begin with a brief review of the research landscape and show that the scholarly efforts concentrate on creating new bot detection methods and characterizing bot actions while less attention has been paid to the effects of human-bot interactions on users. Informed by the critical theory of technology (Feenberg, 1991), we argue that the debate surrounding the threat and mitigation of malicious bots should incorporate at least three interpretations—technological, psychological, and social—of "artificial intelligence." Focusing only on technological interventions is essentially technocratic, and yet the research on the latter two, i.e., psychological and social consequences of human-bot interactions, lags behind.

Drawing from a handful of recent studies that focused on human perceptions of social bots, we show that exposure to potential bot deception activates common perceptual and cognitive biases for human users, especially in the political context. We further re-examine the experimental results of Yan et al. (2021), which demonstrated that users' accuracy at identifying bots was subject to the partisan personas of the profiles being examined and the political leaning of the users. Using this as a case study, we show how the psychological consequences of human-bot interactions may affect social bot research. We also report different user preferences for proposals to counter bots from our survey study and discuss the social implications of human-bot interactions in the current political climate.

THE STATE OF SOCIAL BOT RESEARCH

To illustrate the landscape of research regarding social bots, we conducted a scientometric analysis. We collected related publication records from www.dimensions.ai, which indexes over 127 million publications and allows users to search through keywords. Here, we obtained information on publications that had either "social bot," "bot detection," or "Twitter bot" in their titles or abstracts from 2013 to 2022. The last keyword is included because most bot-related research focuses on Twitter likely due to the accessibility of its data.

The initial search resulted in 729 records. We manually inspected them and removed those focusing on irrelevant topics such as web bots and chatbots. The duplicates and pre-prints of the published manuscripts were removed as well, leading to 432 records in our final analytical sample. The number of publications from each year is shown in Figure 62.1(A). We can see a drastic increase in publications from 2015 to 2020; then the trend appears to plateau.

Each publication in the analytical sample is further classified as either "detection," "characterization," "instrument," "human-bot interaction," "human perception," or "other." We categorize the papers based on the following criterion. For the "detection" category, the

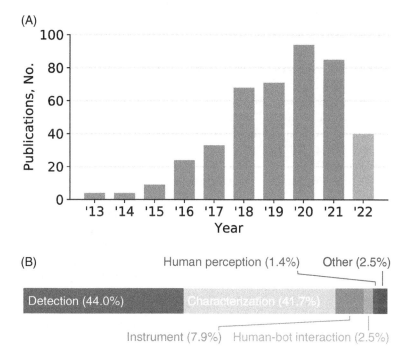

Figure 62.1   (A) Yearly numbers of publications regarding social bots from 2013 to 2022
(the number from 2022 reflects the status as of May 2022); (B) Percentages
of publications in different categories

authors propose and evaluate new bot detection methods. For the "characterization" category, the authors clearly state that the studies aim at observing and delineating the behaviors and actions of social bots in various contexts such as elections and public health crises. In the "instrument" papers, social bots are not the target, instead, they serve as experiment instruments (e.g., Chen et al., 2021). For detection, characterization, and instrument papers, social media users are not the subject being examined. Publications about "human-bot interaction" and "human perception," as the category names suggest, study how humans interact with and perceive social bots, respectively. In these studies, the researchers turn their focus to human users and sometimes directly engage with them through surveys and experiments. Topics of the "other" papers include cultural commentaries on bot phenomena, ethical considerations regarding bots, and discussions about emerging policies. When a manuscript includes more than one theme, we categorize the manuscript based on its core contribution stated in the abstract. We show the percentage of publications in each thematic category in Figure 62.1(B).

ADVANCEMENT OF BOT DETECTION

As shown in Figure 62.1(B), 44% of the publications regarding social bots attempt to propose new detection methods. The volume of the scholarship also reflects the difficulty and the changing nature of the task. In the early days, automated behaviors often manifested as a large number of repeated posts or mentions that were relatively easy to notice (Ratkiewicz et al., 2011). However, the behaviors and tactics of malicious bots have been constantly evolving. For instance, they can follow human circadian habits and be sporadically activated by monitoring the spikes of the information flow (Mønsted et al., 2017). Sometimes they are given various well-designed idiosyncrasies that vary in demographics, temporal patterns, and activity levels, as well as following and conversation strategies (Freitas et al., 2015). Using natural language processing (NLP) tools, they can identify keywords and then participate in popular conversations (Hwang et al., 2012). Recent reports suggest that bot creators start to adopt fake human photos produced by state-of-the-art generative adversarial networks (GAN) as account profiles (Yang & Menczer, 2022). Such fake photos are difficult to identify even for humans (Nightingale & Farid, 2022).

For bots exhibiting mechanistic behaviors, heuristic rules such as identifying accounts posting content at an unusually high frequency might be sufficient (Gorodnichenko et al., 2021). However, it is nontrivial to build a rule-based system that can capture the complex behavioral patterns of different bot classes. More commonly, researchers resort to supervised ML models (Cresci, 2020; Orabi et al., 2020), which require samples of accounts labeled as either humans or bots. The labels often come from human annotation (Varol et al., 2017) and sometimes from automated methods such as trapping bots using honey pots (Lee et al., 2011).

The next step is to capture the account characteristics that can help distinguish bots and humans. Researchers have adopted various ML models from traditional ones such as random forest (Yang et al., 2019) to more advanced neural networks that are customized to different data modalities. For instance, Mazza et al. (2019) use long short-term memory (LSTM) trained on timestamp data of retweets to detect bots based on irregular temporal patterns. The semantics of the textual content posted by different accounts contain vital information that is inaccessible through traditional methods such as word frequency counting. Therefore, many researchers apply newly developed NLP techniques such as LSTM (Kudugunta & Ferrara, 2018) and transformers (Heidari & Jones, 2020) to improve detection accuracy. Similarly, the structure of the following and follower network of an account is exploited through graph embedding techniques (Karpov & Glazkova, 2021) and graph convolution networks (Shangbin, Feng, et al., 2021). Additionally, some studies apply reinforcement learning methods hoping to capture the evolving behaviors of bots (Lingam et al., 2019) and some use GAN to augment the training data (Deng et al., 2020). The deployment of these advanced techniques also reflects the evolution of machine learning as a field that moves from statistical models to neural network-based models.

CHARACTERIZATION OF BOT ACTIONS AND BEHAVIORS

Another common theme of bot-related research, as Figure 62.1 suggests, is to characterize their actions and behaviors. These reports show that malicious bots are involved in all types of online discussions, especially controversial ones such as climate change (Marlow et al., 2021), cryptocurrency (Nizzoli et al., 2020), and stock prices (Fan et al., 2020). Research of this type notes multiple instances of the interference of social bots in major political events, including US elections (Bessi & Ferrara, 2016; Gorodnichenko et al., 2021), French elections (Ferrara, 2017), the Brexit referendum (Bastos & Mercea, 2018; Gorodnichenko et al., 2021), and so on. Debates around public health topics such as vaccines (Broniatowski et al., 2018) and the COVID-19 pandemic (Shi et al., 2020) also attract social bots.

Various behavioral patterns have been observed in the actions of malicious social bots.

The most common one is to simply generate a large volume of posts to amplify certain narratives and sway public attention (Keller et al., 2020; Marlow et al., 2021). They also disseminate low-credibility information strategically by getting involved in the early stage of the spreading process and targeting popular users through mentions and replies (Shao et al., 2018). In terms of content, malicious bots are found to engage other accounts with negative and inflammatory language (Stella et al., 2018) or hate speech (Uyheng & Carley, 2020). Journalistic investigations also show that celebrities, online influencers, and companies may purchase massive bot followers to inflate fake popularity for commercial gains (Confessore et al., 2018).

LACK OF RESEARCH ON BOT EFFECTS

The fact that over 85% of all social bot research focuses on bot detection and characterization entails that the current scholarly attention is devoted to technology-assisted surveillance and detection of *potential* threats. However, some crucial questions remain—if bots pose imminent threats, how threatening are they? If social bots are produced and deployed to deceive and manipulate, are these malicious endeavors successful? How vulnerable are real users when facing such deception and manipulation?

These questions can be partially answered through research on human-bot interactions and their effects on user perceptions. However, as the scientometric analysis has shown, this research direction is yet to be fully explored (Figure 62.1). In our search, only a handful of publications so far explicitly investigate human-bot interactions (2.5%) and human perceptions of social bots (1.4%). In the former case, observational studies reveal how bots and humans selectively amplify the messages from each other (Duan et al., 2022), how sentiment is exchanged between bots and humans (Kušen & Strembeck, 2019), and what types of users are more likely to engage bots (Wald et al., 2013). In the latter case, survey-based studies directly explore human perceptions toward bot accounts in political contexts (Wischnewski et al., 2021; Yan et al., 2021), how media coverage on social bots shapes people's perceived threat of bots (Schmuck & von Sikorski, 2020), and what traits make users more vulnerable to deceptive bots (Kenny et al., 2022).

NEED FOR MORE HUMAN-CENTERED BOT RESEARCH

As previous scholarship suggests that social media have created an attention economy (Ciampaglia et al., 2015), the efforts of using bots to sway public attention are essentially to manage labor and social resources through the deceptive use of technology. In response, the efforts of AI-assisted bot detection and surveillance attempt to resist such deceptive control, also by realizing the potential of technology. This competition per se appears to be analogous to the early philosophical debate that centered around whether automation would release workers from their traditional jobs or be used to strengthen managerial control (Feenberg, 1991). It is beyond the scope of this chapter to diagnose to what end such an analogy holds, but it is worth re-stating what Feenberg (1991) commented in *Critical Theory of Technology* that the issue was more than technological potential versus social control—"Engineers must get beyond the notion that there is always a 'technical fix' and come to terms with the complexity of the social system in which their tools will be employed" (p. 96).

This comment resonates in the present context, as we argue that relying on computer-assisted bot detection is not and will never be enough. One example of why the complexity of the social system makes the technical fix of bots inadequate is the ambiguous definition of bots. Scholars disagree on the extent to which automation is involved so that an account can be classified as a bot (Gorwa & Guilbeault, 2020). While bot accounts try to mimic humans, the behaviors of authentic users can be repetitive and even perceived as robotic because they are constrained by strong social influence and technological affordances. In other words, human accounts can exhibit the characteristics of automation and organic usage simultaneously, just like bot accounts. The complexity of social behaviors makes the subject of study a moving target.

While the debates on the definition of social bots continue, investigating evolving public perceptions of bots provides a complementary view. More importantly, such an assessment can grant further countermeasures and solid public opinion support. In fact, public awareness of bot threats has been rising, as evidenced in a 2018 Pew research survey: two-thirds of social media users were aware of social bots, and four-fifths of whom believed that bots had negative effects (Stocking & Sumida, 2018). However, unlike other deceptive attempts such as phishing emails, the deception social bots induce could take effect through indirect interactions. When viewing social media posts, it is difficult for users to know if a large portion of the retweets and likes are from bots, regardless of the content or its poster. This so-called "networked manipulation," creates inflated popularity without people noticing (Ferrara et al., 2016). This very nature of bots could make their *perceived* effects rather than their actual actions more pernicious, calling for in-depth investigations.

There are also practical reasons why we need more research on human-bot interactions and assessment of their effects on user perceptions. For example, investigating the cues by which social media users successfully tell bots and authentic accounts apart can help the platforms improve user experience. Accordingly, tutorials on profile creation can be given to users who do not want to be mistaken as bots. Investigating reasons why users continue to knowingly interact with bots can shed light on what is deemed as acceptable usage of bots and whether it is advisable to integrate them as a native feature of social media like Telegram. Whereas examining users who mistake bots for humans and keep engaging them can help us understand why people are vulnerable to bot deception.

These studies are also vital for building bot detection systems. Human-annotated training data is the foundation of any supervised ML model. However, the finding that laymen struggle with identifying bots and that they may be biased when facing certain profiles (Yan et al., 2021) suggests that the existing training data might suffer from these issues. No matter how advanced the ML models are, the biases and errors in the training data will propagate through the pipeline and affect downstream research. Therefore, we believe that researchers, especially ML practitioners, should be aware of the human factor and properly address the potential issues for better outcomes.

PARTISAN POLITICAL BOTS AND POLICY PREFERENCES

One of the reasons to advance human-centered social bot research, as mentioned earlier, is to understand public opinion for different countermeasures. In this section, we report some unpublished results of Yan et al. (2021) regarding the public preferences for different bot intervention initiatives. To briefly review the study, Yan et al. (2021) was an experiment where participants (N = 656) first answered a pre-test survey, then participated in a series of bot recognition tasks, and finally answered a post-test survey. In the recognition tasks, participants were instructed to view ten bot-like Twitter profiles and ten human-like ones; after viewing each profile, participants were asked if the profile was a bot or not.

The report of Yan et al. (2021) focuses on how the partisan identities of participants impair the judgment of users when trying to discern bots from authentic human users. The main findings suggest that profiles with conservative political personas are more confusing. More specifically, Democratic participants are more likely to confuse conservative human profiles as bots and Republican participants are more likely to misrecognize conservative bot profiles as humans. The results of this study in part explain how human-bot interactions may exacerbate existing political polarization and inform future training for bot annotators.

The brief recap of the study design also contextualizes the following finding: after exposure to potential deception in the bot recognition tasks, participants reported preferences for much more stringent and top-down countermeasures, as shown in Figure 62.2. In the post-recognition task questionnaire, participants were asked to rank seven different proposed ways to mitigate bot threats. Among all the choices, 62.5% of participants included either "Laws and regulations that penalize the mass manufactures of social bots" or "Policies and regulations towards social media companies" as one of their top three choices. In comparison, bot detection initiated either by the industry itself or by other third parties (e.g., academic research) ranked second (48.9%), despite the fact that this is what current research efforts have been mostly devoted to. Social media literacy education-related measures were the third-tier choice (39.0%). Interestingly, approximately one in five participants (21.6%) also ranked "Not much to be done, because it is the new normal" as one of their preferred countermeasures.

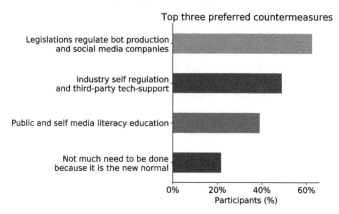

Note: Participants ranked a total of seven countermeasures and the results are collapsed into four categories in the illustration. The figure shows the percentage of participants who ranked the proposed countermeasures in the top three of their preferred choices.

Figure 62.2   Preferences of countermeasures

The results show that the public prefers more top-down countermeasures over other moderate approaches. What underpins this preference may be a rather high level of threat perceptions about bots, since the public has become more aware of them (Stocking & Sumida, 2018) and their potential of manipulating existing political orders (e.g., Bessi & Ferrara, 2016; Ferrera et al., 2020; Duan et al., 2022). Such threat perceptions have long been linked to authoritarianism (Adorno et al., 1950; Feldman & Stenner, 1997). Stenner (2009) argued that authoritarianism, partly reflected in the "relentless" cheerleading for authority, is a predisposition activated by experiences or perceptions of threats to existing social norms. The needs for more authoritative treatments against social bots suggest that AI-empowered political manipulation may be one of many factors that contribute to the rising support for authoritarianism globally. On the other hand, bot deception also breeds political inertia as many participants find there are no effective countermeasures.

We acknowledge that participants reported their preferences for policies and countermeasures in a condition where their senses of bot deception were primed and heightened. Also, since group thinking has its limitations, public opinion should not dictate the choices of individual scholars or the policymaking processes. Nevertheless, the results presented in Figure 62.2 can still inform research and policy choices through a critical reading. As we argued above, the current public reaction toward bots may be the result of strong threat perceptions. Although media literacy campaigns related to social media bots are not a preferred solution, they might be more effective than legislation to clear the threat perceptions and ultimately restore the public trust in social media and the use of automation in content creation.

CONCLUSION

In this chapter, we first evaluated the status of social bot-related research through a systematic bibliography analysis. The results show a strong technocratic bias: most research efforts have been devoted to detecting and characterizing bots through technological means. In the meantime, the public favored legal penalties against bot operators and regulations against social media companies. Our reading of the current public preferences is that they are the result of strong threat perceptions about social bots. These perceptions might not only stem from bots per se but also the fear of AI being used in online manipulation. Yet, there is little effort to address this fear and close the gap between social bot research and public needs. The lack of scientific communication may be typical in all AI-related research. As we argue that social bots are not only a technological issue but also a social one, more collective efforts need to be made to understand the user perceptions of bots and engage the public with updates on research progress as well as media literacy interventions.

FURTHER READING

Cresci, S. (2020). A decade of social bot detection. *Communications of the ACM, 63*(10), 72–83. https://doi.org/10.1145/3409116
Yan, H. Y., Yang, K.-C., Menczer, F., & Shanahan, J. (2021). Asymmetrical perceptions of partisan political bots. *New Media & Society, 23*(10), 3016–3037. https://doi.org/10.1177/1461444820942744

REFERENCES

Adorno, T. W., Frenkel-Brunswik, E., Levinson, D. J., & Sanford, R. N. (1950). *The authoritarian personality.* New York: Harper & Row.
Bastos, M., & Mercea, D. (2018). The public accountability of social platforms: Lessons from a study on bots and trolls in the Brexit campaign. *Philosophical Transactions of the Royal Society A: Mathematical, Physical and Engineering Sciences, 376*(2128), 20180003. https://doi.org/10.1098/rsta.2018.0003
Bessi, A., & Ferrara, E. (2016). Social bots distort the 2016 U.S. Presidential election online discussion. *First Monday.* https://doi.org/10.5210/fm.v21i11.7090
Boshmaf, Y., Muslukhov, I., Beznosov, K., & Ripeanu, M. (2011). The socialbot network: When bots socialize for fame and money. *Proceedings of the 27th Annual Computer Security Applications Conference*, 93–102. https://doi.org/10.1145/2076732.2076746
Broniatowski, D. A., Jamison, A. M., Qi, S., AlKulaib, L., Chen, T., Benton, A., Quinn, S. C., & Dredze, M. (2018). Weaponized Health Communication: Twitter bots and Russian trolls amplify the vaccine debate. *American Journal of Public Health, 108*(10), 1378–1384. https://doi.org/10.2105/AJPH.2018.304567
Ciampaglia, G. L., Flammini, A., & Menczer, F. (2015). The production of information in the attention economy. *Scientific Reports, 5*(1), 9452. https://doi.org/10.1038/srep09452
Chen, W., Pacheco, D., Yang, K. C., & Menczer, F. (2021). Neutral bots probe political bias on social media. *Nature Communications, 12*(1), 1–10.
Confessore, N., Dance, G. J. X., Harris, R., & Hansen, M. (2018, January 27). The follower factory. *The New York Times.* https://www.nytimes.com/interactive/2018/01/27/technology/social-media-bots.html
Cresci, S. (2020). A decade of social bot detection. *Communications of the ACM, 63*(10), 72–83. https://doi.org/10.1145/3409116
Deng, X., Dai, Z., Sun, M., & Lv, T. (2020). Variational autoencoder based enhanced behavior characteristics classification for social robot detection. In S. Yu, P. Mueller, & J. Qian (Eds.), *Security and privacy in digital economy* (pp. 232–248). Springer. https://doi.org/10.1007/978-981-15-9129-7_17
Duan, Z., Li, J., Lukito, J., Yang, K. C., Chen, F., Shah, D. V., & Yang, S. (2022). Algorithmic agents in the hybrid media system: Social bots, selective amplification, and partisan news about COVID-19. *Human Communication Research.*

Fan, R., Talavera, O., & Tran, V. (2020). Social media bots and stock markets. *European Financial Management*, *26*(3), 753–777. https://doi.org/10.1111/eufm.12245

Feenberg, A. (1991). *Critical theory of technology*. Oxford: Oxford University Press.

Feldman, S., & Stenner, K. (1997). Perceived threat and authoritarianism. *Political Psychology*, *18*(4), 741–770.

Ferrara, E. (2017). Disinformation and social bot operations in the run up to the 2017 French presidential election. *First Monday*. https://doi.org/10.5210/fm.v22i8.8005

Ferrara, E., Chang, H., Chen, E., Muric, G., & Patel, J. (2020). Characterizing social media manipulation in the 2020 U.S. presidential election. *First Monday*. https://doi.org/10.5210/fm.v25i11.11431

Ferrara, E., Varol, O., Davis, C., Menczer, F., & Flammini, A. (2016). The rise of social bots. *Communications of the ACM*, *59*(7), 96–104. https://doi.org/10.1145/2818717

Freitas, C., Benevenuto, F., Ghosh, S., & Veloso, A. (2015). Reverse engineering socialbot infiltration strategies in Twitter. *2015 IEEE/ACM International Conference on Advances in Social Networks Analysis and Mining (ASONAM)*, 25–32. https://doi.org/10.1145/2808797.2809292

Gorodnichenko, Y., Pham, T., & Talavera, O. (2021). Social media, sentiment and public opinions: Evidence from #Brexit and #USElection. *European Economic Review*, *136*, 103772. https://doi.org/10.1016/j.euroecorev.2021.103772

Gorwa, R., & Guilbeault, D. (2020). Unpacking the social media bot: A typology to guide research and policy. *Policy & Internet*, *12*(2), 225–248. https://doi.org/10.1002/poi3.184

Heidari, M., & Jones, J. H. (2020). Using BERT to extract topic-independent sentiment features for social media bot detection. *2020 11th IEEE Annual Ubiquitous Computing, Electronics & Mobile Communication Conference (UEMCON)*, 0542–0547. https://doi.org/10.1109/UEMCON51285.2020.9298158

Hwang, T., Pearce, I., & Nanis, M. (2012). Socialbots: Voices from the fronts. *Interactions*, *19*(2), 38–45. https://doi.org/10.1145/2090150.2090161

Karpov, I., & Glazkova, E. (2021). Detecting automatically managed accounts in online social networks: Graph embeddings approach. In W. M. P. van der Aalst, V. Batagelj, A. Buzmakov, D. I. Ignatov, A. Kalenkova, M. Khachay, O. Koltsova, A. Kutuzov, S. O. Kuznetsov, I. A. Lomazova, N. Loukachevitch, I. Makarov, A. Napoli, A. Panchenko, P. M. Pardalos, M. Pelillo, A. V. Savchenko, & E. Tutubalina (Eds.), *Recent trends in analysis of images, social networks and texts* (pp. 11–21). Springer International Publishing. https://doi.org/10.1007/978-3-030-71214-3_2

Keller, F. B., Schoch, D., Stier, S., & Yang, J. (2020). Political astroturfing on Twitter: How to coordinate a disinformation campaign. *Political Communication*, *37*(2), 256–280. https://doi.org/10.1080/10584609.2019.1661888

Kenny, R., Fischhoff, B., Davis, A., Carley, K. M., & Canfield, C. (2022). Duped by bots: Why some are better than others at detecting fake social media personas. *Human Factors*, 00187208211072642. https://doi.org/10.1177/00187208211072642

Kudugunta, S., & Ferrara, E. (2018). Deep neural networks for bot detection. *Information Sciences*, *467*, 312–322. https://doi.org/10.1016/j.ins.2018.08.019

Kušen, E., & Strembeck, M. (2019). Something draws near, I can feel it: An analysis of human and bot emotion-exchange motifs on Twitter. *Online Social Networks and Media*, *10–11*, 1–17. https://doi.org/10.1016/j.osnem.2019.04.001

Lee, K., Eoff, B., & Caverlee, J. (2011). Seven months with the devils: A long-term study of content polluters on Twitter. *Proceedings of the International AAAI Conference on Web and Social Media*, *5*(1), 185–192.

Lingam, G., Rout, R. R., & Somayajulu, D. V. L. N. (2019). Adaptive deep Q-learning model for detecting social bots and influential users in online social networks. *Applied Intelligence*, *49*(11), 3947–3964. https://doi.org/10.1007/s10489-019-01488-3

Lokot, T., & Diakopoulos, N. (2016). News bots. *Digital Journalism*, *4*(6), 682–699. https://doi.org/10.1080/21670811.2015.1081822

Marlow, T., Miller, S., & Roberts, J. T. (2021). Bots and online climate discourses: Twitter discourse on President Trump's announcement of U.S. withdrawal from the Paris Agreement. *Climate Policy*, *21*(6), 765–777. https://doi.org/10.1080/14693062.2020.1870098

Mazza, M., Cresci, S., Avvenuti, M., Quattrociocchi, W., & Tesconi, M. (2019). RTbust: Exploiting temporal patterns for botnet detection on Twitter. *Proceedings of the 10th ACM Conference on Web Science*, 183–192. https://doi.org/10.1145/3292522.3326015

Mønsted, B., Sapieżyński, P., Ferrara, E., & Lehmann, S. (2017). Evidence of complex contagion of information in social media: An experiment using Twitter bots. *PLOS ONE, 12*(9), e0184148. https://doi.org/10.1371/journal.pone.0184148

Nightingale, S. J., & Farid, H. (2022). AI-synthesized faces are indistinguishable from real faces and more trustworthy. *Proceedings of the National Academy of Sciences, 119*(8), e2120481119. https://doi.org/10.1073/pnas.2120481119

Nizzoli, L., Tardelli, S., Avvenuti, M., Cresci, S., Tesconi, M., & Ferrara, E. (2020). Charting the landscape of online cryptocurrency manipulation. *IEEE Access, 8*, 113230–113245. https://doi.org/10.1109/ACCESS.2020.3003370

Orabi, M., Mouheb, D., Al Aghbari, Z., & Kamel, I. (2020). Detection of bots in social media: A systematic review. *Information Processing & Management, 57*(4), 102250. https://doi.org/10.1016/j.ipm.2020.102250

Ratkiewicz, J., Conover, M., Meiss, M., Gonçalves, B., Patil, S., Flammini, A., & Menczer, F. (2011). Truthy: Mapping the spread of astroturf in microblog streams. *Proceedings of the 20th International Conference Companion on World Wide Web*, 249–252. https://doi.org/10.1145/1963192.1963301

Schmuck, D., & von Sikorski, C. (2020). Perceived threats from social bots: The media's role in supporting literacy. *Computers in Human Behavior, 113*, 106507. https://doi.org/10.1016/j.chb.2020.106507

Shangbin, F., Herun, W., Ningnan, W., & Minnan, L. (2021). BotRGCN: Twitter bot detection with relational graph convolutional networks. *Proceedings of the 2021 IEEE/ACM International Conference on Advances in Social Networks Analysis and Mining*, 236–239. https://doi.org/10.1145/3487351.3488336

Shao, C., Ciampaglia, G. L., Varol, O., Yang, K.-C., Flammini, A., & Menczer, F. (2018). The spread of low-credibility content by social bots. *Nature Communications, 9*(1), 4787. https://doi.org/10.1038/s41467-018-06930-7

Shi, W., Liu, D., Yang, J., Zhang, J., Wen, S., & Su, J. (2020). Social bots' sentiment engagement in health emergencies: A topic-based analysis of the COVID-19 pandemic discussions on Twitter. *International Journal of Environmental Research and Public Health, 17*(22), 8701. https://doi.org/10.3390/ijerph17228701

Stella, M., Ferrara, E., & Domenico, M. D. (2018). Bots increase exposure to negative and inflammatory content in online social systems. *Proceedings of the National Academy of Sciences, 115*(49), 12435–12440. https://doi.org/10.1073/pnas.1803470115

Stenner, K. (2009). Three kinds of conservatism. *Psychological Inquiry, 20*(2–3), 142–159.

Stocking, G., & Sumida, N. (2018, October 15). *Social media bots draw public's attention and concern.* Pew Research Center. https://www.pewresearch.org/journalism/2018/10/15/social-media-bots-draw-publics-attention-and-concern/

Uyheng, J., & Carley, K. M. (2020). Bots and online hate during the COVID-19 pandemic: Case studies in the United States and the Philippines. *Journal of Computational Social Science, 3*(2), 445–468. https://doi.org/10.1007/s42001-020-00087-4

Varol, O., Ferrara, E., Davis, C., Menczer, F., & Flammini, A. (2017). Online human-bot interactions: Detection, estimation, and characterization. *Proceedings of the International AAAI Conference on Web and Social Media, 11*(1), 280–289.

Wald, R., Khoshgoftaar, T. M., Napolitano, A., & Sumner, C. (2013). Predicting susceptibility to social bots on Twitter. *2013 IEEE 14th International Conference on Information Reuse & Integration (IRI)*, 6–13. https://doi.org/10.1109/IRI.2013.6642447

Wischnewski, M., Bernemann, R., Ngo, T., & Krämer, N. (2021). Disagree? You must be a bot! How beliefs shape Twitter profile perceptions. In *Proceedings of the 2021 CHI Conference on Human Factors in Computing Systems* (pp. 1–11). Association for Computing Machinery. https://doi.org/10.1145/3411764.3445109

Yan, H. Y., Yang, K.-C., Menczer, F., & Shanahan, J. (2021). Asymmetrical perceptions of partisan political bots. *New Media & Society, 23*(10), 3016–3037. https://doi.org/10.1177/1461444820942744

Yang, K.-C., & Menczer, F. (2022, May 23). *How many bots are on Twitter? The question is difficult to answer and misses the point.* The Conversation. http://theconversation.com/how-many-bots-are-on-twitter-the-question-is-difficult-to-answer-and-misses-the-point-183425

Yang, K.-C., Varol, O., Davis, C. A., Ferrara, E., Flammini, A., & Menczer, F. (2019). Arming the public with artificial intelligence to counter social bots. *Human Behavior and Emerging Technologies, 1*(1), 48–61. https://doi.org/10.1002/hbe2.115

63. Introducing robots and AI in human service organizations: what are the implications for employees and service users?

Susanne Tafvelin, Jan Hjelte, Robyn Schimmer,
Maria Forsgren, Vicenç Torra and Andreas Stenling

INTRODUCTION

Technology is not necessarily good, nor bad; nor is it neutral. (Kranzberg, 1986, p. 545)

The acceleration in technological change brings enormous opportunities for work and society. Technology can replace dull, dirty, and dangerous work, as well as making services far cheaper than before (Walsh & Strano, 2018). However, technology and the work practices it enables also bring risks for work and workers, most prominently the erosion of the need for human workers at all. Some studies estimate that automation may eradicate around 50% of all jobs, and although others have challenged these numbers, there is considerable agreement that new technology will significantly change the overall workforce structure (Brynjolfsson et al., 2018).

Robots have been used for a long time in the manufacturing industry, but with their increased ability to perform non-routine tasks, they are becoming increasingly popular in the public sector (SKR, 2019). In addition, recent developments using big data and algorithms have enabled AI to perform work tasks that previously required human judgement or experience such as decision-making, interpretation, and other cognitive skills. Robots and AI are being implemented in work life at an increasing rate to improve efficiency and reduce menial work tasks and heavy workloads. Recent reports suggest that around 30% of work tasks in public organizations could be automated over time (McKinsey, 2017). The implementation of robots and AI may be of particular importance to the public sector, where robots and AI represent one strategy to meet the expected increase in demand for welfare services while at the same time facing a shortage of employees (SKR, 2018).

Although the implementation of robots and AI may benefit organizations in terms of increased efficiency, there are concerns that robots and AI may have a negative impact on work content and work roles for employees. However, for the successful implementation of robots and AI in organizations, employees need to turn to it as a resource, as well. Thus, it has been argued that the increased efficiency expected from robots and AI should benefit employees and employers equally, not employers only (Demerouti, 2022). Furthermore, in public organizations, citizens are also users, and in many cases, they represent vulnerable groups that need to be considered as part of the ethical impact of AI-enabled services.

In this chapter, we aim to critically examine the potential consequences of introducing robots and AI in human service organizations from the perspective of employees and service users. Human service organizations are public welfare organizations found in the social welfare sector, such as social services, education, health care, and elder care (Hasenfeld, 2010; Johnsson & Svensson, 2006). First, we provide an overview of potential consequences for employees from the perspective of work design and management. Second, we explore potential consequences for service users from an ethical perspective. Finally, we draw conclusions on what steps will further deepen our understanding of the impact of robots and AI in organizations.

IMPLICATIONS FOR EMPLOYEES FROM A WORK DESIGN AND MANAGEMENT PERSPECTIVE

The increased implementation of robots and AI in human service organizations has raised concern among employees related to work content and their work roles (Sunt Arbetsliv, 2018). While some professions will benefit from robots and AI, other professions will be impoverished. The probability of getting support or being replaced is related to the educational level that work tasks require (Gardberg et al., 2020). It is therefore not surprising that robots and AI are sometimes perceived as a threat to professional roles. For example, in a Swedish municipality, 12 out of 16 social workers terminated their employment in protest against an implemented robot, and another municipality was reported to the Parliamentary Ombudsmen due to a lack of transparency in the algorithm behind automated decisions for financial aid (Arbetsvärlden, 2020). These examples indicate that the implementation of robots and AI in organizations is controversial and that employees' worries need to be taken into consideration.

Research on the introduction of robots and AI in organizations from a work design and management perspective is still in its infancy, and most published articles are conceptual or theoretical in nature, rather than empirical (Mynak, 2022). Among the empirical studies, several have focused on robots in surgery and how surgeons perceive and use the technology. By tradition, surgeons have been positive towards new technology; however, the experiences of other medical professions remain unknown. Studies also suggest that robots in surgery may reduce work demands and stress, increase performance, and facilitate ergonomics, particularly for inexperienced surgeons (Chandra et al., 2010). However, findings across studies are mixed, with some studies demonstrating both improvements and impairments in the work environment after the introduction of robots (Dalsgaard et al., 2020).

Another line of research has focused on robots and AI in social service organizations. These studies suggest that automated decision-making renders more neutral decisions while at the same time minimizing the risk of corruption (Wihlborg et al., 2016). However, the logic behind implemented algorithms needs to be transparent for workers to perceive them as fair and useful (Christensen & Laegreid, 2018). There are also concerns that employees' professional discretion may be perceived as threatened, with a risk of parallel systems where some information is processed and kept outside the system (Devlieghere & Roose, 2018). This is in line with a recent survey among social workers suggesting that a majority are worried about the development of their profession when automated decision-making is implemented (Scaramuzzino, 2019). In child welfare services, social workers have expressed concern that user meetings have decreased and that the learning and handling of new systems are too time-consuming (Curry et al., 2017). On the other hand, studies also indicate that new technology provides the flexibility to design meetings based on individual needs (Hansen et al., 2018). Studies on managers in social service organizations that have implemented robots and

AI highlight the importance of involving employees when implementing new technology (Ranerup, 2020). Research on social workers thus suggests that robotization can increase efficiency, but at the same time, there is the risk of erosion in social work practice, and social workers' roles will change (Svensson, 2019b).

A conclusion from studies in human service organizations is that the introduction of robots and AI is happening right now with an important window of opportunity to influence this change that may not be present later (Svensson, 2019). This is echoed in the international literature, which has stressed the importance of empirical and theoretical studies evaluating the implementation of new technology and its impact on employees (Gillingham, 2018). One way to systematically study the consequences of the implementation of robots and AI for employees is to apply a work design and management perspective.

A Work Design Perspective

When implementing robots and AI, it is crucial to understand how human workers and machines might best share tasks and the consequences of different choices in this process. For example, if technology deskills work, it is likely to reduce motivation. Individuals mistrust of technology changes how they use that technology, which in turn can influence employee motivation and well-being (Parker & Grote, 2022).

Work design can be summarized in five broad categories of work characteristics: (1) autonomy and control; (2) social and relational aspects of work; (3) job feedback and related work characteristics (e.g., role clarity, opportunities for practice); (4) skill variety and use; and (5) job demands or aspects of the job that require sustained physical and/or psychological effort. Collectively, these characteristics capture key aspects of work design from a range of theories, including the dominant Job Characteristics Model (Hackman & Oldham, 1975), and are essential to consider when analysing risks and to help steer technological development.

One important work characteristic to consider when implementing robots and AI is *autonomy* (Parker & Grote, 2022). Autonomy allows us to manage demands from the environment, enhances motivation, and can support efficient decision-making (Parker & Grote, 2022). However, the introduction of robots and AI, such as automated decision-making, may reduce autonomy and a sense of control if the algorithms suggesting a decision are not transparent. At the same time, it may reduce workload and thereby job demands. Furthermore, many scholars have discussed the dilemma that with increasing levels of automation comes the risk of losing control. For example, operators may not fully understand automated processes but are left to monitor and handle problems as systems fail. Considerable effort has been made to develop principles and methods that neither overload nor underload humans and that secure transparency, predictability, and means for workers to handle complex, emergent situations, in this sense, remaining in control (Grote, 2009). Though increasing impenetrability of automation has spurred the discussion between full automation in contrast to human-centred automation. Some argue that at some point, accountability should shift to system designers and organizations operating the technology (Boos et al., 2013)

Regarding *relational* work characteristics such as interdependence, feedback from others and support, one influential factor is how people coordinated before the introduction of a robot (Parker & Grote, 2022). For example, examining previous patterns of communication in an intensive care unit, Beane and Orlikowski (2015) found that the same robot could both enhance and hinder coordination. Mixed effects have also been seen in relation to *job feedback*. One example of this is how technology may enable direct feedback from doing the work, for example, call centre agents receive responses on their tone when speaking to customers. Regarding skill variety and use, there is a discussion on what the consequences of AI and robots may be, with many researchers predicting growth in highly skilled jobs with few automated components parallel to lower-skilled jobs declining when algorithms take over, thus influencing *skill variety and use*. Finally, workers have reported that their *workload*, especially work pace, has increased to levels difficult to sustain due to the intensification of surveillance systems (Parker & Grote, 2022). However, physical demands are often reduced when automation replaces manual work.

Consequently, technology can affect work characteristics and their influence on employee motivation and well-being both positively and negatively. Although insufficient attention has been given to how technological change such as robots and AI alter work tasks, organizations can actively make choices with the aim of improving the effects of technology on work design informed by psychological needs (Parker & Grote, 2022). Additionally, human response to technology may shape the way it is used and, in this manner, affect work design. More studies are needed with a focus on the impact of technology on work characteristics such as job autonomy and skill use and how these factors interact in their influence on employee motivation, well-being, and performance.

In studies of robots and AI at work, a gender perspective is consistently lacking (Parker & Grote, 2022). However, we do know that the experience of work characteristics such as autonomy, skill use, feedback, relational aspects, and demands affects men and women differently, and thus is gendered. For example, a recent meta-analysis found that females experience demands at work as more distressing than men do and that females perceive less control over their work than men do (Fila et al., 2017). These findings suggest that any changes in work design due to automation may affect the health and well-being of male and female employees in different ways. Therefore, future research needs to consider gender to make sure that the introduction of robots and AI does not introduce gender inequality at work. In addition, the majority of previous studies of automation at work represent European or US contexts, and more studies representing a wider range of settings are needed to clarify to what extent these findings are context dependent.

A Management Perspective

The rapid development of technology and efficient algorithms has also created new opportunities for management functions, and it has become increasingly common for algorithms to perform tasks traditionally carried out by managers (Parent-Rocheleau & Parker, 2022). Algorithmic management refers to "the use of software algorithms to partially or completely execute workforce management functions" (Gagné et al., 2022, p. 9), and many view this delegation of managerial functions to algorithms as one of the most disruptive forms of technological change currently being implemented (Lee, 2018). Although algorithmic management primarily has been implemented within the platform-mediated gig economy, this phenomenon is now being implemented rapidly in traditional work settings (e.g., the public sector; Charbonneau & Doberstein, 2020). Given that leadership and managerial choices can have a profound impact on work design (Parker et al., 2017), there is a need for a better understanding of how these new management functions (e.g., algorithmic management) impact work design and, in turn, employee outcomes when implementing robots and AI in human service organizations.

Common algorithmic management functions used in organizations include the monitoring of employees, goal setting, performance management, scheduling, compensation, and job termination (Parent-Rocheleau & Parker, 2022). The impact of these algorithmic management functions on employees depends greatly on whether their design considers motivational factors, such as ensuring that employees have enough autonomy, skill usage, task variety, social contact, role clarity, and a manageable workload (Gagné et al., 2022). However, research to date indicates that algorithmic management functions mostly have a negative impact on employees' work motivation and well-being (Parent-Rocheleau & Parker, 2022; Gagné et al., 2022). For example, algorithmic management tends to foster the working-for-data phenomenon, leading employees to focus on tasks that are being monitored and quantified rather than tasks that might be more personally valued or meaningful. There is also a risk that monitoring functions reduces employee autonomy because it is experienced as controlling. Furthermore, algorithmic management functions tend to individualize work and thereby reduce feelings of relatedness. For example, it can substantially reduce employees' contact with the manager, which can lead to feelings that the organization does not care about them and a lack of social support. Algorithmic management functions involving comparative feedback and publicly displaying individual team members' ranking can also hamper relatedness because climates where employees compete against each other do not facilitate trust and supportive relationships. On one hand, algorithmic management functions can provide precise and frequent feedback, which may increase employees' sense of competence. However, the feedback often does not provide enough information or is linked to financial rewards, which likely reduces employees' sense of competence and autonomy.

The design of many algorithmic management functions seems to negatively impact employees' basic psychological needs for autonomy, competence, and relatedness through their influence on work design (Gagné et al., 2022). According to self-determination theory (SDT; Ryan & Deci, 2017), the satisfaction of basic psychological needs is the key mechanism underpinning both self-determined work motivation and well-being. When algorithmic management functions are developed and implemented in organizations, theories of work design and human motivation should be incorporated into the design. Furthermore, in line with the theory of sociotechnical systems (STS) (Emery & Trist, 1978), transparency, fairness, and opportunities for human influence are important elements with the potential to enhance the positive influence of algorithmic management on employees (Parent-Rocheleau & Parker, 2022).

IMPLICATIONS FOR USERS FROM AN ETHICAL PERSPECTIVE

The sections above describe the impact of robots and AI from an organizational, internal, perspective. However, implementation will also have external implications, particularly for service users. One of the major external implications is how the ethics of human service organizations change and how this affects service users. One characteristic of human service organizations is that they constitute moral work. The actions they take are not just service to their users (e.g., clients, patients, students) but also a judgement of their social worth in terms of assessment of the need for financial aid, diagnosis, and assessment of the need for elderly care or school grades. The moral context refers not only to what is done but also how it is done. Therefore, ethical and moral issues are also about whether service users should be considered as objects or subjects and whether, and in what way, they should have an influence on decisions about the service they receive (Hasenfeld, 1992). Another characteristic is their need for legitimacy in society. Because human service organizations perform moral work, they need to seek support for their moral position consistently by adapting to institutionalized moral systems in society. These organizations gain societal legitimacy by adapting to rules, guidelines, and policies that are mainly provided by the state and professions (Hasenfeld, 1992). Such moral and ethical principles can refer to general principles for what and how things should be done (deontological orientation) but also the consequences and utility aspects of actions (teleological orientation) (Decker, 2008).

Human service organizations face the challenge of providing the expected service. Here, robots and AI have come to be seen as viable ways to address the challenges in meeting the needs of service users. However, robots and AI pose several ethical challenges in relation to users who need their services. Public organizations have relatively developed ethical rules and principles for their work, but a central issue has been how to embed those principles in an automated context (Turilli, 2007). How such challenges take shape may depend on which ethical perspective provides the starting point. Much of the research has emphasized *ethical universalism* (Vandemeulebroucke et al., 2018). This means that one approaches the issue of ethical challenges for service users of automation and AI by relating them to more general ethical principles (top-down). From this perspective, general moral and ethical values do not follow from or become changed by technology but are rather a fundamental part of practice. Therefore, it is a matter of translating the principles into a digitized and automated context (Friedman & Kahn, 2003). The challenge is to achieve automation that corresponds to general ethical principles and that includes the organization's relationship with service users.

In contrast, proponents of *ethical particularism* believe that ethical reflection should be at the forefront rather than an assessment of whether a particular practice corresponds to general ethical principles. It also emphasizes the contextual dependence of the basic ethical concepts and the specific relationships that exist between professionals and service users in a particular context. Such an approach means that the boundaries are not defined in advance but it opens an ethical discussion about what the use of automation and AI does to the relationships and the inherent values in a specific context (Vandemeulebroucke et al., 2018). Thus, the ethical challenge of a particularist approach concerns arriving at the ethical and moral values that are essential in relation to users who encounter services from a specific organization, but also what happens to the specific ethical practice through robots and AI. Consequently, different ethical approaches highlight different ethical challenges. However, what these ethical challenges mean may also depend on the stage of the automation process. In the following, we will exemplify this in relation to two different stages of the automation process: service design and application.

Ethical Challenges in Different Stages of the Automation Process

In order to implement robots and AI, an information system is required, and this system must at some point be designed, developed, and configured for the specific setting. Although this can theoretically be divided into separate stages, it is more often an integrated process incrementally addressing these issues in parallel. Service design is one such approach that has gained popularity both in the business sector and in the public sector. Stickdorn and

Schneider (2011) describe five principles framing service design: 1) user-centric, 2) co-creative, 3) sequencing, 4) evidencing, and 5) holistic. In short, this means that service design should be approached in a manner that accounts for the whole context in close collaboration with users and that interaction should be tangible and consist of non-complex steps. This is applicable if the robot or AI is implemented through a previously non-digital or digital service (e.g., non-automated e-service).

Understanding the setting, or context, is an essential part of service design (Benyon, 2019). This involves gathering knowledge of the context in which the system will be used, what tasks it should perform and support, and other requirements. Approaching this from a universalistic standpoint would include the collection of ethical guidelines and practices and subsequently transferring this to the new systems as rules. However, this would assume that the system only mirrors the old, manual process. It also assumes that the system is neutral in the sense that it does not itself have any ethical implications for the service process. This idea of technology being neutral suggests that the piece of technology is a mere tool that can be used in whatever way the user wants and that only the user is a moral agent. However, some criticize this idea of technology for being over-simplified. For example, Ihde (1990) presents a relational account of human-technology interaction by suggesting that technology is always part of shaping how humans perceive the world. This will have an impact on ethics as well. Drawing on Ihde's work, Peter-Paul Verbeek (2011) concludes that "The theory of technological mediation reveals an inherent moral dimension in technology design. It shows that technology always help to shape human actions and interpretations on the basis of which (moral) decisions are made". This standpoint, a non-neutral perspective on technology, challenges universalistic ethics as a viable approach. In the case of robots and AI, how the system is designed will depict what decisions are made and not made. Designing such a system would require a different approach from the designer than seeing the system as a mere tool, and rather as a mediator (Verbeek, 2011).

A particularistic approach towards design would instead provide options to deal with the complexity of understanding technology as a mediator. The emphasis on ethical reflection and contextual awareness aligns well with Verbeek's suggestions for ethical design as he highlights the necessity of anticipating meditations (2011, p. 97). It requires the designer to attempt to foresee the types of mediations that could emerge when using the new system. In the case of robots and AI, this would include attempts to imagine and reflect on mediations that could affect ethical decisions. This is a demanding task that requires much from the designer. Technology is not neutral, nor is it deterministic. A specific system is always situated in a specific context, with a unique group of users and, in the case of a human service organization, within certain organizational boundaries. It is not certain whether the same types of mediations will emerge if the same system is implemented in two different organizations. This non-deterministic aspect of technology is part of the challenge of anticipating mediations. One possible route is to merge the understanding of technology with the principles of service design. The principles of service design already put emphasis on context awareness and on a holistic understanding of the whole human-technology system. The principles of user-centrism and co-creation are worth emphasizing. Involving users and stakeholders early in the design process is already common practice in systems design (Benyon, 2019) but could also be a valuable source for anticipating and assessing mediations. Through what Verbeek (2011) calls augmented stakeholder analysis, stakeholders and user representatives can make use of their experience and perspectives to help the designer(s) imagine mediations and possible ethical dilemmas.

Regarding the *application* of robots and AI, a universalistic approach means that an emphasis on translation and assessment of practice based on a fixed list of criteria is at the forefront (cf. Vandemeulebroucke et al., 2018). One example from the field of elderly care is Sharkey and Sharkey (2012). Based on a list of 12 enduring human values with ethical import that are implicated in technology design (Friedman & Kahn, 2003; Friedman et al., 2006), Sharkey and Sharkey (2012) identify six challenges that need to be considered and addressed when using robotic technology in elderly care. The first challenge concerns whether robots risk reducing *social contact* so that the elderly do not have their emotional needs met. The second challenge, *objectification*, means that the use of robots risks contributing to older people experiencing objectification and a feeling of loss of control. In addition, automation can contribute to a reduction of personal *integrity* at the same time that *personal freedom* (autonomy) is limited. It may also contribute to *infantilization* by encouraging them to interact with robots as if they were comrades. Finally, Sharkey and Sharkey (2012) consider that the use of robots in elderly care is a matter of *responsibility*. If robots are placed under the responsibility of the elderly, who is responsible if something goes wrong? How much responsibility can be given to the elderly regarding their wishes and state of mind?

If the approach instead emphasizes a particularistic view on application, it is a reflection of the ethical content in a specific elderly care context that comes to the fore and where robots and AI are integral parts of the context (cf. Vandemeulebroucke et al., 2018). Therefore, the outlined challenges are different. What ethical and moral values are essential in relation to the care of the elderly, and what happens to the care situation when using robots and AI? One example is Coeckelbergh (2016), who questions the so-called doom scenarios that present the use of robots and AI in terms of isolated people to whom machines administer care. The author believes that these scenarios do not lack value but can form the basis for ethical reflection. However, they rest on dubious assumptions. First, they represent a dualistic worldview where human care belongs to the *real* world while robot care belongs to the *virtual* or even *unreal* world. According to the author, this is wrong because technology is no less real than the social world, nor to be regarded as its opposite. Rather, technology is an integral part of healthcare practice, where the two worlds are embedded in each other. Therefore, care practice should be regarded as a mix of both. Second, doom scenarios point to a lack of context built on the assumption that older people have difficulty managing technology. Here the author believes that one must see the relationship between technology and humans as changing. One can already see that the younger older are familiar and feel at home with digital technology. This also means that the question of what is reasonable and ethically acceptable in a specific context can change over time. In the future, it may even be the case that having access to information technology is seen as a human right, and this may also be the case for robots caring for the elderly if they become widespread (Coeckelbergh, 2016). In sum, the implementation of robots and AI in human service organizations call for increased attention to ethics. Given the changing nature of practice in human service organizations, paired with the understanding of technology as non-neutral, we argue that ethics should be addressed from a particularistic perspective.

CONCLUSION

The rapid technological change and implementation of robots and AI will continue to transform work life. Although we have highlighted many negative consequences for employees and ethical challenges for service users in this chapter, focusing too much on the negative aspects is not a sustainable long-term approach. Instead, an approach guided by the belief that the consequences of robots and AI at work are mainly the result of organizational choices and strategies behind technological design and implementation, and that stakeholders can shape these consequences, provides a more fruitful path forward (Parent-Rocheleau & Parker, 2022). Thus, organizational choices and strategies in relation to design and implementation, and the involvement of key stakeholders within and beyond the organization are crucial for the successful implementation and use of robots and AI in human service organizations.

Regarding work design and management, we argue that incorporating theories of work design and human motivation in design and implementation is key to understanding how and why technology impacts employees. Furthermore, technology characterized by transparency, fairness, and opportunities for human control is much more likely to result in positive outcomes compared with technology perceived as non-transparent, unfair, and involving little human control. However, research on the impact of robots and AI on work design and work motivation is scarce, and future research is urgently needed to understand better how technology can be designed and implemented to benefit employees.

In relation to ethical issues, ideas about fairness and inclusion of various stakeholders have also been emphasized in recent years. Ethical thinking has begun to emerge about the implementation of robots and AI in some sort of golden mean that includes values such as fairness and justice, and where ethical principles are those chosen by free and rational people entering into some sort of agreement (cf. Donaldson & Dunfee, 1994; Rawls, 1999). Here, participation and influence are essential parts of an ethical approach. This approach may include various stakeholders who are affected by the organization's efforts. By using existing ethical principles and inviting representatives from relevant interest groups—including service users—to a reflexive dialogue, they are given the opportunity to speak and gain influence over the considerations that are made (Vandemeulebroucke et al., 2018; Wright & Shultz, 2018). The challenge thus becomes rather how an ethical procedure that includes both assessment and reflection should be organized, which stakeholders should be involved, and how to ensure that the experiences of different stakeholders are taken into consideration.

We began this chapter with the quote "Technology is not necessarily good, nor bad; nor is it neutral" (Kranzberg, 1986, p. 545), which still today captures the essence of our knowledge related to the implementation and use of robots and AI in human service organizations. However, as outlined throughout this chapter, research in this area is still in its infancy and there is a need for frameworks regarding work design, human motivation, and ethics that can guide and improve future implementation of robots and AI in human service organizations.

REFERENCES

Arbetsvärlden. (2020). Fackförbund kräver öppenhet kring bidragsalgoritm. Publicerad 15 februari 2020. Hämtad från https://www.arbetsvarlden.se/fackforbund-kraver-oppenhet-kring-bidragsalgoritmer/

Beane, M. (2019). Shadow learning: Building robotic surgical skill when approved means fail. *Administrative Science Quarterly*, 64(1), 87–123.

Beane, M., & Orlikowski, W. (2015). What difference does a robot make? The material enactment of distributed coordination. *Organization Science*, 26(6), 1553–1573.

Benyon, D. (2019). *Designing user experience: A guide to HCI, UX and interaction design* (4th ed.). Pearson Education.

Brynjolfsson, E., Mitchell, T., & Rock, D. (2018, May). What can machines learn, and what does it mean for occupations and the economy? *AEA Papers and Proceedings, 108*, 43–47.

Boos, D., Guenter, H., Grote, G., & Kinder, K. (2013). Controllable accountabilities: The internet of things and its challenges for organisations. *Behaviour & Information Technology, 32*(5), 449–467.

Chandra, V., Nehra, D., Parent, R., Woo, R., Reyes, R., Hernandez-Boussard, T., & Dutta, S. (2010). A comparison of laparoscopic and robotic assisted suturing performance by experts and novices. *Surgery, 147*(6), 830–839.

Charbonneau, É., & Doberstein, C. (2020). An empirical assessment of the intrusiveness and reasonableness of emerging work surveillance technologies in the public sector. *Public Administration Review, 80*(5), 780–791.

Christensen T. & Lægreid P. (2018). An organization approach to public administration. In: Ongaro E., Van Thiel S. (Eds.), *The Palgrave Handbook of Public Administration and Management in Europe.* London: Palgrave Macmillan.

Coeckelbergh, M. (2016). Care robots and the future of ICT-mediated elderly care: A response to doom scenarios. *AI & Society, 31*(4), 455–462.

Curry, S., van Draanen, J., & Freisthler, B. (2017). Perceptions and use of a web-based referral system in child welfare: Differences by caseworker tenure. *Journal of Technology in Human Services, 35*(2), 152–168.

Dalsgaard, T., Jensen, M., Hartwell, D., Mosgaard, B., Jørgensen, A., & Jensen, B. (2020). Robotic surgery is less physically demanding than laparoscopic surgery: Paired cross sectional study. *Annals of Surgery, 271*(1), 106–113.

Decker, M. (2008). Caregiving robots and ethical reflection: The perspective of interdisciplinary technology assessment. *AI & Society, 22*, 315–330.

Demerouti, E. (2022). Turn digitalization and automation to a job resource. *Applied Psychology, 71*(4), 1205–1209.

Devlieghere, J., & Roose, R. (2018). Electronic information systems: In search of responsive social work. *Journal of Social Work, 18*(6), 650–665.

Donaldson, T., & Dunfee, T. (1994). Toward a unified conception of business ethics: Integrative social contracts theory. *The Academy of Management Review, 19*(2), 252–284.

Emery, F., & Trist, E. (1978). Analytical model for sociotechnical systems. In W. Pasmore & J. Sherwood (Eds.), *Sociotechnical systems: A sourcebook* (pp. 120–133). University Associates.

Fila, M., Purl, J., & Griffeth, R. (2017). Job demands, control and support: Meta-analyzing moderator effects of gender, nationality, and occupation. *Human Resource Management Review, 27*(1), 39–60.

Friedman, B., & Kahn, P. (2003). Human values, ethics, and design. In J. Jacko & A. Sears (Eds.), *The human–computer interaction handbook* (pp. 1177–1201). Lawrence Erlbaum Associates.

Friedman, B., Kahn, P., & Borning, A. (2006). Value sensitive design and information systems. In P. Zhang & D. Galletta (Eds.), *Human–computer interaction in management information systems: Foundations* (pp. 348–372). M.E. Sharpe.

Gagné, M., Parker, S., Griffin, M., Dunlop, P., Knight, C., Klonek, F., & Parent-Rocheleau, X. (2022). Understanding and shaping the future of work with self-determination theory. *Nature Reviews Psychology, 1*, 378–392.

Gardberg, M., Heyman, F., Norbäck, P.-J., & Persson, L. (2020). Digitization-based automation and occupational dynamics. *Economics Letters, 189*, 109032.

Gillingham, P. (2018). Decision-making about the adoption of information technology in social welfare agencies: Some key considerations. *European Journal of Social Work, 21*(4), 521–529

Grote, G. (2009). *Management of uncertainty: Theory and application in the design of systems and organizations.* Springer.

Hackman, J. R., & Oldham, G. R. (1975). Development of the job diagnostic survey. *Journal of Applied Psychology, 60*(2), 159–170.

Hackman, J., & Oldham, G. (1980). *Work redesign.* Addison-Wesley.

Hansen, H. T., Lundberg, K., & Syltevik, L.J. (2018). Digitalization, street-level bureaucracy and welfare users´experiences. *Social Policy and Administration, 52*(1), 67–90.

Hasenfeld, Y. (1992). The attributes of human service organizations. In Y. Hasenfeld (Ed.), *Human services as complex organizations* (pp. 3–23). Sage.

Hasenfeld, Y. (2010). The nature of human service organizations. In Y. Hasenfeld (Ed.), *Human services as complex organizations* (pp. 9–32). Sage.

Ihde, D. (1990). *Technology and the lifeworld: From garden to earth.* Indiana University Press.

Johnsson, E., & Svensson, K. (2006). *Omedelbart samarbete – En rapport om polisers handlingsutrymme vid handräckning enligt LVU och LVM.* Växjö universitet.

Kranzberg, M. (1986). Technology and history: "Kranzberg's laws". *Technology and Culture, 27*(3), 544–560. Lunds universitet.

Lee, M. (2018). Understanding perception of algorithmic decisions: Fairness, trust, and emotion in response to algorithmic management. *Big Data & Society, 5*(1), 1–16.

McKinsey. (2017). *A future that works: Automation, employment and productivity.* McKinsey.

MYNAK. (2022). Articiciell intelligens, robotisering och arbetsmiljön. Kunskapssammanställning, *2022*(1).

Parent-Rocheleau, X., & Parker, S. (2022). Algorithms as work designers: How algorithmic management influences the design of jobs. *Human Resource Management Review, 32*(3), Article 100838.

Parker, S., & Grote, G. (2022). Automation, algorithms, and beyond: Why work design matters more than ever in a digital world. *Applied Psychology, 71*(4), 1171–1204.

Parker, S., Van den Broeck, A., & Holman, D. (2017). Work design influences: A synthesis of multilevel factors that affect the design of jobs. *Academy of Management Annals, 11*(1), 267–308.

Ranerup, A. (2020). Translating robotic process automation in social work: Aspirational changes and the role of technology. *Proceedings from the 11th Scandinavian Conference on Information Systems,* 9.

Rawls, J. (1999). *A theory of justice.* Belknap Press.

Ryan, R., & Deci, E. (2017). *Self-determination theory: Basic psychological needs in motivation, social development, and wellness.* Guilford Press.

Scaramuzzino, G. (2019). *Socialarbetare om automatisering i socialt arbete: En webbenkätundersökning.* Research Reports in Social Work, 3. Socialhögskolan.

Sharkey, A., & Sharkey, N. (2012). Granny and the robots: Ethical issues in robot care for the elderly. *Ethics and Information Technology, 14*(1), 27–40.

Stickdorn, M., & Schneider, J. (2011). *This is service design thinking: Basics, tools, cases.* Wiley Press.

SKR. (2018). Automatiserad ärendehantering. Att frigöra tid för värdeskapande arbete. Hämtad från https://skr.se/tjanster/merfranskr/rapporterochskrifter/publikationer/automatiseradarendehantering .27509.html

SKR. (2019). Automatisering av arbete. Möjlighet och utmaningar för kommuner, landsting och regioner. Hämtad från https://skr.se/tjanster/merfranskr/rapporterochskrifter/publikationer/automat iseringavarbete.27511.html

Sunt arbetliv. (2018). Låt robotar göra (delar av) jobbet. Publicerad 3 september 2018. Hämtad från https://www.suntarbetsliv.se/rapporterat/lat-robotar-gora-delar-av-jobbet/

Svensson, L. (2019b). Automatisering – till nytta eller fördärv? *Socialvetenskaplig Tidskrift, 3–4,* 341–362.

Turilli, M. (2007). Ethical protocols design. *Ethics and Information Technology, 9*(1), 49–62.

Vandemeulebroucke, T., Dierckx de Casterlé, B., & Gastmans, C. (2018). The use of care robots in aged care: A systematic review of argument-based ethics literature. *Archives of Gerontology and Geriatrics, 74,* 15–25.

Walsh, S., & Strano, M. (Eds.). (2018). *Robotic systems and autonomous platforms: Advances in materials and manufacturing.* Woodhead Publishing.

Verbeek, P.-P. (2011). *Moralizing technology: Understanding and designing the morality of things.* University of Chicago Press.

Wihlborg, E., Larsson, H., & Hedström, K. (2016). *The computer says no! – A case study on automated decision-making in public authorities.* Conference Proceedings 49th HICSS, IEEE.

Wright, S., & Shultz, A. (2018). The rising tide of artificial intelligence and business automation: Developing an ethical framework. *Business Horizons, 61*(6), 823–832.

64. Critically analyzing autonomous materialities

Mikael Wiberg

INTRODUCTION

The introduction of AI in our contemporary society seems quite straightforward at first glance. The technology is now sufficiently developed to enable several different things. Just to mention a couple of examples, we can see how AI is used for pattern recognition (see, e.g., Nagaraj and Aggarwal, 1985), security checks at airports (Zhang, 2019), intelligent agents (Woolridge and Jennings, 1995), and chatbots (Luo et al., 2019). The advancements made in AI research and development over the last few years have even reached stages where we can shift from the early visions of driverless vehicles (Brown, 2019) and autonomous drones (Raffaello, 2014)) to real-world and full-scale implementations (see, e.g., Logan, 2019), with its related challenges, including, for instance, questions concerning real-world ethics for self-driving cars (Holstein et al., 2021).

On an overarching level, AI comes with the promise of a digital technology intended to make our lives easier through "automation of interaction" (Wiberg and Stolterman, 2022), i.e., to reduce work (human labor), increase precision, and automate (human-machine) interaction (Fröhlich et al., 2020; Stolterman and Wiberg, 2022). At the current moment, we can see how this plays out in practice, from the implementation of AI to support driverless steering of our vehicles, to the making of recommendations on the web (Priyash and Sharma, 2020) AI is framed as a technology that can do several different things for us – autonomously and automatically.

AI is also gaining momentum at the current moment in terms of scale and societal impact. Beyond the early days of small-scale computer lab experiments with AI, we nowadays have full-scale implementations of this technology at a societal level (Will, 2020). As formulated by Xu (2019), we have now entered the third wave of deployment of AI in society (Xu, 2019). In a sense, this full-scale societal implementation, where AI is blended into our everyday lives as it gets fundamentally integrated into online services, social networking platforms, vehicles, smartphones, and so on is a continuation of Mark Weiser's vision of fully embedded smart computational power. As formulated by Weiser (1991) "the most profound technologies are those that disappear. They weave themselves into the fabric of everyday life until they are indistinguishable from it".

While this development sounds promising at first glance, there are also associated risks and challenges with this ongoing development. Related to this there are several calls to foreground AI – to make the invisible character of AI visible and understandable and calls for AI to be designed so that it is trustworthy, reliable, responsible, and ethically sound (see, e.g., Mariarosaria and Floridi, 2018; Luciano, 2019; Wing, 2021).

In line with these efforts, Dignum (2017) has proposed the "ART" – accountable, responsible, transparent – framework for the design of AI along human values (Dignum, 2017, p. 5). In this chapter, I use this framework for a critical study aimed at identifying potential risks associated with a particular instantiation of AI in our contemporary society. In focus here is the use of AI in autonomous buses for public transportation, and in particular, on what this shift implies for the passengers of these buses. The critical perspective applied here goes beyond "getting it right" (as in arriving at design implications for making AI "transparent", e.g., "explainable AI") or ethically sound. Complementary to such efforts is also a need to critically examine AI and its potential associated risks.

Through a critical analysis of the interplay between AI and our physical and social worlds, we can start to understand ongoing shifts in labor – from humans to machines, what these shifts might imply for us, and for how we relate to these systems. Through a critical analysis, we can learn about what it means in general re-distribution of the division of labor, responsibility, trust, and so on, and we can start to understand how these shifts might redefine human-machine relations and even computer-mediated social relations.

In terms of the object of study, I seek to understand AI, not just in context, but as fully entangled with our material and social world. Here I rely on relational perspectives on AI rooted in the interrelated frameworks of entanglement theory (Barad, 2007), materiality (Wiberg, 2018), and the theory of fourth-wave entanglement human-computer interaction (Frauenberger, 2019). Through this perspective, I seek to understand the autonomous buses and their passengers as an "autonomous materiality", where the physical, digital, and social aspects of going with and experiencing a ride with an autonomous bus are approached as a fully integrated, entangled, object of study. Accordingly, the overarching definition of alienation used in this chapter is an existential and relational definition, i.e., about being disentangled from this entanglement of our social, digital, and physical world. Accordingly, the research question for this critical examination is: *What does it mean to live with/surround ourselves with these autonomous materialities? i.e., to what extent are we entangled versus alienated in relation to these autonomous systems?*

Here I examine not only the buses, but also the interplay between the self-driving buses, the AI technology that governs the behavior of these buses, and the passengers, i.e., a socio-technical system, or – an "autonomous materiality". For the analysis of how we are entangled versus alienated, I rely on Marx´s theory of alienation (1964) to critically examine to what extent, and on which levels (namely alienation at the level of product, process, others, and self), where there is a potential risk for passengers feeling alienated in this shift to autonomous buses. Accordingly, and in order to address this socio-technical system from the passenger's viewpoint, I expand on Marx´s original definition of alienation to include existential matters to understand and analyze alienation not only on a social level but also in relation to autonomous buses as a socio-technical system. By combining Marx's four levels of alienation with the three dimensions of the ART framework I identify and contribute 12 critical aspects of such autonomous materialities to consider as we move through this shift toward the implementation of self-driving buses for public transportation as a particular form of these autonomous materialities.

The rest of this chapter is structured as follows. First, I present the background of this work, including a definition of autonomous materialities and an introduction to the theoretical framework used for the analysis. I then present the method and the empirical case, followed by an analysis in which I critically examine some potential risks through the lens of the three dimensions of the ART framework. In particular, I focus on each of these dimensions in relation to Marx´s four levels to identify critical aspects to consider as we move through this shift toward autonomous materialities. Finally, I discuss these identified aspects of being increasingly entangled with these systems versus the risks of being alienated from these systems before concluding the chapter.

BACKGROUND: THE OBJECT OF STUDY AND CENTRAL NOTIONS FOR THE ANALYSIS

In this section, I do two things. First, I discuss and define this notion of "autonomous materialities" as the central object of study. After that, I present the ART framework proposed by Dignum (2017) as a categorization of concerns to be raised about the development and use of AI-driven and autonomous materialities.

The Object of Study: Autonomous Materialities

If first taking a step back, we can see AI and the Internet of Things (IoT) as two trends of technical developments that are becoming increasingly entangled at the current moment. In short, IoT enables material forms of computing, and it enables ways of connecting and working across physical and digital materials through the use of sensors, actuators, and computational power. On the other hand, AI enables us to implement autonomous behaviors for these computationally enhanced physical objects. In short, our physical world is now being re-imagined and re-activated in this computational moment (Robles and Wiberg, 2010).

These computational objects are not just physical and "smart", but these systems can also act "on behalf of" their owners'. Accordingly, and as formulated by Ågerfalk (2020), we need to talk about artificial intelligence from the viewpoint of "agency", i.e., the capabilities of these computational machines "to act autonomously, but on behalf of humans, organizations and institutions" and how these systems are "actively participating in and shaping reality" (Beynon-Davies, 2016). In the context of this chapter, the autonomous buses in focus for my study are autonomous materialities that do not only consist of the physical and digital aspects of the bus, nor this only in combination with its intended use for public transportation, but to fully understand this autonomous system we also need to understand the behavior of these buses, what it means to go with and interact with these buses, and to understand the algorithms that govern the behavior of the bus – from route following to how it signals to its passengers and surroundings if it is about to accelerate, stop, or take other actions.

Theoretically, I take a point of departure in the "material turn" in human-computer interaction (HCI) research (Robles and Wiberg, 2010), including the development of IoT, the integration of embedded computational power in physical objects, and experiments with tangible forms of human-computer interactions. Further on, I rely on recently developed relational approaches to computational materials that seek to understand and analyze these new forms of physical/digital/social assemblages, and how we as humans relate to these technologies. This includes, for example, the materiality of interaction theory (Wiberg, 2018), fourth wave, entanglement HCI theory (Frauenberger, 2019), and so-called "more than human-centered" approaches to design (see e.g. Coulton and Lindley, 2019; Wakkary, 2021) – in short, theoretical accounts on how our physical, digital, and social worlds are increasingly entangled, and the importance of studies of emergent autonomous materialities.

The "ART" Framework: A Set of Central Notions for the Analysis

We are not only entangled in and with these autonomous materialities, but in this development, and as formulated by Dignum (2017), artificial intelligence (AI) is increasingly affecting our lives, and given this impact of AI, there is a need for ethical principles to address these societal concerns. In her paper, Dignum (2017) proposes the "ART" framework where the three aspects of accountability, responsibility, and transparency might serve these needs. Here, Dignum describes these three aspects of the ART framework as follows:

A – "**Accountability** refers to *the need to explain and justify* one's decisions and actions to its partners, users, and others with whom the system interacts. To ensure accountability, decisions must be derivable from and explained by, the decision-making algorithms used".

R – "**Responsibility** refers to *the role of people themselves*, and to the capability of AI systems to answer for one's decision and identify errors or unexpected results. As the chain of responsibility grows means are needed to link the AI system's decisions to the fair use of data and the actions of stakeholders involved in the system's decision".

T – "**Transparency** refers to *the need to describe, inspect and reproduce the mechanisms* through which AI systems make decisions and learn to adapt to their environment, and the governance of the data used or created".

With these three aspects as cornerstones of her framework, she proposes this as also working as "design principles for the development of AI systems that are sensitive to human values" (Dignum, 2017, p. 1). In this chapter, I take the ART design principles, and in particular, the three aspects of accountable, responsible, and transparent AI as points of departure to critically examine what is at risk as we move toward AI-driven autonomous materialities.

METHOD: CRITICALLY ANALYZING AUTONOMOUS MATERIALITIES

The work presented in this chapter is guided by a critical and theoretical analysis. Accordingly, the overarching method has been to make a point of departure in the ART framework, as the proposed guiding framework for A – accountable, R – responsible, and T – transparent AI, and has then used this to examine, and reflect on, the empirical case of the use of autonomous buses for public transportations to identify potential categorical risks as we shift from humans as drivers, to driverless vehicles where the passengers have very limited abilities to interact with and, in such ways, control the behavior of the bus.

As described by Wiberg and Stolterman (2022), the design and implementation of AI systems can be made at different levels, along a scale ranging from very little/no automation to full automation of interaction. Given that human interaction is fully replaced with AI, there might accordingly be a potential risk of alienation. To explore this question, I have in this study used the ART framework proposed by Dignum (2017) in combination with Marx's four levels of alienation (1964) to create a 3×4 analytical lens (ART × the four levels) to identify and examine 12 potential risks of alienation about autonomous buses as the empirical site for this analysis.

To adapt Marx's four levels of alienation from their original empirical context to the context of autonomous buses I have expanded Marx's definition of alienation to include existential alienation, as well as being alienated in relation to socio-technical systems. I then took each level of alienation as described by Marx and paraphrased it to adjust it to this empirical setting. This approach has allowed me to construct an analytical lens to critically examine potential risks of alienation in the context of autonomous buses for public transportation. When I say "risk" in this context I refer to risks associated with Marx's notion of alienation, including, for example, potential risks of being excluded, overseen, but at a distance, isolated, not being in control, and left alone.

Finally, this approach to examine this case theoretically through the use of this 3×4 matrix is also the first experiment with the development and use of one such theoretical construct to critically examine autonomous materialities. I see this 1) as an opportunity to identify a set of potential risks that can then be studied more in-depth through empirical studies, and 2) as an opportunity to theorize and make classifications of different types of risks that can surface. Finally, 3) I see opportunities with this approach to move from more general discussions on ethical AI to more clearly defined areas for further studies.

EMPIRICAL CASE: AUTONOMOUS BUSES FOR PUBLIC TRANSPORTATION

Even though the overarching method here is a critical and theoretical analysis, we still need an empirical point of reference that can serve as a backbone for this study, to give it a clear focus, illustrate its practical value, relevance, and importance, and work as a "reality check" throughout this critical analysis.

For this empirical research site, I rely on our ongoing research project where we study the development and use of autonomous buses for public transportation in a real-world context. The research site is located in Vallastaden, Sweden, where they have just recently started to introduce these buses to the public. These buses are autonomous, having no bus driver, and these buses are pre-programmed to follow a particular schedule and route around the city, including the university campus area. The buses also contain sensors so that they can adjust themselves to the surrounding traffic situation, other cars, vehicles, pedestrians, bicycles, and so on. Figure 64.1 shows a picture of one of these buses in Vallastaden.

In focus for this research project are three important shifts, including 1) a shift in *labor* (work) – from human (driver) to an autonomous vehicle (machine), 2) a shift in *trust* (driving by yourself, or driving mediated through this autonomous vehicle, and "on behalf of" someone), and 3) a shift in *responsibility* (from the active form of "driving" to the passive/passenger mode of "going with the bus").

In this project, there are two perspectives of particular interest here. On the one hand, it has to do with how the matters in focus are fundamentally *entangled*, i.e., how the bus, the sensors, the AI system, and the passengers are fundamentally inseparable as a unit and object of analysis – *autonomous materiality*. Here the focus is on issues of agency, planning/execution of plans, trust, and issues of being "implicated", enrolled, and part of "the system". On the other hand, we have the perspective of potential risks here – about cracks in this "entanglement". Here I consider issues of potential alienation, about not having a bus driver to rely on, not having a human in the center, and not having a human in control of this vehicle.

Source: ridethefuture.se.

Figure 64.1   *An autonomous bus in Vallastaden, Sweden*

Accordingly, the focus is not on the complete "blend" but on the "cracks", distrust, potential breakdowns between, for example, the social system and the technological system, and risks of being left alone rather than being entangled.

In the context of this ongoing research project, we explore these two perspectives and their related issues empirically – through video recordings, interviews, and follow-up discussions with the passengers of these buses we seek to understand what it means to be a passenger on an autonomous bus.

On a more detailed level, our focus in this project is on: 1) the behavior of the autonomous bus; 2) ways of understanding how people behave about the bus; 3) the collective level, including what "public transportation" means in this context, and the driving visions for the future; and finally, 4) in which ways the use of these buses communicates, symbolizes, and works as paradigms for future-oriented sustainable ways of running public transportations. The last point here is also about the associated risks of "greenwashing" and "tech washing" ("AI-washing") this question, that is, to stay with the focus on what this means for public transportation and those affected by it, rather than just finding a context suitable for trying out new AI systems, or selecting this context because it can illustrate the use of new technologies to address issues of sustainability.

THEORY: MARX'S FOUR LEVELS OF ALIENATION

The autonomous buses in Vallastaden have been in service for a couple of years now, and lots of people are getting used to this new form of public transportation. But beyond the everyday use of these buses, we also need to understand how this shift to autonomous vehicles might affect people, not least those who are using these buses. To critically examine this empirical context from this viewpoint, I turn to critical studies of technologies, critical theory, and in particular critical design theory in the area of human-computer interaction (Bardzell and Bardzell, 2013). More specifically, and to get to a close-up examination of the relationship between these autonomous buses and their passengers I will now turn to Marx's "four levels of alienation" (1964). In his article "Economic and Philosophic Manuscripts of 1844", Marx (1964) presented the theory of Alienation in which he argued that workers become estranged from their humanity as a consequence of "*living in* a society in which capitalism is a mode of production".

In going through his theory, I will cover the following sections and paraphrase each part of it, as to adjust it to the object of study for this particular examination. Accordingly, I will here paraphrase this initial quote and say that we are "*living in* an AI-driven society" or that we are "*entangled with* these autonomous materialities".

The Theory of Alienation suggests that an individual loses the ability to determine his or her own life and destiny, as well as the capacity to direct actions and characters of these actions, define relationships with other people, and own those items produced by his or her labor. A capitalist society does this through "the mechanization of an individual". I here expand on this definition of alienation to allow for an examination of how passengers with be alienated in relation to autonomous buses. Accordingly, I add a socio-technical and existential perspective here, where one might also be alienated in relation to technology, and aspects of not being in control or incapable of affecting a situation. This expanded view on alienation goes hand-in-hand with Ågerfalk´s (2020) discussion on AI and agency, and recent theories on materiality that pinpoint socio-technical entanglements. At stake here is the risk of feeling disentangled from the technology (out of control) or being implicated (i.e., that the technology just assumes, makes predictions, or takes decisions without involving the human). According to Marx (1964), there are "four levels of alienation", which include alienation from 1) the product of labor, 2) the process of labor, 3) others, and 4) self. Here I present each level, together with an attempt to paraphrase each level in relation to this extended definition to make this framework applicable to the critical analysis of autonomous materialities.

(1) The Product of Labor

According to Marx, the design and development of a production rest not in the hands of a worker but within the decisions of the capitalists. "A worker does not have control over what he or she intends to produce or the specifications of his or her product".

To paraphrase this, we can say that "The passenger on these buses does not have control over how he or she intends to interact with the autonomous bus [the product]".

(2) The Process of Labor

Marx continues by saying that the production of goods and services "is repetitive and mechanical that offers little to no psychological satisfaction to the worker".

Here, a paraphrase of this would be to say that "The user experience from going with these buses is repetitive and mechanical". But, it can get even worse. If not even being considered in the first place, i.e., the user experience is not even accounted for, and not considered relevant in the first place. If this is the case, it can cause a related problem which Greenfield (2006) calls "withdrawal behavior", i.e., a state caused by a repetitive surrounding that leads to a counter-reaction where we stop caring about what surrounds us, and we turn inwards about others and our surrounding, i.e., a relational alienation.

(3) Others

For the third level, Marx describes how the reduction of labor to a mere market commodity creates the so-called labor market "in which a worker competes against another worker".

To paraphrase this, one might say "in which a passenger is co-located while being isolated from other passengers" or to say that the shift of labor from human to machine creates a situation where "no interaction or coordination with others is necessary" (the opposite to Marx´s original theory, but with the same effect).

(4) Self

Finally, Marx describes "how an individual loses identity and the opportunity for self-development as he or she is forced to sell his or her labor-power as a market commodity".

To paraphrase this requires a shift in perspective. Instead of actively driving a car, the passenger of a self-driving car, or autonomous bus, is rendered as an inactive human, a passenger among other passengers. Here the paraphrase would be about "the individual loses the opportunity to drive and decide where to go as he or she is forced to let go of active driving, and turn him-/herself into a passenger". This shift is not only about losses of identity, and lost opportunity, but also about lost control and lost freedom of choice (about when and where to go, for how long, and at what pace).

Of course, Marx's theory was about industrialization, and how the organization of work in factories alienated the workers from the work. But are we moving through similar processes now? Are there similar or new forms of dependencies, interdependencies, and entanglements at play? The introduction of factories implied a major shift, and in similar ways, we can see how the introduction of AI in society implies a shift at similar scales in how it redefines how we relate to technology, to each other, to ourselves, and the society at large. Accordingly, I would argue, that there is a need to critically analyze these entanglements, these autonomous materialities.

ANALYSIS: ALONG WITH THE 3×4 ANALYTICAL LENS

For this analysis, I combine the three dimensions of the "ART" framework with the four levels of alienation. Accordingly, I get something of a 3×4 matrix or analytical lens that serves the purpose of identifying potential risks along Dignum´s (2017) three dimensions of accountable, responsible, and transparent AI, and Marx´s (1964) four levels of alienation. With this 3×4 matrix as my analytical lens, I examine potential risks at the intersections, i.e., along 12 dimensions. It should be said here that each of these 12 identified dimensions will be empirically followed up and studied in more detail at later stages in this ongoing research project, with the autonomous buses in use, and from the viewpoint of how the passengers experience these autonomous vehicles.

Across the following three sections I now critically examine the autonomous materiality in focus here, i.e., the potential risks the passengers of these autonomous buses are confronted with from the viewpoint of Marx´s four levels of alienation.

A: A Potentially Risky Shift in Accountability

According to Dignum (2017), "accountability refers to the need to explain and justify". If we take this dimension of the ART framework about the four levels of alienation, we can see how this foreground a set of potential risks when the capability to explain and justify is limited.

Here we can see how there is a potentially risky shift in *accountability* concerning 1) *The product*. An autonomous bus as an autonomous physical/digital product is different from a traditional vehicle with a driver, i.e., it is a technical object rather than a socio-technical object. Accordingly, to make this product accountable, so that it can "explain and justify" its actions, and through such terms be trusted, is a complex matter. Researchers and developers are looking into the design of "explainable AI" to enable AI to explain its actions and underlying decision model, but there are also issues more related to its use, including issues of trust, interpretation, and context-sensitive decisions, which lead to 2) *The process*. Risks are here associated with trusting "self-driving" as an accountable *process*. If there is no bus driver in place to see, interact with, and build trust in relation to, this process needs to be established between the passenger and the self-driving bus. This leads to 3) *Others – Who´s held accountable here?* If removing the bus driver from the equation, as we make the shift to autonomous buses, then there is no one else who can explain and justify, no one who can be asked, and no one else to rely on. And finally, 4) *Self – Who am I in this context?* If there is no one in charge, and you alone cannot control the situation, nor interfere, interact, or in other ways affect the situation, then there is a potential risk of being reduced to a "token" in this larger system. As seen here, there are several potential risks of alienation associated with this dimension of autonomous systems.

R: A Potentially Risky Shift in Responsibility

According to Dignum (2017), "responsibility refers to the role of people themselves". If we take this dimension of the ART framework about the four levels of alienation, we can see how this foregrounds some potential risks when the responsibility of humans is shifted to machines.

Here we can see how there is a potentially risky shift in *responsibility* about: 1) *The product* – Dignum (2017) links the issue of responsibility to people, and similarly Frankl (1987) pinpoints that responsibility is bound to individuals, not artifacts. Accordingly, any shift in responsibility from a human to an autonomous bus is potentially risky. If applied, there is a risk of alienation because of course, "who is in control?", 2) *The process – Where are we going?* In shifting from humans to machines there is no person responsible for when and where to go. This is a shift from active forms of driving to schedules and automated route following. The bus leaves "on time", bound for a particular destination – no matter what. 3) *Others – from fellow road users to networks of sensors*. When people are removed then no person is engaged in the process, no one is responsible on board the bus, which again might cause a feeling of being alienated, and finally, 4) *Self – from self-orientation to being left alone with an app*. There is a risk of being alienated when not just being reduced to a "token" in the system, but also when being left alone. On the one hand, "empowered" with a mobile "public transportation" app, but on the other hand, isolated in terms of not being able to control or in other ways engage.

T: A Potentially Risky Shift in Transparency

Finally, Dignum (2017) suggests that "transparency refers to the need to describe, inspect and reproduce the mechanisms through which AI systems make decisions". If we take this dimension of the ART framework about the four levels of alienation, we can see how this foregrounds some potential risks when the ability to describe, inspect and reproduce these mechanisms is limited.

Here we can see how there is a potentially risky shift in *transparency* about 1) *The product*. For these autonomous systems, the ability to "describe, inspect and reproduce" is restrained to affordance-mediated trust in the product, i.e., to u*nderstand the product through its affordances*, i.e., *perceived functionality*, 2) *The process* – similarly, its mechanisms need to be understood through "behavior mediated trust", i.e., how the autonomous bus work, behaves, and operate. 3) *Others* – how well it behaves and performs about others. In short, if it is impossible to interfere with how the bus operates in relation to others, there is a risk of alienation if not being part of this computational process, while at the same time being entangled with the system, and finally, 4) *Self* – a matter of the feeling of being safe, on-time, and getting there. If it is not possible to act, but instead just a matter of continuing the ride until the bus stops or arrives at its final destination and no options for understanding and affecting the mechanisms at play, then again there are risks of alienation along this dimension of transparency.

CONCLUDING DISCUSSION

In this chapter, I have taken a point of departure in the ongoing AI-fication of our society. On a particular level, I have examined how AI comes with a promise of reducing work (human labor) and automating interaction, and how this societal "turn to AI" also implies certain risks of alienation for the human in relation to these highly automated socio-technical systems. Through a critical analysis of autonomous buses used for public transportation, and in particular, through the use of an analytical lens where the ART framework is combined with Marx´s four levels of alienation, I have identified 12 potentially critical aspects to consider in this shift toward such autonomous materialities.

The analysis pinpoints how there are potential risks for alienation across all three dimensions of the ART framework and at all four stages. This calls for a new sensibility when it comes to the further AI-fication of our contemporary society. AI can be many good things for us, but as we shift from human labor to intelligent machines that can do things for us, we should always remember that in this transition, and strive to reduce work, make processes smoother, and reduce our needs to interact, there are also potential risks associated with this "turn to AI". This chapter has identified 12 such potential risks, but the overarching conclusion is also that it is about *potential risks*, and we should always consider this risk/benefit balance.

We design things for us, but these things might also alienate us from the things we care about, the things we want to be actively engaged in. While lots of existing research are now focused on how we are increasingly entangled with technology, this analysis has also pointed at "cracks" in these entanglements, and it has pointed at how we are not only increasingly entangled but how we also run the risk of being disentangled, isolated, and alienated in this transition to an AI-driven society. Critical studies can here be an important tool and perspective for us to spark discussions and reflections about where we are going, where we want to go, and where technology is taking us – right now and in the future.

REFERENCES

Ågerfalk, P. J. "Artificial intelligence as digital agency." *European Journal of Information Systems* 29.1 (2020): 1–8.

Barad, Karen. *Meeting the Universe Halfway*. Duke University Press, 2007.

Bardzell, Jeffrey, and Bardzell, Shaowen. "What is" critical" about critical design?" Proceedings of the SIGCHI conference on human factors in computing systems, 2013.

Beynon-Davies, P. "Instituting facts: Data structures and institutional order." *Information and Organization* 26.1–2 (2016): 28–44.

Braun, Robert. "Autonomous vehicles: From science fiction to sustainable future." In *Mobilities, Literature, Culture*. Palgrave Macmillan, Cham, 2019, pp. 259–280.

Coulton, P., and Lindley, J. G. "More-than-human-centred design: Considering other things." *The Design Journal* 22.4 (2019): 463–481.

D'Andrea, Raffaello. "Guest Editorial Can Drones Deliver?" *IEEE Transactions on Automation Science and Engineering* 11.3 (2014): 647–648.

Dignum, Virginia. "Responsible artificial intelligence: Designing AI for human values." (2017).

Frankl, Viktor E. *Logotherapie und Existenzanalyse*. Piper Munich, 1987.

Frauenberger, Christopher. "Entanglement HCI the next wave?" *ACM Transactions on Computer-Human Interaction (TOCHI)* 27.1 (2019): 1–27.

Fröhlich, P., Baldauf, M., Meneweger, T. et al. "Everyday automation experience: A research agenda." *Personal and Ubiquitous Computing* 24 (2020): 725–734.

Greenfield, A. *Everyware – The dawning age of ubiquitous computing*. New Riders, 2006.

Holstein, Tobias, Dodig-Crnkovic, Gordana, and Pelliccione, Patrizio. "Steps toward real-world ethics for self-driving cars: Beyond the trolley problem." In *Machine Law, Ethics, and Morality in the Age of Artificial Intelligence*. IGI Global, 2021, pp. 85–107.

Kugler, Logan. "Real-world applications for drones." *Communications of the ACM* 62.11 (2019): 19–21.

Luciano, Floridi. "Establishing the rules for building trustworthy AI." *Nature Machine Intelligence* 1.6 (2019): 261–262.

Luo, X., Tong, S., Fang, Z., & Qu, Z. (2019). Machines versus humans: The impact of AI chatbot disclosure on customer purchases.

Marx, Karl. Economic and philosophic manuscripts of 1844, 1964.

Nandhakumar, Nagaraj, and Aggarwal, Jake K. "The artificial intelligence approach to pattern recognition—a perspective and an overview." *Pattern Recognition* 18.6 (1985): 383–389.

Robles, E., and Wiberg, M. "Texturing the 'material turn' in interaction design." In *Proceedings of the 4th International Conference on Tangible and Embodied Interaction*. ACM Press, 2010, pp. 137–144.

Slocombe, Will. "Artificial intelligence, society, and control." In *AI Narratives: A History of Imaginative Thinking about Intelligent Machines*, 2020, p. 213.

Stolterman, E., and Wiberg, M. "User experience (UX) meets artificial intelligence (AI) - designing engaging user experiences through 'automation of interaction'." CHI2022, USA, 2022.

Taddeo, Mariarosaria, and Floridi, Luciano. "How AI can be a force for good." *Science* 361.6404 (2018): 751–752.

Verma, Priyash, and Sharma, Shilpi. "Artificial intelligence-based recommendation system." In *2020 2nd International Conference on Advances in Computing, Communication Control and Networking (ICACCCN)*. IEEE, 2020.

Wakkary, R. *Things We Could Design: For More Than Human-Centered Worlds*. MIT Press, 2021.

Wei, Xu. "Toward human-centered AI: A perspective from human-computer interaction." *Interactions* 26.4 (July-August 2019): 42–46.

Weiser, Mark. "The computer for the 21st century." *Scientific American* 265.3 (1991): 94–105.

Wiberg, Mikael. *The Materiality of Interaction: Notes on the Materials of Interaction Design*. MIT Press, 2018.

Wooldridge, Michael, and Nicholas R. Jennings. "Intelligent agents: Theory and practice." *The Knowledge Engineering Review* 10.2 (1995): 115–152.

Wing, Jeannette M. "Trustworthy AI." *Communications of the ACM* 64.10 (2021): 64–71.

Zhang, Zhou. "Technologies raise the effectiveness of airport security control." In *2019 IEEE 1st International Conference on Civil Aviation Safety and Information Technology*. IEEE, 2019.

65. Exploring critical dichotomies of AI and the Rule of Law

Markus Naarttijärvi

THE RULE OF LAW CHALLENGE OF AI

The Rule of Law is a foundational concept of the modern democratic state. It contains key legal principles to reduce arbitrariness in the exercise of public power, and in doing so promotes legal certainty and individual autonomy, while simultaneously protecting against despotism (Krygier, 2009, p. 51; Meierhenrich, 2021, p. 53; Sajó & Uitz, 2017, p. 315). It is also a concept under challenge from the technological developments of AI and its use in the exercise of public power. When the well-known constitutional research blog *Verfassungsblog* recently arranged a special debate on "The Rule of Law versus the Rule of the Algorithm" the editors were taken by surprise by the contributions from legal experts.

> When we chose the title of this symposium, we thought it might be controversial. We expected that at least some of the authors would argue that algorithmic threats to the Rule of Law were solvable, or that responsibly-implemented algorithms could even help the delivery of justice. None of the experts did. (Meyer-Resende & Straub, 2022)

Indeed, for several years, there have been warning calls from researchers who identify specific, as well as structural and systematic challenges to the Rule of Law raised by the use of AI by public authorities either to automate decisions or form the basis for profiling, risk assessments, or decision support tools. Bayamlıoğlu and Leenes (2018) talk about the "demise of law as a moral enterprise" due to data-driven models implementing rules or legal frameworks, with an accompanying erosion of human autonomy and the values underpinning legal reasoning since the Enlightenment losing ground to probabilistic reasoning and formalization of reasoning. Suksi points to how

> the (unintended or intended) consequence of the on-going development of AI is that algorithms will increasingly take over functions not only in the private sector, but also within public authorities, with the risk of turning the general system of the rule of law into a rule of algorithm. (Suksi, 2021)

Van den Hoven raises the issue of hermeneutical injustice which may occur as individuals are deprived of the conceptual and interpretive tools needed to make sense of their experiences and interactions with society. She connects this to the Rule of Law through the right of contestation and the ability to give an account of yourself, finding that "[a]t its most extreme, the algorithmic system can render the individual disabled as a contester and thereby threaten their legal protection under the rule of law" (van den Hoven, 2021). Questions have been raised about "whether law, and the rule of law, can survive a shift from written texts to digital rules as the fundamental technology of the law" (Kennedy, 2020, p. 229).

These challenges have of course not gone unnoticed in the wider societal discussions of AI. The proposed EU AI regulation ("AI Act") also highlights how the application of AI in the "administration of justice and democratic processes should be classified as high-risk, considering their potentially significant impact on democracy, rule of law, individual freedoms as well as the right to an effective remedy and to a fair trial" (Proposal for a Regulation of the European Parliament and of the Council laying down harmonized rules on artificial intelligence (Artificial Intelligence Act) and amending certain union legislative acts, 2021). In a similar vein, the EU High Level Expert Group has repeatedly stressed the need to take the Rule of Law into account in judging the risks of AI applications, and the need to safeguard the Rule of Law in the deployment of AI-supported public services (EU High Level Expert Group on AI (AI HLEG), 2019).

Part of the problem is that understanding exactly *when* and *how* the rule of law is affected by the continued deployment of AI in a variety of societal settings can be difficult. The Rule of Law is a multidimensional and contested concept (Waldron, 2021), which AI – another vague concept – can challenge in different ways depending on the underlying values and legal principles at stake in each legal context, the design and character of the AI system, and the institutional and procedural environment where it is implemented. To fully capture specific Rule of Law issues surrounding AI implementations, the concept needs to be operationalized for the specific legal, societal, and organizational context where that implementation is taking place, just as the AI system needs to be understood not as a vague umbrella concept, but as a system designed and implemented in a context, for a purpose, based on certain preconceptions about how that purpose can best be reached.

Applying a critical approach to AI in the legal context will, however, still benefit from a process of exploring underlying assumptions that are more structural in character. In this chapter, I will explore certain dichotomies of AI and the Rule of Law. I believe this dichotomic approach can assist in bringing to the surface, and critically examine, assumptions underpinning both concepts. As Heidegger (1977, p. 4) holds, technology is not neutral, and approaching it as neutral makes us blind to its essence and delivers us over to it in the worst possible way. Nor is it simply a means to an end, "[f]or to posit ends and procure and utilize the means to them is a human activity" (Heidegger, 1977, p. 4). We should, in other words, treat AI not only as a technology with specific features and issues but as a set of chosen ends and means, which themselves account for both human assumptions and preconceptions that can be subject to critical examination. The basis for this critical approach will be sought not in specific components of the Rule of Law, but through a teleological approach (Krygier, 2012), asking essentially "what's the point" of the Rule of Law and how can it be reached.

In this chapter, I will explore four critical dichotomies in a particular facet of AI implementation and a specific context; the use of AI in automated decision-making or decision support systems, what Hildebrandt (2020) has labelled *code-driven law*, and I will specifically take on a setting where power is exercised *by the state* in some capacity. This setting is where Rule of Law concerns will be most relevant, but also most clearly articulated. As for the term "AI", which is used and misused in so many contexts that it has been described as more of an ideology than a technology (Lanier, 2022), I will focus mainly here on the use of machine learning for predictive and risk-assessment purposes, but as we will see, some aspects of these dichotomies will be rather agnostic to the specific technology used. First, however, we need to briefly discuss the Rule of Law.

DELINEATING THE RULE OF LAW: SKETCHING THE OUTLINES OF A NEBULOUS CONCEPT

It is not possible here to do justice to the ages of discussions surrounding the Rule of Law as we now understand it, a concept that can arguably be traced back to Plato (Schofield, 2016; Venice Commission, 2011, para. 7). However, there are certain general points of departure we can keep in mind in trying to conceptualize it in this context of AI and code-driven law. First, while differences have long existed between more continental European approaches under the umbrella of the *Rechtsstaat* on the one hand and more Common Law approaches on the other, the Rule of Law has to some extent coalesced into a more unified concept in the last decade (Venice Commission, 2011, para. 35). This current understanding of the Rule of Law is driven by expectations on both the quality and form of legal rules and the institutional protection of the Rule of Law through an independent judiciary and other safeguards. Through its connection with constitutionalism, the Rule of Law is intended to ensure that governing takes place not only *through* law, but *under* the law, and within the limits set by the constitution.

As such, the prime component of the Rule of Law is legality, meaning that government actions should have a clear and foreseeable basis in law. This clarity in turn implicitly connects government actions, through authorizing legal rules, to the deliberations and democratic decision-making underpinning parliamentary decision-making (Naarttijärvi, 2019). Through the requirements of equality and non-discrimination, as well as the protection of human rights, the Rule of Law has developed into a "thicker" concept with more explicit connections to maintaining not just autonomy, but human dignity (Bingham, 2011, p. 67; Venice Commission, 2011, sec. 41).

Arguably, the most established current definition of the Rule of Law is provided by the Council of Europe Commission on Democracy Through Law (the Venice Commission). This is a consulting body of constitutional experts advising on constitutional reforms and making evaluations on the Rule of Law in states around the world. Their definition of the concept of the Rule of Law is an attempt at overcoming the previously mentioned conceptual differences in different legal traditions. It involved expressing the core components of the Rule of Law in a way that could be operationalized in a variety of different legal settings. The Venice Commission definition drew from legal history, legal philosophical foundations, and best practices, and in a field of conceptional confusion provided a sought-after point of reference for both courts of law, governments, and researchers. As with any attempt at defining contested concepts, the Venice Commission definition is not without critics (Iancu, 2019), but it has become influential in the case law of the European Court of Justice and among European Union institutions (see Clayton, 2019). The Venice Commission definition includes the following elements (Venice Commission, 2011, para. 41):

(1) Legality, including a transparent, accountable and democratic process for enacting law;
(2) Legal certainty;
(3) Prohibition of arbitrariness;
(4) Access to justice before independent and impartial courts, including judicial review of administrative acts;
(5) Respect for human rights;
(6) Non-discrimination and equality before the law.

Each of these elements, however, contains a multitude of legal rules, principles, and definitional discussions, as illustrated by component number five "respect for human rights", which contains within it an entire field of legal study. These components are, however, illustrative of the dual dimension of forcing power to be expressed through legal norms in a clear and foreseeable way, while arming individuals with rights and procedures to ensure the proper exercise of that power in accordance with legal limits. In the following, rather than focusing on the specific components of the Rule of Law, I will instead focus on a selection of legal meta-values existing at the core of the concept of the Rule of Law. These will be drawn from the theoretical literature surrounding the Rule of Law and are primarily connected to the previously mentioned functions of the Rule of Law as a concept intended to maintain individual autonomy, human dignity, and democracy by limiting arbitrariness in the exercise of power (Waldron, 2020).

RULE OF LAW AS A CRITICAL PERSPECTIVE: PERILS AND POSSIBILITIES

Adopting the Rule of Law as a critical lens may, to legal academics, invoke a certain sense of irony, as the Critical Legal Studies movement has directed much of their critique *against* the Rule of Law as a concept, viewing it as enabling a suspicious cementation of power relationships under the guise of objectivity and reason (Boyle, 1992; Wacks, 2020, pp. 344–350). At the core of this critique lies the insight that the law can be indeterminate, and thus open to ideological capture. Of course, law as such is political power (as expressed through parliamentary decisions) temporarily "frozen" in its legal form. The Critical Legal Studies movement however held that the *exercise* of law can be politically captured as well through the ideological surrounding of the context where the Rule of Law is applied. The supposed neutrality of the Rule of Law is then reduced to protection of the vested interests of the status quo. The counterargument is that a functioning Rule of Law, through the requirement of legality, may still contribute to bringing whatever suspicious or dodgy goals the powers at be may promote into the light, and subject them to contestation. As Tushnet (2021) argues, whether the critique of the Critical Legal Studies movement is correct or not in claiming the Rule of Law as an ideological project, the culture of justification that the Rule of Law helps maintain must still be intrinsically better than an order based on pure coercion. Whatever weaknesses the Rule of Law holds – both as a concept and ideal or as a practical mechanism – it does at least contribute towards emancipatory ideals. Like democracy, it may be far from perfect, but it's the best we've got. Finally, as far as legal values go, there are also a few others that are as foundational as the Rule of Law. It has been described by Tuori to exist on the deepest levels of the law, thus forming a basis on which to base critical evaluations of surface-level expressions of the law – such as specific statutes or case law (Tuori, 2002). Here, I will turn this critical potential not towards surface-level rules or regulations, but rather towards the technologies and assumptions mediating these surface-level expressions of the law.

FOUR CRITICAL DICHOTOMIES OF AI AND THE RULE OF LAW

Introduction

In the following, I will explore four critical dichotomies of the relationship between AI and the Rule of Law. It is important to note that these are by no means exhaustive, but rather selected as an attempt to illustrate the analytical value they may provide in explaining the interactions between Rule of Law values and the use of AI in this setting.

Justification/Coercion

The success of the Rule of Law as an umbrella of principles in most democratic states can be traced to how it has paved the way for a transition from *coercion* to *justification* as a foundation for public power. As Tushnet (2021, pp. 338–339) explains, those adversely affected by power need a reason to comply or accede, that reason can be fear or coercion, but such an approach is ineffective at scale. The Rule of Law provides part of a reason to accede without coercion by ensuring that policies are not arbitrary, but rather based on a *culture of justification*. This becomes visible under the Rule of Law umbrella through principles such as generality, foreseeability, and non-retroactivity of the law, which allows citizens to know what the law requires and plan accordingly, thus maximizing their freedom and autonomy within the limits of the law (Habermas, 1996, p. 496; Raz, 2009, p. 222). The culture of justification requires the state to be able to answer a fundamental question raised by those adversely affected by power, namely "why is this law for me?" (Dyzenhaus, 2021, p. 417). This implies that the state must be able to provide justifications "based on legal reasons which make sense to subjects of their subjections" (Dyzenhaus, 2021, p. 419).

The justification required will target both procedural and substantive aspects of the exercise of power. In the operation of public law within administrative authorities, justification tends to form a chain flowing from the constitution. A measure or decision needs to be based on legal powers conferred from the constitution to parliament, through law from parliament to public authorities, with decision-making then delegated through the public authority down to first-line administrators (see Matteucci, 2021, p. 109). This procedural justification thus speaks to *who* can legitimately exercise *what* power based on *which* authorization. Statutory rules surrounding the use of AI in the exercise of power thus need to comply with this chain of authorization, which further requires openness about its application and explicit authorization (Brownsword, 2016, p. 138). Through the logic of the Rule of Law and its component of legality, it follows that power-conferring rules will by default confer power to a human being, which cannot be delegated to a machine unless a specific rule allows it (Matteucci, 2021, p. 121).

A second tier of justification focuses on the specific legal rules and principles operating in the context of a measure or decision and the circumstances of the case at hand. This means that an individual subject to a decision or a measure should be informed about not only why the decision-maker is entitled to decide, but how the specific rules governing the decision have been interpreted and applied in the specific case, taking into account individual circumstances. This justification is key not only to discern what norms have been applied – automated systems can quite handily point out relevant rules – but rather why and how those rules are relevant, and how legal principles and circumstances have been taken into account. As the Court of Justice of the European Union recently held in a case relating to the algorithmic profiling of airline passengers under the PNR directive:

> given the opacity which characterises the way in which artificial intelligence technology works, it might be impossible to understand the reason why a given program arrived at a positive match. In those circumstances, use of such technology may deprive the data subjects also of their right to an effective judicial remedy [...], in particular in order to challenge the non-discriminatory nature of the results obtained. (*Ligue des droits humains ASBL v Conseil des ministres*, 2022, p. 195)

This connection between justification and contestation by the individual concerned (or through other institutional safeguards), actualizes a third mode of justification whereby the connection between the measure and its legal basis needs to be defended in relation to independent actors (such as courts) external to the initial decision. Both the initial and secondary justification will in such a review need to fit both the measure and its legal basis within the limits expressed in the constitution through, for example, fundamental rights. Through this third mode of justification, the law also gains dynamism by allowing the evolutive interpretation of statutory law in light of new situations, knowledge, or interests (Bayamlıoğlu & Leenes, 2018, p. 305). As Hildebrandt (2020) points out, the open texture of legal language creates a normativity of contestability, but more so, as "interpretation is construction rather than description and thus requires giving reasons for interpreting a legal norm in one way rather than another". Importantly, the closure of that interpretation under the Rule of Law is performed by independent courts. Justification and contestation thus activate the institutional arrangements whereby the Rule of Law, through the constitution, disperses power over a number of actors to enact limits to the exercise of public power and maintain a balance between values, actors, and levels (cf. Derlén, 2020; Katyal, 2022).

The Rule of Law also contains a positive aspect – the realization of values such as "dignity, integrity, and moral equality of persons and groups" (Selznick, 2017, p. 26). This brings us to how AI implemented in settings of predicting and assessing future risks can subvert that autonomy by causing the normative exercise of power to revert to approaches relying less on justification and more on manipulation or coercion. Research into algorithmic regulation has begun problematizing the extent to which this new mode of regulation can make noncompliance impossible (Hildebrandt, 2016, p. 226). This type of coercion is not based on fear or force, but rather compliance through the engineering of conformity. The normative equivalent of a speed bump (cf. Hildebrandt, 2010), this engineering is built into the architecture of our relationship with the state (Lessig, 2006), mediating our interactions. This type of enforcement largely takes place behind the scenes, but surfaces and becomes visible only in specific interactions, like the biometric scan at the border crossing or the personalized predictive assessment of your application of social benefits. The application of nudging or "hypernudging" practices under the auspices of implied consent (Yeung, 2017) may become equally manipulative in the setting of public administration, while the associated issues with autonomy and equality and the undermining of our moral and political commons are increased (Yeung, 2019). This challenges the very nature of what legality as a component of the Rule of Law tries to uphold.

> The ends of law are justice, legal certainty and purposiveness. A world focused on regulating, influencing, or even enforcing behaviours has little to do with legal normativity. If one cannot disobey a law it is not law but discipline, as Hegel suggested. (Hildebrandt, 2016, p. 226)

Observing the tendency of algorithmic exercises of power to escape legal constraints, McQuillan (2015) adopts the term *algorithmic states of exception*. He connects algorithmic power to how Agamben (2005) conceptualize states of exception as actions that do not rely on a formal external framework for justification. These actions operate outside of the legal order, constituting a suspension of the Rule of Law, while still having the "force-of" law. This highlights the centrality of justification to the legal enterprise as such. The challenge of justification becomes even clearer if we consider a second dichotomy, that between justification and explanation.

Justification of Subsumption/Explanation of Correlation

A common thread in both critical studies of AI and research into AI development is the attempt to solve the issue of *explainability*. The development of "explainable AI" or XAI has been seen as a major developmental hurdle to further the application of AI based on deep learning networks in a variety of settings. The challenges of explainability in relation to these opaquer methods of machine learning appear significant, as

> [d]espite its rapid growth, explainable artificial intelligence is still not a mature and well-established field, often suffering from a lack of formality and not well agreed upon definitions. Consequently, although a great number of machine learning interpretability techniques and studies have been developed in academia, they rarely form a substantial part of machine learning workflows and pipelines. (Linardatos et al., 2020)

To some extent, XAI research separates the concept of explainability and that of justification, with developments towards the latter that aim to justify the result. However, the delineation between explanation and justification in the XAI setting can be somewhat fluid (Henin & Le Métayer, 2021), where justification have been described as taking aim at explaining why a decision is *good*, but not necessarily providing the explanation of the process of reaching the decision (Biran & McKeown, 2017). This type of justification does not "justify in a strict, argumentative or even logical sense, rather it aims at building trust on the user's side and thereby at facilitating the widespread use of DLNs" (Schubbach, 2021, p. 23). The definition of a *good decision* also tends to differ between contexts, with machine learning models aiming at meeting a specific level of predictive power, essentially "what works", rather than basing decisions on specific models developed by humans (Vestby & Vestby, 2019, p. 48). Certain limits to explainability flow specifically from this approach derived of theory or structural models (cf. Burrell, 2016, p. 10). As put by Berk and Bleich in the context of algorithmic crime forecasting, the point is to employ algorithms that maximize an empirical goal, such as forecasting accuracy, as there is no model, concerns about whether the model is correct are irrelevant as the performance of the algorithm is key. "[I]f other things equal, shoe size is a useful predictor of recidivism, then it can be included as a predictor. Why shoe size matters is immaterial" (Berk & Bleich, 2013; see also Hälterlein, 2021). However, this line of argument, that there is no theory involved – only correlations in the data, has been challenged by Numerico (2019, pp. 157–158), who instead argues that

> [t]he theory is opaque and invisible, because it is embedded in the software chosen to program the machine learning tools that are used to make sense of Big Data under consideration. But the theory is there. It is an invisible layer that is implied by the algorithms decision strategies, chosen, maybe even unconsciously, by the programmers.

Numerico shines a well-needed light on the social dimension of AI development and implementation. To the extent these theories can be revealed and articulated, they are likely to differ from the theories underpinning legal justification, which is based on inherent legal theories on legitimate sources of law (e.g. Hart, 2012, pp. 100–110), their interpretation (e.g. Dworkin, 2010, pp. 225–276), legal discourse (e.g. Alexy, 2010, pp. 292–295), justifiability in relation to legal principles or values such as necessity and proportionality (e.g. Alexy, 2002), and in some cases, even moral considerations (Radbruch, 1946).

This highlights how explainability is not justification in any legal sense even though it may be a step in the right direction, and how even the output of a perfectly explainable algorithm does not necessarily imply a legally justified result. While an algorithm employing DLN could identify a statistically relevant correlation given a specific set of data between your shoe size and your risk of recidivism, basing a legal decision on that same correlation is not justifiable unless it can also be subsumed and justified under legal rules making the result normatively acceptable (Bayamlıoğlu & Leenes, 2018, p. 311). Justification further necessitates that the intended decision – while correct under the rules in force – is filtered through a range of legal principles that serves to check for countervailing legal interests that may mediate what the legally correct decision is. Full legal justification would require an explanation as to how a specific correlation was identified, why it is warranted to take into account given the legal rules surrounding decision-making, and if/how relevant legal principles have been taken into account, some of which, like proportionality in fundamental rights contexts, may require a contextual analysis of the individual consequences of the intended decision as a whole (Enqvist & Naarttijärvi, 2022).

Schubbach suggests that since the output of a DLN is "not to be explained as the result of a mechanical and verifiable rule-based calculation", it is analogous to human judgement we simply have to trust (Schubbach, 2021). The comparison to human decision-making is sometimes repeated in the literature surrounding machine learning, with the argument sometimes being made that human decision-making can be inscrutable too, sometimes even more so as we can't control the training data (Vestby & Vestby, 2019). While the analogy to human decision-making may imply that the use of AI for decision-making would be at least no worse than human decisions, this argument fails to convince from a Rule of Law perspective. The Rule of Law is incompatible with a system based on pure trust in decision-makers. Rather, it aims at holding power to account and through the culture of justification maintains that the exercise of power is subject to control by other institutions and by allowing a review of decisions and rules under the constitution. This is why the Rule of Law includes not just principles aimed at the exercise of power as such, but also the institutional setting of that power and the means to control it through access to justice before independent and impartial courts, including judicial review of administrative acts (Venice Commission, 2011, para. 41). Discussions regarding trusting AI systems becomes even more paradoxical considering that the systems we are supposed to trust are often designed to exchange trust in us for control of us through big data analytics with an associated need for further data and surveillance (see Numerico, 2019, p. 163). Explainable AI still serves an important role in understanding and checking for the proper functioning of AI systems, it is, however, no panacea, and we should be wary of mistaking explanation for justification.

It makes sense then that we should demand more from machines than we do from humans. Not only are we on a psychological level, as Carabantes (2020, p. 317) notes, adapted through evolution to make sense of other humans, but through the Rule of Law, we have developed a framework of legal governance specifically intended to counter the effects of human mistakes, biases, abuse, and ambitions of control. While challenges relating to human decision-making remain, the implementation of AI in public decision-making in the absence of a mature surrounding framework of legal governance risks undermining the structural components of the Rule of Law and the achievements it represents as a model for democratic governance.

Power Dispersal/Accountability Dispersal

This brings us to another keystone aspect of the Rule of Law, the diffusion of power among administrative functions and individuals. As Tamanaha (2021) notes, under the Rule of Law, there is no sovereign, "just officeholders who come and go". Indeed, human decision-making may be flawed and include improper use of discretionary powers, but those flaws will be limited by the relative ineffectiveness of lower-level administrative human decision-making (one person can only do so much damage), and the availability of bureaucratic legal institutions establishing control mechanisms for decision-making and holding decision-makers to account. In comparison, AI systems tend to be implemented for the purposes of increasing efficiency and managing tasks at a scale and speed that exceed human decision-making (see Waldman, 2019, pp. 624–626). The flip side to this efficiency is that it may allow for mistakes to quickly propagate. In practice, AI systems implemented in decision-making are likely to aggregate the practical tasks and powers of what would previously have been many different human decision-makers. Instead of diffusing power among many officeholders that each can be held accountable, automation thus tends to concentrate power into systems, while instead dispersing accountability for those systems.

There are several factors contributing to this concentration of power. Within a public authority, a single system may be responsible for making a multitude of decisions based on a common set of data, concentrating both the possible epistemological basis for decisions and the reasoning applied to that data to a single system rather than a multitude of administrators. Concentration may also be the result of the dominant corporations developing AI applications and their dependent ecosystems and accumulation of data that "shapes the development and deployment of AI as well as the debate on its regulation" (Nemitz, 2018, p. 3).

The dispersal of accountability, or the potential for *de-responsibilisation* (Mittelstadt et al., 2016), is similarly shaped by several factors. Accountability in ADM systems is complicated by new actors who exist outside of the formal chain of legal accountability while having a significant influence on the outcome of decision-making. "[A] design team becomes the locus at which law is interpreted, negotiated, and transformed into actionable tools. This gives engineers enormous power, both to choose winners and losers and decide what the law will mean in practice" (Waldman, 2019, p. 627). In terms of accountability, however, the design team is not the only actor that may be responsible for failures (legal or otherwise) in automated decisions by AI systems. They may simultaneously or alternatively be attributable to failures in, for example, procurement, design, coding, translation of legal norms, training, data quality assurance, implementation, interpretation, and/or human oversight. This dispersal of accountability challenges formal accountability structures under the Rule of Law, which are not necessarily adapted for engineers or others wielding technological power in design processes. It may also shield politicians and public administrators wielding formal public power from accountability as failures in leadership or decision-making may be blamed on "mutant algorithms" (Stewart, 2020). This is potentially compounded by shifts from processes of *accountability* to processes of *compliance*, which may serve to frame the law into process-oriented risk reduction in accordance with managerial neo-liberal values of efficiency (Waldman, 2019, p. 628).

These accountability issues are compounded as the implications of AI implementations may mediate citizen interactions with government power without resulting in decisions open for challenge through the mechanisms of the Rule of Law. They may instead be expressed through differences in procedural treatment depending on algorithmic risk assessments, like an algorithmic fast lane incorporated into the back-end administrative systems, if you conform to statistical expectations or continuous controls if you don't. This difference in treatment is not to be confused with discriminatory outcomes, but rather with the varying intensities of surveillance or controls different individuals will be subjected to in their interactions with the state – implying, for example, varying implications on privacy or data protection depending on their algorithmic profile.

Deliberation/Design

In a narrow sense, the requirement of power being exercised through and under the law requires that power can be subsumed under the laws made by democratically elected representatives, providing democratic legitimacy. In a wider sense though, the ideal of autonomy discussed previously is further highlighted through the legality of the democratic processes and deliberations. The Frankfurt School, questioning the ability of the Rule of Law to cope with the influences of capitalism and live up to its ideals, raised the importance of democratic participation to compensate for those weaknesses (Scheuerman, 2021). Whereas the generality of law supplied normative legitimacy in forcing power to be expressed through more universalized interests rather than individualized concerns, Habermas through his *co-implication thesis* held that the Rule of Law and democracy are co-original or mutually imply and enable one another – the idea that there is no Rule of Law properly speaking without democracy, and vice versa (Habermas, 1996). Importantly, Habermas ties this conception of democracy to certain idealized conditions where equality and inclusion are protected through constitutionalism, but also where the process is regulated so that people are treated as free and equal (autonomous) citizens. This optimally results in self-governance through engagement in democratic discourses and communication (Thomassen, 2010). This sets a high bar for autonomy, requiring "that those subject to law as its addressees can at the same time understand themselves as authors of the law" (Habermas, 1996). This implies then that we can all feel that we had a stake and a role in the democratic processes leading up to the legislation underpinning decisions. While this is a lofty goal, it does highlight the connection between legality as a component of the Rule of Law, and democratic processes leading up to statutory rules.

At first glance, the increased reliance on AI in administrative decision-making does not necessarily impact the democratic foundation of the exercise of power – provided, as discussed above, that the automated decision-making itself is supported by law. However, the mediating role of technology in automated and semi-automated decision-making challenges that impression. A recurring theme in research surrounding the use of automation and prediction in public authorities is that discretion in decision-making is not removed, but rather pushed to less visible parts of the administrative structures (Brayne, 2021; Lessig, 2006, p. 138; Naarttijärvi, 2019). This corresponds to how Latour has described the black box of technology design, where choices and values at the design stage will enter into the box, then influence the use of the system, and by extension, the exercise of power, once the box is opened – i.e., the technology deployed (Latour, 1994, p. 36). The translation of legal norms into coded norms will imply a reinterpretation of the choices made in deliberation surrounding the legal norms into a design of code (Mohun & Roberts, 2020). Latour holds that "[t]echnical action is a form of delegation that allows us to mobilize, during interactions, moves made elsewhere, earlier, by other actants" (Latour, 1994, p. 52). In the same vein, we may view the application of law as a mobilization of moves made by a previous actant – the legislator – in a later setting – the application of law within a specified case. This, however, highlights an important distinction, namely *what moves, by what actors*, that are mobilized. As the application of law moves from human decision-makers to automated systems, a different set of moves by a different set of actants are mobilized. The deliberative structures of the legislative process that are mobilized in the exercise of law become intermingled or potentially replaced with the design processes of technological systems of automation, driven by other values and less open to public participation. The extent to which the choices and values underpinning the deliberative process of legal norms and the design process of coded norms are aligned may vary. Participatory design, or design processes integrating ethical, legal, and societal issues through ELS approaches may assist in reducing the potential disconnect (Akata et al., 2020). However, when it comes to public power, design is not deliberation and not subject to the same processes, structures, institutions, or safeguards as democratic processes are, nor does it hold the same legitimacy within the constitutional framework of the state. In essence, for the exercise of public power, we already have a process for participatory design, democracy.

CRITICAL LESSONS

So, what is the added value of these critical dichotomies? As I see it, the Rule of Law tends to be discussed primarily through one or more of its subcomponents, such as legality or non-discrimination, which is easier to apply in a specific setting. As I have argued at the beginning of this chapter, this is often necessary to operationalize the concept for a specific context. However, to assist in a critical study of AI, the dichotomic approach I have explored here has a few strengths. First, it can thematically group existing lines of critique, thereby underpinning a more coherent critical analysis based on more fundamental or structural issues rather than surface-level issues in specific settings. Second, it can aid in deconstructing and articulating assumptions underpinning the use of AI in a specific setting, such as the setting of decision-making in public administration I have outlined here. Even in problematization, there is a risk of ending up in solutionism (see Roberge et al., 2020). Rather than attempting to "translate" AI into a legal setting – focusing, for example, on how AI can reach certain legal thresholds of transparency – the dichotomic instead serves to highlight more fundamental conflicts, thereby reducing the risk of legal research becoming captured in a narrative of facilitation. The specific dichotomies I have used here are not necessarily the most fundamental in terms of their differences, but I believe they can be instructive of the approach and serve as inspiration for further critical examinations of the relationship between AI and law.

REFERENCES

Agamben, G. (2005). *State of exception*. University of Chicago Press.
Akata, Z., Balliet, D., de Rijke, M., Dignum, F., Dignum, V., Eiben, G., Fokkens, A., Grossi, D., Hindriks, K., Hoos, H., Hung, H., Jonker, C., Monz, C., Neerincx, M., Oliehoek, F., Prakken, H., Schlobach, S., van der Gaag, L., van Harmelen, F., ... Welling, M. (2020). A research agenda for hybrid intelligence: Augmenting human intellect with collaborative, adaptive, responsible, and explainable artificial intelligence. *Computer*, *53*(8), 18–28. https://doi.org/10.1109/MC.2020.2996587
Alexy, R. (2002). *A theory of constitutional rights*. Oxford University Press.

Alexy, R. (2010). *A theory of legal argumentation: The theory of rational discourse as theory of legal justification* (1st ed.). Oxford University Press.

Bayamlıoğlu, E., & Leenes, R. (2018). The "rule of law" implications of data-driven decision-making: A techno-regulatory perspective. *Law, Innovation and Technology, 10*(2), 295–313. https://doi.org/10.1080/17579961.2018.1527475

Berk, R. A., & Bleich, J. (2013). Statistical procedures for forecasting criminal behavior: A comparative assessment. *Criminology & Public Policy, 12*(3), 513–544. https://doi.org/10.1111/1745-9133.12047

Bingham, T. (2011). *The rule of law.* Penguin Books.

Biran, O., & McKeown, K. (2017). Human-centric justification of machine learning predictions. *Proceedings of the Twenty-Sixth International Joint Conference on Artificial Intelligence,* 1461–1467. https://doi.org/10.24963/ijcai.2017/202

Boyle, J. (Ed.). (1992). *Critical legal studies.* New York University Press.

Brayne, S. (2021). *Predict and surveil: Data, discretion, and the future of policing.* Oxford University Press.

Brownsword, R. (2016). Technological management and the rule of law. *Law, Innovation and Technology, 8*(1), 100–140. https://doi.org/10.1080/17579961.2016.1161891

Burrell, J. (2016). How the machine "thinks": Understanding opacity in machine learning algorithms. *Big Data & Society, 3*(1), 1–12. https://doi.org/10.1177/2053951715622512

Carabantes, M. (2020). Black-box artificial intelligence: An epistemological and critical analysis. *AI & Society, 35*(2), 309–317. https://doi.org/10.1007/s00146-019-00888-w

Clayton, R. (2019). The Venice Commission and the rule of law crisis. *Public Law,* 450–460.

Derlén, M. (2020). *Konstitutionell rätt* (Andra upplagan). Norstedts Juridik.

Dworkin, R. (2010). *Law's empire* (Repr). Hart.

Dyzenhaus, D. (2021). *The long arc of legality: Hobbes, Kelsen, Hart.* Cambridge University Press.

Enqvist, L., & Naarttijärvi, M. (2023). Discretion, automation, and proportionality. In M. Suksi (Ed.), *Rule of law and automated decision-making.* Springer.

EU High Level Expert Group on AI (AI HLEG). (2019). *Policy and investment recommendations for trustworthy artificial intelligence.* European Commission. https://digital-strategy.ec.europa.eu/en/library/policy-and-investment-recommendations-trustworthy-artificial-intelligence

Habermas, J. (1996). *Between facts and norms: Contributions to a discourse theory of law and democracy.* Polity.

Hälterlein, J. (2021). Epistemologies of predictive policing: Mathematical social science, social physics and machine learning. *Big Data & Society, 8*(1), 205395172110031. https://doi.org/10.1177/20539517211003118

Hart, H. L. A. (2012). *The concept of law* (3rd ed.). Oxford University Press.

Heidegger, M. (1977). *The question concerning technology, and other essays.* Garland Pub.

Henin, C., & Le Métayer, D. (2021). A framework to contest and justify algorithmic decisions. *AI and Ethics, 1*(4), 463–476. https://doi.org/10.1007/s43681-021-00054-3

Hildebrandt, M. (2010). Proactive forensic profiling: Proactive criminalization? In R. A. Duff, L. Farmer, S. E. Marshall, M. Renzo, & V. Tadros (Eds.), *The boundaries of the criminal law.* Oxford University Press.

Hildebrandt, M. (2016). *Smart technologies and the end(s) of law: Novel entanglements of law and technology* (Paperback edition). Edward Elgar Publishing.

Hildebrandt, M. (2020). Code-driven law: Freezing the future and scaling the past. In S. F. Deakin & C. Markou (Eds.), *Is law computable? Critical perspectives on law and artificial intelligence.* Hart Publishing, an imprint of Bloomsbury Publishing.

Iancu, B. (2019). Quod licet Jovi non licet bovi?: The Venice Commission as norm entrepreneur. *Hague Journal on the Rule of Law, 11*(1), 189–221. https://doi.org/10.1007/s40803-019-00088-0

Katyal, S. K. (2022). Democracy & distrust in an era of artificial intelligence. *Daedalus, 151*(2), 322–334. https://doi.org/10.1162/daed_a_01919

Kennedy, R. (2020). The rule of law and algorithmic governance. In W. Barfield (Ed.), *The Cambridge handbook of the law of algorithms* (1st ed., pp. 209–232). Cambridge University Press. https://doi.org/10.1017/9781108680844.012

Krygier, M. (2009). The rule of law: Legality, teleology, sociology. In G. Palombella & N. Walker (Eds.), *Relocating the rule of law.* Bloomsbury Publishing Plc. http://ebookcentral.proquest.com/lib/umeaub-ebooks/detail.action?docID=1772625

Krygier, M. (2012). *Rule of law.* Oxford University Press. https://doi.org/10.1093/oxfordhb/9780199578610.013.0012

Lanier, J. (2022, March 15). AI is an ideology, not a technology. *Wired.* https://www.wired.com/story/opinion-ai-is-an-ideology-not-a-technology/

Latour, B. (1994). On technological mediation. *Common Knowledge, 3*(2), 29–64.

Lessig, L. (2006). *Code: Version 2.0.* Basic Books.

Ligue des droits humains ASBL v Conseil des ministres, Case C-817/19 (ECJ 21 June 2022). https://eur-lex.europa.eu/legal-content/en/TXT/?uri=CELEX:62019CJ0817

Linardatos, P., Papastefanopoulos, V., & Kotsiantis, S. (2020). Explainable AI: A review of machine learning interpretability methods. *Entropy, 23*(1), 18. https://doi.org/10.3390/e23010018

Matteucci, S. C. (2021). Public administration algorithm decision-making and the rule of law. *European Public Law, 27*(1), 103–130.

McQuillan, D. (2015). Algorithmic states of exception. *European Journal of Cultural Studies, 18*(4–5), 564–576. https://doi.org/10.1177/1367549415577389

Meierhenrich, J. (2021). What the rule of law is…and is not. In J. Meierhenrich & M. Loughlin (Eds.), *The Cambridge companion to the rule of law* (1st ed., pp. 569–621). Cambridge University Press. https://doi.org/10.1017/9781108600569.013

Meyer-Resende, M., & Straub, M. (2022, March 28). The rule of law versus the rule of the algorithm. *Verfassungsblog.* https://verfassungsblog.de/rule-of-the-algorithm/

Mittelstadt, B. D., Allo, P., Taddeo, M., Wachter, S., & Floridi, L. (2016). The ethics of algorithms: Mapping the debate. *Big Data & Society, 3*(2), 1–21. https://doi.org/10.1177/2053951716679679

Mohun, J., & Roberts, A. (2020). *Cracking the code: Rulemaking for humans and machines* (OECD Working Papers on Public Governance No. 42; OECD Working Papers on Public Governance, Vol. 42). https://doi.org/10.1787/3afe6ba5-en

Naarttijärvi, M. (2019). Legality and democratic deliberation in black box policing. *Technology and Regulation,* 35–48. https://doi.org/10.26116/techreg.2019.004

Nemitz, P. (2018). Constitutional democracy and technology in the age of artificial intelligence. *Philosophical Transactions of the Royal Society A: Mathematical, Physical and Engineering Sciences, 376*(2133), 20180089. https://doi.org/10.1098/rsta.2018.0089

Numerico, T. (2019). Politics and epistemology of big data: A critical assessment. In D. Berkich & M. V. d'Alfonso (Eds.), *On the cognitive, ethical, and scientific dimensions of artificial intelligence* (Vol. 134, pp. 147–166). Springer International Publishing. https://doi.org/10.1007/978-3-030-01800-9_8

Proposal for a Regulation of the European Parliament and of the Council laying down harmonised rules on artificial intelligence (artificial intelligence act) and amending certain union legislative acts, no. COM/2021/206 final, European Commission (2021).

Radbruch, G. (1946). Gesetzliches Unrecht und übergesetzliches Recht. *Süddeutsche Juristen-Zeitung, 1*(5), 105–108.

Raz, J. (2009). *The authority of law: Essays on law and morality.* Oxford University Press.

Roberge, J., Senneville, M., & Morin, K. (2020). How to translate artificial intelligence? Myths and justifications in public discourse. *Big Data & Society, 7*(1), 205395172091996. https://doi.org/10.1177/2053951720919968

Sajó, A., & Uitz, R. (2017). *The constitution of freedom* (Vol. 1). Oxford University Press. https://doi.org/10.1093/oso/9780198732174.001.0001

Scheuerman, W. E. (2021). The Frankfurt School and the rule of law. In J. Meierhenrich & M. Loughlin (Eds.), *The Cambridge companion to the rule of law* (1st ed., pp. 312–327). Cambridge University Press. https://doi.org/10.1017/9781108600569.018

Schofield, M. (Ed.). (2016). Book 4. In T. Griffith (Trans.), *Plato: Laws* (1st ed., pp. 140–168). Cambridge University Press. https://doi.org/10.1017/CBO9781139020800.008

Schubbach, A. (2021). Judging machines: Philosophical aspects of deep learning. *Synthese, 198*(2), 1807–1827. https://doi.org/10.1007/s11229-019-02167-z

Selznick, P. (2017). Legal cultures and the rule of law. In M. Krygier & A. Czarnota (Eds.), *The rule of law after communism: Problems and prospects in east-central Europe* (1st ed.). Routledge. https://doi.org/10.4324/9781315085319

Stewart, H. (2020, August 26). Boris Johnson blames "mutant algorithm" for exams fiasco. *The Guardian.* https://www.theguardian.com/politics/2020/aug/26/boris-johnson-blames-mutant-algorithm-for-exams-fiasco

Suksi, M. (2021). Administrative due process when using automated decision-making in public administration: Some notes from a Finnish perspective. *Artificial Intelligence and Law, 29*(1), 87–110. https://doi.org/10.1007/s10506-020-09269-x

Thomassen, L. (2010). *Habermas: A guide for the perplexed*. Continuum.

Tuori, K. (2002). *Critical legal positivism*. Ashgate.

Tushnet, M. (2021). Critical legal studies and the rule of law. In J. Meierhenrich & M. Loughlin (Eds.), *The Cambridge companion to the rule of law* (1st ed., pp. 328–339). Cambridge University Press. https://doi.org/10.1017/9781108600569.019

van den Hoven, E. (2021). Hermeneutical injustice and the computational turn in law. *Journal of Cross-Disciplinary Research in Computational Law, 1*(1). https://journalcrcl.org/crcl/article/view/6

Venice Commission. (2011). *Report on the rule of law* (No. 003rev-e; CDL-AD).

Vestby, A., & Vestby, J. (2019). Machine learning and the police: Asking the right questions. *Policing: A Journal of Policy and Practice*, paz035. https://doi.org/10.1093/police/paz035

Wacks, R. (2020). *Understanding jurisprudence: An introduction to legal theory* (6th ed.). Oxford University Press.

Waldman, E. (2019). Power, process, and automated decision-making. *Fordham Law Review, 88*(2), 613–632.

Waldron, J. (2020). The rule of law. In *The Stanford encyclopedia of philosophy*. Metaphysics Research Lab, Stanford University. https://plato.stanford.edu/archives/sum2020/entries/rule-of-law/

Waldron, J. (2021). The rule of law as an essentially contested concept. In J. Meierhenrich & M. Loughlin (Eds.), *The Cambridge companion to the rule of law* (1st ed., pp. 121–136). Cambridge University Press. https://doi.org/10.1017/9781108600569.013

Yeung, K. (2017). "Hypernudge": Big data as a mode of regulation by design. *Information, Communication & Society, 20*(1), 118–136. https://doi.org/10.1080/1369118X.2016.1186713

Yeung, K. (2019). Why worry about decision-making by machine? In K. Yeung (Ed.), *Algorithmic regulation* (pp. 21–48). Oxford University Press. https://doi.org/10.1093/oso/9780198838494.003.0002

66. The use of AI in domestic security practices
Jens Hälterlein

INTRODUCTION

Recent innovations in the AI subfield of machine learning (ML), which is already used in many real-life applications such as virtual assistants, autonomous vehicles and search engines, have made AI a matter of concern not only for consumers, big businesses and other actors of the private sector but also politicians, agencies and practitioners in the security sector. They envision AI as a crucial factor for the future security of societies. In this chapter, I will first outline the broader societal developments that provide the backdrop for the contemporary importance of AI-based security. I will then focus on the technoscientific promises associated with this technology and then, finally, discuss several critical issues. While the distinction between the civil and military use of AI is often precarious and, in many cases, deliberately blurred by public authorities and policymakers, this chapter will only focus on the non-military application of AI. Lethal autonomous weapons, such as weaponized drones, are, hence, outside of its scope. Nor will the chapter address (possible) applications of AI for cybersecurity purposes and security problems that arise through the use of AI in the first place.

THE NEW SECURITY CULTURE

AI-based security is a constitutive part of a new security culture that results from a fundamental change in the perception of insecurity (Furedi, 2009). The final report of the National Commission on Terrorist Attacks upon the United States (2004), which was set up after the terrorist attacks of September 11, 2001, is paradigmatic for this change. One of the central statements of the report concerns the failure of the US security authorities to foresee the attacks and thereby possibly prevent them from happening, which the Commission primarily interprets as a lack of imagination and as a failure to expect the unexpected and act accordingly. Henceforth, the anticipation of possibilistic risks (Amoore, 2013) based on the imagination of worst-case scenarios (Aradau, 2010) should complement probabilistic risk calculations, the construction of which is based on empirical knowledge and statistics. The Commission's call for the exercise of imagination to become routine (ibid.) has drawn many security agencies' attention to 'unknown unknowns' (Daase & Kessler, 2007) and abstract threats 'that are more diverse, less visible and less predictable' (European Council, 2009, p. 30). They now have to identify and proactively address these new uncertainties by either preventing them from becoming a concrete danger in the first place ('pre-emption') or practising how to mitigate damages if the occurrence of a damaging event cannot be prevented ('preparedness'). At the same time, this development reinforced a shift towards pre-crime orientation in policing, which is primarily focused on preventing crime instead of prosecuting offenders (Zedner, 2007). In consequence, the traditional post-crime orientation of the criminal justice system is increasingly overshadowed by the pre-crime logic of security.

The fundamental change in the perception of insecurity is accompanied by an expanded concept of security that sees Western societies and their populations as no longer threatened by a clearly identifiable enemy but rather by a heterogeneous spectrum of threats, ranging from terrorism to disasters and pandemics. Security policy, thus, no longer operates along with the categorical distinction between internal/domestic and external/military security. Moreover, contemporary security culture is not only concerned with fighting the opponent's strengths but also with reducing Western societies' perceived weaknesses and vulnerabilities. It addresses the ambiguity of the technological constitution of a physical and virtual network society (Dillon, 2002): digital infrastructures and information and communication technologies (ICTs) are considered to be the lifelines of high-tech societies and a source of their susceptibility to global terror networks, cyberattacks, natural disasters, major accidents and highly contagious diseases (van der Vleuten et al., 2013). As 'vital systems' (Lakoff & Collier, 2010), they simultaneously foster new forms of vulnerability.

At the same time, however, technologization becomes the new silver bullet of security (Aas et al., 2009; Ceyhan, 2008; Marx, 2001). It is praised by policymakers and officials in security agencies as the ultimate solution 'to address our present problems and fears' (Bigo & Carrera, 2005, p. 3). Driven by the promises made by the security industry, digital – and in many cases AI-based – technologies are already becoming (or are supposed to become) key elements of security practices in various contexts: facial recognition that identifies search-listed criminals and terrorists in real time; body scanners and other sensory devices that detect weapons and dangerous substances at airports; satellite images and biometric passports that enable efficient border management; software that forecasts future crimes and criminals; computer simulations that model the spread of a virus among a population; firewalls and other forms of IT-security that protect critical infrastructures against cyberattacks; and ICTs that enable efficient coordination of emergency and crisis response activities – just to name a few examples. Moreover, these use cases have moved to the centre stage of applied security research. In numerous R&D projects funded by government agencies, social scientists, ethicists, legal scholars, engineers and practitioners cooperate to further develop, test and evaluate technologies that are supposed to address security problems that have been defined by these funding agencies beforehand. Going along with, and in reaction to the growth of policy-driven research and development, security technologies have become a matter of interest for critical scholars from various disciplinary backgrounds, such as surveillance studies, critical security studies and science and technology studies. In these academic contexts, the use of technologies for security purposes has inspired theoretical debates and empirical insights that often leave established paths for analytical inquiries by opening up new perspectives and approaches (Aas et al., 2009; Amicelle et al., 2015; Hälterlein & Ostermeier, 2018). The great importance attributed to AI in our 'techno-security-culture' (Weber & Kämpf, 2020) is essentially based on two technoscientific promises.

TECHNOSCIENTIFIC PROMISES

Automatic Analysis of Mass Data

As a result of 9/11, a massive expansion of secret service surveillance practices took place that led to the mass recording of communication data, financial transactions and movement profiles of suspicious individuals and groups or entire populations (Lyon, 2014). At the same time, law enforcement agencies are increasingly relying on so-called open source intelligence (OSINT), which is publicly accessible information, for example, from social media (Dencik et al., 2018). In addition, existing police video surveillance of public spaces and critical situations (airports, train stations, border controls, protests, major sports events, etc.) is expanded and supplemented by the use of drones and body cams. It is characteristic of these developments that the collection or production of large, heterogeneous amounts of data of previously unknown dimensions ('big data') goes hand in hand with the need to develop new methods for their analysis. 'Connecting the dots' and 'finding the needle in the haystack' have become hard tasks – if not impossible – to perform without the support of advanced analytical tools. AI-based procedures serve these needs as they counteract the limitations of the cognitive abilities and attention span of human security actors with automated processes that promise both greater efficiency and objectivity (Amoore & Piotukh, 2015; Aradau & Blanke, 2015). This development can be illustrated using two examples. In the context of social media and the Internet in general, new forms of crime have developed that conventional methods and instruments of police work can no longer cope with – either due to its sheer quantity (hate speech) or to its disturbing nature (child abuse images). Hence, state authorities show great interest in the development of AI-based methods for the analysis of social media, which has hence become a growing field within computer science lately. Natural language processing (NLP), for instance, is used to automatically assign linguistic utterances in social networks to certain categories that were previously derived from social science models. These NLP algorithms are first 'trained' by the user through the manual categorization of utterances ('mark-up') until a sufficiently large data corpus has been created and are then used to calculate statistical correlations between linguistic features. In the case of video surveillance, on the contrary, the use of technology itself is increasingly seen as labour-intensive and ineffective. Consequently, AI-based video surveillance is usually linked to the expectation of monitoring public spaces and critical situations more efficiently and effectively, even in the face of ever-increasing amounts of visual data to be analysed. Moreover, AI-based video surveillance is not limited to one single purpose. Possible or desired applications range from the verification of a person's identity at border controls (facial recognition), automatic detection of suspicious behaviour (pattern recognition) or left luggage and other potentially dangerous objects (object detection) and the identification or tracking of search-listed criminals and terrorists, through the prosecution of traffic offenders (number plate recognition), to the prediction of malicious intentions based on visual cues (emotion recognition) (Introna & Wood, 2004). Although these existing or projected applications may seem disparate, the common idea that runs through them is that operators are not required to watch the video screens at all times but are notified by the system in case of an event of interest.

However, the availability of mass data not only created the need for AI but also enabled advancements in AI R&D, especially in the subfield of visual analytics that provides the techno-scientific basis for all video surveillance applications. For a long time, one of the fundamental problems was that training data was not available in sufficient quantity. Therefore, until the early 2010s, computer scientists generally got volunteers or colleagues to pose for photos or act in videos. Then, facial recognition algorithms were capable of identifying individuals in controlled environments such as the laboratory where the image of an individual's face is matched to a pre-existing image on a database and both images meet certain professional scientific standards (2010). The accuracy rate of the same algorithms decreased tremendously, however, in more complex situations when there is no standardized image for comparison or when the comparison comes from an uncontrolled environment such as a crowded public space (Adams & Ferryman, 2015). The situation changed with the possibility of using existing, pre-sorted large databases on the internet (YouTube, etc.) for the training and testing of the systems. Moreover, big tech companies started to develop their own facial recognition algorithms, for instance, for automatic 'photo-tagging' in social media or unlocking smartphones. These facial recognition algorithms perform well as they are assisted and improved by their users who provide high-quality images of themselves and others, help to label ('tag') pictures or confirm automatically tagged pictures. It is, therefore, no surprise that security and law enforcement agencies nowadays mainly rely on (or are interested in) commercial facial recognition software instead of investing in genuine in-house developments.

Data-Driven Predictions

The second technoscientific promise contributing to the high expectations of using AI-based methods for security purposes is that AI would enable the prediction of any type of event of interest including terrorist attacks, cyberattacks on critical infrastructures or pandemic outbreaks (Amoore & Goede, 2005). The particular challenge in predicting these low-probability-high-impact events is that their occurrence cannot be calculated based on existing statistical models and probabilistic risk calculations (Opitz & Tellmann, 2015). The reason for this is the lack of corresponding theories that derive such events based on rules, i.e., deductively draw conclusions from the general rule to the individual case, and thus provide the knowledge base to create reliable forecasts. For instance, decades of research in both academia and security authorities have concluded that there is no single profile of an individual that will become a terrorist in the future (Pelzer, 2018). There are simply no known socio-economic, psychological or biographical attributes 'that would allow a clear distinction between individuals who are on violent and non-violent trajectories' (Pelzer, 2018, p. 167). An increased interest in AI-based technologies, therefore, particularly aims at systems that use methods from the field of ML since they would be able to identify previously unknown correlations and patterns in large data samples and, based on this, predict future events independent both of empirical knowledge about a case at hand and subject-matter theories. ML approaches are imagined as being capable to transgress the boundaries of existing knowledge, enabling data analysts to identify seemingly random patterns, for which no explanatory theory exists that could be applied top-down. Based on so-called unsupervised learning (where no known outcomes are provided during the learning process), for instance, an algorithm can assign data to clusters that are not predefined, detect anomalies and discover patterns. The ML algorithm creates specific outputs from the unstructured inputs by looking for similarities and differences in the data set and discovering relationships that are not necessarily known and might not be obvious. A rule-based formulation of predictive models, which always requires prior knowledge of these rules, is potentially becoming obsolete as ML formulates the promise of enabling access to knowledge that is contained in the data but is imperceptible to the human observer (Aradau & Blanke, 2015). In addition, self-learning systems can adapt better to a rapidly changing environment or database. They continuously learn on the job and thus improve their performance instead of having to treat – and therefore ignore – the unexpected as an exception to the rule.

The difference between rule-based or theory-driven on the one hand and ML-based or data-driven approaches to predictive modelling, on the other hand, is crucial in the context of predictive policing. Broadly speaking, predictive policing makes use of information technology, data and analytical techniques in order to identify likely places and times of future crimes or individuals at high risk of becoming a future (re)offender or victim (Perry et al., 2013; Uchida, 2014). A rule-based or theory-driven approach to predictive policing would translate explanatory knowledge about criminal behaviour into the mathematical formula of a predictive model that is then used to make crime forecasts. This approach can be empirical and may follow sociological modes of inquiry (Chan & Bennett Moses, 2015) or it can rely on theory much more explicitly. One of the most common theory-driven approaches to crime forecasting is based on rational choice theory and routine activities theory. Both theories make certain assumptions about the meaning of criminal acts and the reasoning of the human agent performing these actions. In general, crime is seen as purposive, and the criminal offender is regarded as a rational and self-determining being. These theories have been instructive in the forecasting of near-repeat burglary in particular. The term near repeat simply refers to the statistical observation that certain types of crime (property crime in particular) often occur at places close to each other within a short period of time (Bowers et al., 2004). From the viewpoint of rational choice theory and routine activities theory, near repeats can be understood – and consequently also predicted – based on the following explanation: a successful break-in would boost the attractiveness of a follow-up break-in somewhere nearby since both the likelihood of making a worthwhile haul and the risk of getting caught in the act can be better assessed by the offender. Both, the software *Prospective Crime Mapping* which was used by a British police unit in a pilot project (Johnson et al., 2007) as well as the software *PRECOBS* which is widely used by police departments across Germany and Switzerland (Egbert & Leese, 2020), draw heavily from this explanation. An ML-based or data-driven approach to predictive modelling, on the contrary, would, for example, create decision trees to automatically classify data. A decision tree is a representation of decisive rules that takes the visual form of a tree structure. Decision trees can either be manually deducted from expert knowledge or automatically induced from data samples using ML algorithms. The Memphis Police Department claims to have used a decision tree algorithm as part of its *Blue CRUSH* crime prevention strategy (Utsler, 2011). A so-called random forest is a large ensemble of randomized decision trees (usually around 500) that is used to create a predictive model based on the mean of the individual decision rules/predictions. Richard Berk, professor of statistics and criminology at the University of Pennsylvania, used this technique for the analysis of parole decisions and outcomes undertaken for the Philadelphia Department of Adult Probation and Parole (Berk, 2008). The goal of the study was to forecast which individuals under supervision would commit a homicide or attempted homicide within two years after intake and to assign probationers to a high-, moderate- or low-risk category. The two approaches imply certain limits of prediction and thus allow for different scopes of predictive knowledge. When it comes to the creation of a predictive model, a theory-driven approach can draw from a certain repertoire of theoretical explanations but is at the same time bound to the limits of these theories. In the case of the example described earlier, only criminal behaviour that matches the concepts of rational choice and routine activities can be predicted (Kaufmann et al., 2018). These 'criminologies of everyday life' (Garland, 1999) may offer a fairly plausible, albeit simplified explanation of planned or opportunistic crimes. But they fail to adequately account for offenders acting in the heat of the moment, under the influence of alcohol or drugs or simply in ways that do not fit a Western understanding of rationality. ML-based approaches to crime forecasting, on the contrary, are not only questioning the need for and limits of criminological theories but may also produce results that can be impossible to explain from the viewpoint of criminology (Chan & Bennett Moses, 2015). For Richard Berk, for instance, it is not important why certain predictors improve forecasting accuracy:

> For example, if other things equal, shoe size is a useful predictor of recidivism, then it can be included as a predictor. Why shoe size matters is immaterial. In short, we are not seeking to identify risk factors that may or may not make any subject-matter sense. (Berk & Bleich, 2013, p. 517)

This 'epistemological divide' (Hälterlein, 2021) is reflected in the difference between giving intelligible explanations and generating accurate predictions. From the viewpoint of a classical criminological perspective, predictive models always have to account for the human agency behind the causal mechanisms by which the values of a dependent variable are generated as a particular function of independent variables. For ML, in contrast, a predictive model is an abstraction from crime as an intelligible act. It requires no theory about the criminal subject, its reasoning and the (subjective) meaning of its actions. For ML-based crime forecasting to make explicit the causal mechanisms behind predicted outcomes is of no relevance: A useful predictive model only needs to capitalize on the right patterns and correlations, no matter whether this model explains the inert forces of the social world adequately or not. Instead, successful ML-based crime forecasting first and foremost requires an adequate representation of the social world – as given in a sufficiently large and accurate data sample.

However, even in times of 'data abundance' such a successful application seems to remain a difficult task. To date, there are no independent studies that have demonstrated a strong effect of the use of predictive policing software on crime rates. With recent advances in computational power and the availability of large data sets, the possibilities of making accurate crime predictions have surely made considerable progress. However, accurate predictions still require adequate action, which often presents police departments with great problems as several evaluation studies have demonstrated (Gerstner, 2018; Saunders et al., 2016). The overwhelmingly positive reception of these technologies by security actors, hence, results not so much from its actual impact on crime rates but the mere fact that it allows the implementation of proactive security practices (McCulloch & Wilson, 2017). On the other hand, the use of predictive policing software promises the more efficient use of resources, which appears extremely attractive in view of scarce public funds, scarce staff, and the perception of ever-increasing security demands. The same holds for the use of AI-based video surveillance where both public authorities and media tend to present singular success stories instead of discussing scientific evaluations. Möllers and Hälterlein (2013), for instance, analyse the public discourse on 'smart CCTV' in Germany between 2006 and 2010 and show how both advocates and critics of the technology envision its future use as an effective tool for security purposes, thereby leaving aside the poor results of previous test runs and pilot projects. Overall, the lack of proven successes stands in stark contrast to the high expectations placed on AI-based security technologies. This is all the more problematic as the use of these technologies causes a number of legal and social issues that need to be considered when assessing their impact. Three of these societal impacts will be discussed in the following section.

CRITICAL ISSUES

The possibility of performing security work based on the analysis of large, heterogeneous amounts of data pushed forward the collection of new data and expanded access to existing databases (Lyon, 2014). As a result, the boundaries between state surveillance, surveillance capitalism and self-surveillance are becoming increasingly blurred. Since the amounts of data that are necessary for the training of ML algorithms are often not (legally) available to state actors, it is usually private-sector actors who develop new, more powerful AI systems on the basis of user-generated data and then sell them to state actors. Questions of data protection and digital privacy are thus also implicitly becoming questions of security. Moreover, as it is the nature of ML algorithms to be deployed on data with large sample sizes, using AI for security purposes implies a tendency not only to combine existing data sets on criminal offenders but also to create larger data sets that include large N populations by trend, allowing for analysis and identification of new potential risk patterns that were previously unseen. In this 'big brother' version of AI-based policing and security work, the production of intelligence goes hand in hand with the gathering and screening of large data sets (Heath-Kelly, 2017).

Consequently, critical investigations have long focused on the implications of these technologies concerning data protection and the infringements of privacy rights. Lately, however, the spotlight has moved to the ways AI-based security work produces risk identifications, classifications and assessments that reproduce or even reinforce racial profiling and other forms of discriminatory practices. A study by the NGO ProPublica (Angwin et al., 2016) shows that the software *COMPAS*, which is used in some US states to determine the likelihood of recidivism of offenders, systematically rates people of colour worse than white people. Similar effects can be observed as a result of the use of ML-based software in the analysis of passenger data in Australia, which leads to an intensification of the forms of prejudiced categorization and identity attribution typical in the context of controlling migration movements (Ajana, 2015). About 20 years ago, Introna and Wood (2004) already pointed to a strong ethnic and gender bias in one of the systems they examined. This system detected faces labelled as 'male' better than faces labelled as 'female' and faces with a lighter skin colour better than faces with a darker skin colour. Buolamwini and Gebru (2018) showed that this problem still exists. They found that most of the state-of-the-art facial recognition systems perform clearly worse at classifying faces as 'female' and belonging to a 'person of colour' than at classifying faces as 'male' and belonging to a 'white person'. Concerns over bias have since been quoted frequently in calls for moratoriums or bans of facial recognition software in the US and the EU. Other more moderate voices demand that the use of facial recognition software by law enforcement agencies should only be legal with an expertly trained human in the loop (Lynch, 2018).

Whether such a 'human in the loop' could provide for the accountability of security/police work using AI-based technologies, however, is highly questionable. If decisions of the criminal justice system are taken in response to output generated by an algorithmic system, police officers, judges, probation officers and parole boards can only be held accountable if they understand the accomplishment of this output (at least to a certain degree). They have to be able to interpret and evaluate this output according to legal regulations and their own professional standards. A system that allows for these forms of human reasoning is usually called a 'white box' (or sometimes a 'glass box'). Conversely, if a system is inaccessible, input-output relations may be observable, but the inner workings of the system are obscure. In these cases, the system is called a 'black box'. Predictive models, for instance, that are informed by criminological theories are rather easy to grasp for professionals from the criminal justice systems and would hence meet the requirement of model interpretability (Kaufmann et al., 2018). However, such a system can still become a black box if the information on the data and/ or the model is scarce and the source code of the software is a trade secret. With regard to an AI-based system, on the contrary, even providing open source code and training data would not be sufficient to make its output fully understandable, especially not for end-users from the criminal justice system who are often laypersons in computational science (Ananny & Crawford, 2018). Hence, many systems that are based on ML algorithms would cause account-ability problems even when transparency is given. Moreover, in the case of systems that make use of artificial neural networks, even experts in the field are unable to understand the opera-tions of the system in greater detail. As a result, these systems make it difficult to evaluate their operations according to fairness criteria, which in turn would have consequences on the applicability of existing anti-discrimination laws (Leese, 2014).

In view of the effects that the use of AI-based security technologies has on security and policing practices, the legitimacy of these practices remains precarious and becomes the cause of public controversies. In her study of a police pilot project in Tampa (US), Gates (2010) shows how the officially declared failure of facial recognition software after a two-year test phase was not a purely technical problem, but rather the result of a dispute over the legiti-mate exercise of state power. The future success or failure of AI-based security technologies will thus not only depend on their ability to meet these high expectations in terms of efficient analysis of mass data and accurate predictions of events of interest but also on how public controversies are dealt with.

REFERENCES

Aas, K. F., Gundhus, H. O., & Lomell, H. M. (Eds.). (2009). *Technologies of InSecurity: The surveillance of everyday life*. Routledge-Cavendish. https://www.taylorfrancis.com/books/9781134040360 https://doi.org/10.4324/9780203891582

Adams, A. A., & Ferryman, J. M. (2015). The future of video analytics for surveillance and its ethical implications. *Security Journal, 28*(3), 272–289. https://doi.org/10.1057/sj.2012.48

Ajana, B. (2015). Augmented borders: Big Data and the ethics of immigration control. *Journal of Information, Communication and Ethics in Society, 13*(1), 58–78. https://doi.org/10.1108/JICES-01-2014-0005

Amicelle, A., Aradau, C., & Jeandesboz, J. (2015). Questioning security devices: Performativity, resistance, politics. *Security Dialogue, 46*(4), 293–306. https://doi.org/10.1177/0967010615586964

Amoore, L. (2013). *The politics of possibility: Risk and security beyond probability*. Duke University Press. http://site.ebrary.com/lib/alltitles/docDetail.action?docID=10797305

Amoore, L., & Goede, M. de (2005). Governance, risk and dataveillance in the war on terror. *Crime, Law and Social Change, 43*(2–3), 149–173. https://doi.org/10.1007/s10611-005-1717-8

Amoore, L., & Piotukh, V. (2015). Life beyond big data: Governing with little analytics. *Economy and Society, 44*(3), 341–366. https://doi.org/10.1080/03085147.2015.1043793

Ananny, M., & Crawford, K. (2018). Seeing without knowing: Limitations of the transparency ideal and its application to algorithmic accountability. *New Media & Society, 20*(3), 973–989. https://doi.org/10.1177/1461444816676645

Angwin, J., Larson, J., Mattu, S., & Kirchner, L. (2016). *Machine Bias: There's software used across the country to predict future criminals. And it's biased against blacks.* Pro Publica. https://www .propublica.org/article/machine-bias-risk-assessments-in-criminal-sentencing

Aradau, C. (2010). Security that matters: Critical infrastructure and objects of protection. *Security Dialogue, 41*(5), 491–514. https://doi.org/10.1177/0967010610382687

Aradau, C., & Blanke, T. (2015). The (big) data-security assemblage: Knowledge and critique. *Big Data & Society, 2*(2), 205395171560906. https://doi.org/10.1177/2053951715609066

Berk, R. (2008). Forecasting methods in crime and justice. *Annual Review of Law and Social Science, 4*(1), 219–238. https://doi.org/10.1146/annurev.lawsocsci.3.081806.112812

Berk, R., & Bleich, J. (2013). Statistical procedures for forecasting criminal behavior. *Criminology & Public Policy, 12*(3), 513–544. https://doi.org/10.1111/1745-9133.12047

Bigo, D., & Carrera, S. (2005). *From New York to Madrid: Technology as the ultra-solution to the permanent state of fear and emergency in the EU.* Centre for European Policy Studies.

Bowers, K. J., Johnson, S. D., & Pease, K. (2004). Prospective hot-spotting: The future of crime mapping? *British Journal of Criminology, 44*(5), 641–658. https://doi.org/10.1093/bjc/azh036

Buolamwini, J., & Gebru, T. (2018). Gender shades: Intersectional accuracy disparities in commercial gender classification. In S. A. Friedler & C. Wilson (Eds.), *Proceedings of the 1st conference on fairness, accountability and transparency* (Vol. 81, pp. 77–91). PMLR. https://proceedings.mlr.press /v81/buolamwini18a.html

Ceyhan, A. (2008). Technologization of security: Management of uncertainty and risk in the age of biometrics. *Surveillance and Society, 5*(2), 102–123.

Chan, J., & Bennett Moses, L. (2015). Is Big Data challenging criminology? *Theoretical Criminology, 20*(1), 21–39. https://doi.org/10.1177/1362480615586614

Daase, C., & Kessler, O. (2007). Knowns and unknowns in the 'war on terror': Uncertainty and the political construction of danger. *Security Dialogue, 38*(4), 411–434. https://doi.org/10.1177 /0967010607084994

Dencik, L., Hintz, A., & Carey, Z. (2018). Prediction, pre-emption and limits to dissent: Social media and big data uses for policing protests in the United Kingdom. *New Media & Society, 20*(4), 1433–1450. https://doi.org/10.1177/1461444817697722

Dillon, M. (2002). Network society, network-centric warfare and the state of emergency. *Theory, Culture & Society, 19*(4), 71–79. https://doi.org/10.1177/0263276402019004005

Egbert, S., & Leese, M. (2020). *Criminal futures: Predictive policing and everyday police work. Routledge studies in policing and society.* Routledge.

European Council. (2009). *Stockholm programme: An open and secure Europe serving and protecting citizens.* https://ec.europa.eu/anti-trafficking/eu-policy/stockholm-programme-open-and-secure -europe-serving-and-protecting-citizens-0_en

Furedi, F. (2009). Precautionary culture and the rise of possibilistic risk assessment. *Erasmus Law Review, 2*(2), 197–220.

Garland, D. (1999). The commonplace and the catastrophic: Interpretations of crime in late modernity. *Theoretical Criminology, 3*(3), 353–364.

Gates, K. (2010). The Tampa 'smart CCTV' experiment. *Culture Unbound, 2*(1), 67–89. https://doi.org /10.3384/cu.2000.1525.102567

Gerstner, D. (2018). Predictive policing in the context of residential Burglary: An empirical illustration on the basis of a pilot project in Baden-Württemberg, Germany. *European Journal for Security Research, 3*(2), 115–138. https://doi.org/10.1007/s41125-018-0033-0

Hälterlein, J. (2021). Epistemologies of predictive policing: Mathematical social science, social physics and machine learning. *Big Data & Society, 8*(1), 205395172110031. https://doi.org/10.1177 /20539517211003118

Hälterlein, J., & Ostermeier, L. (2018). Special issue: Predictive security technologies. *European Journal for Security Research, 3*(2), 91–94. https://doi.org/10.1007/s41125-018-0034-z

Heath-Kelly, C. (2017). The geography of pre-criminal space: Epidemiological imaginations of radicalisation risk in the UK prevent strategy, 2007–2017. *Critical Studies on Terrorism, 10*(2), 297–319. https://doi.org/10.1080/17539153.2017.1327141

Introna, L., & Wood, D. M. (2004). Picturing algorithmic surveillance: The politics of facial recognition systems. *Surveillance and Society, 2*(2/3), 177–198.

Introna, L., & Nissenbaum, H. (2010). *Facial recognition technology: A survey of policy and implementation issues* (Organisation, Work and Technology Working Paper Series). The Department of Organisation, Work and Technology.

Johnson, S., Birks, D. J., McLaughlin, L., Bowers, K., & Pease, K. G. (2007). *Prospective crime mapping in operational context: Final report. Home Office online report.* Home Office.

Kaufmann, M., Egbert, S., & Leese, M. (2018). Predictive policing and the politics of patterns. *British Journal of Criminology, 48*, 3. https://doi.org/10.1093/bjc/azy060

Lakoff, A., & Collier, S. J. (2010). Infrastructure and event: The political technology of preparedness. In B. Braun & S. Whatmore (Eds.), *Political matter: Technoscience, democracy, and public life* (pp. 243–266). University of Minnesota Press.

Leese, M. (2014). The new profiling: Algorithms, black boxes, and the failure of anti-discriminatory safeguards in the European Union. *Security Dialogue, 45*(5), 494–511. https://doi.org/10.1177/0967010614544204

Lynch, J. (2018, February 12). *Face off: Law enforcement use of facial recognition technology.* https://www.eff.org/wp/law-enforcement-use-face-recognition

Lyon, D. (2014). Surveillance, Snowden, and big data: Capacities, consequences, critique. *Big Data & Society, 1*(2), 205395171454186. https://doi.org/10.1177/2053951714541861

Marx, G. T. (2001). Technology and social control: The search for the illusive silver bullet. In N. J. Smelser & P. B. Baltes (Eds.), *International encyclopedia of the social & behavioral sciences* (pp. 15506–15512). Elsevier.

McCulloch, J., & Wilson, D. (2017). *Pre-crime: Pre-emption, precaution and the future. Routledge frontiers of criminal justice: Vol. 28.* Routledge.

Möllers, N., & Hälterlein, J. (2013). Privacy issues in public discourse: The case of 'smart' CCTV in Germany. *Innovation: The European Journal of Social Science Research, 26*(1–2), 57–70. https://doi.org/10.1080/13511610.2013.723396

National Commission on Terrorist Attacks upon the United States. (2004). *The 9/11 Commission report.* http://govinfo.library.unt.edu/911/report/911Report.pdf

Opitz, S., & Tellmann, U. (2015). Future emergencies: Temporal politics in law and economy. *Theory, Culture & Society, 32*(2), 107–129. https://doi.org/10.1177/0263276414560416

Pelzer, R. (2018). Policing of terrorism using data from social media. *European Journal for Security Research, 3*(2), 163–179. https://doi.org/10.1007/s41125-018-0029-9

Perry, W. L., McInnis, B., Price, C. C., Smith, S. C., & Hollywood, J. S. (2013). *Predictive policing: The role of crime forecasting in law enforcement operations.* RAND Corporation.

Saunders, J., Hunt, P., & Hollywood, J. S. (2016). Predictions put into practice: A quasi-experimental evaluation of Chicago's predictive policing pilot. *Journal of Experimental Criminology, 12*(3), 347–371. https://doi.org/10.1007/s11292-016-9272-0

Uchida, C. D. (2014). Predictive policing. In G. Bruinsma & D. Weisburd (Eds.), *Encyclopedia of criminology and criminal justice* (pp. 3871–3880). Springer.

Utsler, J. (2011). *The crime fighters: How police departments use advanced analytics to keep people safe.* IBM Systems Magazine.

van der Vleuten, E., Högselius, P., Hommels, A., & Kaijser, A. (2013). Europe's critical infrastructure and its vulnerabilities: Promises, problems, paradoxes. In P. Högselius, A. Hommels, A. Kaijser, & E. van der Vleuten (Eds.), *The making of Europe's critical infrastructure: Common connections and shared vulnerabilities* (pp. 3–19). Palgrave Macmillan.

Weber, J., & Kämpf, K. M. (2020). Technosecurity cultures: Introduction. *Science as Culture, 29*(1), 1–10. https://doi.org/10.1080/09505431.2019.1695769

Zedner, L. (2007). Pre-crime and post-criminology? *Theoretical Criminology, 11*(2), 261–281. https://doi.org/10.1177/1362480607075851

67. Methodological reflections on researching the sociotechnical imaginaries of AI in policing

Carrie B. Sanders and Janet Chan

INTRODUCTION: POLICING AND ARTIFICIAL INTELLIGENCE

In the wake of global calls to 'defund the police' (Lum et al., 2021) and improve police accountability, police services are turning to algorithmic technologies and artificial intelligence (AI to appear 'smarter' (Chan & Bennett Moses, 2019; Nissan, 2017) and 'lessen the exposure of police work to flawed decision making based in human subjectivity and bias' (Sandhu & Fussey, 2021, p. 73; van 't Wout et al., 2020). For example, police services are using facial and vehicle recognition technologies and developing policing strategies and practices informed by machine learning programs and predictive analytics (Robertson, Khoo & Song, 2020). As a result, data science practices have come to perform a central role in informing police decision-making such as frontline and investigative practices, and resource allocation.

In her essay on the future of AI in policing, Chan (2021) argued that in spite of its rapid adoption and exponential growth in application, AI is still a relatively new technology in policing. To ensure that it has a positive impact, she suggests that citizens need to be aware of its social benefits/risks and take actions to resist or contest the technology if and when necessary. Even though AI in policing is becoming more commonplace, the human-algorithmic interaction involved in its use remains under-researched (Leese, 2021). The lack of empirical research on the human-algorithmic interaction available on AI in policing undermines the transparency and accountability of policing decisions and operations Krasman, 2019). During a time of considerable public debate about the role of police and the fairness and efficacy of police practices, empirical research into AI in policing is *critical* to ensure there is not a 'technological overreach' or that its use does not 'exacerbate existing racial disparities in crime data' (Browning & Arrigo, 2021, p. 305).

This chapter argues that in order to arrive at independent evaluations of the impact of AI where such systems are introduced, it is important to examine two aspects of technology. First, researchers need to canvass the range of shared understandings of how technology would affect social life and social order (i.e., the 'sociotechnical imaginaries', or 'collectively held, institutionally stabilized, and publicly performed visions of desirable futures, animated by shared understandings of forms of social life and social order attainable through, and supportive of, advances in science and technology' (Jasanoff & Kim, 2015, p. 4)). Second, researchers need to be aware of the methodological challenges in researching the space between collective imaginations and the situated reality of technology-human interaction when technology is implemented. We argue for a reimagining of the power of ethnography, specifically situational analysis (Clarke, 2005), for interrogating the messy complexities of human-algorithmic interactions in AI policing.

AI IN POLICING: A BRIEF OVERVIEW

Police services are actively working to enhance their intelligence capacities through the implementation of data-driven practices and AI. One important application of this is 'predictive policing' software that identifies people at risk of offending or being a victim of crime, as well as identifying 'places and times with an increased risk of crime' (Perry et al., 2013, pp. 8–9). Empirical research available on AI in policing has illustrated how its implementation has not been a smooth process and is hotly contested, with significant concern regarding the appropriate practical and ethical boundaries of its application (Chan, 2021; Chan et al., 2022).

One body of policing research has focused on the *technological* aspects of AI. For example, scholarship has looked at the effect and impact of using algorithmic practices, such as social network analysis and predictive policing, on the control, regulation and suppression of crime (Bright & Whelan, 2020; Burcher, 2020; Chainey et al., 2008; Ratcliffe, 2010). However, research indicated that the technological infrastructure within police services varies significantly, with a range of technological competency and data literacy skills (Evans & Kebbell, 2012; O'Shea & Nicholls, 2003; Weston et al., 2019), as well as poor technological integration and interoperability (Sanders et al., 2015). As Burcher (2020) illustrates, the technological infrastructure of police services impedes the use of social network analysis and the ability of intelligence analysts to produce meaningful analyses (see also Babuta, 2017; Ridgeway, 2017). While this scholarship has provided valuable insights into the platformization (Egbert, 2019) and scientification (Ericson & Shearing, 1986) of policing, it has prioritized *technology* as the object of analysis while either ignoring or paying insufficient attention to the way 'social, economic and political forces' shape the design and use of these technologies (Wyatt, 2008, p. 168). As van 't Wout et al. (2020) explain, the actual decision-making involved in designing algorithms and interpreting analytic outputs remains a *human responsibility*.

Another body of research explores the interpretive, *social* elements of AI in policing. For example, Chan and Bennett Moses (2019) identify the symbolic capital afforded to AI and algorithmic platforms and argue that '[a]djectives associated with data-driven approaches to decision making (such as "smart" analytics) reflect positively on those who employ them'. Such adjectives, Brayne and Christin (2021) argue have been used to justify and legitimize the use of these technologies in policing and criminal courts. This scholarship demonstrates how police services often perceive AI to be apolitical and objective entities that remove subjectivity and bias from police work (Sandhu & Fussey, 2021). Researchers have also studied the way police officers' understandings of, and perceptions toward, AI shape their adoption and use of these technologies. For example, Egbert and Krasmann's (2020, p. 915) analysis of Germany's PRECOBS software showed how predictive software 'still strongly echoes the logic of conventional risk technology' by drawing on past events to identify high-risk areas and employing 'conventional' policing practices (see also Sanders & Chan, 2020; Sanders & Condon, 2017). Alternatively, Brayne (2017) and Sandhu and Fussey (2021) demonstrate how officers' perceptions of predictive policing and their concerns regarding algorithms replacing their discretion and decision-making have led to organizational resistance and poor technological uptake. For example, Ratcliffe et al. (2019), found officers to feel frustrated by the predictions provided by the technology – arguing that the predictions overlooked 'the detailed, contextual, and contingent knowledge that patrolling officers have acquired about their beats' (654). Further, they found that some of the predictions placed officers 'in direct conflict with deeply felt obligations' that were an important piece of their experiential knowledge (654).

Research examining police and intelligence analysts' interactions with automated tools (e.g., automatic data extraction and pattern recognition, predictive analysis, risk assessment and spatial mapping) have identified how algorithms are prone to several biases, such as algorithmic bias and selective adherence, which can result in discriminatory intelligence practices due to a lack of algorithmic fairness, transparency and accountability (Bennett Moses & Chan, 2018; Richardson et al., 2019). While work in the legal and policy landscape highlights these pressing issues, an empirical investigation into human-algorithm-interaction, and algorithmic complications, is severely lacking. In fact, there is little research available on the physical design of analytic platforms and intelligence tools and how they inform the production of police intelligence, nor how they perpetuate – or may be used to redress – biases and discrimination. As Leese (2021) argues, there is a need to critically interrogate how the inputs of humans affect the outputs of predictive models.

What has challenged policing technology scholars is finding a theory/methods framework that is analytically attentive to peoples' interactions and definitions as well as the structural contexts and material realities that influence, shape and guide the construction of social order. In fact, many police studies that use organizational theories have had difficulty conceptualizing the role of technologies because they have not been able to distinguish between the technical and the social without reifying them and treating them as separate and distinct entities (Clarke, 2005; Latour, 1987). Research in science and technology studies (STS), however, shows how the social and technological are co-constituted – with one making up the other (Clarke, 2005). Such scholarship draws attention to the embedded nature of technologies in their contexts of use and how technologies inform, shape and constrain human agency (Oudshoorn & Pinch, 2005; Woolgar, 1991).

There is a small, but growing, body of STS-informed policing research that illuminates how police technologies are not objective and static entities but are instead shaped by the meaning ascribed by users (see Chan, 2001; Innes et al., 2005; Manning, 2001; Sanders & Hannem, 2013; Tanner & Meyer, 2015). Drawing on a 'technologies-in-practice' (Orlikowski & Gash, 1994) theoretical framework, for example, policing researchers identify how the introduction of technology is socially constructed in the sense that a piece of technology – such as AI – is interpreted and understood through social groups (e.g., platoons, police departments) who are influenced by a range of physical, social, technological, political and organizational factors that may change over space and time (Chan, 2003; Lum et al., 2016; Sanders & Lavoie, 2020). By focusing on 'technologies-in-practice' (Orlikowski, 2000), policing researchers identify how the structures inscribed in information technologies shape 'action by facilitating certain outcomes and constraining others' (Orlikowski & Robey, 1991, p. 148). For example, Sanders and Condon's (2017) study of the integration of crime analysis in Canadian policing demonstrates how 'definitional understandings of crime analysis, as well as the division of police labour and the occupational culture of policing, are embedded within analytic technologies that, in turn, facilitate and constrain the production of intelligence' (p. 248).

Such research uncovers the different ways in which police technologies affect and reflect 'the logics, rationalities and modes of reasoning of security practices' while also facilitating and constraining particular modes of action and interpretation (Amicelle et al., 2015, p. 294). For example, Fussey et al.'s (2021) study on facial recognition software demonstrates how 'police operators and algorithmic processes... are mutually and recursively shaping and structuring one another' (p. 342) because 'technological capability is conditioned by police discretion' (p. 341) and police discretion is 'contingent on the operational and technical environment' (p. 341). While this scholarship is empirically rich and has worked to open up the black box of police-technology interaction, it has, at times, left the 'relationship of science and technology to political institutions undertheorized' (Jasanoff & Kim, 2009, p. 120). It is for these reasons that we invite policing scholars to use 'sociotechnical imaginaries' as a theoretical framework for empirically investigating the relationship between science and technology and political power in AI in policing.

SOCIOTECHNICAL IMAGINARIES

Sociotechnical imaginaries are 'collectively imagined forms of social life and social order reflected in the design and fulfillment of nation-specific scientific and/or technological projects' (Jasanoff & Kim, 2009, p. 120). As a theoretical framework, it provides an entry point for studying the co-production of 'technoscientific and political orders', by identifying how different imaginations of social life and order are co-produced along with the goals, priorities, benefits and risks of science and technology (Jasanoff & Kim, 2009, p. 124). It sensitizes researchers to the way 'human subjectivity and agency get bound up with technoscientific advances through adjustments in identities, institutions, and discourses that accompany new representations of things' (Jasanoff & Kim, 2015, p. 14). Sociotechnical imaginaries are situated, culturally particular, future-oriented visions that are 'stable enough to have the possibility of shaping terrains of choices, and thereby of actions' (Sismondo, 2020, p. 505). Although Jasanoff and Kim's definition focuses on 'desirable futures', it can equally be applied to undesirable or dystopian futures, or what they refer to as 'resistant imaginaries'. In this way, multiple visions can co-exist that are malleable and can change over time when new ideas become embedded in social practice. As Jasanoff and Kim (2015) note, 'imaginaries operate as both glue and solvent, able – when widely disseminated and effectively performed – to preserve continuity across the sharpest ruptures of innovation or, in reverse, to upend firm worlds and make them anew' (p. 29).

Sociotechnical imaginaries, as a theoretical construct, can enrich and broaden studies of police technology by enabling an examination of the relationship between science and technology (S&T) and political power. It provides an avenue for researchers to investigate:

> the role of the state in defining the purposes of publicly supported science and technology: what constitutes the public good, which publics should be served by investments in S&T, who should participate in steering science and by what means, and how should controversies be resolved about the pace or direction of research and development? … Only by addressing such questions head-on can one begin to understand why S&T policies take the forms they take, why they often diverge radically across nation states, and how S&T policymaking could better serve democratic interests in an era of globalization. (Jasanoff & Kim, 2009, p. 120)

As such, sociotechnical imaginaries provide a theoretical lens for attending to state power, as they 'describe attainable futures and prescribe futures that states believe ought to be attained' (Jasanoff & Kim, 2009, p. 120). For example, when studying sociotechnical imaginaries in policing, one can explore how those with authority and power, such as police leaders, politicians and IT developers, shape public imagination regarding AI in policing, and how their narratives define public good, and by extension, how they 'delimit, control, or contain risk in projects aimed at furthering goods' (Jasanoff & Kim, 2015, p. 26).

Chan (2021) provides an example of how to conduct an empirical analysis of sociotechnical imaginaries in relation to predictive policing. Drawing on published literature and web-based communications, she identified four exemplars of how predictive policing had been described and analysed: the *utopian* view which represents the 'myths' of predictive policing; the *social science* view which examines the assumptions, evaluations and accountability of predictive policing; the *data scientists* view which discusses the ethics of data science in predictions; and a view from *civil rights community groups* which expresses concerns about the justice implications of predictive policing. The last three views were examples of 'resistant imaginaries'. Chan discusses the ideal-type nature of this analysis. Rather than assuming homogeneity within groups or invariance over time, the framework allows for the agency of groups and individuals as well as the indeterminacy of history.

METHODOLOGICAL IMPLICATIONS

Studying sociotechnical imaginaries calls for the use of 'interpretive research and analytic methods, including discourse analysis of documents, images and representations, ethnography, cases and controversies, utopias and dystopias, and comparisons' (Harvard Kennedy School, 2022). In what follows, we identify some of the methodological challenges associated with studying sociotechnical imaginaries in policing – such as gaining access, collecting rich data and paying analytic attention to *both* structure and agency. We then advocate for the use of Adele Clarke's (1991) situational analysis – which is a form of ethnography that attends to structure and agency in a way that facilitates an empirical analysis of power.

Police services represent 'bounded and formal institutions' that have organizational rules, policies, procedures and cultures that govern action and membership (Warren & Karner, 2010), and which create challenges for researchers to gain research access (Huey & Riccardelli, 2016). For example, many police services in Canada and Australia have internal research offices that researchers must apply to in order to receive permission to conduct research. These offices often require researchers to develop memorandums of understanding and contractual research agreements before gaining access to the service and its members. Such agreements can outline the types of data collection strategies (i.e., interviews, observations, document analysis) permitted, as well as requests to access findings and to control the release of findings to the public (see Weston & Sanders, 2018).

Once granted access to the police service, researchers can face additional challenges in accessing data. For example, researchers often face 'widespread skepticism' and negative stereotypical attitudes about researchers and academics (Foster & Bailey, 2010, p. 97) that can foster a lack of respect for research efforts and create barriers to establishing trust and rapport with participants (Wong, 2009). These challenges are often exacerbated when the researcher is a visible minority, such as a racialized person or woman (Steinheider et al., 2012). Further, the project needs to adopt a mixed methods approach that draws on a range of data sources including policy and organizational documents, interviews, discourse analysis and field observations of policing agents with technology in order to develop a robust and nuanced analysis of 'imaginaries' within policing.

As an analytical framework, sociotechnical imaginaries cut through the agency-structure divide by incorporating psychological and subjective dimensions of human agency with structural realities, such as technological systems, organizational policies and political cultures (Harvard Kennedy School, 2022). They recognize technology and human agency as intricately connected with each other. Yet, unlike other STS theories, such as actor-network theory (Latour, 1987), the relationship between the social and technological is not symmetrical because it is only humans who have the capacity and power to imagine and give meaning to things (Jasanoff & Kim, 2015). Imagination and intentionality, therefore, create an *asymmetrical* relationship. By recognizing the asymmetrical human-technology relation, sociological imaginaries 'look to reveal the topographies of power' (Jasanoff, 2015, p. 19). In this way, sociotechnical imaginaries require researchers to prioritize meaning-making activities while also placing these activities and interactions within their broader political, economic, organizational, situational and technological contexts. As such, it requires a methodology that places analytic attention on the interactions, discourses and technologies involved in the situation of interest.

While interpretive methods, such as comparative case studies, discourse analyses and ethnography, are often used to study sociotechnical imaginaries, they have traditionally had difficulty attending to the co-constituted nature of the social and technological (Kleinknecht, van den Scott & Sanders, 2018). To address such analytic challenges, we believe that ethnographic methods, specifically 'situational analysis' (Clarke, 2005) provide 'analytic leverage' for analysing sociotechnical imaginaries because it allows the researcher to be attentive to the dynamic relationship between humans and materiality (van den Scott et al., 2017). As van den Scott, Sanders and Puddephatt (2017) argue:

> [b]y studying situated actions and knowledges, ethnographers are able to study the unsettled and dynamic aspects of technology in relation to user groups, often in the midst of wider power struggles...it moves us away from the study of static objects toward a sociology of objects that move, but sometimes in ordered ways. (p. 517)

REIMAGINING THE POWER OF ETHNOGRAPHY: A SITUATIONAL ANALYSIS

It is the analytical attention paid to materiality that makes ethnography – and more specifically 'situational analysis' – valuable for studying work, organizations and science and technology. To ensure that data collection and analysis are attentive to materiality and capture the agency-structure interactions, we advocate for the use of Adele Clarke's (2005) situational analysis. Situational analysis regards the *situation* of inquiry as the key unit of analysis and works to identify and take into account all components of the situation, including actors, materiality, discourses and the silent/implicated actors (those actors not directly/ actively involved in the situation). By focusing on both the situation of interest and peoples' meaning-making activities, it invites an analysis of difference that highlights multiple visions and explores how and why some perspectives (i.e., sociotechnical imaginations) win out over others (Clarke & Montini, 1993; Fujimura, 1991). It encourages a constant comparative method and recognizes that technologies, like all materiality, 'structurally condition the interactions within the situation through their specific properties and requirements' (Clarke, 1991, p. 139).

For example, Sanders (as cited in Sanders and van den Scott, 2018) utilized a situational analysis methodology when studying the integration of interoperable radio systems and records management systems among police, fire and emergency medical services. Drawing on interviews, observations, discourse analyses and texts (privacy legislation, organizational documents, technology training documents), her analysis sought to understand how emergency technologies, such as interoperable radios and records management systems, enable or constrain collaborative action among police, fire and paramedics during multi-agency incidents (where more than one service responds) (see Sanders and van den Scott, 2018). She began by mapping out who and what things mattered in a multi-agency emergency (such as police services, volunteer firefighters, paramedics, emergency call-takers, emergency technologies, technology designers, provincial information act and privacy legislation), as well as the discourses, ideas and concepts that shaped how different emergency workers and technology designers thought about emergency technologies and interoperability (such as risk management, professionalism, legitimation, information sharing and surveillance). Using these maps allowed her to identify all the discourses, objects and actors involved in a multi-agency incident, as well as their relations and negotiations. From this analysis, she uncovered how the structural, cultural and operational contexts of police, fire and emergency medical services led to differing definitions and perceptions of technology for police, fire and medical services. Further, her analysis exposed how hierarchical relations and organizational conflicts among police, fire and paramedics played out and were reinforced through the use of emergency technologies.

One accomplishes situational analysis by creating three types of maps that explicitly and intentionally include materiality: situational maps, social worlds/arenas maps and positional maps (Clarke, 1991). Similar to other ethnographic approaches, it utilizes data triangulation by drawing on numerous forms of data, such as field observations, texts (such as organizational documents, standard operating procedures, training documents and IT manuals), technologies, discourses and in-depth interviews to construct its maps. 'These maps are intended to capture and discuss the messy complexities of the situation in their dense relations and permutations. They intentionally work against the usual simplifications so characteristic of scientific work' by identifying the human, technology, laws, policies, discursive and cultural elements in the situation and analyzes the relations among them (Clarke, 2005, p. xxxv). One does not need to do all three forms of mapping to make sense of the situation. Rather, through the making of any map, researchers are pushed to uncover all of the discourses, technologies, policies, laws and actors involved in their situation, and to ask relational questions of the data, such as: What discourses, ideas and concepts shape how policing agents and police technology designers think about and conceive of artificial intelligence?

In this chapter, we have reimagined the usefulness of ethnography, specifically situational analysis, for empirically exploring sociotechnical imaginaries and interrogating the complexities of human-algorithmic interactions in data-driven policing. By focusing on situations and producing multiple maps, situational analysis, we argue, is analytically attentive to power, bridges structure and agency and facilitates in-depth comparative analyses that are capable of uncovering and assessing the robust and nuanced imaginaries shaping the development, integration, regulation and use of AI in policing.

FURTHER READING

Clarke, A. (2005). *Situational analysis: Grounded theory after the postmodern turn.* Sage Publications.
Orlikowski, W. J., & Gash, D. (1994). Technological frames: Making sense of technology in organizations. *ACM Transactions on Information Systems, 12*(2), 174–207.

REFERENCES

Amicelle, A., Aradau, C., & Jeandesboz, J. (2015). Questioning security devices: Performativity, resistance, politics. *Security Dialogue, 46*(4), 293–306. https://doi.org/10.1177/0967010615586964
Babuta, A. (2017). Big data and policing: An assessment of law enforcement requirements, expectations and priorities. *Royal United Services Institute* (Occasional Paper). https://rusi.org/publication/occasional-papers/big-data-and-policing-assessment-law -enforcement-requirements
Bennett Moses, L., & Chan, J. (2018). Algorithmic prediction in policing: Assumptions, evaluation, and accountability. *Policing and Society, 28*(7), 806–822. https://doi.org/10.1080/10439463.2016 .1253695
Brayne, S. (2017). Big data surveillance: The case of policing. *American Sociological Association, 82*(2), 977–1008.
Brayne, S., & Christin, A. (2021). Technologies of crime prediction: The reception of algorithms in policing and criminal courts. *Social Problems, 68*(3), 608–624. https://doi.org/10.1093/socpro/spaa004
Bright, D., & Whelan, C. (2020). *Organised crime and law enforcement: A network perspective.* Routledge. https://doi.org/10.4324/9781315522579
Browning, M., & Arrigo, B. A. (2021). Stop and risk: Policing, data, and the digital age of discrimination. *American Journal of Criminal Justice, 46*(1), 298–316. https://doi.org/10.1007/s12103-020-09557-x
Burcher, M. (2020). *Social network analysis and law enforcement: Applications for intelligence analysis.* Springer.
Chainey, S., Tompson, L., & Uhlig, S. (2008). The utility of hotspot mapping for predicting spatial patterns of crime. *Security Journal, 21,* 4–28. https://doi.org/10.1057/palgrave.sj.8350066
Chan, J. (2001). The technological game: How information technology is transforming police practice. *Criminal Justice, 1,* 139–159. https://doi.org/10.1177/1466802501001002001
Chan, J. (2003). Police and new technologies. In T. Newburn (Ed.), *Handbook of policing* (pp.665–669). Willan Publishing.
Chan, J. (2021). The future of AI in policing: Exploring the sociotechnical imaginaries. In J. L. M. McDaniel & K. G. Pease (Eds.), *Predictive policing and artificial intelligence* (pp. 43–59). Routledge.
Chan, J., Sanders, C., Bennett Moses, L., & Blackmore, H. (2022). Datafication and the practice of intelligence production. *Big Data & Society.* https://doi.org/10.1177/20539517221089310
Chan, J., & Bennett Moses, L. (2019). Can "Big Data" analytics predict policing practice? In S. Hannem, C. Sanders, C. Schneider, A. Doyle, & T. Christensen (Eds.), *Security and risk technologies in criminal justice: Critical perspectives* (pp. 41–86). Canadian Scholars' Press.
Clarke, A. (1991). Social worlds/arenas theory as organizational theory. In D. Maines (Ed.), *Social organization and social process: Essays in honor of Anselm Strauss* (pp. 119–158). Aldine de Gruyter.
Clarke, A. E. (2005). *Situational analysis: Grounded theory after the postmodern turn.* Sage Publications. https://doi.org/10.4135/9781412985833
Clarke, A., & Montini, T., (1993). The many faces of RU486: Tales of situated knowledges and technological contestations. *Science, Technology, & Human Values, 18*(1), 42–78.
Egbert, S. (2019). Predictive policing and the platformization of police work. *Surveillance & Society, 17*(1/2), 83–88. https://doi.org/10.24908/ss.v17i1/2.12920
Egbert, S., & Krasmann, S. (2020). Predictive policing: Not yet, but soon preemptive? *Policing & Society, 30*(8), 905–919. https://doi.org/10.1080/10439463.2019.1611821
Ericson, R., & Shearing, C. (1986). The scientification of police work. In G. Bohme & N. Stehr (Eds.), *The knowledge society: Sociology of science yearbook* (Vol. 10, pp. 129–159). Reidel.

Evans, J., & Kebbell, M. (2012). The effective analyst: A study of what makes an effective crime and intelligence analyst. *Policing & Society, 22*(2), 204–219. https://doi.org/10.1080/10439463.2011.605130

Ferguson, A. (2017). *The rise of big data policing: Surveillance, race, and the future of law enforcement.* New York University Press. https://doi.org/10.2307/j.ctt1pwtb27

Foster, J., & Bailey, S. (2010). Joining forces: Maximizing ways of making a difference in policing. *Policing, 4*(2), 95–103. https://doi.org/10.1093/police/paq007

Fujimura, J. (1991). On methods, ontologies, and representation in the sociology of science: Where do we stand? In D. Maines (Ed.), *Social organization and social process: Essays in honor of Anselm Strauss* (pp. 207–248). New York: Aldine de Gruyter.

Fussey, P., Davies, B., & Innes, M. (2021). 'Assisted' facial recognition and the reinvention of suspicion and discretion in digital policing. *British Journal of Criminology, 61*(2), 325–344. https://doi.org/10.1093/bjc/azaa068

Harvard Kennedy School. (2022). *Methodological pointers.* Program on Science, Technology & Society. https://sts.hks.harvard.edu/research/platforms/imaginaries/ii.methods/methodological-pointers/

Huey, L., & Ricciardelli, R. (2016). From seeds to orchards: Using evidence-based policing to address Canada's policing needs. *Canadian Journal of Criminology and Criminal Justice, 58*(1), 119–33. https://doi.org/10.3138/cjccj2015.E24

Innes, M., Fielding, N., & Cope, N. (2005). The appliance of science? The theory and practice of crime intelligence analysis. *British Journal of Criminology, 45*, 39–57. https://doi.org/10.1093/bjc/azh053

Jasanoff, S., & Kim, S.-H. (2009). Containing the atom: Sociotechnical imaginaries and nuclear regulation in the U.S. and South Korea. *Minerva, 47*(2), 119–146. https://doi.org/10.1007/s11024-009-9124-4

Jasanoff, S., & Kim, S.-H. (2013). Sociotechnical imaginaries and national energy policies. *Science as Culture, 22*(2), 189–196. https://doi.org/10.1080/09505431.2013.786990

Jasanoff, S., & Kim, S.-H. (Eds.). (2015). *Dreamscapes of modernity: Sociotechnical imaginaries and the fabrication of power.* University of Chicago Press.

Kleinknecht, S., van den Scott, L., & Sanders, C. (Eds.). (2018). *Craft of qualitative research.* Canadian Scholars Press.

Latour, B. (1987). *Science in action: How to follow scientists and engineers through society.* Harvard University Press.

Leese, M. (2021). Security as socio-technical practice: Predictive policing and non-automation. *Swiss Political Science Review, 27*(1), 150–157. https://doi.org/10.1111/spsr.12432

Lum, C., Koper, C., & Willis, J. (2016). Understanding the limits of technology's impact on police effectiveness. *Police Quarterly, 20*(2), 135–163. https://doi.org/10.1177/1098611116667279

Lum, C., Koper, C., & Wu, X. (2021). Can we really defund the police? A nine-agency study of police response to calls for service. *Police Quarterly,* 1–26. https://doi.org/10.1177/10986111211035002

Manning, P. (2001). Technology's ways: Information technology, crime analysis and the rationalizing of policing. *Criminal Justice, 1*, 83–103. https://doi.org/10.1177/1466802501001001005

Nissan, E. (2017). Digital technology's and artificial intelligence's present and foreseeable impact on lawyering, judging, policing and law enforcement. *AI & Society, 32*, 441–464. https://doi.org/10.1007/s00146-015-0596-5

Orlikowski, W. J. (2000). Using technology and constituting structures: A practice lens for studying technology in organizations. *Organization Science, 11*(4), 404–428. https://doi.org/10.1287/orsc.11.4.404.14600

Orlikowski, W. J., & Gash, D. (1994). Technological frames: Making sense of technology in organizations. *ACM Transactions on Information Systems, 12*(2), 174–207. https://doi.org/10.1145/196734.196745

Oudshoorn, N., & Pinch, T. (Eds.). (2005). *How users matter: The co-construction of users and technology.* MIT Press.

O'Shea, T. C., & Nicholls, K. (2003). Police crime analysis: A survey of US police departments with 100 or more sworn personnel. *Police Practice and Research, 4*(3), 233–250. https://doi.org/10.1080/1561426032000113852

Perry, W. L., McInnis, B., Price, C. C., Smith, S. C., & Hollywood, J. S. (2013). *Predictive policing: The role of crime forecasting in law enforcement operations.* RAND Corporation. https://www.rand.org/content/dam/rand/pubs/research_reports/RR200/RR233/RAND_RR233.pdf

Ratcliffe, J. (2010). Crime mapping: Spatial and temporal challenges. In A. R. Piquero & D. Weisburd (Eds.), *Handbook of quantitative criminology* (pp. 5–24). Springer. https://doi.org/10.1007/978-0 -387-77650-7_2

Ratcliffe, J., Taylor, R., & Fisher, R. (2019). Conflicts and congruencies between predictive policing and patrol officer's craft. *Policing and Society: An International Journal of Research and Policy, 30*(6), 639–655.

Richardson, R., Schultz, J., & Crawford, K. (2019). Dirty data, bad predictions: How civil rights violations impact police data, predictive policing systems, and justice. *New York University Law Review Online, 94,* 192–233.

Ridgeway, G. (2017). Policing in the era of big data. *Annual Review of Criminology*, 1, 401–419.

Robertson, K., Khoo, C., & Song, Y. (2020). To surveil and predict: A humans rights analysis of algorithmic policing in Canada. *Factual Findings.*

Sanders, C., & Chan, J. (2020). The challenges facing Canadian police in making use of big data analytics. In D. Lyon & D. Murakami Wood (Eds.), *Big data surveillance and security intelligence: The Canadian case* (pp. 180–194). University of British Columbia Press.

Sanders, C., & Condon, C. (2017). Crime analysis and cognitive effects: The practice of policing through flows of data. *Global Crime, 18*(3), 237–255. https://doi.org/10.1080/17440572.2017.1323637

Sanders, C. B., & Hannem, S. (2013). Policing the "risky": Technology and surveillance in everyday patrol work. *Canadian Review of Sociology, 18*(7), 389–410. https://doi.org/10.1111/j.1755-618X .2012.01300.x

Sanders, C., & Lavoie, J. (2020). Boundary objects and technological frames: Officers' perceptions and experiences using mental health screeners on the frontlines. *Policing & Society.* https://doi.org/10 .1080/10439463.2020.1813140.

Sanders, C., Weston, C., & Schott, N. (2015). Police innovations, 'secret squirrels' & accountability: Empirically studying intelligence-led policing in Canada. *British Journal of Criminology, 55*(4), 711–729. https://doi.org/10.1093/BJC/AZV008

Sandhu, A., & Fussey, P. (2021). The 'uberization of policing'? How police negotiate and operationalise predictive policing technology. *Policing & Society, 31*(1), 66–81. https://doi.org/10.1080/10439463 .2020.1803315

Sismondo, S. (2020). Sociotechnical imaginaries: An accidental themed issue. *Social Studies of Science, 50*(4), 505–507. https://doi.org/10.1177/0306312720944753

Steinheider, B., Wuestewald, T., Boyatzis, R. E., & Kroutter, P. (2012). In search of a methodology of collaboration: Understanding researcher-practitioner philosophical differences in policing. *Police Practice & Research: An International Journal, 13*(4), 357–374. https://doi.org/10.1080/15614263 .2012.671620

Tanner, S., & Meyer, M. (2015). Police work and 'new security devices': A view from the beat. *Security Dialogue, 46*(4), 384–400. https://doi.org/10.1177/0967010615584256

van den Scott, L. J., Sanders, C. B., & Puddephatt, A. (2017). Reconceptualizing users through rich ethnographic accounts. In C. Miller, U. Felt, L. Smith-Doerr, & R. Fouche (Eds.), *Handbook of science and technology studies* (4th ed., pp. 501–529). MIT Press.

van 't Wout, E., Pieringer, C., Irribarra, D. T., Asahi, K., & Larroulet, P. (2020). Machine learning for policing: A case study on arrests in Chile. *Policing and Society, 31*(9), 1036–1050. https://doi.org/10 .1080/10439463.2020.1779270

Warren, C., & Karner, R. (2010). *Discovering qualitative methods: Field research, interviews and analysis* (2nd ed.). Oxford University Press.

Weston, C., Bennett Moses, L., & Sanders, C. (2019). The changing role of the law enforcement analyst: Clarifying core competencies for analysts and supervisors through empirical research. *Policing & Society, 30*(5), 532–547. https://doi.org/10.1080/10439463.2018.1564751

Weston, C., & Sanders, C. (2018). Going through the (e)motions: Attending to social location attending to social location and emotionality in observational studies of police. In S. Kleinknecht, L. van den Scott, & C. Sanders (Eds.), *Craft of qualitative research.* Canadian Scholars Press.

Wong, K. C. (2009). Police scholarship in China. *Police Practice & Research: An International Journal, 10*(5/6), 503–519. https://doi.org/10.1080/15614260903378475

Woolgar, S. (1991). Configuring the user: The case of usability trials. In J. Law (Ed.), *The sociology of monsters: Essays on power, technology and domination* (pp. 57–103). Routledge.

Wyatt, S. (2008). Technological determinism is dead; long live technological determinism. In E. J. Hackett, O. Amsterdamska, M. Lynch, & J. Wajcman (Eds.), *The handbook of science and technology studies* (3rd ed., pp. 165–180). MIT Press.

68. Emergence of artificial intelligence in health care: a critical review

Annika M. Svensson and Fabrice Jotterand

INTRODUCTION

AI[1] systems for the collection and analysis of massive amounts of data are in development for virtually all areas of medicine (Esteva et al., 2019, Kulikowski, 2019, Miller & Brown, 2018).

In pathology, radiology, and dermatology, assisted image analysis is already helping clinicians make a diagnosis at the early stages of diseases to increase the chance of a cure (Bera et al., 2019). In direct patient care, AI may be used as virtual nursing assistants[2] for direct monitoring of patients and risk evaluation for certain disorders, although these applications may not be optimal, desirable, or possible to apply for all patients. AI can also be employed for the health surveillance of entire populations and enable data mining to assist in research efforts that can inform clinical practice guidelines.

However, as the AI algorithms are created, errors could be introduced. Furthermore, the input of imbalanced data could produce systematic bias. In AI systems with decreased transparency, such problems could be exceedingly difficult to detect. Other ethical issues raised by the introduction of AI applications include those of autonomy, beneficence, privacy/confidentiality, and informed consent. The surge in the development of AI applications in health care has not been balanced by international governance grounded on ethical principles, although some efforts are in progress (Morley et al., 2022).

Eventually, AI applications could be envisaged to create algorithms that would be obscure to physicians. Watson for Oncology[3] was developed specifically to aid in medical decision support. The stated intent was to personalize treatments for each patient by integrating patient history, treatment, genetics, imaging data, and biomarkers to compare them to the entire universally available clinical and scientific data corpus on the same disorder. Following the cancellation of several major projects allegedly due to problems with the integration of such diverse data, the future of this specific AI system is now uncertain. However, if a similar application emerges in the future, it would likely have a profound impact on health care at both individual and societal levels.

Advanced AI applications could potentially perform many tasks that are currently performed exclusively by physicians. Thus, the implications for the professional role of physicians

---

[1] Artificial intelligence (AI) denotes the use of machines to make predictions similar to what a human being would do, or an agent that reasons and acts "rationally."

[2] AI applications that can monitor vital parameters (blood pressure, pulse, weight), guide intake of medications and initiate interaction with health care providers through chat bots.

[3] Created by IBM, it was used in trials in India and the US, where projects at MD Anderson and Sloane Kettering were canceled.

and changes in the patient-physician relationship need to be considered as AI applications are introduced.

This chapter discusses the possible consequences of the implementation of advanced AI in health care. The first section presents practical and ethical challenges that the establishment of advanced AI health care applications could pose. In the second section, some examples of developing AI applications are critically examined. Finally, we explore the transforming roles of physicians and their professional responsibilities during the implementation of AI applications in health care.

PRACTICAL AND ETHICAL CHALLENGES

Errors and Bias

There are currently no regulations or tools by which the quality of AI systems can be evaluated. If developing AI applications for health care are not designed to be transparent, quality assessment cannot be readily performed. AI systems should never be constructed to create or perform their own quality control; evaluation by an external entity is necessary. For quality control, specific inquiries with known outcomes could be entered into the system and the output checked by humans or another independent AI system.

Random errors could be introduced by humans during the input of data. Furthermore, data of low quality or poorly or non-uniformly formatted data may not be correctly interpreted by the AI.

Standardized criteria for patient data evaluation and categorization prior to entry into charts are currently lacking and may be exceedingly difficult to implement in a busy clinical setting. Historical patient data may not be possible to curate. Loss of such data could lead to bias.

Physicians who work with a developing AI system must be able to continuously perform checks to confirm that the application operates in a safe manner, despite any time pressure. AI systems should be built with transparency so that any erroneous results can be identified, and inaccurate recommendations overridden.

In general, small sample sizes, such as in the evaluation of treatments for rare cancer variants, present a problem with reproducibility. Therefore, training sets should contain as much material as possible. However, issues with data collection, curation, and organization can result in data sets that are not representative of the entire patient population. It is crucial that databases correctly represent the population for which the derived algorithm will be used. Previously, the lack of geo-diversity in ImageNet, a database that provides free image training sets for researchers that train neural networks, was shown to lead to ethnic and gender biases (Shankar et al., 2017). In a medical context, the relative lack of photographs of non-Caucasian individuals in databases and in general on the internet could hamper adequate network learning and lead to misdiagnosis by improperly trained algorithms.

Considering the surge in non-traditional online platforms for the publication of scientific data, and consequently, the amount of data published without peer review, a standardized vetting process should be instituted so that all data from research studies be critically evaluated prior to inclusion into AI systems. People that serve as annotators for medical databases should possess enough specific expertise to determine whether data should be added to the database or not. If AI applications should become self-sufficient, i.e., designed to annotate their own data sources, it would be even more difficult to ensure correct, non-biased content.

Informed Consent and Responsibility

The concept of informed consent[4] is fundamental to the practice of medicine. It involves the conscious act of reviewing, understanding, and analyzing relevant facts and being able to freely decide about treatment. The patient should receive complete information about the diagnosis and different treatment options, including the option to not be treated at all. Any future AI system that would make suggestions about treatment should be transparent about why a certain treatment is selected. Alternative options should be presented in a manner that invites a discussion between the patient and the provider and allows the patient to reach a decision that is optimal considering his or her personal circumstances and desires. The physician in turn must ensure that he or she is able to provide enough information for the patient to make an independent decision.

Any black box elements of advanced AI would also present a problem when it comes to the issues of responsibility and liability.[5] To what extent would a physician who uses an advanced non-transparent AI device be personally responsible for decisions or other actions taken by the AI system? As a comparison, doctors who work as medical directors in US hospital laboratories, with an enormous output of data from mostly black box instruments, are still personally responsible for the operation of the laboratory and for the quality of the data provided to clinicians (Centers for Medicare and Medicaid Services, 2022). In the 2018 case of a woman killed by a self-driving car in Arizona,[6] the company that built the algorithm faced no criminal charges, while the driver of the self-driving car was charged with negligent homicide (Davies & Marshall, 2019).

Autonomy and Confidentiality/Privacy

In the future, advanced AI applications could potentially be used to integrate diverse types of data and results from surveillance methods, including patient charts, social media activity, wearable sensors, and monitors in the patient's home. Patients that are subject to any type of surveillance should be aware of what data is registered and be given the option to opt-out. Information should be provided about how the information is being used. The data should only be utilized for the intended and stated purpose.

As an example, heart failure, a common ailment among the elderly, makes the patient accumulate fluid. Tracking body weight with an AI system may make it possible to notice subtle changes and intensify treatment before the patient notices other symptoms. Thereby, hospital

---

[4] An in-depth discussion of the issue of informed consent is beyond the scope of this chapter.

[5] Specific issues of liability and data protection are not within the scope of this chapter.

[6] In 2018, a woman was killed by a self-driving Uber car in Tempe, Arizona. She was on foot, pushing her bicycle across the road in the evening, far away from any crosswalk. The AI system built by Uber erroneously classified objects as pedestrians only if they were close to a crosswalk. Classifying the woman as a vehicle, the AI system misjudged her speed trajectory so that there was a delay in applying the brakes. While Uber faced no criminal charges, the driver, who was allegedly distracted by her cell phone, was charged with negligent homicide by Arizona prosecutors and is scheduled to go to trial in the spring of 2022.

admission could be avoided. However, if a patient's body weight is registered by an AI device built into the toilet seat of a "smart toilet" (Jennings, 2021) in a nursing home, the patient should be notified that the seat has this capability and be able to choose whether he or she wants to use this feature. Similarly, elderly patients with dementia may be monitored in their homes by cameras, AI with face recognition, and audio devices. However, it should be possible for patients and their families to disable the devices if desired. For every new AI device that emerges on the market, questions about the preservation of patient dignity and privacy should be raised by the physician. It would be the physician's responsibility to inform the patient, assist in opt-out if desired, and offer alternative options. For instance, instead of cameras, motion sensors could be used to maintain a higher degree of privacy.

DEVELOPING AI APPLICATIONS IN HEALTH CARE

Speech Recognition/Prediction of Human Behavior

Natural language processing (NLP)[7] is already in use in health care for a variety of purposes. For instance, a system for translating speech to written text that adjusts to individual speakers' voices by deep learning[8] has been used in hospitals for many years.

Watson and similar systems use NLP to "understand" questions posed in human language, search the entire internet for information, and provide the answer in a format understandable to humans.

In health care, the ability of an AI system to rearrange and assess a clinical chart for completeness and to immediately extract the data necessary to make decisions about diagnosis or treatment would be highly desirable. Furthermore, AI could potentially be used to identify unexpected and difficult-to-diagnose diseases and risk factors where prevention is key by examining chart notes for obscure patterns or sifting through the entire body of literature published on a disease to inform decision-making. A factor that currently limits the performance of AI in the medical context is that the data is unstructured and derived from many diverse types of sources.

Applications in psychiatry

Automated analysis of massive quantities of data is already performed to predict human behavior in less complex settings, such as the personalization of advertisements.

Using NLP, a multitude of digitalized applications for stress handling and cognitive behavior therapy are available through smartphones. In clinical psychiatry, AI could also be used to support physicians in diagnosing diseases, evaluate patients undergoing therapy, and possibly, predict disease trajectory (Andersson et al., 2019). Recently launched AI applications utilize the fact that speech is affected, sometimes in subtle ways, to reflect alterations in the human mind. For instance, a small study suggested that it would be possible to predict which

---

[7]   The ability of a computer system to "understand" the meaning of spoken or written human language and be able to respond in the same manner. Applications involve rule-based modeling of the human language and machine learning.

[8]   A variant of machine learning based on artificial neural networks with multiple layers, originally constructed to resemble the architecture of the human brain.

patients out of a group of high-risk individuals would eventually transition to psychosis (Bedi et al., 2015).

Determining the risk that a patient may commit suicide is a major challenge in psychiatric practice. Currently, patients undergo evaluation through an interview with a physician and through specific risk assessment surveys that provide numeric scores (Chan et al., 2016). These instruments generally have relatively high sensitivity, but low specificity and predictive value. Overall, the evaluations are subjective and dependent on the quality of interaction between the clinician and the patient. AI applications may now emerge to assist suicide prevention and intervention strategies (Bernert et al., 2020; Lejeune et al., 2022; Berrouiguet et al., 2019; Poulin et al., 2014). In a future clinical scenario where such applications would be used, important concerns beyond the evaluation of clinical utility would be the issue of responsibility in cases where the application fails, and how to resolve possible disagreements about diagnosis and treatment between the AI application and an intuitive but subjective physician.

Image Analysis

Clinical specialties that currently use AI-assisted analysis of images involving pattern recognition include pathology, radiology, and dermatology. AI applications developed for specific purposes may equal the diagnostic performance of skilled clinicians and surpass them when it comes to speed (Miller & Brown, 2018).

Diagnosing malignant melanoma[9] by AI image analysis is complicated by the fact that melanotic (pigmented) lesions appear different dependent on their location. For instance, a melanoma located under a fingernail has an atypical appearance, especially in people with a dark complexion. Such lesions may be difficult to diagnose by an AI image analysis algorithm that has encountered very few if any examples of this particular type of lesion in its training set. An experienced physician who is less rule-bound and used to "thinking outside the box" would be more likely to detect it. Such potential problem areas for AI algorithms must be identified and addressed before they lead to errors or bias in clinical practice. In this case, a new data set was created to specifically feature lesions in unusual places (Combalia et al., 2019).

The ISIC[10] Archive is currently the largest public collection of images of skin disorders. Contributors include several large university clinics around the Western world (the US, Australia, and Europe). It should be noted that most of the images are of Caucasians. When the input data lack contributions from certain ethnicities, one cannot expect the system to perform equally well for those groups of people (Zou & Schiebinger, 2018), and action should be taken to correct such bias.

Recently, computer-aided diagnosis (CAD) systems have been launched for use by the public through cell phone apps for the diagnosis of skin disorders. The user captures pictures with their cell phone camera for evaluation by an AI application. One application achieves a sensitivity of 95% (*vide infra*), while specificity is lower (Udrea et al., 2020). The result is provided directly to the patient. In case of suspected malignancy, the patient is prompted to see a doctor. It has been argued that such systems would be particularly helpful in developing countries and other areas where dermatologic clinics are rare and/or expensive to consult and that their use would increase geographic and socioeconomic equity. However, image quality

---

[9]   Malignant melanoma tumors develop from skin cells that produce pigment (melatonin).
[10] International Skin Imaging Collaboration, ISIC Archive (isic-archive.com).

may vary between photographs, some areas of the body may be missed, and a false sense of security or, conversely, fear in case of being prompted to see a doctor, may cause the patient to be lost to follow-up and treatment.

Facial recognition technology (FRT)[11] may be used to monitor patients, for instance, to determine their adherence to medication regimens or, in the case of patients with dementia, ascertain that they do not leave a care facility. FRT could also be employed to diagnose medical and psychiatric disorders and assess pain and other emotions (Martinez-Martin, 2019). It can be used to assist in the diagnosis of certain genetic disorders since many of these patients display specific facial features[12] (Chen et al., 2018; Basel-Vanagaite et al., 2016; Hsieh et al., 2022).

The use of FRT raises multiple ethical issues, including privacy and confidentiality. To further improve the AI applications, patient images need to be included in new training sets; however, informed consent should be collected from patients or their parents regarding such use. Accidental findings may also present a problem in this context since the application might detect additional disorders or conditions that may be entirely unrelated to the investigation at hand. The patient should be aware that this could occur and be able to opt-out of taking part in such information.

Transforming Roles of Physicians

The practice of personalized, evidence-based medicine requires the analysis of complex patient data as well as applicable research studies to optimize the diagnostic process and treatment options for each individual. With increasing expectations and exponential growth of the body of medical literature, the workload for clinical practitioners is rapidly expanding. AI applications to analyze scientific data and assist in decision-making could increase both efficiency and equity, since the outcome would no longer depend on the individual physician's abilities or personal biases, nor would it differ between geographic areas.

Automated AI services for the initial triaging of patients to immediately place them at the appropriate level of care could help increase efficiency and limit cost. Given the omnipresent chatbots in online life, this loss of personal interaction with a health care professional may be acceptable to many patients in uncomplicated contexts such as initial screening. With improving FRT and NLP, an AI application may even learn to interpret the patient's non-verbal communication and tone of voice and adjust communication accordingly.

Exchanges with AI systems might provide a smoother process for patients that need to communicate in a foreign language, or those that have multiple comorbidities and feel time pressure in the doctor's office. In fact, some patients may prefer a non-judgmental chatbot over a physician when discussing sensitive issues (Lucas et al., 2017).

---

[11]   Mapping of a person's facial features followed by conversion into mathematical descriptors that are entered into a database.

[12]   Genetic diagnosis can be supported by a machine learning application, GestaltMatcher, based on a deep neural network containing over 17,000 portraits of patients with over 1100 rare genetic disorders. The application may be able to delineate entirely new syndromes by combining genotype data with images.

However, for many patients, the personal interview not only provides human comfort but may also be more efficient for patients who do not fit into any common disease pattern by optimizing communication and applying intuitive thinking.

Scarce investigations into patient satisfaction with chatbots have shown reluctance related to trust in the chatbot's ability among some users (Nadarzynski et al., 2019; Dennis et al., 2020; Laranjo et al., 2018). In telemedicine, i.e., interaction with a physician by screen, recent surveys showed that most people preferred in-person encounters if that alternative was provided and that patients with a lower educational level tended to be less satisfied with virtual visits (Khan et al., 2022).

Some authors envisage that the use of AI for tedious or mundane tasks would provide more time for physicians to care for their patients. Others have argued that using AI could lead to an overreliance on the algorithms as well as a lessening of skills and self-confidence (Cabitza et al., 2017).

With the introduction of advanced AI both family practitioners and hospitalists might abdicate most of the cognitively challenging tasks (Hyland et al., 2020), psychiatrists might see an AI device surpass them in evaluating subtle cues in patient communication, and skilled surgeons might find themselves operating robotic hands that are more precise than any human hands could be (Bodenstedt et al., 2020). If the system could be transparent and possible to override, the physician would have a key role in that capacity. With a black box device, he or she would serve mainly to provide counseling and support as needed. Such a fundamental shift would inevitably affect the way physicians view their own role, as well as how they are perceived by patients and society.

Medical schools would have to make major adjustments to manage transformation toward the use of high-complexity AI systems in health care. Users must be well educated regarding the systems, in particular, their limitations. However, would there be an incentive for students to undertake traditional medical studies if cognitively complex work were performed by AI algorithms and robots? Will senior physicians be willing to maintain skills that are no longer necessary in their daily work?

We believe that physicians have a duty to honor their fiduciary relationship with their patients. Physicians should be truthful to those under their care, honor their autonomy, and protect them from harm. Furthermore, physicians have a specific responsibility to serve and protect vulnerable patient groups (Svensson & Jotterand, 2022; Hajar, 2017). During the design and implementation of AI systems, they must engage and educate themselves and act as advocates for their patients and for the public. Each step toward increased dependence on AI should be carefully evaluated. We have suggested that health care professionals should work together with other stakeholders including patients, the general public, ethicists, informaticists, and others toward global regulation of AI to ensure that basic ethical principles not be violated and that human control of AI is preserved at all times (Svensson & Jotterand, 2022).

CONCLUSION

AI applications in health care have the potential to increase efficiency, reduce human errors, and help manage escalating costs and physician workload by automation, optimization of workflow, coordination of care, and transfer of certain tasks from highly specialized humans to machines.

However, numerous issues can be envisaged, both with current limited applications and a potential future autonomous AI. The legal regulation of AI applications is beyond the scope of this chapter, but the need for universal surveillance and legislation is imminent. The physician's personal responsibility for the consequences of medical decisions made exclusively by the software must be clarified.

All AI applications must be independently examined and evaluated prior to being released for use. Clinical utility, safety, and freedom from bias must be ensured. Parallel AI systems should be used as backups to lessen the impact of disruptions to a system, provide options to cross-check results, and enable second opinions. Humans should always be able to override the system. Transparency must be ensured, all alternative treatments should be displayed, and informed consent must be obtained. Socioeconomic status and other demographics should not be automatically incorporated into treatment decisions by the AI.

AI could decrease geographical and socioeconomic inequality but must then be made available to all patients; connectivity issues or computer illiteracy should not limit access. Conversely, those who do not wish to be part of the system or be monitored by AI devices should have their wishes respected. Those that decline participation should not be excluded from health care.

Finally, we believe that physicians should take a leading role in the critical evaluation of new AI applications to inform and protect patients. Physicians and other health care workers can also make crucial contributions toward the creation of a moral framework upon which the regulation of AI applications could be based. This will be exceedingly difficult given the moral and cultural diversity in society. Furthermore, the framework must have enough flexibility to efficiently address systems in development. We have previously proposed that the concept of deliberative democracy (Gutmann & Thompson, 2004; Jotterand, 2006, 2016; Jotterand & Alexander, 2011) should provide the basis for such efforts (Svensson & Jotterand, 2022). Maintaining the balance between proactive control of AI against the desire to develop these systems to advance the practice of medicine will be one of the most important challenges of medicine in the future.

REFERENCES

Andersson G., Titov N., Dear B.F., Rozental A. & Carlbring P. Internet-delivered psychological treatments: From innovation to implementation. (2019). *World Psychiatry. 18*(1):20–28. doi: 10.1002/wps.20610. PMID: 30600624; PMCID: PMC6313242.

Basel-Vanagaite L., Wolf L., Orin M., Larizza L., Gervasini C., Krantz I.D. & Deardoff M.A. Recognition of the Cornelia de Lange syndrome phenotype with facial dysmorphology novel analysis. (2016) *Clin Genet.* May;89(5):557–563. doi: 10.1111/cge.12716. Epub 2016 Jan 25. PMID: 26663098.

Bedi G., Carrillo F., Cecchi G.A., Slezak D.F., Sigman M., Mota N.B., Ribeiro S., Javitt D.C., Copelli M. & Corcoran C.M. Automated analysis of free speech predicts psychosis onset in high-risk youths. (2015). *NPJ Schizophr. 26*(1):15030. doi: 10.1038/npjschz.2015.30. PMID: 27336038; PMCID: PMC4849456.

Bera K., Schalper K.A., Rimm D.L., Velcheti V. & Madabhushi A. Artificial intelligence in digital pathology - new tools for diagnosis and precision oncology. (2019). *Nat Rev Clin Oncol.* 16(11):703–715. doi: 10.1038/s41571-019-0252-y. Epub 2019 Aug 9. PMID: 31399699; PMCID: PMC6880861.

Bernert R.A., Hilberg A.M., Melia R., Kim J.P., Shah N.H. & Abnousi F. Artificial intelligence and suicide prevention: A systematic review of machine learning investigations. (2020). *Int J Environ Res Public Health. 15*;17(16):5929. doi: 10.3390/ijerph17165929. PMID: 32824149; PMCID: PMC7460360.

Berrouiguet S., Billot R., Larsen M.E., Lopez-Castroman J., Jaussent I., Walter M., Lenca P., Baca-García E. & Courtet P. An approach for data mining of electronic health record data for suicide risk management: Database analysis for clinical decision support. (2019). *JMIR Ment Health.* 7;6(5):e9766. doi: 10.2196/mental.9766. PMID: 31066693; PMCID: PMC6707587.

Bodenstedt S., Wagner M., Müller-Stich B.P., Weitz J. & Speidel S. Artificial intelligence-assisted surgery: Potential and challenges. (2020). *Visc Med.* 36(6):450–455. doi: 10.1159/000511351. Epub 2020 Nov PMID: 33447600; PMCID: PMC7768095.

Cabitza F., Rasoini R. & Gensini G.F. (2017). Unintended consequences of machine learning in medicine. *JAMA.* Aug 8;*318*(6):517–518. doi: 10.1001/jama.2017.7797. PMID: 28727867.

Centers for Medicare and Medicaid Services. Clinical Laboratory Improvement Amendments. Laboratory Director Responsibilities. https://www.cms.gov/Regulations-and-Guidance/Legislation/CLIA/downloads/brochure7.pdf. Accessed 220520

Chan M.K., Bhatti H., Meader N., Stockton S., Evans J., O'Connor R.C., Kapur N. & Kendall T. Predicting suicide following self-harm: Systematic review of risk factors and risk scales. (2016). *Br J Psychiatry.* 209(4):277–283. doi: 10.1192/bjp.bp.115.170050. Epub 2016 Jun 23. PMID: 27340111.

Chen S., Pan Z.X., Zhu H.J., Wang Q., Yang J.J., Lei Y., Li J.Q. & Pan H. Development of a computer-aided tool for the pattern recognition of facial features in diagnosing Turner syndrome: Comparison of diagnostic accuracy with clinical workers. (2018). *Sci Rep.* 18;8(1):9317. doi: 10.1038/s41598-018-27586-9. PMID: 29915349; PMCID: PMC6006259.

Combalia M., Codella N.C., Rotemberg V., Helba B., Vilaplana V., Reiter O., Halpern A.C., Puig S. & Malvehy J. BCN20000: Dermoscopic lesions in the wild (2019). arXiv preprint arXiv:1908.02288v2. https://doi.org/10.48550/arXiv.1908.02288.

Davies A. & Marshall A. Feds pin Uber crash on human operator, call for better rules. Nov 2019. https://www.wired.com/story/feds-blame-uber-crash-on-human-driver-call-for-better-rules/ accessed 220515.

Dennis A.R, Kim A., Rahimi M., Ayabakan S. User reactions to COVID-19 screening chatbots from reputable providers. (2020). *J Am Med Inform Assoc.* 27(11):1727–1731. https://doi.org/10.1093/jamia/ocaa167

Esteva A., Robicquet A., Ramsundar B., Kuleshov V., DePristo M., Chou K., Cui C., Corrado G., Thrun S. & Dean J.(2019). A guide to deep learning in healthcare. *Nat Med.* 25(1):24–29. doi: 10.1038/s41591-018-0316-z. Epub 2019 Jan 7. PMID: 30617335.

Gutmann A. & Thompson D.F. (2004). *Why Deliberative Democracy?* Princeton, NJ: Princeton University Press.

Hajar R. (2017). The physician's oath: Historical perspectives. *Heart Views: The Official Journal of the Gulf Heart Association,* 18(4):154–159. https://doi.org/10.4103/heartviews.heartviews_131_2.

Hsieh T.C., Bar-Haim A., Moosa S., Ehmke N., Gripp K.W., Pantel J.T., Danyel M., Mensah M.A., Horn D., Rosnev S., Fleischer N., Bonini G., Hustinx A., Schmid A., Knaus A., Javanmardi B., Klinkhammer H., Lesmann H., Sivalingam S., Kamphans T., Meiswinkel W., Ebstein F., Krüger E., Küry S., Bézieau S., Schmidt A., Peters S., Engels H., Mangold E., Kreiß M., Cremer K., Perne C., Betz R.C., Bender T., Grundmann-Hauser K., Haack T.B., Wagner M., Brunet T., Bentzen H.B., Averdunk L., Coetzer K.C., Lyon G.J., Spielmann M., Schaaf C.P., Mundlos S., Nöthen M.M. & Krawitz P.M. GestaltMatcher facilitates rare disease matching using facial phenotype descriptors. (2022). *Nat Genet.* 54(3):349–357. doi: 10.1038/s41588-021-01010-x. Epub 2022 Feb 10. PMID: 35145301.

Hyland S.L., Faltys M., Hüser M., Lyu X., Gumbsch T., Esteban C., Bock C., Horn M., Moor M., Rieck B., Zimmermann M., Bodenham D., Borgwardt K., Rätsch G. & Merz T.M. Early prediction of circulatory failure in the intensive care unit using machine learning. (2020). *Nat Med.* 26(3):364–373. doi: 10.1038/s41591-020-0789-4. Epub 2020 Mar 9. PMID: 32152583.

Jennings K., This smart toilet seat might save your life one day (forbes.com) Feb 3, 2021.

Jotterand F. The politicization of science and technology: Its implications for nanotechnology. (2006). *J Law Med Ethics.* 34(4):658–666. doi: 10.1111/j.1748-720X.2006.00084.x. PMID: 17199806.

Jotterand F. & Alexander A.A. Managing the "known unknowns": Theranostic cancer nanomedicine and informed consent. (2011) In *Biomedical Nanotechnology: Methods and Protocols Methods in Molecular Biology*, vol. 726, ed. S. J. Hurst, 413–429. Dordrecht, the Netherlands: Springer Science Business Media.

Khan S., Llinas E.J., Danoff S.K., Llinas R.H. & Marsh E.B. The telemedicine experience: Using principles of clinical excellence to identify disparities and optimize care. (2022). *Medicine (Baltimore). 11*;101(10):e29017. doi: 10.1097/MD.0000000000029017. PMID: 35451400; PMCID: PMC8913094.

Kulikowski C.A. Beginnings of artificial intelligence in medicine (AIM): Computational artifice assisting scientific inquiry and clinical art - with reflections on present AIM challenges (2019).

Laranjo L., Dunn A.G., Tong H.L., Kocaballi A.B., Chen J., Bashir R., Surian D., Gallego B., Magrabi F., Lau A.Y.S., Coiera E. Conversational agents in healthcare: A systematic review. (2018). *J Am Med Inform Assoc. 25*(9):1248–1258. https://doi.org/10.1093/jamia/ocy072.

Lejeune A., Le Glaz A., Perron P.A., Sebti J., Baca-Garcia E., Walter M., Lemey C. & Berrouiguet S. Artificial intelligence and suicide prevention: A systematic review. (2022). *Eur Psychiatry. 15*;65(1):1–22. doi: 10.1192/j.eurpsy.2022.8. Epub ahead of print. PMID: 35166203; PMCID: PMC8988272.

Lucas G.M., Rizzo A., Gratch J., Scherer S., Stratou G., Boberg J. & Morency L.-P. (2017) Reporting mental health symptoms: Breaking down barriers to care with virtual human interviewers. *Front. Robot.* AI 4:51. doi: 10.3389/frobt.2017.00051.

Martinez-Martin N. What are important ethical implications of using facial recognition technology in health care? (2019). *AMA J Ethics. 1*;21(2):E180–187. doi: 10.1001/amajethics.2019.180. PMID: 30794128; PMCID: PMC6634990.

Miller D.D. & Brown E.W. Artificial intelligence in medical practice: The question to the answer? (2018). *Am J Med. 131*(2):129–133. doi: 10.1016/j.amjmed.2017.10.035. Epub 2017 Nov 7. PMID: 29126825.

Jotterand F. Moral enhancement, neuroessentialism, and moral content. (2016) In *Cognitive Enhancement: Ethical and Policy Implications in International Perspectives*, eds. F. Jotterand, V. Dubljevic, 42–56. New York: Oxford University Press.

Morley J., Murphy L., Mishra A., Joshi I. & Karpathakis K. (2022). Governing data and artificial intelligence for health care: Developing an international understanding. *JMIR Form Res.* Jan 31;6(1):e31623. doi: 10.2196/31623. PMID: 35099403; PMCID: PMC8844981.

Nadarzynski T., Miles O., Cowie A., Ridge D. (2019). Acceptability of artificial intelligence (AI)-led chatbot services in healthcare: A mixed-methods study. *Digital Health*. doi:10.1177/2055207619871808

Poulin C., Shiner B., Thompson P., Vepstas L., Young-Xu Y., Goertzel B., Watts B., Flashman L. & McAllister T. Predicting the risk of suicide by analyzing the text of clinical notes. (2014). *PLoS One. 28*;9(1):e85733. doi: 10.1371/journal.pone.0085733. Erratum in: *PLoS One.* 2014;9(3):e91602. PMID: 24489669; PMCID: PMC3904866.

Shankar S., Halpern Y., Breck E., Atwood J., Wilson J. & Sculley D. No classification without representation: Assessing geodiversity issues in open data sets for the developing world. (2017). arXiv: Machine Learning.

Svensson A.M. & Jotterand F. (2022). Doctor Ex Machina: A critical assessment of the use of artificial intelligence in health care. *J Med Philos. 8*;47(1):155–178. doi: 10.1093/jmp/jhab036. PMID: 35137175.

Udrea A., Mitra G.D., Costea D., Noels E.C., Wakkee M., Siegel D.M., de Carvalho T.M. & Nijsten T.E.C. Accuracy of a smartphone application for triage of skin lesions based on machine learning algorithms. (2020). *J Eur Acad Dermatol Venereol. 34*(3):648–655. doi: 10.1111/jdv.15935. Epub 2019 Oct 8. PMID: 31494983.

Zou J. & Schiebinger L. Comment: AI can be sexist and racist – it's time to make it fair. (2018). *Nature. 559*:324–326. doi: https://doi.org/10.1038/d41586-018-05707-8.

69. The politics of imaginary technologies: innovation ecosystems as political choreographies for promoting care robotics in health care

Jaana Parviainen

INTRODUCTION

Almost a quarter of a century ago, an American robotics guru, Joseph Engelberger (2000), envisaged that a multitasking robot that could care for older adults in home environments would soon be developed and manufactured. To promote this vision, he travelled around the world in the mid-1990s to motivate research teams to embark on his mission towards designing the 'Elderly Caregiver', a personal robot assistant for everyday tasks (Pransky, 2018). Inspired by Engelberger's vision, several robot prototypes have been developed, including Fraunhofer IPA's care robot platform called Care-O-Bot 1 in 1998, SCITOS A5 by METRA-labs in 2010, the Hector robot in 2012, the Hobbit in 2015, the RobuMate robot in 2012, and IFN Robotics's prototype called Ruby in 2018.[1] It seems that none of these robot prototypes have so far led to commercial solutions in the consumer market beyond research purposes. One of the exceptions is the Wakamaru domestic robot, which was launched by Mitsubishi in 2005. Unfortunately, the Mitsubishi company failed to sell a single robot.

Despite the high expectation that AI-driven robots will revolutionise human care, the role of robots in care has, so far, remained marginal in nursing. Monitoring devices, automatic medicine dispensers, robotic pets, mobile telepresence equipment, and hospital logistics are already in use, but they are only capable of simple, colloquial interactions or modest repetitive tasks, not multitasking assistance in daily activities (van Aerschot & Parviainen, 2020). One of the main technical bottlenecks in developing useful robots for home care and nursing homes is the lack of sophisticated robotic limbs that could help older people with dressing, bathing, and toileting. Thus, it is justified to call multitasking care robots 'imaginary technologies' since the most promising care robots are still at the prototype stage.

With the help of national and international policy programs—so-called 'white papers' or roadmaps—R&D funding is channelled for the development of care robotics that is believed to be important in solving social issues, such as problems related to the ageing of the population (e.g. Government of Japan, 2007).

White papers and robot roadmaps remain only declarations without an active group of participants involved in the process of the domestication of imaginary technologies. Compared

---

[1] All these prototypes are mobile assistive robots, designed for smart home environments to advance wellness and quality of life for seniors. Fraunhofer IPA's latest version of its platform, Care-O-Bot 4, was launched in 2015. Both Care-O-Bot 4 and SCITOS A5 are available for research and development (R&D) projects only.

with the domestication of existing technologies by households (Silverstone & Hirsch, 1992), this discursive domestication process (Hartmann, 2020) aims at preparing people and environments for emerging technologies in advance: by creating positive images of these technologies in public, conducting surveys on care robots, providing information to those who will deploy these technologies, and intervening to change the prevailing practices in which the emerging technologies could be embedded within existing systems. In managerial rhetoric, this is called building up 'innovation ecosystems' that should boost different actors to find a functional goal enabling technological evolution (Jackson, 2011). The actors of ecosystems include the material resources (funds, equipment, facilities, etc.) and the human capital (industry researchers, academic scientists, students, faculties, industry representatives, etc.) that together make up the institutional entities participating in an ecosystem (Niemelä et al., 2021).

Building innovation ecosystems around emerging technologies is under the control of governments, tech giants, and interest groups, though the impression created of innovation ecosystems is that they are more local than global, self-organising, and self-sustaining networks that gather business and R&D under trendy hubs to nurture innovations. This ostensible independence is an essential feature because, otherwise, it would be difficult to integrate, for example, universities and academic research into the business objectives of ecosystems. To avoid managerial rhetoric and discuss the power structure of these systems, I classify innovation ecosystems as 'political choreographies' to better capture their global scale and their strategic practice of steering business decisions. Inspired by assemblage thinking, the notion of political choreography is understood as a network that gathers actors and resources around imaginary technologies, creating value for its participants (Parviainen & Coeckelbergh, 2020). The concept helps us to understand the performative strategies that different types of actors involved (research projects, universities, start-ups, investors, media, etc.) in innovation ecosystems use to promote their agendas around care robotics.

The politics of imaginary technologies has enabled us to address the more-than-instrumental role of technologies to clarify the proactive strategies of innovation ecosystems. Innovation ecosystems need performative tools, such as raising hype in media, to strengthen the network's ability to shape public opinion in a way that is favourable to robots. Consequently, the performative acts of innovation ecosystems help to channel venture investments and R&D funding to care robotics, promoting the robotisation of human care. This also means that not all actors involved in ecosystems are fully aware of their role in this network, and the performative tools of ecosystems never have full control over the actors. Nevertheless, the media spectacle of the Sophia robot has shown that robotics does not need to be mature for the consumer market as long as its performative function reassures investors of its future potential in developing AI-based robotics (Parviainen & Coeckelbergh, 2020).

My hypothesis is that many academic actors in the R&D field of care robotics have embraced a societal goal of advancing the utilisation of robots in social and welfare services, thus, acting as prime movers in innovation ecosystems. Using recent examples from the care robotics literature, I analyse two types of interventions in which research projects contributed to the domestication of care robots in nursing. The first intervention is care robot acceptance studies, which focus on caregivers', patients', and citizens' attitudes towards robotics based on hypothetical scenarios, images, or narratives. The second is press releases by scientists in which preliminary research findings are described and revolutionary promises are made, generating robot hype in the media. Both interventions are also closely interwoven. My understanding is that many scholars leading such projects have taken a proactive approach to changing care infrastructures and practices so that new technologies can be introduced into the healthcare system rather than taking a neutral or critical stance towards these technologies.

ACCEPTANCE RESEARCH PROMOTING THE ROBOT INVASION IN NURSING

Robot acceptance models are developed to explain and evaluate the intention to use a particular type of technology, including robots (e.g. Holden & Karsh, 2010; Hebesberger et al., 2017). One central dimension in acceptance is social acceptance, which is defined as individuals' willingness to integrate a robot into everyday life, emphasising the importance of detecting reasons why people accept or reject robotic systems in their environment and what attitudes they express towards robotic aids (Weiss et al., 2011). Regarding care-assisting robots, acceptance studies focus on either evaluating citizens'/patients'/clients' attitudes towards robots (e.g. Bedaf et al., 2018; Hebesberger et al., 2017; Johnson et al., 2014; Körtner et al., 2014; Khosla et al., 2017; Louie et al., 2014; Smarr et al., 2014; Stafford et al., 2014; Takanokura et al., 2021) or how caregivers and professionals accept or reject robotic systems in their working environments (e.g. Bedaf et al., 2018; Coco et al., 2018; Rantanen et al., 2018; Yuan et al., 2022; Wolbring & Yumakulov, 2014). In the case of older adults, most of these studies come to the conclusion that seniors have positive attitudes towards socially assistive robots (e.g. Bedaf et al., 2018; Bettinelli et al., 2015; Hebesberger et al., 2017; Louie et al., 2014). Furthermore, older adults are especially open to using robot assistants if they perform home-based tasks, such as housekeeping, laundry, and offering medication reminders; manipulate objects, such as finding, fetching, reaching for items, or opening and closing drawers; or information management (Smarr et al., 2014). Seniors have shown that they are more willing to accept the presence of the robot than their caregivers, relatives, or health care professionals (Bedaf et al., 2018).

Of the acceptance studies mentioned above, only two of them (Takanokura et al., 2021; Bettinelli et al., 2015) are based on robots available in the consumer market and create more or less realistic settings in which robots are seen and used as part of care practices. Typically, studies on acceptance are based on research designs in which researchers show images or video of real or imaginary robots (D'Onofrio et al., 2018; Pino et al., 2015), provide narratives or descriptions of robots (Coco et al., 2018; Hall et al., 2019; Pew Research Center, 2017; Rantanen et al., 2018; Smarr et al., 2014), or test robot prototypes to elicit respondents' opinions of care robots (e.g. Chen et al., 2017; Khosla et al., 2017; Pino et al., 2015). In some robot acceptance studies, the Wizard of Oz (WoZ) technique is used to simulate imaginary conditions where participants can feel as if a robot responds to their speech or movement in real-time on screen or in labs (Kim et al., 2013). Using the WoZ technique, the robot's movements and speech are steered on the laptop by the operator as if the robot were moving autonomously to induce participants to interact with and pay attention to the robot.

What do these studies say about the use of care robots in the real world? Almost nothing. Some researchers mention the technical limitations of available care robots; for example, in Bedaf et al. (2018), 'the robot in its current form was found to be too limited and participants wished the robot could perform more complex tasks' (p. 592). In addition, there are very few acceptance studies in which robotic devices are compared with conventional technologies to determine the former's effectiveness in completing the examined tasks (Bettinelli et al.,

2015). Hardly any researchers mention reasons why research designs are almost impossible to arrange to provide solid empirical evidence based on a comparative longitudinal study.

The main reason for the absence of such solid evidence is that there are very few care robot types available on the market. It is likely that research teams would acquire care robots for experiments if affordable and functional equipment were available. The strange thing is that scientists remain silent on this fact in their analyses. An overview of the development and sales figures of the global service robotics market in recent years clearly reveals the current situation. Though there are no separate statistics on care robotics, by looking at the value of world trade in service robots for personal and domestic use, we can outline the volume of robots produced to care for older people (International Federation of Robotics [IFR], 2020a). According to the IFR's recent report, the worldwide sales of assistance robots for older adults or handicapped persons were only US\$91 million in 2019 (IFR, 2020b). For instance, the value of Finland's exports of health technology products alone was €2,400 million (2.4 billion) in 2019 (Niemelä et al., 2021).

I am particularly interested in the question of why robot acceptance research is being conducted in huge volume, even though the field of care robotics is not mature enough to provide a reliable picture of its acceptability. For instance, a simple search for 'care robot acceptance' returned 85,000 results on Google Scholar in March 2022. While some of these results may be from non-refereed articles, several are peer-reviewed academic studies. The volume of care robot acceptance studies has begun to produce a growing number of meta-analytic reviews, generating a new level of speculation (Holt-Lunstad et al., 2015; Shishehgar et al., 2018).

I want to emphasise here that these peer-reviewed academic studies on care robot acceptance meet scientific research criteria, so I do not question their methodological reliability. Instead, I am interested in how acceptability research is used to create tools for transforming people's opinions and perceptions of robots so that robots can be implemented in health care in the future. There are at least two strategies. First, acceptance studies provide valuable information to robotics designers about what kind of software and design solutions inspire users' trust in these devices. Second, these studies produce tools for management to persuade people to use robot-driven services over human-based services. That findings from acceptance studies are used to persuade users becomes evident in the descriptions of research purposes and findings when scientists state, for example, 'we investigated how to increase people's acceptance of a social robot by considering the concept of social distance' (Kim et al., 2013, p. 1091), or 'These findings contribute to our understanding of how elderly users accept assistive social agents' (Heerink et al., 2010, p. 361).

A more worrying feature is related to blurring the line between existing technologies and imaginary technologies in health care (Parviainen & Koski, 2023). The speculative field of research on the acceptance of care robots—producing research results in a huge volume—easily generates the impression that care robotics devices are already widely used in elderly care. The creation of such a distorted image is hardly deliberate, but rather an unintended consequence of the amount of research on this subject. Although the ignorance of researchers may not be intentional, their attitudes can be associated with 'wilful blindness' regarding the fact of how few robotic devices are available on the market. By wilful blindness I mean a process of detachment in which some aspects of reality become or remain invisible or irrelevant to researchers (Bovensiepen, 2020). As the field of robot acceptance has become established independently, researchers do not consider it necessary to rethink the rationale for their research. So, I assume that some researchers and their projects involving speculative studies of robot acceptance are conducted to develop innovation ecosystems as actors. They participate by either consciously or unconsciously promoting robot invasions rather than taking a critical stance on whether it is economic, ecological, or humanly reasonable to prepare care service infrastructures and educate health care professionals to be ready for speculative care robotics in the future.

PRESS RELEASES BY SCIENTISTS IN CARE ROBOTICS

Press releases have served as a major source of story ideas for science journalists in both traditional and new media environments. Scholars in critical media research have complained that the media produce sensationalism and highlight controversy over the coverage of science rather than addressing topics of scientific consensus (Brown Jarreau, 2014). However, while scientists often blame the media for focusing on controversy in some cases—most recently regarding research on COVID-19—press releases by scientists about their research projects are shown to be a major point of distortion in the translation of science from research findings to media stories (Brechman et al., 2011). Sensationalism in press releases gives newsrooms novel and controversial topics to report on but press releases reporting on science by highlighting preliminary or controversial results can lead to distorted perceptions of science (Schwartz et al., 2012).

Brown Jarreau (2014) states that scientists are under increasing pressure to promote academic research in public by issuing press releases. A number of Internet news sites have made science press releases more visible and accessible not only to professionals but also to lay readers through social media and blogs. Many scientists are increasingly practising writing for the lay reader and packaging press releases with images, graphics, videos, and headlines designed to help spread the story via traditional and social media. Media visibility is also important because competition for research funding also requires publicity. Many press releases never cross the news threshold, but there are a few that draw the attention of journalists and newsrooms, including a few cases in the field of social robotics, such as the bear-shaped Robear and the Sophia robot.

The Riken-SRK Collaboration Center for Human–Interactive Robot Research in Japan began its press release on the bear-shaped robot with the following sentences on February 15, 2015:

> Scientists from RIKEN and Sumitomo Riko Company Limited have developed a new experimental nursing care robot, ROBEAR, which is capable of performing tasks such as lifting a patient from a bed into a wheelchair or providing assistance to a patient who is able to stand up but requires help to do so. ROBEAR will provide impetus for research on the creation of robots that can supplement Japan's need for new approaches to care-giving. (Riken, 2015a)

The Robear robot—based on earlier versions of Riba-I, announced in 2009, and Riba-II, developed in 2011—was said to be lighter than its predecessors, weighing just 140 kilograms, to incorporate a number of features that enable it to exert force in a gentle way. Professor Toshiharu Mukai, leader of the robot team, said: 'We really hope that this robot will lead to advances in nursing care, relieving the burden on care-givers today. We intend to continue with research toward more practical robots capable of providing powerful yet gentle care to elderly people' (Riken, 2015a). The press release spread widely on international news platforms. Robear quickly achieved iconic status as a patient transfer robot that could solve care problems for older people in the future. For example, *The Guardian* titled a story based on a press release: 'Robear: The Bear-Shaped Nursing Robot Who'll Look after You When You Get Old' (Dredge, 2015). *The Mirror* titled its story: 'Robot BEARS Could Replace Nurses—'Robear' Combines a Friendly Face with Heavy Lifting Power' (Solon, 2015).

Just a month after the Riken (2015a) press release was sent, the Riken Center for Research on Human–Robot Interactions, which developed the robot, was closed on short notice; the statement read: the 'Riken-TRI Collaboration Center for Human–Interactive Robot Research (RTC) finished its scheduled research term and dissolved at the end of March 2015' (Riken, 2015b). Professor Mukai moved to Meijo University, where he has continued to develop the Robear platform, albeit with much more modest goals. The development and commercialisation of the lifting robot Robear have apparently been abandoned. It is likely that at the time of the February press release, the threat of closing the research centre was already known. The international press did not report this turn in Robear's development work. In 2018, *The Guardian* stated that 'Japan Lays Groundwork for Boom in Robot Carers' (Hurst, 2018). The illustrated photo within the 2018 story by *The Guardian* showed a Japanese robot prototype, 'Robear', lifting a woman for a demonstration at Riken-TRI in Nagoya.

The robot as the saviour of the ageing crisis in industrialised countries seemed such a captivating story that the media has begun to recycle the story without checking the facts. Reporters have remained silent on the weaknesses of robot prototypes and the fact that few care robots are used in nursing. The 'robot as saviour' theme has a special kind of news value in which journalists like to focus on their story selection. Humanoid robot figures, familiar from sci-fi movies, have sparked positive perceptions among readers such that robots will soon be used in senior care in some countries, particularly Japan. The Finnish broadcasting company YLE, for example, has repeatedly claimed in its news that robots will soon assist older people in Japan. Although social robots, such as the humanoid robots Nao or Pepper, cannot yet conduct physical and concrete care tasks, including dressing, bathing, and toileting, they are used to illustrate news about providing basic care services for seniors. *The Guardian* reported in 2016 'how a robot could be grandma's new carer', using the toy robot MiRo in its illustration (McMullan, 2016). In 2017, *BBC News* declared that academics say that 'robots could help solve the social care crisis', using the Pepper robot as an example (Richardson, 2017). None of these robot types has the fine motor ability to assist older people in their daily activities.

The Japanese government, in collaboration with the nation's tech industry, has been actively creating a positive image of Japanese robotisation using humanoid robots. The Innovation 25 roadmap of 2007, developed by Prime Minister Shinzo Abe and his cabinet, aimed to reverse the country's declining birth rate by 2025 by highlighting the key role of the nuclear family in reforming Japanese society (Government of Japan, 2007). Innovation 25 sought to address both birth and ageing issues through robotics and technology. The future Japanese family featured in the Innovation 25 roadmap included a mother, a father, two children, and a grandmother and grandfather. The newest member of the family was a household robot, Inobe-Kun, which took care of the housework and assisted the older grandparents. Jennifer Robertson (2018) called the vision of the Innovation 25 roadmap retro-futuristic because the family model appeared to reproduce sci-fi fantasies together with conservative notions of the nuclear family from the 1950s.

The media have played a pivotal role in publicising care robot developments to advance the initiatives of care robot innovation ecosystems towards the future of humanoid robots in care (van Aerschot & Parviainen, 2020; Parviainen & Coeckelbergh, 2020). However, journalists are not necessarily fully aware of their performative role in this network as they promote care robotics as imaginary technologies. Taking a strict view, providing highly speculative information about care robots could even be called *misinformation* if the audience were to judge these depictions as providing a credible image of future care. From an epistemological perspective, misinformation is understood as false or inaccurate information that is communicated regardless of the intention to deceive (O'Connor & Weatherall, 2019). Certainly, the present study cannot show that press releases like the story about the Robear have advanced public misunderstanding of care robot capabilities in human care. Still, there is a need for scholars to research the effects of these science press releases. So far, the aspects of scientific press releases that influence journalists' interests and later public understanding of phenomena (and how they accomplish this) have remained unknown.

Scientists and research teams that issue press releases on their robot experiments can create intentionally or unintentionally high expectations of care robots by building up hype around care robotics. Their goals can strengthen the network of innovation ecosystems to acquire new resources for R&D work and shape public opinion in a way that is favourable to robots. However, they can also be partly blamed for strengthening skewed images of the capabilities of care robots. In transmitting news on robot experiments, journalists should make it clearer, such as in the case of the Robear robot, that this type of robot prototype may never end up in consumer use. It can be considered misleading to present care robots as a solution for responding to the care needs of the growing elderly population when the available devices are mostly interactive robotic pets. Social robots, automatic medicine dispensers, or floor cleaners can hardly help to solve the massive social, ethical, and economic problems created by the diminishing resources and growing care needs of the ageing population.

CONCLUSION

Looking beyond the rhetoric of innovation ecosystems, this chapter has revealed some aspects of how scientific research and its performative communication are connected to promote the acceptance of care robotics in nursing. Using the term political choreography has enabled us to draw attention to the performative undertaking of innovation ecosystems to draw new R&D funding for the development of care robotics and to create hype to overcome public resistance to the equipment. The performative acts of innovation ecosystems, with the help of the media and other actors, channel venture investments and R&D funding to care robotics, promoting the robotisation of human care.

The chapter suggested that the performative roles of scientists and journalists in promoting care robots as actors in innovation ecosystems are not necessarily deliberate but related to their own wilful blindness. As the research on robot acceptance has become established in its own field, it is necessary for scholars to underline that their empirical results are highly speculative and that they discuss mainly imaginary robots or prototypes. The wilful blindness of journalists is related to their failure to check the facts about care robots, as a result, they recycle speculative promises in the media that are distributed by researchers in press releases.

This highly speculative information about care robots could even be called misinformation if the public takes it as a credible picture of the current state of care robots.

So far, the novel field of robot ethics in elderly care has focused on concerns over the effects and impacts of robot care for older people and care professionals in the future. The ethical discussions have so far remained speculative in nature and try to address the positive and negative potential of robotics: the potential to become socially isolated, the risk of ageist discrimination, and the possibility of losing or gaining one's own autonomy or opportunities for self-growth. My suggestion is that critical attention should also be directed at the political, economic, and ecological realities of organising care and the interests behind developing technological commodities. It is time to openly discuss the drivers of care robot initiatives to outline the bigger picture of organising care under conditions of limited resources. The political choreographies framework offers a helpful lens to discuss how critically proactive strategies create hype around care robotics to overcome potential resistance to equipment.

FURTHER READING

Jasanoff, S. (2016). *The ethics of invention: Technology and the human future.* W.W. Norton & Company.
Turkle, S. (2011). *Alone together: Why we expect more from technology and less from each other.* Basic Books.
Winner, L. (2020). *The whale and the reactor: A search for limits in an age of high technology* (2nd ed.). University of Chicago Press.

REFERENCES

Bedaf, S., Marti, P., Amirabdollahian, F., & de Witte, L. (2018). A multi-perspective evaluation of a service robot for seniors: The voice of different stakeholders. *Disability and Rehabilitation: Assistive Technology, 13*(6), 592–599. https://doi.org/10.1080/17483107.2017.1358300

Bettinelli, M., Lei, Y., Beane, M., Mackey, C., & Liesching, T. N. (2015). Does robotic telerounding enhance nurse–physician collaboration satisfaction about care decisions? *Telemedicine and E-Health, 21*(8), 637–643. https://doi.org/10.1089/tmj.2014.0162

Bovensiepen, J. (2020). On the banality of wilful blindness: Ignorance and affect in extractive encounters. *Critique of Anthropology, 40*(4), 490–507. https://doi.org/10.1177/0308275X20959426

Brechman, J. M., Lee, C., & Cappella, J. N. (2011). Distorting genetic research about cancer: From bench science to press release to published news. *Journal of Communication, 61*(3), 496–513. https://doi.org/10.1111/j.1460-2466.2011.01550.x

Brown Jarreau, P. (2014). When quotes matter: Impact of outside quotes in a science press release on news judgment. *Journal of Science Communication, 13*(4), A02. https://doi.org/10.22323/2.13040202

Chen, T. L., Bhattacharjee, T., Beer, J. M., Ting, L. H., Hackney, M. E., Rogers, W. A., & Kemp, C. C. (2017). Older adults' acceptance of a robot for partner dance-based exercise. *PLOS ONE, 12*(10), e0182736. https://doi.org/10.1371/journal.pone.0182736

Coco, K., Kangasniemi, M., & Rantanen, T. (2018). Care personnel's attitudes and fears toward care robots in elderly care: A comparison of data from the care personnel in Finland and Japan. *Journal of Nursing Scholarship, 50*(6), 634–644. https://doi.org/10.1111/jnu.12435

D'Onofrio, G., Sancarlo, D., Oscar, J., Ricciardi, F., Casey, D., Murphy, K., Giuliani, F., & Greco, A. (2018). A multicenter survey about companion robot acceptability in caregivers of patients with dementia. In A. Leone, A. Forleo, L. Francioso, S. Capone, P. Siciliano, & C. Di Natale (Eds.), *Sensors and microsystems* (Vol. 457, pp. 161–178). Springer International Publishing. https://doi.org/10.1007/978-3-319-66802-4_22

Dredge, S. (2015, February 27). Robear: The bear-shaped nursing robot who'll look after you when you get old. *The Guardian.* https://www.theguardian.com/technology/2015/feb/27/robear-bear-shaped-nursing-care-robot

Engelberger, J. (2000). A day in the life of Isaac. *Industrial Robot: An International Journal, 27*(3), 176–180. https://doi.org/10.1108/01439910010371588

Government of Japan. (2007, June 1). Long-term strategic guidelines "Innovation 25" [unofficial translation]. https://japan.kantei.go.jp/innovation/innovation_final.pdf

Hall, A. K., Backonja, U., Painter, I., Cakmak, M., Sung, M., Lau, T., Thompson, H. J., & Demiris, G. (2019). Acceptance and perceived usefulness of robots to assist with activities of daily living and healthcare tasks. *Assistive Technology, 31*(3), 133–140. https://doi.org/10.1080/10400435.2017.1396565

Hartmann, M. (2020). (The domestication of) Nordic domestication? *Nordic Journal of Media Studies, 2*(1), 47–57. https://doi.org/10.2478/njms-2020-0005

Hebesberger, D., Koertner, T., Gisinger, C., & Pripfl, J. (2017). A long-term autonomous robot at a care hospital: A mixed methods study on social acceptance and experiences of staff and older adults. *International Journal of Social Robotics, 9*(3), 417–429. https://doi.org/10.1007/s12369-016-0391-6

Heerink, M., Kröse, B., Evers, V., & Wielinga, B. (2010). Assessing acceptance of assistive social agent technology by older adults: The Almere model. *International Journal of Social Robotics, 2*(4), 361–375. https://doi.org/10.1007/s12369-010-0068-5

Holden, R. J., & Karsh, B.-T. (2010). The technology acceptance model: Its past and its future in health care. *Journal of Biomedical Informatics, 43*(1), 159–172. https://doi.org/10.1016/j.jbi.2009.07.002

Holt-Lunstad, J., Smith, T. B., Baker, M., Harris, T., & Stephenson, D. (2015). Loneliness and social isolation as risk factors for mortality: A meta-analytic review. *Perspectives on Psychological Science, 10*(2), 227–237. https://doi.org/10.1177/1745691614568352

Hurst, D. (2018, February 6). Japan lays groundwork for boom in robot carers. *The Guardian.* https://www.theguardian.com/world/2018/feb/06/japan-robots-will-care-for-80-of-elderly-by-2020

International Federation of Robotics. (2020a). Executive summary world robotics 2020 service robotics. Retrieved May 10, 2022 from https://ifr.org/free-downloads/

International Federation of Robotics. (2020b, October 28). Service robots record: Sales worldwide up 32% [Press Release]. Retrieved May 10, 2022 from https://ifr.org/ifr-press-releases/news/service-robots-record-sales-worldwide-up-32?fbclid=IwAR05ad%2047wiY7Y11tGtyqNtS3ugus_XRHgal6vKSPT3XCtgiBUobAbtdAw-U

Jackson, D. J. (2011). *What is an innovation ecosystem?* National Science Foundation. https://erc-assoc.org/sites/default/files/topics/policy_studies/DJackson_Innovation%20Ecosystem_03-15-11.pdf

Johnson, D. O., Cuijpers, R. H., Juola, J. F., Torta, E., Simonov, M., Frisiello, A., Bazzani, M., Yan, W., Weber, C., Wermter, S., Meins, N., Oberzaucher, J., Panek, P., Edelmayer, G., Mayer, P., & Beck, C. (2014). Socially assistive robots: A comprehensive approach to extending independent living. *International Journal of Social Robotics, 6*(2), 195–211. https://doi.org/10.1007/s12369-013-0217-8

Khosla, R., Nguyen, K., & Chu, M.-T. (2017). Human robot engagement and acceptability in residential aged care. *International Journal of Human–Computer Interaction, 33*(6), 510–522. https://doi.org/10.1080/10447318.2016.1275435

Kim, Y., Kwak, S. S., & Kim, M. (2013). Am I acceptable to you? Effect of a robot's verbal language forms on people's social distance from robots. *Computers in Human Behavior, 29*(3), 1091–1101. https://doi.org/10.1016/j.chb.2012.10.001

Körtner, T., Schmid, A., Batko-Klein, D., & Gisinger, C. (2014). Meeting requirements of older users? Robot prototype trials in a home-like environment. In C. Stephanidis & M. Antona (Eds.), *Universal access in human–computer interaction: Aging and assistive environments* (Vol. 8515, pp. 660–671). Springer International Publishing. https://doi.org/10.1007/978-3-319-07446-7_63

Louie, W.-Y. G., McColl, D., & Nejat, G. (2014). Acceptance and attitudes toward a human–like socially assistive robot by older adults. *Assistive Technology, 26*(3), 140–150. https://doi.org/10.1080/10400435.2013.869703

McMullan, T. (2016, November 6). How a robot could be grandma's new carer. *The Guardian.* https://www.theguardian.com/technology/2016/nov/06/robot-could-be-grandmas-new-care-assistant

Niemelä, M., Heikkinen, S., Koistinen, P., Laakso, K., Melkas, H., & Kyrki, V. (Eds.). (2021). Robots and the future of welfare services – A Finnish roadmap. *Crossover, 4.* http://urn.fi/URN:ISBN:978-952-64-0323-6

O'Connor, C., & Weatherall, J. O. (2019). *The misinformation age: How false beliefs spread*. Yale University Press.

Parviainen, J., & Coeckelbergh, M. (2020). The political choreography of the Sophia robot: Beyond robot rights and citizenship to political performances for the social robotics market. *AI & Society 36*(3), 715–724. https://doi.org/10.1007/s00146-020-01104-w

Parviainen, J., & Koski, A. (2023). "In the future, as robots become more widespread": A phenomenological approach to imaginary technologies in healthcare organisations. In F.-X. Vaujany, J. Aroles, & M. Perezts (Eds.), *The Oxford handbook of phenomenologies and organization studies*, pp. 277–296. Oxford University Press.

Pew Research Center. (2017, October 4). *Americans' attitudes toward robot caregivers*. https://www.pewresearch.org/internet/2017/10/04/americans-attitudes-toward-robot-caregivers/

Pino, M., Boulay, M., Jouen, F., & Rigaud, A.-S. (2015). "Are we ready for robots that care for us?" Attitudes and opinions of older adults toward socially assistive robots. *Frontiers in Aging Neuroscience, 7*. https://doi.org/10.3389/fnagi.2015.00141

Pransky, J. (2018, August 20). The essential interview: Martin Haegele, head of robot and assistive systems, Fraunhofer Institute. *Robotics Business Review*. https://www.roboticsbusinessreview.com/interview/martin-haegele-robot-fraunhofer-essential-interview/

Rantanen, T., Lehto, P., Vuorinen, P., & Coco, K. (2018). The adoption of care robots in home care: A survey on the attitudes of Finnish home care personnel. *Journal of Clinical Nursing, 27*(9–10), 1846–1859. https://doi.org/10.1111/jocn.14355

Richardson, H. (2017, January 30). Robots could help solve social care crisis, say academics. *BBC News*. https://www.bbc.com/news/education-38770516

Riken. (2015a, February 23). *The strong robot with the gentle touch* [Press Release]. https://www.riken.jp/en/news_pubs/research_news/pr/2015/20150223_2/

Riken. (2015b). *RIKEN-TRI collaboration center for human–interactive robot research (RTC) finished*. http://rtc.nagoya.riken.jp/index-e.html

Robertson, J. (2018). *Robo Sapiens Japanicus: Robots, gender, family, and the Japanese nation*. University of California Press.

Schwartz, L. M., Woloshin, S., Andrews, A., & Stukel, T. A. (2012). Influence of medical journal press releases on the quality of associated newspaper coverage: Retrospective cohort study. *BMJ, 344*(1), d8164–d8164. https://doi.org/10.1136/bmj.d8164

Shishehgar, M., Kerr, D., & Blake, J. (2018). A systematic review of research into how robotic technology can help older people. *Smart Health, 7–8*, 1–18. https://doi.org/10.1016/j.smhl.2018.03.002

Silverstone, R., & Hirsch, E. (1992). *Consuming technologies: Media and information in domestic spaces*. Routledge.

Smarr, C.-A., Mitzner, T. L., Beer, J. M., Prakash, A., Chen, T. L., Kemp, C. C., & Rogers, W. A. (2014). Domestic robots for older adults: Attitudes, preferences, and potential. *International Journal of Social Robotics, 6*(2), 229–247. https://doi.org/10.1007/s12369-013-0220-0

Solon, O. (2015, February 24). Robot BEARS could replace nurses – "Robear" combines a friendly face with heavy lifting power. *The Mirror*. https://www.mirror.co.uk/news/technology-science/technology/robot-bears-could-replace-nurses-5222531

Stafford, R. Q., MacDonald, B. A., Jayawardena, C., Wegner, D. M., & Broadbent, E. (2014). Does the robot have a mind? Mind perception and attitudes towards robots predict use of an eldercare robot. *International Journal of Social Robotics, 6*(1), 17–32. https://doi.org/10.1007/s12369-013-0186-y

Takanokura, M., Kurashima, R., Ohhira, T., Kawahara, Y., & Ogiya, M. (2021). Implementation and user acceptance of social service robot for an elderly care program in a daycare facility. *Journal of Ambient Intelligence and Humanized Computing*. https://doi.org/10.1007/s12652-020-02871-6

Van Aerschot, L., & Parviainen, J. (2020). Robots responding to care needs? A multitasking care robot pursued for 25 years, available products offer simple entertainment and instrumental assistance. *Ethics and Information Technology, 22*(3), 247–256. https://doi.org/10.1007/s10676-020-09536-0

Weiss, A., Bernhaupt, R., & Tscheligi, M. (2011). The USUS evaluation framework for user-centered HRI. In K. Dautenhahn & J. Saunders (Eds.), *New frontiers in human–robot interaction* (pp. 89–110). John Benjamins Publishing Company.

Wolbring, G., & Yumakulov, S. (2014). Social robots: Views of staff of a disability service organization. *International Journal of Social Robotics*, 6(3), 457–468. https://doi.org/10.1007/s12369-014-0229-z

Yuan, F., Anderson, J. G., Wyatt, T. H., Lopez, R. P., Crane, M., Montgomery, A., & Zhao, X. (2022). Assessing the acceptability of a humanoid robot for Alzheimer's disease and related dementia care using an online survey. *International Journal of Social Robotics*. https://doi.org/10.1007/s12369-021-00862-x

70. AI in education: landscape, vision and critical ethical challenges in the 21st century
Daniel S. Schiff and Rinat B. Rosenberg-Kima

AI IN EDUCATION: PAST, PRESENT, AND FUTURE

Artificial intelligence in education (AIED) is entering a new stage. While the origin of artificial intelligence (AI) research is often attributed to the 1950s, AIED is a relatively more recent field involving the adoption of AI in educational settings or for educational purposes. In particular, AIED began to develop in the 1970s under the moniker of computer-assisted instruction (CAI) (Carbonell, 1970), which had the general ambition of simulating a human tutor. Along these lines, researchers in the 1980s began to develop intelligent tutoring systems aimed at providing personalized instruction and feedback based on a deep understanding of student learning as inferred from their interaction with the AI system (Corbett et al., 1997). Following the establishment of the International AIED Society in 1997, AI techniques were applied to other related domains, including through educational data mining (EDM) and learning analytics and knowledge (LAK), resulting in the annual international conference on EDM starting in 2008 and the LAK conference starting in 2010.

Further developments in deep learning techniques in the 21st century enabled researchers to advance work related to social AI abilities, including research on natural language processing (NLP) and identification of facial expressions, gestures, posture, and gaze, along with other indicators of human affect (Lemaignan et al., 2016; McDuff et al., 2013). This progress has helped realize the use of computerized social or virtual agents for educational purposes (Goel & Polepeddi, 2016; Rosenberg-Kima et al., 2008). Relatedly, while most implementations of AIED historically involved a computer as the primary interface, these new socially oriented AI abilities, along with progress in the field of robotics, have opened the way for research and development on human-robot interaction (HRI) in education, as demonstrated with the initiation of the annual international conference on HRI in 2006. Figure 70.1 offers a brief history of selected key milestones related to AIED and AI generally.

In the few decades since AIED's origins, research and applications have proliferated and are now increasingly being utilized in real-world settings. There is thus every reason to think that AIED will be as impactful as AI in sectors like transportation, manufacturing, and healthcare. Yet perhaps surprisingly, AIED has not received as much attention in mainstream AI policy discourse (Schiff, 2021a), and ethical issues associated with AIED have only begun to be examined (Holmes et al., 2021). Meanwhile, historical failures of educational technology and a growing number of scandals associated specifically with AIED urge the need for increased attention to this field. As such, and as recent advances in AI generally have triggered widespread discussion of AI's implications, governance, and purpose, it is likewise timely for AIED to be subject to similar consideration and scrutiny.

This article, therefore, seeks to critically examine the role of AIED in the present and future, including by questioning its underlying assumptions and presumed or unexamined

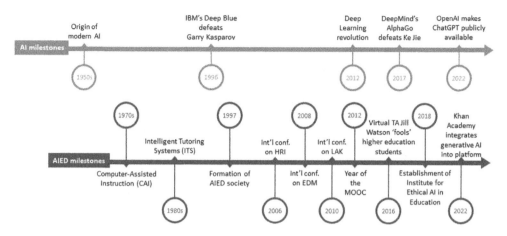

Source: Author.

Figure 70.1   *Key milestones in the history of AIED and AI*

trajectory. We begin by introducing AIED and providing an overview of the growing number of AIED applications in real-world settings. Next, we discuss why AIED applications have successfully scaled or failed to do so, reviewing key challenges related to implementation, governance, research, and ethics. Finally, we take stock of how AI's role in educational systems is unfolding, what ultimate goals and limitations are imagined, and whether the current trajectory of AIED is prudent or begs modification in light of this vision.

EVOLVING APPLICATIONS OF AIED: TEACHING, LEARNING, AND BEYOND

The techniques, applications, and roles of AIED systems have increased since the origin of the field three decades ago. Yet a useful place to start is with the intelligent tutoring system (ITS)—among the most commonly researched tools (Zawacki-Richter et al., 2019) and arguably the "holy grail" of AIED. At their core, ITSs are designed to computerize the teaching and learning process, making explicit the hidden dynamics of education and allowing for the automation of instruction (Self, 1998). They operate by representing content in a discipline (often STEM courses), assessing student engagement and performance on tasks and questions, and identifying the appropriate pedagogical response such as recommending subsequent content to learners (Zhang & Aslan, 2021). ITSs thus theoretically perform many of the core functions associated with teaching. Above all, ITSs are often lauded for their capacity for low-cost and easily-scalable personalization, functionally allowing for one-to-one instruction and the educational benefits that entails (Vincent-Lancrin & Vlies, 2020). Meta-analyses (Kulik & Fletcher, 2016; VanLehn, 2011; Xu et al., 2019) tend to support the capacity of ITS to solve the "2 sigma problem," referring to the ability of individualized tutoring to help students achieve their maximum potential, as compared with conventional group-based instruction that renders differentiation and mastery learning approaches less feasible (Bloom, 1984).

Various elements of ITS—and AIED more broadly—have been adopted to serve learners in a variety of settings, ranging from formal and in-class education to informal, self-guided, after-school, app-based, and online settings. For example, in addition to automated instruction, related functions aimed at learners include automated and personalized assessment (e.g., United States GREs) and feedback (e.g., Duolingo), recommendation of courses (e.g., Coursera), assistive technologies such as speech-to-text, and even academic and career counseling (Schiff, 2021b; Woolf et al., 2013; Zhang & Aslan, 2021). Further, AIED tools might be instantiated quite visibly in computers or online platforms via chatbots and other virtual agents (e.g., Jill Watson) or indeed physically embodied in social robots (e.g., Ozobot); alternatively, they may function more invisibly in the background of learning management systems (e.g., Canvas), intelligent textbooks, and massively online open courses (MOOCs).

Another set of AI systems is targeted at educators and educational administrators, construed broadly. Perhaps most centrally, AIED tools can support teachers by monitoring student learning progress, providing an individual- and classroom-level picture of educational needs (e.g., ASSISTments). Other such functions are largely logistical, like supporting course scheduling and automating teacher communication with parents. Notably, AIED tools are now increasingly used for indirect non-instructional purposes as well as instructional ones, such as to assess student dropout risk and intervention needs (e.g., Course Signals), to assign teachers to schools, inform admissions decisions in higher education, and optimize school operations related to transportation, security, or maintenance (T. Baker & Smith, 2019; Conner & Nelson, 2021; Diebold & Han, 2022).

Figure 70.2 provides an overview of prominent applications and implied purposes of AIED for learners and for teachers and administrators, as well as an incomplete list of underlying techniques, tools, and impacted stakeholders.

IMPLEMENTATION BARRIERS, FAILURE MODES, AND SCANDALS IN AIED

What, if anything, connects these diverse AIED applications? And what accounts for the relative success or failure of different kinds of AIED systems in advancing toward real-world usage? There are several candidate responses. AIED systems may advance because underlying techniques become technically feasible (capability-based reasons), because they fill important gaps in educational systems (needs-based reasons), because they become commercially viable (economic-based reasons), or because they align with certain idealized pathways associated with AI (vision-based). The tension between these drivers and constraints helps to explain differential progress in AIED adoption. Most notably, exciting technical advances, the promise of financial opportunity, and the pursuit of idealized visions may drive the development of AIED that is not especially targeted to serving the needs of students, leading to mismatches and even public-facing failures.

For example, despite numerous efforts to advance sophisticated, affect-aware, human-like tutors, this ambition has not been realized and remains in doubt. AIED systems are still limited in their ability to interpret social and emotional behavior (Belpaeme et al., 2018), and at worst, are accused of perpetuating pseudoscientific practices with historical analogs in physiognomy (Sloane et al., 2022). These limitations are especially apparent when AIED tools like ITS have been scaled beyond demonstration settings to impact large numbers of students. As

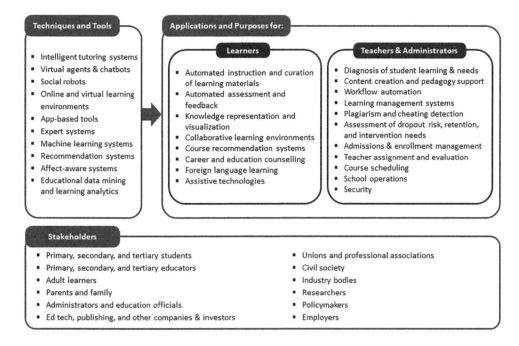

Source: Author.

Figure 70.2 *An overview of AIED stakeholders, techniques, and purposes*

Baker (2016, p. 601) notes, despite decades of research and significant advances employing techniques like Bayesian knowledge tracing and knowledge space theory, the most prominent systems today that model student knowledge rely on simple "heuristics to assess student mastery, such as whether the student gets three [answers] right in a row." Advanced systems, relative to simpler ones (e.g., adaptive assessments) seem to fail to provide a sufficient value to justify the complexities their adoption requires and the risks entailed.

The history of educational technology and AI's promises and overpromises are instructive toward understanding this development trajectory. Notably, many education technology (ed-tech) initiatives, especially in the context of low-income countries, have been marked by efficiency promises and techno-utopian visions that failed to appreciate relevant implementation and policy contexts (Sancho-Gil et al., 2020). Failed projects like One Laptop per Child (OLPC) and newer failures in school system adoption of MOOCs or other ed-tech systems (Rivard, 2013; Warschauer & Ames, 2010) underline this point. Even in countries with more advanced education infrastructure, the bottom-up nature of ed-tech adoption and the prominent role of teacher resistance (Hannafin & Savenye, 1993) delimit the willingness of educators to spend precious time on unproven technologies. Relatedly, while some national education systems are more centralized, allowing for coordinated adoption, many are not. AIED adoption thus often ultimately depends on the individual buy-in, capacity, and vision of individual educators, school leaders, and school systems, who must consider AIED in light of current pedagogical and curricular design as well as funding and policy constraints.

For instance, many ITS are pedagogically premised on variations of mastery learning, where students are allowed sufficient time in a flexible fashion (and with sufficient support) to foster certain competencies before progressing onto subsequent ones (Corbett et al., 1997). While such a strategy pairs nicely with the computerization logic of AIED (and digital platforms like Khan Academy), adoption of mastery learning in school systems is still limited, with modest and sometimes mixed evidence of effectiveness, and a plurality of barriers, including a lack of educator familiarity with mastery approaches (Kulik et al., 1990; Pane et al., 2017). Many schools still rely on whole-class (rather than personalized) learning, traditional textbooks, and the structure of grade bands to demarcate progress. Simply, we lack knowledge on how to even achieve mastery learning and personalized learning using *traditional* tools, much less intelligent ones.

Still, additional challenges are introduced when increasingly socially and emotionally aware AIED systems are introduced. While there is growing interest in these systems (Smakman et al., 2021), research on long-term interaction between students and robots is limited (Woo et al., 2021) and beset by various ethical, technical, and contextual challenges. Stakeholders have raised concerns not only about the potentially pseudoscientific nature of emotion recognition technologies but also about privacy concerns of capturing student physiological data (e.g., tracking eye movements or heart rates) or "nudging" students behaviorally, among numerous other ethical issues (Baker & Hawn, 2021). Additionally, human-human relationships are argued to be essential in educational settings for fostering personal growth, mentorship, productive comparison, and even the capacity to fail safely (Schiff, 2021b). Thus, it is far from clear that even socially sophisticated AIED is suitable to "replace" student-teacher or student-student relationships and the benefits they entail, either now or in the foreseeable future.

Overall, a simplistic notion that AIED systems will deterministically drive low-cost, scalable, highly personalized instruction to upend the current paradigm is based on faulty assumptions; *there is no short path to computerizing away the complexity of educational systems, the social-emotional dynamics of teaching and learning, the broader policy context, the current state of teacher preparation, and so on.* Both technical and sociotechnical trajectories for research have revealed that developing effective and responsible AIED is far more complex than assumed. AIED adoption, if blind to these issues, risks perpetuating old failures associated with educational technology and utopian AI imaginaries, as well as inducing new ones. Indeed, some of these failures have already manifested in the early years and decades of expanded AIED adoption in real-world settings.

One notable example is the A-levels algorithm scandal in the UK's Office of Qualifications and Examinations Regulation (Ofqual). During the Covid-19 pandemic, Ofqual employed an algorithm to adjust teacher predictions about grades that students *would* have received if they had taken examinations. After these adjustments were found to have disproportionately disadvantaged higher-need students, Ofqual's chief resigned and the algorithm was abandoned (Bedingfield, 2020). While some have noted that the algorithm was not especially sophisticated (and thus not really "AI") or have emphasized human failures in decision-making, it is critical to understand that these human decisions are *intrinsic* to the process of adopting and implementing AIED systems.

Other examples of recent AIED experimentation include the use of AIED in K-12 classrooms to examine student facial expressions, moods, and learning behaviors; the widespread adoption of eye-tracking to deter cheating on online exams during the pandemic; and the advancement of AI used in college admissions that draw on student interaction and even social media data (Newton, 2021), despite concerns raised about similar systems used to hire workers. And while some associated harms (e.g., gender or racial/ethnic bias) are relatively salient to many stakeholders, others are relatively subtle and require exploration to understand and demonstrate. Thus, while concerns about some of these systems have come to light, *a likely implication is that an increasing number of AIED systems are leading to ethical violations and producing harms, with these impacts either undetected or unreported.*

CAN ETHICAL FRAMEWORKS AND EMERGING AI GOVERNANCE HELP?

In light of the extended adoption of AIED systems and recent technical advances, and knowledge of the history of mishaps, what is being done to manage the ethical risks and otherwise govern AIED? Though the technical community of scholars engaged in AIED paid relatively little attention to ethics as recently as 2018 (Holmes et al., 2018), a positive development is that the community has now begun to call for ethics in the research agenda, lagging only slightly behind the broader AI ethics community (Holmes et al., 2021). New efforts like The Institute for Ethical AI in Education (formed in 2018) have drawn on stakeholder discussions and interviews to define key ethical principles and associated criteria and requirements for AIED, covering the design, procurement, and implementation of AIED systems. This increased attention is evident in the growing number of scholarly workshops and journal issues focused on ethics, such as a 2021 special issue on the fairness, accountability, transparency, and ethics (FATE) of AIED in the *International Journal of AI in Education*.

Satisfying these calls is no easy task, however, especially for a primarily technical community. It will likely require (at least) new modes of interdisciplinary collaboration with ethics and policy-oriented researchers, a change in structural incentives regarding publication and research priorities, the ability to pilot and evaluate AIED systems in large-scale rather than laboratory settings, thoughtful participation of a diverse array of stakeholders, and venues to facilitate engagement with education technology companies and policymakers (Schiff, 2021a). This challenge of collective governance is exacerbated because AIED is typically driven by academic research followed by industry translation, and then adopted in a bottom-up fashion. Thus, even if both researchers and education technology companies express concern regarding the ethical implications of AIED (Kousa & Niemi, 2022), addressing these concerns will require concerted efforts to promote responsible practices *throughout* the educational ecosystem, especially to safeguard settings with limited capacity and regulatory oversight.

For example, can we expect a teacher or administrator serving low-income students in a resource-poor school to know that they should ask an AIED startup about how their product has been developed and tested, about its differential accuracy across subgroups, about privacy and fairness considerations, and so on? Should we expect the company to have done adequate testing and be sober about the limitations and risks as they promote their product? *There are unfortunately good reasons to be skeptical of the capacity of the broader educational ecosystem to adopt some of the thoughtful practices currently being proposed by the AIED ethics community*, especially given countervailing pressures such as profit motives for providers and efficiency-seeking motives of the public sector. Paradigm shifts are hard.

Might formal governance provide a more realistic alternative? That is, can AIED providers be mandated to perform certain ethical checks, meet certain standards, and provide sufficient transparency to users? Can those who procure AIED systems be similarly required to engage in their own processes for vetting new AI systems, as has been proposed by The Institute for Ethical AI in Education and in line with certain social sectors and countries currently enhancing their AI procurement processes? The development of AI regulation suggests some reasons for worry. Prominent efforts like the EU's developing AI Act only require conformity assessments for certain "high-risk" systems, currently limited in education to those "used for the purpose of determining access" to institutions or for "assessing students" (European Commission, 2021). The challenge of delineating between low-risk and high-risk systems is quite relevant here. It is not clear a priori whether certain AIED applications are truly low risk, and *it has hardly been explored whether even modest impacts from "low-risk" systems might cascade and aggregate over time.* For example, a student, over their lifetime, could be taught inadequately by an ITS developed based on training data from very dissimilar students, punished because of a somewhat faulty plagiarism detection tool, and recommended a less-than-ideal career path or online course. What is the net result of many AIED systems ("low risk" or otherwise) working in concert to a student's (or teacher's) potential detriment?

While emerging and existing regulations surrounding student data and privacy, for example, might also apply, it thus seems likely that many of the diverse usages of AIED presented previously will fall outside of the scope of formal regulation. This is even more true in less-regulated settings like the US, which seems poised to adopt a risk-based classification system but may rely primarily on mere self-regulation, such as voluntary self-assessment using standards (National Institute of Standards and Technology, 2021). Countries without strong regulatory schemes and protections, including many low-income countries where student needs are vast, are even more susceptible to the promotion of AIED systems by unscrupulous external actors (Tzachor et al., 2022). Finally, another reason for the neglect of AIED's ethical and regulatory implications by leading policymakers is the highly emphasized role of education as the sector responsible for producing more AI-capable workers and subsequently driving innovation. Such an emphasis and associated urgency for education's role in building AI capacity arguably draws attention away from the impacts of AI on education itself (Schiff, 2021a), while AI's impacts on sectors like healthcare or transportation are better appreciated. In sum, due to the historical decentralization and self-regulation involved in education technology governance, the failure to imagine AIED's implications by leading policymakers, and the current emphasis on high-risk systems, *it is hardly clear that emerging AI governance is poised to combat the many concerns that are unfolding in AIED.*

QUESTIONS AND RECOMMENDATIONS FOR AIED IN THE 21st CENTURY

This chapter has reviewed the increasingly diverse and complicated landscape of AIED systems, some of the pressures and assumptions driving AIED adoption, a growing list of scandals and ethical risks, and where current efforts in ethical oversight and governance stand. Despite the historical experience and advancing scholarly and practitioner understanding of risks and failures of AI, education technology, and AIED, current efforts to adopt AIED responsibly seem poised to fail to keep pace. In addition to some of these suggestions offered above, this chapter, therefore, offers additional possibilities.

Safe experimentation. Piloting AIED systems is necessary to perform research on AIED's benefits and risks, and an overly precautionary approach can foreclose on urgently needed gains in educational systems. What is needed is *safe* experimentation. AIED research can be gradually applied to larger settings, deeply informed by ethical frameworks, social and policy contexts, and teacher and student needs. Methods like design-based implementation research (Fishman et al., 2013) and engagement with AIED-specific ethical frameworks like that from The Institute for Ethical Al in Education can underpin responsible research projects. Careful research projects, including experiments, can be undertaken before AIED systems are introduced at large scale by the private or public sectors. The AIED community has the opportunity to avoid a "wild west" reputation and instead be a leader in the AI space, a necessity given the vulnerable populations it affects and the scope of AIED's impacts.

Expanded understanding of social and ethical implications. The AI ethics community has devoted a significant portion of its effort to addressing ostensibly technically tractable issues like algorithmic bias, transparency, and privacy, issues for which there are imagined technical "solutions." Yet, there are many more ethical concerns that have received less attention, especially the kinds of murky sociotechnical issues that do not lend themselves to easy solutions. AIED researchers who have explored these issues have the opportunity to both learn from and help mature the broader AI ethics agenda. Associated topics might include the role of AIED in fostering justice within and across school systems or regions, the mental health of students, the well-being of teachers, the ethics of nudging and deception, and many more issues.

Reporting on risks and harms. Relatively little is known about the individual risks of the growing variety of AIED systems, much less their potential harms in combination, over time, for groups versus individuals, and so on. Prominent AIED or education actors should systematically track risks and harms from different types of AIED systems, and catalog this for research, development, implementation, and policy guidance purposes. For example, ethical harms and scandals related to AIED could be reported to the Partnership on AI's AI Incident Database (McGregor, 2020) or through the EU's developing AI database meant to track harms to well-being and human rights. This can foster a more holistic research agenda on AIED's impacts, as well as growing awareness and accountability.

Revisiting the vision for AIED. As noted, much of AIED's research trajectory—as with AI generally—derives from an idealized vision of human-like AI. Yet adopting AIED systems that spin out of this research program, and the program itself, may not be optimal for serving the needs of students, teachers, and other education stakeholders. It is unclear whether we would even want pseudo-conscious AI systems that pretend to portray emotions (much less fully conscious ones) teaching students or emulating teachers. Even so, it remains dubious that AIED will not be used to replace (rather than augment) educators, despite the best intentions. Using AIED to foster personalization and low-cost scaling may be laudable goals, but between the instrumentalized economic logic of efficiency and the idealized technical logic of computerizing human teachers, it may be time for AIED stakeholders to reconsider the long-term vision and course of action, perhaps cantered more closely on real-world contexts and needs.

AIED is a promising and dynamic field, increasingly touching the lives of students and educators, and mirroring the development of AI in key ways in the 21st century. Through historical knowledge, lived experience, and careful examination of the benefits and risks of the diversifying array of AIED systems, we can chart a more careful and beneficial course for the decades to come.

REFERENCES

Baker, R. S. (2016). Stupid Tutoring Systems, Intelligent Humans. *International Journal of Artificial Intelligence in Education*, 26(2), 600–614. https://doi.org/10.1007/s40593-016-0105-0

Baker, R. S., & Hawn, A. (2021). Algorithmic Bias in Education. *International Journal of Artificial Intelligence in Education*. https://doi.org/10.1007/s40593-021-00285-9

Baker, T., & Smith, L. (2019). *Educ-AI-tion Rebooted? Exploring the Future of Artificial Intelligence in Schools and Colleges* (p. 56). Nesta. https://media.nesta.org.uk/documents/Future_of_AI_and_education_v5_WEB.pdf

Bedingfield, W. (2020, August 19). Everything That Went Wrong with the Botched A-Levels Algorithm. *Wired UK*. https://www.wired.co.uk/article/alevel-exam-algorithm

Belpaeme, T., Kennedy, J., Ramachandran, A., Scassellati, B., & Tanaka, F. (2018). Social Robots for Education: A Review. *Science Robotics*, 3(21), eaat5954. https://doi.org/10.1126/scirobotics.aat5954

Bloom, B. S. (1984). The 2 Sigma Problem: The Search for Methods of Group Instruction as Effective as One-to-One Tutoring. *Educational Researcher*, 13(6), 4–16. https://doi.org/10.3102/0013189X013006004

Carbonell, J. R. (1970). AI in CAI: An Artificial-Intelligence Approach to Computer-Assisted Instruction. *IEEE Transactions on Man-Machine Systems*, 11(4), 190–202. https://doi.org/10.1109/TMMS.1970.299942

Conner, T., & Nelson, C. (2021). *Ensuring Equitable AI Adoption in Education: An Initial Framework and Proposed Next Steps* (No. 21-02538–02; p. 14). Oak Ridge Associated Universities and the MITRE Corporation.

Corbett, A. T., Koedinger, K. R., & Anderson, J. R. (1997). Chapter 37—Intelligent Tutoring Systems. In M. G. Helander, T. K. Landauer, & P. V. Prabhu (Eds.), *Handbook of Human-Computer Interaction (Second Edition)* (pp. 849–874). North-Holland. https://doi.org/10.1016/B978-044481862-1.50103-5

Diebold, G., & Han, C. (2022). *How AI Can Improve K-12 Education in the United States* (p. 33). Center for Data Innovation. https://www2.datainnovation.org/2022-ai-education.pdf

European Commission. (2021). *Proposal for a Regulation on a European Approach for Artificial Intelligence* (COM(2021) 206 final; p. 108). European Commission. https://digital-strategy.ec.europa.eu/en/library/proposal-regulation-european-approach-artificial-intelligence

Fishman, B. J., Penuel, W. R., Allen, A.-R., Cheng, B. H., & Sabelli, N. (2013). Design-Based Implementation Research: An Emerging Model for Transforming the Relationship of Research and Practice. *National Society for the Study of Education*, 112(2), 136–156.

Goel, A. K., & Polepeddi, L. (2016). *Jill Watson: A Virtual Teaching Assistant for Online Education*. 21.

Hannafin, R. D., & Savenye, W. C. (1993). Technology in the Classroom: The Teacher's New Role and Resistance to it. *Educational Technology*, 33(6), 26–31.

Holmes, W., Bektik, D., Whitelock, D., & Woolf, B. P. (2018). Ethics in AIED: Who Cares? In C. Penstein Rosé, R. Martínez-Maldonado, H. U. Hoppe, R. Luckin, M. Mavrikis, K. Porayska-Pomsta, B. McLaren, & B. du Boulay (Eds.), *Artificial Intelligence in Education: 19th International Conference, AIED 2018, London, UK, June 27–30, 2018, Proceedings, Part II* (Vol. 10948). Springer International Publishing. https://doi.org/10.1007/978-3-319-93846-2

Holmes, W., Porayska-Pomsta, K., Holstein, K., Sutherland, E., Baker, T., Shum, S. B., Santos, O. C., Rodrigo, M. T., Cukurova, M., Bittencourt, I. I., & Koedinger, K. R. (2021). Ethics of AI in Education: Towards a Community-Wide Framework. *International Journal of Artificial Intelligence in Education*. https://doi.org/10.1007/s40593-021-00239-1

Kousa, P., & Niemi, H. (2022). AI Ethics and Learning: EdTech Companies' Challenges and Solutions. *Interactive Learning Environments*, 1–12. https://doi.org/10.1080/10494820.2022.2043908

Kulik, C.-L. C., Kulik, J. A., & Bangert-Drowns, R. L. (1990). Effectiveness of Mastery Learning Programs: A Meta-Analysis. *Review of Educational Research*, 60(2), 265–299. https://doi.org/10.3102/00346543060002265

Kulik, J. A., & Fletcher, J. D. (2016). Effectiveness of Intelligent Tutoring Systems: A Meta-Analytic Review. *Review of Educational Research, 86*(1), 42–78. https://doi.org/10.3102/0034654315581420

Lemaignan, S., Garcia, F., Jacq, A., & Dillenbourg, P. (2016). From Real-Time Attention Assessment to "with-me-ness" in Human-Robot Interaction. *2016 11th ACM/IEEE International Conference on Human-Robot Interaction (HRI)*, 157–164. https://doi.org/10.1109/HRI.2016.7451747

McDuff, D., Kaliouby, R., Senechal, T., Amr, M., Cohn, J., & Picard, R. (2013). *Affectiva-MIT Facial Expression Dataset (AM-FED): Naturalistic and Spontaneous Facial Expressions Collected*, 881–888. https://www.cv-foundation.org/openaccess/content_cvpr_workshops_2013/W16/html/McDuff_Affectiva-MIT_Facial_Expression_2013_CVPR_paper.html

McGregor, S. (2020). Preventing repeated real world AI failures by cataloging incidents: The AI Incident Database. ArXiv:2011.08512 [Cs]. http://arxiv.org/abs/2011.08512

National Institute of Standards and Technology. (2021). *Summary Analysis of Responses to the NIST Artificial Intelligence Risk Management Framework (AI RMF)—Request for Information (RFI)* (p. 10). National Institute of Standards and Technology. https://www.nist.gov/system/files/documents/2021/10/15/AI%20RMF_RFI%20Summary%20Report.pdf

Newton, D. (2021, April 26). *Artificial Intelligence is Infiltrating Higher Ed, from Admissions to Grading*. The Hechinger Report. http://hechingerreport.org/from-admissions-to-teaching-to-grading-ai-is-infiltrating-higher-education/

Pane, J., Steiner, E., Baird, M., Hamilton, L., & Pane, J. (2017). *Informing Progress: Insights on Personalized Learning Implementation and Effects* (p. 59). RAND Corporation. https://doi.org/10.7249/RR2042

Rivard, R. (2013, July 18). *Udacity Project on "Pause."* Inside Higher Ed. https://www.insidehighered.com/news/2013/07/18/citing-disappointing-student-outcomes-san-jose-state-pauses-work-udacity

Rosenberg-Kima, R. B., Baylor, A. L., Plant, E. A., & Doerr, C. E. (2008). Interface Agents as Social Models for Female Students: The Effects of Agent Visual Presence and Appearance on Female Students' Attitudes and Beliefs. *Computers in Human Behavior, 24*(6), 2741–2756.

Sancho-Gil, J. M., Rivera-Vargas, P., & Miño-Puigcercós, R. (2020). Moving Beyond the Predictable Failure of Ed-Tech Initiatives. *Learning, Media and Technology, 45*(1), 61–75. https://doi.org/10.1080/17439884.2019.1666873

Schiff, D. (2021a). Education for AI, Not AI for Education: The Role of Education and Ethics in National AI Policy Strategies. *International Journal of Artificial Intelligence in Education*. https://doi.org/10.1007/s40593-021-00270-2

Schiff, D. (2021b). Out of the Laboratory and Into the Classroom: The Future of Artificial Intelligence in Education. *AI & Society, 36*(1), 331–348. https://doi.org/10.1007/s00146-020-01033-8

Self, J. (1998). The Defining Characteristics of Intelligent Tutoring Systems Research: ITSs Care, Precisely. *International Journal of Artificial Intelligence in Education (IJAIED), 10*, 350–364.

Sloane, M., Moss, E., & Chowdhury, R. (2022). A Silicon Valley Love Triangle: Hiring Algorithms, Pseudo-Science, and the Quest for Auditability. *Patterns, 3*(2), 100425. https://doi.org/10.1016/j.patter.2021.100425

Smakman, M., Vogt, P., & Konijn, E. A. (2021). Moral Considerations On Social Robots in Education: A Multi-Stakeholder Perspective. *Computers & Education, 174*, 104317. https://doi.org/10.1016/j.compedu.2021.104317

Tzachor, A., Devare, M., King, B., Avin, S., & Ó hÉigeartaigh, S. (2022). Responsible Artificial Intelligence in Agriculture Requires Systemic Understanding of Risks and Externalities. *Nature Machine Intelligence, 4*(2), 104–109. https://doi.org/10.1038/s42256-022-00440-4

VanLehn, K. (2011). The Relative Effectiveness of Human Tutoring, Intelligent Tutoring Systems, and Other Tutoring Systems. *Educational Psychologist, 46*(4), 197–221.

Vincent-Lancrin, S., & Vlies, R. van der. (2020). *Trustworthy Artificial Intelligence (AI) in Education: Promises and challenges*. OECD. https://doi.org/10.1787/a6c90fa9-en

Warschauer, M., & Ames, M. (2010). Can One Laptop per Child Save the World's Poor? *Journal of International Affairs, 64*(1), 33–51.

Woo, H., LeTendre, G. K., Pham-Shouse, T., & Xiong, Y. (2021). The Use of Social Robots in Classrooms: A Review of Field-Based Studies. *Educational Research Review, 33*, 100388. https://doi.org/10.1016/j.edurev.2021.100388

Woolf, B. P., Lane, H. C., Chaudhri, V. K., & Kolodner, J. L. (2013). AI Grand Challenges for Education. *AI Magazine*, *34*(4), 9.

Xu, Z., Wijekumar, K. (Kay), Ramirez, G., Hu, X., & Irey, R. (2019). The Effectiveness of Intelligent Tutoring Systems on K-12 Students' Reading Comprehension: A Meta-Analysis. *British Journal of Educational Technology*, *50*(6), 3119–3137. https://doi.org/10.1111/bjet.12758

Zawacki-Richter, O., Marín, V. I., Bond, M., & Gouverneur, F. (2019). Systematic Review of Research on Artificial Intelligence Applications in Higher Education – Where are the Educators? *International Journal of Educational Technology in Higher Education*, *16*(1), 39. https://doi.org/10.1186/s41239 -019-0171-0

Zhang, K., & Aslan, A. B. (2021). AI Technologies for Education: Recent Research & Future Directions. *Computers and Education: Artificial Intelligence*, *2*, 100025. https://doi.org/10.1016/j.caeai.2021 .100025

71. Critically assessing AI/ML for cultural heritage: potentials and challenges

Anna Foka, Lina Eklund, Anders Sundnes Løvlie and Gabriele Griffin

INTRODUCTION

Today, the term artificial intelligence describes a variety of digital technologies, tools and methods supporting and enabling automated information processing and decision-making beyond human intervention. AI is used on a daily basis to perform many different tasks, such as translating languages and transcribing texts, creating subtitles in videos, detecting cyber-attacks and so on. But what about the implementation of AI for curating cultural data, within the museum and cultural heritage sector more generally? In the last nearly half-century, museums have been subjected to digital transformation due to technological innovations in collections management, curation and public engagement. Concerning digitalisation, expectations are placed high on new technologies such as artificial intelligence (AI), more precisely machine learning (ML) technologies that are only just beginning to be explored by museums and heritage institutions (Tzouganatou 2018: 377–383, 2021; Murphy and Villaespesa 2020; Foka, Attemark and Wahlberg 2022: 66–85).

Can AI be used in the museum and heritage sector to increase the quality and efficiency of people's work through the use of autonomy and adaptivity, allowing humans to be more creative? As AI is a wide field of inquiry, research methods and implementation, several approaches and tools are used, depending on the artefacts and archives in question. Traditions for AI implementation in museums and heritage organisations vary greatly: concepts of reasoning, classification, knowledge representation, curation or learning, utilising natural language or image processing. Recent research has challenged and refined models of practice. Given the nascent state of AI within cultural heritage, critical engagement with AI technologies and their potential for museums is the focus; there is a growing use and interest of AI in museums where museums collaborate with industry partners to harness AI for collections management in creative and effective ways (Ciecko 2020). In the same breath, given the diversity of socio-political context(s) of human memory and culture, the complexity of open access and the lack of funding, museums and heritage stakeholders have approached AI with caution. What this chapter seeks to address is to provide a thorough analysis of this polarity: AI/ML may provide us with highly promising methods and tools, but we also need to address the complexities of implementing them.

In what follows, we review relevant literature on how AI methods and tools are currently used in the heritage and museum sector. While the majority of reviewed literature derives from European, British and North American case studies and practical implementation, we argue that this inquiry is globally relevant. We discuss AI/ML technologies with great potential such as computer vision and natural language processing, as well as the implementation of

815

AI for heritage encounters. We also identify a number of challenges—namely interpretative legacies concerning cultural collections of human memory but also issues of accessibility and lack of necessary technical knowledge. Finally, we suggest ways towards best practice, as we envision the future potential of AI/ML for the museum and heritage sector.

AI USES IN THE HERITAGE SECTOR

Below, we analyse implemented AI methods within the field of heritage such as computer vision and image processing, natural language processing including speech analysis and more. We delve into prominent examples and discuss a variety of implementation complexities that arise from heritage data as well as other technical and epistemic issues.

Computer Vision

Computer vision (CV) helps classify and enrich online collections by auto-generating a description or tags to make images more discoverable (Fontanella 2020: 23–29). Several museums are experimenting with CV approaches. For instance, the National Gallery of Denmark has used off-the-shelf CV software to categorise every single work in the online collection, containing approximately 40,000 digitised works (www.smk.dk/en/article/artifi-cial-intelligence-helps-organise-denmarks-largest-art-collection/). This has enabled online visitors to search for works in new ways, such as by motifs such as people, flowers or chairs; or searching for works done in specific colour schemes or for works that resemble each other. Similarly, Harvard Art Museums uses CV to categorise artwork to make their collections more widely accessible. Several well-known museums have also used CV methods in order to make datasets available for research, including through competitions—such as The Metropolitan Museum of Art and The Museum of Modern Art in New York, and the Rijksmuseum in Amsterdam (Kaggle 2017, 2021)

There are, however, challenges in implementing CV for heritage purposes. The first complexity arises in relation to the images themselves. While image recognition algorithms have achieved impressive performance in classifying and detecting objects in photographic images in recent years, such algorithms still struggle to recognise objects in non-photographic depiction styles such as paintings and drawings; this is sometimes referred to as "the cross-depiction problem" (Boulton and Hall 2019; Cai, Wu, Corradi and Hall 2015; Westlake, Cai and Hall 2016: 825–841). This remains a significant obstacle to the use of image recognition in art collections (Del Chiaro, Bagdanov and Del Bimbo 2019: 420–426; Kadish, Risi and Løvlie 2021). An interesting attempt to circumvent this problem has been presented by Brighton Museum (UK), which has experimented with using off-the-shelf software to offer suggestions for metadata as a "provocation" to inspire human curators to include keywords they otherwise might not have thought of (Bacon 2020).

An additional issue is that algorithms might perpetuate or even amplify existing biases. Ciecko tested a range of off-the-shelf software solutions and found promising results for image classification and object detection, for example, the accuracy of machine vision with an error rate of approximately 4% in 2016, making it on par with humans (Ciecko 2020). However, it seemed that error rates were pointing out bias relating to gender and dominant, Western approaches to culture, as well as sensitive topics such as colonialism. Debates about the ethical challenges relating to image recognition applied to depictions of people—for example, relating to racial and gender biases—have gathered much attention and controversy in recent years (Raji, Gebru, Mitchell, Buolamwini, Lee and Denton 2020: 145–151). Crawford and Paglen (2019) have shown how the central training database ImageNet contains a range of problematic classifications connected with value-laden nouns such as "debtor", "snob", "slut", "Bolshevik" and so on. Automatic image processing, especially relating to the classification and detection of facial features in images are found to entail social biases concerning the misidentification of marginalised groups.

The issue is both technical and epistemic: the gender binary and its classification as a highly racialised tool of colonial power and control. Scholars have recently conceptualised this socio-technical phenomenon as "auto-essentialization" (Scheuerman, Pape and Hanna 2021), the use of automated technologies to re-inscribe the essential notions of difference that were established under colonial rule. They do so by considering the history of gendering embodiment as both face and body, from colonial projects that focus on the normalisation of the European gender binary with sexology, physiognomy and phrenology over the 19th and 20th centuries. These are arguably informing automated facial analysis tools in computer vision that demand attention in rethinking AI/ML for image recognition as mature instantiations of much older technologies (Scheuerman, Pape and Hanna 2021). It is important to further address that systems are trained to recognise features by latching on to aspects of images that humans discern. AI thus *may* reproduce human bias (Banerjee, Bhimireddy, Burns, Celi, Chen, Correa and Gichoya 2021).

If CV is properly implemented, we believe it may help raise central concerns for heritage collections, in particular, those containing images. A technological paradigm based on the assumption that an image can be classified in unambiguous terms by machine-generated keywords will have persistent challenges when applied, for example, to visual art which is characterised by resisting simple and stable interpretations. In order to apply image recognition in a meaningful way that furthers interpretation, technology must be developed to incorporate complex and non-binary, non-stereotypical interpretation.

Document and Language/Speech Analysis: Natural Language Processing

Natural language processing, or NLP, is at the intersection of linguistics and computer science with AI used to analyse and process large amounts of human language. NLP can be defined as the ability of a machine to understand and generate speech. It is an attempt to bridge human communication and computer understanding (Gaia, Boiano and Borda 2019: 309–329). NLP has exploded over the past decade: new interdisciplinary avenues and the growing number of digitised texts of all kinds are the reasons behind its expansion. One prevalent use of NLP deals with pre-processing, concerning the digitisation of written data that is normally done by optical character recognition (OCR). Old documents tend to be idiosyncratic: manuscripts can contain text passages that may be stained, erased, with archaic spelling or unusual and unrecognisable handwriting (Volk, Furrer and Sennrich 2011: 3–22; Romero Serrano, Toselli, Sánchez and Vidal 2011: 90–96). Printed documents such as old newspapers may have a lot of digital "noise", making OCR an expensive and difficult process. Adapting NLP tools to older language varieties can be a process of customisation and adaptation (Borin and Forsberg 2011: 41–61; Rögnvaldsson and Helgadóttir 2011: 63–76). Multiple different usages of NLP in relation to cultural heritage documents concern structural and narrative analysis, detecting topics and finding common content elements (Hendrickx, Généreux and Marquilhas 2011: 135–153), data management, visualisation and retrieval (Berzak, Richter, Ehrler and Shore 2011: 197–212), thus attempting to make heritage documents more flexibly accessible as semantic knowledge bases (Witte, Kappler, Krestel and Lockemann 2011: 213–230)

NLP has also been used in museums and galleries to facilitate audience engagement via speech and artefact information. Museums have been piloting NLP demonstrators, for example, a platform where a user may type a sentence in order to perform different NLP operations, such as activating a chatbot, for more than a decade (Vassos, Malliaraki, Falco, Maggio, Massimetti and Nocentini 2016: 433–437). Emerging free chatbot-creating platforms—for example, Chatfuel, Chatterbot Eliza, among others—and the availability of an open application programming interface (API), a software intermediary that allows two applications to talk to each other, provide possibilities for creating an audience engagement tool with both low effort and low cost (Dale 2016: 811–817). Notable examples of NLP methods to train chatbots include Heinz Nixdorf Museums Forum in Germany (www.hnf.de/en/) as an avatar bot (Kopp, Gesellensetter and Krämer 2005: 329–343).

In March 2017, the Anne Frank House Museum (www.annefrank.org/en/) in Amsterdam launched a Facebook Messenger chatbot. A recent example is the practical design and implementation of an audience development pilot chatbot in Milan involving four historical museums (https://casemuseo.it). Through visualising narrative using a combination of chatbot and gamification platforms, the museums aim to attract teenage audiences (Gaia, Boiano and Borda, 2019: 309–329).

AI Used for Heritage Encounters with the Public

Whereas user modelling is usually not considered AI, one of the most anticipated applications of AI in cultural heritage concerns the personalisation of museum experiences, which has received widespread attention since the 1990s and is now including specific applications such as heritage chatbots (Stock 1993: 197–224; Oberlander, O'Donnell, Mellish and Knott 1998: 11–32). Several recent projects have explored how to design personalised experiences for exhibitions in museum contexts using machine learning methods, such as user modelling and recommender systems (Ryding, Spence, Løvlie and Benford 2021: 1151–1172; Lynch 2000: 60–69; Bowen and Filippini-Fantoni 2004; Casillo, Clarizia, D'Aniello, De Santo, Lombardi and Santaniello 2020: 234–243; Amato, Moscato, Moscato, Pascale and Picariello 2020: 341–347; Kuflik, Stock, Zancanaro, Gorfinkel, Jbara, Kats and Kashtan, 2011: 1–25; Ardissono and Kuflik 2012: 73–99). Work on personalisation in cultural heritage has largely focused on systems that adapt to individual users through user modelling aimed at matching users with relevant content. Other approaches explore using machine analysis of user behaviour in order to support the design of user experiences (Ragusa, Furnari, Battiato, Signorello and Farinella 2020: 150–157).

In a similar vein, Balducci et al. (2020: 142–149) explore the development of "Smart Interactive Experiences" for museum visitors. Caggianese et al. (2020: 361–367) propose "An artificial intelligence powered holographic stand for exploring cultural objects".

A highly publicised example is Send Me SFMOMA, a text messaging service issued by the San Francisco Museum of Modern Art that offers a simple interaction with the museum's digital collection: users can query the database by sending simple phrases like "Send me sunshine" and would receive in return an image from the museum's database that matched the keyword (in this case, "sunshine"). While this type of crude ML is typically not considered to be AI, yet interestingly, the creators of this service further experimented with using tags generated by computer vision software. Results, however, were classified as uninteresting—and instead opted to rely on human-generated tags. Winesmith explains that:

> when computer vision was presented with a piece like photographer Gary Winogrand's *New York* in which a pregnant woman lifts up her arm to hail a taxi, human taggers listed evocative, emotion-laden keywords like *family, pregnant, taxi, New York,* and *street corner.* The computer created much more literal keywords: *person, street, dark, gray.* (Constance 2017)

Another way of AI/ML deployed for personalised engagement is deepfakes: synthetic media that may manipulate and alter sound or image (Kwok and Koh 2021: 1798–1802). The effect of deepfake is twofold and variable: on the one hand, it may bring notable historical events and people to life, enabling a sort of cultural remix such as in the Dalí Museum's deepfake presentation of Salvador Dalí (Lee 2019; https://johanneslarsenmuseet.dk/nyhed/vores-maleri -savner-jer/). Similar experiments have been carried out in other museums such as the Munch Museum and the Johannes Larsen Museum (Benford et al. 2022: 1–16). Deepfakes are also being used for popular entertainment, such as through the popular app Wombo.ai, which allows users to animate their selfies in sync with a popular song. Such applications of deepfake carry the potential to create engaging and playful experiences with art. They also offer a new tool for professionals who have long experimented with ever more sophisticated means of manipulating photo and video material. From a participatory point of view, deepfakes thus also offer a new tool for letting ordinary users repurpose media material, adding to the ever-growing repertoire of "remix culture" (Broca 2010: 121–123).

On the other hand, as this is essentially an application of biometric methods, it calls for building trust, engaging with and including key stakeholders and participatory design. Additionally, using AI-generated avatars for storytelling for society, democracy and humanity is a novelty for heritage enthusiasts and museumgoers. Through examining artworks made with deepfake technology, it was revealed that deepfake could be used to deliver powerful messages by being viewed as both content and medium. Deep fakes rely heavily on a symbiotic circulatory relationship with the Internet for their spreading.

CHALLENGES OF IMPLEMENTING AI IN THE MUSEUM AND HERITAGE SECTOR

Cultural Bias and Cultural Complexity

Post-colonial research questions existing perspectives that dominate cultural heritage in Europe and North America; AI/ML methods and tools may equally be conservative if machine learning processes draw upon existing practices. How can we account for AI when it comes to cultural collections? Cultural heritage collections are: "geographical sites of narrative, telling the stories of diverse pasts of different regions of the world" (Dunn et al. 2019: 253–271). These stories are currently conveyed in a number of conventional ways, for example, by selection and classification in catalogues and labels. These systems of interaction between humans, artefacts and information are deeply contextual and are influenced by socio-material factors such as ownership or possession of artefacts, the museum legacy, its location, the artefacts themselves and curatorial input (Macdonald 2011). At the same time, the word "digital" has penetrated museum physical and conceptual spaces, and, in the process, revolutionised access and possibilities to understand artefacts and immaterial heritage (Geismar 2018). Early histories of large, national museums and their collections are inevitably bound up with the cultural preoccupations of what such societies consider to be important in relation to their own history. These situational specificities transfer over to their digital cultural records and digitising risks reinforcing colonial undertones as well as other systems of oppression which are represented by and in collections (Risam 2018).

This issue coincides with the fact that virtual, hybrid and physical cultural tourism across and beyond Europe ensures that cultural heritage collections are subject to intercultural experiences and international influences (Foka, Westin and Chapman 2018). Cultural heritage can instead be global and interconnected. We must also accept the truths and inequities inherent in most collections: dark provenance, colonial theft, appropriation (Azoulay 2019) and the dominant canons or values they can sustain (Rodríguez-Ortega 2018: 25). However, this requires the incorporation of non-museum data, epistemologies, knowledge and information to create rich narratives about diverse human histories, previously iterated as "selfs" and "others" (Hoobler 2006: 441–460). Many museums are already taking active steps to facilitate wider access and understand those marginalised histories and support greater cultural inclusion.

A study by cognitive scientists on the trustworthiness of faces in European portraits trained an algorithm using 6,608 paintings from two online collections to trace "historical changes in trustworthiness using machine learning analyses of facial clues in paintings" (Safra 2020: 1–7). Results showed the "trustworthiness in portraits increased over the period from 1500–2000 paralleling the decline of interpersonal values and the rise of democratic values in Western Europe". The study is excluding most lived experiences of Europe as datasets are portraits of white men in power, not women or migrants, for example. It has been argued that such uses of AI more generally can bolster perceptions that the data, collections, findings, software and platforms themselves are neutral or objective due to their development by impartial or mathematical approaches. But research reveals algorithms do not only reproduce bias and hierarchies, but they can also amplify them by failing to account for their very existence (Noble 2018; Benjamin 2019).

Accessibility

Another key factor impacting audience experience is the capacity to access and re-use museum collections (Wallace and Deazley 2016). Assumptions that online collections extend access neutrally or democratise heritage access are flawed: even if collections are in the public domain, they may not be open access, searchable or interoperable with other platforms (Thylstrup 2019). If AI may be assumed to solve these problems, yet, implementation also runs the risk of simply perpetuating these problems. We argue here that care must be taken to increase, for example, accessibility for audiences with disabilities. Such ML-driven connectivity of collections and data sources siloed across the cultural heritage sector may facilitate new research in digital art history and humanities as various datasets can be connected to other sources (Zorich 2012). Yet, interoperable cultural heritage data raise questions about the obligations imposed by the General Data Protection Regulation (GDPR), the right to be forgotten and other laws related to privacy and confidentiality (Wallace and Pavis 2020). This poses risks and harms to living individuals through increased interconnectivity of data and metadata, particularly concerning materials digitised by cultural institutions in the European Union, which may be available under open access frameworks to users outside of the EU and not subject to various territorial legal obligations. AI/ML then may improve audience access to physical and digital collections, but must comprehensively consider how to facilitate and continue the work established in the FAIR (Findable, Accessible, Interoperable and Reusable) principles framework: user interface design; interoperability to ensure access across collections and institutions now and in the future; multi-language options and automatic translations; plural narrative development; disability accessibility; and appropriate IPR management, licensing and access permissions. As Tzouganatou (2021) explains, there is a stark tension between openness and privacy at the crossroads of AI and born-digital archives, as automation cannot account for the diversity and plurality of born-digital archives or to meet needs such as different levels of openness of archival collections.

Lack of Technical Competence

Museums often lack digital expertise among their staff. While cultural heritage professionals in Europe in the mid-2010s highlighted a desire for new technology, there exists caution towards overly technological solutions that do not support the basic mission of the museum. Technological experimenting is made possible through cross-cutting initiatives, for example, engaging with stakeholders such as media developers from the private sector. Museums and the companies they work with have various reasons to engage in collaboration and experiment with new technological forms and formats. Just as companies see products, techniques and methods that can "spin out" from museum-based media activities, they may begin to see the museum as a market in itself. We, therefore, argue that there is a two-way process then, where new technology transforms the museum, while at the same time, museum and curatorial impact equally alters the activities of commercial actors, including media formats. In a co-design study between tech experts and museum staff, cultural heritage professionals stated that the mechanisms of new technology and the ways of interacting with it felt beyond their current skill level (Not and Petrelli 2019: 67–120).

Working with more traditional tasks, such as creating a vision or content for a new experience, in collaboration with designers on the other hand was a task they felt confident in. This co-design process made evident how cultural heritage professionals are uneasy with tasks that require technical knowledge. While they were confident in creating a vision for a new visiting experience, technical knowledge was perceived as beyond their skills. In other words, there is a discrepancy between technological development and heritage expertise.

CONCLUSIONS: THE FUTURE OF A "BLACK BOX"?

We conclude that it is evident from current and ongoing research that the use of AI in relation to museum and heritage institutions is promising. It spans a wide variety of areas such as image analysis, classification and restoration; document analysis and recognition; user experience; and application domains including visual art, archaeology, history and music (Fontanella et al. 2020: 23–29). However, widespread adoption of machine learning techniques in cultural heritage, we note critically that such technology is often treated as a "black box" as it can be dependent on the quality and content of datasets to begin with (Fiorucci

2020: 102–108). Accordingly, we expanded such scholarly views to express both the great possibilities and challenges in the AI/ML implementation in the museum and heritage sector. Working with human-made cultural datasets is a complex endeavour to be paired with automation. Museums and heritage stakeholders carry the inherent diversity of humanity in their memory and expression; from something as simple as Netflix hiding media content in other languages, or as alarming as Twitter prioritising lighter faces over darker faces, it is clear that equitable/ethical access to heritage requires algorithms that may be "culture-specific".

Then there exist sector-specific complexities: technical expertise sits outside of the public museum domain and is unaware of such critical perspectives. It is thus important that museum and heritage actors build AI/ML expertise and capacity within the sector. We hope that this will enable museum professionals to navigate ethical issues both when outsourcing development and curating their own collections in order to critically examine what algorithms will or will not do. But museums and the heritage sector cannot do this alone, and there needs to be a deeper exchange between AI experts and critical heritage experts. We argue further that it is important to work with competence-enhancing initiatives in the museum/heritage sector so that heritage professionals can have insight into and thus shape the work with AI in this domain.

AI/ML technologies additionally raise important ethical and practical questions for museums. As such, there is an increasingly pressing need to examine, critique and understand the sustainability, business models and legal and ethical implications of AI within the museum context. Automation and artificial intelligence in any field come with a lot of responsibility, and the question of ethics, inclusion and diversity concerning AI has been brought to the fore before (Cath 2018). Automated systems can exacerbate structural, economic, social and political imbalances unless critical reflections are made during development. AI can be used to influence society and social structures as algorithmic power may produce a truth that is partly material and partly discursive (Beer 2017: 1–13). Last, we ought to remember that AI cannot be "objective", nor, as Kate Crawford has explained, can it be "intelligent" *or* "artificial" (Crawford 2021): it is a product of the human mind and its biases. The research agenda of the future thus requires ongoing work on enhancing critical perspectives for cultural heritage collections, and to carry on being critical when implementing AI/ ML methods and tools in the museum and heritage sector. While the possibilities for curating museums and opening up cultural heritage are endless, algorithms may learn from multiple existing perspectives/biases. Still, we argue, that it can be a worthy enterprise; the cultural heritage field could pioneer some form(s) of unbiased AI that can be then used elsewhere.

REFERENCES

Amato, F., Moscato, F., Moscato, V., Pascale, F., & Picariello, A. (2020). An agent-based approach for recommending cultural tours. *Pattern Recognition Letters*, *131*, 341–347. https://doi.org/10.1016/j.patrec.2020.01.005

Anne Frank House Museum. (2022). http://www.annefrank.org/en/

Ardissono, L., Kuflik, T., & Petrelli, D. (2012). Personalization in cultural heritage: The road travelled and the one ahead. *User Modeling and User-Adapted Interaction*, *22*(1), 73–99. https://doi.org/10.1007/s11257-011-9104-x

Azoulay, A. (2019). *Potential history: Unlearning imperialism*. Verso Books.

Bacon, K. (2020). AI as provocation rather than solution. https://gifting.digital/brighton-museum/

Banerjee, I., Bhimireddy, A. R., Burns, J. L., Celi, L. A., Chen, L. C., Correa, R., & Gichoya, J. W. (2021). Reading race: AI recognises patient's racial identity in medical images. arXiv preprint arXiv:2107.10356.

Balducci, F., Buono, P., Desolda, G., Impedovo, D., & Piccinno, A. (2020). Improving smart interactive experiences in cultural heritage through pattern recognition techniques. *Pattern Recognition Letters*, *131*, 142–149. https://doi.org/10.1016/j.patrec.2019.12.011

Beer, D. (2017). The social power of algorithms. *Information, Communication & Society*, *20*(1), 1–13. https://doi.org/10.1080/1369118X.2016.1216147

Benford, S., Sundnes Løvlie, A., Ryding, K., Rajkowska, P., Bodiaj, E., Paris Darzentas, D., ... Spanjevic, B. (2022, April). Sensitive pictures: Emotional interpretation in the museum. In *CHI conference on human factors in computing systems* (pp. 1–16).

Benjamin, R. (2019). *Race after technology: Abolitionist tools for the new Jim code*. Social Forces.

Berzak, Y., Richter, M., Ehrler, C., & Shore, T. (2011). Information retrieval and visualization for the historical domain. In Sporleder, C., van den Bosch, A., and Zervanou, K. (eds.), *Language technology for cultural heritage* (pp. 197–212). Springer.

Borin, L., & Forsberg, M. (2011). A diachronic computational lexical resource for 800 years of Swedish. In *Language technology for cultural heritage* (pp. 41–61). Springer.

Boulton, P., & Hall, P. (2019). Artistic domain generalisation methods are limited by their deep representations. arXiv preprint arXiv:1907.12622.

Bowen, J. P., & Filippini-Fantoni, S. (2004, March). Personalization and the web from a museum perspective. In *Museums and the web* (Vol. 4). *Archives & Museum Informatics*, Toronto, Canada.

Broca, S. (2010). Lawrence Lessig, remix: Making art and commerce thrive in the hybrid economy. *Quaderni: Communication, Technologies, Pouvoir*, *71*, 121–123. https://doi.org/10.4000/quaderni.535

Caggianese, G., De Pietro, G., Esposito, M., Gallo, L., Minutolo, A., & Neroni, P. (2020). Discovering Leonardo with artificial intelligence and holograms: A user study. *Pattern Recognition Letters*, *131*, 361–367.

Cai, H., Wu, Q., Corradi, T., & Hall, P. (2015). The cross-depiction problem: Computer vision algorithms for recognising objects in artwork and in photographs. arXiv preprint arXiv:1505.00110.

Casillo, M., Clarizia, F., D'Aniello, G., De Santo, M., Lombardi, M., & Santaniello, D. (2020). CHATbot: A cultural heritage aware teller-bot for supporting touristic experiences. *Pattern Recognition Letters*, *131*, 234–243. https://doi.org/10.1016/j.patrec.2020.01.003

Cath, C. (2018). Governing artificial intelligence: ethical, legal and technical opportunities and challenges. *Philosophical Transactions of the Royal Society A: Mathematical, Physical and Engineering Sciences*, *376*(2133), 20180080.

Ciecko, B. (2020). AI sees what? The good, the bad, and the ugly of machine vision for museum collections. *MW2020: Museums and the Web*. https://mw20.museweb.net/paper/ai-sees-what-the-good-the-bad-and-the-ugly-of-machine-vision-for-museum-collections/

Constance G. (2017). How the SFMOMA's artbot responds to text message requests with personally curated art. https://www.vox.com/culture/2017/7/11/15949872/sfmomas-artbot-send-me-text-message

Crawford, K., & Paglen, T. (2019). Excavating AI: The politics of images in machine learning training sets. *AI and Society*. https://doi.org/10.1007/s00146-021-01162-8

Crawford, K. (2021). *The atlas of AI: Power, politics, and the planetary costs of artificial intelligence*. Yale University Press.

Dale, R. (2016). The return of the chatbots. *Natural Language Engineering*, *22*(5), 811–817. https://doi.org/10.1017/S1351324916000243

Del Chiaro, R., Bagdanov, A. D., & Del Bimbo, A. (2019). Webly-supervised zero-shot learning for artwork instance recognition. *Pattern Recognition Letters*, *128*, 420–426.

Dunn, S., Earl, G., Foka, A., & Wootton, W. (2019). Spatial narratives in museums and online: The birth of the digital object itinerary. In *Museums and digital culture* (pp. 253–271). Springer. https://doi.org/10.1007/978-3-319-97457-6

Fiorucci, M., Khoroshiltseva, M., Pontil, M., Traviglia, A., Del Bue, A., & Stuart, S. (2020). Machine learning for cultural heritage: A survey. *Pattern Recognition Letters*, *133*, 102–108. https://doi.org/10.1016/j.patrec.2020.02.017

Foka, A., Westin, J., & Chapman, A. (2018). Introduction to the DHQ special issue: Digital technology in the study of the past. *DHQ: Digital Humanities Quarterly, 3.*

Foka, A., Attemark, J., & Wahlberg, F. (2022). Women's metadata, semantic web ontologies and AI. In *Emerging technologies and museums: Mediating difficult heritage* (pp. 65–88). Bergham Books.

Fontanella, F., Colace, F., Molinara, M., Di Freca, A. S., & Stanco, F. (2020). Pattern recognition and artificial intelligence techniques for cultural heritage. *Pattern Recognition Letters, 138*, 23–29. https://doi.org/10.1016/j.patrec.2020.06.018

Gaia, G., Boiano, S., & Borda, A. (2019). Engaging museum visitors with AI: The case of chatbots. In *Museums and digital culture* (pp. 309–329). Springer. https://doi.org/10.1007/978-3-319-97457-6_15

Geismar, H. (2018). *Museum object lessons for the digital age*. UCL Press.

Heinz Nixdorf Museums Forum, Germany. (2022). http://www.hnf.de/en/

Hendrickx, I., Généreux, M., & Marquilhas, R. (2011). Automatic pragmatic text segmentation of historical letters. In *Language technology for cultural heritage* (pp. 135–153). Springer.

Hollanek, T. (2020). AI transparency: A matter of reconciling design with critique. *AI & Society*, 1–9. https://doi.org/10.1007/s00146-020-01110-y

Hoobler, E. (2006). "To take their heritage in their hands": Indigenous self-representation and decolonization in the community museums of Oaxaca, Mexico. *American Indian Quarterly, 30*(3/4), 441–460.

Kadish, D., Risi, S., & Løvlie, A. S. (2021, July). Improving object detection in art images using only style transfer. In *2021 international joint conference on neural networks (IJCNN)* (pp. 1–8). IEEE.

Kaggle: MOMA, NYC: Title, artist, date, and medium of every artwork in the MoMA collection (2017). https://kaggle.com/momanyc/museum-collection

Kaggle: Rijksmuseum: Images and meta data from Rijksmuseum's collection (2021). https://kaggle.com/lgmoneda/rijksmuseum

Kopp, S., Gesellensetter, L., Krämer, N. C., & Wachsmuth, I. (2005, September). A conversational agent as museum guide–design and evaluation of a real-world application. In *International workshop on intelligent virtual agents* (pp. 329–343). Springer. https://doi.org/10.1007/11550617_28

Kuflik, T., Stock, O., Zancanaro, M., Gorfinkel, A., Jbara, S., Kats, S., … Kashtan, N. (2011). A visitor's guide in an active museum: Presentations, communications, and reflection. *Journal on Computing and Cultural Heritage (JOCCH), 3*(3), 1–25.

Kwok, A. O., & Koh, S. G. (2021). Deepfake: A social construction of technology perspective. *Current Issues in Tourism, 24*(13), 1798–1802. https://doi.org/10.1080/13683500.2020.1738357

Lee, J., & Paddon, M. (2017). Creating the smart museum: The intersection of digital strategy, kiosks and mobile. *MW17: Museums and the Web 2017, Cleveland, OH.*

Lee, D. (2019). Deepfake Salvador Dalí takes selfies with museum visitors. *The Verge.*

Lynch, C. (2000). From automation to transformation. *Educause Review, 35*(1), 60–69.

Macdonald, S. (Ed.). (2011). *A companion to museum studies*. John Wiley & Sons.

Murphy, O., & Villaespesa, E. (2020). AI: A museum planning toolkit. https://themuseumsai.network/toolkit/

Museum Website. *Johannes Larsen Museet* (blog), March 5, 2021. https://johanneslarsenmuseet.dk/nyhed/vores-maleri-savner-jer/

Noble, S. U. (2018). *Algorithms of oppression*. New York University Press.

Not, E., & Petrelli, D. (2019). Empowering cultural heritage professionals with tools for authoring and deploying personalised visitor experiences. *User Modeling and User-Adapted Interaction, 29*(1), 67–120.

Oberlander, J., O'Donnell, M., Mellish, C., & Knott, A. (1998). Conversation in the museum: Experiments in dynamic hypermedia with the intelligent labelling explorer. *New Review of Hypermedia and Multimedia, 4*(1), 11–32. https://doi.org/10.1080/13614569808914693

Raji, I. D., Gebru, T., Mitchell, M., Buolamwini, J., Lee, J., & Denton, E. (2020, February). Saving face: Investigating the ethical concerns of facial recognition auditing. In *Proceedings of the AAAI/ACM conference on AI, ethics, and society* (pp. 145–151). https://doi.org/10.1145/3375627.3375820

Romero, V., Serrano, N., Toselli, A. H., Sánchez, J. A., & Vidal, E. (2011, September). Handwritten text recognition for historical documents. In *Proceedings of the workshop on language technologies for digital humanities and cultural heritage* (pp. 90–96).

Rögnvaldsson, E., & Helgadóttir, S. (2011). Morphosyntactic tagging of Old Icelandic texts and its use in studying syntactic variation and change. In *Language technology for cultural heritage* (pp. 63–76). Springer. https://doi.org/10.1007/978-3-642-20227-8_4

Ryding, K., Spence, J., Løvlie, A. S., & Benford, S. (2021). Interpersonalizing intimate museum experiences. *International Journal of Human–Computer Interaction*, *37*(12), 1151–1172. https://doi .org/10.1080/10447318.2020.1870829

Ragusa, F., Furnari, A., Battiato, S., Signorello, G., & Farinella, G. M. (2020). EGO-CH: Dataset and fundamental tasks for visitors behavioral understanding using egocentric vision. *Pattern Recognition Letters*, *131*, 150–157. https://doi.org/10.48550/arXiv.2002.00899

Risam, R. (2018). *New digital worlds: Postcolonial digital humanities in theory, praxis, and pedagogy.* Northwestern University Press.

Rodríguez-Ortega, N. (2018). Canon, value, and cultural heritage: New processes of assigning value in the postdigital realm. *Multimodal Technologies and Interaction*, *2*(2), 25.

Safra, L., Chevallier, C., Grèzes, J., & Baumard, N. (2020). Tracking historical changes in trustworthiness using machine learning analyses of facial cues in paintings. *Nature communications*, *11*(1), 1–7.

Sansonetti, G., Gasparetti, F., & Micarelli, A. (2019, June). Cross-domain recommendation for enhancing cultural heritage experience. In *Adjunct publication of the 27th conference on user modeling, adaptation and personalization* (pp. 413–415). https://doi.org/10.1145/3314183.3323869

Scheuerman, M. K., Pape, M., & Hanna, A. (2021). Auto-essentialization: Gender in automated facial analysis as extended colonial project. *Big Data & Society*, *8*(2). https://doi.org/10.1177/20539517 211053712

SMK [National Gallery of Denmark]. (2022). Artificial intelligence helps organise Denmark's largest art collection. https://www.smk.dk/en/article/artificial-intelligence-helps-organise-denmarks-largest -art-collection/

Stark, L., & Crawford, K. (2019). The work of art in the age of artificial intelligence: What artists can teach us about the ethics of data practice. *Surveillance & Society*, *17*(3/4), 442–455. https://doi.org /10.24908/ss.v17i3/4.10821

Stock, O. (1993). Alfresco: Enjoying the combination of NLP and hypermedia for information exploration. In *In AAAI workshop on intelligent multimedia interfaces* (pp. 197–224).

The GIFT box: Tools and ways of working to help museums make richer digital experiences for their visitors (blog), 2019. https://gifting.digital/brighton-museum/

The Met Museum. (2019). The Met, Microsoft, and MIT explore the impact of artificial intelligence on how global audiences connect with art | The Metropolitan Museum of Art. https://www.metmuseum .org/press/news/2019/m-x-m-x-m;

The National Gallery of Denmark. Artificial intelligence helps organise Denmark's largest art collection, SMK – National Gallery of Denmark in Copenhagen (Statens Museum for Kunst) (blog), December 12, 2019. https://www.smk.dk/en/article/artificial-intelligence-helps-organise-denmarks -largest-art-collection/

Thylstrup, N. B. (2019). *The politics of mass digitization*. MIT Press.

Tzouganatou, A. (2018). Can heritage bots thrive? Toward future engagement in cultural heritage. *Advances in Archaeological Practice*, *6*(4), 377–383. https://doi.org/10.1017/aap.2018.32

Tzouganatou, A. (2021). Openness and privacy in born-digital archives: Reflecting the role of AI development. *AI & Society*. https://doi.org/10.1007/s00146-021-01361-3

Vassos, S., Malliaraki, E., Falco, F. D., Maggio, J. D., Massimetti, M., Nocentini, M. G., & Testa, A. (2016, November). Art-bots: Toward chat-based conversational experiences in museums. In *International conference on interactive digital storytelling* (pp. 433–437). Springer.

Volk, M., Furrer, L., & Sennrich, R. (2011). Strategies for reducing and correcting OCR errors. In *Language technology for cultural heritage* (pp. 3–22). Springer.

Wallace, A., & Deazley, R. (2016). Display at your own risk: An experimental exhibition of digital cultural heritage. Available at SSRN 3378193.

Wallace, A., & Pavis, M. (2020). SCuLE submission for the EU consultation on digital cultural heritage. Available at SSRN 3721941.

Westlake, N., Cai, H., & Hall, P. (2016, October). Detecting people in artwork with CNNS. In *European conference on computer vision* (pp. 825–841). Springer.

Witte, R., Kappler, T., Krestel, R., & Lockemann, P. C. (2011). Integrating wiki systems, natural language processing, and semantic technologies for cultural heritage data management. In *Language technology for cultural heritage* (pp. 213–230). Springer.

Zorich, D. (2012). Transitioning to a digital world: Art history, its research centers, and digital scholarship. *Journal of Digital Humanities*, *1*(2).

72. AI ethnography

Anne Dippel and Andreas Sudmann

1. INTRODUCTION

One of the central questions of the current upswing of AI is how corresponding technologies (machine learning or rule-based symbolic approaches) and techniques (e.g., convolutional neural networks, unsupervised machine learning) potentially transform scientific methods and practices. What kind of facts are produced and how are truth claims justified by AI technologies? Ethnographic approaches are of three-fold importance in this regard. First, by allowing first-hand participant observations and interviews to be central elements of empirical analysis, they have been a key approach to science and technology studies for decades. Second, they make an important contribution to critical AI studies as presented in the context of this *Handbook* by interweaving different temporalities and modes of action, by considering actants of all kinds, and by creating feedback-loops and thus potentially becoming an important part of how AI is developed and produced. Third, the tools and accounts of AI put ethnographic research under new conditions and help to develop the method itself. In the following, starting from terminological, conceptual (Section 2), and historical (Section 3) considerations, we will present some current approaches to AI ethnography (Section 4), which illustrate the heterogeneous spectrum of this field of research. Subsequently, we will shed light on the question of the potential contribution of ethnographic approaches to fundamental issues and perspectives of critical AI studies (Section 5), the latter also including an examination of the limits and specific problems of an ethnography of AI.

2. CONCEPT/DEFINITION

AI ethnography as a term for a field of research that puts ethnographic approaches and AI in connection can accordingly encompass quite different analytic perspectives. It may mean using ethnographic accounts to study AI technologies, whether in the scientific, industrial, public, or any other domain. It may designate the methodological integration of AI approaches within ethnographic research as a form of computational or digital ethnography. Finally, it could signify using ethnography to collect data or, more generally, gaining insights through ethnographic accounts that can be used to inform the practical development of AI systems – again, across different areas of application.

One of the initial questions of AI ethnography is whether and how it differs from other established forms of ethnography, mainly developed in the fields of anthropology, sociology, and science and technology studies. Indeed, fundamental methodological principles of ethnography "in general" also apply in the context of AI studies: exploring social and cultural practices with a variety of methods to investigate, analyze, and describe perspectives of a given field by "being there" and systematically taking notes and records of all kinds. This encompasses following ethical guidelines as well as established standards to do fieldwork, including participant observation and interviews. The world of AI production is usually a world of scientific and digital work culture, where non-human actors are playing a similarly important role as human ones. Hence, ethnography in this area requires a specific sensitivity toward the involved actants, not only situating the researcher in the position of "studying up" (Nader, 1972, 1977) but also broadening the analytic focus beyond the human as the very center of interest. As most ethnographies are taking a cultural relativist stance that sees positivist descriptions of the world as incompatible with a method that demonstrates the intra-active emergence of phenomena and relies so much on the individual observer and her possibilities of observation, ethnography is almost always characterized by self-reflection (Rabinow et al., 2008; Clifford & Marcus, 2010). This entails descriptions of moments during fieldwork, often framed within vignettes, "thick descriptions" (Geertz, 1973) of qualitatively gained observations and the successive reflection of the researcher's own methodological approaches. Taking seriously the situatedness of the participant observer and their narratological and epistemological choices is part of what it means to understand "what is going on" (Geertz, 1973). In contrast to many theory-driven approaches in academia, ethnography allows the development of theory alongside data acquisition and its subsequent analysis (Clarke & Star, 2008). Therefore, we suggest conceptualizing fieldwork as a form of *situated processuality*. Here, researchers are calibrating themselves and their theoretical perspectives alongside and dependent on the co-creative data acquisition process (Forsythe, 1999, p. 129). As ethnographers slowly get accommodated with the field of research, they learn and gain knowledge, weaving webs of obligations and developing a hermeneutically grounded understanding with others. They co-create the field (Wagner, 1981), informed by a spirit of "learning by doing", as Beaulieu (2016) suggested. With the timely distance to the experiences in the field, hermeneutic circles of source analysis allow us to re-situate and process the gained knowledge while developing theoretical insights and crafting narratives (McGranahan, 2020). AI ethnography differs in the importance of informatic layers of knowledge, especially the importance of code, coding, and algorithmic expertise (Carlson, 2021; Eggel et al., 2021; Franken, 2022). The specific settings of working in AI contexts involve the analysis of technical actants and awareness of the importance of more-than-human actors (De la Cadena & Blaser, 2018) in post-human settings (Braidotti, 2013; Forsythe, 2001; Pickering, 1995; Povinelli, 2016; Star & Griesemer, 1989).

Analyzing AI worlds and worldings (Haraway, 2016; Stewart, 2010), in particular, how machine learning is creating environments, implies the problematization of the very concept of "AI". Since the questioning of central terms like "AI" or "machine learning" is inherent to the field and its community, it is an important terminological effort of AI ethnography not only to work through these critical discussions but also to position itself in relation to them. Against this background, it might be helpful to stress that AI, as a concept, has been and continues to be rejected by many engineers and computer scientists because it seems to imply that it is primarily about approaches to simulating human intelligence (see Star, 1989).

An ethnography of AI can be of use within various disciplinary settings, for example, anthropology, sociology, or media studies, and interdisciplinary fields such as science and technology studies or the emerging field of critical AI studies. Already Diana Forsythe, the pioneer of AI ethnography, stated that conducting interviews and doing participant observation is a challenging task, and stressed that it takes experience and guidance to do it well (Forsythe, 1999, pp. 128–130; Powdermaker, 1966; Wax, 1971; Werner & Schoepfle, 1987). The tools of ethnography allow us to compare the findings with the existing record of ethnographic data across the world. Ethnography situates its discoveries within a wide array of philosophical stances without any hegemonic claims because it is a reflected mode of situated knowledge production. Theory emerges out of empirical observation and the subsequent analysis of data. The description of the field thus "enable[s] the fieldworker to detect consistent patterns of thought and practice and to investigate the relationship between them – an important comparison, since what people do is not always the same as what they say they do" (Forsythe, 1991, p. 128). Being an ethnographer demands empathy and patience. Doing ethnography entails the attitude of a general openness to the fact that nothing can be taken for granted, especially when doing participant observation or leading interviews. Even if handbooks provide a methodological toolkit, it usually takes years of training and intense study of existing literature to become a good ethnographer (ibid).

Subsequently, different disciplinary contexts will inscribe themselves into the perspectives of the ethnographic approaches and thus affect the epistemological outcomes of studies (Pink, 2015). The study of AI is a complex subfield of qualitative research, and the academic scene is thus quite interdisciplinary. Nevertheless, researchers address questions and topics relevant to their disciplinary background. A science and technology studies approach might differ from anthropological frameworks, even if both would focus on practices, communities, and modes of relationalities. Sociological approaches might focus more on how practices and the uses of AI technology are determined by social factors and might also be more related to the respective "own society" (Knoblauch, 2001, p. 124), while a media studies approach could be more interested in the epistemic-aesthetic role of media in relation to the operations of using and developing AI technologies.

Doing AI ethnography can also be a component of a digital ethnography, virtual ethnography, or an ethnography of algorithms (Boellstorff et al., 2012, Domínguez et al., 2007; Hine, 2000; Nardi et al., 2012; Pink, 2015; Seaver, 2017). Again, it is important to specify what attributes like digital or virtual specifically mean in the context of such an analytic approach. In principle, AI ethnography can be conceived as a field of research that addresses specific questions and problems that in so doing differ from general perspectives in digital ethnography, computational anthropology, or other fields. For example, it is important to highlight that artificial neural networks (ANN) are a quasi-analog information technology, which therefore cannot simply be attributed to digital technologies:

> First, … [t]he weighting of the activity between the neurons, i.e., the strength of their connections, is […] mostly represented by floating point numbers (positive and negative) in neural networks. And this representation is so finely structured that the corresponding values can be understood as quasi-analog. Second, it must be emphasized that the masses of interconnected neurons, activated by an input, fire together simultaneously or in parallel, thus ultimately forming a complex emergent system that abolishes the discreteness of the elements it consists of (the layers of neurons and their connection). This extreme or massive parallelism of information processing can indeed count as the essential characteristic of ANN, distinguishing it from the von Neumann architecture of classical digital computers. (Sudmann, 2021, pp. 290–291, see also Sudmann, 2018)

Ethnographers studying the field of AI research and production were able to demonstrate that this kind of study would "delete the social" (Star, 1991), while in fact being entrenched with social and cultural aspects, be it human-machine interactions, modes of communication, the production of code, or networked interactions (see for example Dick, 2011, 2013). Diana Forsythe showed that "knowledge engineers" would conceive humans as "inefficient" when it comes to knowledge production (Forsythe, 1993, p. 454). The idea of humans as being deficient or upholding the primacy of mathematical knowledge and logics over other forms of knowledge has been accompanying the development of AI ever since. Subsequently, critical AI studies are challenged to question the very notion of knowledge produced within the field of AI, suggesting that AI could be conceptualized as alien to human forms of cognition (Dippel, 2019b, 2021).

In addition to "things and actions" (Varis, 2016, p. 57), informatic operations (Sudmann, 2018), race (Benjamin, 2019), gender (Traweek, 1988), affordances, or beliefs about technologies as a form of "media ideologies" (Gershon, 2010, following Silverstein, 1979), as well as ethics and sociotechnical design of responsible innovation (RI) (Hess et al., 2021) play a vital role in the everyday practices of developing and researching "smart" technologies and applications. Therefore, AI ethnography investigates how media technologies shape people's thoughts and actions – and in turn, how people's conceptions, beliefs, and practices inscribe themselves into and in turn configure media technological usage.

AI ethnography is thus not only a research attitude or methodological choice but also a theoretical tool as well as a mode of writing (Blommaert & Dong, 2010; Varis, 2016, pp. 61–62; McGranahan, 2020). Although ethnography is usually qualitative in its methods (Munk et al., 2022), AI ethnography may be more open toward quantitative data acquisition, especially when it comes to research that combines the possibilities of human observation and analysis with the potentials of machine learning algorithms. As Ursula Rao stated, large-scale quantitative studies allow us to gather a heap of data (Rao, 2019, p. 17), and the impact of technologically and AI-assisted modes of governing, engineering, and communication generates a nearly infinite amount of data that would and could be analyzed with the right mix of qualitative and quantitative methodologies.

Given the fact that AI ethnography is dealing with more-than-human and non-human fields (Dippel, 2021a) beyond the realm of any "ethnos", the question of how to properly name such an approach is still under debate. Nevertheless, "ethnography" has become an umbrella term that allows us to easily connect it with the existing body of qualitative data acquisition based on participant observation, interviews, and discourse analysis. However, it seems as if ethnographic research is increasingly interested in exploring how the use of digital tools and technologies of AI can meaningfully expand the repertoire of ethnographic approaches.

3.   HISTORY

The origins of AI ethnography must be seen in relation to its academic contexts, the development of ethnography in general, and the emergence of AI as a field of research at the intersection of science and engineering. Anthropology and sociology have been the main disciplines in which ethnography originally emerged. Early ethnographies were conducted while behavioral, functionalist, and structuralist approaches dominated the fields of social science and humanities. Later, based on ethnographic findings, cultural relativity became influential, suggesting that there are neither universal patterns to be found nor that any understanding of phenomena could be sufficiently convincing without taking the observer's reflection into account. When in the 1960s a certain group of anthropologists, sometimes called "ethnoscientists", experimented with computations according to their interests to find and describe formal cultural laws (Hymes, 1965), the assumptions were greeted with skepticism and were never really pursued in the following decades. A prominent voice of critique in this respect was Clifford Geertz, who also coined the term "thick description":

> Variously called ethnoscience, componential analysis, or cognitive anthropology (a terminological wavering which reflects a deeper uncertainty), this school of thought holds that culture is composed of psychological structures by means of which individuals or groups of individuals guide their behavior. "A society's culture", to quote Goodenough again, this time in a passage which has become the locus classicus of the whole movement, "consists of whatever it is one has to know or believe in order to operate in a manner acceptable to its members". And from this view of what culture is follows a view, equally assured, of what describing it is—the writing out of systematic rules, an ethnographic algorithm, which, if followed, would make it possible so to operate, to pass (physical appearance aside) for a native. (Geertz, 1973, p. 11)

Instead of working on an "ethnoscientific Turing test", anthropology continued to do ethnographic research proving cultural diversity and relativity. Anthropological research on and with AI was not part of the main disciplinary focus. Although automata studies, research within robotics, and AI as part of informatics, developed during the 1970s, there were initially almost no attempts to use ethnographic accounts to explore AI technologies and practices. From the 1980s on, "in-house ethnographers" were working within informatics departments to support research in the field of, for example, medical AI (Hess in Forsythe, 1991). Slowly, the "use of ethnographic methods in design and evaluation" became more apparent (Nardi, 1997). Researchers such as Diana E. Forsythe and Sharon Traweek were among the first who took the chance to apply their anthropological knowledge and expertise in "studying those who study us" (Forsythe, 2001; Traweek, 1988). Roughly at the same time, Susan Leigh Star's work on boundary objects (1989) was significantly influenced by her ethnographic observations of AI research at MIT, specifically in collaboration and conversations with computer scientist Carl Hewitt. It was this group of critical, feminist researchers, deeply influenced by the civil rights movement and the anticapitalistic spirit of the post-1968 era, that contributed to the foundation of a whole new interdisciplinary field: science and technology studies (STS) (Hess & Layne, 1992). STS' insights influence today's AI ethnographies, from workplace cultures (Wenger, 1990; Kling & Scacchi, 1982), distribution of means and social justice (Gerson & Star, 1986; Star, 1992, p. 400), computing environments (Clarke, 1991), seamless spaces (Leigh Star, 1992; see also Vertesi, 2014), "white-washed" and first-world oriented research in science (Fujimura, 1991, later: Calvert & Fujimura, 2009; Fujimura, 2018; Fujimura & Rajagopalan, 2020), Lucy Suchman's studies on human-machine communication (Suchman, 1987), and technologies of accountability (Suchman, 1992) to human-computer-relationalities (Turkle, 1989, 1990, 1995, 2009) and actor-network theory (Bijker & Law, 1992; Callon, 1984, 1986; Law & Rip, 1986; Latour, 1987; Latour & Woolgar, 1986). Constructivist STS evolved while investigating AI in the 1980s, and behaviorist studies emerged as well. For example, Agar and Hobbs conceived of AI as "the investigation of complex formalism" (Agar & Hobbs, 1982, p. 1) and tried to use a kind of "AI formalism" as a descriptive tool for applying it to the study of conversational behavior in ethnographic interviews (ibid.).

What followed, around the end of the 1990s and early 2000s, was an ambivalent period in the history of AI. On the one hand, there has been some progress in machine learning like the invention of long-short-term memory (LSTM) technology by Hochreiter and Schmidhuber (1997) and the establishment and differentiation of models like support vector machines (Cortes & Vapnick, 1995). On the other hand, essential areas of AI research (like NLP and computer vision) were still far away from the level of performance that could be achieved roughly ten or 15 years later.

During this phase, AI ethnography continued to play a rather minor role. Nevertheless, even back then there were some works that at least from an ex-post perspective represent important reference points for writing a history of AI ethnography, from Nicholas Gessler's (1995) research program called "Artificial Culture" to Peter Galison's *Image and Logic* (1997) to Lev Manovich's (2008, 2020) concept of cultural analytics. Of seminal importance is also Michael D. Fischer's book *Applications in Computing for Social Anthropologists* (1994), in which he addresses the issue of the relationship between computing environments and ethnography in general, but also marginally discusses the role of expert systems, yet without assigning them any particular significance for the work of ethnographers.

As has been reviewed in recent historical accounts (Engemann & Sudmann, 2018), the current upswing of machine learning and specifically ANN began around 2008/2009, first in the field of natural language processing and since 2012 in the field of computer vision. However, it took some time for the ethnographic disciplines to respond to these technological breakthroughs. Still, there have been several works in various disciplinary contexts (anthropology, media studies, sociology) that have become very important for current approaches to AI ethnography. These include, for example, the study of ICT (information and communication technologies) and its tools (Gershon, 2010), public life in virtual worlds (Boellstorf, 2008; Nardi, 2010), communities (Coleman et al., 2008; Postill, 2011), cyber and digital ethnographies (Hine, 2000; Lupton, 2014; Marres/Weltjevrede, 2013; Rybas/Gajjala, 2007), new realms of leisure and living such as computer gaming and social media (Boellstorff et al., 2012; Malaby, 2010; Pias, 2017), and the emergence of digital objects and data avatars (Bogost, 2006; Hui, 2016), as well as rethinking indigeneity in digital worlds (Ginsburg, 2008) or discrimination through algorithms and AI technologies (Chun, 2021).

Since the 2010s, digital anthropology had become a major subfield within anthropology (Bender & Zillinger, 2015; Koch, 2017; Horst & Miller, 2006; Madianou & Miller, 2011; Miller, 2012; Miller & Slater, 2000; Miller, 2012b; Pink & Horst, 2015). In addition, anthropology and cultural studies increasingly integrated approaches and concepts from media anthropology (Bareither, 2017), or were working at the intersection of anthropology and media studies informing both theoretical discourses (Dippel, 2017, 2022). Conversely, media studies more and more referred to approaches from sociology and cultural anthropology, especially in terms of methodology, while at the same time advancing the reflection and use of digital methods and media practices in particular (e.g., Schüttpelz & Thielmann, 2013; Gerlitz & Passmann, 2017; Gießmann & Taha, 2017).

Finally, AI and specifically machine learning became a central focus of attention in ethnographic research projects since around 2016, i.e., mostly after the event of AlphaGo's victory. Even the 2017 Routledge *Companion to Digital Ethnography* did not yet contain any reference to machine learning or ANN (Hjorth et al., 2017). One early publication that discusses machine learning, including a somewhat ethnographic perspective, is Mackenzie's book *Machine Learners* in which the author claims that even though "this book is not an ethnography, it has an ethnographic situation" (p. xi).

Today, the impact of computer technologies and the existence of digital cultures and digitization has become part of nearly every field of the social sciences and humanities when it comes to understanding how contemporary phenomena and computers are permeating all aspects of life – from agriculture to zoology, from deep sea mining to probing in outer space. This poses the question of what exactly is *not* digital anthropology, computational social science, or digital humanities. AI ethnography also points to the specific conditions of ethnographic work and its human and more-than-human environment of actants, networks, and emergent interactions of knowledge within situated or procedural modes of cognition.

In times of citizen science (Dippel, 2019a; Fizek & Dippel, 2019) and smart cities (Halpern & Mitchell, 2021), where automated translations, smart systems, Monte Carlo-based computer simulations, and pattern recognition in big data worlds are common, many of the initial critical perspectives on what and how knowledge can be generated through machine learning algorithms seem to be outdated. AI has reached all aspects of social and cultural, even private, life, as Kathleen Richardson's work on sex robots (2015) or Mary L. Grays and Siddharth Suri's book *Ghost Work* (2019) has shown impressively. Algorithms are part of culture (Seaver, 2017). AI has established itself both as a science and an industry, and its outcomes continue to surprise the public, whether AlphaGo is beating Lee Sedol in playing Go, or whether the NASA rover perseverance is landing on Mars and gathering data for astrophysics. AI permeates everyday life and studying AI with ethnographic approaches puts researchers in dependent fieldwork situations when doing fieldwork in laboratories and startup enterprises. To whom do field diaries and recorded interviews in university or entrepreneurial labs belong? To whom belongs the data gathered and analyzed by machine learning algorithms? How are objects of knowledge created today? What helps to understand AI and its spaces of creation beyond established analytical concepts of discursive powers?

The assumption of "humans and computers as clearly bounded creatures whose essential abilities can be discussed and compared in the abstract" (Dick, 2011, p. 496) must be put up for debate in times when the dependency on software grows exponentially, and often in uncontrolled ways (Dick & Vollmar, 2018). Who acts, what does interactivity mean, and where begins *interpassive* living in mediated worlds of technological affordances (Fizek, 2022)? Ethnographies take place in areas "beyond the black box" (Christin, 2020), and as the survey on explainable AI (Adadi & Berrade, 2018) shows, AI ethnography – freed from its positivist origins and enriched with a whole history of critical studies in the humanities and social sciences – has just begun. Its epistemic potential is difficult to assess, and its fields of exploration and development seem to be infinite.

4.   CURRENT APPROACHES

In the following, we would like to present four research projects and their specific focus, illustrating the heterogeneous spectrum of AI ethnography. We have decided to limit our presentation of current projects in the field of AI ethnography to these few examples, mainly to avoid giving the impression of a complete representation of this rapidly growing research field. Indeed, many projects in the field of AI ethnography are currently still in the making (e.g., RAI, 2022; Inkpen et al., 2022; Krassmann & Schmidt, 2022; Vepřek & Carson, 2022). Eventually, the importance of ethnographic studies and quantitative data analysis has reached the field of STEM (Marda & Narayan, 2021) and thus many AI ethnographies are expected to emerge over the next decade within various scientific disciplines and interdisciplinary intersections. Finally, we have decided to present our own research in the section below, primarily because it is the basis of the methodological considerations presented here.

4.1 "The Thick Machine": A "Turing Test for Computational Anthropology"?

Recently, three Danish scholars from the so-called Techno-Anthropological Research Group conceptualized a kind of Turing test for computational anthropology and, in this context, have also speculated on what a Geertzian variation of the Turing test might look like. Such a test would be passed, according to the scholars involved, "if the computer could contribute to interpreting cultural expressions in a way that is indistinguishable from the way an interpretative anthropologist would do it" (Munk et al., 2022, p. 1).

Although the researchers have not developed an AI system that would be able to provide thick descriptions in the sense of Geertz (1973), they at least attribute to their system the ability of "explication", i.e., "doing the initial work of identifying deeper situations where interpretation is not straightforward and, thus, worthwhile" (Munk et al., 2022, p. 1). To this end, they constructed a machine that associates comments on Facebook with various emoji reactions like "wow" or "sad" that the platform has established since 2016. Among other things, the scholars wanted to find out whether the machine could help them differentiate the specific meanings of, for example, a laughing smiley emoji. When is it an ironic or sarcastic laugh and when is it genuine amusement? Within the framework of their research design, they have developed three variants of a "Turing test for computational anthropology" whose concrete test setup is shown in Table 72.1.

According to the research group, the first two "formalistic" imitation games are based on the ethnoscientist idea of an "ethnographic algorithm capable of passing for a native" (p. 10), while the third game was modeled according to the idea of a Geertzian thick description.

To methodically implement the "Thick Machine" project, the researchers trained an artificial neural network on a Facebook dataset consisting of 175000 post-comment pairs (selected from a much larger dataset from the period of January 2012 to January 2018) to predict the right emoji reactions for the respective comments (for the technical details, see p. 5).

As part of their study, the authors clearly identified the limitations of their project in many respects. For example, they admit that the "Thick Machine could never satisfy an ethnoscientific expectation of algorithms as something akin to the 'writing out of systematic rules'" (p. 10). The results of the three different imitation games were nevertheless quite interesting:

Table 72.1   *Three versions of the imitation game for a Turing test in computational anthropology*

Which game?	Imitating who?	By doing what?	Criteria for winning
The naïve ethnoscientist	Users on Facebook	Predicting the user's emoji reactions	High prediction accuracy
The reflexive ethnoscientist	Ethnographers trying to imitate users on Facebook	Predicting emoji reactions in the same way as the ethnographers	Similar pattern of accuracy as the ethnographers
The interpretative ethnographer	Ethnographers trying to identify situations on Facebook that need explication	Showing where emojis are hard to predict	Finds situations where multiple layers of meaning complicate interpretation

Source: Munk et al. (2022, p. 4).

According to the setting of "the naive ethnoscientist", both humans and the computer failed in roughly half of the predictions, but the machine was more precise across different emoji reactions (p. 8). In the case of "the reflexive ethnoscientist", the machine was able to achieve an overall accuracy of 51% in successfully imitating the humans. As with the latter ones, the computer had trouble distinguishing between "sad" and "angry" reactions, but never confused "angry" and "love" reactions. Finally, the imitation game of the "interpretative ethnographer": the assumption here is that correct predictions of emojis refer to un-ambivalent cases, whereas it is precisely the situations where the computer system makes an incorrect prediction that highlight statements that precisely require an interpretive, explicative approach in Geertz's sense.

Here's one of the examples given by the authors:

EXAMPLE 6
Post: "For the Prince, the decision not to be buried next
to the Queen is the natural consequence of not receiving the
same treatment as his spouse when it comes to the title and
function he has always desired, says chief of communications
for the Royal House, Lene Balleby".
Comment: "I will gladly swap problems with him.
Happy to refrain from a royal title in exchange for 8
million a year. Or just the 29 million for the sarcophagus.
Then he can fight my [beep] ex and the system without
getting as much as a penny in return. Get a real problem,
King Carrot".
Reaction: "haha" (machine predicts "angry")

(Munk et al., 2022, p. 12)

According to the Danish scholars, the "haha" articulation in this example could be understood scoffingly. While the machine apparently classifies the comment as "angry", the authors kind of justify the machine's classification by declaring that "you can put up a laugh in a situation where you are actually angry to underline sarcasm or demonstrate contempt" (p. 12). As this example and comment demonstrate, learning algorithms can support heuristic searches for data in need of interpretation, while at the same time, and as admitted by the authors themselves, it's also evident that the AI model itself cannot interpret these selected data.

4.2   David Moats and Nick Seaver: When Data Scientists Engage with Social Science

Ethnographers have been involved in informatics for decades. The body of algorithmic studies has grown substantially in the fields of STS and beyond. Nevertheless, it seems that a communicational gap exists between data science and STS. There are few encounters with disciplinary knowledge systems beyond "boundary work" (Gieryn, 1999) and "boundary objects" (Star, 1989). One important structured attempt to analyze how data scientists react to the ways of thinking in STS has been conducted by David Moats and Nick Seaver in the article "You Social Scientists Love Mind Games", published as part of the Big Data and Society's special issue "Algorithmic normativities" (Larsen & Lee, 2019). Experimenting with the "'divide' between data science and critical algorithm studies", they explore the current state of the art in critical algorithmic studies (Irani, 2015; Iliadis & Russo, 2016; Kitchin, 2014; Lazer &

Pendtlandt, 2009; Lipton & Steinhardt, 2018), situating the approaches within the history of STS research (Hall, 1980; Callon, 1984) and exploring the potentials and limits of interventions in algorithmic practices by setting up an experiment and letting data scientists encounter critical algorithmic research.

The dialogic intervention was based on exchanging emails. It started with specific questions on social scientific vocabulary and explanatory models and was understood by the authors in the tradition of a "breaching experiment" (Garfinkel, 1963, 2011). The outcome can be seen as a fruitful starting point for any future analysis that tries to integrate AI ethnography into the production of AI itself. Moats and Seaver demonstrate that the "divide" between academic cultures starts with how they understand language. Their argument aligns with the *Weltanschauungstheorie* or linguistic relativism known as the Sapir–Whorf hypothesis (Koerner, 1992):

> The background linguistic system (…) of each language is not merely a reproducing instrument for voicing ideas but rather is itself a shaper of ideas, the program and guide for the individual's mental activity, for this analysis of impressions, for his [i.e., their] synthesis of his [i.e., their] mental stock in trade. (Whorf, 1940, p. 212; Koerner, 1992, p. 181)

Terminologies and epistemologies would differ substantially. Creating a dialogue that could bridge the gap turned out to be difficult due to the tight work schedules of data scientists. In their perspective, any attempt to find translational spaces for common vocabulary would be perceived as a loss of time, the valuable time they need for their research. In addition to these findings, experimental dialogues within classroom settings showed that the *reflexivity* of STS approaches became an apparent problem of debating and dialogue.

Given the societal challenges posed by AI technologies, and their transformative potential, the effort to find a common understanding in the future is of utmost importance. It bears potential for new research, paving the way for constructive collaborations between data and social sciences, as well as the humanities. Critical AI studies with such a perspective, i.e., by finding new ways of communication, could also have a political and ethical impact on how AI is deployed and made.

4.3   Anne Dippel, Ludic Infrastructures, and Big Data Games in Physics

From 2013 on, Anne Dippel has been doing long-term ethnography within various fields of physics. Primarily, she worked on computer simulations of experimental systems and measurements, from Monte Carlo-based simulations and machine learning-driven analysis of high-energy physics at the European Organization for Nuclear Research (CERN) to event-based simulations of quantum mechanical experiments (Juelich Super Computing Centre and University of Vienna) (Dippel, 2017; Dippel & Warnke, 2022). During fieldwork, the ethnographer realized that the established analytical frameworks on work environments and practices must be recalibrated with regard to big data and machine learning-oriented fields of research. Dippel analyzed the prevailing importance of ludic infrastructures, i.e., the interplay of mainly competitive, aleatoric, mimetic mechanisms in a rule-based closed system of scientific knowledge production, playful practices – from word plays and puns to tinkering and having fun while doing science – and game-like frameworks when dealing with big data, such as demonstrations of how neural networks are used to understand high-energy physics data analysis on the application "TensorFlow playground" (http://playground.tensorflow.org).

In high-energy physics, physical events must be identified that are:

both rare and obscured by the wide variety of processes that can mimic the signal. This is a veritable case of finding a needle in a haystack, for which the conventional approach of selecting events by using cuts on individual kinematic variables can be far from optimal. (Bhat, 2011, p. 283)

With the advanced capacities of computation and developments in AI research, machine learning algorithms were introduced into the multivariate analysis (MVA) of experimental events to classify particles and reduce errors in data analysis from the 1980s onwards. Since then, neural networks were successfully trained and played, for example, a vital role in the discovery of the Higgs Boson in 2012 at the Large Hadron Collider of CERN. In her fieldwork, Dippel observed how traditional fields of science are slowly permeated by informatics and computer scientific language, post-Fordistic work-time structures, and techno-utopian imaginaries. To solve problems, high-energy physicists collaborate, for example, with computer scientists. In turn, AI research profits from publicly funded big science projects such as the experiments conducted at the Large Hadron Collider of CERN (Dippel, 2017).

Understanding physics through a games and play helped her to interpret, for example, machine learning challenges and competitions beyond the framework of neoliberal work modes and established approaches of actor-network theory to understand laboratory life (Knorr-Cetina, 1999, Latour & Woolgar, 1986). This focus not only allowed a connection with adjacent fields of media studies and game studies but also contributed to re-situate the global critical perspectives on post-industrial and capitalist modes of production and the possibilities and limits of subversion with and through play beyond established frameworks of actor-network theory and anthropology of science and work cultures (Dippel, 2021b, 2022).

4.4 Project: How Is Artificial Intelligence Changing Science? Research in the Era of Learning Algorithms (Echterhölter, Schröter, Sudmann, and Waibel, Since 2019/2021)

Another research project, which draws on approaches from AI ethnography, is addressing the question of how AI technologies are changing research and science. Following a so-called planning grant, a transdisciplinary research group of media studies, history of science, and computer science successfully obtained a main grant from the Volkswagen Foundation in December 2021 and officially started its work in August 2022.

In particular, the group is interested in how AI technologies affect the methods and practices in AI communities in various disciplines and wants to investigate more closely the extent to which current approaches to AI can be used to gain new forms of knowledge and insights. Three so-called focus disciplines are at the center of attention: social sciences, environmental sciences, and film studies. In doing so, the project is expected to achieve several research objectives. First, producing an in-depth study of sociology from the perspective of the history of science and examining the use of data and the definition of classification criteria in historical statistical operations. Second, conducting a media archeological study of the specific technological procedures of AI used in the selected focus projects. Which technologies are used exactly? How have these developed historically? What are their specific strengths and weaknesses? Third, investigating, based on a media ethnographic approach, how the technology is actually used in the focus projects and to shed light on the infrastructural role of media as well as on the relationship of infrastructures and media. The methodical use of AI technologies will be observed and analyzed decidedly as media practices, i.e., with a view to processes of storing, generating, processing, distributing, and presenting information.

Fourth, developing a machine learning-based AI system for analyzing and summarizing scientific texts and lectures, which themselves deal with the use of AI-based methods in various fields.

Within the framework of the planning grant, the project group has created an extensive database on the use of AI in research disciplines at European universities, which will be continuously updated. Four workshops have already been held during the planning grant, in which central challenges and problems of AI meta-research were discussed, not least from a theoretical-methodological point of view. As part of an exploratory essay, an attempt was also made to contour the research question of the project and differentiate it according to its essential dimensions and aspects.

Regarding the current AI discourse, the research group starts from the observation that the transformation of the sciences by AI seems to be always already presupposed, instead of first carefully examining across disciplinary boundaries and from different analytical perspectives whether AI procedures carry the potential to act as a driving force of an epistemic rupture or paradigm shift in Kuhn's sense (1962).

A first case study has explored from a media archeological perspective the extremely data-intensive field of high-energy particle physics. The goal was to compare the data and media practices related to the detection of the omega-minus baryon in the 1960s with those that enabled the discovery of the Higgs boson in 2012. In the first case, the scientific discovery relied very much on stereoscopic photography and early digital photo analysis alongside pattern recognition done by trained human observers (Galison, 1992, pp. 319–320). The search for the Higgs boson relied on machine learning methods due to the enormous amount of data that would overtax any human pattern recognition. What is particularly interesting from a media theoretical perspective is that the ML systems were themselves trained with computer simulations that modeled the types of events predicted by the theory. As the example shows, for critical research on contemporary AI that makes use of ethnographic accounts, a historical approach is at the same time indispensable, especially in view of the always-given need to gain a profound conceptual understanding of the technology that is at the center of the epistemological interest.

5.   CONTRIBUTIONS TO CRITICAL AI STUDIES AND RESEARCH IN AI

An important aspect of ethnographic accounts has always been their capacity to shed light on what has remained unnoticed in everyday life. Different approaches from action anthropology to engaged sociology also allowed researchers to get into dialogue with the actors of the field based on these very observations and insights. Thus, ethnography opens insights about the field that are ideally also new for the actors of the observed field and enables a different form of self-observation for them.

It depends on the efforts of dialogue between data scientists and scholars from the fields of social sciences and humanities to what extent ethnographic research will be able to make an important contribution to dealing with problems of critical AI research that have recently been central in the AI discourse (algorithmic biases, algorithmic opacity, etc.). Of course, on the one hand, ethnography can only to a limited extent be helpful in solving the problems that are currently discussed in the context of machine learning. Nevertheless, on the other hand, ethnographic approaches can make a substantial contribution insofar as they can observe the strategies for dealing with these problems and reflect on them together with the actors in the field.

To illustrate this, the discussion of the opacity of data-driven AI technology is a good example. In fundamental terms, the information processing processes of ANN are intransparent. In contrast to biological brains, the activity of each neuron can be observed and precisely measured within the simulation of neural networks, but there is no way, at least not at present, to adequately understand this activity both as an individual process and in the context of the massive parallelism of the information processing in the network, i.e., to interrelate input, output, and the operations of information processing intelligently, so that the nature and manner of the internal operations could be explained functionally (Sudmann, 2017, 2020). Against this background, concepts such as "Explainable AI" or "Open AI" are simply misleading because they falsely suggest that one can eliminate the fundamental opacity of ANN. Nevertheless, ethnography can be of considerable value in examining the problems arising from the opacity of ANN, as Angèle Christin (2020) has recently pointed out, by focusing on the "multiple enrollments, refractions and mediations taking place between social actors and algorithms" (p. 15), but also by turning to the relationship of media (mediators), practices, and infrastructures related to algorithms and big data.

And such an approach includes the question of how ethnographic perspectives can contribute to interdisciplinary research that seeks to live up to the claim of critical AI research. This points back to fundamental discussions of the critical potential of ethnographic research itself. Finally, it raises the question of whether ethnography can only make a noteworthy contribution to the field of critical AI studies if it declares itself decidedly to be a critical project, as it has been the claim of a critical ethnography for decades (Foley & Valenzuela, 2005). At the same time, Diana Forsythe is precisely an illustrative example of how a critical ethnography does not have to call itself as such to make an interventionist interest explicit. Whether one emphasizes the "critical" in critical AI ethnography or not, it remains to be noted that, especially in the last decade, feminist, queer, and decolonial approaches have significantly shaped the reflections both on ethnographic research and developments in computation, especially in the field of machine learning and data analysis. In addition, and as this *Handbook* shows, a similar development can be observed in the still-young research field of critical AI studies.

Nevertheless, there are inherent limits to how researchers can position themselves critically in relation to the field they are studying and the actors they are observing as part of their ethnographic studies, especially when they are working in relations of dependency within labs or companies and have to sign disclosure agreements for having the possibility to even start research – or when their research takes place in authoritarian countries that deploy AI for their totalitarian modes of governmentality. When actors allow researchers into their field, they want to trust that they will not have to regret having granted access to the field at some point in the study. Of course, this problem exists with basically every form of ethnography, but it is especially relevant concerning controversial and socially relevant fields like AI. In turn, accepting the actors and their views in the field does not mean dealing uncritically with the observations and collected data, but it is first about negotiating the conditions of the possibility of a critical research perspective together with the actors and establishing a trustworthy relationship of transparency and sincerity.

Hence, it can perhaps be argued that the essential critical potential of ethnographic research lies primarily in the fact that it is precisely not subordinated to a particular critical view (of the field). Ethnography is primarily a hypothesis-generating process to research and not, or significantly less so, a hypothesis-confirming approach. This is one of the reasons why an ethnography can only be conditionally subordinated to a specific critical perspective that conceptually structures the research and guides the analytic gaze along certain trajectories. On the contrary, ethnography always means questioning one's own positions in the field, even if they are decidedly critical and interventionist.

The tense relationship between critique and ethnography is inscribed in the specific uses of resources, statements, and reports from the field that position themselves as a critical reflection of the very field one observes. In the case of AI ethnography, there are, for example, many reports or documentation shedding a critical light on the working conditions of the big tech industry and their AI infrastructures and practices that can also be regarded as a form of autoethnography (Stanley, 2021; Hanna & Baker, 2022). Such reports and experiences must themselves be critically appreciated because they are primarily sources, not research itself.

After all, the question remains to what extent a critical ethnography or critical AI studies need to mark itself as such at all. Any self-description of research as critical could be understood in such a way that all other research, without this label, is stigmatized as uncritical. On the other hand, the self-assertion of critical research can be important to make clear that research always has a political dimension and that it is also a matter of linking one's own research with an interventionist claim.

6.   SUMMARY

As has been described here with reference to the work of Forsythe and others, AI ethnography is anything but a new phenomenon. Nevertheless, it is a research field that has only recently gained considerable relevance and visibility in the wake of the general boom in machine learning. Studying AI with ethnographic methods allows us to connect current research in computer science with various epistemic perspectives, from posthumanist approaches to media theoretical ones. For many years, AI ethnographic research has dealt almost exclusively with symbolic, rule-based AI. In this respect, a major challenge of the present is to develop approaches tailored to the specific problems of machine learning as the current paradigm of intelligent machinery. Ultimately, the ethnography of AI as a practice will be evaluated by the extent to which it provides insights about AI that are unobtainable or nearly unobtainable by other approaches. At the same time, methods of AI will be critically evaluated based on whether they can support the work of ethnographers. It is these experimental possibilities and subsequently the chances for new insights that make the field so appealing.

ACKNOWLEDGMENTS/FUNDING

The authors would like to thank Alan F. Backwell and Libuše Vepřek for advice during the research for this chapter.

Andreas Sudmann's work on this chapter is part of the research project *How is artificial intelligence changing science. Research in the era of learning algorithms*, funded by the VW Foundation since 2019 (planning grant), 2021 (full grant).

REFERENCES

Adadi, A., & Berrade, M. (2018). Peeking inside the black-box: A survey on explainable artificial intelligence (XAI). *IEEE Access, 6*, 52138–52160.

Agar, M., & Hobbs, J. R. (1982). Interpreting discourse: Coherence and the analysis of ethnographic interviews. *Discourse Processes*, 5(1), 1–32. https://doi.org/10.1080/01638538209544529.

Bogost, I. (2006). *Unit operations: An approach to videogame criticism*. MIT Press.

Calvert, J., & Fujimura J. (2009). Calculating life? A sociological perspective on systems biology. *EMBO Reports*, 10, 546–649.

Christin, A. (2020). The Ethnographer and the algorithm: Beyond the black box. *Theory & Society*, 49(5–6), 897–918. http://www.angelechristin.com/wp-content/uploads/2020/08/Christin2020_Article_TheEthnographerAndTheAlgorithm.pdf.

Bareither, C. (2017). *Gewalt im Computerspiel. Facetten eines Vergnügens*. transcript.

Beaulieu, A. (2016). Vectors for fieldwork. In L. Hjorth, H. Horst, A. Galloway, & G. Bell (Eds.), *The Routledge companion to digital ethnography* (pp. 29–39). Routledge.

Bender, C., & Zillinger, M. (Eds.). (2015). *Handbuch der Medienethnographie*. Berlin.

Blackwell, A. F., Blythe, M., & Kaye, J. (2017). Undisciplined disciples: Everything you always wanted to know about ethnomethodology but were afraid to ask Yoda. *Personal and Ubiquitous Computing*, 21(3), 571–592. https://doi.org/10.1007/s00779-017-0999-z.

Bijker, W., & Law J. (Eds.). (1992). *Shaping technology/building society: Studies in sociotechnical change*. MIT Press.

Blommaert, J., & Dong, J. (2010). *Ethnographic fieldwork: A beginner's guide*. Multilingual Matters.

Benjamin, R. (2019). *Race after technology*. Polity Press.

Bhat, P. C. (2011). Multivariate analysis in particle physics. *Annual Review of Nuclear and Particle Science*, 61, 281–309.

Boellstorff, T., Nardi, B., Pearce, C., & Taylor, T. L. (2012). *Ethnography and virtual worlds: A handbook of method*. Princeton University Press.

Braidotti, R. (2013). *The posthuman*. Polity Press.

Callon, M. (1984). Some elements of a sociology of translation: Domestication of the scallops and the fishermen of St-Brieuc Bay. *The Sociological Review*, 32(1), 196–233.

Callon, M. Law, J., & Rip, A. (Eds.). (1986). *Mapping the dynamics of science and technology*. Macmillan.

Carlson, R., Eggel, R., Franken, L., Thanner, S., & Vepřek, L. (2021). Approaching code as process: Prototyping ethnographic methodologies. *Kuckuck. Notizen zur Alltagskultur*. Special Issue Code, 1, 13–17.

Carlson, R., & Vepřek, L. H. (2022). *At the "hinge" of future fictions and everyday failings: Ethnographic interventions in AI systems*. Paper presented at the conference Anthropology, AI and the Future of Human Society. Royal Anthropological Institute, June 6th, 2022.

Chun, W. (2021). *Discriminating data: Correlation, neighborhoods, and the new politics of recognition*. MIT Press.

Clarke, A. E., & Star, S. L. (2008). Social worlds/arenas as a theory-methods package. In E. Hackett, O. Amsterdamska, M. L. Lynch, & J. Wacjman (Eds.), *Handbook of science and technology studies* (2nd ed., pp. 113–137). MIT Press.

Clifford, J., & Marcus, G. E. (Eds.). (2010). *Writing culture: The poetics and Politics of ethnography (25th year anniversary ed.)*. University of California Press.

Cortes, C., & Vapnik, V. (1995). Support-vector networks. *Machine Learning*, 20, 273–297. https://doi.org/10.1007/BF00994018.

De La Cadena, M., & Blaser M. (Eds.). (2018). *A world of many worlds*. Duke University Press.

Dick, S. (2011). AfterMath: The work of proof in the age of human–machine collaboration. *Isis,* 102(3), 494–505.

Dick, S. (2015). Of models and machines: Implementing bounded rationality. *Isis,* 106(3), 623–634.

Dick, S., & Vollmar, D. (2018). DLL hell: Software dependencies, failure, and the maintenance of Microsoft Windows. *IEEE Annals of the History of Computing,* 28–51.

Dippel, A. (2017). Das Big Data Game. Zur spielerischen Konstitution kollaborativer Wissensproduktion in der Hochenergiephysik am CERN. *NTM: Zeitschrift für Geschichte der Wissenschaften, Technik und Medizin,* 4, 485–517.

Dippel, A. (2019a). Ludopian visions: On the speculative potential of games in times of algorithmic work and play. In B. Beil, G. S. Freyermuth, & H. C. Schmidt (Eds.), *Playing Utopia: Futures in digital games* (pp. 235–252). Transcript.

Dippel, A. (2019b). 'Metaphors we live by': Three commentaries on artificial intelligence and the human condition. In A. Sudmann (Ed.), *The democratization of artificial intelligence* (pp. 33–42). Transcript.

Dippel, A. (2021a). Provi(de)ncial visions for a more-than-human hypothesise including AI: A response by Anne Dippel to the two previous commentaries. *Arbor: Ciencia, Pensiamento y Cultura,* 197–800.

Dippel, A. (2021b). Trivial Pursuits? Ludic approaches to work environments. *Journal for European Ethnology and Cultural Anthropology,* 6(1), 5–24.

Dippel, A. (2022). *Ludutopia. Elemente einer kulturwissenschaftlichen Spieltheorie. Habilitation.* Friedrich-Schiller-Universität Jena.

Dippel, A., & Warnke, M. (2022). *Tiefen der Täuschung. Computersimulationen und Wirklichkeitserzeugung.* Matthes&Seitz.

Domínguez, D., Beaulieu, A., Estalella, A., Gómez, E., Schnettler, B., & Read, R. (2007). Virtual ethnography. *Forum Qualitative Social Research,* 8(3). http://nbn-resolving.de/urn:nbn:de:0114 -fqs0703E19.

Engemann, C., & Sudmann, A. (Eds.). (2018). *Machine learning: Medien, Infrastrukturen und Technologien der Künstlichen Intelligenz.* Transcript.

Fischer, M. D. (1994). *Applications in computing for social anthropologists.* Routledge.

Fizek, S., & Dippel, A. (2019). Laborious playgrounds: Citizen science games as new modes of work/play in the digital age. In R. Glas, S. Lammes et al., (Eds.), *The playful citizen: Civic engagement in a mediatized culture* (pp. 232–248). Amsterdam University Press.

Fizek, S. (2022). *Playing at a distance: Borderlands of video game aesthetics.* MIT Press.

Franken, L. (2022). Digital data and methods as enlargements of qualitative research processes: Challenges and potentials coming from digital humanities and computational social sciences. *Forum: Qualitative Social Research,* 23(2). https://doi.org/10.17169/fqs-22.2.3818.

Foley, D., & Valenzuela, A. (2005). Critical ethnography. In *The Sage handbook of qualitative research* (pp. 217–234). Sage.

Forsythe, D. E. (1993). The construction of work in artificial intelligence. *Science, Technology, & Human Values,* 18(4), 460–479. https://doi.org/10.1177/016224399301800404.

Forsythe, D. F. (1995). Using ethnography in the design of an explanation system. *Expert Systems with Applications,* 8(4), 403–417.

Forsythe, D. F. (2001). *Studying those who study us: An anthropologist in the world of artificial intelligence.* Stanford University Press.

Fujimura, J. (1987). Constructing 'do-able' problems in cancer research: Articulating alignment. *Social Study of Science,* 17(2), 257–293.

Fujimura, J. (2018). Variations on a chip: Technologies of difference in human genetics research. *Journal of the History of Biology,* 51(4), 841–873. https://doi.org/10.1007/s10739-018-9543-x.

Fujimura, J., & Rajagopalan, R. (2020). Race, ethnicity, ancestry, and genomics in Hawaii: Discourses and practices. *Social Studies of Science,* 50(5), 596–623.

Galison, P. (1997). *Image and logic: A material culture of microphysics.* Chicago University Press.

Garfinkel, H. (1963). *Studies in ethnomethodology.* Blackwell Publishers.

Garfinkel, H. (2011). A conception of and experiments with "trust" as a condition of concerted stable actions. In J. O'Brien, (Ed.), *The production of reality: Essays on social interaction* (5th ed., pp. 379–391). Pine Forge.

Geertz, C. (1973). *The interpretation of cultures*. Basic books.

Gerlitz, C., & Passmann, J. (2017). Popularisierung einer hypothesi Medien-Praktik. *Zeitschrift für Literaturwissenschaft und Linguistik, 47*(3), 375–393. https://doi.org/10.1007/s41244-017-0067-1.

Gershon, I. (2010). Media ideologies: An introduction. *Linguistic Anthropology, 20*(2), 283–293.

Gessler, N. (1995). Ethnography of artificial culture: Specifications, prospects, and constraints. In McDonell et al. (Eds.), *Evolutionary programming IV: Proceedings of the fourth annual conference on evolutionary programming*. https://doi.org/10.7551/mitpress/2887.001.0001.

Gießmann, S., & Taha, N. (Eds.). (2017). *Susan Leigh Star. Grenzobjekte und Medienforschung*. Transcript.

Gieryn, T. F. (1999). *Cultural boundaries of science: Credibility on the line*. University of Chicago Press.

Ginsburg, F. (2008). Rethinking the digital age. In P. Wilson & M. Stewart (Eds.), *Global indigenous media: Cultures, poetics, and politics* (pp. 287–306). Duke University Press.

Gray, M. L., & Suri, S. (2019). *Ghost work: How to stop silicon valley from building a new global underclass*. Houghton Mifflin.

Hall S. (1980). Encoding/decoding. In S. Hall, D. Hobson, A. Lowe, & P. Willis (Eds.), *Culture, media, language: Working papers in cultural studies, 1972–79* (pp. 117–127). Routledge.

Halpern, O., & Mitchell, R. (2021). *The smartness mandate*. MIT Press.

Haraway, D. (2016). *Staying with the trouble: Making Kin in the Chthulucene*. Duke University Press.

Hess, D., & Layne L. (Eds.). (1991). *The anthropology of science and technology*. JAI Press.

Hess, D., Lee, D., Biebl, B., Fränzle, M., Lehnhoff, S., Neema, H., Niehaus, J., Pretschner, A., & Sztipanovits, J. (2021). A comparative, sociotechnical design perspective on responsible innovation: Multidisciplinary research and education on digitized energy and automated vehicles. *Journal of Responsible Innovation, 8*(3), 421–444.

Hine, C. (2000). *Virtual ethnography*. Sage.

Hymes, D. H. (1965). *The use of computers in anthropology* (Vol. 2). The Hague.

Hochreiter, S., & Schmidhuber, J. (1997). Long short-term memory. *Neural Computation, 9*(8), 1735–1780.

Hui, Y. (2016). *On the existence of digital objects*. University of Minnesota Press.

Iliadis, A., & Russo, F. (2016). Critical data studies: An introduction. *Big Data & Society, 3*(2), 1–7.

Inkpen, K., Chappidi, S., Mallari, K. Nushi, B. Ramesh, D., Michellucci, P., Mandava, V., Vepřek, L., & Quinn, G. (2022). Advancing human-AI complementarity: The impact of user expertise and algorithmic tuning on joint decision making. https://arxiv.org/pdf/2208.07960.pdf.

Irani, L. (2015). Hackathons and the making of entrepreneurial citizenship. *Science Technology and Human Values, 40*(5), 799–824.

Kitchin, R. (2014). *The data revolution: Big data, open data, data infrastructures and their consequences*. Sage.

Koerner, E. F. (1992): The Sapir-Whorf hypothesis: A preliminary history and a bibliographical essay. *Journal of Linguistic Anthropology, 2*(2), 173–198.

Knoblauch, H. (2001). Fokussierte Ethnographie: Soziologie, Ethnologie und die neue Welle der Ethnographie. *Sozialer Sinn, 2*(1), 123–141. https://nbn-resolving.org/urn:nbn:de:0168-ssoar-6930.

Knorr-Cetina, K. (1999). *Epistemic cultures: How the sciences make knowledge*. Harvard University Press.

Krasmann, S., & Schmidt, S. (2022). KI und menschliches Sinnverstehen im Recht. Teilprojekt des BMBF-Kompetenznetzwerk "MEHUCO-Meaningful Human Control. Autonome Waffensysteme zwischen Regulation und Reflexion", 2022–2026.

Kuhn, T. S. (1962). *The structure of scientific revolutions*. University of Chicago Press.

Larsen, L., & Frances, F. (Eds.). (2019). Algorithmic normativities. *Big Data and Society, 6*(2).

Latour, B. (1987). *Science in action*. Open University Press.

Latour, B., & Woolgar, S. (1986). *Laboratory life: The social construction of scientific facts*. Princeton University Press.

Lazer, D., Pentland, A. S., Adamic, L., Aral, S., Barabasi, A., Brewer, D., Christakis, N., Contractor, N., Fowler, J., Gutmann, M., Jebara, T., King, G., Macy, M., Roy, D., & Van Alstyne, M. (2009). Life in the network: The coming age of computational social science. *Science, 323*(5915), 721.

Lipton, C., & Steinhardt, J. (2018). *Troubling trends in machine learning scholarship.* Paper presented at ICML 2018: The Debates, Stockholm July 27, 2018. https://doi.org/10.48550/arXiv.1807.03341.

Lupton, D. (2014). Self-tracking cultures: Towards a sociology of personal informatics. *OzCHI '14: Proceedings of the 26th Australian Computer-Human Interaction Conference on Designing Futures: The Future of Design*, 77–86.

MacKenzie, D. A. (2001). *Mechanizing proof: Computing, risk, and trust.* MIT Press.

Marda, V., & Narayan, S. (2021). On the importance of ethnographic methods in AI research. *Nature Machine Intelligence*, 3, 187–189. https://doi.org/10.1038/s42256-021-00323-0.

Marres, N., & Weltjevrede, E. (2013). Scraping the social: Issues in live social research. *Journal of Cultural Economy*, 6(3). Special Issue: The Device: The Social Life of Methods, 313–335.

McGranahan, C. (Ed.). (2020). *Writing anthropology: Essays on craft and commitment.* Duke University Press.

Manovich, L. (2008). The next big thing in humanities, arts, and social science computing: Cultural analytics. *HPC Wire*, July 29. www.hpcwire.com/features/The_Next_Big_Thing_in_Humanities_Arts_and_Social_Science_Computing_Cultural_Analytics.html.

Manovich, L. (2020). *Cultural analytics.* MIT Press.

Moats, D., & Seaver, N. (2019). "You social scientists love mind games": Experimenting in the "divide" between data science and critical algorithm studies. *Big Data & Society*, 6(2). Special Issue: L. Larsen & F. Frances (Eds.), *Algorithmic normativities*, 1–11.

Munk, A. K., Olesen, A. G., & Jacomy, M. (2022). The thick machine: anthropological AI between explanation and explication. *Big Data & Society*, January 2022. https://doi.org/10.1177/20539517211069891.

Nader, L. (1972). Up the anthropologist: Perspectives gained from studying up. In D. Hymes (Ed.), *Reinventing anthropology* (pp. 284–311). Random House.

Nader, L. (1977). Studying up. *Psychology Today*, September 11, 132.

Nardi, B. (1997). The use of ethnographic methods in design and evaluation. In M. G. Helander, T. Landauer, & P. Prabhu (Eds.), *Handbook of human-computer interaction II* (pp. 361–366). Elsevier.

Pias, C. (2017). *Computer – game – worlds.* Diaphanes.

Pickering, A. (1995). *The mangle of practice: Time, agency & science.* University of Chicago Press.

Pink, S., Horst, H., Postill, J., Hjorth, L., Lewis, T., & Tacchi J. (Eds.). (2015). *Digital ethnography: Principles and practice.* Sage.

Povinelli, E. (2016). *Geontologies: A requiem to late liberalism.* Duke University Press.

Powdermaker, H. (1966). *Stranger and friend.* Doubleday.

Rabinow, P., Marcus, G. E., Faubion, J. D., & Rees, T. (Eds.). (2008). *Designs for an anthropology of the contemporary.* Duke University Press.

Rao, U. (2019). Biometric IDs and the remaking of the Indian (welfare) state. *Economic Sociology*, 21(1), 13–21.

Richards, K. (2015). *An anthropology of robots and AI: Annihilation anxiety and machines.* Routledge.

Royer, A. (2020). The short anthropological guide to the study of ethical AI. https://arxiv.org/ftp/arxiv/papers/2010/2010.03362.pdf

Rybas, N., & Gajjala, R. (2007). Developing cyberethnographic research methods for understanding digitally mediated identities. *Forum Qualitative Social Research*, 8(3), Art. 35.

Seaver, N. (2017). Algorithms as culture: Some tactics for the ethnography of algorithmic systems. *Big Data & Society*. https://doi.org/10.1177/2053951717738104

Silverstein, M. (1979). Language structure and linguistic ideology. In P. Cline, W. Hanks, & C. Hofbauer (Eds.), *The elements* (pp. 193–247). Chicago Linguistic Society.

Star, S. L. (1989). The structure of ill-structured solutions: Boundary objects and heterogeneous distributed problem solving. In L. Gasser & M. N. Huhns (Eds.), *Distributed artificial intelligence* (pp. 37–54). Pitman.

Star, S. L., & Griesemer J. (1989). Institutional ecology, "translations" and boundary objects: Amateurs and professionals in Berkeley's museum of vertebrate zoology 1907–1939. *Social Studies of Science*, 19(3), 387–420.

Star, S. L. (1991). The sociology of the invisible: The primacy of work in the writings of Anselm Strauss. In D. Maines (Ed.), *Social organization and social process: Essays in honor of Anselm Strauss* (pp. 265–283). Aldine de Gruyter.

Stewart, K. (2010). Worlding refrains. In M. Gregg & G. Seigworth (Eds.), *The affect theory reader* (pp. 339–353). Duke University Press.

Suchman, L. (1987). *Plans and situated actions: The problem of human-machine communication.* Cambridge University Press.

Suchman, L. (1992). Technologies of accountability: On lizards and airplanes. In G. Button (Ed.), *Technology in working order: Studies of work, interaction and technology* (pp. 113–126). Routledge.

Sudmann, A. (2017). Deep learning als dokumentarische Praxis. *Sprache und Literatur,* 48(2), 155–170.

Sudmann, A. (2018). Szenarien des Postdigitalen. Deep Learning als MedienRevolution. In C. Engemann & A. Sudmann (Eds.), *Machine learning. Medien, Infrastrukturen und Technologien der Künstlichen Intelligenz* (pp. 53–73). Transcript.

Sudmann, A. (2020). Künstliche Neuronale Netzwerke als Black Box. Verfahren der Explainable AI. In P. Klimczak, S. Schilling, & C. Petersen (Eds.), *Medienwissenschaftliche Perspektiven. Maschinen (in) der Kommunikation* (pp. 189–199). Springer.

Sudmann, A. (2021). Artificial neural networks, postdigital infrastructures, and the politics of temporality. In K. Stine & A. Volmar (Eds.), *Media infrastructures and the politics of digital time* (pp. 279–294). Amsterdam University Press.

Traweek, S. (1988). *Beamtimes and lifetimes: The world of high-energy physics.* Harvard University Press.

Turkle, S. (1988). Artificial intelligence and psychoanalysis: A new alliance. *Daedalus,* 117(I), 241–268.

Turkle, S., & Papert S. (1990). Epistemological pluralism: Styles and voices within the computer culture. *Signs,* 16(1), 128–157.

Turkle, S. (1995). *Life on the screen: Identity in the age of the Internet.* Touchstone Book.

Turkle, S. (2009). *Simulation and its discontents.* MIT Press.

Varis, P. (2016). Digital ethnography. In A. Georgakopoulou & T. Spilioti (Eds.), *The Routledge handbook of language and digital communication* (pp. 55–68). Routledge.

Vertesi, J. (2014). Seamful spaces: Heterogeneous infrastructures in interaction. *Science, Technology & Human Values,* 39(2), 264–284.

Wax, R. H. (1971). *Doing fieldwork: Warnings and advice.* University of Chicago Press.

Werner, O., & Schoepfle, G. (1987). *Systematic fieldwork.* Sage.

Whorf, B. L. (1942). Science and linguistics. *Technology Review,* 42(2), 229–231, 247–248.

73. Automating social theory
Ralph Schroeder

INTRODUCTION

This chapter outlines how social theory can be advanced by means of AI. The criterion for success in this respect should be that AI learns by refining the models that are developed and improving these models with ever more comprehensive sources of data (see Mökander and Schroeder, 2021). This is not the place to reopen debates about defining AI or about social theory. For the purposes of this chapter, AI can be defined as learning to learn. And while there is no generally accepted definition of social theory, one starting point is that social science generally, and so also social theory, should aim to be cumulative (Schroeder, 2019). We will come back to these points. One point to highlight immediately, however, is that AI in this chapter does not refer to the task of seeking an artificial general intelligence (or AGI, as it is known in the AI community). Instead, it is to advance social theory by means of current, 'narrow' as they are sometimes called, AI techniques. In short, computational methods such as machine learning and data-driven approaches should learn – and they should cumulatively improve social theory.

One advantage of doing social theory with AI in this way is that social theory has to be made explicit in a particular way: it has to be visualized such that the causal connections are specified (Pearl and McKenzie, 2018) and semanticized or machine readable. It also has to have clear units, an ontology of the social world that includes the time periods and bounded spaces to which these units apply. Further, it has to specify how the units are represented by means of data – and so measured. In other words, the data, and what the data refer to, has to be clear, as do the measures for these datafied objects. As for causality, this is often thought to require statistics. Yet statistics, as Collins has argued, are also theory and must be turned into words (1988: 494–511). Moreover, statistics do not have a monopoly on scientific knowledge. They are one scientific style among others – six, according to Hacking: in addition to statistics (or probability), these are postulation, experiment, modeling, taxonomic, and historicogenetic (2002: 159–199; see also Meyer and Schroeder, 2015, esp. 23 ff.) – all of which can be used to analyze data computationally. These styles, according to Hacking, are self-vindicating, which means that they can be taken for granted when seeking to represent and intervene in the world. Still, regardless of the scientific 'style' or method, thought must be put into the form whereby these styles can be processed by a machine. Automation, or machine-processing data in accordance with this formalized version of social theory, is the starting point for AI: beyond this starting point, or where AI goes beyond simple automation, is the addition of learning to learn, which is another way of saying intelligence (but automation and AI can henceforth be used interchangeably as long AI entails the added learning to learn which is required for intelligence). Here, that intelligence refers to social scientific knowledge. Again, we shall return to these points.

Causality, as mentioned, is often thought to require statistical analysis. But there are major debates about what is to count as a valid causal explanation, including within the machine learning and AI research community (Schölkopf et al., 2021). Here we can also think of the question of whether counterfactual explanations (Morgan and Winship, 2015) in statistics are considered valid. Further, it is unclear whether 'counterfactuals' apply beyond the 'statistical' style of scientific explanation. For the sake of the argument here, these debates do not need to be definitively resolved. What is needed instead is to put all explanations into a format whereby causal explanation is in principle possible; in other words, the causal pathways need to be specified clearly. That includes the scope of the explanation and the data that is available for use in these explanations. The key question with respect to statistical or other scientific styles of analysis is how the explanation contributes to cumulative knowledge, without which learning to learn is not possible. Put differently, the philosophical issues about causality are secondary to the aim of social scientific explanation as long as automation takes place in such a way that causal explanation is in principle enabled. Learning then requires a continual reduction of uncertainty about the phenomena to be explained – combined with a continuous improvement in identifying the most important causes and eliminating less important ones – plus maximizing the overall fit with data (see the figures in Mökander and Schroeder, 2021).

This brings us to another major aim of AI in social science, which is prediction, closely related to thinking about causality. The question of what types of phenomena it is possible for social science to predict will depend on which patterns and relations between them can be identified as more and less stable: if they are stable, the model can be refined. Apart from this stability, there will be new phenomena, which will need to be added to the territory that has already been subject to explanations of past phenomena. A final point related to explanation and prediction is that the knowledge generated may or may not extend to intervening in and manipulating the social world at a greater scale and scope, which is the aim or function of technoscience – as opposed to improving or refining the tools for doing this (Schroeder, 2007: 6–20) and thus the representation of the social world, which 'merely' adds to what is known (cumulation). Further reflection will be needed below in this respect about the extent to which explaining stable patterns in the past – how far back do they need to go? – to enable prediction or forecasting into the future (and how far into the future).

BUILDING BLOCKS AND LEVELS

Against the backdrop of this understanding of how social science works, we can turn to its units or building blocks, the time periods they cover, and thus the objects to which the data belong. In computer science, these units or objects are ontologies (or, in social science, concepts) which are developed, among other things, because databases need labels for objects. The process of labeling data objects increasingly takes place using machine learning. These ontologies, in turn, are evaluated by means of establishing the relations between them – hypothesis testing (Evans and Rzhetsky, 2010). In AI, the development of ontologies has advanced both top-down, via schemata to reproduce the way concepts are linked in language and its logic, and bottom-up, via 'clustering' objects into categories (Mitchell, 2019). Yet in social science, there has been little by way of developing ontologies (but see Hanemann, 1987) since the default has been to ascribe certain attributes to individual agents. This focus on individual agents can be gleaned from examining how the topic of ontology is covered in the philosophy of social science or methods textbooks: individual action is discussed; otherwise, the topic of ontology receives little attention. This is no doubt a legacy of methodological debates, but these legacies should not prevent the development of ontologies that are not based on individuals (as we shall see). In any event, in order for cumulation in AI and CSS to go forward, a more extensive systematization of ontologies (or units of analysis or concepts, and how they interrelate) is needed.

What social science has instead of ontologies are concepts or ideal types that are constantly developed in an interplay with empirical evidence. These could work like ontologies if a) they included the systematic or systemic relations between them and b) their relationship to data, and so to measurement, were clear. In social science, for ontologies or concepts or ideal types to operate like this, it is necessary to specify the period to which they apply and their spatial and other scope conditions. Here, this will be done by taking as units several systems and the dominant institutions within these systems. Further, we will focus on those systems and dominant institutions for which there is social scientific consensus, and which simultaneously provide the greatest fit with the available evidence, which is where cumulation must begin. This alerts us to the fact consensus and fit ideally overlap, and that where there is a failure of overlap, that could owe either to a shifting research front that lacks the units of analysis for new topics – or that there is insufficient consensual ground to begin with for cumulation. However, this insufficient ground could, of course, be the start of a gap analysis for AI-driven social theory.

These starting points, with ontologies and systems and the like, may seem odd in the light of what is conventionally considered social theory, which is theorists or theoretical traditions. But for automating social theory, it does not help to invoke the names of theorists such as Goffman or Habermas, for example, or the labels of traditions such as functionalism or interactionism. Any of these have to be expressed in formal machine-readable language. Still, it will not escape notice in what follows that I will make frequent use of certain social scientists, including Collins, Turner, Turchin, Gellner, and Mann. That is no accident since they have led the way in formalizing social theory and in synthesizing theory. However, as has been noted before (Mökander and Schroeder, 2021), the attachment of names to the project of AI-driven social theory is irrelevant; what matters is that the project is advanced by and embodied in the development of a machinery where the names – including that of this author – appear only in the form of references to take note of previous work in order to build on it. The same applies to the names or labels of software and data sources and other tools, which are similarly incidental.

Still, apart from being dominated by theorists, social theory has also been dominated by conventions about macro- versus micro- and meso-. One instance of reflection on these levels has been Merton's 'theories of the middle range'. But the problem of the macro- micro- link is rarely addressed, with Turner (2002: 585–639) being one exception and Collins (to be discussed shortly) another. 'Theories of the middle range' has come to mean theories that are used for tackling specific questions. Yet tackling specific questions works for statistical or regression analysis and the like but does not contribute to systematic theory development. The problem with 'grand theories', on the other hand, is that they are totalizing 'package deals' that work only within the terms of reference of their own assumptions and often without data or evidence. If, however, social theory is to be subject to machine development, it cannot take the conventional micro- versus macro- or other divisions of phenomena as starting points lest they block translating theory into machine approaches. As for data or evidence, it is of course possible to develop AI theory without these: that would entail merely making logically consistent and machine-readable social theories. (as with top-down AI, which is highly philosophical). Yet this exercise would yield little since an evidence-free constellation of theory would not build on the interlocking of theory with existing findings and so would also not be able to reduce the theoretical elements in play.

Put the other way around, AI technology is indifferent to past conventions and debates in the social sciences except insofar as they represent the state of the art (again, 'cumulation') and can be translated into computational approaches. The social science material needs to be made to fit the logic of machines. At the same time, it is decidedly not the case that scientistic theories from computer science should be imposed on this endeavor – such as complexity, networks, agents, simulation, and the like – partly since, as we shall see, these do not represent the state of the art of social scientific knowledge, including social theory. This difficult negotiation, avoiding disciplinary imperialisms from both sides by means of following the logic of systems and models, needs to be managed. It can also be useful here to contrast social theory with the idea of modeling: modeling can mean quite different things (Page, 2018), but social theories are more systematic than models, going beyond theories of the 'middle range' that are used in modeling. In computer science, modeling can also mean prediction or forecasting (and forecasting can be seen as prediction minus causality, recalling the earlier discussion about causality). But systematized models explaining the social world, plus machine-readable ideas and methods for manipulating data about the social world, plus prediction or forecasting: that is also one way to describe what is meant by AI-driven social theory.

In this context, it can be mentioned again that when AI is used in this chapter, this refers to 'off-the-shelf' computing or currently used commonplace computational ML techniques. When computer scientists talk about AI, they may be talking about the latest innovations that develop machines that can think (as noted earlier). But when social scientists work on social theory in the manner described here, they use large-scale datasets and existing software tools to figure out how best to analyze and combine data sources. They also often use statistics and supervised and unsupervised learning, again, with existing tools. The current main gap is in formalizing social theory, which is poorly advanced in social science except (as we shall see) in certain domains. Put differently, social theory is not tied to technological advances; instead, there are plenty of areas where the combinations of ML plus big data remain to be implemented.

This allows us to turn finally to concrete building blocks. As we have seen at the micro-level, the building blocks of theory have often taken to be individual actors. Yet, as Collins (2004) has argued, the units of analysis for micro-social interactions should not be individuals but rather situations. Hence the units here are also not, as in many computational social science efforts, 'agents', as with agent-based modeling. Instead, individuals become social beings through social interaction with others, or via 'interaction ritual chains' (Collins, 2004). In other words, these are not individuals but rather aggregations of situations and the rules that emerge from repeated interactions. By capturing data from these interactions, AI can learn how people become social (Collins, 1992: 155–184). This involves analyzing how individuals react to how they are perceived by others, how they incorporate this perception of themselves into their self-understanding (a la Mead), and so on. Hence social 'individuals', reconstructed by AI, could interact with each other, and these social individuals could further be aggregated into the organizations or dominant institutions in certain systems.

It would go beyond the scope to detail how this aggregation of micro-social interaction can be taken further since the focus will be on macro-theory. Still, it can be sketched briefly how the micro- macro- linkage sometimes works in the three systems: first, in the economic realm or system, people seek, in everyday encounters, to maximize their emotional energy, and these interactions aggregate into status groups, thus resulting in stratification (Collins, 2004: 258–296). Economic stratification arises from encounters or situations and how status is being sought. However, most everyday encounters are routine and do not aggregate into macro-social change in stratification: this disconnect is one example of the still incomplete working out of substantive micro- macro- linkages. Another example from the political system is the limited conditions under which the aggregation of micro-interactions can lead to larger-scale political change, as with revolutions (Collins, 1999: 37–69). The same applies to scientific-intellectual or cultural change: a change of direction requires the aggregation of intellectual encounters via networks that are mobilized into movements (Frickel and Gross, 2005). As an aside, computational social science can be seen as one such scientific or intellectual movement in the development of the social sciences, driven not just by researcher movements but also the technologies that they use to advance their agenda (Meyer and Schroeder, 2015).

SYSTEMS AND THE RELATIONS WITHIN AND BETWEEN THEM

With this, we can turn to the macro-level, where there is considerable agreement over the substance if not the terminology of different systems in social theory: 'systems' itself has been used by thinkers like Parsons and Luhmann. In this chapter, economic, political, and cultural systems will be used but without assuming 'functionalism' or 'evolutionism' that is typically entailed by these thinkers. Terms other than 'system' could equally be used here, such as the 'sources of social power' (Mann, 1986) or 'social orders' (Gellner, 1988; Schroeder, 2013). Rejecting functionalism means that conflict within and between systems is possible, as are movements or stratified hierarchical orders. The rejection of evolutionism, as we shall see, further entails a break inaugurated by the modern period, since when a new differentiation of systems has taken place, and thence the logics within and between these new systems or orders must be identified. Still, these systems can be brought together into a unified whole so that they can be subject to automated techniques, which therefore must also work at the intersections between systems.

Before we get to these intersections, each system, as mentioned, has a dominant institution, or the main ontological unit within the system. To start with, the dominant modern institution of the political system is the nation-state, the most powerful container of social interaction (Giddens, 1985). This 'container' is an 'actor' only under certain circumstances, but it is a unit that has many data sources attached to it. The dominant modern institution in the economic system is the disembedded market (Schroeder, 2013), where the units of economic action are many atomized (and in this sense individual) interactions, seen by economists as maximizing. These interactions or exchanges ultimately aggregate into equilibria between supply and demand, with different models for this (Morgan, 2012). Economic sociologists have identified the mechanisms at work (Hamilton and Feenstra, 1998) and which parts of the economic system do not function as markets (Schroeder, 2013: 103–109). And as we saw, the units here are not individuals as such but patterns of maximizing status-seeking in encounters. Finally, in the cultural system, technoscience is the dominant modern institution, transforming the physical or natural and hence also the social environment. This institution has autonomy from the other two systems and from other parts of culture (such as religion) as these other parts of culture are not cumulative in relation to transforming the environment. Technoscience thus consists not just of knowledge production but also of large technological infrastructures (Schroeder, 2007) where the key constraint is the 'reverse salient' (Hughes, 1987) or bottleneck of this large technological system. In the case of energy infrastructure, that inescapable bottleneck has become the planetary boundaries (Rockstroem et al., 2009) of the system, with severe resource constraints because of a heating planet.

In each system then, the dominant institutions are shaped by certain patterns (again, we will come to the interactions between systems in a moment). In the modern political system, the main pattern is that there has been a push from below to gain more control vis-à-vis political elites. In other words, the direction of travel has been the extension and deepening of rights – civil, political, and most recently, social rights, and how they apply to ever greater parts of the population and to more diverse groups. Political elites (parties, political leaders, and other representatives) have had to meet this demand for more rights mostly within the unit of the nation-state ('mostly', because human rights and the like also operate transnationally), becoming more harnessed to providing rights as they do so. It needs to be added that this is not a unilinear process and operates via contention. A key measure for social rights is the extent of tax capture from society, which translates into how generously these rights are provided. In the economic system, the main pattern is GDP growth arising from the factors of production within the overall balance of demand and supply, which generates unequal – stratified – distribution among the population. And finally, the pattern of technoscience in the cultural system is the ever-greater capability (non-zero sum) in transforming the environment, but a zero-sum game insofar as the environment is finite.

Nation-state units can be subdivided into democracies and non-democracies (authoritarian states) that currently exhaust the range globally from a 'systems' perspective (Stichweh, 2021). It needs to be mentioned that these two types exhaust the political system at the nation-state level but in terms of the relations between them, it is also necessary to distinguish between 'great powers' and the rest. The system that these great powers seek to shape and how they are shaped by it is a separate geopolitical system or a system of military power (Mann, 1987). The geopolitical or military set of relations will have to be left to one side here for reasons of space (but see Mökander and Schroeder, 2021). But apart from this spatially separate system with separate military relations, if we narrow our periodization to the post-war period and our units to democracies, this means that the effect of military relations on relations between them (though not between them and the rest of the world) can be largely 'bracketed' out.

This brings us back to periodization, and one way to tackle the issue is to contrast the position here with evolutionary thought: the three systems and their dominant institutions that have been described have only taken shape in modern societies. One problem with theories like Turner's (1995) and Turchin's (2019) is that they seek laws across human history. They elicit evolutionary or timeless laws, but these have been applied mainly to certain processes such as state formation. Turner, an evolutionist, contrasts his own explanation of macro-dynamics, 'in terms of timeless, generic and universal laws about a few fundamental forces' - against 'the most prominent…macro-level analysis' which is 'historical…a descriptive scenario about causal sequences among specific empirical/historical events' which make them 'indeterminate' (1995: 3–4). I disagree: to be sure, timeless and universal laws can be useful for scientific explanations. But analysis with historical periodizations or breaks is not more 'indeterminate' or contingent, as Turner argues, but quite the reverse: imposing a structure on human history, including breaks, allows social science to be more determinative (for example, Gellner, 1988). And while an approach with a modern 'cut-off' may be less parsimonious and in this respect less powerfully scientific, it fits better with the data (Turner's theory is not data-driven) and so with the empirical reality of system differentiation and the distinctiveness of units in certain periods. In this sense, the approach here leads to more powerfully scientific explanations with fewer 'laws' than Turner's – albeit for shorter periods and sometimes restricted to a certain group of nation-states. Though for the post-war period, the most determinative process (bar the use of nuclear weapons) applies to the whole globe with the technoscientific transformation of the environment and its 'boomerang effect' on the planet. In any event, this disagreement about periodization and laws will ultimately be put to the test: fewer 'laws' (or patterns or regularities in the data, if that is preferred) or factors – or more parsimonious explanations over greater temporal and spatial reaches – can be weighed against better fit with the available data.

Again, the evolutionary approach prevents us from recognizing that modern social structure has become differentiated in new ways and how, in modern orders or systems, the dominant institutions work in different ways. The 'big ditch' or break between modernity and pre-modernity, wherever and whenever located, can be found both in the data and in the consensus at least among the macro-social theorists drawn upon here (such as Gellner, 1988; Mann, 2013: 421–423; Schroeder, 2013, 2022). Then there is another break after the two world wars, which ruptured these systems, so that afterward, if we restrict the scope further to high-income democracies, they work differently and stabilize only in the post-war period in terms of how rights, markets, and impact of the transformation of the environment were institutionalized, including the relations between them. A further and final divide can then be made within the post-war period for an 'Age of Limits' (starting in the mid-1970s or so) after the post-war 'Golden Age' (Schroeder, 2013) because, since then, the intersection between the three systems has become different again: in the Age of Limits, the three systems constrain each other. This additional break and new constraint is reflected in the time-series data and in the spatial units – at least with respect to the environment: it was only after the 'Golden Age' that the 'boomerang effect', of the constraints on how the technoscientific institution transforms the environment, was recognized, with its inescapable effect on the whole globe or planet, even if the post-war period inaugurated the unprecedented intensification or 'acceleration' (McNeill and Engelke, 2014) of this process, and thus provides continuity through the two periods.

These two breaks also relate to the political system. If the post-war period first expanded the push for rights during the Golden Age, since then, in the Age of Limits (Schroeder, 2013), these rights have both expanded but also been constrained due to the relative slowdown of economic growth – an inter-systemic relation we shall come to in a moment – relative to the growing costs of social rights among an expanding population that benefits from them. How the struggle for rights within nation-states – again, the political system is the arena for the struggle for the expansion of rights between elites and civil society – expanded and then stalled can be modeled: the main inputs for the roughly three-quarters of a century of the post-war period were the rise and then a relative decline in economic growth rates, resulting in greater and then lesser responsiveness to expanding, especially social (welfare), rights. We can add external pressures such as economic globalization and migration leading to internal exclusionism, again stalling social rights. These two (one internal, one inter-systemic) factors can be hypothesized to make for the varieties of politics: whether other factors compete with them in importance could be tested.

The ability to identify patterns of social change and the determinants within each of the three systems and their dominant institutions is relatively straightforward. The relation between the three systems is not. That is because the systems are orthogonal; as we have seen, the dominant institution in each works in a different way. That makes the relations complicated:

- The relation between the technoscientific and the economic system is that the environment is transformed by technoscience, but this transformation both enables and constrains – in the Age of Limits – growth in the economic system. The enabling part has been theorized – how innovation, and also the use of energy, spurred economic growth. As for constraints, however, while the planet's probable future temperature rise is known, how this has affected and will affect economic growth is subject to uncertainty. In the past, the temperature rise was not known to constrain economic growth, especially as the effect of growth on the environment (as mentioned) only accelerated three-quarters of a century ago, even if it was initiated during the industrial revolution. The relatively short period of dramatic impact explains why course correction, which takes many years and the effect of which is difficult to measure, will entail further uncertainty. The certainty is that some kind of major course correction will be required, either by drastic changes in economic growth or changes in the technological infrastructure for energy uses.
- The relation between the political system and the technoscientific system is that the latter enables greater control by the former (bureaucratization and surveillance) and that politics has limited possibilities of steering technoscientific research and technological infrastructures.
- As for the relations between the economic and political systems, economic growth has begun to slow in an 'Age of Limits' (Schroeder, 2013) when living standards in Europe and North America (or high-income democracies) are no longer rising as they did during the post-war Golden Age. In the US, for example, real household income has not grown since the 1970s even as inequality has widened. How economic growth is distributed across the globe and across national populations varies, but its measurement is standardized by GDP measures and via Gini indexes for inequality. The relation to the political system is that the state regulates the economy and redistributes more than a third and sometimes close to half of all economic resources (via taxation), but the state's capacity to do so is constrained by the amount of growth in the economy (recall here also the relation to the technoscientific system) and the constraint of political legitimacy on the other. Thus the state can shape inequality, especially via the provision of welfare services – in other words, the expansion of social rights (which fall within the political system) – but this shaping is constrained by markets, making the relation between the economic system and political system a two-way connection (the hypothesis here concerns the struggle for rights, though the alternative, that economic growth provides legitimacy and so stability for governments, has been the main – functionalist – alternative).

The struggle for the extension of social rights with these new limits thus comes up against certain elites favoring economic globalization and immigration, versus citizens or civil society seeking protection for rights within the nation-state. Domestic and external (market) constraints are thus linked. This link between the economic and political systems is different for high-income democracies and may not apply to non-democratic and low-income states (which are subject to different patterns that go beyond the scope here). But these systemic and inter-system relations also apply only to the post-war period, after the break when inter-state relations strongly impacted economies and states, as with the effect of wars on inequality (Scheidel, 2018) and state capacity (as analyzed by Tilly, Goldstone, Mann, and others, see Collins, 1999: 1–18). And again, for high-income democracies and the relations between them (and not between them and other nation-states), these can be left out for the post-war period (since the effect of wars just mentioned no longer applies). Finally, I have sketched some of the main patterns within and between the systems; the point of automating the analysis would be to test these patterns against other hypothesized patterns, rank them in terms of fit with the data and the overall fit, extend their scale and scope, and incorporate more data, and so on, in an iterative process (see figures in Mökander and Schroeder, 2021).

COMPUTATIONAL ANALYSES

This sketch of the ontological units of the social world and its systems and relations has only addressed the macro-level and has done so only in outline and within limited periods and geographical scope of the units. The work of testing these systemic relations can be envisaged as an effort that requires drawing together various data sources (such as Our World in Data 2022; a longer list of data sources can be found in Schroeder [2022]) and iterative refining of hypotheses about them to identify the main factors or causal pathways, only some of which have been sketched. Such data analysis will, in keeping with the theory proposed, require a certain type of research organization, including the research technologies for analyzing these data. It will also require applying the six different scientific styles to the three – autonomous and orthogonal – systems and the relations between them. The styles of science are not mutually incompatible or unintelligible, and part of the effort in automating social theory will be to see how they can be not only borne to bear but also combined. For example, for understanding the social impact of climate change, a combination of probability plus modeling could be used such that the analysis of the large technological system for transforming the environment's resources into energy (the technoscientific infrastructure that interlocks with the natural environment for this purpose) is combined with extrapolations of future patterns of economic growth plus projections for population size within the market system. Or again, for the state, the dominant institution in the political system, the historicogenetic style can be used, charting the resources of the state devoted to social rights (the Global Welfare Dataset [2022] needs to be added to Our World in Data above for this measurement), which can also be related to rates of economic growth in the market system. Markets, the dominant institution in the economic system, require the style of postulation for market equilibria, plus modeling how these equilibria affect stratification.

Learning takes place when the rules (algorithms) involved in these styles are interrelated so that the data can be integrated into overall models. To do this, the relations – intra- and inter-systemic – can be translated rather mechanically in the first instance into hypotheses: rates of growth, positive and negative reinforcements, degrees of openness and closedness of economies and states, and the like. After aligning time periods and spaces of the relevant units, the next task is to show how the measures for the relations between units are such that the measures from one unit translate into those of others – which is central to explanation. In this chapter, again, only certain relations within and between systems have been identified, but in the full model, these explanations would need to be ranked alongside others in terms of their 'primacy' (in inverted commas, because the number of causes that should be ranked in this way is open). In the case of the causes or explanations of the development within the political system, for example, these are first, elite response, and second, the strength of pressure 'from below', leading to extensions in the expansion of rights gained from and provided by the state.

An interdependent set of dynamic interrelated parts: how can learning take place in the relations between systems? What is aimed at in the case of modeling these inter-systemic relations is not a 'super-system', but rather the shifts in the relations between systems. One way to think about inter-systemic relations is whether 'primacy' can be applied to one or other systems or inter-systemic relations in different periods – against the backdrop that this 'primacy' is premised on the autonomy of the systems. Further, this learning about patterns apart from the various component parts could consist of refining the techniques that have been described – the use of visualizations and models to advance data-driven computational techniques – and integrating them into learning models (AI). This integration could include thinking about how AI research technologies themselves become a shared focus of attention among computational social scientists such that they seek to develop the tools specifically for high-consensus rapid-discovery science (Collins and Sanderson, 2016: 8–12) as applied to the advance of social theory; in this case, modeling the systemic and inter-systemic relations in machine readable ways. Such a shared understanding of the symbols for the manipulation of data would fit with how other sciences advance.

The aim would be to maximize the overall fit of the model, even if it consists of three orthogonal systems and the relations between them (see the figures in Mökander and Schroeder, 2021). They can also be nested levels (see figure 9.2 in Schroeder, 2013: 200). The outermost time-space envelope is the environment, operating under the constraint of planetary boundaries and how economic growth has continued to push up the temperature of the globe over a period of 300 years and mostly since the post-war great acceleration (McNeill and Engelke, 2014) mentioned earlier. Again, on this basis, forecasts can be made assuming population growth, economic growth, and the requisite energy needs for these. The second nested level is economic growth and inequality in disembedded markets: here, as mentioned, apart from the post-war break, another break is needed for high-income democracies after the 'Golden Age'. The third nested level consists of nation-states, where, in the same period, the pattern can be hypothesized for the expansion and then plateauing or regression of rights in terms of their inclusiveness and their scale since the end of the Golden Age, and how these patterns obtain for various high-income democratic nation-states.

The three nested levels – nested, in that 'primacy' works from the outermost level – from the environmental, via its constraints on market growth, and to the constraint on the expansion of rights – can also be seen as the inter-systemic relations applied to different spatial sizes of units interacting over different periods. Optimizing the fit of this overall model (note, again, not a 'super system') of how these patterns interrelate comes up against translatability of the units of measurement: how much temperature rise translates into what percentage restriction on economic growth? How much additional economic growth translates into the provision (or lack of it) of social rights per person or for different strata? And even for such a short-term period – the post-war three-quarters of a century with one break for the end of the golden age – aligning these patterns incorporating the relations between high-income democracies and the more global scope of markets and technoscience – poses challenges.

KNOWLEDGE ADVANCES AND DISCIPLINARY DIVIDES

Disciplinary and sub-disciplinary specialisms and the variety of theory traditions will stand in the way of this project. Further, there are many concurrent efforts in computational social science that are not oriented to cumulative theory-building and which start and end at the micro-level. Integrating and harnessing them toward a more synthetic understanding and explanation of the social world is urgent – if only to avoid duplication of effort. A sociology of knowledge of the technoscientific organization of this effort and where gaps need to be filled could be useful in this respect. This chapter has taken steps in that direction, sketching a unifying program for AI and social theory, where 'unifying' does not mean the unity of science (a grander aim) but merely making theory formalized and calculable and showing possibilities for integrating datasets about the social world. This research program, combining machine-readable formalized expressions of social theory with large-scale data sources, can lead to advances in social scientific knowledge. It can also lead to forecasts which have, again, for disciplinary reasons, been narrower to date: economics has, for example, prioritized short-term forecasts, and political science often tries to forecast elections. And so on. The effort described here is indifferent to these traditional disciplinary concerns or practical aims; what matters is theoretical coherence and fit with data, plus learning.

To be sure, there will be objections to this project from disciplines that already provide various theories, including economics, international relations, psychology, and anthropology. There will also be objections from those who claim that scientistic theories like evolution or complexity provide better explanations. In this chapter, an agnostic view has been taken: the validity of social theory does not rest on disciplinary boundaries (even if we can be sanguine about why they persist) but rather on the analysis of data and where there is consensus or the lack thereof. As for scientific knowledge, the view taken here has been that scientific knowledge is separate from other types of knowledge – without prejudging which particular scientific domain should supply social theories. Another objection might be that only creative human minds are capable of synthesizing the explanation of the social world, rather than machines. However, that objection only needs to be stated explicitly to be seen as faulty: some inputs will be human, but they will be refined by machines and shaped by ongoing patterns of cumulation.

Further, what is proposed here does not rule out qualitative analysis (if that is what is meant by creativity, including 'meaning'): as long as the meaning of theory or of what theory seeks to explain can be formalized and patterns can be incorporated into models, qualitative and quantitative analysis can go hand in hand. Yet another objection could be that there is bound to be bias in AI-driven social scientific knowledge. But this problem, as exemplified by how certain parts of the population may be captured disproportionally by data that could reinforce existing disadvantages, is well-known in AI and admits to working toward solutions. As Esposito (2022) has argued, the problem is not too much bias, but too little bias with respect to the need to specify clearly what kinds of aims AI communication – or here, AI-driven social scientific knowledge cumulation – should serve. This also applies to the bias toward certain topics due to the availability of digital data, as with how Twitter studies have been overrepresented in research on digital media, or by how economic growth is measured by GDP with all the shortcomings that this entails: the question should be how, given the aims of cumulative knowledge, these gaps can be overcome by means of specifying which aims of knowledge can be served (and which ones will have to prioritized less because of the lack of available data).

Again, identifying, and so steering the aim that the technoscientific institutionalization and implementation of AI-driven social scientific knowledge cumulation should serve, could be a reflexive and rewarding task for scholars of the role of AI in society (though quite a 'niche' – albeit crucial for research – task, making research more effective).

The purpose of AI-driven social theory is to refine our explanation of the social world, not (in the first instance at least) to manipulate it, though that could be a longer-term byproduct. And manipulation takes place within constraints: it can easily be imagined, for example, that there is an excellent model for the most effective way to achieve economic growth. Implementing it would be another matter. As Schumpeter pointed out, there is a difference between invention and innovation: innovation puts science into practice. The purpose here has been to systematize social science knowledge so that there is a better fit with the evidence, which is some distance away from innovations that apply this knowledge to social engineering. Here is also a clue as to why social theory is a special type of knowledge: while causal explanations (often multiple regressions) do better at analyzing specific patterns of social change (theories of the middle range), cumulative theory does better at picking out overall patterns and 'fit'.

Theory can thus be seen as a general-purpose technology, albeit for a relatively narrow range of units, a means for allowing models to 'travel' across domains. These models can be applied to the social world globally as well as to forecasting, but such modeling is weak insofar as the various interactions within and between systems become more indeterminate over time – except when facing hard constraints such as climate change – and the implementation of models to steer social systems is a remote prospect. Modeling the past is more straightforward, but past patterns come up against the limits whereby the period and geography of the units covered will constrain the degree of usefulness for forecasting. Still, the systemic dynamics that have been sketched here can be extended into the future, as has been done, for example, in the forecasts for the next 50–100 years of GDP growth and their convergence or divergence for different parts of the world (by Grinin and Korotayev, 2015: 194–98) or the course of political stability and violence over the same period for the US (Turchin, 2021). These forecasts, and how they could be combined, go beyond the scope of this chapter, but they are continuous with the ideas about automating social theory put forward here.

This brings us to a final objection: that automating social theory to undertake theory refinement and forecasting is a less essential task for academic social science, which should focus instead on current – perhaps 'middle range' – problems. Be that as it may, actors in the private and public sectors, including cultural industries and the military, will develop such forecasting models – regardless of whether they measure up to the most accurate social theory or not. These forecasting efforts will not adhere to the criteria of cumulative social scientific knowledge but rather focus on narrower commercial or strategic purposes. Moreover, they may be based on proprietary data. These efforts will take place in parallel but also intersect with cumulative academic social scientific theory and knowledge. The difference between cumulation and these narrower efforts alerts us to the fact that whereas social theory is constrained by social reality and representing it ever more comprehensively, modeling, for practical purposes, is not constrained in this way. Put differently, practical forecasts are aimed at particular social problems whereas academic or social scientific social theory is aimed at capturing as much of social reality (scale) as possible with the greatest theoretical coherence (scope). Whether there will be mutual learning between these academic and non-academic efforts, and between academic disciplines, including computer science, remains to be seen.

ACKNOWLEDGMENTS

I would like to thank Jakob Mökander, Andreas Jungherr, Steve Hoffman, and Jaana Parviainen for their helpful comments on earlier versions of this chapter. The usual disclaimers apply.

REFERENCES

Collins, R. (1988). *Theoretical Sociology*. San Diego: Harcourt Brace Jovanovich.
Collins, R. (1992). *Sociological Insight: An Introduction to Non-obvious Sociology*. Oxford: Oxford University Press.
Collins, R. (1999). *Macrohistory: Essays in the Sociology of the Long Run*. Stanford: Stanford University Press.
Collins, R. (2004). *Interaction Ritual Chains*. Princeton: Princeton University Press.
Collins, R. and Sanderson, S. (2016). *Conflict Sociology: A Sociological Classic Updated*. Abingdon: Routledge.
Esposito, E. (2022). *Artificial Communication*. Cambridge, MA: MIT Press.
Evans, J. and Rzhetsky, A. (2010). Philosophy of science: Machine science. *Science*, 329(5990), 399–400. https://doi.org/10.1126/science.1189416
Frickel, S. and Gross, N. (2005). A general theory of scientific/intellectual movements. *American Sociological Review*, 70(2), 204–232.
Gellner, E. (1988). *Plough, Sword and Book: The Structure of Human History*. London: Collins Harvill.
Giddens, A. (1985). *The Nation-state and Violence*. Cambridge: Polity Press.
Global Welfare Dataset. (2022). https://emw.ku.edu.tr/global-welfare-dataset-glow/
Grinin, L. and Korotayev, A. (2015). *Great Divergence and Great Convergence: A Global Perspective*. Cham: Springer.
Hacking, I. (2002). *Historical Ontology*. Cambridge, MA: Harvard University Press.
Hanemann, R. (1987). *Computer-assisted Theory Building: Modelling Dynamic Social Systems*. Beverly Hills: Sage.
Hamilton, G. and Feenstra, R. (1998). The organization of economies, in M. Brinton and V. Nee (eds), *The New Institutionalism in Sociology*. New York: Russell Sage Foundation, pp. 153–180.
Hughes, T. (1987). The evolution of large technological systems, in W. Bijker, T. Hughes and T. Pinch (eds), *The Social Construction of Technological Systems*. Cambridge, MA: MIT Press, pp. 51–82.
Mann, M. (1986). *The Sources of Social Power, Volume I: A History of Power from the Beginning to 1760 AD*. Cambridge: Cambridge University Press.
McNeill, J.R. and Engelke, P. (2014). *The Great Acceleration: An Environmental History of the Anthropocene since 1945*. Cambridge, MA: Harvard University Press.
Meyer, E.T. and Schroeder, R. (2015). *Knowledge Machines: Digital Transformations of the Sciences and Humanities*. Cambridge, MA: MIT Press.
Mitchell, M. (2019). *Artificial Intelligence: A Guide for to Thinking Humans*. New York: Farrar, Straus and Giroux.
Morgan, M.S. (2012). *The World in the Model: How Economists Work and Think*. Cambridge: Cambridge University Press.
Morgan, S.L. and Winship, C. (2015). *Counterfactuals and Causal Inference*. Cambridge: Cambridge University Press.
Mökander, J. and Schroeder, R. (2021). AI and social theory. *AI & Society*, 1–15. https://doi.org/10.1007/s00146-021-01222-z
Our World in Data. (2022). https://ourworldindata.org/
Page, S. (2018). *The Model Thinker: What You Need to Know to Make Data Work for You*. New York: Basic Books.
Pearl, J. and McKenzie, D. (2018). *The Book of Why: The New Science of Cause and Effect*. London: Allen Lane.
Rockstroem, J. et al. (2009). A safe operating space for humanity. *Nature*, 461, 472–475.

Scheidel, W. (2018). *The Great Leveler: Violence and the History of Inequality from the Stone Age to the Twenty-first Century*. Princeton: Princeton University Press.

Schölkopf, B. et al. (2021). Toward causal representation learning. *Proceedings of the IEEE*, 109(5), 612–634. https://doi.org/10.1109/JPROC.2021.3058954

Schroeder, R. (2007). *Rethinking Science, Technology and Social Change*. Stanford: Stanford University Press.

Schroeder, R. (2013). *An Age of Limits: Social Theory for the 21st Century*. Basingstoke: Palgrave Macmillan.

Schroeder, R. (2019). Cumulation and big data in the social sciences. *Information, Communication and Society*. https://doi.org/10.1080/1369118X.2019.1594334

Schroeder, R. (2022). Computational and data-driven Gellnerian social theory: From the transition to modernity to a disenchanted future, in P. Skalnik (ed), *Gellner and Contemporary Social Science*. Basingstoke: MacMillan.

Stichweh, R. (2021). Individual and collective inclusion and exclusion in political systems, in A. Ahlers, D. Krichewsky, E. Moser and R. Stichweh (eds), *Democratic and Authoritarian Political Systems in 21st Century World Society*. Bielefeld: Transcript Verlag, pp. 13–38.

Turchin, P. (2019). *Historical Dynamics: Why States Rise and Fall*. Princeton: Princeton University Press.

Turchin, P. (2021). Multipath forecasting: The aftermath of the 2020 American crisis. https://osf.io/preprints/socarxiv/f37jy/

Turner, J. (1995). *Macrodynamics: Toward a Theory on the Organization of Human Populations*. New Brunswick: Rutgers University Press.

Turner, J. (2002). *The Structure of Sociological Theory*. Belmont: Wadsworth Publishing.

74. Artificial intelligence and scientific problem choice at the nexus of industry and academia
Steve G. Hoffman

INTRODUCTION

Academic capitalism is a defining feature of the 21st-century research university. A search for pots of gold, some big and some small, is its hallmark. Commercialization schemes have been particularly prolific within the American higher education system over the last several decades, given the size and strength of private research universities in the US and the state-centeredness of many European and Asian institutions (Nickolai, Hoffman, & Trautner, 2012). Nevertheless, scholars of academic capitalism and university-industry relations (UIRs) have documented commercialization schemes and associated entrepreneurial practices not only in the US and Europe but also in African, Asian, Australian, Indian, and Canadian universities and colleges (Cantwell & Kauppinen, 2014; Metcalfe, 2010; Johnson & Hirt, 2011). Some scholars, therefore, have proposed that academic capitalism is a transnational trend (Kauppinen, 2015), even if important economic and political localisms characterize its institutionalization within different national, regional, and unit-level contexts (Centellas, 2010; Fochler, 2016b; Hoffman, 2011).

The commercialization of university-based research is not particularly new to academic scientists working in artificial intelligence (AI). Although funded primarily by government science agencies throughout its modern history, and in particular by the United States military, industry investment, "challenge grants," and related knowledge capitalization schemes have played a prominent role within AI research practice since its inception as an academic research domain in the mid-20th century (Edwards, 1996; Crevier, 1993). The most notable "summer" of industry investment in AI came from the heat of expert systems techniques in the 1980s (Collins, 1990; Brock, 2018). With the cooling of the hype around expert systems, corporate investments continued to provide a consistent, if sometimes stingy and fickle, resource base for AI, especially in case-based reasoning systems used in the education, health, and related professions throughout the 1990s and early-2000s. However, the last several years have been called the "Great AI Awakening" (Lewis-Kraus, 2016), a period in which popular and philosophical hyperbole, journalistic hype, impressive technical breakthroughs, and large-scale private and public investments have combined to flow attention and resources toward university labs working on "big data" information processing, predictive machine learning techniques (Joyce et al., 2021; Popkin, 2019), and most recently, generative AI like ChatGPT and DALL-E. This, in turn, has reinvigorated a critical focus on the problem of research problem choice at the nexus of industry and academia.

Whereas the influence of industry and commercial interests is quite flagrant in pharmaceutical and related health research fields, especially in the United States (Prainsack, 2020; Sismondo, 2009), academic AI research typically looks more like university-based bioscience and biotech research (Cooper, 2009; Vallas & Kleinman, 2008). That is, the impact of knowledge capitalization on scientific problem choice in academic AI has tended to be uneven, sometimes contradictory, and often quite subtle (Hoffman, 2011). Some lab groups have carefully tuned their lab practice and scientific problem choice to consumer and industry-oriented technology markets. Others seek refuge in Ivory Tower bunkers, continuing to cultivate long-standing ties with government science agencies to defend turf against the pro-capitalist infidels. Most AI scientists, however, are opportunistic rather than ideological. They are strategic in how they weave in and out of the increasingly porous boundaries that separate university from industry-based research. Furthermore, academics who seek industry funding and commercial technologies are usually multivocal, able to appeal to multiple audiences and diverse forms of evaluative worth across academia, government, and industry interests (Fochler, 2016b; Shore & McLauchlan, 2012; Birch, 2020). A key strategy used by many such labs is to cultivate diverse research "portfolios" that simultaneously pursue a variety of investment opportunities and research objectives (Rushforth, Franssen, & de Rijcke, 2019). Some lab projects may focus primarily on problems and techniques related to commercial applications whereas others trade in a more theoretical, exploratory, or promissory register (Hoffman, 2021). While academic labs may pursue many goals simultaneously, the range of problems pursued comes to deeply mark everyday lab practice, epistemic culture, methodological convention, and the knowledge claims that AI scientists make with their developing systems (Hoffman, 2015, 2017; Ensmenger, 2012).

Strategic choices grow epistemic forms that anchor day-to-day research practice to leverage reputational position among funders with whom they have placed their bets (Jeon, 2019; Kleinman, 1998). These choices deeply shape the array of problems that researchers perceive as "doable" projects (Fujimura, 1987). Grant writing requires focused attention, time, and expenditure of intellectual capital, which go to the heart of academic labor power. Research problems are typically laid out during the planning stages through grant applications. Therefore, choices made during planning have downstream consequences for subsequent project outcomes and knowledge products.

Problem choice can be especially tricky when a lab relies on industry funding that is short-term and fickle, requiring a nimble orientation to research questions and forms of research practice that can quickly adapt to new funding opportunities as they rise and fall (Hoffman, 2021; for parallel examples in biotech and environmental science labs, see Fochler, 2016a; Jeon, 2019). In high-tech fields of research funding for the technological infrastructure needed to carry out new projects is the key to whether a line of research continues or not. If a lab group can continue to develop new technical systems (or to be more exact, make claims to build technologies that credible members of their research field and investors publicly acknowledge as an example of AI), publish knowledge claims based on these new systems, raise funds to pay staff, and keep processing students toward degrees, then the game can continue.

Much of my research on AI lab research shows how focused attention also creates silences. Questions around "impact," for example, can supplant concerns for empirical accuracy (Hoffman, 2017; Winsberg, 2006). The big questions that vexed the founding figures of academic AI – What is intelligence? How do we recognize it? Can it be simulated in a machine? – can get ignored or even shamed. Those questions that do not demonstrate clear market potential, or that prove resistant to a quick fix, are the ones that are ignored or left on the scrap heap of aborted starts. Yet, science agency labs are no panacea for Mertonian scientific purity either. They, too, are opportunistic and may be limited to small groups of specialists invested in their esoteric branch of the knowledge tree. Regardless of their position, however, academic

AI scientists develop methodological conventions and make claims to their guiding sense of academic mission, contributions to knowledge, and scientific integrity. They are constantly re-braiding what ought to count as "good" science and "interesting" work, as they search the terrain where they think the latest rainbow ends.

WELCOME TO THE DEEP REASONING GROUP AND THE CLEVER MINDS LAB

To gain an appreciation for how differently situated academic lab groups have responded to university pressures toward entrepreneurial research, I conducted long-term ethnographic observations, interviews, and textual analysis of research publications at two neighboring but differently situated AI labs at a single private research university in the American Midwest. The primary years of data collection transpired between 2004 and 2007, with occasional updates from lab members and lab website content through 2021.

The Deep Reasoning Group,[1] or DRG, works on knowledge representation and qualitative reasoning systems. Although not adverse to taking advantage of industry funding for smaller projects that have industry or commercial applications, members of the DRG preferred multi-year grants from the Defense Advanced Research Projects Agency (DARPA), the Office of Naval Research (ONR), the National Science Foundation (NSF), or the US Department of Homeland Security (DHS). The head of the DRG, Derek, reasoned that science agency grants tend to cover longer time horizons, typically between three and five years, and when crafted correctly, come with relatively few expectations for providing "field deliverables." A few DRG projects acquired industry funding, although these were small grants focused on short-term projects that Derek considered peripheral to his lab's portfolio. In contrast, the neighboring AI lab – the Clever Minds Lab, or CML – relied almost entirely on industry-based funding.

The CML worked on an eclectic array of information technologies that grew out of the lab head's training in case-based reasoning (CBR). CBR developed out of expert systems and is part and parcel of a four-decade-long shift within academic AI toward formal and informal industry ties through consulting, licensing, on-campus commercial start-ups, and technology incubators. These ties deeply shaped the CML's choice of research problems and overall research portfolio. They paved the path for more recent developments in commercially oriented ML, forging what Gulson and Webb (2021) call "established research feedback loops" (3). The CML engages in a range of formal and informal collaborative exchanges with industry actors and corporate firms, which provides what lab members referred to as the "problem spaces" within which members derive a pragmatic and commercially oriented approach to doing academic research. The CML relied primarily on small and medium-sized grants from telecommunication firms, consumer product and advertising, social media companies, the arts and entertainment industry, venture capital investment, and to a lesser extent, municipal government agencies promoting economic development through seed grants. The CML included several projects that were moving through the stages of knowledge capitalization,

---

[1]   All personal names and organizational affiliations are pseudonyms. In most of my publications on these two labs, I refer to individual members of the Clever Minds Lab with names that begin with the letter C, as in Charles. Members of the Deep Reasoning Group have pseudonyms that begin with D, such as Derek or David. Sergio Sismondo suggested this convention several years ago and I like it.

including patent applications, an on-campus commercial incubator with a small staff focused on marketing, start-ups for the most commercially viable technologies, and related "knowledge translation" schemes.

My introduction to the DRG and CML conveyed that these were quite different spaces for doing quite different kinds of AI research. Although the two labs are housed within the same department of computer science and on the same floor, they could hardly look or feel more divergent. The DRG, for its part, presents as a prototypic academic department with bookshelves set amidst walls adorned with research posters that had been presented at various academic conferences. The DRG is a neat, tidy, and quiet place. Communal space was limited to a few lounge chairs in a small meeting area surrounded by closed-door offices. When I met with lab head Derek to propose my observational study, his impulse was to erect some clear parameters to my access. First and foremost, he did not want me to slow down the progress of his students. He recalled a story about an AI lab in the UK that had been the subject of a sociology graduate student's thesis. When lab members read the work, they felt betrayed by the negative portrayal of their internal relationships. Derek admitted, however, that this lab had been "filled with strong personalities…it would have been impossible to describe them without putting something embarrassing in print." I tried my best to assure him by discussing my research methods and goals, pledging that I was not interested in producing a journalistic exposé. He especially appreciated the idea of confidentiality. At my first lab-wide meeting a few days later, Derek introduced me to the group and highlighted that each member's participation was voluntary, and their identity would be kept anonymous: "For those of you who are not used to dealing with social scientists, there is something called confidentiality. They are very good about taking your names and affiliations out of anything that is written about you in reports."

The CML, just down the hall, felt like a different world entirely. Instead of research posters and bookshelves, the walls were filled with vintage sci-fi movie posters and computer screens running engaging information systems designed by lab members (e.g., an automated live news show hosted by the video game character Alex Vance ran on a large monitor mounted on the entryway wall). Open-door offices surrounded a very large communal table typically occupied by several graduate student members of the lab. A few bookshelves were littered with piles of dissected computer parts, wiring, and tools, suggesting recent surgical reconstructions. In contrast to Derek's friendly but reserved welcome, the head of CML was downright exuberant about my proposal to observe him and his lab members. Charles emphasized the CML's "transparency" and welcomed my regular input on lab projects. He set me up with a shared office space. He suggested I concentrate full-time on his lab since they had many exciting projects in the works. He even chafed at the idea that I disguise his or his lab's identity due to human subject protocols. He saw this as an opportunity for exposure. A few days later, Charles introduced me at a lab meeting by joking that the CML was my "aboriginal tribe." I demurred, "Yes! Tell me your strange ways." This would not be the only joke about my presence. The following week, Charles told a group of visiting representatives from a private telecommunications firm that I occasionally took graduate students into a small room to perform experiments. The main joke in those early days was that I was a spy sent from a Big Tech company.[2] Under the guise of a sociologist, I could ask all manner of silly questions. But they were on to me. I was, in fact, stealing good ideas on behalf of a corporate titan.

---

[2]   The actual joke involved a specific company, which has been replaced with generic terminology.

The ways that these two AI labs welcomed me into their fold signaled their divergent orientation to scientific problem choice. Derek and the DRG welcomed me as a fellow academic researcher, establishing boundaries and expectations around how my inquiry might impact their own. He drew upon a precedent for my lab study to establish what not to do while leaning into the bureaucratic, subjects-rights idiom of Human Subjects Review to establish some guidance. Derek expressed the concerns of a paternal lab director who was hospitable to the research goals of a fellow scientist if they remained within agreed-upon, rationalized procedures. My access was clear, formal, and limited. The lab felt then and later like a serious kind of place, elevated and insulated by its rigor and sense of scholarly purpose. As I was to learn over the ensuing years of observation and analysis, this neatly reflected the DRG's research practice and problem choice. The lab was highly successful at acquiring federal science agency grants. These largely buffered Derek, his students and staff, and the lab's developing technologies from the volatility of commercial markets and fickle investments in the latest technological fads. In general, the DRG organized its scientific problem choice in a top-down, tightly organized fashion. Derek carefully steered his lab's research objectives, closely tethered to cumulative progress based on a theoretical framework he had established with a colleague in the psychology department. The head of the lab did not invite deliberation over the theoretical assumptions animating his approach to AI. Instead, he carefully chose staff and students that aligned with his interests and were pre-invested in his institutional reputation as a leader in the field. The result was a highly coherent portfolio of research projects characterized by a steady stream of cumulative contributions and dependable federal agency grants. The top-down approach to scientific problem choice tended to close off from consideration alternative theoretical pathways before they could even be raised. The DRG's knowledge claims and technologies, though well-respected, reserved their impact for a quite small and closed-off group of specialist interlocutors.

Derek's cautious welcome to the DRG evoked his lab's priority around maintaining a focused attention space for exploring the questions animating his group's scientific problem space. This was a place not merely for tinkering on machines but for disciplined and cumulative thinking. The sort of lab where group conversation is a prelude to individual contemplation. A full-time staff researcher once compared the DRG with the CML by stating, "We are the kind of place that does science rather than build applications." David, a graduate student at the DRG who entertained the possibility of joining the CML when he first enrolled, explained his decision as follows:

> in grad school…you are trying to do things that you don't know whether they are going to be useful or not…I feel like that is more of a constraint for [the] corporate world…But I didn't want to worry about how applicable my stuff was going to be so much as how interesting it was and how innovative.

Charles and the CML, in contrast, welcomed me into a far more informal and looser milieu with warmth, humor, and exuberance. The space itself put emphasis on informality and collaborative exchange, suggesting a rather more inductive orientation to scientific problem choice. Charles indicated his understanding of my own research goals by playfully indexing a trope of cultural anthropology – Malinowski among the Trobriand – and medical experimentation. Though gracious to an extreme, his jokes also expressed a subtle uneasiness with the very idea that he was to become a scientific subject. The joke that proved most lasting, however, was that I was a Big Tech spy. This both made light of and expressed anxiety around just how open or "transparent" the CML should be as members navigated the fraught waters of their commercially oriented academic research. Similar jokes that teased around these kinds of tensions became commonplace. Years later, Charles deadpanned in response to a frustrating meeting with a university administrator, "Oh forget it. Maybe I'll just give up this whole professor thing and go work for [Big Tech]."[3] The lab was simultaneously a light and heady place – confident, boastful, yet anxious. Excitingly open, a little edgy, and very fun, yet haunted by uncertainties about which paths would yield the most golden coin.

Welcoming rituals separate and pull together, marking inside and outside along with insiders and outsiders (Malinowski, 2002 [1922]: 4–5). The kidding and joking that characterized my time at the CML played on a similarly Janus-faced register, simultaneously friendly and antagonistic, welcoming and displacing (Radcliffe-Brown, 1940). Jokes often promote the personal embarrassment of an individual to fortify collective memberships. More generally, jokes provide a "meta-communication" that frames the activity at hand within an implicit message that "this is just play" (Bateson, 2000 [1972]). In his poking fun at the conventions of ethnography and medical science, Charles conveyed his understanding that neither tribalism nor medical procedure were what was happening. The idea that I might be a spy for a Big Tech company had a similar underlying sentiment, while also indicating the CML's concerns around proprietary knowledge and the boundary work involved when "incubating" innovations with market potential. Finally, by "playing along" with the jokes at the CML, I took an opportunity to assure my subjects by evoking what Erving Goffman referred to as "disdainful detachment" (1961: 110) with my putative role as an objectifying observer. I was trying to signal that there was nothing to worry about in my transient membership. Rest assured! I would never stoop to citing mid-20th-century ethnographers to help make sense of my findings about the lab's group culture.

Like the DRG, the CML's welcome was revealing of the group's epistemic form. I came to see that the lab's emphasis on openness and collaboration was a concerted effort to put the idea of a spontaneous and flexible "distributed mind" into small group practice. This priority on flexibility and adaptation was constantly tuned and re-tuned to funding opportunities as they arose. This was a lab characterized by shifting alliances, short-term investments, and the desire for a big score. The lab's frequently stated skepticism toward theoretical orthodoxy in AI, loose epistemological standards, and careful focus on the potential "impact" of its systems made practical sense given this resource niche. Their epistemic form reflected the volatile resource base they relied upon and their heterogeneous network of external interlocutors.

CONCLUSION (OR, THE PROBLEM OF SCIENTIFIC PROBLEM CHOICE)

The problem I pursued in my ethnography of the DRG and CML was the problem of scientific problem choice. Critical analyses of scientific problem choice have a rich history in the sociology of science and science and technology studies (Gieryn, 1978; Ziman, 1981; Zuckerman, 1978; Fujimura, 1987; Webster, 1994). This tradition has typically focused on the way that methodological standards and research priorities are deeply shaped by institutional pressures and contextual factors. More recent scholarship has focused on the agency of academic scientists as they respond to competing institutional incentives, developing a rather precarious

---

[3]   Similar to the joke that I was a Big Tech spy, Charles actually referenced a specific company.

balance of obligations that tethers the tight rope of student learning, a university's public good mission, and administrative pressures to be more entrepreneurial with research outputs (Holloway, 2015). The lab studies tradition in STS comes out of a somewhat different agenda, demonstrating how day-to-day lab decision making and the epistemic practices that produce objectified knowledge is not, itself, particularly rational and planned. Rather, scientific practice is associational, indexical, and iterative (Latour & Woolgar, 1986 [1979]; Knorr Cetina, 1999; Traweek, 1988). Nevertheless, the STS emphasis on science-in-the-making converges with studies of scientific problem choice where it demonstrates that science is situated within particular "patterns of familiarity" (Shapin, 2008, p. 286) reflective of heterogenous networks of interlocutors, funders, and boundary technologies.

My research revealed the patterning of social organization and the kinds of knowledge produced by academic AI labs working within different resource ecologies. My work has identified the different forms of epistemic value evinced by AI scientists as they manage the ambiguities at the "edge of knowledge," how AI scientists enact multiple and often contradictory repertoires of basic and applied science in daily practice, and how the cultural logics of commercialization can carry across research units seemingly distant from direct industry influence.

A deep shortcoming of many critical analyses of academic capitalism is that scholars gloss over the details of everyday research practice, eager to point out where direct and formal evidence of the corporate corruption of higher education can be identified (Mirowski, 2011; Krimsky, 2003; Blumenthal, Gluck, Louis, Stoto, & Wise, 1986). This work has also tended to rely heavily on *ex-post facto* interviews and surveys that ask subjects to reflect upon and reconstruct decisions and processes outside of the dynamic interactions that gave rise to those decisions and processes (Slaughter & Rhoades, 2004). In addition to yielding a somewhat distant caricature of everyday scientific decision making, the move can also render opaque the subtle but pernicious ways in which scientific problem choice can be informally "steered" by industry interests (Abraham & Ballinger, 2012; Kleinman, 2003; Subramaniam, Perrucci, & Whitlock, 2014). As Gulson and Webb (2021) report, much of this is about "concentrating attention" or "steering the mind share," not direct control over any particular research group or project:

> The influence of technology companies appears more evident in encouraging researchers to investigate broad topics of interest for the companies…For a relatively small amount of money – small for the corporation, not the researcher! – there is the possibility of creating new academic fields of interest that converge with corporate aims. (6)

What the organizational theorist (and early AI scientist) Herbert Simon referred to as "premise controls" operate less at the level of coercion and more at the level of what questions appear to be practically doable or available for asking (see March & Simon, 1993 [1958]: 186–187). The action is in how scientists come to believe that some projects are practical, doable, "good," or "interesting" in the first place.

As I argue with colleagues in a recent essay on the sociology of AI (Hoffman et al., 2022), much hinges on who the intended users of new technology systems are imagined to be. For example, while it may be more profitable to create AI systems that generate risk profiles for renters, similar systems could be used to profile landlords that neglect repairs or fail to return security deposits. Many AI systems focus on tracking criminal behavior in poor neighborhoods but could just as well focus on informing citizens where racial profiling and violence against minorities are most likely to occur. In other words, as research groups forge strategies for navigating their preferred funding ecologies, some problems are attended to while others are neglected. Silences are produced with each utterance. For example, the resource instability of the CML yielded a highly adventurous selection of technical problems that pushed the lab's science into new and rarely explored problem areas and empirical domains. Nearly all these domains, however, focused on for-profit enterprises and managerial problems. What's more is that the most ambitious projects, those that raised canonical questions about the nature of intelligence, were choked off when they failed to produce obvious commercial applications (Hoffman, 2017, 2021).

It is also important that critical analyses of AI move past a latent nostalgia for mid-20th-century federalized science arrangements. The DRG pursued longer-term research problems supported by public science agencies but did so in a strikingly myopic fashion. Furthermore, their technologies and knowledge claims were tuned to a highly insulated audience of technical experts, the most influential of whom were interested in AI techniques that could enhance military capabilities. We need to be clear-eyed about the benefits and drawbacks of federalized science programs if our future in AI is to primarily manifest public benefits rather than private gains and more efficient corporate, administrative, and military technologies.

REFERENCES

Abraham, J., & Ballinger, R. (2012). The neoliberal regulatory state, industry interests, and the ideological penetration of scientific knowledge: Deconstructing the redefininition of carcinogens in pharmaceuticals. *Science, Technology, & Human Values, 37*(5), 443–477.

Bateson, G. (2000 [1972]). *Steps to an Ecology of Mind*. Chicago, IL: University of Chicago Press.

Birch, K. (2020). Technoscience rent: Toward a theory of rentiership for technoscientific capitalism. *Science, Technology, & Human Values, 45*(1), 3–33.

Blumenthal, D., Gluck, M., Louis, K. S., Stoto, M. A., & Wise, D. (1986). University-industry research relationships in biotechnology: Implications for the university. *Science, 232*(4756), 1361–1366.

Brock, D. C. (2018). Learning from artificial intelligence's previous awakenings: The history of expert systems. *AI Magazine, 39*(3), 3–15.

Cantwell, B., & Kauppinen, I. (Eds.). (2014). *Academic Capitalism in the Age of Globalization*. Baltimore, MD: Johns Hopkins University Press.

Centellas, K. M. (2010). The localism of Bolivian science: Tradition, policy, and projects. *Latin American Perspectives, 37*(172), 160–175.

Collins, H. M. (1990). *Artificial Experts: Social Knowledge and Intelligent Machines*. Cambridge, MA: The MIT Press.

Cooper, M. H. (2009). Commericalization of the university and problem choice by academic biological scientists. *Science, Technology, & Human Values, 34*(5), 629–653.

Crevier, D. (1993). *AI: The Tumultuous History of the Search for Artificial Intelligence*. New York, NY: Basic Books.

Edwards, P. (1996). *The Closed World: Computers and the Politics of Discourse in Cold War America*. Cambridge, MA: The MIT Press.

Ensmenger, N. (2012). Is chess the drosophila of artificial intelligence? A social history of an algorithm. *Social Studies of Science, 42*(1), 5–30.

Fochler, M. (2016a). Beyond and between academia and business: How Austrian biotechnology researchers describe high-tech startup companies as spaces of knowledge production. *Social Studies of Science, 46*(2), 259–281.

Fochler, M. (2016b). Variants of epistemic capitalism: Knowledge production and the accumulation of worth in commercial biotechnology and the academic life sciences. *Science, Technology, & Human Values, 41*(5), 922–948.

Fujimura, J. H. (1987). Constructing 'Do-able' problems in cancer research: Articulating alignment. *Social Studies of Science (Sage), 17*(2), 257–293.

Gieryn, T. F. (1978). Problem retention and problem choice in science. *Sociological Inquiry, 48*(3–4), 96–115.

Goffman, E. (1961). *Encounters: Two Studies in the Sociology of Interaction.* Indianapolis, IN: Bobbs-Merrill.

Gulson, K. N., & Webb, P. T. (2021). Steering the mind share: Technology companies, policy and Artificial Intelligence research in universities. *Discourse: Studies in the Cultural Politics of Education,* 1–13.

Hoffman, S. G. (2011). The new tools of the science trade: Contested knowledge production and the conceptual vocabularies of academic capitalism. *Social Anthropology, 19*(4), 439–462.

Hoffman, S. G. (2015). Thinking science with thinking machines: The multiple realities of basic and applied knowledge in a research border zone. *Social Studies of Science, 45*(2), 242–269.

Hoffman, S. G. (2017). Managing ambiguities at the edge of knowledge: Research strategy and artificial intelligence labs in an era of academic capitalism. *Science, Technology, & Human Values, 42*(4), 703–740.

Hoffman, S. G. (2021). A story of nimble knowledge production in an era of academic capitalism. *Theory & Society, 50*(4), 541–575.

Hoffman, S. G., Joyce, K., Alegria, S., Bell, S. E., Cruz, T. M., Noble, S. U., ... Smith-Doerr, L. (2022). Five big ideas about AI. *Contexts, 21*(3), 8–15.

Holloway, K. J. (2015). Normalizing complaint scientists and the challenge of commercialization. *Science, Technology & Human Values, 40*(5), 744–765.

Jeon, J. (2019). Invisibilizing politics: Accepting and legitimating ignorance in environmental sciences. *Social Studies of Science, 49*(6), 839–862.

Johnson, A. T., & Hirt, J. B. (2011). Reshaping academic capitalism to meet development priorities: The case of public universities in Kenya. *Higher Education, 61*(4), 483–499.

Joyce, K., Smith-Doerr, L., Alegria, S., Bell, S., Cruz, T., Hoffman, S. G., ... Shestakofsky, B. (2021). Toward a sociology of artificial intelligence: A call for research on inequalities and structural change. *Socius, 7,* 2378023121999581.

Kauppinen, I. (2015). Towards a theory of transnational academic capitalism. *British Journal of Sociology of Education, 36*(2), 336–353.

Kleinman, D. L. (1998). Untangling context: Understanding a university laboratory in the commercial world. *Science, Technology & Human Values, 23*(3), 285–314.

Kleinman, D. L. (2003). *Impure Cultures: University Biology and the World of Commerce.* Madison, WI: University of Wisconsin Press.

Knorr Cetina, K. (1999). *Epistemic Cultures: How the Sciences Make Knowledge.* Cambridge, MA: Harvard University Press.

Krimsky, S. (2003). *Science in the Private Interest: Has the Lure of Profits Corrupted Biomedical Research?* Lanham, MD: Rowman & Littlefield Publishers.

Latour, B., & Woolgar, S. (1986 [1979]). *Laboratory Life: The Construction of Scientific Facts.* Princeton, NJ: Princeton University Press.

Lewis-Kraus, G. (2016). The great A.I. Awakening. *The New York Times Magazine.* Retrieved from https://www.nytimes.com/2016/12/14/magazine/the-great-ai-awakening.html.

Malinowski, B. (2002 [1922]). *Argonauts of the Western Pacific: An Account of Native Enterprise and Adventure in the Archipelagoes of Melanesian New Guinea.* Routledge.

March, J. G., & Simon, H. A. (1993 [1958]). *Organizations.* New York, NY: Wiley.

Metcalfe, A. S. (2010). Revisiting academic capitalism in Canada: No longer the exception. *The Journal of Higher Education, 81*(4), 489–514.

Mirowski, P. (2011). *Science-Mart: Privatizing American Science.* Cambridge, MA: Harvard University Press.

Nickolai, D. H., Hoffman, S. G., & Trautner, M. N. (2012). Can a knowledge sanctuary also be an economic engine? The marketization of higher education as institutional boundary work. *Sociology Compass, 6*(3), 205–218.

Popkin, G. (2019). Plug into industry. *Nature, 565*(7741), 665–667.

Prainsack, B. (2020). The political economy of digital data: Introduction to the special issue. *Policy Studies, 41*(5), 439–446.

Radcliffe-Brown, A. R. (1940). On joking relationships. *Africa, 13*(3), 195–210.
Rushforth, A., Franssen, T., & de Rijcke, S. (2019). Portfolios of worth: Capitalizing on basic and clinical problems in biomedical research groups. *Science, Technology, & Human Values, 44*(2), 209–236.
Shapin, S. (2008). *The Scientific Life: A Moral History of a Late Modern Vocation.* Chicago, IL and London: University of Chicago Press.
Shore, C., & McLauchlan, L. (2012). 'Third mission' activities, commercialisation and academic entrepreneurs. *Social Anthropology, 20*(3), 267–286. https://doi.org/10.1111/j.1469-8676.2012.00207.x.
Sismondo, S. (2009). Ghosts in the machine publication planning in the medical sciences. *Social Studies of Science, 39*(2), 171–198.
Slaughter, S., & Rhoades, G. (2004). *Academic Capitalism and the New Economy: Markets, State, and Higher Education.* Baltimore, MD: The Johns Hopkins University Press.
Subramaniam, M., Perrucci, R., & Whitlock, D. (2014). Intellectual closure: A theoretical framework linking knowledge, power, and the corporate university. *Critical Sociology, 40*(3), 411–430. https://doi.org/10.1177/0896920512463412.
Traweek, S. (1988). *Beamtimes and Lifetimes: The World of High Energy Physicists.* Cambridge, MA: Harvard University Press.
Vallas, S. P., & Kleinman, D. L. (2008). Contradiction, convergence and the knowledge economy: The confluence of academic and commercial biotechnology. *Socio-Economic Review, 6*(2), 283–311.
Webster, A. (1994). University-corporate ties and the construction of research agendas. *Sociology, 28*(1), 123–142.
Winsberg, E. (2006). Models of success versus success of models: Reliability without truth. *Synthese, 152*, 1–19.
Ziman, J. (1981). What are the options? Social determinants of personal research plants. *Minerva, 19*(1), 1–42.
Zuckerman, H. (1978). Theory choice and problem choice in science. *Sociological Inquiry, 48*(3, 4), 65–95.

75. Myths, techno solutionism and artificial intelligence: reclaiming AI materiality and its massive environmental costs

Benedetta Brevini

INTRODUCTION

The UN's climate change summit – COP27 – which took place in November 2022 in Egypt warned once again that the planet is "sending a distress signal". The most recent State of the Global Climate Report 2022 by the UN painted a "chronicle of climate chaos", concluding that the past eight years were on track to be the warmest on record (Global Climate Report, 2022)/ The scientists writing the report estimated that global temperatures have now risen by 1.15°C since pre-industrial times, warning of the other wide-ranging impacts of climate change, including the acceleration of sea level rise, record glacier mass losses and record-breaking heatwaves.

The Intergovernmental Panel on Climate Change (IPCC) has also been sounding the alarm for years and it is now clear that if we want to meet the Paris Agreement target of keeping global warming below the 1.5°C threshold, we will need to cut emissions globally by 50% in the next decade (IPCC, 2022). Although, we are globally on a trajectory to 3°C warming (UN Environment Programme, 2019).

Several reports around the world made huge strides towards a greener planet during the pandemic given our inability to drive to work or travel, and yet, despite global lockdowns, greenhouse gas emissions have remained stubbornly high. While emissions fell by as much as 17% in April 2020, as the world's economy recovered, emissions rebounded; with the UN indicating 2020 saw just a 7% decline in carbon dioxide relative to 2019 (United Nations News, 2020).

How did this happen? Although transportation and industrial activity declined, we became more tightly bound to communication and computational systems than ever before, meaning a heavily increased consumption of electricity.

According to the World Energy Outlook 2019, globally, 64% of the global electricity energy mix comes from fossil fuels (coal 38%, gas 23%, oil 3%: IEA 2019). Of course, *data-driven communication systems* rely on snowballing amounts of energy to function. It is crucial to ponder on these data in light of our increased reliance on data-driven communication systems.

Since fossil fuels are the largest source of greenhouse gas emissions, without fundamental shifts to renewable resources in global electricity production, we shall not be able to prevent incalculable climate catastrophes.

In the work I undertook with Graham Murdock for the book *Carbon Capitalism and Communication: Confronting Climate Crisis* (2017) we explained how important it is to expand communication scholarship that places the climate emergency at centre stage. This is what we set out to do with our discipline, political economy of communication, thus stressing the critical questions of this tradition: What are the political, economic and ideological power moulding data-driven communication systems? Who owns the critical infrastructures on which these systems run? From this scholarly perspective, communication systems cannot be interpreted only as sites of public discussion where meaning is created. We should understand communication systems as machines and infrastructures that deplete scarce resources in their production, consumption and disposal, thus increasing the amounts of energy in their use, and exacerbating the climate crisis (Brevini and Murdock, 2017).

Embracing an understanding of AI from a political economy of communication perspective (Brevini, 2020, 2021), this chapter establishes a research trajectory that emphasizes the materiality of AI, thus unveiling (and dispelling) powerful hypes and mythologies on AI. It thus explores the multifaceted ways in which AI is impacting the climate emergency and concludes by offering a set of solutions to limit the direct challenges that AI poses to our planet.

FROM DATA-DRIVEN COMMUNICATION SYSTEMS TO AI: DEFINING AI IN POLITICAL ECONOMY

Many AI applications are already so embedded in our everyday life that we no longer notice them. They are now employed in every sector of social, political and economic relevance. They are used to translate languages, guide agricultural businesses, assess climate threats, advise corporations on HR and investments, fly drones, diagnose diseases and protect borders.

From the AI-enabled camera that helps control traffic, the facial recognition scan at airports, the latest smartphone applications recommending music videos on YouTube and the smart homes powered by Amazon Alexa.

The AI industry is dominated by a handful of companies, mainly from the US and China (Brevini, 2021; Cognylitica, 2020; Ernst, 2020). In both the leading countries, AI applications are controlled by "Digital Lords" (Brevini, 2020a), the tech giants who have become to dominate technology developments, both in the West (Google, Microsoft, Apple, Facebook/Meta and Amazon) and in China (Baidu, Tencent, Alibaba). In the last decade after continuous acquisitions of startups and new market entries, the market of AI has become progressively more concentrated. (Brevini, 2021; Verdegem, 2022).[1] Besides the United States and China, many countries in the northern hemisphere have invested heavily in funding for AI technologies and intellectual property. France, Israel, the United Kingdom, South Korea and Japan have all joined the race for AI (Cognilytica, 2020).

As scholars have amply documented, for decades, the study of artificial intelligence (AI) and the study of communication have proceeded along different trajectories (Guzman and Lewis, 2019).

In popular discourse, AI is defined as the ability of machines to mimic and perform human cognitive functions. These include reasoning, learning, problem-solving, decision-making and even the attempt to match elements of human behaviour such as creativity. Moving towards a more comprehensive framework, established scholarship within human-machine communication (HMC) has understood AI agents not as mere AI technologies, but as communicative agents by focusing on the study of the "creation of meaning among humans and machines"

---

[1]　For an in-depth discussion of the connection between the unprecedented uptake of AI and data capitalism, see the volume "Is AI good for the planet" (2021), chapter 2.

(Guzman and Lewis, 2019: 1) and the refinement and development of theory related to people's interactions with technologies such as agents and robots (Lindgren and Holmström, 2020; Spence, 2019).

However, in previous work, I argued for a more comprehensive framework to understand AI which is deeply rooted in the political economy of communication, therefore, concerned with the political, economic, social and ideological structures in which AI is developed (Brevini, 2020, 2021). To understand AI from this perspective means to emphasize the unequal distribution of power and the social and ideological arrangements whereby such inequalities are maintained and reproduced (Murdock and Golding, 1974).

Such an approach entails an understanding of AI in its materiality (Lievrouw, 2014), placing an emphasis on its physical character, as a collection of technologies, machines and infrastructures that demand amounts of energy to compute, analyse and categorise. This in turn allows an analysis that can delve into the environmental costs, inequalities and harms of communication technologies which are often neglected by mainstream scholarship on AI.

HOW MYTHOLOGIES ON AI OBFUSCATE THE ENVIRONMENTAL HARMS THEY GENERATE

Before delving into details about the ways in which AI impacts the climate crisis, I want to ponder on the reasons for the policy silence (Freedman, 2010) on various aspects of the environmental harms produced by AI.

Consistently with a political economy of communication framework (Brevini, 2020b, 2021), I have looked at AI "myths", as powerful ideological devices that normalise conventional wisdom into "common sense" (Gramsci, 1971; Mosco, 2004; Brevini, 2020b), thus favouring established relations of power. Through this process, the values of powerful elites are naturalised, becoming the default position against which all things are assessed and compared. Thus, myths can influence and shape policymaking, as Wyatt notes: "Sometimes today's imaginary becomes tomorrow's lived reality" (Wyatt, 2004: 244).

It is through the legitimation of dominant narratives (Brevini and Schlosberg, 2016) that "common sense" can direct attention from the public, construct and promote digital developments and communication policy and legitimate modes of governance that would not have been possible without the establishment of such a narrative (Brevini and Schlosberg, 2016). There are three crucial ways myths are used in the context of legitimising the status quo. First, they are used as weapons to control political debates. Second, they are used to depoliticise discourses that would otherwise show their contested political character. Third, they are a crucial component of hegemonies, thus making it difficult for a counter-hegemonic discourse to arise (Brevini, 2020b, 2021).

Since its beginnings in the 1950s, AI has been portrayed as the magic tool to rescue the global capitalist system from its dramatic failures (Brevini, 2020; Natale and Ballatore, 2020; Elish and boyd, 2018). It has been surrounded by evocative claims about the imminent creation of a machine capable of surpassing the potential of humankind (Brevini, 2020; Natale and Ballatore, 2020; Elish and boyd, 2018).

Take, for example, a now-famous report entitled *Harnessing Artificial Intelligence for the Earth*, published in January 2018 by the World Economic Forum, comparing the AI revolution to the impact of electricity on humanity:

> AI is becoming the "electricity" of the Fourth Industrial Revolution, as innovators embed intelligence into more devices, application and interconnected systems. Beyond productivity gains, AI also promises to enable humans to develop intelligence not yet reached, opening the door to new discoveries. (WEF, 2018: 5)

Furthermore, it is not surprising that AI also promises to tackle the most urgent emergency: the climate crisis that the earth is facing. A famous report entitled *Harnessing Artificial Intelligence for the Earth*, published in January 2018 by the World Economic Forum, reiterated that the solution to the world's most pressing environmental challenges is to employ technological innovations and more specifically AI (World Economic Forum, 2018).

"We have a unique opportunity to harness this Fourth Industrial Revolution, and the societal shifts it triggers, to help address environmental issues and redesign how we manage our shared global environment" (World Economic Forum 2018: 3). "The intelligence and productivity gains that AI will deliver can unlock new solutions to society's most pressing environmental challenges: climate change, biodiversity, ocean health, water management, air pollution, and resilience, among others" (ibid, 19).

These mythologies on AI help construct a dominant narrative that reasserts the myth of a "technology fix" (Harvey, 2005) where AI is portrayed as a divine hand that can disrupt inequalities and power asymmetries, without the need to challenge the status quo. As a result, tech solutionism (Sætra, 2022: 103), the myth that technology can provide an easy fix to world inequalities, becomes "common sense": virtually any social problem can be subject to a technical and technological fix (Kurzweil, 1985).

The development of digital technology, we are reassured, will empower people out of radical inequalities, while naturalising market-based solutions to every issue of governance. Of course, the employment technological myths have a long history in the legitimation of a socio-political order (Mosco, 2004; Freedman, 2004; Brevini, 2020; Bory, 2020).

For example, "techno solutionism myths" kept getting stronger throughout the 1970s, 1980s and 1990s, "more attuned to the climate of Thatcherism and Reaganism" (ibid, 21) than to a Keynesian state's framework. The neoliberal Clinton administration of the 1990s was an aggressive supporter of the technocratic "information revolution" and "techno solutionism". In 1994, congress passed the National Information Infrastructure Bill, which launched the worldwide famous "information superhighway", championed by Al Gore in numerous speeches around the world. Another crucial futurologist of the time stressed once again the link between technological determinism and neoliberal ideologies. Francis Fukuyama's influential book, *The End of History* (1992), proclaimed that the end of the Cold War demonstrated the collapse of any reasonable alternative to neoliberalism. Moreover, in order to reinstate the alliance between neoliberalism and technology, in *The Great Disruption* (2017), Fukuyama argues:

> A society built around information tends to produce more of the two things people value most in a modern democracy – freedom and equality. Freedom of choice has exploded, in everything from cable channels to low-cost shopping outlets to friends met on the Internet. Hierarchies of all sorts, political and corporate, have come under pressure and begun to crumble. (Fukuyama, 2017: 4)

As Elish and boyd's research (2018) elucidated, "through the manufacturing of hype and promise, the business community has helped produce rhetoric around these technologies that extend far past the current methodological capabilities" (Elish & boyd, 2018: 58).

In exploring public discourse shaping the popular imagination around possible AI futures, Goode (2018) observes that contemporary discourse is

> skewed heavily towards specific voices – predominantly male science fiction authors and techno-centric scientists, futurists and entrepreneurs – and the field of AI and robotics is all too easily presented as a kind of sublime spectacle of inevitability (…) that does little to offer lay citizens the sense that they can be actively involved in shaping its future. (Goode, 2018: 204)

Through this process of legitimation and repetition of these mythologies on AI, the values of powerful elites are turned into a default position where AI becomes the magic, artificial, divine hand that will rescue society. These mythologies thus radically exclude the emergence of a counter-hegemonic narrative that re-centres the focus on the *materiality* of the machines, infrastructure and devices that are crucial for AI to function (Brevini, 2020, 2021).

Instead, we must analyse AI as technologies, machines and infrastructures if we want to address the question of its environmental costs, thus placing the climate emergency at centre stage.

HOW AI IMPACTS THE CLIMATE CRISIS

In order to understand the multiple environmental costs associated with AI we should begin with an analysis of the life cycle of AI and its global supply, starting with a kind of "extractivism" (Smart, 2017) and disregard for social and environmental justice that AI currently requires to produce, transport, train and dispose (Brevini, 2021).

In order to produce the material devices needed for AI to run, we need to start exploring its planetary costs by considering the extraction of rare metals and mineral sources that are needed following the logics of colonialism.

In her work on digital developments with humanitarian structures, Mirca Madianou (2019) has developed the notion of "technocolonialism" in order to analyse how "the convergence of digital developments with humanitarian structures and market forces reinvigorate and rework colonial legacies" (2019a: 2). Here, I am employing technocolonialism to reaffirm how the same "tenacity of colonial genealogies and inequalities" (Madianou, 2020: 1) characterise the global supply chains of AI, as the extractive nature of technocolonialism resides in the minerals that need to be mined to make the hardware for AI applications. (Smart, 2017). So, for example, the European Communication has stressed that the demand for lithium in the EU, mainly in batteries, is projected to rise by 3500% by 2050 (EC, 2022).

Moving to the second phase of the global supply chain, the production and training of AI models also show high environmental costs.

A study published in 2019 by the College of Information and Computer Sciences at the University of Massachusetts Amherst (Strubell et al., 2019) quantifies the energy consumed by running artificial intelligence programs. In the case examined by the study, a common AI training model in linguistics emitted more than 284 tonnes of equivalent carbon dioxide (ibid). This is comparable to five times the lifetime emissions of the average American car.[2] It is also comparable to roughly 100 return flights from London to NYC. Meanwhile, the converged com-

---

[2]   This study assessed the energy consumption necessary to train four large neural networks, a type of AI used for processing language. It should be noted that these types of language-processing AIs are at the basis of the algorithms that, for example, are used by Google Translate or Open AI.

munication systems upon which AI relies generate a plethora of environmental problems of their own, most notably energy consumption and emissions, material toxicity and electronic waste (Brevini and Murdock, 2017). According to the International Energy Agency, if the energy demand continues to accelerate at the current pace, the residential electricity needed to power electronics will rise to 30% of global consumption by 2022 and 45% by 2030 (Maxwell, 2015).

Artificial intelligence relies on data to work. At present, cloud computing eats up energy at a rate somewhere between the national consumption of Japan and that of India (Greenpeace International, 2011; Murdock and Brevini, 2019). Today, data centres' energy usage averages 200 terawatt hours (TWh) each year (Jones, 2018; International Energy Agency, 2017) more than the national energy consumption of some countries, including Iran. Moreover, the information and communications technology (ICT) sector, which includes mobile phone networks, digital devices and televisions, amounts to 2% of global emissions (Jones, 2018). Greenhouse gas emissions from the information and communication industry could grow from roughly 1–1.6% in 2007 to exceed 14% worldwide by 2040, accounting for more than half of the current relative contributions of the whole transportation sector.

Moreover, data centres require large, continuous supplies of water for their cooling systems, raising serious policy issues in places like the US and Australia where years of drought have ravaged communities (Mosco, 2017). As the website of Google's DeepMind website explains (Evans and Gao, 2016):

> One of the primary sources of energy use in the data centre environment is cooling (…). Our data centres – which contain servers powering Google Search, Gmail, YouTube, etc. – also generate a lot of heat that must be removed to keep the servers running. This cooling is typically accomplished via large industrial equipment such as pumps, chillers and cooling towers.

According to DeepMind, the solution to this problem is of course machine learning (ibid), which is also extremely energy-consuming and generative of carbon emissions.

At the end of the global supply chain, we should also consider the problem of the disposal of the devices employed in AI.

When communication machines are discarded, they become electronic waste or e-waste, saddling local municipalities with the challenge of safe disposal. This task is so burdensome that it is frequently offshored, and many countries with developing economies have become digital dumping grounds for more privileged nations (Brevini and Murdock, 2017).

Finally, while promising to solve the climate emergency, AI companies are marketing their offers and services to coal, oil and gas companies, thus compromising efforts to reduce emissions and divest from fossil fuels. A new report on the future of AI in the oil and gas market published by Zion Market Research (Zion Market Research, 2019) found that the sector of AI in oil and gas is expected to reach around US$4.01 billion globally by 2025 from 1.75 billion in 2018. AI companies around the world are pushing their capabilities to the oil and gas sectors to increase their efficiencies, optimise their operations and increase productivity: in other words, they are selling their services to increase the pace and productivity of excavation and drilling. Exxon Mobil, for example, signed a partnership in February this year with Microsoft to deploy AI programs, while oil and gas exploration in the fragile ecosystem of Brazil has seen recent employment of AI technology by state oil giant Petrobras; similarly, European oil major Royal Dutch Shell has signed a partnership with AI company C3 (Joppa and Herweijer, 2018).

PLACING THE CLIMATE EMERGENCY AT THE CENTRE OF SCHOLARSHIP

New developments of AI place escalating demands on energy, water and resources in their production, transportation and use, reinforcing a culture of hyper-consumerism, and adding to the accumulating amounts of waste and pollution already generated by accelerating rates of digital obsolescence and disposal (see Brevini, 2021; Gabrys, 2013). Instead of embracing the mythologies of AI that portray it as the magic wand that will fix the world and capitalism problems, we should start quantifying and considering the environmental costs and damages of the current acceleration of AI.

We need to ask who should own and control the essential infrastructures that power data communication and AI and make sure to place the climate emergency at the centre of the debate on sustainable development. How can we shape the future of AI to be one of collective well-being and minimised climate impact?

Progress is being made at global fora and national levels as international agreements, legislative frameworks, position papers and guidelines are being drawn up by the European Union and Council of Europe, and UNESCO (2021) has just adopted a new Recommendation on the Ethics of Artificial Intelligence.

Despite this, however, it seems that global discussions on the climate emergency – for example, in the context of UN COP – are yet to soundly connect environmental with AI policy discussions, and more research is needed to ascertain the environmental damage caused by artificial intelligence.

As this chapter showed, if we consider the material basis of AI and look at its techno-colonialist character, we are able to account for all its environmental costs. They start with mineral extractions, water, energy and natural resources necessary for hardware and machine production; additional resource depletion is generated by the distribution, transportation and post-consumption of material technology to end with major e-waste disposal needs. Added to this is the major environmental cost of data extraction, computing and analysis.

We know that many corporations now audit the production conditions of subcontractors' factories, but there is still an urgent need to demand accountability for those who own clouds and data centres. One crucial intervention could be a government-mandated green certification for server farms and centres to achieve zero emissions. Given AI's increasing computing capabilities, the disclosure of its carbon footprint could be a first step in the right direction. This could take the form of a tech carbon footprint label, which would provide information about the raw materials used, the carbon costs involved and what recycling options are available, resulting in stronger public awareness about the implications of adopting a piece of smart technology.

Making transparent the energy used to produce, transport, assemble and deliver the technology we use daily would enable policymakers to make more informed decisions and the public to make more informed choices. Added to this could be policy interventions that request manufacturers to lengthen the lifespan of smart devices and provide spare parts to replace faulty components.

Additionally, global policymaking should encourage educational programmes to enhance green tech literacy, raising awareness of the costs of hyper-consumerism and the importance of responsible energy consumption. Green tech literacy programmes should include interventions banning the production of products that are too data-demanding and energy-depleting.

For example, the recent request by the EU commissioner to lower the default quality of video stream services by Netflix, YouTube and Amazon to preserve bandwidth during the corona-virus lockdowns was a good practice in this direction. As the recent global pandemic crisis has shown, governments around the world can act fast when urgent action is needed for the public good. What is needed now is to embrace a green agenda for AI that puts the climate emergency at centre stage and should not be delayed any longer.

FURTHER READING

Brevini, B. (2021) *Is AI good for the planet?* Cambridge: Polity.
Brevini, B. and Murdock, G. (2017) *Carbon capitalism and communication: Confronting climate crisis*. Cham: Palgrave.
Gabrys, J. (2011) *Digital rubbish: A natural history of electronics*. University of Michigan Press.
Maxwell, R. and Miller, T. (2020) *How green is your smartphone?* Cambridge: Polity.
Techno Solutionism for Sustainable Development. (2023, in press) Edited by H. Sætra. New York: Routledge.

REFERENCES

Bory, P. (2020) *The internet myth: From the internet imaginary to network ideologies*. London: University of Westminster Press.
Brevini, B. (2020) Black boxes, not green: Mythologizing artificial intelligence and omitting the environment. *Big Data & Society*, 7(2), 205395172093514. doi:10.1177/2053951720935141.
Brevini, B. (2020a) *Conclusion in "Amazon: Understanding a global communication giant"*. New York: Routledge.
Brevini, B. (2020b) Creating the technological saviour: Discourses on AI in Europe and the legitimation of super capitalism. In P. Verdegem (Ed.), *AI for Everyone?* (p. 145).
Brevini, B. (2021) *Is AI good for the planet?* Cambridge: Polity.
Brevini, B. and Murdock, G. (2017) *Carbon capitalism and communication confronting climate crisis*. London and New York: Palgrave Macmillan.
Cognilytica. (2020) Worldwide country AI strategies and competitiveness 2020. Cognilytica, February 7. https://www.cognilytica.com/download/worldwide-country-ai-strategies-and-competitiveness-2020-cgr-str20.
Ernst, D. (2020) Competing in artificial intelligence chips: China's challenge amid technology war. Centre for International Governance Innovation, March 26. https://www.cigionline.org/publications/competing-artificial-intelligence-chips-chinas-challenge-amid-technology-war.
European Commission. (2022) Communication from the Commission to the European Parliament and the Council "Strategic Foresight Report Twinning the green and digital transitions in the new geopolitical context".
Evans, R. and Gao, J. (2016) DeepMind AI reduces Google data centre cooling bill by 40%. Deepmind. https://deepmind.com/blog/article/deepmind-ai-reduces-google-data-centre-cooling-bill-40.
Fukuyama, F. (1992) *The end of history and the last man*. New York: Simon & Schuster.
Gabrys, J. (2013) Plastic and the work of the biodegradable. In J. Gabrys, G. Hawkins and M. Michael (Eds.), *Accumulation: The material politics of plastic* (pp. 208–227). London: Routledge.
Gössling, S. and Humpe, A. (2020) The global scale, distribution and growth of aviation: Implications for climate change. *Global Environmental Change*, 65, 1–12. https://doi.org/10.1016/j.gloenvcha.2020.102194.
Global Commission. 2018 report of the global commission on the economy and climate. https://newclimateeconomy.report/.

Greenpeace International. (2011) How dirty is your data? A look at the energy choices that power cloud computing. Corrected version, May 24. https://www.greenpeace.org/static/planet4-international-stateless/2011/04/4cceba18-dirty-data-report-greenpeace.pdf.

Guzman, A. L. and Lewis, S. C. (2019) Artificial intelligence and communication: A human–machine communication research agenda. *New Media & Society*, 22(1), 70–86. https://doi.org/10.1177/1461444819858691.

Harvey, D. (2005) *The new imperialism*. Oxford: Oxford University Press.

IEA. (2017) *Digitalisation and energy*. IEA: Paris. https://www.iea.org/reports/digitalisation-and-energy.

IEA. (2019) *World energy outlook 2019*. IEA: Paris. https://www.iea.org/reports/world-energy-outlook-2019.

IEA. (2020) *Global energy review 2020*. IEA: Paris https://www.iea.org/reports/global-energy-review-2020.

IPCC (Intergovernmental Panel on Climate Change) (2022) The intergovernmental panel on climate change. https://www.ipcc.ch/report/sixth-assessment-report-working-group-ii/.

Lievrouw, L. A. (2014) Materiality and media in communication and technology studies: An unfinished project. *Media Technologies: Essays on Communication, Materiality, and Society*, 21–51.

Lindgren, S. and Holmström, J. (2020) A social science perspective on artificial intelligence: Building blocks for a research agenda. *Journal of Digital Social Research (JDSR)*, 2(3).

Madianou, M. (2019) Technocolonialism: Digital innovation and data practices in the humanitarian response to the refugee crisis. *Social Media and Society,* 5(3). https://doi.org/10.1177/2056305119863146.

Maxwell, R. and Miller, T. (2015) High-tech consumerism, a global catastrophe happening on our watch. The Conversation, September 11. https://theconversation.com/high-tech-consumerism-a-global-catastrophe-happening-on-our-watch-43476.

Milkround. (2021) Gen Z lead the way through lockdown with tech skills that boost productivity. Accessed February 8, 2022. https://www.milkround.com/advice/gen-z-lead-the-way-through-lockdon-with-tech-skills-that-boost-productivity.

Mosco, V. (2004) *The digital sublime: Myth, power, and cyberspace*. Cambridge, MA: MIT Press.

Mosco, V. (2017) The next internet. In *Carbon capitalism and communication* (1st ed.). Sydney: Palgrave Macmillan.

Murdock, G. and Golding, P. (1974) For a political economy of mass communications. In R. Miliband and J. Saville (Eds.). https://socialistregister.com/index.php/srv/article/view/5355/2256.

Sætra, H. S. (2022) *AI for the sustainable development goals*. Boca Raton, FL: CRC Press.

Smart, S. (2017) Resistance against mining extractivism in Chile. *Critical Planning*, 23.

Strubell, E., Ganesh, A. and McCallum, A. (2019) Energy and policy considerations for deep learning in NLP. Cornell University. arXiv:1906.02243.

UN News. (2020) Carbon dioxide levels hit new record; COVID impact 'a tiny blip', WMO says. United Nations. https://news.un.org/en/story/2020/11/1078322.

United Nations Environment Programme. (2019) *Emissions gap report 2019*. Nairobi: UNEP.

Verdegem, P. (2022) Dismantling AI capitalism: The commons as an alternative to the power concentration of Big Tech. *AI & Society*. https://doi.org/10.1007/s00146-022-01437-8.

World Economic Forum. (2018) Harnessing artificial intelligence for the Earth. WE Forum. https://www3.weforum.org/docs/Harnessing_Artificial_Intelligence_for_the_Earth_report_2018.pdf.

Zion Market Research. (2019) Global AI in oil and gas market. Intrado GlobeNewsare. https://www.globenewswire.com/newsrelease/2019/07/18/1884499/0/en/Global-AI-In-Oil-and-Gas-Market-Will-Reach-to-USD-4-01-Billion-By-2025-Zion-Market-Research.html. https://socialistregister.com/index.php/srv/article/view/5355/2256.

United Nations. (2020) United Nations news 2020. https://news.un.org/en/story/2020/11/1078322.

76. AI governance and civil society: the need for critical engagement

Megan LePere-Schloop and Sandy Zook

INTRODUCTION

Artificial intelligence (AI) is part of a broader system of knowledge production where power is not evenly distributed (Adams 2021; Mohamed, Png, and Isaac 2020). In this system, knowledge production that relies on 'rational' statistical and computational methods are privileged, helping to explain why AI systems broadly—and machine learning algorithms specifically—are increasingly integrated into public and private sector decision-making (Gandy 2010; O'Neil 2016). Experts anticipate that new AI developments may transform power, welfare, and wealth at a scale comparable to the industrial and nuclear revolutions (Grace et al. 2018), while critical work asserts that AI is altering what it means to be human (Adams 2021). Individuals, organizations and institutions around the world are developing approaches to AI governance (Dafoe 2018; Jobin, Ienca, and Vayena 2019; Schiff et al. 2020; World Economic Forum 2021), which a 2018 Oxford report describes as 'devising global norms, policies, and institutions to best ensure the beneficial development and use of advanced AI' (Dafoe 2018, 1).

In recent years, critical scholarship has called attention to significant shortcomings of prominent approaches to AI governance (Adams 2021; Erman and Furendal 2022; Ganesh and Moss 2022; Schiff et al. 2020; Stark, Greene, and Hoffmann 2021; Ulnicane et al. 2021). One common critique is that AI governance needs to center the full diversity of people affected by AI, not simply technocratic elites. Another overarching critique is the need to attend to the ways that broader systems of knowledge production reproduce inequality by foregrounding 'Western rationality'[1] to shape AI governance. However, critical technology scholars often provide broad prescriptions on the need to center AI stakeholders and disrupt power structures without elaborating on strategies for doing so.

Civil Society provides the space and structure to facilitate engagement of AI stakeholders and shift power, particularly through civil society organizations (CSOs) focused on technical training, policy advocacy, issue education, and deliberative discourse. Utilizing a typology of civil society roles (Levine Daniel and Fyall 2019; Moulton and Eckerd 2012), we situate the potential opportunities for civil society to contribute to critical AI governance discourses. Similar to critical scholarship elucidating critiques of AI governance, we also draw on critical civil society scholarship to identify important barriers and pitfalls of CSO efforts to redistribute power and amplify marginalized perspectives within these systems.

In this chapter, we argue that critical technology and civil society scholarship need greater integration to address challenges and generate more robust research and discussions around

---

[1] 'Western rationality' is the prioritization of Western (i.e., European and North American) notions of knowledge production, values and institutions—such as, democratic political systems and capitalist economic systems. This results in prioritization of 'Western rationality' over non-Western and/or localized contexts.

civil society's role in AI governance. We begin the work of integration by identifying insights from civil society research that enhance our understanding of three AI governance challenges and corresponding civil society roles. Specifically, we discuss how CSOs can help diversify the ranks of the technocratic elite through direct service provision; develop innovative goods, services, and networks for AI governance through direct service provision and bridging; and integrate AI stakeholders to reimagine AI governance through bridging and policy advocacy. This work contributes to critical research on AI governance (Adams 2021; Ganesh and Moss 2022; Stark, Greene, and Hoffmann 2021; Ulnicane et al. 2021) and the emergent body of work on the intersection of AI and civil society (Duberry 2019; LePere-Schloop et al. 2022).

AI GOVERNANCE

AI governance is in a pre-paradigmatic state, meaning that actors are currently jostling for power and position while working to identify key terms and concepts, as well as determining how and what questions are pertinent to the development of the field. Calls to address AI governance are increasingly prominent (Jobin, Ienca, and Vayena 2019; Schiff et al. 2020; World Economic Forum 2021). While the need for AI governance is clear, the solutions around which corporations, global institutions, and governments are converging raise important critiques.

Critical scholarship highlights the shortcomings of AI governance mechanisms, best practices, and discourse for their inability to foreground justice and redistribute power. Stark, Greene, and Hoffman (2021) identify five broad categories of convergent AI governance mechanisms: governance through tools, principles, regulations and standards, human rights, and securitization. AI governance through tools focuses on algorithm design solutions implemented by technocratic elites, while AI governance through principles asks Big Tech firms to adhere to statements of shared values for AI design and deployment. AI governance by regulations and standards recognizes a place for third-party oversight of technocratic elites and Big Tech firms, while human rights-based approaches suggest extending protections for individuals through the framework of international human rights law. Securitization connects AI governance to the strategic priorities of nation-states and coalitions thereof. These convergent AI governance mechanisms reproduce the power of technocratic elites, Big Tech firms, and the Global North by foregrounding notions of 'Western rationality' and marginalizing AI stakeholders outside of the Global North, Big Tech firms and the ranks of the technocratic elite (Adams 2021; Mohamed, Png, and Isaac 2020). As such, these AI governance mechanisms reproduce unjust social structures and undemocratic norms (Erman and Furendal 2022; Ganesh and Moss 2022; Stark, Greene, and Hoffmann 2021).

Across the five categories of AI governance mechanisms, critical perspectives underscore the need for broader and deeper engagement of AI stakeholders and recognition that AI systems are embedded in social structures where power is not equally distributed. For example, Stark et al (2021) highlight the need to engage AI stakeholders in more than algorithmic design processes as prescribed by tool, principle, and standards-based governance mechanisms. The authors further challenge the problem definitions at the heart of human rights and securitization approaches to AI governance because they foreground actors and priorities of the Global North. Similarly, Anghie (2007) has critiqued the human rights framework as prioritizing political over economic rights, enabling the ongoing exploitation of populations in the Global South. Securitization, like AI governance, is framed as a technical problem, exacerbating digital inequality between the Global North and South (Chowdhury 2019). Alternative approaches in AI governance center diverse stakeholders' socially and historically grounded experiences to shape the discourse, problem definition and solution identification undergirding AI governance (Adams 2021; Ganesh and Moss 2022; Mohamed, Png, and Isaac 2020; Stark, Greene, and Hoffmann 2021).

This brief overview of AI governance and associated critiques highlights both the current importance and the need for deeper engagement of stakeholders and consideration of power and inequality in AI governance. We argue that civil society has important roles to play in realizing this shift, but that it also faces critical challenges. We next define civil society and clarify the roles it can potentially play in AI governance.

CIVIL SOCIETY

Civil society[2] permeates every country globally—regardless of political regime, and social and economic context. The size and scope of civil society, however, varies across countries based on these contexts, but consists of a complex array of individuals, groups and organizations occupying the space between government and private sector (i.e., for-profit corporations). For the purposes of this chapter, we adopt the World Bank definition of civil society—used and replicated by a variety of different international institutions—'the wide array of non-governmental and not for profit organizations that have a presence in public life, express the interests and values of their members and others, based on ethical, cultural, political, scientific, religious or philanthropic considerations' (World Bank 2022).

For the purposes of examining civil society's roles in AI governance, we further home our scope to formal and legally registered civil society organizations CSOs. These organizations are by definition: separate from and not controlled by government; have a set of policies and/or by-laws overseen by a governing body, such that the organization is self-governed; and have complete or substantial profit-distribution limits with some type of clearly stated social purpose (Salamon and Sokolowski 2016).

A well-established body of theoretical and empirical research helps us understand the distinguishing characteristics of CSOs and the roles they play in society, and vis-à-vis the government and for-profit sectors. Traditional civil society theory utilizes Weisbrod's (1977) public good theory and Hansmann's (1980) contract failure theory—asserting that CSOs utilize collective action, acting altruistically through trust and connection with the populations they serve. As such, civil society assumes several roles, acting as intermediaries between the government, private sector and society—as bridges, collaborators, advocates and wielding soft power to influence actors and policy (Levine Daniel and Fyall 2019; Nye 1990). Building on these early theories, subsequent research has sought to develop typologies of civil society's role as an intermediary (i.e., public-private partnerships, three failures theory, government-nonprofit typologies).

---

[2]   Depending on the institutional context, civil society comprises and/or is identified by many different names, including the third sector, nongovernmental sector or nonprofit sector. Similar to the civil society sector, organizations within civil society are identified by several names, depending on institutional context. Examples include: civil society organizations, nongovernmental organizations, nonprofits, or social purpose organizations. For the purpose of this chapter we will use the terms civil society and civil society organizations (CSOs).

Focusing on civil society's role as connectors and implementers within the AI governance infrastructure, we selected Moulton and Eckerd (2012) typology for civil society roles within a policy implementation infrastructure. We consolidate this framework to focus on three primary roles of civil society (Moulton and Eckerd's roles in italics):

- Direct *Service Provision:* Civil Society provides goods and services, and/or implements policy alone or in partnership with other sectors. This includes *innovation,* including the provision of new or improved goods or services, new processes for delivery, or new organizational structures and methods to delivering products and services (Monroe-White and Zook 2018).
- Policy Advocacy: While Moulton and Eckerd (2012) specifically identify *Political Advocacy,* we broaden this to include the array of advocacy activities civil society engages with across sectors. This includes wielding soft power to influence actors (Nye 1990). Soft power is non-monetary, non-military power—examples include Freedom House's Democracy Index, or public information campaigns to raise public awareness and pressure organizations to be better stewards of the public good.
- Bridging: *Social Capital Creation* and *Individual Expression* and *Citizen Engagement* represent relational, values-based approaches civil society use to engage individuals and groups in participation, community building and democratic processes.

Civil society is traditionally portrayed as altruistic, acting on behalf of the public good and bridging access to goods and services for specific populations excluded from provision in other sectors. Emergent research, however, scrutinizes civil society from various critical perspectives (i.e., critical race theory, LGBTQ+/queer theory, feminist theory, theory of racialized organizations, decolonization). These critical perspectives highlight that civil society theory is grounded in neo-liberal democratic, capitalist systems of the Global North (Mercer 2002). The critiques from these perspectives align with similar critical perspectives on AI governance, in that civil society can indeed succumb to pitfalls that reinforce unjust systems and institutional norms. This includes being co-opted and coerced by government, the for-profit sector and other civil society actors.

One such example from civil society that has significant parallels to AI governance problems is resource dependency theory and associated power imbalances. Resource dependency arises when organizations depend on external resource providers, resulting in resource providers wielding power over the operations of recipient organizations (Pfeffer and Salancik 2003). Many CSOs rely on donations and grants, and research finds that resource dependency can affect the strategy and operations of CSOs (AbouAssi 2013; Barman 2008; Bouchard and Raufflet 2019). For example, North-South international development partnerships characterize Global South actors as resource dependent on Global North funders (AbouAssi 2013; Elbers and Arts 2011). This results in fiscal and structural power imbalances, whereby Global North institutions set rules for receiving funding, as well as the scope and nature of development activities, thus enforcing Global North institutions, ideologies, and definitions, overriding the importance of local institutional contexts (AbouAssi 2013; Edwards and Hulme 1996).

Resource dependency leads to three primary challenges for CSOs. First, CSOs may become more responsive to funders, than local populations (AbouAssi 2013; O'Brien and Evans 2017). This leads to top-down mandates and foregrounding of 'Western rationality' over local contexts. Second, in response to donor demands for funding accountability and proof of impact,

CSOs may frame their work paternalistically—focusing on resource guarding and viewing local populations as beneficiaries and recipients—rather than local populations as partners and collaborators. Third, resource dependency can result in CSO being co-opted or coerced by organizations with greater power. CSOs in this case lose their agency to enact inclusive development projects and their autonomy to act as bridges to local populations.

Counter to these narratives, critical perspectives utilize a decolonization lens to assert that Global South organizations bring a variety of financial and non-financial resources to North-South partnerships, including legitimacy, local knowledge, and connections to local populations (O'Brien and Evans 2017). Thus, critical perspectives seek to reassess, redefine, and realign power, inclusive of local non-financial resources. Strategies for combating the foregrounding of 'Western rationality', acting paternalistically, and co-optation and coercion emphasize inclusive, participatory governance models for CSOs—similar to discussions we observe in critical AI governance.

Using the framing from this section, we examine the potential roles civil society can occupy in AI governance, incorporating appropriate critical perspectives to identify potential pitfalls for civil society actors. In the next section, we engage and interweave critical perspectives in AI governance and civil society research to identify avenues for civil society to contribute to and advance inclusive perspectives in AI governance.

ROLES AND CHALLENGES FOR CIVIL SOCIETY IN AI GOVERNANCE

Critical scholarship examines how AI governance mechanisms and discourse reproduce the hegemony of technocratic elites, Big Tech firms, and the Global North. Diversifying the stakeholders engaged in AI governance decision-making and re-framing AI governance discourse around issues of equity, justice, and social change can help disrupt the status quo.

CSOs have multiple roles to play in disrupting the status quo. In this section, we identify three AI governance challenges and corresponding civil society roles based on Moulton and Eckerd's (2012) typology:

- Diversifying the ranks of the technocratic elite by providing technical training and career support to under-represented groups (direct service provision).
- Developing innovative goods, services, and networks for AI governance including algorithm risk assessment tools and professional associations (direct service provision and bridging).
- Integrating AI stakeholders to reimagine AI governance by educating the public and organizing collective action to shape corporate and public policy, as well as defining challenges in terms of equity, justice and social change (bridging and policy advocacy).

While we discuss each of the three challenges and corresponding roles in turn, Figure 76.1 highlights their overlapping and interconnected nature. Diversifying technocratic ranks aids in developing innovative goods and services for AI governance. What is more, many of the technocratic elites innovating goods and services for AI governance left Big Tech because their perspectives were marginalized. Finally, diversifying the ranks of the technocratic elite helps integrate diverse stakeholders in AI governance, and the integration of diverse perspectives

Figure 76.1   *Overlapping narratives of inclusive AI governance*

outside of Big Tech goes hand in hand with the development of innovative AI governance solutions. Progress in any one area, provides opportunities for synergy with the other areas.

Diversifying the Ranks of the Technocratic Elite to Shape AI Governance

At present, AI governance discourse often frames the issue as a technical problem with correspondingly technical solutions, both of which center technocratic elites and Big Tech firms (Stark, Greene, and Hoffmann 2021). While technocratic elites and Big Tech firms are distributed around the globe, a recent report finds that the flow of AI talent is mediated by the Global North and that the US is the global 'hub' for AI research and education (Gagné 2018). The diversity of the US tech sector (or lack thereof), therefore has global implications for AI Governance. Women, Hispanics and African-Americans are under-represented in the US tech sector compared to companies overall across industries (US EEOC 2014). Because current AI Governance discourse and the mechanisms it promotes help White, male, technocratic elites working in the Global North maintain economic, political, and social power, they have little incentive to advance alternative discourses and mechanisms.

While not a panacea, efforts to foster greater diversity in the tech sector could help center a wider range of human perspectives and priorities. Research on representative bureaucracy suggests that the socio-demographic characteristics of individuals in front-line and managerial roles (i.e. team leaders and programmers involved in algorithm design) shape decisions in ways that benefit the social identity groups they represent, and equity and justice goals more broadly (Groeneveld and Meier 2022). In Big Tech, this insight is reflected in the fact that firms often draw upon civil liberty experts and individuals with diverse identities, such as Timnit Gebru, when creating ethical AI research and review boards (Bordelon 2022; Suarez 2021).

CSOs can support diversification of the tech sector by providing free and/or accessible technical training to marginalized groups. For example, Ada Academy is a Seattle-based CSO school that provides free training in software development to women and gender diverse people (Ada Academy 2019). While this work is important, critical scholarship on civil society also highlights a pitfall that could undermine the effect that Ada Academy and similar CSOs could have on AI Governance; namely, resource dependency. As previously discussed in our section on Civil Society, resource dependency arises when organizations depend on external resource providers, which gives these resource providers power over organizational operations (Pfeffer and Salancik 2003). According to their 2021 Annual Report, thirty-two percent of Ada Academy's revenue came from corporate sponsorship, most of which was provided by Big Tech firms (Lindsey et al. 2021). To the extent that Ada Academy and similar CSOs depend on Big Tech firms and/or donations from technocratic elites, resource dependence may lead them to avoid providing training and fostering discourse around AI Governance that runs counter to the preferences of Big Tech.

Diversifying the ranks of the technocratic elite calls on civil society predominantly in the service delivery role. AI experts with diverse identities are playing leading roles in AI governance, and CSOs are providing technical training to help bring more diverse perspectives into Big Tech. Resource dependency, however, could disrupt this work, as CSOs providing technical training often rely on funding and partnerships with Big Tech.

Developing Innovative Goods, Services, and Professional Networks for AI Governance

Even if Big Tech becomes more diverse, this does not guarantee that firms will attend to AI perspectives that do not align with their preferred AI governance solutions. Civil society thus also has an important role to play in innovating goods and services for AI governance outside of Big Tech.

In fact, as corporations including Google have moved to disband ethical AI boards and research groups, some disillusioned employees have created socially minded nonprofits and social enterprises (both types of CSOs) to combat challenges exacerbated by Big Tech (Grant and Eidelson 2022). Unfortunately, many examples of this exodus include AI experts from diverse background who found their voices marginalized in Big Tech firms. This includes Timnit Gebru, who identifies as a refugee and Black woman, who left Google to join the CSO Distributed AI Research; Rumman Chowdhury, who left Big Tech to form Parity AI, a company that helps organizations manage risk by assessing their AI algorithms; and, Krishna Gade, who left Facebook to form Fidler, helping organizations understand and improve their AI transparency (Hao 2021; Suarez 2021).

In its current pre-paradigmatic state, technocratic elites are also developing professional associations organized around critical AI governance, such as the Ethical AI Governance Group (EAIGG no date). CSOs like EAIGG provide networking opportunities to technology professionals, entrepreneurs, and investors interested in responsible AI, helping them to develop professional social capital. These CSOs are also mapping the infrastructure of organizations doing work in areas related to their mission, making it easier for actors from civil society, government, and for-profit firms to connect on the shared interest of AI governance.

Unfortunately, resource dependency may also be a challenge to CSOs providing innovative goods and services for AI governance. To the extent that these organizations are overly dependent on contracts with certain clients, especially Big Tech firms, CSOs can suffer from mission drift as they adapt to the preferences of key clients. Professional associations like EAIGG can similarly be shaped by the influence of Big Tech to the extent that they rely on sponsorships or access to firms for membership recruitment.

This section reflects CSOs service delivery role and its bridging role in AI governance, facilitating social capital creation and individual self-expression through professional association. Civil society must be mindful of resource dependence and the challenges faced by defunct AI ethics departments and boards, so that their mission and goals are not co-opted by clients and sponsors.

Integrating Diverse Stakeholders to Reimagine AI Governance Discourses

While CSOs have important roles to play as innovators of good and services, and as bridges connecting professionals and organizations invested in AI governance, these efforts have an important limitation: they tend to center technocratic elites and exclude other AI stakeholders. In this section, we discuss the critical role that CSOs can play in centering marginalized stakeholders in AI governance.

Globally, organizations from all sectors—from Big Tech to multi-lateral organizations (i.e., United Nations, World Economic Forum), international CSOs to central governments- are publishing AI governance handbooks, manuals, and policy agendas. Each seeks to identify and define key terminology around AI governance—transparency, safety, ethics, accountability—as well as elucidate ethical standards and identify policy and regulatory opportunities. Each seeks to seize space and power within the AI governance discourse, either within a specific country or region or on the global stage.

To date, defining and implementing AI governance has predominantly occurred with Global North organizations leading—even controlling—the discourse. This means that definitions, concepts and discussions predominantly reflect neo-liberal democratic norms and 'Western rationality' (Adams 2021; Mohamed, Png, and Isaac 2020). CSOs can build and incorporate bottom-up approaches to AI governance dialogue, to draw out context-rich conceptualizations and definitions of key terms from marginalized perspectives. Decolonial perspectives in AI governance highlight the context-specific nature of terms, such as ethics, accountability and transparency, which illuminate context-specific challenges within the AI governance infrastructure (Mohamed, Png, and Isaac 2020). For example, context shapes understandings and issues related to data ethics and transparency. The Global South produces data, but often that data is owned and harvested by Global North corporations and governments, with Global South governments and populations having little to no power or ownership over the data they produce (Stark, Greene, and Hoffmann 2021).

As efforts to globally map the AI infrastructure emerge, such as where tech employees work and the headquarters of AI corporations (e.g., AI Ethicist, EAIGG and Knowledge 4 All [K4All]), they highlight the disparities between the Global North and South. Organizations working on AI governance issues exist in every world region; however, comparing K4All's map of the Global South to similar maps of the Global North provides a stark contrast of opportunities and infrastructure relevant to AI governance (Knowledge 4 All Foundation Ltd. n.d.). Similarly, AI Talent mapped employees and AI conferences by country, finding strong concentrations of employment and conferences in the Global North (Gagné 2018). Many Global South countries had missing or incomplete data due to challenges and bias in the data collection process. These data collection challenges have ramifications for identifying and integrating AI stakeholders in non-Western contexts into AI governance. Namely, by using Western systems for communication and networking, such as LinkedIn, to identify AI professionals, efforts to invite and include stakeholders in AI governance discourse will be biased. This also points to the importance of continuing to invest in education to diversify the ranks of the technocratic elite—to make it easier to identify, locate and engage critical populations in AI governance.

Challenges to integrate technocrats from non-Western contexts also permeate challenges for more inclusive, participatory discourse with non-technocratic elites. Fortunately, there are examples of CSOs based in the Global South seeking to break down the barriers—for technocrats and citizens. For example, Coding Rights, a Brazilian CSO asserts a feminist lens to AI governance through their program Not my AI (Coding Rights n.d.), providing a forum for both technocratic elites and women in Brazil to voice concerns and challenges with AI. Coding Rights leverages this program by acting as a bridge to marginalized actors, as well as utilizing their positionality for rights-based policy advocacy.

Civil society has long played a bridging role by facilitating participatory governance, including education, integration, advocacy and mobilization, such that diverse stakeholders and populations may contribute effectively to governance discourses (Fischer 2012). Many examples exist of civil society utilizing participatory governance models to engage marginalized populations in highly technical governance challenges within Global South contexts, including smart cities (Komninos and Kakderi 2019; Lim and Yigitcanlar 2022), and various poverty reduction programs (Schneider 1999; Speer 2012).

For this challenge, civil society's roles include policy advocacy and bridging. The policy advocacy role involves wielding soft power to draw attention to important and emergent challenges in AI governance. By supporting AI stakeholders in building social capital, facilitating individual expression, and priming specific populations for engaging in the AI governance discourse, CSOs can play an important bridging role. The challenge will be to facilitate stakeholders working together without acting paternalistically, or becoming co-opted by a single group or population, to the detriment of others.

CONCLUSION

CSOs are, and need to be, engaged in AI governance: providing and supporting opportunities to diversify the ranks of the technocratic elite; developing innovative goods, services, and networks; and advocating and collaborating to shape AI discourse and policy at the local, regional, and international levels. Emergent participatory governance models provide evidence-based support that civil society can effectively mobilize diverse populations in highly technical and entrenched governance challenges, similar to AI governance.

It is important to note that, while this chapter focuses on the roles that CSOs can play in disrupting the status quo and addressing AI governance challenges, there are significant limits to CSO power and influence. Voluntary action, soft power and normative pressure are central to civil society, which can significantly constrain the impact of CSOs. For example, while CSOs can help train a more diverse technical workforce and support individuals developing innovative AI governance solutions through professional associations, Big Tech firms can choose not to prioritize diversity in hiring and/or refuse to engage with CSOs around new AI governance approaches. By playing roles highlighted in this chapter, CSOs can complement, but not substitute for, the ethical behaviour or firms and top-down AI regulation.

To date, critical perspectives on AI governance and the role of civil society have developed in parallel, with few examples of cross-pollination. While research nods to civil society as a potential collaborator—a bridge to access affected communities—these acknowledgements lack specificity in who should be included and the types of roles civil society can occupy (Gutierrez and Bryant 2022; Wieringa 2020). Continued efforts to integrate AI governance and civil society research provide fruitful avenues for developing well-rounded theories and frameworks moving forward.

REFERENCES

AbouAssi, Khaldoun. 2013. 'Hands in the Pockets of Mercurial Donors: NGO Response to Shifting Funding Priorities.' *Nonprofit and Voluntary Sector Quarterly* 42(3): 584–602.

Ada Academy. 2019. 'Ada Developers Academy.' https://adadevelopersacademy.org/ (May 17, 2022).

Adams, Rachel. 2021. 'Can Artificial Intelligence Be Decolonized?' *Interdisciplinary Science Reviews* 46(1–2): 176–97.

Anghie, Antony. 2007. *Imperialism, Sovereignty and the Making of International Law*. Cambridge University Press.

Barman, Emily. 2008. 'With Strings Attached: Nonprofits and the Adoption of Donor Choice.' *Nonprofit and Voluntary Sector Quarterly* 37(1): 39–56.

Bordelon, Brendan. 2022. 'Civil Liberties Advocates Decamp to Tech Industry.' *POLITICO*. https://politi.co/3J9pBAw (May 19, 2022).

Bouchard, Mathieu, and Emmanuel Raufflet. 2019. 'Domesticating the Beast: A 'Resource Profile' Framework of Power Relations in Nonprofit–Business Collaboration.' *Nonprofit and Voluntary Sector Quarterly*: 24.

Chowdhury, Rumman. 2019. 'AI Ethics and Algorithmic Colonialism.' *IGSF*. https://www.mcgill.ca/igsf/channels/event/rumman-chowdhury-ai-ethics-and-algorithmic-colonialism-300414 (July 25, 2022).

Coding Rights. n.d. 'Not My A.I.' *Coding Rights*. https://notmy.ai/about/ (May 20, 2022).

Dafoe, Allan. 2018. *AI Governance: A Research Agenda*. Centre for the Governance of AI: University of Oxford. http://www.fhi.ox.ac.uk/wp-content/uploads/GovAI-Agenda.pdf.

Duberry, Jérôme. 2019. *Global Environmental Governance in the Information Age: Civil Society Organizations and Digital Media*. 1st ed. Routledge. https://www.taylorfrancis.com/books/9781351613545 (May 11, 2022).

EAIGG. no date. 'ETHICAL AI GOVERNANCE GROUP.' *ETHICAL AI GOVERNANCE GROUP*. https://www.eaigg.org (May 20, 2022).

Edwards, Michael, and David Hulme. 1996. 'Too Close for Comfort? The Impact of Official Aid on Nongovernmental Organizations.' *World Development* 24(6): 961–73.

Elbers, Willem, and Bas Arts. 2011. 'Keeping Body and Soul Together: Southern NGOs' Strategic Responses to Donor Constraints.' *International Review of Administrative Sciences* 77(4): 713–32.

Erman, Eva, and Markus Furendal. 2022. 'The Global Governance of Artificial Intelligence: Some Normative Concerns.' *Moral Philosophy and Politics* 0(0). https://www.degruyter.com/document/doi/10.1515/mopp-2020-0046/html (May 11, 2022).

Fischer, Frank. 2012. 'Participatory Governance: From Theory To Practice.' In *The Oxford Handbook of Governance*, https://www.oxfordhandbooks.com/view/10.1093/oxfordhb/9780199560530.001.0001/oxfordhb-9780199560530-e-32 (May 20, 2022).

Gagné, Jean-François. 2018. 'Global AI Talent Pool Report 2018.' *jfgagne*. https://jfgagne.ai/talent/ (May 19, 2022).

Gandy, Oscar H. 2010. 'Engaging Rational Discrimination: Exploring Reasons for Placing Regulatory Constraints on Decision Support Systems.' *Ethics and Information Technology* 12(1): 29–42.

Ganesh, Maya Indira, and Emanuel Moss. 2022. 'Resistance and Refusal to Algorithmic Harms: Varieties of 'Knowledge Projects.' *Media International Australia* 183(1): 90–106.

Grace, Katja et al. 2018. 'Viewpoint: When Will AI Exceed Human Performance? Evidence from AI Experts.' *Journal of Artificial Intelligence Research* 62: 729–54.

Grant, Nico, and Josh Eidelson. 2022. 'Two of Google's Ethical AI Staffers Leave to Join Ousted Colleague's Institute.' *Yahoo News*. https://www.yahoo.com/now/two-googles-ethical-ai-staffers-200000349.html (May 20, 2022).

Groeneveld, Sandra, and Kenneth J. Meier. 2022. 'Theorizing Status Distance: Rethinking the Micro Theories of Representation and Diversity in Public Organizations.' *Administration & Society* 54(2): 248–76.

Gutierrez, Miren, and John Bryant. 2022. 'The Fading Gloss of Data Science: Towards an Agenda That Faces the Challenges of Big Data for Development and Humanitarian Action.' *Development* 65(1): 80–93.

Hansmann, Henry B. 1980. 'The Role of Nonprofit Enterprise.' *Yale Law Journal* 89(5): 835–902.

Hao, Karen. 2021. 'Worried about Your Firm's AI Ethics? These Startups Are Here to Help.' *MIT Technology Review.* https://www.technologyreview.com/2021/01/15/1016183/ai-ethics-startups/ (May 20, 2022).

Jobin, Anna, Marcello Ienca, and Effy Vayena. 2019. 'The Global Landscape of AI Ethics Guidelines.' *Nature Machine Intelligence* 1(9): 389–99.

Knowledge 4 All Foundation Ltd. n.d. 'Global South Map of Emerging Areas in Artificial Intelligence.' https://www.k4all.org/project/aiecosystem/ (May 20, 2022).

Komninos, Nicos, and Christina Kakderi. 2019. *Smart Cities in the Post-Algorithmic Era: Integrating Technologies, Platforms and Governance.* Edward Elgar Publishing.

LePere-Schloop, Megan et al. 2022. 'Mapping Civil Society in the Digital Age: Critical Reflections From a Project Based in the Global South.' *Nonprofit and Voluntary Sector Quarterly* 51(3): 587–605.

Levine Daniel, Jamie, and Rachel Fyall. 2019. 'The Intersection of Nonprofit Roles and Public Policy Implementation.' *Public Performance & Management Review* 42(6): 1351–71.

Lim, Seng Boon, and Tan Yigitcanlar. 2022. 'Participatory Governance of Smart Cities: Insights from e-Participation of Putrajaya and Petaling Jaya, Malaysia.' *Smart Cities* 5(1): 71–89.

Lindsey, Bethany et al. 2021. *ADA Developers Academy Annual Report 2021.* ADA Developers Academy. Annual Report.

Mercer, Claire. 2002. 'NGOs, Civil Society and Democratization: A Critical Review of the Literature.' *Progress in Development Studies* 2(1): 5–22.

Mohamed, Shakir, Marie-Therese Png, and William Isaac. 2020. 'Decolonial AI: Decolonial Theory as Sociotechnical Foresight in Artificial Intelligence.' *Philosophy & Technology* 33(4): 659–84.

Monroe-White, Thema, and Sandy Zook. 2018. 'Social Enterprise Innovation: A Quantitative Analysis of Global Patterns.' *VOLUNTAS: International Journal of Voluntary and Nonprofit Organizations* 29(3): 496–510.

Moulton, Stephanie, and Adam Eckerd. 2012. 'Preserving the Publicness of the Nonprofit Sector: Resources, Roles, and Public Values.' *Nonprofit and Voluntary Sector Quarterly* 41(4): 656–85.

Nye, Joseph S. 1990. 'Soft Power.' *Foreign Policy* (80): 153–71.

O'Brien, Nina F., and Sandra K. Evans. 2017. 'Civil Society Partnerships: Power Imbalance and Mutual Dependence in NGO Partnerships.' *VOLUNTAS: International Journal of Voluntary and Nonprofit Organizations* 28(4): 1399–1421.

O'Neil, Cathy. 2016. *Weapons of Math Destruction: How Big Data Increases Inequality and Threatens Democracy.* Crown.

Pfeffer, Jeffrey, and Gerald R. Salancik. 2003. *The External Control of Organizations: A Resource Dependence Perspective.* Stanford University Press.

Salamon, Lester M., and S. Wojciech Sokolowski. 2016. 'Beyond Nonprofits: Re-Conceptualizing the Third Sector.' *VOLUNTAS: International Journal of Voluntary and Nonprofit Organizations* 27(4): 1515–45.

Schiff, Daniel, Justin Biddle, Jason Borenstein, and Kelly Laas. 2020. 'What's Next for AI Ethics, Policy, and Governance? A Global Overview.' In *Proceedings of the AAAI/ACM Conference on AI, Ethics, and Society*, New York NY USA: ACM, 153–58. https://dl.acm.org/doi/10.1145/3375627.3375804 (May 16, 2022).

Schneider, Hartmut. 1999. 'Participatory Governance for Poverty Reduction.' *Journal of International Development* 11(4): 521–34.

Speer, Johanna. 2012. 'Participatory Governance Reform: A Good Strategy for Increasing Government Responsiveness and Improving Public Services?' *World Development* 40(12): 2379–98.

Stark, Luke, Daniel Greene, and Anna Lauren Hoffmann. 2021. 'Critical Perspectives on Governance Mechanisms for AI/ML Systems.' In *The Cultural Life of Machine Learning*, eds. Jonathan Roberge and Michael Castelle. Cham: Springer International Publishing, 257–80. https://link.springer.com/10.1007/978-3-030-56286-1_9 (May 11, 2022).

Suarez, Cyndi. 2021. 'Why Civil Society Needs to Pay Attention to AI.' *Non Profit News | Nonprofit Quarterly.* https://nonprofitquarterly.org/civil-society-pay-attention-to-ai-2/ (May 20, 2022).

Ulnicane, Inga et al. 2021. 'Framing Governance for a Contested Emerging Technology:Insights from AI Policy.' *Policy and Society* 40(2): 158–77.

US EEOC. 2014. *Diversity in High-Tech.* US Equal Employment Opportunity Commission. Special Report. https://www.eeoc.gov/special-report/diversity-high-tech (May 17, 2022).

Weisbrod, Burton A. 1977. *The Voluntary Nonprofit Sector: An Economic Analysis.* Lexington, MA: Heath & Co.

Wieringa, Maranke. 2020. 'What to Account for When Accounting for Algorithms: A Systematic Literature Review on Algorithmic Accountability.' In *Proceedings of the 2020 Conference on Fairness, Accountability, and Transparency,* Barcelona Spain: ACM, 1–18. https://dl.acm.org/doi/10.1145/3351095.3372833 (May 11, 2022).

World Bank. 2022. 'Civil Society.' *World Bank.* https://www.worldbank.org/en/about/partners/civil-society/overview (May 19, 2022).

World Economic Forum. 2021. *The AI Governance Journey: Development and Opportunities.* World Economic Forum. Insight Report.

Index